CASES AND COMMENTS

ON

CRIMINAL LAW

FIFTH EDITION

By

ANDRE A. MOENSSENS
Professor of Law,
University of Richmond

FRED E. INBAU
John Henry Wigmore Professor of Law Emeritus,
Northwestern University

and

RONALD J. BACIGAL
Professor of Law,
University of Richmond

Westbury, New York
THE FOUNDATION PRESS, INC.
1992

Library of Congress Cataloging-in-Publication Data

Moenssens, Andre A.
    Cases and comments on criminal law / by Andre A. Moenssens, Fred
E. Inbau, and Ronald J. Bacigal. — 5th ed.
        p.   cm. — (University casebook series)
    Fred E. Inbau's name appears first on 4th ed.
    Includes index.
    ISBN 0–88277–937–0
    1. Criminal law—United States—Cases. I. Inbau, Fred Edward.
II. Bacigal, Ronald J. III. Title. IV. Series.
KF9218.M63   1992
345.73—dc20
[347.305]   91–26932

 TEXT IS PRINTED ON 10% POST
CONSUMER RECYCLED PAPER

M., I. & B. Cs. Crim.Law 5th Ed. UCB
2nd Reprint—1996

PREFACE

The 1992 fifth edition of *Cases and Comments on Criminal Law* introduces significant changes from the earlier editions. Not only has the subject content been updated by the inclusion of many modern cases, both as principal cases and in the accompanying notes, but the subject matter has been entirely rearranged according to a different organizational framework that begins the study of criminal law by focusing on general concepts of criminality. Only after these concepts have been developed in the cases and note materials, do we reach the study of specific crimes and defenses to criminal liability.

We continue to believe that it is important for beginning law students to quickly gain an in-depth understanding of the constitutional restraints upon criminal law legislation. We have kept the materials on due process, the right of privacy, equal protection under the law, and on cruel and unusual punishment, in one chapter, to permit easy omission of the materials if study time is not available or their use in a separate course is desired.

In the selection of many modern cases for inclusion as new principal cases and in the notes, the authors have sought to maintain a careful balance between those dealing with criminal law developments in modern code states and the cases evidencing a concern for the traditional common law concepts, which are important both for their historical perspective and because they are still very much the law in many jurisdictions.

Following the increasing emphasis now being given to the crime of conspiracy, additional materials have been included to develop further that area of the law, particularly in connection with RICO and other federal conspiracy statutes.

It is in the defenses to crime that the past few years have seen the greatest number of new concepts that are being advanced in the cases and legal literature. The 1992 edition includes mention of the proliferation of "syndrome" defenses, including the "battered woman" syndrome in self defense, and, among the special defenses seeking to diminish criminal responsibility, the "post-traumatic stress disorder," multiple personality disorder, the premenstrual syndrome defense, and the whole host of other types of diminished capacity-type defenses proffered by psychiatric or psychological experts in modern cases. The materials on the insanity defense also reflect the impact of the recent movements to abolish, limit or modify that defense.

Other significant changes deal with the continued controversy over whether the felony-murder rule should be retained, the expansion of the sex offenses coupled with the widespread adoption of "rape shield" statutes and the use of "rape trauma syndrome" evidence by prosecutors seeking to bolster their cases. The burgeoning of regulatory and property offenses is also highlighted.

As in the past, our book starts with an outline of criminal procedure. We believe it essential that a beginning student have an insight into the criminal law processes as a prerequisite to proper understanding of many of the cases on substantive criminal law. The book ends with an Appendix containing pertinent provisions of the United States Constitution and its Amendments. Since these provisions are referred to in many cases, especially in the latter part of the book, the student has ready access to their precise wording.

We express our appreciation to the American Law Institute for permitting us to reprint portions of the Model Penal Code, and to the many authors of law review articles who gave us permission to use excerpts from their thoughtful and scholarly articles.

Many of the court opinions reproduced in this casebook have been condensed, and their footnotes were either omitted completely or reduced in number; otherwise the book would be of unmanageable size. The omissions of case opinion textual material are indicated by either of two symbols: . . . (generally for omissions of parts of paragraphs) and * * * (generally indicative of omitted paragraphs).

In our notes and comments, and indeed, the reported cases themselves, whenever the word "he" and other masculine pronouns appear, they are used generically for the sake of brevity and should be considered, in appropriate instances, to include both females as well as males.

A.A.M.
F.E.I.
R.J.B.

December, 1991

SUMMARY OF CONTENTS

*

TABLE OF CONTENTS

TABLE OF CONTENTS

TABLE OF CONTENTS

PART II. CRIMES

*

TABLE OF CASES

Principal cases are in italic type. Non-principal cases are in roman type. References are to Pages.

xix

TABLE OF CASES

*

CASES AND COMMENTS
ON
CRIMINAL LAW

*

Part I

THE CRIMINAL JUSTICE SYSTEM
LEGAL CONCEPTS OF CRIMINALITY

Chapter 1

OVERVIEW OF CRIMINAL PROCEDURE

The procedure followed in a criminal case is not the same for all states, but the differences are rather slight as regards basic concepts and principles. In essential respects there is also very little difference between the procedure of the state courts and that which exists in the federal courts.

The following outline of criminal procedure is here presented for the purpose of familiarizing the beginning law student with the basic procedures that are involved or referred to in the case reports he will be encountering in subsequent chapters.

A. PROCEDURE BETWEEN ARREST AND TRIAL

In most states there is a statutory provision to the effect that an arrested person must be taken without unnecessary delay before the nearest judge or magistrate. What happens after presentation to the judge or magistrate will depend upon whether the arrested person is accused of a felony or a misdemeanor. If the charge is a misdemeanor, the judge or magistrate will sometimes have the power and authority to hear the case himself, and he may proceed with the trial unless the accused demands trial by jury or a continuance is requested or ordered for some reason. If the offense charged is a felony, the judge or magistrate before whom the accused is brought will ordinarily lack the constitutional or legislative authority to conduct trials for crimes of that degree of seriousness, and in such instances he only conducts what is known as a "preliminary hearing," which will be subsequently described.

1. THE RIGHT TO BAIL

After arrest, the first decision made by a court is, frequently, whether the accused is entitled to release on bail. Subject to some exceptions for persons charged with death penalty offenses, persons on parole and others, an accused is entitled to have the court set bail. Bail is fixed at a specific dollar amount. If the accused places cash or property worth that amount with the clerk of court, he will be at

1

liberty pending his trial. If the accused appears at the required proceedings, bail is refunded but failure to appear results in forfeiture of bail. In some states, professional bail bondsmen will, in effect, deposit bail in exchange for a non-refundable fee from the defendant. In other states, a defendant is allowed to deposit a portion of his bail (usually equivalent to the bondsman's fee, i.e., 10%), most of which is refunded if the defendant honors his obligation to appear. Moreover, courts generally have the power to allow release without any deposit— merely accepting the defendant's signature on a bond that makes him liable for the amount of bail if he fails to appear. Such defendants, usually those thought to be highly likely to appear for trial, are said to be released on "recognizance," "signature," or "individual bond." Finally, an accused has no right to have bail set at an amount he can meet. A number of defendants will fail to "make" bail and remain in jail pending trial.

2. PROBABLE CAUSE TO DETAIN AND THE HABEAS CORPUS WRIT

After a person has been arrested as a suspect by the police or upon authorization of a prosecutor, and remains deprived of his liberty, he is entitled, as a constitutional right, to a prompt, though limited judicial hearing on the question of probable cause *to detain*. At this kind of hearing, normal rules of evidence are not applicable and counsel for the accused is not required. This procedure is akin to that used when, prior to arrest, the prosecutor seeks an arrest warrant from a court.

In the event an arrested person is not formally charged with an offense and is not taken before a judge or other magistrate without unnecessary delay he, or rather someone on his behalf, may petition a judge for a "writ of habeas corpus" and thereby attempt to secure his release or at least compel the police to file a specific charge against him. In the latter event he may then seek his release on bond. If the court issues the writ, the police or other custodians of the arrested person are required, either immediately or at an early designated time, to bring him into court (that is, "you have the body," which is the literal meaning of the term habeas corpus), and to explain to the court the reason or justification for holding the accused person in custody.

Upon the police showing adequate cause, a court may continue the hearing in order to give the police a little more time to conduct a further investigation before making the formal charge against the arrestee. Many times, however, the police are required to file their charges immediately or release the prisoner. In some jurisdictions the prosecutor makes the decision as to whether the initial charge shall be filed.

3. PRELIMINARY HEARING

Following the filing in court of a police accusation against a person, or after an accusation has been filed by a prosecuting attorney in the form of an "information" detailing the charge, the accused is entitled to a preliminary hearing. This is a relatively informal judicial proceeding during which a determination is made as to whether there are reasonable grounds for believing the accused person committed the offense—as to whether it is fair, under the circumstances, to require him to stand a regular trial. If after such a hearing the judge or magistrate decides that the accusation is without probable cause, the accused will be discharged. This discharge, however, will not bar a grand jury indictment if subsequently developed evidence (or the same evidence presented on the preliminary hearing) satisfies the grand jury that the accusation is well founded.

If the preliminary hearing judge or magistrate decides that the accusation is a reasonable one, the accused will be "bound over" to the grand jury—that is, held in jail until the charge against him is presented for grand jury consideration. If the offense is a bailable one, however, the accused may be released after a bond of a certain amount is given to ensure his presence until the grand jury has acted in the matter. (The nature and composition of a grand jury and the difference between it and a petit or trial jury is described later in this chapter.)

In some jurisdictions, as subsequently detailed, once the magistrate has found probable cause, the prosecutor may bypass the grand jury and file a felony "information" upon which the accused will be tried.

4. THE RIGHT TO AN ATTORNEY

The Sixth Amendment to the Constitution of the United States provides that "in all criminal prosecutions, the accused shall enjoy the right . . . to have the assistance of Counsel for his defense." And the Supreme Court of the United States has held that where incarceration may be a consequence of the prosecution, the defendant is entitled to appointed counsel in the event he cannot afford one. A preliminary hearing, of course, is a part of the "criminal prosecution."

5. CORONER'S INQUEST AND MEDICAL EXAMINER SYSTEM

At this point in a discussion of criminal procedure, mention should be made of a proceeding peculiar to homicide cases, which comes into operation soon after a killing or discovered death. This is the "coroner's inquest."

The coroner's inquest is a very old proceeding and its function was and still is to determine the cause of death. The verdict of the coroner's jury, which is made up, in some states, of six laymen selected by the coroner or one of his deputies, is not binding on the prosecuting attorney, grand jury or court. In effect, it is merely an advisory finding which can be either accepted or completely ignored. For instance, even though a coroner's jury returns a verdict of accidental death, a grand jury, either upon its own initiative or upon evidence presented by the prosecutor, may find that death resulted because of someone's criminal act and charge that person with the offense.

In some jurisdictions the office of coroner has been replaced by what is known as a medical examiner system. Whereas the coroner is usually an elected official (who may or may not be a physician), a medical examiner must be a physician appointed by a state or county officer or agency; moreover, in many jurisdictions he must be a forensic pathologist, specially trained for the position. He, in turn, has the power of appointing assistants who are physicians already trained for the purpose or at least in the process of receiving such training.

6. THE GRAND JURY

Misdemeanors are usually prosecuted upon an information filed by the prosecuting attorney after he has received and considered the sworn complaint of the victim or of some other person with knowledge of the facts. For felonies, however, many states require that the matter must first be submitted to a "grand jury." Then, after hearing the alleged facts related by the victim or other persons, the grand jury determines whether there are reasonable grounds for proceeding to an actual trial of the person charged.

A grand jury is usually composed of 23 citizen-voters, 16 of whom constitute a quorum. The votes of 12 members are necessary to the return of an "indictment." This indictment is also known as a "true bill."

The Constitution of the United States does not require that state prosecutors use a grand jury to charge felony offenses, and there is an increasing tendency to enact statutes that permit the prosecution to charge felonies by filing an "information." Ordinarily a person charged by information must have a preliminary hearing before he can be tried for the charge. A defendant charged by a grand jury, however, may not have a right to a preliminary hearing because it is thought that his rights are adequately safeguarded by his fellow citizens who serve on the grand jury.

One highly significant and increasing modern purpose of the grand jury is to investigate complex crimes. The grand jury has the right to subpoena witnesses, to ask them questions, and to require the production of books and records. It may exercise these rights before any charge is filed and before the specific crime or its perpetrator is known. Police agencies usually do not possess this authority to compel the production of evidence and it is generally conceded that such a right is required for effective investigation of much financial crime, official corruption, and organized crime.

The consideration of a felony charge by a grand jury is in no sense of the word a trial. Only the state's evidence is presented and considered; the suspected offender is usually not even heard nor is his lawyer present to offer evidence in his behalf. Some state laws, however, now provide that the suspect has a right to appear before the grand jury if he elects to do so, but very few suspects exercise that option. Other laws provide that a "target" of the grand jury investigation has the right to have counsel with him if he is summoned to appear before the grand jury.

7. THE ARRAIGNMENT AND PLEA

Following an indictment, the next step in felony cases is the appearance of the accused person before a judge who is empowered to try felony cases. The indictment is read to the defendant or the essence of its contents is made known to him; in other words, he is advised of the criminal charges made against him. If he pleads guilty, the judge can sentence him immediately or take the matter under advisement for a decision at an early date. If the accused pleads not guilty, a date is then set for his actual trial.

In some states, and in the federal system, the defendant may enter a plea of "nolo contendere," a plea which has the same effect as a plea of guilty, except that the admission thereby made cannot be used as evidence in any other action.

8. PRE–TRIAL MOTIONS

After the formal charge has been made against the accused, he may, in advance of trial, seek to terminate the prosecution's case, or at least seek to prepare a better defense, by utilizing a procedure known as making or filing a *motion*. A motion is merely a request for a court ruling or order that will afford the defendant the assistance or remedy he is thereby seeking. Some of the more frequently used motions are the following:

Motion to Quash the Indictment. With this motion the defendant may question the legal sufficiency of the indictment. If the court decides that the indictment adequately charges a criminal offense, and that it was obtained in accordance with the prescribed legal procedures, the motion will be overruled; otherwise the indictment will be considered invalid and "quashed." Even after an indictment has been thus rejected and set aside, the prosecutor may proceed to obtain another and proper indictment. Moreover, the prosecution is entitled to appeal from a court order quashing an indictment; at this stage of the proceedings the defendant has not been placed in jeopardy, and consequently a subsequent indictment and trial would not constitute a violation of his constitutional privilege against double jeopardy.

Motion for a Bill of Particulars. Although the indictment, if valid, will ordinarily contain all the allegations of fact necessary for the defendant to prepare his defense, he may, by a motion for a "bill of particulars," obtain further details respecting the accusation.

In addition to the motion for a bill of particulars, there now exists an expanded right, accorded to both the prosecution and the defense, to learn what evidence the other side intends to use. It is known as a *Motion for Discovery*, whereby both parties seek to learn not only the details of the crime but also the names of the other side's witnesses and what they are expected to say.

Motion for a Change of Venue. A defendant may attempt to avoid trial before a particular judge or in the city, county, or district where the crime occurred by seeking a "change of venue." In instances where this appears to be necessary in order that the defendant may receive a fair trial, the motion for a change of venue will be granted.

Motion to Suppress Evidence. A defendant has the privilege of filing with the court, normally in advance of trial, a "motion to suppress" evidence that he contends has been obtained from him in an unconstitutional manner. The evidence in question may be, on the one hand, a tangible item such as a gun, narcotics, or stolen property or, on the other hand, an intangible item such as a confession or the testimony of eyewitnesses who are expected to identify the accused as the offender. If the court is satisfied that the evidence has been illegally obtained, it will order the evidence suppressed, which means that it cannot be used at the trial. If the court decides that the evidence was lawfully obtained, it is usable against the defendant at the trial.

B. THE TRIAL

In all states, and in the federal system, the accused is entitled to a "speedy trial." This right to an early trial is guaranteed by the various constitutions, and the constitutional provisions are generally supplemented by legislative enactments that particularize and specifically limit the pre-trial detention period. In Illinois, for instance, once a person is jailed upon a criminal charge, he must be tried within 120 days, unless the delay has been occasioned by him, or is necessitated by a hearing to determine his mental competency to stand trial. If the accused is out on bail, he can demand trial within 160 days. In either instance, however, if the court determines that the prosecution has exercised, without success, due diligence to obtain evidence material to the case, and that there are reasonable grounds to believe that such evidence will be forthcoming, the time for trial may be extended for another 60 days. Such time limits vary from state to state, but the consistent rule is that unless the accused person is tried within the specified period of time he must be released and is thereafter immune from prosecution for that offense.

The federal courts are governed by the Speedy Trial Act of 1974, which is a statutory scheme that provides time periods within which federal trials must begin. Since July 1, 1979, subject to narrow exceptions, a federal trial must commence within sixty days of arraignment. Even under the new federal act, some circumstances permit the accused to waive his right to a trial within the statutory period.

1. JURY TRIAL—TRIAL BY JUDGE ALONE

A person accused of a "serious crime", which is considered to be one for which there may be incarceration beyond six months, is entitled to trial by jury, as a matter of constitutional right. However, he may waive this right and elect to be tried by a judge alone. In some jurisdictions the defendant has an absolute right to this waiver; in other states and in the federal system, it is conditioned upon the concurrence of the judge and the prosecution.

If the case is tried without a jury—also called a "bench trial"—the judge hears the evidence and decides for himself whether the defendant is guilty or not guilty. Where the trial is by a jury, the jury determines the facts and the judge serves more or less as an umpire or referee; it is his function to determine what testimony or evidence is legally "admissible," that is, to decide what should be heard or considered by the jury. But the ultimate decision as to whether the defendant is guilty is one to be made by the jury alone.

2. JURY SELECTION

In the selection of the jurors, usually twelve in number, who hear the defendant's case, most states permit his attorney as well as the prosecuting attorney to question a larger number of citizens who have been chosen for jury service from the list of registered voters. In the federal system and a growing number of states, however, most trial judges will do practically all of the questioning, with very little opportunity for questioning accorded the prosecutor and defense counsel. Nevertheless, each lawyer has a certain number of "peremptory challenges" which means that he can arbitrarily refuse to accept as jurors a certain number of those who appear as prospective jurors. In some states, by statutory provision, the defendant in larceny cases has ten such challenges and the state has an equal number; in a murder case the defendant and the state each have twenty peremptory challenges; and in minor criminal cases, such as petit larceny, the challenges are five in number for each side. And in all cases, if any prospective juror's answers to the questions of either attorney reveal a prejudice or bias that prevents him from being a fair and impartial juror, the judge, either on his own initiative or at the suggestion of either counsel, will dismiss that person from jury service. Although the desired result is not always achieved, the avowed purpose of this practice of permitting lawyers to question prospective jurors is to obtain twelve jurors who will be fair to both sides of the case.

As a safeguard against a juror becoming ill or disabled for some other reason, in many states, and within the federal system, provision is made for alternate jurors (usually two) who will hear all the evidence but not participate in the deliberation of the jury unless there is a replacement of one of the original jurors.

3. OPENING STATEMENTS

After the jury is selected, both the prosecuting attorney and the defense lawyer are entitled to make "opening statements" in which each outlines what he intends to prove. The purpose of this is to acquaint the jurors with each side of the case, so that it will be easier for them to follow the evidence as it is presented.

4. THE PROSECUTION'S EVIDENCE

After the opening statements the prosecuting attorney produces the prosecution's testimony and evidence. He has the burden of proving the state's case "beyond a reasonable doubt." If at the close of the prosecution's case the judge is of the opinion that reasonable jurors could not conclude that the charge against the defendant has been proved, he will "direct a verdict" of acquittal. That ends the matter and the defendant goes free—forever immune from further prosecution for the crime, just the same as if a jury had heard all the evidence and found him not guilty.

5. THE DEFENDANT'S EVIDENCE

If at the close of the prosecution's case the court does not direct the jury to find the defendant not guilty, the defendant may, if he wishes, present evidence in refutation. He himself may or may not testify, and if he chooses not to appear as a witness, the prosecuting attorney is not permitted to comment upon that fact to the jury. The basis for this principle whereby the defendant is not obligated to speak in his own behalf is the constitutional privilege that protects a person from self-incrimination.

The prosecution is given an opportunity to rebut the defendant's evidence, if any, and the presentation of testimony usually ends at that point. Then, once more, defense counsel will try to persuade the court to "direct a verdict" in favor of the defendant. If the court decides to let the case go to the jury, the prosecuting attorney and defense counsel make their closing arguments.

The defense and the prosecution have the right to subpoena witnesses and require them to testify at trial or to produce records if such evidence would be of value at trial. It is possible in certain case situations to enforce subpoenas against out-of-state witnesses and, in some instances, against witnesses in foreign countries.

The prosecution has the obligation in most, if not all, cases to notify the defense of any evidence that would be of significance in exculpating the accused or in mitigating his sentence, if the prosecution is aware of this evidence.

6. CLOSING ARGUMENTS

In their closing arguments the prosecutor and defense counsel review and analyze the evidence and attempt to persuade the jury to render a favorable verdict.

7. INSTRUCTIONS OF THE COURT TO THE JURY

After the closing arguments are completed, or in some jurisdictions before the closing arguments, the judge will read and give to the jury certain written instructions as to the legal principles that should be applied to the facts of the case as determined by the jury. The judge also gives the jury certain written forms of possible verdicts. The jury then retires to the jury room where they are given an adequate opportunity to deliberate upon the matter, away from everyone, including the judge himself.

8. THE VERDICT OF THE JURY

When the jurors have reached a decision, they advise the bailiff that they have reached a verdict and then return to the courtroom. The foreman, usually selected by the jurors themselves to serve as their leader and spokesman, announces the verdict of the jury. Jury participation in the case is then at an end.

If the defendant is acquitted, he is free forever from any further prosecution by that particular state or jurisdiction for the crime for which he was tried. If he is found guilty, then, in most types of cases and in most jurisdictions, it becomes the function of the trial judge to fix the sentence within the legislatively prescribed limitations.

In the event the jurors are unable to agree upon a verdict—and it must be unanimous in most states—the jury, commonly referred to as a "hung jury," is discharged, and a new trial date may be set for a retrial of the case before another jury. The retrial does not constitute a violation of the constitutional protection against double jeopardy—trying a person twice for the same offense—because there actually has not been a first trial; in other words, it has been terminated by the failure of the jury to agree upon a verdict.

9. THE MOTION FOR A NEW TRIAL

After a verdict of guilty there are still certain opportunities provided the defendant to obtain his freedom. He may file a "motion for a new trial," in which he alleges certain "errors" committed in the course of his trial; if the trial judge agrees, the conviction is set aside and the defendant may be tried again by a new jury and usually before a different judge. Where this motion for a new trial is "overruled" or "denied," the judge will then proceed to sentence the defendant.

The defendant may also seek a new trial on the grounds of newly discovered evidence favorable to him. Such motions are rarely granted.

The defendant must establish that he was not aware of the evidence, that he could not have discovered the evidence by exercising due diligence, and that the evidence would probably change the result of the trial.

10. THE SENTENCE

In cases tried without a jury, the judge, of course, will determine the sentence to be imposed. In jury cases the practice varies among the states, with most of them following the practice of confining the jury function to a determination of guilt or innocence and permitting the judge to fix the penalty. For the crimes of murder and rape, however, most of the states place both responsibilities upon the jury.

In some states there are statutory provisions that prescribe that upon conviction of a felony, the defendant must be sentenced for a specified minimum-maximum term in the penitentiary—for example, one year to ten years for burglary. In many states a judge is permitted to set a minimum-maximum period anywhere within the minimum-maximum term prescribed by the legislature. In other words, the sentence given for grand larceny may be one to ten years, the statutory range, or one to two, nine to ten, or any other combination between one and ten. The minimum-maximum term means that the defendant cannot be released before serving the minimum period, less "time off for good behavior," nor can he be kept in the penitentiary longer than the maximum period, less "time off for good behavior." In between this minimum-maximum period the convict is eligible for "parole." The determination of the appropriate time of his release within that period is to be made by a "parole board," whose judgment in that respect is based upon the extent of the convict's rehabilitation, the security risk involved, and similar factors.

In instances where imprisonment is fixed at a specified number of years, rather than for an indeterminate period, the law usually provides that the convicted person must serve one-third of the sentence before becoming eligible for parole.

In recent years there has been an increase in two new forms of incarceration. "Work release" allows an inmate to work at a job and return to custody during nonworking hours. "Periodic imprisonment" allows an inmate his freedom except for certain specified periods, e.g., weekends.

Recently some states have adopted a plan that limits the sentencing discretion of judges and the release powers of parole boards, or even abolishes parole boards. Under this new system the judge is required to set a specific term according to more or less strict guidelines. The sentence may be reduced by "good time" allowance (for "good behavior") in prison, which is calculated by a set formula. When the inmate serves his sentence less "good time," he is automatically released.

C. AFTER THE TRIAL

---

1. PROBATION

In certain types of cases, a judge is empowered, by statute, to grant "probation" to a convicted person. This means that instead of sending the defendant to the penitentiary the court permits him to remain at liberty but upon certain conditions prescribed by law and by the judge. His background must first be investigated by a probation officer for the purpose of determining whether he is the kind of person who may have "learned his lesson" by the mere fact of being caught and convicted, or whether he could be rehabilitated outside of prison better than behind prison walls. In other words, would any useful purpose be served for him or society by sending him to prison?

Among the conditions of a defendant's probation, the court may require him to make restitution of money stolen, or reparations to a person he physically injured. Some state statutes provide that for a period of up to six months in misdemeanor cases, and up to five years in felony cases, a defendant on probation will be subjected to the supervision of a probation officer and, in general, must remain on "good behavior" during the period fixed by the court. A failure to abide by the conditions prescribed by the court will subject the defendant to a sentence in the same manner and form as though he had been denied probation and sentenced immediately after his conviction for the offense.

2. PAROLE

A penitentiary sentence of a specified term or number of years does not necessarily mean that a convicted person will remain in the penitentiary for that particular period of time. Under certain conditions and circumstances he may be released earlier "on parole," which means a release under supervision until the expiration of his sentence or until the expiration of a period otherwise specified by law. For instance, a person sentenced "for life" is, in some states eligible for release "on parole" at the end of twenty years, with a subsequent five year period of parole supervision. One sentenced for a fixed number of years, for example 14 years for murder, may be eligible for parole in some states after he has served one-third that period of time. And a person who has been given an indeterminate minimum-maximum sentence, such as to 5 to 10 years for grand larceny, may be eligible for a parole after he has served the 5 year minimum, less time off for good behavior.

The manner of computing time off for good behavior, or "good time," varies among the states. Some states have a system based on yearly credits; under this arrangement, the amount of the credit granted increases as the amount of time served by the obedient prisoner increases. Accordingly, one month off is granted for good behavior in the first year, two months for the second year, and so on up to a maxium of six months off for good behavior in the sixth year and in each succeeding year. The inmate is allowed to accumulate these credits. Thus, under this system, a prisoner who received a minimum-maximum sentence of 3 to 5 years and who served "good time", would be eligible for parole after serving 2 years and 6 months of his sentence.

A violation of the conditions of the parole will subject the parolee to possible return to prison for the remainder of his unexpired sentence.

As previously noted, some states have practically abolished parole by providing mandatory release dates, less time off for good behavior, which means that there can be no parole release prior to that date.

In states maintaining the conventional parole system, revocation of probation or parole cannot be arbitrary. In either case there must be a hearing. The hearing need not be like a full scale trial, i.e., there is no jury, but it must be a fair determination of whether the conditions of probation and parole were violated.

3. THE APPEAL

After sentence has been pronounced, the defendant may appeal his conviction to a reviewing court. The reviewing court will examine all or part of the written record of what happened at the trial, and consider the written and oral arguments of both the defense attorney and the prosecutor. It will then render a written decision and opinion which will either reverse or affirm the trial court conviction and state the reasons for the decision. If the trial court's decision is "reversed and remanded", it means that the defendant's conviction is nullified, although he may be tried over again by another jury. A decision of "reversed" ordinarily means that in addition to an improper trial there appears to be insufficient competent evidence upon which to try the defendant again, and consequently the prosecuting attorney may not make a second attempt to win a conviction.

A decision of the state's highest court affirming a conviction is, in nearly all instances, a final disposition of the case, and there is nothing else the convicted person can do but submit to the judgment of the trial court. But if the appeal involved a *federal* constitutional question or issue the defendant is entitled to seek a review of the state appellate court decision by the Supreme Court of the United States. Such requests, known as petitions for a *writ of certiorari,* are rarely granted, however.

The courts may allow the defendant to remain free on bail pending appeal or they may increase the amount of bail or revoke bail entirely while the case is on appeal.

Whenever a defendant has succeeded in obtaining a reversal of his conviction, he may be retried unless the highest court to review the case has reversed for insufficiency of evidence. The reasons that a second trial after a reversal of a conviction for trial error does not constitute double jeopardy are three-fold, according to the courts which have been confronted with the issue. First of all, by appealing his conviction the accused is considered to "waive" his right not to be tried twice. Secondly, there is a strong societal interest in a final adjudication of the guilt or innocence of the accused. Thirdly, a retrial is in effect a continuation of the original proceeding.

Only the defendant has a right to appeal the result of a trial; to permit the prosecution to appeal from a verdict of acquittal or a trial judge's finding of not guilty has been held to violate the constitutional protection against double jeopardy.

In a growing number of jurisdictions, however, the prosecution is being accorded the right to appeal certain decisions of a pre-trial nature. It is not unusual today for the law to permit prosecution appeals from a trial court order dismissing the charge against a defendant, or from an order suppressing a confession or other evidence alleged to have been illegally obtained.

The prosecution generally has the same right of appeal as the defense from an adverse decision of an intermediate appeals court. Many states and the federal government have two kinds of reviewing courts. The first, usually called a court of appeals, hears most appeals. The losing party may then ask the second court, usually called the supreme court, to rehear the appeal. This second court, the highest court, may rehear the appeal and render a final decision or it may simply refuse to rehear the case.

D. OTHER POST–CONVICTION REMEDIES

In addition to the appeal itself, nearly all states in recent years have provided additional post-conviction remedies by which a defendant may attack his conviction. Such "collateral" remedies are known, variously, as proceedings in habeas corpus, post-conviction petitions, or by other titles. A defendant may thereby seek a re-litigation, in a trial court, of an issue that had been considered and decided on the direct appeal; or he may attempt to raise an entirely new issue. Moreover, the decision with respect to a collateral attack may be the subject of an appeal to a reviewing court.

Even after a conviction is upheld against collateral attack in the state courts, if a federal constitutional question had been presented, the convicted person has yet another remedy available—the *federal* writ of habeas corpus. The Supreme Court of the United States has held that a state court judgment of conviction resulting from a trial which involved a substantial error of federal constitutional dimension is void, and a prisoner held pursuant to a void judgment is unlawfully confined and subject to release by a federal court upon a writ of habeas corpus. However, the Court has imposed some limitations upon this right. A state prisoner who claims that evidence used against him at trial was obtained in violation of constitutional rules governing arrest, search and seizure, cannot present those claims in a federal habeas corpus proceeding if he had the opportunity to make them in the state court.

In considering a petition for habeas corpus, a federal district court judge may order another "evidentiary hearing." And he has the power to remand the case to the state court for a new trial or for the outright release of the defendant, depending upon the kind of error committed and the evidence still available to the state. But his decision is appealable to higher federal courts.

NOTE

A brief comparison, in outline form, between English and American criminal procedure appears in a pamphlet entitled "British Criminal Law," published by the Criminal Law Section of the American Bar Association for use at the Association's London Meeting in 1957, and reproduced in 50 J.CrimL., C. & P.S. 59 (1959). Also see, for other comparisons between English and American criminal procedure: Fellman, The Defendant's Rights Under English Law (1966); Karlen, Sawer & Wise, Anglo-American Criminal Justice (1967); and Kaufman, Criminal Procedure in England and the United States: Comparison in Initiating Prosecutions, 49 Fordham L.Rev. 26 (1980).

For an incisive, brief comparison, made in 1958, between the United States, England, Germany, Italy and Sweden, see Hartshorne, Court Procedure Compared, 41 J.Am.Jud.Soc'y 166 (1958). In his article Judge Hartshorne points out some interesting facts, such as the following: In Sweden, a court will try both the civil and criminal aspects of a case at the same time; in Italy, as is also true in some other countries, there is practically no cross-examination of witnesses, since the lawyers must submit to the judge every question they wish to ask of a witness, whereupon the judge decides whether the question should be modified or perhaps even asked at all; in some of these countries the defendant's past criminal record is before the court for consideration; and in Sweden and Germany there is no jury, as we know it, but a trial body composed of both professional and lay judges who sit as a "jury," deliberate together, and make their findings as a group. After considering a number of differences between American procedure and that of other countries, Judge Hartshorne concludes: "We must not be too sure that simply because we have been accustomed to doing a certain thing in a certain way that that way is the only way it should be done. In fact, the writer discussed many of these Swedish differences in procedure with some of the most estimable and broadminded Swedish citizens, and they were quite as convinced that their system was correct, as an American is that the American system is correct. Naturally, we have a predilection for our own system, because that is what we are used to, and have come to consider to be the only right way to do things. But clearly there are certain advantages in other ways of accomplishing the same result. Whether these advantages outweigh the advantages inhering in our system is another question. But the point is that we must not be hasty in our criticism, before we have considered objectively the merits of older, though to us strange, procedures."

An extensive update analysis of British criminal procedure is contained in the 1981 report of the Royal Commission on Criminal Procedure and its supporting volume "The Investigation and Prosecution of Criminal Offences in

England and Wales: The Law and Procedure." Both documents were published by Her Majesty's Stationery Office as Cmnd. 8092 and 8092–1.

The early English procedures for disposing of criminal accusations by such devices as trial by ordeal, trial by compurgation, and trial by battle, are discussed in 31 Tul.L.Rev. 68 (1956).

As regards Soviet Russia, see Berman, Soviet Criminal Law and Procedure (2d ed. 1972); Bassiouni and Savitski (Eds.), The Criminal Justice System of the USSR (1979); and Gorgone, Soviet Criminal Procedure Legislation: A Dissenting Perspective, 28 Amer.J.Comp.L. 577 (1980).

For an extensive discussion of modern Chinese law, see The Chinese Criminal Code Symposium by Jerome Alan Cohen, et al, 73 J.Crim.L. & Criminology 135–317 (1982). It covers the subjects of China's Criminal Codes; The Criminal Law of the People's Republic of China; The Criminal Procedure Law of the People's Republic of China; Criminal Justice in Post-Mao China: Some Preliminary Observations; A Comparison of the Chinese and Soviet Codes of Criminal Law and Procedure; and The People's Republic of China and The Presumption of Innocence.

A comparative treatment of certain aspects of criminal procedure in the United States, England, Canada, France, Norway, Japan, Germany, and Israel is contained in Sowle (Ed.), Police Power and Individual Freedom (1962), which is a reproduction of a series of articles originally published during 1960 and 1961 in the Journal of Criminal Law, Criminology and Police Science (Vol. 51, 129–188, 385–441: and Vol. 52, 1–74, 245–292). Also see Steenhuis, Andenaes, Bishop, and Kaiser, Developments in Criminal Law and Penal Systems in Holland, Norway, Sweden and West Germany, [1977] Crim.L.Rev. 404; Schrager, Recent Developments in the Law Relating to Confessions: England, Canada and Australia, 26 McGill L.J. 435 (1981); Volkmann-Schluck, Continental European Criminal Procedures: True or Illusive Model?, 9 Amer.J.Crim.L. 1 (1981); Shaschnow, Exclusionary Rule: Comparison of Israeli and United States Approaches, 93 Military L.Rev. 57 (Summer 1981); Perris, Admissibility of Evidence Obtained Illegally: A Comparative Analysis, 13 Ottawa L.Rev. 309 (1981); and Darby, Lessons in Comparative Criminal Procedure: France and the United States, 19 San Diego L.Rev. 277 (1982).

Among other publications, see Meyer, German Criminal Procedure: The Position of the Defendant in Court, 41 A.B.A.J. 592 (1955); Berg, Criminal Procedure: France, England, and the United States, 8 De Paul L.Rev. 256 (1959); and Abe, Criminal Procedure in Japan, 48 J.Crim.L., C. & P.S. 359 (1957); Pugh, Administration of Criminal Justice in France: An Introductory Analysis, 23 La.L.Rev. 1 (1962); Bratholm, Pagripelse og varetektsfengsel, pp. 379–97 (1957) (summary of law with respect to arrest and detention before trial in Norway, Sweden and Denmark); Goldstein and Marcus, Myth Judicial Supervision in Three "Inquisitional" Systems: France, Italy, and Germany, 87 Yale L.J. 240 (1977); Langbeim and Weinreb, Continental Criminal Procedure: "Myth" and Reality (A Response), 87 Yale L.J. 1549 (1978); Goldstein and Marcus, Comment on Continental Criminal Procedure, 87 Yale L.J. 1570 (1978); Robinson, Arrest, Prosecution and Police Power in the Federal Republic of Germany, 4 Duq.U.L.Rev. 225 (1965); Jescheck, Principles of German Criminal Law in Comparison with American Law, 56 Va.L.Rev. 239 (1970); Langbein, Comparative Criminal Procedure: Germany (1977); Symposium: The New German Penal Law, reproduced in 24 Amer.J.Comp.L. 589 (1976). Also see The Criminal Justice System of the Federal Republic of Germany, proceeding from the Conference sponsored by The American National Section of the Association Internationale de Droit Penal (1981).

For a coordinated series of publications in the field of comparative criminal law, see the following, under the sponsorship of the Comparative Criminal Law Project of New York University: Mueller (Ed.), Essays in Criminal Science (1961); Mueller & Wise, International Criminal Law (1965); and Andenaes (transl. by Ogle), The General Part of the Criminal Law of Norway (1965). Also see the series under the title The Comparative Study of the Administration of Justice (consisting primarily of reprints from other law journals), edited by Professor Francis C. Sullivan; and The American Series of Foreign Penal Codes, published by F. B. Rothman Co.

Chapter 2

ESSENTIAL CONCEPTS OF CRIMINALITY

A. THE PROHIBITED CONDUCT—"ACTUS REUS"

---

1. VOLUNTARY ACT

PEOPLE v. DECINA
Court of Appeals of New York, 1956.
2 N.Y.2d 133, 157 N.Y.S.2d 558, 138 N.E.2d 799.

FROESSEL, JUDGE. At about 3:30 p.m. on March 14, 1955, a bright, sunny day, defendant was driving, alone in his car, in a northerly direction on Delaware Avenue in the city of Buffalo. The portion of Delaware Avenue here involved is 60 feet wide. At a point south of an overhead viaduct of the Erie Railroad, defendant's car swerved to the left, across the center line in the street, so that it was completely in the south lane, traveling 35 to 40 miles per hour.

It then veered sharply to the right, crossing Delaware Avenue and mounting the easterly curb at a point beneath the viaduct and continued thereafter at a speed estimated to have been about 50 or 60 miles per hour or more. During this latter swerve, a pedestrian testified that he saw defendant's hand above his head; another witness said he saw defendant's left arm bent over the wheel, and his right hand extended towards the right door.

A group of six schoolgirls were walking north on the easterly sidewalk of Delaware Avenue, two in front and four slightly in the rear, when defendant's car struck them from behind. One of the girls escaped injury by jumping against the wall of the viaduct. The bodies of the children struck were propelled northward onto the street and the lawn in front of a coal company, located to the north of the Erie viaduct on Delaware Avenue. Three of the children, 6 to 12 years old, were found dead on arrival by the medical examiner, and a fourth child, 7 years old, died in a hospital two days later as a result of injuries sustained in the accident.

After striking the children, defendant's car continued on the easterly sidewalk, and then swerved back onto Delaware Avenue once more. It continued in a northerly direction passing under a second viaduct before it again veered to the right and remounted the easterly curb, striking and breaking a metal lamppost. With its horn blowing steadily—apparently because defendant was "stooped over" the steering wheel—the car proceeded on the sidewalk until it finally crashed through a 7¼-inch brick wall of a grocery store, injuring at least one customer and causing considerable property damage.

When the car came to a halt in the store, with its horn still blowing, several fires had been ignited. Defendant was stooped over in the car and was "bobbing a little". To one witness he appeared dazed, to another unconscious, lying back with his hands off the wheel. Various people present shouted to defendant to turn off the ignition of his car, and "within a matter of seconds the horn stopped blowing and the car did shut off."

Defendant was pulled out of the car by a number of bystanders and laid down on the sidewalk. To a policeman who came on the scene shortly he appeared "injured, dazed"; another witness said that "he looked as though he was knocked out, and his arm seemed to be bleeding". An injured customer in the store, after receiving first aid, pressed defendant for an explanation of the accident and he told her: "I blacked out from the bridge".

When the police arrived, defendant attempted to rise, staggered and appeared dazed and unsteady. When informed that he was under arrest, and would have to accompany the police to the station house, he resisted and, when he tried to get away, was handcuffed. The foregoing evidence was adduced by the People, and is virtually undisputed—defendant did not take the stand nor did he produce any witnesses.

From the police station defendant was taken to the E.J. Meyer Memorial Hospital. . . .

[There,] defendant proceeded to relate to Dr. Wechter his past medical history, namely, that at the age of 7 he was struck by an auto and suffered a marked loss of hearing. In 1946 he was treated in this same hospital for an illness during which he had some convulsions. Several burr holes were made in his skull and a brain abscess was drained. Following this operation defendant had no convulsions from 1946 through 1950. In 1950 he had four convulsions, caused by scar tissue on the brain. From 1950 to 1954 he experienced about 10 or 20 seizures a year, in which his right hand would jump although he remained fully conscious. In 1954, he had 4 or 5 generalized seizures with loss of consciousness, the last being in September, 1954, a few months before the accident. Thereafter he had more hospitalization, a spinal tap, consultation with a neurologist, and took medication daily to help prevent seizures.

On the basis of this medical history, Dr. Wechter made a diagnosis of Jacksonian epilepsy, and was of the opinion that defendant had a seizure at the time of the accident. Other members of the hospital staff performed blood tests and took an electroencephalogram during defendant's three-day stay there. The testimony of Dr. Wechter is the only testimony before the trial court showing that defendant had epilepsy, suffered an attack at the time of the accident, and had knowledge of his susceptibility to such attacks.

Defendant was indicted and charged with violating section 1053–a of the Penal Law, Consol.Laws, c. 40.[1] . . .

We turn first to the subject of defendant's cross appeal, namely, that his demurrer should have been sustained, since the *indictment* here does not charge a crime. The indictment states essentially that defendant, *knowing* "that he was subject to epileptic attacks or other disorder rendering him likely to lose consciousness for a considerable period of time", was culpably negligent "in that he *consciously* undertook to and *did operate* his Buick sedan on a public highway" (emphasis supplied) and "while so doing" suffered such an attack which caused said automobile "to travel at a fast and reckless rate of speed, jumping the curb and driving over the sidewalk" causing the death of 4 persons. In our opinion, this clearly states a violation of section 1053–a of the Penal Law. The statute does not require that a defendant must deliberately intend to kill a human being, for that would be murder. Nor does the statute require that he knowingly and consciously follow the precise path that leads to death and destruction. It is sufficient, we have said, when his conduct manifests a "disregard of the consequences which may ensue from the act, and indifference to the rights of others. No clearer definition, applicable to the hundreds of varying circumstances that may arise, can be given. Under a given state of facts, whether negligence is culpable is a question of judgment.". . .

Assuming the truth of the indictment, as we must on a demurrer, this defendant knew he was subject to epileptic attacks and seizures that might strike *at any time.* He also knew that a moving motor vehicle uncontrolled on a public highway is a highly dangerous instrumentality capable of unrestrained destruction. With this *knowledge,* and without anyone accompanying him, he deliberately took a chance by making a conscious choice of a course of action, in disregard of the consequences which he knew might follow from his conscious act, and which in this case did ensue. How can we say as a matter of law that this did not amount to culpable negligence within the meaning of section 1053–a?

To hold otherwise would be to say that a man may freely indulge himself in liquor in the same hope that it will not affect his driving, and if it later develops that ensuing intoxication causes dangerous and reckless driving resulting in death, his unconsciousness or involuntariness at that time would relieve him from prosecution under the statute. His awareness of a condition which he knows may produce such consequences as here, and his disregard of the consequences, renders him liable for culpable negligence, as the courts below have properly held. . . . To have a sudden sleeping spell, an unexpected heart or other disabling attack, without any prior knowledge or warning thereof,

---

1. "Any person who operates or drives any vehicle of any kind in a reckless or culpably negligent manner, whereby a human being is killed, is guilty of criminal negligence in the operation of a vehicle resulting in death". (A person convicted of violating § 1053–a is punishable by imprisonment up to 5 years, or a fine up to $1,000, or both. § 1053–b.)

is an altogether different situation, . . . and there is simply no basis for comparing such cases with the flagrant disregard manifested here. . . .

Accordingly, the Appellate Division properly sustained the lower court's order overruling the demurrer, as well as its denial of the motion in arrest of judgment on the same ground. . . .

DESMOND, JUDGE (dissenting in part). . . . The indictment charges that defendant knowing that "he was subject to epileptic attacks or other disorder rendering him likely to lose consciousness" suffered "an attack and loss of consciousness which caused the said automobile operated by the said defendant to travel at a fast and reckless rate of speed" and to jump a curb and run onto the sidewalk "thereby striking and causing the death" of 4 children. Horrible as this occurrence was and whatever necessity it may show for new licensing and driving laws, nevertheless this indictment charges no crime known to the New York statutes. Our duty is to dismiss it.

Section 1053–a of the Penal Law describes the crime of "criminal negligence in the operation of a vehicle resulting in death". Declared to be guilty of that crime is "A person who operates or drives any vehicle of any kind in a reckless or culpably negligent manner, whereby a human being is killed". The essentials of the crime are, therefore, first, vehicle *operation* in a culpably negligent *manner,* and second, the resulting death of a person. This indictment asserts that defendant violated section 1053–a, but it then proceeds in the language quoted in the next-above paragraph of this opinion to describe the way in which defendant is supposed to have offended against that statute. That descriptive matter (an inseparable and controlling ingredient of the indictment, . . .) shows that defendant did *not* violate section 1053–a. No *operation* of an automobile in a reckless manner is charged against defendant. The excessive speed of the car and its jumping the curb were "caused", says the indictment itself, by defendant's prior "attack and loss of consciousness". Therefore, what defendant is accused of is *not* reckless or culpably negligent driving, which necessarily connotes and involves consciousness and volition. The fatal assault by this car was after and because of defendant's failure of consciousness. To say that one drove a car in a reckless manner in that his unconscious condition caused the car to travel recklessly is to make two mutually contradictory assertions. One cannot be "reckless" while unconscious. One cannot while unconscious "operate" a car in a culpably negligent manner or in any other "manner". The statute makes criminal a particular kind of knowing, voluntary, immediate operation. It does not touch at all the involuntary presence of an unconscious person at the wheel of an uncontrolled vehicle. To negative the possibility of applying section 1053–a to these alleged facts we do not even have to resort to the rule that all criminal statutes are closely and strictly construed in favor of the citizen and that no act or omission is criminal unless specifically and in terms so labeled by a clearly worded statute, . . .

Tested by its history section 1053–a has the same meaning: penalization of conscious operation of a vehicle in a culpably negligent manner. It is significant that until this case . . . no attempt was ever made to penalize, either under section 1053–a or as manslaughter, the wrong done by one whose foreseeable blackout while driving had consequences fatal to another person.

The purpose of and occasion for the enactment of section 1053–a is well known (see Governor's Bill Jacket on L.1936 ch. 733). It was passed to give a new label to, and to fix a lesser punishment for, the culpably negligent automobile driving which had formerly been prosecuted under section 1052 of the Penal Law defining manslaughter in the second degree. It had been found difficult to get manslaughter convictions against death-dealing motorists. But neither of the two statutes has ever been thought until now to make it a crime to drive a car when one is subject to attacks or seizures such as are incident to certain forms and levels of epilepsy and other diseases and conditions.

Now let us test by its consequences this new construction of section 1053–a. Numerous are the diseases and other conditions of a human being which make it possible or even likely that the afflicted person will lose control of his automobile. Epilepsy, coronary involvements, circulatory diseases, nephritis, uremic poisoning, diabetes, Meniere's syndrome, a tendency to fits of sneezing, locking of the knee, muscular contractions—any of these common conditions may cause loss of control of a vehicle for a period long enough to cause a fatal accident. An automobile traveling at only 30 miles an hour goes 44 feet in a second. Just what is the court holding here? No less than this: that a driver whose brief blackout lets his car run amuck and kill another has killed that other by reckless driving. But any such "recklessness" consists necessarily not of the erratic behavior of the automobile while its driver is unconscious, but of his driving at all when he knew he was subject to such attacks. Thus, it must be that such a blackout-prone driver is guilty of reckless driving whenever and as soon as he steps into the driver's seat of a vehicle. Every time he drives, accident or no accident, he is subject to criminal prosecution for reckless driving or to revocation of his operator's license. And how many of this State's 5,000,000 licensed operators are subject to such penalties for merely driving the cars they are licensed to drive? No one knows how many citizens or how many or what kind of physical conditions will be gathered in under this practically limitless coverage of section 1053–a of the Penal Law and section 58 and subdivision 3 of section 71 of the Vehicle and Traffic Law. It is no answer that prosecutors and juries will be reasonable or compassionate. A criminal statute whose reach is so unpredictable violates constitutional rights, as we shall now show.

When section 1053–a was new it was assailed as unconstitutional on the ground that the language "operate or drives any vehicle of any kind in a reckless or culpably negligent manner" was too indefinite since a driver could only guess as to what acts or omissions were meant. Constitutionality was upheld in People v. Gardner, . . . The then

Justice Lewis, later of this court, wrote in People v. Gardner that the statutory language was sufficiently explicit since "reckless driving" and "culpable negligence" had been judicially defined in manslaughter cases as meaning the operation of an automobile in such a way as to show a disregard of the consequences, . . . The *manner* in which a car is driven may be investigated by a jury, grand or trial, to see whether the manner was such as to show a reckless disregard of consequences. But giving section 1053–a the new meaning assigned to it permits punishment of one who did not drive in any forbidden manner but should not have driven at all, according to the present theory. No motorist suffering from any serious malady or infirmity can with impunity drive any automobile at any time or place, since no one can know what physical conditions make it "reckless" or "culpably negligent" to drive an automobile. Such a construction of a criminal statute offends against due process and against justice and fairness. The courts are bound to reject such conclusions when, as here, it is clearly possible to ascribe a different but reasonable meaning, . . .

A whole new approach may be necessary to the problem of issuing or refusing drivers' licenses to epileptics and persons similarly afflicted . . . But the absence of adequate licensing controls cannot in law or in justice be supplied by criminal prosecutions of drivers who have violated neither the language nor the intendment of any criminal law.

Entirely without pertinence here is any consideration of driving while intoxicated or while sleepy, since those are conditions presently known to the driver, not mere future possibilities or probabilities.

The demurrer should be sustained and the indictment dismissed.

CONWAY, CH. J., DYE and BURKE, JJ., concur with FROESSEL, J.; DESMOND, J., concurs in part and dissents in part in an opinion in which FULD and VAN VOORHIS, JJ., concur.

Order affirmed.

NOTES

1. The speaking of words can be the voluntary "act" upon which a prosecution can be based. This will be discussed later when studying the inchoate (or substantive) crime of solicitation to commit a crime. When a prosecution is based on spoken words, can the accused defend by claiming a First Amendment freedom of speech?

2. Possession of something which it is illegal to possess can also serve as the "act" in criminal prosecutions, provided the possession is knowing.

2. INACTION

COMMONWEALTH v. KONZ

Supreme Court of Pennsylvania, 1982.
498 Pa. 639, 450 A.2d 638.

FLAHERTY, JUSTICE.

This is an appeal from an order of the Superior Court which reversed a decision of the Court of Common Pleas of the Thirty-First Judicial District granting a Motion in Arrest of Judgment to the appellants, Dorothy A. Konz and Stephen R.C. Erikson, subsequent to their being found guilty of involuntary manslaughter in a trial by jury. The prosecution of Dorothy Konz arose from her failure to comply with an alleged duty to seek medical assistance for Reverend David G. Konz, her husband, when he was stricken with a diabetic crisis which proved fatal. The prosecution of Erikson rested upon his alleged role as an accomplice in that breach of duty.

Viewed in the light most favorable to the Commonwealth, as verdict winner, the following facts were established at trial. In September, 1973, Reverend Konz, while serving as a teacher, counselor, and chaplain at United Wesleyan College, became acquainted with Erikson, a student at the College. A close friendship, based on their common interest in religion, formed between Erikson and Reverend Konz as the former became a regular visitor at the latter's residence.

Reverend Konz was a thirty-four year old diabetic and had, for seventeen years, administered to himself daily doses of insulin. On March 4, 1974, however, following an encounter on campus with a visiting evangelist speaker, Reverend Konz publicly proclaimed his desire to discontinue insulin treatment in reliance on the belief that God would heal the diabetic condition. He assured the president of the College and members of the student body that he would carefully monitor his condition and would, if necessary, take insulin. On only one or two occasions did the Reverend thereafter administer insulin. On March 18, 1974, however, Erikson and Reverend Konz formed a pact to pray together to enable the latter to resist the temptation to administer insulin.

Mrs. Konz was informed of the prayer pact, and, on the morning of Saturday, March 23, 1974, when her husband evidenced symptoms of insulin debt, she removed his insulin from the refrigerator and concealed it. Later that day, the Reverend attempted to obtain insulin from the refrigerator, and, upon discovering that the medicine had been removed, strongly indicated that it should be returned. He then attempted to proceed from room to room but his passage was blocked by Erikson. Harsh words were exchanged, and Erikson, after kneeling in prayer, forced the Reverend into a bedroom where, accompanied by Mrs. Konz, Erikson and the Reverend conversed for approximately one half hour. During that time, the Reverend tried to telephone police to obtain assistance but was prevented from doing so by Erikson and Mrs. Konz, who, during a struggle with the Reverend, rendered at least that telephone permanently inoperable. Immediately after this confrontation, the Reverend, his wife, and Erikson returned amicably to the kitchen for coffee, and no further request for insulin was ever made. In addition, the Reverend approached his aunt who resided in the same household and stated, in an apparent reference to the preceding confrontation with Erikson, that "It's all settled now," and told her that there was no cause for concern. He also told his eleven year old daughter that "Everything is fine," and indicated to her that he did not intend to take insulin. The Reverend then departed from the house, accompanied by Erikson, and returned an hour later. As the day progressed, Reverend Konz cancelled his speaking commitment for the following day and drove his wife to an institution having hospital facilities to pick up a close friend who was a practical nurse. Late on Saturday night, while waiting inside the institution for the nurse to complete her duties, the Reverend appeared very fatigued and complained that he was developing an upset stomach. Both of these conditions were symptomatic of lack of insulin, but neither the Reverend nor his wife requested that insulin, which was available at the institution, be administered. With regard to the Reverend's condition at that time, the nurse observed that he travelled with unimpaired mobility, and that he was conversant, rational, and cognizant of his environs. Nevertheless, he made no mention of a need for insulin, and the nurse made no inquiry as to such a need because the Reverend had on a previous day become very upset at her inquiry as to his diabetic condition.

Upon returning home from this errand, Reverend Konz experienced increasing illness, vomiting intermittently Saturday night and Sunday morning, and remained in bed all day Sunday except for trips into the bathroom. On Sunday afternoon visitors arrived at the Konz residence. The Reverend, recognizing their voices, called to them from his room to inquire whether they wished to see him; having been informed of the Reverend's nausea, however, the visitors declined to stay. As the Reverend's condition worsened and he became restless, his wife and Erikson administered cracked ice but did not summon medical aid. The Konz's eleven year-old daughter then inquired as to why a doctor had not been summoned but Mrs. Konz responded that her husband was "going to be getting better." Late Sunday night or early Monday morning everyone in the household fell asleep. On Monday morning at approximately 6 AM, while the others were still asleep, Reverend Konz died of diabetic ketoacidosis.

Appellants were found guilty by a jury of the crime of involuntary manslaughter pursuant to Section 2504 of the Pennsylvania Crimes Code, which provides: "A person is guilty of involuntary manslaughter when as a direct result of the doing of an unlawful act in a reckless or grossly negligent manner, or the doing of a lawful act in a reckless or grossly negligent manner, he causes the death of another person." To impose criminal liability for an omission as opposed to an act, the omission must be "expressly made sufficient by the law defining the offense," or "a duty to perform the omitted act [must be] otherwise imposed by law." . . . The determinative issue on appeal, therefore, is whether Mrs. Konz had a duty to seek medical attention for her spouse. Under the circumstances of this case, we find no such duty to have been present; hence, the conviction of Mrs. Konz, and that of Erkison as her accomplice, cannot be sustained.

Courts have, in limited circumstances, departed from the long-standing common law rule that one human being is under no *legal* compulsion to take action to aid another human being. One such circumstance is where there exists a requisite status of relationship between the parties, as is present in the relationship of parent to child. Hence, a parent has been held guilty of involuntary manslaughter for failure to seek medical assistance for his sick child. The inherent dependency of a child upon his parent to obtain medical aid, i.e., the incapacity of a child to evaluate his condition and summon aid by himself, supports imposition of such a duty upon the parent.

The Commonwealth argues that the marital relationship gives rise to a similar duty to aid one's spouse. Spouses, however, do not generally suffer the same incapacity as do children with respect to the ability to comprehend their states of health and obtain medical assistance. We reject, therefore, the holding of the Superior Court that the marital relationship gives rise to an unrestricted duty for one spouse to summon medical aid whenever the other is in a serious or immediate need of medical attention. Recognition of such a duty would place lay persons in peril of criminal prosecution while compelling them to medically diagnose the seriousness of their spouses' illnesses and injuries. In addition, it would impose an obligation for a spouse to take action at a time when the stricken individual competently chooses *not* to receive assistance. The marital relationship gives rise to an expectation of reliance between spouses, and to a belief that one's spouse should be trusted to respect, rather than ignore, one's expressed preferences. That expectation would be frustrated by imposition of a broad duty to seek aid, since one's spouse would then be forced to ignore the expectation that the preference to forego assistance will be honored.

Since there is no precedent in this Commonwealth addressing the existence of the particular spousal duty in question, it is to be noted that certain other jurisdictions have regarded the marital relationship as sufficient, in itself, to invoke a limited duty for one spouse to seek medical care for the other. In Westrup v. Commonwealth, 123 Ky. 95, 93 S.W. 646 (1906), the defendant's pregnant wife insisted that she did not want medical aid for the birth of their child. Soon after giving birth, however, she suffered complications; the defendant then summoned a physician, but the physician was unable, at that point, to prevent the wife's death. Finding that the defendant had acted in good faith and at his wife's competent request in not obtaining aid sooner, the court found no breach of duty to the wife. Reversing the conviction, the court stated:

> Where the husband neglects to provide necessaries for his wife, or medical attention in case of her illness, he will be guilty of involuntary manslaughter, provided it appears that she was in a *helpless state and unable to appeal elsewhere for aid,* and that the death, though not intended nor anticipated by him, was the natural and reasonable consequence of his negligence. (Emphasis added.)

Hence, prior to his wife's lapsing into an unexpected and helpless condition, the defendant was not obliged to override the mature conscious and rational decision of his wife to forego assistance.

A limited spousal duty was similarly recognized in State v. Mally, 139 Mont. 599, 366 P.2d 868 (1961), wherein the defendant's wife was in poor physical condition prior to the occurrence of an accident in which both of her arms were fractured. After the accident, defendant allowed his wife to lay in a semi-comatose condition while she decried the need for aid for two days before he summoned a physician, and this delay caused her death. Affirming defendant's involuntary manslaughter conviction, the court stated:

> We are aware that the large majority of homicide cases involving a failure to provide medical aid involve a parent-child relationship. This is undoubtedly due to the fact that a person of mature years is not generally in a helpless condition. However, fact situations do arise, such as the instant case, wherein it is apparent *that an adult is as helpless as the newborn.* The record is replete with evidence that [decedent] could not have *consciously or rationally denied medical aid.* (Emphasis added.)

Unlike the foregoing cases, however, the instant case is not one wherein there is evidence of the stricken spouse having unintentionally entered a helpless state, or of having been less than competent to consciously and rationally deny medical aid. Rather, the record supports only the conclusion that subsequent to the incident on Saturday, March 23, 1974, when Reverend Konz was briefly restrained in a bedroom by Erikson, the Reverend was in such mental condition as to fairly understand and appreciate his situation and had ample opportunity to request assistance but chose, instead, to forego medical treatment. Hence, assuming that one spouse owes the other a duty to seek aid when the latter is unwillingly rendered incompetent to evaluate the need for aid, or helpless to obtain it, that duty would not have been breached under the facts presented.

Subsequent to being restrained by Erikson in a bedroom for one half hour on the Saturday preceding his death, Reverend Konz elected on numerous occasions not to obtain insulin. The record does not support the inference raised by the Superior Court that the Reverend was, against his will, and until his death, continuously held incommunicado as an isolated captive of Erikson and Mrs. Konz while being denied the opportunity to secure medical assistance.

After announcing that the confrontation with Erikson was "settled," Reverend Konz could easily have addressed a request for insulin to his aunt, to his daughter, to the clergyman to whom he spoke to cancel a speaking engagement for Sunday, to persons at the hospital facility to which he drove Saturday night, to the nurse with whom he conversed late Saturday night, or to visitors at his home on Sunday. The Reverend not only remained silent as to a desire for insulin, however, but even took the initiative to reassure his aunt and daughter that there was no cause for concern. This course of behavior is inconsistent with any conclusion other than that the Reverend, by Saturday evening had become firmly resolved to abstain from the administration of insulin. Had the Reverend been dissatisfied with his treatment, as a diabetic would be in the event of being forcibly denied insulin, he presumably would have attempted to obtain the medication or to call his dissatisfaction to the attention of persons with whom he came in contact. Yet, the record is devoid of any evidence that such an effort was made. Nor can the Reverend's acquiescence be attributed to a lack of mental competency to comprehend and militate against his plight. The testimony of the nurse with whom the Reverend conversed on Saturday night, as well as the Reverend's reaction to the presence of visitors in his home on Sunday, indicate clearly that the Reverend was in an alert and rational condition. Hence, the conclusion is inescapable that Reverend Konz, having been a diabetic for seventeen years, was aware of the importance of insulin to the preservation of his life but competently chose to forego treatment. Under this circumstance, we find no breach of duty to have been incurred by Mrs. Konz in her failure to seek medical aid for her husband.

Order reversed and appellants discharged.

NIX, J., files a concurring opinion.

McDERMOTT, J., files a dissenting opinion in which LARSEN, J., joins.

NIX, JUSTICE, concurring.

This case raises the possibility of criminal liability as to both defendants as a consequence of their affirmative acts of Saturday, March 23, 1974. As to Mrs. Konz, it also raises the question of possible criminal liability for her *failure to act* between the events of Saturday evening and Monday morning (when Rev. Konz died) in view of the relationship she shared with the decedent. For the reasons that follow, I am satisfied the instant record does not support criminal liability under either theory.

In this appeal there is no causal connection between the acts of appellants and the death of Rev. Konz. The record is clear that the appellants' prevention of the decedent's attempt to administer insulin on Saturday was in no way causally connected with the death on Monday morning. Subsequent to the events of Saturday, the Reverend had numerous opportunities to seek help if he wanted an insulin injection. His conscious decision to continue to forego insulin after the events of Saturday constituted an intervening, superseding cause, thus cutting off any connection between appellants' affirmative actions on Saturday and Rev. Konz's death on Monday.

The more difficult question presented is whether there is a duty upon a spouse to seek medical aid for the other partner in contravention of the conscious decision of the ill spouse. The majority correctly notes that this is not a situation where one spouse is unable, because of a weakened condition, "to evaluate the need for [medical] aid, or helpless to obtain it,. . . ."

Without determining whether a healthy spouse has to seek medical aid for a physically infirm spouse in spite of the conscious choice of the ill spouse, it is clear that if such a duty were required it could not be operative in this case. The knowledge requisite to show criminal responsibility for failure to act must include knowledge of the risk of danger or life. Since the wife here had no superior knowledge of medicine and apparently shared her husband's religious views, the knowledge essential to the establishment of an affirmative duty is lacking and the requisite mental state does not exist.

Thus, I concur in the result.

MCDERMOTT, JUSTICE, dissenting.

I dissent from the Court's decision, which disregards the jury's verdict, as well as our own maxim that, upon appeal, the evidence adduced at trial must be viewed in the light most favorable to the verdict winner.

The Reverend David Konz, the deceased in this case, was an ordained minister. His ministry was in the academic world: professor, chaplin [sic] and counselor at the United Wesleyan College. He lived with his wife, appellant Dorothy Konz, and five children in West Bethlehem, Pennsylvania. While in the Marine Corps, he discovered he was a diabetic and for seventeen of his thirty-seven years he required quotidian injections of insulin.

In early March of 1974, Reverend Konz attended an evangelical prayer meeting. At that meeting, he was inspired to believe that his long standing burden of diabetes was lifted. On March 4, 1974, Reverend Konz proclaimed in church his desire to withdraw from insulin and trust in the efficacy of his faith to heal his diabetes.

His academic and religious confreres reminded him of the wisdom that God works through His creation; that Heaven cannot be stormed, God tempted, nor His will substituted. Reverend Konz later assured the president of the college, members of the student body and others that he would do nothing foolish, would carefully monitor his condition, and would take insulin, if warranted, during the withdrawal period.

For about three weeks, he put his faith to test and took insulin only once or twice. On March 18, 1974, Reverend Konz and appellant Stephen Erikson, a frequent visitor in the Konz home, made a pact to pray together to enable the decedent to resist the temptation to administer insulin to himself.

At the end of March, the crisis came. Reverend Konz' symptoms escalated, his resolve yielded and he sought the medicine. It is then that this case took its bizarre twist. Appellants, his companions in prayer, denied him the insulin by removing it from the refrigerator and hiding it. They forced him physically into his bedroom and deliberately ripped out the phone so that he could not call the police, as he threatened, or summon other help. They made him the unwilling prisoner of the resolve he had abandoned. Appellants' determination, *their* faith and *their* hope were substituted for his. From the evidence as accepted by the jury there can be no question that appellants recklessly sacrificed the life of David Konz for *their* belief. They purposely isolated him and denied him access to help; they watched and ministered to his last extremity and brought ice packs to tide him over the gap between *their* faith and the miracle. He had pain and vomited. Visitors were told simply that he was resting. Wherever he went, one of the appellants went also. Help, but a needle point away, was discouraged and denied. His eleven year-old daughter, a witness to his forcible imprisonment, asked why a physician was not summoned. Reverend Konz died at 6:00 a.m. on Monday, March 25, 1974, the victim of a ruthless, reckless determination that he be cured.[1]

The majority has adopted the view that Reverend Konz died because he wanted to; that this careful father of five children, whose last visit to the world was to take his daughter shopping for shoes, simply died for a blessing he knew had failed. Unless the rule that the verdict-winner is entitled to all favorable inferences has meaning only in weariness or whim, the verdict of the jury in this case must be sustained. The jury resolved against appellants all the inferences now adopted in appellants' favor by the majority. They saw and heard all the evidence and, under an appropriate and lawful charge by the trial court, they found appellants guilty of involuntary manslaughter, as set forth in Section 2504 of the Crimes Code:

> A person is guilty of involuntary manslaughter when as a direct result of the doing of an unlawful act in a reckless or grossly negligent manner, he causes the death of another person.

I believe that, on the evidence recited above, the jury could properly have found that the affirmative actions of appellants in purposely depriving Reverend Konz of his life-sustaining insulin, in violently restraining his attempts to obtain assistance, and in deliberately isolating him from others from whom he might have sought aid satisfies the factual requirements of Section 2504. The jury was certainly not obliged to view the situation as the majority chooses to frame it, i.e., that there could be no "conclusion other than that the Reverend . . .

1. Although Dorothy Konz was aware of her husband's death as early as 7:30   a.m. Monday, she did not attempt to notify the authorities until 5:00 p.m.

became firmly resolved to abstain from the administration of insulin," regardless of the consequences.[2]

The majority's "inescapable" conclusion is rendered all the more astonishing in light of the charge of the trial judge, who put the issue squarely before the jury:

> In this regard it is the law that a rational person has a right to refuse medical treatment, and he has a right to refuse it for any reason whatsoever, and that includes religious convictions. *If Reverend Konz did refuse treatment or did not want treatment and refused the taking of insulin and that this was his choice, the defendants are clearly entitled to a verdict of not guilty.* And on this point I charge you *it is incumbent upon the Commonwealth to prove beyond a reasonable doubt that Reverend Konz did so refuse. . . .*

(Emphasis supplied). The jury's verdict demonstrates without a doubt that it did not credit the proposition, upon which the majority relies, that Reverend Konz chose to forgo insulin and medical treatment. This court is in no position to second-guess the fact-finder on such a clear issue of fact.

It does not matter what the relationship between appellants and decedent may have been, spouse or friend, in the real world beyond the situation precipitating the crisis which cost Reverend Konz his life. What appellants' duties might be under different circumstances or in another context is not relevant. Appellants created their own circumstances and context and lived them out in a reckless, even ruthless, fashion. They did not simply stand by while Reverend Konz expired.[3] Despite the majority's creative re-interpretation of the facts, the record shows deliberate steps taken by appellants to keep from Reverend Konz the vital substance which he *needed and wanted* to save his life. The jury, having been carefully instructed as to the elements of involuntary manslaughter, properly could have found on this record that appellants' actions were reckless or grossly negligent and that they directly caused Reverend Konz' death. No more is required to sustain a conviction under Section 2504.[4]

I would affirm the order of the Superior Court, reinstating the jury's verdict.

LARSEN, J., joins in this dissenting opinion.

---

2. The majority draws its "inescapable" conclusion that Reverend Konz chose "to forgo treatment" from thin air. There is nothing whatsoever in the record to suggest that Reverend Konz stopped taking insulin in order to end his life, or even that he preferred death to life as a diabetic. In fact, the evidence is strongly to the contrary.

3. The jury's verdict shows that we are not presented here with a case concerning the right to die or euthanasia or "mercy-killing," in which appellants simply acquiesced in Reverend Konz' decision to die. Nor is this a situation in which appellants merely failed to seek medical assistance for the deceased. The jury faced these issues squarely and resolved them against appellants.

4. Indeed, in less charitable hands the charge might have risen higher than involuntary manslaughter.

NOTES

1. If a person who is under a legal obligation to care for an infant of tender years wilfully withholds needful food or any other needful thing, though not with intent to kill, and by reason thereof the child dies, a homicide is committed. If death is the direct consequence of the malicious omission of the performance of a duty, such as of a mother to feed her child, this is a case of murder; but if the omission is not wilful, and arose out of neglect only, it is manslaughter. See Biddle v. Commonwealth, 206 Va. 14, 141 S.E.2d 710 (1965). See also, Commonwealth v. Gallison, 383 Mass. 659, 421 N.E.2d 757 (1981), holding that a parent's failure to get medical help for an infant child may be manslaughter, and Singleton v. State, 33 Ala.App. 536, 35 So.2d 375 (1948), holding it can possibly be murder as well. See also, People v. Robbins, 83 A.D.2d 271, 443 N.Y.S.2d 1016 (4th Dept.1981). In Vaughan v. Commonwealth, 7 Va.App. 665, 376 S.E.2d 801 (1989), the court held that a sixteen-year-old woman who had just given unattended childbirth had a legal duty to give postpartum care to the baby.

Does the same duty rest on a babysitter, caretaker, relative, or landlord? See, e.g., Jones v. United States, 308 F.2d 307 (D.C.Cir.1962).

2. In People v. Beardsley, 150 Mich. 206, 113 N.W. 1128 (1907), defendant arranged for Blanche, a woman friend, to visit him in his apartment while his wife was out of town. They both got drunk and at some time during the weekend the woman asked a store clerk to bring her some morphine tablets. When defendant surprised her taking some of them, he struck the box from her hands and crushed some of the tablets which fell on the floor with his foot, though she picked up and swallowed two tablets. The woman went into a stupor and defendant and the clerk took her to a basement apartment. He asked the downstairs tenant to look after her and let her out the back when she woke up. The tenant became alarmed later that evening and called a doctor, who determined that she was dead. After defendant's conviction of manslaughter on a theory that he owed to the victim a duty which he had failed to perform, he appealed. In reversing the conviction, the court said, in part:

> "The law recognizes that under some circumstances the omission of a duty owed by one individual to another, where such omission results in the death of the one to whom the duty is owing, will make the other chargeable with manslaughter. . . . This rule of law is always based upon the proposition that the duty neglected must be a legal duty, and not a mere moral obligation. It must be a duty imposed by law or by contract, and the omission to perform the duty must be the immediate and direct cause of death. . . .

> "Although the literature upon the subject is quite meagre and the cases few . . . one authority has briefly and correctly stated the rule . . .: 'If a person who sustains to another the legal relation of protector, as husband to wife, parent to child, master to seaman, etc., knowing such person to be in peril, willfully and negligently fails to make such reasonable and proper efforts to rescue him as he might have done, without jeopardizing his own life, or the lives of others, he is guilty of manslaughter at least, if by reason of his omission of duty the dependent person dies.' 'So one who from domestic relationship, public duty, voluntary choice, or otherwise, has the custody and care of a human being, helpless either from imprisonment, infancy, sickness,

age, imbecility, or other incapacity of mind or body is bound to execute the charge with proper diligence, and will be held guilty of manslaughter, if by capable negligence he lets the helpless creature die.' 21 Am. & Eng.Enc. of Law (2d Ed.) p. 192. . . .

* * *

". . . Seeking for a proper determination of the case at bar by the application of the legal principles involved, we must eliminate from the case all consideration of mere moral obligation, and discover whether respondent was under a legal duty toward Blanche Burns at the time of her death, knowing her to be in peril of her life, which required him to make all reasonable and proper efforts to save her, the omission to perform which duty would make him responsible for her death. . . . If we hold that such legal duty rested upon respondent, it must arise by implication from the facts and circumstances already recited. The record in this case discloses that the deceased was a woman past 30 years of age. She had been twice married. She was accustomed to visiting saloons and to the use of intoxicants. She previously had made assignations with this man in Detroit at least twice. There is no evidence or claim from this record that any duress, fraud or deceit had been practiced upon her. On the contrary, it appears that she went upon this carouse with respondent voluntarily, and so continued to remain with him. Her entire conduct indicates that she had ample experience in such affairs.

"It is urged by the prosecutor that the respondent 'stood towards this woman for the time being in the place of her natural guardian and protector, and as such owed her a clear legal duty which he completely failed to perform.' . . . The fact that this woman was in his house created no such legal duty as exists in law and is due from a husband towards his wife, as seems to be intimated by the prosecutor's brief. Such an inference would be very repugnant to our moral sense. Respondent had assumed either in fact or by implication no care or control over his companion. Had this been a case where two men under like circumstances had voluntarily gone on a debauch together, and one had attempted suicide, no one would claim that this doctrine of legal duty could be invoked to hold the other criminally responsible for omitting to make effort to rescue his companion. How can the fact that in this case one of the parties was a woman change the principle of law applicable to it? Deriving and applying the law in this case from the principle of decided cases, we do not find that such legal duty as is contended for existed in fact or by implication on the part of respondent toward the deceased. . . ."

3. Husband is convicted of first degree rape upon his daughter because of a sexual relationship that had been going on for some time, and wife is convicted of being an accomplice to the first degree rape because she knew of the relationship between her husband and her daughter. Wife had done nothing to protect the child and did not intervene on the child's behalf. Does wife have a legal duty to make an effort to prevent the rape? See, Knox v. Commonwealth, 735 S.W.2d 711 (Ky.1987).

4. The duty to act may be imposed by statute. Under 26 U.S.C.A. § 7203 a person who is required by the Internal Revenue Act to file tax returns "who willfully fails to . . . make such a return" shall be guilty of a misdemeanor.

B. MENTAL STATE—"MENS REA"

1. SPECIFIC AND GENERAL INTENT

THACKER v. COMMONWEALTH

Supreme Court of Virginia, 1922.
134 Va. 767, 114 S.E. 504.

WEST, J. This writ of error is to a judgment upon the verdict of a jury finding John Thacker, the accused, guilty of attempting to murder Mrs. J.A. Ratrie, and fixing his punishment at two years in the penitentiary.

* * *

The only assignment of error is the refusal of the trial court to set aside the verdict as contrary to the law and the evidence.

The accused, in company with two other young men, Doc Campbell and Paul Kelly, was attending a church festival in Alleghany county, at which all three became intoxicated. They left the church between 10 and 11 o'clock at night, and walked down the county road about 1½ miles, when they came to a sharp curve. Located in this curve was a tent in which the said Mrs. J.A. Ratrie, her husband, four children, and a servant were camping for the summer. The husband, though absent, was expected home that night, and Mrs. Ratrie, upon retiring, had placed a lighted lamp on a trunk by the head of her bed. After 11 o'clock she was awakened by the shots of a pistol and loud talking in the road nearby, and heard a man say, "I am going to shoot that God-damned light out;" and another voice said, "Don't shoot the light out." The accused and his friends then appeared at the back of the tent, where the flaps of the tent were open, and said they were from Bath county and had lost their way, and asked Mrs. Ratrie if she could take care of them all night. She informed them she was camping for the summer, and had no room for them. One of the three thanked her, and they turned away, but after passing around the tent the accused used some vulgar language and did some cursing and singing. When they got back in the road, the accused said again he was going to shoot the light out, and fired three shots, two of which went through the tent, one passing through the head of the bed in which Mrs. Ratrie was lying, just missing her head and the head of her baby, who was sleeping with her. The accused did not know Mrs. Ratrie, and had never seen her before. He testified he did not know any of the parties in the tent, and had no ill will against either of them; that he simply shot at the light, without any intent to harm Mrs. Ratrie or any one else; that he would not have shot had he been sober, and regretted his action.

The foregoing are the admitted facts in the case.

An attempt to commit a crime is composed of two elements: (1) The intent to commit it; and (2) a direct, ineffectual act done towards its commission. The act must reach far enough towards the accomplishment of the desired result to amount to the commencement of the consummation.

The law can presume the intention so far as realized in the act, but not an intention beyond what was so realized. The law does not presume, because an assault was made with a weapon likely to produce death, that it was an assault with the intent to murder. And where it takes a particular intent to constitute a crime, that particular intent must be proved either by direct or circumstantial evidence, which would warrant the inference of the intent with which the act was done.

When a statute makes an offense to consist of an act combined with a particular intent, that intent is just as necessary to be proved as the act itself, and must be found as a matter of fact before a conviction can be had; and no intent in law or mere legal presumption, differing from the intent in fact, can be allowed to supply the place of the latter.

* * *

Mr. Bishop, in his Criminal Law, vol. 1 (8th Ed.), at section 729, says:

"When the law makes an act, whether more or less evil in itself, punishable, though done simply from general malevolence, if one takes what, were all accomplished, would be a step towards it, yet if he does not mean to do the whole, no court can justly hold him answerable for more than he does. And when the thing done does not constitute a substantive crime, there is no ground for treating it as an attempt. So that necessarily an act prompted by general malevolence, or by a specific design to do something else, is not an attempt to commit a crime not intended. * * * When we say that a man attempted to do a given wrong, we mean that he intended to do specifically it, and proceeded a certain way in the doing. The intent in the mind covers the thing in full; the act covers it only in part. Thus (section 730) to commit murder, one need not intend to take life, but to be guilty of an attempt to murder, he must so intend. It is not sufficient that his act, had it proved fatal, would have been murder. Section 736. We have seen that the unintended taking of life may be murder, yet there can be no attempt to murder without the specific intent to commit it—a rule the latter branch whereof appears probably in a few of the states to have been interfered with by statutes (citing Texas cases). For example, if one from a housetop recklessly throws down a billet of wood upon the sidewalk where persons are constantly passing, and it falls upon a person passing by and kills him, this would be the common-law murder, but if, instead of killing, it inflicts only a slight injury, the party could not be convicted of an assault with attempt to commit murder, since, in fact, the murder was not intended."

The application of the foregoing principles to the facts of the instant case shows clearly, as we think, that the judgment complained of is erroneous. While it might possibly be said that the firing of the shot into the head of Mrs. Ratrie's bed was an act done towards the commission of the offense charged, the evidence falls far short of proving that it was fired with the intent to murder her.

However averse we may be to disturb the verdict of the jury, our obligation to the law compels us to do so.

The judgment [of guilty of attempting to murder] will be reversed, the verdict of the jury set aside, and the case remanded for a new trial therein, if the commonwealth shall be so advised.

Reversed.

STATE v. ROCKER

Supreme Court of Hawaii, 1970.
52 Hawaii 336, 475 P.2d 684.

RICHARDSON, CHIEF JUSTICE. Defendants-appellants, having waived a jury trial, were tried in the circuit court of the second circuit and found guilty as charged for violation of HRS § 727–1 for creating a common nuisance. The complaint read: "That Richard Barry Rocker and Joseph Cava [defendants] at Puu Olai, Makena, District of Makawao, County of Maui, State of Hawaii, on the 26th day of February, 1969, did openly sun bathe in the nude, which was offensive and against common decency or common morality, thereby committing the offense of common nuisance, contrary to the provisions of Section 727–1 of the Hawaii Revised Statutes."

It is undisputed that on February 26, 1969, police officers of the Maui Police Department received a phone call from an anonymous person and, thereafter, on the day of the call, proceeded to the Puu Olai beach at Makena to look for nude sunbathers. On reaching their destination, the police surveyed the beach from a ridge using both their naked eyes and binoculars and saw the defendants lying on the beach completely nude, one on his stomach and the other on his back. The officers then approached the defendants and arrested them for indecent exposure. It was admitted by the police officers that defendants were not at any time engaged in any activity other than sunbathing. At the time of the arrest there were several other people on the beach where the defendants were nude. Defendant Rocker was nude at the Puu Olai beach on other days before and after he was arrested on February 26, 1969. Defendant Cava likewise frequently sunbathed in the nude at the same beach prior to his arrest on February 26, 1969.

I. *Indecent Exposure: Elements*

The first issue we are asked to decide on this appeal is whether defendants created a common nuisance by sunbathing in the nude on a public beach.

The statute (HRS § 727-1) reads as follows:

The offense of common nuisance is the endangering of the public personal safety or health, or doing, causing or promoting, maintaining or continuing what is offensive, or annoying and vexatious, or plainly hurtful to the public; or is a public outrage against common decency or common morality; or tends plainly and directly to the corruption of the morals, honesty, and good habits of the people; the same being without authority or justification by law:

As for example: * * *

* * *

Open lewdness or lascivious behavior, or indecent exposure;

* * *

HRS § 727-1, unlike statutes of most states, incorporates indecent exposure as an example of what the legislature has defined to constitute common nuisances. The statute does not specifically delineate the elements of the crime of indecent exposure, and although reference to the common law or to cases decided in other jurisdictions based upon statutes different from ours may be helpful, neither is controlling. The question of whether sunbathing in the nude on a public beach is punishable as a common nuisance is one of construction of our statute.

* * *

. . . To create a common nuisance there must be an indecent exposure of the person in a public place where it may be seen by others if they pass by, and it need actually be seen by one person only.

However, to answer the specific questions presented to us on this appeal and to clarify and examine our construction of the statute in light of recent decisions in this and other jurisdictions, a further discussion of the elements of the crime of indecent exposure is needed.

A. *Intent*

Sunbathing in the nude is not per se illegal. It must be coupled with the intent to indecently expose oneself. Intent is an element of the crime of common nuisance defined by HRS § 727-1. The King v. Grieve, 6 Haw. 740 (1883). The intent necessary is a general intent, not a specific intent; i.e., it is not necessary that the exposure be made with the intent that some particular person see it, but only that the exposure was made where it was likely to be observed by others. Thus, the intent may be inferred from the conduct of the accused and the circumstances and environment of the occurrence. The criminal intent necessary for a conviction of indecent exposure is usually established by some action by which the defendant either (1) draws attention to his exposed condition or (2) by a display in a place so public that it must be presumed it was intended to be seen by others.

The defendants argue that there is no circumstantial evidence in the record from which a trier of fact could conclude that the element of intent had been proved beyond a reasonable doubt. The issue, therefore, is whether defendants' nude sunbathing at Puu Olai beach at Makena, Maui, was at a place *so public* that a trier of fact could infer it was intended to be seen by others. The prosecution offered testimony of one of the arresting police officers that the beach was a popular location for fishermen and was in fact one of his favorite fishing spots. Defendants testified that the public in general used the beach, that it was used by fishermen and local residents, and that they observed between 20 and 25 people on the beach over a two-month period. Although the Puu Olai beach is isolated by a hill and a ledge, away from the view of the public road and adjoining beaches, it is accessible by a well-worn path and known to be a favorite location of fishermen to cast and throw fish nets. In view of this and other evidence in the record, we cannot agree with defendants' argument that the trier of fact could not find the beach so public as to justify an inference of intent on the part of defendants to be seen by others.

* * *

III. *Motion for Acquittal: Test on Appeal*

The third issue raised on this appeal is whether the trial court erred in denying the defendants' motion for judgment of acquittal at the end of the prosecution's case. Rule 29(a), Motion for Judgment of Acquittal, of the Hawaii Rules of Criminal Procedure states in relevant part:

> The court on motion of a defendant or of its own motion shall order the entry of judgment of acquittal of one or more offenses charged in the indictment or information after the evidence on either side is closed if the evidence is insufficient to sustain a conviction of such offense or offenses.

* * *

This court will not disturb the ruling of a lower court if the evidence of the prosecution is such that "a reasonable mind might fairly conclude guilt beyond a reasonable doubt." As discussed under section I of this opinion, the elements of the crime of indecent exposure that the prosecution must prove in order to establish a prima facie case against the defendants are that (1) the defendants expose themselves, (2) in a public place where it may be seen by others and (3) under circumstances that a trier of fact could infer a general intent of the defendants to offend the community's common sense of decency, propriety, and morality.

At the close of the prosecution's case it had been established that the defendants were seen by two police officers sunbathing in the nude at Puu Olai beach, a beach isolated by a hill and a ledge but accessible by a well worn path. One of the officers testified that the beach was a popular location for fishermen and was in fact one of his favorite fishing spots. From these facts the trial judge ruled that a prima facie case had been established and denied the defendants' motion for acquittal. We affirm this ruling. There was sufficient evidence at the close of the prosecution's case to justify an inference beyond a reasonable doubt that the Puu Olai beach was so public that the defendants could be attributed with the necessary knowledge to know that their acts under the circumstances were likely to offend members of the general public.

* * *

Affirmed.

LEVINSON, JUSTICE (dissenting).

* * *

III. THE EVIDENCE ADDUED BY THE GOVERNMENT AT THE CLOSE OF THE PROSECUTION'S CASE WAS INSUFFICIENT TO SUSTAIN A CONVICTION OF THE OFFENSE CHARGED.

Before proceeding to my analysis of the insufficiency of the evidence offered by the prosecution I feel compelled to state the facts in the record at the close of the prosecution's case. I do this because I believe that the majority has failed to segregate clearly the prosecution's evidence from that offered by the defense and has omitted stating a key fact which I believe raises a reasonable doubt as to the defendants' guilt.

A. *The Evidence in the Record at the Close of the Prosecution's Case-in-Chief.*

The State's case consisted solely of the testimony of the two arresting police officers. They both testified that the Puu Olai beach is isolated by a hill and a ledge, away from the view of the public road and adjoining beach. The beach is accessible by two trails. One is a well-worn path leading over the hill. The other is a trail on the Wailuku side of the beach, which is not well-used and connects the beach to a small road. The officers testified to being able to see, with the naked eye, the nudity of the defendants, from the crest of the hill.

One of the officers, George Matsunaga, testified that this beach was one of his favorite fishing spots and that it was a popular location for other fishermen. He also stated that the fishermen went to the beach in the "day or night." On examination by the court, Officer Matsunaga admitted that he had never seen the beach used for picnics or family recreation, and the only non-fishermen that he recalled having observed on this beach were what he called "hippie type characters." It was on this evidence alone that the State rested its case.

B. *Intent to Be Seen by Others.*

My reading of the majority opinion leads me to conclude that in order to prove a prima facie case against the defendants it was necessary for the prosecution to demonstrate that the defendants possessed a general intent to expose themselves in a place where it would be likely that they would be observed by others. To prove this, it would be enough for the prosecution to establish the defendants' awareness of sufficient facts and circumstances from which a trier of fact could infer such intent beyond a reasonable doubt. From the evidence in the record at the close of the prosecution's case I do not think that a trier of fact could be justified in inferring beyond a reasonable doubt that the defendants possessed the necessary general intent to be seen by others.

Although there was testimony that the beach was visited by fishermen there was no link established between the visits by the fishermen and visits to the beach by the defendants. Officer Matsunaga, one of the fishermen who used the beach, did not testify to ever having observed the defendants on this beach prior to arresting them. Thus, this evidence could not be used to support an inference that the defendants were aware that this beach was used by fishermen and therefore public.

Nor could a trier of fact infer beyond a reasonable doubt that the defendants were aware of the "well-worn" path leading over the hill to the beach and therefore knew that they were sunbathing in an area readily accessible to the public. One of the police officers testified that the beach was accessible by another trail which was *not* "well-used." There was no other evidence that would eliminate as a reasonable doubt the possibility that the defendants had used this other path and therefore inferred from its unused nature that the public would not be likely to see them. . . .

* * *

Since the prosecution failed to prove a prima facie case against the defendants the motion for acquittal was erroneously denied. I would reverse the convictions.

NOTES

1. The California Supreme Court, in In re Smith, 7 Cal.3d 362, 102 Cal. Rptr. 335, 497 P.2d 807 (1972), has ruled that nude sunbathing on an isolated beach without any other sexual act being performed, does not satisfy the requirements of the crime prohibiting the willful or lewd exposure of the private parts of the body. However, the Tenth Circuit Court of Appeals, in United States v. Hymans, 463 F.2d 615 (10th Cir.1972), upheld a conviction of male and female defendants who had engaged in "skinny dipping" in a national forest and were arrested while they were sunning themselves on the bank, eating watermelons. The court said it was not "persuaded by such nostalgic authorities as James Whitcomb Riley's 'The Old Swimming Hole', or Mark Twain's 'Adventures of Huckleberry Finn'."

2. In People v. Hardy, 77 Misc.2d 1092, 357 N.Y.S.2d 970 (1974), the court held that nude sunbathing on a public beach by the defendant, along with several other persons, did not in itself violate the New York public exposure statute (N.Y.Pen.Laws § 245.00): "Since no evidence was introduced establishing that defendant had intentionally exposed her private parts in a public place in a 'lewd' manner's or otherwise committed a 'lewd act,' her guilt was not established beyond a reasonable doubt."

In Duvallon v. State, 404 So.2d 196 (Fla.App.1981), defendant was protesting what she considered judicial and police corruption, and picketed in front of the state's capitol and across from its Supreme Court building "dressed" in a 44.5" × 28" piece of cardboard suspended by a cord around her neck. She was arrested and charged with exposure of sexual organs. In reversing her conviction, the court said, "We find no evidence in the present record that the petitioner exposed or exhibited her sexual organs in [a lewd and lascivious] manner. The arresting officer testified that the placard allowed exposure of her bare backside and the sides of her breasts, but he saw nothing lewd or lascivious about her conduct. The petitioner's behavior was, at a minimum, bizarre, but it falls short of being a vulgar and indecent exposure of her sexual organs."

3. One of the key elements of public exposure is that the exhibition be done from a place where the conduct in question may reasonably be expected to be viewed by others. This includes a person who, in his own home, exposes his penis either in front of the window or by an open door. People v. Garrison, 82 Ill.2d 444, 45 Ill.Dec. 132, 412 N.E.2d 483 (1980). See also, Anno. 96 A.L.R.3d 692. In State v. Muller, 365 So.2d 464 (La.1978), however, the court said that a supermarket is not "any location or place open to the view of the public or the people at large such as a street, highway, neutral ground, sidewalk, park, beach, river bank or other place or location viewable therefrom" under La.Rev. Stat. § 14:106 which defines the crime of obscenity and proscribes exposure of the sexual organs in such places.

CHEEK v. UNITED STATES

Supreme Court of the United States, 1991.
___ U.S. ___, 111 S.Ct. 604, 112 L.Ed.2d 617.

JUSTICE WHITE delivered the opinion of the Court.

*   *   *

I

Petitioner John L. Cheek has been a pilot for American Airlines since 1973. He filed federal income tax returns through 1979 but thereafter ceased to file returns. He also claimed an increasing number of withholding allowances—eventually claiming 60 allowances by mid–1980—and for the years 1981 to 1984 indicated on his W–4 forms that he was exempt from federal income taxes. In 1983, petitioner unsuccessfully sought a refund of all tax withheld by his employer in 1982. Petitioner's income during this period at all times far exceeded the minimum necessary to trigger the statutory filing requirement.

As a result of his activities, petitioner was indicted for 10 violations of federal law. He was charged with six counts of willfully failing to file a federal income tax return for the years 1980, 1981, and 1983 through 1986, in violation of 26 U.S.C. § 7203. He was further charged with three counts of willfully attempting to evade his income taxes for the years 1980, 1981, and 1983 in violation of 26 U.S.C. § 7201. In those years, American Airlines withheld substantially less than the amount of tax petitioner owed because of the numerous allowances and exempt status he claimed on his W–4 forms. The tax offenses with which petitioner was charged are specific intent crimes that require the defendant to have acted willfully.

At trial, the evidence established that between 1982 and 1986, petitioner was involved in at least four civil cases that challenged various aspects of the federal income tax system. In all four of those cases, the plaintiffs were informed by the courts that many of their arguments, including that they were not taxpayers within the meaning of the tax laws, that wages are not income, that the Sixteenth Amendment does not authorize the imposition of an income tax on individuals, and that the Sixteenth Amendment is unenforceable, were frivolous or had been repeatedly rejected by the courts. During this time period, petitioner also attended at least two criminal trials of persons charged with tax offenses. In addition, there was evidence that in 1980 or 1981 an attorney had advised Cheek that the courts had rejected as frivolous the claim that wages are not income.

Cheek represented himself at trial and testified in his defense. He admitted that he had not filed personal income tax returns during the years in question. He testified that as early as 1978, he had begun attending seminars sponsored by, and following the advice of, a group that believes, among other things, that the federal tax system is unconstitutional. Some of the speakers at these meetings were lawyers who purported to give professional opinions about the invalidity of the federal income tax laws. Cheek produced a letter from an attorney stating that the Sixteenth Amendment did not authorize a tax on wages and salaries but only on gain or profit. Petitioner's defense was that, based on the indoctrination he received from this group and from his own study, he sincerely believed that the tax laws were being unconstitutionally enforced and that his actions during the 1980–1986 period were lawful. He therefore argued that he had acted without the willfulness required for conviction of the various offenses with which he was charged.

In the course of its instructions, the trial court advised the jury that to prove "willfulness" the Government must prove the voluntary and intentional violation of a known legal duty, a burden that could not be proved by showing mistake, ignorance, or negligence. The court further advised the jury that an objectively reasonable good-faith misunderstanding of the law would negate willfulness but mere disagreement with the law would not. The court described Cheek's beliefs about the income tax system and instructed the jury that if it found that Cheek "honestly and reasonably believed that he was not required to pay income taxes or to file tax returns," a not guilty verdict should be returned.

After several hours of deliberation, the jury sent a note to the judge that stated in part:

> " 'We have a basic disagreement between some of us as to if Mr. Cheek honestly & reasonably believed that he was not required to pay income taxes.

*   *   *

" 'Page 32 [the relevant jury instruction] discusses good faith misunderstanding & disagreement. Is there any additional clarification you can give us on this point?' "

The District Judge responded with a supplemental instruction containing the following statements:

"[A] person's opinion that the tax laws violate his constitutional rights does not constitute a good faith misunderstanding of the law. Furthermore, a person's disagreement with the government's tax collection systems and policies does not constitute a good faith misunderstanding of the law."

At the end of the first day of deliberation, the jury sent out another note saying that it still could not reach a verdict because " '[w]e are divided on the issue as to if Mr. Cheek honestly & reasonably believed that he was not required to pay income tax.' " When the jury resumed its deliberations, the District Judge gave the jury an additional instruction. This instruction stated in part that "[a]n honest but unreasonable belief is not a defense and does not negate willfulness," and that "[a]dvice or research resulting in the conclusion that wages of a privately employed person are not income or that the tax laws are unconstitutional is not objectively reasonable and cannot serve as the basis for a good faith misunderstanding of the law defense." The court also instructed the jury that "[p]ersistent refusal to acknowledge the law does not constitute a good faith misunderstanding of the law." Approximately two hours later, the jury returned a verdict finding petitioner guilty on all counts.

Petitioner appealed his convictions, arguing that the District Court erred by instructing the jury that only an objectively reasonable misunderstanding of the law negates the statutory willfulness requirement. The United States Court of Appeals for the Seventh Circuit rejected that contention and affirmed the convictions. In prior cases, the Seventh Circuit had made clear that good-faith misunderstanding of the law negates willfulness only if the defendant's beliefs are objectively reasonable; in the Seventh Circuit, even actual ignorance is not a defense unless the defendant's ignorance was itself objectively reasonable. . . .

II

The general rule that ignorance of the law or a mistake of law is no defense to criminal prosecution is deeply rooted in the American legal system. Based on the notion that the law is definite and knowable, the common law presumed that every person knew the law. This common-law rule has been applied by the Court in numerous cases construing criminal statutes.

The proliferation of statutes and regulations has sometimes made it difficult for the average citizen to know and comprehend the extent of the duties and obligations imposed by the tax laws. Congress has accordingly softened the impact of the common-law presumption by making specific intent to violate the law an element of certain federal criminal tax offenses. Thus, the Court almost 60 years ago interpreted the statutory term "willfully" as used in the federal criminal tax statutes as carving out an exception to the traditional rule. This special treatment of criminal tax offenses is largely due to the complexity of the tax laws. In United States v. Murdock, 290 U.S. 389 (1933), the Court recognized that:

> "Congress did not intend that a person, by reason of a bona fide misunderstanding as to his liability for the tax, as to his duty to make a return, or as to the adequacy of the records he maintained, should become a criminal by his mere failure to measure up to the prescribed standard of conduct."

The Court held that the defendant was entitled to an instruction with respect to whether he acted in good faith based on his actual belief. In *Murdock,* the Court interpreted the term "willfully" as used in the criminal tax statutes generally to mean "an act done with a bad purpose," or with "an evil motive."

Subsequent decisions have refined this proposition. In United States v. Bishop, 412 U.S. 346 (1973), we described the term "willfully" as connoting "a voluntary, intentional violation of a known legal duty," and did so with specific reference to the "bad faith or evil intent" language employed in *Murdock.* Still later, United States v. Pomponio, 429 U.S. 10 (1976) (*per curiam*), addressed a situation in which several defendants had been charged with willfully filing false tax returns. The jury was given an instruction on willfulness similar to the standard set forth in *Bishop.* In addition, it was instructed that " '[g]ood motive alone is never a defense where the act done or omitted is a crime.' " The defendants were convicted but the Court of Appeals reversed, concluding that the latter instruction was improper because the statute required a finding of bad purpose or evil motive.

We reversed the Court of Appeals, stating that "the Court of Appeals incorrectly assumed that the reference to an 'evil motive' in *United States v. Bishop,* supra, and prior cases," "requires proof of any motive other than an intentional violation of a known legal duty." As "the other Courts of Appeals that have considered the question have recognized, willfulness in this context simply means a voluntary, intentional violation of a known legal duty." We concluded that after instructing the jury on willfulness, "[a]n additional instruction on good faith was unnecessary." Taken together, *Bishop* and *Pomponio* conclusively establish that the standard for the statutory willfulness requirement is the "voluntary, intentional violation of a known legal duty."

III

Cheek accepts the *Pomponio* definition of willfulness, but asserts that the District Court's instructions and the Court of Appeals' opinion departed from that definition. In particular, he challenges the ruling that a good-faith misunderstanding of the law or a good-faith belief that one is not violating the law, if it is to negate willfulness, must be objectively reasonable. We agree that the Court of Appeals and the District Court erred in this respect.

A

Willfulness, as construed by our prior decisions in criminal tax cases, requires the Government to prove that the law imposed a duty on the defendant, that the defendant knew of this duty, and that he voluntarily and intentionally violated that duty. We deal first with the case where the issue is whether the defendant knew of the duty purportedly imposed by the provision of the statute or regulation he is accused of violating, a case in which there is no claim that the provision at issue is invalid. In such a case, if the Government proves actual knowledge of the pertinent legal duty, the prosecution, without more, has satisfied the knowledge component of the willfulness requirement. But carrying this burden requires negating a defendant's claim of ignorance of the law or a claim that because of a misunderstanding of the law, he had a good-faith belief that he was not violating any of the provisions of the tax laws. This is so because one cannot be aware that the law imposes a duty upon him and yet be ignorant of it, misunderstand the law, or believe that the duty does not exist. In the end, the issue is whether, based on all the evidence, the Government has proved that the defendant was aware of the duty at issue, which cannot be true if the jury credits a good-faith misunderstanding and belief submission, whether or not the claimed belief or misunderstanding is objectively reasonable.

In this case, if Cheek asserted that he truly believed that the Internal Revenue Code did not purport to treat wages as income, and the jury believed him, the Government would not have carried its burden to prove willfulness, however unreasonable a court might deem such a belief. Of course, in deciding whether to credit Cheek's good-faith belief claim, the jury would be free to consider any admissible evidence from any source showing that Cheek was aware of his duty to file a return and to treat wages as income, including evidence showing his awareness of the relevant provisions of the Code or regulations, of court decisions rejecting his interpretation of the tax law, of authoritative rulings of the Internal Revenue Service, or of any contents of the personal income tax return forms and accompanying instructions that made it plain that wages should be returned as income.

We thus disagree with the Court of Appeals' requirement that a claimed good-faith belief must be objectively reasonable if it is to be considered as possibly negating the Government's evidence purporting to show a defendant's awareness of the legal duty at issue. Knowledge and belief are characteristically questions for the factfinder, in this case the jury. Characterizing a particular belief as not objectively reasonable transforms the inquiry into a legal one and would prevent the jury from considering it. It would of course be proper to exclude evidence having no relevance or probative value with respect to willfulness; but it is not contrary to common sense, let alone impossible, for a defendant to be ignorant of his duty based on an irrational belief that he has no duty, and forbidding the jury to consider evidence that might negate willfulness would raise a serious question under the Sixth Amendment's jury trial provision. It is common ground that this Court, where possible, interprets congressional enactments so as to avoid raising serious constitutional questions.

It was therefore error to instruct the jury to disregard evidence of Cheek's understanding that, within the meaning of the tax laws, he was not a person required to file a return or to pay income taxes and that wages are not taxable income, as incredible as such misunderstandings of and beliefs about the law might be. Of course, the more unreasonable the asserted beliefs or misunderstandings are, the more likely the jury will consider them to be nothing more than simple disagreement with known legal duties imposed by the tax laws and will find that the Government has carried its burden of proving knowledge.

B

Cheek asserted in the trial court that he should be acquitted because he believed in good faith that the income tax law is unconstitutional as applied to him and thus could not legally impose any duty upon him of which he should have been aware. Such a submission is unsound, not because Cheek's constitutional arguments are not objectively reasonable or frivolous, which they surely are, but because the *Murdock–Pomponio* line of cases does not support such a position. Those cases construed the willfulness requirement in the criminal provisions of the Internal Revenue Code to require proof of knowledge of the law. This was because in "our complex tax system, uncertainty often arises even among taxpayers who earnestly wish to follow the law" and " '[i]t is not the purpose of the law to penalize frank difference of opinion or innocent errors made despite the exercise of reasonable care.' "

Claims that some of the provisions of the tax code are unconstitutional are submissions of a different order. They do not arise from innocent mistakes caused by the complexity of the Internal Revenue Code. Rather, they reveal full knowledge of the provisions at issue and a studied conclusion, however wrong, that those provisions are invalid and unenforceable. Thus in this case, Cheek paid his taxes for years, but after attending various seminars and based on his own study, he concluded that the income tax laws could not constitutionally require him to pay a tax.

We do not believe that Congress contemplated that such a taxpayer, without risking criminal prosecution, could ignore the duties imposed upon him by the Internal Revenue Code and refuse to utilize the mechanisms provided by Congress to present his claims of invalidity to the courts and to abide by their decisions. There is no doubt that

Cheek, from year to year, was free to pay the tax that the law purported to require, file for a refund and, if denied, present his claims of invalidity, constitutional or otherwise, to the courts. Also, without paying the tax, he could have challenged claims of tax deficiencies in the Tax Court, 26 U.S.C. § 6213, with the right to appeal to a higher court if unsuccessful. § 7482(a)(1). Cheek took neither course in some years, and when he did was unwilling to accept the outcome. As we see it, he is in no position to claim that his good-faith belief about the validity of the Internal Revenue Code negates willfulness or provides a defense to criminal prosecution under §§ 7201 and 7203. Of course, Cheek was free in this very case to present his claims of invalidity and have them adjudicated, but like defendants in criminal cases in other contexts, who "willfully" refuse to comply with the duties placed upon them by the law, he must take the risk of being wrong.

We thus hold that in a case like this, a defendant's views about the validity of the tax statutes are irrelevant to the issue of willfulness, need not be heard by the jury, and if they are, an instruction to disregard them would be proper. For this purpose, it makes no difference whether the claims of invalidity are frivolous or have substance. It was therefore not error in this case for the District Judge to instruct the jury not to consider Cheek's claims that the tax laws were unconstitutional. However, it was error for the court to instruct the jury that petitioner's asserted beliefs that wages are not income and that he was not a taxpayer within the meaning of the Internal Revenue Code should not be considered by the jury in determining whether Cheek had acted willfully.

IV

For the reasons set forth in the opinion above, the judgment of the Court of Appeals is vacated, and the case is remanded for further proceedings consistent with this opinion.

It is so ordered.

* * *

[JUSTICE SCALIA'S concurring opinion is omitted.]

JUSTICE BLACKMUN, with whom JUSTICE MARSHALL joins, dissenting.

It seems to me that we are concerned in this case not with "the complexity of the tax laws," but with the income tax law in its most elementary and basic aspect: Is a wage earner a taxpayer and are wages income?

The Court acknowledges that the conclusively established standard for willfulness under the applicable statutes is the "voluntary, intentional violation of a known legal duty." That being so, it is incomprehensible to me how, in this day, more than 70 years after the institution of our present federal income tax system with the passage of the Revenue Act of 1913, 38 Stat. 166, any taxpayer of competent mentality can assert as his defense to charges of statutory willfulness the proposition that the wage he receives for his labor is not income, irrespective of a cult that says otherwise and advises the gullible to resist income tax collections. One might note in passing that this particular taxpayer, after all, was a licensed pilot for one of our major commercial airlines; he presumably was a person of at least minimum intellectual competence.

The District Court's instruction that an objectively reasonable and good faith misunderstanding of the law negates willfulness lends further, rather than less, protection to this defendant, for it added an additional hurdle for the prosecution to overcome. Petitioner should be grateful for this further protection, rather than be opposed to it.

This Court's opinion today, I fear, will encourage taxpayers to cling to frivolous views of the law in the hope of convincing a jury of their sincerity. If that ensues, I suspect we have gone beyond the limits of common sense.

While I may not agree with every word the Court of Appeals has enunciated in its opinion, I would affirm its judgment in this case. I therefore dissent.

---

2. MODEL PENAL CODE APPROACH

Section 2.02. General Requirements of Culpability.

(1) *Minimum Requirements of Culpability.* Except as provided in Section 2.05, a person is not guilty of an offense unless he acted purposely, knowingly, recklessly or negligently, as the law may require, with respect to each material element of the offense.

(2) *Kinds of Culpability Defined.*

   (a) *Purposely.*

A person acts purposely with respect to a material element of an offense when:

      (i) if the element involves the nature of his conduct or a result thereof, it is his conscious object to engage in conduct of that nature or to cause such a result; and

      (ii) if the element involves the attendant circumstances, he is aware of the existence of such circumstances or he believes or hopes that they exist.

   (b) *Knowingly.*

A person acts knowingly with respect to a material element of an offense when:

      (i) if the element involves the nature of his conduct or the attendant circumstances, he is aware that his conduct is of that nature or that such circumstances exist; and

(ii) if the element involves a result of his conduct, he is aware that it is practically certain that his conduct will cause such a result.

(c) *Recklessly.*

A person acts recklessly with respect to a material element of an offense when he consciously disregards a substantial and unjustifiable risk that the material element exists or will result from his conduct. The risk must be of such a nature and degree that, considering the nature and purpose of the actor's conduct and the circumstances known to him, its disregard involves a gross deviation from the standard of conduct that a law-abiding person would observe in the actor's situation.

(d) *Negligently.*

A person acts negligently with respect to a material element of an offense when he should be aware of a substantial and unjustifiable risk that the material element exists or will result from his conduct. The risk must be of such a nature and degree that the actor's failure to perceive it, considering the nature and purpose of his conduct and the circumstances known to him, involves a gross deviation from the standard of care that a reasonable person would observe in the actor's situation.

(3) *Culpability Required Unless Otherwise Provided.* When the culpability sufficient to establish a material element of an offense is not prescribed by law, such element is established if a person acts purposely, knowingly or recklessly with respect thereto.

(4) *Prescribed Culpability Requirement Applies to All Material Elements.* When the law defining an offense prescribes the kind of culpability that is sufficient for the commission of an offense, without distinguishing among the material elements thereof, such provision shall apply to all the material elements of the offense, unless a contrary purpose plainly appears.

(5) *Substitutes for Negligence, Recklessness and Knowledge.* When the law provides that negligence suffices to establish an element of an offense, such element also is established if a person acts purposely, knowingly or recklessly. When recklessness suffices to establish an element, such element also is established if a person acts purposely or knowingly. When acting knowingly suffices to establish an element, such element also is established if a person acts purposely.

(6) *Requirement of Purpose Satisfied if Purpose Is Conditional.* When a particular purpose is an element of an offense, the element is established although such purpose is conditional, unless the condition negatives the harm or evil sought to be prevented by the law defining the offense.

(7) *Requirement of Knowledge Satisfied by Knowledge of High Probability.* When knowledge of the existence of a particular fact is an element of an offense, such knowledge is established if a person is aware of a high probability of its existence, unless he actually believes that it does not exist.

(8) *Requirement of Wilfulness Satisfied by Acting Knowingly.* A requirement that an offense be committed wilfully is satisfied if a person acts knowingly with respect to the material elements of the offense, unless a purpose to impose further requirements appears.

(9) *Culpability as to Illegality of Conduct.* Neither knowledge nor recklessness or negligence as to whether conduct constitutes an offense or as to the existence, meaning or application of the law determining the elements of an offense is an element of such offense, unless the definition of the offense or the Code so provides.

(10) *Culpability as Determinant of Grade of Offense.* When the grade or degree of an offense depends on whether the offense is committed purposely, knowingly, recklessly or negligently, its grade or degree shall be the lowest for which the determinative kind of culpability is established with respect to any material element of the offense.

3. TRANSFERRED INTENT

EX PARTE WEEMS

Supreme Court of Alabama, 1984.
463 So.2d 170.

FAULKNER, JUSTICE.

We granted certiorari to review the Court of Criminal Appeals' decision affirming petitioner's murder conviction.

On the night of the killing, petitioner, Jared Jerome Weems, had been at a "gambling house" next door to the East North Cafe in Dothan, where he had won about $160.00. While in the house he purchased two cartons of cigarettes. When he left, he encountered a man outside the house who asked him for a pack of cigarettes. When Weems refused, the man slapped him and attempted to cut him with a knife, whereupon Weems fled. Weems had never seen the man before the altercation, but was later told that the man had recently come to Dothan from Florida.

Later that evening Weems returned to the area to retrieve his mother's car, which he had been driving. When he got to the car he discovered that during the course of the evening he had lost the car keys. He surmised that he had probably lost the keys during the altercation with the man from Florida. In an attempt to locate the keys, he decided to go into the East North Cafe to ask if anyone had found them. Fearing the possibility of another encounter with the man from Florida, Weems decided to take into the cafe the gun which his mother kept in the car glove box.

Upon entering the cafe, he surveyed the patrons and determined that the man from Florida was not there. He noticed that a friend of his, Christine Wilson, whom he referred to as "Mama Chris", was at the cafe that night. Weems went over to talk to her. When Weems arrived at the table where Wilson was sitting, he realized that he still had the pistol in his hand. Weems testified that while he was in the process of putting the pistol away, it discharged and hit Ms. Wilson.

Numerous people who were in the cafe at the time of the shooting testified. Their accounts were substantially similar to Weems's and to each other's. Typical of the accounts of the shooting given at the trial was the one given by the bartender, Linton McIntyre. McIntyre testified that he was standing behind the counter facing the victim when she was shot. Neither he nor any of the other witnesses saw the shot being fired. When McIntyre heard the shot he looked in that direction and heard Wilson tell Weems, "Mister, you done shot me." McIntyre testified that Weems replied, "Mama Chris, if you are shot let me take you to the hospital." There was some confusion in the cafe as to whether Wilson had been shot or whether she had had a heart attack, because her wound did not bleed. McIntyre testified that Weems left "a couple of minutes" later.

On appeal, Weems argued that because he did not intend to kill Wilson, his conviction for murder was inappropriate. The Court of Criminal Appeals concluded that, although Weems may not have intended to shoot Wilson, there was evidence to support a finding that he had intended to shoot Sylvester Goodson, the man sitting at the table with the victim. The court noted that Weems did not know the man with whom he had had the altercation earlier and that it was "very likely that Weems thought Goodson was his attacker." The court based its conclusion that Weems was attempting to shoot Goodson on the fact that the trajectory of the bullet was parallel to the ground and the fact that the bullet was traveling in Goodson's direction. The court concluded that it was unlikely that Weems was attempting to place the gun under his belt since the trajectory of the bullet was parallel to the ground and that Goodson must have been the intended target, because the bullet was traveling toward him.

The problem with the Court of Criminal Appeals' transferred intent theory is that there was no more evidence that Weems was attempting to kill Goodson than there was that he intended to kill Wilson. Weems knew Goodson. He testified that Goodson was not the man who attacked him. There was no testimony given by any of the occurrence witnesses to the effect that there had been any sort of disagreement that evening, or on any previous occasion, between Weems and Goodson. It is patently obvious that intent to kill cannot be proved from the trajectory of the bullet alone. Obviously, whenever a person is shot, he is in the path of the bullet which hits him. If being in the path of the bullet were sufficient to prove intent, there would be no accidental shootings. Since there was no evidence of intent to kill Goodson other than the naked fact that Goodson was in the bullet's path, the conviction cannot be upheld on the theory that Weems was trying to shoot Goodson when Wilson was killed.

Indeed, the state does not even contend that Weems was trying to shoot Goodson. It argues that, "It is uncontradicted that the killing of 'Mama Chris' was accidental; nonetheless, ample evidence was produced whereby a jury could easily infer Mr. Weems entered the East North Cafe with a cocked, loaded pistol, intending to shoot someone."

In support of its position, the state relies primarily on Sashington v. State, 56 Ala.App. 698, 325 So.2d 205 (1975). The victim in that case was celebrating his 65th birthday with a party at his home when he was shot. The defendant, a guest at the party, lived in a trailer about 150 yards from the victim's house. A fight occurred during the party involving the defendant's father and brother. Another individual was standing in the front yard waving a shotgun. The defendant went home and returned with a shotgun. One shot was fired from the defendant's gun in the direction of the front porch, killing the victim. The victim was a friend of the defendant, and the defendant argued that he had not intended to kill him. Additionally, the defendant argued that he had not intended to kill anyone. In holding the evidence presented a jury question as to intent to kill someone, the Court of Criminal Appeals relied on the transferred intent theory. It stated, "To be guilty of murder, one has to have the intention to kill a human being, but it does not have to be the person who is killed."

Under Alabama law an accidental killing may support a conviction for murder, manslaughter, or negligent homicide, depending on the circumstances of the case. An accidental death may constitute murder if, "[u]nder circumstances manifesting extreme indifference to human life, [the defendant] recklessly engages in conduct which creates a grave risk of death" to the victim and thereby causes the victim's death. Section 13A–6–2(a)(2); Code 1975. On the other hand, if the defendant's conduct in bringing about the victim's death is simply "reckless," the defendant is guilty of manslaughter. Section 13A–6–3(a)(1). If the death results from "criminal negligence," the defendant is guilty of criminally negligent homicide. Section 13A–6–4(a).

Alabama's homicide statutes were derived from the Model Penal Code. In providing that homicide committed "recklessly under circumstances manifesting extreme indifference to human life" constitutes murder, the drafters of the model code were attempting to define a degree of recklessness "that cannot be fairly distinguished from homicides committed purposely or knowingly." Model Penal Code and Commentaries, § 210.02, Comment 4 (1980). That standard was designed to encompass the category of murder traditionally referred to as "depraved heart" or "universal malice" killings. Examples of such acts include shooting into an occupied house or into a moving automobile or piloting a speedboat through a group of swimmers.

Recklessly causing another's death may give rise to the lesser included offense of manslaughter. A defendant who recklessly causes another's death commits manslaughter if he "consciously disregard[ed] a substantial and unjustifiable risk that his conduct would cause that result." Model Penal Code and Commentaries, § 210.03, Comment 4 (1980). The difference between the circumstances which will support a murder conviction and the degree of risk contemplated by the manslaughter statute is one of degree, not kind. From a comparison of Sections 210.03 and 210.02 of the Model Code, it appears that the degree of recklessness which will support a manslaughter conviction involves a circumstance which is a "gross deviation from the standard of conduct that a law-abiding person would observe in the actor's situation," but is not so high that it cannot be "fairly distinguished from" the mental state required in intentional homicides. Compare Comment 4 to § 210.02 with Comment 4 to § 210.03.

If the homicide is brought about by "criminal negligence," the defendant is guilty of criminally negligent homicide. The essential difference between "recklessness," as that term is used in the murder and manslaughter statutes, and "criminal negligence" is that a reckless defendant is one who has "consciously disregarded" a substantial and unjustifiable risk, whereas a negligent actor needs only to disregard a risk of which he "should have been aware." Model Penal Code and Commentaries § 210.04, Comment 1.

In this case there was ample evidence that the defendant consciously disregarded a substantial and unjustifiable risk by carrying the pistol into the cafe. In so doing, Weems committed a "gross deviation" from the standard of conduct which would have been observed by a law-abiding person. The evidence would have supported a conviction for manslaughter, therefore. The degree of recklessness exhibited by Weems can, however, be distinguished from the extreme indifference to human life displayed by a person who commits an intentional homicide. These facts would, therefore, support a conviction of manslaughter, but not murder.

In our opinion, the facts of this case are distinguishable from Sashington v. State, 56 Ala.App. 698, 325 So.2d 205 (1975), which is relied on by the state. There was evidence in *Sashington* to support a finding that the defendant was attempting to shoot someone else when he killed the victim. Here, the state concedes that "the killing of 'Mama Chris' was accidental." Although Weems was grossly reckless, his disregard for the safety of those around him did not rise to a level of disregard for the value of human life that would be tantamount to proof of an intentional killing. The facts of this case appear to present a clear case of manslaughter.

Reversed and remanded.

TORBERT, C.J., and JONES, SHORES and EMBRY, JJ., concur.

BEATTY and ADAMS, JJ., dissent.

MADDOX and ALMON, JJ., not sitting.

NOTES

1. In State v. Gandy, 283 S.C. 571, 324 S.E.2d 65 (1984), the court said: "Where a defendant intends to kill or seriously injure one person, but kills another, a defendant may be found guilty of murder or manslaughter. If malice is found at the time of the killing, even if a third party is killed rather than the intended victim, the defendant is guilty of murder. . . . This result is sometimes described as the function of the doctrine of 'transferred intent' whereby the actor's intent to kill his intended victim is said to be transferred to his actual victim."

What justifies such a doctrine?

2. If A and B are assailants engaged in a gun battle with C, who is shooting back in self-defense, and in the gun battle an innocent bystander located roughly behind C is killed, can A be convicted of the homicide under the doctrine of transferred intent even if it is impossible to establish who fired the bullet that killed the bystander? See, Riddick v. Commonwealth, 226 Va. 244, 308 S.E.2d 117 (1983).

3. After an altercation between A and B, A fled with the promise that he will be back to kill B. Sometime later, A and two of his friends drive by B's house, at a time when B and several other friends are sitting on the front porch. As A drives by the house, he yells, "I'm going to kill you." When the car returns, all of the people who are on the porch run inside; A fires two shots into the home through a closed window shade, killing a woman inside. The woman was never in any altercation with A. A is charged with intentional murder which states: "A person commits the crime of murder if: (1) With intent to cause the death of that person or of another person. . . ." "To be guilty of murder one must have the intention to kill a human being but it does not have to be toward the person who was killed." Can A be found guilty of intentional murder upon proof of a general intent to kill, or must the prosecutor prove a specific intent to kill? See, Dubose v. State, 563 So.2d 18 (Ala.Crim. App.1990), where the court affirmed a conviction of intentional murder.

4. A throws a rock into B's window, intending to frighten B and damage B's property. By accident, the rock knocks over a burning oil lamp which starts a blaze that destroys B's home. Can A be convicted of the arson of B's home under the transferred intent doctrine?

4. STRICT LIABILITY AND LACK OF CRIMINAL INTENT AS A DEFENSE

COMMONWEALTH v. OLSHEFSKI

Pennsylvania District and County Court, 1948.
64 Pa.D. & C. 343 (1946).

KREISHER, P.J., September 9, 1948.—On February 6, 1948, John Fisher, a driver for above-named defendant, at the direction of defendant, purchased a load of coal at the Gilberton Coal Company colliery and had the same loaded upon a truck owned by defendant, which had a "U" tag on it, and which, under The Vehicle Code of May 1, 1929, P.L. 905, is permitted to weigh 15,000 pounds plus five percent, or a gross weight of 15,750 pounds. The load was weighed by a licensed weighmaster at the colliery and the weight was given at 15,200 pounds. Fisher drove the truck to the home of defendant, who was out of town at the time and then placed the weigh slip from the colliery in the compartment of the truck. The following day defendant went to the Danville National Bank to do some banking business and observed the Pennsylvania State Police at the northern end of the river bridge checking on trucks. He then returned to his home and drove his truck with the load of coal to the northern end of the river bridge on his way to the borough water department scales for the purpose of having it weighed. He states that he was selling the coal in Danville, and pursuant to the requirements of an ordinance in Danville, he had to have a Danville weigh slip. Before reaching the water department's scales a State policeman stopped him and he was directed to the scales where his load was weighed by the officer and the weigh slip was signed by a licensed weighmaster, showing that his gross weight was 16,015, and that he was, therefore, overloaded 265 pounds. The officer lodged an information for his violation of The Vehicle Code. Defendant waived a hearing and the matter is now before us for disposition. . . .

It is also contended by counsel for defendant that this prosecution should be dismissed for the reason that defendant had in his possession a weigh bill for this particular load by a duly licensed weighmaster, which was weighed the day before, showing that the gross weight of the truck and the load was within the load allowed by law for this particular truck, and that defendant, relying upon this weigh bill, voluntarily drove to where he knew the police were weighing trucks, and was of the belief that his load was a legal load, and therefore, because of this belief, he is not guilty of the crime charged.

In criminal law we have two distinct types of crimes: The one type of crime being the common-law crimes, which are designated as crimes mala in se, which means that they are crimes because the act is bad in and of itself. The other type of crime which did not exist at common law covers those acts which are made criminal by statute, and are termed crimes mala prohibita, and simply means that they are crimes not because they are bad in and of themselves, but merely because the legislative authority makes the act criminal and penal.

In crimes that are mala in se, two elements are necessary for the commission of the crime, viz., the mental element and the physical element. In this type of crime intent is a necessary element, but in statutory crimes, which are simply mala prohibita, the mental element is not necessary for the commission of the crime, and one who does an act in violation of the statute and is caught and prosecuted, is guilty of the crime irrespective of his intent or belief. The power of the legislature to punish an act as a crime, even though it is not bad in and of itself, is an absolute power of the legislature, the only restriction being the constitutional restrictions, and it is the duty of the court to enforce these enactments irrespective of what the court might personally think about the prosecution or the wisdom of the act.

Except for constitutional limitations, the power of the State legislature is absolute. It may punish any act which in its judgment requires punishment, provided it violates no constitutional restriction, and its enactments must be enforced by the courts. The courts cannot review the discretion of the legislature, or pass upon the expediency, wisdom, or propriety of legislative action in matters within its powers. Neither can the courts pass upon the action of a prosecuting officer who prosecutes a person for the violation of a statute which is violated by that person, even though the court might be of the opinion that the officer should have not instituted the prosecution.

If the testimony shows, as in this case, that defendant violated the law, and is prosecuted for that violation, then the court is bound to enforce the legislative enactments, and cannot in good conscience set itself up as the legislature and excuse one person who has violated the law and find another person guilty for the same violation. It is true that this rule of law may seem harsh and unjustifiable, but the court is powerless to correct it, and, therefore, under our duty as judge, we are obliged to hold that this defendant violated The Vehicle Code by having his truck overloaded, and that he is guilty as charged. . . .

EX PARTE MARLEY

Supreme Court of California, 1946.
29 Cal.2d 525, 175 P.2d 832.

SCHAUER, JUSTICE. Petitioner, the proprietor of a meat market, was convicted of a violation of section 12023 of the Business and Professions Code, and sentenced to ninety days in the county jail. The mentioned section provides as follows: "Every person who by himself or his employee or agent, or as the employee or agent of another, sells any commodity, at, by, or according to gross weight or measure, or at, by, as, of, or according to any weight, measure or count which is greater than the true net weight, . . . is guilty of a misdemeanor." Petitioner seeks release through habeas corpus on the ground that the quoted statute is unconstitutional as it is sought to be applied to the facts here shown. With his position we are compelled to disagree.

The record discloses that on or about March 22, 1945, an employee of the Office of Price Administration, named Mrs. Punteney, accompanied openly by one other woman (named Mrs. Sampson) and surreptitiously by two men (one of them named Delaney), all of the same calling, appeared at the counter of petitioner's meat market in Los Angeles County and requested of petitioner's clerk and employe, one Dennis, that the latter sell her one veal steak and four or five lamb chops. Dennis weighed the selections, told Mrs. Punteney and Mrs. Sampson the respective prices, and wrapped the meat. Mrs. Punteney then showed Dennis her "identification" and summoned Delaney "who was waiting outside the door," and together they checked the weight of the meat, which was found to be less than that which would correspond, according to Office of Price Administration price charts posted in the market, to the prices charged. About two weeks later Delaney signed the complaint upon which petitioner's conviction is based. Dennis was also named as a defendant, was convicted, and was penalized by a $100 fine. It is undisputed that petitioner did not participate personally in the transaction here involved, was absent from the premises at the time it occurred, and had at no time instructed Dennis to give short weight.

The general rule of law as repeatedly enunciated and emphasized by the courts of California and of other jurisdictions is that a master or principal before he can be held criminally responsible for the act of an employe or agent must be proved to have "Knowingly and intentionally aided, advised, or encouraged the criminal act." . . .

In limited qualification of the general rule, however, legislative bodies in California as well as in other jurisdictions have adopted various statutes positively forbidding certain acts and imposing criminal liability upon the master if the act is knowingly performed by his servant within the scope of the latter's authority. Such statutes have dealt with the sale of intoxicating liquor . . .; of pure foods and drugs . . .; and with the operating of gaming establishments and of saloons, and have been upheld by the courts. Other instances in which criminal responsibility has been imposed despite lack of specific knowledge, direction or encouragement by the employer of the criminal act on the part of the servant are listed in Commonwealth v. Mixer (1910), 207 Mass. 141, 93 N.E. 249. Examples are the driving of an unregistered automobile . . .; being present where gaming implements are found . . .; obstructing a highway . . .; being present where implements for smoking opium are found . . .; and the killing for sale of an animal under a designated age. . . .

Such exceptions are also recognized in the statement of the prevailing principles in C.J.S. Criminal Law, § 84, at page 150, by the observation that "Under statutes positively forbidding certain acts irrespective of the motive or intent of the actor, a principal or master may be criminally liable for his agent's or employee's act done within the scope of his employment. . . ."

And in the field of weights and measures, the rule is, as stated in 68 Corpus Juris 165–166, sections 24, 25, that where, as here, the statute provides that "whoever, himself or by a servant or agent, is guilty of giving false or insufficient weight or measure shall be punishable, evidence of giving short weight by defendant's servant in his absence warrants a conviction of defendant. . . . [W]here qualifying words such as knowingly, intentionally, or fraudulently are omitted from provisions creating the offense it is held that guilty knowledge and intent are not elements of the offense. . . . These statutes make the seller the guarantor of the weight and quantity of the commodity sold without regard to his intent or knowledge." . . . The principle upon which such holdings are based is expressed as follows in State v. Weisberg (1943) . . . at page 95 of 74 Ohio App., at page 872 of 55 N.E.2d: "There are many acts that are so destructive of the social order, or where the ability of the state to establish the element of criminal intent would be so extremely difficult if not impossible of proof, that in the interest of justice the legislature has provided that the doing of the act constitutes a crime, regardless of knowledge or criminal intent on the part of the defendant.

"In these cases it is the duty of the defendant to know what the facts are that are involved or result from his acts or conduct. Statutes punishing the sale of adulterated foods or prohibiting the sale of intoxicating liquor to minors are most frequently found in this class of cases. The use of false weights could well come within this field of the law."

In the Beggs case, . . . 69 Cal.2d Supp. 819, 160 P.2d 600, the defendants had, in violation of section 26510 of the Health and Safety Code, sold sacks of onions which they represented to be of the weight stated on the respective labels of such sacks which defendants themselves had purchased but which actually, without defendants' knowledge, weighed less. Judge Bishop, authorizing the opinion for the Appellate Department of the Superior Court, applied and followed the stated exception to the general rule (requiring intent as a prerequisite to criminal liability) and in so doing observed . . . that "Neither knowledge nor an intent to defraud is made a condition of the statute, with the result that the act of selling misbranded goods constitutes the offense, though done, as it doubtless was in the case before us, both in happy ignorance of the fact that the legend on the sacks was incorrect and without any intention of defrauding anyone. This conclusion is supported by cases analogous to ours, decided in this state [Citations]."

Petitioner complains that he was denied due process and the equal protection of the laws in that he was not permitted to prove that he came within the provisions of subdivisions 4 and 6 of section 26 of the Penal Code. Such provisions are, in material part, as follows: "All persons are capable of committing crimes except those belonging to the following classes: . . . Four. Persons who committed the act . . . under an ignorance or mistake of fact, which disproves any criminal intent . . . Six. Persons who committed the act . . . through misfortune or by accident, when it appears that there was no evil design, intention, or culpable negligence." Without any implication as to the legal propriety of his claim, as such, it is to be noted that the petitioner was properly allowed to introduce evidence tending to show that the prohibited act (the short weight element of the sale) was committed by the clerk by accident or mistake of fact, but on this issue the finding was adverse to the two defendants. The facts that petitioner was not present when the short weight sales were made and that he had not instructed the clerk to sell short weight, do not bring petitioner within the code provisions above quoted. He shows no other evidence or offer of evidence to that end. Whether some hypothetical situation (such, for example, as a conspiracy by a clerk with others deliberately to injure an employer) not shown by the record here, might properly be shown and be held to bring an employer within the purview of the code provisions, we do not, upon this application for habeas corpus, in the light of the record, have occasion to determine.

Inasmuch as the Legislature of this state has seen fit, in the exercise of its power, to impose upon petitioner criminal liability for the offense which was committed by his employe, we cannot, in the light of the authorities above cited, hold that the statute as written, or as applied here, invades a constitutional right of the petitioner. The seemingly (upon the record before us) disproportionate severity of the penalty assessed by the trial judge against this petitioner, as compared to that meted out against his codefendant, who was the primary actor, does not constitute a legal basis for intervention by habeas corpus. The writ of habeas corpus heretofore issued is discharged and petitioner is remanded to custody.

CARTER, JUSTICE. I dissent. Broadly speaking this case brings into sharp focus the clash between conflicting social philosophies which are reflected in the interpretation of constitutional and statutory provisions. That is, should the burden be placed upon an innocent and blameless employer, engaged in a business not in itself harmful to the public, of risking conviction of a crime and service of a jail sentence because of the mistake, intentional or not, of his employee? The majority opinion answers this question in the affirmative. With this conclusion I cannot agree. In my opinion there are no considerations of public policy or general welfare which warrant such a departure from the long established rule that criminal intent is a necessary element of a crime. Various situations can be imagined which render intolerable, and shocking to one's sense of justice, the construction placed by the majority opinion on the statute here involved. Similar statutes could be passed relating to the sale of railroad tickets or the cashing of checks which would make criminally liable the officers of a railway or banking corporation for an error made by an employee in overcharging a customer for a ticket or short changing a customer in the cashing of a check. Upon the occurrence of such an event in a remote section of the state where the railroad or bank was operating, the president and other officers of the railroad or bank who might reside in a metropolitan area hundreds of miles from the place where the crime was committed could be arrested and sent to jail for an alleged violation committed by a ticket clerk or bank teller. Likewise a merchant, who had been inducted into military service and who left his business in charge of a manager, could be sent to jail for violation of such a statute committed during his absence in military service when he had no knowledge whatever of what was taking place in his place of business. In such a case there is nothing an employer can do to protect himself, as the act of the employee is one which depends entirely upon use of his own faculties and senses and it is impossible for the employer to determine with any degree of accuracy whether the faculties and senses of the employee are functioning properly and accurately during all his working hours. These considerations, in my opinion, outweigh any benefit or advantage which may be gained to the public by an interpretation of a statute which places upon an innocent and blameless employer criminal responsibility for an act of his employee.

The specific issue here involved is the correct construction of section 12023 of the Business and Professions Code quoted in the majority opinion. Should it be construed to mean (1) that the master or principal (petitioner here) is criminally liable thereunder even though he is wholly innocent of fault or blame—did not authorize, assent to, direct or acquiesce in the act of his employee, or (2) that he shall not be denounced a criminal unless he authorized, assented to, directed or acquiesced in the unlawful act of his employee?

It is clear that the section is reasonably susceptible of the second construction; it certainly is at least equally amenable to either the first or the second interpretation. The statute condemns unlawful action of a principal by his agent. In other words, the unlawful action of the agent must be authorized specifically not generally under the broad authority to sell his principal's merchandise. It will be remembered that the statute condemns the unlawful act by oneself or by agent. "By oneself" means "alone" "unaided." (Webster's New Int. Dict., p. 367.) That expression followed by "or by an agent" must indicate that in the latter case the principal is acting not alone. He has procured and had the aid of his employee. They are acting together—in concert. He is still the one who must commit the unlawful act before he is guilty but he has assistance, that is, he instructs his agents to physically commit the act denounced. But even if the scales hang equally the second construction is compelled by numerous factors.

In a comprehensive discussion of the law with respect to criminal liability without fault Professor Francis Bowes Sayre, in suggesting tests for the construction of statutes purporting to impose such liability, says: "How then can one determine practically which offenses do and which do not require mens rea, where the statute creating the offense is entirely silent as to requisite knowledge? Although no hard and fast lines can be drawn, two cardinal principles stand out upon which the determination must turn.

"The first relates to the character of the offense. All criminal enactments in a sense serve the double purpose of singling out wrongdoers for the purpose of punishment or correction and of regulating the social order. But often the importance of the one far outweighs the other. Crimes created primarily for the purpose of singling out individual wrongdoers for punishment or correction are the ones commonly requiring mens rea; police offenses of a merely regulatory nature are frequently enforceable irrespective of any guilty intent.

"The second criterion depends upon the possible penalty. If this be serious, particularly if the offense be punishable by imprisonment, the individual interest of the defendant weighs too heavily to allow conviction without proof of a guilty mind. To subject defendants entirely free from moral blameworthiness to the possibility of prison sentences is revolting to the community sense of justice; and no law which violates this fundamental instinct can long endure. Crimes punishable with prison sentences, therefore, ordinarily require proof of a guilty intent." (33 Col.L.Rev. 55, 72). In the instant case a violation of the statute is a misdemeanor. (Bus. & Prof.Code, § 12023, supra.) And a misdemeanor is punishable by a fine not exceeding $500 or by imprisonment in the county jail not exceeding six months, or by both (Pen.Code, § 19). . . .

There are cases involving various statutes where the innocent employer is held criminally liable for the acts of his employee. (See 43 L.R.A., N.S., 11; 33 Col.L.Rev. 55, 84). Where an employee sells liquor to a minor he is making the very decision that he has been employed to make, that is, deciding when he should sell and whether a particular customer is a minor. The employer in effect confers upon him the authority to violate or not violate the law in selling the liquor. But it is not to be supposed that the employer would authorize the employee to give short of the correct weight in the sale of merchandise. In the pure and adulterated food cases the employer has possession and control of the merchandise and is not asked to warrant at his peril the integrity of an employee. . . .

In my opinion the petitioner should be discharged from custody.

MORISSETTE v. UNITED STATES

Supreme Court of the United States, 1952.
342 U.S. 246, 72 S.Ct. 240.

MR. JUSTICE JACKSON delivered the opinion of the Court. . . .

On a large tract of uninhabited and untilled land in a wooded and sparsely populated area of Michigan, the Government established a practice bombing range over which the Air Force dropped simulated bombs at ground targets. These bombs consisted of a metal cylinder about forty inches long and eight inches across, filled with sand and enough black powder to cause a smoke puff by which the strike could be located. At various places about the range signs read "Danger—Keep Out—Bombing Range." Nevertheless, the range was known as good deer country and was extensively hunted.

Spent bomb casings were cleared from the targets and thrown into piles "so that they will be out of the way." They were not stacked or piled in any order but were dumped in heaps, some of which had been accumulating for four years or upwards, were exposed to the weather and rusting away.

Morissette, in December of 1948, went hunting in this area but did not get a deer. He thought to meet expenses of the trip by salvaging some of these casings. He loaded three tons of them on his truck and took them to a nearby farm, where they were flattened by driving a tractor over them. After expending this labor and trucking them to market in Flint, he realized $84.

Morissette, by occupation, is a fruit stand operator in summer and a trucker and scrap iron collector in winter. An honorably discharged veteran of World War II, he enjoys a good name among his neighbors and has had no blemish on his record more disreputable than a conviction for reckless driving.

The loading, crushing and transporting of these casings were all in broad daylight, in full view of passers-by, without the slightest effort at concealment. When an investigation was started, Morissette voluntarily, promptly and candidly told the whole story to the authorities, saying that he had no intention of stealing but thought the property was abandoned, unwanted and considered of no value to the Government. He was indicted, however, on the charge that he "did unlawfully, wilfully and knowingly steal and convert" property of the United States of the value of $84, in violation of 18 U.S.C. § 641, 18 U.S.C.A. § 641, which provides that "whoever embezzles, steals, purloins, or knowingly converts" government property is punishable by fine and imprisonment. Morissette was convicted and sentenced to imprisonment for two months or to pay a fine of $200. The Court of Appeals affirmed, one judge dissenting.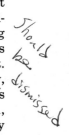

On his trial, Morissette, as he had at all times told investigating officers, testified that from appearances he believed the casings were cast-off and abandoned, that he did not intend to steal the property, and took it with no wrongful or criminal intent. The trial court, however, was unimpressed, and ruled: "[H]e took it because he thought it was abandoned and he knew he was on government property. . . . That is no defense. . . . I don't think anybody can have the defense they thought the property was abandoned on another man's piece of property." The court stated: "I will not permit you to show this man thought it was abandoned. . . . I hold in this case that there is no question of abandoned property." The court refused to submit or to allow counsel to argue to the jury whether Morissette acted with innocent intention. It charged: "And I instruct you that if you believe the testimony of the government in this case, he intended to take it. . . . He had no right to take this property. . . . [A]nd it is no defense to claim that it was abandoned, because it was on private property. . . . And I instruct you to this effect: That if this young man took this property (and he says he did), without any permission (he says he did), that was on the property of the United States Government (he says it was), that it was of the value of one cent or more (and evidently it was), that he is guilty of the offense charged here. If you believe the government, he is guilty. . . . The question on intent is whether or not he intended to take the property. He says he did. Therefore, if you believe either side, he is guilty." Petitioner's counsel contended, "But the taking must have been with a felonious intent." The court ruled, however: "That is presumed by his own act."

The Court of Appeals suggested that "greater restraint in expression should have been exercised", but affirmed the conviction because "As we have interpreted the statute, appellant was guilty of its violation beyond a shadow of doubt, as evidenced even by his own admissions." Its construction of the statute is that it creates several separate and distinct offenses, one being knowing conversion of government property. The court ruled that this particular offense requires no element of criminal intent. This conclusion was thought to be required by the failure of Congress to express such a requisite and this Court's decisions in United States v. Behrman, and United States v. Balint.

In those cases this Court did construe mere omission from a criminal enactment of any mention of criminal intent as dispensing with it. If they be deemed precedents for principles of construction generally applicable to federal penal statutes, they authorize this conviction. . . .

The contention that an injury can amount to a crime only when inflicted by intention is no provincial or transient notion. It is as universal and persistent in mature systems of law as belief in freedom of the human will and a consequent ability and duty of the normal individual to choose between good and evil. A relation between some mental element and punishment for a harmful act is almost as instinctive as the child's familiar exculpatory "But I didn't mean to," and has afforded the rational basis for a tardy and unfinished substitution of deterrence and reformation in place of retaliation and vengeance as the motivation for public prosecution. Unqualified acceptance of this doctrine by English common law in the Eighteenth Century was indicated by Blackstone's sweeping statement that to constitute any crime there must first be a "vicious will." Common-law commentators of the Nineteenth Century early pronounced the same principle. . . .

Crime as a compound concept, generally constituted only from concurrence of an evil-meaning mind with an evil-doing hand, was congenial to an intense individualism and took deep and early root in American soil. As the states codified the common law of crimes, even if their enactments were silent on the subject, their courts assumed that the omission did not signify disapproval of the principle but merely recognized that intent was so inherent in the idea of the offense that it required no statutory affirmation. Courts, with little hesitation or division, found an implication of the requirement as to offenses that were taken over from the common law. The unanimity with which they have adhered to the central thought that wrongdoing must be conscious to be criminal is emphasized by the variety, disparity and confusion of their definitions of the requisite but elusive mental element. However, courts of various jurisdictions, and for the purposes of different offenses, have devised working formulae, if not scientific ones, for the instruction of juries around such terms as "felonious intent," "criminal intent," "malice aforethought," "guilty knowledge," "fraudulent intent," "wilfulness," "*scienter*," to denote guilty knowledge or "*mens rea*," to signify an evil purpose or mental culpability. By use or combination of these various tokens, they have sought to protect those who were not blameworthy in mind from conviction of infamous common-law crimes.

However, the Balint and Behrman offenses belong to a category of another character, with very different antecedents and origins. The crimes there involved depend on no mental element but consist only of forbidden acts or omissions. This, while not expressed by the Court, is made clear from examination of a century-old but accelerating tendency, discernible both here and in England, to call into existence new duties and crimes which disregard any ingredient of intent. The industrial revolution multiplied the number of workmen exposed to injury from increasingly powerful and complex mechanisms, driven by freshly discovered sources of energy, requiring higher precautions by employers. Traffic of velocities, volumes and varieties unheard of came to subject the wayfarer to intolerable casualty risks if owners and drivers were not to observe new cares and uniformities of conduct. Congestion of cities and crowding of quarters called for health and welfare regulations undreamed of in simpler times. Wide distribution of goods became an instrument of wide distribution of harm when those who dispersed food, drink, drugs, and even securities, did not comply with reasonable standards of quality, integrity, disclosure and care. Such dangers have engendered increasingly numerous and detailed regulations which heighten the duties of those in control of particular industries, trades, properties or activities that affect public health, safety or welfare.

While many of these duties are sanctioned by a more strict civil liability, lawmakers, whether wisely or not,[1] have sought to make such regulations more effective by invoking criminal sanctions to be applied by the familiar technique of criminal prosecutions and convictions. This has confronted the courts with a multitude of prosecutions, based

1. Consequences of a general abolition of intent as an ingredient of serious crimes have aroused the concern of responsible and disinterested students of penology. Of course, they would not justify judicial disregard of a clear command to that effect from Congress, but they do admonish us to caution in assuming that Congress, without clear expression, intends in any instance to do so.

Radin, Intent, Criminal, 8 Encyc.Soc.Sci. 126, 130, says, ". . . as long as in popular belief intention and the freedom of the will are taken as axiomatic, no penal system that negates the mental element can find general acceptance. It is vital to retain public support of methods of dealing with crime." Again, "The question of criminal intent will probably always have something of an academic taint. Nevertheless, the fact remains that the determination of the boundary between intent and negligence spells freedom or condemnation for thousands of individuals. The watchfulness of the jurist justifies itself at present in its insistence upon the examination of the mind of each individual offender."

Sayre, Public Welfare Offenses, 33 Col.L. Rev. 55, 56, says: "To inflict substantial punishment upon one who is morally entirely innocent, who caused injury through reasonable mistake or pure accident, would so outrage the feelings of the community as to nullify its own enforcement."

Hall, Prolegomena to a Science of Criminal Law, 89 U. of Pa.L.Rev. 549, 569, appears somewhat less disturbed by the trend, if properly limited, but, as to so-called public welfare crimes, suggests that "There is no reason to continue to believe that the present mode of dealing with these offenses is the best solution obtainable, or that we must be content with this sacrifice of established principles. *The raising of a presumption of knowledge might be an improvement.*" (Italics added.)

In Felton v. United States, 96 U.S. 699, 703, 24 L.Ed. 875, the Court said, "But the law at the same time is not so unreasonable as to attach culpability, and consequently to impose punishment, where there is no intention to evade its provisions. . . ."

on statutes or administrative regulations, for what have been aptly called "public welfare offenses." These cases do not fit neatly into any of such accepted classifications of common-law offenses, such as those against the state, the person, property, or public morals. Many of these offenses are not in the nature of positive aggressions or invasions, with which the common law so often dealt, but are in the nature of neglect where the law requires care, or inaction where it imposes a duty. Many violations of such regulations result in no direct or immediate injury to person or property but merely create the danger or probability of it which the law seeks to minimize. While such offenses do not threaten the security of the state in the manner of treason, they may be regarded as offenses against its authority, for their occurrence impairs the efficiency of controls deemed essential to the social order as presently constituted. In this respect, whatever the intent of the violator, the injury is the same, and the consequences are injurious or not according to fortuity. Hence, legislation applicable to such offenses, as a matter of policy, does not specify intent as a necessary element. The accused, if he does not will the violation, usually is in a position to prevent it with no more care than society might reasonably expect and no more exertion than it might reasonably exact from one who assumed his responsibilities. Also, penalties commonly are relatively small, and conviction does no grave damage to an offender's reputation. Under such considerations, courts have turned to construing statutes and regulations which make no mention of intent as dispensing with it and holding that the guilty act alone makes out the crime. This has not, however, been without expressions of misgiving.

The pilot of the movement in this country appears to be a holding that a tavernkeeper could be convicted for selling liquor to an habitual drunkard even if he did not know the buyer to be such. . . . Later came Massachusetts holdings that convictions for selling adulterated milk in violation of statutes forbidding such sales require no allegation or proof that defendant knew of the adulteration. . . . Departures from the common-law tradition, mainly of these general classes, were reviewed and their rationale appraised by Chief Justice Cooley, as follows: "I agree that as a rule there can be no crime without a criminal intent, but this is not by any means a universal rule. . . . Many statutes which are in the nature of police regulations, as this is, impose criminal penalties irrespective of any intent to violate them, the purpose being to require a degree of diligence for the protection of the public which shall render violation impossible." . . .

Neither this Court nor, so far as we are aware, any other has undertaken to delineate a precise line or set forth comprehensive criteria for distinguishing between crimes that require a mental element and crimes that do not. We attempt no closed definition, for the law on the subject is neither settled nor static. The conclusion reached in the Balint and Behrman cases has our approval and adherence for the circumstances to which it was there applied. A quite different question here is whether we will expand the doctrine of crimes without intent to include those charged here.

Stealing, larceny, and its variants and equivalents, were among the earliest offenses known to the law that existed before legislation; they are invasions of rights of property which stir a sense of insecurity in the whole community and arouse public demand for retribution, the penalty is high and, when a sufficient amount is involved, the infamy is that of a felony, which, says Maitland, is ". . . as bad a word as you can give to man or thing." State courts of last resort, on whom fall the heaviest burden of interpreting criminal law in this country, have consistently retained the requirement of intent in larceny-type offenses. If any state has deviated, the exception has neither been called to our attention nor disclosed by our research.

Congress, therefore, omitted any express prescription of criminal intent from the enactment before us in the light of an unbroken course of judicial decision in all constituent states of the Union holding intent inherent in this class of offense even when not expressed in a statute. Congressional silence as to mental elements in an Act merely adopting into federal statutory law a concept of crime already so well defined in common law and statutory interpretation by the states may warrant quite contrary inferences than the same silence in creating an offense new to general law, for whose definition the courts have no guidance except the Act. Because the offenses before this Court in the Balint and Behrman cases were of this latter class, we cannot accept them as authority for eliminating intent from offenses incorporated from the common law. Nor do exhaustive studies of state court cases disclose any well-considered decisions applying the doctrine of crime without intent to such enacted common-law offenses. . . .[2]

The Government asks us by a feat of construction radically to change the weights and balances in the scales of justice. The purpose and obvious effect of doing away with the requirement of a guilty intent is to ease the prosecution's path to conviction, to strip the defendant of such benefit as he derived at common law from innocence of evil purpose, and to circumscribe the freedom heretofore allowed juries. Such a manifest impairment of the immunities of the individual should not be extended to common-law crimes on judicial initiative. . . .

We hold that mere omission from § 641 of any mention of intent will not be construed as eliminating that element from the crimes denounced.

It is suggested, however, that the history and purposes of § 641 imply something more affirmative as to elimination of intent from at

---

2. Sayre, Public Welfare Offenses, 33 Col.L.Rev. 55, 73, 84, cites and classifies a large number of cases and concludes that they fall roughly into subdivisions of (1) illegal sales of intoxicating liquor, (2) sales of impure or adulterated food or drugs, (3) sales of misbranded articles, (4) violations of antinarcotic Acts, (5) criminal nuisances, (6) violations of traffic regulations, (7) violations of motor-vehicle laws, and (8) violations of general police regulations, passed for the safety, health or well-being of the community.

least one of the offenses charged under it in this case. The argument does not contest that criminal intent is retained in the offenses of embezzlement, stealing and purloining, as incorporated into this section. But it is urged that Congress joined with those, as a new, separate and distinct offense, knowingly to convert government property, under circumstances which imply that it is an offense in which the mental element of intent is not necessary.

Congress has been alert to what often is a decisive function of some mental element in crime. It has seen fit to prescribe that an evil state of mind, described variously in one or more such terms as "intentional," "wilful," "knowing," "fraudulent" or "malicious," will make criminal an otherwise indifferent act, or increase the degree of the offense or its punishment. Also, it has at times required a specific intent or purpose which will require some specialized knowledge or design for some evil beyond the common-law intent to do injury. The law under some circumstances recognizes good faith or blameless intent as a defense, partial defense, or as an element to be considered in mitigation of punishment. . . . In view of the care that has been bestowed upon the subject, it is significant that we have not found, nor has our attention been directed to, any instance in which Congress has expressly eliminated the mental element from a crime taken over from the common law.

Congress, by the language of this section, has been at pains to incriminate only "knowing" conversions. But, at common law there are unwitting acts which constitute conversions. In the civil tort, except for recovery of exemplary damages, the defendant's knowledge, intent, motive, mistake, and good faith are generally irrelevant. If one takes property which turns out to belong to another, his innocent intent will not shield him from making restitution or indemnity, for his well-meaning may not be allowed to deprive another of his own.

Had the statute applied to conversions without qualification, it would have made crimes of all unwitting, inadvertent and unintended conversions. Knowledge, of course, is not identical with intent and may not have been the most apt words of limitation. But knowing conversion requires more than knowledge that defendant was taking the property into his possession. He must have had knowledge of the facts, though not necessarily the law, that made the taking a conversion. In the case before us, whether the mental element that Congress required be spoken of as knowledge or as intent, would not seem to alter its bearing on guilt. For it is not apparent how Morissette could have knowingly or intentionally converted property that he did not know could be converted, as would be the case if it was in fact abandoned or if he truly believed it to be abandoned and unwanted property.

It is said, and at first blush the claim has plausibility, that, if we construe the statute to require a mental element as part of criminal conversion, it becomes a meaningless duplication of the offense of stealing, and that conversion can be given meaning only by interpreting it to disregard intention. But here again a broader view of the evolution of these crimes throws a different light on the legislation.

It is not surprising if there is considerable overlapping in the embezzlement, stealing, purloining and knowing conversion grouped in this statute. What has concerned codifiers of the larceny-type offense is that gaps or crevices have separated particular crimes of this general class and guilty men have escaped through the breaches. The books contain a surfeit of cases drawing fine distinctions between slightly different circumstances under which one may obtain wrongful advantages from another's property. The codifiers wanted to reach all such instances. . . . Knowing conversion adds significantly to the range of protection of government property without interpreting it to punish unwitting conversions. . . .

We find no grounds for inferring any affirmative instruction from Congress to eliminate intent from any offense with which this defendant was charged.

As we read the record, this case was tried on the theory that even if criminal intent were essential its presence (a) should be decided by the court (b) as a presumption of law, apparently conclusive, (c) predicated upon the isolated act of taking rather than upon all of the circumstances. In each of these respects we believe the trial court was in error. . . .

We think presumptive intent has no place in this case. A conclusive presumption which testimony could not overthrow would effectively eliminate intent as an ingredient of the offense. A presumption which would permit but not require the jury to assume intent from an isolated fact would prejudge a conclusion which the jury should reach of its own volition. A presumption which would permit the jury to make an assumption which all the evidence considered together does not logically establish would give to a proven fact an artificial and fictional effect. In either case, this presumption would conflict with the overriding presumption of innocence with which the law endows the accused and which extends to every element of the crime. Such incriminating presumptions are not to be improvised by the judiciary. Even congressional power to facilitate convictions by substituting presumptions for proof is not without limit. Tot v. United States, 319 U.S. 463, 63 S.Ct. 1241, 87 L.Ed. 1519.

Moreover, the conclusion supplied by presumption in this instance was one of intent to steal the casings, and it was based on the mere fact that defendant took them. The court thought the only question was, "Did he intend to take the property?" That the removal of them was a conscious and intentional act was admitted. But that isolated fact is not an adequate basis on which the jury should find the criminal intent to steal or knowingly convert, that is, *wrongfully* to deprive another of possession of property. Whether that intent existed, the jury must determine, not only from the act of taking, but from that together with defendant's testimony and all of the surrounding circumstances.

Of course, the jury, considering Morissette's awareness that these casings were on government property, his failure to seek any permission for their removal and his self-interest as a witness, might have disbelieved his profession of innocent intent and concluded that his assertion of a belief that the casings were abandoned was an afterthought. Had the jury convicted on proper instructions it would be the end of the matter. But juries are not found by what seems inescapable logic to judges. They might have concluded that the heaps of spent casings left in the hinterland to rust away presented an appearance of unwanted and abandoned junk, and that lack of any conscious deprivation of property or intentional injury was indicated by Morissette's good character, the openness of the taking, crushing and transporting of the casings, and the candor with which it was all admitted. They might have refused to brand Morissette as a thief. Had they done so, that too would have been the end of the matter.

Reversed.

NOTES

1. In People v. Whitlow, 89 Ill.2d 322, 60 Ill.Dec. 587, 433 N.E.2d 629 (1982), the court said that a statute creating a felony offense—here, securities law provisions—does not impose absolute liability unless the legislative intent to do so is clearly expressed.

2. In Aaron v. Securities & Exchange Com., 446 U.S. 680, 100 S.Ct. 1945, 64 L.Ed.2d 611 (1980), a civil case, the Supreme Court addressed the issue of which mental state is required to enjoin violations of the Act. The Court concluded that under section 77q(a)(1), *scienter* is an essential element of the offense. It was defined as a "mental state embracing intent to deceive, manipulate, or defraud." Although *scienter* was thus defined with reference to intent, the court indicated that the term also includes knowledge: "The language of section 17(a)(1), which makes it unlawful to 'employ any device, scheme, or artifice to defraud,' plainly evinces an intent on the part of Congress to proscribe only knowing or intentional misconduct."

3. See also Liparota v. United States, 471 U.S. 419, 105 S.Ct. 2084, 85 L.Ed.2d 434 (1985), a conviction of unlawfully acquiring and possessing food stamps, wherein the United States Supreme Court held that the federal statute governing food stamp frauds (7 U.S.C.A. § 2024(b)) requires proof that the defendant knew that his acquisition or possession of food stamps was in a manner unauthorized by statute or regulations.

UNITED STATES v. PARK

Supreme Court of the United States, 1975.
421 U.S. 658, 95 S.Ct. 1903.

MR. CHIEF JUSTICE BURGER delivered the opinion of the Court.

* * *

Acme Markets, Inc., is a national retail food chain with approximately 36,000 employees, 874 retail outlets, 12 general warehouses, and four special warehouses. Its headquarters, including the office of the president, respondent Park, who is chief executive officer of the corporation, are located in Philadelphia, Pennsylvania. In a five-count information . . . the Government charged Acme and respondent with violations of the Federal Food, Drug and Cosmetic Act. Each count of the information alleged that the defendants had received food that had been shipped in interstate commerce and that, while the food was being held for sale in Acme's Baltimore warehouse following shipment in interstate commerce, they caused it to be held in a building accessible to rodents and to be exposed to contamination by rodents. These acts were alleged to have resulted in the food being adulterated . . . in violation of 21 U.S.C.A. § 331(k).[1]

Acme pleaded guilty to each count of the information. Respondent pleaded not guilty. The evidence at trial [2] demonstrated that in April 1970 the Food and Drug Administration (FDA) advised respondent by letter of insanitary conditions in Acme's Philadelphia warehouse. In 1971 FDA found that similar conditions existed in the firm's Baltimore warehouse. An FDA consumer safety officer testified concerning evidence of rodent infestation and other insanitary conditions discovered during a 12–day inspection of the Baltimore warehouse in November and December 1971.[3] He also related that a second inspection of the warehouse had been conducted in March 1972. On that occasion the inspectors found that there had been improvement in the sanitary conditions, but that "there was still evidence of rodent activity in the building and in the warehouse and we found some rodent-contaminated lots of food items."

The Government also presented testimony by the Chief of Compliance of FDA's Baltimore office, who informed respondent by letter of the conditions at the Baltimore warehouse after the first inspection.

1. 21 U.S.C.A. § 331(k), provides:

"The following acts and the causing thereof are prohibited:

* * *

(k) The alteration, mutilation, destruction, obliteration, or removal of the whole or any part of the labeling of, or the doing of any other act with respect to, a food, drug, device, or cosmetic, if such act is done while such article is held for sale (whether or not the first sale) after shipment in interstate commerce and results in such article being adulterated or misbranded."

2. The parties stipulated in effect that the items of food described in the information had been shipped in interstate commerce and were being held for sale in Acme's Baltimore warehouse.

3. The witness testified with respect to the inspection of the basement of the "old building" in the warehouse complex:

"We found extensive evidence of rodent infestation in the form of rat and mouse pellets throughout the entire perimeter area and along the wall.

"We also found that the doors leading to the basement area from the rail siding had openings at the bottom or openings beneath part of the door that came down at the bottom large enough to admit rodent entry. There were also roden[t] pellets found on a number of different packages of boxes of various items stored in the basement, and looking at this document, I see there were also broken windows along the rail siding." On the first floor of the "old building," the inspectors found:

"Thirty mouse pellets on the floor along walls and on the ledge in the hanging meat room. There were at least twenty mouse pellets beside bales of lime Jello and one of the bales had a chewed rodent hole in the product. . . ."

There was testimony by Acme's Baltimore division vice president, who had responded to the letter on behalf of Acme and respondent and who described the steps taken to remedy the insanitary conditions discovered by both inspections. The Government's final witness, Acme's vice president for legal affairs and assistant secretary, identified respondent as the president and chief executive officer of the company and read a bylaw prescribing the duties of the chief executive officer.[4] He testified that respondent functioned by delegating "normal operating duties," including sanitation, but that he retained "certain things, which are the big, broad, principles of the operation of the company," and had "the responsibility of seeing that they all work together."

At the close of the Government's case-in-chief, respondent moved for a judgment of acquittal on the ground that "the evidence in chief has shown that Mr. Park is not personally concerned in this Food and Drug violation." The trial judge denied the motion, stating that United States v. Dotterweich, 320 U.S. 277, 64 S.Ct. 134 was controlling.

Respondent was the only defense witness. He testified that, although all of Acme's employees were in a sense under his general direction, the company had an "organizational structure for responsibilities for certain functions" according to which different phases of its operation were "assigned to individuals who, in turn, have staff and departments under them." He identified those individuals responsible for sanitation and related that upon receipt of the January 1972 FDA letter, he had conferred with the vice president for legal affairs, who informed him that the Baltimore division vice president "was investigating the situation immediately and would be taking corrective action and would be preparing a summary of the corrective action to reply to the letter." Respondent stated that he did not "believe there was anything [he] could have done more constructively than what [he] found was being done."

On cross-examination, respondent conceded that providing sanitary conditions for food offered for sale to the public was something that he was "responsible for in the entire operation of the company," and he stated that it was one of many phases of the company that he assigned to "dependable subordinates." Respondent was asked about and, over the objections of his counsel, admitted receiving, the April 1970 letter addressed to him from FDA regarding insanitary conditions at Acme's Philadelphia warehouse.[5] He acknowledged that, with the exception of

4. The bylaw provided in pertinent part:

"The Chairman of the board of directors or the president shall be the chief executive officer of the company as the board of directors may from time to time determine. He shall, subject to the board of directors, have general and active supervision of the affairs, business, offices and employees of the company. . . .

"He shall, from time to time, in his discretion or at the order of the board, report the operations and affairs of the company. He shall also perform such other duties and have such other powers as may be assigned to him from time to time by the board of directors."

5. The April 1970 letter informed respondent of the following "objectionable conditions" in Acme's Philadelphia warehouse:

the division vice president, the same individuals had responsibility for sanitation in both Baltimore and Philadelphia. Finally, in response to questions concerning the Philadelphia and Baltimore incidents, respondent admitted that the Baltimore problem indicated the system for handling sanitation "wasn't working perfectly" and that as Acme's chief executive officer he was responsible for "any result which occurs in our company."

At the close of the evidence, respondent's renewed motion for a judgment of acquittal was denied. The relevant portion of the trial judge's instructions to the jury challenged by respondent is set out in the margin.[6] Respondent's counsel objected to the instructions on the ground that they failed fairly to reflect our decision in United States v. Dotterweich, 320 U.S. 277, 64 S.Ct. 134, and to define " 'responsible relationship.' " The trial judge overruled the objection. The jury found respondent guilty on all counts of the information, and he was subsequently sentenced to pay a fine of $50 on each count.

The Court of Appeals reversed the conviction and remanded for a new trial. That court viewed the Government as arguing "that the conviction may be predicated solely upon a showing that . . . [respondent] was the President of the offending corporation," and it stated that as "a general proposition, some act of commission or omission is an essential element of every crime." It reasoned that, although our decision in United States v. Dotterweich, had construed the statutory

"1. Potential rodent entry ways were noted via ill fitting doors and door ir-repair at Southwest corner of warehouse; at dock at old salvage room and at receiving and shipping doors which were observed to be open most of the time.

"2. Rodent nesting, rodent excreta pellets, rodent stained bale bagging and rodent gnawed holes were noted among bales of flour stored in warehouse.

"3. Potential rodent harborage was noted in discarded paper, rope, sawdust and other debris piled in corner of shipping and receiving dock near bakery and warehouse doors. Rodent excreta pellets were observed among bags of sawdust (or wood shavings)."

6. "In order to find the Defendant guilty on any count of the Information, you must find beyond a reasonable doubt on each count.

* * *

"Thirdly, that John R. Park held a position of authority in the operation of the business of Acme Markets, Incorporated.

"However, you need not concern yourselves with the first two elements of the case. The main issue for your determination is only with the third element, whether the Defendant held a position of authority and responsibility in the business of Acme Markets.

. . .

"The statute makes individuals, as well as corporations, liable for violations. An individual is liable if it is clear, beyond a reasonable doubt, that the elements of the adulteration of the food as to travel in interstate commerce are present. As I have instructed you in this case, they are, and that the individual had a responsible relation to the situation, even though he may not have participated personally.

"The individual is or could be liable under the statute, even if he did not consciously do wrong. However, the fact that the Defendant is pres[id]ent and is a chief executive officer of the Acme Markets does not require a finding of guilt. Though, he need not have personally participated in the situation, he must have had a responsible relationship to the issue. The issue is, in this case, whether the Defendant, John R. Park, by virtue of his position in the company, had a position of authority and responsibility in the situation out of which these charges arose."

provisions under which respondent was tried to dispense with the traditional element of " 'awareness of some wrongdoing,' " the Court had not construed them as dispensing with the element of "wrongful action." The Court of Appeals concluded that the trial judge's instructions "might well have left the jury with the erroneous impression that Park could be found guilty in the absence of 'wrongful action' on his part," and that proof of this element was required by due process. It held, with one dissent, that the instructions did not "correctly state the law of the case," and directed that on retrial the jury be instructed as to "wrongful action," which might be "gross negligence and inattention in discharging . . . corporate duties and obligations or any of a host of other acts of commission or omission which would 'cause' the contamination of food."

The Court of Appeals also held that the admission in evidence of the April 1970 FDA warning to respondent was error warranting reversal, based on its conclusion that, "as this case was submitted to the jury and in light of the sole issue presented," there was no need for the evidence and thus that its prejudicial effect outweighed its relevancy.

* * *

I

The question presented in United States v. Dotterweich, supra, was whether "the manager of a corporation, as well as the corporation itself, may be prosecuted under the Federal Food, Drug, and Cosmetic Act of 1938 for the introduction of misbranded and adulterated articles into interstate commerce." In *Dotterweich,* a jury had disagreed as to the corporation, a jobber purchasing drugs from manufacturers and shipping them in interstate commerce under its own label, but had convicted Dotterweich, the corporation's president and general manager. The Court of Appeals reversed the conviction on the ground that only the drug dealer, whether corporation or individual, was subject to the criminal provisions of the Act, and that where the dealer was a corporation, an individual connected therewith might be held personally only if he was operating the corporation "as his 'alter ego.' "

In reversing the Court of Appeals, this Court looked to the purposes of the Act and noted that they "touch phases of the lives and health of the people which, in the circumstances of modern industrialism, are largely beyond self-protection." It observed that the Act is of "a now familiar type" which "dispenses with the conventional requirement for criminal conduct—awareness of some wrongdoing. In the interest of the larger good it puts the burden of acting at hazard upon a person otherwise innocent but standing in responsible relation to a public danger."

Central to the Court's conclusion that individuals other than proprietors are subject to the criminal provisions of the Act was the reality that "the only way in which a corporation can act is through the individuals who act on its behalf." The Court also noted that corporate officers had been subject to criminal liability under the Federal Food and Drugs Act of 1906, and it observed that a contrary result under the 1938 legislation would be incompatible with the expressed intent of Congress to "enlarge and stiffen the penal net" and to discourage a view of the Act's criminal penalties as a " 'license fee for the conduct of an illegitimate business.' "

At the same time, however, the Court was aware of the concern which was the motivating factor in the Court of Appeals' decision, that literal enforcement "might operate too harshly by sweeping within its condemnation any person however remotely entangled in the proscribed shipment." A limiting principle, in the form of "settled doctrines of criminal law" defining those who "are responsible for the commission of a misdemeanor", was available. In this context, the Court concluded, those doctrines dictated that the offense was committed "by all who have . . . a responsible share in the furtherance of the transaction which the statute outlaws".

The Court recognized that, because the Act dispenses with the need to prove "consciousness of wrongdoing", it may result in hardship even as applied to those who share "[a] responsibility in the business process resulting in" a violation. It regarded as "too treacherous" an attempt "to define or even to indicate by way of illustration the class of employees which stands in such a responsible relation." The question of responsibility, the Court said, depends "on the evidence produced at the trial and its submission—assuming the evidence warrants it—to the jury under appropriate guidance." The Court added: "In such matters the good sense of prosecutors, the wise guidance of trial judges, and the ultimate judgment of juries must be trusted."

II

The rule that corporate employees who have "a responsible share in the furtherance of the transaction which the statute outlaws" are subject to the criminal provisions of the Act was not formulated in a vacuum. Cases under the Federal Food and Drugs Act of 1906 reflected the view both that knowledge or intent were not required to be proved in prosecutions under its criminal provisions, and that responsible corporate agents could be subjected to the liability thereby imposed. Moreover, the principle had been recognized that a corporate agent, through whose act, default, or omission the corporation committed a crime, was himself guilty individually of that crime. The principle had been applied whether or not the crime required "consciousness of wrongdoing", and it had been applied not only to those corporate agents who themselves committed the criminal act, but also to those who by virtue of their managerial positions or other similar relation to the actor could be deemed responsible for its commission.

In the latter class of cases, the liability of managerial officers did not depend on their knowledge of, or personal participation in, the act made criminal by the statute. Rather, where the statute under which they were prosecuted dispensed with "consciousness of wrongdoing", and omission or failure to act was deemed a sufficient basis for a responsible corporate agent's liability. It was enough in such cases, that, by virtue of the relationship he bore to the corporation, the agent had the power to have prevented the act complained of.

The rationale of the interpretation given the Act in *Dotterweich,* as holding criminally accountable the persons whose failure to exercise the authority and supervisory responsibility reposed in them by the business organization resulted in the violation complained of, has been confirmed in our subsequent cases. Thus, the Court has reaffirmed the proposition that "the public interest in the purity of its food is so great as to warrant the imposition of the highest standard of care on distributors". In order to make "distributors of food the strictest censors of their merchandise", the Act punishes "neglect where the law requires care, or inaction where it imposes a duty." Morissette v. United States [Casebook, p. 634]. "The accused, if he does not will the violation, usually is in a position to prevent it with no more care than society might reasonably expect and no more exertion than it might reasonably exact from one who assumed his responsibilities." Similarly, in cases decided after *Dotterweich,* the courts of appeals have recognized that those corporate agents vested with the responsibility, and power commensurate with that responsibility, to devise whatever measures are necessary to ensure compliance with the Act bear a "responsible relationship" to, or have a "responsible share" in, violations.

Thus *Dotterweich* and the cases which have followed reveal that in providing sanctions which reach and touch the individuals who execute the corporate mission—and this is by no means necessarily confined to a single corporate agent or employee—the Act imposes not only a positive duty to seek out and remedy violations when they occur but also, and primarily, a duty to implement measures that will insure that violations will not occur. The requirements of foresight and vigilance imposed on responsible corporate agents are beyond question demanding, and perhaps onerous, but they are no more stringent than the public has a right to expect of those who voluntarily assume positions of authority in business enterprises whose services and products affect the health and well-being of the public that supports them.

The Act does not, as we observed in *Dotterweich,* make criminal liability turn on "awareness of some wrongdoing" or "conscious fraud". The duty imposed by Congress on responsible corporate agents is, we emphasize, one that requires the highest standard of foresight and vigilance, but the Act, in its criminal aspect, does not require that which is objectively impossible. The theory upon which responsible corporate agents are held criminally accountable for "causing" violations of the Act permits a claim that a defendant was "powerless" to prevent or correct the violation to "be raised defensively at a trial on the merits." If such a claim is made, the defendant has the burden of coming forward with evidence, but this does not alter the Government's ultimate burden of proving beyond a reasonable doubt the defendant's guilt, including his power, in light of the duty imposed by the Act, to prevent or correct the prohibited condition. Congress has seen fit to enforce the accountability of responsible corporate agents dealing with products which may affect the health of consumers by penal sanctions cast in rigorous terms, and the obligation of the courts is to give them effect so long as they do not violate the Constitution.

III

We cannot agree with the Court of Appeals that it was incumbent upon the District Court to instruct the jury that the Government had the burden of establishing "wrongful action" in the sense in which the Court of Appeals used that phrase. The concept of a "responsible relationship" to, or a "responsible share" in, a violation of the Act indeed imports some measure of blameworthiness; but it is equally clear that the Government establishes a prima facie case when it introduces evidence sufficient to warrant a finding by the trier of the facts that the defendant had, by reason of his position in the corporation, responsibility and authority either to prevent in the first instance, or promptly to correct, the violation complained of, and that he failed to do so. The failure thus to fulfill the duty imposed by the interaction of the corporate agent's authority and the statute furnishes a sufficient causal link. The considerations which prompted the imposition of this duty, and the scope of the duty, provide the measure of culpability.

Turning to the jury charge in this case, it is of course arguable that isolated parts can be read as intimating that a finding of guilt could be predicated solely on respondent's corporate position. But this is not the way we review jury instructions, because "a single instruction to a jury may not be judged in artificial isolation, but must be viewed in the context of the overall charge."

Reading the entire charge satisfies us that the jury's attention was adequately focused on the issue of respondent's authority with respect to the conditions that formed the basis of the alleged violations. Viewed as a whole, the charge did not permit the jury to find guilt solely on the basis of respondent's position in the corporation; rather, it fairly advised the jury that to find guilt it must find respondent "had a responsible relation to the situation," and "by virtue of his position . . . had authority and responsibility" to deal with the situation. The situation referred to could only be "food . . . held in unsanitary conditions in a warehouse with the result that it consisted, in part, of filth or . . . may have been contaminated with filth."

. . . The record in this case reveals that the jury could not have failed to be aware that the main issue for determination was not respondent's position in the corporate hierarchy, but rather his accountability, because of the responsibility and authority of his position, for the conditions which gave rise to the charges against him.

* * *

IV

Our conclusion that the Court of Appeals erred in its reading of the jury charge suggests as well our disagreement with that court concerning the admissibility of evidence demonstrating that respondent was advised by FDA in 1970 of insanitary conditions in Acme's Philadelphia warehouse. We are satisfied that the Act imposes the highest standard of care and permits conviction of responsible corporate officials who, in light of this standard of care, have the power to prevent or correct violations of its provisions. Implicit in the Court's admonition that "the ultimate judgment of juries must be trusted", United States v. Dotterweich, supra, however, is the realization that they may demand more than corporate bylaws to find culpability.

Respondent testified in his defense that he had employed a system in which he relied upon his subordinates and that he was ultimately responsible for this system. He testified further that he had found these subordinates to be "dependable" and had "great confidence" in them. By this and other testimony respondent evidently sought to persuade the jury that, as the president of a large corporation, he had no choice but to delegate duties to those in whom he reposed confidence, that he had no reason to suspect his subordinates were failing to insure compliance with the Act, and that, once violations were unearthed, acting through those subordinates he did everything possible to correct them.

. . . the testimony clearly created the "need" for rebuttal evidence. That evidence was not offered to show that respondent had a propensity to commit criminal acts, or, that the crime charged had been committed; its purpose was to demonstrate that respondent was on notice that he could not rely on his system of delegation to subordinates to prevent or correct insanitary conditions at Acme's warehouses, and that he must have been aware of the deficiencies of this system before the Baltimore violations were discovered. The evidence was therefore relevant since it served to rebut respondent's defense that he had justifiably relied upon subordinates to handle sanitation matters. C. McCormick, Evidence § 190, at 450–452 (2d ed. 1972). And, particularly in light of the difficult task of juries in prosecutions under the Act, we conclude that its relevance and persuasiveness outweighed any prejudicial effect.

Reversed.

MR. JUSTICE STEWART, with whom MR. JUSTICE MARSHALL and MR. JUSTICE POWELL join, dissenting.

Although agreeing with much of what is said in the Court's opinion, I dissent from the opinion and judgment, because the jury instructions in this case were not consistent with the law as the Court today expounds it.

As I understand the Court's opinion, it holds that in order to sustain a conviction under § 301(k) of the Food, Drug, and Cosmetic Act the prosecution must at least show that by reason of an individual's corporate position and responsibilities, he had a duty to use care to maintain the physical integrity of the corporation's food products. A jury may then draw the inference that when the food is found to be in such condition as to violate the statute's prohibitions, that condition was "caused" by a breach of the standard of care imposed upon the responsible official. This is the language of negligence, and I agree with it.

To affirm this conviction, however, the Court must approve the instructions given to the members of the jury who were entrusted with determining whether the respondent was innocent or guilty. Those instructions did not conform to the standards that the Court itself sets out today.

The trial judge instructed the jury to find Park guilty if it found beyond a reasonable doubt that Park "had a responsible relation to the situation . . . The issue is, in this case, whether the Defendant, John R. Park, by virtue of his position in the company, had a position of authority and responsibility in the situation out of which these charges arose." Requiring, as it did, a verdict of guilty upon a finding of "responsibility," this instruction standing alone could have been construed as a direction to convict if the jury found Park "responsible" for the condition in the sense that his position as chief executive officer gave him formal responsibility within the structure of the corporation. But the trial judge went on specifically to caution the jury not to attach such a meaning to his instruction saying that "the fact that the Defendant is present [sic] and is a chief executive officer of the Acme Markets does not require a finding of guilt." "Responsibility" as used by the trial judge therefore had whatever meaning the jury in its unguided discretion chose to give it.

The instructions, therefore, expressed nothing more than a tautology. They told the jury: "You must find the defendant guilty if you find that he is to be held accountable for this adulterated food." In other words: "You must find the defendant guilty if you conclude that he is guilty." The trial judge recognized the infirmities in these instructions, but he reluctantly concluded that he was required to give such a charge under United States v. Dotterweich, which, he thought, in declining to define "responsible relation" had declined to specify the minimum standard of liability for criminal guilt.[7]

As the Court today recognized, the *Dotterweich* case did not deal with what kind of conduct must be proved to support a finding of criminal guilt under the Act. *Dotterweich* was concerned, rather, with the statutory definition of "person"—with what kind of corporate

---

7. In response to a request for further illumination of what he meant by "responsible relationship" the District Judge said:

"Let me say this, simply as to the definition of the 'responsible relationship.' Dotterweich and subsequent cases have indicated this really is a jury question. It says it is not even subject to being defined by the Court. As I have indicated to counsel, I am quite candid in stating that I do not agree with the decision; therefore, I am going to stick by it."

employees were even "subject to the criminal provisions of the Act." Ante, at 1910. The Court held that those employees with a "responsible relation" to the violative transaction or condition were subject to the Act's criminal provisions, but all that the Court had to say with respect to the kind of conduct that can constitute criminal guilt was that the Act "dispenses with the conventional requirement for criminal conduct—awareness of some wrongdoing."

In approving the instructions to the jury in this case—instructions based upon what the Court concedes was a misunderstanding of *Dotterweich*—the Court approves a conspicuous departure from the long and firmly established division of functions between judge and jury in the administration of criminal justice. As the Court put the matter more than 80 years ago:

> "We must hold firmly to the doctrine that in the courts of the United States it is the duty of juries in criminal cases to take the law from the court, and apply that law to the facts as they find them to be from the evidence. Upon the court rests the responsibility of declaring the law; upon the jury, the responsibility of applying the law so declared to the facts as they, upon their conscience, believe them to be. Under any other system, the courts, although established in order to declare the law, would for every practical purpose be eliminated from our system of government as instrumentalities devised for protection equally of society and of individuals in their essential rights. When that occurs our government will cease to be a government of laws and become a government of men. Liberty regulated by law is the underlying principle of our institutions."

More recently the Court declared unconstitutional a procedure whereby a jury, having acquitted a defendant of a misdemeanor, was instructed to impose upon him such costs of the prosecution as it deemed appropriate to his degree of "responsibility." Giaccio v. Pennsylvania, 382 U.S. 399, 86 S.Ct. 518 (1966). The state statute under which the procedure was authorized was invalidated because it left "to the jury such broad and unlimited power in imposing costs on acquitted defendants that the jurors must make determinations of the crucial issue upon their own notions of what the law should be instead of what it is." . . .

These cases no more than embody a principle fundamental to our jurisprudence: that a jury is to decide the facts and apply to them the law as explained by the trial judge. Were it otherwise, trial by jury would be no more rational and no more responsive to the accumulated wisdom of the law than trial by ordeal. It is the function of jury instructions, in short, to establish in any trial the objective standards that a jury is to apply as it performs its own function of finding the facts.

To be sure, "the day [is] long past when [courts] parsed instructions and engaged in nice semantic distinctions." But this Court has never before abandoned the view that jury instructions must contain a statement of the applicable law sufficiently precise to enable the jury to be guided by something other than its rough notions of social justice. And while it might be argued that the issue before the jury in this case was a "mixed" question of both law and fact, this has never meant that a jury is to be left wholly at sea, without any guidance as to the standard of conduct the law requires. The instructions given by the trial court in this case, it must be emphasized, were a virtual nullity, a mere authorization to convict if the jury thought it appropriate. Such instructions—regardless of the blameworthiness of the defendant's conduct, regardless of the social value of the Food, Drug, and Cosmetic Act, and regardless of the importance of convicting those who violate it— have no place in our jurisprudence.

We deal here with a criminal conviction, not a civil forfeiture. It is true that the crime was but a misdemeanor and the penalty in this case light. But under the statute even a first conviction can result in imprisonment for a year, and a subsequent offense is a felony carrying a punishment of up to three years in prison. So the standardless conviction approved today can serve in another case tomorrow to support a felony conviction and a substantial prison sentence. However highly the Court may regard the social objectives of the Food, Drug and Cosmetic Act, that regard cannot serve to justify a criminal conviction so wholly alien to fundamental principles of our law.

The *Dotterweich* case stands for two propositions, and I accept them both. First, "any person" within the meaning of 21 U.S.C.A. § 333 may include any corporate officer or employee "standing in responsible relation" to a condition or transaction forbidden by the Act. Second, a person may be convicted of a criminal offense under the Act even in the absence of "the conventional requirement for criminal conduct—awareness of some wrongdoing."

But before a person can be convicted of a criminal violation of this Act, a jury must find—and must be clearly instructed that it must find—evidence beyond a reasonable doubt that he engaged in wrongful conduct amounting at least to common-law negligence. There were no such instructions, and clearly, therefore, no such finding in this case.

For these reasons, I cannot join the Court in affirming Park's criminal conviction.

NOTES

1. The *Park* case has been implemented by two circuit court cases: United States v. Y. Hata & Co., Ltd., 535 F.2d 508 (9th Cir.1976) and United States v. Starr, 535 F.2d 512 (9th Cir.1976).

Among the various federal statutes imposing personal criminal liability are: Federal Food, Drug and Cosmetic Act § 303, 21 U.S.C.A. § 333; Antitrust Laws, 15 U.S.C.A. § 24; Securities Laws, 15 U.S.C.A. § 77x; Tax Laws, 15 U.S.

C.A. § 7203; Clean Air Act, 42 U.S.C.A. § 1857c–8(c)(1); Federal Water Pollution Act, 33 U.S.C.A. § 1319(c)(1); Occupational Safety and Health Act, 29 U.S.C.A. § 666(g); Flammable Fabrics Act, 15 U.S.C.A. § 1196; Hazardous Substances Act, 15 U.S.C.A. § 1264; Economic Poison Control Act, 7 U.S.C.A. § 135f; Pesticide Control Act, 7 U.S.C.A. § 136*l*(b); Employee Retirement Income Security Act, 29 U.S.C.A. § 1131; Labor Reporting and Disclosure Act, 29 U.S.C.A. § 501(c); and Labor Management Relations Act, 29 U.S.C.A. § 216.

2.   Professor Jerome Hall in his book, General Principles of Criminal Law (2d ed. 1960), devotes a chapter to the problems of strict liability. In connection with proposed substitutes for strict liability, he suggests the following (at pp. 351–353):

"Any current estimate of strict liability must take account of the vastly improved procedural and administrative facilities that now abound. Summary judicial hearings have been greatly improved; various techniques for arriving at judgments by conference, requiring mere recordation in court, are available; administration and administrative law have been greatly improved and expanded in the past quarter of a century. In short, the sole *raison d'être* of strict liability no longer exists—the problem posed by statistics can now be met by available legal institutions. . . . The continued recital of the rationalizations of a century ago loses any modicum of persuasiveness when the insistent claims of principle can be satisfied.

"The elimination of punitive strict liability would not restrict the inducements made by prosecutors to obtain pleas of guilty to the relevant criminal charges. The general features of contemporary criminal procedure, characterized by the disposal of the greatest part of the business by prosecutors and judges sitting without juries, would obtain here too. The bulk of the problem of protecting public welfare would be transferred to licensing and administrative agencies, . . . leaving the willful violations to be disposed of by specialized criminal courts or by special procedure. Against these unscrupulous individuals, the criminal law, sharpened to allow adequate dealing with crimes that are very serious in modern conditions, would be used much more frequently than in the past. On the other hand, the trial of reputable persons in a criminal court would be discontinued. Instead, sound legislation, . . . inspection, licensing, information, . . . investigation by boards, informal conferences, and publicity would provide much more likely means of influencing legitimate business.

"For the incompetents who simply cannot conform to decent standards, even after warning, information and counsel by regulatory boards, there is no alternative save to bar them from the pursuit of activities which are harmful to the public—whether that is driving an automobile, supplying milk or operating a public bar. It is undoubtedly true that the penal law functions much less onerously than would revocation of a license to do business. But this does not support the continuance of an anomalous strict 'penal' liability. The community is entitled to protection from inefficient persons who engage in potentially dangerous vocations or activities. They are certainly not restrained or improved by the perfunctory imposition of petty fines, nor for that matter by much severer penalties. The only proper recourse in some cases (very few, presumably, by comparison with those who improve their course of business after notice and assistance are received) must be the termination of the business or other activity. To make that depend on criminal behavior is to confuse immorality with inefficiency. To confine revocation of a license to the former is to ignore a major cause of injury to important social interests."

3.　See also, Edwards, Mens Rea in Statutory Offenses (1955); Remington & Helstad, The Mental Element in Crime—A Legislative Problem, 1952 Wis.L. Rev. 644; and Packer, Mens Rea and the Supreme Court, 1962 Sup.Ct.Rev. (Kurland ed.) 107; Haddad, The Mental Attitude Requirement in Criminal Law—and Some Exceptions, 59 J.Crim.L., C. & P.S. 4 (1968).

4.　For a collection of cases involving a variety of public welfare statutes and ordinances see the American Law Institute's Model Penal Code (Tent.Draft # 4) commentary at pp. 141–145. For an extensive list of some of the earlier cases, see Sayre, Public Welfare Offense, 33 Colum.L.Rev. 55, 84–88 (1933). In their more unusual varieties, strict liability offenses include the types of crimes Professor Allen refers to when he says, "The killing of domesticated pigeons, the fencing of saltpeter caves against wandering cattle, . . . and the issue of daylight savings versus standard time have all at one place or another been made problems of the criminal law." Allen, Book Review, 66 Yale L.J. 1120, 1121 (1957).

5.　See Noble v. State, 248 Ind. 101, 223 N.E.2d 755 (1967), for a remarkable attempt to impose a heavy prison sentence upon a notary public without proof of fault and without permitting the defense of reasonable and good faith mistake.

BRAUN v. STATE

Court of Appeals of Maryland, 1962.
230 Md. 82, 185 A.2d 905.

BRUNE, CHIEF JUDGE.　The appellant was tried in the Criminal Court of Baltimore before the court, sitting without a jury, on a charge of bigamy, was found guilty, and was sentenced to five years' imprisonment. . . .

The appellant's main contention is that when he entered into the marriage with his second wife in Maryland in 1961, he believed that his first wife had divorced him, that he, therefore, lacked any wrongful intent and hence was not guilty of bigamy. He was prosecuted under § 18 of Art. 27 of the Code (1957) which provides in part:

"Whosoever being married and not having obtained an annulment or a divorce a vinculo matrimonii * * *, the first husband or wife (as the case may be) being alive, shall marry any person, shall undergo a confinement in the penitentiary for * * * not less than eighteen months nor more than nine years; provided, that nothing herein contained shall extend to any person whose husband or wife shall be continuously remaining beyond the seas seven years together, or shall be absent * * * seven years together, in any part within the United States or elsewhere, the one of them not knowing the other to be living at that time."

Most American jurisdictions which have considered the question hold that the fact that the defendant may have believed in good faith that there had been a prior divorce or that a prior divorce was valid is no defense to a charge of bigamy if in fact there has been no divorce or it is invalid. . . . Most American jurisdictions also follow a similar rule where the defendant in good faith, but mistakenly, believes his or her first spouse to be dead. . . . There are some authorities contrary to the majority view, which largely follow Reg. v. Tolson, [1889] 23 Q.B.D. 168. In that case it was held by nine of the judges, with five dissenting, that the defendant's belief in good faith and on reasonable grounds at the time of her second marriage that her first husband, who had deserted her more than seven years earlier, was dead, constituted a defense to a charge of bigamy under the statute of 24 & 25 Victoria, c. 100, s. 57, which is similar to our present statute against bigamy. Tolson was, however, limited by Rex v. Wheat, [1921] 2 K.B. 119, which involved the same statute. There the court unanimously held that a mistaken belief that a divorce had been granted afforded no defense, and distinguished Tolson. . . .

This court has not previously been called upon directly to decide in a prosecution for bigamy whether or not a belief on the part of the defendant that he and his first wife have been divorced constitutes a good defense. Expressions of this court in prior cases point clearly to a view in accord with that held by the majority of American cases and also that of Rex v. Wheat, supra.

There is quite a full discussion of the subject of a mistaken belief based upon a mistake of law in Geisselman v. Geisselman, 134 Md. 453, 107 A. 185 (1919) which was a divorce case. The first wife had been convicted of a crime and sentenced to imprisonment. The husband thought that this left him free to remarry, and he proceeded to do so in Maryland, and the second marriage was consummated. He was indicted for bigamy, pleaded guilty and was paroled. He sued for a divorce from his first wife, but his bill was dismissed on the ground of recrimination. The decree of dismissal was affirmed. This court held that the husband's mistake of law did not excuse him from the charge of adultery. In reaching this conclusion the court relied largely on the analogy to bigamy cases and dismissed a number of authorities in other jurisdictions, including Reg. v. Tolson, supra. It reviewed a number of authorities and found the majority rule in this country to be opposed to Tolson, and declined to adopt the minority or Tolson view. This court, after referring to American authorities, said (134 Md. at 458, 107 A. at 187): "There would seem to be no doubt that under the above authorities, and others might be cited, the appellant could not have escaped conviction for bigamy * * *." The court left open the possibility that under some circumstances a bona fide mistake of fact under which a man had married a woman other than his real wife and had cohabited with her might be a bar on the ground of recrimination to his obtaining relief in a suit against his first wife if he was justified in his mistaken belief and had not been negligent or lax in endeavoring to ascertain the actual facts before entering into the second marriage (134 Md. at 462, 107 A. at 188), but held that in the Geisselman case the mistake was one of law and not one of fact, and took the general rule that a mistake of law will not excuse one charged with adultery.

In Slansky v. State, 192 Md. 94, 63 A.2d 599, a man had gone to another state and had there obtained a divorce from his first wife. A few days later he married his second wife in Maryland and was thereafter prosecuted for and convicted of bigamy. He relied upon the divorce obtained elsewhere, but under advisory instructions from the court (which were not challenged) as to the effect of the decree of another state and with regard to domicil the defendant was found guilty. His principal contention on appeal was that full faith and credit had been denied to the decree of a court of a sister state (Nevada). The conviction was affirmed largely on Williams v. North Carolina, 325 U.S. 226, 65 S.Ct. 1092, 89 L.Ed. 1577, since there was evidence in the Maryland trial court upon which the jury could properly find that the defendant had not acquired a domicil in the other state. This court stated (192 Md. at 110, 63 A.2d at 606): "Appellant assumed the risk that Maryland might justifiably find that he had not been domiciled in Nevada." This court did not directly pass upon the question of the defendant's belief in the validity of the Nevada divorce, but seems to have assumed in the statement just quoted that it was not material. . . .

The problem of statutory construction is primarily whether or not a requirement of *mens rea* to establish guilt should be read into the statute. . . . Jenkins v. State, 215 Md. 70, 137 A.2d 115 . . . cited and reviewed many authorities. That case involved possession of narcotics. It was held unnecessary under the statute there involved for the State to prove that the defendant knew that the contents of a package, which he admittedly had in his possession, consisted of a narcotic (cannabis). In Geisselman this Court quoted with approval a statement that in the United States, "the crime of [bigamy] is considered to be on a par with various police regulations where criminal intent is unnecessary." In the light of the majority American rule and of the prior expressions of this Court—particularly in the Geisselman case, both that just quoted and that with regard to the social purposes underlying the bigamy statute—and in view of the fact that honest belief is not one of the exceptions from liability enumerated in the statute itself, we think that even if the appellant had entertained a bona fide belief that his first wife had divorced him before his second marriage, and even if this erroneous belief were to be regarded as a mistake of fact and not of law (which we do not decide), this would not constitute a defense to the charge of bigamy under our statute. . . .

Judgment affirmed.

PEOPLE v. STUART

Supreme Court of California, 1956.
47 Cal.2d 167, 302 P.2d 5.

TRAYNOR, JUSTICE. Defendant was charged by information with manslaughter, Pen.Code, § 192, and the violation of section 380 of the Penal Code. He was convicted of both offenses by the court sitting without a jury. His motions for a new trial and for dismissal, Pen. Code, § 1385, were denied, sentence was suspended, and he was placed on probation for two years. He appeals from the judgment of conviction and the order denying his motion for a new trial.

Defendant was licensed as a pharmacist by this state in 1946 and has practiced here since that time. He holds a B.S. degree in chemistry from Long Island University and a B.S. degree in pharmacy from Columbia University. In April, 1954, he was employed as a pharmacist by the Ethical Drug Company in Los Angeles.

On July 16, 1954, he filled a prescription for Irvin Sills. It had been written by Dr. D.M. Goldstein for Sills' eight-day-old child. It called for "Sodium phenobarbital, grains eight. Sodium citrate, drams three. Simple Syrup, ounces two. Aqua pepperment, ounces one. Aqua *distilate* QS, ounces four." . . . Sills returned home, put a teaspoonful of the prescription in the baby's milk and gave it to the baby. The baby died a few hours later.

Defendant stipulated that there was nitrate in the prescription bottle and that "the cause of death was methemoglobinemia caused by the ingestion of nitrite." When he compounded the prescription, there was a bottle containing sodium nitrite on the shelf near a bottle labeled sodium citrate. He testified that at no time during his employment at the Ethical Drug Company had he filled any prescription calling for sodium nitrite and that he had taken the prescribed three drams of sodium citrate from the bottle so labeled.

* * *

An analysis made by the staff of the head toxicologist for the Los Angeles County Coroner of the contents of the bottle given to Sills disclosed that it contained 1.33 drams of sodium citrate and 1.23 of sodium nitrite. An analysis made by Biochemical Procedures, Incorporated, a laboratory, of a sample of the contents of the bottle labeled sodium citrate disclosed that it contained 38.9 milligrams of nitrite per gram of material. Charles Covet, one of the owners of the Ethical Drug Company, testified that on the 17th or 18th of October, 1954, he emptied the contents of the sodium citrate bottle, washed the bottle but not its cap, and put in new sodium citrate. A subsequent analysis of rinsings from the cap gave strong positive tests for nitrite. Covet also testified that when he purchased an interest in the company in April, 1950, the bottle labeled sodium citrate was part of the inventory, that no one had put additional sodium citrate into the bottle from that time until he refilled it after the death of the Sills child and that he had never seen any other supply of sodium citrate in the store.

There is nothing in the record to indicate that the contents of the bottle labeled sodium citrate could have been identified as containing sodium nitrite without laboratory analysis. There was testimony that at first glance sodium citrate and sodium nitrite are identical in appearance, that in form either may consist of small colorless crystals or white crystalline powder, that the granulation of the crystals may vary with the manufacturer, and that there may be a slight difference in color between the two. The substance from the bottle labeled sodium citrate was exhibited to the court, but no attempt was made to compare it with unadulterated sodium citrate or sodium nitrite. A chemist with Biochemical Procedures, Incorporated, testified that the mixture did not appear to be homogeneous but that from visual observation alone he could not identify the crystals as one substance or the other. Defendant testified that he had no occasion before July 16th to examine or fill any prescription from the sodium citrate bottle.

No evidence whatever was introduced that would justify an inference that defendant knew or should have known that the bottle labeled sodium citrate contained sodium nitrite. On the contrary, the undisputed evidence shows conclusively that defendant was morally entirely innocent and that only because of a reasonable mistake or unavoidable accident was the prescription filled with a substance containing sodium nitrite. Section 20 of the Penal Code makes the union of act and intent or criminal negligence an invariable element of every crime unless it is excluded expressly or by necessary implication. Moreover, section 26 of the Penal Code lists among the persons incapable of committing crimes "[p]ersons who committed the act or made the omission charged under an ignorance or mistake of fact, which disproves any criminal intent", subd. 4, and "[p]ersons who committed the act or made the omission charged through misfortune or by accident, when it appears that there was no evil design, intention, or culpable negligence." Subd. 6; see also Pen.Code, §§ 195, 199. The question is thus presented whether a person can be convicted of manslaughter or a violation of section 380 of the Penal Code in the absence of any evidence of criminal intent or criminal negligence.

The answer to this question as it relates to the conviction of manslaughter depends on whether or not defendant committed an "unlawful act" within the meaning of section 192 of the Penal Code when he filled the prescription. The Attorney General contends that even if he had no criminal intent and was not criminally negligent, defendant violated section 26280 of the Health and Safety Code and therefore committed an unlawful act within the meaning of section 192 of the Penal Code.

Section 26280 of the Health and Safety Code provides: "The manufacture, production, preparation, compounding, packing, selling, offering for sale, advertising or keeping for sale within the State of California * * * of any drug or device which is adulterated or misbranded is prohibited." In view of the analyses of the contents of the prescription bottle and the bottle labeled sodium citrate and defendant's stipulation, there can be no doubt that he prepared, compounded, and sold an adulterated and misbranded drug.

Because of the great danger to the public health and safety that the preparation, compounding, or sale of adulterated or misbranded drugs entails, the public interest in demanding that those who prepare, compound, or sell drugs make certain that they are not adulterated or misbranded, and the belief that although an occasional nonculpable offender may be punished, it is necessary to incur that risk by imposing strict liability to prevent the escape of great numbers of culpable offenders, public welfare statutes like section 26280 are not ordinarily governed by section 20 of the Penal Code and therefore call for the sanctions imposed even though the prohibited acts are committed without criminal intent or criminal negligence. . . .

It does not follow, however, that such acts, committed without criminal intent or criminal negligence, are unlawful acts within the meaning of section 192 of the Penal Code, for it is settled that this section is governed by section 20 of the Penal Code. Thus, in People v. Penny, 44 Cal.2d 861, 877–880, 285 P.2d 926, 936, we held that "there was nothing to show that the Legislature intended to except section 192 of the Penal Code from the operation of section 20 of the same code" and that the phrase "without due caution and circumspection" in section 192 was therefore the equivalent of criminal negligence. Since section 20 also applies to the phrase "unlawful act," the act in question must be committed with criminal intent or criminal negligence to be an unlawful act within the meaning of section 192. By virtue of its application to both phrases, section 20 precludes the incongruity of imposing on the morally innocent the same penalty, Pen.Code, § 193, appropriate only for the culpable. Words such as "unlawful act, not amounting to felony" have been included in most definitions of manslaughter since the time of Blackstone (4 Bl.Comm.Homicide * 191; see Riesenfeld, Negligent Homicide: A Study in Statutory Interpretation, 25 Cal.L.Rev. 21–22) and even since the time of Lord Hale, "unlawful act" as it pertains to manslaughter has been interpreted as meaning an act that aside from its unlawfulness was of such a dangerous nature as to justify a conviction of manslaughter if done intentionally or without due caution. To be an unlawful act within the meaning of section 192, therefore, the act in question must be dangerous to human life or safety and meet the conditions of section 20.

It follows, therefore, that only if defendant had intentionally or through criminal negligence prepared, compounded, or sold an adulterated or misbranded drug, would his violation of section 26280 of the Health and Safety Code be an unlawful act within the meaning of section 192 of the Penal Code. . . .

* * *

The judgment and order are reversed.

PEOPLE v. HERNANDEZ

Supreme Court of California, 1964.
61 Cal.2d 529, 39 Cal.Rptr. 361, 393 P.2d 673.

PEEK, JUSTICE. By information defendant was charged with statutory rape. (Pen.Code, § 261, subd. 1.) Following his plea of not guilty he was convicted as charged by the court sitting without a jury and the offense determined to be a misdemeanor.

Section 261 of the Penal Code provides in part as follows: "Rape is an act of sexual intercourse, accomplished with a female not the wife of the perpetrator, under either of the following circumstances: 1. Where the female is under the age of 18 years; * * *.' "

The sole contention raised on appeal is that the trial court erred in refusing to permit defendant to present evidence going to his guilt for the purpose of showing that he had in good faith a reasonable belief that the prosecutrix was 18 years or more of age.

The undisputed facts show that the defendant and the prosecuting witness were not married and had been companions for several months prior to January 3, 1961—the date of the commission of the alleged offense. Upon that date the prosecutrix was 17 years and 9 months of age and voluntarily engaged in an act of sexual intercourse with defendant.

In support of his contention defendant relies upon Penal Code § 20, which provides that "there must exist a union, or joint operation of act and intent, or criminal negligence" to constitute the commission of a crime. He further relies upon section 26 of that code which provides that one is not capable of committing a crime who commits an act under an ignorance or mistake of fact which disapproves any criminal intent.

Thus the sole issue relates to the question of intent and knowledge entertained by the defendant at the time of the commission of the crime charged.

Consent of the female is often an unrealistic and unfortunate standard for branding sexual intercourse a crime as serious as forcible rape. Yet the consent standard has been deemed to be required by important policy goals. We are dealing here, of course, with statutory rape where, in one sense, the lack of consent of the female is not an element of the offense. In a broader sense, however, the lack of consent is deemed to remain an element but the law makes a conclusive presumption of the lack thereof because she is presumed too innocent and naive to understand the implications and nature of her act. (People v. Griffen . . .) The law's concern with her capacity or lack thereof to so understand is explained in part by a popular conception of the social, moral and personal values which are preserved by the abstinence from sexual indulgence on the part of a young woman. An unwise disposition of her sexual favor is deemed to do harm both to herself and the social mores by which the community's conduct patterns are established. Hence the law of statutory rape intervenes in an effort to avoid such a disposition. This goal, moreover, is not accomplished by penalizing the naive female but by imposing criminal sanctions against the male, who is conclusively presumed to be responsible for the occurrence. . . .

The assumption that age alone will bring an understanding of the sexual act to a young woman is of doubtful validity. Both learning from the cultural group to which she is a member and her actual sexual experiences will determine her level of comprehension. The sexually experienced 15–year–old may be far more acutely aware of the implications of sexual intercourse than her sheltered cousin who is beyond the age of consent. A girl who belongs to a group whose members indulge in sexual intercourse at an early age is likely to rapidly acquire an insight into the rewards and penalties of sexual indulgence. Nevertheless, even in circumstances where a girl's actual comprehension contradicts the law's presumption, the male is deemed criminally responsible for the act, although himself young and naive and responding to advances which may have been made to him.

The law as presently constituted does not concern itself with the relative culpability of the male and female participants in the prohibited sexual act. Even where the young woman is knowledgeable it does not impose sanctions upon her. The knowledgeable young man, on the other hand, is penalized and there are none who would claim that under any construction of the law this should be otherwise. However, the issue raised by the rejected offer of proof in the instant case goes to the culpability of the young man who acts *without* knowledge that an essential factual element exists and has, on the other hand, a positive, reasonable belief that it does not exist.

The primordial concept of *mens rea*, the guilty mind, expresses the principle that it is not conduct alone but conduct accompanied by certain specific mental states which concerns, or should concern the law. In a broad sense the concept may be said to relate to such important doctrines as justification, excuse, mistake, necessity and mental capacity, but in the final analysis it means simply that there must be a "joint operation of act and intent," as expressed in section 20 of the Penal Code, to constitute the commission of a criminal offense. The statutory law, however, furnishes no assistance to the courts beyond that, and the casebooks are filled to overflowing with the courts' struggles to determine just what state of mind should be considered relevant in particular contexts. In numerous instances culpability has been completely eliminated as a necessary element of criminal conduct in spite of the admonition of section 20 to the contrary . . . (membership in organizations advocating criminal syndicalism); . . . (violation of Corporate Securities Act); . . . (sale of liquor). More recently, however, this court has moved away from the imposition of criminal sanctions in the absence of culpability where the governing statute, by implication or otherwise, expresses no legislative intent or policy to be served by imposing strict liability. . . .

Statutory rape has long furnished a fertile battleground upon which to argue that the lack of knowledgeable conduct is a proper defense. The law in this state now rests, as it did in 1896, with this court's decision in People v. Ratz, . . . where it is stated: "The claim here made is not a new one. It has frequently been pressed upon the attention of courts, but in no case, so far as our examination goes, has it met with favor. The object and purpose of the law are too plain to need comment, the crime too infamous to bear discussion. The protection of society, of the family, and of the infant, demand that one who has carnal intercourse under such circumstances shall do so in peril of the fact, and he will not be heard against the evidence to urge his belief that the victim of his outrage had passed the period which would make his act a crime." The age of consent at the time of the Ratz decision was 14 years, and it is noteworthy that the purpose of the rule, as there announced, was to afford protection to young females therein described as "infants." The decision on which the court in Ratz relied was The Queen v. Prince, L.R. 2 Crown Cas. 154. However England has now, by statute, departed from the strict rule, and excludes as a crime an act of sexual intercourse with a female between the ages of 13 and 16 years if the perpetrator is under the age of 24 years, has not previously been charged with a like offense, and believes the female "to be of the age of sixteen or over and has reasonable cause for the belief." . . .[1]

The rationale of the Ratz decision, rather than purporting to eliminate intent as an element of the crime, holds that the wrongdoer must assume the risk; that, subjectively, when the act is committed, he consciously intends to proceed regardless of the age of the female and the consequences of his act, and that the circumstances involving the female, whether she be a day or a decade less than the statutory age, are irrelevant. There can be no dispute that a criminal intent exists when the perpetrator proceeds with utter disregard of, or in the lack of grounds for, a belief that the female has reached the age of consent. But if he participates in a mutual act of sexual intercourse, believing his partner to be beyond the age of consent, with reasonable grounds for such belief, where is his criminal intent? In such circumstances he has not consciously taken any risk. Instead he has subjectively eliminated the risk by satisfying himself on reasonable evidence that the crime cannot be committed. If it occurs that he has been misled, we cannot realistically conclude that for such reason alone the intent with which he undertook the act suddenly becomes more heinous.

While the specific contentions herein made have been dealt with and rejected both within and without this state, the courts have uniformly failed to satisfactorily explain the nature of the criminal intent present in the mind of one who in good faith believes he has obtained a lawful consent before engaging in the prohibited act. As in the Ratz case the courts often justify convictions on policy reasons

---

1. The American Law Institute in its model Penal Code (1962) provides in part as follows at pages 149 and 150:

"Section 213.6. Provisions Generally Applicable (Article 213 [Sexual Offenses].)

"(1) *Mistake as to Age.* Whenever in this Article the criminality of conduct depends upon a child's being below the age of 10, it is no defense that the actor did not know the child's age, or reasonably believed the child to be older than 10. When criminality depends upon the child's being below a critical age other than 10, it is a defense for the actor to prove that he reasonably believed the child to be above the critical age."

which, in effect, eliminate the element of intent. The Legislature, of course, by making intent an element of the crime, has established the prevailing policy from which it alone can properly advise us to depart.

We have recently given recognition to the legislative declarations in sections 20 and 26 of the Penal Code, and departed from prior decisional law which had failed to accord full effect to those sections as applied to charges of bigamy. (People v. Vogel, . . .) We held there that a good faith belief that a former wife had obtained a divorce was a valid defense to a charge of bigamy arising out of a second marriage when the first marriage had not in fact been terminated. Pertinent to the instant contention that defendant's intent did not suddenly become more criminal because it later developed that he had been misled by the prosecutrix, are the following comments appearing in Vogel at page 804 of 46 Cal.2d, at page 854 of 299 P.2d: "Nor would it be reasonable to hold that a person is guilty of bigamy who remarries in good faith in reliance on a judgment of divorce or annulment that is subsequently found not to be the 'judgment of a competent Court' * * *. Since it is often difficult for laymen to know when a judgment is not that of a competent court, we cannot reasonably expect them always to have such knowledge and make them criminals if their bona fide belief proves to be erroneous." Certainly it cannot be a greater wrong to entertain a bona fide but erroneous belief that a valid consent to an act of sexual intercourse has been obtained.

Equally applicable to the instant case are the following remarks, also appearing at page 804 of 46 Cal.2d, at page 855 of 299 P.2d of the Vogel decision: "The severe penalty imposed for bigamy, the serious loss of reputation conviction entails, * * * and the fact that it has been regarded for centuries as a crime involving moral turpitude, make it extremely unlikely that the Legislature meant to include the morally innocent to make sure the guilty did not escape."

We are persuaded that the reluctance to accord to a charge of statutory rape the defense of a lack of criminal intent has no greater justification than in the case of other statutory crimes, where the Legislature has made identical provision with respect to intent. " 'At common law an honest and reasonable belief in the existence of circumstances, which, if true, would make the act for which the person is indicted an innocent act, has always been held to be a good defense. * * * So far as I am aware it has never been suggested that these exceptions do not equally apply to the case of statutory offenses unless they are excluded expressly or by necessary implication.' " . . . Our departure from the views expressed in Ratz is in no manner indicative of a withdrawal from the sound policy that it is in the public interest to protect the sexually naive female from exploitation. No responsible person would hesitate to condemn as untenable a claimed good faith belief in the age of consent of an "infant" female whose obviously tender years preclude the existence of reasonable grounds for that belief. However, the prosecutrix in the instant case was but three months short of 18 years of age and there is nothing in the record to indicate that the purposes of the law as stated in Ratz can be better served by foreclosing the defense of a lack of intent. This is not to say that the granting of consent by even a sexually sophisticated girl known to be less than the statutory age is a defense. We hold only that in the absence of a legislative direction otherwise, a charge of statutory rape is defensible wherein a criminal intent is lacking.

For the foregoing reasons People v. Ratz, supra, and People v. Griffin, supra, are overruled, and People v. Sheffield, 9 Cal.App. 130, 98 P. 67, is disapproved to the extent that such decisions are inconsistent with the views expressed herein. . . .

The judgment is reversed.

NOTES

1. Haddad, The Mental Attitude Requirement in Criminal Law—And Some Exceptions, 59 J.Crim.L., C. & P.S., 4, 15 (1968), suggests, in relation to prosecutions for bigamy:

> Strict liability in these cases is indefensible, whatever be the nature of the underlying mistake of fact. Defendants would not have been engaged in any legal or moral wrong had the facts been as they reasonably believed them to be; hence the principle of substituted intent is unavailable. Penalties from blameless defendants may be heavy, but they are unlikely to deter people who reasonably believe that they are free to marry, so that it makes little sense to say that the stability of the family depends upon a strict-liability standard. Even if such a standard would prevent more bigamous marriages than would a negligence standard, any *in terrorem* effect would also deter people whose marriages would not be bigamous from marrying because they lacked absolute certainty that the first spouse was dead or that a decree existed. This would be a significant deprivation of an important human right. Nor is there proof that juries would be deceived frequently by false claims of reasonable mistake of fact.

Yet, according to LaFave & Scott, Criminal Law (1972), at p. 358, "the prevailing view of the crime of bigamy is that none of the following constitutes a valid defense: reasonable belief that the first spouse is dead; reasonable belief that the first marriage was illegal; reasonable belief that the decree concerning the first marriage was a divorce decree; or reasonable belief that a foreign divorce would be recognized in the jurisdiction."

2. The offense of carnal knowledge with a female under the age of consent, commonly called "statutory rape," has been dealt with in the same manner as the offense of bigamy, as far as the mistaken belief of an offender that the girl was above the age of consent is concerned. Most jurisdictions treat the offense as a strict liability crime. A minority of jurisdictions allow the reasonable mistake as to age defense, either by judicial fiat, as in the *Hernandez* case, or by statute. The Illinois Criminal Code, for instance, provides in Ill.Rev.Stat. ch. 38, § 12–17 that

> (b) It shall be a defense under subsection (b) of Section 12–15 and subsection (d) of Section 12–16 of this Code that the accused reasonably believed the person to be 17 years of age or over.

3. In connection with Williams v. North Carolina, 325 U.S. 226, 65 S.Ct. 1092 (1945), where the Supreme Court permitted criminal punishments to be imposed by one state upon persons who relied upon a judicial determination of the courts of another state as to their marital status, consider Needham v. State, 55 Okl.Crim.App. 430, 32 P.2d 92 (1934):

"It is next contended the court erred in refusing to permit defendants to introduce proof that defendant Needham had consulted attorneys, including the county attorney, and been advised by them that if he employed a regular licensed physician to conduct his sanitarium that he would not be violating the law.

"The court very properly denied defendants an opportunity to make this proof.

"It is well established that an accused cannot prove as a defense that he acted upon the advice of counsel in committing the act complained of, because if such were the law it would be placing the advice of counsel above the law itself. Each person charged with an offense must know what the law is, and he acts at his own peril. . . .

"Counsel for defendants admit they cannot find any authorities to support their contention. This is not surprising, since there probably are no such cases."

To the same effect, see Hunter v. State, 158 Tenn. 63, 12 S.W.2d 361 (1928).

4. A former provision of the Los Angeles Municipal Code stated that it was unlawful for "any convicted person" to be or remain in that city for more than 5 days without registering with local authorities. The ordinance defined "convicted persons" as "any person who . . . has been or hereafter is convicted of an offense punishable as a felony in the State of California, or who has been or who is hereafter convicted of any offense in any place other than the State of California, which offense, if committed in the State of California, would have been punishable as a felony." The appellant in Lambert v. California, 355 U.S. 225, 78 S.Ct. 240 (1957), at the time of her arrest had been a resident of Los Angeles for over 7 years. Within that period she had been convicted in Los Angeles of forgery, an offense which California punishes as a felony. Though thus convicted, she had not, at the time of her arrest on suspicion of another offense, registered in accordance with the Code provisions. She was tried for failure to register and convicted. The court fined her $250 and placed her on probation for 3 years. Her conviction was affirmed by the appellate division of the Superior Court of California for Los Angeles County.

Mr. Justice Douglas spoke for a five-man majority:

". . . [W]e . . . hold that the registration provisions of the Code as sought to be applied here violate the Due Process requirement of the Fourteenth Amendment.

". . . No element of willfulness is by terms included in the ordinance nor read into it by the California court as a condition necessary for a conviction.

"We must assume that appellant had no actual knowledge of the requirement that she register under this ordinance, as she offered proof of this defense which was refused. The question is whether a registration act of this character violates due process where it is applied to a person who has no actual knowledge of his duty to register, and where no showing is made of the probability of such knowledge.

"We do not go with Blackstone in saying that 'a vicious will' is necessary to constitute a crime, 4 Bl.Comm. 21, for conduct alone without regard to the intent of the doer is often sufficient. There is wide latitude in the lawmakers to declare an offense and to exclude elements of knowledge and diligence from its definition. . . . But we deal here with conduct that is wholly passive— mere failure to register. It is unlike the commission of acts, or the failure to act under circumstances that should alert the doer to the consequences of his deed. . . . The rule that 'ignorance of the law will not excuse' . . . is deep in our law, as is the principle that of all the powers of local government, the police power is 'one of the least limitable.' . . . On the other hand, due process places some limits on its exercise. Engrained in our concept of due process is the requirement of notice. Notice is sometimes essential so that the citizen has the chance to defend charges. Notice is required before property interests are disturbed, before assessments are made, before penalties are assessed. Notice is required in a myriad of situations where a penalty or forfeiture might be suffered for more failure to act. Recent cases illustrating the point are . . . These cases involved only property interests in civil litigation. But the principle is equally appropriate where a person, wholly passive and unaware of any wrongdoing, is brought to the bar of justice for condemnation in a criminal case.

"Registration laws are common and their range is wide. . . . Many such laws are akin to licensing statutes in that they pertain to the regulation of business activities. But the present ordinance is entirely different. Violation of its provisions is unaccompanied by any activity whatever, mere presence in the city being the test. Moreover, circumstances which might move one to inquire as to the necessity of registration are completely lacking. At most the ordinance is but a law enforcement technique designed for the convenience of law enforcement agencies through which a list of the names and addresses of felons then residing in a given community is compiled. The disclosure is merely a compilation of former convictions already publicly recorded in the jurisdiction where obtained. Nevertheless, this appellant on first becoming aware of her duty to register was given no opportunity to comply with the law and avoid its penalty, even though her default was entirely innocent. She could but suffer the consequences of the ordinance, namely, conviction with the imposition of heavy criminal penalties thereunder. We believe that actual knowledge of the duty to register or proof of the probability of such knowledge and subsequent failure to comply are necessary before a conviction under the ordinance can stand. As Holmes wrote in The Common Law, 'A law which punished conduct which would not be blameworthy in the average member of the community would be too severe for that community to bear.' Id., at 50. Its severity lies in the absence of an opportunity either to avoid the consequences of the law or to defend any prosecution brought under it. Where a person did not know of the duty to register and where there was no proof of the probability of such knowledge, he may not be convicted consistently with due process. Were it otherwise, the evil would be as great as it is when the law is written in print too fine to read or in a language foreign to the community."

Shortly after *Lambert,* Professor Mueller wrote:

"The Supreme Court has clearly told us that it detests the misuse of criminal sanctions in the case of a morally blameless defendant . . . Absolute criminal liability is beginning to end in America." Mueller, On Common Law Mens Rea, 42 Minn.L.Rev. 1043 (1958).

The prophecy has not been fulfilled, perhaps because Mrs. Lambert's mistake was that she did not know of the existence of a penal law, a different sort of mistake from those involved in the other cases treated in this section. *Lambert* has come to stand only for the proposition that where an affirmative duty is imposed on a citizen which he would have no reason to suppose exists, and where a violation of that duty requires no affirmative act, the lawmakers must see that the law's promulgation takes those circumstances into account. See United States v. Juzwiak, 258 F.2d 844 (2d Cir.1958), and Reyes v. United States, 258 F.2d 774 (9th Cir.1958).

The administrative difficulties of proving that the defendant knew of the existence of a penal statute dictates that ignorance of the penal law generally be disallowed as a defense. But is the defendant any more culpable if he is in good faith ignorant of the existence of a statute rather than of the nature of his conduct?

5. Smith v. California, 361 U.S. 147, 80 S.Ct. 215 (1959), is a Supreme Court decision that strikes down a statute on the grounds that it dispenses with mens rea. The Court condemned an ordinance that permitted conviction of a bookseller who sold an obscene book without knowledge of its contents. Subjecting sellers to such treatment, it was thought, would limit the distribution of books that were not, in fact, obscene and thereby inhibit the exercise of free speech. Contrast the extent to which policy considerations, as opposed to legal maxims and mechanical rules, were factors in the decisions in *Braun* and *Hernandez,* supra. See Hogan, Mens Rea in Bigamy in Maryland: An Obituary?, 23 Md.L.Rev. 224 (1963) and Myers, Reasonable Mistake of Age: A Needed Defense to Statutory Rape, 64 Mich.L.Rev. 105 (1966).

6. Consider the following, from Hall, Principles of Criminal Law (2d ed. 1960), at p. 365: ". . . mistake of fact is a defense if, because of the mistake, *mens rea* is lacking." With respect to the larger issue of the mens rea requirement generally, consult Hall, ibid 70–212.

PEOPLE v. CASH
Supreme Court of Michigan, 1984.
419 Mich. 230, 351 N.W.2d 822.

WILLIAMS, CHIEF JUSTICE.

The main issue presented in this case requires us to reconsider whether a reasonable mistake of fact as to a complainant's age is a defense to a statutory rape charge. Over 61 years ago, this Court enunciated a rule rejecting such a defense in People v. Gengels, 218 Mich. 632, 188 N.W. 398 (1922), which involved a similar charge under the former statutory rape statute. We reaffirm the *Gengels* rule and likewise reject this defense in cases brought under § 520d(1)(a) of the third-degree criminal sexual conduct statute.[1]

1. The statutory rape statute in effect at the time of *Gengels,* which prohibited carnal knowledge of a female under 16, M.C.L. § 750.520; M.S.A. § 28.788, was repealed by 1974 P.A. 266 and replaced by the new criminal sexual conduct statute, M.C.L. § 750.520a *et seq.;* M.S.A. § 28.788(1) et seq. The purpose of the new statute was to codify, consolidate, define, and prescribe punishment for a number of sexually assaultive crimes under one heading. See People v. Johnson, 406 Mich. 320, 327–330, 279 N.W.2d 534 (1979). In furtherance of this goal, the Legislature created four degrees of criminal sexual conduct, the first three of which comprise the "new" statutory rape law. Under the new law, sexual penetration or contact with a

This appeal raises two additional issues: (1) whether the trial court abused its discretion in not permitting cross-examination of the complainant or her mother regarding the complainant's lifestyle; and (2) whether the prosecution's argument and introduction of evidence concerning a forcible rape denied defendant a fair trial. We answer each of these issues in the negative, and therefore we affirm defendant's conviction.

I. FACTS

On the evening of September 23, 1979, the complainant, who was one month shy of her 16th birthday, met the defendant at a Greyhound bus station in Detroit. The complainant was running away from home at the time. After talking with complainant for a couple of hours and gaining her trust, defendant persuaded complainant to accompany him on a drive in his car. They drove to a motel in Marshall, Michigan, where two separate acts of sexual intercourse took place. The complainant managed to leave the motel room undetected after defendant fell asleep, and awakened the person in charge of the motel, who in turn called the police. The defendant was charged with two counts of third-degree criminal sexual conduct, namely, engaging in sexual penetration with a person between the ages of 13 and 16 years. Documents found in the court file indicate that at the time of the offense, the defendant was 30 years old.

At the preliminary examination, complainant admitted that she told defendant that she was 17 years old. The defendant had also indicated to the police at the time of his arrest that the complainant told him she was 17. The complainant was described by defendant as being 5'8" tall and weighing about 165 pounds.

Prior to trial, defendant brought a motion requesting that the jury be instructed that a reasonable mistake as to the complainant's age is a defense, or, in the alternative, that the charges be dismissed on the ground that the complainant is collaterally estopped from asserting that she was 16 since at the time of the offense she stated that she was 17. Following a hearing, the trial court denied defendant's motion and entered its opinion and order to that effect.

. . . At trial, the complainant testified that she had voluntarily, though reluctantly, engaged in sexual intercourse with defendant out of fear that defendant would otherwise harm her. Defendant tried to impeach the complainant with questions about her lifestyle to show that she was "street-wise", but the trial court prohibited this cross-examination. Defendant was also prohibited from questioning complainant's mother as to her daughter's lifestyle.

person under 13 years old is distinguished from sexual penetration with a person between the ages of 13 and 16. We are concerned in the present case only with the latter age group, although we note that the same policy considerations advanced here could apply with even greater force to the under–13 age group.

Sergeant Max Faurot of the Calhoun County Sheriff's Department was called to testify for the prosecution. The relevant portions of that testimony follow:

"Q. Do you recall whether or not you were dispatched to Marshall Heights Motel at some point on the morning of September 24th?

"A. Yes, I was.

"Q. Do you know with regards to what?

"A. Yes, my dispatcher advised that she had a call from the motel that there had been a rape. That there had been a rape at that location, that the suspect was around and in one of the motel rooms, and that the victim was in the office with the manager of the motel."

The trial court instructed the jury that the defense theory was one of mistake of fact and that defendant reasonably believed that complainant had reached the age of consent. Over defendant's objection, the court later instructed the jury that "[i]t is no defense that the defendant believed that [the complainant] was 16 years old or older at the time of the alleged act".

The defendant was found guilty by the jury of third-degree criminal sexual conduct, M.C.L. § 750.520d(1)(a); M.S.A. § 28.788(4)(1)(a), and was sentenced to a term of from 5 to 15 years in prison. The Court of Appeals affirmed defendant's conviction in an unpublished per curiam opinion. We granted leave to appeal on August 10, 1982. 414 Mich. 868, 323 N.W.2d 910.

II. REASONABLE–MISTAKE–OF–AGE DEFENSE

A. *The Gengels Decision*

This Court first stated that a good-faith or reasonable mistake as to the complainant's age is not a defense to a statutory rape charge in People v. Gengels, 218 Mich. 632, 188 N.W. 398 (1922), nearly 61 years ago. In that case, the defendant was convicted under the predecessor to the current criminal sexual conduct statute of carnally knowing a female child under 16 years of age. The defendant testified that the complainant told him that she was 18 years old. This Court reversed the defendant's conviction and granted a new trial on the ground that the prosecutor had impermissibly impeached the defendant by collateral evidence of similar acts. While recognizing that such evidence may be admissible where guilt of a particular crime depends on intent, the Court noted:

"But in the crime charged here proof of the intent goes with proof of the act of sexual intercourse with a girl under the age of consent. It is not necessary for the prosecution to prove want of consent. Proof of consent is no defense, for a female child under the statutory age is legally incapable of consenting. Neither is it any defense that the accused believed from the statement of his victim or others that she had reached the age of consent. 33 Cyc, p. 1438, and cases cited." *Gengels,* supra, p. 641, 188 N.W. 398.

The *Gengels* decision has only been cited once in this state's courts for the proposition that mistake of age is not a defense to a statutory rape charge. People v. Doyle, 16 Mich.App. 242, 167 N.W.2d 907 (1969), *lv. den.* 382 Mich. 753 (1969). In *Doyle,* the defendant was charged with taking indecent liberties with a female under 16 years of age. The Court of Appeals observed that "[c]urrent social and moral values make more realistic the California view that a reasonable and honest mistake of age is a valid defense to a charge of statutory rape, *People v. Hernandez.* The Court, however, concluded that it was bound to follow the *Gengels* rule and therefore refused to adopt the mistake-of-age defense in indecent liberties cases. Neither in *Gengels* nor in *Doyle* was the constitutionality of the rule prohibiting the defense of a reasonable mistake of age to a statutory rape charge squarely presented.

B.   *Is Gengels Still Viable?*

This Court for the first time has the opportunity to review the rule announced in *Gengels* and determine whether it is still viable under the successor provision of the third-degree criminal sexual conduct statute and, if so, whether it comports with a defendant's right to due process.

The statute reads, in relevant part:

"(1) A person is guilty of criminal sexual conduct in the third degree if the person engages in sexual penetration with another person and if any of the following circumstances exists:

"(a) That other person is at least 13 years of age and under 16 years of age." M.C.L. § 750.520d; M.S.A. § 28.788(4).

"Sexual penetration" is defined as:

"[S]exual intercourse, cunnilingus, fellatio, anal intercourse, or any other intrusion, however slight, of any part of a person's body or of any object into the genital or anal openings of another person's body, but emission of semen is not required." M.C.L. § 750.520a(h); M.S.A. § 28.788(1)(h).

In the present case, defendant directly attacks the constitutionality of the above statute on due process grounds for imposing criminal liability without requiring proof of specific criminal intent, *i.e.,* that the accused know that the victim is below the statutory age of consent. In particular, he argues that the crime of statutory rape is rooted in the common law and, as with other common-law offenses, the element of intent must be implied within the statutory definition of a crime, absent clear legislative language to the contrary. We are urged by defendant to construe the statute's silence with respect to the element of intent as not negating the defense of a reasonable mistake of fact as to the complainant's age.

In support of his argument, defendant relies primarily on two out-of-state cases which represent the minority view that, in a statutory rape prosecution, an accused's reasonable, though mistaken, belief that the complainant was of the age of consent is a valid defense.[2] People v. Hernandez, 61 Cal.2d 529, 39 Cal.Rptr. 361, 393 P.2d 673 (1964); State v. Guest, 583 P.2d 836 (Alas., 1978). In both these cases, the Court engrafted a *mens rea* element onto the statutes in question where they were otherwise silent as to any requisite criminal intent.

The vast majority of states, as well as the federal courts, which have considered this identical issue have rejected defendant's arguments and do not recognize the defense of a reasonable mistake of age to a statutory rape charge. For the reasons discussed below, we agree with the majority's position.

After careful examination of the statute in the instant case and its legislative history, we are persuaded that the Legislature, in enacting the new criminal sexual conduct code, 1974 P.A. 266, intended to omit the defense of a reasonable mistake of age from its definition of third-degree criminal sexual conduct involving a 13– to 16–year–old, and we follow the legislative intention.

First, a general rule of statutory construction is that the Legislature is "presumed to know of and legislate in harmony with existing laws". The Legislature must have been aware of our earlier decision rejecting the reasonable-mistake-of-age defense under the old statutory rape statute. Had the Legislature desired to revise the existing law by allowing for a reasonable-mistake-of-age defense, it could have done so, but it did not do so. This is further supported by the fact that under another provision of the same section of the statute, concerning the mentally ill or physically helpless rape victim, the Legislature specifically provided for the defense of a reasonable mistake of fact by adding the language that the actor "knows or has reason to know" of the victim's condition where the prior statute contained no requirement of intent. The Legislature's failure to include similar language under the section of the statute in question indicates to us the Legislature's intent to adhere to the *Gengels* rule that the actual, and not the apparent, age of the complainant governs in statutory rape offenses.

2. See generally Anno: Mistake or Lack of Information as to Victim's Age as Defense to Statutory Rape, 8 A.L.R.3d 1100.

A few states have adopted, by statute, the reasonable-mistake-of-age defense in statutory rape cases. See, e.g., Alas.Rev. Stat. § 11.41.445(b); Ariz.Rev.Stat.Ann. § 13–1407(B); Ark.Stat.Ann. § 41–1802(3); Ill.Ann.Stat. ch. 38, § 11–4(c) (Smith–Hurd); Ky.Rev.Stat. § 510.030; Mont.Rev. Codes Ann. § 45–5–506(1); Wash.Rev.Code § 9A.44.030(2).

This defense has also been adopted in limited fashion in the 1962 Proposed Draft of the Model Penal Code § 213.6(1), which reads:

"(1) *Mistake as to Age.* Whenever in this Article the criminality of conduct depends on a child's being below the age of 10, it is no defense that the actor did not know the child's age, or reasonably believed the child to be older than 10. When criminality depends on the child's being below a critical age other than 10, it is a defense for the actor to prove that he reasonably believed the child to be above the critical age."

Second, while the crime of statutory rape has its origins in the English common law, Michigan's new criminal sexual conduct statute represents a major attempt by the Legislature to redefine the law of sexually assaultive crimes, including that of statutory rape. It is well established that the Legislature may, pursuant to its police powers, define criminal offenses without requiring proof of a specific criminal intent and so provide that the perpetrator proceed at his own peril regardless of his defense of ignorance or an honest mistake of fact. In the case of statutory rape, such legislation, in the nature of "strict liability" offenses, has been upheld as a matter of public policy because of the need to protect children below a specified age from sexual intercourse on the presumption that their immaturity and innocence prevents them from appreciating the full magnitude and consequences of their conduct.

Analysis of the statutory scheme adopted by the Legislature to define criminal sexual conduct further reveals that the Legislature cannot reasonably be said to have intended that a defense based on reasonable mistake of fact concerning the victim's age be available to persons charged under the act.

We are dealing with a statute, passed by the Legislature just nine years ago, which shows, on its face, that the age of the victim was carefully considered in defining and establishing the severity of the criminal conduct. The age of the victim is balanced against the nature of the sexual conduct to establish a graduated system of punishment.

Under the prior rape or carnal knowledge statute, sexual penetration of a female under the age of 16 was defined as rape, punishable by life imprisonment or any term of years. In 1974, when the Legislature revised the law of criminal sexual conduct, it could have retained this definition of "statutory rape" and could have continued to punish it as criminal sexual conduct in the first degree, i.e., by life imprisonment or any term of years. The Legislature chose not to do so. The Legislature, alternatively, could have completely decriminalized consensual sexual activity with a person between the ages of 13 and 16, or, for that matter, it could have made age irrelevant. But it chose not to do so.[3] What the Legislature did choose to do was to create a system of definitions and punishments which considers the age of the victim, the type of sexual contact, and several limited situations in which the relationship of authority between victim and defendant warrant, in the legislative judgment, an increase in punishment.

Thus, the Legislature has determined that sexual penetration of a victim under 13 years of age is first-degree criminal sexual conduct which is punishable by life imprisonment or any term of years. But sexual penetration of a victim 13 or older, but under 16 years of age, is third-degree criminal sexual conduct, with a maximum punishment of

---

3. The Legislature also could have followed the lead of those states which had previously adopted, by statute, the reasonable mistake of age defense in statutory rape cases. See, e.g., Ill.Ann.Stat., ch. 38, § 11–4(c) (Smith–Hurd). See also the 1962 Proposed Draft of the Model Penal Code § 213.6(1).

15 years in prison. However, if the victim is at least 13, but less than 16 years of age, and is a member of the defendant's household or related to the defendant, a person who engages in sexual penetration of that victim is guilty of first-degree criminal sexual conduct and may receive a maximum sentence of life imprisonment.

These discrete choices made by the Legislature evidence careful consideration of age and a deliberate determination to retain the law of statutory rape where the prohibited conduct occurred and the victim was within the protected age group.

One critic has argued that the exclusion of a reasonable-mistake-of-age defense in statutory rape cases is no longer justified given the increased age of consent, the realities of modern society that young teens are more sexually mature, and the seriousness of the penalty as compared with other strict liability offenses. We are not convinced that the policy behind the statutory rape laws of protecting children from sexual exploitation and possible physical or psychological harm from engaging in sexual intercourse is outmoded. Indeed, the United States Supreme Court recently acknowledged the state's authority to regulate the sexual behavior of minors in order to promote their physical and mental well-being, even under a gender-based statutory rape law.[4]

C. *Is the Defense of a Reasonable Mistake of Age Constitutionally Mandated?*

Contrary to defendant's contention, the mistake-of-age defense, at least with regard to statutory rape crimes, is not constitutionally mandated. We quote with approval the following language from Nelson v. Moriarty, 484 F.2d 1034, 1035–1036 (CA 1, 1973):

> "Petitioner claims that his honest belief that the prosecutrix of the statutory rape charge was over sixteen years of age should constitute a defense, of constitutional dimensions, to statutory rape. The effect of *mens rea* and mistake on state criminal law has generally been left to the discretion of the states. * * * The Supreme Court has never held that an honest mistake as to the age of the prosecutrix is a constitutional defense to statutory rape, * * * and nothing in the Court's recent decisions clarifying the scope of procreative privacy, * * * suggests that a state may no longer place the risk of mistake as to the prosecutrix's age on the person engaging in sexual intercourse with a partner who may be young enough to fall within the protection of the statute. Petitioner's argument is without merit."

Moreover, given the already highly emotional setting of a statutory rape trial, the allowance of a mistake-of-age defense would only cause additional undue focus on the complainant by the

---

4. See Michael M. v. Superior Court of Sonoma County, 450 U.S. 464, 472, fn. 8, 101 S.Ct. 1200, 1209, fn. 8, 67 L.Ed.2d 437 (1981), wherein the court upheld, against an equal protection challenge, California's statutory rape law which exclusively punished male perpetrators.

jury's scrutinizing her appearance and any other visible signs of maturity. The obvious problem is that because early adolescents tend to grow at a rapid rate, by the time of trial a relatively undeveloped young girl or boy may have transformed into a young woman or man. A better procedure would be to permit any mitigating and ameliorating evidence in support of a defendant's mistaken belief as to the complainant's age to be considered by the trial judge at the time of sentencing.

We again note that our decision is in line with the preponderant majority of jurisdictions, both state and federal, which do not recognize the reasonable-mistake-of-age defense for statutory rape offenses and have likewise upheld against due process challenges their respective statutes' imposition of criminal liability without the necessity of proving the defendant's knowledge that the victim was below the designated age. Accordingly, we reaffirm our earlier opinion in *Gengels* and reject the reasonable-mistake-of-age defense for cases brought under § 520d(1)(a) of the third-degree criminal sexual conduct statute.

* * *

V. CONCLUSION

We find that the Legislature intentionally omitted the defense of a reasonable mistake of age from its statutory definition of third-degree criminal sexual conduct involving a 13– to 16–year–old. Moreover, we hold that this defense is not constitutionally compelled.

* * *

Accordingly, we affirm defendant's conviction.

BOYLE, CAVANAGH, BRICKLEY and RYAN, JJ., concur.

KAVANAGH, JUSTICE.

Defendant was convicted by a jury of criminal sexual conduct in the third degree, M.C.L. § 750.520d(1)(a); M.S.A. § 28.788(4)(1)(a), on March 7, 1980. Prior to trial, defendant moved to be allowed to present the defense of mistake of age, arguing that consciousness of wrongdoing is an essential element of criminal liability. Defendant's motion was denied. Defendant's entire defense at trial was mistake of fact. He claimed that he honestly believed that the prosecutrix was 17 years of age at the time of the offense. The Court of Appeals affirmed defendant's conviction in an unpublished per curiam opinion.

Michigan has a long history of insistence on the establishment of *mens rea* in felony cases. In Pond v. People, 8 Mich. 150, 174 (1860), Justice Campbell observed:

"A criminal intent is a necessary ingredient of every crime. And therefore it is well remarked by Baron Parke in Regina v. Thurborn, 2 C & K 832, that 'as the rule of law, founded on justice and reason, is that *actus non facit reum, nisi mens sit rea,* the guilt of the accused must depend on the circumstances as they appear to him.' And Mr. Bishop has expressed the same rule very clearly, by declaring that 'in all cases where a party, without fault or carelessness, is misled concerning facts, and acts as he would be justified in doing if the facts were what he believed them to be, he is legally as he is morally innocent: 1 Bish Cr L, § 242.' "

Justice Fitzgerald adverted to this principle in quoting Gegan, Criminal Homicide in Revised New York Penal Law, 12 N.Y.L.Forum 565, 586 (1966), in *People v. Aaron,* 409 Mich. 672, 708, 299 N.W.2d 304 (1980):

> " 'If one had to choose the most basic principle of the criminal law in general * * * it would be that criminal liability for causing a particular result is not justified in the absence of some culpable mental state in respect to that result * * *.' "

Disallowing a defense of reasonable mistake of fact obviates proof of *mens rea.* While this practice has been approved in misdemeanor cases, we are cited no case, nor has our research uncovered one, wherein this Court has sanctioned it in felony cases.

Recognizing the defense of a reasonable mistake of age to a charge of statutory rape, however, does not imply that the defendant must have in fact known the person was under age. Instead, when the defense is raised, the factfinder need only determine whether the defendant honestly believed that the prosecutrix was an adult and, if so, whether the belief was reasonable.

Reasonable mistake of age should not be confused with the rule that a person under the statutory age is legally incapable of consent. Consent of the underage person is not the issue here. It is the defendant's state of mind. The gravamen of the charged offense is voluntary intercourse with an underage person. Just as proof of coercion of a defendant would defeat the charge, so should defendant's reasonable mistake of the fact of age. In neither instance could there be *mens rea,* for in each case there would be no free election to do the thing forbidden.

LEVIN, J., concurs.

C. THE CAUSAL CONNECTION

STATE v. FRAZIER

Supreme Court of Missouri, 1936.
339 Mo. 966, 98 S.W.2d 707.

ELLISON, JUDGE. The appellant was convicted of manslaughter and his punishment assessed at a fine of $400 and 6 months in the county jail, for the killing of Daniel I. Gross in Fredericktown in August, 1934. . . . The deceased was a hemophiliac, or "bleeder." The appellant struck him on the jaw once with his fist. A slight laceration on the inside of the mouth resulted which produced a hemorrhage lasting ten days and ending in death. The State's evidence showed the appellant's assault upon the deceased was unprovoked. The evidence for the appellant was that he acted in self-defense; and his theory further was that Gross' death was not caused by the blow struck, but by his disease, aforesaid, and the failure to treat it properly. * * *

The appellant swore he did cross the street diagonally . . . and that the deceased, who was standing in the doorway of his shop, called out and cursed him. Appellant thereupon came back and walked up to the deceased, asking what was the matter. The deceased assaulted him. Appellant warded off the blows and pushed the deceased back. The deceased took off his glasses, renewed the attack, and then, uttering foul epithets, retreated into the store and got a book. Appellant started away, the deceased followed and hit him with the book and appellant hit the deceased an ordinary blow in self-defense. He swore he did not know the deceased was a hemophiliac.

Regarding the evidence showing the physical condition of the deceased and the effect upon him of the blow struck by the appellant: He was 36 years old and had been afflicted with hemophilia since birth. He had been under treatment for that disease about 2 years before when he bumped his knee on a table, and was in the Veterans' Hospital in St. Louis for a short time. He was below the average in height and overweight, or fat, as some of the witnesses said, and rather pale or anemic. He walked with a slow draggy or hobbling gait.

The two young women . . . who were called as witnesses by the appellant testified that after the difficulty had ended they walked on by the shop and saw the deceased standing in the doorway spitting out a little blood. R.O. Buzbee, deputy sheriff, said he had occasion about noon that day to go to the deceased's shop, and found him standing inside the door. He was bleeding from the mouth and his jaw was puffed up and discolored. Mrs. F.T. Gross, mother of the deceased, said she saw him that night about 6 o'clock. His face, jaw, and lips were swollen. His lip was in very bad condition. He went to bed about 8:30 or 9 o'clock that night, but remained in bed only overnight, taking care of himself. He was confined to his bed in his last sickness from September 5, 5 days later, and died on September 10. One of the defendant's witnesses testified to seeing him at a picnic in Fredericktown on Labor Day, which was September 3. He was standing by one of the booths.

Dr. W.H. Barron, a physician at Fredericktown for 30 years' practice, treated him in his last illness. He had known him for 15 years and intimately for 6 or 8 years, having been his physician on the occasion of his illness 2 years before. The deceased came to his office in the morning of September 1. His left jaw was badly swollen. An examination disclosed that he had an abrasion or laceration on the inside of his lip. It was an opening in the mucous membrane about one-eighth inch deep, but did not cut into the muscular tissue. The wound was bleeding slowly but not excessively. His face was swollen and rather pale. The doctor did not treat him on this occasion.

Three or four days later the mother of the deceased called at the doctor's office and the latter prescribed treatment for him which included rest in bed, quietude, light foods, cold packs on the face, and a drug called ergot. The doctor did not see the patient on this occasion. Several days later on September 8 Dr. Barron was called to see the deceased in the latter's home. The swollen condition of his jaw was about the same and he was pale and weak. Lots of blood was coming from the mouth and also from the intestines and kidneys. He was expectorating clots of blood coming from the abrasion in his lip. Part of this blood was swallowed and going into the intestinal tract. The patient was vomiting some. On September 10 the doctor was called to the deceased's bedside again. The pallor in his face was more marked and he was going into a state of coma. The pulse at the wrist was barely perceptible. He could not expectorate and the blood from the wound was going into his throat. He died in half an hour.

Dr. Barron gave it as his professional opinion that the death of Gross was caused by hemorrhage from the laceration in his mouth, the latter appearing to be the result of some sort of violence. He described hemophilia as an hereditary condition of the blood such as prevents coagulation thereof and thereby permits hemorrhages to continue unchecked. He further said these hemorrhages could occur spontaneously, without violence, but were usually more aggravated when resulting from trauma. It was his opinion that the injury to the left jaw of the deceased would not have caused him to bleed to death if he had not been a hemophiliac. He said the disease was incurable but that there were treatments for it. The treatments he prescribed were recognized, he said. . . .

*   *   *

Appellant complains further that the proof was insufficient to support the verdict against him because all the evidence showed: (1) That he struck in self-defense; (2) and that the death of Gross was caused solely by the disease of hemophilia, and not by the blow struck. Appellant is entirely wrong in saying all the evidence shows he acted in self-defense. The testimony of two eyewitnesses, Messrs. Anthony and Bess, was that he walked rapidly up to Gross and hit him before a word had been spoken or a demonstration made by Gross. But it is true the undisputed evidence establishes that appellant struck only a single, moderate blow with his fist against Gross' jaw, which was not calculated to produce death or great bodily harm.

Dr. Barron, the attending physician, gave it as his professional opinion that the death of Gross was caused by hemorrhage from the laceration in his mouth, and the evidence is clear that the laceration was produced by the blow struck by appellant. But it was the doctor's further opinion that the blow on the jaw would not have caused the deceased to bleed to death if he had not been a hemophiliac. He also testified the hemorrhages from hemophilia might occur spontaneously, and admitted that he had learned the patient was bleeding rather freely from the kidneys, and, it seems, also through the intestinal tract, during the last 3 days of his sickness. He made no examination of these parts, and the foregoing information came to him only as it was communicated with the case history. He found no evidence of violence in the region of these organs, and stated blood from the wound in the mouth when swallowed might find its way into the intestines. He also said the mere fact that a person might pass blood wouldn't be an indication of bleeding at the kidneys. And yet the record shows that, when asked on cross-examination whether the hemorrhage that caused Gross' death was from the intestines, the kidneys, or the mouth, he said he didn't know; and he also said that without making tests he couldn't determine where the blood came from.

This somewhat equivocal testimony from Dr. Barron seems to leave the way open for a possible inference that hemorrhages starting spontaneously in the kidneys and intestinal tract, and being wholly independent of the hemorrhage from the laceration in the mouth of the deceased, may have caused his death. But, on the other hand, the doctor affirmatively expressed the opinion as a physician that Gross' death was caused by the hemorrhage from the laceration in his mouth (which, in turn, was caused by the blow he received), and he further said the passage of blood through the organs of elimination might occur because the blood had been swallowed. It is therefore clear there is no foundation for appellant's contention that *all* the evidence showed Gross' death was caused solely by hemophilia. And for the reasons just stated we are further of the opinion that the doctor's testimony was not so equivocal as to be self-destructive and make it impossible for a jury to find whether the deceased died from the hemorrhage in his mouth or from a different hemorrhage independently starting in his kidneys and intestinal tract. The more natural construction of what he said, it seems to us, is that, while he could not be sure without making certain tests which he did not make, yet his professional opinion was that Gross' death resulted from the hemorrhage in his mouth. His opinion as an expert on the question was competent and substantial evidence, and absolute certainty was not required of him.

Remembering the appellant was convicted of manslaughter, two questions remain: (1) Was it an adequate defense that the appellant did not know the deceased was a hemophiliac, and struck only one moderate blow with his fist, which ordinarily would not have been dangerous to life? (2) Is he to be excused because the blow producing the hemorrhage would not have resulted fatally if deceased had not been a hemophiliac? Both these questions must be answered in the negative. Section 3988, R.S.Mo.1929, Mo.St.Ann. § 3988, p. 2793, provides that "every killing of a human being by the act, procurement or culpable negligence of another, not herein declared to be murder or excusable or justifiable homicide, shall be deemed manslaughter." If one commits an unlawful assault and battery upon another without malice and death results, the assailant is guilty of manslaughter, although death was not intended and the assault was not of a character likely to result fatally.

Neither is it an excuse that appellant did not know the deceased was a hemophiliac, and that death would not have resulted but for that affliction. On this point 13 R.C.L. § 55, p. 750, says: "The law declares that one who inflicts an injury on another and thereby accelerates his death shall be held criminally responsible therefor, although death would not have resulted from the injury but for the diseased or wounded condition of the person so injured." And the doctrine is more fully set out in 29 C.J. § 57, p. 1082, as follows: "If the deceased was in feeble health and died from the combined effects of the injury and of his disease, or if the injury accelerated the death from the disease, he who inflicted the injury is liable, although the injury alone would not have been fatal. The same rule applies, although the disease itself would probably have been fatal, if the injury accelerated death. It is immaterial that defendant did not know that the deceased was in the feeble condition which facilitated the killing, or that he did not reasonably anticipate that his act would cause death."

The last seven assignments of error in the motion for new trial severally complain of instructions given. Only a few of these are specific enough to comply with the requirements of the new trial statute. . . .

* * *

Specific complaint is made of instruction No. 4 that it assumed the deceased died as a result of injuries inflicted by the appellant. The instruction in substance told the jury if the appellant struck a blow causing injury to Gross, and that the blow was of such force and nature as to have brought about or caused his death, then the fact that Gross may not thereafter have received proper medical treatment would not relieve appellant. The opening part of the instruction does assume the facts that a blow was struck, and that the blow caused injury. It says: "If you find from the evidence beyond a reasonable doubt, that the Defendant wilfully and knowingly struck *the blow that caused an injury to Daniel I. Gross.*" But it does not assume, as the assignment charges, that Gross died as a result of injuries inflicted by appellant. On the contrary, it required the jury to find "that said blow was of such force and of such nature as to have brought about or caused the death of said Gross." And the concluding lines of the instruction informed them they must "be satisfied from all the evidence, beyond a reasonable doubt, that said Gross did die as a result of an injury which was inflicted by this defendant."

* * *

Finding no reversible error, the judgment and sentence below are affirmed.

PEOPLE v. LOVE

Supreme Court of Illinois, 1978.
71 Ill.2d 74, 15 Ill.Dec. 628, 373 N.E.2d 1312.

MORAN, JUSTICE. Following a bench trial in the circuit court of Cook County, defendant, Tyrone Love, was convicted of the voluntary manslaughter of his wife, Sharon. On appeal, the appellate court reversed the conviction on grounds that the State failed to establish beyond a reasonable doubt that the defendant's conduct caused the injury which contributed to his wife's ultimate death. This court granted the State leave to appeal.

Gloria Fly, an eyewitness to the fight, testified on behalf of the State. She stated that during the late afternoon of December 11, 1972, she visited defendant's wife at the Love apartment. While Ms. Fly was with Sharon in the kitchen, Sharon asked the defendant for a "spoon of drugs." Defendant refused and stated that he did not know where drugs could be obtained. At that, Sharon began to berate defendant and to call him names. She threw a glass cup at the defendant; the cup missed him, shattered against the door and cut the defendant. He cursed his wife and slapped her face. A fight ensued. Defendant hit Sharon on the shoulder with his fist, causing her to fall against the dining room doors and onto the floor. He then began to kick her. The witness indicated that the defendant drew his foot back slightly and administered kicks to his wife's right side in the area of the abdomen approximately two inches above the hip, and to her vaginal area. The witness estimated the defendant kicked his wife for a period of 10 to 15 minutes, during which time his wife cursed him and called out for help. At one point, she tried, unsuccessfully, to crawl away. She also attempted to hit the defendant with a record rack, but defendant took it away from her and hit her with it, cutting her on the side of the head. He grabbed her by the arm and hair and dragged her into the living room. At that point, the witness gathered up Sharon's two-year-old son and took the child across the courtyard to a relative's home. Defendant departed from the apartment, leaving his wife on the living room floor.

Approximately 30 to 60 minutes later, Ms. Fly returned to the Love apartment, where she found Sharon sitting in the kitchen, crying and holding her stomach. Sharon began to vomit a thick substance. About an hour later, Ms. Fly, with the assistance of others, took Sharon to Billings Hospital. The attending physician attempted to persuade Sharon to stay at the hospital but she refused. Ms. Fly testified that, upon their return to the apartment, Sharon continued to vomit and cough for approximately 2½ hours before being taken by ambulance to Osteopathic Hospital. As doctors there examined Sharon, she evidenced pain when pressure was applied to her abdomen. She regurgitated pills given her. Sometime subsequent to 3 a.m., Ms. Fly returned with Sharon to the Love apartment, and stayed with her through the early morning hours.

Sharon's mother, Leslie Edinburg, testified that she visited her daughter on the morning of December 12 and observed her daughter with a gash on the head, bent over, and holding her left side. Later that day, Ms. Edinburg returned and took Sharon to Michael Reese Hospital. While there, Sharon began vomiting a greenish fluid and was doubled up with pain. Doctors operated immediately. Ms. Edinburg stated that, prior to December 11, her daughter was in fine health.

Dr. Harry Richter, a surgeon, testified that he supervised the care of Sharon at the hospital and was present at her operation on December 12. Prior to this operation, his examination of Sharon revealed that she had suffered an injury, suggesting progressive internal bleeding in her abdomen. Surgery revealed the source of the bleeding to be a lacerated spleen which was surgically removed. Dr. Richter observed the spleen upon its removal and described it as looking like "an apple that's been cracked open." Dr. Richter did not recall any other signs of internal trauma. He stated that the condition of the spleen was the result of a traumatic injury, but could not identify the character of the injury other than to describe it as being like a "military injury," i.e., a major abdominal injury caused by an external force and one which was many hours old at the time it was first observed. Sharon remained hospitalized until her death on December 29, 1972. During this period, she had two other operations—a tracheotomy on December 17, to ease her breathing, and an exploratory surgery on December 29. Dr. Richter stated that the cause of Sharon's death was a combination of pneumonia, edema, lung abscesses, and post-operative complications. He considered pneumonia to be a common result following a splenectomy. He stated that the onset of the factors causing Sharon's death occurred prior to the first operation, but that, in his opinion, the original trauma had triggered the sequence of events which led to Sharon's death.

On cross-examination, Dr. Richter described the location of the spleen as being in the upper left quadrant of the abdominal cavity and noted that the spleen can be torn by broken ribs. Defense counsel inquired whether Sharon had any broken ribs, to which Dr. Richter responded that he did not personally know but understood that the X ray report indicated that there were some broken ribs. On redirect examination by the State, Dr. Richter again indicated that he had no personal knowledge of broken ribs. When further questioned, he stated that he was told the X rays indicated three broken ribs. Defense counsel objected on grounds that the doctor's remarks were hearsay. The court overruled counsel's objection and held that the doctor could state what the X rays showed if, in fact, he relied on them in making his diagnosis. The X rays were not introduced into evidence, and no testimony was elicited by the State to indicate whether the doctor relied on that information in making his diagnosis.

Dr. Alexander O. Custodio, a pathologist employed by the coroner of Cook County, testified that he had performed an autopsy upon the decedent on December 30, 1972. In the course of his internal examination, he found extensive bilateral pneumonia and mild peritonitis. Aside from the surgical removal of the spleen, Dr. Custodio did not notice any other signs of trauma. Pathologically, Dr. Custodio stated, surgery and pneumonia are separate entities, but, clinically speaking, they can be related in that surgery predisposes the patient to pneumonia. Dr. Custodio could not with any degree of certainty pinpoint when the decedent contracted pneumonia other than to state that she had had it a few days before her death. Dr. Custodio agreed that the decedent's death was caused by extensive bilateral pneumonia and mild peritonitis due to the exploratory laparotomy and splenectomy.

At trial, defendant testified that he and his brother, Ronald, left the Love apartment at 4:30 p.m. on December 11 to go to the movies. They returned to the apartment between 10 and 10:30 p.m., at which time Sharon requested that defendant obtain drugs for her. When he refused, Sharon threw an object at him. Defendant stated that he slapped her twice and left the apartment to spend the night at Ronald's. He denied that he kicked her. Defendant's brother testified, corroborating defendant's testimony as to the events of December 11. He, too, denied defendant kicked Sharon.

In reversing defendant's conviction, the appellate court held that inasmuch as there was no evidence to indicate that decedent was kicked or externally injured in the area of the spleen, the trier of fact was, as a matter of law, incapable of determining, without the assistance of medical testimony, whether the defendant's conduct caused the spleen to rupture.

The State contends that the appellate court erred in reversing defendant's conviction; that no additional medical testimony was required inasmuch as the evidence introduced at trial was more than sufficient to prove beyond a reasonable doubt that defendant's conduct caused the decedent's spleen to rupture. The State concludes that the appellate court substituted its judgment for that of the trier of fact.

By cross-argument, the defendant contends that the State failed to prove beyond a reasonable doubt the causal relationship between the defendant's conduct and the pneumonia which ultimately led to Sharon's death: Defendant also asserts that the trial court erred in considering Dr. Richter's testimony concerning broken ribs. Due to the appellate court's view of the case, it did not reach the defendant's latter contention.

We find that the appellate court erred in reversing the defendant's conviction. The evidence at trial clearly established that decedent was severely beaten. The eyewitness testified that the defendant repeatedly administered kicks to the abdominal and vaginal regions for approximately 10 to 15 minutes. Although the witness indicated to the court that the kicks were administered to the right side of the abdomen, approximately two inches above the victim's hip, there was also testimony that the decedent demonstrated pain throughout her abdominal region. From Ms. Fly's description of the fight, it can be reasonably inferred that the defendant acted with a substantial amount of force, evidenced by his repeated kicking, his causing the decedent to fall against the dining room doors, his striking her over the head with the record rack, and his dragging her from one room to another by her hair and arm. Following the fight and until decedent's final admission to the hospital, she demonstrated abdominal pains and discomfort, vomiting and coughing. Decedent's mother testified that, prior to December 11, 1972, her daughter was in fine health. Dr. Richter testified that when he examined Sharon upon her arrival at Michael Reese Hospital, he found evidence suggesting progressive internal bleeding, that her stomach was exquisitely tender to palpation, and that the ordinary, normal sounds of the abdomen were absent. Surgery revealed a lacerated, bleeding spleen. Dr. Richter indicated that the condition of the decedent's spleen was the result of a traumatic injury caused by an external force of some kind.

Defendant's contention that further medical testimony was required to establish causation between the defendant's act and the decedent's injury is unpersuasive. The medical evidence, as related above, clearly established the decedent's injury to be the result of an external force applied to the abdominal region. Apart from the defendant's conduct, there is no evidence of any other external force to the decedent's abdomen.

In cases where the evidence suggests one or more acts which might have caused the injury, some of which are disconnected from any act of the defendant, medical testimony may be necessary to assist the trier of fact in determining whether the defendant's act or course of conduct constituted a contributing factor. But when, as here, the evidence reasonably and sufficiently connects the defendant's acts to the victim's subsequent state of ill-being, and where there is no evidence suggesting an act or cause of injury apart from the defendant's conduct, further medical testimony is not required to establish that the defendant's acts were sufficient to cause the injury.

* * *

Defendant, in his brief, argues that the record suggests two alternative explanations for the ruptured spleen. He hypothesizes that decedent suffered from drug addiction and that this addiction resulted in an embolization of the spleen which caused it to rupture. He further hypothesizes that the deceased could have caused the injury to herself. As to the first of these contentions, there is no evidence that decedent was a drug addict, and, further, medical testimony indicated that the injury was caused by an external force, not by an internal disorder. With respect to defendant's second theory, there is no suggestion in the record to indicate that decedent caused the injury herself. On the contrary, evidence indicates that decedent was in the same state of ill-being from the time of the beating until the time of her admission to Michael Reese Hospital.

By way of cross-argument, defendant posits that the evidence was insufficient to establish the causal relationship between the splenectomy and the deceased's ultimate death caused mainly by pneumonia. With respect to this argument, the appellate court held, "[T]he record as a whole supports causation between [deceased's] pneumonia and the surgical removal of her spleen." We concur in this conclusion. The record clearly establishes that the splenectomy predisposed the decedent to pneumonia. Although Dr. Richter stated that the combination of factors which resulted in Sharon's death existed prior to her first operation, he opined that the original trauma triggered the sequence of events which ultimately led to her death. Dr. Custodio, too, related that the surgery would predispose the body to pneumonia, and he agreed that the cause of death was extensive bilateral pneumonia and mild peritonitis due to the exploratory laparotomy and the splenectomy. Defendant is liable for the decedent's death even though his acts are not the sole and immediate cause. Accordingly, we find that the State sufficiently proved that the defendant's conduct contributed to his wife's subsequent death.

* * *

COMMONWEALTH v. ROOT

Supreme Court of Pennsylvania, 1961.
403 Pa. 571, 170 A.2d 310.

CHARLES ALVIN JONES, CHIEF JUSTICE.   The appellant was found guilty of involuntary manslaughter for the death of his competitor in the course of an automobile race between them on a highway. The trial court overruled the defendant's demurrer to the Commonwealth's evidence and, after verdict, denied his motion in arrest of judgment. On appeal from the judgment of sentence entered on the jury's verdict, the Superior Court affirmed. We granted allocatur because of the important question present as to whether the defendant's unlawful and reckless conduct was a sufficiently direct cause of the death to warrant his being charged with criminal homicide.

The testimony, which is uncontradicted in material part, discloses that, on the night of the fatal accident, the defendant accepted the deceased's challenge to engage in an automobile race; that the racing took place on a rural 3–lane highway; that the night was clear and dry, and traffic light; that the speed limit on the highway was 50 miles per hour; that, immediately prior to the accident, the two automobiles were being operated at varying speeds of from 70 to 90 miles per hour; that the accident occurred in a no-passing zone on the approach to a bridge where the highway narrowed to two directionally-opposite lanes; that, at the time of the accident, the defendant was in the lead and was proceeding in his right hand lane of travel; that the deceased, in an attempt to pass the defendant's automobile, when a truck was closely approaching from the opposite direction, swerved his car to the left, crossed the highway's white dividing line and drove his automobile on the wrong side of the highway head-on into the oncoming truck with resultant fatal effect to himself.

This evidence would of course amply support a conviction of the defendant for speeding, reckless driving and, perhaps, other violations of The Vehicle Code of May 1, 1929, P.L. 905, as amended. In fact, it may be noted, in passing, that the Act of January 8, 1960, . . . makes automobile racing on a highway an independent crime punishable by fine or imprisonment or both up to $500 and three years in jail. As the highway racing in the instant case occurred prior to the enactment of the Act of 1960, . . . that statute is, of course, not presently applicable. In any event, unlawful or reckless conduct is only one ingredient of the crime of involuntary manslaughter. Another essential and distinctly separate element of the crime is that the unlawful or reckless conduct charged to the defendant was the *direct* cause of the death in issue. The first ingredient is obviously present in this case but, just as plainly, the second is not.

While precedent is to be found for application of the tort law concept of "proximate cause" in fixing responsibility for criminal homicide, the want of any rational basis for its use in determining criminal liability can no longer be properly disregarded. When proximate cause was first borrowed from the field of tort law and applied to homicide prosecutions in Pennsylvania, the concept connoted a much more direct causal relation in producing the alleged culpable result than it does today. Proximate cause, as an essential element of a tort founded in negligence, has undergone in recent times, and is still undergoing, a marked extension. More specifically, this area of civil law has been progressively liberalized in favor of claims for damages for personal injuries to which careless conduct of others can in some way be associated. To persist in applying the tort liability concept of proximate cause to prosecutions for criminal homicide after the marked expansion of *civil* liability of defendants in tort actions for negligence would be to extend possible *criminal* liability to persons chargeable with unlawful or reckless conduct in circumstances not generally considered to present the likelihood of a resultant death. * * *

The instant case is one of first impression in this State; and our research has not disclosed a single instance where a district attorney has ever before attempted to prosecute for involuntary manslaughter on facts similar to those established by the record now before us. . . .

Legal theory which makes guilt or innocence of criminal homicide depend upon such accidental and fortuitous circumstances as are now embraced by modern tort law's encompassing concept of proximate cause is too harsh to be just. . . .

Even if the tort liability concept of proximate cause were to be deemed applicable, the defendant's conviction of involuntary manslaughter in the instant case could not be sustained under the evidence. . . .

The Superior Court, in affirming the defendant's conviction in this case, approved the charge above mentioned, despite a number of decisions in involuntary manslaughter cases holding that the conduct of the deceased victim must be considered in order to determine whether the defendant's reckless acts were the proximate (i.e., sufficiently direct) cause of his death. . . . The Superior Court dispensed with this decisional authority . . . It did so on the ground that there can be more than one proximate cause of death. The point is wholly irrelevant. Of course there can be more than one proximate cause of death just as there can also be more than one *direct* cause of death. For example, in the so-called "shield" cases where a felon interposes the person of an innocent victim between himself and a pursuing officer, if the officer should fire his gun at the felon to prevent his escape and fatally wound the person used as a shield, the different acts of the policeman and the felon would each be a direct cause of the victim's death.

If the tort liability concept of proximate cause were to be applied in a criminal homicide prosecution, then the conduct of the person whose death is the basis of the indictment would have to be considered, not to prove that it was merely an *additional* proximate cause of the death, but to determine under fundamental and long recognized law applicable to proximate cause, whether the subsequent wrongful act *superseded* the original conduct chargeable to the defendant. If it did in fact supervene, then the original act is so insulated from the ensuing death as not to be its proximate cause.

Under the uncontradicted evidence in this case, the conduct of the defendant was not the proximate cause of the decedent's death as a matter of law. In Kline v. Moyer and Albert, 1937 . . ., the rule is stated as follows: "Where a second actor has become aware of the existence of a potential danger created by the negligence of an original tort-feasor, and thereafter, by an independent act of negligence, brings about an accident, the first tort-feasor is relieved of liability, because the condition created by him was merely a circumstance of the accident and not its proximate cause." . . .

In the case now before us, the deceased was aware of the dangerous condition created by the defendant's reckless conduct in driving his automobile at an excessive rate of speed along the highway but, despite such knowledge, he recklessly chose to swerve his car to the left and into the path of an oncoming truck, thereby bringing about the head-on collision which caused his own death. . . .

The judgment of sentence is reversed and the defendant's motion in arrest of judgment granted.

The concurring opinion of BELL, JUSTICE is omitted.

EAGEN, JUSTICE (dissenting). The opinion of the learned Chief Justice admits, under the uncontradicted facts, that the defendant, at the time of the fatal accident involved, was engaged in an unlawful and reckless course of conduct. Racing an automobile at 90 miles per hour, trying to prevent another automobile going in the same direction from passing him, in a no-passing zone on a two-lane public highway, is certainly all of that. Admittedly also, there can be more than one direct cause of an unlawful death. To me, this is self-evident. But, says the majority opinion, the defendant's recklessness was not a direct cause of the death. With this, I cannot agree.

If the defendant did not engage in the unlawful race and so operate his automobile in such a reckless manner, this accident would never have occurred. He helped create the dangerous event. He was a vital part of it. The victim's acts were a natural reaction to the stimulus of the situation. The race, the attempt to pass the other car and forge ahead, the reckless speed, all of these factors the defendant himself helped create. He was part and parcel of them. That the victim's response was normal under the circumstances, that his reaction should have been expected and was clearly foreseeable, is to me beyond argument. That the defendant's recklessness was a substantial factor is obvious. All of this, in my opinion, makes his unlawful conduct a direct cause of the resulting collision.

* * *

Professor Joseph Beale, late renowned member of the Harvard Law School faculty, in an article entitled, The Proximate Consequence of an Act, 33 Harv.L.Rev. 633, 646, said, "Though there is an active force intervening after defendant's act, the result will nevertheless be proximate if the defendant's act actually caused the intervening force. In such a case the defendant's force is really continuing an active operation *by means of the force it stimulated into activity*." Professor Beale, at 658, sums up the requirements of proximity of result in this manner: "1. The defendant must have acted (or failed to act in violation of a duty). 2. The force thus created must (a) have remained active itself or created another *force* which remained active until it directly caused the result; or (b) have created a new active *risk* of being acted upon by the active force that caused the result." 2 Bishop, New Criminal Law § 424 (1913), says: "He whose act causes in any way, directly or indirectly, the death of another, kills him, within the meaning of felonious homicide. It is a rule of both reason and the law that whenever one's will contributes to impel a physical force, whether another's, his own, or a combined force, proceeding from whatever different sources, he is responsible for the result, the same as though his hand, unaided, had produced it."

But, says the majority opinion, these are principles of tort law and should not in these days be applied to the criminal law. But such has been the case since the time of Blackstone. These same principles have always been germane to both crimes and tort. They have been repeatedly so applied throughout the years and were employed in a criminal case in Pennsylvania as long as one hundred and seventeen years ago. See, Commonwealth v. Hare, 1844, 2 Clark 467. In that case, two separate bands of men were fighting each other with firearms in a public street and, as a result, an innocent citizen was shot and killed.

The person firing the fatal shot could not be ascertained. Hare, one of the rioters, was convicted of homicide and the judgment was affirmed. Can anyone question the logic or correctness of this decision? Under the rationale of the majority opinion, what would be the result in the Hare case? Certainly, under its reasoning, if the truck driver met death under the circumstances the case at hand presents, the defendant would not be legally responsible. Again with this conclusion, I cannot agree.

While the victim's foolhardiness in this case contributed to his own death, he was not the only one responsible and it is not he alone with whom we are concerned. It is the people of the Commonwealth who are harmed by the kind of conduct the defendant pursued. Their interests must be kept in mind.

I, therefore, dissent and would accordingly affirm the judgment of conviction.

NOTES

1. The appropriate standard of causation to be applied in negligent vehicular homicide cases in Massachusetts is that employed in tort law, the Massachusetts Supreme Judicial Court held in Commonwealth v. Berggren, 398 Mass. 338, 496 N.E.2d 660 (1986). The court held that the homicide statute could be applied, under this standard, to a defendant who led a policeman on a high speed chase that ended when the policeman lost control of his vehicle and was killed. The court said:

"The defendant essentially contends that since he was one hundred yards ahead of the patrolman's cruiser and was unaware of the accident, his conduct cannot be viewed as directly traceable to the resulting death of the patrolman. The defendant, however, was speeding on a motorcycle at night on roads which his attorney at oral argument before this court characterized as 'winding' and 'narrow.' He knew the patrolman was following him, but intentionally did not stop and continued on at high speeds for six miles. From the fact that the defendant was 'in fear of his license,' it may be reasonably inferred that he was aware that he had committed at least one motor vehicle violation. Under these circumstances, the defendant's acts were hardly a remote link in the chain of events leading to the patrolman's death. . . . The officer's pursuit was certainly foreseeable, as was, tragically, the likelihood of serious injury or death to the defendant himself, to the patrolman, or to some third party."

The vehicular homicide statutes of Washington and Maryland, among others, employ tort concepts of causation requiring a causal connection between driving while intoxicated and the fatal accident. Under Washington law the state must prove that the impairment due to alcohol is a proximate cause of the fatal accident. State v. MacMaster, 113 Wash.2d 226, 778 P.2d 1037 (1989). Under Maryland law the state must prove that the accident causing the fatal death of another was a result of the driver's negligent driving while intoxicated, but the mere fact of intoxication is not enough, said the court in Webber v. State, 320 Md. 238, 577 A.2d 58 (1990); to avoid a "strict liability" result, there must be "a causal relationship between the intoxicated motorist's negligence and the death of another." Contrast this with People v. Garner, 781 P.2d 87

(Colo.1989), where the court said that proof of a causal connection between drinking and a fatal collision is not required; all that is needed is a showing that defendant's voluntary act of driving while intoxicated resulted in the death of another.

2. Consider a case situation involving the death of a participant in the "game" of "Russian Roulette." May the surviving participants be held guilty of manslaughter? Such a conviction was upheld in Commonwealth v. Atencio, 345 Mass. 627, 189 N.E.2d 223 (1963), in which the court distinguished the Root case on the ground that "skill" is involved in a "drag race," whereas "Russian Roulette" involves only a matter of chance and someone is very likely to be killed. In Commonwealth v. Malone, 354 Pa. 180, 47 A.2d 445 (1946), the defendant's conviction for murder was affirmed when it was shown he had placed a gun against the decedent and pulled the trigger three times. He erroneously believed that he had placed the bullet in such a manner that the gun would not fire.

3. Does the discontinuance of respirator support for a person who has been severely injured in an accident while a passenger in defendant's car relieve the defendant of liability for first-degree manslaughter while driving under the influence of drugs? See Eby v. State, 702 P.2d 1047 (Okl.Crim.App. 1985). See also State v. Inger, 292 N.W.2d 119 (Iowa 1980), holding that premature removal of a life support system does not relieve a defendant of criminal liability if the defendant was responsible for causing the trauma that placed the doctors in the position to exercise judgment as to whether the victim was dead.

4. In Commonwealth v. Cheeks, 423 Pa. 67, 223 A.2d 291 (1966), the victim of a robbery and stabbing was taken to the hospital where he required surgery. Following the operation and after coming out of the anesthesia, the victim was disoriented, resisted treatment, demonstrated delirium tremens, and hallucinations. He also extracted the "Levin" tube which was inserted through the nostril to the stomach on four occasions, as a result of which he ultimately died. In affirming the conviction of murder, the majority of the court said: "The fact that the victim, while in weakened physical condition and disoriented mental state, pulled out the tubes and created the immediate situation, which resulted in his death, is not such an intervening and independent act sufficient to break the chain of causation of events between the stabbing and the death."

5. In State v. Preslar, 48 N.C. 421 (1856), the defendant and his wife had quarrelled, and the defendant inflicted a severe beating upon her. She left the house and sat down in the yard. A short time later, she walked to the home of her father. Instead of entering the house, however, she laid down on a bedquilt in the woods, telling her son, who had accompanied her, that she would wait until morning to go inside. The next morning she was unable to walk, from the effects of exposure. She died the next day. The defendant was convicted of murder, but the conviction was set aside on appeal. The court stated that "if, to avoid the rage of a brutal husband, a wife is compelled to expose herself, by wading through a swamp, or jumping into a river, the husband is responsible for the consequences." The court further stated, however, that "if she exposes herself thus, without necessity, and of her own accord, we know of no principle of law, by which he is held responsible. . . ."

Consider the language of the Supreme Court of Missouri in State v. Glover, 330 Mo. 709, 50 S.W.2d 1049 (1932), where the defendant was convicted of first degree murder as a result of the death of a fireman who died fighting a fire allegedly set by the defendant for the purpose of collecting insurance proceeds on the premises and contents:

"If the appellant had reason to think members of the fire department of Kansas City and citizens generally would congregate at the drug store to fight the fire, and thus would place themselves within perilous range of the flames and potentially destructive forces that had been set at work, the ensuing homicide was a natural and probable consequence of the arson; and the fact that the deceased fireman came after the fire began to burn did not break the causal relation between the arson and the homicide or constitute an independent intervening cause."

See also State v. Leopold, 110 Conn. 55, 147 A. 118 (1929), where defendant was convicted of the murder of two boys who died in a fire maliciously set by the defendant. The boys, in the building when the fire was set, had ample opportunity to escape; however, after starting to leave (or in fact leaving the building), they returned to save some property and as a result died in the fire. The Supreme Court of Connecticut noted that the boys' efforts to save property from destruction was "such a natural and ordinary course of conduct that it cannot be said to break the sequence of cause and effect."

In People v. Kibbe, 35 N.Y.2d 407, 362 N.Y.S.2d 848, 321 N.E.2d 773 (1974), the defendants stole money from a helplessly drunken victim and left him in near zero temperatures on a rural two-lane highway, having stripped him of his outer clothing with his trousers down around his ankles and shoeless. Sometime later, the victim was killed when he was struck by a vehicle driven by one Blake. Is Blake's act an independent intervening act, cutting the chain of causation? The Court said, "Under the conditions surrounding Blake's operation of his truck (i.e., the fact that he had his low beams on as the two cars approached; that there was no artificial lighting on the highway; and that there was insufficient time in which to react to Stafford's [the victim] presence in his lane, we do not think it may be said that any supervening wrongful act occurred to relieve the defendants from the directly foreseeable consequences of their actions."

6. In Clark v. Commonwealth, 90 Va. 360, 18 S.E. 440 (1893), the court said, "If the prisoner willfully inflicted upon the deceased a dangerous wound, one that was calculated to endanger and destroy life, and death ensued therefrom within a year and a day, the prisoner is none the less responsible for the results although it may appear that the deceased might have recovered but for the aggravation of the wound by skillful or improper treatment.

"But if, on the other hand, a wound or beating was inflicted upon the deceased which was not mortal, and the deceased, while laboring under the effect of the violence, became sick of a disease not caused by such violence, from which disease death ensued within a year and a day, the party charged with the homicide was not criminally responsible for the death, although it also appeared that the symptoms of the disease were aggravated, and the fatal progress quickened, by the enfeebled or irritated condition of the deceased, caused by the violence: Livingston v. Commonwealth, 14 Grat. (55 Va.) 592 (1857)."

Compare the foregoing with the result reached in People v. Flenon, 42 Mich.App. 457, 202 N.W.2d 471 (1972), where the defendant shot his victim in the leg (a non-mortal wound), necessitating amputation above the knee. The victim was discharged from the hospital several weeks later, but within a short time thereafter was readmitted to the hospital. He died from serum hepatitis contracted as a result of exposure to the disease while receiving blood transfusions during the course of the amputation operation. Defendant was convicted of homicide and the Court of Appeals of Michigan affirmed, holding that the defendant could prevail only if it be determined that the contraction of serum hepatitis was due to gross medical negligence. Short of that, it must be considered, said the court, that the consequences of a defendant's attack upon a victim are foreseeable. Since doctors are not infallible, ordinary medical negligence must be considered as foreseeable.

While the rule that ordinary medical negligence is deemed not to be an independent intervening act sufficient to cut off the chain of causation leading from the initial wrongful act of the defendant to the ultimate death is well established, should the rule be applied where, as in *Flenon,* the original wound inflicted was non-mortal?

7. During a bar holdup, the robbers line up the victims along a wall and proceed to take money from the cash register. While this is going on, a lady among the victims topples over and falls to the floor. The defendants, on seeing this, run out the front of the bar and disappear. It is later determined that the lady suffered cardiac arrest, having had a history of heart disease in the past, due to fright during the holdup. Are the robbers guilty of murder? See State v. McKeiver, 89 N.J.Super. 52, 213 A.2d 320 (1965); State v. Chavers, 294 So.2d 489 (La.1974); Phillips v. State, 289 So.2d 447 (Fla.App.1974).

Defendant snatches the victim's purse, causing her to fall. The fall caused the victim to suffer a broken hip. The broken hip required treatment by surgery. During the surgery, the victim suffered cardiac arrest. Is defendant guilty of murder or any form of homicide?

If a victim of a kidnaping and rape kills herself by ingesting poison because she is overwhelmed by shame due to the depravities to which defendant subjected her, is her death proximately caused by kidnaper-defendant? See, Stephenson v. State, 205 Ind. 141, 179 N.E. 633 (1932).

NOTE: THE YEAR–AND–A–DAY RULE

At common law, when a death occurred after the infliction of a mortal wound, the person inflicting the wound could be charged with the criminal homicide only if death occurred within a year and a day from the infliction of the wound. What is the purpose of such a rule? The rule is still retained in a number of jurisdictions. See Elliott v. Mills, 335 P.2d 1104 (Okl.Crim.App. 1959); State v. Minster, 302 Md. 240, 486 A.2d 1197 (1985) [Any change should be left to the legislature; while modern medicine may be said to have removed the reason for the rule, there is still a need to make certain of the connection between a defendant's act and the death.]; State v. Young, 77 N.J. 245, 390 A.2d 556 (1978).

The rule has been modified in some states by statute or court decision. See, e.g., State v. Hefler, 310 N.C. 135, 310 S.E.2d 310 (1984), where the court examined precedent and concluded that the rule had been applied only in murder cases and that the apparent reason for the rule was the uncertainty of medical science in determining the cause of death because of the long lapse of time between the injury and death. Taking judicial notice of the rapid development of the state of knowledge in forensic pathology, with the availability of sophisticated medical tests, analyses, and diagnoses, the court saw no reason to continue the rule for involuntary manslaughter cases. The court said, in part: "We must let the light of scientific development illuminate the legal issues of today. It would be incongruous indeed that medical science has developed to the point that it may prolong human life for long periods if that same development be utilized to bar conviction of a killer by prolonging the life of his victim." The court expressly refused to express an opinion on whether the rule should continue in murder cases. Also abolishing the year-and-a-day rule, see Commonwealth v. Ladd, 402 Pa. 164, 166 A.2d 501 (1960).

When three criminals shot a service station attendant, the victim remained in a coma for a year and eight months until he died. In response to this particular crime, the Washington legislature, by statute, replaced the old year-and-a-day rule with a new statutory provision that permits murder to be charged if the victim dies within three years and a day from the attack. The perpetrators were then charged with murder, but the Washington Supreme Court, in State v. Edwards, 104 Wash.2d 63, 701 P.2d 508 (1985) considered this statute as *ex post facto* legislation as to these defendants. While some courts have characterized the year-and-a-day rule as procedural or one of evidence law which can therefore be abolished without running afoul of the protection against *ex post facto* laws, the Washington court determined causation to be an element of the crime of murder.

A Florida court discarded the year-and-a-day rule, holding that it was not an element of the offense of murder but was merely a rule of evidence which, in the age of modern medical technology, had lost whatever relevance it might once have enjoyed. Jones v. Dugger, 518 So.2d 295 (Fla.App.1987). In State v. Cross, 260 Ga. 845, 401 S.E.2d 510 (1991), a majority of the Georgia Supreme Court held that the legislature's silence on the issue in the adoption of the state's 1968 comprehensive criminal code abrogated the common law year-and-a-day rule.

D. BURDEN OF PROOF

----

1. FROM THE COMMON LAW TO THE CONSTITUTION

IN RE WINSHIP

Supreme Court of the United States, 1970.
397 U.S. 358, 90 S.Ct. 1068.

BRENNAN, J.

* * *

The requirement that guilt of a criminal charge be established by proof beyond a reasonable doubt dates at least from our early years as a Nation. The "demand for a higher degree of persuasion in criminal cases was recurrently expressed from ancient times, though its crystallization into the formula 'beyond a reasonable doubt' seems to have occurred as late at 1798. It is now accepted in common law jurisdictions as the measure of persuasion by which the prosecution must convince the trier of all the essential elements of guilt." McCormick, Evidence, § 321, at 681–682 (1954). Although virtually unanimous adherence to the reasonable-doubt standard in common-law jurisdictions may not conclusively establish it as a requirement of due process, such adherence does "reflect a profound judgment about the way in which law should be enforced and justice administered." . . .

Expressions in many opinions of this Court indicate that it has long been assumed that proof of a criminal charge beyond a reasonable doubt is constitutionally required [citing authorities].

* * *

The reasonable-doubt standard plays a vital role in the American scheme of criminal procedure. It is a prime instrument for reducing the risk of convictions resting on factual error. The standard provides concrete substance for the presumption of innocence—that bedrock "axiomatic and elementary" principle whose "enforcement lies at the foundation of the administration of our criminal law." . . .

The requirement of proof beyond a reasonable doubt has this vital role in our criminal procedure for cogent reasons. The accused during a criminal prosecution has at stake interests of immense importance, both because of the possibility that he may lose his liberty upon conviction and because of the certainty that he would be stigmatized by that conviction. Accordingly, a society that values the good name and freedom of every individual should not condemn a man for commission of a crime when there is reasonable doubt about his guilt. As we said in Speiser v. Randall, 357 U.S. 513, 525 . . .: "There is always in litigation a margin of error, representing error in factfinding, which both parties must take into account. Where one party has at stake an interest of transcending value—as a criminal defendant his liberty—this margin of error is reduced as to him by the process of placing on the other party the burden of . . . persuading the factfinder at the conclusion of the trial of his guilt beyond a reasonable doubt. Due process commands that no man shall lose his liberty unless the Gove-ment has borne the burden of . . . convincing the factfinder of his guilt. To this end, the reasonable-doubt standard is indispensable. . . .

Moreover, use of the reasonable-doubt standard is indispensable to command the respect and confidence of the community in applications of the criminal law. It is critical that the moral force of the criminal law not be diluted by a standard of proof which leaves people in doubt whether innocent men are being condemned. It is also important in our free society that every individual going about his ordinary affairs have confidence that his government cannot adjudge him guilty of a criminal offense without convincing a proper factfinder of his guilt with utmost certainty.

———

[In his concurring opinion, JUSTICE HARLAN observed, in part:]

. . . In a civil suit between two private parties for money damages . . . we view it as no more serious in general for there to be an erroneous verdict in the defendant's favor than for there to be an erroneous verdict in the plaintiff's favor. A preponderance of the evidence standard therefore seems peculiarly appropriate for, as explained most sensibly, it simply requires that trier of fact "to believe that the existence of a fact is more probable than its nonexistence before [he] may find in favor of the party who has the burden to persuade the [judge] of the fact's existence."

In a criminal case, on the other hand, we do not view the social disutility of convicting an innocent man as equivalent to the disutility of acquitting someone who is guilty. . . .

In this context, I view the requirement of proof beyond a reasonable doubt in a criminal case as bottomed on a fundamental value determination of our society that it is far worse to convict an innocent man than to let a guilty man go free. It is only because of the nearly complete and longstanding acceptance of the reasonable-doubt standard by the States in criminal trials that the Court has not before today had to hold explicitly that due process, as an expression of fundamental procedural fairness, requires a more stringent standard for criminal trials than for ordinary civil litigation. . . .

[MR. JUSTICE BLACK'S dissenting opinion is omitted.]

NOTES

1. Although the concept of requiring proof of guilt beyond a "reasonable doubt" is firmly embedded in our criminal justice system, the meaning of the term has been and continues to be a troublesome one, and particularly with respect to the trial judge's instructions to the jury. The California legislature, in Section 1096 of its Penal Code, has sought to define it by stating, essentially, that what is required of a jury verdict of guilty is "an abiding conviction, to a moral certainty, of the truth of the charge." On the other hand the Supreme Court of Pennsylvania has held that the use of the words "moral certainty" merely "serves to confuse and befog the jury instead of enlightening them." Commonwealth v. Kloiber, 378 Pa. 412, 106 A.2d 820 (1954). The United States Court of Military Appeals has defined reasonable doubt as "a doubt based on reason." United States v. Kloh, 10 U.S.C.M.A. 329, 27 C.M.R. 403 (1959). In England the Court of Criminal Appeals experimented with the expression that reasonable doubt means the jury must "feel sure" about a verdict of guilty, R. v. Summers, 36 Cr.App.R. 15, [1952] 1 All Eng.R. 1059, but this too was found to be in need of clarification in a subsequent case, R. v. Hepworth [1955] 2 All Eng. R. 918. The Illinois Supreme Court, after exploring the possibility of assisting jurors in applying the "beyond a reasonable doubt" requirement, finally concluded that the term "needs no definition" and that trial judges should not give instructions "resulting in an elaboration of it." People v. Schuele, 326 Ill. 366, 372, 157 N.E. 215, 217 (1927). Wigmore, in his treatise on Evidence (§ 2497, 3d ed. 1940) expressed a similar viewpoint.

With respect to the application of the "reasonable doubt" requirement by trial courts, see Allen & DeGrazzia, The Constitutional Requirement of Proof Beyond a Reasonable Doubt in Criminal Cases: A Comment Upon Incipient Chaos in the Lower Courts, 20 Amer.Crim.L.Rev. 1 (1982).

2. Consider the words of Chief Justice Carrico of the Virginia Supreme Court who, while addressing lawyers, made this statement about the presumption of innocence:

"The second thing . . . was the shocking revelation that a large segment of the public misconceived certain basic rights which we, as lawyers, assumed everyone understood. For example, a national survey revealed that 50% of our citizenry believed a person accused of crime must prove himself or herself innocent. Worse yet, 49.9% of those who had served on juries harbored this mistaken belief.

"It takes but little imagination to understand why there is lack of respect for courts and lawyers when the public is so grossly misinformed concerning such a fundamental principle of law as the presumption of innocence. With half the people believing the defense must prove innocence, they cannot help but wonder why so many acquittals occur, and they cannot be faulted when they blame lawyers and judges for what they perceive as an obvious breakdown in the system." (Virginia Bar News, p. 26 [Aug. 1987].)

What special burdens does this place upon criminal defense lawyers? How does a lawyer overcome the common understanding on the part of the public, reflected in the opinions polls, that "where there's smoke there's fire," and "the police wouldn't have brought him to court if he weren't guilty"?

3. In countries whose criminal justice system is based on English common law, charges may be brought against an individual when there is "probable cause" the person has committed an offense. "Probable cause" is not a particularly high standard of proof—one prosecuting authorities ordinarily have no difficulty meeting. By contrast, in the civil law countries, significantly more proof of guilt is required before a person may be formally charged with an offense. Does this mean that in such countries, it would be even more difficult to maintain the presumption of innocence throughout a trial?

For a very thoughtful and thorough analysis of the presumption of innocence and its meaning in the context of a justice system that has its roots in European civil law, see Quigley, The Soviet Conception of the Presumption of Innocence, 29 Santa Clara L.Rev. 301 (1989).

2. PRESUMPTIONS AND SHIFTING THE BURDEN OF PROOF

PATTERSON v. NEW YORK

Supreme Court of the United States, 1977.
432 U.S. 197, 97 S.Ct. 2319.

MR. JUSTICE WHITE delivered the opinion of the Court.

The question here is the constitutionality under the Fourteenth Amendment's Due Process Clause of burdening the defendant in a New York State murder trial with proving the affirmative defense of extreme emotional disturbance as defined by New York law.

After a brief and unstable marriage, the appellant, Gordon Patterson, became estranged from his wife, Roberta. Roberta resumed an association with John Northrup, a neighbor to whom she had been engaged prior to her marriage to appellant. On December 27, 1970, Patterson borrowed a rifle from an acquaintance and went to the residence of his father-in-law. There, he observed his wife through a window in a state of semiundress in the presence of John Northrup. He entered the house and killed Northrup by shooting him twice in the head.

Patterson was charged with second-degree murder. In New York there are two elements of this crime: (1) "intent to cause the death of another person"; and (2) "caus[ing] the death of such person or of a third person." N.Y.Penal Law § 125.25 (McKinney). Malice aforethought is not an element of the crime. In addition, the State permits a person accused of murder to raise an affirmative defense that he "acted under the influence of extreme emotional disturbance for which there was a reasonable explanation or excuse."

New York also recognizes the crime of manslaughter. A person is guilty of manslaughter if he intentionally kills another person "under circumstances which do not constitute murder because he acts under the influence of extreme emotional disturbance." Appellant confessed before trial to killing Northrup, but at trial he raised the defense of extreme emotional disturbance.

The jury was instructed as to the elements of the crime of murder. Focusing on the element of intent, the trial court charged,

> "Before you, considering all of the evidence, can convict this defendant or any one of murder, you must believe and decide that the People have established beyond a reasonable doubt that he intended, in firing the gun, to kill either the victim himself or some other human being. . . ."

The jury was further instructed, consistently with New York law, that the defendant had the burden of proving his affirmative defense by a preponderance of the evidence. The jury was told that if it found beyond a reasonable doubt that appellant had intentionally killed Northrup but that appellant had demonstrated by a preponderance of the evidence that he had acted under the influence of extreme emotional disturbance, it must find appellant guilty of manslaughter instead of murder.

The jury found appellant guilty of murder. Judgment was entered on the verdict, and the Appellate Division affirmed. While appeal to the New York Court of Appeals was pending, this Court decided *Mullaney v. Wilbur*, 421 U.S. 684, 95 S.Ct. 1881 (1975), in which the Court declared Maine's murder statute unconstitutional. Under the Maine statute, a person accused of murder could rebut the statutory presumption that he committed the offense with "malice aforethought" by proving that he acted in the heat of passion on sudden provocation. The Court held that this scheme improperly shifted the burden of persuasion from the prosecutor to the defendant and was therefore a violation of due process. In the Court of Appeals appellant urged that New York's murder statute is functionally equivalent to the one struck down in *Mullaney* and that therefore his conviction should be reversed.

The Court of Appeals rejected appellant's argument, holding that the New York murder statute is consistent with due process. . . . We affirm.

It goes without saying that preventing and dealing with crime is much more the business of the States than it is of the Federal Government, and that we should not lightly construe the Constitution so as to intrude upon the administration of justice by the individual States. . . .

In determining whether New York's allocation to the defendant of proving the mitigating circumstances of severe emotional disturbance is consistent with due process, it is therefore relevant to note that this defense is a considerably expanded version of the common law defense of heat of passion on sudden provocation and that at common law the burden of proving the latter, as well as other affirmative defenses— indeed, "all . . . circumstances of justification, excuse or alleviation"—rested on the defendant. This was the rule when the Fifth Amendment was adopted, and it was the American rule when the Fourteenth Amendment was ratified. Commonwealth v. York, 50 Mass. 93 (1845).

In 1895 the common law view was abandoned with respect to the insanity defense in federal prosecutions. Davis v. United States, 160 U.S. 469, 16 S.Ct. 353 (1895). This ruling had wide impact on the practice in the federal courts with respect to the burden of proving various affirmative defenses, and the prosecution in a majority of jurisdictions in this country sooner or later came to shoulder the burden of proving the sanity of the accused and of disproving the facts constituting other affirmative defenses, including provocation. *Davis* was not a constitutional ruling, however, as Leland v. Oregon, 343 U.S. 790, 72 S.Ct. 1002 (1958), made clear.

At issue in Leland v. Oregon was the constitutionality under the Due Process Clause of the Oregon rule that the defense of insanity must be proved by the defendant beyond a reasonable doubt. Noting that *Davis* "obviously established no constitutional doctrine," the Court refused to strike down the Oregon scheme, saying that the burden of proving all elements of the crime beyond reasonable doubt, including the elements of premeditation and deliberation, was placed on the State under Oregon procedures and remained there throughout the trial. To convict, the jury was required to find each element of the crime beyond reasonable doubt, based on all the evidence, including the evidence going to the issue of insanity. Only then was the jury "to consider separately the issue of legal sanity *per se*. . . ." This practice did not offend the Due Process Clause even though among the 20 States then placing the burden of proving his insanity on the defendant, Oregon was alone in requiring him to convince the jury beyond a reasonable doubt.

In 1970, the Court declared [in Winship] that the Due Process Clause "protects the accused against conviction except upon proof beyond a reasonable doubt of every fact necessary to constitute the crime with which he is charged." Five years later, in Mullaney v. Wilbur, supra, the Court further announced that under the Maine law of homicide, the burden could not constitutionally be placed on the defendant of proving by a preponderance of the evidence that the killing had occurred in the heat of passion on sudden provocation. The Chief Justice and Mr. Justice Rehnquist, concurring, expressed their understanding that the *Mullaney* decision did not call into question the ruling in Leland v. Oregon, supra, with respect to the proof of insanity.

* * *

We cannot conclude that Patterson's conviction under the New York law deprived him of due process of law. The crime of murder is defined by the statute, which represents a recent revision of the State criminal code, as causing the death of another person with intent to do so. The death, the intent to kill, and causation are the facts that the State is required to prove beyond reasonable doubt if a person is to be convicted of murder. No further facts are either presumed or inferred in order to constitute the crime. The statute does provide an affirmative defense—that the defendant acted under the influence of extreme emotional disturbance for which there was a reasonable explanation—which, if proved by a preponderance of the evidence, would reduce the crime to manslaughter, an offense defined in a separate section of the statute. It is plain enough that if the intentional killing is shown, the State intends to deal with the defendant as a murderer unless he demonstrates the mitigating circumstances.

* * *

We are unwilling to reconsider *Leland* . . . But even if we were to hold that a State must prove sanity to convict once that fact is put in issue, it would not necessarily follow that a State must prove beyond a reasonable doubt every fact, the existence or nonexistence of which it is willing to recognize as an exculpatory or mitigating circumstance affecting the degree of culpability or the severity of the punishment. Here, in revising its criminal code, New York provided the affirmative defense of extreme emotional disturbance, a substantially expanded version of the older heat of passion concept; but it was willing to do so only if the facts making out the defense were established by the defendant with sufficient certainty. The State was itself unwilling to undertake to establish the absence of those facts beyond reasonable doubt, perhaps fearing that proof would be too difficult and that too many persons deserving treatment as murderers would escape that punishment if the evidence need merely raise a reasonable doubt about the defendant's emotional state. It has been said that the new criminal code of New York contains some 25 affirmative defenses which exculpate or mitigate but which must be established by the defendant to be operative. The Due Process Clause, as we see it, does not put New York to the choice of abandoning those defenses or undertaking to disprove their existence in order to convict for a crime which otherwise is within its constitutional powers to sanction by substantial punishment.

The requirement of proof beyond reasonable doubt in a criminal case is "bottomed on a fundamental value determination of our society that it is far worse to convict an innocent man than to let a guilty man go free." The social cost of placing the burden on the prosecution to prove guilt beyond a reasonable doubt is thus an increased risk that the guilty will go free. While it is clear that our society has willingly chosen to bear a substantial burden in order to protect the innocent, it is equally clear that the risk it must bear is not without limits; and Justice Harlan's aphorism provides little guidance for determining what those limits are. Due process does not require that every conceivable step be taken, at whatever cost, to eliminate the possibility of convicting an innocent person. Punishment of those found guilty by a jury, for example, is not forbidden merely because there is a remote possibility in some instances that an innocent person might go to jail.

It is said that the common law rule permits a State to punish one as a murderer when it is as likely as not that he acted in the heat of passion or under severe emotional distress and when, if he did, he is guilty only of manslaughter. But this has always been the case in those jurisdictions adhering to the traditional rule. It is also very likely true that fewer convictions for murder would occur if New York were required to negative the affirmative defense at issue here. But in each instance of a murder conviction under the present law New York will have proved beyond reasonable doubt that the defendant has intentionally killed another person, an act which it is not disputed the State may constitutionally criminalize and punish. . . .

We thus decline to adopt as a constitutional imperative, operative country-wide, that a State must disprove beyond reasonable doubt every fact constituting any and all affirmative defenses related to the culpability of an accused. Traditionally, due process has required that only the most basic procedural safeguards be observed; more subtle balancing of society's interests against those of the accused have been left to the legislative branch. We therefore will not disturb the balance struck in previous cases holding that the Due Process Clause requires the prosecution to prove beyond reasonable doubt all of the elements included in the definition of the offense of which the defendant is charged. Proof of the nonexistence of all affirmative defenses has never been constitutionally required; and we perceive no reason to fashion such a rule in this case and apply it to the statutory defense at issue here. . . .

It is urged that Mullaney v. Wilbur necessarily invalidates Patterson's conviction. In *Mullaney* the charge was murder, which the Maine statute defined as the unlawful killing of a human being "with malice aforethought either express or implied." The trial court instructed the jury that the words "malice aforethought" were most important "because malice aforethought is an essential and indispensable element of the crime of murder." Malice, as the statute indicated and as the court instructed, could be implied and was to be implied from "any deliberate, cruel act committed by one person against another suddenly or without a considerable provocation," in which event an intentional killing was murder unless by a preponderance of the evidence it was shown that the act was committed "in the heat of passion upon sudden provocation." The instructions emphasized that " 'malice aforethought and heat of passion on sudden provocation are two inconsistent things'; thus, by proving the latter the defendant would negate the former."

Mullaney's conviction, which followed, was affirmed. The Maine Supreme Judicial Court held that murder and manslaughter were varying degrees of the crime of felonious homicide and that the presumption of malice arising from the unlawful killing was a mere policy presumption operating to cast on the defendant the burden of proving provocation if he was to be found guilty of manslaughter rather than murder—a burden which the Maine law had allocated to him at least since the mid–1800's.

The Court of Appeals for the First Circuit then ordered that a writ of habeas corpus issue, holding that the presumption unconstitutionally shifted to the defendant the burden of proof with respect to an essential element of the crime. The Maine Supreme Judicial Court disputed this interpretation of Maine law in State v. Lafferty, 309 A.2d 647 (1973), declaring that malice aforethought, in the sense of premeditation, was not an element of the crime of murder and that the federal court had erroneously equated the presumption of malice with a presumption of premeditation.

> "Maine law does not rely on a presumption of 'premeditation' (as Wilbur v. Mullaney assumed) to prove an essential element of unlawful homicide punishable as murder. Proof beyond reasonable doubt of 'malice aforethought' (in the sense of 'premeditation') is not essential to conviction. . . . [T]he failure of the State to prove 'premeditation' in this context is not fatal to such a prosecution because, by legal definition under Maine law, a killing becomes unlawful and punishable as 'murder' on proof of 'any deliberate cruel act, committed by one person against another, suddenly *without any, or without a considerable provocation.* ' State v. Neal, 37 Me. 468, 470 (1854). *Neal* has been frequently cited with approval by our Court." State v. Lafferty, supra, at 664–665. (Emphasis added; footnote omitted.)

When the judgment of the First Circuit was vacated for reconsideration in the light of *Lafferty*, that court reaffirmed its view that Mullaney's conviction was unconstitutional. This Court, accepting the Maine court's interpretation of the Maine law, unanimously agreed with the Court of Appeals that Mullaney's due process rights had been invaded by the presumption casting upon him the burden of proving by preponderance of the evidence that he had acted in the heat of passion upon sudden provocation.

Mullaney's holding, it is argued, is that the State may not permit the blameworthiness of an act or the severity of punishment authorized for its commission to depend on the presence or absence of an identified fact without assuming the burden of proving the presence or absence of that fact, as the case may be, beyond reasonable doubt. In our view, the *Mullaney* holding should not be so broadly read.

Mullaney surely held that a State must prove every ingredient of an offense beyond a reasonable doubt, and that it may not shift the burden of proof to the defendant by presuming that ingredient upon proof of the other elements of the offense. This is true even though the State's practice, as in Maine, had been traditionally to the contrary. Such shifting of the burden of persuasion with respect to a fact which the State deems so important that it must be either proved or presumed is impermissible under the Due Process Clause.

It was unnecessary to go further in *Mullaney*. The Maine Supreme Court made it clear that malice aforethought, which was mentioned in the statutory definition of the crime, was not equivalent to premeditation and that the presumption of malice traditionally arising in intentional homicide cases carried no factual meaning insofar as premeditation was concerned. Even so, a killing became murder in Maine when it resulted from a deliberate, cruel act committed by one person against another, "suddenly, and without any, or without considerable, provocation." State v. Lafferty, supra. Premeditation was not within the definition of murder; but malice, in the sense of the absence of provocation, was part of the definition of that crime. Yet malice, i.e., lack of provocation, was presumed and could be rebutted by the defendant only by proving by a preponderance of the evidence that he acted with heat of passion upon sudden provocation. In *Mullaney* we held that however traditional this mode of proceeding might have been, it is contrary to the Due Process Clause as construed in *Winship*.

As we have explained, nothing was presumed or implied against Patterson; and his conviction is not invalid under any of our prior cases. The judgment of the New York Court of Appeals is

Affirmed.

Mr. Justice Rehnquist took no part in the consideration or decision of this case.

MR. JUSTICE POWELL, with whom MR. JUSTICE BRENNAN and MR. JUSTICE MARSHALL join, dissenting.

In the name of preserving legislative flexibility, the Court today drains In re Winship, supra, of much of its vitality. Legislatures do require broad discretion in the drafting of criminal laws, but the Court surrenders to the legislative branch a significant part of its responsibility to protect the presumption of innocence. . . .

Maine's homicide laws embodied the common-law distinctions along with the colorful common-law language. Murder was defined in the statute as the unlawful killing of a human being "with malice aforethought, either express or implied." Manslaughter was a killing "in the heat of passion, on sudden provocation, without express or implied malice aforethought. . . ." And the Maine Supreme Judicial Court had held that instructions concerning express malice (in the sense of premeditation) were unnecessary. The only inquiry for the jury in deciding whether a homicide amounted to murder or manslaughter was the inquiry into heat of passion on sudden provocation.

Our holding in *Mullaney* found no constitutional defect in these statutory provisions. Rather, the defect in Maine practice lay in its allocation of the burden of persuasion with respect to the crucial factor distinguishing murder from manslaughter. In Maine, juries were instructed that if the prosecution proved that the homicide was both intentional and unlawful, the crime was to be considered murder unless the *defendant* proved by a preponderance of the evidence that he acted in the heat of passion on sudden provocation. Only if the defendant carried this burden would the offense be reduced to manslaughter.

New York's present homicide laws had their genesis in lingering dissatisfaction with certain aspects of the common-law framework that this Court confronted in *Mullaney*. Critics charged that the archaic language tended to obscure the factors of real importance in the jury's decision. Also, only a limited range of aggravations would lead to mitigation under the common-law formula, usually only those resulting from direct provocation by the victim himself. It was thought that actors whose emotions were stirred by other forms of outrageous conduct, even conduct by someone other than the ultimate victim, also should be punished as manslaughterers rather than murderers. Moreover, the common-law formula was generally applied with rather strict objectivity. Only provocations that might cause the hypothetical reasonable man to lose control could be considered. And even provocations of that sort were inadequate to reduce the crime to manslaughter if enough time had passed for the reasonable man's passions to cool, regardless of whether the actor's own thermometer had registered any decline.

The American Law Institute took the lead in moving to remedy these difficulties. As part of its commendable undertaking to prepare a Model Penal Code, it endeavored to bring modern insights to bear on the law of homicide. The result was a proposal to replace "heat of passion" with the moderately broader concept of "extreme mental or emotional disturbance. . . ."

At about this time the New York Legislature undertook the preparation of a new criminal code, . . . The new code adopted virtually word-for-word the ALI formula for distinguishing murder from manslaughter. . . . There is no mention of malice aforethought, no attempt to give a name to the state of mind that exists when extreme emotional disturbance is not present. . . .

Despite these changes, the major factor that distinguishes murder from manslaughter in New York—"extreme emotional disturbance"—is undeniably the modern equivalent of "heat of passion. . . ."

But in one important respect the New York drafters chose to parallel Maine's practice precisely, departing markedly from the ALI recommendation. Under the Model Penal Code the prosecution must prove the absence of emotional disturbance beyond a reasonable doubt once the issue is properly raised. In New York, however, extreme emotional disturbance constitutes an affirmative defense rather than a simple defense. Consequently the defendant bears not only the burden of production on this issue; he has the burden of persuasion as well.

Mullaney held invalid Maine's requirement that the defendant prove heat of passion. The Court today, without disavowing the unanimous holding of *Mullaney,* approves New York's requirement that the defendant prove extreme emotional disturbance. The Court manages to run a constitutional boundary line through the barely visible space that separates Maine's law from New York's. It does so on the basis of distinctions in language that are formalistic rather than substantive.

This result is achieved by a narrowly literal parsing of the holding in *Winship:* "the Due Process Clause protects the accused against conviction except upon proof beyond a reasonable doubt of every fact necessary to constitute the crime with which he is charged." The only "facts" necessary to constitute a crime are said to be those that appear on the face of the statute as a part of the definition of the crime. Maine's statute was invalid, the Court reasons, because it "defined [murder] as the unlawful killing of a human being 'with malice aforethought either express or implied.' " "[M]alice," the Court reiterates, "in the sense of the absence of provocation, was part of the definition of that crime." *Winship* was violated only because this "fact"—malice— was "presumed" unless the defendant persuaded the jury otherwise by showing that he acted in the heat of passion. New York, in form presuming no affirmative "fact" against Patterson, and blessed with a statute drafted in the leaner language of the 20th century, escapes constitutional scrutiny unscathed even though the effect on the defendant of New York's placement of the burden of persuasion is exactly the same as Maine's.

This explanation of the *Mullaney* holding bears little resemblance to the basic rationale of that decision. But this is not the cause of greatest concern. The test the Court today establishes allows a legislature to shift, virtually at will, the burden of persuasion with respect to any factor in a criminal case, so long as it is careful not to mention the nonexistence of that factor in the statutory language that defines the crime * * *

. . . What *Winship* and *Mullaney* had sought to teach about the limits a free society places on its procedures to safeguard the liberty of its citizens becomes a rather simplistic lesson in statutory draftman-ship. Nothing in the Court's opinion prevents a legislature from applying this new learning to many of the classical elements of the crimes it punishes. . . .

The Court understandably manifests some uneasiness that its for-malistic approach will give legislatures too much latitude in shifting the burden of persuasion. And so it issues a warning that "there are obviously constitutional limits beyond which the States may not go in this regard." The Court thereby concedes that legislative abuses may occur and that they must be curbed by the judicial branch. But if the State is careful to conform to the drafting formulas articulated today, the constitutional limits are anything but "obvious." This decision simply leaves us without a conceptual framework for distinguishing abuses from legitimate legislative adjustments of the burden of persua-sion in criminal cases. * * *

NOTES

1. In Mullaney v. Wilbur, 421 U.S. 684, 95 S.Ct. 1881 (1975), the Court held that, to obtain a murder conviction under the Maine statutes, the prosecu-tion must prove beyond a reasonable doubt the absence of the heat of passion on sudden provocation.

Consider how courts interpret Mullaney v. Wilbur and Patterson v. New York in the light of the federal murder statute (18 U.S.C.A. § 1111), which requires proof of malice. In United States v. Lofton, 776 F.2d 918 (10th Cir. 1985), defendant shot her husband in the aftermath of his sexual abuse of their daughter. In reversing a second degree murder conviction, the court stated that Mullaney requires a clear and unambiguous statement, in the form of a jury instruction, that the Government must prove the absence of heat of passion beyond a reasonable doubt. Similarly, see United States v. Lesina, 833 F.2d 156 (9th Cir.1987).

Contrast these cases with United States v. Molina–Uribe, 853 F.2d 1193 (5th Cir.1988), cert. denied 489 U.S. 1022, 109 S.Ct. 1145 (1989). Here the court held that not instructing the jury that the government must prove that defendant acted in the absence of heat of passion was not impermissibly burden-shifting. Can these cases be reconciled?

2. Assume that a state statute provides that anyone convicted of certain felonies is subject to a mandatory minimum sentence of five years if the sentencing judge finds, on the basis of the evidence presented at trial and that also brought forth at the sentencing hearing, by a preponderance of the evidence, that the defendant "visibly possessed a firearm" during the commis-sion of the offense. Does this quantum of proof requirement violate the Mullaney decision? Or does Patterson apply? What if the state made the visibly possession of a firearm an element of an offense?

See, McMillan v. Pennsylvania, 477 U.S. 79, 106 S.Ct. 2411, 91 L.Ed.2d 67 (1986), wherein Justice Rehnquist's opinion for the 5–to–4 majority of the Court reasoned that the state's provision on the weight to be given to a factor at sentencing does not translate that provision into an "element" of some hypo-thetical offense. But Justice Stevens concluded that due process under Patterson required proof beyond a reasonable doubt for conduct which exposes a criminal defendant to a greater stigma or punishment.

MARTIN v. OHIO

Supreme Court of the United States, 1987.
480 U.S. 228, 107 S.Ct. 1098, 94 L.Ed.2d 267.

JUSTICE WHITE delivered the opinion of the Court.

The Ohio Code provides that "[e]very person accused of an offense is presumed innocent until proven guilty beyond a reasonable doubt, and the burden of proof for all elements of the offense is upon the prosecution. The burden of going forward with the evidence of an affirmative defense, and the burden of proof by a preponderance of the evidence, for an affirmative defense, is upon the accused." Ohio Rev. Code Ann. § 2901.05(A) (1982). An affirmative defense is one involving "an excuse or justification peculiarly within the knowledge of the accused, on which he can fairly be required to adduce supporting evidence." Ohio Rev.Code Ann. § 2901.05(C)(2) (1982). The Ohio courts have "long determined that self-defense is an affirmative defense," and that the defendant has the burden of proving it as required by § 2901.05(A).

As defined by the trial court in its instructions in this case, the elements of self-defense that the defendant must prove are (1) that the defendant was not at fault in creating the situation giving rise to the argument; (2) the defendant had an honest belief that she was in imminent danger of death or great bodily harm and that her only means of escape from such danger was in the use of such force; and (3) the defendant must not have violated any duty to retreat or avoid danger. App. 19. The question before us is whether the Due Process Clause of the Fourteenth Amendment forbids placing the burden of proving self-defense on the defendant when she is charged by the State of Ohio with committing the crime of aggravated murder, which, as relevant to this case, is defined by the Revised Code of Ohio as "purposely, and with prior calculation and design, caus[ing] the death of another." Ohio Rev.Code Ann. § 2903.01 (1982).

The facts of the case, taken from the opinions of the courts below, may be succinctly stated. On July 21, 1983, petitioner Earline Martin and her husband, Walter Martin, argued over grocery money. Petitioner claimed that her husband struck her in the head during the argument. Petitioner's version of what then transpired was that she went upstairs, put on a robe, and later came back down with her husband's gun which she intended to dispose of. Her husband saw something in her hand and questioned her about it. He came at her, she lost her head and fired the gun at him. Five or six shots were fired, three of them striking and killing Mr. Martin. She was charged with and tried for aggravated murder. She pleaded self-defense and testified in her own defense. The judge charged the jury with respect to the elements of the crime and of self-defense and rejected petitioner's Due Process

Clause challenge to the charge placing on her the burden of proving self-defense. The jury found her guilty.

Both the Ohio Court of Appeals and the Supreme Court of Ohio affirmed the conviction. Both rejected the constitutional challenge to the instruction requiring petitioner to prove self-defense. The latter court, relying upon our opinion in *Patterson v. New York* (1977), concluded that, the State was required to prove the three elements of aggravated murder but that *Patterson* did not require it to disprove self-defense, which is a separate issue that did not require Mrs. Martin to disprove any element of the offense with which she was charged. . . .

In re Winship (1970), declared that the Due Process Clause "protects the accused against conviction except upon proof beyond a reasonable doubt of every fact necessary to constitute the crime with which he is charged." A few years later, we held that *Winship*'s mandate was fully satisfied where the State of New York had proved beyond reasonable doubt, each of the elements of murder, but placed on the defendant the burden of proving the affirmative defense of extreme emotional disturbance, which, if proved, would have reduced the crime from murder to manslaughter. We there emphasized the preeminent role of the States in preventing and dealing with crime and the reluctance of the Court to disturb a State's decision with respect to the definition of criminal conduct and the procedures by which the criminal laws are to be enforced in the courts, including the burden of producing evidence and allocating the burden of persuasion. New York had the authority to define murder as the intentional killing of another person. It had chosen, however, to reduce the crime to manslaughter if the defendant proved by a preponderance of the evidence that he had acted under the influence of extreme emotional distress. To convict of murder, the jury was required to find beyond a reasonable doubt, based on all the evidence, including that related to the defendant's mental state at the time of the crime, each of the elements of murder and also to conclude that the defendant had not proved his affirmative defense. The jury convicted Patterson, and we held there was no violation of the Fourteenth Amendment as construed in *Winship*. Referring to *Leland v. Oregon* (1952) and *Rivera v. Delaware*, 429 U.S. 877, 97 S.Ct. 226, 50 L.Ed.2d 160 (1976), we added that New York "did no more than *Leland* and *Rivera* permitted it to do without violating the Due Process Clause" and declined to reconsider those cases. It was also observed that "the fact that a majority of the States have now assumed the burden of disproving affirmative defenses—for whatever reasons—[does not] mean that those States that strike a different balance are in violation of the Constitution."

As in *Patterson,* the jury was here instructed that to convict it must find, in light of all the evidence, that each of elements of the crime of aggravated murder must be proved by the State beyond reasonable doubt and that the burden of proof with respect to these elements did not shift. To find guilt, the jury had to be convinced that none of the evidence, whether offered by the State or by Martin in connection with her plea of self-defense, raised a reasonable doubt that Martin had killed her husband, that she had the specific purpose and intent to cause his death, or that she had done so with prior calculation and design. It was also told, however, that it could acquit if it found by a preponderance of the evidence that Martin had not precipitated the confrontation, that she had an honest belief that she was in imminent danger of death or great bodily harm, and that she had satisfied any duty to retreat or avoid danger. The jury convicted Martin.

We agree with the State and its Supreme Court that this conviction did not violate the Due Process Clause. The State did not . . . seek to shift to Martin the burden of proving any of those elements, and the jury's verdict reflects that none of her self-defense evidence raised a reasonable doubt about the state's proof that she purposefully killed with prior calculation and design. She nevertheless had the opportunity under state law and the instructions given to justify the killing and show herself to be blameless by proving that she acted in self-defense. The jury thought she had failed to do so, and Ohio is as entitled to punish Martin as one guilty of murder as New York was to punish Patterson.

It would be quite different if the jury had been instructed that self-defense evidence could not be considered in determining whether there was a reasonable doubt about the state's case, i.e., that self-defense evidence must be put aside for all purposes unless it satisfied the preponderance standard. Such instruction would relieve the state of its burden and plainly run afoul of *Winship*'s mandate. The instructions in this case could be clearer in this respect, but when read as a whole, we think they are adequate to convey to the jury that all of the evidence, including the evidence going to self-defense, must be considered in deciding whether there was a reasonable doubt about the sufficiency of the state's proof of the elements of the crime.

We are thus not moved by assertions that the elements of aggravated murder and self-defense overlap in the sense that evidence to prove the latter will often tend to negate the former. It may be that most encounters in which self-defense is claimed arise suddenly and involve no prior plan or specific purpose to take life. In those cases, evidence offered to support the defense may negate a purposeful killing by prior calculation and design, but Ohio does not shift to the defendant the burden of disproving any element of the state's case. When the prosecution has made out a *prima facie* case and survives a motion to acquit, the jury may nevertheless not convict if the evidence offered by the defendant raises any reasonable doubt about the existence of any fact necessary for the finding of guilt. Evidence creating a reasonable doubt could easily fall far short of proving self-defense by a preponderance of the evidence. Of course, if such doubt is not raised in the jury's mind and each juror is convinced that the defendant purposely and with prior calculation and design took life, the killing will still be excused if the elements of the defense are satisfactorily established. We note here, but need not rely on it, the observation of the Supreme

Court of Ohio that "Appellant did not dispute the existence of [the elements of aggravated murder], but rather sought to justify her actions on grounds she acted in self-defense." *

*   *   *

As we noted in *Patterson,* the common law rule was that affirmative defenses, including self-defense, were matters for the defendant to prove. This was the rule when the Fifth Amendment was adopted, and it was the American rule when the Fourteenth Amendment was ratified. Indeed, well into this century, a number of States followed the common law rule and required a defendant to shoulder the burden of proving that he acted in self-defense. We are aware that all but two of the States, Ohio and South Carolina, have abandoned the common law rule and require the prosecution to prove the absence of self-defense when it is properly raised by the defendant. But the question remains whether those States are in violation of the Constitution; and, as we observed in *Patterson,* that question is not answered by cataloging the practices of other States. We are no more convinced that the Ohio practice of requiring self-defense to be proved by the defendant is unconstitutional than we are that the Constitution requires the prosecution to prove the sanity of a defendant who pleads not guilty by reason of insanity. We have had the opportunity to depart from *Leland v. Oregon* but have refused to do so. *Rivera v. Delaware* (1976). These cases were important to the *Patterson* decision and they, along with *Patterson,* are authority for our decision today.

The judgment of the Ohio Supreme Court is accordingly

Affirmed.

JUSTICE POWELL, with whom JUSTICE BRENNAN and JUSTICE MARSHALL join, and with whom JUSTICE BLACKMUN joins with respect to Parts I and III, dissenting.

Today the Court holds that a defendant can be convicted of aggravated murder even though the jury may have a reasonable doubt whether the accused acted in self-defense, and thus, whether he is guilty of a crime. Because I think this decision is inconsistent with both precedent and fundamental fairness, I dissent.

I

*   *   *

In *Patterson,* the Court upheld a state statute that shifted the burden of proof for an affirmative defense to the accused. New York law required the prosecutor to prove all of the statutorily defined

---

* The dissent believes that the self-defense instruction might have led the jury to believe that the defendant had the burden of proving prior calculation and design. Indeed, its position is that *no* instruction could be clear enough not to mislead the jury. As is evident from the test, we disagree. We do not harbor the dissent's mistrust of the jury; and the instructions were sufficiently clear to convey to the jury that the state's burden of proving prior calculation did not shift and that self-defense evidence had to be considered in determining whether the state's burden had been discharged. We do not depart from *Patterson v. New York,* in this respect, or in any other.

elements of murder beyond a reasonable doubt, but permitted a defendant to reduce the charge to manslaughter by showing that he acted while suffering an "extreme emotional disturbance." The Court found that this burden-shifting did not violate due process, largely because the affirmative defense did "not serve to negative any facts of the crime which the State is to prove in order to convict of murder." The clear implication of this ruling is that when an affirmative defense *does* negate an element of the crime, the state may not shift the burden. In such a case, *In re Winship* (1970), requires the state to prove the nonexistence of the defense beyond a reasonable doubt.

The reason for treating a defense that negates an element of the crime differently from other affirmative defenses is plain. If the jury is told that the prosecution has the burden of proving all the elements of a crime, but then also is instructed that the defendant has the burden of *dis* proving one of those same elements, there is a danger that the jurors will resolve the inconsistency in a way that lessens the presumption of innocence. For example, the jury might reasonably believe that by raising the defense, the accused has assumed the ultimate burden of proving that particular element. Or, it might reconcile the instructions simply by balancing the evidence that supports the prosecutor's case against the evidence supporting the affirmative defense, and conclude that the state has satisfied its burden if the prosecution's version is more persuasive. In either case, the jury is given the unmistakable but erroneous impression that the defendant shares the risk of nonpersuasion as to a fact necessary for conviction.[1]

Given these principles, the Court's reliance on *Patterson* is puzzling. Under Ohio law, the element of "prior calculation and design" is satisfied only when the accused has engaged in a "definite process of reasoning *in advance* of the killing," *i.e.,* when he has given the plan at least some "studied consideration." In contrast, when a defendant such as Martin raises a claim of self-defense, the jury also is instructed that the accused must prove that she "had an honest belief that she was in *imminent* danger of death or great bodily harm." In many cases, a defendant who finds himself in immediate danger and reacts with deadly force will not have formed a prior intent to kill. . . . Under *Patterson,* this conclusion should suggest that Ohio is precluded from

---

1. Indeed, this type of instruction has an inherently illogical aspect. It makes no sense to say that the prosecution has the burden of proving an element beyond a reasonable doubt *and* that the defense has the burden of proving the contrary by a preponderance of the evidence. If the jury finds that the prosecutor has *not* met his burden, it of course will have no occasion to consider the affirmative defense. And if the jury finds that each element of the crime *has* been proved beyond a reasonable doubt, it necessarily has decided that the defendant has not disproved an element of the crime. In either situation the instructions on the affirmative defense are surplusage. Because a reasonable jury will attempt to ascribe some significance to the court's instructions, the likelihood that it will impermissibly shift the burden is increased.

Of course, whether the jury will in fact improperly shift the burden away from the state is uncertain. But it is "settled law . . . that when there exists a reasonable possibility that the jury relied on an unconstitutional understanding of the law in reaching a guilty verdict, that verdict must be set aside." *Francis v. Franklin* (1985).

shifting the burden as to self-defense. The Court nevertheless concludes that Martin was properly required to prove self-defense, simply because "Ohio does not shift to the defendant the burden of disproving any element of the state's case."

The Court gives no explanation for this apparent rejection of *Patterson.* The only justification advanced for the Court's decision is that the jury could have used the evidence of self-defense to find that the state failed to carry its burden of proof. Because the jurors were free to consider both Martin's and the state's evidence, the argument goes, the verdict of guilt necessarily means that they were convinced that the defendant acted with prior calculation and design, and were unpersuaded that she acted in self-defense. The Court thus seems to conclude that as long as the jury is told that the state has the burden of proving all elements of the crime, the overlap between the offense and defense is immaterial.

This reasoning is flawed in two respects. First, it simply ignores the problem that arises from inconsistent jury instructions in a criminal case. The Court's holding implicitly assumes that the jury in fact understands that the ultimate burden remains with the prosecutor at all times, despite a conflicting instruction that places the burden on the accused to disprove the same element. But as pointed out above, the *Patterson* distinction between defenses that negate an element of the crime and those that do not is based on the legitimate concern that the jury *will* mistakenly lower the state's burden. In short, the Court's rationale fails to explain why the overlap in this case does not create the risk that *Patterson* suggested was unacceptable.

Second, the Court significantly, and without explanation, extends the deference granted to state legislatures in this area. Today's decision could be read to say that virtually all state attempts to shift the burden of proof for affirmative defenses will be upheld, regardless of the relationship between the elements of the defense and the elements of the crime. As I understand it, *Patterson* allowed burden-shifting because evidence of an extreme emotional disturbance did not negate the *mens rea* of the underlying offense. After today's decision, however, even if proof of the defense *does* negate an element of the offense, burden-shifting still may be permitted because the jury can consider the defendant's evidence when reaching its verdict.

I agree, of course, that States must have substantial leeway in defining their criminal laws and administering their criminal justice systems. But none of our precedents suggests that courts must give complete deference to a State's judgment about whether a shift in the burden of proof is consistent with the presumption of innocence. In the past we have emphasized that in some circumstances it may be necessary to look beyond the text of the State's burden-shifting laws to satisfy ourselves that the requirements of *Winship* have been satisfied. In *Mullaney v. Wilbur* (1975) we explicitly noted the danger of granting the State unchecked discretion to shift the burden as to any element of proof in a criminal case. The Court today fails to discuss or even cite *Mullaney,* despite our unanimous agreement in that case that this danger would justify judicial intervention in some cases. Even *Patterson,* from which I dissented, recognized that "there are obviously constitutional limits beyond which the States may not go [in labeling elements of a crime as an affirmative defense]." Today, however, the Court simply asserts that Ohio law properly allocates the burdens, without giving any indication of where those limits lie.

* * *

II

Although I believe that this case is wrongly decided even under the principles set forth in *Patterson,* my differences with the Court's approach are more fundamental. I continue to believe that the better method for deciding when a state may shift the burden of proof is outlined in the Court's opinion in *Mullaney* and in my dissenting opinion in *Patterson.* In *Mullaney,* we emphasized that the state's obligation to prove certain facts beyond a reasonable doubt was not necessarily restricted to legislative distinctions between offenses and affirmative defenses. The boundaries of the state's authority in this respect were elaborated in the *Patterson* dissent, where I proposed a two-part inquiry:

> "The Due Process Clause requires that the prosecutor bear the burden of persuasion beyond a reasonable doubt only if the factor at issue makes a substantial difference in punishment and stigma. The requirement of course applies *a fortiori* if the factor makes the difference between guilt and innocence. . . . It also must be shown that in the Anglo–American legal tradition the factor in question historically has held that level of importance. If either branch of the test is not met, then the legislature retains its traditional authority over matters of proof." 432 U.S., at 226–227, 97 S.Ct., at 2335 (footnotes omitted).

* * *

There are at least two benefits to this approach. First, it ensures that the critical facts necessary to sustain a conviction will be proved by the state. Because the Court would be willing to look beyond the text of a state statute, legislatures would have no incentive to redefine essential elements of an offense to make them part of an affirmative defense, thereby shifting the burden of proof in a manner inconsistent with *Winship* and *Mullaney.* Second, it would leave the states free in all other respects to recognize new factors that may mitigate the degree of criminality or punishment, without requiring that they also bear the burden of disproving these defenses. . . .

Under this analysis, it plainly is impermissible to require the accused to prove self-defense. If petitioner could have carried her burden, the result would have been decisively different as to both guilt and punishment. There also is no dispute that self-defense historically is one of the primary justifications for otherwise unlawful conduct. Thus, while I acknowledge that the two-part test may be difficult to apply at times, it is hard to imagine a more clear-cut application than the one presented here.

III

In its willingness to defer to the State's legislative definitions of crimes and defenses, the Court apparently has failed to recognize the practical effect of its decision. Martin alleged that she was innocent because she acted in self-defense, a complete justification under Ohio law. Because she had the burden of proof on this issue, the jury could have believed that it was just as likely as not that Martin's conduct was justified, and yet still have voted to convict. In other words, even though the jury may have had a substantial doubt whether Martin committed a crime, she was found guilty under Ohio law. I do not agree that the Court's authority to review state legislative choices is so limited that it justifies increasing the risk of convicting a person who may not be blameworthy. . . . .

SANDSTROM v. MONTANA

Supreme Court of the United States, 1979.
442 U.S. 510, 99 S.Ct. 2450.

MR. JUSTICE BRENNAN delivered the opinion of the Court.

The question presented is whether, in a case in which intent is an element of the crime charged, the jury instruction, "the law presumes that a person intends the ordinary consequences of his voluntary acts," violates the Fourteenth Amendment's requirement that the State prove every element of a criminal offense beyond a reasonable doubt.

I

On November 22, 1976, 18–year–old David Sandstrom confessed to the slaying of Annie Jessen. Based upon the confession and corroborating evidence, petitioner was charged on December 2 with "deliberate homicide," Mont.Code Ann. § 45–5–102 (1978), in that he "purposely or knowingly caused the death of Annie Jessen." [1] At trial, Sandstrom's attorney informed the jury that, although his client admitted killing Jessen, he did not do so "purposely or knowingly," and was therefore not guilty of "deliberate homicide" but of a lesser crime. The basic

---

1. The statute provides:

"45–5–101. Criminal homicide. (1) A person commits the offense of criminal homicide if he purposely, knowingly, or negligently causes the death of another human being.

"(2) Criminal homicide is deliberate homicide, mitigated deliberate homicide, or negligent homicide.

"45–5–102. Deliberate homicide. (1) Except as provided in 45–5–103(1), criminal homicide constitutes deliberate homicide if:

"(a) it is committed purposely or knowingly. . . ."

support for this contention was the testimony of two court-appointed mental health experts, each of whom described for the jury petitioner's mental state at the time of the incident. Sandstrom's attorney argued that this testimony demonstrated that petitioner, due to a personality disorder aggravated by alcohol consumption, did not kill Annie Jessen "purposely or knowingly."

The prosecution requested the trial judge to instruct the jury that "[t]he law presumes that a person intends the ordinary consequences of his voluntary acts." Petitioner's counsel objected, arguing that "the instruction has the effect of shifting the burden of proof on the issue of" purpose or knowledge to the defense, and that "that is impermissible under the Federal Constitution, due process of law." He offered to provide a number of federal decisions in support of the objection, including this Court's holding in Mullaney v. Wilbur (1975), but was told by the judge: "You can give those to the Supreme Court. The objection is overruled." The instruction was delivered, the jury found petitioner guilty of deliberate homicide, *id.,* at 38, and petitioner was sentenced to 100 years in prison.

Sandstrom appealed to the Supreme Court of Montana, again contending that the instruction shifted to the defendant the burden of disproving an element of the crime charged in violation of Mullaney v. Wilbur, In re Winship, and Patterson v. New York. The Montana court conceded that these cases did prohibit shifting the burden of proof to the defendant by means of a presumption, but held that the cases "do not prohibit allocation of *some* burden of proof to a defendant under certain circumstances." Since in the court's view, "[d]efendant's sole burden under instruction No. 5 was to produce *some* evidence that he did not intend the ordinary consequences of his voluntary acts, not to disprove that he acted 'purposely' or 'knowingly,' . . . the instruction does not violate due process standards as defined by the United States or Montana Constitution. . . ." (emphasis added.)

Both federal and state courts have held, under a variety of rationales, that the giving of an instruction similar to that challenged here is fatal to the validity of a criminal conviction. We granted certiorari, to decide the important question of the instruction's constitutionality. We reverse.

II

The threshold inquiry in ascertaining the constitutional analysis applicable to this kind of jury instruction is to determine the nature of the presumption it describes. That determination requires careful attention to the words actually spoken to the jury, for whether a defendant has been accorded his constitutional rights depends upon the way in which a reasonable juror could have interpreted the instruction.

Respondent argues, first, that the instruction merely described a permissive inference—that is, it allowed but did not require the jury to draw conclusions about defendant's intent from his actions—and that such inferences are constitutional. These arguments need not detain us long, for even respondent admits that "it's possible" that the jury believed they were required to apply the presumption. Sandstrom's jurors were told that "[t]he law presumes that a person intends the ordinary consequences of his voluntary acts." They were not told that they had a choice, or that they might infer that conclusion; they were told only that the law presumed it. It is clear that a reasonable juror could easily have viewed such an instruction as mandatory. . . .

In the alternative, respondent urges that, even if viewed as a mandatory presumption rather than as a permissive inference, the presumption did not conclusively establish intent but rather could be rebutted. On this view, the instruction required the jury, if satisfied as to the facts which trigger the presumption, to find intent *unless* the defendant offered evidence to the contrary. Moreover, according to the State, all the defendant had to do to rebut the presumption was produce "some" contrary evidence; he did not have to "prove" that he lacked the required mental state. Thus, "[a]t most, it placed a *burden of production* on the petitioner," but "did not shift to petitioner the *burden of persuasion* with respect to any element of the offense. . . ." (emphasis added). Again, respondent contends that presumptions with this limited effect pass constitutional muster.

We need not review respondent's constitutional argument on this point either, however, for we reject this characterization of the presumption as well. Respondent concedes there is a "risk" that the jury, once having found petitioner's act voluntary, would interpret the instruction as automatically directing a finding of intent. Moreover, the State also concedes that numerous courts "have differed as to the effect of the presumption when given as a jury instruction without further explanation as to its use by the jury," and that some have found it to shift more than the burden of production, and even to have conclusive effect. Nonetheless, the State contends that the only authoritative reading of the effect of the presumption resides in the Supreme Court of Montana. And the State argues that by holding that "[d]efendant's sole burden under instruction No. 5 was to produce *some* evidence that he did not intend the ordinary consequences of his voluntary acts, not to disprove that he acted 'purposely' or 'knowingly,' " (emphasis added), the Montana Supreme Court decisively established that the presumption at most affected only the burden of going forward with evidence of intent—that is, the burden of production.

The Supreme Court of Montana is, of course, the final authority on the legal weight to be given a presumption under Montana law, but it is not the final authority on the interpretation which a jury could have given the instruction. If Montana intended its presumption to have only the effect described by its Supreme Court, then we are convinced that a reasonable juror could well have been misled by the instruction given, and could have believed that the presumption was not limited to requiring the defendant to satisfy only a burden of production. Petitioner's jury was told that "*[t]he law presumes* that a person intends the ordinary consequences of his voluntary acts." They were not told that the presumption could be rebutted, as the Montana Supreme Court held, by the defendant's simple presentation of "some" evidence; nor even that it could be rebutted at all. Given the common definition of "presume" as "to suppose to be true without proof," Webster's New Collegiate Dictionary 911 (1974), and given the lack of qualifying instructions as to the legal effect of the presumption, we cannot discount the possibility that the jury may have interpreted the instruction in either of two more stringent ways.

First, a reasonable jury could well have interpreted the presumption as "conclusive," that is, not technically as a presumption at all, but rather as an irrebuttable direction by the court to find intent once convinced of the facts triggering the presumption. Alternatively, the jury may have interpreted the instruction as a direction to find intent upon proof of the defendant's voluntary actions (and their "ordinary" consequences), unless *the defendant* proved the contrary by some quantum of proof which may well have been considerably greater than "some" evidence—thus effectively shifting the burden of persuasion on the element of intent. Numerous federal and state courts have warned that instructions of the type given here can be interpreted in just these ways. . . . And although the Montana Supreme Court held to the contrary in this case, Montana's own Rules of Evidence expressly state that the presumption at issue here may be overcome only "by a preponderance of evidence contrary to the presumption." Montana Rule of Evidence 301(b)(2). Such a requirement shifts not only the burden of production, but also the ultimate burden of persuasion on the issue of intent. . . .

III

In *Winship,* this Court stated:

> "Lest there remain any doubt about the constitutional stature of the reasonable-doubt standard, we explicitly hold that the Due Process Clause protects the accused against conviction except upon proof beyond a reasonable doubt *of every fact* necessary to constitute the crime with which he is charged." (emphasis added).

The petitioner here was charged with and convicted of deliberate homicide, committed purposely or knowingly, under Mont.Code Ann. § 45–5–102(a) (1978). It is clear that under Montana law, whether the crime was committed purposely or knowingly is a fact necessary to constitute the crime of deliberate homicide. Indeed, it was the lone element of the offense at issue in Sandstrom's trial, as he confessed to causing the death of the victim, told the jury that knowledge and purpose were the only questions he was controverting, and introduced evidence solely on those points. Moreover, it is conceded that proof of defendant's "intent" would be sufficient to establish this element. Thus, the question before this Court is whether the challenged jury instruction had the effect of relieving the State of the burden of proof enunciated in *Winship* on the critical question of petitioner's state of mind. We conclude that under either of the two possible interpretations of the instruction set out above, precisely that effect would result, and that the instruction therefore represents constitutional error.

We consider first the validity of a conclusive presumption. This Court has considered such a presumption on at least two prior occasions. In Morissette v. United States (1952), the defendant was charged with willful and knowing theft of Government property. Although his attorney argued that for his client to be found guilty, "the taking must have been with felonious intent," the trial judge ruled that "[t]hat is presumed by his own act." After first concluding that intent was in fact an element of the crime charged, and after declaring that "[w]here intent of the accused is an ingredient of the crime charged, its existence is . . . a jury issue," *Morissette* held:

> "*It follows that the trial court may not withdraw or prejudge the issue by instruction that the law raises a presumption of intent from an act.* It often is tempting to cast in terms of a 'presumption' a conclusion which a court thinks probable from given facts. . . . [But] [w]e think presumptive intent has no place in this case. *A conclusive presumption which testimony could not overthrow would effectively eliminate intent as an ingredient of the offense.* A presumption which would permit but not require the jury to assume intent from an isolated fact would prejudge a conclusion which the jury should reach of its own volition. A presumption which would permit the jury to make an assumption which all the evidence considered together does not logically establish would give to a proven fact an artificial and fictional effect. In either case, *this presumption would conflict with the overriding presumption of innocence with which the law endows the accused and which extends to every element of the crime.*" (Emphasis added; footnote omitted.)

Just last Term, in United States v. United States Gypsum Co., 438 U.S. 422 (1978), we reaffirmed the holding of *Morissette*. In that case defendants, who were charged with criminal violations of the Sherman Act, challenged the following jury instruction:

> "The law presumes that a person intends the necessary and natural consequences of his acts. Therefore, if the effect of the exchanges of pricing information was to raise, fix, maintain, and stabilize prices, then the parties to them are presumed, as a matter of law, to have intended that result."

After again determining that the offense included the element of intent, we held:

> "[A] defendant's state of mind or *intent is an element of a criminal antitrust offense which . . . cannot be taken from the*

trier of fact through reliance on a legal presumption of wrongful intent from proof of an effect on prices. . . .

"Although an effect on prices may well support an inference that the defendant had knowledge of the probability of such a consequence at the time he acted, the jury must remain free to consider additional evidence before accepting or rejecting the inference. . . . [U]ltimately the decision on the issue of intent must be left to the trier of fact alone. The instruction given invaded this factfinding function." (emphasis added.)

As in *Morissette* and *United States Gypsum Co.,* a conclusive presumption in this case would "conflict with the overriding presumption of innocence with which the law endows the accused and which extends to every element of the crime," and would "invade [the] factfinding function" which in a criminal case the law assigns solely to the jury. The instruction announced to David Sandstrom's jury may well have had exactly these consequences. Upon finding proof of one element of the crime (causing death), and of facts insufficient to establish the second (the voluntariness and "ordinary consequences" of defendant's action), Sandstrom's jurors could reasonably have concluded that they were directed to find against defendant on the element of intent. The State was thus not forced to prove "beyond a reasonable doubt . . . every fact necessary to constitute the crime . . . charged," and defendant was deprived of his constitutional rights as explicated in *Winship.*

A presumption which, although not conclusive, had the effect of shifting the burden of persuasion to the defendant, would have suffered from similar infirmities. If Sandstrom's jury interpreted the presumption in that manner, it could have concluded that upon proof by the State of the slaying, and of additional facts not themselves establishing the element of intent, the burden was shifted to the defendant to prove that he lacked the requisite mental state. Such a presumption was found constitutionally deficient in Mullaney v. Wilbur, 421 U.S. 684 (1975). In *Mullaney,* the charge was murder, which under Maine law required proof not only of intent but of malice. The trial court charged the jury that " 'malice aforethought is an essential and indispensable element of the crime of murder.' " However, it also instructed that if the prosecution established that the homicide was both intentional and unlawful, malice aforethought was to be implied unless the defendant proved by a fair preponderance of the evidence that he acted in the heat of passion on sudden provocation. Ibid. As we recounted just two Terms ago in Patterson v. New York, "[t]his Court . . . unanimously agreed with the Court of Appeals that Wilbur's due process rights had been invaded by the presumption casting upon him the burden of proving by a preponderance of the evidence that he had acted in the heat of passion upon sudden provocation." And *Patterson* reaffirmed that "a State must prove every ingredient of an offense beyond a reasonable doubt, and . . . may not shift the burden of proof to the defendant" by means of such a presumption.

Because David Sandstrom's jury may have interpreted the judge's instruction as constituting either a burden-shifting presumption like that in *Mullaney,* or a conclusive presumption like those in *Morissette* and *United States Gypsum Co.,* and because either interpretation would have deprived defendant of his right to the due process of law, we hold the instruction given in this case unconstitutional.

* * *

[The concurring opinion of MR. JUSTICE REHNQUIST, with whom THE CHIEF JUSTICE joins, is omitted.]

NOTES

1. In *Sandstrom,* the Court left open the question of whether a jury instruction that "the law presumes that a person intends the ordinary consequences of his voluntary acts," could ever be harmless error. Holding that it could not be in the case of Connecticut v. Johnson, 460 U.S. 73, 103 S.Ct. 969 (1983), the Court's plurality opinion recognized some exceptions:

"There may be rare situations in which the reviewing court can be confident that a *Sandstrom* error did not play any role in the jury's verdict. For example, if the erroneous instruction was given in connection with an offense for which the defendant was acquitted and if the instruction had no bearing on the offense for which he was convicted, it would be appropriate to find the error harmless. In addition, a *Sandstrom* error may be harmless if the defendant conceded the issue of intent. . . ."

Such a concession might be by the defendant's presentation of an alibi defense, or defenses of insanity or self-defense. But the Court left it to the lower courts to determine whether, by raising a particular defense or by his other actions, a defendant has himself taken the issue of intent away from the jury.

2. In Francis v. Franklin, 471 U.S. 307, 105 S.Ct. 1965, 85 L.Ed.2d 344 (1985), the defendant in a murder prosecution had shot and killed a person in the neighborhood of a dentist's office where the defendant had obtained treatment. The killing occurred at the moment the victim, a resident in a nearby home, slammed the front door shut as defendant asked for the key to the victim's car. Defendant's pistol fired and a bullet pierced the door hitting the victim in the chest. Defendant argued that he lacked the intent to commit malice-murder and claimed that the killing was an accident. The trial court instructed the jury on the issue of intent as follows: "The acts of a person of sound mind and discretion are presumed to be the product of a person's will, but the presumption may be rebutted. A person of sound mind and discretion is presumed to intend the natural and probable consequences of his acts, but the presumption may be rebutted. A person will not be presumed to act with criminal intention but the trier of facts . . . may find criminal intention upon a consideration of the words, conduct, demeanor, motive and all of the circumstances connected with the act for which the accused is prosecuted." The court also instructed the jury in the presumption of innocence and the state's burden of proof. After conviction and sentencing to death, the state courts affirmed, but on subsequent federal habeas corpus, a five-to-four majority of the United States Supreme Court affirmed the Court of Appeals' reversal of the conviction.

The majority held that the instruction on intent, when read in the context of a jury charge as a whole, violated the 14th Amendment's requirement that the state prove every element of a criminal offense beyond a reasonable doubt. It said that a jury instruction creating a mandatory presumption whereby the jury must infer the presumed fact if the prosecution proves certain predicate facts violates the Due Process clause if it relieves the State of the burden of persuasion on an element of an offense, and that if a specific portion of a jury charge, considered in isolation, could reasonably have been understood as creating such a presumption, the potentially offending words must be considered in the context of the charge as a whole. Looking at the instructions given in that context, the Court found a reasonable juror could have understood that the first two sentences of the presumption created a mandatory presumption that shifted to the defendant the burden of persuasion on the element of intent once the state had proved the predicate facts. Telling the jury the presumption may be rebutted does not cure the infirmity in the charge, the Court added. The error was also held not to be harmless in the context of *Sandstrom*.

3. See also, Rose v. Clark, 478 U.S. 570, 106 S.Ct. 3101, 92 L.Ed.2d 460 (1986), where the Court decided that the harmless error rule could be applied to a jury instruction that violates the principles of *Sandstrom*. Justice Powell held that the harmless error standard, under which a reviewing court should not set aside an otherwise valid conviction if the court may confidently say on the whole record that the constitutional error in question was harmless beyond a reasonable doubt, should be applied to an erroneous "malice" instruction that all homicides are presumed to be malicious in the absence of evidence which would rebut the implied presumption.

4. The issue of the validity of presumptions prevails, of course, in all types of criminal cases. A good illustration is Leary v. United States, 395 U.S. 6, 89 S.Ct. 1532 (1969) (appeal after remand 431 F.2d 85 (5th Cir.1970)), which involved a prosecution for the violation of federal statutes governing traffic in marijuana. The defendant, Dr. Timothy Leary, and several other persons had been to Mexico. As they reentered the United States, Leary's car and the occupants were searched and small amounts of marijuana were found. The federal prosecution relied upon a statutory provision declaring that possession of marijuana was sufficient evidence that it had been illegally transported into the United States. Leary's conviction was reversed upon a Supreme Court finding that the presumption was invalid because of the fact that there were many other ways he might have acquired the marijuana other than by illegally transporting it into the country. In contrast, however, is the case of Turner v. United States, 396 U.S. 398, 90 S.Ct. 642 (1970), in which the Supreme Court held the presumption to be valid with respect to the possession of heroin, because of its unavailability except by importation. Nevertheless, in *Turner* the Court held that the presumption was not applicable to cocaine, because it is produced in the United States in sizeable quantity for medicinal purposes and therefore may be obtainable other than by importation.

Consider the following as a test of the validity of a presumption: "a rational connection between the fact proved and the ultimate fact presumed," a test which was enunciated by the Supreme Court in Tot v. United States, 319 U.S. 463, 63 S.Ct. 1241 (1943). In the dissenting opinion in People v. Hildebrandt, 308 N.Y. 397, 126 N.E.2d 377 (1955), the following language was used with respect to the presence or absence of that rational connection in a specific case: "The basic test is whether common experience supports the *probability, not the certainty* that if the first fact is true, the second is also true. . . ."

STATE v. LEVERETT

Supreme Court of Montana, 1990.
—— Mont. ——, 799 P.2d 119.

TURNAGE, CHIEF JUSTICE.

* * *

Late in the afternoon of September 24, 1988, appellant Leverett was involved in an automobile accident near the curve where Sixth Avenue North leads into Division Street in downtown Billings, Montana. After rounding the curve, Leverett's car crossed from the outside lane of traffic through the inside lane and two oncoming lanes and crashed into a parked car. Somewhere near the centerline, his vehicle struck a pedestrian who died the next morning of injuries. Following the accident, the appellant underwent field sobriety tests and a breath test. The breath test registered his blood alcohol content at .121. The State subsequently charged Leverett with negligent homicide, and a jury found him guilty.

Leverett now appeals his conviction and raises a number of issues related to the evidence and jury instructions concerning intoxication. We decline to discuss every issue raised by the appellant because one is sufficient to reverse his conviction and remand the case for a new trial. The District Court's jury instruction that a blood alcohol level greater than .10 raised a mandatory rebuttable presumption that the appellant was under the influence of alcohol violated his right to due process under the Fourteenth Amendment of the United States Constitution.

Instruction No. 11 tracked verbatim § 61–8–401, MCA, providing in pertinent part:

> Upon the trial of any civil or criminal action or proceeding arising out of acts alleged to have been committed by any person driving or in actual physical control of a vehicle while under the influence of alcohol, the concentration of alcohol in the person's blood at the time alleged, as shown by chemical analysis of the person's blood, urine, breath, or other bodily substance, shall give rise to the following presumptions:
>
> * * *
>
> (c) If there was at that time an alcohol concentration of 0.10 or more, it shall be presumed that the person was under the influence of alcohol. Such presumption is rebuttable.
>
> The provisions of subsections A–C do not limit the introduction of any other competent evidence bearing upon the issue of whether the person was under the influence of alcohol.

Jury Instruction No. 12 quoted § 30–1–201(31), MCA, stating:

> "Presumption" or "presumed" means that the trier of fact must find the existence of the fact presumed unless and until evidence is introduced which would support a finding of its nonexistence.

The current analysis of whether a jury instruction containing an evidentiary presumption in a criminal case violated the defendant's due process rights follows a procedure established by the United States Supreme Court in *Sandstrom v. Montana* (1979), and *Ulster County Court v. Allen* (1979). The United States Supreme Court has most recently reaffirmed that procedure in Francis v. Franklin (1985), 471 U.S. 307, 105 S.Ct. 1965, 85 L.Ed.2d 344.

In analyzing evidentiary presumptions in a criminal case, the reviewing court must focus on the particular language used to charge the jury and determine whether a reasonable juror could have interpreted the challenged instruction as an unconstitutional presumption.

> Analysis must focus initially on the specific language challenged, but the inquiry does not end there. If a specific portion of the jury charge, considered in isolation, could reasonably have been understood as creating [an unconstitutional presumption], the potentially offending words must be considered in the context of the charge as a whole. Other instructions might explain the particular infirm language to the extent that a reasonable juror could not have considered the charge to have created an unconstitutional presumption.

Francis, 471 U.S. at 315, 105 S.Ct. at 1971, 85 L.Ed.2d at 354 (citation omitted).

We begin our analysis with a preliminary matter which the United States Supreme Court has not explicitly addressed: whether the challenged presumption must go to an essential element of the crime charged. The United States Supreme Court has consistently reiterated the premise that its holdings on unconstitutional presumptions apply only to presumptions of facts which must be proved before the defendant can be found guilty. . . . This Court has specifically held that presumptions which create affirmative defenses do not go to an element of the crime charged and, therefore, do not violate due process.

In the present case, in view of the wording of the information and Instruction No. 5, the presumption of intoxication does go to an element of the crime charged. "A person commits the offense of negligent homicide if he negligently causes the death of another human being." Section 45–5–104, MCA. A person is criminally negligent under the negligent homicide statute when he

> consciously disregards a risk that the [death] will occur . . . or when he disregards a risk of which he should be aware that the [death] will occur. . . . The risk must be of such a nature and degree that to disregard it involves a gross deviation from the standard of conduct that a reasonable person would observe in the actor's situation. "Gross deviation" means a deviation that is considerably greater than lack of ordinary care.

Section 45–2–101(37), MCA. In two previous negligent homicide cases, this Court held that driving under the influence of alcohol may be tantamount to criminal negligence. More important to our present analysis is the language of the instructions to the jury. Instruction No. 5 followed the language of the information filed against the appellant:

> You are instructed that the specific charge in this case reads as follows: . . .
>
> *The facts constituting the offense are:*
>
> That the defendant CLIFFORD R. LEVERETT negligently caused the death of Ronald Lee Scheetz as defined at MCA Section 45–2–101(37) (1987) by driving his motor vehicle . . . into a pedestrian, Ronald Scheetz at an unsafe rate of speed *and with a blood alcohol concentration in excess of .10.* . . .

(Emphasis added.) From this instruction, a reasonable juror may have concluded that a finding of intoxication was necessary for conviction.

Under the United States Supreme Court's analysis, we must undertake a step-by-step classification of the presumption used in this case to determine whether it violated the appellant's right to due process. The first step in this classification is to determine whether a reasonable juror would understand it to be a mandatory or permissive presumption.

. . . A permissive presumption does not violate due process so long as a rational connection exists between the predicate and presumed fact. A mandatory presumption, on the other hand, may or may not be constitutional depending on its type and function.

In determining whether a reasonable juror would have viewed Instruction Nos. 11 and 12 as mandatory or permissive, we note that most jurisdictions considering similar jury charges have found that they create mandatory presumptions unless the language of the inference is unambiguously permissive. See e.g. State v. McDonald (S.D. 1988), 421 N.W.2d 492, 496; Barnes v. People (Colo.1987), 735 P.2d 869, 874; Commonwealth v. Moreira (1982), 385 Mass. 792, 434 N.E.2d 196, 200; State v. Vick (1981), 104 Wis.2d 678, 312 N.W.2d 489, 497; State v. Dacey (1980), 138 Vt. 491, 418 A.2d 856, 859; State v. Berch (Iowa 1974), 222 N.W.2d 741, 746; but see Commonwealth v. DiFrancesco (1974), 458 Pa. 188, 329 A.2d 204, 211; Hillery v. State (1983), 165 Ga. App. 127, 299 S.E.2d 421, 422. Here, the challenged instructions clearly are not permissive. Instruction No. 11 states that "it *shall be* presumed." Instruction No. 12 states that "the trier of fact *must find.*" By their plain language, the instructions create a mandatory presumption of intoxication.

The next classification step is to determine whether the mandatory presumption is conclusive or rebuttable.

. . . A conclusive presumption eliminates the defendant's right to challenge the presumed fact and violates due process if it goes to an element of the crime charged.

The present presumption of intoxication is plainly not conclusive. Instruction No. 11 specifically provides that the presumption is rebuttable and does not limit the defendant's ability to introduce contrary evidence. A reasonable juror could not have found anything but a mandatory rebuttable presumption of intoxication.

As the United States Supreme Court made clear in *Francis,* a mandatory rebuttable presumption is generally just as unconstitutional as a conclusive presumption because it commonly shifts the burden of persuasion to the defendant.

* * *

The final step in classifying the presumption of intoxication is one not yet reached by any United States Supreme Court decision. Mandatory rebuttable presumptions may be divided into those which shift the burden of persuasion to the defendant and those which shift the burden of production to the defendant. The former type is represented by affirmative defenses which require the defendant to meet some specified degree of persuasion to overcome the presumption. Affirmative defenses do not violate due process so long as they do not supplant the traditional elements of the crime charged.

The burden-of-production shifting presumptions, however, are much more problematic. They generally go to an element of the crime charged and allow the defendant to overcome the presumption by introducing any contrary evidence. The United States Supreme Court has not yet been faced with the question of whether such presumptions violate due process, but the Court has indicated in dicta that they may be constitutional in some instances:

> To the extent that a presumption imposes an extremely low burden of production—e.g., being satisfied by "any" evidence— it may well be that its impact is no greater than that of a permissive inference, and it may be proper to analyze it as such.

Ulster County, 442 U.S. at 157, n. 16, 99 S.Ct. at 2225, n. 16, 60 L.Ed.2d at 792, n. 16. It would appear, however, that the United States Supreme Court's supposition would not apply to the present case because the presumption of intoxication was presented to the jury.

Were we not looking through the eyes of a reasonable juror, we might understand Instruction No. 12 to make the presumption of intoxication a burden-of-production shifting presumption. Instruction No. 12 states:

> "Presumption" or "presumed" means that the trier of fact must find the existence of the fact presumed unless and until evidence is introduced which would support a finding of its nonexistence.

The "unless or until" language indicates that the presumption might be overcome as soon as the defendant introduced any contrary evidence.

If this is a burden-of-production presumption, we must ask why it was given as a jury instruction. Such presumptions may serve several purposes, none of which appear to be constitutional when the presumption is presented to the jury. A burden-of-production presumption may establish the State's prima facie case against the defendant's motion for a directed verdict or it may streamline the prosecution by eliminating collateral issues, such as affirmative defenses, until raised by the defendant. See 1 Weinstein's Evidence, ¶ 300[02] (1989). As a procedural device, the presumption presents a question of law for the court. A question of law has no place in the jury charge. In the present case, the appellant presented considerable evidence that he was not intoxicated at the time of the accident. As soon as he presented his first witness on the issue, the presumption of intoxication had served its purpose as a procedural device and should have been eliminated for the case.

Like any other presumption, a burden-of-production presumption may also represent scientific, statistical, or common-knowledge evidence linking the predicate and presumed facts. See 1 Weinstein's Evidence, ¶ 300[02] (1989). Montana's presumption of intoxication is apparently based on evidence demonstrating that a person with a blood-alcohol level of greater than .10 cannot safely operate a motor vehicle. However, even if the presumption's only function is to point out that well recognized relationship to the jury, it still should not be presented to the jury in a manner which places a burden of production on the defendant. If the defendant came forward with no contrary evidence, the presumption would act as a directed verdict for the State on the issue of intoxication. That would be contrary to the due process axiom that the criminal defendant is entitled to sit silent and go free if the prosecution fails to prove every element of the crime beyond a reasonable doubt. If, on the other hand, the defendant does not present contrary evidence, as he did in this case, the presumption is overcome. Presenting the presumption to the jury then serves no purpose except to imply that the defendant has some burden of proof on an element of the crime. The danger of that implication was particularly great in this case because Instruction No. 12 was not unmistakably clear that the appellant could overcome the presumption by producing any evidence that he was not intoxicated.

A reasonable juror could easily have interpreted Instruction No. 12 as shifting the burden of persuasion to the appellant and not as merely shifting the burden of production. The instruction required the jury to find intoxication "unless and until evidence is introduced which would support a finding of its nonexistence." It did not state what quantum of evidence was necessary to support a finding of its nonexistence. A reasonable juror may have believed that the appellant not only had to introduce contrary evidence, but that he had an affirmative duty to convince the jury that he was not intoxicated. As noted above, under *Francis,* such a mandatory rebuttable presumption which shifts the burden of persuasion to the defendant violates due process.

An unconstitutional mandatory presumption charged to the jury cannot be cured by other instructions giving a correct statement of the law. The reviewing court cannot determine whether the jury improperly relied upon the unconstitutional instructions or properly relied on the correct instructions but found the defendant guilty anyway. It is, therefore, no answer to say that Instruction Nos. 3 and 8 informed the jury that the defendant was cloaked in a presumption of innocence throughout the proceeding and that the State could overcome that presumption only by proving every element of negligent homicide beyond a reasonable doubt.

A resort to harmless error analysis also fails to save the unconstitutional instructions. Although at one time the United States Supreme Court refused to apply harmless error analysis to unconstitutional presumptions, *Sandstrom,* 442 U.S. at 526–27, 99 S.Ct. at 2460–61, 61 L.Ed.2d at 52–53, in *Rose v. Clark* the Court adopted the same harmless error test applied to other types of constitutional errors.

> [I]f the defendant had counsel and was tried by an impartial adjudicator, there is a strong presumption that any other errors that may have occurred are subject to harmless error analysis. . . . Where a reviewing court can find that the record developed at trial establishes guilt beyond a reasonable doubt, . . . the judgment should be affirmed.

Rose (1986), 478 U.S. 570, 579, 106 S.Ct. 3101, 3106, 92 L.Ed.2d 460, 471. A finding of guilt beyond a reasonable doubt does not require that defendant conceded the presumed fact. The question is to be determined from the entire record. *Rose,* 478 U.S. at 583, 106 S.Ct. at 3109, 92 L.Ed.2d at 474.

Here the record indicates that intoxication was a hotly debated trial issue. Several witnesses testified that the appellant had little to drink and did not appear to be intoxicated immediately before or after the accident. Two police officers, however, testified that the appellant later failed field sobriety tests. Both parties presented expert witnesses who testified for and against the accuracy of the breath test which registered .121. The evidence also conflicted on the appellant's driving immediately prior to the accident and on how the accident occurred. The recorded evidence is not so clear that we can now step into the shoes of the jury and find the appellant guilty beyond a reasonable doubt. Compare People v. Hickox (Colo.App.1987), 751 P.2d 645, 647– 48 (presumption of intoxication held unconstitutional but harmless because the record contained overwhelming evidence of intoxication).

Our holding that the jury instructions on the presumption of intoxication were unconstitutional does not reach the statute itself. By its plain language, § 61–8–401, MCA, creates a mandatory rebuttable presumption of intoxication. When the 1983 Legislature amended the statute to make the presumption rebuttable, it considered the implications of *Sandstrom* and apparently decided that the statute was constitutional because the presumption was rebuttable. Consideration of H.B. 540 Before the Senate Judiciary Comm., 48th Leg., (February 10, 1983) at 3–4, and Exhibit A at 5–6 (Testimony of Asst. Att'y. Gen. Steve Johnson). In *Francis,* the United States Supreme Court nullified that theory by holding that even mandatory rebuttable presumptions are unconstitutional. Like every other state in the union, Montana adopted the presumption of intoxication to fulfill federal highway funding requirements. See 23 U.S.C. § 408(e)(1)(C); 23 C.F.R. § 1204.4, Highway Safety Program Guideline No. 8, IB. A number of states have saved their unconstitutional statutory versions of the presumption by reading indisputably mandatory language as permissive; in effect, the courts have held that "shall" means "may." See e.g. Barnes v. People (Colo.1987), 735 P.2d 869, 873; State v. Dacey (1980), 138 Vt. 491, 418 A.2d 856, 859.

We do not find it necessary to go to such lengths to avoid striking down the statute. The introductory language of § 61–8–401, MCA, provides that it applies to "any civil or criminal action or proceeding. . . ." In some of the many contexts in which the presumption of intoxication might come into play, it may be constitutional; in others, it may not. That determination will depend on the purpose of the presumption, the type of proceeding, and the particular language used to convey the presumption to the jury. Under our holding today, the presumption of intoxication violates the criminal defendant's right to due process only if the presumption goes to an element of the crime charged and a reasonable juror could read the presumption as mandatory.

The solution to the due process problems of using presumptions in jury charges is not, as was attempted in this case, to make them burden-of-production shifting presumptions. The solution is to make the presumptions unambiguously permissive.

> Because [a] permissive presumption leaves the trier of fact free to credit or reject the inference and does not shift the burden of proof, it affects the application of the "beyond a reasonable doubt" standard only if, under the facts of the case, there is no rational way the trier could make the connection permitted by the inference. For only in that situation is there any risk that an explanation of the permissible inference to a jury, or its use by a jury, has caused the presumptively rational factfinder to make an erroneous factual determination.

Ulster County, 442 U.S. at 157, 99 S.Ct. at 2225, 60 L.Ed.2d at 792. While Montana has not yet done so, a large number of jurisdictions have followed the federal courts in adopting evidentiary rules which require that all presumptions presented to juries be clearly permissive. See 1 Weinstein's Evidence, ¶ 303[08] (1989). In the present case, had the language of Instruction Nos. 11 and 12 been modified to make the presumption unmistakably permissive, the instructions would have passed constitutional muster.

* * *

By copy of this opinion, we ask the Supreme Court Commission on Rules of Evidence to consider the advisability of adopting a rule of evidence addressed to presumptions in criminal cases. See Uniform

Rules of Evidence, Rule 303 (1974); also 1 Weinstein's Evidence, ¶ 303 (1989).

The case is reversed and remanded for a new trial.

HARRISON, WEBER and HUNT, JJ., concur.

HONZEL, DISTRICT JUDGE, sitting for BARZ, J.

MIZNER, DISTRICT JUDGE, sitting for SHEEHY, J.

GULBRANDSON, (RET.) JUSTICE, sitting for MCDONOUGH, J.

ORDER

The State of Montana has filed a petition for rehearing of the Court's September 18, 1990, Opinion in this matter. Defendant and appellant has filed his objection thereto.

Having considered the matter, the Court wishes to reemphasize that the Information filed against Leverett alleged that he drove his motor vehicle into a pedestrian at an unsafe rate of speed *and with a blood alcohol concentration in excess of .10,* and that Jury Instruction No. 10 provided that an alcohol concentration of .10 or more shall be presumed to indicate that the person was under the influence of alcohol. Our decision does not propose any expansion of the holdings of Sandstrom v. Montana (1979), 442 U.S. 510, 99 S.Ct. 2450, 61 L.Ed.2d 39.

The petition for rehearing is DENIED.

/s/ J.A. Turnage
Chief Justice

/s/ John Conway Harrison

/s/ William E. Hunt, Sr.

/s/ Fred J. Weber
Justices

/s/ Thomas C. Honzel
Hon. Thomas C. Honzel,
District Judge, sitting in
place of Justice Diane G.
Barz

/s/ Ted L. Mizner
Hon. Ted L. Mizner, District
Judge, sitting in place of
Justice John C. Sheehy

/s/ L.C. Gulbrandson
Hon. L.C. Gulbrandson,
Retired Justice, sitting in
place of Justice R.C.
McDonough

NOTE

See also, Wilhelm v. State, 568 So.2d 1 (Fla.1990) for a similar decision. The issue was the validity of an instruction that if the jury found that defendant had .10% or more by weight of alcohol in his blood, prima facie evidence was established that the defendant was under the influence of alcoholic beverages to the extent that his normal faculties were impaired. Did the instruction create an unconstitutional mandatory rebuttable presumption? The court said, in part:

" 'Prima facie' is a technical legal term without a common meaning for the lay person. Confronted with such a term in the jury instructions, and provided with no definition, a reasonable juror would be forced to guess as to its meaning from the context in which it was used. In this case, that context is an explanation in the jury instructions of what the jury can and cannot 'presume.' Further, there was no language in the instruction immediately following that challenged which instructed the jury that evidence of blood-alcohol content as it related to intoxication could be rebutted by the defendant. Although such language would not have cured the instruction, its absence makes it possible that the jury understood the instruction not only as a mandatory presumption, but one which is irrebuttable."

Chapter 3

THE POWER TO CREATE CRIMES AND ITS LIMITATIONS

A. SOURCES OF THE CRIMINAL LAW

1. THE COMMON LAW

"*Penn:* I desire you would let me know by what law it is you prosecute me, and upon what law you ground my indictment.

"*Rec.:* Upon the common-law.

"*Penn:* Where is that common law?

"*Rec.:* You must not think that I am able to run up so many years, and over so many adjudged cases, which we call common law, to answer your curiosity.

"*Penn:* This answer I am sure is very short of my question, for if it be common, it should not be so hard to produce.

"*Rec.:* The question is, whether you are Guilty of this Indictment?

"*Penn:* The question is not, whether I am Guilty of this Indictment, but whether this Indictment be legal. It is too general and imperfect an answer, to say it is the common law, unless we knew both where and what it is. For where there is no law, there is no transgression; and that law which is not in being, is so far from being common, that it is no law at all.

"*Rec.:* You are an impertinent fellow, will you teach the court what the law is? It is '*Lex non scripta,*' that which many have studied 30 or 40 years to know, and would you have me tell you in a moment?

"*Penn:* Certainly, if the common law be so hard to understand it is far from being common."

Trial of William Penn, 6 How.St.Trials 951, 958 (1670).

SHAW v. DIRECTOR OF PUBLIC PROSECUTIONS
House of Lords, 1961.
2 W.L.R. 897, 45 Cr.App.R. 113, 2 All E.R. 446.

[The appellant, Frederick Charles Shaw, pleaded not guilty at the Central Criminal Court, before Judge Maxwell Turner and a jury, on an indictment containing the following three counts: (1) "Conspiracy to corrupt public morals. Particulars of Offence. . . . conspired with certain persons who inserted advertisements in issues of a magazine entitled 'Ladies' Directory' numbered 7, 7 revised, 8, 9, 10 and a supplement thereto, and with certain other persons whose names are unknown, by means of the said magazine and the said advertisements to induce readers thereof to resort to the said advertisers for the purposes of fornication and of taking part in or witnessing other disgusting and immoral acts and exhibitions, with intent thereby to debauch and corrupt the morals as well of youth as of divers other liege subjects of Our Lady The Queen and to raise and create in their minds inordinate and lustful desires"; (2) living on the earnings of prostitution, contrary to section 30 of the Sexual Offences Act, 1956; and (3) publishing an obscene article, the Ladies' Directory, contrary to section 2 of the Obscene Publications Act, 1959.

The Ladies' Directory was a booklet of some 28 pages, most of which were taken up with the names and addresses of women who were prostitutes, together with a number of photographs of nude female figures, and the matter published left no doubt that the advertisers could be got in touch with at the telephone numbers given and were offering their services for sexual intercourse and, in some cases, for the practice of sexual perversions.

The appellant did not give evidence, but he had admitted publication and his avowed object in publishing was to assist prostitutes to ply their trade when, as a result of the Street Offences Act, 1959, they were no longer able to solicit in the streets. There was evidence that on October 22, 1959, prior to publication, he had taken advice as to whether publication would be legal, and had shown a police officer at Scotland Yard the first issue of the booklet and asked him if it would be all right to publish; apparently he had arranged that the Director of Public Prosecutions should see a copy. There was also evidence that he had assured the owner of a kiosk, whom he had asked to sell the booklet, that it would not be published unless it was legal. When later he was asked by a police officer if he was the Shaw who had published the Ladies' Directory he said: "Yes," and "I publish this and distribute it for 5s. each to help the prostitutes who advertise in it," but would not state how much he charged for advertisements, saying that he ran it as a business and that his solicitor thought it was all right. There was evidence that advertisers paid 25 guineas for the front cover, 15 guineas for the back cover, and inside, 10 guineas for a full-page advertisement, 8 guineas for a half-page photograph, and 2 guineas for a small printed advertisement; the amount paid by prostitutes advertising in issue No. 9 was calculated to be £250 19s., but there was no evidence as to how much of that was profit. The appellant charged 2s. 6d. to sellers for the booklet and it was sold to the public for 5s. Evidence was given by five prostitutes that they had paid for the advertisements out of their earnings as prostitutes, that the advertisements were good at bringing clients in and as to the ages of the persons resorting to them; they also gave evidence as to the meaning of certain abbreviations and about the sexual perversions referred to in their advertisements, and there was police evidence as to the objects found at their addresses.

After the close of the evidence for the prosecution, counsel for the appellant submitted that the conspiracy alleged in count 1 disclosed no offence. . . .

Judge Maxwell Turner ruled that a conspiracy to debauch and corrupt public morals was a common law misdemeanour and was indictable at common law and that the particulars of the offences set out in count 1 were particulars of such a conspiracy, if the jury found the facts alleged to be true.

The jury convicted the appellant on all three counts and he was sentenced to nine months' imprisonment.]

[*Opinion of the Court of Criminal Appeal*] The appellant appealed against his conviction on all three counts to the Court of Criminal Appeal. On count 1 it was contended, in effect, that there was no such offence at common law as a conspiracy to corrupt public morals unless the acts alleged were offences against the criminal law or amounted to a civil wrong and that, as the acts alleged in the indictment were not in either of those classes, the conspiracy alleged disclosed no offence. . . .

Conspiracy is an offence which takes many different forms but in the present appeal the matter was greatly simplified when Mr. Buzzard, on behalf of the prosecution, made it clear that the form of conspiracy, which he had alleged at the trial and to which he adhered, was a conspiracy to commit an unlawful act, and not a conspiracy to commit a lawful act by unlaw means. He reserved the right to contend, should it be necessary, that a conspiracy to corrupt the morals of a particular individual was an indictable offence by reason of the conspiracy, even if such corruption if done by one person would not be an offence. The unlawful act which he alleged was said to be a common law misdemeanour, namely, the corruption of public morals. His proposition was two-fold: at common law any act calculated or intended to corrupt the morals of the public or a portion thereof in general, as opposed to the morals of a particular individual or individuals, is indictable as a substantive offence. Secondly, an act calculated or intended to outrage public decency is also indictable as a substantive offence. Both parts of this proposition were naturally contested by Mr. Rees Davies and the main issue before us on this first count is whether the first of Mr. Buzzard's propositions is well-founded.

We were referred to a large number of cases, but before alluding to any of them in detail we may usefully refer to the speech of Lord Sumner in Bowman v. Secular Society Ltd. in which is set out an illuminating survey of this branch of the law from the beginning of the seventeenth century. He said: The time of Charles II was one of notorious laxity both in faith and morals, and for a time it seemed as if the old safeguards were in abeyance or had been swept away. Immorality and irreligion were cognisable in the Ecclesiastical Courts, but spiritual censures had lost their sting and those civil courts were extinct, which had specially dealt with such matters viewed as offences against civil order. The Court of King's Bench stepped in to fill the gap."

The first reported occasion on which the Court of King's Bench thus stepped in appears to be Rex v. Sidley. Amongst other acts alleged against Sir Charles Sidley were his exposure of his naked body upon a balcony in Covent Garden before a large gathering of people and making water on the persons below. In addition he was said to have thrown down bottles upon such persons' heads. This latter conduct was plainly within the jurisdiction of the Court of King's Bench but there was evidently an issue whether the other conduct was such as could be dealt with in that court. In the short report of the case there appears the statement that "this court is custos morum of all the King's subjects and that it is high time to punish such profane conduct." In 1708, in Reg. v. Read, the court expressed a different view when considering a charge of publishing an obscene libel, but the judgment in the defendant's favour was only a "judgment nisi," that is, a provisional judgment. Not long afterwards the case of Rex v. Curl came before the Court of King's Bench, in which the charge against the accused was that of publishing an obscene libel. Reliance was naturally placed on *Read's* case by defending counsel, but the Attorney-General's argument to the contrary prevailed: "What I insist upon is, that this is an offence at common law, as it tends to corrupt the morals of the King's subjects, and is against the peace of the King. . . . I do not insist that every immoral act is indictable, such as telling a lie, or the like; but if it is destructive of morality in general, if it does, or may, affect all the King's subjects, it then is an offence of a public nature." Lord Raymond C. J., in giving judgment, said: ". . . if it reflects on religion, virtue, or morality, if it tends to disturb the civil order of society, I think it is a temporal offence." After the case had been adjourned the court "gave it as their unanimous opinion, that this was a temporal offence. They said it was plain that the force used in *Sidley's* case was but a small ingredient in the judgment of the court who fined him £2,000. And if the force was all they went upon there was no occasion to talk of the court's being censor morum of the King's subjects. They said that if *Read's* case was to be adjudged, they should rule it otherwise: and therefore in this case they gave judgment for the King."

* * *

In our opinion, having regard to the long line of cases to which we have been referred, it is an established principle of common law that conduct calculated or intended to corrupt public morals (as opposed to the morals of a particular individual) is an indictable misdemeanour. As the reports show, the conduct to which that principle is applicable may vary considerably, but the principle itself does not, and in our view the facts of the present case fall plainly within it.

The contrary view put forward by Mr. Rees Davies may be summarised as follows: He accepted for the purposes of his argument the claim of the Court of King's Bench to be custos morum but he contended that acting in that role the court had, so to speak, from time to time declared particular conduct to be an offence, thereby creating an offence rather than applying existing law to particular facts. He went on to contend that Parliament in the last 100 years had concerned itself with legislation on issues of morality, decency and the like, that such legislation must be taken to be in effect a comprehensive code, and that there is no longer any occasion for the court to create new offences in its capacity as custos morum. We are unable to agree with this argument, which fails to give sufficient weight to the repeated statements of the established principle of common law to which we have already referred. The courts in the relevant cases were not creating new offences or making new law: they were applying existing law to new facts.

It is perhaps worth adding that the principle itself is not in any way affected or qualified by the fact that in the course of time public opinion as expressed in juries' verdicts may change in regard to matters of public decency and morality. This was emphasized by Lord Sumner in *Bowman's* case: "The fact that opinion grounded on experience has moved one way does not in law preclude the possibility of its moving on fresh experience in the other; nor does it bind succeeding generations, when conditions have again changed. After all, the question whether a given opinion is a danger to society is a question of the times and is a question of fact." * * *

In the present case the issue involved in this first count was fully argued in the absence of a jury, and the judge's ruling was in the following terms: "In my opinion a conspiracy to debauch and corrupt public morals is a common law misdemeanour and is indictable at common law." We agree with this ruling. If the principle to which we have referred is part of the common law of this country, it must follow that a conspiracy of the type alleged is an indictable offence.

[Opinion of the HOUSE OF LORDS.]

VISCOUNT SIMONDS. My Lords . . . the first count in the indictment is "Conspiracy to corrupt public morals," and the particulars of offence will have sufficiently appeared. I am concerned only to assert what was vigorously denied by counsel for the appellant, that such an offence is known to the common law, and that it was open to the jury to find on the facts of this case that the appellant was guilty of such an offence. I must say categorically that, if it were not so, Her Majesty's courts would strangely have failed in their duty as servants and guardians of the common law. Need I say, my Lords, that I am no advocate of the right of the judges to create new criminal offences? I will repeat well-known words: "Amongst many other points of happiness and freedom which your Majesty's subjects have enjoyed there is none which they have accounted more dear and precious than this, to be guided and governed by certain rules of law which giveth both to the head and members that which of right belongeth to them and not by any arbitrary or uncertain form of government." These words are as true today as they were in the seventeenth century and command the allegiance of us all. But I am at a loss to understand how it can be said either that the law does not recognise a conspiracy to corrupt public morals or that, though there may not be an exact precedent for such a conspiracy as this case reveals, it does not fall fairly within the general words by which it is described. I do not propose to examine all the relevant authorities. That will be done by my noble and learned friend. The fallacy in the argument that was addressed to us lay in the attempt to exclude from the scope of general words acts well calculated to corrupt public morals just because they had not been committed or had not been brought to the notice of the court before. It is not thus that the common law has developed. We are perhaps more accustomed to hear this matter discussed upon the question whether such and such a transaction is contrary to public policy. At once the controversy arises. On the one hand it is said that it is not possible in the twentieth century for the court to create a new head of public policy, on the other it is said that this is but a new example of a well-established head. In the sphere of criminal law I entertain no doubt that there remains in the courts of law a residual power to enforce the supreme and fundamental purpose of the law, to conserve not only the safety and order but also the moral welfare of the State, and that it is their duty to guard it against attacks which may be the more insidious because they are novel and unprepared for. That is the broad head (call it public policy if you wish) within which the present indictment falls. It matters little what label is given to the offending act. To one of your Lordships it may appear an affront to public decency, to another, considering that it may succeed in its obvious intention of provoking libidinous desires, it will seem a corruption of public morals. Yet others may deem it aptly described as the creation of a public mischief or the undermining of moral conduct. The same act will not in all ages be regarded in the same way. The law must be related to the changing standards of life, not yielding to every shifting impulse of the popular will but having regard to fundamental assessments of human values and the purposes of society. Today a denial of the fundamental Christian doctrine, which in past centuries would have been regarded by the ecclesiastical courts as heresy and by the common law as blasphemy, will no longer be an offence if the decencies of controversy are observed. When Lord Mansfield, speaking long after the Star Chamber had been abolished, said that the Court of King's Bench was the custos morum of the people and had the superintendency of offences contra bonos mores, he was asserting, as I now assert, that there is in that court a residual power, where no statute has yet intervened to supersede the common law, to superintend those offences which are prejudicial to the public welfare. Such occasions will be rare, for Parliament has not been slow to legislate when attention has been sufficiently aroused. But gaps remain and will always remain since no one can foresee every way in which the wickedness of man may disrupt the order of society. Let me take a single instance . . . Let it be supposed that at some future, perhaps, early date, homosexual practices between adult consenting males are no longer a crime. Would it not be an offence if even without obscenity, such practices were publicly advocated and encouraged by pamphlet and advertisement? Or must we wait until Parliament finds time to deal with such conduct? I say, my Lords, that if the common law is powerless in such an event, then we should no longer do her reverence. But I say that her hand is still powerful and that it is for Her Majesty's judges to play the part which Lord Mansfield pointed out to them.

I have so far paid little regard to the fact that the charge here is of conspiracy. But, if I have correctly described the conduct of the appellant, it is an irresistible inference that a conspiracy between him and others to do such acts is indictable. * * *

I will say a final word upon an aspect of the case which was urged by counsel. No one doubts—and I have put it in the forefront of this opinion—that certainty is a most desirable attribute of the criminal and civil law alike. Nevertheless there are matters which must ultimately depend on the opinion of a jury. In the civil law I will take an example which comes perhaps nearest to the criminal law—the tort of negligence. It is for a jury to decide not only whether the defendant has committed the act complained of but whether in doing it he has fallen short of the standard of care which the circumstances require. Till their verdict is given it is uncertain what the law requires. The same branch of the civil law supplies another interesting analogy. For, though in the Factory Acts and the regulations made under them, the measure of care required of an employer is defined in the greatest detail, no one supposes that he may not be guilty of negligence in a manner unforeseen and unprovided for. That will be a matter for the jury to decide. There are still, as has recently been said, "unravished remnants of the common law."

So in the case of a charge of conspiracy to corrupt public morals the uncertainty that necessarily arises from the vagueness of general words can only be resolved by the opinion of twelve chosen men and women. I am content to leave it to them.

The appeal on both counts should, in my opinion, be dismissed.

LORD REID [In dissent] * * *

In my opinion there is no such general offence known to the law as conspiracy to corrupt public morals. Undoubtedly there is an offence of criminal conspiracy and undoubtedly it is of fairly wide scope. In my view its scope cannot be determined without having regard first to the history of the matter and then to the broad general principles which have generally been thought to underlie our system of law and government and in particular our system of criminal law.

It appears to be generally accepted that the offence of criminal conspiracy was the creature of the Star Chamber. So far as I am able to judge the summary in Kenny's Outlines of Criminal Law, section 59, 17th ed., p. 88, is a fair one. There it is said that the criminal side of conspiracy was "emphasised by the Star Chamber which recognised its possibilities as an engine of government and moulded it into a substantive offence of wide scope whose attractions were such that its princi-

ples were gradually adopted by the common law courts . . .." The
Star Chamber perhaps had more merits than its detractors will admit
but its methods and principles were superseded and what it did is of no
authority today. The question is how far the common law courts in
fact went in borrowing from it. * * *

There are two competing views. One is that conspiring to corrupt
public morals is only one facet of a still more general offence, conspiracy to effect public mischief; and that, like the categories of negligence,
the categories of public mischief are never closed. The other is that,
whatever may have been done two or three centuries ago, we ought not
now to extend the doctrine further than it has already been carried by
the common law courts. Of course I do not mean that it should only be
applied in circumstances precisely similar to those in some decided
case. Decisions are always authority for other cases which are reasonably analogous and are not properly distinguishable. But we ought not
to extend the doctrine to new fields.

I agree [with the viewpoint that]: "There appear to be great
theoretical objections to any general rule that agreement may make
punishable that which ought not to be punished in the absence of
agreement." And I think, or at least I hope, that it is now established
that the courts cannot create new offences by individuals. So far at
least I have the authority of Lord Goddard C. J. in delivering the
opinion of the court in *Newland:* "The dictum [in Rex v. Higgins] was
that all offences of a public nature, that is, all such acts or attempts as
tend to the prejudice of the public are indictable, but no other member
of the court stated the law in such wide terms. It is the breadth of that
dictum that was so strongly criticised by Sir Fitzjames Stephen in the
passage in his History of the Criminal Law (vol. 3, p. 359) . . . and
also by Dr. Stallybrass in the Law Quarterly Review, vol. 34, p. 183. In
effect it would leave it to the judges to declare new crimes and enable
them to hold anything which they considered prejudicial to the community to be a misdemeanour. However beneficial that might have been
in days when Parliament met seldom, or at least only at long intervals
it surely is now the province of the legislature and not of the judiciary
to create new criminal offences." Every argument against creating
new offences by an individual appears to me to be equally valid against
creating new offences by a combination of individuals. * * *

Finally I must advert to the consequences of holding that this very
general offence exists. It has always been thought to be of primary
importance that our law, and particularly our criminal law, should be
certain: that a man should be able to know what conduct is and what is
not criminal, particularly when heavy penalties are involved. Some
suggestion was made that it does not matter if this offence is very wide:
no one would ever prosecute and if they did no jury would ever convict
if the breach was venial. Indeed, the suggestion goes even further:
that the meaning and application of the words "deprave" and "corrupt"
(the traditional words in obscene libel now enacted in the 1959 Act) or
the words "debauch" and "corrupt" in this indictment ought to be

entirely for the jury, so that any conduct of this kind is criminal if in the end a jury think it so. In other words, you cannot tell what is criminal except by guessing what view a jury will take, and juries' views may vary and may change with the passing of time. Normally, the meaning of words is a question of law for the court. For example, it is not left to a jury to determine the meaning of negligence: they have to consider on evidence and on their own knowledge a much more specific question—Would a reasonable man have done what this man did? I know that in obscene libel the jury has great latitude but I think that it is an understatement to say that this has not been found wholly satisfactory. If the trial judge's charge in the present case was right, if a jury is entitled to water down the strong words "deprave," "corrupt" or "debauch" so as merely to mean lead astray morally, then it seems to me that the court has transferred to the jury the whole of its functions as censor morum, the law will be whatever any jury may happen to think it ought to be, and this branch of the law will have lost all the certainty which we rightly prize in other branches of our law.

[Opinions of Lords Tucker, Morris of Borth-y-Gest, and Hodson omitted.]

Appeal dismissed.

NOTES

1. For an excellent analysis of the problems raised by the *Shaw* case, see Brownlie and Williams, Judicial Legislation In Criminal Law, 42 Can. Bar Rev. 561 (1964). And see Gordon, Crimes Without Laws?, 11 Jur.Rev. 214 (1966).

2. In Commonwealth v. Mochan, 177 Pa.Super. 454, 110 A.2d 788 (1955), the defendant was convicted of "devising" and "contriving to debauch and corrupt the morals and manners" of the "good citizens" of Pennsylvania, and, in particular, one Louise Zivkovich, by making lewd and obscene phone calls to her on a party line. The conviction was sustained on appeal against the contention that such an offense was unknown to the common law. In dissenting from the affirmance of the conviction, Judge Woodside said: "There is no doubt that the common law is a part of the law of this Commonwealth, and we punish many acts under the common law. But after nearly two hundred years of constitutional government in which the legislature and not the courts have been charged by the people with the responsibility of deciding which acts do and which do not injure the public to the extent which requires punishment, it seems to me we are making an unwarranted invasion of the legislative field when we arrogate that responsibility to ourselves by declaring now, for the first time, that certain acts are a crime." Does this mean that a conviction for an offense for which there was a precedent in the English law prior to the adoption of the Pennsylvania constitution would be upheld now? Would the same result follow if the English precedent was one set *after* the adoption of the Pennsylvania constitution?

In two Connecticut cases decided in 1962 two different telephone callers of the type represented by Mochan were prosecuted under two separate statutes, one for a "breach of the peace," the other for "disorderly conduct." The conduct was held to constitute a "breach of the peace" in State v. Protopapas, 23 Conn.Sup. 471, 184 A.2d 558 (1962), on the ground that "peace" referred to that of individuals as well as that of the general public. But in State v. Robinson, 23 Conn.Sup. 430, 184 A.2d 188 (1962), the same court held that this did not constitute "disorderly conduct."

In Anniskette v. State, 489 P.2d 1012 (Alaska 1971), the defendant telephoned a police officer and called him a "no good goddam cop". This was held not to violate a statute prohibiting the use of "obscene and profane language . . . to the disturbance or annoyance of another".

Consider the following provision of the U.S.Code (Title 47, 223);

Whoever—

(1) in the District of Columbia or in interstate or foreign communication by means of telephone—

(A) makes any comment, request, suggestion or proposal which is obscene, lewd, lascivious, filthy, or indecent;

(B) makes a telephone call, whether or not conversation ensues, without disclosing his identity and with intent to annoy, abuse, threaten, or harass any person at the called number;

(C) makes or causes the telephone of another repeatedly or continuously to ring, with intent to harass any person at the called number; or

(D) makes repeated telephone calls, during which conversation ensues, solely to harass any person at the called number; or

(2) knowingly permits any telephone under his control to be used for any purpose prohibited by this section, shall be fined not more than $50,000 or imprisoned not more than six months, or both. * * *

3. Consider the case of the "Peeping Tom" in Frey v. Fedoruk [1950] Can. Sup.Ct. 517, 3 D.L.R. 513, which held that "window peeping" was not an offense at common law. See discussion in Thompson, Common Law Crimes Against Public Morals, 49 J.Crim.L., C. & P.S. 350 (1958).

2. STATUTES AND JUDICIAL CONSTRUCTION

"The judicial function is that of interpretation; it does not include the power of amendment under the guise of interpretation."

Justice Sutherland, in 300 U.S. 379, 404 (1937).

CAMINETTI v. U.S.

DIGGS v. U.S.

HAYS v. U.S.

Supreme Court of the United States, 1916.
242 U.S. 470, 37 S.Ct. 192.

MR. JUSTICE DAY delivered the opinion of the court:

These three cases were argued together, and may be disposed of in a single opinion. In each of the cases there was a conviction and sentence for violation of the so-called White Slave Traffic Act of June

25, 1910 (36 Stat. at L. 825, chap. 395, Comp.Stat.1913, § 8813),[1] the judgments were affirmed by the circuit courts of appeals, and writs of certiorari bring the cases here.

In the *Caminetti* Case, the petitioner was indicted in the United States district court for the northern district of California, upon the 6th day of May, 1913, for alleged violations of the act. The indictment was in four counts, the first of which charged him with transporting and causing to be transported, and aiding and assisting in obtaining transportation for a certain woman from Sacramento, California, to Reno, Nevada, in interstate commerce, for the purpose of debauchery, and for an immoral purpose, to wit, that the aforesaid woman should be and become his mistress and concubine. A verdict of not guilty was returned as to the other three counts of this indictment. As to the first count, defendant was found guilty and sentenced to imprisonment for eighteen months and to pay a fine of $1,500. Upon writ of error to the United States circuit court of appeals for the ninth circuit, that judgment was affirmed. . . .

Diggs was indicted at the same time as was Caminetti. . . . The first count charged the defendant with transporting and causing to be transported, and aiding and assisting in obtaining transportation for, a certain woman from Sacramento, California, to Reno, Nevada, for the purpose of debauchery, and for an immoral purpose, to wit, that the aforesaid woman should be and become his concubine and mistress. The second count charged him with a like offense as to another woman (the companion of Caminetti) in transportation, etc., from Sacramento to Reno, that she might become the mistress and concubine of Caminetti. The third count charged him (Diggs) with procuring a ticket for the first-mentioned woman from Sacramento to Reno in interstate commerce, with the intent that she should become his concubine and mistress. The fourth count made a like charge as to the girl companion

1. The White Slave Traffic Act, U.S. C.A., Title 18, § 2421, currently provides as follows:

"Whoever knowingly transports in interstate or foreign commerce, or in the District of Columbia or in any Territory or Possession of the United States, any woman or girl for the purpose of prostitution or debauchery, or for any other immoral purpose, or with the intent and purpose to induce, entice, or compel such woman or girl to become a prostitute or to give herself up to debauchery, or to engage in any other immoral practice; or

"Whoever knowingly procures or obtains any ticket or tickets, or any form of transportation or evidence of the right thereto, to be used by any woman or girl in interstate or foreign commerce, or in the District of Columbia or any Territory or Possession of the United States, in going to any place for the purpose of prostitution or debauchery, or for any other immoral purpose, or with the intent or purpose on the part of such person to induce, entice, or compel her to give herself up to the practice of prostitution, or to give herself up to debauchery, or any other immoral practice, whereby any such woman or girl shall be transported in interstate or foreign commerce, or in the District of Columbia or any Territory or Possession of the United States." [In 1986 the Mann Act was amended to read:

"Whoever knowingly transports any individual in interstate or foreign commerce, or in any Territory or Possession of the United States, with intent that such individual engage in prostitution, or in any sexual activity for which any person can be charged with a criminal offense, shall be fined under this title or imprisoned not more than five years, or both."]

of Caminetti. Upon trial and verdict of guilty on these four counts, he was sentenced to imprisonment for two years and to pay a fine of $2,000. As in the *Caminetti* Case, that judgment was affirmed by the circuit court of appeals. . . .

In the *Hays* Case, upon June 26th, 1914, an indictment was returned in the United States district court for the western district of Oklahoma against Hays and another, charging violations of the act. The first count charged the said defendants with having, on March 17th, 1914, persuaded, induced, enticed, and coerced a certain woman, unmarried and under the age of eighteen years, from Oklahoma City, Oklahoma, to the city of Wichita, Kansas, in interstate commerce and travel, for the purpose and with intent then and there to induce and coerce the said woman, and intending that she should be induced and coerced to engage in prostitution, debauchery, and other immoral practices, and did then and there, in furtherance of such purposes, procure and furnish a railway ticket entitling her to passage over the line of railway, to wit, the Atchison, Topeka & Santa Fe Railway, and did then and there and thereby, knowingly entice and cause the said women to go and to be carried and transported as a passenger in interstate commerce upon said line of railway. The second count charged that on the same date the defendants persuaded, induced, enticed, and coerced the same woman to be transported from Oklahoma City to Wichita, Kansas, with the purpose and intent to induce and coerce her to engage in prostitution, debauchery, and other immoral practices at and within the state of Kansas, and that they enticed her and caused her to go and be carried and transported as a passenger in interstate commerce from Oklahoma City, Oklahoma, to Wichita, Kansas, upon a line and route of a common carrier, to wit: The Atchison, Topeka & Santa Fe Railway. Defendants were found guilty by a jury upon both counts, and Hays was sentenced to imprisonment for eighteen months. Upon writ of error to the circuit court of appeals for the eighth circuit, judgment was affirmed. . . .

It is contended that the act of Congress is intended to reach only "commercialized vice," or the traffic in women for gain, and that the conduct for which the several petitioners were indicted and convicted, however, reprehensible in morals, is not within the purview of the statute when properly construed in the light of its history and the purposes intended to be accomplished by its enactment. In none of the cases was it charged or proved that the transportation was for gain or for the purpose of furnishing women for prostitution for hire, and it is insisted that, such being the case, the acts charged and proved, upon which conviction was had, do not come within the statute.

It is elementary that the meaning of a statute must, in the first instance, be sought in the language in which the act is framed, and if that is plain, and if the law is within the constitutional authority of the law-making body which passed it, the sole function of the courts is to enforce it according to its terms. . . .

Where the language is plain and admits of no more than one meaning, the duty of interpretation does not arise, and the rules which are to aid doubtful meanings need no discussion. . . . There is no ambiguity in the terms of this act. It is specifically made an offense to knowingly transport or cause to be transported, etc., in interstate commerce, any woman or girl for the purpose of prostitution or debauchery, or for "any other immoral purpose," or with the intent and purpose to induce any such woman or girl to become a prostitute or to give herself up to debauchery, or to engage in any other immoral practice.

Statutory words are uniformly presumed, unless the contrary appears, to be used in their ordinary and usual sense, and with the meaning commonly attributed to them. To cause a woman or girl to be transported for the purposes of debauchery, and for an immoral purpose, to wit, becoming a concubine or mistress, for which Caminetti and Diggs were convicted; or to transport an unmarried woman, under eighteen years of age, with the intent to induce her to engage in prostitution, debauchery, and other immoral practices, for which Hays was convicted, would seem by the very statement of the facts to embrace transportation for purposes denounced by the act, and therefore fairly within its meaning.

While such immoral purpose would be more culpable in morals and attributed to baser motives if accompanied with the expectation of pecuniary gain, such considerations do not prevent the lesser offense against morals of furnishing transportation in order that a woman may be debauched, or become a mistress or a concubine, from being the execution of purposes within the meaning of this law. To say the contrary would shock the common understanding of what constitutes an immoral purpose when those terms are applied, as here, to sexual relations.

In United States v. Bitty . . ., it was held that the act of Congress against the importation of alien women and girls for the purpose of prostitution "and any other immoral purpose" included the importation of an alien woman to live in concubinage with the person importing her. In that case this court said:

"All will admit that full effect must be given to the intention of Congress as gathered from the words of the statute. There can be no doubt as to what class was aimed at by the clause forbidding the importation of alien women for purposes of 'prostitution.' It refers to women who, for hire or without hire, offer their bodies to indiscriminate intercourse with men. The lives and example of such persons are in hostility to 'the idea of the family, as consisting in and springing from the union for life of one man and one woman in the holy estate of matrimony; the sure foundation of all that is stable and noble in our civilization; the best guaranty of that reverent morality which is the source of all beneficent progress in social and political improvement.'

. . . Now the addition in the last statute of the words, 'or for any other immoral purpose,' after the word 'prostitution,' must have been made for some practical object.   Those added words show beyond question that Congress had in view the protection of society against another class of alien women other than those who might be brought here merely for purposes of 'prostitution.'   In forbidding the importation of alien women 'for any other immoral purpose,' Congress evidently thought that there were purposes in connection with the importations of alien women which, as in the case of importations for prostitution, were to be deemed immoral.   It may be admitted that, in accordance with the familiar rule of *ejusdem generis,* the immoral purpose referred to by the words 'any other immoral purpose' must be one of the same general class or kind as the particular purpose of 'prostitution' specified in the same clause of the statute.   2 Lewis' Sutherland Stat.Constr. § 423, and authorities cited.   But that rule cannot avail the accused in this case; for the immoral purpose charged in the indictment is of the same general class or kind as the one that controls in the importation of an alien woman for the purpose strictly of prostitution.   The prostitute may, in the popular sense, be more degraded in character than the concubine, but the latter none the less must be held to lead an immoral life, if any regard whatever be had to the views that are almost universally held in this country as to the relations which may rightfully, from the standpoint of morality, exist between man and woman in the matter of sexual intercourse."

This definition of an immoral purpose was given prior to the enactment of the act now under consideration, and must be presumed to have been known to Congress when it enacted the law here involved. . . .

But it is contended that though the words are so plain that they cannot be misapprehended when given their usual and ordinary interpretation, and although the sections in which they appear do not in terms limit the offense defined and punished to acts of "commercialized vice," or the furnishing or procuring of transportation of women for debauchery, prostitution, or immoral practices for hire, such limited purpose is to be attributed to Congress and engrafted upon the act in view of the language of § 8 and the report which accompanied the law upon its introduction into and subsequent passage by the House of Representatives.

In this connection, it may be observed that while the title of an act cannot overcome the meaning of plain and unambiguous words used in its body . . ., the title of this act embraces the regulation of interstate commerce "by prohibiting the transportation therein for immoral purposes of women and girls, and for other purposes."   It is true that § 8 of the act provides that it shall be known and referred to as the "White Slave Traffic Act," and the report accompanying the introduction of the same into the House of Representatives set forth the fact that a material portion of the legislation suggested was to meet conditions which had arisen in the past few years, and that the legislation was needed to put a stop to a villainous interstate and international traffic in women and girls. Still, the name given to an act by way of designation or description, or the report which accompanies it, cannot change the plain import of its words. If the words are plain, they give meaning to the act, and it is neither the duty nor the privilege of the courts to enter speculative fields in search of a different meaning.

Reports to Congress accompanying the introduction of proposed laws may aid the courts in reaching the true meaning of the legislature in cases of doubtful interpretation. . . . But, as we have already said, and it has been so often affirmed as to become a recognized rule, when words are free from doubt they must be taken as the final expression of the legislative intent, and are not to be added to or subtracted from by considerations drawn from titles or designating names or reports accompanying their introduction, or from any extraneous source. In other words, the language being plain, and not leading to absurd or wholly impracticable consequences, it is the sole evidence of the ultimate legislative intent. . . .

The fact, if it be so, that the act as it is written opens the door to blackmailing operations upon a large scale, is no reason why the courts should refuse to enforce it according to its terms, if within the constitutional authority of Congress. Such considerations are more appropriately addressed to the legislative branch of the government, which alone had authority to enact and may, if it sees fit, amend the law.

It is further insisted that a different construction of the act than is to be gathered from reading it is necessary in order to save it from constitutional objections, fatal to its validity. The act has its constitutional sanction in the power of Congress over interstate commerce. The broad character of that authority was declared once for all in the judgment pronounced by this court, speaking by Chief Justice Marshall, . . . and has since been steadily adhered to and applied to a variety of new conditions as they have arisen.

It may be conceded, for the purpose of the argument, that Congress has no power to punish one who travels in interstate commerce merely because he has the intention of committing an illegal or immoral act at the conclusion of the journey. But this act is not concerned with such instances. It seeks to reach and punish the movement in interstate commerce of women and girls with a view to the accomplishment of the unlawful purposes prohibited.

The transportation of passengers in interstate commerce, it has long been settled, is within the regulatory power of Congress, under the commerce clause of the Constitution, and the authority of Congress to keep the channels of interstate commerce free from immoral and injurious uses has been frequently sustained, and is no longer open to question. . . .

The judgment in each of the cases is affirmed.

MR. JUSTICE MCKENNA, with whom concurred the CHIEF JUSTICE and MR. JUSTICE CLARKE, dissenting:

Undoubtedly, in the investigation of the meaning of a statute we resort first to its words, and, when clear, they are decisive. The principle has attractive and seemingly disposing simplicity, but that it is not easy of application, or, at least, encounters other principles, many cases demonstrate. The words of a statute may be uncertain in their signification or in their application. If the words be ambiguous, the problem they present is to be resolved by their definition; the subject matter and the lexicons become our guides. But here, even, we are not exempt from putting ourselves in the place of the legislators. If the words be clear in meaning, but the objects to which they are addressed be uncertain, the problem then is to determine the uncertainty. And for this a realization of conditions that provoked the statute must inform our judgment. Let us apply these observations to the present case.

The transportation which is made unlawful is of a woman or girl "to become a prostitute or to give herself up to debauchery, or to engage in any other immoral practice." Our present concern is with the words "any other immoral practice," which, it is asserted, have a special office. The words are clear enough as general descriptions; they fail in particular designation; they are class words, not specifications. Are they controlled by those which precede them? If not, they are broader in generalization and include those that precede them, making them unnecessary and confusing. To what conclusion would this lead us? "Immoral" is a very comprehensive word. It means a dereliction of morals. In such sense it covers every form of vice, every form of conduct that is contrary to good order. It will hardly be contended that in this sweeping sense it is used in the statute. But, if not used in such sense, to what is it limited and by what limited? If it be admitted that it is limited at all, that ends the imperative effect assigned to it in the opinion of the court. But not insisting quite on that, we ask again, By what is it limited? By its context, necessarily, and the purpose of the statute.

For the context I must refer to the statute; of the purpose of the statute Congress itself has given us illumination. It devotes a section to the declaration that the "act shall be known and referred to as the 'White Slave Traffic Act.'" And its prominence gives it prevalence in the construction of the statute. It cannot be pushed aside or subordinated by indefinite words in other sentences, limited even there by the context. It is a peremptory rule of construction that all parts of a statute must be taken into account in ascertaining its meaning, and it cannot be said that § 8 has no object. Even if it gives only a title to the act, it has especial weight. . . . But it gives more than a title; it makes distinctive the purpose of the statute. The designation "white slave traffic" has the sufficiency of an axiom. If apprehended, there is no uncertainty as to the conduct it describes. It is commercialized vice, immoralities having a mercenary purpose, and this is confirmed by other circumstances.

The author of the bill was Mr. Mann, and in reporting it from the House committee on interstate and foreign commerce he declared for the committee that it was not the purpose of the bill to interfere with or usurp in any way the police power of the states, and further, that it was not the intention of the bill to regulate prostitution or the places where prostitution or immorality was practised, which were said to be matters wholly within the power of the states,[2] and over which the Federal government had no jurisdiction. And further explaining the bill, it was said that the sections of the act had been "so drawn that they are limited to the cases in which there is an act of transportation in interstate commerce of women for the purposes of prostitution." and again:

"The White Slave Trade.—A material portion of the legislation suggested and proposed is necessary to meet conditions which have arisen within the past few years. The legislation is needed to put a stop to a villainous interstate and international traffic in women and girls. The legislation is not needed or intended as an aid to the states in the exercise of the police powers in the suppression or regulation of

2. State statutory coverage of prostitution and related activities is extensive. Although these statutes vary greatly in their wording, they are fairly uniform with respect to the specific matters dealt with. For purposes of illustration, the Wisconsin provisions, which are uncommonly succinct, are set forth below:

§ 944.30. *Prostitution.* Any female who intentionally does any of the following may be fined not more than $500 or imprisoned not more than one year or both:

(1) Has or offers to have non-marital sexual intercourse for money; or

(2) Commits or offers to commit an act of sexual perversion for money; or

(3) Is an inmate of a place of prostitution.

§ 944.31. *Patronizing Prostitutes.* Any male who enters or remains in any place of prostitution with intent to have non-marital sexual intercourse or to commit an act of sexual perversion may be fined not more than $100 or imprisoned not more than 3 months or both.

§ 944.32. *Soliciting Prostitutes.* Whoever intentionally solicits or causes any female to practice prostitution or establishes any female in a place of prostitution may be fined not more than $1,000 or imprisoned not more than 5 years or both. If the female is under the age of 18, the defendant may be fined not more than $2,000 or imprisoned not more than 10 years or both.

§ 944.33. *Pandering.* (1) Whoever does any of the following may be fined not more than $200 or imprisoned not more than 6 months or both:

(a) Solicits another to have non-marital sexual intercourse or to commit an act of sexual perversion with a female he knows is a prostitute; or

(b) With intent to facilitate another in having non-marital intercourse or committing an act of sexual perversion with a prostitute, directs or transports him to a prostitute or directs or transports a prostitute to him.

(2) If the accused received compensation from the earnings of the prostitute, he may be fined not more than $5,000 or imprisoned not more than 10 years or both. . . .

§ 944.34. *Keeping Place of Prostitution.* Whoever intentionally does any of the following may be fined not more than $5,000 or imprisoned not more than 5 years or both:

(1) Keeps a place of prostitution; or

(2) Grants the use or allows the continued use of a place as a place of prostitution. [Eds.]

immorality in general. It does not attempt to regulate the practice of voluntary prostitution, but aims solely to prevent panderers and procurers from compelling thousands of women and girls against their will and desire to enter and continue in a life of prostitution."   . . .

In other words, it is vice as a business at which the law is directed, using interstate commerce as a facility to procure or distribute its victims.

In 1912 the sense of the Department of Justice was taken of the act in a case where a woman of twenty-four years went from Illinois, where she lived, to Minnesota, at the solicitation and expense of a man. She was there met by him and engaged with him in immoral practices like those for which petitioners were convicted. The assistant district attorney forwarded her statement to the Attorney General, with the comment that the element of traffic was absent from the transaction and that therefore, in his opinion, it was not "within the spirit and intent of the Mann Act." Replying, the Attorney General expressed his concurrence in the view of his subordinate.

Of course, neither the declarations of the report of the committee on interstate commerce of the House nor the opinion of the Attorney General are conclusive of the meaning of the law, but they are highly persuasive. The opinion was by one skilled in the rules and methods employed in the interpretation or construction of laws, and informed, besides, of the conditions to which the act was addressed. The report was by the committee charged with the duty of investigating the necessity for the act, and to inform the House of the results of that investigation, both of evil and remedy. The report of the committee has, therefore, a higher quality than debates on the floor of the House. The representations of the latter may indeed be ascribed to the exaggerations of advocacy or opposition. The report of a committee is the execution of a duty and has the sanction of duty. There is a presumption, therefore, that the measure it recommends has the purpose it declares and will accomplish it as declared.

This being the purpose, the words of the statute should be construed to execute it, and they may be so construed even if their literal meaning be otherwise. . . . .

There is much in the present case to tempt to a violation of the rule. Any measure that protects the purity of women from assault or enticement to degradation finds an instant advocate in our best emotions; but the judicial function cannot yield to emotion—it must, with poise of mind, consider and decide. It should not shut its eyes to the facts of the world and assume not to know what everybody else knows. And everybody knows that there is a difference between the occasional immoralities of men and women and that systematized and mercenary immorality epitomized in the statute's graphic phrase "white slave traffic." And it was such immorality that was in the legislative mind, and not the other. The other is occasional, not habitual,—inconspicuous,—does not offensively obtrude upon public notice. Interstate commerce is not its instrument as it is of the other, nor is prostitution its object or its end. It may, indeed, in instances, find a convenience in crossing state lines, but this is its accident, not its aid.

There is danger in extending a statute beyond its purpose, even if justified by a strict adherence to its words. The purpose is studied, all effects measured, not left at random,—one evil practice prevented, opportunity given to another. The present case warns against ascribing such improvidence to the statute under review. Blackmailers of both sexes have arisen, using the terrors of the construction now sanctioned by this court as a help—indeed, the means—for their brigandage. The result is grave and should give us pause. It certainly will not be denied that legal authority justifies the rejection of a construction which leads to mischievous consequences, if the statute be susceptible of another construction. . . .

NOTES

Although the objective of the legislatures is to state precisely the meaning of the expressions contained in their codes and statutes, the courts are often required to attempt clarification in litigated cases. Following are several illustrations of the basic problem.

1. A federal statute prohibits interstate travel with intent to carry on "extortion" in violation of the laws of the state in which it is committed. X and Y entered the state of Pennsylvania for the purpose of "shaking down" homosexuals, by getting wealthy persons with homosexual interests into compromising situations and threatening to expose them unless certain sums of money were given to X and Y.

In Pennsylvania an offense of this type is "blackmail"; a separate statute deals with "extortion," but its coverage is confined to activities involving public officials.

Does the Pennsylvania differentiation between "blackmail" and "extortion" render the federal statute inapplicable to X and Y?

In United States v. Nardello, 393 U.S. 286, 89 S.Ct. 534 (1969), the Supreme Court held that the federal statute was designed to be of material assistance to the States in combatting pernicious undertakings which cross state lines, and it was not Congress' intention to limit its coverage to state classifications. The Court pointed out that many states prohibit such conduct by various designations such as theft, coercion, and even robbery. In any event "extortion" covers "shakedown" activities as here involved.

2. An Arizona statute provided as follows:

"A person is guilty of a misdemeanor who:

"1. Writes, composes, prints, publishes, sells, distributes, keeps for sale, gives, loans or exhibits an obscene or indecent writing, paper or book to any person, or designs, copies, draws, engraves, paints or otherwise prepares an obscene or indecent picture or print. * * *"

The defendant in State v. Locks, 91 Ariz. 394, 372 P.2d 724 (1962), was charged with its violation by "wilfully and unlawfully" keeping for sale, selling and exhibiting obscene and indecent pictures and written materials. He contended that the statute was unconstitutional because of the lack of a "scienter" requirement in the statute—in other words it did not provide for proof of guilty knowledge that the materials were indeed obscene.

In upholding the defendant's conviction the Arizona Supreme Court said:

"If, as defendant here contends, the Arizona obscenity statute is in fact without the scienter requirement, then the statute must fall. . . . However, the Supreme Court of the United States has often recognized '* * * the basic constitutional principle that the construction of state laws is the exclusive responsibility of the state courts. * * *'

"The principal device employed . . . in saving [a statute] has been the rule that whenever possible a statute should be construed as to render it constitutional. Representative of this approach is the opinion in Demetropoulos v. Commonwealth [342 Mass. 658, 175 N.E.2d 259 (1961)]. * * *

"On the other hand the Supreme Courts of Indiana, Missouri, and Washington have struck down statutes similar to [our statute].

"We choose to follow the lead of the majority of those courts which have ruled on this question and construe [our statute] as impliedly requiring scienter. * * *

"Accordingly, we hold that the element of scienter is implicit in the Arizona obscenity statute; [it] must be read as if prefaced by 'whoever wilfully and knowingly'; and that 'knowingly' means with knowledge of the obscene nature of the materials involved."

3. With regard to the general principles governing the interpretation of criminal statutes, consider the views of Professor Livingston Hall in his article "Strict or Liberal Construction of Penal Statutes", 48 Harv.L.Rev. 748 (1935):

I. Introduction

"Doctrines of strict or liberal construction have a peculiarly important place in the interpretation of criminal statutes. The extraordinary vitality of the old common-law rule of strict construction, statutes in about a third of the states substituting more liberal rules of construction in place of the common-law rule, and the absence of other guides to the 'intent of the legislature' in so many cases, unite to contribute to the influence of such doctrines at the present time. . . .

"Undoubtedly precedent—the hundreds of cases stating and usually applying the common-law rule of strict construction of penal statutes—is one of the most powerful forces shaping the attitude of the courts today toward this problem. . . . [However,] the unrestrained application of this rule, particularly in regard to the extreme technicality invoked to find an 'ambiguity' which would call for its application, led to the formulation . . . of a counter-irritant, thus stated by Chief Justice Marshall: '. . . though penal laws are to be construed strictly, they are not to be construed so strictly as to defeat the obvious intention of the legislature. . . . The intention of the legislature is to be collected from the words they employ. Where there is no ambiguity in the words, there is no room for construction. . . .

"The numerous examples of legislative frustration which the common-law rule produced finally led to direct action by the legislatures of many states to overthrow, in whole or in part, the older rule . . . Various types of statutes were tried. The most common . . . specifically abrogates the common-law rule of strict construction, providing instead that all penal statutes 'are to be construed according to the fair import of their terms, with a view to effect their objects and to promote justice'. . . . Another type of statute, without specifically abrogating the old rule, provides that statutes shall be 'liberally construed', either to carry out 'the true intent and meaning of the legislature' . . . or 'with a view to effecting their objects and promoting justice'. . . .

II. The Rationale of the Legal Rules

"*For Strict Construction.* Potentially the most serious argument is that the rule is founded 'on the plain principle that the power of punishment is vested in the legislative, not in the judicial department.' For if this were true, a liberal construction statute would be an unconstitutional delegation of legislative power to the judiciary. But this objection is clearly unsound. Liberal construction does not involve going beyond the intention of the legislature. . . . Where liberal construction statutes have been passed, courts have never raised this objection to their enforcement. . . .

"It has further been claimed that as the state makes the laws, they should be most strongly construed against it. But the contract analogy is weak, for the state is presumably acting in the public interest in enacting criminal statutes, and need not in every case be subjected to a rule of interpretation designed to secure justice between private parties. . . .

"Obviously, the original reason for the growth of this rule, to mitigate the extension of capital felonies, no longer applies to all penal statutes; . . . this has often been recognized in states where the rule has been abrogated. . . .

"There remains for consideration only Mr. Justice Holmes' statement in McBoyle v. United States [1] that it is 'reasonable' for penal statutes to be construed to give 'fair warning' of 'what the law intends to do if a certain line is passed' in language 'that the common world will understand'. Why such a warning should be needed in murder and theft, two crimes as to which Mr. Justice Holmes himself admits that 'it is not likely that a criminal will carefully consider the text of the law before he murders or steals,' or especially in transporting stolen property, as in the McBoyle case itself, . . . is far from self-evident. Even if 'fair warning' had been called for in the particular case, as it undoubtedly is in many crimes, it was unnecessary to lay down a general rule. Simply because a liberal construction might work injustice in some cases is no proper reason for inflicting on the people the rule of strict construction in all cases.

"*For Liberal Construction.* The argument for liberal construction of nonpenal statutes has been put forcibly by Dean Pound nearly 20 years ago in an article concluding: 'The public cannot be relied upon permanently to tolerate judicial obstruction or nullification of the social policies to which more and more it is compelled to be committed.' [2] This argument is equally applicable to penal statutes, except insofar as 'political liberty requires clear and exact definition of the offense.' The public is already impatient with the refined, and for practical purposes unnecessary, distinctions embodied in the penal codes. Strict construction of . . . statutes has completed the degradation of the

1. 283 U.S. 25, 51 S.Ct. 340 (1931). The Court held that an airplane was not "an automobile, automobile truck, automobile wagon, motorcycle, or any other self-propelled vehicle not running on rails" and hence did not come under the National Motor Vehicle Theft Act, . . .

2. Pound, Common Law and Legislation, 21 Harv.L.Rev. 383, 407 (1908).

substantive criminal law [in the mind of the average man]. . . . An attitude of liberal construction goes far, on the other hand, to make the law appear rational. . . .

III. Guides to Rational Construction

"The conclusions which may be drawn from the foregoing are twofold: first, that there is no sound reason for a general doctrine of strict construction of penal statutes, and *prima facie* all such should have as liberal a construction as statutes generally, and second, that certain penal statutes should be strictly construed to avoid injustice. These exceptions range themselves into a few fairly well defined categories.

"*Effect of a Disproportionate Penalty.* A statute imposing a penalty which the court regards as disproportionately heavy for the acts committed can hardly escape a strict construction. . . . [T]he history of the past four hundred years has amply proved that under such circumstances courts, juries, and even prosecutors will cooperate to defeat a clearly avowed 'legislative will' by any available means.

. . . It would serve only to perpetuate an unnecessary conflict between principle and decision to ignore this tendency; hence, a cautious modification of the rule of liberal construction here seems proper. . . .

"*Effect of Honest Attempt at Compliance.* Where an honest attempt is commonly made by those to whom the law applies to ascertain the precise limits of the legal sanction imposed, particularly in the regulation of business practices for the social welfare, indefiniteness is usually fatal to the enforcement of the law. It is unfair to those affected to inflict punishment, which is *ex post facto* by nature, for acts whose criminality was not readily apparent before the commission of the crime, where the honest motives of the defendant cannot be questioned, as is true in many crimes.. . . .

"It is difficult to lay down a practical guide defining this class of crime. . . . The gist of this exception is the tendency of a liberal construction to mislead persons acting in good faith and honestly attempting to comply with the law, and a general exception in these terms should prove sufficient.

"*Effect of Changed Conditions.* The spasmodic attempt to enforce old legislation which is inapplicable to changed social or economic conditions presents another instance in which the doctrine of strict construction provides some measure of needed protection against administrative tyranny. The dead hand of the past, where it bars rather than leads social progress, must be narrowly limited in scope until outright repeal becomes possible. . . .

"Strict construction of statutes inapplicable because of changed social or economic conditions does not do violence to the intent of the legislature in the true sense. Although usually perpetual in form, statutes are passed in the light of conditions at the time, and there would seem no proper ground for inferring that the legislators of one generation ever intended to insist upon a broad interpretation of their statutes where they run clearly contrary to the social and economic policies of a subsequent generation.

IV. Reform of the Present Rules

"If the foregoing argument is sound, there is urgent need of reform in the construction of penal statutes. . . .

"Undoubtedly the most effective way to secure reform in this field, as in most others, is by new legislation. The whole problem of statutory interpretation calls for the finest exercise of judgment, and the standards to be applied are necessarily somewhat indefinite. About all that can be done is to free the courts from the binding force of the old rule and lay down a rule of liberal construction sufficiently flexible to allow them to avoid the injustice occasionally inherent in such a rule without having to violate the legislative standard to do so.

"The following form of statute is offered as a suggested model:

'Sec. 1. The rule of the common law that penal statutes shall be strictly construed shall not apply to any penal statute now in force or hereafter enacted in this state. All such statutes shall be construed liberally, without regard to any distinction between the construction of penal and nonpenal statutes, except as specifically provided in Section 2 of this Act.

'Sec. 2. A penal statute may be construed strictly where such construction is necessary (1) to make the words of the statute not misleading to persons acting in good faith and honestly attempting to comply with all provisions of the law regulating their conduct; or (2) to prevent the imposition of a penalty which is so disproportionate to other penalties imposed by law or which is so clearly inappropriate in view of changed social or economic conditions in the state that it is reasonable to believe that the legislature did not intend such a result.' "

3. ADMINISTRATIVE REGULATIONS

UNITED STATES v. GRIMAUD

Supreme Court of the United States, 1911.
220 U.S. 506, 31 S.Ct. 480.

MR. JUSTICE LAMAR delivered the opinion of the court.

The defendants were indicted for grazing sheep on the Sierra Forest Reserve without having obtained the permission required by the regulations adopted by the Secretary of Agriculture. They demurred on the ground that the Forest Reserve Act of 1891 was unconstitutional, in so far as it delegated to the Secretary of Agriculture power to make rules and regulations and made a violation thereof a penal offense. Their several demurrers were sustained. The Government brought the case here under that clause of the Criminal Appeals Act . . . which allows a writ of error where the "decision complained of was based upon the invalidity of the statute."

The Federal courts have been divided on the question as to whether violations of those regulations of the Secretary of Agriculture constitute a crime.

From the various acts relating to the establishment and management of forest reservations it appears that they were intended "to improve and protect the forest and to secure favorable conditions of water flows." It was declared that the acts should not be "construed to prohibit the egress and ingress of actual settlers" residing therein nor "to prohibit any person from entering the reservation for all proper and lawful purposes, including that of prospecting, and locating and developing mineral resources; provided that such persons comply with the rules and regulations covering such forest reservation." It was also declared that the Secretary "may make such rules and regulations and establish such service as will insure the objects of such reservation, namely, to regulate their occupancy and use and to preserve the forests thereon from destruction; *and any violation of the provisions of this act or such rules and regulations shall be punished*" . . . [by a fine of not more than five hundred dollars and imprisonment for not more than twelve months or both, at the discretion of the court].

Under these acts, therefore, any use of the reservation for grazing or other lawful purpose was required to be subject to the rules and regulations established by the Secretary of Agriculture. To pasture sheep and cattle on the reservation, at will and without restraint, might interfere seriously with the accomplishment of the purposes for which they were established. But a limited and regulated use for pasturage might not be inconsistent with the object sought to be attained by the statute. The determination of such questions, however, was a matter of administrative detail. What might be harmless in one forest might be harmful to another. What might be injurious at one stage of timber growth, or at one season of the year, might not be so at another.

In the nature of things it was impracticable for Congress to provide general regulations for these various and varying details of management. Each reservation had its peculiar and special features; and in authorizing the Secretary of Agriculture to meet these local conditions Congress was merely conferring administrative functions upon an agent, and not delegating to him legislative power. The authority actually given was much less than what has been granted to municipalities by virtue of which they make by-laws, ordinances and regulations for the government of towns and cities. Such ordinances do not declare general rules with reference to rights of persons and property, nor do they create or regulate obligations and liabilities, nor declare what shall be crimes nor fix penalties therefor.

By whatever name they are called they refer to matters of local management and local police. . . . They are "not of legislative character in the highest sense of the term; and as an owner may delegate to his principal agent the right to employ subordinates, giving them a limited discretion, so it would seem that Congress might rightfully entrust to the local legislature [authorities] the determination of minor matters.". . .

It must be admitted that it is difficult to define the line which separates legislative power to make laws, from administrative authority to make regulations. This difficulty has often been recognized, and was referred to by Chief Justice Marshall in Wayman v. Southard, . . ., where he was considering the authority of courts to make rules. He there said: "It will not be contended that Congress can delegate to the courts, or to any other tribunals, powers which are strictly and exclusively legislative. But Congress may certainly delegate to others, powers which the legislature may rightfully exercise itself." What were these non-legislative powers which Congress *could* exercise but which might also be delegated to others was not determined, for he said: "The line has not been exactly drawn which separates those important subjects, which *must* be entirely regulated by the legislature itself, from those of less interest, in which a general provision may be made, and power given to those who are to act under such general provisions to fill up the details."

From the beginning of the Government various acts have been passed conferring upon executive officers power to make rules and regulations—not for the government of their departments, but for administering the laws which did govern. None of these statutes could confer legislative power. But when Congress had legislated and indicated its will, it could give to those who were to act under such general provisions "power to fill up the details" by the establishment of administrative rules and regulations, the violation of which could be punished by fine or imprisonment fixed by Congress, or by penalties fixed by Congress or measured by the injury done.

Thus it is unlawful to charge unreasonable rates or to discriminate between shippers, and the Interstate Commerce Commission has been given authority to make reasonable rates and to administer the law against discrimination. . . . Congress provided that after a given date only cars with drawbars of uniform height should be used in interstate commerce, and then constitutionally left to the Commission the administrative duty of fixing a uniform standard. . . . In Union Bridge Co. v. United States, 204 U.S. 364, 27 S.Ct. 367; In re Kollock, 165 U.S. 526, 17 S.Ct. 444; Buttfield v. Stranahan, 192 U.S. 470, 24 S.Ct. 349, it appeared from the statutes involved that Congress had either expressly or by necessary implication made it unlawful, if not criminal, to obstruct navigable streams; to sell unbranded oleomargarine; or to import unwholesome teas. With this unlawfulness as a predicate the executive officers were authorized to make rules and regulations appropriate to the several matters covered by the various acts. A violation of these rules was then made an offense punishable as prescribed by Congress. But in making these regulations the officers did not legislate. They did not go outside of the circle of that which the act itself had affirmatively required to be done, or treated as unlawful if done. But confining themselves within the field covered by the statute they could adopt regulations of the nature they had thus been generally authorized to make, in order to administer the law and carry the statute into effect.

The defendants rely on United States v. Eaton, . . ., where the act authorized the Commissioner to make rules for carrying the statute into effect, but imposed no penalty for failure to observe his regulations. Another section (5) required that the dealer should keep books showing certain facts, and providing that he should conduct his business under such surveillance of officers as the Commissioner might by regulation require. Another section declared that if any dealer should knowingly omit to do any of the things "required by law" he should pay a penalty of a thousand dollars. Eaton failed to keep the books required by the regulations. But there was no charge that he omitted "anything required by law," unless it could be held that the books called for by the regulations were "required by law." The court construed the act as a whole and proceeded on the theory that while a violation of the regulations might have been punished as an offense if Congress had so enacted, it had, in fact, made no such provision so far as concerned the particular charge then under consideration. Congress required the dealer to keep books rendering return of materials and products, but imposed no penalty for failing so to do. The Commissioner went much further and required the dealer to keep books showing oleomargarine received, from whom received and to whom the same was sold. It was sought to punish the defendant for failing to keep the books required by the regulations. Manifestly this was putting the regulations above the statute. The court showed that when Congress enacted that a certain sort of book should be kept, the Commissioner could not go further and require additional books; or, if he did make such regulation, there was no provision in the statute by which a failure to comply therewith could be punished. It said that, "if Congress intended to make it an offense for wholesale dealers to omit to keep books and render returns required by regulations of the Commissioner, it would have done so distinctly"—implying that if it had done so distinctly the violation of the regulations would have been an offense.

But the very thing which was omitted in the Oleomargarine Act has been distinctly done in the Forest Reserve Act, which, in terms, provides that "any violation of the provisions of this act or such rules and regulations of the Secretary shall be punished as prescribed in section 5388 of the Revised Statutes as amended." * * *

It is true that there is no act of Congress which, in express terms, declares that it shall be unlawful to graze sheep on a forest reserve. But the statutes, from which we have quoted, declare, that the privilege of using reserves for "all proper and lawful purposes" is subject to the proviso that the person so using them shall comply "with the rules and regulations covering such forest reservation." The same act makes it an offense to violate those regulations, that is, to use them otherwise than in accordance with the rules established by the Secretary.. . . .

If, after the passage of the act and the promulgation of the rule, the defendants drove and grazed their sheep upon the reserve, in violation of the regulations, they were making an unlawful use of the Government's property. In doing so they thereby made themselves liable to the penalty imposed by Congress. * * *

The Secretary of Agriculture could not make rules and regulations for any and every purpose. As to those here involved, they all relate to matters clearly indicated and authorized by Congress. The subjects as to which the Secretary can regulate are defined. The lands are set apart as a forest reserve. He is required to make provision to protect them from depredations and from harmful uses. He is authorized "to regulate the occupancy and use and to preserve the forests from destruction." A violation of reasonable rules regulating the use and occupancy of the property is made a crime, not by the Secretary, but by Congress. The statute, not the Secretary, fixes the penalty.

The indictment charges, and the demurrer admits, that Rule 45 was promulgated for the purpose of regulating the occupancy and use of the public forest reservation and preserving the forest. The Secretary did not exercise the legislative power of declaring the penalty or fixing the punishment for grazing sheep without a permit, but the punishment is imposed by the act itself. The offense is not against the Secretary, but, as the indictment properly concludes, "contrary to the laws of the United States and the peace and dignity thereof." The demurrers should have been overruled. The affirmances by a divided court heretofore entered are set aside and the judgments in both cases

Reversed.

NOTES

1. Suppose that the statute provided that a violation of an administrative regulation should be a crime, but left it to the agency to determine the penalty? Would it make a difference if the legislature provided a *maximum* penalty, but authorized the agency to impose a lesser one? See Zuber v. Southern Railway Co., 9 Ga.App. 539, 71 S.E. 937 (1911); Schwenk, The Administrative Crime, Its Creation And Punishment By Administrative Agencies, 42 Mich.L.Rev. 51 (1943).

2. On the question of the construction of administrative regulations which define and punish a criminal offense, consider the following:

"This delegation to the Price Administrator of the power to provide in detail against circumvention and evasion, as to which Congress has imposed criminal sanctions, creates a grave responsibility. In a very literal sense the liberties and fortunes of others may depend upon his definitions and specifications regarding evasion. Hence to these provisions must be applied the same strict rule of construction that is applied to statutes defining criminal action. In other words, the Administrator's provisions must be explicit and unambiguous in order to sustain a criminal prosecution; they must adequately inform those who are subject to their terms what conduct will be considered evasive so as to bring the criminal penalties of the Act into operation. . . . The dividing line between unlawful evasion and lawful action cannot be left to conjecture. The elements of evasive conduct should be so clearly expressed by the Administrator that the ordinary person can know in advance how to avoid an unlawful course of action. * * * A prosecutor in framing an indictment, a court in interpreting the Administrator's regulations or a jury in judging guilt cannot supply that which the Administrator failed to do by express word or fair implication. Not even the Administrator's interpretation of his own regulations can cure an omission or add certainty and definiteness to otherwise vague language. The prohibited conduct must, for criminal purposes, be set forth with clarity in the regulations and orders which he is authorized by Congress to promulgate under the Act. Congress has warned the public to look to that source alone to discover what conduct is evasive and hence likely to create criminal liability." M. Kraus & Bros., Inc. v. United States, 327 U.S. 614, 621–22, 66 S.Ct. 705, 707–08 (1946).

4. THE FEDERAL–STATE DICHOTOMY

(a) THE CONSTITUTION AND FEDERAL "COMMON LAW"

*   *   *

ARTICLE I

Section 1. All legislative Powers herein granted shall be vested in a Congress of the United States, which shall consist of a Senate and House of Representatives.

*   *   *

Section 8. The Congress shall have Power To lay and collect Taxes, Duties, Imposts and Excises, to pay the Debts and provide for the common Defence and general Welfare of the United States; but all Duties, Imposts and Excises shall be uniform throughout the United States;

To borrow Money on the credit of the United States;

To regulate Commerce with foreign Nations, and among the several States, and with the Indian Tribes;

To establish an uniform Rule of Naturalization, and uniform Laws on the subject of Bankruptcies throughout the United States;

To coin Money, regulate the Value thereof, and of foreign Coin, and fix the Standard of Weights and Measures;

To provide for the Punishment of counterfeiting the Securities and current Coin of the United States;

To establish Post Offices and post Roads; *   *   *

To define and punish Piracies and Felonies committed on the high Seas, and Offences against the Law of Nations;

To declare War, grant Letters of Marque and Reprisal, and make Rules concerning Captures on Land and Water;

To raise and support Armies, but no Appropriation of Money to that Use shall be for a longer Term than two Years;

To provide and maintain a Navy;

To make Rules for the Government and Regulation of the land and naval Forces; *   *   *

To exercise exclusive Legislation in all Cases whatsoever, over such District (not exceeding ten Miles square) as may, by Cession of particular States, and the Acceptance of Congress, become the Seat of the Government of the United States, and to exercise like Authority over all Places purchased by the Consent of the Legislature of the State in which the Same shall be, for the Erection of Forts, Magazines, Arsenals, dock-Yards, and other needful Buildings;—And

To make all Laws which shall be necessary and proper for carrying into Execution the foregoing Powers, and all other Powers vested by this Constitution in the Government of the United States, or in any Department or Officer thereof. * * *

ARTICLE [XIV]

Section 1. All persons born or naturalized in the United States, and subject to the jurisdiction thereof, are citizens of the United States and of the State wherein they reside. No State shall make or enforce any law which shall abridge the privileges or immunities of citizens of the United States; nor shall any State deprive any person of life, liberty, or property, without due process of law; nor deny to any person within its jurisdiction the equal protection of the laws.
    * * *
Section 5. The Congress shall have power to enforce, by appropriate legislation, the provisions of this article.

THE UNITED STATES v. HUDSON AND GOODWIN
Supreme Court of the United States, 1812.
11 U.S. (7 Cranch) 32.

This was a case certified from the Circuit Court for the District of *Connecticut,* in which, upon argument of a general demurrer to an *indictment* for a libel on the President and Congress of the United States, contained in the *Connecticut Courant,* of the 7th of May, 1806, charging them with having in secret voted two millions of dollars as a present to Bonaparte for leave to make a treaty with Spain, the judges of that Court were divided in opinion upon the question, *whether the Circuit Court of the United States had a common law jurisdiction in cases of libel.*

The Court having taken time to consider, the following opinion was delivered (on the last day of the term, all the judges being present) by JOHNSON, J.

The only question which this case presents is, whether the Circuit Courts of the United States can exercise a common law jurisdiction in criminal cases. We state it thus broadly because a decision on a case of libel will apply to every case in which jurisdiction is not vested in those courts by statute.

Although this question is brought up now for the first time to be decided by this Court, we consider it as having been long since settled in public opinion. In no other case for many years has this jurisdiction been asserted; and the general acquiescence of legal men shews the prevalence of opinion in favor of the negative of the proposition.

The course of reasoning which leads to this conclusion is simple, obvious, and admits of but little illustration. The powers of the general Government are made up of concessions from the several states— whatever is not expressly given to the former, the latter expressly reserve. The judicial power of the United States is a constituent part of those concessions—that power is to be exercised by Courts organized for the purpose, and brought into existence by an effort of the legislative power of the Union. Of all the Courts which the United States may, under their general powers, constitute, one only, the Supreme Court, possesses jurisdiction derived immediately from the Constitution, and of which the legislative power cannot deprive it. All other Courts created by the general Government possess no jurisdiction but what is given them by the power that creates them, and can be vested with none but what the power ceded to the general Government will authorize them to confer.

It is not necessary to inquire whether the general Government, in any and what extent, possesses the power of conferring on its Courts a jurisdiction in cases similar to the present; it is enough that such jurisdiction has not been conferred by any legislative act, if it does not result to those Courts as a consequence of their creation.

And such is the opinion of a majority of this court: For, the power which Congress possess to create Courts of inferior jurisdiction, necessarily implies the power to limit the jurisdiction of those Courts to particular objects; and when a Court is created, and its operations confined to certain specific objects, with what propriety can it assume to itself a jurisdiction—much more extended—in its nature very indefinite—applicable to a great variety of subjects—varying in every State in the Union—and with regard to which there exists no definite criterion of distribution between the district and Circuit Courts of the same district?

The only ground on which it has ever been contended that this jurisdiction could be maintained is, that, upon the formation of any political body, an implied power to preserve its own existence and promote the end and object of its creation, necessarily results to it. But, without examining how far this consideration is applicable to the peculiar character of our constitution, it may be remarked that it is a principle by no means peculiar to the common law. It is coeval, probably, with the first formation of a limited Government; belongs to a system of universal law, and may as well support the assumption of many other powers as those more peculiarly acknowledged by the common law of England.

But if admitted as applicable to the state of things in this country, the consequence would not result from it which is here contended for. If it may communicate certain implied powers to the general Government, it would not follow that the Courts of that Government are vested with jurisdiction over any particular act done by an individual in supposed violation of the peace and dignity of the sovereign power.

The legislative authority of the Union must first make an act a crime, affix a punishment to it, and declare the Court that shall have jurisdiction of the offence.

Certain implied powers must necessarily result to our Courts of justice from the nature of their institution. But jurisdiction of crimes against the state is not among those powers. To fine for contempt— imprison for contumacy—inforce the observance of order, &c. are powers which cannot be dispensed with in a Court, because they are necessary to the exercise of all others: and so far our Courts no doubt possess powers not immediately derived from statute; but all exercise of criminal law cases we are of opinion is not within their implied powers.

(b) DIRECT FEDERAL INTEREST OFFENSES

SONZINSKY v. UNITED STATES

Supreme Court of the United States, 1937.
300 U.S. 506, 57 S.Ct. 554.

MR. JUSTICE STONE delivered the opinion of the Court.

The question for decision is whether § 2 of the National Firearms Act of June 26, 1934, . . . 26 U.S.C.A., §§ 1132–1132q, which imposes a $200 annual license tax on dealers in firearms, is a constitutional exercise of the legislative power of Congress.

Petitioner was convicted by the District Court for Eastern Illinois on two counts of an indictment, the first charging him with violation of § 2, by dealing in firearms without payment of the tax. On appeal the Court of Appeals set aside the conviction on the second count and affirmed on the first. 86 F.2d 486. On petition of the accused we granted certiorari, limited to the question of the constitutional validity of the statute in its application under the first count in the indictment.

Section 2 of the National Firearms Act requires every dealer in firearms to register with the Collector of Internal Revenue in the district where he carries on business, and to pay a special excise tax of $200 a year. Importers or manufacturers are taxed $500 a year. Section 3 imposes a tax of $200 on each transfer of a firearm, payable by the transferor, and § 4 prescribes regulations for the identification of purchases. The term "firearm" is defined by § 1 as meaning a shotgun or a rifle having a barrel less than eighteen inches in length, or any other weapon, except a pistol or revolver, from which a shot is discharged by an explosive, if capable of being concealed on the person, or a machine gun, and includes a muffler or silencer for any firearm.

* * *

In the exercise of its constitutional power to lay taxes, Congress may select the subjects of taxation, choosing some and omitting others. . . . Its power extends to the imposition of excise taxes upon the doing of business. . . . Petitioner does not deny that Congress may tax his business as a dealer in firearms. He insists that the present levy is not a true tax, but a penalty imposed for the purpose of suppressing traffic in a certain noxious type of firearms, the local regulation of which is reserved to the states because not granted to the national government. To establish its penal and prohibitive character, he relies on the amounts of the tax imposed by § 2 on dealers, manufacturers and importers, and of the tax imposed by § 3 on each transfer of a "firearm," payable by the transferor. The cumulative effect on the distribution of a limited class of firearms, of relatively small value, by the successive imposition of different taxes, one on the business of the importer or manufacturer, another on that of the dealer, and a third on the transfer to a buyer, is said to be prohibitive in effect and to disclose unmistakably the legislative purpose to regulate rather than to tax.

The case is not one where the statute contains regulatory provisions related to a purported tax in such a way as has enabled this Court to say in other cases that the latter is a penalty resorted to as a means of enforcing the regulations. . . . Nor is the subject of the tax described or treated as criminal by the taxing statute. . . . Here § 2 contains no regulation other than the mere registration provisions, which are obviously supportable as in aid of a revenue purpose. On its face it is only a taxing measure, and we are asked to say that the tax, by virtue of its deterrent effect on the activities taxed, operates as a regulation which is beyond the congressional power.

Every tax is in some measure regulatory. To some extent it interposes an economic impediment to the activity taxed as compared with others not taxed. But a tax is not any the less a tax because it has a regulatory effect, . . . and it has long been established that an Act of Congress which on its face purports to be an exercise of the taxing power is not any the less so because the tax is burdensome or tends to restrict or suppress the thing taxed. . . .

Inquiry into the hidden motives which may move Congress to exercise a power constitutionally conferred upon it is beyond the competency of courts. . . . They will not undertake, by collateral inquiry as to the measure of the regulatory effect of a tax, to ascribe to Congress an attempt, under the guise of taxation, to exercise another power denied by the Federal Constitution. . . .

Here the annual tax of $200 is productive of some revenue.[1] We are not free to speculate as to the motives which moved Congress to impose it, or as to the extent to which it may operate to restrict the activities taxed. As it is not attended by an offensive regulation, and since it operates as a tax, it is within the national taxing power. . . .

Affirmed.

1. The $200 tax was paid by 27 dealers in 1934, and by 22 dealers in 1935. Annual Report of the Commissioner of Internal Revenue, Fiscal Year Ended June 30, 1935, pp. 129–131; id., Fiscal Year Ended June 30, 1936, pp. 139–141.

NOTE

The judiciary has taken the position that, given the broad grant of constitutional power vested in Congress to collect taxes, it will not restrain an exercise of the taxing power because of the onerous and burdensome results to taxpayers. McCray v. United States, 195 U.S. 27, 24 S.Ct. 769 (1904). Congress, not the courts, has the right to select the objects of taxation and the measures for implementing the collection process. Thus, without inquiring into the reasons underlying Congress' decision to select a particular subject for taxation the courts will not limit any tax unless there are provisions in the tax statute extraneous to a constitutionally authorized taxing need. United States v. Kahriger, 345 U.S. 22, 73 S.Ct. 510 (1953).

In this manner, the courts have recognized Congress' power to collect taxes whether the business involved is lawful or unlawful, Wainer v. United States, 299 U.S. 92, 57 S.Ct. 79 (1936), although the method of reporting the income subject to taxation may generate Fifth Amendment self incrimination problems. See Marchetti v. United States, 390 U.S. 39, 88 S.Ct. 697 (1968). Consequently, the taxing power has been upheld in a wide variety of situations. E.g., United States v. Singer, 82 U.S. (15 Wall.) 111 (1872) (distilled spirits); United States v. Gullett, 322 F.Supp. 272 (D.Colo.1971) (transfer of firearms); United States v. Gross, 313 F.Supp. 1330 (D.Ind.1970), affirmed 451 F.2d 1355 (7th Cir. 1971) (firearms dealers). But compare Harper v. Virginia State Bd. of Elections, 383 U.S. 663, 86 S.Ct. 1079 (1966) (state poll tax unconstitutional).

UNITED STATES v. SHARPNACK

Supreme Court of the United States, 1958.
355 U.S. 286, 78 S.Ct. 291.

MR. JUSTICE BURTON delivered the opinion of the Court. The issue in this case is whether the Assimilative Crimes Act of 1948 . . . is constitutional insofar as it makes applicable to a federal enclave a subsequently enacted criminal law of the State in which the enclave is situated. For the reasons hereafter stated, we hold that it is constitutional.

* * *

The 1948 Assimilative Crimes Act was enacted . . . and reads as follows:

"§ 13. Laws of States adopted for areas within Federal jurisdiction.

"Whoever within or upon any of the places now existing or hereafter reserved or acquired . . . is guilty of any act not made punishable by any enactment of Congress, would be punishable if committed or omitted within the jurisdiction of the State, Territory, Possession, or District in which such place is situated, by the laws thereof in force at the time of such act or omission, shall be guilty of a like offense and subject to a like punishment." . . .

In the absence of restriction in the cessions of the respective enclaves to the United States, the power of Congress to exercise legislative jurisdiction over them is clearly stated in Article I, § 8, cl. 17, and Article IV, § 3, cl. 2, of the Constitution.[1] . . . The first Federal Crimes Act, enacted in 1790, . . . defined a number of federal crimes and referred to federal enclaves. The need for dealing more extensively with criminal offenses in the enclaves was evident, and one natural solution was to adopt for each enclave the offenses made punishable by the State in which it was situated. . . .

* * *

The application of the Assimilative Crimes Act to subsequently adopted state legislation, under the limitations here prescribed, is a reasonable exercise of congressional legislative power and discretion.

[The majority's reasons in support of the decision and the opposing views of the dissent have been omitted. The differences only concerned the constitutionality of the law as it relates to subsequently enacted state legislation. In the casebook our only objective is to acquaint students with the existence of the Assimilative Crimes Act.]

(c) The "Necessary and Proper" Offenses

In conjunction with the specific authority to create laws in a number of enumerated areas, the Necessary and Proper clause of the Constitution, U.S. Const. Art. 1, § 8, cl. 18, provides Congress with the power to legislate in areas that will facilitate the execution of the powers vested in the federal government. In Logan v. United States, 144 U.S. 263, 12 S.Ct. 617 (1892), the Supreme Court recognized the applicability of this clause. There, taking cognizance of the propriety of the civil rights conspiracy statute, the Court upheld the right of federal authorities to protect prisoners in their custody:

> Among the powers which the Constitution expressly confers upon Congress is the power to make all laws necessary and proper for carrying into execution the powers specifically granted to it, and all other powers vested by the Constitution in the government of the United States, or in any department or officer thereof. In the exercise of this general power of legislation, Congress may use any means, appearing to it most eligible and appropriate, which are adapted to the end to be accomplished, and are consistent with the letter and the spirit of the Constitution.

> Although the Constitution contains no grant, general or specific, to Congress of the power to provide for the punishment of crimes, except piracies and felonies on the high seas, offences against the law of nations, treason, and counterfeiting the securities and current coin of the United States, no one doubts the power of Congress to provide for the punishment of

---

1. "The Congress shall have Power to dispose of and make all needful Rules and Regulations respecting the Territory or other Property belonging to the United States; and nothing in this Constitution shall be so construed as to Prejudice any Claims of the United States, or of any particular State." U.S. Const.

all crimes and offences against the United States, whether committed within one of the States of the Union, or within territory over which Congress has plenary and exclusive jurisdiction.

To accomplish this end, Congress has the right to enact laws for the arrest and commitment of those accused of any such crime or offence, and for holding them in safe custody until indictment and trial; and persons arrested and held pursuant to such laws are in the exclusive custody of the United States, and are not subject to the judicial process or executive warrant of any State. The United States, having the absolute right to hold such prisoners, have an equal duty to protect them, while so held, against assault or injury from any quarter. The existence of that duty on the part of the government necessarily implies a corresponding right of the prisoners to be so protected; and this right of the prisoners is a right secured to them by the Constitution and laws of the United States.

Therefore, notwithstanding the fact that the Constitution may not specifically grant Congress the power to regulate conduct in certain areas, where a given piece of legislation may be characterized as an incident of sovereignty which inheres in the government, it will be upheld under the Necessary and Proper Clause. Congress, thus, has the power to create, define and punish offenses whenever it is necessary and proper, by law, to do so to effectuate the objects of government.

UNITED STATES v. STATES

United States Court of Appeals, Eighth Circuit, 1973.
488 F.2d 761.

MATTHES, SENIOR CIRCUIT JUDGE. * * *

Before trial appellants moved to dismiss [their] indictment [under the mail fraud statute] asserting that it failed to allege that anyone had been defrauded of any money or property, and consequently failed to state an offense against the United States. . . . [After their motion was denied] appellants waived a jury and a bench trial resulted in their convictions. Their appeals challenge the court's action in entertaining the charge.

* * *

The indictment charges that the defendants devised a scheme to defraud the voters and residents of the third and nineteenth wards of the City of St. Louis and the Board of Election Commissioners of the City of St. Louis by the use of fraudulent voter registrations and applications for absentee ballots. It is alleged that the purpose of the scheme to defraud was to influence the outcome of the election of the Republican Committeeman for the nineteenth ward and the Democratic Committeeman for the third ward "for the purpose of securing and controlling said political offices and the political influence and financial benefits of said offices   *   *   *." It is further alleged that as part of the scheme to defraud, the defendants submitted false and fraudulent voter registration affidavits bearing the names of false and fictitious persons with false addresses and caused the St. Louis Board of Election Commissioners to place absentee ballots for the fictitious persons in an authorized depository for mail matter.

* * *

At the outset of their claim for reversal the appellants submit that the very language of 18 U.S.C.A. § 1341 mandates a holding that there is an offense under the statute only if money or property is involved in the scheme to defraud. Appellants argue that the first phrase of § 1341, dealing with "any scheme or artifice to defraud," must be read in conjunction with the second phrase, concerning "obtaining money or property by means of false or fraudulent pretenses, representations, or promises," which was added to the statute by a subsequent amendment.* Appellants suggest that the second phrase was added to the predecessor of § 1341 because Congress believed that the "scheme to defraud" language included only frauds perpetrated without misrepresentations. They argue that the explicit "money or property" limitation in the added passage reveals that Congress believed that the first phrase in the original legislation dealt only with schemes to defraud of money or property.

But no case or legislative history is cited by the appellants supporting such an interpretation of legislative intent, nor does there appear to be any authority justifying such a construction of the statute. Moreover, not only does the appellants' conjunctive construction of the two phrases place a very strained and limited meaning on the broad wording of the first phrase, but a reading of the statute as a whole reveals that the two phrases in question are part of an uninterrupted listing of a series of obviously diverse schemes which result in criminal sanctions if the mails are used. The more natural construction of the wording in the statute is to view the two phrases independently, rather than complementary of one another. Indeed, numerous courts have construed the "scheme or artifice to defraud" language of § 1341 without reference to the "obtaining money or property" phrase.

* * *

* § 1341. Frauds and swindles

Whoever, having devised or intending to devise any scheme or artifice to defraud, or for obtaining money or property by means of false or fraudulent pretenses, representations, or promises, or to sell, dispose of, loan, exchange, alter, give away, distribute, supply, or furnish or procure for unlawful use any counterfeit or spurious coin, obligation, security, or other article, or anything represented to be or intimated or held out to be such counterfeit or spurious article, for the purpose of executing such scheme or artifice or attempting to do so, places in any post office or authorized depository for mail matter, any matter or thing whatever to be sent or delivered by the Postal Service, or takes or receives therefrom, any such matter or thing, or knowingly causes to be delivered by mail according to the direction thereon, or at the place at which it is directed to be delivered by the person to whom it is addressed, any such matter or thing, shall be fined not more than $1,000 or imprisoned not more than five years, or both.

Consequently, we hold that the language of the statute on its face does not preclude a finding that a "scheme or artifice to defraud" need not concern money or property. Since the statutory wording itself does not conclusively resolve the issue presented by the appellants, and since the legislative history does not deal with the scope and meaning of the provision of the statute in issue, we examine judicial opinions construing § 1341 for assistance in definitely determining whether the statute should apply to the facts of this case.

Initially, it should be noted that the concept of fraud in § 1341 is to be construed very broadly. . . . In Blachly v. United States [380 F.2d 665 (5th Cir. 1967)], the court observed:

> 'The crime of mail fraud is broad in scope. * * * The fraudulent aspect of the scheme to 'defraud' is measured by a nontechnical standard. * * * Law puts its imprimatur on the accepted moral standards and condemns conduct which fails to match, the 'reflection of moral uprightness, of fundamental honesty, fair play and right dealing in the general and business life of the members of society.' This is indeed broad. For as Judge Holmes once observed, '[t]he law does not define fraud; it needs no definition. It is as old as falsehood and as versable as human ingenuity.' "

Likewise, the definition of fraud in § 1341 is to be broadly and liberally construed to further the purpose of the statute; namely, to prohibit the misuse of the mails to further fraudulent enterprises. Accordingly, many courts have construed the term "scheme or artifice to defraud" to include within its ambit widely diverse schemes. [For instance, a divorce mill granting decrees of questionable validity; bribery of public officials; bribery of an oil company employee to gain the company's geophysical maps; mailing an extortion note; and ballot tampering by election officials.] * * *

There are also cases concerning bribery schemes which support the view that money or tangible property need not be involved in the scheme to defraud in order for the mail fraud statute to be invoked. Beginning with Shushan v. United States, the term "scheme or artifice to defraud" [included] an operation to bribe and corrupt public officials in order to gain advantages and special treatment. In *Shushan* there is the implication that a scheme to gain personal favors from public officials is a scheme to defraud the public, although the interest lost by the public can be described no more concretely than as an intangible right to the proper and honest administration of government. "[T]here must be a purpose to do wrong which is inconsistent with moral uprightness." This concept, that a scheme to defraud of certain intangible rights is grounds for prosecution under § 1341 if the mails are used, is more explicitly stated in United States v. Faser . . . (1969). In *Faser,* the defendants were indicted under the mail fraud statute after they accepted bribes to deposit public funds in a certain bank. There, as here, the defendants contended the indictment failed to state an offense because it did not allege that someone was actually defrauded out of something tangible that can be measured in terms of money or property. In rejecting that argument the court specifically discussed whether a fraudulent scheme must entail money or property in order for there to be an offense under § 1341. As an alternative ground for overruling the motion to dismiss, the court stated:

> "[I]t is further the opinion of this Court that the thing out of which it is charged that the State was defrauded need not necessarily be that which can be measured in terms of money or property. It is the opinion of this Court that it is a violation of the statute in question if a person defrauds the State out of the 'loyal and faithful services of an employee.' * * *

> "Thus it seems quite clear that even if the thing out of which the State was allegedly defrauded was not susceptible of measurement in terms of money or physical property, a valid indictment may still result therefrom."

. . . In [a number of cases the courts have] upheld the mail fraud indictment on the ground that the mails had been used in a scheme to defraud a corporation of the "honest and faithful services" of one or more employees. . . . These cases serve as persuasive authority for the proposition that in a prosecution for use of the mails to further and execute a vote fraud scheme the indictment states an offense even though it does not contain allegations that anyone was defrauded of any property or money. Nevertheless, the appellants argue that the application of the mail fraud statute to the facts of this case will result in a "policing" of state election procedure, and that Congress has never explicitly authorized such widespread intervention into state affairs. The appellants' argument misinterprets the purpose of the mail fraud legislation. The focus of the statute is upon the misuse of the Postal Service, not the regulation of state affairs, and Congress clearly has the authority to regulate such misuse of the mails. [In Badders v. United States (1916), the court said:] "The overt act of putting a letter into the postoffice of the United States is a matter that Congress may regulate. * * * Whatever the limits to its power, it may forbid any such acts done in furtherance of a scheme it regards as contrary to public policy, whether it can forbid the scheme or not." The purpose of 18 U.S.C. § 1341 is to prevent the Postal Service from being used to carry out fraudulent schemes, regardless of what is the exact nature of the scheme and regardless of whether it happens to be forbidden by state law. . . . "Congress definitely intends that the misuse of the mails shall be controlled even though it be its policy to leave the control of elections to the several States."

The appellants' argument presents no justification for refusing to apply the mail fraud statutes to the facts of this case. The prosecution of appellants in federal court for mail fraud does not interfere with the state's enforcement of its election laws. There are no grounds for dismissing the indictment under the principles of comity or the abstention doctrine or under any other principle of federalism.

* * *

Affirmed.

ROSS, CIRCUIT JUDGE (concurring).

I reluctantly concur. The law, as capably expressed by Judge Matthes, leaves us no other alternative.

However, I cannot believe that it was the original intent of Congress that the Federal Government should take over the prosecution of every state crime involving fraud just because the mails have been used in furtherance of that crime. The facts in this case show that this election fraud was purely a state matter. It should have been prosecuted in state court. [The federal government's decision to prosecute this case] relieved the state of its duty to police the violation of its local election laws and helped create a precedent which will encourage the same sort of unwarranted federal preemption in the future.

(d) THE COMMERCE CLAUSE OFFENSES

PEREZ v. UNITED STATES

Supreme Court of the United States, 1971.
402 U.S. 146, 91 S.Ct. 1357.

MR. JUSTICE DOUGLAS delivered the opinion of the Court.

The question in this case is whether Title II of the Consumer Credit Protection Act, 18 U.S.C.A. § 891 et seq., as construed and applied to petitioner, is a permissible exercise by Congress of its powers under the Commerce Clause of the Constitution. Petitioner's conviction after trial by jury and his sentence were affirmed by the Court of Appeals, one judge dissenting. We granted the petition for a writ of certiorari because of the importance of the question presented. We affirm that judgment.

Petitioner is one of the species commonly known as "loan sharks" which Congress found are in large part under the control of "organized crime." [1] "Extortionate credit transactions" are defined as those char-

---

1. Section 201(a) of Title II contains the following findings by Congress:

"(1) Organized crime is interstate and international in character. Its activities involve many billions of dollars each year. It is directly responsible for murders, willful injuries to person and property, corruption of officials, and terrorization of countless citizens. A substantial part of the income of organized crime is generated by extortionate credit transactions.

"(2) Extortionate credit transactions are characterized by the use, or the express or implicit threat of the use, of violence or other criminal means to cause harm to person, reputation, or property as a means of enforcing repayment. Among the factors which have rendered past efforts at prosecution almost wholly ineffective has been the existence of exclusionary rules of evidence stricter than necessary for the protection of constitutional rights.

"(3) Extortionate credit transactions are carried on to a substantial extent in interstate and foreign commerce and through the means and instrumentalities of such commerce. Even where extortionate credit transactions are purely

acterized by the use or threat of the use of "violence or other criminal means" in enforcement.[2] There was ample evidence showing petitioner was a "loan shark" who used the threat of violence as a method of collection. He loaned money to one Miranda, owner of a new butcher shop, making a $1,000 advance to be repaid in installments of $105 per week for 14 weeks. After paying at this rate for six or eight weeks, petitioner increased the weekly payment to $130. In two months Miranda asked for an additional loan of $2,000 which was made, the agreement being that Miranda was to pay $205 a week. In a few weeks petitioner increased the weekly payment to $330. When Miranda objected, petitioner told him about a customer who refused to pay and ended up in a hospital. So Miranda paid. In a few months petitioner increased his demands to $500 weekly which Miranda paid, only to be advised that at the end of the week petitioner would need $1,000. Miranda made that payment by not paying his suppliers; but faced with a $1,000 payment the next week, he sold his butcher shop. Petitioner pursued Miranda, first making threats to Miranda's wife and then telling Miranda he could have him castrated. When Miranda did not make more payments, petitioner said he was turning over his collections to people who would not be nice but who would put him in the hospital if he did not pay. Negotiations went on, Miranda finally saying he could only pay $25 a week. Petitioner said that was not enough, that Miranda should steal or sell drugs if necessary to get the money to pay the loan, and that if he went to jail it would be better than going to a hospital with a broken back or legs. He added, "I could have sent you to the hospital, you and your family, any moment I want with my people."

Petitioner's arrest followed. Miranda, his wife and an employee gave the evidence against petitioner who did not testify or call any witnesses. Petitioner's attack was on the constitutionality of the Act, starting with a motion to dismiss the indictment.

The constitutional question is a substantial one.

Two "loan shark" amendments to the bill that became this Act were proposed in the House—one by Congressman Poff of Virginia, 114 Cong.Rec. 1605–1606 and another one by Congressman McDade of Pennsylvania. Id., at 1609–1610.

The House debates include a long article from the New York Times Magazine for January 28, 1968, on the connection between the "loan

intrastate in character, they nevertheless directly affect interstate and foreign commerce."

2. Section 891 of 18 U.S.C.A. (1964 ed., Supp. V) provides in part:

"(6) An extortionate extension of credit is any extension of credit with respect to which it is the understanding of the creditor and the debtor at the time it is made that delay in making repayment or failure to make repayment could result in the use of violence or other criminal means to cause harm to the person, reputation, or property of any person.

"(7) An extortionate means is any means which involves the use, or an express or implicit threat of use, of violence or other criminal means to cause harm to the person, reputation, or property of any person."

shark" and organized crime. The gruesome and stirring episodes related have the following as a prelude:

> "The loan shark, then, is the indispensable 'money-mover' of the underworld. He takes 'black' money tainted by its derivation from the gambling or narcotics rackets and turns it 'white' by funneling it into channels of legitimate trade. In so doing, he exacts usurious interest that doubles the black-white money in no time; and, by his special decrees, by his imposition of impossible penalties, he greases the way for the underworld takeover of entire businesses."

There were objections on constitutional grounds. Congressman Eckhardt of Texas said:

> "Should it become law, the amendment would take a long stride by the Federal Government toward occupying the field of general criminal law and toward exercising a general Federal police power; and it would permit prosecution in Federal as well as State courts of a typically State offense.
>
> . . .
>
> "I believe that Alexander Hamilton, though a federalist, would be astonished that such a deep entrenchment on the rights of the States in performing their most fundamental function should come from the more conservative quarter of the House." Id., at 1610.

Senator Proxmire presented to the Senate the Conference Report approving essentially the "loan shark" provision suggested by Congressman McDade, saying:

> "Once again these provisions raised serious questions of Federal-State responsibilities. Nonetheless, because of the importance of the problem, the Senate conferees agreed to the House provision. Organized crime operates on a national scale. One of the principal sources of revenue of organized crime comes from loan sharking. If we are to win the battle against organized crime we must strike at their source of revenue and give the Justice Department additional tools to deal with the problem. The problems simply cannot be solved by the States alone. We must bring into play the full resources of the Federal Government." Id., at 14490.

The Commerce Clause reaches, in the main, three categories of problems. First, the use of channels of interstate or foreign commerce which Congress deems are being misused, as, for example, the shipment of stolen goods (18 U.S.C.A. §§ 2312–2315) or of persons who have been kidnaped (18 U.S.C.A. § 1201). Second, protection of the instrumentalities of interstate commerce, as, for example, the destruction of an aircraft (18 U.S.C.A. § 32), or persons or things in commerce, as, for example, thefts from interstate shipments (18 U.S.C.A. § 659). Third, those activities affecting commerce. It is with this last category that we are here concerned.

Chief Justice Marshall in Gibbons v. Ogden, 9 Wheat. 1, 195, said:

"The genius and character of the whole government seem to be, that its action is to be applied to all the external concerns of the nation, and to those internal concerns which affect the States generally; but not to those which are completely within a particular State, which do not affect other States, and with which it is not necessary to interfere, for the purpose of executing some of the general powers of the government. The completely internal commerce of a State, then, may be considered as reserve for the State itself."

Decisions which followed departed from that view; but by the time of United States v. Darby, 312 U.S. 100, 61 S.Ct. 451 and Wickard v. Filburn, 317 U.S. 111, 63 S.Ct. 82 the broader view of the Commerce Clause announced by Chief Justice Marshall had been restored. Chief Justice Stone wrote for a unanimous Court in 1942 that Congress could provide for the regulation of the price of intrastate milk, the sale of which, in competition with interstate milk, affects the price structure and federal regulation of the latter. The commerce power, he said, "extends to those activities intrastate which so affect interstate commerce, or the exertion of the power of Congress over it, as to make regulation of them appropriate means to the attainment of a legitimate end, the effective execution of the granted power to regulate interstate commerce."

Wickard v. Filburn, 317 U.S. 111, 63 S.Ct. 82, soon followed in which a unanimous Court held that wheat grown wholly for home consumption was constitutionally within the scope of federal regulation of wheat production because, though never marketed interstate, it supplied the need of the grower which otherwise would be satisfied by his purchases in the open market. We said:

"[E]ven if appellee's activity be local and though it may not be regarded as commerce, it may still, whatever its nature, be reached by Congress if it exerts a substantial economic effect on interstate commerce, and this irrespective of whether such effect is what might at some earlier time have been defined as 'direct' or 'indirect.' " 317 U.S., at 125, 63 S.Ct., at 89.

In United States v. Darby, 312 U.S. 100, 61 S.Ct. 451, the decision sustaining an Act of Congress which prohibited the employment of workers in the production of goods "for interstate commerce" at other than prescribed wages and hours, *a class of activities* was held properly regulated by Congress without proof that the particular intrastate activity against which a sanction was laid had an effect on commerce. A unanimous Court said:

"Congress has sometimes left it to the courts to determine whether the intrastate activities have the prohibited effect on the commerce, as in the Sherman Act. It has sometimes left it to an administrative board or agency to determine whether the activities sought to be regulated or prohibited have such effect, as in the case of the Interstate Commerce Act, and the National Labor Relations Act, or whether they come within the statutory definition of the prohibited Act, as in the Federal Trade Commission Act. And sometimes Congress itself has said that a particular activity affects the commerce, as it did in the present Act, the Safety Appliance Act and the Railway Labor Act. In passing on the validity of legislation of the *class* last mentioned the only function of courts is to determine whether the particular activity regulated or prohibited is within the reach of the federal power."

That case is particularly relevant here because it involved a criminal prosecution, a unanimous Court holding that the Act was "sufficiently definite to meet constitutional demands." Petitioner is clearly *a member of the class* which engages in "extortionate credit transactions" as defined by Congress and the description of that class has the required definiteness.

It was the "class of activities" test which we employed in Atlanta Motel v. United States, 379 U.S. 241, 85 S.Ct. 348, to sustain an Act of Congress requiring hotel or motel accommodations for Negro guests. The Act declared that " 'any inn, hotel, motel, or other establishment which provides lodging to transient guests' affects commerce *per se*." That exercise of power under the Commerce Clause was sustained.

> "[O]ur people have become increasingly mobile with millions of people of all races traveling from State to State; . . . Negroes in particular have been the subject of discrimination in transient accommodations, having to travel great distances to secure the same; . . . often they have been unable to obtain accommodations and have had to call upon friends to put them up overnight . . . and . . . these conditions had become so acute as to require the listing of available lodging for Negroes in a special guidebook. . . . "

In a companion case, Katzenbach v. McClung, 379 U.S. 294, 85 S.Ct. 377, we ruled on the constitutionality of the restaurant provision of the same Civil Rights Act which regulated the restaurant "if . . . it serves or offers to serve interstate travelers or a substantial portion of the food which it serves . . . has moved in commerce." Apart from the effect on the flow of food in commerce to restaurants, we spoke of the restrictive effect of the exclusion of Negroes from restaurants on interstate travel by Negroes.

> "[T]here was an impressive array of testimony that discrimination in restaurants had a direct and highly restrictive effect upon interstate travel by Negroes. This resulted, it was said, because discriminatory practices prevent Negroes from buying prepared food served on the premises while on a trip,

except in isolated and unkempt restaurants and under most unsatisfactory and often unpleasant conditions. This obviously discourages travel and obstructs interstate commerce for one can hardly travel without eating. Likewise it was said, that discrimination deterred professional, as well as skilled, people from moving into areas where such practices occurred and thereby caused industry to be reluctant to establish there."

In emphasis of our position that it was the *class of activities* regulated that was the measure, we acknowledged that Congress appropriately considered the "total incidence" of the practice on commerce.

Where the *class of activities* is regulated and that *class* is within the reach of federal power, the courts have no power "to excise, as trivial, individual instances" of the class. Maryland v. Wirtz, 392 U.S. 183, 193, 88 S.Ct. 2017.

Extortionate credit transactions, though purely intrastate, may in the judgment of Congress affect interstate commerce. In an analogous situation, Mr. Justice Holmes, speaking for a unanimous Court, said: "[W]hen it is necessary in order to prevent an evil to make the law embrace more than the precise thing to be prevented it may do so." Westfall v. United States, 274 U.S. 256, 259, 47 S.Ct. 629. In that case an officer of a state bank which was a member of the Federal Reserve System issued a fraudulent certificate of deposit and paid it from the funds of the state bank. It was argued that there was no loss to the Reserve Bank. Mr. Justice Holmes replied, "But every fraud like the one before us weakens the member bank and therefore weakens the System." In the setting of the present case there is a tie-in between local loan sharks and intrastate crime.

The findings by Congress are quite adequate on that ground. The McDade Amendment in the House, as already noted, was the one ultimately adopted. As stated by Congressman McDade it grew out of a "profound study of organized crime, its ramifications and its implications" undertaken by some 22 Congressmen in 1966–1967. 114 Cong. Rec. 14391. The results of that study were included in a report, The Urban Poor and Organized Crime, submitted to the House on August 29, 1967, which revealed that "organized crime takes over $350 million a year from America's poor through loan-sharking alone." See 113 Cong.Rec. 24460–24464. Congressman McDade also relied on The Challenge of Crime in a Free Society, A Report by the President's Commission on Law Enforcement and Administration of Justice (February 1967) which stated that loan sharking was "the second largest source of revenue for organized crime," and is one way by which the underworld obtains control of legitimate businesses.

The Congress also knew about New York's Report, An Investigation of the Loan Shark Racket (1965). See 114 Cong.Rec. 1428–1431. That report shows the loan shark racket is controlled by organized criminal syndicates, either directly or in partnership with independent operators; that in most instances the racket is organized into three echelons, with the top underworld "bosses" providing the money to their principal "lieutenants," who in turn distribute the money to the "operators" who make the actual individual loans; that loan sharks serve as a source of funds to bookmakers, narcotics dealers, and other racketeers; that victims of the racket include all classes, rich and poor, businessmen and laborers; that the victims are often coerced into the commission of criminal acts in order to repay their loans; that through loan sharking the organized underworld has obtained control of legitimate businesses, including securities brokerages and banks which are then exploited; and that "[e]ven where extortionate credit transactions are purely intrastate in character, they nevertheless directly affect interstate and foreign commerce."

Shortly before the Conference bill was adopted by Congress a Senate Committee had held hearings on loan sharking and that testimony was made available to members of the House.

The essence of all these reports and hearings was summarized and embodied in formal congressional findings. They supplied Congress with the knowledge that the loan shark racket provides organized crime with its second most lucrative source of revenue, exacts millions from the pockets of people, coerces its victims into the commission of crimes against property, and causes the takeover by racketeers of legitimate businesses.

We have mentioned in detail the economic, financial, and social setting of the problem as revealed to Congress. We do so not to infer that Congress need make particularized findings in order to legislate. We relate the history of the Act in detail to answer the impassioned plea of petitioner that all that is involved in loan sharking is a traditionally local activity. It appears, instead, that loan sharking in its national setting is one way organized interstate crime holds its guns to the heads of the poor and the rich alike and syphons funds from numerous localities to finance its national operations.

Affirmed.

MR. JUSTICE STEWART, dissenting.

Congress surely has power under the Commerce Clause to enact criminal laws to protect the instrumentalities of interstate commerce, to prohibit the misuse of the channels or facilities of interstate commerce, and to prohibit or regulate those intrastate activities that have a demonstrably substantial effect on interstate commerce. But under the statute before us a man can be convicted without any proof of interstate movement, of the use of the facilities of interstate commerce, or of facts showing that his conduct affected interstate commerce. I think the Framers of the Constitution never intended that the National Government might define as a crime and prosecute such wholly local activity through the enactment of federal criminal laws.

In order to sustain this law we would, in my view, have to be able at the least to say that Congress could rationally have concluded that loan sharking is an activity with interstate attributes that distinguish it in some substantial respect from other local crime. But it is not enough to say that loan sharking is a national problem, for all crime is a national problem. It is not enough to say that some loan sharking has interstate characteristics, for any crime may have an interstate setting. And the circumstance that loan sharking has an adverse impact on interstate business is not a distinguishing attribute, for interstate business suffers from almost all criminal activity, be it shoplifting or violence in the streets.

Because I am unable to discern any rational distinction between loan sharking and other local crime, I cannot escape the conclusion that this statute was beyond the power of Congress to enact. The definition and prosecution of local, intrastate crime are reserved to the States under the Ninth and Tenth Amendments.

NOTES

1. The rationale of the loan sharking statute is that Congress can legislate effectively against interstate loan sharking only by including within the sweep of the statute all activities, whether local, or interstate, within the class. The same approach has been followed in Title 18, § 1511, which makes the obstruction of state laws a federal offense if the obstruction is part of an organized gambling conspiracy. What policy considerations might Congress have had in mind when it followed this approach, rather than the approach of the Hobbs Act, which requires some allegation and *proof* of interstate involvement, no matter how minimal, in each case?

2. The Court's opinion in *Perez* classifies one category of interstate commerce offenses as the "misuse" of channels of interstate or foreign commerce. Title 18, § 2312 (the Dyer Act) prohibits the transportation in interstate or foreign commerce of a motor vehicle, knowing the same to have been stolen. Originally enacted in aid of local law enforcement, the provision has now come full circle since most such cases are originally made by local police officers who turn them over to the FBI.

When Congress legislates under the Commerce Clause in aid of local law enforcement the federal violations are rarely prosecuted to conclusion. For example, Title 18, § 1073 prohibits travel in interstate or foreign commerce to avoid testimony, prosecution or confinement under state laws. Under federal guidelines arrests are made by agents of the FBI only (1) upon request of local authorities, and (2) only where process has been issued. In the year 1961 1,878 arrests were made and only one case was prosecuted in the federal courts. For the rationale of this policy see Kennedy, Three Weapons Against Organized Crime, 8 Crime & Del. 321, 323 (1962).

UNITED STATES v. DeMET

United States Court of Appeals, Seventh Circuit, 1973.
486 F.2d 816.

FAIRCHILD, CIRCUIT JUDGE. Defendant was convicted by a jury of obstructing, delaying and affecting commerce and the movement of articles in commerce by extortion in violation of 18 U.S.C. § 1951, commonly called the Hobbs Act.[1] On this appeal defendant asserts error in . . . insufficiency of the evidence as to extortion and effect on interstate commerce . . .. We have considered these contentions, find none meritorious and affirm the conviction.

Viewing the evidence in a light most favorable to support the verdict, the following facts appear:

Louis King owned a Chicago cocktail lounge called "The Scene" during the period covered by the indictment, November, 1969 to February, 1970. King purchased some of the beer for his business from the Chicago branch of Anheuser-Busch. It was brewed outside Illinois. Some of the liquor he purchased came from distilleries in other states or countries.

During the period of the indictment, defendant was a Chicago police officer and vice coordinator assigned to the district where the Scene was located.

In late November or early December, 1969, defendant and several other police officers visited the Scene. They sat at the bar and defendant asked King how it was going and whether King had any problems. King described how a police sergeant would come into the lounge on weekend nights and require payment of $10 or $20 in exchange for not enforcing a late night parking ordinance which went into effect one hour before closing. King also told defendant that police officers would come on week nights and unjustifiably accuse him of staying open after hours.

This conversation occurred at about 2:00 A.M. when the lounge was busy. Defendant asked if there was a more quiet place where they could talk. King led defendant to a back room. Once in the room, defendant said, "In order to avoid all this bullshit why don't you pay so much a month." King asked, "Now, what's the mutuels?" To which defendant replied, "Well you tell us." King offered $50.00 a month, a sum which defendant found acceptable. King and his wife made the payment to defendant.

---

1. In pertinent part, § 1951 provides:

"(a) Whoever in any way or degree obstructs, delays, or affects commerce or the movement of any article or commodity in commerce, by robbery or extortion or attempts or conspires so to do, or commits or threatens physical violence to any person or property in furtherance of a plan or purpose to do anything in violation of this section shall be fined not more than $10,000 or imprisoned not more than twenty years, or both.

(b) As used in this section—

(1) . . ..

(2) The term "extortion" means the obtaining of property from another, with his consent, induced by wrongful use of actual or threatened force, violence, or fear, or under color of official right.

(3) The term "commerce" means commerce within the District of Columbia, or any Territory or Possession of the United States; all commerce between any point in a State, Territory, Possession, or the District of Columbia and any point outside thereof; all commerce between points within the same State through any place outside such State; and all other commerce over which the United States has jurisdiction."

King testified that he paid the money to defendant because he feared that if he did not pay it might jeopardize his liquor license and lead to more "harassment."

Just before Christmas 1969, defendant and three other officers all in plain clothes entered the Scene Lounge. During conversation with King one of the officers mentioned that a gift had been given or would be given to the "Commander." One of the officers asked what King was going to give. King displayed a bottle of Grand Metaxa. Then one of the officers asked, "Well what about us?" King replied, "O.K. Stop around Christmas and I will have something for you."

King testified that he inferred from this conversation that if he didn't cooperate he might be charged with liquor violations or risk loss of his license.

Later during the Christmas week, defendant stopped at the Scene between 7:00 and 8:00 P.M. before it had opened for business. He had previously called to make sure someone would be there. King had two cases of liquor and two extra bottles waiting for him when he arrived, and assisted in loading the cases into defendant's car. King estimated the value to be over $300.00.

Sometime between Christmas, 1969 and New Year's Day, King had another conversation with defendant at the police station. King complained to defendant that even though he was paying $50.00 a month, he had been forced to pay $300.00 to a sergeant and a patrolman the previous evening. Defendant professed ignorance of the incident and suggested that they go see the "boss." Defendant and King then went to the district commander's office. Defendant went in to see the commander and, after a few minutes, King was invited into his office.

In the presence of defendant, King related to the commander the incident of the previous night. King then asked, "Why am I paying $50.00 a month when I am brought into the station for after hours and forced to pay $300.00 a month?" The commander replied, "I will take care of this. Don't worry about it."

In January, 1970, defendant again visited King at the Scene in the company of other police officers. Defendant asked to see King for a few minutes. The two then went to a back room. King called his wife; Mrs. King came in and gave defendant $50.00.

Following the payments, the Scene had no further parking problems.

* * *

Alleged Failure to Prove Extortion.

Under § 1951 extortion is defined as "the obtaining of property from another, with his consent, induced by wrongful use of actual or threatened fear, or under color of official right." The government's proof was directed to showing that King feared economic loss should he not comply with defendant's demands.

Defendant contends that the government's proof was an insufficient basis upon which to convict for extortion. Because King admitted his encounters with the defendant were friendly and defendant never said nor intimated he would cause "trouble," defendant contends that King's conduct was not motivated by fear as required by § 1951. Rather, defendant argues, King willingly gave money to defendant because it brought certain advantages (such as non-enforcement of parking restrictions) to which he was not lawfully entitled. Thus, in essence, defendant argues that he was merely receiver of bribes and could therefore not be guilty of extortion.

Fear, as used in § 1951, includes not only fear of physical violence but fear of economic harm, as well. . . . It is not necessary that this fear be a consequence of a direct threat, it is enough that the circumstances surrounding the alleged extortion render the victim's fear reasonable. . . .

Indeed, fear may be present even if confrontations between the victim and the alleged extorter appear friendly:

"The fact that relations between the victims and the extorters were often cordial is not inconsistent with extortion. Knowing that they were at the mercy of the Attorney General's office, it is a fair inference that the victims felt that to save their businesses they had to keep the extorters satisfied." United States v. Hyde (1971).

Finally, it is important to note that the economic loss which the victim fears may be a consequence of action which the alleged extorter has a duty to take:

"It is the wrongful use of an otherwise valid power that converts dutiful action into extortion. If the purpose and effect are to intimidate others, forcing them to pay, the action constitutes extortion. Put another way, it is the right to impartial determination of the issue on the merits (i.e. whether to enforce the law or whether to picket or strike) that the victim is deprived of when these actions are taken for the purpose of coercing him into paying. The distinction from bribery is therefore the initiative and purpose on the part of the official and the fear and lack of voluntariness on the part of the victim." United States v. Hyde, supra.

While portions of King's testimony taken with other evidence may be consistent with defendant's view that King freely gave money and liquor to obtain advantages, the jury could reasonably infer from all the circumstances, including defendant's official position, that King was in fear of harm to his business, his fear was reasonable, and defendant exploited it to extort money and liquor.

If early morning customers of the Scene had their cars ticketed, they might take their business elsewhere or at least leave earlier. An arrest for staying open after hours could lead to loss of the liquor license. Defendant, the vice coordinator of the district, promised to eliminate these concerns in exchange for a monthly payment. There was support for a finding that King believed that implicit in defendant's offer was the threat of continued "parking problems" and other harassment if the money (and later liquor) was not forthcoming.

In arguing for acquittal, defendant's counsel presented his view of the facts, i.e. that King was a willing participant and that any fear which King felt was unreasonable. The jury was instructed that in order for defendant's conduct to be considered extortion defendant must obtain the money through a wrongful use of fear, including fear of economic harm, and that the fear must be reasonable. Thus the issue of whether King gave money to defendant voluntarily in order to obtain certain advantages or out of fear that if the money was not forthcoming he would be subject to police harassment was squarely presented to the jury.

The jury apparently thought King's conduct was induced by fear and that defendant's conduct constituted extortion. We cannot say the verdict was not supported by substantial evidence.

Alleged Failure to Affect Interstate Commerce.

Extortion is an offense against the United States when the extorter "in any way or degree obstructs, delays or affects commerce or the movement of any article or commodity in commerce, . . ." 18 U.S.C. § 1951(a). In order to satisfy the interstate commerce element, the government offered proof that some of the beer and liquor purchased for the Scene had out of state origins, that in one instance a national corporation shipped its product across state lines to a Chicago warehouse from which it was delivered to the Scene and that in another instance a local company purchased liquor from out of state producers and then resold it to the Scene and others.

Relying primarily on cases applying the Fair Labor Standards Act, defendant argues that by the time the Scene acquired these beverages they were no longer in interstate commerce and that any extortion therefore could have no effect on interstate commerce. Because of differences in the statutes, such decisions are not controlling as to the requisite manner or degree of interference with commerce that may justify conviction under the Hobbs Act. . . .

Although King's business was primarily local, depletion of King's assets by the goods and money extorted, or the cessation of his business if he did not yield and his fears were realized, would tend to reduce the demand for and amount of beer and liquor moving into Illinois. The effect on interstate commerce would exist, though small by most standards, and only indirectly caused by defendant's acts. There are obvious questions as to the most desirable division between the states and the federal government of the function of enforcing good order, but given the existence of an impact of defendant's conduct on interstate commerce, the question is whether the Hobbs Act must be construed as stopping some margin short of full application of the commerce power.

"The commerce clause endows Congress with full and plenary power to do anything and everything necessary to protect interstate commerce—The specific question is whether in the statute involved the Congress has seen fit to exercise all of its power." Walling v. Goldblatt Bros. (1942).

When a law purports to regulate activities "in commerce" something less than the full commerce power is exercised. On the other hand, a law which regulates matters "affecting" interstate commerce is within, though a more nearly full application of, the commerce power.

Section 1951 clearly contemplates a full application of the commerce power. It proscribes extortion which "in any way or degree obstructs, delays, or affects commerce or the movement of any article or commodity in commerce . . .." In United States v. Stirone, 361 U.S. 212, 215, 80 S.Ct. 270, 272, 4 L.Ed.2d 252, 255 (1960), the Supreme Court said of the Hobbs Act:

> " 'That Act speaks in broad language, manifesting a purpose to use all the constitutional power Congress has to punish interference with interstate commerce by extortion, robbery or physical violence.' The Act outlaws such interference 'in any way or degree.' "[2]

Because Congress has seen fit to exercise its full power under the commerce clause, extortionate conduct having an arguably *de minimis* effect on commerce may nevertheless be punished. Battaglia v. United States (1967) (extortion resulted in a pool table from an out-of-state source being kept from use); United States v. Augello (1971) (assets of drive-in restaurant which purchased mostly from an out-of-state concern depleted by $100; proprietor, in addition, gave $200 from his personal funds.). . . .

Where the victim of extortion, as here, customarily obtains inventory which has come from outside the state, obstruction and delay of, and effect upon commerce may, for the purpose of the Hobbs Act, be found in curtailment of the victim's potential as a buyer of such goods. This may be traced either through the depletion of his assets by his fulfillment of the extortionate demands or the harm which would follow if the threats were carried out.

* * *

The judgment is affirmed.

––––––––

SWYGERT, CHIEF JUDGE, concurring.

Several years ago I took issue by dissent with a holding of this court that a depletion of corporate reserves comprised an "interference

2. We have considered the Supreme Court's 1971 interpretation of the Travel Act as a less than full application of the commerce power, and the policy factors the Court suggests Congress may have considered, Rewis v. United States, 401 U.S. 808, 812 (1971). The two statutes are differently structured. We do not conclude that we are authorized, in a Hobbs Act case, to create a formula under which an impact on interstate commerce is to be dismissed as *de minimis*.

with interstate commerce" within the meaning of the Hobbs Act where a corporation was engaged in interstate commerce. My concern was centered on the unlimited reach of the doctrine espoused by the majority:

> "If a depletion of reserves is all that is necessary to show the requisite affect on commerce, then a threat of any kind to extract money made to a person who happens to operate a business engaged to any extent in interstate commerce comes within the statute's proscription. Under this rationale, a retail store owner, for example, would be afforded federal protection from extortion, regardless of the nature or the likely affect of the threat, simply because his stock of merchandise had in some measure moved in interstate commerce."

Exactly what I apprehended in 1968 has today come to pass. My misgivings, however, did not persuade my brethren in *Amabile* [395 F.2d 47, 54], and I stand by the decision reached in this case as the law of the circuit.

I would also narrow what some might read to be the holding of the majority on the question of extortion under the Hobbs Act. DeMet was prosecuted below for a violation of that portion of the Hobbs Act which makes illegal "the obtaining of property from another, with his consent, induced by wrongful use of actual or threatened fear." As my colleagues recognize, the proof of the Government was directed to demonstrating a fear of economic loss on the part of King. Proof of fear may not have been necessary had the Government chosen to rely on another provision to the Hobbs Act, namely, that prohibiting "the obtaining of property from another, with his consent, . . . *under color of official right.*" (emphasis supplied). It is, of course, hardly appropriate to render a decision on that issue in this case, and I express no views on it.*

NOTES

1. Only a minimal connection between the extortion and interstate commerce is required under the Hobbs Act, noted the majority in United States v. Wright, 797 F.2d 245 (5th Cir.1986). In *Wright*, a city attorney in Louisiana and a defense attorney who was formerly an assistant city attorney, operated a scheme of extortion whereby the clients of the defense attorney were not prosecuted for drunken driving. What is the interstate commerce nexus required for federal jurisdiction under the Hobbs Act? The court said:

> ". . . [T]he district court relied on the testimony of a government witness, Robert Voas, qualified as an expert in the field of alcohol and highway safety. Mr. Voas testified that the consumption of alcohol is

---

* It is worthy of note, however, that an argument has been made in the literature that this provision renders criminal any reception of money (not rightfully due) "under color of official right" by a police officer or other public official, without reference to whether the facts which surround the receipt characterize the action as bribery or extortion. See Stern, Prosecutions of Local Political Corruption Under the Hobbs Act: The Unnecessary Distinction Between Bribery and Extortion. 3 Seton Hall L.Rev. 1 (1971).

'a major, perhaps the major factor causing highway accidents.' His experience evaluating law enforcement techniques in the area of DWI led him to conclude that the more serious an automobile accident is, the more likely it is that a drinking driver is involved. . . . It was Voas' opinion that the higher risk can be reduced either by treating the drinking driver or by suspending or revoking his driving privileges. . . . Failure to prosecute cases where the evidence is sufficient to sustain a conviction has a demoralizing effect on police officers to the point that they tend to make fewer arrests. Finally Voas testified that alcoholism is a tremendous problem in the United States, costing the nation one hundred billion dollars per year in medical expenses and lost working time, and that people with drinking problems who finally do seek help often do so because they have been arrested and prosecuted on a charge of drunk driving.

"The district court, clearly acting within its prerogative, credited this testimony, and relied on it to find that the government had proved the interstate commerce element of a Hobbs Act crime. . . . The district court's findings to support its conclusion on interstate commerce are not clearly erroneous, and we are powerless to disturb them."

The dissenting judge didn't believe that every case of small-town corruption was an appropriate target for cranking up the federal prosecution machinery, and while a minimal connection between the extortion and the effect on interstate commerce is undoubtedly sufficient, he did not think that the tenuous connection between local DWI prosecutions in Louisiana and interstate commerce amounted to a sufficient nexus.

2.   Commerce may be affected either as a direct result of the extortionate transaction or by a depletion of the resources of a business operating in interstate commerce. The latter theory is predicated on the notion that the business would have been in a position to purchase more or better quality merchandise from out of state if the extortionate payment had not been made. For example, in United States v. Tropiano, 418 F.2d 1069 (2d Cir. 1969), certiorari denied 397 U.S. 1021, 90 S.Ct. 1258 (1970), defendants, engaged in the rubbish removal business, were charged with threatening to harm certain individuals engaged in the same business for soliciting accounts in the city in which defendants operated. At trial, the government's sole evidence in support of the interstate commerce aspect of the offense was the fact that the victim purchased refuse removal trucks from an out of state corporation. In response to defendants' claim that this proof was insufficient, the court said:

"[The victim's] surrender of his right to solicit additional customers in [the city] automatically limited his future orders for receptacles for new customers and the trucks required to serve such customers."

In United States v. Pranno, 385 F.2d 387 (7th Cir. 1967), certiorari denied 390 U.S. 944, 88 S.Ct. 1028 (1968), the court affirmed the Hobbs Act conviction of two defendants who extorted a large sum from the owner and contractor of a proposed manufacturing plant by threatening to withhold a building permit. Because the extortionate demands were met, the permit was granted and the construction of the plant was not delayed. The movement of construction materials in interstate commerce was not, therefore, actually affected. The court, nevertheless, held that "it was only necessary to prove that delay *would*

have been caused had the owner and contractor refused payment. . . ."
(emphasis added).

Pranno is consistent with the cases which have considered similar situations. For example, in United States v. Hyde, 448 F.2d 815 (5th Cir. 1971), cert. denied 404 U.S. 1058, 92 S.Ct. 736 (1972), defendant claimed that the extorted companies had not commenced interstate operations until several months after payment was made. This claim was rejected on the ground that the interstate commerce element can be established by expectation at the time of the extortionate transaction:

"The companies were formed, and registration for a stock sale was sought, with a stated purpose of going into the activities that support a finding of interstate commerce. Neither the statute nor the Constitution requires that the company be engaged in an interstate transaction at the moment of the extortion to support federal jurisdiction."

See also United States v. Murphy, 768 F.2d 1518 (7th Cir. 1985), a Hobbs Act prosecution of an associate judge of a county circuit court convicted after being snared in an elaborate sting operation conducted in Cook County, Illinois, and known as "Operation Greylord." The case is included in a later Chapter.

3. For a case which appears to extend the Hobbs Act coverage to its outer limits, consider United States v. Staszcuk, 517 F.2d 53 (7th Cir. 1975), cert. denied 423 U.S. 837, 96 S.Ct. 65. The defendant, a Chicago alderman, was convicted of extorting $9000 for a favorable zoning ruling with respect to the planned construction of an animal hospital. The commerce clause connection was based upon the fact that the building contractor needed various materials such as a furnace, plate glass, plumbing, and electrical fixtures which would be purchased from out-of-state suppliers.

4. Does the extraordinarily broad reading of the Hobbs Act trench upon state's rights? See Note, The Scope of Federal Criminal Jurisdiction Under the Commerce Clause, 1972 U.Ill.L.F. 805, 822:

"[I]t should be noted that the use of the commerce clause as an expansive basis for federal intervention in the area of crime control has not been opposed by the states, though similar federal intervention in economic affairs faced heavy resistance. State acquiescence, if not encouragement, can be attributed to several factors: the federal government has not preempted state powers; federal intervention has helped states deal with problems serious enough to override the usual states' rights fears; and the federal government has entered this area gradually, reluctantly, and primarily with programs aimed at organized crime, a problem generally felt to be incapable of solution by the states acting alone."

(e) CIVIL RIGHTS OFFENSES

A number of statutes, both federal and state, make it a criminal offense to deprive a person of his constitutional rights. Foremost are the following two federal enactments.

Section 241 of Title 18 of the United States Code provides:

"If two or more persons conspire to injure, oppress, threaten, or intimidate any citizen in the free exercise or enjoyment of any right or privilege secured to him by the Constitution or laws of the United States, or because of his having so exercised the same: or

"If two or more persons go in disguise on the highway, or on the premises of another, with intent to prevent or hinder his free exercise or enjoyment of any right or privilege so secured—

"They shall be fined not more than $10,000 or imprisoned not more than ten years, or both; and if death results, they shall be subject to imprisonment for any term of years or for life."

A companion provision, Section 242, reads:

"Whoever, under color of any law, statute, ordinance, regulation, or custom, willfully subjects any inhabitant of any State, Territory, or District to the deprivation of any rights, privileges, or immunities secured or protected by the Constitution or laws of the United States, or to different punishments, pains, or penalties, on account of such inhabitant being an alien, or by reason of his color, or race, than are prescribed for the punishment of citizens, shall be fined not more than $1,000 or imprisoned not more than one year, or both; and if death results shall be subject to imprisonment for any term of years or for life."

There is also the Federal Civil Rights Act of 1871 (42 U.S.C. § 1983), under which a civil action may be brought by any person who has been deprived of his constitutional rights by a person who acts "under color of any statute, ordinance, regulation, custom, or usage of any State or territory." The language of the statute obviously confines its application to agents of state governments. However, the United States Supreme Court has held (in a 6 to 3 decision) that federal law enforcement officials may be subject to a civil action in the federal courts where such officials violate a person's Fourth Amendment protection against unreasonable searches and seizures. The dissenting justices were of the view that congressional authorization was needed for according such civil actions against federal officers. Bivens v. Six Unknown Named Agents of Federal Bureau of Narcotics, 403 U.S. 388, 91 S.Ct. 1999 (1971).

NOTE: FEDERAL PROSECUTORIAL DISCRETION AND STATE LAW ENFORCEMENT

The relationship of federal and state law enforcement authorities in acting upon offenses and offenders within a common sphere is a delicate and critical one. Apart from an early article, Schwartz, Federal Criminal Jurisdiction and Prosecutorial Discretion, 13 Law & Contemp.Prob. 64, 69 (1948), little has been written on the subject.

Two areas deserve focus. The first is the notion that primary and plenary law enforcement is the task of the states. The second is the growing reach of federal jurisdiction—by Congressional enactment and judicial construction—in areas where state jurisdiction has not been satisfactorily used, e.g., extortion, theft, bribery, especially in organized crime and official corruption cases.

In these circumstances, how does the federal prosecutor—newly armed with broadened jurisdictional powers, all-encompassing immunity statutes, and federal resources—define his area of activity and avoid federal-state tensions by supplanting, in whole or in part, the state prosecutor and police? Does vigorous federal prosecution of essentially local offenses weaken local law enforcement in the long run by encouraging lethargy or inactivity on the part of the local prosecutor who has other resource allocation problems, e.g., violent street crime, narcotics and the so-called "victimless" offenses in the area of gambling, prostitution and drunkenness?

What standards should a federal prosecutor employ to guide his prosecutorial discretion in the overlap area? Perhaps the threshold consideration for the federal prosecutor is to determine whether he has—or can obtain—the resources and manpower to broaden his prosecutorial base and, at the same time, continue to deter the commission of uniquely federal offenses. Assuming that he can, the question is reduced to whether he should branch out into the area of overlap between state and federal jurisdiction.

A key yardstick for measuring the degree to which the federal government should enter into this area is the quality of the local prosecutor's office. While some part of this evaluation may be subjective, factors such as community confidence in local authorities, as reflected by the media, the extent of local resources devoted to the prosecutor's office and the relationship between that office and local judges are relatively objective considerations in the overall determination. Moreover, where the same political party that controls a large part of the local government also controls the prosecutor's office, it is inconceivable, either because of pursestring control or political association, that local officials can always deal satisfactorily with the problems of official corruption. And where corruption appears in the local prosecutor's own investigative force—the community police—it is virtually impossible for him to take any extensive action because of the cohesion within the police fraternity. In instances such as this, an independent investigative agency, such as the FBI, is essential.

Thus, there may be some legitimate areas of prosecutorial concern in which the local officials are unwilling or unable to act. It is in these areas that the federal prosecutor must employ the existing federal statutes—and some degree of imagination—to combat and deter crime. But the decision to enter into this area depends upon a balancing of the factors outlined above in the particular circumstances of the jurisdiction over which the federal prosecutor presides. Are there any other factors that should be considered in reaching this ultimate decision?

Consider also the following case:

WAYTE v. UNITED STATES

Supreme Court of the United States, 1985.
470 U.S. 598, 105 S.Ct. 1524, 84 L.Ed.2d 547.

JUSTICE POWELL delivered the opinion of the Court.

The question presented is whether a passive enforcement policy under which the Government prosecutes only those who report themselves as having violated the law, or who are reported by others, violates the First and Fifth Amendments.

I

On July 2, 1980, pursuant to his authority under § 3 of the Military Selective Service Act, 50 U.S.C.App. § 453,[1] the President issued Presidential Proclamation No. 4771, 3 CFR 82 (1981). This proclamation directed male citizens and certain male residents born during 1960 to register with the Selective Service System during the week of July 21, 1980. Petitioner fell within that class but did not register. Instead, he wrote several letters to Government officials, including the President, stating that he had not registered and did not intend to do so.

Petitioner's letters were added to a Selective Service file of young men who advised that they had failed to register or who were reported by others as having failed to register. For reasons we discuss, Selective Service adopted a policy of passive enforcement under which it would investigate and prosecute only the cases of nonregistration contained in this file. In furtherance of this policy, Selective Service sent a letter on June 17, 1981 to each reported violator who had not registered and for whom it had an address. The letter explained the duty to register, stated that Selective Service had information that the person was required to register but had not done so, requested that he either comply with the law by filling out an enclosed registration card or explain why he was not subject to registration, and warned that a violation could result in criminal prosecution and specified penalties. Petitioner received a copy of this letter but did not respond.

On July 20, 1981, Selective Service transmitted to the Department of Justice, for investigation and potential prosecution, the names of petitioner and 133 other young men identified under its passive enforcement system—all of whom had not registered in response to the Service's June letter. At two later dates, it referred the names of 152 more young men similarly identified. After screening out the names of those who appeared not to be in the class required to register, the Department of Justice referred the remaining names to the Federal Bureau of Investigation for additional inquiry and to the United States

---

1. Section 3 provides in pertinent part:

"[I]t shall be the duty of every male citizen of the United States, and every other male person residing in the United States, who, on the day or days fixed for the first or any subsequent registration, is between the ages of eighteen and twenty-six, to present himself for and submit to registration at such time or times and place or places, and in such manner, as shall be determined by proclamation of the President and by rules and regulations prescribed hereunder."

The United States requires only that young men *register* for military service while most other major countries of the world require actual service. The International Institute for Strategic Studies, The Military Balance 1983–1984 (1983); see Selective Service System v. Minnesota Public Service Research Group, 468 U.S. 841, n. 2, 104 S.Ct. 3348, 3351, n. 2, 82 L.Ed.2d 632 (1984) (Powell, J., concurring in part and concurring in judgment).

Attorneys for the districts in which the nonregistrants resided. Petitioner's name was one of those referred.

Pursuant to Department of Justice policy, those referred were not immediately prosecuted. Instead, the appropriate United States Attorney was required to notify identified nonregistrants by registered mail that, unless they registered within a specified time, prosecution would be considered. In addition, an FBI agent was usually sent to interview the nonregistrant before prosecution was instituted. This effort to persuade nonregistrants to change their minds became known as the "beg" policy. Under it, young men who registered late were not prosecuted, while those who never registered were investigated further by the Government. Pursuant to the "beg" policy, the United States Attorney for the Central District of California sent petitioner a letter on October 15, 1981 urging him to register or face possible prosecution. Again petitioner failed to respond.

On December 9, 1981, the Department of Justice instructed all United States Attorneys not to begin seeking indictments against nonregistrants until further notice. On January 7, 1982, the President announced a grace period to afford nonregistrants a further opportunity to register without penalty. This grace period extended until February 28, 1982. Petitioner still did not register.

Over the next few months, the Department decided to begin prosecuting those young men who, despite the grace period and "beg" policy, continued to refuse to register. It recognized that under the passive enforcement system those prosecuted were "liable to be vocal proponents of nonregistration" or persons "with religious or moral objections." It also recognized that prosecutions would "undoubtedly result in allegations that the [case was] brought in retribution for the nonregistrant's exercise of his first amendment rights." The Department was advised, however, that Selective Service could not develop a more "active" enforcement system for quite some time. Because of this, the Department decided to begin seeking indictments under the passive system without further delay. On May 21, 1982, United States Attorneys were notified to begin prosecution of nonregistrants. On June 28, 1982, FBI agents interviewed petitioner and he continued to refuse to register. Accordingly, on July 22, 1982, an indictment was returned against him for knowingly and willfully failing to register with the Selective Service. . . . This was one of the first indictments returned against any individual under the passive policy.

II

Petitioner moved to dismiss the indictment on the ground of selective prosecution. He contended that he and the other indicted nonregistrants [2] were "vocal" opponents of the registration program

---

2. The record indicates that only 13 of the 286 young men Selective Service referred to the Department of Justice had been indicted at the time the District Court considered this case. As of March 31, 1984, three more men had been indicted.

who had been impermissibly targeted (out of an estimated 674,000 nonregistrants [3] for prosecution on the basis of their exercise of First Amendment rights. . . .

On November 15, 1982, the District Court dismissed the indictment on the ground that the Government had failed to rebut petitioner's prima facie case of selective prosecution. Following precedents of the Court of Appeals for the Ninth Circuit, the District Court found that in order to establish a prima facie case petitioner had to prove that (i) others similarly situated generally had not been prosecuted for conduct similar to petitioner's and (ii) the Government's discriminatory selection was based on impermissible grounds such as race, religion, or exercise of First Amendment rights. Petitioner satisfied the first requirement, the District Court held, because he had shown that all those prosecuted were "vocal" nonregistrants and because "[t]he inference is strong that the Government could have located non-vocal nonregistrants, but chose not to." The District Court found the second requirement satisfied for three reasons. First, the passive enforcement program was " 'inherently suspect' " because " 'it focuse[d] upon the vocal offender . . . [and was] vulnerable to the charge that those chosen for prosecution [were] being punished for their expression of ideas, a constitutionally protected right.' " Second, the Government's awareness that a disproportionate number of vocal nonregistrants would be prosecuted under the passive enforcement system indicated that petitioner was prosecuted because of his exercise of First Amendment rights. Finally, the involvement of high Government officials in the prosecution decisions "strongly suggest[ed] impermissible selective prosecution." The District Court then held that the Government had failed to rebut the prima facie case.

The Court of Appeals reversed. Applying the same test, it found the first requirement satisfied but not the second. . . . As to the second requirement, the Court of Appeals held that petitioner had to show that the Government focused its investigation on him *because of* his protest activities. Petitioner's evidence, however, showed only that the Government was aware that the passive enforcement system would result in prosecutions primarily of two types of men—religious and moral objectors and vocal objectors—and that the Government recognized that the latter type would probably make claims of selective prosecution. Finding no evidence of impermissible governmental motivation, the court held that the District Court's finding of a prima facie case of selective prosecution was clearly erroneous. The Court of

The approximately 270 not indicted either registered, were found not to be subject to registration requirements, could not be found, or were under continuing investigation. The record does not indicate how many fell into each category.

3. On July 28, 1982, Selective Service stated that 8,365,000 young men had registered out of the estimated 9,039,000 who were required to do so. Selective Service Prosecutions: Oversight Hearing before the Subcommittee on Courts, Civil Liberties, and the Administration of Justice of the House Committee on the Judiciary, 97th Cong., 2d Sess., 10 (1982). This amounted to a nonregistration rate of approximately 7.5 percent.

Appeals also found two legitimate explanations for the Government's passive enforcement system: (i) the identities of nonreported nonregistrants were not known, and (ii) nonregistrants who expressed their refusal to register made clear their willful violation of the law.

* * *

III

In our criminal justice system, the Government retains "broad discretion" as to whom to prosecute. "[S]o long as the prosecutor has probable cause to believe that the accused committed an offense defined by statute, the decision whether or not to prosecute, and what charge to file or bring before a grand jury, generally rests entirely in his discretion." Bordenkircher v. Hayes, 434 U.S. 357, 364, 98 S.Ct. 663, 668, 54 L.Ed.2d 604 (1978). This broad discretion rests largely on the recognition that the decision to prosecute is particularly ill-suited to judicial review. Such factors as the strength of the case, the prosecution's general deterrence value, the Government's enforcement priorities, and the case's relationship to the Government's overall enforcement plan are not readily susceptible to the kind of analysis the courts are competent to undertake. Judicial supervision in this area, moreover, entails systemic costs of particular concern. Examining the basis of a prosecution delays the criminal proceeding, threatens to chill law enforcement by subjecting the prosecutor's motives and decisionmaking to outside inquiry, and may undermine prosecutorial effectiveness by revealing the Government's enforcement policy. All these are substantial concerns that make the courts properly hesitant to examine the decision whether to prosecute.

As we have noted in a slightly different context, however, although prosecutorial discretion is broad, it is not " 'unfettered.' Selectivity in the enforcement of criminal laws is . . . subject to constitutional constraints." United States v. Batchelder, 442 U.S. 114, 125, 99 S.Ct. 2198, 2205, 60 L.Ed.2d 755 (1979). In particular, the decision to prosecute may not be " 'deliberately based upon an unjustifiable standard such as race, religion, or other arbitrary classification,' " Bordenkircher v. Hayes, supra, including the exercise of protected statutory and constitutional rights.

It is appropriate to judge selective prosecution claims according to ordinary equal protection standards. Under our prior cases, these standards require petitioner to show both that the passive enforcement system had a discriminatory effect and that it was motivated by a discriminatory purpose. All petitioner has shown here is that those eventually prosecuted, along with many not prosecuted, reported themselves as having violated the law. He has not shown that the enforcement policy selected nonregistrants for prosecution on the basis of their speech. Indeed, he could not have done so given the way the "beg" policy was carried out. The Government did not prosecute those who reported themselves but later registered. Nor did it prosecute those who protested registration but did not report themselves or were not reported by others. In fact, the Government did not even investigate those who wrote letters to Selective Service criticizing registration unless their letters stated affirmatively that they had refused to comply with the law. The Government, on the other hand, did prosecute people who reported themselves or were reported by others but who did not publicly protest. These facts demonstrate that the Government treated all reported nonregistrants similarly. It did not subject vocal nonregistrants to any special burden. Indeed, those prosecuted in effect selected themselves for prosecution by refusing to register after being reported and warned by the Government.

Even if the passive policy had a discriminatory effect, petitioner has not shown that the Government intended such a result. The evidence he presented demonstrated only that the Government was aware that the passive enforcement policy would result in prosecution of vocal objectors and that they would probably make selective prosecution claims. As we have noted, however, " '[d]iscriminatory purpose' . . . implies more than . . . intent as awareness of consequences. It implies that the decisionmaker . . . selected or reaffirmed a particular course of action at least in part 'because of,' not merely 'in spite of,' its adverse effects upon an identifiable group." In the present case, petitioner has not shown that the Government prosecuted him *because of* his protest activities. Absent such a showing, his claim of selective prosecution fails.

* * *

[The Court's discussion of First Amendment grounds is omitted.]

V

We conclude that the Government's passive enforcement system together with its "beg" policy violated neither the First nor Fifth Amendments. Accordingly, we affirm the judgment of the Court of Appeals.

It is so ordered.

[JUSTICE MARSHALL, dissenting, with whom JUSTICE BRENNAN joined, believed that the case hinged on an entirely different issue, one of the right to discovery of documents from the Government, rather than the issue addressed by the Court's majority. For that reason, the opinion is omitted.]

B. PROBLEMS IN DEFINING CRIMINAL CONDUCT

1. DEFINING "DEATH" AND "LIFE"

(a) THE RIGHT TO DIE

CRUZAN v. DIRECTOR, MISSOURI DEPARTMENT OF HEALTH

Supreme Court of the United States, 1990.
___ U.S. ___, 110 S.Ct. 2841, 111 L.Ed.2d 224.

CHIEF JUSTICE REHNQUIST delivered the opinion of the Court.

Petitioner Nancy Beth Cruzan was rendered incompetent as a result of severe injuries sustained during an automobile accident. Co-petitioners Lester and Joyce Cruzan, Nancy's parents and co-guardians, sought a court order directing the withdrawal of their daughter's artificial feeding and hydration equipment after it became apparent that she had virtually no chance of recovering her cognitive faculties. The Supreme Court of Missouri held that because there was no clear and convincing evidence of Nancy's desire to have life-sustaining treatment withdrawn under such circumstances, her parents lacked authority to effectuate such a request. We granted certiorari and now affirm.

On the night of January 11, 1983, Nancy Cruzan lost control of her car as she traveled down Elm Road in Jasper County, Missouri. The vehicle overturned, and Cruzan was discovered lying face down in a ditch without detectable respiratory or cardiac function. Paramedics were able to restore her breathing and heartbeat at the accident site, and she was transported to a hospital in an unconscious state. An attending neurosurgeon diagnosed her as having sustained probable cerebral contusions compounded by significant anoxia (lack of oxygen). The Missouri trial court in this case found that permanent brain damage generally results after 6 minutes in an anoxic state; it was estimated that Cruzan was deprived of oxygen from 12 to 14 minutes. She remained in a coma for approximately three weeks and then progressed to an unconscious state in which she was able to orally ingest some nutrition. In order to ease feeding and further the recovery, surgeons implanted a gastrostomy feeding and hydration tube in Cruzan with the consent of her then husband. Subsequent rehabilitative efforts proved unavailing. She now lies in a Missouri state hospital in what is commonly referred to as a persistent vegetative state: generally, a condition in which a person exhibits motor reflexes but evinces no indications of significant cognitive function.[1] The State of Missouri is bearing the cost of her care.

---

1. The State Supreme Court, adopting much of the trial court's findings, de- scribed Nancy Cruzan's medical condition as follows:

After it had become apparent that Nancy Cruzan had virtually no chance of regaining her mental faculties her parents asked hospital employees to terminate the artificial nutrition and hydration procedures. All agree that such a removal would cause her death. The employees refused to honor the request without court approval. The parents then sought and received authorization from the state trial court for termination. The court found that a person in Nancy's condition had a fundamental right under the State and Federal Constitutions to refuse or direct the withdrawal of "death prolonging procedures." The court also found that Nancy's "expressed thoughts at age twenty-five in somewhat serious conversation with a housemate friend that if sick or injured she would not wish to continue her life unless she could live at least halfway normally suggests that given her present condition she would not wish to continue on with her nutrition and hydration."

The Supreme Court of Missouri reversed by a divided vote. . . .

". . . (1) [H]er respiration and circulation are not artificially maintained and are within the normal limits of a thirty-year-old female; (2) she is oblivious to her environment except for reflexive responses to sound and perhaps painful stimuli; (3) she suffered anoxia of the brain resulting in a massive enlargement of the ventricles filling with cerebrospinal fluid in the area where the brain has degenerated and [her] cerebral cortical atrophy is irreversible, permanent, progressive and ongoing; (4) her highest cognitive brain function is exhibited by her grimacing perhaps in recognition of ordinarily painful stimuli, indicating the experience of pain and apparent response to sound; (5) she is a spastic quadriplegic; (6) her four extremities are contracted with irreversible muscular and tendon damage to all extremities; (7) she has no cognitive or reflexive ability to swallow food or water to maintain her daily essential needs and . . . she will never recover her ability to swallow sufficient [sic] to satisfy her needs. In sum, Nancy is diagnosed as in a persistent vegetative state. She is not dead. She is not terminally ill. Medical experts testified that she could live another thirty years." Cruzan v. Harmon, 760 S.W.2d 408, 411 (Mo.1988) (en banc) (quotations omitted; footnote omitted).

In observing that Cruzan was not dead, the court referred to the following Missouri statute:

"For all legal purposes, the occurrence of human death shall be determined in accordance with the usual and customary standards of medical practice, provided that death shall not be determined to have occurred unless the following minimal conditions have been met:

"(1) When respiration and circulation are not artificially maintained, there is an irreversible cessation of spontaneous respiration and circulation; or

"(2) When respiration and circulation are artificially maintained, and there is total and irreversible cessation of all brain function, including the brain stem and that such determination is made by a licensed physician." Mo.Rev.Stat. § 194.005 (1986).

Since Cruzan's respiration and circulation were not being artificially maintained, she obviously fit within the first proviso of the statute.

Dr. Fred Plum, the creator of the term "persistent vegetative state" and a renowned expert on the subject, has described the "vegetative state" in the following terms:

"'Vegetative state describes a body which is functioning entirely in terms of its internal controls. It maintains temperature. It maintains heart beat and pulmonary ventilation. It maintains digestive activity. It maintains reflex activity of muscles and nerves for low level conditioned responses. But there is no behavioral evidence of either self-awareness or awareness of the surroundings in a learned manner.'" In re Jobes, 108 N.J. 394, 403, 529 A.2d 434, 438 (1987).

See also Brief for American Medical Association et al., as Amici Curiae, 6 ("The persistent vegetative state can best be understood as one of the conditions in which patients have suffered a loss of consciousness").

We granted certiorari to consider the question of whether Cruzan has a right under the United States Constitution which would require the hospital to withdraw life-sustaining treatment from her under these circumstances.

At common law, even the touching of one person by another without consent and without legal justification was a battery. . . . This notion of bodily integrity has been embodied in the requirement that informed consent is generally required for medical treatment. Justice Cardozo, while on the Court of Appeals of New York, aptly described this doctrine: "Every human being of adult years and sound mind has a right to determine what shall be done with his own body; and a surgeon who performs an operation without his patient's consent commits an assault, for which he is liable in damages." Schloendorff v. Society of New York Hospital, 211 N.Y. 125, 129–30, 105 N.E. 92, 93 (1914). The informed consent doctrine has become firmly entrenched in American tort law.

The logical corollary of the doctrine of informed consent is that the patient generally possesses the right not to consent, that is, to refuse treatment. Until about 15 years ago and the seminal decision in In re Quinlan, 70 N.J. 10, 355 A.2d 647, cert. denied sub nom., Garger v. New Jersey, 429 U.S. 922, 97 S.Ct. 319, 50 L.Ed.2d 289 (1976), the number of right-to-refuse-treatment decisions were relatively few. Most of the earlier cases involved patients who refused medical treatment forbidden by their religious beliefs, thus implicating First Amendment rights as well as common law rights of self-determination. More recently, however, with the advance of medical technology capable of sustaining life well past the point where natural forces would have brought certain death in earlier times, cases involving the right to refuse life-sustaining treatment have burgeoned.

In the *Quinlan* case, young Karen Quinlan suffered severe brain damage as the result of anoxia, and entered a persistent vegetative state. Karen's father sought judicial approval to disconnect his daughter's respirator. The New Jersey Supreme Court granted the relief, holding that Karen had a right of privacy grounded in the Federal Constitution to terminate treatment. Recognizing that this right was not absolute, however, the court balanced it against asserted state interests. Noting that the State's interest "weakens and the individual's right to privacy grows as the degree of bodily invasion increases and the prognosis dims," the court concluded that the state interests had to give way in that case. The court also concluded that the "only practical way" to prevent the loss of Karen's privacy right due to her incompetence was to allow her guardian and family to decide "whether she would exercise it in these circumstances."

After *Quinlan*, however, most courts have based a right to refuse treatment either solely on the common law right to informed consent or on both the common law right and a constitutional privacy right. See

L. Tribe, American Constitutional Law § 15–11, p. 1365 (2d ed. 1988). . . .

In In re Storar, 52 N.Y.2d 363, 438 N.Y.S.2d 266, 420 N.E.2d 64, cert. denied, 454 U.S. 858, 102 S.Ct. 309, 70 L.Ed.2d 153 (1981), the New York Court of Appeals declined to base a right to refuse treatment on a constitutional privacy right. Instead, it found such a right "adequately supported" by the informed consent doctrine. In *In re Eichner* (decided with *In re Storar,* supra) an 83–year–old man who had suffered brain damage from anoxia entered a vegetative state and was thus incompetent to consent to the removal of his respirator. The court, however, found it unnecessary to reach the question of whether his rights could be exercised by others since it found the evidence clear and convincing from statements made by the patient when competent that he "did not want to be maintained in a vegetative coma by use of a respirator." In the companion *Storar* case, a 52–year–old man suffering from bladder cancer had been profoundly retarded during most of his life. Implicitly rejecting the approach taken in *Saikewicz,* supra, the court reasoned that due to such life-long incompetency, "it is unrealistic to attempt to determine whether he would want to continue potentially life prolonging treatment if he were competent." As the evidence showed that the patient's required blood transfusions did not involve excessive pain and without them his mental and physical abilities would deteriorate, the court concluded that it should not "allow an incompetent patient to bleed to death because someone, even someone as close as a parent or sibling, feels that this is best for one with an incurable disease."

Many of the later cases build on the principles established in *Quinlan,* . . . and *Storar/Eichner.* For instance, in In re Conroy, 98 N.J. 321, 486 A.2d 1209 (1985), the same court that decided *Quinlan* considered whether a nasogastric feeding tube could be removed from an 84–year–old incompetent nursing-home resident suffering irreversible mental and physical ailments. While recognizing that a federal right of privacy might apply in the case, the court, contrary to its approach in *Quinlan,* decided to base its decision on the common-law right to self-determination and informed consent. "On balance, the right to self-determination ordinarily outweighs any countervailing state interests, and competent persons generally are permitted to refuse medical treatment, even at the risk of death. Most of the cases that have held otherwise, unless they involved the interest in protecting innocent third parties, have concerned the patient's competency to make a rational and considered choice."

Reasoning that the right of self-determination should not be lost merely because an individual is unable to sense a violation of it, the court held that incompetent individuals retain a right to refuse treatment. It also held that such a right could be exercised by a surrogate decisionmaker using a "subjective" standard when there was clear evidence that the incompetent person would have exercised it. Where such evidence was lacking, the court held that an individual's right could still be invoked in certain circumstances under objective "best interest" standards. Thus, if some trustworthy evidence existed that the individual would have wanted to terminate treatment, but not enough to clearly establish a person's wishes for purposes of the subjective standard, and the burden of a prolonged life from the experience of pain and suffering markedly outweighed its satisfactions, treatment could be terminated under a "limited-objective" standard. Where no trustworthy evidence existed, and a person's suffering would make the administration of life-sustaining treatment inhumane, a "pure-objective" standard could be used to terminate treatment. If none of these conditions obtained, the court held it was best to err in favor of preserving life.

The court also rejected certain categorical distinctions that had been drawn in prior refusal-of-treatment cases as lacking substance for decision purposes: the distinction between actively hastening death by terminating treatment and passively allowing a person to die of a disease; between treating individuals as an initial matter versus withdrawing treatment afterwards; between ordinary versus extraordinary treatment; and between treatment by artificial feeding versus other forms of life-sustaining medical procedures. As to the last item, the court acknowledged the "emotional significance" of food, but noted that feeding by implanted tubes is a "medical procedur[e] with inherent risks and possible side effects, instituted by skilled health-care providers to compensate for impaired physical functioning" which analytically was equivalent to artificial breathing using a respirator.[2]

In contrast to *Conroy,* the Court of Appeals of New York recently refused to accept less than the clearly expressed wishes of a patient before permitting the exercise of her right to refuse treatment by a surrogate decisionmaker. In re Westchester County Medical Center on behalf of O'Connor, 72 N.Y.2d 517, 534 N.Y.S.2d 886, 531 N.E.2d 607 (1988) (*O'Connor*). There, the court, over the objection of the patient's family members, granted an order to insert a feeding tube into a 77–year–old woman rendered incompetent as a result of several strokes. While continuing to recognize a common-law right to refuse treatment, the court rejected the substituted judgment approach for asserting it "because it is inconsistent with our fundamental commitment to the notion that no person or court should substitute its judgment as to what

---

2. In a later trilogy of cases, the New Jersey Supreme Court stressed that the analytic framework adopted in *Conroy* was limited to elderly, incompetent patients with shortened life expectancies, and established alternative approaches to deal with a different set of situations. See In re Farrell, 108 N.J. 335, 529 A.2d 404 (1987) (37–year–old competent mother with terminal illness had right to removal of respirator based on common law and constitutional principles which overrode competing state interests); In re Peter, 108 N.J. 365, 529 A.2d 419 (1987) (65–year–old woman in persistent vegetative state had right to re- moval of nasogastric feeding tube—under *Conroy* subjective test, power of attorney and hearsay testimony constituted clear and convincing proof of patient's intent to have treatment withdrawn); In re Jobes, 108 N.J. 394, 529 A.2d 434 (1987) (31–year–old woman in persistent vegetative state entitled to removal of jejunostomy feeding tube—even though hearsay testimony regarding patient's intent insufficient to meet clear and convincing standard of proof, under *Quinlan,* family or close friends entitled to make a substituted judgment for patient).

would be an acceptable quality of life for another. Consequently, we adhere to the view that, despite its pitfalls and inevitable uncertainties, the inquiry must always be narrowed to the patient's expressed intent, with every effort made to minimize the opportunity for error." . . .

* * *

As these cases demonstrate, the common-law doctrine of informed consent is viewed as generally encompassing the right of a competent individual to refuse medical treatment. Beyond that, these decisions demonstrate both similarity and diversity in their approach to decision of what all agree is a perplexing question with unusually strong moral and ethical overtones. State courts have available to them for decision a number of sources—state constitutions, statutes, and common law—which are not available to us. In this Court, the question is simply and starkly whether the United States Constitution prohibits Missouri from choosing the rule of decision which it did. This is the first case in which we have been squarely presented with the issue of whether the United States Constitution grants what is in common parlance referred to as a "right to die." . . .

The Fourteenth Amendment provides that no State shall "deprive any person of life, liberty, or property, without due process of law." The principle that a competent person has a constitutionally protected liberty interest in refusing unwanted medical treatment may be inferred from our prior decisions. . . .

Just this Term, in the course of holding that a State's procedures for administering antipsychotic medication to prisoners were sufficient to satisfy due process concerns, we recognized that prisoners possess "a significant liberty interest in avoiding the unwanted administration of antipsychotic drugs under the Due Process Clause of the Fourteenth Amendment." Washington v. Harper, ___ U.S. ___, ___, 110 S.Ct. 1028, 1036, 108 L.Ed.2d 178 (1990); . . . Still other cases support the recognition of a general liberty interest in refusing medical treatment.

But determining that a person has a "liberty interest" under the Due Process Clause does not end the inquiry;[3] "whether respondent's constitutional rights have been violated must be determined by balancing his liberty interests against the relevant state interests." Youngberg v. Romeo, 457 U.S. 307, 321, 102 S.Ct. 2452, 2461, 73 L.Ed.2d 28 (1982).

Petitioners insist that under the general holdings of our cases, the forced administration of life-sustaining medical treatment, and even of artificially-delivered food and water essential to life, would implicate a competent person's liberty interest. Although we think the logic of the cases discussed above would embrace such a liberty interest, the dramatic consequences involved in refusal of such treatment would inform

---

3. Although many state courts have held that a right to refuse treatment is encompassed by a generalized constitutional right of privacy, we have never so held. We believe this issue is more properly ana-lyzed in terms of a Fourteenth Amendment liberty interest. See Bowers v. Hardwick, 478 U.S. 186, 194–195, 106 S.Ct. 2841, 2846, 92 L.Ed.2d 140 (1986).

the inquiry as to whether the deprivation of that interest is constitutionally permissible. But for purposes of this case, we assume that the United States Constitution would grant a competent person a constitutionally protected right to refuse lifesaving hydration and nutrition.

Petitioners go on to assert that an incompetent person should possess the same right in this respect as is possessed by a competent person. . . .

The difficulty with petitioners' claim is that in a sense it begs the question: an incompetent person is not able to make an informed and voluntary choice to exercise a hypothetical right to refuse treatment or any other right. Such a "right" must be exercised for her, if at all, by some sort of surrogate. Here, Missouri has in effect recognized that under certain circumstances a surrogate may act for the patient in electing to have hydration and nutrition withdrawn in such a way as to cause death, but it has established a procedural safeguard to assure that the action of the surrogate conforms as best it may to the wishes expressed by the patient while competent. Missouri requires that evidence of the incompetent's wishes as to the withdrawal of treatment be proved by clear and convincing evidence. The question, then, is whether the United States Constitution forbids the establishment of this procedural requirement by the State. We hold that it does not.

Whether or not Missouri's clear and convincing evidence requirement comports with the United States Constitution depends in part on what interests the State may properly seek to protect in this situation. Missouri relies on its interest in the protection and preservation of human life, and there can be no gainsaying this interest. As a general matter, the States—indeed, all civilized nations—demonstrate their commitment to life by treating homicide as serious crime. Moreover, the majority of States in this country have laws imposing criminal penalties on one who assists another to commit suicide.[4] We do not think a State is required to remain neutral in the face of an informed and voluntary decision by a physically-able adult to starve to death.

But in the context presented here, a State has more particular interests at stake. The choice between life and death is a deeply personal decision of obvious and overwhelming finality. We believe Missouri may legitimately seek to safeguard the personal element of this choice through the imposition of heightened evidentiary requirements. It cannot be disputed that the Due Process Clause protects an interest in life as well as an interest in refusing life-sustaining medical treatment. Not all incompetent patients will have loved ones available to serve as surrogate decision-makers. And even where family members are present, "[t]here will, of course, be some unfortunate situations in which family members will not act to protect a patient." In re Jobes, 108 N.J. 394, 419, 529 A.2d 434, 477 (1987). A State is entitled to

4. See Smith, All's Well That Ends Well: Toward a Policy of Assisted Rational Suicide or Merely Enlightened Self–Determination?, 22 U.C.Davis L.Rev. 275, 290–291, n. 106 (1989) (compiling statutes).

guard against potential abuses in such situations. Similarly, a State is entitled to consider that a judicial proceeding to make a determination regarding an incompetent's wishes may very well not be an adversarial one, with the added guarantee of accurate factfinding that the adversary process brings with it. Finally, we think a State may properly decline to make judgments about the "quality" of life that a particular individual may enjoy, and simply assert an unqualified interest in the preservation of human life to be weighed against the constitutionally protected interests of the individual.

In our view, Missouri has permissibly sought to advance these interests through the adoption of a "clear and convincing" standard of proof to govern such proceedings. . . . Further, this level of proof, or an even higher one, has traditionally been imposed in cases involving allegations of civil fraud, and in a variety of other kinds of civil cases involving such issues as . . . lost wills, oral contracts to make bequests, and the like.

We think it self-evident that the interests at stake in the instant proceedings are more substantial, both on an individual and societal level, than those involved in a run-of-the-mine civil dispute. But not only does the standard of proof reflect the importance of a particular adjudication, it also serves as a societal judgment about how the risk of error should be distributed between the litigants. The more stringent the burden of proof a party must bear, the more that party bears the risk of an erroneous decision. We believe that Missouri may permissibly place an increased risk of an erroneous decision on those seeking to terminate an incompetent individual's life-sustaining treatment. An erroneous decision not to terminate results in a maintenance of the status quo; the possibility of subsequent developments such as advancements in medical science, the discovery of new evidence regarding the patient's intent, changes in the law, or simply the unexpected death of the patient despite the administration of life-sustaining treatment, at least create the potential that a wrong decision will eventually be corrected or its impact mitigated. An erroneous decision to withdraw life-sustaining treatment, however, is not susceptible of correction. . . .

It is also worth noting that most, if not all, States simply forbid oral testimony entirely in determining the wishes of parties in transactions which, while important, simply do not have the consequences that a decision to terminate a person's life does. At common law and by statute in most States, the parol evidence rule prevents the variations of the terms of a written contract by oral testimony. The statute of frauds makes unenforceable oral contracts to leave property by will, and statutes regulating the making of wills universally require that those instruments be in writing. See 2 A. Corbin, Contracts § 398, pp. 360–361 (1950); 2 W. Page, Law of Wills §§ 19.3–19.5, pp. 61–71 (1960). There is no doubt that statutes requiring wills to be in writing, and statutes of frauds which require that a contract to make a will be in writing, on occasion frustrate the effectuation of the intent of a particular decedent, just as Missouri's requirement of proof in this case may have frustrated the effectuation of the not-fully-expressed desires of Nancy Cruzan. But the Constitution does not require general rules to work faultlessly; no general rule can.

In sum, we conclude that a State may apply a clear and convincing evidence standard in proceedings where a guardian seeks to discontinue nutrition and hydration of a person diagnosed to be in a persistent vegetative state. We note that many courts which have adopted some sort of substituted judgment procedure in situations like this, whether they limit consideration of evidence to the prior expressed wishes of the incompetent individual, or whether they allow more general proof of what the individual's decision would have been, require a clear and convincing standard of proof for such evidence.

The Supreme Court of Missouri held that in this case the testimony adduced at trial did not amount to clear and convincing proof of the patient's desire to have hydration and nutrition withdrawn. In so doing, it reversed a decision of the Missouri trial court which had found that the evidence "suggest[ed]" Nancy Cruzan would not have desired to continue such measures, but which had not adopted the standard of "clear and convincing evidence" enunciated by the Supreme Court. The testimony adduced at trial consisted primarily of Nancy Cruzan's statements made to a housemate about a year before her accident that she would not want to live should she face life as a "vegetable," and other observations to the same effect. The observations did not deal in terms with withdrawal of medical treatment or of hydration and nutrition. We cannot say that the Supreme Court of Missouri committed constitutional error in reaching the conclusion that it did.

Petitioners alternatively contend that Missouri must accept the "substituted judgment" of close family members even in the absence of substantial proof that their views reflect the views of the patient. . . .

No doubt is engendered by anything in this record but that Nancy Cruzan's mother and father are loving and caring parents. If the State were required by the United States Constitution to repose a right of "substituted judgment" with anyone, the Cruzans would surely qualify. But we do not think the Due Process Clause requires the State to repose judgment on these matters with anyone but the patient herself. Close family members may have a strong feeling—a feeling not at all ignoble or unworthy, but not entirely disinterested, either—that they do not wish to witness the continuation of the life of a loved one which they regard as hopeless, meaningless, and even degrading. But there is no automatic assurance that the view of close family members will necessarily be the same as the patient's would have been had she been confronted with the prospect of her situation while competent. All of the reasons previously discussed for allowing Missouri to require clear and convincing evidence of the patient's wishes lead us to conclude that the State may choose to defer only to those wishes, rather than confide the decision to close family members.

The judgment of the Supreme Court of Missouri is

Affirmed.

JUSTICE O'CONNOR, concurring.

I agree that a protected liberty interest in refusing unwanted medical treatment may be inferred from our prior decisions, see ante at 2851, and that the refusal of artificially delivered food and water is encompassed within that liberty interest. I write separately to clarify why I believe this to be so.

* * *

. . . Artificial feeding cannot readily be distinguished from other forms of medical treatment. See, e.g., Council on Ethical and Judicial Affairs, American Medical Association, AMA Ethical Opinion 2.20, Withholding or Withdrawing Life–Prolonging Medical Treatment, Current Opinions 13 (1989); The Hastings Center, Guidelines on the Termination of Life–Sustaining Treatment and the Care of the Dying 59 (1987). Whether or not the techniques used to pass food and water into the patient's alimentary tract are termed "medical treatment," it is clear they all involve some degree of intrusion and restraint. Feeding a patient by means of a nasogastric tube requires a physician to pass a long flexible tube through the patient's nose, throat and esophagus and into the stomach. Because of the discomfort such a tube causes, "[m]any patients need to be restrained forcibly and their hands put into large mittens to prevent them from removing the tube." Major, The Medical Procedures for Providing Food and Water: Indications and Effects, in By No Extraordinary Means: The Choice to Forgo Life–Sustaining Food and Water 25 (J. Lynn ed. 1986). A gastrostomy tube (as was used to provide food and water to Nancy Cruzan, or jejunostomy tube must be surgically implanted into the stomach or small intestine. Requiring a competent adult to endure such procedures against her will burdens the patient's liberty, dignity, and freedom to determine the course of her own treatment. Accordingly, the liberty guaranteed by the Due Process Clause must protect, if it protects anything, an individual's deeply personal decision to reject medical treatment, including the artificial delivery of food and water.

I also write separately to emphasize that the Court does not today decide the issue whether a State must also give effect to the decisions of a surrogate decisionmaker. In my view, such a duty may well be constitutionally required to protect the patient's liberty interest in refusing medical treatment. Few individuals provide explicit oral or written instructions regarding their intent to refuse medical treatment should they become incompetent.[1] States which decline to consider any

1. See 2 President's Commission for the Study of Ethical Problems in Medicine and Biomedical and Behavioral Research, Making Health Care Decisions 241–242 (1982) (36% of those surveyed gave instructions regarding how they would like to be treated if they ever became too sick to make decisions; 23% put those instructions in writing) (Lou Harris Poll, September 1982); American Medical Association Surveys of

evidence other than such instructions may frequently fail to honor a patient's intent. Such failures might be avoided if the State considered an equally probative source of evidence: the patient's appointment of a proxy to make health care decisions on her behalf. Delegating the authority to make medical decisions to a family member or friend is becoming a common method of planning for the future. Several States have recognized the practical wisdom of such a procedure by enacting durable power of attorney statutes that specifically authorize an individual to appoint a surrogate to make medical treatment decisions.[2] Some state courts have suggested that an agent appointed pursuant to a general durable power of attorney statute would also be empowered to make health care decisions on behalf of the patient.[3] Other States allow an individual to designate a proxy to carry out the intent of a living will.[4] These procedures for surrogate decisionmaking, which

Physician and Public Opinion on Health Care Issues 29–30 (1988) (56% of those surveyed had told family members their wishes concerning the use of life-sustaining treatment if they entered an irreversible coma; 15% had filled out a living will specifying those wishes).

2. At least 13 states and the District of Columbia have durable power of attorney statutes expressly authorizing the appointment of proxies for making health care decisions. See Alaska Stat.Ann. §§ 13.26.335, 13.26.344(*l*) (Supp.1989); Cal. Civ.Code § 2500 (Supp.1990); D.C.Code § 21–2205 (1989); Idaho Code § 39–4505 (Supp.1989); Ill.Rev.Stat., ch. 110½, ¶¶ 804–1 to 804–12 (Supp.1988); Kan.Stat. Ann. § 58–625 (Supp.1989); Me.Rev.Stat. Ann., Tit. 18–A, § 5–501 (Supp.1989); Nev. Rev.Stat. § 449.800 (Supp.1989); Ohio Rev. Code Ann. § 1337.11 et seq. (Supp.1989); Ore.Rev.Stat. § 127.510 (1989); Pa.Con. Stat.Ann., Tit. 20, § 5603(h) (Purdon Supp. 1989); R.I.Gen.Laws § 23–4.10–1 et seq. (1989); Tex.Rev.Civ.Stat.Ann. § 4590h–1 (Vernon Supp.1990); Vt.Stat.Ann., Tit. 14, § 3451 et seq. (1989).

3. All 50 states and the District of Columbia have general durable power of attorney statutes. See Ala.Code § 26–1–2 (1986); Alaska Stat.Ann. §§ 13.26.350 to 13.26.356 (Supp.1989); Ariz.Rev.Stat.Ann. § 14–5501 (1975); Ark.Code Ann. §§ 28–68–201 to 28–68–203 (1987); Cal.Civ.Code Ann. § 2400 (West Supp.1990); Colo.Rev. Stat. § 15–14–501 et seq. (1987); Conn.Gen. Stat. § 45–69*o* (Supp.1989); Del.Code Ann., Tit. 12, §§ 4901–4905 (1987); D.C.Code § 21–2081 et seq. (1989); Fla.Stat. § 709.08 (1989); Ga.Code Ann. § 10–6–36 (1989); Haw.Rev.Stat. §§ 551D–1 to 551D–7 (Supp. 1989); Idaho Code § 15–5–501 et seq. (Supp.1989); Ill.Rev.Stat., ch. 110½, ¶ 802–6 (1987); Ind.Code §§ 30–2–11–1 to 30–2–

11–7 (1988); Iowa Code § 633.705 (Supp. 1989); Kan.Stat.Ann. § 58–610 (1983); Ky. Rev.Stat.Ann. § 386.093 (Baldwin 1983); La.Civ.Code Ann. § 3027 (West Supp.1990); Me.Rev.Stat.Ann., Tit. 18–A, § 5–501 et seq. (Supp.1989); Md.Est. & Trusts Code Ann. §§ 13–601 to 13–602 (1974) (as interpreted by the Attorney General, see 73 Op. Md.Atty.Gen. No. 88–046 (Oct. 17, 1988)); Mass.Gen.Laws ch. 201B, § 1 to 201B, § 7 (1988); Mich.Comp.Laws §§ 700.495, 700.497 (1980); Minn.Stat. § 523.01 et seq. (1988); Miss.Code Ann. § 87–3–13 (Supp. 1989); Mo.Rev.Stat. § 404.700 (Supp.1990); Mont.Code Ann. §§ 72–5–501 to 72–5–502 (1989); Neb.Rev.Stat. §§ 30–2664 to 30–2672, 30–2667 (1985); Nev.Rev.Stat. § 111.460 et seq. (1986); N.H.Rev.Stat. Ann. § 506:6 et seq. (Supp.1989); N.J.Stat. Ann. § 46:2B–8 (1989); N.M.Stat.Ann. § 45–5–501 et seq. (1989); N.Y.Gen.Oblig. Law § 5–1602 (McKinney 1989); N.C.Gen. Stat. § 32A–1 et seq. (1987); N.D.Cent. Code §§ 30.1–30–01 to 30.1–30–05 (Supp. 1989); Ohio Rev.Code Ann. § 1337.09 (Supp.1989); Okla.Stat., Tit. 58, §§ 1071–1077 (Supp.1989); Ore.Rev.Stat. § 127.005 (1989); Pa.Con.Stat.Ann., Tit. 20, §§ 5601 et seq., 5602(a)(9) (Purdon Supp.1989); R.I. Gen.Laws § 34–22–6.1 (1984); S.C.Code §§ 62–5–501 to 62–5–502 (1987); S.D.Codified Laws § 59–7–2.1 (1978); Tenn.Code Ann. § 34–6–101 et seq. (1984); Tex.Prob. Code Ann. § 36A (Supp.1990); Utah Code Ann. § 75–5–501 et seq. (1978); Vt.Stat. Ann., Tit. 14, § 3051 et seq. (1989); Va. Code § 11–9.1 et seq. (1989); Wash.Rev. Code § 11.94.020 (1989); W.Va.Code § 39–4–1 et seq. (Supp.1989); Wis.Stat. § 243.07 (1987–1988) (as interpreted by the Attorney General, see Wis.Op.Atty.Gen. 35–88 (1988); Wyo.Stat. § 3–5–101 et seq. (1985).

4. Thirteen states have living will statutes authorizing the appointment of

appear to be rapidly gaining in acceptance, may be a valuable additional safeguard of the patient's interest in directing his medical care. Moreover, as patients are likely to select a family member as a surrogate, giving effect to a proxy's decisions may also protect the "freedom of personal choice in matters of . . . family life." Cleveland Board of Education v. LaFleur, 414 U.S. 632, 639, 94 S.Ct. 791, 796, 39 L.Ed.2d 52 (1974).

Today's decision, holding only that the Constitution permits a State to require clear and convincing evidence of Nancy Cruzan's desire to have artificial hydration and nutrition withdrawn, does not preclude a future determination that the Constitution requires the States to implement the decisions of a patient's duly appointed surrogate. Nor does it prevent States from developing other approaches for protecting an incompetent individual's liberty interest in refusing medical treatment. As is evident from the Court's survey of state court decisions, no national consensus has yet emerged on the best solution for this difficult and sensitive problem. Today we decide only that one State's practice does not violate the Constitution; the more challenging task of crafting appropriate procedures for safeguarding incompetents' liberty interests is entrusted to the "laboratory" of the States.

The opinion of JUSTICE SCALIA, concurring, is omitted.

[Only very limited excerpts of the dissenting opinions are included. The entire opinions are worthy of careful study for the interested student.]

JUSTICE BRENNAN, with whom JUSTICE MARSHALL and JUSTICE BLACKMUN join, dissenting.

"Medical technology has effectively created a twilight zone of suspended animation where death commences while life, in some form, continues. Some patients, however, want no part of a life sustained only by medical technology. Instead, they prefer a plan of medical treatment that allows nature to take its course and permits them to die with dignity."

Nancy Cruzan has dwelt in that twilight zone for six years. She is oblivious to her surroundings and will remain so. Her body twitches only reflexively, without consciousness. The areas of her brain that once thought, felt, and experienced sensations have degenerated badly and are continuing to do so. The cavities remaining are filling with cerebro-spinal fluid. The "'cerebral cortical atrophy is irreversible, permanent, progressive and ongoing.'" "Nancy will never interact meaningfully with her environment again. She will remain in a persistent vegetative state until her death." Because she cannot swal-

healthcare proxies. See Ark.Code Ann. § 20–17–202 (Supp.1989); Del.Code Ann., Tit. 16, § 2502 (1983); Fla.Stat. § 765.05(2) (1989); Idaho Code § 39–4504 (Supp.1989); Ind.Code § 16–8–11–14(g)(2) (1988); Iowa Code § 144A.7(1)(a) (1989); La.R.S.Ann., 40:1299.58.1, 40:1299.58.3(C) (West Supp. 1990); Minn.Stat. § 145B.01 et seq. (Supp. 1989); Texas Health & Safety Code Ann. § 672.003(d) (Supp.1990); Utah Code Ann. §§ 75–2–1105, 75–2–1106 (Supp.1989); Va. Code § 54.1–2986(2) (1988); 1987 Wash. Laws, ch. 162 § 1, Sec. (1)(b); Wyo.Stat. § 35–22–102 (1988).

low, her nutrition and hydration are delivered through a tube surgically implanted in her stomach.

A grown woman at the time of the accident, Nancy had previously expressed her wish to forgo continuing medical care under circumstances such as these. Her family and her friends are convinced that this is what she would want. A guardian ad litem appointed by the trial court is also convinced that this is what Nancy would want. Yet the Missouri Supreme Court, alone among state courts deciding such a question, has determined that an irreversibly vegetative patient will remain a passive prisoner of medical technology—for Nancy, perhaps for the next 30 years.

Today the Court, while tentatively accepting that there is some degree of constitutionally protected liberty interest in avoiding unwanted medical treatment, including life-sustaining medical treatment such as artificial nutrition and hydration, affirms the decision of the Missouri Supreme Court. The majority opinion, as I read it, would affirm that decision on the ground that a State may require "clear and convincing" evidence of Nancy Cruzan's prior decision to forgo life-sustaining treatment under circumstances such as hers in order to ensure that her actual wishes are honored. Because I believe that Nancy Cruzan has a fundamental right to be free of unwanted artificial nutrition and hydration, which right is not outweighed by any interests of the State, and because I find that the improperly biased procedural obstacles imposed by the Missouri Supreme Court impermissibly burden that right, I respectfully dissent. Nancy Cruzan is entitled to choose to die with dignity.

* * *

I respectfully dissent.

JUSTICE STEVENS, dissenting.

Our Constitution is born of the proposition that all legitimate governments must secure the equal right of every person to "Life, Liberty, and the pursuit of Happiness." [1] In the ordinary case we quite naturally assume that these three ends are compatible, mutually enhancing, and perhaps even coincident.

The Court would make an exception here. It permits the State's abstract, undifferentiated interest in the preservation of life to overwhelm the best interests of Nancy Beth Cruzan, interests which would, according to an undisputed finding, be served by allowing her guardians to exercise her constitutional right to discontinue medical treatment.

1. It is stated in the Declaration of Independence that:

"We hold these truths to be self-evident, that all men are created equal, that they are endowed by their Creator with certain unalienable Rights, that among these are Life, Liberty and the pursuit of Happiness.—That to secure these rights, Governments are instituted among Men, deriving their just powers from the consent of the governed,—That whenever any Form of Government becomes destructive of these ends, it is the Right of the People to alter or to abolish it, and to institute new Government, laying its foundation on such principles and organizing its powers in such form, as to them shall seem most likely to effect their Safety and Happiness."

Ironically, the Court reaches this conclusion despite endorsing three significant propositions which should save it from any such dilemma. First, a competent individual's decision to refuse life-sustaining medical procedures is an aspect of liberty protected by the Due Process Clause of the Fourteenth Amendment. Second, upon a proper evidentiary showing, a qualified guardian may make that decision on behalf of an incompetent ward. Third, in answering the important question presented by this tragic case, it is wise "not to attempt by any general statement, to cover every possible phase of the subject." Together, these considerations suggest that Nancy Cruzan's liberty to be free from medical treatment must be understood in light of the facts and circumstances particular to her.

I would so hold: in my view, the Constitution requires the State to care for Nancy Cruzan's life in a way that gives appropriate respect to her own best interests.

*   *   *

III

It is perhaps predictable that courts might undervalue the liberty at stake here. Because death is so profoundly personal, public reflection upon it is unusual. As this sad case shows, however, such reflection must become more common if we are to deal responsibly with the modern circumstances of death. Medical advances have altered the physiological conditions of death in ways that may be alarming: highly invasive treatment may perpetuate human existence through a merger of body and machine that some might reasonably regard as an insult to life rather than as its continuation. But those same advances, and the reorganization of medical care accompanying the new science and technology, have also transformed the political and social conditions of death: people are less likely to die at home, and more likely to die in relatively public places, such as hospitals or nursing homes.

Ultimate questions that might once have been dealt with in intimacy by a family and its physician have now become the concern of institutions. When the institution is a state hospital, as it is in this case, the government itself becomes involved. Dying nonetheless remains a part of the life which characteristically has its place in the home.

*   *   *

The more precise constitutional significance of death is difficult to describe; not much may be said with confidence about death unless it is said from faith, and that alone is reason enough to protect the freedom to conform choices about death to individual conscience. We may also, however, justly assume that death is not life's simple opposite, or its necessary terminus, but rather its completion. Our ethical tradition has long regarded an appreciation of mortality as essential to understanding life's significance. It may, in fact, be impossible to live for anything without being prepared to die for something. Certainly there was no disdain for life in Nathan Hale's most famous declaration or in Patrick Henry's; their words instead bespeak a passion for life that forever preserves their own lives in the memories of their countrymen. From such "honored dead we take increased devotion to that cause for which they gave the last full measure of devotion." [2]

These considerations cast into stark relief the injustice, and unconstitutionality, of Missouri's treatment of Nancy Beth Cruzan. Nancy Cruzan's death, when it comes, cannot be an historic act of heroism; it will inevitably be the consequence of her tragic accident. But Nancy Cruzan's interest in life, no less than that of any other person, includes an interest in how she will be thought of after her death by those whose opinions mattered to her. There can be no doubt that her life made her dear to her family, and to others. How she dies will affect how that life is remembered. The trial court's order authorizing Nancy's parents to cease their daughter's treatment would have permitted the family that cares for Nancy to bring to a close her tragedy and her death. Missouri's objection to that order subordinates Nancy's body, her family, and the lasting significance of her life to the State's own interests. The decision we review thereby interferes with constitutional interests of the highest order.

*   *   *

My disagreement with the Court is thus unrelated to its endorsement of the clear and convincing standard of proof for cases of this kind. Indeed, I agree that the controlling facts must be established with unmistakable clarity. The critical question, however, is not how to prove the controlling facts but rather what proven facts should be controlling. In my view, the constitutional answer is clear: the best interests of the individual, especially when buttressed by the interests of all related third parties, must prevail over any general state policy that simply ignores those interests. Indeed, the only apparent *secular* basis for the State's interest in life is the policy's persuasive impact upon people other than Nancy and her family. . . .

Only because Missouri has arrogated to itself the power to define life, and only because the Court permits this usurpation, are Nancy Cruzan's life and liberty put into disquieting conflict. If Nancy Cruzan's life were defined by reference to her own interests, so that her life expired when her biological existence ceased serving *any* of her own interests, then her constitutionally protected interest in freedom from unwanted treatment would not come into conflict with her constitutionally protected interest in life. Conversely, if there were *any* evidence that Nancy Cruzan herself defined life to encompass every form of biological persistence by a human being, so that the continuation of treatment would serve Nancy's own liberty, then once again there would be no conflict between life and liberty. The opposition of life and liberty in this case are thus not the result of Nancy Cruzan's tragic

2. A. Lincoln, Gettysburg Address, 1 Documents of American History (H. Commager ed.) (9th ed. 1973).

accident, but are instead the artificial consequence of Missouri's effort, and this Court's willingness, to abstract Nancy Cruzan's life from Nancy Cruzan's person.

IV

* * *

V

In this case, as is no doubt true in many others, the predicament confronted by the healthy members of the Cruzan family merely adds emphasis to the best interests finding made by the trial judge. Each of us has an interest in the kind of memories that will survive after death. To that end, individual decisions are often motivated by their impact on others. A member of the kind of family identified in the trial court's findings in this case would likely have not only a normal interest in minimizing the burden that her own illness imposes on others, but also an interest in having their memories of her filled predominantly with thoughts about her past vitality rather than her current condition. The meaning and completion of her life should be controlled by persons who have her best interests at heart—not by a state legislature concerned only with the "preservation of human life."

The Cruzan family's continuing concern provides a concrete reminder that Nancy Cruzan's interests did not disappear with her vitality or her consciousness. However commendable may be the State's interest in human life, it cannot pursue that interest by appropriating Nancy Cruzan's life as a symbol for its own purposes. Lives do not exist in abstraction from persons, and to pretend otherwise is not to honor but to desecrate the State's responsibility for protecting life. A State that seeks to demonstrate its commitment to life may do so by aiding those who are actively struggling for life and health. In this endeavor, unfortunately, no State can lack for opportunities: there can be no need to make an example of tragic cases like that of Nancy Cruzan.

I respectfully dissent.

NOTES

1. After the decision in *Cruzan,* the Kansas City probate court conducted a new hearing and considered new evidence of three former co-workers who recalled specific conversations in which Nancy Cruzan had expressed the thought that she would never want to "live" in a vegetable-like condition. Accordingly, in an order entered on December 14, 1990, the judge found there was the required clear and convincing evidence and ordered that Cruzan's food and water be cut off. See, "Cruzan's Death Doesn't Still Debate," ABA Journal, p. 26 (March, 1991).

2. In In re Longeway, 133 Ill.2d 33, 139 Ill.Dec. 780, 549 N.E.2d 292 (1989), the court found authority in the Illinois Probate Act and the common law to permit withholding medical treatment from a 76–year old incompetent and permanently comatose woman. The patient had left no will nor was there a

power of attorney. Skirting federal and state constitutional privacy rights, the boundaries of which the majority of the Illinois Supreme Court found unclear, it found authority to deal with such topics in the common law concept to refuse medical treatment which, it said, includes artificial nutrition and hydration, and applied probate act concepts to permit a surrogate to act on behalf of an incompetent ward. In setting out the procedure, the court said:

> The first step in allowing an incompetent patient to refuse artificial nutrition and hydration through a surrogate is to define, as best we can, what kind of an incompetent patient is eligible for surrogate exercise of this right. First, we wish to state emphatically that we do not condone suicide or active euthanasia in this State. Accordingly, an incompetent patient must be terminally ill before his right to refuse artificial sustenance may be exercised. We note that the Living Will Act (Ill.Rev.Stat.1987, ch. 110½, par. 702(h)) defines "terminal condition" as an incurable and irreversible condition which is such that death is imminent and the application of death-delaying procedures serves only to prolong the dying process. We find that it is appropriate to apply this definition to the requirement we have just stated that the incompetent patient must be terminally ill. Second, such patient must be diagnosed as irreversibly comatose, or in a persistently vegetative state. . . .

> Finally, the accuracy of the diagnosis must be safe-guarded. Consequently, the patient's attending physician along with at least two other consulting physicians must concur in the diagnosis.

> The next step is to balance an eligible patient's right to discontinue sustenance against any interests the State may have in continuing it. The cases identify four countervailing State interests: "(1) the preservation of life; (2) the protection of the interests of innocent third parties; (3) the prevention of suicide; and (4) maintaining the ethical integrity of the medical profession." Normally, none of these interests will override a patient's refusal of artificially administered food and water. Adequate safeguards exist to protect life and third parties, and to prevent suicide. Moreover, the ethical integrity of the medical profession can be ensured by not compelling (by court order or any other means) any medical facility or its staff to act contrary to their moral principles. The patient can be transferred to a different facility or a new physician can be appointed to carry out the patient's wishes, if the current staff or physician cannot.

> The next step is to detail how the patient's wishes can be ascertained. Obviously, a patient who is irreversibly comatose or in a vegetative state will be incompetent, unable to communicate his intent. The courts have generally employed one of two theories in ascertaining an incompetent patient's wishes: "best interests" or "substituted judgment."

> The best-interests approach has been utilized by several courts dealing with this issue. Under the best-interests test, a surrogate decisionmaker chooses for the incompetent patient which medical procedures would be in the patient's best interests. The criteria used include relief from suffering, preservation or restoration of functioning, and quality and extent of sustained life. The problem with the best-interests test is that it lets another make a determination of a

patient's quality of life, thereby undermining the foundation of self-determination and inviolability of the person upon which the right to refuse medical treatment stands. A dilemma arises, of course, when the patient is an infant or life-long incompetent who never could have made a reasoned judgment about his quality of life. While not passing on the viability of the best-interests theory in Illinois, we decline to adopt it in this case because we believe the record demonstrates the relevancy of the substituted-judgment theory. Furthermore, the substituted-judgment theory has already been implicitly adopted in Illinois by our legislature in the Powers of Attorney for Health Care Law. The Law states: "Your agent will have authority * * * to obtain or terminate any type of health care, including withdrawal of food and water * * * if your agent believes such action *would be consistent with your intent and desires.*" (Emphasis added.) Ill.Rev.Stat.1987, ch. 110½, par. 804–10.

Under substituted judgment, a surrogate decision-maker attempts to establish, with as much accuracy as possible, what decision the patient would make if he were competent to do so. Employing this theory, the surrogate first tries to determine if the patient had expressed explicit intent regarding this type of medical treatment prior to becoming incompetent. Where no clear intent exists, the patient's personal value system must guide the surrogate: * * *

In this case, Mrs. Longeway's guardian must substitute her judgment for that of Longeway's, based upon other clear and convincing evidence of Longeway's intent. The guidelines quoted above from *Jobes* should aid in ascertaining Longeway's desires and in reaching a decision. On remand, the court should not hesitate to admit any reliable and relevant evidence if it will aid in judging Longeway's intent.

The final step in a patient's exercise of the right to refuse life-sustaining treatment is to determine the role of the court. The majority of the cases addressing the issue do not specifically require a court order to withdraw artificial life support. Nevertheless, we feel that to halt artificial sustenance, the intervention of a judge is proper for several reasons.

First, Illinois has a strong public policy of preserving the sanctity of human life, even if in an imperfect state. Health care professionals serve patients best by maintaining a presumption in favor of sustaining life, while recognizing that competent patients are entitled to choose to forego any treatments, including those that sustain life. Because we agree that a presumption exists favoring life, we find that scrutiny by a judge is appropriate in these cases. Furthermore, since the key element in deciding to refuse or withdraw artificial sustenance is determining the patient's intent, we require proof of this element by clear and convincing evidence.

Second, court intervention is necessary to guard against the remote, yet real possibility that greed may taint the judgment of the surrogate decisionmaker. We stress that the record in the case before us reveals no such problems and we do not imply that greed is present here. We can foresee other cases, however, where the surrogate decisionmaker stands to profit from the patient's demise and covets ill-gotten wealth to the point of fatal attraction. Generally, no penetrating investigation will be required. Nevertheless, the judge is free to inquire as to the beneficiaries and extent of the patient's estate, if it appears necessary to do so.

Third, the courts have a *parens patriae* power which enables them to protect the estate and person of incompetents. Moreover, if the surrogate decisionmaker is a court-appointed guardian, procedural due process questions involving deprivation of life may arise. . . .

We recognize that some will consider court intervention objectionable. The medical profession may rightfully resent judicial intrusion into its domain. The slow, deliberate nature of the court system may frustrate the family and loved ones of the patient. Although we feel that the courts can act expeditiously in clear-cut uncontested cases, we acknowledge these objections and the difficulty in reaching a balanced approach to this dilemma. For this reason, we, like most courts that have pondered these issues, invite the legislature to address this problem. . . .

3. The topic of the right to die has generated innumerable articles and books. Among the voluminous literature, Alan Meisel's book "The Right to Die" was named the most outstanding book in the legal and accounting practice category for 1989 by The Association of American Publishers.

For some comments that pre-date *Cruzan*, see Gurney, Is There a Right to Die: A Study of the Law of Euthanasia, 3 Cumber.Law L.Rev. 235 (1972); Louisell, Euthanasia, and Biathanasia: On Dying and Killing, 22 Cath.U.L.Rev. 723 (1973); Vodiga, Euthanasia and the Right to Die—Moral, Ethical, and Legal Perspectives, 51 Chi.Kent L.Rev. 1 (1974); Robertson, Involuntary Euthanasia of Defective Newborns: A Legal Analysis, 27 Stan.L.Rev. 213 (1975). Ellis III, Letting Defective Babies Die: Who Decides?, 7 Am.J.L. & Med. 393 (1982); Ward, Euthanasia: A Medical and Legal Overview, 49 Kan.B.A.J. 317 (1980); Hill, Euthanasia: The Right To Be "Let" Alone, 7 S.U.L.Rev. 101 (1980); Ufford, Brain Death—Termination of Heroic Efforts to Save Life—Who Decides?, 19 Washburn L.J. 225 (1980); Note, *In re Quinlan* Revisited: The Judicial Role in Protecting the Privacy Rights of Dying Incompetents, 15 Hastings Const.L.Q. 479 (1988); Weber, Substituted Judgment Doctrine: A Critical Analysis, 1 Issues in L. & Med. 131 (1985).

4. The seminal case is Matter of Karen Ann Quinlan, 70 N.J. 10, 355 A.2d 647 (1976). After removal of the life support systems, Miss Quinlan remained in a vegetative coma and finally died in June of 1985.

5. Consider this UPI release which appeared in the press:

"Medical Vegetable" Survives Coma, Starts New Life

Union, Ill. (UPI)—Carol Dusold Rogman, 28, was called a "medical vegetable" nine years ago.

A doctor told her mother there was no hope and that "all we could do is try to starve her by taking the intravenous out." But Mrs. Dusold refused to give up the hope her daughter's life could be saved.

Today the woman is married and has a 19–month–old son.

Carol Dusold was in a coma for four months after severely bruising her brain stem and breaking her left arm in an auto accident when she was 19.

The Dundee Community High School Homecoming Queen wasted away to 65 pounds, her body frozen in a grotesque position. And after regaining consciousness, it took almost a year to learn to walk and talk again.

"I was glad I had a mother like I had. I realize now how much she must have loved me and cared for me and had a deep feeling for me.

"She was so determined that I was going to make it.

"She kept telling me, 'You're going to make it,' and that she needed me at home because my father was dead and my brother was in the service. Nobody was home except my mother.

"I had the determination to pull through. I don't know if it was for my mother, or for the religious beliefs I had, but I pulled through and I'm here to help whoever needs it," Mrs. Rogman said.

Neither she nor her mother resented the doctors who advised her life-supporting treatments be ended, she said.

"I don't blame them one bit. It wasn't their fault. They did the best they could because they had no knowledge of whatever was going on, except from former experiences.

"You couldn't expect a miracle. Although we did, we shouldn't have."

She still limps, has a slight speech impediment and has a little trouble with her permanently curled left hand, but Mrs. Rogman said she really doesn't "see all the harm that came out of" the accident.

Concerning other similar cases, such as the Karen Quinlan case in New Jersey, Mrs. Rogman said "I really don't think they should shut the machine off, because you never know what is going to happen. Because miracles do happen. I know for a fact."

(b) SUICIDE

Suicide is the intentional killing of oneself. At common law it was a felony, punishable by forfeiture of goods and ignominous burial; attempted suicide was a misdemeanor. Since forfeiture of goods as a punishment for crime has largely been abandoned, and ignominous burial is no longer practiced, it might be said that the successful suicide has not committed any offense, since he cannot be punished. Some states still punish the unsuccessful (attempted) suicide by statute.

IN RE JOSEPH G.

Supreme Court of California, 1983.
34 Cal.3d 429, 194 Cal.Rptr. 163, 667 P.2d 1176.

MOSK, JUSTICE.

Joseph G., a minor, was charged in a juvenile court petition to declare him a ward of the court, with murder, and aiding and abetting a suicide. At the contested adjudication hearing, the court sustained the petition as to the murder count but dismissed the aiding and abetting charge as inapplicable; the court further found that the murder was in the first degree.

In the case before us a genuine suicide pact was partially fulfilled by driving a car over a cliff; the primary issue is whether the survivor, who drove the vehicle, is guilty of aiding and abetting the suicide rather than the murder of his deceased partner. We conclude that, under the unusual, inexplicable and tragic circumstances of this case, the minor's actions fall more properly within the statutory definition of the former (Pen.Code, § 401).

I.

The minor and his friend, Jeff W., both 16 years old, drove to the Fillmore library one evening and joined a number of their friends who had congregated there. During the course of the two hours they spent at the library talking, mention was made of a car turnout on a curve over-looking a 300 to 350–foot precipice on a country road known as "the cliff." Both the minor and Jeff declared that they intended to "fly off the cliff" and that they meant to kill themselves. The others were skeptical but the minor affirmed their seriousness, stating "You don't believe us that we are going to do it. We are going to do it. You can read it in the paper tomorrow." The minor gave one of the girls his baseball hat, saying firmly that this was the last time he would see her. Jeff repeatedly encouraged the minor by urging, "let's go, let's go" whenever the minor spoke. One other youth attempted to get in the car with Jeff and the minor but they refused to allow him to join them "because we don't want to be responsible for you." Jeff and the minor shook hands with their friends and departed.

The pair then drove to a gas station and put air in a front tire of the car, which had been damaged earlier in the evening; the fender and passenger door were dented and the tire was very low in air pressure, nearly flat. Two of their fellow students, Keith C. and Craig B., drove up and spoke with Jeff and the minor. The minor said, "Shake my hand and stay cool." Jeff urged, "Let's go," shook their hands and said, "Remember you shook my hand." The minor then drove off in the direction of the cliff with Jeff in the passenger seat; Keith and Craig surreptitiously followed them out of curiosity. The minor and Jeff proceeded up the hill past the cliff, turned around and drove down around the curve and over the steep cliff.

Two other vehicles were parked in the turnout, from which vantage point their occupants watched the minor's car plummeting down the hill at an estimated 50 mph. The car veered off the road without swerving or changing course; the witnesses heard the car accelerate and then drive straight off the cliff. No one saw brakelights flash. The impact of the crash killed Jeff and caused severe injuries to the minor, resulting in the amputation of a foot.

* * *

II.

The minor maintains that, under the peculiar circumstances presented here, he can be convicted only of aiding and abetting a suicide and not of murder. We begin by reviewing the development of the law relevant to suicide and related crimes.

At common law suicide was a felony, punished by forfeiture of property to the king and ignominious burial. Essentially, suicide was considered a form of murder. Under American law, suicide has never been punished and the ancient English attitude has been expressly rejected. Rather than classifying suicide as criminal, suicide in the United States "has continued to be considered an expression of mental illness." As one commentator has noted, "punishing suicide is contrary to modern penal and psychological theory." (Victoroff, The Suicidal Patient: Recognition, Intervention, Management (1982) pp. 173–174 (hereafter referred to as Victoroff).)

Currently no state, including California, has a statute making a successful suicide a crime, nor does the Model Penal Code recognize suicide as a crime. Contemporary England, by abolishing its criminal penalties for suicide, has also adopted this more modern approach.

Attempted suicide was also a crime at common law. A few American jurisdictions have adopted this view, but most, including California, attach no criminal liability to one who makes a suicide attempt. . . .

The law has, however, retained culpability for aiding, abetting and advising suicide. At common law, an aider and abettor was guilty of murder by construction of law because he was a principal in the second degree to the self-murder of the other. Most states provide, either by statute or case law, criminal sanctions for aiding suicide, but few adopt the extreme common law position that such conduct is murder. Some jurisdictions instead classify aiding suicide as a unique type of manslaughter.[1] But the predominant statutory scheme, and the one adopted in California, is to create a sui generis crime of aiding and abetting suicide.[2] This latter structure reflects a fundamental shift in the understanding of the law. Since public morals are no longer imposed upon the would-be suicide, the traditional rationale that would support the proscription of assisting suicide as the assistance of a crime is accordingly eroded. The modern trend reflected by this statutory scheme is therefore to mitigate the punishment for assisting a suicide by removing it from the harsh consequences of homicide law and giving

1. Alaska Stat., § 11.41.120; Ariz.Rev. Stat.Ann., § 13–1103; Ark.Stat.Ann., § 41–1504; Colo.Rev.Stat., § 18–3–104; Conn.Gen.Stat., § 53a–56; Fla.Stat.Ann., § 782.08; Hawaii Rev.Stat., § 707–702; N.Y.Penal Law, § 125.15; Ore.Rev.Stat., § 163.125. (See Englehardt & Malloy, Suicide and Assisting Suicide: A Critique of Legal Sanctions (1982) 36 Sw.L.J. 1003, 1019 at fn. 71 (hereafter cited as Englehardt & Malloy).)

2. State statutes which criminalize assisting suicide as a specific offense include: Cal.Pen.Code, § 401; Del.Code Ann., tit. 11, § 645; Ind.Stat.Ann. § 35–42–1–2; Kan.Stat.Ann., § 21–3406; Me.Rev.Stat. Ann., tit. 17–A, § 204; Minn.Stat.Ann., § 609.215; Miss.Code Ann., § 97–3–49; Mo.Ann.Stat., § 565.021; Mont.Code Ann. § 45–5–105; Neb.Rev.Stat., § 28–307; N.H. Stat.Ann., § 603.4; N.J.Stat.Ann., § 2C:11–6; N.M.Stat.Ann., § 30–2–4; N.Y. Penal Law, § 120.30; Okla.Stat.Ann., tit. 21, §§ 813–818; 18 Pa.Const.Stat.Ann., § 2505; P.R.Laws Ann., tit. 33, § 1385; S.D.Codified Laws Ann., § 22–16–37; Tex. Pen.Code Ann., § 22.08; Wash.Rev.Code Ann., § 9A.36.060; Wis.Stat.Ann., § 940.12 (see Englehardt & Malloy, supra, 36 Sw. L.J. at p. 1019, fn. 72).

it a separate criminal classification more carefully tailored to the actual culpability of the aider and abettor.

The California aiding statute, in effect since 1873, provides simply that "Every person who deliberately aids, or advises or encourages another to commit suicide, is guilty of a felony." (Pen.Code, § 401.) This statute, although creating a felony, places California among the most lenient jurisdictions in its punishment for those who assist suicide. The sole California decision which even peripherally considers criminal liability for assisting suicide under this statute is People v. Matlock (1959) 51 Cal.2d 682, 336 P.2d 505. Although by no means entirely dispositive of the issue presented here, the opinion is reviewed in some depth because of the paucity of apposite decisions.

The defendant in *Matlock* was convicted of murder and robbery. Although admitting that he strangled the victim and took his money, the defendant claimed he did so solely at the victim's insistence. According to the defendant, the victim, who had only six months to live and had been recently convicted of a federal crime, sought a way to die but could not commit suicide without forfeiting the benefits of his insurance policy; the victim therefore induced the defendant to kill him and take his property so that it would appear to be a robbery-murder.

. . . Relying on the Oregon decision in People v. Bouse (1953) 199 Or. 676, 264 P.2d 800 (overruled on other issues in State v. Brewton (1964) 238 Or. 590, 395 P.2d 874, 878), we held that the defendant's active participation in the final overt act causing the victim's death, i.e., strangling him, precluded the application of the aiding suicide statute.

In *Bouse,* the defendant's wife drowned in a bathtub; there was evidence that she had told the defendant she wanted to die and that he attempted suicide shortly after her death. On the evidence, the jury could have found that the defendant held his wife's head underwater, despite her struggles, until she died, thereby committing murder. On the other hand, the jury might have found that the defendant merely ran the water and assisted his wife into the tub, and was therefore guilty of only manslaughter under the Oregon assisting statute. In upholding the manslaughter instruction, the court reasoned that the latter statute "does not contemplate active participation by one in the overt act directly causing death. It contemplates some participation in the events leading up to the commission of the final overt act, such as furnishing the means for bringing about death—the gun, the knife, the poison, or providing the water, for the use of the person who himself commits the act of self-murder. But where a person actually performs, or actively assists in performing, the overt act resulting in death, such as shooting or stabbing the victim, administering the poison, or holding one under water until death takes place by drowning, his act constitutes murder, and it is wholly immaterial whether this act is committed pursuant to an agreement with the victim, such as a mutual suicide pact."

* * *

Under *Matlock* and *Bouse,* the key to distinguishing between the crimes of murder and of assisting suicide is the active or passive role of the defendant in the suicide. If the defendant merely furnishes the means, he is guilty of aiding a suicide; if he actively participates in the death of the suicide victim, he is guilty of murder. If this literal formulation were to be applied mechanically to the facts in the case at hand, it would be difficult not to conclude that the minor, by driving the car, "actively participated" in the death of his friend Jeff. It must be remembered, however, that *Matlock* did not involve a suicide pact but instead dealt with the more straightforward situation in which a suicide victim is killed as a result of direct injury that the defendant inflicts on him, i.e., strangling. The reasoning which justified the application of the active/passive distinction in *Matlock* is therefore not wholly apposite to the peculiar facts shown here. The present case requires us instead to consider an entirely distinct situation to determine whether the minor's actions fall most appropriately within the conduct sought to be proscribed by Penal Code section 401.

* * *

Traditionally under the common law the survivor of a suicide pact was held to be guilty of murder. . . . It has been suggested that "the reason for imposing criminal liability upon a surviving party to a suicide pact is the 'support' such a pact presents . . . [¶] Besides the notion of 'support,' . . . [s]urviving a suicide pact gives rise to a presumption . . . that the participant may have entered into the pact in less than good faith. Survival, either because one party backed out at the last minute or because the poison, or other agent, did not have the desired effect, suggests that the pact may have been employed to induce the other person to take his own life. . . .

Under the facts presented here, these concerns are not particularly appropriate. First, the trial judge was satisfied there was a genuine suicide pact between Jeff and the minor. By "genuine," we mean simply that the pact was freely entered into and was not induced by force, duress or deception. There is no evidence in the present case that Jeff's participation in the pact was anything but fully voluntary and uncoerced. Second, because of the instrumentality used there was no danger of fraud: the potential consequences for the minor of driving the car off the cliff were identical to the potential consequences for Jeff, his passenger. Finally, the suicide and the attempted suicide were committed simultaneously by the same act.

These factors clearly distinguish the present case from the murder-suicide pact situation in which one party to the agreement actively kills the other (e.g., by shooting, poison, etc.) and then is to kill himself. The active participant in that scenario has the opportunity to renege on the agreement after killing the other or to feign agreement only for the purpose of disposing of his companion and without any true intention to commit suicide himself. By contrast, in the case at hand the minor and Jeff, because of the instrumentality chosen, necessarily were to commit their suicidal acts simultaneously and were subject to identical risks of death. The potential for fraud is thus absent in a genuine suicide pact executed simultaneously by both parties by means of the same instrumentality. The traditional rationale for holding the survivor of the pact guilty of murder is thus not appropriate in this limited factual situation.

The anomaly of classifying the minor's actions herein as murder is further illustrated by consideration of Jeff's potential criminal liability had he survived. If Jeff, the passenger, had survived and the minor had been killed, Jeff would be guilty, at most, of a violation of Penal Code section 401. In order to commit suicide by this means, i.e., a car, only one of the parties to the pact, the driver, can be said to "control" the instrumentality. To make the distinction between criminal liability for first degree murder and merely aiding and abetting suicide turn on the fortuitous circumstance of which of the pair was actually driving serves no rational purpose. The illogic of such a distinction has been similarly recognized in the classic example of the parties to the pact agreeing to commit suicide by gassing themselves in a closed room. If the party who turns on the gas survives, he is guilty of murder; if on the other hand, the other person survives, that person's criminal liability is only that of an aider and abettor. . . .

In light of the foregoing analysis we decline to ritualistically apply the active/passive distinction of *Matlock* to the genuine suicide pact situation in which the suicides are undertaken simultaneously by a single instrumentality. Given the inapplicability of *Matlock,* the actions of the minor constitute no more than a violation of Penal Code section 401.

The order declaring the minor a ward of the court is reversed and the cause is remanded to the trial court for further proceedings not inconsistent with this opinion.

NOTE

1. In the article by Englehardt, Jr. and Malloy, "Suicide and Assisting Suicide: A Critique of Legal Sanctions," 36 Southwestern L.J. 1003 (1982), the authors explore the recent statutory enactments on "The Right to Die" and cases, to raise the issue whether penalties for passively assisted suicide ought to be maintained, and concludes that suicide and aiding and abetting suicide should be legislatively defined as non-criminal.

2. Is a decision to have artificial feeding tubes of an incurable ill person removed, assisting a person in committing suicide? Justice Scalia, in his concurring opinion in Cruzan v. Director, Missouri Department of Health (1990), supra, said in part:

At common law in England, a suicide—defined as one who "deliberately puts an end to his own existence, or commits any unlawful malicious act, the consequence of which is his own death," 4 W. Blackstone, Commentaries *189—was criminally liable. Although the

States abolished the penalties imposed by the common law (i.e., forfeiture and ignominious burial), they did so to spare the innocent family, and not to legitimize the act. Case law at the time of the Fourteenth Amendment generally held that assisting suicide was a criminal offense. See Marzen, O'Dowd, Crone, & Balch, Suicide: A Constitutional Right?, 24 Duquesne L.Rev. 1, 76 (1985) ("In short, twenty-one of the thirty-seven states, and eighteen of the thirty ratifying states prohibited assisting suicide. Only eight of the states, and seven of the ratifying states, definitely did not"). The System of Penal Law presented to the House of Representatives by Representative Livingston in 1828 would have criminalized assisted suicide. The Field Penal Code, adopted by the Dakota Territory in 1877, proscribed attempted suicide and assisted suicide. And most States that did not explicitly prohibit assisted suicide in 1868 recognized, when the issue arose in the 50 years following the Fourteenth Amendment's ratification, that assisted and (in some cases) attempted suicide were unlawful. Thus, "there is no significant support for the claim that a right to suicide is so rooted in our tradition that it may be deemed 'fundamental' or 'implicit in the concept of ordered liberty.'" Id., at 100 (quoting Palko v. Connecticut, 302 U.S. 319, 325, 58 S.Ct. 149, 152, 82 L.Ed. 288 (1937)).

Petitioners rely on three distinctions to separate Nancy Cruzan's case from ordinary suicide: (1) that she is permanently incapacitated and in pain; (2) that she would bring on her death not by any affirmative act but by merely declining treatment that provides nourishment; and (3) that preventing her from effectuating her presumed wish to die requires violation of her bodily integrity. None of these suffices. Suicide was not excused even when committed "to avoid those ills which [persons] had not the fortitude to endure." 4 Blackstone, supra, at *189. "The life of those to whom life has become a burden—of those who are hopelessly diseased or fatally wounded—nay, even the lives of criminals condemned to death, are under the protection of the law, equally as the lives of those who are in the full tide of life's enjoyment, and anxious to continue to live." Blackburn v. State, 23 Ohio St. 146, 163 (1873). Thus, a man who prepared a poison, and placed it within reach of his wife, "to put an end to her suffering" from a terminal illness was convicted of murder, People v. Roberts, 211 Mich. 187, 178 N.W. 690, 693 (1920); the "incurable suffering of the suicide, as a legal question, could hardly affect the degree of criminality. . . ." Note, 30 Yale L.J. 408, 412 (1921) (discussing *Roberts*). Nor would the imminence of the patient's death have affected liability. "The lives of all are equally under the protection of the law, and under that protection to their last moment. . . . [Assisted suicide] is declared by the law to be murder, irrespective of the wishes or the condition of the party to whom the poison is administered. . . ." *Blackburn*, supra, at 163; see also Commonwealth v. Bowen, 13 Mass. 356, 360 (1816).

The second asserted distinction—suggested by the recent cases canvassed by the Court concerning the right to refuse treatment, ante, at 2846–2850—relies on the dichotomy between action and inaction. Suicide, it is said, consists of an affirmative act to end one's life; refusing treatment is not an affirmative act "causing" death, but merely a passive acceptance of the natural process of dying. I readily acknowledge that the distinction between action and inaction has some bearing upon the legislative judgment of what ought to be prevented as suicide—though even there it would seem to me unreasonable to draw the line precisely between action and inaction, rather than between various forms of inaction. It would not make much sense to say that one may not kill oneself by walking into the sea, but may sit on the beach until submerged by the incoming tide; or that one may not intentionally lock oneself into a cold storage locker, but may refrain from coming indoors when the temperature drops below freezing. Even as a legislative matter, in other words, the intelligent line does not fall between action and inaction but between those forms of inaction that consist of abstaining from "ordinary" care and those that consist of abstaining from "excessive" or "heroic" measures. Unlike action vs. inaction, that is not a line to be discerned by logic or legal analysis, and we should not pretend that it is.

But to return to the principal point for present purposes: the irrelevance of the action-inaction distinction. Starving oneself to death is no different from putting a gun to one's temple as far as the common-law definition of suicide is concerned; the cause of death in both cases is the suicide's conscious decision to pu[t] an end to his own existence. Of course the common law rejected the action-inaction distinction in other contexts involving the taking of human life as well. In the prosecution of a parent for the starvation death of her infant, it was no defense that the infant's death was "caused" by no action of the parent but by the natural process of starvation, or by the infant's natural inability to provide for itself. A physician, moreover, could be criminally liable for failure to provide care that could have extended the patient's life, even if death was immediately caused by the underlying disease that the physician failed to treat.

It is not surprising, therefore, that the early cases considering the claimed right to refuse medical treatment dismissed as specious the nice distinction between "passively submitting to death and actively seeking it. The distinction may be merely verbal, as it would be if an adult sought death by starvation instead of a drug. If the State may interrupt one mode of self-destruction, it may with equal authority interfere with the other." John F. Kennedy Memorial Hosp. v. Heston, 58 N.J. 576, 581–582, 279 A.2d 670, 672–673 (1971).

The third asserted basis of distinction—that frustrating Nancy Cruzan's wish to die in the present case requires interference with her bodily integrity—is likewise inadequate, because such interference is impermissible only if one begs the question whether her refusal to undergo the treatment on her own is suicide. It has always been lawful not only for the State, but even for private citizens, to interfere with bodily integrity to prevent a felony. That general rule has of course been applied to suicide. At common law, even a private person's use of force to prevent suicide was privileged. It is not even reasonable, much less required by the Constitution, to maintain that although the State has the right to prevent a person from slashing his wrists it does not have the power to apply physical force to prevent him from doing so, nor the power, should he succeed, to apply, coercively if necessary, medical measures to stop the flow of blood. The state-run hospital, I am certain, is not liable under 42 U.S.C.

M., I. & B. Cs. Crim.Law 5th Ed. UCB—7

§ 1983 for violation of constitutional rights, nor the private hospital liable under general tort law, if, in a State where suicide is unlawful, it pumps out the stomach of a person who has intentionally taken an overdose of barbiturates, despite that person's wishes to the contrary.

The dissents of Justices Brennan and Stevens make a plausible case for our intervention here only by embracing—the latter explicitly and the former by implication—a political principle that the States are free to adopt, but that is demonstrably not imposed by the Constitution. "The State," says Justice Brennan, "has no legitimate general interest in someone's life, completely abstracted from the interest of the person living that life, that could outweigh the person's choice *to avoid medical treatment.*" (emphasis added). The italicized phrase sounds moderate enough, and is all that is needed to cover the present case—but the proposition cannot *logically* be so limited. One who accepts it must also accept, I think, that the State has no such legitimate interest that could outweigh "the person's choice *to put an end to her life.*" . . . For insofar as balancing the relative interests of the State and the individual is concerned, there is nothing distinctive about accepting death through the refusal of "medical treatment," as opposed to accepting it through the refusal of food, or through the failure to shut off the engine and get out of the car after parking in one's garage after work. Suppose that Nancy Cruzan were in precisely the condition she is in today, except that she could be fed and digest food and water *without* artificial assistance. How is the State's "interest" in keeping her alive thereby increased, or her interest in deciding whether she wants to continue living reduced? It seems to me, in other words, that Justice Brennan's position ultimately rests upon the proposition that it is none of the State's business if a person wants to commit suicide. Justice Stevens is explicit on the point: "Choices about death touch the core of liberty. . . . [N]ot much may be said with confidence about death unless it is said from faith, and that alone is reason enough to protect the freedom to conform choices about death to individual conscience." This is a view that some societies have held, and that our States are free to adopt if they wish. But it is not a view imposed by our constitutional traditions, in which the power of the State to prohibit suicide is unquestionable.

* * *

3. If a person commits suicide in Japan, and does so for a "higher cause," then the act of suicide is considered praiseworthy. This has been illustrated by examples of suicide dive bombers who crash their planes on enemy ships to sink the vessels, and by persons who publicly commit suicide to protest the sex scandals in the highest echelons of government. On the other hand, if a person commits suicide for a personal motive, as where a student jumps from a high-rise building with his books because he cannot stand the pressures of university life, then the act of committing suicide brings great shame and humiliation upon his family. It may even expose the deceased's family to punishment in the form of fines if the suicide also causes damage or loss to society. In one reported case, a person committed suicide by jumping in front of a commuter train, and thereby disrupted and halted all commuter train traffic for three hours while the victim's bodily remains were scraped off the tracks; the family may be assessed fines to compensate society for the disruption of public transportation.

(c) When Does Death Occur?

Important legal issues arise when a vital organ is removed, for transplant purposes, from a crime victim who is considered medically "dead." Consider the following case situations:

Police arrive at a crime scene where they find a young man lying in a pool of blood with a bullet in his brain. Upon arrival at the hospital, the victim is comatose and given "one chance in a million" to survive after having been hooked up to life support systems which kept his heart beating. Two days later doctors decide the victim is dead because his brain stopped functioning and they proceed to remove his still beating heart to rush it to a university medical school where it is transplanted into the chest of a person with a defective heart. The person who fired the shot into the young man's brain is indicted for murder. Was there proof that a criminal death occurred?

A like instance was reported in 1974 in Trial Magazine (Jan.–Feb.) under the headline "Unusual Death". The story reads:

"A Santa Rosa, California judge has ruled that a 12–year–old girl died because her heart was removed for transplant purposes and not because of brain injuries suffered in an auto accident.

"The judge's decision resulted in an acquittal for a man charged with manslaughter in connection with the girl's death.

"A doctor from the Stanford Medical Center had testified that the girl was the victim of 'cerebral death' or 'brain death syndrome,' i.e., her brain was not performing its normal function.

"Three other physicians concluded that without the life-support systems, the girl would have died within three hours of the accident, and with the support systems, she might have lived a week.

"The defendant's lawyer argued that death is defined as 'a total stoppage of the circulation of blood and a cessation of the animal and vital functions of the body such as respiration and pulsation.'

"In his ruling, the judge said that the evidence showed that the girl had 'a healthy body' and 'was in good shape except for her brain.' He said, furthermore, that a person is not legally dead until he ceases to exist."

Some states hold that death occurs when the end of life is confirmed by the cessation of all electrical impulses in the brain—the so-called "flat EEG." Other states still adhere to the common law view that death occurs only when there is a cessation of breathing and a stopping of the heart.

For an example of a modern "definition of death" statute, see Code of Virginia, § 54.1–2972, which reads as follows:

"A person shall be medically and legally dead if:

"1. In the opinion of a physician duly authorized to practice medicine in this Commonwealth, based on the ordinary standards of medical practice, there is the absence of spontaneous respiratory and spontaneous cardiac functions and, because of the disease or condition which directly or indirectly caused these functions to cease, or because of the passage of time since these functions ceased, attempts at resuscitation would not, in the opinion of such physician, be successful in restoring spontaneous life-sustaining functions, and, in such event, death shall be deemed to have occurred at the time these functions ceased; or

"2. In the opinion of a physician, who shall be duly licensed and a specialist in the field of neurology, neurosurgery, or electroencephalography, when based on the ordinary standards of medical practice, there is the absence of spontaneous brain functions and spontaneous respiratory functions and, in the opinion of another physician and such neurospecialist, based on the ordinary standards of medical practice and considering the absence of spontaneous brain functions and spontaneous respiratory functions and the patient's medical record, further attempts at resuscitation or continued supportive maintenance would not be successful in restoring such spontaneous functions, and, in such event, death shall be deemed to have occurred at the time when these conditions first coincide.

Death, as defined in subdivision 2 hereof, shall be pronounced by one of the two physicians and recorded in the patient's medical record and attested by the other physician. One of two physicians pronouncing or attesting to brain death may be the attending physician regardless of his specialty so long as at least one of the physicians is a neurospecialist.

Either of these alternative definitions of death may be utilized for all purposes in the Commonwealth, including the trial of civil and criminal cases."

For a commentary on the foregoing statute, see, "Telling the Time of Human Death by Statute: An Essential and Progressive Trend," 31 Wash. & Lee L.Rev. 521 (1974). See also, Gorman, "Medical Diagnosis Versus Legal Determination of Death," 30 J.For.Sci. 150 (1985).

(d) WHEN DOES LIFE BEGIN?

KEELER v. SUPERIOR COURT
Supreme Court of California, 1970.
2 Cal.3d 619, 87 Cal.Rptr. 481, 470 P.2d 617.

MOSK, JUSTICE.

In this proceeding for writ of prohibition we are called upon to decide whether an unborn but viable fetus is a "human being" within the meaning of the California statute defining murder (Pen.Code, § 187). We conclude that the Legislature did not intend such a meaning, and that for us to construe the statute to the contrary and apply it to this petitioner would exceed our judicial power and deny petitioner due process of law.

The evidence received at the preliminary examination may be summarized as follows: Petitioner and Teresa Keeler obtained an interlocutory decree of divorce on September 27, 1968. They had been married for 16 years. Unknown to petitioner, Mrs. Keeler was then pregnant by one Ernest Vogt, whom she had met earlier that summer. She subsequently began living with Vogt in Stockton, but concealed the fact from petitioner. Petitioner was given custody of their two daughters, aged 12 and 13 years, and under the decree Mrs. Keeler had the right to take the girls on alternate weekends.

On February 23, 1969, Mrs. Keeler was driving on a narrow mountain road in Amador County after delivering the girls to their home. She met petitioner driving in the opposite direction; he blocked the road with his car, and she pulled over to the side. He walked to her vehicle and began speaking to her. He seemed calm, and she rolled down her window to hear him. He said, "I hear you're pregnant. If you are you had better stay away from the girls and from here." She did not reply, and he opened the car door; as she later testified, "He assisted me out of the car. * * * [I]t wasn't roughly at this time." Petitioner then looked at her abdomen and became "extremely upset." He said, "You sure are. I'm going to stomp it out of you." He pushed her against the car, shoved his knee into her abdomen, and struck her in the face with several blows. She fainted, and when she regained consciousness petitioner had departed.

Mrs. Keeler drove back to Stockton, and the police and medical assistance were summoned. . . . A Caesarian section was performed and the fetus was examined *in utero*. Its head was found to be severely fractured, and it was delivered stillborn. The pathologist gave as his opinion that the cause of death was skull fracture with consequent cerebral hemorrhaging, that death would have been immediate, and that the injury could have been the result of force applied to the mother's abdomen. There was no air in the fetus' lungs, and the umbilical cord was intact.

Upon delivery the fetus weighed five pounds and was 18 inches in length. Both Mrs. Keeler and her obstetrician testified that fetal movements had been observed prior to February 23, 1969. The evidence was in conflict as to the estimated age of the fetus; the expert testimony on the point, however, concluded "with reasonable medical certainty" that the fetus had developed to the stage of viability, i.e., that in the event of premature birth on the date in question it would have had a 75 percent to 96 percent chance of survival.

An information was filed charging petitioner, in Count I, with committing the crime of murder (Pen.Code, § 187) in that he did "unlawfully kill a human being, to wit Baby Girl VOGT, with malice aforethought." . . . His motion to set aside the information for lack of probable cause (Pen.Code, § 995) was denied, and he now seeks a writ of prohibition; . . .

I

Penal Code section 187 provides: "Murder is the unlawful killing of a human being, with malice aforethought." The dispositive question is whether the fetus which petitioner is accused of killing was, on February 23, 1969, a "human being" within the meaning of this statute. If it was not, petitioner cannot be charged with its "murder" and prohibition will lie.

Section 187 was enacted as part of the Penal Code of 1872. Inasmuch as the provision has not been amended since that date, we must determine the intent of the Legislature at the time of its enactment. But section 187 was, in turn, taken verbatim from the first California statute defining murder, part of the Crimes and Punishments Act of 1850. (Stats.1850, ch. 99, § 19, p. 231.) Penal Code section 5 (also enacted in 1872) declares: "The provisions of this Code, so far as they are substantially the same as existing statutes, must be construed as continuations thereof, and not as new enactments." We begin, accordingly, by inquiring into the intent of the Legislature in 1850 when it first defined murder as the unlawful and malicious killing of a "human being."

It will be presumed, of course, that in enacting a statute the Legislature was familiar with the relevant rules of the common law, and, when it couches its enactment in common law language, that its intent was to continue those rules in statutory form. This is particularly appropriate in considering the work of the first session of our Legislature: its precedents were necessarily drawn from the common law, as modified in certain respects by the Constitution and by legislation of our sister states.

We therefore undertake a brief review of the origins and development of the common law of abortional homicide. . . . From that inquiry it appears that by the year 1850—the date with which we are concerned—an infant could not be the subject of homicide at common law *unless it had been born alive.* Perhaps the most influential statement of the "born alive" rule is that of Coke, in mid–17th century: "If a woman be quick with childe, and by a potion or otherwise killeth it in her wombe, or if a man beat her, whereby the childe dyeth in her body, and she is delivered of a dead childe, this is a great misprision [i.e., misdemeanor], and no murder; but if the childe be born alive and dyeth of the potion, battery, or other cause, this is murder; for in law it is accounted a reasonable creature, *in rerum natura,* when it is born alive." (3 Coke, Institutes *58 (1648).) In short, "By Coke's time, the common law regarded abortion as murder only if the foetus is (1) quickened, (2) born alive, (3) lives for a brief interval, and (4) then dies." Whatever intrinsic defects there may have been in Coke's work, the common law accepted his views as authoritative. . . .

* * *

By the year 1850 this rule of the common law had long been accepted in the United States. . . .

While it was thus "well settled" in American case law that the killing of an unborn child was not homicide, a number of state legislatures in the first half of the 19th century undertook to modify the common law in this respect. The movement began when New York abandoned the common law of abortion in 1830. The revisers' notes on that legislation recognized the existing rule, but nevertheless proposed a special feticide statute which, as enacted, provided that "The wilful killing of an unborn quick child, by any injury to the mother of such child, which would be murder if it resulted in the death of such mother, shall be deemed manslaughter in the first degree." (N.Y.Rev.Stat.1829, pt. IV, ch. 1, tit. 2, § 8.) At the same time the New York Legislature enacted a companion section (§ 9) which, although punishing a violation thereof as second degree manslaughter, was in essence an "abortion law" similar to those in force in most states today.

In the years between 1830 and 1850 at least five other states followed New York and enacted, as companion provisions, (1) a statute declaring feticide to be a crime, punishable as manslaughter, and (2) a statute prohibiting abortion. In California, however, the pattern was not repeated. Much of the Crimes and Punishments Act of 1850 was based on existing New York statute law; but although a section proscribing abortion was included in the new Act (§ 45), the Legislature declined to adopt any provision defining and punishing a special crime of feticide.

We conclude that in declaring murder to be the unlawful and malicious killing of a "human being" the Legislature of 1850 intended that term to have the settled common law meaning of a person who had been born alive, and did not intend the act of feticide—as distinguished from abortion—to be an offense under the laws of California.

Nothing occurred between the years 1850 and 1872 to suggest that in adopting the new Penal Code on the latter date the Legislature entertained any different intent. The case law of our sister states, for example, remained consonant with the common law. . . .

Any lingering doubt on this subject must be laid to rest by a consideration of the legislative history of the Penal Code of 1872. The Act establishing the California Code Commission (Stats.1870, ch. 516, § 2, p. 774) required the commissioners to revise all statutes then in force, correct errors and omissions, and "recommend all such enactments as shall, in the judgment of the Commission, be necessary to supply the defects of and give completeness to the existing legislation of the State * * *." In discharging this duty the statutory schemes of our sister states were carefully examined, and we must assume the commissioners had knowledge of the feticide laws noted hereinabove. Yet the commissioners proposed no such law for California, and none has been adopted to this day.

That such an omission was not an oversight clearly appears, moreover, from the commissioners' explanatory notes to Penal Code section 187. After quoting the definitions of murder given by Coke, Blackstone, and Hawkins, the commissioners conclude: "A child within its mother's womb is not a 'human being' within the meaning of that term as used in defining murder. The rule is that it must be born.—" Rex vs. Brain, 6 Car. & P., p. 349. That every part of it must have come from the mother before the killing of it will constitute a felonious homicide. . . .

* * *

It is the policy of this state to construe a penal statute as favorably to the defendant as its language and the circumstances of its application may reasonably permit; just as in the case of a question of fact, the defendant is entitled to the benefit of every reasonable doubt as to the true interpretation of words or the construction of language used in a statute. We hold that in adopting the definition of murder in Penal Code section 187 the Legislature intended to exclude from its reach the act of killing an unborn fetus.

II

The People urge, however, that the sciences of obstetrics and pediatrics have greatly progressed since 1872, to the point where with proper medical care a normally developed fetus prematurely born at 28 weeks or more has an excellent chance of survival, i.e., is "viable"; that the common law requirement of live birth to prove the fetus had become a "human being" who may be the victim of murder is no longer in accord with scientific fact, since an unborn but viable fetus is now fully capable of independent life; and that one who unlawfully and maliciously terminates such a life should therefore be liable to prosecution for murder under section 187. We may grant the premises of this argument; indeed, we neither deny nor denigrate the vast progress of medicine in the century since the enactment of the Penal Code. But we cannot join in the conclusion sought to be deduced: we cannot hold this petitioner to answer for murder by reason of his alleged act of killing an unborn—even thought viable—fetus. To such a charge there are two insuperable obstacles, one "jurisdictional" and the other constitutional.

Penal Code section 6 declares in relevant part that "No act or omission" accomplished after the code has taken effect "is criminal or punishable, except as prescribed or authorized by this Code, or by some of the statutes which it specifies as continuing in force and as not affected by its provisions, or by some ordinance, municipal, county, or township regulation * * *." This section embodies a fundamental principle of our tripartite form of government, i.e., that subject to the constitutional prohibition against cruel and unusual punishment, the power to define crimes and fix penalties is vested exclusively in the legislative branch. Stated differently, there are no common law crimes in California. In order that a public offense be committed, some statute, ordinance or regulation prior in time to the commission of the act must denounce it; likewise with excuses or justifications—if no statutory excuse or justification apply as to the commission of the particular offense, neither the common law nor the so-called "unwritten law" may legally supply it.

* * *

Applying these rules to the case at bar, we would undoubtedly act in excess of the judicial power if we were to adopt the People's proposed construction of section 187. As we have shown, the Legislature has defined the crime of murder in California to apply only to the unlawful and malicious killing of one who has been born alive. We recognize that the killing of an unborn but viable fetus may be deemed by some to be an offense of similar nature and gravity; but as Chief Justice Marshall warned long ago, "It would be dangerous, indeed, to carry the principle, that a case which is within the reason or mischief of a statute, is within its provisions, so far as to punish a crime not enumerated in the statute, because it is of equal atrocity, or of kindred character, with those which are enumerated." (United States v. Wiltberger (1820) 18 U.S. (5 Wheat.) 76, 96, 5 L.Ed. 37.) Whether to thus extend liability for murder in California is a determination solely within the province of the Legislature. For a court to simply declare, by judicial fiat, that the time has now come to prosecute under section 187 one who kills an unborn but viable fetus would indeed be to rewrite the statute under the guise of construing it. . . .

The second obstacle to the proposed judicial enlargement of section 187 is the guarantee of due process of law. Assuming *arguendo* that we have the power to adopt the new construction of this statute as the law of California, such a ruling, by constitutional command, could operate only prospectively, and thus could not in any event reach the conduct of petitioner on February 23, 1969.

The first essential of due process is fair warning of the act which is made punishable as a crime. "That the terms of a penal statute creating a new offense must be sufficiently explicit to inform those who are subject to it what conduct on their part will render them liable to its penalties, is a well-recognized requirement, consonant alike with ordinary notions of fair play and the settled rules of law." (Connally v. General Constr. Co. (1926) 269 U.S. 385, 391, 46 S.Ct. 126, 127, 70 L.Ed. 322.) "No one may be required at peril of life, liberty or property to speculate as to the meaning of penal statutes. All are entitled to be informed as to what the State commands or forbids." (Lanzetta v. New Jersey (1939) 306 U.S. 451, 453, 59 S.Ct. 618, 619, 83 L.Ed. 888.) The law of California is in full accord.

This requirement of fair warning is reflected in the constitutional prohibition against the enactment of ex post facto laws (U.S. Const., art. I, §§ 9, 10; Cal. Const., art. I, § 16). When a new penal statute is applied retrospectively to make punishable an act which was not criminal at the time it was performed, the defendant has been given no advance notice consistent with due process. And precisely the same effect occurs when such an act is made punishable under a preexisting statute but by means of an unforeseeable *judicial* enlargement thereof. . . .

* * *

. . . In the present case, it will be remembered, petitioner's avowed goal was not primarily to kill the fetus while it was inside his wife's body, but rather to "stomp it out of" her; although one presumably cannot be done without the other, petitioner's choice of words is significant and strongly implies an "intent thereby to procure the miscarriage" of his wife in violation of section 274.

Turning to the case law, we find no reported decision of the California courts which should have given petitioner notice that the killing of an unborn but viable fetus was prohibited by section 187. . . .

Properly understood, the often cited case of People v. Chavez (1947) 77 Cal.App.2d 621, 176 P.2d 92, does not derogate from this rule. There the defendant was charged with the murder of her newborn child, and convicted of manslaughter. She testified that the baby dropped from her womb into the toilet bowl; that she picked it up two or three minutes later, and cut but did not tie the umbilical cord; that the baby was limp and made no cry; and that after 15 minutes she wrapped it in a newspaper and concealed it, where it was found dead the next day. The autopsy surgeon testified that the baby was a full-term, nine-month child, weighing six and one-half pounds and appearing normal in every respect; that the body had very little blood in it, indicating the child had bled to death through the untied umbilical cord; that such a process would have taken about an hour; and that in his opinion "the child was born alive, based on conditions he found and the fact that the lungs contained air and the blood was extravasated or pushed back into the tissues, indicating heart action."

On appeal, the defendant emphasized that a doctor called by the defense had suggested other tests which the autopsy surgeon could have performed to determine the matter of live birth; on this basis, it was contended that the question of whether the infant was born alive "rests entirely on pure speculation." The Court of Appeal found only an insignificant conflict in that regard and focused its attention instead on testimony of the autopsy surgeon admitting the possibility that the evidence of heart and lung action could have resulted from the child's breathing "after presentation of the head but before the birth was completed".

The court cited the mid–19th century English infanticide cases mentioned hereinabove, and noted that the decisions had not reached uniformity on whether breathing, heart action, severance of the umbilical cord, or some combination of these or other factors established the status of "human being" for purposes of the law of homicide. The court then adverted to the state of modern medical knowledge, discussed the phenomenon of viability, and held that "a viable child *in the process of being born* is a human being within the meaning of the homicide statutes, whether or not the process has been fully completed. It should at least be considered a human being where it is a living baby and where in the natural course of events *a birth which is already started* would naturally be successfully completed." (Italics added.) Since the testimony of the autopsy surgeon left no doubt in that case that a live birth had at least begun, the court found "the evidence is sufficient here to support the implied finding of the jury that this child *was born alive and became a human being within the meaning of the homicide statutes.*" (Italics added.)

Chavez thus stands for the proposition—to which we adhere—that a viable fetus "in the process of being born" is a human being within the meaning of the homicide statutes. But it stands for no more; in particular it does not hold that a fetus, however viable, which is *not* "in the process of being born" is nevertheless a "human being" in the law of homicide. On the contrary, the opinion is replete with references to the common law requirement that the child be "born alive," however that term is defined, and must accordingly be deemed to reaffirm that requirement as part of the law of California.

* * *

We conclude that the judicial enlargement of section 187 now urged upon us by the People would not have been foreseeable to this petitioner, and hence that its adoption at this time would deny him due process of law.

Let a peremptory writ of prohibition issue restraining respondent court from taking any further proceedings on Count I of the information, charging petitioner with the crime of murder.

McComb, Peters, and Tobriner, JJ., and Peek, J. pro tem., concur.

Burke, Acting Chief Justice (dissenting).

The majority hold that "Baby Girl" Vogt, who, according to medical testimony, had reached the 35th week of development, had a 96 percent chance of survival, and was "definitely" alive and viable at the time of her death, nevertheless was not a "human being" under California's homicide statutes. In my view, in so holding, the majority ignore significant common law precedents, frustrate the express intent of the Legislature, and defy reason, logic and common sense.

* * *

The majority cast a passing glance at the common law concept of quickening, but fail to explain the significance of that concept: At common law, the quickened fetus *was* considered to be a human being, a second life separate and apart from its mother. . . .

Modern scholars have confirmed this aspect of common law jurisprudence. As Means observes, "The common law itself prohibited abortion after quickening and hanging a pregnant felon after quickening, *because the life of a second human being would thereby be taken,* although it did not call the offense murder or manslaughter." (Italics added; Means, The Law of New York Concerning Abortion and the Status of the Foetus, 1664–1968: A Case of Cessation of Constitutionality (1968) 14 N.Y.L.F. 411, 504.)

This reasoning explains why the killing of a quickened child was considered "a great misprision," although the killing of an unquickened child was no crime at all at common law (Means, *supra,* at p. 420). Moreover, although the common law did not apply the labels of "murder" or "manslaughter" to the killing of a quickened fetus, it appears that at common law this "great misprision" was severely punished. . . .

In my view, we cannot assume that the Legislature intended a person such as defendant charged with the malicious slaying of a fully viable child, to suffer only the mild penalties imposed upon common abortionists who, ordinarily, procure only the miscarriage of a nonviable fetus or embryo. To do so would completely ignore the important common law distinction between the quickened and unquickened child.

Of course, I do not suggest that we should interpret the term "human being" in our homicide statutes in terms of the common law concept of quickening. At one time, that concept had a value in differentiating, as accurately as was then scientifically possible, between life and nonlife. The analogous concept of viability is clearly more satisfactory, for it has a well defined and medically determinable meaning denoting the ability of the fetus to live or survive apart from its mother.

The majority opinion suggests that we are confined to common law concepts, and to the common law definition of murder or manslaughter. However, the Legislature, in Penal Code sections 187 and 192, has defined those offenses for us: homicide is the unlawful killing of a "human being." Those words need not be frozen in place as of any particular time, but must be fairly and reasonably interpreted by this court to promote justice and to carry out the evident purposes of the Legislature in adopting a homicide statute. . . .

. . . The true doctrine is that the common law by its own principles adapts itself to varying conditions, and modifies its own rules so as to serve the ends of justice under the different circumstances, a principle adopted into our code by section 3510 of the Civ.Code: 'When the reason of a rule ceases, so should the rule itself.' "

. . . Consequently, nothing should prevent this court from holding that Baby Girl Vogt was a human ("belonging or relating to ban; characteristic of man") being ("existence, as opp. to nonexistence; specif. life") under California's homicide statutes.

We commonly conceive of human existence as a spectrum stretching from birth to death. However, if this court properly might expand the definition of "human being" at one end of that spectrum, we may do so at the other end. Consider the following example: All would agree that "Shooting or otherwise damaging a corpse is not homicide.

* * *" (Perkins, Criminal Law (2d ed. 1969) ch. 2, § 1, p. 31.) In other words, a corpse is not considered to be a "human being" and thus cannot be the subject of a "killing" as those terms are used in homicide statutes. However, it is readily apparent that our concepts of what constitutes a "corpse" have been and are being continually modified by advances in the field of medicine, including new techniques for life revival, restoration and resuscitation such as artificial respiration, open heart massage, transfusions, transplants and a variety of life-restoring stimulants, drugs and new surgical methods. Would this court ignore these developments and exonerate the killer of an apparently "drowned" child merely because that child would have been pronounced dead in 1648 or 1850? Obviously not. Whether a homicide occurred in that case would be determined by medical testimony regarding the capability of the child to have survived prior to the defendant's act. And that is precisely the test which this court should adopt in the instant case.

The common law reluctance to characterize the killing of a quickened fetus as a homicide was based solely upon a presumption that the fetus would have been born dead. This presumption seems to have persisted in this country at least as late as 1876. Based upon the state of the medical art in the 17th, 18th and 19th centuries, that presumption may have been well-founded. However, as we approach the 21st century, it has become apparent that "This presumption is not only contrary to common experience and the ordinary course of nature, but it is contrary to the usual rule with respect to presumptions followed in this state."

There are no accurate statistics disclosing fetal death rates in "common law England," although the foregoing presumption of death indicates a significantly high death experience. On the other hand, in California the fetal death rate in 1968 is estimated to be 12 deaths in 1,000, a ratio which would have given Baby Girl Vogt a 98.8 percent chance of survival. (California Statistical Abstract (1969) Table E–3, p. 65.) If, as I have contended, the term "human being" in our homicide statutes is a fluid concept to be defined in accordance with present conditions, then there can be no question that the term should include the fully viable fetus.

The majority suggest that to do so would improperly create some new offense. However, the offense of murder is no new offense. Contrary to the majority opinion, the Legislature has not "defined the crime of murder in California to apply only to the unlawful and malicious killing one who has been born alive." Instead, the Legislature simply used the broad term "human being" and directed the courts to construe that term according to its "fair import" with a view to effect the objects of the homicide statutes and promote justice. (Pen.Code, § 4.) What justice will be promoted, what objects effectuated, by construing "human being" as excluding Baby Girl Vogt and her unfortunate successors? Was defendant's brutal act of stomping her to death any less an act of homicide than the murder of a newly born baby? No one doubts that the term "human being" would include the elderly or dying persons whose potential for life has nearly lapsed; their proximity to death is deemed immaterial. There is no sound reason for denying the viable fetus, with its unbounded potential for life, the same status.

The majority also suggest that such an interpretation of our homicide statutes would deny defendant "fair warning" that his act was punishable as a crime. Aside from the absurdity of the underlying premise that defendant consulted Coke, Blackstone or Hale before kicking Baby Girl Vogt to death, it is clear that defendant had adequate notice that his act could constitute homicide. Due process only precludes prosecution under a new statute insufficiently explicit regarding the specific conduct proscribed, or under a pre-existing statute "by means of an unforeseeable *judicial* enlargement thereof."

Our homicide statutes have been in effect in this state since 1850. The fact that the California courts have not been called upon to determine the precise question before us does not render "unforeseeable" a decision which determines that a viable fetus is a "human being" under those statutes. Can defendant really claim surprise that a 5–pound, 18–inch, 34–week-old, living, viable child is considered to be a human being?

The fact is that the foregoing construction of our homicide statutes easily could have been anticipated from strong dicta in People v. Chavez, wherein the court reviewed common law precedents but disapproved their requirement that the child be born alive and completely separated from its mother. The court in *Chavez* held that a viable child killed during, but prior to completion of, the birth process, was a human being under the homicide statutes. However, the court did not hold that partial birth was a prerequisite, for the court expressly set forth its holding "Without drawing a line of distinction applicable to all cases * * *." In dicta, the court discussed the question when an unborn infant becomes a human being under the homicide statutes, as follows: "There is not much change in the child itself between a moment before and a moment after its expulsion from the body of its mother, and normally, while still dependent upon its mother, the child for some time before it is born, has not only the possibility but a strong probability of an ability to live an independent life. * * * While before birth or removal it is in a sense dependent upon its mother for life, there is another sense in which it has started an independent existence after it has reached a state of development where it is capable of living and where it will, in the normal course of nature and with ordinary care, continue to live and grow as a separate being. While it may not be possible to draw an exact line applicable to all cases, the rules of law should recognize and make some attempt to follow the natural and scientific facts to which they relate. * * * [It]t would be a mere fiction to hold that a child is not a human being because the process of birth has not been fully completed, when it has reached that state of viability when the destruction of the life of its mother would not end its existence and when, if separated from the mother naturally or by artificial means, it will live and grow in the normal manner."

* * *

The trial court's denial of defendant's motion to set aside the information was proper, and the peremptory writ of prohibition should be denied.

SULLIVAN, J., concurs.

Rehearing denied; BURKE and SULLIVAN, JJ., dissenting.

NOTE

1. Consider the following excerpt of Justice Blackmun's opinion for the Court in Roe v. Wade, 410 U.S. 113, 93 S.Ct. 705, 35 L.Ed.2d 147 (1973), to be more fully discussed later in the Section on The Right of Privacy; after concluding that the definition of "person" does not include the unborn, the opinion states this in connection with when life begins:

Texas urges that, apart from the Fourteenth Amendment, life begins at conception and is present throughout pregnancy, and that, therefore, the State has a compelling interest in protecting that life from and after conception. We need not resolve the difficult question of when life begins. When those trained in the respective disciplines of medicine, philosophy, and theology are unable to arrive at any consensus, the judiciary, at this point in the development of man's knowledge, is not in a position to speculate as to the answer.

It should be sufficient to note briefly the wide divergence of thinking on this most sensitive and difficult question. There has always been strong support for the view that life does not begin until live birth. This was the belief of the Stoics. It appears to be the predominant, though not the unanimous, attitude of the Jewish faith. It may be taken to represent also the position of a large segment of the Protestant community, insofar as that can be ascertained; organized groups that have taken a formal position on the abortion issue have generally regarded abortion as a matter for the conscience of the individual and her family. As we have noted, the common law found greater significance in quickening. Physicians and their scientific colleagues have regarded that event with less interest and have tended to focus either upon conception or upon live birth or upon the interim point at which the fetus becomes "viable," that is, potentially able to live outside the mother's womb, albeit with artificial aid. Viability is usually placed at about seven months (28 weeks) but may occur earlier, even at 24 weeks. The Aristotelian theory of "mediate animation," that held sway throughout the Middle Ages and the Renaissance in Europe, continued to be official Roman Catholic dogma until the 19th century, despite opposition to this "ensoulment" theory from those in the Church who would recognize the existence of life from the moment of conception. The latter is now, of course, the official belief of the Catholic Church. As one of the briefs *amicus* discloses, this is a view strongly held by many non-Catholics as well, and by many physicians. Substantial problems for precise definition of this view are posed, however, by new embryological data that purport to indicate that conception is a "process" over time, rather than an event, and by new medical techniques such as menstrual extraction, the "morning-after" pill, implantation of embryos, artificial insemination, and even artificial wombs.

In areas other than criminal abortion the law has been reluctant to endorse any theory that life, as we recognize it, begins before live birth or to accord legal rights to the unborn except in narrowly defined situations and except when the rights are contingent upon live birth. For example, the traditional rule of tort law had denied recovery for prenatal injuries even though the child was born alive. That rule has been changed in almost every jurisdiction. In most States recovery is said to be permitted only if the fetus was viable, or at least quick, when the injuries were sustained, though few courts have squarely so held. In a recent development, generally opposed by the commentators, some States permit the parents of a stillborn child to maintain an action for wrongful death because of prenatal injuries. Such an action, however, would appear to be one to vindicate the parents' interest and is thus consistent with the view that the fetus, at most, represents only the potentiality of life. Similarly, unborn children have been recognized as acquiring rights or interests by way of inheritance or other devolution of property, and have been represented by guardians *ad litem*. Perfection of the interests involved, again, has generally been contingent upon live birth. In short, the unborn have never been recognized in the law as persons in the whole sense.

2. The New York Penal Code provides, in § 125.05 where definitions applicable to homicide prosecutions are contained, that ". . . 1. 'Person,' when referring to the victim of a homicide, means a human being who has been born and is alive."

3. Holding that a viable fetus is not a "human being" for purposes of the aggravated vehicular homicide statute of the State of Kansas, see State v. Trudell, 243 Kan. 29, 755 P.2d 511 (1988). While the state's wrongful death statute had been interpreted liberally to give parents of a viable fetus a right to maintain a wrongful death action despite any specific statutory language in the act, the Kansas Supreme Court said that criminal statutes, with their punitive effects, must be construed more narrowly. If the common law rule, requiring a live birth, is to be changed, the legislative branch is the proper forum to resolve such an issue. See also, in that regard, the discussion in Chapter 5–A–(3), infra, on the destruction of the unborn child.

2.   DEFINING "DANGEROUS" AND "DEADLY"

The desire to punish dangerous behavior furnishes serious drafting challenges to a legislator. Dangerous conduct requires that we spell out, with some degree of precision and clarity, the type of act (conduct) that is prohibited, while at the same time also incorporating the mental state required for criminality. In view of the many offenses which seek to punish certain "dangerous" behavior or the use of "deadly" or "dangerous" weapons, definitional problems abound. Even when the statute contains definitions, courts still face problems of construction. But the problems are greatly magnified when a statute defining a crime uses general characterizations without definitional legislative assistance. Sometimes, the uncertainty as to what conduct is prohibited may impair the validity of the statute on constitutional grounds. (See, infra in this chapter, discussions on vagueness and overbreadth.) Here, however, we deal not with the unconstitutional failure to define clearly what is prohibited; rather, we explore the difficulties encountered in seeking to spell out what conduct is criminal.

COMMONWEALTH v. DAVIS

Appeals Court of Massachusetts, Hampden, 1980.
10 Mass.App.Ct. 190, 406 N.E.2d 417.

GREANEY, JUSTICE.

On December 16, 1978, the defendant and the victim quarrelled at the "Diamond Mine" Lounge in Holyoke. An encounter ensued, in the course of which the defendant bit off a piece of the victim's left ear. The defendant was indicted for the crimes of mayhem (G.L. c. 265, § 14), and assault and battery by means of a dangerous weapon "to wit, [t]eeth" (G.L. c. 265, § 15A). A Superior Court jury convicted him on both indictments, and he has appealed, assigning as error: . . .; and (2) the denial of his motion for a directed verdict on so much of indictment no. 79–705 as charged the use of a dangerous weapon, contending that human teeth cannot constitute a dangerous weapon. We hold that . . . the motion for a directed verdict should have been allowed as to that portion of the assault and battery indictment that charged the use of teeth as a dangerous weapon.

* * *

2. We turn now to the question whether human teeth or parts of the body should be excluded from consideration by the fact finder as instrumentalities which can be used as dangerous weapons in indictments framed under G.L. c. 265, § 15A (inserted by St.1927, c. 187, § 1). Section 15A punishes assaults and batteries committed by "means of a dangerous weapon" but does not expressly define the term "dangerous weapon." Instead, the meaning of the term was evolved through case law. Recently in Commonwealth v. Appleby, ___ Mass. ___, 402 N.E.2d 1051 (1980) the Supreme Judicial Court stated that the concept of a dangerous weapon as used in § 15A embraces two classes of objects— "dangerous weapons per se" (those specially designed and constructed to produce death or great bodily harm; and objects which are not dangerous per se but which can be used in a dangerous fashion to inflict serious harm. A wide variety of objects have been held to fall within the latter category. See Commonwealth v. Farrell, 322 Mass. 606, 615, 78 N.E.2d 697 (1948) (lighted cigarette); Commonwealth v. Tarrant, 2 Mass.App. 483, 486–487, 314 N.E.2d 448 (1974), Id., 367 Mass. 411, 326 N.E.2d 710 (1975) ("kitchen-type" knife and German shepherd dog); Commonwealth v. LeBlanc, 3 Mass.App. 780, 334 N.E.2d 647 (1975) (automobile door used to strike police officer); United States v. Johnson, 324 F.2d 264, 266 (4th Cir.1963) (chair brought down upon victim's head); United States v. Loman, 551 F.2d 164, 169 (7th Cir.), cert. denied, 433 U.S. 912, 97 S.Ct. 2982, 53 L.Ed.2d 1097 (1977) (walking stick used with enough force to break it); People v. White, 212 Cal.App. 2d 464, 465, 28 Cal.Rptr. 67 (1963) (a rock); Commonwealth v. Branham, 71 Ky. (8 Bush.) 387, 388 (1871) (a chisel used for stabbing); Bennett v. State, 237 Md. 212, 216, 205 A.2d 393 (1964) (microphone cord tied around victim's neck); People v. Buford, 69 Mich.App. 27, 30, 244 N.W.2d 351 (1976) (dictum) (automobile, broomstick, flashlight and

lighter fluid all may be dangerous as used); State v. Howard, 125 N.J. Super. 39, 45, 308 A.2d 366 (App.Div.1973) (straight razor); State v. Martinez, 57 N.M. 174, 176, 256 P.2d 791 (1953) (a knife with a blade two inches long); Regan v. State, 46 Wis. 256, 258, 50 N.W. 287 (1879) (large stones). We recognize that our cases have held that questions as to whether instrumentalities which are not dangerous per se have been used in a dangerous fashion are generally reserved to the fact finder to be decided on the basis of the circumstances surrounding the crime, the nature, size and shape of the object, and the manner in which it is handled or controlled. However, for the reasons now discussed we think that human teeth and other parts of the human body should be removed from consideration as dangerous weapons in § 15A indictments, even on a case-by-case basis.

First, all the Massachusetts cases which have considered the use of neutral objects as potential weapons in the commission of assault crimes have considered instrumentalities apart from the defendant's person. The *Farrell, Tarrant* and *Appleby* decisions considered a lighted cigarette, an attack dog, and a riding crop, respectively. Even when the act of "kicking" underlies the charge of assault with a "dangerous weapon," the shoe or boot, not the foot, is the object which is considered as the "weapon" subjecting the assailant to a charge of aggravated assault. . . . Since the adoption of § 15A, there has been no decision reported in this State which holds that human hands, feet or teeth alone can constitute a dangerous weapon. This suggests that for over fifty years prosecutors have not considered assault cases involving the use of hands, feet, fingers or teeth as incidents where "dangerous weapons" were employed. It also suggests that prosecutors have been reluctant to read our judicial precedent on the subject as inviting indictments pressing factual contentions that parts of the body can be used as weapons. Rather, where serious or disabling injuries are inflicted, and the requisite intent is present, district attorneys typically bring indictments under § 14 (mayhem) or § 15 (assault with intent to maim or disfigure) of c. 265; otherwise § 13A (assault and battery) is used as the prosecutorial tool to vindicate society's interest. Thus in the context of the practical application of the statute the concept of neutral objects used as dangerous weapons has been confined to independent nonhuman instrumentalities. These considerations, in light of the fact that fifty-three years have elapsed since the Legislature enacted § 15A, call, in our view, for the exercise of judicial restraint in expanding the concept beyond its traditional scope.

Second, the notion that parts of the body may be used as dangerous weapons has not been generally accepted elsewhere. The clear weight of authority is to the effect that bodily parts alone cannot constitute a dangerous weapon for the purpose of an aggravated assault based on the alleged use of such a weapon. This is so, irrespective of the degree of harm inflicted. See Ransom v. State, 460 P.2d at 172; Dickson v. State, 230 Ark. 491, 492, 323 S.W.2d 432 (1959); Reed v. Commonwealth, 248 S.W.2d 911, 914 (Ky.1952); State v. Calvin, 209 La. 257,

265–266, 24 So.2d 467 (1945); People v. VanDiver, 80 Mich.App. 352, 356–357, 263 N.W.2d 370 (1977); People v. Vollmer, 299 N.Y. 347, 350, 87 N.E.2d 291 (1949); Bean v. State, 77 Okl.Cr. 73, 81–84, 138 P.2d 563 (1943); State v. Wier, 22 Or.App. 549, 540 P.2d 394 (1975); State v. Hariott, 210 S.C. 290, 299–300, 42 S.E.2d 385 (1947).

State v. Calvin, supra, the sole reported decision dealing with the question whether teeth may constitute a dangerous weapon, is particularly instructive. In that case there was evidence that the defendant had bitten the victim, and the trial judge had charged the jury that since "a person's bare fist could be classed and used as a dangerous weapon, . . . a person's teeth could be classed as a dangerous weapon." The Supreme Court of Louisiana, applying a definition of "dangerous weapon" ("any . . . instrumentality, which, in the manner used, is calculated or likely to produce death or great bodily harm") virtually identical to that set forth in *Commonwealth v. Farrell,* supra, held that charge to be error: . . .

Third, in the absence of reconsideration by the Legislature of the term "dangerous weapon" or of the gist of the crime defined in § 15A, we see no compelling reason to stretch the term "weapon" to allow prosecution under § 15A of actions that are ordinarily prosecuted in other ways. Almost every attack which involves the use of a part of the body to inflict serious injury has been and remains punishable under one or the other of the felonious assault statutes apart from § 15A. Thus, an attack such as an attempt to strangle falls under G.L. c. 265, § 15 (assault with intent to murder), or under § 29 of the same chapter (assault with intent to commit a felony, i.e., to kill). Attacks without weapons which result in injuries to particular parts of the body or which cause disabling or disfiguring injuries are prosecuted under the first portion of G.L. c. 265, § 14, as mayhem, or under § 15, as assault with intent to maim. If weapons, chemicals, or substances are used to maim or disfigure, the indictment is brought under the second portion of § 14 which "allows conviction of mayhem for a more general range of injury." The mental state required for conviction of mayhem or assault with intent to maim is satisfied by direct or inferential proof that the assault was intentional, unjustified, and made with the reasonable appreciation on the assailant's part that a disabling or disfiguring injury would result. Bending § 15A to include an assault of the type that occurred in the present case would result in needless duplicity and would frustrate what we perceive to be the legislative intent in separating felonious assaults. On similar analysis, the Court of Appeals of Michigan has held, in a well-reasoned opinion based on the intent of the Legislature in that State, that "the term 'dangerous weapon' cannot be construed to include the bare hands." People v. VanDiver, 80 Mich. App. at 357, 263 N.W.2d at 373.

* * *

We think, essentially for the reasons of public policy stated, that a broadening of the definition of a dangerous weapon in the context discussed should occur, if it occurs, through deliberative legislative action.

. . . The judgment on indictment no. 79–705 is reversed, and so much of the verdict is set aside as found the defendant guilty of the use of a dangerous weapon. The case is remanded to the Superior Court for the defendant's resentencing on indictment no. 79–705 as if for assault and battery.

So ordered.

UNITED STATES v. MOORE
United States Court of Appeals, Eighth Circuit, 1988.
846 F.2d 1163.

TIMBERS, CIRCUIT JUDGE.

Appellant James Vernell Moore appeals from a judgment entered September 25, 1987 . . ., following Moore's conviction by a jury on June 24, 1987 of two counts of assault with a deadly and [1] dangerous weapon upon federal correctional officers engaged in their official duties, in violation of 18 U.S.C. §§ 111 (1982) and 1114 (Supp. IV 1986). . . .

Moore had tested positive for antibodies for the Human Immunodeficiency Virus ("HIV virus") which are considered to be indicative of the presence of Acquired Immune Deficiency Syndrome ("AIDS"). After learning that he had tested positive for the HIV virus, Moore bit two correctional officers during a struggle. The indictment charged that the deadly and dangerous weapon Moore used was his own mouth and teeth.

On appeal, Moore claims, first, that the evidence at trial was insufficient to sustain a finding that Moore's mouth and teeth were a deadly and dangerous weapon; . . .

We hold that the evidence at trial was sufficient to sustain a finding that Moore's mouth and teeth were a deadly and dangerous weapon because that evidence supported a finding that Moore used his teeth in a manner likely to inflict serious bodily harm—even if he had not been infected with the HIV virus. . . .

We affirm.

I.

We shall summarize only those facts and prior proceedings believed necessary to an understanding of the issues raised on appeal.

At the time of the incident which is the subject of this appeal, Moore was an inmate at the Federal Medical Center ("FMC") in Rochester, Minnesota. On November 25 and December 3, 1986, Dr.

---

1. It should be noted that, although the statutory language is in the disjunctive—"deadly *or* dangerous weapon", the indictment charged in the conjunctive—"deadly *and* dangerous weapon" (emphasis added). In this opinion we shall use the conjunctive language adopted by the parties.

Clifford Gastineau had Moore tested for the HIV virus because his long time heroin addiction placed him in a risk category for AIDS. In mid-December, Dr. Gastineau advised Moore that the tests were positive and that the disease could be fatal. He told Moore that the disease could be transmitted by way of blood or semen and counseled him to avoid unprotected intercourse and not to share needles, razor blades or toothbrushes.

On January 7, 1987, Lieutenant Ronald E. McCullough, a correctional officer at the FMC, called Moore to his office as part of his investigation of a report that Moore had been smoking in a non-smoking area in the FMC's medical surgical unit. Moore refused to answer questions. When McCullough told Moore he would have to be placed in seclusion and administrative detention, Moore refused to move. McCullough called for assistance. Correctional officer Timothy Voigt arrived. He told Moore to stand so that he could be handcuffed. Moore said "I won't be cuffed." McCullough called two additional correctional officers who arrived and attempted to lift Moore from his chair. Moore reacted violently.

In the ensuing struggle, Moore kneed McCullough in the groin twice, attempted to bite him on the hand, and did bite him on the left knee and hip without breaking the skin. Moore held his mouth over the bite on the leg for several seconds. He also bit Voigt on the right leg, holding his mouth against the bite from five to seven seconds. Dr. Gastineau testified that during the struggle a mild abrasion appeared at the point on Voigt's thigh where Moore had bitten him. This abrasion apparently resulted from friction with the fabric of Voigt's pants.[2] The abrasion may have come into contact with a wet patch on Voigt's pants which possibly was made by Moore's saliva. During the struggle, Moore threatened to kill the officers.

On January 10, 1987, Moore told Debra Alberts, a nurse at the FMC, that he had "wanted to hurt them bad, wanted to kill the bastards." He also said that he "hopes the wounds that he inflicted on the officers when he bit them were bad enough that they get the disease that he has."

On April 9, 1987, Moore was indicted. The indictment charged that Moore willfully had assaulted McCullough and Voigt, federal correctional officers engaged in their official duties, by means of a deadly and dangerous weapon, i.e., Moore's mouth and teeth. The indictment specifically charged that Moore was "a person then having been tested positively for the [HIV] antibody". Although Moore also

2. The parties dispute whether this bite punctured Voigt's skin. Moore, citing Dr. Gastineau's testimony, asserts that the bite failed to penetrate the fabric of Voigt's pants. The government, citing Voigt's testimony, asserts that Moore bit deeply into Voigt's thigh, puncturing Voigt's skin in three places. Voigt's subsequent testimony indicates, however, that the bleeding at the site of this wound was due to an abrasion caused by the friction of his pants rubbing against his legs. Thus the "puncture" wounds he describes apparently were indentations that in themselves did not cause bleeding.

had tested positive for hepatitis, the indictment did not refer to this disease.

At trial, Dr. Gastineau testified that the medical profession knew of no "well-proven instances in which a human bite has resulted in transmission of the [HIV] virus to the bitten person." He agreed with a medical manual that stated there is no evidence that AIDS can be transmitted through any contact that does not involve the exchange of bodily fluids and that, while the virus has appeared in minute amounts in saliva, it has never been shown to have been spread through contact with saliva. He said that theoretically "one cannot exclude the possibility" of transmission through biting. Later he added, however, "it seems that in medicine everything is conceivable or possible." He testified about a case of a person who had been bitten deeply by a person with AIDS and had tested negative 18 months later.

Dr. Gastineau also testified that, apart from the matter of AIDS, a human bite can be dangerous. He said that when a human bite is of a more damaging nature than the ones inflicted by Moore and "where the skin is really broken to greater depths", it can be "much more dangerous than a dog bite." He also said that "there are probably 30 to 50 variet[ies] of germs in the human mouth that together, all of them acting in concert, could cause serious infection." He characterized a human bite as "a very dangerous form of aggression" and "one of the most dangerous of all forms of bites".

On June 24, 1987, the jury found Moore guilty on both counts of the indictment. The jury had been instructed on the lesser included offense of assaulting a federal officer. The court declined to instruct the jury that the government was required to prove that AIDS could be transmitted by way of a bite in order to prove that Moore's mouth and teeth were a deadly and dangerous weapon. Moore was sentenced to concurrent five-year prison terms, which were to run consecutively to the seven-year federal prison sentence he was serving at the time of the incident.

II.

In reviewing the sufficiency of the evidence to determine whether it supports the conviction, we must view the evidence in the light most favorable to the government, grant the government the benefit of all inferences that reasonably may be drawn from the evidence, and uphold the conviction if there is substantial evidence to support it.

The question of what constitutes a "deadly and dangerous weapon" is a question of fact for the jury. We previously have defined a "deadly and dangerous weapon" as an object "used in a manner likely to endanger life or inflict serious bodily harm." United States v. Hollow, 747 F.2d 481, 482 (8th Cir.1984). "Serious bodily harm" has been defined as something more than minor injury, but not necessarily injury creating a substantial likelihood of death. See United States v. Webster, 620 F.2d 640, 641–42 (7th Cir.1980); United States v. Johnson,

324 F.2d 264, 267 (4th Cir.1963). In *Webster,* a case arising under 18 U.S.C. § 113 (1982), the court stated that the phrase contains "words in general use by laymen" and that "[t]here is no indication that Congress in adopting such commonly used terms intended to include only the very highest degree of serious bodily injury."

As a practical matter, it often is difficult to determine whether a particular object is a deadly and dangerous weapon. Almost any weapon, as used or attempted to be used, may endanger life or inflict great bodily harm; as such, in appropriate circumstances, it may be a dangerous and deadly weapon. Moreover, the object need not be inherently dangerous, or a "weapon" by definition, such as a gun or a knife, to be found to be a dangerous and deadly weapon. Courts frequently have considered various kinds of objects to be deadly and dangerous, including such normally innocuous objects as (1) a chair; (2) a walking stick; (3) a broken beer bottle and pool cue; (4) an automobile; and (5) mop handles. In short, what constitutes a dangerous weapon depends not on the nature of the object itself but on its capacity, given the manner of its use, to . . . endanger life or inflict great bodily harm.

As a corollary, it is not necessary that the object, as used by a defendant, actually cause great bodily harm, as long as it has the capacity to inflict such harm in the way it was used. . . .

Courts also have held that in appropriate circumstances a part of the body may be a dangerous weapon. United States v. Parman, 461 F.2d 1203, 1204 n. 1 (D.C.Cir.1971) (indictment charged assault with a deadly weapon, the deadly weapon being "biting with teeth"); State v. Born, 280 Minn. 306, 159 N.W.2d 283 (1968) (fists or feet in certain circumstances may be dangerous weapons when used to inflict injury).

III.

In light of the law on what may be considered a deadly and dangerous weapon, we conclude that the evidence in the instant case was sufficient to support the jury's finding that Moore used his mouth and teeth as a deadly and dangerous weapon. As stated above, Dr. Gastineau testified that a human bite is potentially "more dangerous than a dog bite"; that it is capable of causing "serious infection"; and that it can be "a very dangerous form of aggression". We reaffirm that this potential for "serious infection" is a form of "serious bodily harm" . . . especially since we use the term in its general lay meaning and do not limit it to only the highest degree of injury. We therefore hold that Dr. Gastineau's testimony, viewed in the light most favorable to the government, was substantial evidence supporting the jury's finding that Moore used his mouth and teeth in a manner likely to inflict serious bodily harm.

It is true that Dr. Gastineau testified that he was describing a bite "more damaging" than those actually inflicted by Moore. As stated above, however, it is the *capacity* for harm in the weapon and its use that is significant, not the *actual* harm inflicted. It may be that Moore did not transmit any of the "30 to 50" varieties of germs he might have transmitted to the officers. He nevertheless used his mouth and teeth in a way that *could* have transmitted disease. It was only a fortuity that he did not do so. The instant case is similar to *Johnson,* where it was only fortuity which prevented the defendant from causing serious bodily injury when he struck the victim in the head with a chair. Since a human bite has the capacity to inflict serious bodily harm, we hold that the human mouth and teeth are a deadly and dangerous weapon in circumstances like those in the instant case, even if the harm actually inflicted was not severe.

The gravamen of Moore's claim is that on the evidence the only way the government could establish that his mouth and teeth were used as a deadly and dangerous weapon was for it to establish that AIDS can be transmitted by biting. As Moore points out, Dr. Gastineau's testimony, which was the only evidence on the transmissibility of the HIV virus, established only a remote or theoretical possibility that the virus could be transmitted through biting. He asserts that the government did not try the case on the theory that *any* human bite— regardless of the presence of the HIV virus—was a deadly and dangerous weapon. His assertion rests on the facts that the indictment charged that Moore, "a person then having been tested positively for the [HIV] antibody, did willfully and forcibly assault" the two officers "by means of a deadly and dangerous weapon, namely, his mouth and teeth"; that the indictment failed to make any similar charge with respect to his hepatitis infection; and that the government introduced a substantial amount of evidence at trial concerning the transmissibility of AIDS by way of biting.

We reject Moore's massive emphasis on the AIDS aspect of this case. As stated above, the record, viewed in the light most favorable to the government, contained sufficient evidence to allow the jury to find that Moore's mouth and teeth were used as a deadly and dangerous weapon, even if Moore was *not* infected with AIDS. As the district court correctly held, moreover, the reference to AIDS in the indictment was mere surplusage and did not limit the government to one theory of the case at trial.

Although there is sufficient evidence in the record that the human mouth and teeth may be used as a deadly and dangerous weapon, we nevertheless wish to emphasize that the medical evidence in the record was insufficient to establish that AIDS may be transmitted by a bite. The evidence established that there are no well-proven cases of AIDS transmission by way of a bite; that contact with saliva has never been shown to transmit the disease; and that in one case a person who had been deeply bitten by a person with AIDS tested negative several months later. Indeed, a recent study has indicated that saliva actually may contain substances that *protect* the body from AIDS. New York Times, May 6, 1988, at A 16, col. 4. While Dr. Gastineau testified "in medicine everything is conceivable", in a legal context the possibility of

AIDS transmission by means of a bite is too remote to support a finding that the mouth and teeth may be considered a deadly and dangerous weapon in this respect.

In short, we hold that the evidence was sufficient to support the finding that Moore's mouth and teeth were a deadly and dangerous weapon, regardless of the presence or absence of AIDS.

* * *

NOTE

For an analysis of "dangerous" weapons and the use of teeth, and a comment on the *Moore* decision, see the Note, Deadly and Dangerous Weapons and AIDS: The *Moore* Analysis is Likely to be Dangerous, 74 Iowa L.Rev. 951 (1989).

Chapter 4

CONSTITUTIONAL LIMITATIONS ON DEFINING CRIMINAL CONDUCT

A. SCOPE OF THE POLICE POWER

COMMONWEALTH v. BONADIO

Supreme Court of Pennsylvania, 1980.
490 Pa. 91, 415 A.2d 47.

FLAHERTY, JUSTICE. This is an appeal from an Order of the Court of Common Pleas of Allegheny County granting appellees' Motion to Quash an Information on the ground that the Voluntary Deviate Sexual Intercourse Statute [1] is unconstitutional. Appellees were arrested at an "adult" pornographic theater on charges of voluntary deviate sexual intercourse and/or conspiracy to perform the same.

The Commonwealth's position is that the statute in question is a valid exercise of the police power pursuant to the authority of states to regulate public health, safety, welfare, and morals. Yet, the police power is not unlimited, as was stated by the United States Supreme Court in Lawton v. Steele, 152 U.S. 133, 137, 14 S.Ct. 499, 501 (1894).

> "To justify the State in thus interposing its authority in behalf of the public, it must appear, first, that the *interests of the public generally,* as distinguished from those of a particular class, require such interference; and, second, that the means are reasonably necessary for the accomplishment of the purpose, and *not unduly oppressive upon individuals.*" (Emphasis added.)

The threshold question in determining whether the statute in question is a valid exercise of the police power is to decide whether it benefits the public generally. The state clearly has a proper role to perform in protecting the public from inadvertent offensive displays of sexual behavior, in preventing people from being forced against their will to submit to sexual contact, in protecting minors from being sexually used by adults, and in eliminating cruelty to animals. To

---

1. The relevant portions of the statute are the following:

"A person who engages in deviate sexual intercourse under circumstances not covered by section 3123 of this title (related to involuntary deviate sexual intercourse) is guilty of a misdemeanor of the second degree." Act of December 6, 1972, P.L.1482, No. 334 § 1, 18 Pa.C.S.A. § 3124 (1973).

" 'Deviate sexual intercourse.' Sexual intercourse per os or per anus between human beings who are not husband and wife, and any form of sexual intercourse with an animal." Act of December 6, 1972, P.L.1482, No. 334, § 1, 18 Pa.C.S.A. § 3101 (1973).

268

assure these protections, a broad range of criminal statutes constitute valid police power exercises, including proscriptions of indecent exposure, open lewdness, rape, *involuntary* deviate sexual intercourse, indecent assault, statutory rape, corruption of minors, and cruelty to animals. The statute in question serves none of the foregoing purposes and it is nugatory to suggest that it promotes a state interest in the institution of marriage. The Voluntary Deviate Sexual Intercourse Statute has only one possible purpose: to regulate the private conduct of consenting adults. Such a purpose, we believe, exceeds the valid bounds of the police power while infringing the right to equal protection of the laws guaranteed by the Constitution of the United States and of this Commonwealth.

With respect to regulation of morals, the police power should properly be exercised to protect each individual's right to be free from interference in defining and pursuing his own morality but not to enforce a majority morality on persons whose conduct *does not harm others*. "No harm to the secular interests of the community is involved in atypical sex practice in private between consenting adult partners." Model Penal Code § 207.5—Sodomy & Related Offenses. Comment (Tent.Draft No. 4, 1955). Many issues that are considered to be matters of morals are subject to debate, and no sufficient state interest justifies legislation of norms simply because a particular belief is followed by a number of people, or even a majority. Indeed, what is considered to be "moral" changes with the times and is dependent upon societal background. Spiritual leadership, not the government, has the responsibility for striving to improve the morality of individuals. Enactment of the Voluntary Deviate Sexual Intercourse Statute, despite the fact that it provides punishment for what many believe to be abhorrent crimes against nature and perceived sins against God, is not properly in the realm of the temporal police power.

The concepts underlying our view of the police power in the case before us were once summarized as follows by the great philosopher, John Stuart Mill, in his eminent and apposite work, On Liberty (1859):

> [T]he sole end for which mankind are warranted, individually or collectively, in interfering with the liberty of action of any of their number, is self-protection . . . . [T]he only purpose for which power can be rightfully exercised over any member of a civilised community, against his will, is to prevent harm to others. His own good, either physical or moral is not a sufficient warrant. He cannot rightfully be compelled to do or forbear because it will be better for him to do so, because it will make him happier, because, in the opinions of others, to do so would be wise, or even right. These are good reasons for remonstrating with him, or reasoning with him, or persuading him, or entreating him, but not for compelling him, or visiting him with any evil in case he do otherwise. To justify that, the conduct from which it is desired to deter him must be calculated to produce evil to some one else. *The only part of the*

*conduct of any one, for which he is amenable to society, is that
which concerns others.   In the part which merely concerns
himself, his independence is, of right, absolute.   Over himself,
over his own body and mind, the individual is sovereign.*

It is, perhaps, hardly necessary to say that this doctrine is
meant to apply to human beings in the maturity of their
faculties. . . .

But there is a sphere of action in which society as distinguished from the individual, has, if any, only an indirect
interest; comprehending all that portion of a person's life and
conduct which affects only himself, or if it also affects others,
only with their free, voluntary, and undeceived consent and
participation. . . .

This, then, is the appropriate region of human liberty.   It
comprises, first, the inward domain of consciousness; demanding liberty of conscience, in the most comprehensive sense;
liberty of thought and feeling; absolute freedom of opinion and
sentiment on all subjects, practical or speculative, scientific,
moral, or theological . . .   Secondly, the principle requires
liberty of tastes and pursuits; of framing the plan of our life to
suit our own character; of doing as we like, subject to such
consequences as may follow: without impediment from our
fellow-creatures, *so long as what we do does not harm them,
even though they should think our conduct foolish, perverse, or
wrong.*   Thirdly, from this liberty of each individual, follows
the liberty, within the same limits of combination among
individuals; freedom to unite, for any purpose not involving
harm to others: the persons combining being supposed to be of
full age, and not forced or deceived.

No society in which these liberties are not, on the whole,
respected, is free, whatever may be its form of government;
. . . *The only freedom which deserves the name, is that of
pursuing our own good in our own way, so long as we do not
attempt to deprive others of theirs,* or impede their efforts to
obtain it.   Each is the proper guardian of his own health,
whether bodily, or mental or spiritual.   Mankind are greater
gainers by suffering each other to live as seems good to
themselves, than by compelling each to live as seems good to
the rest.   (Emphasis Supplied)

This philosophy, as applied to the issue of regulation of sexual morality
presently before the Court, or employed to delimit the police power
generally, properly circumscribes state power over the individual.

Not only does the statute in question exceed the proper bounds of
the police power, but, in addition, it offends the Constitution by creating a classification based on marital status (making deviate acts criminal only when performed between unmarried persons) where such
differential treatment is not supported by a sufficient state interest and

thereby denies equal protection of the laws. Assuming, without deciding, that no fundamental interest is at stake (i.e., the right of privacy), so that strict scrutiny of the classification is not required, the classification still denies equal protection under the following standard:

> The Equal Protection Clause of [the state and federal] constitutions does not deny the State the power to treat different classes of persons in different ways, but does deny the right to legislate that different treatment be accorded to persons placed by a statute into different classes on the basis of criteria wholly unrelated to the objective of the particular statute. The classification must be reasonable, not arbitrary, and must rest upon some ground of difference having a fair and substantial relation to the object of the legislation so that all persons similarly circumstanced shall be treated alike.

Moyer v. Phillips, 462 Pa. 395, 400–401, 341 A.2d 441, 443 (1975).

The Commonwealth submits that the classification is justified on the ground that the legislature intended to forbid, generally, voluntary "deviate" sexual intercourse, but created an exception for persons whose exclusion is claimed to further a state interest in promoting the privacy inherent in the marital relationship. We do not find such a justification for the classification to be reasonable or to have a fair and substantial relation to the object of the legislation. Viewing the statute as exceeding the proper bounds of the police power, however, since none of the previously discussed valid legislative interests in regulating sexual conduct are promoted by the statute, the classification itself could not bear a substantial relation to a valid legislative objective. Furthermore, even if the subject of the statute's regulation were properly within the police power, the marital status of voluntarily participating adults would bear no rational relationship to whether a sexual act should be legal or criminal. In *Eisenstadt v. Baird*, 405 U.S. 438, 453, 92 S.Ct. 1029, 1038 . . . the Supreme Court of the United States stated: "[T]he State could not, consistently with the Equal Protection Clause, outlaw distribution [of contraceptives] to unmarried but not to married persons. In each case the evil, as perceived by the State, would be identical, and the underinclusion would be invidious." Similarly, to suggest that deviate acts are heinous if performed by unmarried persons but acceptable when done by married persons lacks even a rational basis, for requiring less moral behavior of married persons than is expected of unmarried persons is without basis in logic. If the statute regulated sexual acts so affecting others that proscription by law would be justified, then they should be proscribed for all people, not just the unmarried.

Order affirmed.

EAGEN, CHIEF JUSTICE, concurring.

I am convinced the statute violates the constitutional right of equal protection and for this reason I concur in the result reached by Mr. Justice Flaherty.

Larsen and Kauffman, JJ., join in this opinion.

Larsen, Justice, concurring.

I join Mr. Chief Justice Eagen's concurring opinion. Additionally, I would like to point out that *all* public sexual intercourse should be illegal, not just those public sex acts entered into by single persons.

Roberts, Justice, dissenting.

The record plainly demonstrates that these appellants engaged in the proscribed conduct on a stage before a public audience and in plain view of the arresting officers. Thus there is no basis, constitutional or otherwise, for the majority's hasty invalidation of our Legislature's Crimes Code. Accordingly, I would reverse the order of the Court of Common Pleas of Allegheny County and allow the prosecution to proceed.

O'Brien, J., joins in this dissenting opinion.

Nix, Justice, dissenting.

The majority tries to justify its novel and shocking ruling by suggesting that they are defending the individual from state intervention on questions of morality and personal conscience. Regrettably this theory ignores the facts of the case before the court. This is not a case of private, intimate conduct between consenting adults.

Appellees, Mildred Kannitz, known on the stage as "Dawn Delight" and Shanne Wimbel are "exotic" dancers. Appellees, Patrick Gagliano and Michael Bonadio are employees of the Penthouse Theater in downtown Pittsburgh, in which Ms. Delight and Ms. Wimbel perform. In March of last year, plainclothes police officers went to the Penthouse Theater, paid an admission fee, entered the theater, and viewed the performances of Ms. Delight and Ms. Wimbel. During the course of these performances Ms. Delight and Ms. Wimbel engaged in sexual acts with members of the audience. The police officers arrested the two performers, the patrons who participated in the sexual acts, as well as the theater's cashier, Bonadio, and the theater's manager, Gagliano. Ms. Delight and Ms. Wimbel were each charged by information with one count each of voluntary deviate sexual intercourse pursuant to 18 Pa.C.S.A. § 3124. Messrs. Bonadio and Gagliano were charged with one count each of criminal conspiracy.

The majority attempts to avoid the privacy issue [1] by reasoning that there was not a valid exercise of the state's police power in the prohibition of this type of conduct. The absurdity of such a position does not require demonstration. Here we have a public display of the most depraved type of sexual behavior for pay. Any member of the public who pays the fee can witness and participate in this conduct. That the majority would suggest that this is beyond the state's power to

---

1. The court below declared the statute constitutionally infirm as an invasion of privacy. The assertion of a privacy right, however, is completely out of place in light of the present factual predicate. Argu- ments regarding *private* sexual conduct are totally irrelevant in the instant appeal, where the sexual activity involved was *public*.

regulate public health, safety, welfare, and morals is incredible. I assume that regulation of prostitution and hard core pornography are also now prohibited by today's ruling.

Finally, the majority's conclusion that the statute violates equal protection presents a "red herring." Concern over the marital exception contained within the voluntary deviate sexual intercourse statute, is misplaced, for the heart of this exception is the intimacy and warmth of a *private* marital sexual relationship. Here the sexual acts were performed in *public* and in return for monetary compensation. It is therefore clear that the marital status of the participants in this conduct would not have affected their culpability. To suggest that the marital exception was intended to insulate a marital couple who performed deviate sexual acts for public display for pay would distort the obvious legislative objective in providing for this exception. The marital exception was designed to protect the intimacy and privacy of the marital unit. It did not give married couples the license to publicly engage in lewd and lascivious public acts.

NOTE

John Stuart Mill's essay, quoted in the *Bonadio* decision, represents an almost classical position that there are limits on the power of the government to interfere with an individual's exercise of choices. He also advocates that the enforcement of the prevailing moral codes is not, absent other considerations, a sufficient justification for criminalization of conduct that deviates from the "norm" of the majority.

For a critique of Mill's views, see Sir James Fitzjames Stephen work *Liberty, Equality, Fraternity* (1874). Stephen admits that in the use of the criminal law to enforce accepted norms of morality, restraint ought to be exercised, but he believes that the moral coercion of public opinion is the engine that protects the cohesiveness of a society. He states that to "try to regulate the internal affairs of a family, the relations of love or friendship, or many things of the same sort, by law or by the coercion of public opinion, is like trying to pull an eyelash out of a man's eye with a pair of tongs." It will put out an eye, but will not remove the eyelash. But the importance of trying to promote virtue and restrain unconventional conduct that is branded as "immoral" by the majority through the use of the criminal laws, said Stephen, is that "in extreme cases it brands gross acts of vice with the deepest mark of infamy which can be impressed upon them, and that in this manner it protects the public and accepted standard of morals from being grossly and openly violated." He concludes by saying that the use of the criminal law for that purpose "affirms in a singularly emphatic manner a principle which is absolutely inconsistent with and contradictory to Mr. Mill's—the principle, namely, that there are acts of wickedness so gross and outrageous that, self-protection apart, they must be prevented as far as possible at any cost to the offender, and punished, if they occur, with exemplary severity."

In 1957, an English Committee on Homosexual Offenses and Prostitution issued what is known as the Wolfenden Report. In discussing the proper scope of the criminal law, the Committee said that the function of the criminal law should be "to preserve public order and decency, to protect the citizen from what is offensive or injurious, and to provide sufficient safeguards against exploitation and corruption of others, particularly those who are specially vulnerable because they are young, weak in body or mind, inexperienced, or in a state of special physical, official or economic dependence." In recommending that private homosexual behavior between consenting adults be decriminalized, the report continued, however:

> "It is not, in our view, the function of the law to intervene in the private lives of citizens, or to seek to enforce any particular pattern of behavior, further than is necessary to carry out the purposes we have outlined."

> ". . . Unless a deliberate attempt is to be made by society, acting through the agency of the law, to equate the sphere of crime with that of sin, there must remain a realm of private morality and immorality which is, in brief and crude terms, not the law's business. To say this is not to condone or encourage private immorality."

Expressing disagreement with the Wolfenden Committee's statement that it is not a proper function of the criminal law to enforce conventional morality, see Lord Patrick Devlin's critique in Devlin, The Enforcement of Morals (1965). Advocating the Mill libertarian position, see Hart, Law, Liberty and Morality (1963). See also, Dworkin, Lord Devlin and the Enforcement of Morals, 75 Yale L.J. 986 (1966), and the more recent work by Feinberg, *Harm to Others* (1984).

B. DUE PROCESS, VAGUENESS, OVERBREADTH AND THE FIRST AMENDMENT

PAPACHRISTOU v. CITY OF JACKSONVILLE

Supreme Court of the United States, 1972.
405 U.S. 156, 92 S.Ct. 839, 31 L.Ed.2d 110.

MR. JUSTICE DOUGLAS delivered the opinion of the Court.

This case involves eight defendants who were convicted in a Florida municipal court of violating a Jacksonville, Florida, vagrancy ordinance.[1] Their convictions, entailing fines and jail sentences (some of which were suspended), were affirmed by the Florida Circuit Court in a consolidated appeal, and their petition for certiorari was denied by the District Court of Appeals, . . . The case is here on a petition for

---

1. Jacksonville Ordinance Code § 26–57 provided at the time of these arrests and convictions as follows:

"Rogues and vagabonds, or dissolute persons who go about begging, common gamblers, persons who use juggling or unlawful games or plays, common drunkards, common night walkers, thieves, pilferers or pickpockets, traders in stolen property, lewd, wanton and lascivious persons, keepers of gambling places, common railers and brawlers, persons wandering or strolling around from place to place without any lawful purpose or object, habitual loafers, disor-

derly persons, persons neglecting all lawful business and habitually spending their time by frequenting houses of ill fame, gaming houses, or places where alcoholic beverages are sold or served, persons able to work but habitually living upon the earnings of their wives or minor children shall be deemed vagrants and, upon conviction in the Municipal Court shall be punished [90 days imprisonment, $500 fine, or both.]

We are advised that at present the Jacksonville vagrancy ordinance is § 330.107 and identical with the earlier one except that "juggling" has been eliminated.

certiorari, which we granted. . . .　For reasons which will appear, we reverse.[2]

At issue are five consolidated cases.　Margaret Papachristou, Betty Calloway, Eugene Eddie Melton, and Leonard Johnson were all arrested early on a Sunday morning, and charged with vagrancy—"prowling by auto."

Jimmy Lee Smith and Milton Henry were charged with vagrancy—"vagabonds."

Henry Edward Heath and a co-defendant were arrested for vagrancy—"loitering" and "common thief."

Thomas Owen Campbell was charged with vagrancy—"common thief."

Hugh Brown was charged with vagrancy—"disorderly loitering on street" and "disorderly conduct—resisting arrest with violence."

The facts are stipulated.　Papachristou and Calloway are white females.　Melton and Johnson are black males.　Papachristou was enrolled in a job-training program sponsored by the State Employment Service at Florida Junior College in Jacksonville.　Calloway was a typing and shorthand teacher at a state mental institution located near Jacksonville.　She was the owner of the automobile in which the four defendants were arrested.　Melton was a Vietnam war veteran who had been released from the Navy after nine months in a veterans' hospital. On the date of his arrest he was a part-time computer helper while attending college as a full-time student in Jacksonville.　Johnson was a tow-motor operator in a grocery chain warehouse and was a lifelong resident of Jacksonville.

At the time of their arrest the four of them were riding in Calloway's car on the main thoroughfare in Jacksonville.　They had left a restaurant owned by Johnson's uncle where they had eaten and were on their way to a night club.　The arresting officers denied that the racial mixture in the car played any part in the decision to make the arrest.　The arrest they said, was made because the defendants had stopped near a used-car lot which had been broken into several times.

---

2. Florida also has a vagrancy statute . . . which reads quite closely on the Jacksonville ordinance. . . . [It] makes the commission of any Florida misdemeanor a Class D offense against the City of Jacksonville. In 1971 Florida made minor amendments to its statute.

[The statute] was declared unconstitutionally overbroad in Lazarus v. Faircloth, D.C., 301 F.Supp. 266. The Court said: "All loitering, loafing, or idling on the streets and highways of a city, even though habitual, is not necessarily detrimental to the public welfare nor is it under all circumstances an interference with travel upon them. It may be and often is entirely innocuous. The statute draws no distinction between conduct that is calculated to harm and that which is essentially innocent." See also Smith v. Florida, 405 U.S. 172, 92 S.Ct. 848, 31 L.Ed.2d 122 (1972).

The Florida disorderly conduct ordinance, covering "loitering about any hotel, block, barroom, dramshop, gambling house or disorderly house, or wandering about the streets either by night or by day without any known lawful means of support or without being able to give a satisfactory account of themselves" has also been held void for "excessive broadness and vagueness" by the Florida Supreme Court, Headley v. Selkowitz, 171 So.2d 368, 370.

There was, however, no evidence of any breaking and entering on the night in question.

Of these four charged with "prowling by auto" none had been previously arrested except Papachristou who had once been convicted of a municipal offense.

Jimmy Lee Smith and Milton Henry (who is not a petitioner) were arrested between 9 and 10 a.m. on a weekday in downtown Jacksonville, while waiting for a friend who was to lend them a car so they could apply for a job at a produce company. Smith was a part-time produce worker and part-time organizer for a Negro political group. He had a common-law wife and three children supported by him and his wife. He had been arrested several times but convicted only once. Smith's companion, Henry, was an 18–year–old high school student with no previous record of arrest.

This morning it was cold, and Smith had no jacket, so they went briefly into a dry cleaning shop to wait, but left when requested to do so. They thereafter walked back and forth two or three times over a two-block stretch looking for their friend. The store owners, who apparently were wary of Smith and his companion, summoned two police officers who searched the men and found neither had a weapon. But they were arrested because the officers said they had no identification and because the officers did not believe their story.

Heath and a codefendant were arrested for "loitering" and for "common thief." Both were residents of Jacksonville, Heath having lived there all his life and being employed at an automobile and body shop. Heath had previously been arrested but his codefendant had no arrest record. Heath and his companion were arrested when they drove up to a residence shared by Heath's girlfriend and some other girls. Some police officers were already there in the process of arresting another man. When Heath and his companion started backing out of the driveway, the officers signaled to them to stop and asked them to get out of the car, which they did. Thereupon they and the automobile were searched. Although no contraband or incriminating evidence was found, they were both arrested, Heath being charged with being a "common thief" because he was reputed to be a thief. The codefendant was charged with "loitering" because he was standing in the driveway, an act which the officers admitted was done only at their command.

Campbell was arrested as he reached his home very early one morning and was charged with "common thief." He was stopped by officers because he was traveling at a high rate of speed, yet no speeding charge was placed against him.

Brown was arrested when he was observed leaving a downtown, Jacksonville, hotel by a police officer seated in a cruiser. The police testified he was reputed to be a thief, narcotics pusher, and generally opprobrious character. The officer called Brown over to the car, intending at that time to arrest him unless he had a good explanation for being on the street. Brown walked over to the police cruiser, as commanded, and the officer began to search him, apparently preparatory to placing him in the car. In the process of the search he came on two small packets which were later found to contain heroin. When the officer touched the pocket where the packets were, Brown began to resist. He was charged with "disorderly loitering on the street" and "disorderly conduct—resisting arrest with violence." While he was also charged with a narcotics violation, that charge was *nolled*.

Jacksonville's ordinance and Florida's statute were "derived from early English law," . . . and employ "archaic language" in their definitions of vagrants. The history is an often-told tale. The breakup of feudal estates in England led to labor shortages which in turn resulted in the Statutes of Laborers, designed to stabilize the labor force by prohibiting increases in wages and prohibiting the movement of workers from their home areas in search of improved conditions. Later vagrancy laws became criminal aspects of the poor laws. The series of laws passed in England on the subject became increasingly severe. But "the theory of the Elizabethan poor laws no longer fits the facts," . . . The conditions which spawned these laws may be gone, but the archaic classifications remain.

This ordinance is void-for-vagueness, both in the sense that it "fails to give a person of ordinary intelligence fair notice that his contemplated conduct is forbidden by the statute," . . . and because it encourages arbitrary and erratic arrests and convictions . . .

Living under a rule of law entails various suppositions, one of which is that "All [persons] are entitled to be informed as to what the State commands or forbids." Lanzetta v. New Jersey, . . .

Lanzetta is one of a well-recognized group of cases insisting that the law give fair notice of the offending conduct. . . . In the field of regulatory statutes governing business activities, where the acts limited are in a narrow category, greater leeway is allowed. . . .

The poor among us, the minorities, the average householder are not in business and not alerted to the regulatory schemes of vagrancy laws; and we assume they would have no understanding of their meaning and impact if they read them. Nor are they protected from being caught in the vagrancy net by the necessity of having a specific intent to commit an unlawful act. . . .

The Jacksonville ordinance makes criminal activities which by modern standards are normally innocent. "Nightwalking" is one. Florida construes the ordinance not to make criminal one night's wandering, . . . only the "habitual" wanderer or as the ordinance describes it "common night walkers." We know, however, from experience that sleepless people often walk at night, perhaps hopeful that sleep-inducing relaxation will result.

Luis Munoz–Marin, former Governor of Puerto Rico, commented once that "loafing" was a national virtue in his Commonwealth and that it should be encouraged. It is, however, a crime in Jacksonville.

"Persons able to work but habitually living on the earnings of their wives or minor children"—like habitually living "without visible means of support"—might implicate unemployed pillars of the community who have married rich wives.

"Persons able to work but habitually living on the earnings of their wives or minor children" may also embrace unemployed people out of the labor market, by reason of a recession or disemployed by reason of technological or so-called structural displacements.

Persons "wandering or strolling" from place to place have been extolled by Walt Whitman and Vachel Lindsay. The qualification "without any lawful purpose or object" may be a trap for innocent acts. Persons "neglecting all lawful business and habitually spending their time by frequenting . . . places where alcoholic beverages are sold or served" would literally embrace many members of golf clubs and city clubs.

Walkers and strollers and wanderers may be going to or coming from a burglary. Loafers or loiterers may be "casing" a place for a holdup. Letting one's wife support him is an intra-family matter, and normally of no concern to the police. Yet it may, of course, be the setting for numerous crimes.

The difficulty is that these activities are historically part of the amenities of life as we have known it. They are not mentioned in the Constitution or in the Bill of Rights. These unwritten amenities have been in part responsible for giving our people the feeling of independence and self-confidence, the feeling of creativity. These amenities have dignified the right of dissent and have honored the right to be nonconformists and the right to defy submissiveness. They have encouraged lives of high spirits rather than hushed, suffocating silence.

They are embedded in Walt Whitman's writings especially in his Song of the Open Road. They are reflected too, in the spirit of Vachel Lindsay's I Want to go Wandering and by Henry D. Thoreau.

This aspect of the vagrancy ordinance before us is suggested by what this Court said in 1875 about a broad criminal statute enacted by Congress: "It would certainly be dangerous if the legislature could set a net large enough to catch all possible offenders, and leave it to the courts to step inside and say who could be rightfully detained, and who should be set at large." . . .

While that was a federal case, the due process implications are equally applicable to the States and to this vagrancy ordinance. Here the net cast is large, not to give the courts the power to pick and choose but to increase the arsenal of the police. . . .

* * *

Where the list of crimes is so all-inclusive and generalized as that one in this ordinance, those convicted may be punished for no more than vindicating affronts to police authority: . . .

Another aspect of the ordinance's vagueness appears when we focus, not on the lack of notice given a potential offender, but on the effect of the unfettered discretion it places in the hands of the Jacksonville police. Caleb Foote, an early student of this subject, has called the vagrancy-type law as offering "punishment by analogy." Such crimes, though long common in Russia, are not compatible with our constitutional system. We allow our police to make arrests only on "probable cause," a Fourth and Fourteenth Amendment standard applicable to the States as well as to the Federal Government. Arresting a person on suspicion, like arresting a person for investigation, is foreign to our system, even when the arrest is for past criminality. Future criminality, however, is the common justification for the presence of vagrancy statutes. . . . Florida has indeed construed her vagrancy statute "as necessary regulations," *inter alia,* "to deter vagabondage and prevent crimes." . . .

A direction by a legislature to the police to arrest all "suspicious" persons would not pass constitutional muster. A vagrancy prosecution may be merely the cloak for a conviction which could not be obtained on the real but undisclosed grounds for the arrest. . . .

Those generally implicated by the imprecise terms of the ordinance—poor people, nonconformists, dissenters, idlers—may be required to comport themselves according to the life-style deemed appropriate by the Jacksonville police and the courts. Where, as here, there are no standards governing the exercise of the discretion granted by the ordinance, the scheme permits and encourages an arbitrary and discriminatory enforcement of the law. It furnishes a convenient tool for "harsh and discriminatory enforcement by prosecuting officials, against particular groups deemed to merit their displeasure." . . . It results in a regime in which the poor and the unpopular are permitted to "stand on a public sidewalk . . . only at the whim of any police officer." . . .

A presumption that people who might walk or loaf or loiter or stroll or frequent houses where liquor is sold, or who are supported by their wives or who look suspicious to the police are to become future criminals is too precarious for a rule of law. The implicit presumption in these generalized vagrancy standards—that crime is being nipped in the bud—is too extravagant to deserve extended treatment. Of course, vagrancy statutes are useful to the police. Of course they are nets making easy the round-up of so-called undesirables. But the rule of law implies equality and justice in its application. Vagrancy laws of the Jacksonville type teach that the scales of justice are so tipped that even-handed administration of the law is not possible. The rule of law, evenly applied to minorities as well as majorities, to the poor as well as the rich, is the great mucilage that holds society together.

NOTES

1. What makes an indefinite law constitutionally "vague" is hard to define, as evidenced by Mr. Justice Frankfurter's attempt in his dissent in Winters v. New York, 333 U.S. 507, 68 S.Ct. 665, 92 L.Ed. 840 (1948):

"[Indefiniteness] is not a quantitative concept. It is not even a techni- cal concept of definite components. It is itself an indefinite concept. There is no such thing as 'indefiniteness' in the abstract, by which the sufficiency of the requirement expressed by the term may be ascer- tained. The requirement is fair notice that conduct may entail punish- ment. But whether notice is or is not 'fair' depends upon the subject matter to which it relates. Unlike the abstract stuff of mathematics, or the quantitatively ascertainable elements of much of natural sci- ence, legislation is greatly concerned with the multiform psychological complexities of individual and social conduct. Accordingly, the de- mands upon legislation, and its responses, are variable and multiform. That which may appear to be too vague and even meaningless as to one subject matter may be as definite as another subject matter of legislation permits, . . .

"In these matters legislatures are confronted with a dilemma. If a law is framed with narrow particularity, too easy opportunities are afforded to nullify the purposes of the legislation. If the legislation is drafted in terms so vague that no ascertainable line is drawn in advance between innocent and condemned conduct, the purpose of the legislation cannot be enforced because no purpose is defined. . . . the reconciliation of these two contradictories is necessarily an empiric enterprise largely depending on the nature of the particular legislative problem."

2. A statute prohibits a person from peeping through doors, windows, or similar places of another while on another's premises with intent or purpose to spy on such person or to invade his privacy, or going onto another's premises for that purpose. Is such a statute unconstitutionally vague? See Lemon v. State, 235 Ga. 74, 218 S.E.2d 818 (1975).

A statute makes it a misdemeanor when a person "intentionally interferes with a person recognized to be a law enforcement official seeking to effect an arrest or detention of himself or another regardless of whether there is a legal basis for the arrest." Unconstitutionally vague? See, State v. Bradshaw, 541 P.2d 800 (Utah 1975).

A statute makes it unlawful for a known prostitute to "repeatedly stop or attempt to stop any pedestrian or motor vehicle by hailing, whistling, waving of arms or any other bodily gesture, while such person is on any public sidewalk or street. . . ." Constitutional? See, Detroit v. Bowden, 6 Mich.App. 514, 149 N.W.2d 771 (1967).

3. A 128–year–old statute provided: "If any man and woman not being married to each other, lewdly and viciously associate and cohabit together or if any man or woman, married or unmarried, is guilty of open and gross lewdness, and designedly makes an open and indecent or obscene exposure of his or her person, or of the person of another, every such person shall be imprisoned in the county jail not exceeding six months, or be fined not exceeding two hundred dollars." Is this statute sufficiently precise to meet constitutional challenge? See, State v. Kueny, 215 N.W.2d 215 (Iowa 1974). See also, Courtemanche v.

State, 507 S.W.2d 545 (Tex.Crim.App.1974) holding unconstitutional as being void for vagueness a statute which proscribes lewd or vulgar entertainment, or lewd, immoral or offensive conduct where beer is sold. But see Johnson v. Phoenix City Court, 24 Ariz.App. 63, 535 P.2d 1067 (1975).

4. A Kansas statute punishes "any fondling or touching of the person of either the child or the offender done or submitted to with the intent to arouse or to satisfy the sexual desires of either the child or the offender or both," when these acts are done with a child under the age of 16. Is this statute unconstitutionally vague? See State v. Conley, 216 Kan. 66, 531 P.2d 36 (1975).

5. Is a statute which proscribes members of the opposite sex from occupying the same bedroom at a hotel for "any immoral purposes" unconstitutionally vague? See State v. Sanders, 37 N.C.App. 53, 245 S.E.2d 397 (1978).

6. A Sunday closing law exempts stores that have no more than four employees on duty at any one time on Sunday. Is such statute sufficiently precise? Does "employees" include the owner of a business, members of his family, whether paid or unpaid, a clean-up man, bag boy, or security guard? See Simonetti v. City of Birmingham, 55 Ala.App. 163, 314 So.2d 83 (1975), cert. denied 294 Ala. 192, 314 So.2d 99.

7. In State v. Allen, 304 N.W.2d 203 (Iowa 1981), the Supreme Court of Iowa held that a trial court erred when it held unconstitutionally vague the state's statute on incest, as applied to a defendant who had sexual intercourse with his wife's half-sister. The statute speaks only in terms of relationships by "blood or affinity to the fourth degree" and is silent on the issue of half-blood relatives, but the court determined that the law's reference to civil law methods of computing affinity eliminates what vagueness there might be said to be. The court said:

> ". . . [T]he degree of kinship is determined by counting upward from one of the persons in question to the nearest common ancestor, and then down to the other person, calling it one degree for each generation in the ascending as well as descending line. Under this rule a woman's sister is related to her by consanguinity in the second degree. The sister is thus related to the woman's husband by affinity in the second degree. These relationships are not changed merely by the fact that the blood relationship in a given case is by half blood. . . . Persons related by half blood necessarily have a common ancestor, and the degree of their relationship is established through that ancestor. No requirement exists that they have a second ancestor in common. Thus, unless a statute provides otherwise, a woman's half sister is related to her by consanguinity in the second degree. The half sister is accordingly related to the woman's husband by affinity in the second degree. . . ."

8. Is a statute that prohibits the operation of a place of public entertainment that permits "lewd" dancing or in which "lewd" pictures are accessible to public view unconstitutionally vague? See State v. Crater, 388 So.2d 802 (La. 1980). How about an ordinance that provides that "it shall be unlawful . . . to commit any indecent, immodest or filthy act in the presence of any person or in such a situation that persons passing might ordinarily see the same"? Unconstitutionally vague? See State v. Metzger, 211 Neb. 593, 319 N.W.2d 459 (1982).

COATES v. CITY OF CINCINNATI

Supreme Court of the United States, 1971.
402 U.S. 611, 91 S.Ct. 1686, 29 L.Ed.2d 214.

MR. JUSTICE STEWART delivered the opinion of the Court.

A Cincinnati, Ohio, ordinance makes it a criminal offense for "three or more persons to assemble . . . on any of the sidewalks . . . and there conduct themselves in a manner annoying to persons passing by. . . ." The issue before us is whether this ordinance is unconstitutional on its face.

The appellants were convicted of violating the ordinance, and the convictions were ultimately affirmed by a closely divided vote in the Supreme Court of Ohio, upholding the constitutional validity of the ordinance. . . . The record brought before the reviewing courts tells us no more than that the appellant Coates was a student involved in a demonstration and the other appellants were pickets involved in a labor dispute. For throughout this litigation it has been the appellants' position that the ordinance on its face violates the First and Fourteenth Amendments of the Constitution. . . .

In rejecting this claim and affirming the convictions the Ohio Supreme Court did not give the ordinance any construction at variance with the apparent plain import of its language. The court simply stated:

"The ordinance prohibits, *inter alia,* 'conduct . . . annoying to persons passing by.' The word 'annoying' is a widely used and well understood word; it is not necessary to guess its meaning. 'Annoying' is the present participle of the transitive verb 'annoy' which means to trouble, to vex, to impede, to incommode, to provoke, to harass or to irritate.

"We conclude, as did the Supreme Court of the United States in Cameron v. Johnson, . . . in which the issue of the vagueness of a statute was presented, that the ordinance 'clearly and precisely delineates its reach in words of common understanding. It is a "precise and narrowly drawn regulatory statute [ordinance] evincing a legislative judgment that certain specific conduct be . . . proscribed." ' " . . .

Beyond this, the only construction put upon the ordinance by the state court was its unexplained conclusion that "the standard of conduct which it specifies is not dependent upon each complainant's sensitivity." But the court did not indicate upon whose sensitivity a violation does depend—the sensitivity of the judge or jury, the sensitivity of the arresting officer, or the sensitivity of a hypothetical reasonable man.

We are thus relegated, at best, to the words of the ordinance itself. If three or more people meet together on a sidewalk or street corner, they must conduct themselves so as not to annoy any police officer or other person who should happen to pass by. In our opinion this ordinance is unconstitutionally vague because it subjects the exercise of the right of assembly to an unascertainable standard, and unconstitutionally broad because it authorizes the punishment of constitutionally protected conduct.

Conduct that annoys some people does not annoy others. Thus, the ordinance is vague, not in the sense that it requires a person to conform his conduct to an imprecise but comprehensible normative standard, but rather in the sense that no standard of conduct is specified at all. As a result, "men of common intelligence must necessarily guess at its meaning." . . .

It is said that the ordinance is broad enough to encompass many types of conduct clearly within the city's constitutional power to prohibit. And so, indeed, it is. The city is free to prevent people from blocking sidewalks, obstructing traffic, littering streets, committing assaults, or engaging in countless other forms of antisocial conduct. It can do so through the enactment and enforcement of ordinances directed with reasonable specificity toward the conduct to be prohibited. . . . It cannot constitutionally do so through the enactment and enforcement of an ordinance whose violation may entirely depend upon whether or not a policeman is annoyed.

But the vice of the ordinance lies not alone in its violation of the due process standard of vagueness. The ordinance also violates the constitutional right of free assembly and association. Our decisions establish that mere public intolerance or animosity cannot be the basis for abridgment of these constitutional freedoms. . . . The First and Fourteenth Amendments do not permit a State to make criminal the exercise of the right of assembly simply because its exercise may be "annoying" to some people. If this were not the rule, the right of the people to gather in public places for social or political purposes would be continually subject to summary suspension through the good-faith enforcement of a prohibition against annoying conduct. And such a prohibition, in addition, contains an obvious invitation to discriminatory enforcement against those whose association together is "annoying" because their ideas, their lifestyle, or their physical appearance is resented by the majority of their fellow citizens.

The ordinance before us makes a crime out of what under the Constitution cannot be a crime. It is aimed directly at activity protected by the Constitution. We need not lament that we do not have before us the details of the conduct found to be annoying. It is the ordinance on its face that sets the standard of conduct and warns against transgression. The details of the offense could no more serve to validate this ordinance than could the details of an offense charged under an ordinance suspending unconditionally the right of assembly and free speech.

The judgment is reversed.

Mr. Justice Black.

*   *   *

This Court has long held that laws so vague that a person of common understanding cannot know what is forbidden are unconstitutional on their face. . . . Likewise, laws which broadly forbid conduct or activities which are protected by the Federal Constitution, such as, for instance, the discussion of political matters, are void on their face. . . . On the other hand, laws which plainly forbid conduct which is constitutionally within the power of the State to forbid but also restrict constitutionally protected conduct may be void either on their face or merely as applied in certain instances. As my Brother White states in his opinion (with which I substantially agree), this is one of those numerous cases where the law could be held unconstitutional because it prohibits both conduct which the Constitution safeguards and conduct which the State may constitutionally punish. Thus, the First Amendment which forbids the State to abridge freedom of speech, would invalidate this city ordinance if it were used to punish the making of a political speech, even if that speech were to annoy other persons. In contrast, however, the ordinance could properly be applied to prohibit the gathering of persons in the mouths of alleys to annoy passersby by throwing rocks or by some other conduct not at all connected with speech. It is a matter of no little difficulty to determine when a law can be held void on its face and when such summary action is inappropriate. This difficulty has been aggravated in this case, because the record fails to show in what conduct these defendants had engaged to annoy other people. In my view, a record showing the facts surrounding the conviction is essential to adjudicate the important constitutional issues in this case. I would therefore vacate the judgment and remand the case with instructions that the trial court give both parties an opportunity to supplement the record so that we may determine whether the conduct actually punished is the kind of conduct which it is within the power of the State to punish.

MR. JUSTICE WHITE, with whom THE CHIEF JUSTICE and MR. JUSTICE BLACKMUN join, dissenting.

The claim in this case, in part, is that the Cincinnati ordinance is so vague that it may not constitutionally be applied to any conduct. But the ordinance prohibits persons from assembling with others and "conduct[ing] themselves in a manner annoying to persons passing by. . . ." Cincinnati Code of Ordinances § 901–L6. Any man of average comprehension should know that some kinds of conduct, such as assault or blocking passage on the street, will annoy others and are clearly covered by the "annoying conduct" standard of the ordinance. It would be frivolous to say that these and many other kinds of conduct are not within the foreseeable reach of the law.

It is possible that a whole range of other acts, defined with unconstitutional imprecision, is forbidden by the ordinance. But as a general rule, when a criminal charge is based on conduct constitutionally subject to proscription and clearly forbidden by a statute, it is no defense that the law would be unconstitutionally vague if applied to other behavior. Such a statute is not vague on its face. It may be vague as applied in some circumstances, but ruling on such a challenge obviously requires knowledge of the conduct with which a defendant is charged.

In Williams v. United States, 341 U.S. 97 (1951), a police officer was charged under federal statutes with extracting confessions by force and thus, under color of law, depriving the prisoner there involved of rights, privileges, and immunities secured or protected by the Constitution and laws of the United States, contrary to 18 U.S.C.A. § 242. The defendant there urged that the standard—rights, privileges, and immunities secured by the Constitution—was impermissibly vague and, more particularly, that the Court was often so closely divided on illegal-confession issues that no defendant could be expected to know when he was violating the law. The Court's response was that, while application of the statute to less obvious methods of coercion might raise doubts about the adequacy of the standard of guilt, in the case before it, it was "plain as a pikestaff that the present confessions would not be allowed in evidence whatever the school of thought concerning the scope and meaning of the Due Process Clause." The claim of facial vagueness was thus rejected.

So too in United States v. National Dairy Corp., where we considered a statute forbidding sales of goods at "unreasonably" low prices to injure or eliminate a competitor, 15 U.S.C.A. § 13a, we thought the statute gave a seller adequate notice that sales below cost were illegal. The statute was therefore not facially vague, although it might be difficult to tell whether certain other kinds of conduct fell within this language. We said: "In determining the sufficiency of the notice a statute must of necessity be examined in the light of the conduct with which a defendant is charged." . . . This approach is consistent with the host of cases holding that "one to whom application of a statute is constitutional will not be heard to attack the statute on the ground that impliedly it might also be taken as applying to other persons or other situations in which its application might be unconstitutional." . . .

Our cases, however, including *National Dairy,* recognize a different approach where the statute at issue purports to regulate or proscribe rights of speech or press protected by the First Amendment. . . . Although a statute may be neither vague, overbroad, nor otherwise invalid as applied to the conduct charged against a particular defendant, he is permitted to raise its vagueness or unconstitutional overbreadth as applied to others. And if the law is found deficient in one of these respects, it may not be applied to him either, until and unless a satisfactory limiting construction is placed on the statute. . . . The statute, in effect, is stricken down on its face. This result is deemed justified since the otherwise continued existence of the statute in unnarrowed form would tend to suppress constitutionally protected rights. . . .

Even accepting the overbreadth doctrine with respect to statutes clearly reaching speech, the Cincinnati ordinance does not purport to bar or regulate speech as such. It prohibits persons from assembling and "conduct[ing]" themselves in a manner annoying to other persons. Even if the assembled defendants in this case were demonstrating and picketing, we have long recognized that picketing is not solely a communicative endeavor and has aspects which the State is entitled to regulate even though there is incidental impact on speech. In Cox v. Louisiana (1965), the Court held valid on its face a statute forbidding picketing and parading near a courthouse. This was deemed a valid regulation of conduct rather than pure speech. The conduct reached by the statute was "subject to regulation even though [it was] intertwined with expression and association." The Court then went on to consider the statute as applied to the facts of record.

In the case before us, I would deal with the Cincinnati ordinance as we would with the ordinary criminal statute. The ordinance clearly reaches certain conduct but may be illegally vague with respect to other conduct. The statute is not infirm on its face and since we have no information from this record as to what conduct was charged against these defendants, we are in no position to judge the statute as applied. That the ordinance may confer wide discretion in a wide range of circumstances is irrelevant when he may be dealing with conduct at its core.

I would therefore affirm the judgment of the Ohio Supreme Court.

VILLAGE OF HOFFMAN ESTATES v. FLIPSIDE, HOFFMAN ESTATES, INC.

Supreme Court of the United States, 1982.
455 U.S. 489, 102 S.Ct. 1186, 71 L.Ed.2d 362.

JUSTICE MARSHALL delivered the opinion of the Court.

This case presents a pre-enforcement facial challenge to a drug paraphernalia ordinance on the ground that it is unconstitutionally vague and overbroad. The ordinance in question requires a business to obtain a license if it sells any items that are "designed or marketed for use with illegal cannabis or drugs." The United States Court of Appeals for the Seventh Circuit held that the ordinance is vague on its face. We noted probable jurisdiction, and now reverse.

I

For more than three years prior to May 1, 1978, appellee The Flipside, Hoffman Estates, Inc. (Flipside) sold a variety of merchandise, including phonographic records, smoking accessories, novelty devices and jewelry, in its store located in the village of Hoffman Estates, Illinois (the village).[1] On February 20, 1978, the village enacted an

---

1. More specifically, the District Court found:

"[Flipside] sold literature that included 'A Child's Garden of Grass,' 'Marijuana Grower's Guide,' and magazines such as

ordinance regulating drug paraphernalia, to be effective May 1, 1978. The ordinance makes it unlawful for any person "to sell any items, effect, paraphernalia, accessory or thing which is designed or marketed for use with illegal cannabis or drugs, as defined by Illinois Revised Statutes, without obtaining a license therefor." The license fee is $150.00. A business must also file affidavits that the licensee and its employees have not been convicted of a drug-related offense. Moreover, the business must keep a record of each sale of a regulated item, including the name and address of the purchaser, to be open to police inspection. No regulated item may be sold to a minor. A violation is subject to a fine of not less than $10.00 and not more than $500.00, and each day that a violation continues gives rise to a separate offense. A series of licensing guidelines prepared by the village attorney define "Paper," "Roach Clips," "Pipes" and "Paraphernalia," the sale of which is required to be licensed.

After an administrative inquiry, the village determined that Flipside and one other store appeared to be in violation of the ordinance. The village attorney notified Flipside of the existence of the ordinance, and made a copy of the ordinance and guidelines available to Flipside. Flipside's owner asked for guidance concerning which items were covered by the ordinance; the village attorney advised him to remove items in a certain section of the store "for his protection," and he did so. The items included, according to Flipside's description, a clamp, chain ornaments, an "alligator" clip, key chains, necklaces, earrings, cigarette holders, glove stretchers, scales, strainers, a pulverizer, squeeze bottles, pipes, water pipes, pins, an herb sifter, mirrors, vials, cigarette rolling papers, and tobacco snuff. On May 30, 1978, instead of applying for a license or seeking clarification via the administrative procedures that the village had established for its licensing ordinances, Flipside filed this lawsuit in the United States District Court for the Northern District of Illinois.

The complaint alleged, inter alia, that the ordinance is unconstitutionally vague and overbroad, and requested injunctive and declaratory relief and damages. The District Court, . . . issued an opinion upholding the constitutionality of the ordinance, and awarded judgment to the village defendants.

The Court of Appeals reversed, on the ground that the ordinance is unconstitutionally vague on its face. . . .

'National Lampoon,' 'Rolling Stone,' and 'High Times.' The novelty devices and tobacco-related items plaintiff sold in its store ranged from small commodities such as clamps, chain ornaments and earrings through cigarette holders, scales, pipes of various types and sizes, to large water pipes, some designed for individual use, some which as many as four persons can use with flexible plastic tubes. Plaintiff also sold a large number of cigarette rolling papers in a variety of colors. One of plaintiff's displayed items was a mirror, about seven by nine inches with the word 'Cocaine' painted on its surface in a purple color. Plaintiff sold cigarette holders, 'alligator clips,' herb sifters, vials, and a variety of tobacco snuff." 485 F.Supp. 400, 403 (N.D.Ill. 1980).

II

In a facial challenge to the overbreadth and vagueness of a law [2], a court's first task is to determine whether the enactment reaches a substantial amount of constitutionally protected conduct.[3] If it does not, then the overbreadth challenge must fail. The court should then examine the facial vagueness challenge and, assuming the enactment implicates no constitutionally protected conduct, should uphold the challenge only if the enactment is impermissibly vague in all of its applications. A plaintiff who engages in some conduct that is clearly proscribed cannot complain of the vagueness of the law as applied to the conduct of others.[4] A court should therefore examine the complainant's conduct before analyzing other hypothetical applications of the law.

The Court of Appeals in this case did not explicitly consider whether the ordinance reaches constitutionally protected conduct and is overbroad, nor whether the ordinance is vague in all of its applications. Instead, the court determined that the ordinance is void for vagueness because it is unclear in *some* of its applications to the conduct of Flipside and of other hypothetical parties. Under a proper analysis, however, the ordinance is not facially invalid.

*   *   *

IV

A

A law that does not reach constitutionally protected conduct and therefore satisfies the overbreadth test may nevertheless be challenged on its face as unduly vague, in violation of due process. To succeed, however, the complainant must demonstrate that the law is impermissibly vague in all of its applications. Flipside makes no such showing.

The standards for evaluating vagueness were enunciated in *Grayned v. City of Rockford,* 408 U.S. 104, 108, 92 S.Ct. 2294, 2298 (1972):

> "Vague laws offend several important values. First, because we assume that man is free to steer between lawful and unlawful conduct, we insist that laws give the person of ordinary intelligence a reasonable opportunity to know what is pro-

2. A "facial" challenge, in this context, means a claim that the law is "invalid *in toto*—and therefore incapable of any valid application." In evaluating a facial challenge to a state law, a federal court must, of course, consider any limiting construction that a state court or enforcement agency has proffered.

3. In making that determination, a court should evaluate the ambiguous as well as the unambiguous scope of the en-

actment. To this extent, the vagueness of a law affects overbreadth analysis. The Court has long recognized that ambiguous meanings cause citizens to " 'steer far wider of the unlawful zone' . . . than if the boundaries of the forbidden areas were clearly marked." . . .

4. "[V]agueness challenges to statutes which do not involve First Amendment freedoms must be examined in the light of the facts of the case at hand." . . .

hibited so that he may act accordingly. Vague laws may trap the innocent by not providing fair warning. Second, if arbitrary and discriminatory enforcement is to be prevented, laws must provide explicit standards for those who apply them. A vague law impermissibly delegates basic policy matters to policemen, judges, and juries for resolution on an *ad hoc* and subjective basis, with the attendant dangers of arbitrary and discriminatory applications." (footnotes omitted).

These standards should not, of course, be mechanically applied. The degree of vagueness that the Constitution tolerates—as well as the relative importance of fair notice and fair enforcement—depend in part on the nature of the enactment. Thus, economic regulation is subject to a less strict vagueness test because its subject-matter is often more narrow, and because businesses, which face economic demands to plan behavior carefully, can be expected to consult relevant legislation in advance of action. Indeed, the regulated enterprise may have the ability to clarify the meaning of the regulation by its own inquiry, or by resort to an administrative process. The Court has also expressed greater tolerance of enactments with civil rather than criminal penalties because the consequences of imprecision are qualitatively less severe. And the Court has recognized that a scienter requirement may mitigate a law's vagueness, especially with respect to the adequacy of notice to the complainant that his conduct is proscribed.

* * *

B

This ordinance simply regulates business behavior and contains a scienter requirement with respect to the alternative "marketed for use" standard. The ordinance nominally imposes only civil penalties. However, the village concedes that the ordinance is "quasi-criminal," and its prohibitory and stigmatizing effect may warrant a relatively strict test. Flipside's facial challenge fails because, under the test appropriate to either a quasi-criminal or a criminal law, the ordinance is sufficiently clear as applied to Flipside.

The ordinance requires Flipside to obtain a license if it sells "any items, effect, paraphernalia, accessory or thing which is designed or marketed for use with illegal cannabis or drugs, as defined by the Illinois Revised Statutes." . . .

1. *"Designed for Use"*

The Court of Appeals objected that "designed . . . for use" is ambiguous with respect to whether items must be inherently suited only for drug use; whether the retailer's intent or manner of display is relevant; and whether the intent of a third party, the manufacturer, is critical, since the manufacturer is the "designer." For the reasons that follow, we conclude that this language is not unconstitutionally vague on its face.

The Court of Appeals' speculation about the meaning of "design" is largely unfounded. The guidelines refer to "paper of colorful design" and to other specific items as conclusively "designed" or not "designed" for illegal use. A principal meaning of "design" is "To fashion according to a plan." Webster's New International Dictionary of the English Language 707 (2d ed. 1957). It is therefore plain that the standard encompasses at least an item that is principally used with illegal drugs by virtue of its objective features, i.e., features designed by the manufacturer. A business person of ordinary intelligence would understand that this term refers to the design of the manufacturer, not the intent of the retailer or customer. . . .

The ordinance and guidelines do contain ambiguities. Nevertheless, the "designed for use" standard is sufficiently clear to cover at least some of the items that Flipside sold. The ordinance, through the guidelines, explicitly regulates "roach clips." Flipside's co-operator admitted that the store sold such items, and the village Chief of Police testified that he had never seen a "roach clip" used for any purpose other than to smoke cannabis. The chief also testified that a specially-designed pipe that Flipside marketed is typically used to smoke marijuana. Whether further guidelines, administrative rules, or enforcement policy will clarify the more ambiguous scope of the standard in other respects is of no concern in this facial challenge.

2. *"Marketed for Use"*

Whatever ambiguities the "designed . . . for use" standard may engender, the alternative "marketed for use" standard is transparently clear: it describes a retailer's intentional display and marketing of merchandise. The guidelines refer to the display of paraphernalia, and to the proximity of covered items to otherwise uncovered items. A retail store therefore must obtain a license if it deliberately displays its wares in a manner that appeals to or encourages illegal drug use. The standard requires scienter, since a retailer could scarcely "market" items "for" a particular use without intending that use.

Under this test, Flipside had ample warning that its marketing activities required a license. Flipside displayed the magazine "High Times" and books entitled "Marijuana Grower's Guide," "Children's Garden of Grass," and "The Pleasures of Cocaine," physically close to pipes and colored rolling papers, in clear violation of the guidelines. . . .

V

The Court of Appeals also held that the ordinance provides insufficient standards for enforcement. Specifically, the court feared that the ordinance might be used to harass individuals with alternative lifestyles and views. In reviewing a business regulation for facial vagueness, however, the principal inquiry is whether the law affords fair warning of what is proscribed. Moreover, this emphasis is almost inescapable in reviewing a pre-enforcement challenge to a law. Here, no evidence has been, or could be, introduced to indicate whether the ordinance has been enforced in a discriminatory manner or with the aim of inhibiting unpopular speech. The language of the ordinance is sufficiently clear that the speculative danger of arbitrary enforcement does not render the ordinance void for vagueness.

We do not suggest that the risk of discriminatory enforcement is insignificant here. Testimony of the village attorney who drafted the ordinance, the village president, and the police chief revealed confusion over whether the ordinance applies to certain items, as well as extensive reliance on the "judgment" of police officers to give meaning to the ordinance and to enforce it fairly. At this state, however, we are not prepared to hold that this risk jeopardizes the entire ordinance.

Nor do we assume that the village will take no further steps to minimize the dangers of arbitrary enforcement. The village may adopt administrative regulations that will sufficiently narrow potentially vague or arbitrary interpretations of the ordinance. In economic regulation especially, such administrative regulation will often suffice to clarify a standard with an otherwise uncertain scope. We also find it significant that the village, in testimony below, primarily relied on the "marketing" aspect of the standard, which does not require the more ambiguous item-by-item analysis of whether paraphernalia are "designed for" illegal drug use, and which therefore presents a lesser risk of discriminatory enforcement. "Although it is possible that specific future applications . . . may engender concrete problems of constitutional dimension, it will be time enough to consider any such problems when they arise."

VI

Many American communities have recently enacted laws regulating or prohibiting the sale of drug paraphernalia. Whether these laws are wise or effective is not, of course, the province of this Court. We hold only that such legislation is not facially overbroad or vague if it does not reach constitutionally protected conduct and is reasonably clear in its application to the complainant.

Accordingly, the judgment of the Court of Appeals is reversed, and the case is remanded for further proceedings consistent with this opinion.

It is so ordered.

Justice Stevens took no part in the consideration or decision of this case.

APPENDIX

Village of Hoffman Estates Ordinance No. 969–1978

An Ordinance Amending the Municipal Code of the Village of Hoffman Estates by Providing for Regulation of Items

Designed or Marketed for Use With Illegal Cannabis or Drugs

Whereas, certain items designed or marketed for use with illegal drugs are being retailed within the Village of Hoffman Estates, Cook County, Illinois, and

Whereas, it is recognized that such items are legal retail items and that their sale cannot be banned, and

Whereas, there is evidence that these items are designed or marketed for use with illegal cannabis or drugs and it is in the best interests of the health, safety and welfare of the citizens of the Village of Hoffman Estates to regulate within the Village the sale of items designed or marketed for use with illegal cannabis or drugs.

Now Therefore, Be It Ordained by the President and Board of Trustees of the Village of Hoffman Estates, Cook County, Illinois as follows:

Section 1: That the Hoffman Estates Municipal Code be amended by adding thereto an additional section, Section 8–7–16, which additional section shall read as follows:

Sec. 8–7–16—*Items Designed or Marketed for Use With Illegal Cannabis or Drugs*

A. License Required:

It shall be unlawful for any person or persons as principal, clerk, agent or servant to sell any items, effect, paraphernalia, accessory or thing which is designed or marketed for use with illegal cannabis or drugs, as defined by Illinois Revised Statutes, without obtaining a license therefor. Such licenses shall be in addition to any or all other licenses held by applicant.

B. Application:

Application to sell any item, effect, paraphernalia, accessory or thing which is designed or marketed for use with illegal cannabis or drugs shall, in addition to requirements of Article 8–1, be accompanied by affidavits by applicant and each and every employee authorized to sell such items that such person has never been convicted of a drug-related offense.

C. Minors:

It shall be unlawful to sell or give items as described in Section 8–7–16A in any form to any male or female child under eighteen years of age.

D. Records:

Every licensee must keep a record of every item, effect, paraphernalia, accessory or thing which is designed or marketed for
use with illegal cannabis or drugs which is sold and this record
shall be open to the inspection of any police officer at any time
during the hours of business. Such record shall contain the
name and address of the purchaser, the name and quantity of
the product, the date and time of the sale, and the licensee or
agent of the licensee's signature, such records shall be retained
for not less than two (2) years.

E. Regulations:

The applicant shall comply with all applicable regulations of
the Department of Health Services and the Police Department.

Section 2: That the Hoffman Estates Municipal Code be amended by
adding to Sec. 8–2–1 Fees: Merchants (Products) the additional language as follows:

Items designed or marketed for use with illegal cannabis or
drugs $150.00

Section 3: Penalty. Any person violating any provision of this ordinance shall be fined not less than ten dollars ($10.00) nor more than
five hundred dollars ($500.00) for the first offense and succeeding
offenses during the same calendar year and each day that such violation shall continue shall be deemed a separate and distinct offense.

* * *

[The opinion of Mr. Justice White, concurring in the judgment, is
omitted.]

NOTES

1. A Kentucky statute provided that "a person is guilty of disorderly
conduct if, with intent to cause public inconvenience, annoyance or alarm, or
recklessly creating a risk thereof, he . . . congregates with other persons in a
public place and refuses to comply with a lawful order of the police to disperse
. . .". In Colten v. Kentucky, 407 U.S. 104, 92 S.Ct. 1953, 32 L.Ed.2d 584
(1972), a police officer requested the defendant several times to leave a con-
gested roadside where a friend of his in another car was being ticketed for a
traffic offense. Defendant refused, was arrested for disorderly conduct, and
convicted. The majority of the Court held that the statute was not impermissibly vague or broad. It laid down these basic principles:

"The root of the vagueness doctrine is a rough idea of fairness. It
is not a principle designed to convert into a constitutional dilemma the
practical difficulties in drawing criminal statutes both general enough
to take into account a variety of human conduct and sufficiently
specific to provide fair warning that certain kinds of conduct are
prohibited. We agree with the Kentucky court when it said: 'We
believe that citizens who desire to obey the statute will have no
difficulty in understanding it . . .'

2. In Plummer v. Columbus, 414 U.S. 2, 94 S.Ct. 17, 38 L.Ed.2d 3 (1973), the defendant was convicted of violating a city code provision which prohibits any person from abusing another by using menacing, insulting, slanderous or profane language. The Supreme Court held that even though as applied to the defendant, the ordinance might be neither vague, nor overbroad, nor otherwise constitutionally infirm, he nevertheless could raise its vagueness or constitutional overbreadth as applied to others. In holding the ordinance facially unconstitutional in the absence of a satisfactory limiting construction by the state courts, the defendant's conviction was reversed.

In Hynes v. Mayor of Oradell, 425 U.S. 610, 96 S.Ct. 1755, 48 L.Ed.2d 243 (1976), a municipal ordinance required door-to-door canvassers to give advance notice of their intent to do so to the police department. The ordinance was held invalid for vagueness in that it covers "recognized charitable causes" without explaining which causes are so recognized. Other constitutional defects were noted as well.

3. For an Annotation on the validity and construction of statutes and ordinances prohibiting profanity or profane swearing or cursing, see 5 A.L.R.4th 956.

ROSE v. LOCKE

Supreme Court of the United States, 1975.
423 U.S. 48, 96 S.Ct. 243.

PER CURIAM. Respondent was convicted in the Criminal Court for Knox County, Tenn., of having committed a "crime against nature" in violation of Tenn.Code Ann. § 39–707 (1955).[1] The evidence showed that he had entered the apartment of a female neighbor late at night on the pretext of using the telephone. Once inside, he produced a butcher knife, forced his neighbor to partially disrobe, and compelled her to submit to his twice performing cunnilingus upon her. He was sentenced to five to seven years' imprisonment. The Tennessee Court of Criminal Appeals affirmed the conviction, rejecting respondent's claim that the Tennessee statute's proscription of "crimes against nature" did not encompass cunnilingus, as well as his contention that the statute was unconstitutionally vague. The Supreme Court of Tennessee denied review.

Respondent renewed his constitutional claim in a petition for a writ of habeas corpus filed in the District Court for the Eastern District of Tennessee. The District Court denied respondent's petition. . . .

Respondent appealed to the Court of Appeals for the Sixth Circuit, and that court sustained his constitutional challenge. . . .

It is settled that the fair-warning requirement embodied in the Due Process Clause prohibits the States from holding an individual "criminally responsible for conduct which he could not reasonably understand to be proscribed." But this prohibition against excessive vagueness does not invalidate every statute which a reviewing court believes could

---

1. "39–707. Crimes against nature— Penalty.—Crimes against nature, either with mankind or any beast, are punishable by imprisonment in the penitentiary not less than five (5) years nor more than fifteen (15) years."

have been drafted with greater precision. Many statutes will have some inherent vagueness, for "[i]n most English words and phrases there lurk uncertainties." Even trained lawyers may find it necessary to consult legal dictionaries, treatises, and judicial opinions before they may say with any certainty what some statutes may compel or forbid. All the Due Process Clause requires is that the law give sufficient warning that men may conduct themselves so as to avoid that which is forbidden.

Viewed against this standard, the phrase "crimes against nature" is no more vague than many other terms used to describe criminal offenses at common law and now codified in state and federal penal codes. The phrase has been in use among English-speaking people for many centuries, see 4 W. Blackstone, Commentaries 216, and a substantial number of jurisdictions in this country continue to utilize it. Anyone who cared to do so could certainly determine what particular acts have been considered crimes against nature, and there can be no contention that the respondent's acts were ones never before considered as such.

Respondent argued that the vice in the Tennessee statute derives from the fact that jurisdictions differ as to whether "crime against nature" is to be narrowly applied to only those acts constituting the common-law offense of sodomy, or is to be broadly interpreted to encompass additional forms of sexual aberration. We do not understand him to contend that the broad interpretation is itself impermissibly vague; nor do we think he could successfully do so. We have twice before upheld statutes against similar challenges. In State v. Crawford, 478 S.W.2d 314 (1972), the Supreme Court of Missouri rejected a claim that its crime-against-nature statute was so devoid of definition as to be unconstitutional, pointing out that its provision was derived from early English law and broadly embraced sodomy, bestiality, buggery, fellatio, and cunnilingus within its terms. We dismissed the appeal from this judgment as failing to present a substantial federal question. And in [another case] we held that a Florida statute proscribing "the abominable and detestable crime against nature" was not unconstitutionally vague, despite the fact that the State Supreme Court had recently changed its mind about the statute's permissible scope.

The Court of Appeals . . . apparently believed these cases turned upon the fact that the state courts had previously construed their statutes to cover the same acts with which the defendants therein were charged. But although [previous cases] demonstrated that the existence of previous applications of a particular statute to one set of facts forecloses lack-of-fair-warning challenges to subsequent prosecutions of factually identical conduct, it did not hold that such applications were a prerequisite to a statute's withstanding constitutional attack. If that were the case it would be extremely difficult ever to mount an effective prosecution based upon the broader of two reasonable constructions of newly enacted or previously unapplied statutes, even though a neighboring jurisdiction had been applying the broader construction of its identically worded provision for years.

Respondent seems to argue instead that because some jurisdictions have taken a narrow view of "crime against nature" and some a broader interpretation, it could not be determined which approach Tennessee would take, making it therefore impossible for him to know if § 39–707 covered forced cunnilingus. But even assuming the correctness of such an argument if there were no indication which interpretation Tennessee might adopt, it is not available here. Respondent is simply mistaken in his view of Tennessee law. As early as 1955 Tennessee had expressly rejected a claim that "crime against nature" did not cover fellatio, repudiating those jurisdictions which had taken a narrow restrictive definition of the offense. And four years later the Tennessee Supreme Court reiterated its view of the coverage intended by § 39–707. Emphasizing that the Tennessee statute's proscription encompasses the broad meaning, the court quoted from a Maine decision it had earlier cited with approval to the effect that " 'the prohibition brings all unnatural copulation with mankind or a beast, including sodomy, within its scope.' " Sherrill v. State, 204 Tenn. 427, 429, 321 S.W.2d 811, 812 (1959), quoting from State v. Cyr, 135 Me. 513, 198 A. 743 (1938). And the Maine statute, which the Tennessee court had at that point twice equated with its own, had been applied to cunnilingus before either Tennessee decision. Thus, we think the Tennessee Supreme Court had given sufficiently clear notice that § 39–707 would receive the broader of two plausible interpretations, and would be applied to acts such as those committed here when such a case arose.

This also serves to distinguish this case from Bouie v. City of Columbia, 378 U.S. 347, 84 S.Ct. 1697 (1964), a decision the Court of Appeals thought controlling. In *Bouie,* the Court held that an unforeseeable judicial enlargement of a criminal statute narrow and precise on its face violated the Due Process Clause. It pointed out that such a process may lull "the potential defendant into a false sense of security, giving him no reason even to suspect that conduct clearly outside the scope of the statute as written will be retroactively brought within it by an act of judicial construction." But as we have noted, respondent can make no claim that § 39–707 afforded no notice that his conduct might be within its scope. Other jurisdictions had already reasonably construed identical statutory language to apply to such acts. And given the Tennessee court's clear pronouncements that its statute was intended to effect broad coverage, there was nothing to indicate, clearly or otherwise, that respondent's acts were outside the scope of § 39–707. . . . Accordingly, the petition for certiorari and respondent's motion to proceed *in forma pauperis* are granted, and the judgment of the Court of Appeals is reversed.

Judgment of Court of Appeals reversed.

So ordered.

MR. JUSTICE BRENNAN, with whom MR. JUSTICE MARSHALL concurs, dissenting.

I dissent from the Court's summary reversal. The offense of "crimes against nature" at common law was narrowly limited to copulation *per anum*. American jurisdictions, however, expanded the term—some broadly and some narrowly—to include other sexual "aberrations." Of particular significance for this case, as the Court of Appeals accurately stated, "courts have differed widely in construing the reach of 'crimes against nature' to cunnilingus."

The Court holds, however, that because "[o]ther jurisdictions had already reasonably construed identical statutory language to apply to [cunnilingus] . . . given the Tennessee court's clear pronouncements that its statute was intended to effect broad coverage, there was nothing to indicate, clearly or otherwise, that respondent's acts were outside the scope of § 39–707." In other words the traditional test of vagueness—whether the statute gives fair warning that one's conduct is criminal—is supplanted by a test of whether there is anything in the statute "to indicate, clearly or otherwise, that respondent's acts were outside the scope of" the statute. This stands the test of unconstitutional vagueness on its head. And this startling change in vagueness law is accompanied by the equally startling holding that, although the Tennessee courts had not previously construed "crimes against nature" to include cunnilingus, respondent cannot be heard to claim that § 39–707, therefore afforded no notice that his conduct fell within its scope, because he was on notice that Tennessee courts favored a broad reach of "crimes against nature" and other state courts favoring a broad reach had construed their state statutes to include cunnilingus.

Yet these extraordinary distortions of the principle that the Due Process Clause prohibits the States from holding an individual criminally responsible for conduct when the statute did not give fair warning that the conduct was criminal, are perpetrated without plenary review affording the parties an opportunity to brief and argue the issues orally. It is difficult to recall a more patent instance of judicial irresponsibility. For without plenary review the Court announces today, contrary to our prior decisions, that even when the statute he is charged with violating fails of itself to give fair warning, one acts at his peril if the state court has indicated a tendency to construe the pertinent statute broadly, and some other state court of like persuasion has construed its state statute to embrace the conduct made the subject of the charge. I simply cannot comprehend how the fact that one state court has judicially construed its otherwise vague criminal statute to include particular conduct can, without explicit adoption of that state court's construction by the courts of the charging State, render an uninterpreted statute of the latter State also sufficiently concrete to withstand a charge of unconstitutional vagueness. But apart from the merits of the proposition, surely the citizens of this country are entitled to plenary review of its soundness before being required to attempt to conform their conduct to this drastically new standard. Today's holding surely flies in the face of the line of our recent decisions that have struck down statutes as vague and overbroad, although other state courts had previously construed their like statutes to withstand challenges of vagueness and overbreadth. See e.g., the "abusive language" decisions of which Gooding v. Wilson, 405 U.S. 518, 92 S.Ct. 1103 (1972), is illustrative.

Nor will the Court's assertions that the Tennessee courts had in any event in effect construed the Tennessee statute to include cunnilingus withstand analysis. The Court relies on a 1955 Tennessee decision that had held that "crimes against nature" include fellatio, the Tennessee court rejecting the contention that the statute was limited to the common-law copulation-*per-anum* scope of the phrase. The Tennessee court in that opinion cited a Maine case, decided in 1938, State v. Cyr, 135 Me. 513, 198 A. 743, where the Maine court had applied a "crimes against nature" statute to fellatio. But the Tennessee court did not also cite a 1950 Maine decision, State v. Townsend, 145 Me. 384, 71 A.2d 517, that applied Maine's "crimes against nature" statute to cunnilingus. Fisher v. State, 197 Tenn. 594, 277 S.W.2d 340 (1955). Four years later, in 1959, in another fellatio case, the Tennessee court again made no mention of *Townsend*, although quoting from *Cyr's* holding that the Maine statute applies to " 'all unnatural copulation with mankind or a beast, including sodomy.' " Sherrill v. State, 204 Tenn. 427, 429, 321 S.W.2d 811, 812 (1959). Despite this significant failure of the Tennessee court to cite *Townsend*, and solely on the strength of the Tennessee court's general "equating" of the Maine statute with the Tennessee statute, this Court holds today that respondent had sufficient notice that the Tennessee statute would receive a "broad" interpretation that would embrace cunnilingus.

This 1974 attempt to bootstrap 1950 Maine law for the first time into the Tennessee statute must obviously fail if the principle of fair warning is to have any meaning. When the Maine court in 1938 applied its statute broadly to all "unnatural copulation," nothing said by the Maine court suggested that that phrase reached cunnilingus. The common-law "crime against nature," limited to copulation *per anum,* required penetration as an essential element. In holding that a "broad" reading of that phrase should encompass all unnatural copulation including fellatio—copulation *per os*—Maine could not reasonably be understood as including cunnilingus in that category. Other jurisdictions, though on their State's particular statutory language, have drawn that distinction. Thus, when the Tennessee court in 1955 adopted the language of Maine's 1938 *Cyr* case, a Tennessee citizen had at most notice of developments in Maine law through 1938. That Maine subsequently in 1950 applied its statute to cunnilingus is irrelevant, for such subsequent developments were not "adopted" by the Tennessee court until the case before us. Indeed, the Tennessee court's failure in its 1955 *Fisher* opinion to cite *Townsend*, Maine's 1950 cunnilingus decision, although citing *Cyr*, Maine's 1938 fellatio decision, more arguably was notice that the Tennessee courts considered fellatio but not cunnilingus as within the nebulous reach of the Tennessee statute.

Moreover, I seriously question the Court's assumption that the "broad interpretation" of the phrase "crime against nature" is not unconstitutionally vague. The Court's assumption rests upon two supposed precedents: (1) this Court's dismissal for want of a substantial federal question of the appeal in Crawford v. Missouri, 409 U.S. 811, 93 S.Ct. 176 (1972), and (2) the Court's *per curiam* opinion in Wainwright v. Stone (1973). That reliance is plainly misplaced.

In *Crawford,* the appellant had been convicted of coercing a mentally retarded individual to perform fellatio on appellant. The Supreme Court of Missouri did not, as the Court implies, for the first time in that case adopt a "broad" construction of its statute and apply that construction in appellant's case. Rather, the Supreme Court of Missouri first noted that the original statute, probably reaching only the common-law "crime against nature," had been legislatively amended in express terms to expand the offense to conduct committed "with the sexual organs or with the mouth," thereby "enlarg[ing] the common law definition of the crime. . . ." Moreover, the court, observing that a "court's construction of statutory language becomes a part of the statute 'as if it had been so amended by the legislature,'" ibid. (citations omitted), stated that in the 60 years since that amendment, the Missouri courts had "adjudicated" that the statute embraced "bestiality, buggery, fellatio . . . and cunnilingus," and that "[a]t least five [Missouri] cases have specifically held that the act charged [against appellant] is within the statute." In light of that prior judicial and legislative construction of the statutory phrase, and its specific prior application to acts identical to the appellant's, the dismissal in *Crawford* simply cannot be treated as holding that the phrase "crime against nature" is not in itself vague.

Wainwright v. Stone, as Mr. Justice Stewart correctly observes, also involved a statute already construed to cover the conduct there in question. . . . The reversal of the Court of Appeals' holding finding the statute unconstitutional was explicitly based on the fact that the state statute had previously been applied to identical conduct, which decisions "require[d] reversal" in *Wainwright* since they put the particular conduct expressly within the statute.

No specter of increasing caseload can possibly justify today's summary disposition of this case. The principle that due process requires that criminal statutes give sufficient warning to enable men to conform their conduct to avoid that which is forbidden is one of the great bulwarks of our scheme of constitutional liberty. The Court's erosion today of that great principle without even plenary review reaches a dangerous level of judicial irresponsibility. I would have denied the petition for certiorari, but now that the writ has been granted would affirm the judgment of the Court of Appeals or at least set the case for oral argument.

MR. JUSTICE STEWART, with whom MR. JUSTICE MARSHALL concurs, dissenting.

I would have denied the petition for certiorari in this case, but, now that the writ has been granted, I would affirm the judgment of the Court of Appeals.

This case is not of a piece with Wainwright v. Stone upon which the Court so heavily relies. There the Florida courts had repeatedly and explicitly ruled that the state law in question prohibited precisely the conduct in which the defendants were found to have engaged. Here, by contrast, the Tennessee courts had never ruled that the act that Locke was found to have committed was covered by the vague and cryptic language of the Tennessee statute, Tenn.Code Ann. § 39–707. The Court today emphasizes that a previous Tennessee court opinion had cited a decision of a Maine court construing a similar statute "broadly," but even the cited Maine decision had not construed the statute to cover the conduct in question here. And a later Tennessee decision would have supported the inference that this conduct was *not* proscribed by the Tennessee statute. Stephens v. State, 489 S.W.2d 542 (1972).

In the *Stone* case, supra, the Florida statute had "been construed to forbid identifiable conduct so that 'interpretation by [the state court] puts these words in the statute as definitely as if it had been so amended by the legislature. . . .'" 414 U.S., at 23, 94 S.Ct., at 192. In the present case, by contrast, the state courts had never held that the statutory language here at issue covered the respondent's conduct.

As the Court of Appeals pointed out, the respondent in this case could, and probably should, be prosecuted for aggravated assault and battery. But I think the Court of Appeals was correct in holding that the Tennessee statute under which the defendant was in fact prosecuted was unconstitutionally vague as here applied.

———

Considerable case law exist on inhibitions that the First Amendment places upon the power of the states to create and define criminal conduct. There also are important other United States Supreme Court cases in this area of the law that trace how the right to freedom of speech and the press impacts on crime creation in the areas of obscenity, the exercise of religious practices, the freedom of association, and the like. A study of these cases is typically undertaken in courses of constitutional law or specialized courses and seminars dealing with the Bill of Rights, or even just the First Amendment alone. For that reason, no treatment of that broad subject is attempted in this casebook. The following case is but one example of the frequent interplay in First Amendment cases between what is constitutionally protected speech, and the difficulties encountered in defining such speech or conduct without running afoul of the constitutional prohibition against vague and overbroad statutes.

———

GOODING, WARDEN v. WILSON

Supreme Court of the United States, 1972.
405 U.S. 518, 92 S.Ct. 1103, 31 L.Ed.2d 408.

MR. JUSTICE BRENNAN delivered the opinion of the Court.

Appellee was convicted in Superior Court, Fulton County, Georgia, on two counts of using opprobrious words and abusive language in violation of Georgia Code § 26–6303, which provides: "Any person who shall, without provocation, use to or of another, and in his presence . . . opprobrious words or abusive language, tending to cause a breach of the peace . . . shall be guilty of a misdemeanor."

* * *

Section 26–6303 punishes only spoken words. It can therefore withstand appellee's attack upon its facial constitutionality only if, as authoritatively construed by the Georgia courts, it is not susceptible of application to speech, although vulgar or offensive, that is protected by the First and Fourteenth Amendments, . . . Only the Georgia courts can supply the requisite construction, since of course "we lack jurisdiction authoritatively to construe state legislation." . . . It matters not that the words appellee used might have been constitutionally prohibited under a narrowly and precisely drawn statute. At least when statutes regulate or proscribe speech and when "no readily apparent construction suggests itself as a vehicle for rehabilitating the statutes in a single prosecution," . . . the transcendent value to all society of constitutionally protected expression is deemed to justify allowing "attacks on overly broad statutes with no requirement that the person making the attack demonstrate that his own conduct could not be regulated by a statute drawn with the requisite narrow specificity," . . . this is deemed necessary because persons whose expression is constitutionally protected may well refrain from exercising their rights for fear of criminal sanctions provided by a statute susceptible of application to protected expression.

* * *

The constitutional guarantees of freedom of speech forbid the States from punishing the use of words or language not within "narrowly limited classes of speech." Chaplinsky v. New Hampshire, . . . Even as to such a class, however, because "the line between speech unconditionally guaranteed and speech which may legitimately be regulated, suppressed, or punished is finely drawn," . . . "[i]n every case the power to regulate must be so exercised as not, in attaining a permissible end, unduly to infringe the protected freedom,". . . . In other words, the statute must be carefully drawn or be authoritatively construed to punish only unprotected speech and not be susceptible of application to protected expression. "Because First Amendment freedoms need breathing space to survive, government may regulate in the area only with narrow specificity." . . .

Appellant does not challenge these principles but contends that the Georgia statute is narrowly drawn to apply only to a constitutionally unprotected class of words—"fighting" words—"those which by their very utterance inflict injury or tend to incite an immediate breach of the peace." . . . In *Chaplinsky,* we sustained a conviction under Chapter 378, § 2, of the Public Laws of New Hampshire, which provided: "No person shall address any offensive, derisive or annoying word to any other person who is lawfully in any street or other public place, nor call him by any offensive or derisive name. . . ." Chaplinsky was convicted for addressing to another on a public sidewalk the words, "You are a God damned racketeer," and "a damned Fascist and the whole government of Rochester are Fascists or agents of Fascists." Chaplinsky challenged the constitutionality of the statute as inhibiting freedom of expression because it was vague and indefinite. The Supreme Court of New Hampshire, however, "long before the words for which Chaplinsky was convicted," sharply limited the statutory language "offensive, derisive or annoying word" to "fighting" words . . .

* * *

Appellant argues that the Georgia appellate courts have by construction limited the proscription of § 26–6303 to "fighting" words, as the New Hampshire Supreme Court limited the New Hampshire statute. . . . We have however, made our own examination of the Georgia cases, both those cited and others discovered in research. That examination brings us to the conclusion, in agreement with the courts below, that the Georgia appellate decisions have not construed § 26–6303 to be limited in application, as in *Chaplinsky,* to words that "have a direct tendency to cause acts of violence by the person to whom, individually, the remark is addressed."

The dictionary definitions of "opprobrious" and "abusive" give them greater reach than "fighting" words. . . .

* * *

Mr. Justice Powell and Mr. Justice Rehnquist, took no part in the consideration or decision of this case.

Mr. Chief Justice Burger, dissenting.

I fully join in Mr. Justice Blackmun's dissent against the bizarre result reached by the Court. It is not merely odd, it is nothing less than remarkable that a court can find a state statute void on its face, not because of its language—which is the traditional test—but because of the way courts of that State have applied the statute in a few isolated cases, decided as long ago as 1905 and generally long before this Court's decision in Chaplinsky v. New Hampshire, . . . Even if all of those cases had been decided yesterday, they do nothing to demonstrate that the narrow language of the Georgia statute has any significant potential for sweeping application to suppress or deter important protected speech.

In part the Court's decision appears to stem from its assumption that a statute should be regarded in the same light as its most vague clause, without regard to any of its other language. . . . The statute at bar, however, does not prohibit language "tending to cause a breach of the peace." Nor does it prohibit the use of "opprobrious words or abusive language" without more. Rather, it prohibits use "to or of another, and in his presence opprobrious words or abusive language, tending to cause a breach of the peace." If words are to bear their common meaning, and are to be considered in context, rather than dissected with surgical precision using a semantical scalpel, this statute has little potential for application outside the realm of "fighting words" which this Court held beyond the protection of the First Amendment in *Chaplinsky.* Indeed, the language used by the *Chaplinsky* Court to describe words properly subject to regulation bears a striking resemblance to that of the Georgia statute, which was enacted many, many years before *Chaplinsky* was decided. And, if the early Georgia cases cited by the majority establish any proposition, it is that the statute, as its language so clearly indicates, is aimed at preventing precisely that type of personal, face-to-face abusive and insulting language likely to provoke a violent retaliation—self help, as we euphemistically call it— which the *Chaplinsky* case recognized could be validly prohibited. The facts of the case now before the Court demonstrate that the Georgia statute is serving that valid and entirely proper purpose. There is no persuasive reason to wipe the statute from the books, unless we want to encourage victims of such verbal assaults to seek their own private redress.

* * *

MR. JUSTICE BLACKMUN, with whom THE CHIEF JUSTICE joins, dissenting.

It seems strange indeed that in this day a man may say to a police officer, who is attempting to restore access to a public building, "White son of a bitch, I'll kill you" and "You son of a bitch, I'll choke you to death," and say to an accompanying officer, "You son of a bitch, if you ever put your hands on me again, I'll cut you all to pieces," and yet constitutionally cannot be prosecuted and convicted under a state statute which makes it a misdemeanor to "use to or of another, and in his presence, opprobrious words or abusive language, tending to cause a breach of the peace. . . ." This, however, is precisely what the Court pronounces as the law today.

The Supreme Court of Georgia, when the conviction was appealed, unanimously held the other way. . . . Surely any adult who can read—and I do not exclude this appellee-defendant from that category—should reasonably expect no other conclusion. The words of Georgia Code § 26–6303 are clear. They are also concise. They are not, in my view, overbroad or incapable of being understood. Except perhaps for the "big" word "opprobrious"—and no point is made of its bigness— any Georgia schoolboy would expect that his defendant's fighting and provocative words to the officers were covered by § 26–6303. Common sense permits no other conclusion. This is demonstrated by the fact that the appellee, and this Court, attacks the statute not as it applies to the appellee, but as it conceivably might apply to others who might utter other words.

The Court reaches its result by saying that the Georgia statute has been interpreted by the State's courts so as to be applicable in practice to otherwise constitutionally protected speech. It follows, says the Court, that the statute is overbroad and therefore is facially unconstitutional and to be struck down in its entirety. Thus Georgia apparently is to be left with no valid statute on its books to meet Wilson's bullying tactic. This result, achieved by what is indeed a very strict construction, will be totally incomprehensible to the State of Georgia, to its courts, and to its citizens.

The Court would justify its conclusion by unearthing a 66–year–old decision, . . ., of the Supreme Court of Georgia, and two intermediate appellate court cases over 55 years old, . . . broadly applying the statute in those less permissive days, and by additional reference to (a) a 1956 Georgia intermediate appellate court decision, . . . which, were it the first and only Georgia case, would surely not support today's decision, and (b) another intermediate appellate court decision . . . (1961), relating not to § 26–6303, but to another statute.

This Court appears to have developed its overbreadth rationale in the years since these early Georgia cases. The State's statute, therefore, is condemned because the State's courts have not had an opportunity to adjust to this Court's modern theories of overbreadth.

I wonder, now that § 26–6303 is voided, just what Georgia can do if it seeks to proscribe what the Court says it still may constitutionally proscribe. The natural thing would be to enact a new statute reading just as § 26–6303 reads. But it, too, presumably would be overbroad unless the legislature would add words to the effect that it means only what this Court says it may mean and no more.

* * *

For me, Chaplinsky v. New Hampshire . . . was good law when it was decided and deserves to remain as good law now. A unanimous Court, including among its members Chief Justice Stone and Justices Black, Reed, Douglas and Murphy, obviously thought it was good law. But I feel that by decisions such as this one . . ., despite its protestations to the contrary, is merely paying lip service to *Chaplinsky*. As the appellee states in a footnote to his brief, p. 14, "Although there is no doubt that the state can punish 'fighting words' this appears to be about all that is left of the decision in *Chaplinsky*." If this is what the overbreadth doctrine means, and if this is what it produces, it urgently needs reexamination. The Court has painted itself into a corner from which it, and the States, can extricate themselves only with difficulty.

C. THE RIGHT TO PRIVACY AND TO EQUAL PROTECTION

GRISWOLD v. CONNECTICUT

Supreme Court of the United States, 1965.
381 U.S. 479, 85 S.Ct. 1678, 14 L.Ed.2d 510.

MR. JUSTICE DOUGLAS delivered the opinion of the Court.

Appellant Griswold is Executive Director of the Planned Parenthood League of Connecticut. Appellant Buxton is a licensed physician and a professor at the Yale Medical School who served as Medical Director for the League at its Center in New Haven—a center open and operating from November 1 to November 10, 1961, when appellants were arrested.

They gave information, instruction, and medical advice to *married persons* as to the means of preventing conception. They examined the wife and prescribed the best contraceptive device or material for her use. Fees were usually charged, although some couples were serviced free.

The statutes whose constitutionality is involved in this appeal are §§ 53–32 and 54–196 of the General Statutes of Connecticut (1958 rev.). The former provides:

"Any person who uses any drug, medicinal article or instrument for the purpose of preventing conception shall be fined not less than fifty dollars or imprisoned not less than sixty days nor more than one year or be both fined and imprisoned."

Section 54–196 provides:

"Any person who assists, abets, counsels, causes, hires or commands another to commit any offense may be prosecuted and punished as if he were the principal offender."

The appellants were found guilty as accessories and fined $100 each, against the claim that the accessory statute as so applied violated the Fourteenth Amendment. . . .

* * *

Coming to the merits, we are met with a wide range of questions that implicate the Due Process Clause of the Fourteenth Amendment. . . . We do not sit as a super-legislature to determine the wisdom, need, and propriety of laws that touch economic problems, business affairs, or social conditions. This law, however, operates directly on an intimate relation of husband and wife and their physician's role in one aspect of that relation.

The association of people is not mentioned in the Constitution nor in the Bill of Rights. The right to educate a child in a school of the parents' choice—whether public or private or parochial—is also not mentioned. Nor is the right to study any particular subject or any foreign language. Yet the First Amendment has been construed to include certain of those rights.

. . . Without those peripheral rights the specific rights would be less secure. . . .

* * *

[The] specific guarantees in the Bill of Rights have penumbras, formed by emanations from those guarantees that help give them life and substance. . . . Various guarantees create zones of privacy. The right of association contained in the penumbra of the First Amendment is one, . . . The Third Amendment in its prohibition against the quartering of soldiers "in any house" in time of peace without the consent of the owner is another facet of that privacy. The Fourth Amendment explicitly affirms the "right of the people to be secure in their persons, houses, papers, and effects, against unreasonable searches and seizures." The Fifth Amendment in its Self–Incrimination Clause enables the citizen to create a zone of privacy which government may not force him to surrender to his detriment. The Ninth Amendment provides: "The enumeration in the Constitution, of certain rights, shall not be construed to deny or disparage others retained by the people."

. . .

The present case, then, concerns a relationship lying within the zone of privacy created by several fundamental constitutional guarantees. And it concerns a law which, in forbidding the *use* of contraceptives rather than regulating their manufacture or sale, seeks to achieve its goals by means having a maximum destructive impact upon that relationship. Such a law cannot stand in light of the familiar principle, so often applied by this Court, that a "governmental purpose to control or prevent activities constitutionally subject to state regulation may not be achieved by means which sweep unnecessarily broadly and thereby invade the area of protected freedoms."

. . . Would we allow the police to search the sacred precincts of marital bedrooms for telltale signs of the use of contraceptives? The very idea is repulsive to the notions of privacy surrounding the marriage relationship.

We deal with a right of privacy older than the Bill of Rights—older than our political parties, older than our school system. Marriage is a coming together for better or for worse, hopefully enduring, and intimate to the degree of being sacred. It is an association that promotes a way of life, not causes; a harmony in living, not political faiths; a bilateral loyalty, not commercial or social projects. Yet it is an association for as noble a purpose as any involved in our prior decisions.

Reversed.

MR. JUSTICE GOLDBERG, whom, THE CHIEF JUSTICE and MR. JUSTICE BRENNAN join, concurring.

I agree with the Court that Connecticut's birth-control law unconstitutionally intrudes upon the right of marital privacy, and I join in its opinion and judgment. Although I have not accepted the view that "due process" as used in the Fourteenth Amendment includes all of the first eight Amendments . . ., I do agree that the concept of liberty protects those personal rights that are fundamental, and is not confined to the specific terms of the Bill of Rights. My conclusion that the concept of liberty is not so restricted and that it embraces the right of marital privacy though that right is not mentioned explicitly in the Constitution is supported both by numerous decisions of this Court, . . . and by the language and history of the Ninth Amendment. In reaching the conclusion that the right of marital privacy is protected, as being within the protected penumbra of specific guarantees of the Bill of Rights, the Court refers to the Ninth Amendment. I add these words to emphasize the relevance of that Amendment to the Court's holding.

* * *

. . . The language and history of the Ninth Amendment reveal that the Framers of the Constitution believed that there are additional fundamental rights, protected from governmental infringement, which exist alongside those fundamental rights specifically mentioned in the first eight constitutional amendments.

The Ninth Amendment reads, "The enumeration in the Constitution, of certain rights, shall not be construed to deny or disparage others retained by the people." The Amendment is almost entirely the work of James Madison. It was introduced in Congress by him and passed the House and Senate with little or no debate and virtually no change in language. It was proffered to quiet expressed fears that a bill of specifically enumerated rights could not be sufficiently broad to cover all essential rights and that the specific mention of certain rights would be interpreted as a denial that others were protected.[1]

* * *

1. Alexander Hamilton was opposed to a bill of rights on the ground that it was unnecessary because the Federal Government was a government of delegated powers and it was not granted the power to intrude upon fundamental personal rights. The Federalist, No. 84 (Cooke ed. 1961), at 578–579.

He also argued,

"I go further, and affirm that bills of rights, in the sense and in the extent in which they are contended for, are not only unnecessary in the proposed constitution, but would even be dangerous. They would contain various exceptions to powers which are not granted; and on this very account, would afford a colourable pretext to claim more than were granted. For why declare that things shall not be done which there is no power to do? Why for instance, should it be said, that the liberty of the press shall not be restrained, when no power is given by which restrictions may be imposed? I will not contend that such a provision would confer a regulating power; but it is evident that it would furnish, to men disposed to usurp, a plausible pretence for claiming that power." The Ninth Amendment and the Tenth Amendment, which provides, "The powers not delegated to the United States by the Constitution, nor prohibited by it to the States, are reserved to the States respectively, or to the people," were apparently also designed in part to meet the above-quoted argument of Hamilton.

In presenting the proposed Amendment, Madison said:

"It has been objected also against a bill of rights, that, by enumerating particular exceptions to the grant of power, it would disparage those rights which were not placed in that enumeration; and it might follow by implication, that those rights which were not singled out, were intended to be assigned into the hands of the General Government, and were consequently insecure. This is one of the most plausible arguments I have ever heard urged against the admission of a bill of rights into this system; but, I conceive, that it may be guarded against. I have attempted it, as gentlemen may see by turning to the last clause of the fourth resolution [the Ninth Amendment]." I Annals of Congress 439 (Gales and Seaton ed. 1834).

Mr. Justice Story wrote of this argument against a bill of rights and the meaning of the Ninth Amendment:

"In regard to ∗ ∗ ∗ [a] suggestion, that the affirmance of certain rights might disparage others, or might lead to argumentative implications in favor of other powers, it might be sufficient to say that such a course of reasoning could never be sustained upon any solid basis ∗ ∗ ∗. But a conclusive answer is, that such an attempt may be interdicted (as it has been) by a positive declaration in such a bill of rights that the enumeration of certain rights shall not be construed to deny or disparage others retained by the people." II Story, Commentaries on the Constitution of the United States 626–627 (5th ed. 1891).

He further stated, referring to the Ninth Amendment:

"This clause was manifestly introduced to prevent any perverse or ingenious misapplication of the well-known maxim, that an affirmation in particular cases implies a negation in all others; and, *e converso,* that a negation in particular cases implies an affirmation in all others." Id., at 651.

These statements of Madison and Story make clear that the Framers did not intend that the first eight amendments be construed to exhaust the basic and fundamental rights which the Constitution guaranteed to the people.

While this Court has had little occasion to interpret the Ninth Amendment, . . . "[i]t cannot be presumed that any clause in the constitution is intended to be without effect." . . . In interpreting the Constitution, "real effect should be given to all the words it uses." . . . The Ninth Amendment to the Constitution may be regarded by some as a recent discovery but since 1791 it has been a basic part of the Constitution which we are sworn to uphold. To hold that a right so basic and fundamental and so deep-rooted in our society as the right of privacy in marriage may be infringed because that right is not guaranteed in so many words by the first eight amendments to the Constitution is to ignore the Ninth Amendment and to give it no effect whatsoever. Moreover, a judicial construction that this fundamental right is not protected by the Constitution because it is not mentioned in explicit terms by one of the first eight amendments or elsewhere in the Constitution would violate the Ninth Amendment, which specifically states that "[t]he enumeration in the Constitution, of certain rights shall not be *construed* to deny or disparage others retained by the people." (Emphasis added.)

A dissenting opinion suggests that my interpretation of the Ninth Amendment somehow "broaden[s] the powers of this Court." . . . With all due respect, I believe that it misses the import of what I am saying. . . . [The] Ninth Amendment shows a belief of the Constitution's authors that fundamental rights exist that are not expressly enumerated in the first eight amendments and an intent that the list of rights included there not be deemed exhaustive. As any student of this Court's opinions knows, this Court has held, often unanimously, that the Fifth and Fourteenth Amendments protect certain fundamental personal liberties from abridgment by the Federal Government or the States. . . . The Ninth Amendment simply shows the intent of the Constitution's authors that other fundamental personal rights should not be denied such protection or disparaged in any other way simply because they are not specifically listed in the first eight constitutional amendments. I do not see how this broadens the authority of the Court; rather it serves to support what this Court has been doing in protecting fundamental rights.

Nor am I turning somersaults with history in arguing that the Ninth Amendment is relevant in a case dealing with a *State's* infringement of a fundamental right. While the Ninth Amendment—and indeed the entire Bill of Rights—originally concerned restrictions upon *federal* power, the subsequently enacted Fourteenth Amendment prohibits the States as well from abridging fundamental personal liberties. And, the Ninth Amendment, in indicating that not all such liberties are specifically mentioned in the first eight amendments, is surely relevant in showing the existence of other fundamental personal rights, now protected from state, as well as federal, infringement. In sum, the Ninth Amendment simply lends strong support to the view that the "liberty" protected by the Fifth and Fourteenth Amendments from infringement by the Federal Government or the States is not restricted to rights specifically mentioned in the first eight amendments. * * *

The entire fabric of the Constitution and the purposes that clearly underlie its specific guarantees demonstrate that the rights to marital privacy and to marry and raise a family are of similar order and magnitude as the fundamental rights specifically protected.

Although the Constitution, does not speak in so many words of the right of privacy in marriage, I cannot believe that it offers these fundamental rights no protection. The fact that no particular provision of the Constitution explicitly forbids the State from disrupting the traditional relation of the family—a relation as old and as fundamental as our entire civilization—surely does not show that the Government was meant to have the power to do so. Rather, as the Ninth Amendment expressly recognizes, there are fundamental personal rights such as this one, which are protected from abridgment by the Government though not specifically mentioned in the Constitution. * * *

Although the Connecticut birth-control law obviously encroaches upon a fundamental personal liberty, the State does not show that the law serves any "subordinating [state] interest which is compelling" or that it is "necessary . . . to the accomplishment of a permissible state policy." The State, at most, argues that there is some rational relation between this statute and what is admittedly a legitimate subject of state concern—the discouraging of extra-marital relations. It says that preventing the use of birth-control devices by married persons helps prevent the indulgence by some in such extra-marital relations. The rationality of this justification is dubious, particularly in light of the admitted widespread availability to all persons in the State of Connecticut, unmarried as well as married, of birth-control devices for the prevention of disease, as distinguished from the prevention of conception, . . . But, in any event, it is clear that the state interest in safeguarding marital fidelity can be served by a more discriminately tailored statute, which does not, like the present one, sweep unnecessarily broadly, reaching far beyond the evil sought to be dealt with and intruding upon the privacy of all married couples. . . . The State of Connecticut does have statutes, the constitutionality of which is beyond doubt, which prohibit adultery and fornication. . . . These statutes demonstrate that means for achieving the same basic purpose of protecting marital fidelity are available to Connecticut without the need to "invade the area of protected freedoms." . . .

In sum, I believe that the right of privacy in the marital relation is fundamental and basic—a personal right "retained by the people" within the meaning of the Ninth Amendment. Connecticut cannot constitutionally abridge this fundamental right, which is protected by the Fourteenth Amendment from infringement by the States. I agree with the Court that petitioners' convictions must therefore be reversed.

* * *

[Justice Harlan's concurring opinion is omitted. He expressed the view that the decision should rest upon the due process clause of the Fourteenth Amendment because he considered the statute violative of the basic values "implicit in the concept of ordered liberty".]

[Justice White's concurring opinion is also omitted. He, too, thought that the basis for the decision should be in violation of due process.]

[Justice Black's dissenting opinion, in which Justice Stewart concurred, is omitted too.]

* * *

MR. JUSTICE STEWART, whom MR. JUSTICE BLACK joins, dissenting.

Since 1879 Connecticut has had on its books a law which forbids the use of contraceptives by anyone. I think this is an uncommonly silly law. As a practical matter, the law is obviously unenforceable, except in the oblique context of the present case. As a philosophical matter, I believe the use of contraceptives in the relationship of marriage should be left to personal and private choice, based upon each individual's moral, ethical, and religious beliefs. As a matter of social policy, I think professional counsel about methods of birth control should be available to all, so that each individual's choice can be meaningfully made. But we are not asked in this case to say whether we think this law is unwise, or even asinine. We are asked to hold that it violates the United States Constitution. And that I cannot do.

In the course of its opinion the Court refers to no less than six Amendments to the Constitution: the First, the Third, the Fourth, the Fifth, the Ninth, and the Fourteenth. But the Court does not say which of these Amendments, if any, it thinks is infringed by this Connecticut law.

We *are* told that the Due Process Clause of the Fourteenth Amendment is not, as such, the "guide" in this case. With that much I agree. There is no claim that this law, duly enacted by the Connecticut Legislature, is unconstitutionally vague. There is no claim that the appellants were denied any of the elements of procedural due process at their trial, so as to make their convictions constitutionally invalid. And, as the Court says, the day has long passed since the Due Process Clause was regarded as a proper instrument for determining "the wisdom, need, and propriety" of state laws . . .

As to the First, Third, Fourth, and Fifth Amendments, I can find nothing in any of them to invalidate this Connecticut law, even assuming that all those Amendments are fully applicable against the States. It has not even been argued that this is a law "respecting an establishment of religion, or prohibiting the free exercise thereof." And surely, unless the solemn process of constitutional adjudication is to descend to the level of a play on words, there is not involved here any abridgment of "the freedom of speech, or of the press; or the right of the people peaceably to assemble, and to petition the Government for a redress of grievances." No soldier has been quartered in any house. There has been no search, and no seizure. Nobody has been compelled to be a witness against himself.

The Court, also quotes the Ninth Amendment, and my Brother Goldberg's concurring opinion relies heavily upon it. But to say that the Ninth Amendment has anything to do with this case is to turn somersaults with history. The Ninth Amendment, like its companion, the Tenth, which this Court held "states but a truism that all is retained which has not been surrendered" . . . was framed by James Madison and adopted by the States simply to make clear that the adoption of the Bill of Rights did not alter the plan that the *Federal* Government was to be a government of express and limited powers, and that all rights and powers not delegated to it were retained by the people and the individual States. Until today no member of this Court has ever suggested that the Ninth Amendment meant anything else, and the idea that a federal court could ever use the Ninth Amendment to annul a law passed by the elected representatives of the people of the State of Connecticut would have caused James Madison no little wonder.

What provision of the Constitution, then, does make this state law invalid? The Court says it is the right of privacy "created by several fundamental constitutional guarantees." With all deference, I can find no such general right of privacy in the Bill of Rights, in any other part of the Constitution, or in any case ever before decided by this Court.

At the oral argument in this case we were told that the Connecticut law does not "conform to current community standards." But it is not the function of this Court to decide cases on the basis of community standards. We are here to decide cases "agreeably to the Constitution and laws of the United States." It is the essence of judicial duty to subordinate our own personal views, our own ideas of what legislation is wise and what is not. If, as I should surely hope, the law before us does not reflect the standards of the people of Connecticut, the people of Connecticut can freely exercise their true Ninth and Tenth Amendment rights to persuade their elected representatives to repeal it. That is the constitutional way to take this law off the books.

NOTES

1. In City of Chicago v. Wilson, 75 Ill.2d 525, 27 Ill.Dec. 458, 389 N.E.2d 522 (1978), defendant was arrested for violating a section of the Chicago Municipal Code which prohibits a person from wearing clothing of the opposite sex with the intent to conceal his or her sex. He was a transsexual preparing for a sex-reassignment operation and preoperative therapy required that he cross-dress. The Illinois Supreme Court reversed the conviction, holding that the ordinance was unconstitutional as applied to the defendant. The court recognized that there exist unspecified constitutionally protected freedoms which include the freedom to choose one's appearance. The ability of the state to regulate one's appearance uncontrolled by constitutional restraints "is fundamentally inconsistent with values of privacy, self-identity, autonomy and personal integrity that . . . the constitution was designed to protect." Although the state may infringe upon a person's right of privacy, the court asserted that the state's justification for intrusion must be stronger in the context of regulation which "controls the dress of the citizens at large," as opposed to regulation "in the context of an organized government activity." When these principles are applied to the defendant, the court found little justification against cross-dressing. We cannot "assume that individuals who cross-dress . . . as a means of . . . therapy are prone to commit crimes," the court said. It also found no evidence that this preoperative therapy violates public morals.

What would the result be if the defendant were a transvestite rather than a transsexual? Are a transvestite's constitutional rights to cross-dress less worthy of protection than a transsexual's?

2. A person lives in a home with her son and two grandsons in a neighborhood zoned for single family dwellings. A housing ordinance defines "family" in such a way that the grandsons do not qualify. If the person refuses to remove her grandsons from the home, can she be convicted of violating the ordinance over her claim that her constitutional right of privacy is infringed? The Supreme Court said "no" in Moore v. City of East Cleveland, Ohio, 431 U.S. 494, 97 S.Ct. 1932, 52 L.Ed.2d 531 (1977). The majority opinion held the ordinance unconstitutional because it had, at best, only a tenuous relationship to the objectives cited by the city: avoiding overcrowding, traffic congestion, and an undue financial burden on the school system. Considering the strong constitutional protection of the sanctity of the family which it had established in numerous previous decisions, the Court's plurality opinion felt this also included the family choice involved in this case. "Family," the Court said, is not confined within an arbitrary boundary drawn at the limits of the nuclear family.

3. A state statute makes it mandatory for physicians who prescribe, and pharmacists who dispense, certain controlled legitimate dangerous drugs to use an official form, a copy of which has to be filed with the State Health Department, where pertinent data, including names of the doctors, pharmacists, and patients, are recorded on tapes for computer processing. In such situations, is the "doctor-patient relationship" one of the zones of privacy accorded constitutional protection? Is the statute an unconstitutional impairment of the physicians' right to practice medicine free from unwarranted state interference? Answering both questions in the negative, a unanimous Supreme Court, in Whalen v. Roe, 429 U.S. 589, 97 S.Ct. 869, 51 L.Ed.2d 64 (1977), reversed a District Court decision that had held the statute unconstitutional. At the conclusion of the opinion, the Court stated:

> . . . We are not unaware of the threat to privacy implicit in the accumulation of vast amounts of personal information in computerized data banks or other massive government files. The collection of taxes, the distribution of welfare and social security benefits, the supervision of public health, the direction of our Armed Forces, and the enforcement of the criminal laws all require the orderly preservation of great quantities of information, much of which is personal in character and potentially embarrassing or harmful if disclosed. The right to collect and use such data for public purposes is typically accompanied by a concomitant statutory or regulatory duty to avoid unwarranted disclosures. Recognizing that in some circumstances that duty arguably has its roots in the Constitution, nevertheless New York's statutory scheme, and its implementing administrative procedures, evidence a proper concern with, and protection of, the individual's interest in privacy. We therefore need not, and do not, decide any question which might be presented by the unwarranted disclosure of accumulated private data—whether intentional or unintentional—or by a system that did not contain comparable security provisions. We simply hold that this record does not establish an invasion of any right or liberty protected by the Fourteenth Amendment.

4. In Stanley v. Georgia, 394 U.S. 557, 89 S.Ct. 1243, 22 L.Ed.2d 542 (1969), the Court held that the mere private possession of obscene matter cannot constitutionally be made a crime. Although obscene matter is not protected by the First Amendment freedom of the press guarantee, the Court said that when this obscene matter is located in the privacy of one's own home, the "right

takes on an added dimension." The Court held that even though the states are free to regulate, or even ban, obscenity, "that power simply does not extend to mere possession by the individual in the privacy of his own home."

In light of *Stanley*, is it constitutionally permissible for a statute to provide criminal penalties for the simple possession of marijuana in one's home? See, e.g., People v. Shepard, 50 N.Y.2d 640, 431 N.Y.S.2d 363, 409 N.E.2d 840 (1980).

5. Is it an invasion of one's privacy for male officers to search a female, or for male inmates to be subjected to body searches by female guards? See Sterling v. Cupp, 290 Or. 611, 625 P.2d 123 (1981).

EISENSTADT v. BAIRD

Supreme Court of the United States, 1972.
405 U.S. 438, 92 S.Ct. 1029, 31 L.Ed.2d 349.

MR. JUSTICE BRENNAN delivered the opinion of the Court.

Appellee William Baird was convicted at a bench trial in the Massachusetts Superior Court under Massachusetts General Laws Ann., c. 272, § 21, first, for exhibiting contraceptive articles in the course of delivering a lecture on contraception to a group of students at Boston University and, second, for giving a young woman a package of Emko vaginal foam at the close of his address. The Massachusetts Supreme Judicial Court unanimously set aside the conviction for exhibiting contraceptives on the ground that it violated Baird's First Amendment rights, but by a four-to-three vote sustained the conviction for giving away the foam. Commonwealth v. Baird, 355 Mass. 746, 247 N.E.2d 574 (1969). Baird subsequently filed a petition for a federal writ of habeas corpus, which the District Court dismissed. On appeal, however, the Court of Appeals for the First Circuit vacated the dismissal and remanded the action with directions to grant the writ discharging Baird. This appeal by the Sheriff of Suffolk County, Massachusetts, followed, and we noted probable jurisdiction. We affirm.

Massachusetts General Laws Ann., c. 272, § 21, under which Baird was convicted, provides a maximum five-year term of imprisonment for "whoever . . . gives away . . . any drug, medicine, instrument or article whatever for the prevention of conception," except as authorized in § 21A. Under § 21A, "[a] registered physician may administer to or prescribe for any married person drugs or articles intended for the prevention of pregnancy or conception. [And a] registered pharmacist actually engaged in the business of pharmacy may furnish such drugs or articles to any married person presenting a prescription from a registered physician." As interpreted by the State Supreme Judicial Court, these provisions make it a felony for anyone, other than a registered physician or pharmacist acting in accordance with the terms of § 21A, to dispense any article with the intention that it be used for the prevention of conception. The statutory scheme distinguishes among three distinct classes of distributees—*first*, married persons may obtain contraceptives to prevent pregnancy, but only from doctors or druggists on prescription; *second*, single persons may not obtain contraceptives from anyone to prevent pregnancy; and *third*, married or single persons may obtain contraceptives from anyone to prevent, not pregnancy, but the spread of disease. This construction of state law is, of course binding on us.

The legislative purposes that the statute is meant to serve are not altogether clear. In Commonwealth v. Baird, supra, the Supreme Judicial Court noted only the State's interest in protecting the health of its citizens: . . . In a subsequent decision, Sturgis v. Attorney General, 358 Mass. 37, 260 N.E.2d 687, 690 (1970), the court, however, found "a second and more compelling ground for upholding the statute"— namely, to protect morals through "regulating the private sexual lives of single persons." The Court of Appeals, for reasons that will appear, did not consider the promotion of health or the protection of morals through the deterrence of fornication to be the legislative aim. Instead, the court concluded that the statutory goal was to limit contraception in and of itself—a purpose that the court held conflicted "with fundamental human rights" under Griswold v. Connecticut, 381 U.S. 479 (1965), where this Court struck down Connecticut's prohibition against the use of contraceptives as an unconstitutional infringement of the right of marital privacy.

We agree that the goals of deterring premarital sex and regulating the distribution of potentially harmful articles cannot reasonably be regarded as legislative aims of §§ 21 and 21A. And we hold that the statute, viewed as a prohibition on contraception *per se,* violates the rights of single persons under the Equal Protection Clause of the Fourteenth Amendment.

I

[The portion of the opinion in which the Court decided that Baird had standing to assert the rights of unmarried persons is omitted.]

II

The basic principles governing application of the Equal Protection Clause of the Fourteenth Amendment are familiar. As The Chief Justice only recently explained in Reed v. Reed, 404 U.S. 71, 75–76 (1971):

"In applying that clause, this Court has consistently recognized that the Fourteenth Amendment does not deny to States the power to treat different classes of persons in different ways. The Equal Protection Clause of that amendment does, however, deny to States the power to legislate that different treatment be accorded to persons placed by a statute into different classes on the basis of criteria wholly unrelated to the objective of that statute. A classification 'must be reasonable, not arbitrary, and must rest upon some ground of difference having a fair and substantial relation to the object of the legislation, so that all persons similarly circumstanced shall be treated alike."

The question for our determination in this case is whether there is some ground of difference that rationally explains the different treatment accorded married and unmarried persons under Massachusetts General Laws Ann., c. 272, §§ 21 and 21A. For the reasons that follow, we conclude that no such ground exists.

First. Section 21 stems from Mass.Stat.1879, c. 159, § 1, which prohibited, without exception, distribution of articles intended to be used as contraceptives. In Commonwealth v. Allison, 227 Mass. 57, 62, 116 N.E. 265, 266 (1917), the Massachusetts Supreme Judicial Court explained that the law's "plain purpose is to protect purity, to preserve chastity, to encourage continence and self restraint, to defend the sanctity of the home, and thus to engender in the State and nation a virile and virtuous race of men and women." Although the State clearly abandoned that purpose with the enactment of § 21A, at least insofar as the illicit sexual activities of married persons are concerned, the court reiterated in Sturgis v. Attorney General, supra, that the object of the legislation is to discourage premarital sexual intercourse. Conceding that the State could, consistently with the Equal Protection Clause, regard the problems of extramarital and premarital sexual relations as "[e]vils . . . of different dimensions and proportions, requiring different remedies," we cannot agree that the deterrence of premarital sex may reasonably be regarded as the purpose of the Massachusetts law.

It would be plainly unreasonable to assume that Massachusetts has prescribed pregnancy and the birth of an unwanted child as punishment for fornication, which is a misdemeanor under Massachusetts General Laws Ann., c. 272, § 18. Aside from the scheme of values that assumption would attribute to the State, it is abundantly clear that the effect of the ban on distribution of contraceptives to unmarried persons has at best a marginal relation to the proffered objective. What Mr. Justice Goldberg said in Griswold v. Connecticut, concerning the effect of Connecticut's prohibition on the use of contraceptives in discouraging extramarital sexual relations, is equally applicable here. "The rationality of this justification is dubious, particularly in light of the admitted widespread availability to all persons in the State of Connecticut, unmarried as well as married, of birth-control devices for the prevention of disease, as distinguished from the prevention of conception." Like Connecticut's laws, §§ 21 and 21A do not at all regulate the distribution of contraceptives when they are to be used to prevent, not pregnancy, but the spread of disease. Nor, in making contraceptives available to married persons without regard to their intended use, does Massachusetts attempt to deter married persons from engaging in illicit sexual relations with unmarried persons. Even on the assumption that the fear of pregnancy operates as a deterrent to fornication, the Massachusetts statute is thus so riddled with exceptions that deterrence of premarital sex cannot reasonably be regarded as its aim.

Moreover, §§ 21 and 21A on their face have a dubious relation to the State's criminal prohibition on fornication. As the Court of Appeals explained, "Fornication is a misdemeanor [in Massachusetts], entailing a thirty dollar fine, or three months in jail. Violation of the present statute is a felony, punishable by five years in prison. We find it hard to believe that the legislature adopted a statute carrying a five-year penalty for its possible, obviously by no means fully effective, deterrence of the commission of a ninety-day misdemeanor." Even conceding the legislature a full measure of discretion in fashioning means to prevent fornication, and recognizing that the State may seek to deter prohibited conduct by punishing more severely those who facilitate than those who actually engage in its commission, we, like the Court of Appeals, cannot believe that in this instance Massachusetts has chosen to expose the aider and abettor who simply *gives away* a contraceptive to *20* times the *90–day* sentence of the offender himself. The very terms of the State's criminal statutes, coupled with the *de minimis* effect of §§ 21 and 21A in deterring fornication, thus compel the conclusion that such deterrence cannot reasonably be taken as the purpose of the ban on distribution of contraceptives to unmarried persons.

Second. Section 21A was added to the Massachusetts General Laws by Stat.1966, c. 265, § 1. The Supreme Judicial Court in Commonwealth v. Baird, supra, held that the purpose of the amendment was to serve the health needs of the community by regulating the distribution of potentially harmful articles. It is plain that Massachusetts had no such purpose in mind before the enactment of § 21A. As the Court of Appeals remarked, "Consistent with the fact that the statute was contained in a chapter dealing with 'Crimes Against Chastity, Morality, Decency and Good Order,' it was cast only in terms of morals. A physician was forbidden to prescribe contraceptives even when needed for the protection of health. Commonwealth v. Gardner, 1938, 300 Mass. 372, 15 N.E.2d 222." 429 F.2d at 1401. Nor did the Court of Appeals "believe that the legislature [in enacting § 21A] suddenly reversed its field and developed an interest in health. Rather, it merely made what it thought to be the precise accommodation necessary to escape the *Griswold* ruling." Ibid.

Again, we must agree with the Court of Appeals. If health were the rationale of § 21A, the statute would be both discriminatory and overbroad. . . .: "If the prohibition [on distribution to unmarried persons] . . . is to be taken to mean that the same physician who can prescribe for married patients does not have sufficient skill to protect the health of patients who lack a marriage certificate, or who may be currently divorced, it is illogical to the point of irrationality." 429 F.2d, at 1401. Furthermore, we must join the Court of Appeals in noting that not all contraceptives are potentially dangerous. As a result, if the Massachusetts statute were a health measure, it would not only invidiously discriminate against the unmarried, but also be overbroad with respect to the married, a fact that the Supreme Judicial Court itself seems to have conceded in Sturgis v. Attorney General [supra], where it noted that "it may well be that certain contraceptive medication and devices constitute no hazard to health, in which event it could be argued that the statute swept too broadly in its prohibition."

. . .

But if further proof that the Massachusetts statute is not a health measure is necessary, the argument of Justice Spiegel, who also dissented in Commonwealth v. Baird [supra], is conclusive: "It is at best a strained conception to say that the Legislature intended to prevent the distribution of articles 'which may have undesirable, if not dangerous, physical consequences.' If that was the Legislature's goal, § 21 is not required" in view of the federal and state laws *already* regulating the distribution of harmful drugs. We conclude, accordingly, that, despite the statute's superficial earmarks as a health measure, health, on the face of the statute, may no more reasonably be regarded as its purpose than the deterrence of premarital sexual relations.

Third. If the Massachusetts statute cannot be upheld as a deterrent to fornication or as a health measure, may it, nevertheless, be sustained simply as a prohibition on contraception? The Court of Appeals analysis "led inevitably to the conclusion that, so far as morals are concerned, it is contraceptives per se that are considered immoral—to the extent that *Griswold* will permit such a declaration." The Court of Appeals went on to hold:

> "To say that contraceptives are immoral as such, and are to be forbidden to unmarried persons who will nevertheless persist in having intercourse, means that such persons must risk for themselves an unwanted pregnancy, for the child, illegitimacy, and for society, a possible obligation of support. Such a view of morality is not only the very mirror image of sensible legislation; we consider that it conflicts with fundamental human rights. In the absence of demonstrated harm, we hold it is beyond the competency of the state."

We need not and do not, however, decide that important question in this case because, whatever the rights of the individual to access to contraceptives may be, the rights must be the same for the unmarried and the married alike.

If under *Griswold* the distribution of contraceptives to married persons cannot be prohibited, a ban on distribution to unmarried persons would be equally impermissible. It is true that in *Griswold* the right of privacy in question inhered in the marital relationship. Yet the marital couple is not an independent entity with a mind and heart of its own, but an association of two individuals each with a separate intellectual and emotional makeup. If the right of privacy means anything it is the right of the *individual*, married or single, to be free from unwarranted governmental intrusion into matters so fundamentally affecting a person as the decision whether to bear or beget a child.

On the other hand, if *Griswold* is no bar to a prohibition on the distribution of contraceptives, the State could not, consistently with the Equal Protection Clause, outlaw distribution to unmarried but not to married persons. In each case the evil, as perceived by the State, would be identical, and the underinclusion would be invidious. Mr. Justice Jackson, concurring in Railway Express Agency v. New York, 336 U.S. 106, 112–113 (1949), made the point:

> "The framers of the Constitution knew, and we should not forget today, that there is no more effective practical guaranty against arbitrary and unreasonable government than to require that the principles of law which officials would impose upon a minority must be imposed generally. Conversely, nothing opens the door to arbitrary action so effectively as to allow those officials to pick and choose only a few to whom they will apply legislation and thus to escape the political retribution that might be visited upon them if larger numbers were affected. Courts can take no better measure to assure that laws will be just than to require that laws be equal in operation."

Although Mr. Justice Jackson's comments had reference to administrative regulations, the principle he affirmed has equal application to the legislation here. We hold that by providing dissimilar treatment for married and unmarried persons who are similarly situated, Massachusetts General Laws, violate the Equal Protection Clause. The judgment of the Court of Appeals is

Affirmed.

Mr. Justice Powell and Mr. Justice Rehnquist took no part in the consideration or decision of this case.

[The concurring opinion of Mr. Justice Douglas, which rests on the First Amendment, is omitted.]

Mr. Justice White, with whom Mr. Justice Blackmun joins, concurring in the result.

In Griswold v. Connecticut we reversed criminal convictions for advising married persons with respect to the use of contraceptives. As there applied, the Connecticut law, which forbade using contraceptives or giving advice on the subject, unduly invaded a zone of marital privacy protected by the Bill of Rights. . . .

Appellee Baird was indicted for giving away Emko Vaginal Foam, a "medicine and article for the prevention of conception. . . ." The State did not purport to charge or convict Baird for distributing to an unmarried person. No proof was offered as to the marital status of the recipient. The gravamen of the offense charged was that Baird had no license and therefore no authority to distribute to anyone. As the Supreme Judicial Court of Massachusetts noted, the constitutional validity of Baird's conviction rested upon his lack of status as a "distributor and not . . . the marital status of the recipient." Commonwealth v. Baird [supra]. The Federal District Court was of the same view.

I assume that a State's interest in the health of its citizens empowers it to restrict to medical channels the distribution of products whose use should be accompanied by medical advice. I also do not doubt that various contraceptive medicines and articles are properly available only on prescription, and I therefore have no difficulty with the Massachusetts court's characterization of the statute at issue here as expressing "a legitimate interest in preventing the distribution of articles designed to prevent conception which may have undesirable, if not dangerous, physical consequences." Had Baird distributed a supply of the so-called "pill," I would sustain his conviction under this statute. Requiring a prescription to obtain potentially dangerous contraceptive material may place a substantial burden upon the right recognized in *Griswold,* but that burden is justified by a strong state interest and does not, as did the statute at issue in *Griswold,* sweep unnecessarily broadly or seek "to achieve its goals by means having a maximum destructive impact upon" a protected relationship.

Baird, however, was found guilty of giving away vaginal foam. Inquiry into the validity of this conviction does not come to an end merely because some contraceptives are harmful and their distribution may be restricted. Our general reluctance to question a State's judgment on matters of public health must give way where, as here, the restriction at issue burdens the constitutional rights of married persons to use contraceptives. In these circumstances we may not accept on faith the State's classification of a particular contraceptive as dangerous to health. Due regard for protecting constitutional rights requires that the record contain evidence that a restriction on distribution of vaginal foam is essential to achieve the statutory purpose, or the relevant facts concerning the product must be such as to fall within the range of judicial notice.

Neither requirement is met here. Nothing in the record even suggests that the distribution of vaginal foam should be accompanied by medical advice in order to protect the user's health. Nor does the opinion of the Massachusetts court or the State's brief filed here marshal facts demonstrating that the hazards of using vaginal foam are common knowledge or so incontrovertible that they may be noticed judicially. On the contrary, the State acknowledges that Emko is a product widely available without prescription. Given Griswold v. Connecticut, supra, and absent proof of the probable hazards of using vaginal foam, we could not sustain appellee's conviction had it been for selling or giving away foam to a married person. Just as in *Griswold,* where the right of married persons to use contraceptives was "diluted or adversely affected" by permitting a conviction for giving advice as to its exercise, so here, to sanction a medical restriction upon distribution of a contraceptive not proved hazardous to health would impair the exercise of the constitutional right.

That Baird could not be convicted for distributing Emko to a married person disposes of this case. Assuming, *arguendo,* that the result would be otherwise had the recipient been unmarried, nothing has been placed in the record to indicate her marital status. The State has maintained that marital status is irrelevant because an unlicensed person cannot legally dispense vaginal foam either to married or unmarried persons. This approach is plainly erroneous and requires the reversal of Baird's conviction; for on the facts of this case, it deprives us of knowing whether Baird was in fact convicted for making a constitutionally protected distribution of Emko to a married person.

The principle established in Stromberg v. California, 283 U.S. 359 (1931), and consistently adhered to is that a conviction cannot stand where the "record fail[s] to prove that the conviction was not founded upon a theory which could not constitutionally support a verdict." To uphold a conviction even "though we cannot know that it did not rest on the invalid constitutional ground . . . would be to countenance a procedure which would cause a serious impairment of constitutional rights."

Because this case can be disposed of on the basis of settled constitutional doctrine, I perceive no reason for reaching the novel constitutional question whether a State may restrict or forbid the distribution of contraceptives to the unmarried.

Mr. Chief Justice Burger, dissenting.

The judgment of the Supreme Judicial Court of Massachusetts in sustaining appellee's conviction for dispensing medicinal material without a license seems eminently correct to me and I would not disturb it. . . .

The opinion of the Court today brushes aside appellee's status as an unlicensed layman by concluding that the Massachusetts Legislature was not really concerned with the protection of health when it passed this statute. Mr. Justice White acknowledges the statutory concern with the protection of health, but finds the restriction on distributors overly broad because the State has failed to adduce facts showing the health hazards of the particular substance dispensed by appellee as distinguished from other contraceptives. Mr. Justice Douglas' concurring opinion does not directly challenge the power of Massachusetts to prohibit laymen from dispensing contraceptives, but considers that appellee rather than dispensing the substance was resorting to a "time-honored teaching technique" by utilizing a "visual aid" as an adjunct to his protected speech. I am puzzled by this third characterization of the case. If the suggestion is that appellee was merely displaying the contraceptive material without relinquishing his ownership of it, then the argument must be that the prosecution failed to prove that appellee had "given away" the contraceptive material. But appellee does not challenge the sufficiency of the evidence, and himself summarizes the record as showing that "at the close of his lecture he invited members of the audience . . . to come and help themselves." On the other hand, if the concurring opinion means that the First Amendment protects the distribution of all articles "not dangerous *per se*" when the distribution is coupled with some form of speech, then I must confess that I have misread certain cases in the area.

My disagreement with the opinion of the Court and that of Mr. Justice White goes far beyond mere puzzlement, however, for these opinions seriously invade the constitutional prerogatives of the States and regrettably hark back to the heyday of substantive due process.

In affirming appellee's conviction, the highest tribunal in Massachusetts held that the statutory requirement that contraceptives be dispensed only through medical channels served the legitimate interest of the State in protecting the health of its citizens. The Court today blithely hurdles this authoritative state pronouncement and concludes that the statute has no such purpose. Three basic arguments are advanced: First, since the distribution of contraceptives was prohibited as a moral matter in Massachusetts prior to 1966, it is impossible to believe that the legislature was concerned with health when it lifted the complete ban but insisted on medical supervision. I fail to see why the historical predominance of an unacceptable legislative purpose makes incredible the emergence of a new and valid one. The second argument, finding its origin in a dissenting opinion in the Supreme Judicial Court of Massachusetts, rejects a health purpose because, "[i]f there is need to have a physician prescribe . . . contraceptives, that need is as great for unmarried persons as for married persons." 355 Mass. 746, 758, 247 N.E.2d 574, 581. This argument confuses the validity of the restriction on distributors with the validity of the further restriction on distributees, a part of the statute not properly before the Court. Assuming the legislature too broadly restricted the class of persons who could obtain contraceptives, it hardly follows that it saw no need to protect the health of all persons to whom they are made available. Third, the Court sees no health purpose underlying the restriction on distributors because other state and federal laws regulate the distribution of harmful drugs. I know of no rule that all enactments relating to a particular purpose must be neatly consolidated in one package in the statute books for, if so, the United States Code will not pass muster. . . .

* * *

Mr. Justice White, while acknowledging a valid legislative purpose of protecting health, concludes that the State lacks power to regulate the distribution of the contraceptive involved in this case as a means of protecting health. The opinion grants that appellee's conviction would be valid if he had given away a potentially harmful substance, but rejects the State's placing this particular contraceptive in that category. So far as I am aware, this Court has never before challenged the police power of a State to protect the public from the risks of possibly spurious and deleterious substances sold within its borders. Moreover, a statutory classification is not invalid

"simply because some innocent articles or transactions may be found within the proscribed class. The inquiry must be whether, considering the end in view, the statute passes the bounds of reason and assumes the character of a merely arbitrary fiat."

But since the Massachusetts statute seeks to protect health by regulating contraceptives, the opinion invokes Griswold v. Connecticut, and puts the statutory classification to an unprecedented test: either the record must contain evidence supporting the classification or the health hazards of the particular contraceptive must be judicially noticeable. This is indeed a novel constitutional doctrine and not surprisingly no authority is cited for it.

Since the potential harmfulness of this particular medicinal substance has never been placed in issue in the state or federal courts, the State can hardly be faulted for its failure to build a record on this point. And it totally mystifies me, why in the absence of some evidence in the record, the factual underpinnings of the statutory classification must be "incontrovertible" or a matter of "common knowledge."

The actual hazards of introducing a particular foreign substance into the human body are frequently controverted, and I cannot believe that unanimity of expert opinion is a prerequisite to a State's exercise of its police power, no matter what the subject matter of the regulation. Even assuming no present dispute among medical authorities, we cannot ignore that it has become commonplace for a drug or food additive to be universally regarded as harmless on one day and to be condemned as perilous on the next. It is inappropriate for this Court to overrule a legislative classification by relying on the present consensus among leading authorities. The commands of the Constitution cannot fluctuate with the shifting tides of scientific opinion.

Even if it were conclusively established once and for all that the product dispensed by appellee is not actually or potentially dangerous in the somatic sense, I would still be unable to agree that the restriction on dispensing it falls outside the State's power to regulate in the area of health. The choice of a means of birth control, although a highly personal matter, is also a health matter in a very real sense, and I see nothing arbitrary in a requirement of medical supervision. It is generally acknowledged that contraceptives vary in degree of effectiveness and potential harmfulness. There may be compelling health reasons for certain women to choose the most effective means of birth control available, no matter how harmless the less effective alternatives. Others might be advised not to use a highly effective means of contraception because of their peculiar susceptibility to an adverse side effect. Moreover, there may be information known to the medical profession that a particular brand of contraceptive is to be preferred or avoided, or that it has not been adequately tested. Nonetheless, the concurring opinion would hold, as a constitutional matter, that a State must allow someone without medical training the same power to distribute this medicinal substance as is enjoyed by a physician.

It is revealing, I think, that those portions of the majority and concurring opinions rejecting the statutory limitation on distributors rely on no particular provision of the Constitution. I see nothing in the Fourteenth Amendment or any other part of the Constitution that even vaguely suggests that these medicinal forms of contraceptives must be available in the open market. I do not challenge Griswold v. Connecticut, supra, despite its tenuous moorings to the text of the Constitution, but I cannot view it as controlling authority for this case. The Court was there confronted with a statute flatly prohibiting the use of contraceptives, not one regulating their distribution. I simply cannot believe that the limitation on the class of lawful distributors has significantly impaired the right to use contraceptives in Massachusetts. By relying on *Griswold* in the present context, the Court has passed beyond the penumbras of the specific guarantees into the uncircumscribed area of personal predilections.

The need for dissemination of information on birth control is not impinged in the slightest by limiting the distribution of medicinal substances to medical and pharmaceutical channels as Massachusetts has done by statute. The appellee has succeeded, it seems, in cloaking his activities in some new permutation of the First Amendment although his conviction rests in fact and law on dispensing a medicinal substance without a license. I am constrained to suggest that if the Constitution can be strained to invalidate the Massachusetts statute underlying appellee's conviction, we could quite as well employ it for the protection of a "curbstone quack," reminiscent of the "medicine man" of times past, who attracted a crowd of the curious with a soapbox lecture and then plied them with "free samples" of some unproved remedy. Massachusetts presumably outlawed such activities long ago, but today's holding seems to invite their return.

MICHAEL M. v. SUPERIOR COURT OF SONOMA COUNTY

Supreme Court of the United States, 1981.
450 U.S. 464, 101 S.Ct. 1200, 67 L.Ed.2d 437.

JUSTICE REHNQUIST announced the judgment of the Court and delivered an opinion in which THE CHIEF JUSTICE, JUSTICE STEWART, and JUSTICE POWELL joined.

The question presented in this case is whether California's "statutory rape" law, § 261.5 of the California Penal Code, violates the Equal Protection Clause of the Fourteenth Amendment. Section 261.5 defines unlawful sexual intercourse as "an act of sexual intercourse accomplished with a female not the wife of the perpetrator, where the female is under the age of 18 years." The statute thus makes men alone criminally liable for the act of sexual intercourse.

In July 1978, a complaint was filed in the Municipal Court of Sonoma County, Cal., alleging that petitioner, then a 17½ year old male, had had unlawful sexual intercourse with a female under the age of 18, in violation of § 261.5. The evidence, adduced at a preliminary hearing showed that at approximately midnight on June 3, 1978, petitioner and two friends approached Sharon, a 16½ year old female, and her sister as they waited at a bus stop. Petitioner and Sharon, who had already been drinking, moved away from the others and began to kiss. After being struck in the face for rebuffing petitioner's initial advances, Sharon submitted to sexual intercourse with petitioner. Prior to trial, petitioner sought to set aside the information on both state and federal constitutional grounds, asserting that § 261.5 unlawfully discriminated on the basis of gender. The trial court and the California Court of Appeal denied petitioner's request for relief and petitioner sought review in the Supreme Court of California.

The Supreme Court held that "Section 261.5 discriminates on the basis of sex because only females may be victims, and only males may violate the section." The court then subjected the classification to "strict scrutiny," stating that it must be justified by a compelling state interest. It found that the classification was "supported not by mere social convention but by the immutable physiological fact that it is the female exclusively who can become pregnant." Canvassing "the tragic human cost of illegitimate teenage pregnancies," including the large number of teenage abortions, the increased medical risk associated with teenage pregnancies, and the social consequences of teenage child bearing, the court concluded that the state has a compelling interest in preventing such pregnancies. Because males alone can "physiologically cause the result which the law properly seeks to avoid" the court further held that the gender classification was readily justified as a means of identifying offender and victim. For the reasons stated below, we affirm the judgment of the California Supreme Court.

As is evident from our opinions, the Court has had some difficulty in agreeing upon the proper approach and analysis in cases involving challenges to gender-based classifications. The issues posted by such challenges range from issues of standing, to the appropriate standard of judicial review for the substantive classification. Unlike the California Supreme Court, we have not held that gender-based classifications are "inherently suspect" and thus we do not apply so-called "strict scrutiny" to those classifications. Our cases have held, however, that the traditional minimum rationality test takes on a somewhat "sharper focus" when gender-based classifications are challenged. In Reed v. Reed, 404 U.S. 71, 92 S.Ct. 251 (1971), for example, the Court stated that a gender-based classification will be upheld if it bears a "fair and substantial relationship" to legitimate state ends, while in Craig v. Boren, 429 U.S. at 197, 97 S.Ct. at 457, the Court restated the test to require the classification to bear a "substantial relationship" to "important governmental objectives."

Underlying these decisions is the principle that a legislature may not "make overbroad generalizations based on sex which are entirely unrelated to any differences between men and women or which demean the ability or social status of the affected class." But because the Equal Protection Clause does not "demand that a statute necessarily apply

equally to all persons" or require "things which are different in fact
. . . to be treated in law as though they were the same," this Court
has consistently upheld statutes where the gender classification is not
invidious, but rather realistically reflects the fact that the sexes are not
similarly situated in certain circumstances. As the Court has stated, a
legislature may "provide for the special problems of women."

Applying those principles to this case, the fact that the California
Legislature criminalized the act of illicit sexual intercourse with a
minor female is a sure indication of its intent or purpose to discourage
that conduct. Precisely why the legislature desired that result is of
course somewhat less clear. . . . Here, for example, the individual
legislators may have voted for the statute for a variety of reasons.
Some legislators may have been concerned about preventing teenage
pregnancies, others about protecting young females from physical injury or from the loss of "chastity," and still others about promoting
various religious and moral attitudes towards premarital sex.

The justification for the statute offered by the State, and accepted
by the Supreme Court of California, is that the legislature sought to
prevent illegitimate teenage pregnancies. That finding, of course, is
entitled to great deference. And although our cases establish that the
State's asserted reason for the enactment of a statute may be rejected,
"if it could not have been a goal of the legislation," this is not such a
case.

We are satisfied not only that the prevention of illegitimate pregnancy is at least one of the "purposes" of the statute, but that the State
has a strong interest in preventing such pregnancy. At the risk of
stating the obvious, teenage pregnancies, which have increased dramatically over the last two decades, have significant social, medical and
economic consequences for both the mother and her child, and the
State. Of particular concern to the State is that approximately half of
all teenage pregnancies end in abortion. And of those children who are
born, their illegitimacy makes them likely candidates to become wards
of the State.

We need not be medical doctors to discern that young men and
young women are not similarly situated with respect to the problems
and the risks of sexual intercourse. Only women may become pregnant
and they suffer disproportionately the profound physical, emotional and
psychological consequences of sexual activity. The statute at issue here
protects women from sexual intercourse at an age when those consequences are particularly severe.

The question thus boils down to whether a State may attack the
problem of sexual intercourse and teenage pregnancy directly by
prohibiting a male from having sexual intercourse with a minor female.
We hold that such a statute is sufficiently related to the State's
objectives to pass constitutional muster.

Because virtually all of the significant harmful and inescapably
identifiable consequences of teenage pregnancy fall on the young fe-

male, a legislature acts well within its authority when it elects to punish only the participant who, by nature, suffers few of the consequences of his conduct. It is hardly unreasonable for a legislature acting to protect minor females to exclude them from punishment. Moreover, the risk of pregnancy itself constitutes a substantial deterrence to young females. No similar natural sanctions deter males. A criminal sanction imposed solely on males thus serves to roughly "equalize" the deterrents on the sexes.

We are unable to accept petitioner's contention that the statute is impermissibly underinclusive and must, in order to pass judicial scrutiny, be *broadened* so as to hold the female as criminally liable as the male. It is argued that this statute is not *necessary* to deter teenage pregnancy because a gender-neutral statute, where both male and female would be subject to prosecution, would serve that goal equally well. The relevant inquiry, however, is not whether the statute is drawn as precisely as it might have been, but whether the line chosen by the California Legislature is within constitutional limitations.

* * *

We similarly reject petitioner's argument that § 261.5 is impermissibly overbroad because it makes unlawful sexual intercourse with prepubescent females, who are, by definition, incapable of becoming pregnant. Quite apart from the fact that the statute could well be justified on the grounds that very young females are particularly susceptible to physical injury from sexual intercourse, it is ludicrous to suggest that the Constitution requires the California Legislature to limit the scope of its rape statute to older teenagers and exclude young girls.

* * *

In upholding the California statute we also recognize that this is not a case where a statute is being challenged on the grounds that it "invidiously discriminates" against females. To the contrary, the statute places a burden on males which is not shared by females. But we find nothing to suggest that men, because of past discrimination or peculiar disadvantages, are in need of the special solicitude of the courts. . . .

Accordingly, the judgment of the California Supreme Court is affirmed.

Affirmed.

JUSTICE STEWART, concurring.

Section 261.5, on its face, classifies on the basis of sex. A male who engages in sexual intercourse with an underage female who is not his wife violates the statute; a female who engages in sexual intercourse with an underage male who is not her husband does not. The petitioner contends that this state law, which punishes only males for the conduct in question, violates his Fourteenth Amendment right to the equal protection of the law. The Court today correctly rejects that contention.

A

At the outset, it should be noted that the statutory discrimination, when viewed as part of the wider scheme of California law, is not as clearcut as might at first appear. Females are not freed from criminal liability in California for engaging in sexual activity that may be harmful. It is unlawful, for example, for any person, of either sex, to molest, annoy, or contribute to the delinquency of anyone under 18 years of age. All persons are prohibited from committing "any lewd or lascivious act," including consensual intercourse, with a child under 14. And members of both sexes may be convicted for engaging in deviant sexual acts with anyone under 18. Finally, females may be brought within the proscription of § 261.5 itself, since a female may be charged with aiding and abetting its violation.

Section 261.5 is thus but one part of a broad statutory scheme that protects all minors from the problems and risks attendant upon adolescent sexual activity. . . .

B

The Constitution is violated when government, state or federal, invidiously classifies similarly situated people on the basis of the immutable characteristics with which they were born. Thus, detrimental racial classifications by government always violate the Constitution, for the simple reason that, so far as the Constitution is concerned, people of different races are always similarly situated. By contrast, while detrimental gender classifications by government often violate the Constitution, they do not always do so, for the reason that there are differences between males and females that the Constitution necessarily recognizes. In this case we deal with the most basic of these differences: females can become pregnant as the result of sexual intercourse; males cannot.

*   *   *

Applying these principles to the classification enacted by the California Legislature, it is readily apparent that § 261.5 does not violate the Equal Protection Clause. Young women and men are not similarly situated with respect to the problems and risk associated with intercourse and pregnancy, and the statute is realistically related to the legitimate state purpose of reducing those problems and risks.

C

As the California Supreme Court's catalogue shows, the pregnant unmarried female confronts problems more numerous and more severe than any faced by her male partner. She alone endures the medical risks of pregnancy or abortion. She suffers disproportionately the social, educational, and emotional consequences of pregnancy. Recognizing this disproportion, California has attempted to protect teenage females by prohibiting males from participating in the act necessary for conception.

* * *

In short, the Equal Protection Clause does not mean that the physiological differences between men and women must be disregarded. While those differences must never be permitted to become a pretext for invidious discrimination, no such discrimination is presented by this case. The Constitution surely does not require a State to pretend that demonstrable differences between men and women do not really exist.

The opinion of JUSTICE BLACKMUN, concurring in the judgment, is omitted.

JUSTICE BRENNAN, with whom JUSTICES WHITE and MARSHALL join, dissenting.

I

It is disturbing to find the Court so splintered on a case that presents such a straightforward issue: whether the admittedly gender-based classification in Cal.Penal Code § 261.5 bears a sufficient relationship to the State's asserted goal of preventing teenage pregnancies to survive the "mid-level" constitutional scrutiny mandated by Craig v. Boren (1976). Applying the analytical framework provided by our precedents, I am convinced that there is only one proper resolution of this issue: the classification must be declared unconstitutional. I fear that the plurality and Justices Stewart and Blackmun reach the opposite result by placing too much emphasis on the desirability of achieving the State's asserted statutory goal—prevention of teenage pregnancy—and not enough emphasis on the fundamental question of whether the sex-based discrimination in the California statute is *substantially* related to the achievement of that goal.

II

After some uncertainty as to the proper framework for analyzing equal protection challenges to statutes containing gender-based classifications, this Court settled upon the proposition that a statute containing a gender-based classification cannot withstand constitutional challenge unless the classification is substantially related to the achievement of an important governmental objective. This analysis applies whether the classification discriminates against males or against females. The burden is on the government to prove both the importance of its asserted objective and the substantial relationship between the classification and that objective. And the State cannot meet that burden without showing that a gender-neutral statute would be a less effective means of achieving that goal.[1]

1. Gender-based statutory rape laws were struck down in *Navedo v. Preisser*, 630 F.2d 636 (CA8 1980), *United States v. Hicks*, 625 F.2d 216 (CA9 1980), and Meloon v. Helgemoe, 564 F.2d 602 (CA1 1977), cert. denied, 436 U.S. 950, 98 S.Ct. 2858 (1978), precisely because the government failed to meet this burden of proof.

The State of California vigorously asserts that the "important governmental objective" to be served by § 261.5 is the prevention of teenage pregnancy. It claims that its statute furthers this goal by deterring sexual activity by males—the class of persons it considers more responsible for causing those pregnancies. But even assuming that prevention of teenage pregnancy is an important governmental objective and that it is in fact an objective of § 261.5, California still has the burden of proving that there are fewer teenage pregnancies under its gender-based statutory rape law than there would be if the law were gender-neutral. To meet this burden, the State must show that because its statutory rape law punishes only males, and not females, it more effectively deters minor females from having sexual intercourse.

The plurality assumes that a gender-neutral statute would be less effective than § 261.5 in deterring sexual activity because a gender-neutral statute would create significant enforcement problems. . . .

However, a State's bare assertion that its gender-based statutory classification substantially furthers an important governmental interest is not enough to meet its burden of proof. . . . Rather, the State must produce evidence that will persuade the Court that its assertion is true.

The State has not produced such evidence in this case. Moreover, there are at least two serious flaws in the State's assertion that law enforcement problems created by a gender-neutral statutory rape law would make such a statute less effective than a gender-based statute in deterring sexual activity.

First, the experience of other jurisdictions, and California itself, belies the plurality's conclusion that a gender-neutral statutory rape law "may well be incapable of enforcement." There are now at least 37 States that have enacted gender-neutral statutory rape laws. Although most of these laws protect young persons (of either sex) from the sexual exploitation of older individuals, the laws of Arizona, Florida, and Illinois permit prosecution of both minor females and minor males for engaging in mutual sexual conduct.[2] California has introduced no evidence that those states have been handicapped by the enforcement problems the plurality finds so persuasive. Surely, if those States could provide such evidence, we might expect that California would have introduced it.

In addition, the California Legislature in recent years has revised other sections of the Penal Code to make them gender-neutral. For example, Cal.Penal Code §§ 286(b)(1) and 288a(b)(1), prohibiting sodomy and oral copulation with a "person who is under 18 years of age," could cause two minor homosexuals to be subjected to criminal sanctions for

---

2. See Ariz.Rev.Stat.Ann. § 13–1405; Fla.Stat.Ann. § 794.05; Ill.Ann.Stat. ch. 38, § 11–5. In addition, eight other States permit both parties to be prosecuted when one of the participants to a consensual act of sexual intercourse is under the age of 16.

engaging in mutually consensual conduct. Again, the State has introduced no evidence to explain why a gender-neutral statutory rape law would be any more difficult to enforce than those statutes.

The second flaw in the State's assertion is that even assuming that a gender-neutral statute would be more difficult to enforce, the State has still not shown that those enforcement problems would make such a statute less effective than a gender-based statute in deterring minor females from engaging in sexual intercourse. Common sense, however, suggests that a gender-neutral statutory rape law is potentially a *greater* deterrent of sexual activity than a gender-based law, for the simple reason that a gender-neutral law subjects both men and women to criminal sanctions and thus arguably has a deterrent effect on twice as many potential violators. Even if fewer persons were prosecuted under the gender-neutral law, as the State suggests, it would still be true that twice as many persons would be *subject* to arrest. The State's failure to prove that a gender-neutral law would be a less effective deterrent than a gender-based law, like the State's failure to prove that a gender-neutral law would be difficult to enforce, should have led this Court to invalidate § 261.5.

III

Until very recently, no California court or commentator had suggested that the purpose of California's statutory rape law was to protect young women from the risk of pregnancy. Indeed, the historical development of § 261.5 demonstrates that the law was initially enacted on the premise that young women, in contrast to young men, were to be deemed legally incapable of consenting to an act of sexual intercourse. Because their chastity was considered particularly precious, those young women were felt to be uniquely in need of the State's protection. In contrast, young men were assumed to be capable of making such decisions for themselves; the law therefore did not offer them any special protection.

It is perhaps because the gender classification in California's statutory rape law was initially designed to further these outmoded sexual stereotypes, rather than to reduce the incidence of teenage pregnancies, that the State has been unable to demonstrate a substantial relationship between the classification and its newly asserted goal. But whatever the reason, the State has not shown that Cal.Penal Code § 261.5 is any more effective than a gender-neutral law would be in determining minor females from engaging in sexual intercourse. It has therefore not met its burden of proving that the statutory classification is substantially related to the achievement of its asserted goal.

I would hold that § 261.5 violates the Equal Protection Clause of the Fourteenth Amendment and I would reverse the judgment of the California Supreme Court.

JUSTICE STEVENS, dissenting.

Local custom and belief—rather than statutory laws of venerable but doubtful ancestry—will determine the volume of sexual activity among unmarried teenages. The empirical evidence cited by the plurality demonstrates the futility of the notion that a statutory prohibition will significantly affect the volume of that activity or provide a meaningful solution to the problems created by it. Nevertheless, as a matter of constitutional power, unlike my Brother Brennan, I would have no doubt about the validity of a state law prohibiting all unmarried teenages from engaging in sexual intercourse. The societal interests in reducing the incidence of venereal disease and teenage pregnancy are sufficient, in my judgment, to justify a prohibition of conduct that increases the risk of those harms.

My conclusion that a nondiscriminatory prohibition would be constitutional does not help me answer the question whether a prohibition applicable to only half of the joint participants in the risk-creating conduct is also valid. It cannot be true that the validity of a total ban is an adequate justification for a selective prohibition; otherwise, the constitutional objection to discriminatory rules would be meaningless. The question in this case is whether the difference between males and females justifies this statutory discrimination based entirely on sex.

The fact that the Court did not immediately acknowledge that the capacity to become pregnant is what primarily differentiates the female from the male does not impeach the validity of the plurality's newly-found wisdom. I think the plurality is quite correct in making the assumption that the joint act that this law seeks to prohibit creates a greater risk of harm for the female than for the male. But the plurality surely cannot believe that the risk of pregnancy confronted by the female—any more than the risk of venereal disease confronted by males as well as females—has provided an effective deterrent to voluntary female participation in the risk-creating conduct. Yet the plurality's decision seems to rest on the assumption that the California Legislature acted on the basis of that rather fanciful notion.

In my judgment, the fact that a class of persons is especially vulnerable to a risk that a statute is designed to avoid is a reason for making the statute applicable to that class. The argument that a special need for protection provides a rational explanation for an exemption is one I simply do not comprehend.

In this case, the fact that a female confronts a greater risk of harm than a male is a reason for applying the prohibition to her—not a reason for granting her a license to use her own judgment on whether or not to assume the risk. Surely, if we examine the problem from the point of view of society's interest in preventing the risk-creating conduct from occurring at all, it is irrational to exempt 50% of the potential violators. And, if we view the government's interest as that of a *parens patriae* seeking to protect its subjects from harming themselves, the discrimination is actually perverse. Would a rational parent making rules for the conduct of twin children of opposite sex simultaneously forbid the son and authorize the daughter to engage in conduct that is especially harmful to the daughter? That is the effect of this statutory classification.

If pregnancy or some other special harm is suffered by one of the two participants in the prohibited act, that special harm no doubt would constitute a legitimate mitigating factor in deciding what, if any, punishment might be appropriate in a given case. But from the standpoint of fashioning a general preventive rule—or, indeed, in determining appropriate punishment when neither party in fact has suffered any special harm—I regard a total exemption for the members of the more endangered class as utterly irrational.

In my opinion, the only acceptable justification for a general rule requiring disparate treatment of the two participants in a joint act must be a legislative judgment that one is more guilty than the other. The risk-creating conduct that this statute is designed to prevent requires the participation of two persons—one male and one female. In many situations it is probably true that one is the aggressor and the other is either an unwilling, or at least a less willing, participant in the joint act. If a statute authorized punishment of only one participant and required the prosecutor to prove that that participant had been the aggressor, I assume that the discrimination would be valid. Although the question is less clear, I also assume, for the purpose of deciding this case, that it would be permissible to punish only the male participant, if one element of the offense were proof that he had been the aggressor, or at least in some respects the more responsible participant in the joint act. The statute at issue in this case, however, requires no such proof. The question raised by this statute is whether the State, consistently with the Federal Constitution, may always punish the male and never the female when they are equally responsible or when the female is the more responsible of the two.

It would seem to me that an impartial lawmaker could give only one answer to that question. The fact that the California Legislature has decided to apply its prohibition only to the male may reflect a legislative judgment that in the typical case the male is actually the more guilty party. Any such judgment must, in turn, assume that the decision to engage in the risk-creating conduct is always—or at least typically—a male decision. If that assumption is valid, the statutory classification should also be valid. But what is the support for the assumption? It is not contained in the record of this case or in any legislative history or scholarly study that has been called to our attention. I think it is supported to some extent by traditional attitudes toward male-female relationships. But the possibility that such an habitual attitude may reflect nothing more than an irrational prejudice makes it an insufficient justification for discriminatory treatment that is otherwise blatantly unfair. For, as I read this statute, it requires that one, and only one, of two equally guilty wrongdoers be stigmatized by a criminal conviction.

I cannot accept the State's argument that the constitutionality of the discriminatory rule can be saved by an assumption that prosecutors will commonly invoke this statute only in cases that actually involve a forcible rape, but one that cannot be established by proof beyond a reasonable doubt. That assumption implies that a State has a legitimate interest in convicting a defendant on evidence that is constitutionally insufficient. . . .

Nor do I find at all persuasive the suggestion that this discrimination is adequately justified by the desire to encourage females to inform against their male partners. Even if the concept of a wholesale informant's exemption were an acceptable enforcement device, what is the justification for defining the exempt class entirely by reference to sex rather than by reference to a more neutral criterion such as relative innocence? Indeed, if the exempt class is to be composed entirely of members of one sex, what is there to support the view that the statutory purpose will be better served by granting the informing license to females rather than to males? If a discarded male partner informs on a promiscuous female, a timely threat of prosecution might well prevent the precise harm the statute is intended to minimize.

Finally, even if my logic is faulty and there actually is some speculative basis for treating equally guilty males and females differently, I still believe that any such speculative justification would be outweighed by the paramount interest in evenhanded enforcement of the law. A rule that authorizes punishment of only one of two equally guilty wrongdoers violates the essence of the constitutional requirement that the sovereign must govern impartially.

I respectfully dissent.

NOTES

1. In footnote 1 of the Court's plurality opinion in the leading case, Justice Rehnquist cited cases from 21 state and two federal circuit courts of appeal which had concluded that statutory rape laws are constitutional. The Texas Supreme Court avoided the constitutional issue in Ex parte Groves, 571 S.W.2d 888 (Tex.Crim.App.1978), by construing the statutory rape statute to protect both male and female victims. Is that a sounder approach?

2. In Tatro v. State, 372 So.2d 283 (Miss.1979), a majority of the Mississippi Supreme Court held unconstitutional, on equal protection grounds, a state law criminalizing conduct by a "male person" who handles, touches, or rubs any child under the age of 14 for the purpose of gratifying his sexual desires. The court found no valid reason for this "patent discrimination against males," inasmuch as women clearly could perform the same acts. The court also noted that the state failed to show "that such unequal treatment serves any traditional, governmental or public policy or is based upon a rational distinction based upon sex." The dissenting opinion argued that the majority should have saved the statute by striking the word "male" so as to make the statute sex-neutral. Should courts use that approach?

3. A defendant was convicted of violating the Mann Act by causing a woman to travel to Nevada for the purpose of prostitution, an activity which is

legal in that state. Can he claim that the Mann Act is unconstitutional because it violates the right of a female to travel to the State of Nevada to seek legal employment? See United States v. Pelton, 578 F.2d 701 (8th Cir.1978), opining that the argument's strength appeared to "lie in its ingenuity rather than in any degree of legal cogency." Why?

4. Are prostitution statutes unconstitutionally invalid because they discriminate against women? See e.g., State v. Gaither, 236 Ga. 497, 224 S.E.2d 378 (1976); State v. Mertes, 60 Wis.2d 414, 210 N.W.2d 741 (1973); State v. Butler, 331 So.2d 425 (La.1976); Commonwealth v. King, 374 Mass. 5, 372 N.E.2d 196 (1977). On the constitutionality of assault and battery laws which provide protection to females only, or which provide greater penalties for males than for females, see Anno., 5 A.L.R. 4th 708.

5. The conviction of a woman for being "a common scold" was voided in State v. Palendrano, 120 N.J.Super. 336, 293 A.2d 747 (1972). Among the grounds for the decision was the element of unequal protection, since only a woman, and not a man, could be subject to prosecution, whereas a man might be just as "troublesome and angry" by "wrangling" among his neighbors.

Is there an equal protection violation in a regulation that requires a woman visitor to an all-male prison to wear a brassiere? See Holdman v. Olim, 59 Hawaii 346, 581 P.2d 1164 (1978).

6. The European Convention on Human Rights, in its Article 14, provides:

"The enjoyment of the rights and freedoms set forth in this Convention shall be secured without discrimination on any ground such as sex, race, colour, language, religion, political or other opinion, national or social origin, association with a national minority, property, birth or other status."

ROE v. WADE

Supreme Court of the United States, 1973.
410 U.S. 113, 93 S.Ct. 705, 35 L.Ed.2d 147.

[The majority and minority opinions in this case occupied 64 pages in the official U.S. reporter, so they obviously had to be condensed extensively for casebook usage. Although the following excerpts deal primarily with the right of privacy issue, we have retained certain tangentially related ones, for the reason that the subject of abortion is not treated elsewhere in the casebook. Students with a greater interest in the subject than is here presented will have access, of course, to the unabridged opinions themselves.]

MR. JUSTICE BLACKMUN delivered the opinion of the Court.

* * *

The Texas statutes that concern us here . . . make it a crime to "procure an abortion," as therein defined, or to attempt one, except with respect to "an abortion procured or attempted by medical advice for the purpose of saving the life of the mother." Similar statutes are in existence in a majority of the States. . . .

* * *

Jane Roe, a single woman who was residing in Dallas County, Texas, instituted this federal action in March 1970 against the District

Attorney of the county. She sought a declaratory judgment that the Texas criminal abortion statutes were unconstitutional on their face, and an injunction restraining the defendant from enforcing the statutes.

Roe alleged that she was unmarried and pregnant; that she wished to terminate her pregnancy by an abortion "performed by a competent, licensed physician, under safe, clinical conditions"; that she was unable to get a "legal" abortion in Texas because her life did not appear to be threatened by the continuation of her pregnancy; and that she could not afford to travel to another jurisdiction in order to secure a legal abortion under safe conditions. She claimed that the Texas statutes were unconstitutionally vague and that they abridged her right of personal privacy, protected by the First, Fourth, Fifth, Ninth, and Fourteenth Amendments. By an amendment to her complaint Roe purported to sue "on behalf of herself and all other women" similarly situated.

* * *

The principal thrust of appellant's attack on the Texas statutes is that they improperly invade a right, said to be possessed by the pregnant woman, to choose to terminate her pregnancy. Appellant would discover this right in the concept of personal "liberty" embodied in the Fourteenth Amendment's Due Process Clause; or in personal, marital, familial, and sexual privacy said to be protected by the Bill of Rights or its penumbras, . . . Before addressing this claim, we feel it desirable briefly to survey, in several aspects, the history of abortion, for such insight as that history may afford us, and then to examine the state purposes and interests behind the criminal abortion laws.

It perhaps is not generally appreciated that the restrictive criminal abortion laws in effect in a majority of States today are of relatively recent vintage. Those laws, generally proscribing abortion or its attempt at any time during pregnancy except when necessary to preserve the pregnant woman's life, are not of ancient or even of common law origin. Instead, they derive from statutory changes effected, for the most part, in the latter half of the 19th century.

1. *Ancient Attitudes.* These are not capable of precise determination. We are told that at the time of the Persian Empire abortifacients were known and that criminal abortions were severely punished. We are also told, however, that abortion was practiced in Greek times as well as in the Roman Era, and that "it was resorted to without scruple." The Ephesian, Soranos, often described as the greatest of the ancient gynecologists, appears to have been generally opposed to Rome's prevailing pre-abortion practices. He found it necessary to think first of the life of the mother, and he resorted to abortion when, upon this standard, he felt the procedure advisable. Greek and Roman law afforded little protection to the unborn. If abortion was prosecuted in some places, it seems to have been based on a concept of a violation

of the father's right to his offspring. Ancient religion did not bar abortion.

    2. *The Hippocratic Oath.* What then of the famous Oath that has stood so long as the ethical guide of the medical profession and that bears the name of the great Greek (460 (?)–377 (?) B.C.), who has been described as the Father of Medicine, the "wisest and the greatest practitioner of his art," and the "most important and most complete medical personality of antiquity," who dominated the medical schools of this time, and who typified the sum of the medical knowledge of the past? The Oath varies somewhat according to the particular translation, but in any translation the content is clear: "I will give no deadly medicine to anyone if asked, nor suggest any such counsel; and in like manner I will not give to a woman a pessary to produce abortion," or "I will neither give a deadly drug to anybody if asked for it, nor will I make a suggestion to this effect. Similarly, I will not give to a woman an abortive remedy."

    Although the Oath is not mentioned in any of the principal briefs in this case, . . . it represents the apex of the development of strict ethical concepts in medicine, and its influence endures to this day. Why did not the authority of Hippocrates dissuade abortion practice in his time and that of Rome? The late Dr. Edelstein provides us with a theory: . . . The Oath was not uncontested even in Hippocrates' day; only the Pythagorean school of philosphers frowned upon the related act of suicide. Most Greek thinkers, on the other hand, commended abortion, at least prior to viability. . . . For the Pythagoreans, however, it was a matter of dogma. For them the embryo was animate from the moment of conception, and abortion meant destruction of a living being. The abortion clause of the Oath, therefore, "echoes Pythagorean doctrines," and "[i]n no other stratum of Greek opinion were such views held or proposed in the same spirit of uncompromising austerity."

    Edelstein then concludes that the Oath originated in a group representing only a small segment of Greek opinion and that it certainly was not accepted by all ancient physicians. He points out that medical writings down to Galen (130–200 A.D.) "give evidence of the violation of almost every one of its injunctions." But with the end of antiquity a decided change took place. Resistance against suicide and against abortion became common. The Oath came to be popular. The emerging teachings of Christianity were in agreement with the Pythagorean ethic. The Oath "became the nucleus of all medical ethics" and "was applauded as the embodiment of truth." Thus, suggests Dr. Edelstein, it is "a Pythagorean manifesto and not the expression of an absolute standard of medical conduct."

    This, it seems to us, is a satisfactory and acceptable explanation of the Hippocratic Oath's apparent rigidity. It enables us to understand, in historical context, a long accepted and revered statement of medical ethics.

3. *The Common Law.* It is undisputed that at the common law, abortion performed *before* "quickening"—the first recognizable movement of the fetus *in utero*, appearing usually from the 16th to the 18th week of pregnancy—was not an indictable offense. The absence of a common law crime for pre-quickening abortion appears to have developed from a confluence of earlier philosophical, theological, and civil and canon law concepts of when life begins. These disciplines variously approached the question in terms of the point at which the embryo or fetus became "formed" or recognizably human, or in terms of when a "person" came into being, that is, infused with a "soul" or "animated." A loose consensus evolved in early English law that these events occurred at some point between conception and live birth. This was "mediate animation." Although Christian theology and the canon law came to fix the point of animation at 40 days for a male and 80 days for a female, a view that persisted until the 19th century, there was otherwise little agreement about the precise time of formation or animation. There was agreement, however, that prior to this point the fetus was to be regarded as part of the mother and its destruction, therefore, was not homicide. Due to continued uncertainty about the precise time when animation occurred, to the lack of any empirical basis for the 40–80 day view, and perhaps to Acquinas' definition of movement as one of the two first principles of life, Bracton focused upon quickening as the critical point. The significance of quickening was echoed by later common law scholars and found its way into the received common law in this country.

Whether abortion of a *quick* fetus was a felony at common law, or even a lesser crime, is still disputed. Bracton, writing early in the 13th century, thought it homicide. But the later and predominant view, following the great common law scholars, has been that it was at most a lesser offense. In a frequently cited passage, Coke took the position that abortion of a woman "quick with childe" is "a great misprision and no murder." Blackstone followed, saying that while abortion after quickening had once been considered manslaughter (though not murder), "modern law" took a less severe view. A recent review of the common law precedents argues, however, that those precedents contradict Coke and that even post-quickening abortion was never established as a common law crime. This is of some importance because while most American courts ruled, in holding or dictum, that abortion of an unquickened fetus was not criminal under their received common law, others followed Coke in stating that abortion of a quick fetus was a "misprision," a term they translated to mean "misdemeanor." That their reliance on Coke on this aspect of the law was uncritical and, apparently in all the reported cases, dictum (due probably to the paucity of common law prosecutions for post-quickening abortion), makes it now appear doubtful that abortion was ever firmly established as a common law crime even with respect to the destruction of a quick fetus.

4. *The English Statutory Law.* England's first criminal abortion statute . . . came in 1803. It made abortion of a quick fetus, § 1, a capital crime, but in § 2 it provided lesser penalties for the felony of abortion before quickening, and thus preserved the quickening distinction. This contrast was continued in the general revision of 1828 . . . It disappeared, however, together with the death penalty, in 1837 . . . and did not reappear in the Offenses Against the Person Act of 1861 . . . that formed the core of English anti-abortion law until the liberalizing reforms of 1967. * * *

[The 1967 Abortion Act] permits a licensed physician to perform an abortion where two other licensed physicians agree (a) "that the continuance of the pregnancy would involve risk to the life of the pregnant woman, or of injury to the physical or mental health of the pregnant woman or any existing children of her family, greater than if the pregnancy were terminated," or (b) "that there is a substantial risk that if the child were born it would suffer from such physical or mental abnormalities as to be seriously handicapped." The Act also provides that, in making this determination, "account may be taken of the pregnant woman's actual or reasonably foreseeable environment." It also permits a physician, without the concurrence of others, to terminate a pregnancy where he is of the good faith opinion that the abortion "is immediately necessary to save the life or to prevent grave permanent injury to the physical or mental health of the pregnant woman."

5. *The American Law.* In this country the law in effect in all but a few States until mid–19th century was the pre-existing English common law. Connecticut, the first State to enact abortion legislation, adopted in 1821 that part of [the early English act] that related to a woman "quick with child." The death penalty was not imposed. Abortion before quickening was made a crime in that State only in 1860. In 1828 New York enacted legislation that, in two respects, was to serve as a model for early anti-abortion statutes. First, while barring destruction of an unquickened fetus as well as a quick fetus, it made the former only a misdemeanor, but the latter second-degree manslaughter. Second, it incorporated a concept of therapeutic abortion by providing that an abortion was excused if it "shall have been necessary to preserve the life of such mother, or shall have been advised by two physicians to be necessary for such purpose." By 1840, when Texas had received the common law, only eight American States had statutes dealing with abortion. It was not until after the War Between the States that legislation began generally to replace the common law. Most of these initial statutes dealt severely with abortion after quickening but were lenient with it before quickening. Most punished attempts equally with completed abortions. While many statutes included the exception for an abortion thought by one or more physicians to be necessary to save the mother's life, that provision soon disappeared and the typical law required that the procedure actually be necessary for that purpose.

Gradually, in the middle and late 19th century the quickening distinction disappeared from the statutory law of most States and the degree of the offense and the penalties were increased. By the end of the 1950's a large majority of the States banned abortion, however and whenever performed, unless done to save or preserve the life of the mother. The exceptions, Alabama and the District of Columbia, permitted abortion to preserve the mother's health. Three other States permitted abortions that were not "unlawfully" performed or that were not "without lawful justification," leaving interpretation of those standards to the courts. In the past several years, however, a trend toward liberalization of abortion statutes has resulted in adoption, by about one-third of the States, of less stringent laws, most of them patterned after the ALI Model Penal Code, . . .

It is thus apparent that at common law, at the time of the adoption of our Constitution, and throughout the major portion of the 19th century, abortion was viewed with less disfavor than under most American statutes currently in effect. Phrasing it another way, a woman enjoyed a substantially broader right to terminate a pregnancy than she does in most States today. At least with respect to the early stage of pregnancy, and very possibly without such a limitation, the opportunity to make this choice was present in this country well into the 19th century. Even later, the law continued for some time to treat less punitively an abortion procured in early pregnancy.

6. *The Position of the American Medical Association.* The anti-abortion mood prevalent in this country in the late 19th century was shared by the medical profession. Indeed, the attitude of the profession may have played a significant role in the enactment of stringent criminal abortion legislation during that period. * * *

. . . [In 1967 the AMA's] Committee on Human Reproduction urged the adoption of a stated policy of opposition to induced abortion except when there is "documented medical evidence" of a threat to the health or life of the mother, or that the child "may be born with incapacitating physical deformity or mental deficiency," or that a pregnancy "resulting from legally established statutory or forcible rape or incest may constitute a threat to the mental or physical health of the patient," and two other physicians "chosen because of their recognized professional competency have examined the patient and have concurred in writing," and the procedure "is performed in a hospital accredited by the Joint Commission on Accreditation of Hospitals." The providing of medical information by physicians to state legislatures in their consideration of legislation regarding therapeutic abortion was "to be considered consistent with the principles of ethics of the American Medical Association." This recommendation was adopted by the House of Delegates. . . .

In 1970, after the introduction of a variety of proposed resolutions, and of a report from its Board of Trustees, a reference committee noted "polarization of the medical profession on this controversial issue";

division among those who had testified; a difference of opinion among AMA councils and committees; "the remarkable shift in testimony" in six months, felt to be influenced "by the rapid changes in state laws and by the judicial decisions which tend to make abortion more freely available;" and a feeling "that this trend will continue." On June 25, 1970, the House of Delegates adopted preambles and most of the resolutions proposed by the reference committee. The preambles emphasized "the best interests of the patient," "sound clinical judgment," and "informed patient consent," in contrast to "mere acquiescence to the patient's demand." The resolutions asserted that abortion is a medical procedure that should be performed by a licensed physician in an accredited hospital only after consultation with two other physicians and in conformity with state law, and that no party to the procedure should be required to violate personally held moral principles. . . . The AMA Judicial Council rendered a complementary opinion. * * *

[Omitted here are the reported position of the American Public Health Association, and that of the American Bar Association. The latter organization's House of Delegates in 1972 approved the Uniform Abortion Act drafted by the Conference of Commissioners on Uniform State Laws. It appears in footnote 40 of the court's opinion.] * * *

Three reasons have been advanced to explain historically the enactment of criminal abortion laws in the 19th century and to justify their continued existence.

It has been argued occasionally that these laws were the product of a Victorian social concern to discourage illicit sexual conduct. Texas, however, does not advance this justification in the present case, and it appears that no court or commentator has taken the argument seriously. . . .

A second reason is concerned with abortion as a medical procedure. When most criminal abortion laws were first enacted, the procedure was a hazardous one for the woman. This was particularly true prior to the development of antisepsis. Antiseptic techniques, of course, were based on discoveries by Lister, Pasteur, and others first announced in 1867, but were not generally accepted and employed until about the turn of the century. Abortion mortality was high. Even after 1900, and perhaps until as late as the development of antibiotics in the 1940's, standard modern techniques such as dilation and curettage were not nearly so safe as they are today. Thus it has been argued that a State's real concern in enacting a criminal abortion law was to protect the pregnant woman, that is, to restrain her from submitting to a procedure that placed her life in serious jeopardy.

Modern medical techniques have altered this situation. Appellants and various *amici* refer to medical data indicating that abortion in early pregnancy, that is, prior to the end of first trimester, although not without its risk, is now relatively safe. Mortality rates for women undergoing early abortions, where the procedure is legal, appear to be as low as or lower than the rates for normal childbirth. Consequently, any interest of the State in protecting the woman from an inherently hazardous procedure, except when it would be equally dangerous for her to forgo it, has largely disappeared. Of course, important state interests in the area of health and medical standards do remain. The State has a legitimate interest in seeing to it that abortion, like any other medical procedure, is performed under circumstances that insure maximum safety for the patient. . . . The prevalence of high mortality rates at illegal "abortion mills" strengthens, rather than weakens, the State's interest in regulating the conditions under which abortions are performed. Moreover, the risk to the woman increases as her pregnancy continues. Thus the State retains a definite interest in protecting the woman's own health and safety when an abortion is proposed at a late stage of pregnancy.

The third reason is the State's interest—some phrase it in terms of duty—in protecting prenatal life. Some of the argument for this justification rests on the theory that a new human life is present from the moment of conception. The State's interest and general obligation to protect life then extends, it is argued, to prenatal life. Only when the life of the pregnant mother herself is at stake, balanced against the life she carries within her, should the interest of the embryo or fetus not prevail. Logically, of course, a legitimate state interest in this area need not stand or fall on acceptance of the belief that life begins at conception or at some other point prior to live birth. In assessing the State's interest, recognition may be given to the less rigid claim that as long as at least *potential* life is involved, the State may assert interests beyond the protection of the pregnant woman alone.

Parties challenging state abortion laws have sharply disputed in some courts the contention that a purpose of these laws, when enacted, was to protect prenatal life. Pointing to the absence of legislative history to support the contention, they claim that most state laws were designed solely to protect the woman. . . . Proponents of this view point out that in many States, including Texas, by statute or judicial interpretation, the pregnant woman herself could not be prosecuted for self-abortion or for cooperating in an abortion performed upon her by another. They claim that adoption of the "quickening" distinction through received common law and state statutes tacitly recognizes the greater health hazards inherent in late abortion and impliedly repudiates the theory that life begins at conception.

It is with these interests, and the weight to be attached to them, that this case is concerned.

The Constitution does not explicitly mention any right of privacy. In a line of decisions, however, going back perhaps as far as [1891] . . ., the Court has recognized that a right of personal privacy, or a guarantee of certain areas or zones of privacy, does exist under the Constitution. In varying contexts the Court or individual Justices have indeed found at least the roots of that right in the First Amendment,

. . .; in the Fourth and Fifth Amendments, . . .; in the penumbras of the Bill of Rights, . . .; in the Ninth Amendment, . . .; or in the concept of liberty guaranteed by the first section of the Fourteenth Amendment, . . . These decisions make it clear that only personal rights that can be deemed "fundamental" or "implicit in the concept of ordered liberty," . . . are included in this guarantee of personal privacy. They also make it clear that the right has some extension to activities relating to marriage, . . . procreation, . . . contraception, . . . family relationships, . . . and child rearing and education, . . .

This right of privacy, whether it be founded in the Fourteenth Amendment's concept of personal liberty and restrictions upon state action, as we feel it is, or, as the District Court determined, in the Ninth Amendment's reservation of rights to the people, is broad enough to encompass a woman's decision whether or not to terminate her pregnancy. The detriment that the State would impose upon the pregnant woman by denying this choice altogether is apparent. Specific and direct harm medically diagnosable even in early pregnancy may be involved. Maternity, or additional offspring, may force upon the woman a distressful life and future. Psychological harm may be imminent. Mental and physical health may be taxed by child care. There is also the distress, for all concerned, associated with the unwanted child, and there is the problem of bringing a child into a family already unable, psychologically and otherwise, to care for it. In other cases, as in this one, the additional difficulties and continuing stigma of unwed motherhood may be involved. All these are factors the woman and her responsible physician necessarily will consider in consultation.

On the basis of elements such as these, appellants and some *amici* argue that the woman's right is absolute and that she is entitled to terminate her pregnancy at whatever time, in whatever way, and for whatever reason she alone chooses. With this we do not agree. Appellants' arguments that Texas either has no valid interest at all in regulating the abortion decision, or no interest strong enough to support any limitation upon the woman's sole determination, is unpersuasive. The Court's decisions recognizing a right of privacy also acknowledge that some state regulation in areas protected by that right is appropriate. As noted above, a state may properly assert important interests in safeguarding health, in maintaining medical standards, and in protecting potential life. At some point in pregnancy, these respective interests become sufficiently compelling to sustain regulation of the factors that govern the abortion decision. The privacy right involved, therefore, cannot be said to be absolute. . . .

The appellee and certain *amici* argue that the fetus is a "person" within the language and meaning of the Fourteenth Amendment. In support of this they outline at length and in detail the well-known facts of fetal development. If this suggestion of personhood is established, the appellant's case, of course, collapses, for the fetus' right to life is then guaranteed specifically by the Amendment. The appellant conceded as much on reargument. On the other hand, the appellee conceded on reargument that no case could be cited that holds that a fetus is a person within the meaning of the Fourteenth Amendment.

The Constitution does not define "person" in so many words. Section 1 of the Fourteenth Amendment contains three references to "person." The first, in defining "citizens," speaks of "persons born or naturalized in the United States." The word also appears both in the Due Process Clause and in the Equal Protection Clause. "Person" is used in other places in the Constitution: in the listing of qualifications for representatives and senators [etc.], and in the Fifth, Twelfth, and Twenty-second Amendments as well as in §§ 2 and 3 of the Fourteenth Amendment. But in nearly all these instances, the use of the word is such that it has application only postnatally. None indicates, with any assurance, that it has any possible pre-natal application.

All this, together with our observation, supra, that throughout the major portion of the 19th century prevailing legal abortion practices were far freer than they are today, persuades us that the word "person," as used in the Fourteenth Amendment, does not include the unborn. . . .

This conclusion, however, does not of itself fully answer the contentions raised by Texas, and we pass on to other considerations.

The pregnant woman cannot be isolated in her privacy. She carries an embryo, and, later, a fetus, if one accepts the medical definitions of the developing young in the human uterus. The situation therefore is inherently different from marital intimacy, or bedroom possession of obscene material, or marriage, or procreation, or education. . . . As we have intimated above, it is reasonable and appropriate for a State to decide that at some point in time another interest, that of health of the mother or that of potential human life, becomes significantly involved. The woman's privacy is no longer sole and any right of privacy she possesses must be measured accordingly.

[At this point Justice Blackmun discusses the issue of when life begins, already included in Section B–1–(a) of this chapter.]

* * *

In view of all this, we do not agree that, by adopting one theory of life, Texas may override the rights of the pregnant woman that are at stake. We repeat, however, that the State does have an important and legitimate interest in preserving and protecting the health of the pregnant woman, whether she be a resident of the State or a nonresident who seeks medical consultation and treatment there, and that it has still *another* important and legitimate interest in protecting the potentiality of human life. These interests are separate and distinct. Each grows in substantiality as the woman approaches term and, at a point during pregnancy, each becomes "compelling."

With respect to the State's important and legitimate interest in the health of the mother, the "compelling" point, in the light of present medical knowledge, is at approximately the end of the first trimester. This is so because of the now established medical fact, referred to above that until the end of the first trimester mortality in abortion is less than mortality in normal childbirth. It follows that, from and after this point, a State may regulate the abortion procedure to the extent that the regulation reasonably relates to the preservation and protection of maternal health. Examples of permissible state regulation in this area are requirements as to the qualifications of the person who is to perform the abortion; as to the licensure of that person; as to the facility in which the procedure is to be performed, that is, whether it must be a hospital or may be a clinic or some other place of less-than-hospital status; as to the licensing of the facility; and the like.

This means, on the other hand, that, for the period of pregnancy prior to this "compelling" point, the attending physician, in consultation with his patient, is free to determine, without regulation by the State, that in his medical judgment the patient's pregnancy should be terminated. If that decision is reached, the judgment may be effectuated by any abortion free of interference by the State.

With respect to the State's important and legitimate interest in potential life, the "compelling" point is at viability. This is so because the fetus then presumably has the capability of meaningful life outside the mother's womb. State regulation protective of fetal life after viability thus has both logical and biological justifications. If the State is interested in protecting fetal life after viability, it may go so far as to proscribe abortion during that period except when it is necessary to preserve the life or health of the mother.

Measured against these standards, the Texas Penal Code, in restricting legal abortions to those "procured or attempted by medical advice for the purpose of saving the life of the mother," sweeps too broadly. The statute makes no distinction between abortions performed early in pregnancy and those performed later, and it limits to a single reason, "saving" the mother's life, the legal justification for the procedure. The statute, therefore, cannot survive the constitutional attack made upon it here. * * *

To summarize and to repeat:

1. A state criminal abortion statute of the current Texas type, that excepts from criminality only a *life saving* procedure on behalf of the mother, without regard to pregnancy stage and without recognition of the other interests involved, is violative of the Due Process Clause of the Fourteenth Amendment.

(a) For the stage prior to approximately the end of the first trimester, the abortion decision and its effectuation must be left to the medical judgment of the pregnant woman's attending physician.

(b) For the stage subsequent to approximately the end of the first trimester, the State, in promoting its interest in the health of the mother, may, if it chooses, regulate the abortion procedure in ways that are reasonably related to maternal health.

(c) For the stage subsequent to viability the State, in promoting its interest in the potentiality of human life, may, if it chooses, regulate, and even proscribe, abortion except where it is necessary, in appropriate medical judgment, for the preservation of the life or health of the mother.

2. The State may define the term "physician" . . . to mean only a physician currently licensed by the State, and may proscribe any abortion by a person who is not a physician as so defined. * * *

[The concurring opinions of Chief Justice Burger and of Justices Douglas and Stewart are omitted.]

MR. JUSTICE REHNQUIST, dissenting.

The Court's opinion brings to the decision of this troubling question both extensive historical fact and a wealth of legal scholarship. While its opinion thus commands my respect, I find myself nonetheless in fundamental disagreement with those parts of it which invalidate the Texas statute in question, and therefore dissent.

The Court's opinion decides that a State may impose virtually no restriction on the performance of abortions during the first trimester of pregnancy. Our previous decisions indicate that a necessary predicate for such an opinion is a plaintiff who was in her first trimester of pregnancy at some time during the pendency of her law suit. While a party may vindicate his own constitutional rights, he may not seek vindication for the rights of others. . . . The Court's statement of facts in this case makes clear, however, that the record in no way indicates the presence of such a plaintiff. We know only that plaintiff Roe at the time of filing her complaint was a pregnant woman; for aught that appears in this record, she may have been in her *last* trimester of pregnancy as of the date the complaint was filed.

Nothing in the Court's opinion indicates that Texas might not constitutionally apply its proscription of abortion as written to a woman in that stage of pregnancy. Nonetheless, the Court uses her complaint against the Texas statute as a fulcrum for deciding that States may impose virtually no restrictions on medical abortions performed during the *first* trimester of pregnancy. In deciding such a hypothetical lawsuit the Court departs from the longstanding admonition that it should never "formulate a rule of constitutional law broader than is required by the precise facts to which it is to be applied." . . .

Even if there were a plaintiff in this case capable of litigating the issue which the Court decides, I would reach a conclusion opposite to that reached by the Court. I have difficulty in concluding as the Court does, that the right of "privacy" is involved in this case. Texas by the statute here challenged bars the performance of a medical abortion by a licensed physician on a plaintiff such as Roe. A transaction resulting in an operation such as this is not "private" in the ordinary usage of that word. Nor is the "privacy" which the Court finds here even a distant relative of the freedom from searches and seizures protected by the Fourth Amendment to the Constitution which the Court has referred to as embodying a right to privacy. . . .

If the Court means by the term "privacy" no more than that the claim of a person to be free from unwanted state regulation of consensual transactions may be a form of "liberty" protected by the Fourteenth Amendment, there is no doubt that similar claims have been upheld in our earlier decisions on the basis of that liberty. I agree with the statement of Mr. Justice Stewart in his concurring opinion that the "liberty," against deprivation of which without due process the Fourteenth Amendment protects, embraces more than the rights found in the Bill of Rights. But that liberty is not guaranteed absolutely against deprivation, but only against deprivation without due process of law. The test traditionally applied in the area of social and economic legislation is whether or not a law such as that challenged has a rational relation to a valid state objective. . . . The Due Process Clause of the Fourteenth Amendment undoubtedly does place a limit on legislative power to enact laws such as this, albeit a broad one. If the Texas statute were to prohibit an abortion even where the mother's life is in jeopardy, I have little doubt that such a statute would lack a rational relation to a valid state objective. . . . But the Court's sweeping invalidation of any restrictions on abortion during the first trimester is impossible to justify under that standard, and the conscious weighing of competing factors which the Court's opinion apparently substitutes for the established test is far more appropriate to a legislative judgment than to a judicial one. * * *

The fact that a majority of the States, reflecting after all the majority sentiment in those States, have had restrictions on abortions for at least a century seems to me as strong an indication there is that the asserted right to an abortion is not "so rooted in the traditions and conscience of our people as to be ranked as fundamental." . . . Even today, when society's views on abortion are changing, the very existence of the debate is evidence that the "right" to an abortion is not so universally accepted as the appellants would have us believe.

To reach its result the Court necessarily has had to find within the Scope of the Fourteenth Amendment a right that was apparently completely unknown to the drafters of the Amendment. As early as 1821, the first state law dealing directly with abortion was enacted by the Connecticut legislature. . . . By the time of the adoption of the Fourteenth Amendment in 1868 there were at least 36 laws enacted by state or territorial legislatures limiting abortion. While many States have amended or updated their laws, 21 of the laws on the books in 1868 remain in effect today. Indeed, the Texas statute struck down today was, as the majority notes, first enacted in 1857 and "has remained substantially unchanged to the present time."

There apparently was no question concerning the validity of this provision or of any of the other state statutes when the Fourteenth Amendment was adopted. The only conclusion possible from this history is that the drafters did not intend to have the Fourteenth Amendment withdraw from the States the power to legislate with respect to this matter.

* * *

Mr. Justice White, with whom Mr. Justice Rehnquist joins, dissenting.

At the heart of the controversy in these cases are those recurring pregnancies that pose no danger whatsoever to the life or health of the mother but are nevertheless unwanted for any one or more of a variety of reasons—convenience, family planning, economics, dislike of children, the embarrassment of illegitimacy, etc. The common claim before us is that for any one of such reasons, or for no reason at all, and without asserting or claiming any threat to life or health, any woman is entitled to an abortion at her request if she is able to find a medical advisor willing to undertake the procedure.

The Court for the most part sustains this position: During the period prior to the time the fetus becomes viable, the Constitution of the United States values the convenience, whim or caprice of the putative mother more than the life or potential life of the fetus; the Constitution, therefore, guarantees the right to an abortion as against any state law or policy seeking to protect the fetus from an abortion not prompted by more compelling reasons of the mother.

With all due respect, I dissent. I find nothing in the language or history of the Constitution to support the Court's judgment. The Court simply fashions and announces a new constitutional right for pregnant mothers and with scarcely any reason or authority for its action, invests that right with sufficient substance to override most existing state abortion statutes. The upshot is that the people and the legislatures of the 50 States are constitutionally disentitled to weigh the relative importance of the continued existence and development of the fetus on the one hand against a spectrum of possible impacts on the mother on the other hand. As an exercise of raw judicial power, the Court perhaps has authority to do what it does today; but in my view its judgment is an improvident and extravagant exercise of the power of judicial review which the Constitution extends to this Court.

The Court apparently values the convenience of the pregnant mother more than the continued existence and development of the life or potential life which she carries. Whether or not I might agree with that marshalling of values, I can in no event join the Court's judgment because I find no constitutional warrant for imposing such an order of priorities on the people and legislatures of the States. In a sensitive area such as this, involving as it does issues over which reasonable men may easily and heatedly differ, I cannot accept the Court's exercise of its clear power of choice by interposing a constitutional barrier to state efforts to protect human life and by investing mothers and doctors with the constitutionally protected right to exterminate it. This issue, for the most part, should be left with the people and to the political processes the people have devised to govern their affairs.

It is my view, therefore, that the Texas statute is not constitutionally infirm because it denies abortions to those who seek to serve only their convenience rather than to protect their life or health. Nor is this plaintiff, who claims no threat to her mental or physical health, entitled to assert the possible rights of those women whose pregnancy assertedly implicates their health. . . .

NOTES

1. In the companion case of Doe v. Bolton, 410 U.S. 179, 93 S.Ct. 739, 35 L.Ed.2d 201 (1973) not only did a majority of the court re-affirm what had been decided in *Roe* but it also declared unconstitutional a 1968 Georgia "therapeutic abortion" statute because the Court found invalid certain conditions that were attached to the performance of the abortions authorized by the statute. The conditions prescribed in the statute were: (1) that the abortion be performed in a hospital accredited by a "Joint Commission on Accreditation of Hospitals"; (2) that the procedure be approved by the hospital staff abortion committee; (3) that the performing physician's judgment be confirmed by the independent examination of two other licensed physicians; and (4) that the woman be a resident of Georgia. The Court found (1) objectionable because Georgia placed no restriction on the performance of nonabortion surgery in hospitals without the commission's accreditation, and there was no showing that there was a particular need for it in abortion cases; (2) was "unduly restrictive of the patient's rights and needs"; (3) had no rational connection with a patient's needs and unduly infringed upon the physician's right to practice; and (4) was not based upon any policy of preserving state-supported facilities for Georgia's residents, since the restriction also applied to private hospitals and to privately retained physicians.

2. Shortly after the Supreme Court's decision in Roe v. Wade, the Pennsylvania legislature enacted "The Abortion Control Act." Among the provisions in this comprehensive statute was one which provided that "whoever, intentionally and willfully, took the life of a premature infant aborted alive was guilty of murder in the second degree." Another provision declared that if the fetus was determined to be viable, or if there was sufficient reason to believe that the fetus may be viable, the person performing the abortion was required to exercise the same care to preserve the life and health of the fetus as would be required in the case of a fetus intended to be born alive, and was required to adopt the abortion technique providing the best opportunity for the fetus to be aborted alive, so long as a different technique was not necessary in order to preserve the life or health of the mother.

The foregoing statutory provision was held to be unconstitutional by the United States Supreme Court in Colautti v. Franklin, 439 U.S. 379, 99 S.Ct. 675, 58 L.Ed.2d 596 (1979), on the ground that it was "ambiguous, and that its uncertainty is aggravated by the absence of a scienter requirement with respect to the finding of viability," in violation of due process.

3. May a state require a doctor performing an abortion to protect the potential life of a fetus? That issue was decided in the negative by the U.S. Supreme Court in Beal v. Franklin, 428 U.S. 901, 96 S.Ct. 3201 (1976) order vacating.

4. The Supreme Court has dealt with issues relating to financial assistance and medicaid support of desired nontherapeutic abortions in Beal v. Doe, 432 U.S. 438, 97 S.Ct. 2366, 53 L.Ed.2d 464 (1977); Maher v. Roe, 432 U.S. 464, 97 S.Ct. 2376, 53 L.Ed.2d 484 (1977), and Poelker v. Doe, 432 U.S. 519, 97 S.Ct. 2391, 53 L.Ed.2d 528 (1977), all decided the same day.

The foregoing line of cases held that public funds could not be required to perform abortions. However, Nyberg v. Virginia, 667 F.2d 754 (8th Cir.1982), held that willing staff physicians had a right to perform abortions in a publicly funded hospital. *Nyberg* emphasized the difference between direct funding of abortions and allowing qualified doctors to voluntarily perform abortions at a publicly owned hospital.

5. In Planned Parenthood of Central Missouri v. Danforth, 428 U.S. 52, 96 S.Ct. 2831, 49 L.Ed.2d 788 (1976), the Court dealt with a statute which required:

(a) that a woman must consent in writing and certify that her consent is informed and freely given if she is to undergo an abortion during the first twelve weeks of pregnancy;

(b) the written consent of the woman's spouse, unless a physician certifies that abortion is necessary to preserve her life;

(c) the written consent of the parent or guardian if the woman is an unmarried minor;

(d) the physician to exercise professional care to save the life of the fetus, and failure to do so was deemed manslaughter;

(e) that an infant who survives an abortion (not performed to save the mother's life or health) is a ward of the state whose parents have lost all rights to him or her;

The statute also prohibited, after the first twelve weeks, the use of saline amniocentesis to achieve an abortion.

The Court upheld the requirement of written consent from the woman seeking abortion but overturned both the spousal and parental consent provision. The Court found that a State could not delegate a veto power to spouse or parent which the state itself did not have, and that the rights of the woman, who physically bears the child outweighs any right of her spouse or, in most cases, her parents. The Court implied, however, that a state might require parental consent for very young or immature females. The prohibition of the saline method was invalidated because it banned the most common (68%–80%) abortion technique while allowing more dangerous methods, thus inhibiting abortions by means of an unreasonable regulation. The requirement that the physician attempt to preserve the life of the fetus was held overbroad since it applied to pregnancies in which the fetus had not become viable.

6. In H.L. v. Matheson, 450 U.S. 398, 101 S.Ct. 1164, 67 L.Ed.2d 388 (1981), the Supreme Court confronted the issue whether a state statute which requires a physician to notify, if possible, the parents of a dependent, unmarried minor girl prior to performing an abortion on the girl violates federal constitutional guarantees. In Bellotti v. Baird, 443 U.S. 622, 99 S.Ct. 3035, 61 L.Ed.2d 797 (1979) the Court had struck down a Massachusetts statute requiring parental or judicial consent before an abortion could be performed on any unmarried minor, holding that "the statute was unconstitutional for failure to allow mature minors to decide to undergo abortions without parental consent." In *Matheson,* however, the Court found that as applied to immature and dependent minors, the state statute served the important considerations of family

integrity and protecting adolescents which it had identified as valid state interests in the 1979 *Baird* case. In upholding the Utah parental notification requirement, the Matheson Court found, additionally, that the statute served a further significant state interest by providing an opportunity for parents to supply essential medical and other information to a physician.

7. In Thornburgh v. American College of Obstetricians & Gynecologists, 476 U.S. 747, 106 S.Ct. 2169, 90 L.Ed.2d 779 (1986), the Supreme Court struck down Pennsylvania's 1982 Abortion Control Act as unconstitutional, holding that a state may not discourage a woman from having an abortion under the pretext of "informed consent" legislation. Provisions of the act required a woman to be advised prior to the abortion of the medical risks, be given a description of the fetus, and warned of possible negative mental and physical consequences of an abortion. Physicians would also have been required to inform the woman of the father's support obligations and to refer her to social services that might be available to assist her to bear the child. The Court also rejected reporting requirements that would have identified the physician, the personal and medical data on the woman, and the reasons for the abortion. Also rejected were provisions that physicians must use abortion methods most likely to permit the fetus to remain alive and that a second physician be present to promote the life of the fetus.

The Court's 5–to–4 decision reaffirmed women's rights to choose an abortion, established in Roe v. Wade. Chief Justice Burger dissented, believing that the state had a legitimate interest justifying the act. Justice O'Connor dissented, arguing that the majority should have dealt only with the preliminary injunction issue. Neither of them, however, rejected the fundamental right to an abortion, as did dissenting Justices White and Rehnquist.

The *Thornburgh* ruling was influenced by several other recent Supreme Court decisions. In Akron v. Akron Center for Reproductive Health, Inc., 462 U.S. 416, 103 S.Ct. 2481, 76 L.Ed.2d 687 (1983), the Court reaffirmed Roe v. Wade and held informational requirements invalid. Planned Parenthood Association of Kansas City, Mo., Inc. v. Ashcroft, 462 U.S. 476, 103 S.Ct. 2517, 76 L.Ed.2d 733 (1983), however, upheld the requirement that a second physician be present to attend to a viable fetus, because the legislation allowed for a waiver of the requirement if delay in arrival of the second physician jeopardized the mother's health. The act invalidated in *Thornburgh* made no allowance for emergency exceptions. A criminal case, Simopoulos v. Virginia, 462 U.S. 506, 103 S.Ct. 2532, 76 L.Ed.2d 755 (1983), dealt with the prosecution of a physician who performed a second-trimester abortion in his unlicensed clinic rather than the statutorily required licensed hospital or clinic. The Supreme Court affirmed the conviction stating that the state's interest in protecting the woman's health became compelling during the second trimester. Virginia's requirement that second-trimester abortions be performed only in licensed facilities was upheld.

In Webster v. Reproductive Health Services, 492 U.S. 490, 109 S.Ct. 3040, 106 L.Ed.2d 410 (1989), a five-member majority of the Court stopped short of overruling Roe v. Wade, but indicated a willingness to uphold a wide range of state laws restricting abortion. Only Justice Scalia indicated he would have voted to overturn the Roe case. In Webster, the Court upheld a Missouri statute that imposes significant restrictions on the availability of abortions, by prohibiting the use of public facilities and public employees to perform or assist in the performance of abortions. This holding is consistent with other holdings, said Chief Justice Rehnquist, that teach that the state has no obligation to commit any resources to facilitate abortions. On the issue of fetal viability testing, which the statute required, he stated that the statute only required such tests to be done as are necessary in accordance with the exercise of the physician's professional judgment. The Chief Justice also criticized the trimester framework set out in Roe as "overly rigid" and unworkable. With respect to the preamble of the Missouri statute, which states that life begins at conception, the Court's majority noted that this only sets forth the value judgment made by the Missouri legislature, but does not actually regulate abortion.

Later decisions have been equally splintered. In Hodgson v. Minnesota, ___ U.S. ___, 110 S.Ct. 2926, 111 L.Ed.2d 344 (1990), the Court upheld the Minnesota statute 49-hour waiting period between notification of the parents of a minor's intention to obtain an abortion and the performance of that abortion. This period of time does not result in an unreasonable delay and is therefore constitutional, said the Court. The requirement of a two-parent notification, unless the pregnant minor obtains a judicial bypass, was also upheld. However, the requirement that *both* parents be notified of the minor's intent to obtain an abortion, whether or not both wish to be notified or have assumed responsibilities for upbringing the child, does not reasonably further the legitimate state's interest, and is therefore unconstitutional. In Ohio v. Akron Center for Reproductive Health, ___ U.S. ___, 110 S.Ct. 2972, 111 L.Ed.2d 405 (1990), the validity of the judicial by-pass of the statutory requirement that the parents be notified by the physician who will perform the abortion was at issue. The Court upheld the procedure as complying with due process, even though the procedure might take 22 days in a rare case.

BOWERS v. HARDWICK

Supreme Court of the United States, 1986.
478 U.S. 186, 106 S.Ct. 2841, 92 L.Ed.2d 140.

JUSTICE WHITE delivered the opinion of the Court.

In August 1982, respondent was charged with violating the Georgia statute criminalizing sodomy by committing that act with another adult male in the bedroom of respondent's home. After a preliminary hearing, the District Attorney decided not to present the matter to the grand jury unless further evidence developed.

Respondent then brought suit in the Federal District Court, challenging the constitutionality of the statute insofar as it criminalized consensual sodomy. He asserted that he was a practicing homosexual, that the Georgia sodomy statute, as administered by the defendants placed him in imminent danger of arrest, and that the statute for several reasons violates the Federal Constitution. The District Court granted the defendants' motion to dismiss for failure to state a claim,
. . .

A divided panel of the Court of Appeals for the Eleventh Circuit reversed. . . . Relying on our decisions in Griswold v. Connecticut (1965), Eisenstadt v. Baird (1972), Stanley v. Georgia (1969), and Roe v. Wade (1973), the court went on to hold that the Georgia statute violated respondent's fundamental rights because his homosexual activity is a private and intimate association that is beyond the reach of state regulation by reason of the Ninth Amendment and the Due Process Clause of the Fourteenth Amendment. The case was remanded for trial, at which to prevail, the State would have to prove that the statute is supported by a compelling interest and is the most narrowly drawn means of achieving that end.

Because other Courts of Appeals have arrived at judgments contrary to that of the Eleventh Circuit in this case, we granted the State's petition for certiorari questioning the holding that its sodomy statute violates the fundamental rights of homosexuals. We agree with the State that the Court of Appeals erred, and hence reverse its judgment.

This case does not require a judgment on whether laws against sodomy between consenting adults in general, or between homosexuals in particular, are wise or desirable. It raises no question about the right or propriety of state legislative decisions to repeal their laws that criminalize homosexual sodomy, or of state court decisions invalidating those laws on state constitutional grounds. The issue presented is whether the Federal Constitution confers a fundamental right upon homosexuals to engage in sodomy and hence invalidates the laws of the many States that still make such conduct illegal and have done so for a very long time. The case also calls for some judgment about the limits of the Court's role in carrying out its constitutional mandate.

We first register our disagreement with the Court of Appeals and with respondent that the Court's prior cases have construed the Constitution to confer a right of privacy that extends to homosexual sodomy and for all intents and purposes have decided this case. . . .

Accepting the decisions in these cases and the above description of them, we think it evident that none of the rights announced in those cases bears any resemblance to the claimed constitutional right of homosexuals to engage in acts of sodomy that is asserted in this case. No connection between family, marriage, or procreation on the one hand and homosexual activity on the other has been demonstrated, either by the Court of Appeals or by respondent. Moreover, any claim that these cases nevertheless stand for the proposition that any kind of private sexual conduct between consenting adults is constitutionally insulated from state proscription is unsupportable. Indeed, the Court's opinion in *Carey* twice asserted that the privacy right which the *Griswold* line of cases found to be one of the protections provided by the Due Process Clause, did not reach so far.

Precedent aside, however, respondent would have us announce, as the Court of Appeals did, a fundamental right to engage in homosexual sodomy. This we are quite unwilling to do. It is true that despite the language of the Due Process Clauses of the Fifth and Fourteenth Amendments, which appears to focus only on the processes by which life, liberty, or property is taken, the cases are legion in which those Clauses have been interpreted to have substantive content, subsuming rights that to a great extent are immune from federal or state regulation or proscription. Among such cases are those recognizing rights that have little or no textual support in the constitutional language. . . .

Striving to assure itself and the public that announcing rights not readily identifiable in the Constitution's text involves much more than the imposition of the Justices' own choice of values on the States and the Federal Government, the Court has sought to identify the nature of the rights qualifying for heightened judicial protection. In Palko v. Connecticut (1937), it was said that this category includes those fundamental liberties that are "implicit in the concept of ordered liberty," such that "neither liberty nor justice would exist if [they] were sacrificed." A different description of fundamental liberties appeared in Moore v. East Cleveland (1977) (opinion of POWELL, J.), where they are characterized as those liberties that are "deeply rooted in this Nation's history and tradition."

It is obvious to us that neither of these formulations would extend a fundamental right to homosexuals to engage in acts of consensual sodomy. Proscriptions against that conduct have ancient roots. Sodomy was a criminal offense at common law and was forbidden by the laws of the original thirteen States when they ratified the Bill of Rights. In 1868, when the Fourteenth Amendment was ratified, all but 5 of the 37 States in the Union had criminal sodomy laws. In fact, until 1961, all 50 States outlawed sodomy, and today, 24 States and the District of Columbia continue to provide criminal penalties for sodomy performed in private and between consenting adults. Against this background, to claim that a right to engage in such conduct is "deeply rooted in this Nation's history and tradition" or "implicit in the concept of ordered liberty" is, at best, facetious.

Nor are we inclined to take a more expansive view of our authority to discover new fundamental rights imbedded in the Due Process Clause. The Court is most vulnerable and comes nearest to illegitimacy when it deals with judge-made constitutional law having little or no cognizable roots in the language or design of the Constitution. . . .

Respondent, however, asserts that the result should be different where the homosexual conduct occurs in the privacy of the home. He relies on Stanley v. Georgia (1969), where the Court held that the First Amendment prevents conviction for possessing and reading obscene material in the privacy of his home: "If the First Amendment means anything, it means that a State has no business telling a man, sitting alone in his house, what books he may read or what films he may watch."

Stanley did protect conduct that would not have been protected outside the home, and it partially prevented the enforcement of state obscenity laws; but the decision was firmly grounded in the First Amendment. The right pressed upon us here has no similar support in the text of the Constitution, and it does not qualify for recognition under the prevailing principles for construing the Fourteenth Amendment. Its limits are also difficult to discern. Plainly enough, otherwise illegal conduct is not always immunized whenever it occurs in the home. Victimless crimes, such as the possession and use of illegal drugs, do not escape the law where they are committed at home. *Stanley* itself recognized that its holding offered no protection for the possession in the home of drugs, firearms, or stolen goods. And if respondent's submission is limited to the voluntary sexual conduct between consenting adults, it would be difficult, except by fiat, to limit the claimed right to homosexual conduct while leaving exposed to prosecution adultery, incest, and other sexual crimes even though they are committed in the home. We are unwilling to start down that road.

Even if the conduct at issue here is not a fundamental right, respondent asserts that there must be a rational basis for the law and that there is none in this case other than the presumed belief of a majority of the electorate in Georgia that homosexual sodomy is immoral and unacceptable. This is said to be an inadequate rationale to support the law. The law, however, is constantly based on notions of morality, and if all laws representing essentially moral choices are to be invalidated under the Due Process Clause, the courts will be very busy indeed. Even respondent makes no such claim, but insists that majority sentiments about the morality of homosexuality should be declared inadequate. We do not agree, and are unpersuaded that the sodomy laws of some 25 States should be invalidated on this basis.

Accordingly, the judgment of the Court of Appeals is

Reversed.

CHIEF JUSTICE BURGER concurring.

I join the Court's opinion, but I write separately to underscore my view that in constitutional terms there is no such thing as a fundamental right to commit homosexual sodomy.

As the Court notes, the proscriptions against sodomy have very "ancient roots." Decisions of individuals relating to homosexual conduct have been subject to state intervention throughout the history of Western Civilization. Condemnation of those practices is firmly rooted in Judaeo–Christian moral and ethical standards. Homosexual sodomy was a capital crime under Roman law. During the English Reformation when powers of the ecclesiastical courts were transferred to the King's Courts, the first English statute criminalizing sodomy was passed. Blackstone described "the infamous crime against nature" as an offense of "deeper malignity" than rape, and heinous act "the very mention of which is a disgrace to human nature," and "a crime not fit to be named." The common law of England, including its prohibition of sodomy, became the received law of Georgia and the other Colonies. In 1816 the Georgia Legislature passed the statute at issue here, and that statute has been continuously in force in one form or another since that time. To hold that the act of homosexual sodomy is somehow protected as a fundamental right would be to cast aside millennia of moral teaching.

This is essentially not a question of personal "preferences" but rather of the legislative authority of the State. I find nothing in the Constitution depriving a State of the power to enact the statute challenged here.

[Justice Powell's concurring opinion is omitted.]

JUSTICE BLACKMUN, with whom JUSTICE BRENNAN, JUSTICE MARSHALL, and JUSTICE STEVENS join, dissenting.

This case is no more about "a fundamental right to engage in homosexual sodomy," as the Court purports to declare, than Stanley v. Georgia (1969), was about a fundamental right to watch obscene movies, or Katz v. United States, 389 U.S. 347, 88 S.Ct. 507, 19 L.Ed.2d 576 (1967), was about a fundamental right to place interstate bets from a telephone booth. Rather, this case is about "the most comprehensive of rights and the right most valued by civilized men," namely, "the right to be let alone." Olmstead v. United States, 277 U.S. 438, 478, 48 S.Ct. 564, 572, 72 L.Ed. 944 (1928) (Brandeis, J., dissenting).

The statute at issue, denies individuals the right to decide for themselves whether to engage in particular forms of private, consensual sexual activity. The Court concludes that § 16–6–2 is valid essentially because "the laws of . . . many States . . . still make such conduct illegal and have done so for a very long time." But the fact that the moral judgments expressed by statutes like § 16–6–2 may be "natural and familiar . . . ought not to conclude our judgment upon the question whether statutes embodying them conflict with the Constitution of the United States." Like Justice Holmes, I believe that "[i]t is revolting to have no better reason for a rule of law than that so it was laid down in the time of Henry IV. It is still more revolting if the grounds upon which it was laid down have vanished long since, and the rule simply persists from blind imitation of the past." Holmes, The Path of the Law, 10 Harv.L.Rev. 457, 469 (1897). I believe we must analyze respondent's claim in the light of the values that underlie the constitutional right to privacy. If that right means anything, it means that, before Georgia can prosecute its citizens for making choices about the most intimate aspects of their lives, it must do more than assert that the choice they have made is an " 'abominable crime not fit to be named among Christians.' "

I

In its haste to reverse the Court of Appeals and hold that the Constitution does not "confe[r] a fundamental right upon homosexuals to engage in sodomy," the Court relegates the actual statute being challenged to a footnote and ignores the procedural posture of the case before it. A fair reading of the statute and of the complaint clearly reveals that the majority has distorted the question this case presents.

First, the Court's almost obsessive focus on homosexual activity is particularly hard to justify in light of the broad language Georgia has used. Unlike the Court, the Georgia Legislature has not proceeded on the assumption that homosexuals are so different from other citizens that their lives may be controlled in a way that would not be tolerated if it limited the choices of those other citizens. Rather, Georgia has provided that "[a] person commits the offense of sodomy when he performs or submits to any sexual act involving the sex organs of one person and the mouth or anus of another." The sex or status of the persons who engage in the act is irrelevant as a matter of state law. In fact, to the extent I can discern a legislative purpose for Georgia's 1968 enactment of § 16–6–2, that purpose seems to have been to broaden the coverage of the law to reach heterosexual as well as homosexual activity. . . . Michael Hardwick's standing may rest in significant part on Georgia's apparent willingness to enforce against homosexuals a law it seems not to have any desire to enforce against heterosexuals. But his claim that § 16–6–2 involves an unconstitutional intrusion into his privacy and his right of intimate association does not depend in any way on his sexual orientation.

Second, I disagree with the Court's refusal to consider whether § 16–6–2 runs afoul of the Eighth or Ninth Amendments or the Equal Protection Clause of the Fourteenth Amendment. Respondent's complaint expressly invoked the Ninth Amendment, and he relied heavily before this Court on Griswold v. Connecticut, which identifies that Amendment as one of the specific constitutional provisions giving "life and substance" to our understanding of privacy. More importantly, the procedural posture of the case requires that we affirm the Court of Appeals' judgment if there is *any* ground on which respondent may be entitled to relief. This case is before us on petitioner's motion to dismiss for failure to state a claim, Fed.Rule Civ.Proc. 12(b)(6). It is a well settled principle of law that "a complaint should not be dismissed merely because a plaintiff's allegations do not support the particular legal theory he advances, for the court is under a duty to examine the complaint to determine if the allegations provide for relief on any possible theory." Thus, even if respondent did not advance claims based on the Eighth or Ninth Amendments, or on the Equal Protection Clause, his complaint should not be dismissed if any of those provisions could entitle him to relief. I need not reach either the Eighth Amendment or the Equal Protection Clause issues because I believe that Hardwick has stated a cognizable claim that § 16–6–2 interferes with constitutionally protected interests in privacy and freedom of intimate association. . . . The Court's cramped reading of the issue before it makes for a short opinion, but it does little to make for a persuasive one.

II

Our cases long have recognized that the Constitution embodies a promise that a certain private sphere of individual liberty will be kept largely beyond the reach of government. In construing the right to privacy, the Court has proceeded along two somewhat distinct, albeit complementary, lines. First, it has recognized a privacy interest with reference to certain *decisions* that are properly for the individual to make. Second, it has recognized a privacy interest with reference to certain *places* without regard for the particular activities in which the individuals who occupy them are engaged. The case before us implicates both the decisional and the spatial aspects of the right to privacy.

A

The Court concludes today that none of our prior cases dealing with various decisions that individuals are entitled to make free of governmental interference "bears any resemblance to the claimed constitutional right of homosexuals to engage in acts of sodomy that is asserted in this case." While it is true that these cases may be characterized by their connection to protection of the family, the Court's conclusion that they extend no further than this boundary ignores the warning in Moore v. East Cleveland (1977) (plurality opinion), against "clos[ing] our eyes to the basic reasons why certain rights associated with the family have been accorded shelter under the Fourteenth Amendment's Due Process Clause." We protect those rights not because they contribute, in some direct and material way, to the general public welfare, but because they form so central a part of an individual's life. "[T]he concept of privacy embodies the 'moral fact that a person belongs to himself and not others nor to society as a whole.'" And so we protect the decision whether to marry precisely because marriage "is an association that promotes a way of life, not causes; a harmony in living, not political faiths; a bilateral loyalty, not commercial or social projects." We protect the decision whether to have a child because parenthood alters so dramatically an individual's self-definition, not because of demographic considerations or the Bible's command to be fruitful and multiply. And we protect the family because it contributes so powerfully to the happiness of individuals, not because of a preference for stereotypical households. . . .

Only the most willful blindness could obscure the fact that sexual intimacy is "a sensitive, key relationship of human existence, central to family life, community welfare, and the development of human personality," Paris Adult Theatre I v. Slaton, 413 U.S. 49, 63, 93 S.Ct. 2628, 2638, 37 L.Ed.2d 446 (1973). The fact that individuals define themselves in a significant way through their intimate sexual relationships with others suggests, in a Nation as diverse as ours, that there may be many "right" ways of conducting those relationships, and that much of the richness of a relationship will come from the freedom an individual has to *choose* the form and nature of these intensely personal bonds.

In a variety of circumstances we have recognized that a necessary corollary of giving individuals freedom to choose how to conduct their lives is acceptance of the fact that different individuals will make different choices. For example, in holding that the clearly important state interest in public education should give way to a competing claim by the Amish to the effect that extended formal schooling threatened their way of life, the Court declared: "There can be no assumption that today's majority is 'right' and the Amish and others like them are 'wrong.' A way of life that is odd or even erratic but interferes with no rights or interests of others is not to be condemned because it is different." Wisconsin v. Yoder, 406 U.S. 205, 223–224, 92 S.Ct. 1526, 1537, 32 L.Ed.2d 15 (1972). The Court claims that its decision today merely refuses to recognize a fundamental right to engage in homosexual sodomy; what the Court really has refused to recognize is the fundamental interest all individuals have in controlling the nature of their intimate associations with others.

B

The behavior for which Hardwick faces prosecution occurred in his own home, a place to which the Fourth Amendment attaches special significance. The Court's treatment of this aspect of the case is symptomatic of its overall refusal to consider the broad principles that have informed our treatment of privacy in specific cases. Just as the right to privacy is more than the mere aggregation of a number of entitlements to engage in specific behavior, so too, protecting the physical integrity of the home is more than merely a means of protecting specific activities that often take place there. Even when our understanding of the contours of the right to privacy depends on "reference to a 'place,' " "the essence of a Fourth Amendment violation is 'not the breaking of [a person's] doors, and the rummaging of his drawers,' but rather is 'the invasion of his indefeasible right of personal security, personal liberty and private property.' "

The Court's interpretation of the pivotal case of Stanley v. Georgia is entirely unconvincing. Stanley held that Georgia's undoubted power to punish the public distribution of constitutionally unprotected, obscene material did not permit the State to punish the private possession of such material. According to the majority here, Stanley relied entirely on the First Amendment, and thus, it is claimed, sheds no light on cases not involving printed materials. But that is not what Stanley said. Rather, the Stanley Court anchored its holding in the Fourth Amendment's special protection for the individual in his home:

" 'The makers of our Constitution undertook to secure conditions favorable to the pursuit of happiness. They recognized the significance of man's spiritual nature, of his feelings and of his intellect. They knew that only a part of the pain, pleasure and satisfactions of life are to be found in material things. They sought to protect Americans in their beliefs, their thoughts, their emotions and their sensations.'

* * *

"These are the rights that appellant is asserting in the case before us. He is asserting the right to read or observe what he pleases—the right to satisfy his intellectual and emotional needs in the privacy of his own home."

The central place that *Stanley* gives Justice Brandeis' dissent in *Olmstead,* a case raising *no* First Amendment claim, shows that *Stanley* rested as much on the Court's understanding of the Fourth Amendment as it did on the First. Indeed, in Paris Adult Theatre I v. Slaton the Court suggested that reliance on the Fourth Amendment not only supported the Court's outcome in *Stanley* but actually was *necessary* to it: "If obscene material unprotected by the First Amendment in itself carried with it a 'penumbra' of constitutionally protected privacy, this Court would not have found it necessary to decide *Stanley* on the narrow basis of the 'privacy of the home,' which was hardly more than a reaffirmation that 'a man's home is his castle.'" "The right of the people to be secure in their . . . houses," expressly guaranteed by the Fourth Amendment, is perhaps the most "textual" of the various constitutional provisions that inform our understanding of the right to privacy, and thus I cannot agree with the Court's statement that "[t]he right pressed upon us here has no support in the text of the Constitution." Indeed, the right of an individual to conduct intimate relationships in the intimacy of his or her own home seems to me to be the heart of the Constitution's protection of privacy.

III

The Court's failure to comprehend the magnitude of the liberty interests at stake in this case leads it to slight the question whether petitioner, on behalf of the State, has justified Georgia's infringement on these interests. I believe that neither of the two general justifications for § 16–6–2 that petitioner has advanced warrants dismissing respondent's challenge for failure to state a claim.

First, petitioner asserts that the acts made criminal by the statute may have serious adverse consequences for "the general public health and welfare," such as spreading communicable diseases or fostering other criminal activity. Inasmuch as this case was dismissed by the District Court on the pleadings, it is not surprising that the record before us is barren of any evidence to support petitioner's claim. In light of the state of the record, I see no justification for the Court's attempt to equate the private, consensual sexual activity at issue here with the "possession in the home of drugs, firearms, or stolen goods," to which *Stanley* refused to extend its protection. None of the behavior so mentioned in *Stanley* can properly be viewed as "[v]ictimless," drugs and weapons are inherently dangerous, and for property to be "stolen," someone must have been wrongfully deprived of it. Nothing in the record before the Court provides any justification for finding the activity forbidden by § 16–6–2 to be physically dangerous, either to the persons engaged in it or to others.

The core of petitioner's defense of § 16–6–2, however, is that respondent and others who engage in the conduct prohibited by § 16–6–2 interfere with Georgia's exercise of the "'right of the Nation and of the States to maintain a decent society.'" Essentially, petitioner argues, and the Court agrees that the fact that the acts described in § 16–6–2 "for hundreds of years, if not thousands, have been uniformly condemned as immoral" is a sufficient reason to permit a State to ban them today. I cannot agree that either the length of time a majority has held its convictions or the passions with which it defends them can withdraw legislation from this Court's scrutiny. As Justice Jackson wrote so eloquently for the Court in West Virginia Board of Education v. Barnette, 319 U.S. 624, 641–642, 63 S.Ct. 1178, 1187, 87 L.Ed. 1628 (1943), "we apply the limitations of the Constitution with no fear that freedom to be intellectually and spiritually diverse or even contrary will disintegrate the social organization. . . . [F]reedom to differ is not limited to things that do not matter much. That would be a mere shadow of freedom. The test of its substance is the right to differ as to things that touch the heart of the existing order." It is precisely because the issue raised by this case touches the heart of what makes individuals what they are that we should be especially sensitive to the rights of those whose choices upset the majority.

The assertion that "traditional Judeo–Christian values proscribe" the conduct involved, cannot provide an adequate justification for § 16–6–2. That certain, but by no means all, religious groups condemn the behavior at issue gives the State no license to impose their judgments on the entire citizenry. The legitimacy of secular legislation depends instead on whether the State can advance some justification for its law beyond its conformity to religious doctrine. Thus, far from buttressing his case, petitioner's invocation of Leviticus, Romans, St. Thomas Aquinas, and sodomy's heretical status during the Middle Ages undermines his suggestion that § 16–6–2 represents a legitimate use of secular coercive power.[1] A State can no more punish private behavior because of religious intolerance than it can punish such behavior because of racial animus. "The Constitution cannot control such prejudices, but neither can it tolerate them. Private biases may be outside the reach of the law, but the law, cannot, directly or indirectly give them effect." Palmore v. Sidoti, 466 U.S. 429, 433, 104 S.Ct. 1879, 1882, 80 L.Ed.2d 421 (1984). No matter how uncomfortable a certain group may make the majority of this Court, we have held that "[m]ere public intolerance or animosity cannot constitutionally justify the deprivation of a person's physical liberty."

*   *   *

---

1. The theological nature of the origin of Anglo–American antisodomy statutes is patent. It was not until 1533 that sodomy was made a secular offense in England. 25 Hen. VIII, cap. 6. Until that time, the offense was, in Sir James Stephen's words, "merely ecclesiastical." 2 J. Stephen, A History of the Criminal Law of England 430 (1883). Pollock and Maitland similarly observed that "[t]he crime against nature . . . was so closely connected with heresy that the vulgar had but one name for both." 2 F. Pollock & F. Maitland, The History of English Law 554 (1895). The transfer of jurisdiction over prosecutions for sodomy to the secular courts seems primarily due to the alteration of ecclesiastical jurisdiction attendant on England's break with the Roman Catholic Church, rather than to any new understanding of the sovereign's interest in preventing or punishing the behavior involved. Cf. E. Coke, The Third Part of the Institutes of the Laws of England, ch. 10 (4th ed. 1797).

This case involves no real interference with the rights of others, for the mere knowledge that other individuals do not adhere to one's value system cannot be a legally cognizable interest, let alone an interest that can justify invading the houses, hearts, and minds of citizens who choose to live their lives differently.

IV

It took but three years for the Court to see the error in its analysis in Minersville School District v. Gobitis, 310 U.S. 586, 60 S.Ct. 1010, 84 L.Ed. 1375 (1940), and to recognize that the threat to national cohesion posed by a refusal to salute the flag was vastly outweighed by the threat to those same values posed by compelling such a salute. I can only hope that here, too, the Court soon will reconsider its analysis and conclude that depriving individuals of the right to choose for themselves how to conduct their intimate relationships poses a far greater threat to the values most deeply rooted in our Nation's history than tolerance of nonconformity could ever do. Because I think the Court today betrays those values, I dissent.

JUSTICE STEVENS, with whom JUSTICE BRENNAN and JUSTICE MARSHALL join, dissenting.

Like the statute that is challenged in this case, the rationale of the Court's opinion applies equally to the prohibited conduct regardless of whether the parties who engage in it are married or unmarried, or are of the same or different sexes. Sodomy was condemned as an odious and sinful type of behavior during the formative period of the common law. That condemnation was equally damning for heterosexual and homosexual sodomy. Moreover, it provided no special exemption for married couples. The license to cohabit and to produce legitimate offspring simply did not include any permission to engage in sexual conduct that was considered a "crime against nature."

The history of the Georgia statute before us clearly reveals this traditional prohibition of heterosexual, as well as homosexual, sodomy. Indeed, at one point in the 20th century, Georgia's law was construed to permit certain sexual conduct between homosexual women even though such conduct was prohibited between heterosexuals. The history of the statutes cited by the majority as proof for the proposition that sodomy is not constitutionally protected, similarly reveals a prohibition on heterosexual, as well as homosexual, sodomy.

Because the Georgia statute expresses the traditional view that sodomy is an immoral kind of conduct regardless of the identity of the persons who engage in it, I believe that a proper analysis of its constitutionality requires consideration of two questions: First, may a State totally prohibit the described conduct by means of a neutral law applying without exception to all persons subject to its jurisdiction? If not may the State save the statute by announcing that it will only enforce the law against homosexuals? The two questions merit separate discussion.

I

Our prior cases make two propositions abundantly clear. First, the fact that the governing majority in a State has traditionally viewed a particular practice as immoral is not a sufficient reason for upholding a law prohibiting the practice; neither history nor tradition could save a law prohibiting miscegenation from constitutional attack. Second, individual decisions by married persons, concerning the intimacies of their physical relationship, even when not intended to produce offspring, are a form of "liberty" protected by the Due Process Clause of the Fourteenth Amendment. Moreover, this protection extends to intimate choices by unmarried as well as married persons.

In consideration of claims of this kind, the Court has emphasized the individual interest in privacy, but its decisions have actually been animated by an even more fundamental concern. As I wrote some years ago:

"These cases do not deal with the individual's interest in protection from unwarranted public attention, comment, or exploitation. They deal, rather, with the individual's right to make certain unusually important decisions that will affect his own, or his family's, destiny. The Court has referred to such decisions as implicating 'basic values,' as being 'fundamental,' and as being dignified by history and tradition. The character of the Court's language in these cases brings to mind the origins of the American heritage of freedom—the abiding interest in individual liberty that makes certain state intrusions on the citizen's right to decide how he will live his own life intolerable. Guided by history, our tradition of respect for the dignity of individual choice in matters of conscience and the restraints implicit in the federal system, federal judges have accepted the responsibility for recognition and protection of these rights in appropriate cases."

Society has every right to encourage its individual members to follow particular traditions in expressing affection for one another and in gratifying their personal desires. It, of course, may prohibit an individual from imposing his will on another to satisfy his own selfish interests. It also may prevent an individual from interfering with, or violating, a legally sanctioned and protected relationship, such as marriage. And it may explain the relative advantages and disadvantages of different forms of intimate expression. But when individual married couples are isolated from observation by others, the way in which they voluntarily choose to conduct their intimate relations is a matter for them—not the State—to decide. The essential "liberty" that animated the development of the law in cases like *Griswold, Eisenstadt,* and *Carey* surely embraces the right to engage in nonreproductive, sexual conduct that others may consider offensive or immoral.

Paradoxical as it may seem, our prior cases thus establish that a State may not prohibit sodomy within "the sacred precincts of marital bedrooms," or, indeed, between unmarried heterosexual adults. In all events, it is perfectly clear that the State of Georgia may not totally prohibit the conduct proscribed by § 16–6–2 of the Georgia Criminal Code.

II

If the Georgia statute cannot be enforced as it is written—if the conduct it seeks to prohibit is a protected form of liberty for the vast majority of Georgia's citizens—the State must assume the burden of justifying a selective application of its law. Either the persons to whom Georgia seeks to apply its statute do not have the same interest in "liberty" that others have, or there must be a reason why the State may be permitted to apply a generally applicable law to certain persons that it does not apply to others.

The first possibility is plainly unacceptable. Although the meaning of the principle that "all men are created equal" is not always clear, it surely must mean that every free citizen has the same interest in "liberty" that the members of the majority share. From the standpoint of the individual, the homosexual and the heterosexual have the same interest in deciding how he will live his own life, and more narrowly, how he will conduct himself in his personal and voluntary associations with his companions. State intrusion into the private conduct of either is equally burdensome.

The second possibility is similarly unacceptable. A policy of selective application must be supported by a neutral and legitimate interest—something more substantial than a habitual dislike for, or ignorance about, the disfavored group. Neither the State nor the Court has identified any such interest in this case. The Court has posited as a justification for the Georgia statute "the presumed belief of a majority of the electorate in Georgia that homosexual sodomy is immoral and unacceptable." But the Georgia electorate has expressed no such belief—instead, its representatives enacted a law that presumably reflects the belief that *all sodomy* is immoral and unacceptable. Unless the Court is prepared to conclude that such a law is constitutional, it may not rely on the work product of the Georgia Legislature to support its holding. For the Georgia statute does not single out homosexuals as a separate class meriting special disfavored treatment.

Nor, indeed, does the Georgia prosecutor even believe that all homosexuals who violate this statute should be punished. This conclusion is evident from the fact that the respondent in this very case has formally acknowledged in his complaint and in court that he has engaged, and intends to continue to engage, in the prohibited conduct, yet the State has elected not to process criminal charges against him. As JUSTICE POWELL points out, moreover, Georgia's prohibition on private, consensual sodomy has not been enforced for decades. The record of nonenforcement, in this case and in the last several decades, belies the Attorney General's representations about the importance of the State's selective application of its generally applicable law.

Both the Georgia statute and the Georgia prosecutor thus completely fail to provide the Court with any support for the conclusion that homosexual sodomy, *simpliciter,* is considered unacceptable conduct in that State, and that the burden of justifying a selective application of the generally applicable law has been met.

III

The Court orders the dismissal of respondent's complaint even though the State's statute prohibits all sodomy; even though that prohibition is concededly unconstitutional with respect to heterosexuals; and even though the State's *post hoc* explanations for selective application are belied by the State's own actions. At the very least, I think it clear at this early stage of the litigation that respondent has alleged a constitutional claim sufficient to withstand a motion to dismiss.

I respectfully dissent.

NOTES

1. In People v. Onofre, 51 N.Y.2d 476, 434 N.Y.S.2d 947, 415 N.E.2d 936 (1980), cert. denied 451 U.S. 987, 101 S.Ct. 2323 (1981), the New York Court of Appeals struck down as an unconstitutional invasion of the right of privacy, New York's penal law that makes consensual sodomy a crime. In doing so, the court's majority relied principally on federal constitutional rights, the *Griswold* and Eisenstadt v. Baird cases and other United States Supreme Court decisions.

Does the fact that the United States Supreme Court denied the petition for a writ of certiorari indicate approval with the New York Court's interpretation of federal constitutional principles? What is the status of a decision such as the *Onofre* case in the aftermath of Bowers v. Hardwick?

2. In People v. Uplinger, 58 N.Y.2d 936, 460 N.Y.S.2d 514, 447 N.E.2d 62 (1983), the New York Court of Appeals, relying on the *Onofre* decision, struck down a statute that prohibits loitering "in a public place for the purpose of engaging or soliciting another person to engage, in deviate sexual intercourse, or other sexual behavior of a deviate nature." The majority noted that the purpose of the statute was "to punish conduct anticipatory to the act of consensual sodomy." Inasmuch as the acts that are contemplated have been decriminalized in the *Onofre* decision, the court saw no reason to continue punishing loitering for that purpose.

The United States Supreme Court granted certiorari to review the case of New York v. Uplinger, but then, in 1984, in a per curiam order, over three dissents, dismissed the writ of certiorari as improvidently granted. See 467 U.S. 246, 104 S.Ct. 2332, 81 L.Ed.2d 201 (1984).

3. In Carey v. Population Services International, 431 U.S. 678, 97 S.Ct. 2010 (1977), the Court affirmed the invalidation of the New York Education Law sections which make it a crime (1) for any person to sell or distribute any contraceptive of any kind to a minor under 16; (2) for anyone other than a

licensed pharmacist to distribute contraceptives to persons 16 or over; and (3) for anyone, including licensed pharmacists to advertise or display contraceptives. As is customary in cases on this issue, the views of the various members of the Court are widely divergent. Six different opinions were written in this case. (The opinion of the Court was written by Mr. Justice Brennan; one portion thereof, however, was concurred in by only three additional justices.)

4. Article 8 of the European Convention on Human Rights provides:

1. Everyone has the right to respect for his private and family life, his home and his correspondence.

2. There shall be no interference by a public authority with the exercise of this right except such as is in accordance with the law and is necessary in a democratic society in the interests of national security, public safety or the economic well-being of the country, for the prevention of disorder or crime, for the protection of health or morals, or for the protection of the rights and freedoms of others.

D. THE PROHIBITION AGAINST CRUEL AND UNUSUAL PUNISHMENT

1. PUNISHMENT FOR NARCOTIC ADDICTION AND ALCOHOLISM

ROBINSON v. CALIFORNIA

Supreme Court of the United States, 1962.
370 U.S. 660, 82 S.Ct. 1417, 8 L.Ed.2d 758.

MR. JUSTICE STEWART delivered the opinion of the Court.

A California statute makes it a criminal offense for a person to "be addicted to the use of narcotics." [1] This appeal draws into question the constitutionality of that provision of the state law, as construed by the California courts in the present case.

The appellant was convicted after a jury trial in the Municipal Court of Los Angeles. The evidence against him was given by two Los Angeles police officers. Officer Brown testified that he had had occasion to examine the appellant's arms one evening on a street in Los Angeles some four months before the trial. The officer testified that at that time he had observed "scar tissue and discoloration on the inside"

---

1. The statute is § 11721 of the California Health and Safety Code. It provides:

"No person shall use, or be under the influence of, or be addicted to the use of narcotics, excepting when administered by or under the direction of a person licensed by the State to prescribe and administer narcotics. It shall be the burden of the defense to show that it comes within the exception. Any person convicted of violating any provision of this section is guilty of a misdemeanor and shall be sentenced to serve a term of not less than 90 days nor more than one year in the county jail. The court may place a person convicted hereunder on probation for a period not to exceed five years and shall in all cases in which probation is granted require as a condition thereof that such person be confined in the county jail for at least 90 days. In no event does the court have the power to absolve a person who violates this section from the obligation of spending at least 90 days in confinement in the county jail."

of the appellant's right arm, and "what appeared to be numerous needle marks and a scab which was approximately three inches below the crook of the elbow" on the appellant's left arm. The officer also testified that the appellant under questioning had admitted to the occasional use of narcotics.

Officer Lindquist testified that he had examined the appellant the following morning in the Central Jail in Los Angeles. The officer stated that at that time he had observed discolorations and scabs on the appellant's arms, and he identified photographs which had been taken of the appellant's arms shortly after his arrest the night before. Based upon more than ten years of experience as a member of the Narcotic Division of the Los Angeles Police Department, the witness gave his opinion that "these marks and the discoloration were the result of the injection of hypodermic needles into the tissue into the vein that was not sterile." He stated that the scabs were several days old at the time of his examination, and that the appellant was neither under the influence of narcotics nor suffering withdrawal symptoms at the time he saw him. This witness also testified that the appellant had admitted using narcotics in the past.

The appellant testified in his own behalf, denying the alleged conversations with the police officers and denying that he had ever used narcotics or been addicted to their use. He explained the marks on his arms as resulting from an allergic condition contracted during his military service. His testimony was corroborated by two witnesses.

The trial judge instructed the jury that the statute made it a misdemeanor for a person "either to use narcotics, or to be addicted to the use of narcotics * * * That portion of the statute referring to the 'use' of narcotics is based upon the 'act' of using. That portion of the statute referring to 'addicted to the use' of narcotics is based upon a condition or status. They are not identical. * * * To be addicted to the use of narcotics is said to be a status or condition and not an act. It is a continuing offense and differs from most other offenses in the fact that [it] is chronic rather than acute; that it continues after it is complete and subjects the offender to arrest at any time before he reforms. The existence of such a chronic condition may be ascertained from a single examination, if the characteristic reactions of that condition be found present."

The judge further instructed the jury that the appellant could be convicted under a general verdict if the jury agreed *either* that he was of the "status" *or* had committed the "act" denounced by the statute. "All that the People must show is either that the defendant did use a narcotic in Los Angeles County, or that while in the City of Los Angeles he was addicted to the use of narcotics * * *."

Under these instructions the jury returned a verdict finding the appellant "guilty of the offense charged." An appeal was taken to the Appellate Department of the Los Angeles County Superior Court, "the highest court of a State in which a decision could be had" in this case. . . . Although expressing some doubt as to the constitutionality of "the crime of being a narcotic addict," the reviewing court in an unreported opinion affirmed the judgment of conviction, citing two of its own previous unreported decisions which had upheld the constitutionality of the statute. We noted probable jurisdiction of this appeal . . . because it squarely presents the issue whether the statute as construed by the California courts in this case is repugnant to the Fourteenth Amendment of the Constitution.

The broad power of a State to regulate the narcotic drugs traffic within its borders is not here in issue. More than forty years ago, in Whipple v. Martinson, 256 U.S. 41, 41 S.Ct. 425, 65 L.Ed. 819, this Court explicitly recognized the validity of that power: "There can be no question of the authority of the state in the exercise of its police power to regulate the administration, sale, prescription and use of dangerous and habit-forming drugs * * *. The right to exercise this power is so manifest in the interest of the public health and welfare, that it is unnecessary to enter upon a discussion of it beyond saying that it is too firmly established to be successfully called in question." . . .

Such regulation, it can be assumed, could take a variety of valid forms. A State might impose criminal sanctions, for example, against the unauthorized manufacture, prescription, sale, purchase, or possession of narcotics within its borders. In the interest of discouraging the violation of such laws, or in the interest of the general health or welfare of its inhabitants, a State might establish a program of compulsory treatment for those addicted to narcotics.[2] Such a program of treatment might require periods of involuntary confinement. And penal sanctions might be imposed for failure to comply with established compulsory treatment procedures. . . . Or a State might choose to attack the evils of narcotics traffic on broader fronts also—through public health education, for example, or by efforts to ameliorate the economic and social conditions under which those evils might be thought to flourish. In short, the range of valid choice which a State might make in this area is undoubtedly a wide one, and the wisdom of any particular choice within the allowable spectrum is not for us to decide. Upon that premise we turn to the California law in issue here.

It would be possible to construe the statute under which the appellant was convicted as one which is operative only upon proof of the actual use of narcotics within the State's jurisdiction. But the California courts have not so construed this law. Although there was evidence in the present case that the appellant had used narcotics in Los Angeles, the jury were instructed that they could convict him even if they disbelieved that evidence. The appellant could be convicted, they were told, if they found simply that the appellant's "status" or "chronic condition" was that of being "addicted to the use of narcotics."

---

2. California appears to have established just such a program in §§ 5350–5361 of its Welfare and Institutions Code. The record contains no explanation of why the civil procedures authorized by this legislation were not utilized in the present case.

And it is impossible to know from the jury's verdict that the defendant was not convicted upon precisely such a finding.

The instructions of the trial court, implicitly approved on appeal, amounted to "a ruling on a question of state law that is as binding on us as though the precise words had been written" into the statute. Terminiello v. Chicago, 337 U.S. 1, 4, 69 S.Ct. 894, 895, 93 L.Ed. 1131. "We can only take the statute as the state courts read it." Id., at 6, 69 S.Ct. at 896. Indeed, in their brief in this Court counsel for the State have emphasized that it is "the proof of addiction by circumstantial evidence * * * by the tell-tale track of needle marks and scabs over the veins of his arms, that remains the gist of the section."

This statute, therefore, is not one which punishes a person for the use of narcotics, for their purchase, sale or possession, or for antisocial or disorderly behavior resulting from their administration. It is not a law which even purports to provide or require medical treatment. Rather, we deal with a statute which makes the "status" of narcotic addiction a criminal offense, for which the offender may be prosecuted "at any time before he reforms". California has said that a person can be continuously guilty of this offense, whether or not he has ever used or possessed any narcotics within the State, and whether or not he has been guilty of any antisocial behavior there.

It is unlikely that any State at this moment in history would attempt to make it a criminal offense for a person to be mentally ill, or a leper, or to be afflicted with a venereal disease. A State might determine that the general health and welfare require that the victims of these and other human afflictions be dealt with by compulsory treatment, involving quarantine, confinement, or sequestration. But, in the light of contemporary human knowledge, a law which made a criminal offense of such a disease would doubtless be universally thought to be an infliction of cruel and unusual punishment in violation of the Eighth and Fourteenth Amendments. . . .

We cannot but consider the statute before us as of the same category. In this Court counsel for the State recognized that narcotic addiction is an illness. Indeed, it is apparently an illness which may be contracted innocently or involuntarily.[3] We hold that a state law which imprisons a person thus afflicted as a criminal, even though he has never touched any narcotic drug within the State or been guilty of any irregular behavior there, inflicts a cruel and unusual punishment in violation of the Fourteenth Amendment. To be sure, imprisonment for ninety days is not, in the abstract, a punishment which is either cruel or unusual. But the question cannot be considered in the abstract. Even one day in prison would be a cruel and unusual punishment for the "crime" of having a common cold.

3. Not only may addiction innocently result from the use of medically prescribed narcotics, but a person may even be a narcotics addict from the moment of his birth. [citation here to many supporting authorities.]

We are not unmindful that the vicious evils of the narcotics traffic have occasioned the grave concern of government. There are, as we have said, countless fronts on which those evils may be legitimately attacked. We deal in this case only with an individual provision of a particularized local law as it has so far been interpreted by the California courts.

Reversed.

[Mr. Justice Frankfurter took no part in the case. Mr. Justice Douglas' concurring opinion is omitted.]

MR. JUSTICE HARLAN, concurring. I am not prepared to hold that on the present state of medical knowledge it is completely irrational and hence unconstitutional for a State to conclude that narcotics addiction is something other than an illness nor that it amounts to cruel and unusual punishment for the State to subject narcotics addicts to its criminal law. Insofar as addiction may be identified with the use or possession of narcotics within the State (or, I would suppose, without the State), in violation of local statutes prohibiting such acts, it may surely be reached by the State's criminal law. But in this case the trial court's instructions permitted the jury to find the appellant guilty on no more proof than that he was present in California while he was addicted to narcotics. Since addiction alone cannot reasonably be thought to amount to more than a compelling propensity to use narcotics, the effect of this instruction was to authorize criminal punishment for a bare desire to commit a criminal act.

If the California statute reaches this type of conduct, and for present purposes we must accept the trial court's construction as binding, . . . it is an arbitrary imposition which exceeds the power that a State may exercise in enacting its criminal law. Accordingly, I agree that the application of the California statute was unconstitutional in this case and join the judgment of reversal.

MR. JUSTICE CLARK, dissenting. The Court finds § 11721 of California's Health and Safety Code, making it an offense to "be addicted to the use of narcotics," violative of due process as "a cruel and unusual punishment." I cannot agree.

The statute must first be placed in perspective. California has a comprehensive and enlightened program for the control of narcotism based on the overriding policy of prevention and cure. It is the product of an extensive investigation made in the mid-Fifties by a committee of distinguished scientists, doctors, law enforcement officers and laymen appointed by the then Attorney General, now Governor, of California. The committee filed a detailed study entitled "Report on Narcotic Addiction" which was given considerable attention. No recommendation was made therein for the repeal of § 11721, and the State Legislature in its discretion continued the policy of that section.

Apart from prohibiting specific acts such as the purchase, possession and sale of narcotics, California has taken certain legislative steps in regard to the status of being a narcotic addict—a condition commonly recognized as a threat to the State and to the individual. The Code deals with this problem in realistic stages. At its incipiency narcotic addiction is handled under § 11721 of the Health and Safety Code which is at issue here. It provides that a person found to be addicted to the use of narcotics shall serve a term in the county jail of not less than 90 days nor more than one year, with the minimum 90–day confinement applying in all cases without exception. Provision is made for parole with periodic tests to detect readdiction.

The trial court defined "addicted to narcotics" as used in § 11721 in the following charge to the jury:

> "The word 'addicted' means, strongly disposed to some taste or practice or habituated, especially to drugs. In order to inquire as to whether a person is addicted to the use of narcotics is in effect an inquiry as to his habit in that regard. Does he use them habitually? To use them often or daily is, according to the ordinary acceptance of those words, to use them habitually."

There was no suggestion that the term "narcotic addict" as here used included a person who acted without volition or who had lost the power of self-control. Although the section is penal in appearance—perhaps a carry-over from a less sophisticated approach—its present provisions are quite similar to those for civil commitment and treatment of addicts who have lost the power of self-control, and its present purpose is reflected in a statement which closely follows § 11721: "The rehabilitation of narcotic addicts and the prevention of continued addiction to narcotics is a matter of statewide concern." California Health and Safety Code, § 11728.

Where narcotic addiction has progressed beyond the incipient, volitional stage, California provides for commitment of three months to two years in a state hospital. California Welfare and Institutions Code, § 5355. For the purposes of this provision, a narcotic addict is defined as

> "any person who habitually takes or otherwise uses *to the extent of having lost the power of self-control* any opium, morphine, cocaine, or other narcotic drug as defined in Article 1 of Chapter 1 of Division 10 of the Health and Safety Code." California Welfare and Institutions Code, § 5350. (Emphasis supplied.)

This proceeding is clearly civil in nature with a purpose of rehabilitation and cure. Significantly, if it is found that a person committed under § 5355 will not receive substantial benefit from further hospital treatment and is not dangerous to society, he may be discharged—but only after a minimum confinement of three months, § 5355.1.

Thus, the "criminal" provision applies to the incipient narcotic addict who retains self-control, requiring confinement of three months to one year and parole with frequent tests to detect renewed use of drugs. Its overriding purpose is to cure the less seriously addicted person by preventing further use. On the other hand, the "civil" commitment provision deals with addicts who have lost the power of self-control, requiring hospitalization up to two years. Each deals with a different type of addict but with a common purpose. This is most apparent when the sections overlap: if after civil commitment of an addict it is found that hospital treatment will not be helpful, the addict is confined for a minimum period of three months in the same manner as is the volitional addict under the "criminal" provision.

In the instant case the proceedings against the petitioner were brought under the volitional-addict section. There was testimony that he had been using drugs only four months with three to four relatively mild doses a week. At arrest and trial he appeared normal. His testimony was clear and concise, being simply that he had never used drugs. The scabs and pocks on his arms and body were caused, he said, by "overseas shots" administered during army service preparatory to foreign assignment. He was very articulate in his testimony but the jury did not believe him, apparently because he had told the clinical expert while being examined after arrest that he had been using drugs, as I have stated above. The officer who arrested him also testified to like statements and to scabs—some 10 or 15 days old—showing narcotic injections. There was no evidence in the record of withdrawal symptoms. Obviously he could not have been committed under § 5355 as one who had completely "lost the power of self-control." The jury was instructed that narcotic "addiction" as used in § 11721 meant strongly disposed to a taste or practice or habit of its use, indicated by the use of narcotics often or daily. A general verdict was returned against petitioner, and he was ordered confined for 90 days to be followed by a two-year parole during which he was required to take periodic Nalline tests.

The majority strikes down the conviction primarily on the grounds that petitioner was denied due process by the imposition of criminal penalties for nothing more than being in a status. This viewpoint is premised upon the theme that § 11721 is a "criminal" provision authorizing a punishment, for the majority admits that "a State might establish a program of compulsory treatment for those addicted to narcotics" which "might require periods of involuntary confinement." I submit that California has done exactly that. The majority's error is in instructing the California Legislature that hospitalization is the *only treatment* for narcotics addiction—that anything less is a punishment denying due process. California has found otherwise after a study which I suggest was more extensive than that conducted by the Court. Even in California's program for hospital commitment of nonvolitional narcotic addicts—which the majority approves—it is recognized that some addicts will not respond to or do not need hospital treatment. As to these persons its provisions are identical to those of § 11721— confinement for a period of not less than 90 days. Section 11721 provides this confinement as treatment for the volitional addicts to whom its provisions apply, in addition to parole with frequent tests to detect and prevent further use of drugs. The fact that § 11721 might be labeled "criminal" seems irrelevant,[4] not only to the majority's own "treatment" test but to the "concept of ordered liberty" to which the States must attain under the Fourteenth Amendment. The test is the overall purpose and effect of a State's act, and I submit that California's program relative to narcotic addicts—including both the "criminal" and "civil" provisions—is inherently one of treatment and lies well within the power of a State.

However, the case in support of the judgment below need not rest solely on this reading of California law. For even if the overall statutory scheme is ignored and a purpose and effect of punishment is attached to § 11721, that provision still does not violate the Fourteenth Amendment. The majority acknowledges, as it must, that a State can punish persons who purchase, possess or use narcotics. Although none of these acts are harmful to society *in themselves,* the State constitutionally may attempt to deter and prevent them through punishment because of the grave threat of future harmful conduct which they pose. Narcotics addiction—including the incipient, volitional addiction to which this provision speaks—is no different. California courts have taken judicial notice that "the inordinate use of a narcotic drug tends to create an irresistible craving and forms a habit for its continued use until one becomes an addict, and he respects no convention or obligation and will lie, steal, or use any other base means to gratify his passion for the drug, being lost to all considerations of duty or social position." . . . Can this Court deny the legislative and judicial judgment of California that incipient, volitional narcotic addiction poses a threat of serious crime similar to the threat inherent in the purchase or possession of narcotics? And if such a threat is inherent in addiction, can this Court say that California is powerless to deter it by punishment?

It is no answer to suggest that we are dealing with an involuntary status and thus penal sanctions will be ineffective and unfair. The section at issue applies only to persons who use narcotics often or even daily but not to the point of losing self-control. When dealing with involuntary addicts California moves only through § 5355 of its Welfare and Institutions Code which clearly is not penal. Even if it could be argued that § 11721 may not be limited to volitional addicts, the petitioner in the instant case undeniably retained the power of self-control and thus to him the statute would be constitutional. Moreover, "status" offenses have long been known and recognized in the criminal law. A ready example is drunkenness, which plainly is as involuntary after addiction to alcohol as is the taking of drugs.

Nor is the conjecture relevant that petitioner may have acquired his habit under lawful circumstances. There was no suggestion by him

---

4. Any reliance upon the "stigma" of a misdemeanor conviction in this context is misplaced, as it would hardly be different from the stigma of a civil commitment for narcotics addiction.

to this effect at trial, and surely the State need not rebut all possible lawful sources of addiction as part of its prima facie case.

The argument that the statute constitutes a cruel and unusual punishment is governed by the discussion above. Properly construed, the statute provides a treatment rather than a punishment. But even if interpreted as penal, the sanction of incarceration for 3 to 12 months is not unreasonable when applied to a person who has voluntarily placed himself in a condition posing a serious threat to the State. Under either theory, its provisions for 3 to 12 months' confinement can hardly be deemed unreasonable when compared to the provisions for 3 to 24 months' confinement under § 5355 which the majority approves.

I would affirm the judgment.

Mr. Justice White, dissenting. If appellant's conviction rested upon sheer status, condition or illness or if he was convicted for being an addict who had lost his power of self-control, I would have other thoughts about this case. But this record presents neither situation. And I believe the Court has departed from its wise rule of not deciding constitutional questions except where necessary and from its equally sound practice of construing state statutes, where possible, in a manner saving their constitutionality.

I am not at all ready to place the use of narcotics beyond the reach of the States' criminal laws. I do not consider appellant's conviction to be a punishment for having an illness or for simply being in some status or condition, but rather a conviction for the regular, repeated or habitual use of narcotics immediately prior to his arrest and in violation of the California law. As defined by the trial court, addiction *is* the regular use of narcotics and can be proved only by evidence of such use. To find addiction in this case the jury had to believe that appellant had frequently used narcotics in the recent past.[5] California is entitled to have its statute and the record so read, particularly where the State's only purpose in allowing prosecutions for addiction was to supersede its own venue requirements applicable to prosecutions for the use of narcotics and in effect to allow convictions for use where there is no precise evidence of the county where the use took place.

Nor do I find any indications in this record that California would apply to § 11721 to the case of the helpless addict. I agree with my Brother Clark that there was no evidence at all that appellant had lost the power to control his acts. There was no evidence of any use within

---

5. This is not a case where a defendant is convicted "even though he has never touched any narcotic drug within the State or been guilty of any irregular behavior there." The evidence was that appellant lived and worked in Los Angeles. He admitted before trial that he had used narcotics for three or four months, three or four times a week, usually at his place with his friends. He stated to the police that he had last used narcotics at 54th and Central in the City of Los Angeles on January 27, 8 days before his arrest. According to the State's expert, no needle mark or scab found on appellant's arms was newer than 3 days old and the most recent mark might have been as old as 10 days, which was consistent with appellant's own pretrial admissions. The State's evidence was that appellant had used narcotics at least 7 times in the 15 days immediately preceding his arrest.

3 days prior to appellant's arrest. The most recent marks might have been 3 days old or they might have been 10 days old. The appellant admitted before trial that he had last used narcotics 8 days before his arrest. At the trial he denied having taken narcotics at all. The uncontroverted evidence was that appellant was not under the influence of narcotics at the time of his arrest nor did he have withdrawal symptoms. He was an incipient addict, a redeemable user, and the State chose to send him to jail for 90 days rather than to attempt to confine him by civil proceedings under another statute which requires a finding that the addict has lost the power of self-control. In my opinion, on this record, it was within the power of the State of California to confine him by criminal proceedings for the use of narcotics or for regular use amounting to habitual use.[6]

The Court clearly does not rest its decision upon the narrow ground that the jury was not expressly instructed not to convict if it believed appellant's use of narcotics was beyond his control. The Court recognizes no degrees of addiction. The Fourteenth Amendment is today held to bar any prosecution for addiction regardless of the degree or frequency of use, and the Court's opinion bristles with indications of further consequences. If it is "cruel and unusual punishment" to convict appellant for addiction, it is difficult to understand why it would be any less offensive to the Fourteenth Amendment to convict him for use on the same evidence of use which proved he was an addict. It is significant that in purporting to reaffirm the power of the States to deal with the narcotics traffic, the Court does not include among the obvious powers of the State the power to punish for the use of narcotics. I cannot think that the omission was inadvertent.

The Court has not merely tidied up California's law by removing some irritating vestige of an outmoded approach to the control of narcotics. At the very least, it has effectively removed California's power to deal effectively with the recurring case under the statute where there is ample evidence of use but no evidence of the precise location of use. Beyond this it has cast serious doubt upon the power of any State to forbid the use of narcotics under threat of criminal punishment. I cannot believe that the Court would forbid the application of the criminal laws to the use of narcotics under any circumstances. But the States, as well as the Federal Government, are now on notice. They will have to await a final answer in another case.

Finally, I deem this application of "cruel and unusual punishment" so novel that I suspect the Court was hard put to find a way to ascribe to the Framers of the Constitution the result reached today rather than to its own notions of ordered liberty. If this case involved economic regulation, the present Court's allergy to substantive due process would surely save the statute and prevent the Court from imposing its own philosophical predilections upon state legislatures or Congress. I fail to

6. Health and Safety Code § 11391 expressly permits and contemplates the medical treatment of narcotics addicts confined to jail.

see why the Court deems it more appropriate to write into the Constitution its own abstract notions of how best to handle the narcotics problem, for it obviously cannot match either the States or Congress in expert understanding.

I respectfully dissent.

NOTES

1. In 1965 the California legislature transferred the provisions for the commitment and treatment of addicts from the Penal Code to the Welfare and Institutions Code. See People v. Reynoso, 64 Cal.2d 432, 50 Cal.Rptr. 468, 412 P.2d 812 (1966).

2. In State v. Margo, 40 N.J. 188, 191 A.2d 43 (1963) the court distinguished a New Jersey statute making it a criminal offense "to use" or be "under the influence of narcotics" from the one in Robinson by saying that addiction was something distinct from being under the influence. (The case does not reveal that defendant was a confirmed addict, although there were needle scars on his arm.) The court said "*Our statute does not punish for an unsatisfied craving for drugs.* Rather it *denounces the state of being under the influence* . . . the statute deals with being under the influence . . . to obviate an issue as to whether the drug was taken here or in another jurisdiction." And the court added that if a person could be prosecuted for use, because it is an anti-social act, he can be prosecuted for being under the influence, which offends society's interest in the same way.

In Watson v. United States, 141 U.S.App.D.C. 335, 439 F.2d 442 (1968), the defendant, an addict, had been convicted of having purchased and of having facilitated the concealment sale of heroin. (Under the federal statute possession is "sufficient evidence to authorize conviction unless the defendant explains the possession to the satisfaction of the jury"). The D.C. Court of Appeals, en banc, affirmed the conviction but remanded the case for resentencing, with consideration to be given to the National Addict Rehabilitation Act. In a footnote (# 15) the court referred a 5th circuit case which cautioned that in view of the rehabilitation procedures in that Act great caution should be exhibited in any "extension of *Robinson* ". Nevertheless the D.C. Court of Appeals had this to say:

". . . if *Robinson's* deployment of the Eighth Amendment as a barrier to California's making addiction a crime means anything, it must also mean in all logic that (1) Congress either did not intend to expose the non-trafficking addict possessor to criminal punishment, or (2) its effort to do so is as unavailing constitutionally as that of the California legislature."

In his concurring opinion one of the judges (457–458) said that "today's opinion leads clearly to the conclusion that the federal narcotics laws involved in this case do not apply to nontrafficking addicts in possession of narcotics for their own use."

See also, Anno., Drug Addiction or Related Mental State as Defense to Criminal Charge, 73 A.L.R.3d 16.

3. If a nontrafficking addict cannot be prosecuted for use or possession, as *Watson,* supra, seems to hold, what about prosecutions for the crimes addicts commit in order to support their habits?

In Wheeler v. United States, a decision of the District of Columbia Court of Appeals, 276 A.2d 722 (D.C.App.1971), the defendant was prosecuted for violating a provision of the District of Columbia's Criminal Code which prohibits the possession of narcotics paraphernalia. He argued that in view of *Robinson* he could not be convicted for conduct incidental to the conviction. In rejecting this contention the court pointed out that Congress, in the preamble to the rehabilitation act, stated that "The Congress intends that Federal Criminal laws shall be enforced against drug users . . . and [the act] shall not be used to substitute treatment for punishment in cases of crimes committed by drug users". The court said that it would be "a paradox if the eighth amendment must be read today as invalidating the measures enacted by Congress to deter narcotics users from persisting in habits ruinous to their health and character as well to protect the public from dangerous crimes committed by them".

4. If narcotic addiction is not punishable criminally, may a chronic alcoholic be found guilty for violating a law prohibiting public intoxication?

In Powell v. Texas, 392 U.S. 514, 88 S.Ct. 2145, 20 L.Ed.2d 1254 (1968), the Supreme Court, in a 5–4 decision, held that the conviction for public intoxication of a person who was to some degree compelled to drink did not amount to "cruel and unusual punishment" where it did not appear that he was unable to stay off the streets on the occasion in question.

The Minnesota Supreme Court, in State v. Fearon, 283 Minn. 90, 166 N.W. 2d 720 (1969), held that since a chronic alcoholic does not drink by choice he cannot be punished for his subsequent drunkenness in a public place. For a general review of the case law, see 40 A.L.R.3d 321.

5. The American Medical Association, in its Manual on Alcoholism, rev'd 1977, p. 4, states that "Alcoholism is an illness characterized by significant impairment that is directly associated with persistent and excessive use of alcohol. Impairment may involve physiological, psychological or social dysfunction." The National Council on Alcoholism, in the Dec. issue, 1976, of Annals of Internal Medicine, stated that "Alcoholism is a chronic, progressive and potentially fatal disease. It is characterized by tolerance and physical dependency, pathological organ changes, or both, all of which are the direct consequences of the alcohol ingested."

6. Can a woman who has used drugs during pregnancy and subsequently delivers a drug-exposed baby be charged with criminal neglect? With delivery of drugs to a minor? If the baby is still-born, can the woman be charged with involuntary manslaughter? See Massardo McGinnis, Prosecution of Mothers of Drug–Exposed Babies; Constitutional and Criminal Theory, 139 U.Pa.L.Rev. 505 (1990). See also, Fetal Drug or Alcohol Addiction Syndrome: A Case of Prenatal Child Abuse?, 25 Willamette L.Rev. 223 (1989); Paltrow, When Becoming Pregnant Is A Crime, 9 Crim. Justice Ethics 41 (1990); Of Woman's First Disobedience: Forsaking a Duty of Care to Her Fetus—Is This a Mother's Crime?, 53 Brooklyn L.Rev. 807 (1987).

2. THE DEATH PENALTY

GREGG v. GEORGIA

Supreme Court of the United States, 1976.
428 U.S. 153, 96 S.Ct. 2909, 49 L.Ed.2d 859.

Judgment of the Court, and opinion of MR. JUSTICE STEWART, MR. JUSTICE POWELL, and MR. JUSTICE STEVENS, announced by MR. JUSTICE STEWART.

The issue in this case is whether the imposition of the sentence of death for the crime of murder under the law of Georgia violates the Eighth and Fourteenth Amendments.

I

The petitioner, Troy Gregg, was charged with committing armed robbery and murder. In accordance with Georgia procedure in capital cases, the trial was in two stages, a guilt stage and a sentencing stage. The evidence at the guilt trial established that on November 21, 1973, the petitioner and a traveling companion, Floyd Allen, while hitchhiking north in Florida were picked up by Fred Simmons and Bob Moore. Their car broke down, but they continued north after Simmons purchased another vehicle with some of the cash he was carrying. While still in Florida, they picked up another hitchhiker, Dennis Weaver, who rode with them to Atlanta, where he was let out about 11 p.m. A short time later the four men interrupted their journey for a rest stop along the highway. The next morning the bodies of Simmons and Moore were discovered in a ditch nearby.

On November 23, after reading about the shootings in an Atlanta newspaper, Weaver communicated with the Gwinnett County police and related information concerning the journey with the victims, including a description of the car. The next afternoon, the petitioner and Allen, while in Simmons' car, were arrested in Asheville, N.C. In the search incident to the arrest a .25–caliber pistol, later shown to be that used to kill Simmons and Moore, was found in the petitioner's pocket. After receiving the warnings required by Miranda v. Arizona, 384 U.S. 436, 86 S.Ct. 1602 (1966), and signing a written waiver of his rights, the petitioner signed a statement in which he admitted shooting, then robbing Simmons and Moore. He justified the slayings on grounds of self-defense. The next day, while being transferred to Lawrenceville, Ga., the petitioner and Allen were taken to the scene of the shootings. Upon arriving there, Allen recounted the events leading to the slayings. His version of these events was as follows: After Simmons and Moore left the car, the petitioner stated that he intended to rob them. The petitioner then took his pistol in hand and positioned himself on the car to improve his aim. As Simmons and Moore came up an embankment toward the car, the petitioner fired three shots and the two men fell near a ditch. The petitioner, at close range, then fired a shot into the head of each. He robbed them of valuables and drove away with Allen.

A medical examiner testified that Simmons died from a bullet wound in the eye and that Moore died from bullet wounds in the cheek and in the back of the head. He further testified that both men had several bruises and abrasions about the face and head which probably were sustained either from the fall into the ditch or from being dragged or pushed along the embankment. Although Allen did not testify, a police detective recounted the substance of Allen's statements about the slayings and indicated that directly after Allen had made these statements the petitioner had admitted that Allen's account was accurate. The petitioner testified in his own defense. He confirmed that Allen had made the statements described by the detective, but denied their truth or ever having admitted to their accuracy. He indicated that he had shot Simmons and Moore because of fear and in self-defense, testifying they had attacked Allen and him, one wielding a pipe and the other a knife.

The trial judge submitted the murder charges to the jury on both felony-murder and nonfelony-murder theories. He also instructed on the issue of self-defense but declined to instruct on manslaughter. He submitted the robbery case to the jury on both an armed-robbery theory and on the lesser included offense of robbery by intimidation. The jury found the petitioner guilty of two counts of armed robbery and two counts of murder.

At the penalty stage, which took place before the same jury, neither the prosecutor nor the petitioner's lawyer offered any additional evidence. Both counsel, however, made lengthy arguments dealing generally with the propriety of capital punishment under the circumstances and with the weight of the evidence of guilt. The trial judge instructed the jury that it could recommend either a death sentence or a life prison sentence on each count. The judge further charged the jury that in determining what sentence was appropriate the jury was free to consider the facts and circumstances, if any, presented by the parties in mitigation or aggravation.

Finally, the judge instructed the jury that it "would not be authorized to consider [imposing] the penalty of death" unless it first found beyond a reasonable doubt one of these aggravating circumstances:

> "One—That the offense of murder was committed while the offender was engaged in the commission of two other capital felonies, to-wit the armed robbery of [Simmons and Moore].

> "Two—That the offender committed the offense of murder for the purpose of receiving money and the automobile described in the indictment.

> "Three—The offense of murder was outrageously and wantonly vile, horrible and inhuman, in that they [*sic*] involved the depravity of [the] mind of the defendant."

Finding the first and second of these circumstances, the jury returned verdicts of death on each count.

The Supreme Court of Georgia affirmed the convictions and the imposition of the death sentences for murder. After reviewing the trial transcript and the record, including the evidence, and comparing the evidence and sentence in similar cases in accordance with the requirements of Georgia law, the court concluded that, considering the nature of the crime and the defendant, the sentences of death had not resulted from prejudice or any other arbitrary factor and were not excessive or disproportionate to the penalty applied in similar cases. The death sentences imposed for armed robbery, however, were vacated on the grounds that the death penalty had rarely been imposed in Georgia for that offense and that the jury improperly considered the murders as aggravating circumstances for the robberies after having considered the armed robberies as aggravating circumstances for the murders.

* * *

II

Before considering the issues presented it is necessary to understand the Georgia statutory scheme for the imposition of the death penalty. The Georgia statute, as amended after our decision in Furman v. Georgia, 408 U.S. 238, 92 S.Ct. 2726 (1972), retains the death penalty for six categories of crime: murder, kidnaping for ransom or where the victim is harmed, armed robbery, rape, treason, and aircraft hijacking. The capital defendant's guilt or innocence is determined in the traditional manner, either by a trial judge or a jury, in the first stage of a bifurcated trial.

If trial is by jury, the trial judge is required to charge lesser included offenses when they are supported by any view of the evidence. After a verdict, finding, or plea of guilty to a capital crime, a presentence hearing is conducted before whoever made the determination of guilt. The sentencing procedures are essentially the same in both bench and jury trials. At the hearing:

> "[T]he judge [or jury] shall hear additional evidence in extenuation, mitigation and aggravation of punishment, including the record of any prior criminal convictions and pleas of guilty or pleas of nolo contendere of the defendant, or the absence of any prior conviction and pleas: Provided, however, that only such evidence in aggravation as the State has made known to the defendant prior to his trial shall be admissible. The judge [or jury] shall also hear argument by the defendant or his counsel and the prosecuting attorney . . . regarding the punishment to be imposed."

The defendant is accorded substantial latitude as to the types of evidence that he may introduce. Evidence considered during the guilt stage may be considered during the sentencing stage without being resubmitted.

In the assessment of the appropriate sentence to be imposed the judge is also required to consider or to include in his instructions to the jury "any mitigating circumstances or aggravating circumstances otherwise authorized by law and any of [10] statutory aggravating circumstances which may be supported by the evidence. . . ." The scope of the nonstatutory aggravating or mitigating circumstances is not delineated in the statute. Before a convicted defendant may be sentenced to death, however, except in cases of treason or aircraft hijacking, the jury, or the trial judge in cases tried without a jury, must find beyond a reasonable doubt one of the 10 aggravating circumstances specified in the statute.[1] The sentence of death may be imposed only if the jury (or judge) finds one of the statutory aggravating circumstances and then elects to impose that sentence. If the verdict is death, the jury or judge

---

1. The statute provides in part:

"(a) The death penalty may be imposed for the offenses of aircraft hijacking or treason, in any case.

"(b) In all cases of other offenses for which the death penalty may be authorized, the judge shall consider, or he shall include in his instructions to the jury for it to consider, any mitigating circumstances or aggravating circumstances otherwise authorized by law and any of the following statutory aggravating circumstances which may be supported by the evidence:

"(1) The offense of murder, rape, armed robbery, or kidnapping was committed by a person with a prior record of conviction for a capital felony, or the offense of murder was committed by a person who has a substantial history of serious assaultive criminal convictions.

"(2) The offense of murder, rape, armed robbery, or kidnapping was committed while the offender was engaged in the commission of another capital felony, or aggravated battery, or the offense of murder was committed while the offender was engaged in the commission of burglary or arson in the first degree.

"(3) The offender by his act of murder, armed robbery, or kidnapping knowingly created a great risk of death to more than one person in a public place by means of a weapon or device which would normally be hazardous to the lives of more than one person.

"(4) The offender committed the offense of murder for himself or another, for the purpose of receiving money or any other thing of monetary value.

"(5) The murder of a judicial officer, former judicial officer, district attorney or solicitor or former district attorney or solicitor during or because of the exercise of his official duty.

"(6) The offender caused or directed another to commit murder or committed murder as an agent or employee of another person.

"(7) The offense of murder, rape, armed robbery, or kidnapping was outrageously or wantonly vile, horrible or inhuman in that it involved torture, depravity of mind, or an aggravated battery to the victim.

"(8) The offense of murder was committed against any peace officer, corrections employee or fireman while engaged in the performance of his official duties.

"(9) The offense of murder was committed by a person in, or who has escaped from, the lawful custody of a peace officer or place of lawful confinement.

"(10) The murder was committed for the purpose of avoiding, interfering with, or preventing a lawful arrest or custody in a place of lawful confinement, of himself or another.

"(c) The statutory instructions as determined by the trial judge to be warranted by the evidence shall be given in charge and in writing to the jury for its deliberation. The jury, if its verdict be a recommendation of death, shall designate in writing, signed by the foreman of the jury, the aggravating circumstance or circumstances which it found beyond a reasonable doubt. In non-jury cases the judge shall make such designation. Except in cases of treason or aircraft hijacking, unless at least one of the statutory aggravating circumstances enumerated in section 27–2534.1(b) is so found, the death penalty shall not be imposed." § 27–2534.1 (Supp.1975).

* * *

must specify the aggravating circumstance(s) found. In jury cases, the trial judge is bound by the jury's recommended sentence.

In addition to the conventional appellate process available in all criminal cases, provision is made for special expedited direct review by the Supreme Court of Georgia of the appropriateness of imposing the sentence of death in the particular case. The court is directed to consider "the punishment as well as any errors enumerated by way of appeal," and to determine:

"(1) Whether the sentence of death was imposed under the influence of passion, prejudice, or any other arbitrary factor, and

"(2) Whether, in cases other than treason or aircraft hijacking, the evidence supports the jury's or judge's finding of a statutory aggravating circumstance as enumerated in section 27.2534.1(b), and

"(3) Whether the sentence of death is excessive or disproportionate to the penalty imposed in similar cases, considering both the crime and the defendant."

If the court affirms a death sentence, it is required to include in its decision reference to similar cases that it has taken into consideration.

A transcript and complete record of the trial, as well as a separate report by the trial judge, are transmitted to the court for its use in reviewing the sentence. The report is in the form of a 6½–page questionnaire, designed to elicit information about the defendant, the crime, and the circumstances of the trial. It requires the trial judge to characterize the trial in several ways designed to test for arbitrariness and disproportionality of sentence. Included in the report are responses to detailed questions concerning the quality of the defendant's representation, whether race played a role in the trial, and, whether, in the trial court's judgment, there was any doubt about the defendant's guilt or the appropriateness of the sentence. A copy of the report is served upon defense counsel. Under its special review authority, the court may either affirm the death sentence or remand the case for resentencing. In cases in which the death sentence is affirmed there remains the possibility of executive clemency.

III

We address initially the basic contention that the punishment of death for the crime of murder is, under all circumstances, "cruel and unusual" in violation of the Eighth and Fourteenth Amendments of the Constitution. . . .

The Court on a number of occasions has both assumed and asserted the constitutionality of capital punishment. In several cases that assumption provided a necessary foundation for the decision, as the Court was asked to decide whether a particular method of carrying out a capital sentence would be allowed to stand under the Eighth Amendment. But until Furman v. Georgia (1972) the Court never confronted squarely the fundamental claim that the punishment of death always, regardless of the enormity of the offense or the procedure followed in imposing the sentence, is cruel and unusual punishment in violation of the Constitution. Although this issue was presented and addressed in *Furman*, it was not resolved by the Court. Four Justices would have held that capital punishment is not unconstitutional *per se;* two Justices would have reached the opposite conclusion; and three Justices, while agreeing that the statutes then before the Court were invalid as applied, left open the question whether such punishment may ever be imposed. We now hold that the punishment of death does not invariably violate the Constitution. * * *

The imposition of the death penalty for the crime of murder has a long history of acceptance both in the United States and in England.

Four years ago, the petitioners in *Furman* and its companion cases predicated their argument primarily upon the asserted proposition that standards of decency had evolved to the point where capital punishment no longer could be tolerated. The petitioners in those cases said, in effect, that the evolutionary process had come to an end, and that standards of decency required that the Eighth Amendment be construed finally as prohibiting capital punishment for any crime regardless of its depravity and impact on society. This view was accepted by two Justices. Three other Justices were unwilling to go so far; focusing on the procedures by which convicted defendants were selected for the death penalty rather than on the actual punishment inflicted, they joined in the conclusion that the statutes before the Court were constitionally invalid.

The petitioners in the capital cases before the Court today renew the "standards of decency" argument, but developments during the four years since *Furman* have undercut substantially the assumptions upon which their argument rested. Despite the continuing debate, dating back to the 19th century, over the morality and utility of capital punishment, it is now evident that a large proportion of American society continues to regard it as an appropriate and necessary criminal sanction.

The most marked indication of society's endorsement of the death penalty for murder is the legislative response to *Furman*. The legislatures of at least 35 States have enacted new statutes that provide for the death penalty for at least some crimes that result in the death of another person. And the Congress of the United States, in 1974, enacted a statute providing the death penalty for aircraft piracy that results in death. . . .

In the only statewide referendum occurring since *Furman* and brought to our attention, the people of California adopted a constitutional amendment that authorized capital punishment, in effect negating a prior ruling by the Supreme Court of California in People v. Anderson, 6 Cal.3d 628, 493 P.2d 880, cert. denied, 406 U.S. 958, 92

S.Ct. 2060 (1972), that the death penalty violated the California Constitution.

The jury also is a significant and reliable objective index of contemporary values because it is so directly involved. The Court has said that "one of the most important functions any jury can perform in making . . . a selection [between life imprisonment and death for a defendant convicted in a capital case] is to maintain a link between contemporary community values and the penal system." Witherspoon v. Illinois, 391 U.S. 510, 519 n. 15, 88 S.Ct. 1770, 1775 (1968). It may be true that evolving standards have influenced juries in recent decades to be more discriminating in imposing the sentence of death. But the relative infrequency of jury verdicts imposing the death sentence does not indicate rejection of capital punishment *per se*. . . .   Indeed, the actions of juries in many States since *Furman* are fully compatible with the legislative judgments, reflected in the new statutes, as to the continued utility and necessity of capital punishment in appropriate cases. At the close of 1974 at least 254 persons had been sentenced to death since *Furman,* and by the end of March 1976, more than 460 persons were subject to death sentences.

As we have seen, however, the Eighth Amendment demands more than that a challenged punishment be acceptable to contemporary society. The Court also must ask whether it comports with the basic concept of human dignity at the core of the Amendment. Trop v. Dulles, 356 U.S., at 100, 78 S.Ct., at 597 (plurality opinion). Although we cannot "invalidate a category of penalties because we deem less severe penalties adequate to serve the ends of penology," Furman v. Georgia, supra, 408 U.S., at 451, 92 S.Ct., at 2834 (Powell, J., dissenting), the sanction imposed cannot be so totally without penological justification that it results in the gratuitous infliction of suffering.

The death penalty is said to serve two principal social purposes: retribution and deterrence of capital crimes by prospective offenders.

In part, capital punishment is an expression of society's moral outrage at particularly offensive conduct. This function may be unappealing to many, but it is essential in an ordered society that asks its citizens to rely on legal processes rather than self-help to vindicate their wrongs. . . .   "Retribution is no longer the dominant objective of the criminal law," Williams v. New York, 337 U.S. 241, 248, 69 S.Ct. 1079, 1084 (1949), but neither is it a forbidden objective nor one inconsistent with our respect for the dignity of men. Indeed, the decision that capital punishment may be the appropriate sanction in extreme cases is an expression of the community's belief that certain crimes are themselves so grievous an affront to humanity that the only adequate response may be the penalty of death.

Statistical attempts to evaluate the worth of the death penalty as a deterrent to crimes by potential offenders have occasioned a great deal of debate. The results simply have been inconclusive. . . .

In sum, we cannot say that the judgment of the Georgia Legislature that capital punishment may be necessary in some cases is clearly wrong. Considerations of federalism, as well as respect for the ability of a legislature to evaluate, in terms of its particular State, the moral consensus concerning the death penalty and its social utility as a sanction, require us to conclude, in the absence of more convincing evidence that the infliction of death as a punishment for murder is not without justification and thus is not unconstitutionally severe.

Finally, we must consider whether the punishment of death is disproportionate in relation to the crime for which it is imposed. There is no question that death as a punishment is unique in its severity and irrevocability. When a defendant's life is at stake, the Court has been particularly sensitive to insure that every safeguard is observed. But we are concerned here only with the imposition of capital punishment for the crime of murder, and when a life has been taken deliberately by the offender,[2] we cannot say that the punishment is invariably disproportionate to the crime. It is an extreme sanction, suitable to the most extreme of crimes.

We hold that the death penalty is not a form of punishment that may never be imposed, regardless of the circumstances of the offense, regardless of the character of the offender, and regardless of the procedure followed in reaching the decision to impose it.

IV

We now consider whether Georgia may impose the death penalty on the petitioner in this case.

A

While *Furman* did not hold that the infliction of the death penalty *per se* violates the Constitution's ban on cruel and unusual punishments, it did recognize that the penalty of death is different in kind from any other punishment imposed under our system of criminal justice. Because of the uniqueness of the death penalty, *Furman* held that it could not be imposed under sentencing procedures that created a substantial risk that it would be inflicted in an arbitrary and capricious manner. . . .

While some have suggested that standards to guide a capital jury's sentencing deliberations are impossible to formulate, the fact is that such standards have been developed. When the drafters of the Model Penal Code faced this problem, they concluded "that it is within the realm of possibility to point to the main circumstances of aggravation and of mitigation that should be weighed *and weighed against each other* when they are presented in a concrete case." ALI, Model Penal

---

2. We do not address here the question whether the taking of the criminal's life is a proportionate sanction where no victim has been deprived of life—for example, when capital punishment is imposed for rape, kidnaping, or armed robbery that does not result in the death of any human being.

Code § 201.6, Comment 3, p. 71 (Tent.Draft No. 9, 1959 (emphasis in original). While such standards are by necessity somewhat general, they do provide guidance to the sentencing authority and thereby reduce the likelihood that it will impose a sentence that fairly can be called capricious or arbitrary. Where the sentencing authority is required to specify the factors it relied upon in reaching its decision, the further safeguard of meaningful appellate review is available to ensure that death sentences are not imposed capriciously or in a freakish manner.

In summary, the concerns expressed in *Furman* that the penalty of death not be imposed in an arbitrary or capricious manner can be met by a carefully drafted statute that ensures that the sentencing authority is given adequate information and guidance. As a general proposition these concerns are best met by a system that provides for a bifurcated proceeding at which the sentencing authority is apprised of the information relevant to the imposition of sentence and provided with standards to guide its use of the information.

We do not intend to suggest that only the above-described procedures would be permissible under *Furman* or that any sentencing system constructed along these general lines would inevitably satisfy the concerns of *Furman,* for each distinct system must be examined on an individual basis. Rather, we have embarked upon this general exposition to make clear that it is possible to construct capital-sentencing systems capable of meeting *Furman's* constitutional concerns.

B

We now turn to consideration of the constitutionality of Georgia's capital-sentencing procedures. In the wake of *Furman,* Georgia amended its capital punishment statute, but chose not to narrow the scope of its murder provisions. See Part II, supra. Thus, now as before *Furman,* in Georgia "[a] person commits murder when he unlawfully and with malice aforethought, either express or implied, causes the death of another human being." All persons convicted of murder "shall be punished by death or by imprisonment for life."

Georgia did act, however, to narrow the class of murderers subject to capital punishment by specifying 10 statutory aggravating circumstances, one of which must be found by the jury to exist beyond a reasonable doubt before a death sentence can ever be imposed. In addition, the jury is authorized to consider any other appropriate aggravating or mitigating circumstances. The jury is not required to find any mitigating circumstance in order to make a recommendation of mercy that is binding on the trial court, but it must find a *statutory* aggravating circumstance before recommending a sentence of death.
* * *

In short, Georgia's new sentencing procedures require as a prerequisite to the imposition of the death penalty, specific jury findings as to the circumstances of the crime or the character of the defendant.

Moreover, to guard further against a situation comparable to that presented in *Furman*, the Supreme Court of Georgia compares each death sentence with the sentences imposed on similarly situated defendants to ensure that the sentence of death in a particular case is not disproportionate. On their face these procedures seem to satisfy the concerns of *Furman*. . . .

The petitioner contends, however, that the changes in the Georgia sentencing procedures are only cosmetic, that the arbitrariness and capriciousness condemned by *Furman* continue to exist in Georgia— both in traditional practices that still remain and in the new sentencing procedures adopted in response to *Furman*.

1

First, the petitioner focuses on the opportunities for discretionary action that are inherent in the processing of any murder case under Georgia law. He notes that the state prosecutor has unfettered authority to select those persons whom he wishes to prosecute for a capital offense and to plea bargain with them. Further, at the trial the jury may choose to convict a defendant of a lesser included offense rather than find him guilty of a crime punishable by death, even if the evidence would support a capital verdict. And finally, a defendant who is convicted and sentenced to die may have his sentence commuted by the Governor of the State and the Georgia Board of Pardons and Paroles.

The existence of these discretionary stages is not determinative of the issues before us. . . .

2

The petitioner further contends that the capital-sentencing procedures adopted by Georgia in response to *Furman* do not eliminate the dangers of arbitrariness and caprice in jury sentencing that were held in *Furman* to be violative of the Eighth and Fourteenth Amendments. He claims that the statute is so broad and vague as to leave juries free to act as arbitrarily and capriciously as they wish in deciding whether to impose the death penalty. . . .

. . . We think that the Georgia court wisely has chosen not to impose unnecessary restrictions on the evidence that can be offered at such a hearing and to approve open and far-ranging argument. So long as the evidence introduced and the arguments made at the pre-sentence hearing do not prejudice a defendant, it is preferable not to impose restrictions. We think it desirable for the jury to have as much information before it as possible when it makes the sentencing decision.

3

Finally, the Georgia statute has an additional provision designed to assure that the death penalty will not be imposed on a capriciously selected group of convicted defendants. The new sentencing procedures require that the State Supreme Court review every death sentence to determine whether it was imposed under the influence of passion, prejudice, or any other arbitrary factor, whether the evidence supports the findings of a statutory aggravating circumstance, and "[w]hether the sentence of death is excessive or disproportionate to the penalty imposed in similar cases, considering both the crime and the defendant." In performing its sentence-review function, the Georgia court has held that "if the death penalty is only rarely imposed for an act or it is substantially out of line with sentences imposed for other acts it will be set aside as excessive." . . .

It is apparent that the Supreme Court of Georgia has taken its review responsibilities seriously. . . .

The provision for appellate review in the Georgia capital-sentencing system serves as a check against the random or arbitrary imposition of the death penalty. In particular, the proportionality review substantially eliminates the possibility that a person will be sentenced to die by the action of an aberrant jury. If a time comes when juries generally do not impose the death sentence in a certain kind of murder case, the appellate review procedures assure that no defendant convicted under such circumstances will suffer a sentence of death.

V

The basic concern of *Furman* centered on those defendants who were being condemned to death capriciously and arbitrarily. Under the procedures before the Court in that case, sentencing authorities were not directed to give attention to the nature or circumstances of the crime committed or to the character or record of the defendant. Left unguided, juries imposed the death sentence in a way that could only be called freakish. The new Georgia sentencing procedures, by contrast, focus the jury's attention on the particularized nature of the crime and the particularized characteristics of the individual defendant. While the jury is permitted to consider any aggravating or mitigating circumstances, it must find and identify at least one statutory aggravating factor before it may impose a penalty of death. In this way the jury's discretion is channeled. No longer can a jury wantonly and freakishly impose the death sentence; it is always circumscribed by the legislative guidelines. In addition, the review function of the Supreme Court of Georgia affords additional assurance that the concerns that prompted our decision in *Furman* are not present to any significant degree in the Georgia procedure applied here.

For the reasons expressed in this opinion, we hold that the statutory system under which Gregg was sentenced to death does not violate the Constitution. Accordingly, the judgment of the Georgia Supreme Court is affirmed.

[The concurring opinion of Mr. Justice White, with whom the Chief Justice and Mr. Justice Rehnquist join, is omitted. The statements of the Chief Justice and Mr. Justice Rehnquist, as well as the brief concurrence by Mr. Justice Blackmun, are also omitted.]

MR. JUSTICE BRENNAN, dissenting.

The Cruel and Unusual Punishments Clause "must draw its meaning from the evolving standards of decency that mark the progress of a maturing society." The opinions of Mr. Justice Stewart, Mr. Justice Powell, and Mr. Justice Stevens today hold that "evolving standards of decency" require focus not on the essence of the death penalty itself but primarily upon the procedures employed by the State to single out persons to suffer the penalty of death. Those opinions hold further that, so viewed, the Clause invalidates the mandatory infliction of the death penalty but not its infliction under sentencing procedures that Mr. Justice Stewart, Mr. Justice Powell, and Mr. Justice Stevens conclude adequately safeguard against the risk that the death penalty was imposed in an arbitrary and capricious manner.

In Furman v. Georgia (concurring opinion), I read "evolving standards of decency" as requiring focus upon the essence of the death penalty itself and not primarily or solely upon the procedures under which the determination to inflict the penalty upon a particular person was made. . . . That continues to be my view. For the Clause forbidding cruel and unusual punishments under our constitutional system of government embodies in unique degree moral principles restraining the punishments that our civilized society may impose on those persons who transgress its laws. Thus, I too say: "For myself, I do not hesitate to assert the proposition that the only way the law has progressed from the days of the rack, the screw and the wheel is the development of moral concepts, or, as stated by the Supreme Court . . . the application of 'evolving standards of decency' . . . ."

This Court inescapably has the duty, as the ultimate arbiter of the meaning of our Constitution, to say whether, when individuals condemned to death stand before our Bar, "moral concepts" require us to hold that the law has progressed to the point where we should declare that the punishment of death, like punishments on the rack, the screw, and the wheel, is no longer morally tolerable in our civilized society. My opinion in Furman v. Georgia concluded that our civilization and the law had progressed to this point and that therefore the punishment of death, for whatever crime and under all circumstances, is "cruel and unusual" in violation of the Eighth and Fourteenth Amendments of the Constitution. I shall not again canvass the reasons that led to that conclusion. I emphasize only that foremost among the "moral concepts" recognized in our cases and inherent in the Clause is the primary moral principle that the State, even as it punishes, must treat its citizens in a manner consistent with their intrinsic worth as human beings—a punishment must not be so severe as to be degrading to human dignity. . . .

*   *   *

The fatal constitutional infirmity in the punishment of death is that it treats "members of the human race as nonhumans, as objects to be toyed with and discarded. [It is] thus inconsistent with the fundamental premise of the Clause that even the vilest criminal remains a human being possessed of common human dignity." As such it is a penalty that "subjects the individual to a fate forbidden by the principle of civilized treatment guaranteed by the [Clause]." I therefore would hold, on that ground alone, that death is today a cruel and unusual punishment prohibited by the Clause. "Justice of this kind is obviously no less shocking than the crime itself, and the new 'official' murder, far from offering redress for the offense committed against society, adds instead a second defilement to the first." * * *

Mr. Justice Marshall, dissenting.

In Furman v. Georgia, (concurring opinion), I set forth at some length my views on the basic issue presented to the Court in these cases. The death penalty, I concluded, is a cruel and unusual punishment prohibited by the Eighth and Fourteenth Amendments. That continues to be my view.

I have no intention of retracing the "long and tedious journey," that led to my conclusion in *Furman.* My sole purposes here are to consider the suggestion that my conclusion in *Furman* has been undercut by developments since then. . . .

Since the decision in *Furman,* the legislatures of 35 States have enacted new statutes authorizing the imposition of the death sentence for certain crimes, and Congress has enacted a law providing the death penalty for air piracy resulting in death. I would be less than candid if I did not acknowledge that these developments have a significant bearing on a realistic assessment of the moral acceptability of the death penalty to the American people. But if the constitutionality of the death penalty turns, as I have urged, on the opinion of an *informed* citizenry, then even the enactment of new death statutes cannot be viewed as conclusive. In *Furman,* I observed that the American people are largely unaware of the information critical to a judgment on the morality of the death penalty, and concluded that if they were better informed they would consider it shocking, unjust, and unacceptable. A recent study, conducted after the enactment of the post-*Furman* statutes, has confirmed that the American people know little about the death penalty, and that the opinions of an informed public would differ significantly from those of a public unaware of the consequences and effects of the death penalty.

* * *

The contentions [presented in the majority opinion]—that society's expression of moral outrage through the imposition of the death penalty pre-empts the citizenry from taking the law into its own hands and reinforces moral values—are not retributive in the purest sense. They are essentially utilitarian in that they portray the death penalty as valuable because of its beneficial results. These justifications for the death penalty are inadequate because the penalty is, quite clearly I think, not necessary to the accomplishment of those results.

There remains for consideration, however, what might be termed the purely retributive justification for the death penalty—that the death penalty is appropriate, not because of its beneficial effect on society, but because the taking of the murderer's life is itself morally good. Some of the language of the opinion of my Brothers Stewart, Powell, and Stevens . . . appears positively to embrace this notion of retribution for its own sake as a justification for capital punishment. They state:

> "[T]he decision that capital punishment may be the appropriate sanction in extreme cases is an expression of the community's belief that certain crimes are themselves so grievous an affront to humanity that the only adequate response may be the penalty of death."

*   *   *

Of course, it may be that these statements are intended as no more than observations as to the popular demands that it is thought must be responded to in order to prevent anarchy. But the implication of the statements appears to me to be quite different—namely, that society's judgment that the murderer "deserves" death must be respected not simply because the preservation of order requires it, but because it is appropriate that society make the judgment and carry it out. It is this latter notion, in particular, that I consider to be fundamentally at odds with the Eighth Amendment. The mere fact that the community demands the murderer's life in return for the evil he has done cannot sustain the death penalty, for as Justices Stewart, Powell, and Stevens remind us, "the Eighth Amendment demands more than that a challenged punishment be acceptable to contemporary society." To be sustained under the Eighth Amendment, the death penalty must "compor[t] with the basic concept of human dignity at the core of the Amendment," ibid.; the objective in imposing it must be "[consistent] with our respect for the dignity of [other] men." Under these standards, the taking of life "because the wrongdoer deserves it" surely must fall, for such a punishment has as its very basis the total denial of the wrongdoer's dignity and worth.

The death penalty, unnecessary to promote the goal of deterrence or to further any legitimate notion of retribution, is an excessive penalty forbidden by the Eighth and Fourteenth Amendments. I respectfully dissent from the Court's judgment upholding the sentences of death imposed upon the petitioners in these cases.

NOTES

1. *Gregg* was one of a series of cases handed down the same day. In Proffitt v. Florida, 428 U.S. 242, 96 S.Ct. 2960, 49 L.Ed.2d 913 (1976), the Court sustained imposition of the death penalty under a Florida capital crimes scheme similar to Georgia's except that the jury role on sentencing is advisory.

Mr. Justice Powell, writing the Court's plurality opinion, distinguished the two schemes thusly:

"On their face these procedures, like those used in Georgia appear to meet the constitutional deficiencies identified in *Furman*. The sentencing authority in Florida, the trial judge, is directed to weigh eight aggravating factors against seven mitigating factors to determine whether the death penalty shall be imposed. This determination requires the trial judge to focus on the circumstances of the crime and the character of the individual defendant. He must, *inter alia*, consider whether the defendant has a prior criminal record, whether the defendant acted under duress or under the influence of extreme mental or emotional disturbance, whether the defendant's role in the crime was that of a minor accomplice, and whether the defendant's youth argues in favor of a more lenient sentence than might otherwise be imposed. The trial judge must also determine whether the crime was committed in the course of one of several enumerated felonies, whether it was committed for pecuniary gain, whether it was committed to assist in an escape from custody or to prevent a lawful arrest, and whether the crime was especially heinous, atrocious, or cruel. To answer these questions, which are not unlike those considered by a Georgia sentencing jury, . . . the sentencing judge must focus on the individual circumstances of each homicide and each defendant.

"The basic difference between the Florida system and the Georgia system is that in Florida the sentence is determined by the trial judge rather than by the jury. This Court has pointed out that jury sentencing in a capital case can perform an important societal function, Witherspoon v. Illinois, 391 U.S. 510, 519 n. 15, 88 S.Ct. 1770, 1775, but it has never suggested that jury sentencing is constitutionally required. And it would appear that judicial sentencing should lead, if anything, to even greater consistency in the imposition at the trial court level of capital punishment, since a trial judge is more experienced in sentencing than a jury, and therefore is better able to impose sentences similar to those imposed in analogous cases.

"The Florida capital-sentencing procedures thus seek to assure that the death penalty will not be imposed in an arbitrary or capricious manner. Moreover, to the extent that any risk to the contrary exists, it is minimized by Florida's appellate review system, under which the evidence of the aggravating and mitigating circumstances is reviewed and reweighed by the Supreme Court of Florida 'to determine independently whether the imposition of the ultimate penalty is warranted.' Songer v. State, 322 So.2d 481, 484 (1975). . . . The Supreme Court of Florida, like that of Georgia, has not hesitated to vacate a death sentence when it has determined that the sentence should not have been imposed. Indeed, it has vacated eight of the 21 death sentences that it has reviewed to date.

"Under Florida's capital-sentencing procedures, in sum, trial judges are given specific and detailed guidance to assist them in deciding whether to impose a death penalty or imprisonment for life. Moreover, their decisions are reviewed to ensure that they are consistent with other sentences imposed in similar circumstances. Thus, in Florida, as in Georgia, it is no longer true that there is ' "no meaningful basis for distinguishing the few cases in which [the death penalty] is imposed from the many cases where it is not." ' On its face the Florida system thus satisfies the constitutional deficiencies identified in *Furman*."

The Court also sustained the Texas death penalty statute procedures in Jurek v. Texas, 428 U.S. 262, 96 S.Ct. 2950, 49 L.Ed.2d 929 (1976):

"While Texas has not adopted a list of statutory aggravating circumstances the existence of which can justify the imposition of the death penalty as have Georgia and Florida, its action in narrowing the categories of murders for which a death sentence may never be imposed serves much the same purpose. In fact, each of the five classes of murders made capital by the Texas statute is encompassed in Georgia and Florida by one or more of their statutory aggravating circumstances. For example, the Texas statute requires the jury at the guilt determining stage to consider whether the crime was committed in the course of a particular felony, whether it was committed for hire, or whether the defendant was an inmate of a penal institution at the time of its commission. Thus, in essence, the Texas statute requires that the jury find the existence of a statutory aggravating circumstance before the death penalty may be imposed. So far as consideration of aggravating circumstances is concerned, therefore, the principal difference between Texas and the other two States is that the death penalty is an available sentencing option—even potentially—for a smaller class of murders in Texas. Otherwise the statutes are similar. Each requires the sentencing authority to focus on the particularized nature of the crime.

* * *

"We conclude that Texas' capital-sentencing procedures, like those of Georgia and Florida, do not violate the Eighth and Fourteenth Amendments. By narrowing its definition of capital murder, Texas has essentially said that there must be at least one statutory aggravating circumstance in a first-degree murder case before a death sentence may even be considered. By authorizing the defense to bring before the jury at the separate sentencing hearing whatever mitigating circumstances relating to the individual defendant can be adduced, Texas has ensured that the sentencing jury will have adequate guidance to enable it to perform its sentencing function. By providing prompt judicial review of the jury's decision in a court with statewide jurisdiction, Texas has provided a means to promote the evenhanded, rational, and consistent imposition of death sentences under law. Because this system serves to assure that sentences of death will not be 'wantonly' or 'freakishly' imposed, it does not violate the Constitution."

2. In Woodson v. North Carolina, 428 U.S. 280, 96 S.Ct. 2978, 49 L.Ed.2d 944 (1976), however, the Court struck down the North Carolina capital punishment scheme. That state had previously provided that the jury could, in its unbridled discretion, impose the death penalty for certain crimes, but subsequent to *Furman* had changed its statute to make the death penalty mandatory in first-degree murder cases. Petitioners' convictions under this new statutory scheme were reversed. The court said, in part:

* * *

"Although it seems beyond dispute that, at the time of the *Furman* decision in 1972, mandatory death penalty statutes had been renounced by American juries and legislatures, there remains the question whether the mandatory statutes adopted by North Carolina and a number of other States following *Furman* evince a sudden reversal of societal values regarding the imposition of capital punishment. In view of the persistent and unswerving legislative rejection of mandatory death penalty statutes beginning in 1838 and continuing for more than 130 years until *Furman*, it seems evident that the post-*Furman* enactments reflect attempts by the States to retain the death penalty in a form consistent with the Constitution, rather than a renewed societal acceptance of mandatory death sentencing.

* * *

". . . [O]ne of the most significant developments in our society's treatment of capital punishment has been the rejection of the common-law practice of inexorably imposing a death sentence upon every person convicted of a specified offense. North Carolina's mandatory death penalty statute for first-degree murder departs markedly from contemporary standards respecting the imposition of the punishment of death and thus cannot be applied consistently with the Eighth and Fourteenth Amendments' requirement that the State's power to punish 'be exercised within the limits of civilized standards.'

"A separate deficiency of North Carolina's mandatory death sentence statute is its failure to provide a constitutionally tolerable response to *Furman*'s rejection of unbridled jury discretion in the imposition of capital sentences. Central to the limited holding in *Furman* was the conviction that the vesting of standardless sentencing power in the jury violated the Eighth and Fourteenth Amendments. It is argued that North Carolina has remedied the inadequacies of the death penalty statutes held unconstitutional in *Furman* by withdrawing all sentencing discretion from juries in capital cases. But when one considers the long and consistent American experience with the death penalty in first-degree murder cases, it becomes evident that mandatory statutes enacted in response to *Furman* have simply papered over the problem of unguided and unchecked jury discretion.

* * *

"A third constitutional shortcoming of the North Carolina statute is its failure to allow the particularized consideration of relevant aspects of the character and record of each convicted defendant before the imposition upon him of a sentence of death. . . . A process that accords no significance to relevant facets of the character and record of the individual offender or the circumstances of the particular offense excludes from consideration in fixing the ultimate punishment of death the possibility of compassionate or mitigating factors stemming from the diverse frailties of humankind. It treats all persons convicted of a designated offense not as uniquely individual human beings, but as members of a faceless, undifferentiated mass to be subjected to the blind infliction of the penalty of death * * *."

Louisiana's death penalty statute, enacted in the wake of *Furman*, was also invalidated by the Court in Roberts v. Louisiana, 428 U.S. 325, 96 S.Ct. 3001 (1976). The Louisiana statute required imposition of the death penalty for five different types of homicide, if the jury should find that the defendant specifically intended to kill or do great bodily harm. The *Roberts* homicide was a felony-murder (killing during the commission of an armed robbery). Despite the narrower definition of murder than under the North Carolina scheme reviewed in *Woodson*, the plurality opinion identified these reasons for the statute's invalidity:

"The constitutional vice of mandatory death sentence statutes—lack of focus on the circumstances of the particular offense and the character and propensities of the offender—is not resolved by Louisiana's limitation of first-degree murder to various categories of killings. The diversity of circumstances presented in cases falling within the single category of killings during the commission of a specified felony, as well as the variety of possible offenders involved in such crimes, underscores the rigidity of Louisiana's enactment and its similarity to the North Carolina statute. Even the other more narrowly drawn categories of first-degree murder in the Louisiana law afford no meaningful opportunity for consideration of mitigating factors presented by the circumstances of the particular crime or by the attributes of the individual offender."

3. In Coker v. Georgia, 433 U.S. 584, 97 S.Ct. 2861, 53 L.Ed.2d 982 (1977) the Supreme Court struck down a death sentence for the crime of rape as grossly disproportionate and excessive punishment forbidden by the Eighth Amendment. The rape and armed robbery had been committed by an escaped felon and the death sentence had been imposed because of that aggravated factor. Mr. Justice White, in authoring the plurality opinion, stressed that the Eighth Amendment bars not only those punishments that are barbaric, but also those that are excessive in relation to the crime committed. A punishment is excessive and therefore unconstitutional if it "(1) makes no measurable contribution to acceptable goals of punishment and hence is nothing more than a purposeless and needless imposition of pain and suffering; or (2) is grossly out of proportion to the severity of the crime."

While rape is deserving of serious punishment, the Court's opinion suggested that the imposition of the death sentence for the rape, even though committed by a person with prior felony convictions, was excessive where under Georgia law a deliberate killer cannot be sentenced to death absent aggravating circumstances. It seemed incongruous to the Court that a rapist who does not take life should be punished more severely than a deliberate killer.

4. See also, Gardner v. Florida, 430 U.S. 349, 97 S.Ct. 1197, 51 L.Ed.2d 393 (1977), where the United States Supreme Court vacated a death sentence and remanded to the state supreme court because of the manner in which the sentence was imposed.

5. See also, Lockett v. Ohio, 438 U.S. 586, 98 S.Ct. 2954, 57 L.Ed.2d 973 (1978), where a plurality of the Court held state law provisions unconstitutional which did not permit a defendant to argue that he was only a minor participant in a homicide, and that he had no prior criminal record. The Court said that "the eighth and 14th amendments require that the sentencer, in all but the rarest of capital cases, not be precluded from considering as a mitigating factor, any aspect of a defendant's character or record and any of the circumstances of the offense that the defendant proffers as a basis for a sentence less than death." See also, in this regard, Bell v. Ohio, 438 U.S. 637, 98 S.Ct. 2977 (1978).

6. In Beck v. Alabama, 447 U.S. 625, 100 S.Ct. 2382, 65 L.Ed.2d 392 (1980), defendant and an accomplice committed a robbery during which the accomplice unexpectedly struck and killed the victim with a knife. The defendant freely admitted his intent to commit the robbery, but denied he had any intent to murder the victim. The state death penalty statute, however, prevented a jury instruction which would have allowed a conviction for the lesser included offense of felony-murder. The United States Supreme Court reversed both the verdict and the sentence, holding that the jury should have been permitted to consider whether the defendant was guilty of the lesser included non-capital offense of felony-murder. However, in Schad v. Arizona, ___ U.S. ___, 111 S.Ct. 2491, 115 L.Ed.2d 555 (1991), a first degree murder prosecution wherein the case was submitted to the jury under instructions that did not require unanimity on the available theories (premeditated murder and felony murder), *Beck* was said not to have been violated.

7. The Supreme Court denies certiorari in a great number of petitions from state convictions imposing capital punishment. In Coleman v. Balkcom,

451 U.S. 949, 101 S.Ct. 2031, 68 L.Ed.2d 334 (1981), 29 Cr.L. 4034. Mr. Justice Rehnquist dissented from the denial of certiorari. He said the Court should grant review in a greater number of death row cases, not to free more inmates from the imposition of the death penalty, but to insulate death sentences from further attack. He said that while hundreds of defendants have been condemned to death since the Gregg v. Georgia decision in 1976, only one defendant who did not want to die (John Spenkelink) was actually executed. Justice Rehnquist characterized this as "a mockery of our criminal justice system" in which the Supreme Court participates by sending a "signal to the lower state and federal courts that the actual imposition of the death sentence is to be avoided at all costs." Such a state of affairs frustrates the purposes of retribution and deterrence, he said. Mr. Justice Stevens concurred in the majority's denial of certiorari and criticized Mr. Justice Rehnquist's proposal as one that might result in an improper allocation of the Supreme Court's limited resources, since the Court could easily spend half its time with capital cases if it were to grant the many certiorari petitions of death row inmates. But even if the Court were to take that step, said Justice Stevens, that would still not achieve Justice Rehnquist's purpose, "(b)ecause this Court is not equipped to process all of these cases as expeditiously as the several district courts." It would therefore be "most unlikely that this innovative proposal would dramatically accelerate the execution of the persons on death row."

8. In Godfrey v. Georgia, 446 U.S. 420, 100 S.Ct. 1759, 64 L.Ed.2d 398 (1980), the Supreme Court dealt again with the Georgia death statute under which a person convicted of murder may be sentenced to death if it is found beyond a reasonable doubt that the offense was "outrageously or wantonly vile, horrible or inhuman in that it involved torture, depravity of mind, or an aggravated battery to the victim." This provision was held to be unconstitutionally vague as applied to a murder that did not involve torture nor an aggravated battery, and in which the defendant's mental state was not shown to be more depraved than that of any person guilty of murder.

9. In Mills v. Maryland, 486 U.S. 367, 108 S.Ct. 1860, 100 L.Ed.2d 384 (1988) the Court held, in a 5–to–4 decision, that Maryland's statutory scheme was unconstitutional in requiring that the jurors unanimously found specific mitigating circumstances present in the case, before an individual juror could consider that circumstance in deciding whether to impose the death penalty. And in McKoy v. North Carolina, 494 U.S. 433, 110 S.Ct. 1227, 108 L.Ed.2d 369 (1990), it was held that individual jurors cannot be limited to considering those mitigating factors which the jury unanimously determines to exist.

10. Continuing to fine-tune the constitutional problems presented by aggravating and mitigating circumstances, the Court decided, in Blystone v. Pennsylvania, 494 U.S. 299, 110 S.Ct. 1078, 108 L.Ed.2d 255 (1990), that while mandatory capital punishment schemes have been out since Woodson v. North Carolina and Roberts v. Louisiana, the mere fact that a statute has a mandatory feature to it, does not mean it is automatically unconstitutional. The Court continued to allow a jury to take into account all relevant mitigating circumstances and requiring them to find at least one aggravating factor that outweighed mitigating circumstances before imposing the death penalty.

Similarly, the Court held in Clemons v. Mississippi, 494 U.S. 738, 110 S.Ct. 1441, 108 L.Ed.2d 725 (1990), that an appellate court could properly hold a death sentence constitutional where it was based, in part, on improperly defined aggravating circumstances, if the reviewing court engaged in a reweighing of aggravating and mitigating circumstances, and determined that the error was harmless. Previously, in Maynard v. Cartwright, 486 U.S. 356, 108 S.Ct. 1853, 100 L.Ed.2d 372 (1988) the Court had struck down Oklahoma's death penalty statute as unconstitutionally vague where it permitted juries to find as an aggravating factor that the killing was "especially heinous, atrocious, or cruel." The words "especially heinous, cruel or depraved," however, were acceptable to a majority of the Court in Walton v. Arizona, 497 U.S. ___, 110 S.Ct. 3047, 111 L.Ed.2d 511 (1990), where the state supreme court had first determined the meaning of the words. See also, the decisions in Franklin v. Lynaugh, 487 U.S. 164, 108 S.Ct. 2320, 101 L.Ed.2d 155 (1988), and the earlier cases of Booth v. Maryland, 482 U.S. 496, 107 S.Ct. 2529, 96 L.Ed.2d 440 (1987) and Pulley v. Harris, 465 U.S. 37, 104 S.Ct. 871, 79 L.Ed.2d 29 (1984). In Payne v. Tennessee, ___ U.S. ___, 111 S.Ct. 2597, 115 L.Ed.2d 720 (1991), the Court overruled Booth v. Maryland, holding by a 6–3 majority, that "victim impact statements" may be admitted at the penalty phase of a capital trial.

EDDINGS v. OKLAHOMA

Supreme Court of the United States, 1982.
455 U.S. 104, 102 S.Ct. 869, 71 L.Ed.2d 1.

JUSTICE POWELL delivered the opinion of the Court.

Petitioner Monty Lee Eddings was convicted of first degree murder and sentenced to death. Because this sentence was imposed without "the type of individualized consideration of mitigating factors . . . required by the Eighth and Fourteenth Amendments in capital cases," we reverse.

I

On April 4, 1977, Eddings, a 16 year old youth, and several younger companions ran away from their Missouri homes. They travelled in a car owned by Eddings' brother, and drove without destination or purpose in a southwesterly direction eventually reaching the Oklahoma turnpike. Eddings had in the car a shotgun and several rifles he had taken from his father. After he momentarily lost control of the car, he was signalled to pull over by Officer Crabtree of the Oklahoma Highway Patrol. Eddings did so, and when the Officer approached the car, Eddings stuck a loaded shotgun out of the window and fired, killing the Officer.

Because Eddings was a juvenile, the State moved to have him certified to stand trial as an adult. Finding that there was prosecutive merit to the complaint and that Eddings was not amenable to rehabilitation within the juvenile system, the trial court granted the motion. The ruling was affirmed on appeal. Eddings was then charged with murder in the first degree, and the District Court of Creek County found him guilty upon his plea of nolo contendere.

The Oklahoma death penalty statute provides, in pertinent part:

"Upon conviction . . . of guilt of a defendant of murder in the first degree, the court shall conduct a separate sentencing proceeding to determine whether the defendant should be sentenced to death or life imprisonment. . . . In the sentencing proceeding, evidence may be presented as to *any mitigating circumstances* or as to any of the aggravating circumstances enumerated in this act." Okla.Stat., Tit. 21, § 701.10 (emphasis added).

Section 701.12 lists seven separate aggravating circumstances; the statute nowhere defines what is meant by "any mitigating circumstances."

At the sentencing hearing, the State alleged three of the aggravating circumstances enumerated in the statute: that the murder was especially heinous, atrocious, or cruel, that the crime was committed for the purpose of avoiding or preventing a lawful arrest, and that there was a probability that the defendant would commit criminal acts of violence that would constitute a continuing threat to society.

In mitigation, Eddings presented substantial evidence at the hearing of his troubled youth. The testimony of his supervising Juvenile Officer indicated that Eddings had been raised without proper guidance. His parents were divorced when he was 5 years old, and until he was 14 Eddings lived with his mother without rules or supervision. There is the suggestion that Eddings' mother was an alcoholic and possibly a prostitute. By the time Eddings was 14 he no longer could be controlled, and his mother sent him to live with his father. But neither could the father control the boy. Attempts to reason and talk gave way to physical punishment. The Juvenile Officer testified that Eddings was frightened and bitter, that his father overreacted and used excessive physical punishment: "Mr. Eddings found the only thing that he thought was effectful with the boy was actual punishment, or physical violence—hitting with a strap or something like this."

Testimony from other witnesses indicated that Eddings was emotionally disturbed in general and at the time of the crime, and that his mental and emotional development were at a level several years below his age. A state psychologist stated that Eddings had a sociopathic or anti-social personality and that approximately 30% of youths suffering from such a disorder grew out of it as they aged. App. 137 and 139. A sociologist specializing in juvenile offenders testified that Eddings was treatable. A psychiatrist testified that Eddings could be rehabilitated by intensive therapy over a 15 to 20 year period. He testified further that Eddings "did pull the trigger, he did kill someone, but I don't even think he knew that he was doing it." The psychiatrist suggested that, if treated, Eddings would no longer pose a serious threat to society.

At the conclusion of all the evidence, the trial judge weighed the evidence of aggravating and mitigating circumstances. . . . Finding that the only mitigating circumstance was Eddings' youth and finding further that this circumstance could not outweigh the aggravating circumstances present, the judge sentenced Eddings to death.

The Court of Criminal Appeals affirmed the sentence of death. . . .

II

In Lockett v. Ohio (1978), Chief Justice Burger, writing for the plurality, stated the rule that we apply today: [1]

> "[W]e conclude that the Eighth and Fourteenth Amendments require that the sentencer . . . not be precluded from considering, *as a mitigating factor,* any aspect of a defendant's character or record and any of the circumstances of the offense that the defendant proffers as a basis for a sentence less than death." (emphasis in original).

Recognizing "that the imposition of death by public authority is . . . profoundly different from all other penalties," the plurality held that the sentencer must be free to give "independent mitigating weight to aspects of the defendant's character and record and to circumstances of the offense proffered in mitigation. . . ." Because the Ohio death penalty statute only permitted consideration of three mitigating circumstances, the Court found the statute to be invalid.

As The Chief Justice explained, the rule in *Lockett* is the product of a considerable history reflecting the law's effort to develop a system of capital punishment at once consistent and principled but also humane and sensible to the uniqueness of the individual. Since the early days of the common law, the legal system has struggled to accommodate these twin objectives. Thus, the common law began by treating all criminal homicides as capital offenses, with a mandatory sentence of death. Later it allowed exceptions, first through an exclusion for those entitled to claim benefit of clergy and then by limiting capital punishment to murders upon "malice prepensed." In this country we attempted to soften the rigor of the system of mandatory death sentences we inherited from England, first by grading murder into different degrees of which only murder of the first degree was a capital offense and then by committing use of the death penalty to the absolute discretion of the jury. By the time of our decision in Furman v. Georgia (1972), the country had moved so far from a mandatory system that the imposition of capital punishment frequently had become arbitrary and capricious.

* * *

Thus, the rule in *Lockett* followed from the earlier decisions of the Court and from the Court's insistence that capital punishment be imposed fairly, and with reasonable consistency, or not at all. By requiring that the sentencer be permitted to focus "on the characteristics óf the person who committed the crime," the rule in *Lockett* recognizes that "justice . . . requires . . . that there be taken into account the circumstances of the offense together with the character and propensities of the offender." By holding that the sentencer in

---

1. Because we decide this case on the basis of Lockett v. Ohio, we do not reach the question of whether—in light of con- temporary standards—the Eighth Amendment forbids the execution of a defendant who was 16 at the time of the offense.

capital cases must be permitted to consider any relevant mitigating factor, the rule in *Lockett* recognizes that a consistency produced by ignoring individual differences is a false consistency.

III

We now apply the rule in *Lockett* to the circumstances of this case. The trial judge stated that "in following the law," he could not "consider the fact of this young man's violent background." There is no dispute that by "violent background" the trial judge was referring to the mitigating evidence of Eddings' family history. From this statement it is clear that the trial judge did not evaluate the evidence in mitigation and find it wanting as a matter of fact, rather he found that *as a matter of law* he was unable even to consider the evidence.

The Court of Criminal Appeals took the same approach. It found that the evidence in mitigation was not relevant because it did not tend to provide a legal excuse from criminal responsibility. . . .

We find that the limitations placed by these courts upon the mitigating evidence they would consider violated the rule in *Lockett*. Just as the state may not by statute preclude the sentencer from considering any mitigating factor, neither may the sentencer, refuse to consider, *as a matter of law*, any relevant mitigating evidence. In this instance, it was as if the trial judge had instructed a jury to disregard the mitigating evidence Eddings proffered on his behalf. The sentencer, and the Court of Criminal Appeals on review, may determine the weight to be given relevant mitigating evidence. But they may not give it no weight by excluding such evidence from their consideration.

Nor do we doubt that the evidence Eddings offered was relevant mitigating evidence. Eddings was a youth of 16 years at the time of the murder. Evidence of a difficult family history and of emotional disturbance is typically introduced by defendants in mitigation. In some cases, such evidence properly may be given little weight. But when the defendant was 16 years old at the time of the offense there can be no doubt that evidence of a turbulent family history, of beatings by a harsh father, and of severe emotional disturbance is particularly relevant.

*　　*　　*

We are not unaware of the extent to which minors engage increasingly in violent crime. Nor do we suggest an absence of legal responsibility where crime is committed by a minor. We are concerned here only with the manner of the imposition of the ultimate penalty: the death sentence imposed for the crime of murder upon an emotionally disturbed youth with a disturbed child's immaturity.

On remand, the state courts must consider all relevant mitigating evidence and weigh it against the evidence of the aggravating circumstances. We do not weigh the evidence for them. Accordingly, the judgment is reversed to the extent that it sustains the imposition of the death penalty, and the case is remanded for further proceedings not inconsistent with this opinion.

So ordered.

JUSTICE BRENNAN, concurring.

I join the Court's opinion without, however, departing from my view that the death penalty is in all circumstances cruel and unusual punishment prohibited by the Eighth and Fourteenth Amendments.

The opinion of JUSTICE O'CONNOR, concurring, is omitted.

CHIEF JUSTICE BURGER, with whom JUSTICE WHITE, JUSTICE BLACK-MUN, and JUSTICE REHNQUIST join, dissenting.

It is important at the outset to remember—as the Court does not— the narrow question on which we granted certiorari. We took care to limit our consideration to whether the Eighth and Fourteenth Amendments prohibit the imposition of a death sentence on an offender because he was 16 years old in 1977 at the time he committed the offense; review of all other questions raised in the petition for certiorari was denied. Yet the Court today goes beyond the issue on which review was sought—and granted—to decide the case on a point raised for the first time in petitioner's brief to this Court. This claim was neither presented to the Oklahoma courts nor presented to this Court in the petition for certiorari. Relying on this "eleventh-hour" claim, the Court strains to construct a plausible legal theory to support its mandate for the relief granted.

I

In Lockett v. Ohio, (1978), we considered whether Ohio violated the Eighth and Fourteenth Amendments by sentencing Lockett to death under a statute that "narrowly limit[ed] the sentencer's discretion to consider the circumstances of the crime and the record and character of the offense as mitigating factors." The statute at issue required the trial court to impose the death penalty upon Lockett's conviction for "aggravated murder with specifications," unless it found "that (1) the victim had induced or facilitated the offense, (2) it was unlikely that Lockett would have committed the offense but for the fact that she 'was under duress, coercion, or strong provocation,' or (3) the offense was 'primarily the product of [Lockett's] psychosis or mental deficiency.' " It was plain that although guilty of felony homicide under Ohio law, Lockett had played a relatively minor role in a robbery which resulted in a homicide actually perpetrated by the hand of another. Lockett had previously committed no major offenses; in addition, a psychological report described her "prognosis for rehabilitation" as "favorable." However, since she was not found to have acted under duress, did not suffer from "psychosis," and was not "mentally deficient," the sentencing judge concluded that he had " 'no alternative, whether [he] like[d] the law or not' but to impose the death penalty."

* * *

In contrast to the Ohio statute at issue in *Lockett,* the Oklahoma death penalty statute provides:

> "In the sentencing proceeding, evidence may be presented as to *any* mitigating circumstances or as to any of the aggravating circumstances enumerated in this act."

The statute further provides that

> "[u]nless at least one of the statutory aggravating circumstances enumerated in this act is [found to exist beyond a reasonable doubt] or if it is found that any such aggravating circumstance is outweighed by the finding of one or more mitigating circumstances, the death penalty shall not be imposed."

This provision, of course, instructs the sentencer to weigh the mitigating evidence introduced by a defendant against the aggravating circumstances proven by the state.

The Oklahoma statute thus contains provisions virtually identical to those cited with approval in *Lockett,* as examples of proper legislation which highlighted the Ohio statute's "constitutional infirmities." Indeed, the Court does not contend that the Oklahoma sentencing provisions are inconsistent with *Lockett.* Moreover, the Court recognizes that, as mandated by the Oklahoma statute, Eddings was permitted to present "substantial evidence at the [sentencing] hearing of his troubled youth."

In its attempt to make out a violation of *Lockett,* the Court relies entirely on a single sentence of the trial court's opinion delivered from the bench at the close of the sentencing hearing. After discussing the aggravated nature of petitioner's offense, and noting that he had "given very serious consideration to the youth of the Defendant when this particular crime was committed," the trial judge said that he could not

> "be persuaded entirely by the . . . fact that the youth was sixteen years old when this heinous crime was committed. Nor can the Court in following the law, in my opinion, consider the fact of this young man's violent background."

From this statement, the Court concludes "it is clear that the trial judge did not evaluate the evidence in mitigation and find it wanting as a matter of fact, rather he found that *as a matter of law* he was unable even to consider the evidence." This is simply not a correct characterization of the sentencing judge's action.

* * *

To be sure, neither the Court of Criminal Appeals nor the trial court labelled Eddings' family background and personality disturbance as "mitigating factors." It is plain to me, however, that this was purely a matter of semantics associated with the rational belief that "evidence in mitigation" must rise to a certain level of persuasiveness before it can be said to constitute a "mitigating circumstance." . . .

II

It can never be less than the most painful of our duties to pass on capital cases, and the more so in a case such as this one. However, there comes a time in every case when a court must "bite the bullet."

Whether the Court's remand will serve any useful purpose remains to be seen, for petitioner has already been given an opportunity to introduce whatever evidence he considered relevant to the sentencing determination. Two Oklahoma courts have weighed that evidence and found it insufficient to offset the aggravating circumstances shown by the state. The Court's opinion makes clear that some Justices who join it would not have imposed the death penalty had they sat as the sentencing authority. Indeed, I am not sure I would have done so. But the Constitution does not authorize us to determine whether sentences imposed by state courts are sentences we consider "appropriate"; our only authority is to decide whether they are constitutional under the Eighth Amendment. . . .

Because the sentencing proceedings in this case were in no sense inconsistent with Lockett v. Ohio, I would decide the sole issue on which we granted certiorari, and affirm the judgment.

NOTES

1. In *Eddings,* the Supreme Court avoided the question of whether juveniles should be exempt from the death penalty. Those who say that age should not be an absolute bar to execution rely on the theories of deterring others from violent crimes and of protecting society from juveniles who can not likely be rehabilitated. The other viewpoint is that youthful offenders are more amenable to rehabilitation and do not fully comprehend the nature of their acts. Also, about two-thirds of the 287 juveniles executed to date are black. This suggestion of racial discrimination provides another argument for excluding juveniles from the death penalty. See, in this regard, Anders & Brody, Should Juvenile Murderers Be Sentenced To Death?, A.B.A.J., June 1, 1986, at 32.

At its February, 1983 meeting in New Orleans, La., the Criminal Justice Section Council of the American Bar Association, by a 12–7 vote, concurred with a recommendation of its Juvenile Justice Committee that the death penalty be prohibited as a sentence for acts committed by persons under the age of 18. According to its report, the youngest person among the 13,600 legal executions in American history was 10 years old, with a total of 32 persons executed for crimes they committed while they were age 15 or younger. About 285 of the then executed persons had committed the offense while under the age of 18.

In Thompson v. Oklahoma, 487 U.S. 815, 108 S.Ct. 2687, 101 L.Ed.2d 702 (1988), the defendant was only fifteen at the time of the crime. A plurality of the Court (Justice Stevens, joined by Justices Brennan, Marshall, and Blackmun) expressed the belief that under today's standards of decency, the execution of a youth under sixteen would violate the provision against cruel and unusual punishment. Justice O'Connor shared this belief also, but chose to join the decision to reverse on a narrower procedural ground. The dissenters

(Justice Scalia, joined by Chief Justice Rehnquist and Justice White) felt that some lower age might be a more appropriate cut-off point. The following year, in Stanford v. Kentucky, 492 U.S. 361, 109 S.Ct. 2969, 106 L.Ed.2d 306 (1989), the Court sanctioned imposition of the death penalty on a defendant who was sixteen years old when the crime occurred.

2. Should a capital murder defendant's good behavior in jail between the time of his arrest and trial be considered as a mitigating factor in his sentencing? In Skipper v. South Carolina, 476 U.S. 1, 106 S.Ct. 1669, 90 L.Ed. 2d 1 (1986), a majority of the Court held that the defendant's adjustment to incarceration was indicative of future behavior and should be considered as a mitigating factor in the sentencing consideration.

ENMUND v. FLORIDA

Supreme Court of the United States, 1982.
458 U.S. 782, 102 S.Ct. 3368, 73 L.Ed.2d 1140.

JUSTICE WHITE delivered the opinion of the Court.

I

The facts of this case, taken principally from the opinion of the Florida Supreme Court, are as follows. On April 1, 1975, at approximately 7:45 a.m., Thomas and Eunice Kersey, aged 86 and 74, were robbed and fatally shot at their farmhouse in central Florida. The evidence showed that Sampson and Jeanette Armstrong had gone to the back door of the Kersey house and asked for water for an overheated car. When Mr. Kersey came out of the house, Sampson Armstrong grabbed him, pointed a gun at him, and told Jeanette Armstrong to take his money. Mr. Kersey cried for help, and his wife came out of the house with a gun and shot Jeanette Armstrong, wounding her. Sampson Armstrong, and perhaps Jeanette Armstrong, then shot and killed both of the Kerseys, dragged them into the kitchen, and took their money and fled.

Two witnesses testified that they drove past the Kersey house between 7:30 and 7:40 a.m. and saw a large cream or yellow-colored car parked beside the road about 200 yards from the house and that a man was sitting in the car. Another witness testified that at approximately 6:45 a.m. he saw Ida Jean Shaw, petitioner's common-law wife and Jeanette Armstrong's mother, driving a yellow Buick with a vinyl top which belonged to her and petitioner Earl Enmund. Enmund was a passenger in the car along with an unidentified woman. At about 8 a.m. the same witness saw the car return at a high rate of speed. Enmund was driving, Ida Jean Shaw was in the front seat, and one of the other two people in the car was lying down across the back seat.

Enmund, Sampson Armstrong, and Jeanette Armstrong were indicted for the first-degree murder and robbery of the Kerseys. Enmund and Sampson Armstrong were tried together. The prosecutor maintained in his closing argument that "Sampson Armstrong killed the old people." The judge instructed the jury that "[t]he killing of a human being while engaged in the perpetration of or in the attempt to perpetrate the offense of robbery is murder in the first degree even though there is no premeditated design or intent to kill." He went on to instruct them that

> "In order to obtain a conviction of first degree murder while engaging in the perpetration of or in the attempted perpetration of the crime of robbery, the evidence must establish beyond a reasonable doubt that the defendant was actually present and was actively aiding and abetting the robbery or attempted robbery, and that the unlawful killing occurred in the perpetration of or in the attempted perpetration of the robbery."

The jury found both Enmund and Sampson Armstrong guilty of two counts of first-degree murder and one count of robbery. A separate sentencing hearing was held and the jury recommended the death penalty for both defendants under the Florida procedure whereby the jury advises the trial judge whether to impose the death penalty. See Fla.Stat. § 921.141(2) (Supp.1981). The trial judge then sentenced Enmund to death on the two counts of first-degree murder. Enmund appealed, and the Florida Supreme Court remanded for written findings as required by Fla.Stat. § 921.141(3) (Supp.1981). The trial judge found four statutory aggravating circumstances: the capital felony was committed while Enmund was engaged in or was an accomplice in the commission of an armed robbery, the capital felony was committed for pecuniary gain, it was especially heinous, atrocious, or cruel, and Enmund was previously convicted of a felony involving the use or threat of violence, . . . The court found that "*none* of the statutory mitigating circumstances applied" to Enmund and that the aggravating circumstances outweighed the mitigating circumstances. Enmund was therefore sentenced to death on each of the murder counts.

The Florida Supreme Court affirmed Enmund's conviction and sentences. . . .

*   *   *

We granted Enmund's petition for certiorari, presenting the question whether death is a valid penalty under the Eighth and Fourteenth Amendments "for one who neither took life, attempted to take life, nor intended to take life."

II

As recounted above, the Florida Supreme Court held that the record supported no more than the inference that Enmund was the person in the car by the side of the road at the time of the killings, waiting to help the robbers escape. This was enough under Florida law to make Enmund a constructive aider and abettor and hence a principal in first-degree murder upon whom the death penalty could be imposed. . . . We have concluded that imposition of the death penalty in these circumstances is inconsistent with the Eighth and Fourteenth Amendments.

A

The Cruel and Unusual Punishment Clause of the Eighth Amendment is directed, in part, "against all punishments which by their excessive length or severity are greatly disproportioned to the offenses charged." Weems v. United States (1910). This Court most recently held a punishment excessive in relation to the crime charged in Coker v. Georgia (1977). There the plurality opinion concluded that the imposition of the death penalty for the rape of an adult woman "is grossly disproportionate and excessive punishment for the crime of rape and is therefore forbidden by the Eighth Amendment as cruel and unusual punishment." . . .

B

The *Coker* plurality observed that "[a]t no time in the last 50 years have a majority of the States authorized death as a punishment for rape." More importantly, in reenacting death penalty laws in order to satisfy the criteria established in Furman v. Georgia (1972), only three states provided the death penalty for the rape of an adult woman in their revised statutes. The plurality therefore concluded that "[t]he current judgment with respect to the death penalty for rape is not wholly unanimous among state legislatures, but it obviously weighs very heavily on the side of rejecting capital punishment as a suitable penalty for raping an adult woman."

Thirty-six state and federal jurisdictions presently authorize the death penalty. Of these, only nine jurisdictions authorize imposition of the death penalty solely for participation in a robbery in which another robber takes life. Of the remaining 27 jurisdictions, in three felony murder is not a capital crime. Eleven states require some culpable mental state with respect to the homicide as a prerequisite to conviction of a crime for which the death penalty is authorized. Of these 11 states, 8 make knowing, intentional, purposeful, or premeditated killing an element of capital murder. Three other states require proof of a culpable mental state short of intent, such as recklessness or extreme indifference to human life, before the death penalty may be imposed. In these 11 states, therefore, the actors in a felony murder are not subject to the death penalty without proof of their mental state, proof which was not required with respect to Enmund either under the trial court's instructions or under the law announced by the Florida Supreme Court.

Four additional jurisdictions do not permit a defendant such as Enmund to be put to death. Of these, one state flatly prohibits capital punishment in cases where the defendant did not actually commit murder. Two jurisdictions preclude the death penalty in cases such as this one where the defendant "was a principal in the offense, which was committed by another, but his participation was relatively minor, although not so minor as to constitute a defense to prosecution." One other state limits the death penalty in felony murders to narrow circumstances not involved here.

Nine of the remaining states deal with the imposition of the death penalty for a vicarious felony murder in their capital sentencing statutes. In each of these states, a defendant may not be executed *solely* for participating in a felony in which a person was killed if the defendant did not actually cause the victim's death. For a defendant to be executed in these states, typically the statutory aggravating circumstances which are present must outweigh mitigating factors. To be sure, a vicarious felony murderer may be sentenced to death in these jurisdictions absent an intent to kill if sufficient aggravating circumstances are present. However, six of these nine states make it a statutory *mitigating* circumstance that the defendant was an accomplice in a capital felony committed by another person and his participation was relatively minor. By making minimal participation in a capital felony committed by another person a mitigating circumstance, these sentencing statutes reduce the likelihood that a person will be executed for vicarious felony murder. The remaining three jurisdictions exclude felony murder from their lists of aggravating circumstances that will support a death sentence. In each of these nine states, a non-triggerman guilty of felony murder cannot be sentenced to death for the felony murder absent aggravating circumstances above and beyond the felony murder itself.

Thus only a small minority of jurisdictions—nine—allow the death penalty to be imposed solely because the defendant somehow participated in a robbery in the course of which a murder was committed. Even if the nine states are included where such a defendant could be executed for an unintended felony murder if sufficient aggravating circumstances are present to outweigh mitigating circumstances— which often include the defendant's minimal participation in the murder—only about a third of American jurisdictions would ever permit a defendant who somehow participated in a robbery where a murder occurred to be sentenced to die. Moreover, of the eight states which have enacted new death-penalty statutes since 1978, only one authorizes capital punishment in such circumstances. While the current legislative judgment with respect to imposition of the death penalty where a defendant did not take life, attempt to take it, or intend to take life is neither "wholly unanimous among state legislatures," nor as compelling as the legislative judgments considered in *Coker,* it nevertheless weighs on the side of rejecting capital punishment for the crime at issue.

* * *

III

Although the judgments of legislatures, juries and prosecutors weigh heavily in the balance, it is for us ultimately to judge whether the Eighth Amendment permits imposition of the death penalty on one such as Enmund who aids and abets a felony in the course of which a murder is committed by others but who does not himself kill, attempt to kill, or intend that a killing take place or that lethal force will be employed. We have concluded, along with most legislatures and juries, that it does not.

* * *

Here the robbers did commit murder; but they were subjected to the death penalty only because they killed as well as robbed. The question before us is not the disproportionality of death as a penalty for murder, but rather the validity of capital punishment for Enmund's own conduct. The focus must be on *his* culpability, not on that of those who committed the robbery and shot the victims, for we insist on "individualized consideration as a constitutional requirement in imposing the death sentence," which means that we must focus on "relevant facets of the character and record of the individual offender." . . . Enmund did not kill or intend to kill and thus his culpability is plainly different from that of the robbers who killed; yet the state treated them alike and attributed to Enmund the culpability of those who killed the Kerseys. This was impermissible under the Eighth Amendment.

* * *

For purposes of imposing the death penalty, Enmund's criminal culpability must be limited to his participation in the robbery, and his punishment must be tailored to his personal responsibility and moral guilt. Putting Enmund to death to avenge two killings that he did not commit and had no intention of committing or causing does not measurably contribute to the retributive end of ensuring that the criminal gets his just deserts. This is the judgment of most of the legislatures that have recently addressed the matter, and we have no reason to disagree with that judgment for purposes of construing and applying the Eighth Amendment.

IV

Because the Florida Supreme Court affirmed the death penalty in this case in the absence of proof that Enmund killed or attempted to kill, and regardless of whether Enmund intended or contemplated that life would be taken, we reverse the judgment upholding the death penalty and remand for further proceedings not inconsistent with this opinion.

So Ordered.

JUSTICE BRENNAN, concurring.

I join the Court's opinion. However, I adhere to my view that the death penalty is in all circumstances cruel and unusual punishment prohibited by the Eighth and Fourteenth Amendments.

JUSTICE O'CONNOR, with whom THE CHIEF JUSTICE, JUSTICE POWELL, and JUSTICE REHNQUIST join, dissenting.

Today the Court holds that the Eighth Amendment prohibits a State from executing a convicted felony murderer. I dissent from this holding not only because I believe that it is not supported by the analysis in our previous cases, but also because today's holding interferes with state criteria for assessing legal guilt by recasting intent as a matter of federal constitutional law.

I

The evidence at trial showed that at approximately 7:30 a.m. on April 1, 1975, Sampson and Jeanette Armstrong approached the backdoor of Thomas and Eunice Kersey's farmhouse on the pretext of obtaining water for their overheated car. When Thomas Kersey retrieved a water jug to help the Armstrongs, Sampson Armstrong grabbed him, held a gun to him, and told Jeanette Armstrong to take his wallet. Hearing her husband's cries for help, Eunice Kersey came around the side of the house with a gun and shot Jeanette Armstrong. Sampson Armstrong, and perhaps Jeanette Armstrong, returned the fire, killing both of the Kerseys. The Armstrongs dragged the bodies into the kitchen, took Thomas Kersey's money, and fled to a nearby car, where the petitioner Earl Enmund, was waiting to help the Armstrongs escape.

Ida Jean Shaw testified that on March 31 the petitioner and the two Armstrongs were staying at her house. When she awoke on April 1, the day of the murders, the petitioner, Jeanette, and Sampson, as well as Shaw's 1969 yellow Buick, were gone. A little after eight o'clock, either the petitioner or Sampson Armstrong entered the house and told her that Jeanette had been shot. After learning that Jeanette had been shot during a robbery, Shaw asked the petitioner "why he did it." Enmund answered that he had decided to rob Thomas Kersey after he had seen Kersey's money a few weeks earlier. At the same time, Sampson Armstrong volunteered that he had made sure that the Kerseys were dead.

Ida Jean Shaw also testified that, pursuant to the petitioner's and Sampson Armstrong's instructions, she had disposed of a .22 caliber pistol that she normally kept in her car, as well as a .38 caliber pistol belonging to the Armstrongs. The murder weapons were never recovered.

In his closing argument, the prosecutor did not argue that Earl Enmund had killed the Kerseys. Instead, he maintained that the petitioner had initiated and planned the armed robbery, and was in the car during the killings. According to the prosecutor, "Sampson Armstrong killed the old people."

After deliberating for four hours, the jury found Sampson Armstrong and the petitioner each guilty of two counts of first degree murder and one count of robbery. The jury then heard evidence pertaining to the appropriate sentence for the two defendants, and recommended the death penalty for each defendant on each of the murder counts.

In its sentencing findings, the trial court found four statutory aggravating circumstances regarding the petitioner's involvement in the murder: (1) the petitioner previously had been convicted of a felony involving the use of violence (an armed robbery in 1957), (2) the murders were committed during the course of a robbery, (3) the murders were committed for pecuniary gain, and (4) the murders were especially heinous, atrocious, or cruel because the Kerseys had been shot in a prone position in an effort to eliminate them as witnesses.

The trial court also found that "*none* of the statutory mitigating circumstances applied" to the petitioner. (emphasis in original). Most notably, the court concluded that the evidence clearly showed that the petitioner was an accomplice to the capital felony and that his participation had not been "relatively minor," but had been major in that he "planned the capital felony and actively participated in an attempt to avoid detection by disposing of the murder weapons."

* * *

On appeal, the Florida Supreme Court affirmed the petitioner's convictions and sentences. In challenging his convictions for first degree murder, the petitioner claimed that there was no evidence that he had committed premeditated murder, or that he had been present aiding and abetting the robbery when the Kerseys were shot. He argued that since the jury properly could have concluded only that he was in the car on the highway when the murders were committed, he could be found guilty at most of second degree murder under the State's felony murder rule.

The court rejected this argument.

* * *

II

Earl Enmund's claim in this Court is that the death sentence imposed by the Florida trial court, and affirmed by the Florida Supreme Court, is unconstitutionally disproportionate to the role he played in the robbery and murders of the Kerseys. In particular, he contends that because he had no actual intent to kill the victims—in effect, because his behavior and intent were no more blameworthy than that of any robber—capital punishment is too extreme a penalty.

. . . . Thus, it is necessary to examine the concept of proportionality as enunciated in this Court's cases to determine whether the penalty imposed on Earl Enmund is unconstitutionally disproportionate to his crimes.

A

The Eighth Amendment concept of proportionality was first fully expressed in Weems v. United States (1910). In that case, defendant Weems was sentenced to fifteen years at hard labor for falsifying a public document. After remarking that "it is a precept of justice that punishment for crime should be graduated and proportioned to offense," and after comparing Weems' punishment to the punishments for other crimes, the Court concluded that the sentence was cruel and unusual.

Not until two-thirds of a century later, in Coker v. Georgia (1977), did the Court declare another punishment to be unconstitutionally disproportionate to the crime. . . .

* * *

In addition to ascertaining "contemporary standards," the plurality opinion also considered qualitative factors bearing on the question whether the death penalty was disproportionate, for "the Constitution contemplates that in the end our own judgment will be brought to bear on the question of the acceptability of the death penalty under the Eighth Amendment." The plurality acknowledged that a rapist is almost as blameworthy as a murderer, . . . Despite the enormity of the crime of rape, however, the Court concluded that the death penalty was "grossly out of proportion to the severity of the crime," in part because the harm caused by a rape "does not compare with murder, which does involve the unjustified taking of human life."

* * *

B

* * *

As the petitioner acknowledges, the felony murder doctrine, and its corresponding capital penalty, originated hundreds of years ago, and was a fixture of English common law until 1957 when Parliament declared that an unintentional killing during a felony would be classified as manslaughter. The common law rule was transplanted to the American Colonies, and its use continued largely unabated into the Twentieth Century, although legislative reforms often restricted capital felony murder to enumerated violent felonies.

* * *

The Court's curious method of counting the States that authorize imposition of the death penalty for felony murder cannot hide the fact that 24 States permit a sentencer to impose the death penalty even though the felony murderer has neither killed nor intended to kill his victim. While the Court acknowledges that nine state statutes follow the Florida death penalty scheme, it also concedes that 15 other statutes permit imposition of the death penalty where the defendant neither intended to kill or actually killed the victims. Not all of the statutes list the same aggravating circumstances. Nevertheless, the question before the Court is not whether a particular species of death penalty statute is unconstitutional, but whether a scheme that permits imposition of the death penalty, absent a finding that the defendant either killed or intended to kill the victims, is unconstitutional. In short, the Court's peculiar statutory analysis cannot withstand closer scrutiny.

Thus, in nearly half of the States, and in two-thirds of the States that permit the death penalty for murder, a defendant who neither killed the victim nor specifically intended that the victim die may be sentenced to death for his participation in the robbery-murder. Far from "weigh[ing] very heavily on the side of rejecting capital punishment as a suitable penalty for" felony murder, these legislative judgments indicate that our "evolving standards of decency" still embrace capital punishment for this crime. For this reason, I conclude that the petitioner has failed to meet the standards in *Coker* and *Woodson* . . . In short, the death penalty for felony murder does not fall short of our national "standards of decency."

C

As I noted earlier, the Eighth Amendment concept of proportionality involves more than merely a measurement of contemporary standards of decency. It requires in addition that the penalty imposed in a capital case be proportional to the harm caused and the defendant's blameworthiness. . . .

Although the Court disingenuously seeks to characterize Enmund as only a "robber," it cannot be disputed that he is responsible, along with Sampson and Jeanette Armstrong, for the murders of the Kerseys. There is no dispute that their lives were unjustifiably taken, and that the petitioner, as one who aided and abetted the armed robbery, is legally liable for their deaths. Quite unlike the defendant in *Coker,* the petitioner cannot claim that the penalty imposed is "grossly out of proportion" to the harm for which he admittedly is at least partly responsible.

* * *

In sum, the petitioner and the Court have failed to show that contemporary standards, as reflected in both jury determinations and legislative enactments, preclude imposition of the death penalty for accomplice felony murder. . . . Finally, because of the unique and complex mixture of facts involving a defendant's actions, knowledge, motives, and participation during the commission of a felony murder, I believe that the factfinder is best able to assess the defendant's blameworthiness. Accordingly, I conclude that the death penalty is not disproportionate to the crime of felony murder, even though the defendant did not actually kill or intend to kill his victims.

* * *

NOTES

1. Must the finding that the defendant murdered or intended to murder be made by the judge or jury? The *Enmund* test of individualizing the defendant's punishment according to his personal responsibility and guilt may be determined at any point in a state's criminal process, even at the appellate level. The factual finding that the defendant himself killed, attempted to kill, or intended a killing need not be limited to a jury determination, but must be determined at some point in the state's judicial system. The Court explained

these standards in Cabana v. Bullock, 474 U.S. 376, 106 S.Ct. 689, 88 L.Ed.2d 704 (1986). There the defendant had initially held the victim while a robbery accomplice struck the victim in the face with a bottle. The accomplice then beat the victim and used a concrete block to crush the victim's head. Because the lower courts had not factually determined that the defendant himself had killed, attempted to kill or intended the killing, the death sentence was vacated and the case remanded, the state being given the option of imposing the alternative life imprisonment or make the required *Enmund* determination.

2. In Tison v. Arizona, 481 U.S. 137, 107 S.Ct. 1676, 95 L.Ed.2d 127 (1987), the father of the defendants, who had previously killed in an attempt to escape from prison, induced the defendants, his sons, ages 19 and 20, and another brother to bring weapons to their father and another prison inmate. In assisting in the escape, they helped to kidnap and rob a family passing in their automobile, and stood by without interfering while their father and the other escapee murdered the family. The Court said that imposition of the death penalty was not contrary to *Enmund*. Justice O'Connor's majority opinion described *Enmund* as prohibiting only the death penalty for minor participants in an armed robbery who did not kill, were not present when the killing occurred, and did not have the required mental state for an intentional killing. Here, by contrast, the jury could have found the sons were major participants in the crime. The case was, however, remanded for some additional fact findings.

In Booth v. Maryland, 482 U.S. 496, 107 S.Ct. 2529, 96 L.Ed.2d 440 (1987), the jury sentenced the defendant to death after considering a presentence report which included a victim impact statement. Such statements typically describe the personal characteristics of the victim and the emotional impact of the crimes on the family. A majority of the Court decided that victim impact statements are inadmissible at the sentencing stage of a capital murder as irrelevant and as creating a constitutionally unacceptable risk that the jury may impose the death penalty in an arbitrary and capricious manner.

3. In former times the death sentence was disproportionally imposed on blacks, particularly in the Southern states. Consider the statistics presented by Professor Anthony Amsterdam of Stanford University, in The Death Penalty Report, Vol. 1, No. 1, published by the National College for Criminal Defense, College of Law, University of Houston (Sept. 1980). Of the 652 inmates on death row at the time of Amsterdam's study, 351 were whites, 247 blacks, 27 with Spanish surnames, 5 "others" and 22 "unknown." Of the total number awaiting execution, 7 were females. Illustrative of the state statistics in point, in Georgia there were 42 blacks and 38 whites; in Florida, 59 blacks and 89 whites; in South Carolina, 3 blacks and 8 whites; in Texas 47 blacks and 65 whites. In Alabama the figures were 18 blacks and 9 whites, and in Arkansas 5 blacks and 6 whites.

Suppose a trial judge refuses to ask potential jurors in capital cases whether the fact that the defendant is black and the victim white would prejudice them against the defendant. Would this deprive the defendant of a fair and impartial trial? In Turner v. Murray, 476 U.S. 28, 106 S.Ct. 1683, 90 L.Ed.2d 27 (1986), a black man killed a white jewelry store owner during a robbery. The Virginia state trial judge did not allow the defense to question the potential jurors regarding racial prejudice. The Court rules that in interracial crimes the defendant is entitled to question the prospective jurors regarding racial prejudice, where the defendant specifically requests the inquiry. Justice Brennan criticized the "Solomonic" decision in this case for a remand for a new sentencing hearing, without a reversal of the conviction. He felt that reversal would be the only effective means of insuring an impartial jury for defendants involved in interracial crimes.

In McCleskey v. Kemp, 481 U.S. 279, 107 S.Ct. 1756, 95 L.Ed.2d 262 (1987), the defendant argued that a complicated statistical study of all murder cases in Georgia, which showed that the death penalty was imposed more frequently in cases where the victim was white and the defendant black, demonstrated the unconstitutionality of the statute. The majority was unconvinced by the statistical evidence. Justice Powell, writing for the Court, said that every capital case was unique, and before invalidating the exercise of discretion vested in the decision-makers, "we would demand exceptionally clear proof before we would infer that the discretion has been abused."

4. Is a jury impartial if every prospective juror who expresses reservations about imposing a death sentence is automatically excluded? Will such a practice result in a jury composed of people who more likely than not will return a death sentence? The defendant in Witherspoon v. Illinois, 391 U.S. 510, 88 S.Ct. 1770, 20 L.Ed.2d 776 (1968) argued that when 47 veniremen were quickly disqualified because of personal objections to capital punishment, the result was a "hanging" jury biased in favor of the death penalty. The Supreme Court agreed and reversed.

The *Witherspoon* test for excluding jurors in capital cases was that the juror make it "unmistakenly clear" that he/she would "automatically" reject the death penalty despite its appropriateness for the crime charged. The language used in *Witherspoon* has been replaced and now a juror may be rejected for cause when his beliefs about capital punishment would "prevent or substantially impair the performance of his duties as a juror in accordance with his instructions and oath." Adams v. Texas, 448 U.S. 38, 100 S.Ct. 2521, 65 L.Ed.2d 581 (1980). This more recent language was restated in Wainwright v. Witt, 469 U.S. 412, 105 S.Ct. 844, 83 L.Ed.2d 841 (1985).

5. Of the methods of execution, more than 100 countries continue to execute by various means ranging from stoning to the garroting. In one, for murderers and adulterers, the condemned person is tied to a stake in the village square and a government-paid executioner throws the first few stones until the condemned person is unconscious. Then the crowd joins in. In some others, the condemned person sits hooded and upright in a chair with a metal collar around his neck. A screw in the collar is gradually tightened until death occurs by either a severed spine or by strangulation.

FORD v. WAINWRIGHT

Supreme Court of the United States, 1986.
477 U.S. 399, 106 S.Ct. 2595, 91 L.Ed.2d 335.

JUSTICE MARSHALL announced the judgment of the Court and delivered the opinion of the Court with respect to Parts I and II and an opinion in Parts III, IV and V, in which JUSTICE BRENNAN, JUSTICE BLACKMUN, and JUSTICE STEVENS join.

For centuries no jurisdiction has countenanced the execution of the insane, yet this Court has never decided whether the Constitution forbids the practice. Today we keep faith with our common-law heritage in holding that it does.

I

Alvin Bernard Ford was convicted of murder in 1974 and sentenced to death. There is no suggestion that he was incompetent at the time of his offense, at trial, or at sentencing. In early 1982, however, Ford began to manifest gradual changes in behavior. They began as an occasional peculiar idea or confused perception, but became more serious over time. After reading in the newspaper that the Ku Klux Klan had held a rally in nearby Jacksonville, Florida, Ford developed an obsession focused upon the Klan. His letters to various people reveal endless brooding about his "Klan work," and an increasingly pervasive delusion that he had become the target of a complex conspiracy, involving the Klan and assorted others, designed to force him to commit suicide. He believed that the prison guards, part of the conspiracy, had been killing people and putting the bodies in the concrete enclosures used for beds. Later, he began to believe that his women relatives were being tortured and sexually abused somewhere in the prison. This notion developed into a delusion that the people who were tormenting him at the prison had taken members of Ford's family hostage. The hostage delusion took firm hold and expanded, until Ford was reporting that 135 of his friends and family were being held hostage in the prison, and that only he could help them. By "day 287" of the "hostage crisis," the list of hostages had expanded to include "senators, Senator Kennedy, and many other leaders." In a letter to the Attorney General of Florida, written in 1983, Ford appeared to assume authority for ending the "crisis," claiming to have fired a number of prison officials. He began to refer to himself as "Pope John Paul, III," and reported having appointed nine new justices to the Florida Supreme Court.

Counsel for Ford asked a psychiatrist who had examined Ford earlier, Dr. Jamal Amin, to continue seeing him and to recommend appropriate treatment. On the basis of roughly 14 months of evaluation, taped conversations between Ford and his attorneys, letters written by Ford, interviews with Ford's acquaintances, and various medical records, Dr. Amin concluded in 1983 that Ford suffered from "a severe, uncontrollable, mental disease which closely resembles 'Paranoid Schizophrenia With Suicide Potential' "—a "major mental disorder . . . severe enough to substantially affect Mr. Ford's present ability to assist in the defense of his life."

Ford subsequently refused to see Dr. Amin again, believing him to have joined the conspiracy against him, and Ford's counsel sought assistance from Dr. Harold Kaufman, who interviewed Ford in November 1983. Ford told Dr. Kaufman that "I know there is some sort of death penalty, but I'm free to go whenever I want because it would be illegal and the executioner would be executed." When asked if he would be executed, Ford replied, "I can't be executed because of the landmark case. I won. Ford v. State will prevent executions all over." These statements appeared amidst long streams of seemingly unrelated thoughts in rapid succession.   Dr. Kaufman concluded that Ford had no understanding of why he was being executed, made no connection between the homicide of which he had been convicted and the death penalty, and indeed sincerely believed that he would not be executed because he owned the prisons and could control the Governor through mind waves.   Dr. Kaufman found that there was "no reasonable possibility that Mr. Ford was dissembling, malingering or otherwise putting on a performance. . . ."   The following month, in an interview with his attorneys, Ford regressed further into nearly complete incomprehensibility, speaking only in a code characterized by intermittent use of the word "one," making statements such as "Hands one, face one.   Mafia one.   God one, father one, Pope one.   Pope one. Leader one."

Counsel for Ford invoked the procedures of Florida law governing the determination of competency of a condemned inmate, Fla.Stat. § 922.07 (1985).   Following the procedures set forth in the statute, the Governor of Florida appointed a panel of three psychiatrists to evaluate whether, under § 922.07(2), Ford had "the mental capacity to understand the nature of the death penalty and the reasons why it was imposed upon him."   At a single meeting, the three psychiatrists together interviewed Ford for approximately 30 minutes.   Each doctor then filed a separate two- or three-page report with the Governor, to whom the statute delegates the final decision.   One doctor concluded that Ford suffered from "psychosis with paranoia" but had "enough cognitive functioning to understand the nature and the effects of the death penalty, and why it is to be imposed on him."   Another found that, although Ford was "psychotic," he did "know fully what can happen to him."   The third concluded that Ford had a "severe adaptational disorder," but did "comprehend his total situation including being sentenced to death, and all of the implications of that penalty." He believed that Ford's disorder, "although severe, seem[ed] contrived and recently learned."   Thus, the interview produced three different diagnoses, but accord on the question of sanity as defined by state law.

The Governor's decision was announced on April 30, 1984, when, without explanation or statement, he signed a death warrant for Ford's execution.   Ford's attorneys unsuccessfully sought a hearing in state court to determine anew Ford's competency to suffer execution.   Counsel then filed a petition for habeas corpus in the United States District Court for the Southern District of Florida, seeking an evidentiary hearing on the question of Ford's sanity, proffering the conflicting findings of the Governor-appointed commission and subsequent challenges to their methods by other psychiatrists.   The District Court denied the petition without a hearing.   The Court of Appeals . . . addressed the merits of Ford's claim and a divided panel affirmed the District Court's denial of the writ.   This Court granted Ford's petition for certiorari in order to resolve the important issue whether the Eighth Amendment prohibits the execution of the insane and, if so, whether the District Court should have held a hearing on petitioner's claim.

II

* * *

There is now little room for doubt that the Eighth Amendment's ban on cruel and unusual punishment embraces, at a minimum, those modes or acts of punishment that had been considered cruel and unusual at the time that the Bill of Rights was adopted. . . .

Moreover, the Eighth Amendment's proscriptions are not limited to those practices condemned by the common law in 1789. Not bound by the sparing humanitarian concessions of our forebears, the Amendment also recognizes the "evolving standards of decency that mark the progress of a maturing society." Trop v. Dulles (1958) (plurality opinion). In addition to considering the barbarous methods generally outlawed in the 18th century, therefore, this Court takes into account objective evidence of contemporary values before determining whether a particular punishment comports with the fundamental human dignity that the Amendment protects.

A

We begin, then, with the common law. The bar against executing a prisoner who has lost his sanity bears impressive historical credentials; the practice consistently has been branded "savage and inhuman." 4 W. Blackstone, Commentaries *24–25 (1769) (hereinafter Blackstone). Blackstone explained:

> "[I]diots and lunatics are not chargeable for their own acts, if committed when under these incapacities: no, not even for treason itself. Also, if a man in his sound memory commits a capital offence, and before arraignment for it, he becomes mad, he ought not to be arraigned for it: because he is not able to plead to it with that advice and caution that he ought. And if, after he has pleaded, the prisoner becomes mad, he shall not be tried: for how can he make his defence? If, after he be tried and found guilty, he loses his senses before judgment, judgment shall not be pronounced; and if, after judgment, he becomes of nonsane memory, execution shall be stayed: for peradventure, says the humanity of the English law, had the prisoner been of sound memory, he might have alleged something in stay of judgment or execution."

Sir Edward Coke had earlier expressed the same view of the common law of England: "[B]y intendment of Law the execution of the offender is for example, . . . but so it is not when a mad man is executed, but should be a miserable spectacle, both against Law, and of extreme inhumanity and cruelty, and can be no example to others." E. Coke, Third Institute 6 (6th ed. 1680) (hereinafter Coke). Other recorders of the common law concurred.

As is often true of common-law principles, the reasons for the rule are less sure and less uniform than the rule itself. One explanation is that the execution of an insane person simply offends humanity; another, that it provides no example to others and thus contributes nothing to whatever deterrence value is intended to be served by capital punishment. Other commentators postulate religious underpinnings: that it is uncharitable to dispatch an offender "into another world, when he is not of a capacity to fit himself for it". It is also said that execution serves no purposes in these cases because madness is its own punishment: *furiosus solo furore punitur.* More recent commentators opine that the community's quest for "retribution"—the need to offset a criminal act by a punishment of equivalent "moral quality"—is not served by execution of an insane person, which has a "lesser value" than that of the crime for which he is to be punished. Unanimity of rationale, therefore, we do not find. "But whatever the reason of the law is, it is plain the law is so." We know of virtually no authority condoning the execution of the insane at English common law.

Further indications suggest that this solid proscription was carried to America, where it was early observed that "the judge is bound" to stay the execution upon insanity of the prisoner.

B

This ancestral legacy has not outlived its time. Today, no State in the Union permits the execution of the insane. It is clear that the ancient and humane limitation upon the State's ability to execute its sentences has as firm a hold upon the jurisprudence of today as it had centuries ago in England. The various reasons put forth in support of the common-law restriction have no less logical, moral, and practical force than they did when first voiced. . . . Faced with such widespread evidence of a restriction upon sovereign power, this Court is compelled to conclude that the Eighth Amendment prohibits a State from carrying out a sentence of death upon a prisoner who is insane. Whether its aim be to protect the condemned from fear and pain without comfort of understanding, or to protect the dignity of society itself from the barbarity of exacting mindless vengeance, the restriction finds enforcement in the Eighth Amendment.

III

* * *

IV

A

The first deficiency in Florida's procedure lies in its failure to include the prisoner in the truth-seeking process. Notwithstanding this Court's longstanding pronouncement that "[t]he fundamental requisite of due process of law is the opportunity to be heard," state practice does not permit any material relevant to the ultimate decision to be submitted on behalf of the prisoner facing execution. In all other proceedings leading to the execution of an accused, we have said that the factfinder must "have before it all possible relevant information about the individual defendant whose fate it must determine." And we have forbidden States to limit the capital defendant's submission of relevant evidence in mitigation of the sentence. It would be odd were we now to abandon our insistence upon unfettered presentation of relevant information, before the final fact antecedent to execution has been found.

Rather, consistent with the heightened concern for fairness and accuracy that has characterized our review of the process requisite to the taking of a human life, we believe that any procedure that precludes the prisoner or his counsel from presenting material relevant to his sanity or bars consideration of that material by the factfinder is necessarily inadequate. "[T]he minimum assurance that the life-and-death guess will be a truly informed guess requires respect for the basic ingredient of due process, namely, an opportunity to be allowed to substantiate a claim before it is rejected."

We recently had occasion to underscore the value to be derived from a factfinder's consideration of differing psychiatric opinions when resolving contested issues of mental state. In Ake v. Oklahoma, 470 U.S. 68, 105 S.Ct. 1087, 84 L.Ed.2d 53 (1985), we recognized that, because "psychiatrists disagree widely and frequently on what constitutes mental illness [and] on the appropriate diagnosis to be attached to given behavior and symptoms," the factfinder must resolve differences in opinion within the psychiatric profession "on the basis of the evidence offered by each party" when a defendant's sanity is at issue in a criminal trial. The same holds true after conviction; without any adversarial assistance from the prisoner's representative—especially when the psychiatric opinion he proffers is based on much more extensive evaluation than that of the state-appointed commission—the factfinder loses the substantial benefit of potentially probative information. The result is a much greater likelihood of an erroneous decision.

B

A related flaw in the Florida procedure is the denial of any opportunity to challenge or impeach the state-appointed psychiatrists' opinions. . . . Cross-examination of the psychiatrists, or perhaps a less formal equivalent, would contribute markedly to the process of seeking truth in sanity disputes by bringing to light the bases for each expert's beliefs, the precise factors underlying those beliefs, any history of error or caprice of the examiner, any personal bias with respect to the issue of capital punishment, the expert's degree of certainty about his or her own conclusions, and the precise meaning of ambiguous words used in the report. Without some questioning of the experts concerning their technical conclusions, a factfinder simply cannot be expected to evaluate the various opinions, particularly when they are themselves inconsistent. The failure of the Florida procedure to afford the prisoner's representative any opportunity to clarify or challenge the state experts' opinions or methods creates a significant possibility that the ultimate decision made in reliance on those experts will be distorted.

C

Perhaps the most striking defect in the procedures of Fla.Stat. § 922.07, as noted earlier, is the State's placement of the decision wholly within the executive branch. Under this procedure, the person who appoints the experts and ultimately decides whether the State will be able to carry out the sentence that it has long sought is the Governor, whose subordinates have been responsible for initiating every stage of the prosecution of the condemned from arrest through sentencing. The commander of the State's corps of prosecutors cannot be said to have the neutrality that is necessary for reliability in the factfinding proceeding.

Historically, delay of execution on account of insanity was not a matter of executive clemency (*ex mandato regis*) or judicial discretion (*ex arbitrio legis*); rather, it was required by law (*ex necessitate legis*). 1 N. Walker, Crime and Insanity in England 196 (1968). Thus, history affords no better basis than does logic for placing the final determination of a fact, critical to the trigger of a constitutional limitation upon the State's power, in the hands of the State's own chief executive. In no other circumstance of which we are aware is the vindication of a constitutional right entrusted to the unreviewable discretion of an administrative tribunal.

V

A

Having identified various failings of the Florida scheme, we must conclude that the State's procedures for determining sanity are inadequate to preclude federal redetermination of the constitutional issue. We do not here suggest that only a full trial on the issue of sanity will suffice to protect the federal interests; we leave to the State the task of developing appropriate ways to enforce the constitutional restriction upon its execution of sentences. It may be that some high threshold showing on behalf of the prisoner will be found a necessary means to control the number of nonmeritorious or repetitive claims of insanity. . . . Other legitimate pragmatic considerations may also supply the boundaries of the procedural safeguards that feasibly can be provided.

Yet the lodestar of any effort to devise a procedure must be the overriding dual imperative of providing redress for those with substantial claims and of encouraging accuracy in the factfinding determination. The stakes are high, and the "evidence" will always be imprecise.

It is all the more important that the adversary presentation of relevant information be as unrestricted as possible. Also essential is that the manner of selecting and using the experts responsible for producing that "evidence" be conducive to the formation of neutral, sound, and professional judgments as to the prisoner's ability to comprehend the nature of the penalty. Fidelity to these principles is the solemn obligation of a civilized society.

B

Today we have explicitly recognized in our law a principle that has long resided there. It is no less abhorrent today than it has been for centuries to exact in penance the life of one whose mental illness prevents him from comprehending the reasons for the penalty or its implications. In light of the clear need for trustworthiness in any factual finding that will prevent or permit the carrying out of an execution, we hold that Fla.Stat. § 922.07 provides inadequate assurances of accuracy to satisfy the requirements of Townsend v. Sain, 372 U.S. 293, 83 S.Ct. 745, 9 L.Ed.2d 770 (1963). Having been denied a factfinding procedure "adequate to afford a full and fair hearing" on the critical issue, petitioner is entitled to an evidentiary hearing in the District Court, *de novo,* on the question of his competence to be executed.

The judgment of the Court of Appeals is reversed, and the case remanded for further proceedings consistent with this opinion.

It is so ordered.

[The opinion of JUSTICE POWELL, concurring in part and concurring in the judgment, is omitted.]

JUSTICE O'CONNOR, with whom JUSTICE WHITE joins, concurring in the result in part and dissenting in part.

I am in full agreement with JUSTICE REHNQUIST's conclusion that the Eighth Amendment does not create a substantive right not to be executed while insane. Accordingly, I do not join the Court's reasoning or opinion. Because, however, the conclusion is for me inescapable that Florida positive law has created a protected liberty interest in avoiding execution while incompetent, and because Florida does not provide even those minimal procedural protections required by due process in this area, I would vacate the judgment and remand to the Court of Appeals with directions that the case be returned to the Florida system so that a hearing can be held in a manner consistent with the requirements of the Due Process Clause. . . .

* * *

JUSTICE REHNQUIST, with whom THE CHIEF JUSTICE joins, dissenting.

The Court today holds that the Eighth Amendment prohibits a State from carrying out a lawfully imposed sentence of death upon a person who is currently insane. This holding is based almost entirely on two unremarkable observations. First, the Court states that it "know[s] of virtually no authority condoning the execution of the insane at English common law." Second, it notes that "Today, no State in the Union permits the execution of the insane." Armed with these facts, and shielded by the claim that it is simply "keep[ing] faith with our common-law heritage," the Court proceeds to cast aside settled precedent and to significantly alter both the common-law and current practice of not executing the insane. It manages this feat by carefully ignoring the fact that the Florida scheme it finds unconstitutional, in which the Governor is assigned the ultimate responsibility of deciding whether a condemned prisoner is currently insane, is fully consistent with the "common-law heritage" and current practice on which the Court purports to rely.

The Court places great weight on the "impressive historical credentials" of the common-law bar against executing a prisoner who has lost his sanity. What it fails to mention, however, is the equally important and unchallenged fact that at common law it was the *executive* who passed upon the sanity of the condemned. See 1 N. Walker, Crime and Insanity in England 194–203 (1968). So when the Court today creates a constitutional right to a determination of sanity outside of the executive branch, it does so not in keeping with but at the expense of "our common-law heritage."

In Solesbee v. Balkcom, 339 U.S. 9, 70 S.Ct. 457, 94 L.Ed. 604 (1950), a condemned prisoner claimed that he had a constitutional right to a judicial determination of his sanity. There, as here, the State did not approve the execution of insane persons and vested in the Governor the responsibility for determining, with the aid of experts, the sanity *vel non* of persons sentenced to death. In rejecting the prisoner's claim, this Court stated:

> "Postponement of execution because of insanity bears a close affinity not to trial for a crime but rather to reprieves of sentences in general. The power to reprieve has usually sprung from the same source as the power to pardon. Power of executive clemency in this country undoubtedly derived from the practice as it had existed in England. Such power has traditionally rested in governors or the President, although some of that power is often delegated to agencies such as pardon or parole boards. Seldom, if ever, has this power of executive clemency been subjected to review by the courts."

Despite references to "evolving standards of decency," and "the jurisprudence of today," the Court points to no change since *Solesbee* in the States' approach to determining the sanity of a condemned prisoner. Current statutes quite often provide that initiation of inquiry into and/or final determination of post-sentencing insanity is a matter for the executive or the prisoner's custodian. The Court's profession of "faith to our common-law heritage" and "evolving standards of decency" is thus at best a half-truth. It is Florida's scheme—which combines a prohibition against execution of the insane with executive-branch procedures for evaluating claims of insanity—that is more faithful to both traditional and modern practice. And no matter how longstanding and universal, laws providing that the State should not execute persons the executive finds insane are not themselves sufficient to create an Eighth Amendment right that sweeps away as inadequate the procedures for determining sanity crafted by those very laws.

. . . Even the sole dissenter in *Solesbee*, JUSTICE FRANKFURTER, agreed that if the Constitution afforded condemned prisoners no substantive right not to be executed when insane, then the State would be free to place on the Governor the responsibility for determining sanity.

Petitioner argues that *Solesbee* is no longer controlling because it was decided "at a time when due process analysis still turned on the right-privilege distinction." But as petitioner concedes, his due process claim turns on a showing that the Florida statute at issue here created an individual right not to be executed while insane. Even a cursory reading of the statute reveals that the only right it creates in a condemned prisoner is to inform the Governor that the prisoner may be insane. Fla.Stat. § 922.07(1) (1985). The only legitimate expectation it creates is that "*[i]f the Governor decides* that the convicted person does not have the mental capacity to understand the nature of the death penalty and why it was imposed on him, he shall have him committed to a Department of Corrections mental health treatment facility." § 922.07(3) (emphasis added). Our recent cases in this area of the law may not be wholly consistent with one another. I do not think this state of the law requires the conclusion that Florida has granted petitioner the sort of entitlement that gives rise to the procedural protections for which he contends.

In any event, I see no reason to reject the *Solesbee* Court's conclusion that wholly executive procedures can satisfy due process in the context of a post-trial, post-appeal, post-collateral-attack challenge to a State's effort to carry out a lawfully imposed sentence. Creating a constitutional right to a judicial determination of sanity before that sentence may be carried out, whether through the Eighth Amendment or the Due Process Clause, needlessly complicates and postpones still further any finality in this area of the law. The defendant has already had a full trial on the issue of guilt, and a trial on the issue of penalty; the requirement of still a third adjudication offers an invitation to those who have nothing to lose by accepting it to advance entirely spurious claims of insanity. A claim of insanity may be made at any time before sentence and, once rejected, may be raised again; a prisoner found sane two days before execution might claim to have lost his sanity the next day, thus necessitating another judicial determination of his sanity and presumably another stay of his execution.

Since no State sanctions execution of the insane, the real battle being fought in this case is over what procedures must accompany the inquiry into sanity. The Court reaches the result it does by examining the common law, creating a constitutional right that no State seeks to violate, and then concluding that the common-law procedures are inadequate to protect the newly created by common-law based right. I find it unnecessary to "constitutionalize" the already uniform view that the insane should not be executed, and inappropriate to "selectively incorporate" the common-law practice. I therefore dissent.

NOTE

In Penry v. Lynaugh, 492 U.S. 302, 109 S.Ct. 2934, 106 L.Ed.2d 256 (1989), the Court observed that whether a particular criminal penalty is cruel and unusual punishment changes in accordance with "evolving standards of decency that mark the progress of a maturing society." Perceiving no national consensus against the practice, the Court held that the execution of the mentally retarded is not, as of now, barred by the Eighth Amendment.

3. DISPROPORTIONALITY OF SENTENCES

RUMMEL v. ESTELLE, CORRECTIONS DIRECTOR

Supreme Court of the United States, 1980.
445 U.S. 263, 100 S.Ct. 1133, 63 L.Ed.2d 382.

MR. JUSTICE REHNQUIST delivered the opinion of the Court.

Petitioner William James Rummel is presently serving a life sentence imposed by the State of Texas in 1973 under its "recidivist statute," formerly Art. 63 of its Penal Code, which provided that "[w]hoever shall have been three times convicted of a felony less than capital shall on such third conviction be imprisoned for life in the penitentiary." . . .

I

In 1964 the State of Texas charged Rummel with fraudulent use of a credit card to obtain $80 worth of goods or services. Because the amount in question was greater than $50, the charged offense was a felony punishable by a minimum of 2 years and a maximum of 10 years in the Texas Department of Corrections. Rummel eventually pleaded guilty to the charge and was sentenced to three years' confinement in a state penitentiary.

In 1969 the State of Texas charged Rummel with passing a forged check in the amount of $28.36, a crime punishable by imprisonment in a penitentiary for not less than two nor more than five years. Rummel pleaded guilty to this offense and was sentenced to four years' imprisonment.

In 1973 Rummel was charged with obtaining $120.75 by false pretenses. Because the amount obtained was greater than $50, the charged offense was designated "felony theft," which, by itself, was punishable by confinement in a penitentiary for not less than 2 nor more than 10 years. The prosecution chose, however, to proceed against Rummel under Texas' recidivist statute, and cited in the indictment his 1964 and 1969 convictions as requiring imposition of a life sentence if Rummel were convicted of the charged offense. A jury convicted Rummel of felony theft and also found as true the allegation that he had been convicted of two prior felonies. As a result, on April 26, 1973, the trial court imposed upon Rummel the life sentence mandated by Art. 63.

The Texas appellate courts rejected Rummel's direct appeal as well as his subsequent collateral attacks on his imprisonment. Rummel then filed a petition for a writ of habeas corpus in the United States District Court for the Western District of Texas. In that petition, he claimed, *inter alia,* that his life sentence was so disproportionate to the crimes he had committed as to constitute cruel and unusual punishment. The District Court rejected this claim, . . .

A divided panel of the Court of Appeals reversed. The majority relied upon this Court's decision in Weems v. United States, 217 U.S. 349 (1910), and a decision of the United States Court of Appeals for the Fourth Circuit, Hart v. Coiner, 483 F.2d 136 (1973), cert. denied, 415 U.S. 983 (1974), in holding that Rummel's life sentence was "so grossly disproportionate" to his offenses as to constitute cruel and unusual punishment.

Rummel's case was reheard by the Court of Appeals sitting en banc. That court vacated the panel opinion and affirmed the District Court's denial of habeas corpus relief on Rummel's Eighth Amendment claim. Of particular importance to the majority of the Court of Appeals en banc was the probability that Rummel would be eligible for parole within 12 years of his initial confinement. Six members of the Court of Appeals dissented, arguing that Rummel had no enforceable right to parole and that *Weems* and *Hart* compelled a finding that Rummel's life sentence was unconstitutional.

II

Initially, we believe it important to set forth two propositions that Rummel does not contest. First, Rummel does not challenge the constitutionality of Texas' recidivist statute as a general proposition. . . .

Second, Rummel does not challenge Texas' authority to punish each of his offenses as felonies, that is, by imprisoning him in a state penitentiary. . . . Rummel's challenge thus focuses only on the State's authority to impose a sentence of life imprisonment, as opposed to a substantial term of years, for his third felony.

This Court has on occasion stated that the Eighth Amendment prohibits imposition of a sentence that is grossly disproportionate to the severity of the crime. In recent years this proposition has appeared most frequently in opinions dealing with the death penalty. Rummel cites these latter opinions dealing with capital punishment as compelling the conclusion that his sentence is disproportionate to his offenses. But as Mr. Justice Stewart noted in *Furman:*

"The penalty of death differs from all other forms of criminal punishment, not in degree but in kind. It is unique in its total irrevocability. It is unique in its rejection of rehabilitation of the convict as a basic purpose of criminal justice. And it is unique, finally, in its absolute renunciation of all that is embodied in our concept of humanity."

This theme, the unique nature of the death penalty for purposes of Eighth Amendment analysis, has been repeated time and time again in our opinions. . . . Because a sentence of death differs in kind from any sentence of imprisonment, no matter how long, our decisions applying the prohibition of cruel and unusual punishments to capital cases are of limited assistance in deciding the constitutionality of the punishment meted out to Rummel.

Outside the context of capital punishment, successful challenges to the proportionality of particular sentences have been exceedingly rare. In Weems v. United States, supra, a case coming to this Court from the Supreme Court of the Philippine Islands, petitioner successfully attacked the imposition of a punishment known as *"cadena temporal"* for the crime of falsifying a public record. Although the Court in *Weems* invalidated the sentence after weighing "the mischief and the remedy," its finding of disproportionality cannot be wrenched from the extreme facts of that case. As for the "mischief," Weems was convicted of falsifying a public document, a crime apparently complete upon the knowing entry of a single item of false information in a public record, "though there be no one injured, though there be no fraud or purpose of it, no gain or desire of it." The mandatory "remedy" for this offense was *cadena temporal,* a punishment described graphically by the Court:

"Its minimum degree is confinement in a penal institution for twelve years and one day, a chain at the ankle and wrist of the offender, hard and painful labor, no assistance from friend or relative, no marital authority or parental rights or rights of property, no participation even in the family council. These parts of his penalty endure for the term of imprisonment. From other parts there is no intermission. His prison bars and chains are removed, it is true, after twelve years, but he goes from them to a perpetual limitation of his liberty. He is forever kept under the shadow of his crime, forever kept within voice and view of the criminal magistrate, not being able to change his domicil without giving notice to the 'authority immediately in charge of his surveillance,' and without permission in writing."

Although Rummel argues that the length of Weems' imprisonment was, by itself, a basis for the Court's decision, the Court's opinion does not support such a simple conclusion. The opinion consistently referred jointly to the length of imprisonment and its "accessories" or "accompaniments." Indeed, the Court expressly rejected an argument made on behalf of the United States that "the provision for imprisonment in the

Philippine Code is separable from the accessory punishment, and that the latter may be declared illegal, leaving the former to have application." According to the Court, "[t]he Philippine Code unites the penalities of *cadena temporal,* principal and accessory, and it is not in our power to separate them. . . ." Thus, we do not believe that *Weems* can be applied without regard to its peculiar facts: the triviality of the charged offense, the impressive length of the minimum term of imprisonment, and the extraordinary nature of the "accessories" included within the punishment of *cadena temporal.*

Given the unique nature of the punishments considered in *Weems* and in the death penalty cases, one could argue without fear of contradiction by any decision of this Court that for crimes concededly classified and classifiable as felonies, that is, as punishable by significant terms of imprisonment in a state penitentiary, the length of the sentence actually imposed is purely a matter of legislative prerogative.[1] Only six years after *Weems,* for example, Mr. Justice Holmes wrote for a unanimous Court in brushing aside a proportionality challenge to concurrent sentences of five years' imprisonment and cumulative fines of $1,000 on each of seven counts of mail fraud. See Badders v. United States, 240 U.S. 391 (1916). According to the Court, there was simply "no ground for declaring the punishment unconstitutional."

Such reluctance to review legislatively mandated terms of imprisonment is implicit in our more recent decisions as well. . . .

In an attempt to provide us with objective criteria against which we might measure the proportionality of his life sentence, Rummel points to certain characteristics of his offenses that allegedly render them "petty." He cites, for example, the absence of violence in his crimes. But the presence or absence of violence does not always affect the strength of society's interest in deterring a particular crime or in punishing a particular criminal. A high official in a large corporation can commit undeniably serious crimes in the area of antitrust, bribery, or clean air or water standards without coming close to engaging in any "violent" or short-term "life-threatening" behavior. Additionally, Rummel cites the "small" amount of money taken in each of his crimes. But to recognize that the State of Texas could have imprisoned Rummel for life if he had stolen $5,000, $50,000, or $500,000, rather than the $120.75 that a jury convicted him of stealing, is virtually to concede that the lines to be drawn are indeed "subjective," and therefore properly within the province of legislatures, not courts. Moreover, if Rummel had attempted to defraud his victim of $50,000, but had failed, no money whatsoever would have changed hands; yet Rummel would be no less blameworthy, only less skillful, than if he had succeeded.

* * *

Nearly 70 years ago, and only 2 years after *Weems,* this Court rejected an Eighth Amendment claim that seems factually indistin-

---

1. This is not to say that a proportionality principle would not come into play in the extreme example mentioned by the dissent, if a legislature made overtime parking a felony punishable by life imprisonment.

guishable from that advanced by Rummel in the present case. In Graham v. West Virginia, 224 U.S. 616 (1912), this Court considered the case of an apparently incorrigible horsethief who was sentenced to life imprisonment under West Virginia's recidivist statute. In 1898 Graham had been convicted of stealing "one bay mare" valued at $50; in 1901 he had been convicted of "feloniously and burglariously" entering a stable in order to steal "one brown horse, named Harry, of the value of $100"; finally, in 1907 he was convicted of stealing "one red roan horse" valued at $75 and various tack and accessories valued at $85. Upon conviction of this last crime, Graham received the life sentence mandated by West Virginia's recidivist statute. This Court did not tarry long on Graham's Eighth Amendment claim, noting only that it could not be maintained "that cruel and unusual punishment [had] been inflicted."

Undaunted by earlier cases like *Graham* and *Badders,* Rummel attempts to ground his proportionality attack on an alleged "nationwide" trend away from mandatory life sentences and toward "lighter, discretionary sentences." According to Rummel, "[n]o jurisdiction in the United States or the Free World punishes habitual offenders as harshly as Texas." In support of this proposition, Rummel offers detailed charts and tables documenting the history of recidivist statutes in the United States since 1776.

* * *

Rummel's charts and tables do appear to indicate that he might have received more lenient treatment in almost any State other than Texas, West Virginia, or Washington. The distinctions, however, are subtle rather than gross. A number of States impose a mandatory life sentence upon conviction of four felonies rather than three. Other States require one or more of the felonies to be "violent" to support a life sentence. Still other States leave the imposition of a life sentence after three felonies within the discretion of a judge or jury. It is one thing for a court to compare those States that impose capital punishment for a specific offense with those States that do not. It is quite another thing for a court to attempt to evaluate the position of any particular recidivist scheme within Rummel's complex matrix.

Nor do Rummel's extensive charts even begin to reflect the complexity of the comparison he asks this Court to make. Texas, we are told, has a relatively liberal policy of granting "good time" credits to its prisoners, a policy that historically has allowed a prisoner serving a life sentence to become eligible for parole in as little as 12 years. We agree with Rummel that his inability to enforce any "right" to parole precludes us from treating his life sentence as if it were equivalent to a sentence of 12 years. Nevertheless, because parole is "an established variation on imprisonment of convicted criminals," a proper assessment of Texas' treatment of Rummel could hardly ignore the possibility that he will not actually be imprisoned for the rest of his life. If nothing else, the possibility of parole, however slim, serves to distinguish Rummel from a person sentenced under a recidivist statute like Mississippi's, which provides for a sentence of life without parole upon conviction of three felonies including at least one violent felony.

*   *   *

III

The most casual review of the various criminal justice systems now in force in the 50 States of the Union shows that the line dividing felony theft from petty larceny, a line usually based on the value of the property taken, varies markedly from one State to another. We believe that Texas is entitled to make its own judgment as to where such lines lie, subject only to those strictures of the Eighth Amendment that can be informed by objective factors. Moreover, given Rummel's record, Texas was not required to treat him in the same manner as it might treat him were this his first "petty property offense." Having twice imprisoned him for felonies, Texas was entitled to place upon Rummel the onus of one who is simply unable to bring his conduct within the social norms prescribed by the criminal law of the State.

The purpose of a recidivist statute such as that involved here is not to simplify the task of prosecutors, judges, or juries. Its primary goals are to deter repeat offenders and, at some point in the life of one who repeatedly commits criminal offenses serious enough to be punished as felonies, to segregate that person from the rest of society for an extended period of time. This segregation and its duration are based not merely on that person's most recent offense but also on the propensities he has demonstrated over a period of time during which he has been convicted of and sentenced for other crimes. Like the line dividing felony theft from petty larceny, the point at which a recidivist will be deemed to have demonstrated the necessary propensities and the amount of time that the recidivist will be isolated from society are matters largely within the discretion of the punishing jurisdiction.

We therefore hold that the mandatory life sentence imposed upon this petitioner does not constitute cruel and unusual punishment under the Eighth and Fourteenth Amendments. The judgment of the Court of Appeals will be

Affirmed.

The opinion of JUSTICE STEWART, concurring, is omitted.

MR. JUSTICE POWELL, with whom MR. JUSTICE BRENNAN, MR. JUSTICE MARSHALL, and MR. JUSTICE STEVENS join, dissenting.

The question in this case is whether petitioner was subjected to cruel and unusual punishment in contravention of the Eighth Amendment, made applicable to the States by the Fourteenth Amendment, when he received a mandatory life sentence upon his conviction for a third property-related felony. Today, the Court holds that petitioner has not been punished unconstitutionally. I dissent.

I

* * *

This Court today affirms the Fifth Circuit's decision. I dissent because I believe that (i) the penalty for a noncapital offense may be unconstitutionally disproportionate, (ii) the possibility of parole should not be considered in assessing the nature of the punishment, (iii) a mandatory life sentence is grossly disproportionate as applied to petitioner, and (iv) the conclusion that this petitioner has suffered a violation of his Eighth Amendment rights is compatible with principles of judicial restraint and federalism.

II

A

The Eighth Amendment prohibits "cruel and unusual punishments." That language came from Art. I, § 9, of the Virginia Declaration of Rights, which provided that "excessive bail ought not to be required, nor excessive fines imposed, nor cruel and unusual punishment inflicted." The words of the Virginia Declaration were taken from the English Bill of Rights of 1689. See Granucci, "Nor Cruel and Unusual Punishments Inflicted": The Original Meaning, 57 Calif.L. Rev. 839, 840 (1969).

Although the legislative history of the Eighth Amendment is not extensive, we can be certain that the Framers intended to proscribe inhumane methods of punishment. When the Virginia delegates met to consider the Federal Constitution, for example, Patrick Henry specifically noted the absence of the provisions contained within the Virginia Declaration. Henry feared that without a "cruel and unusual punishments" clause, Congress "may introduce the practice . . . of torturing, to extort a confession of the crime." Indeed, during debate in the First Congress on the adoption of the Bill of Rights, one Congressman objected to adoption of the Eighth Amendment precisely because "villains often deserve whipping, and perhaps having their ears cut off."

In two 19th–century cases, the Court considered constitutional challenges to forms of capital punishment. In Wilkerson v. Utah, 99 U.S. 130, 135 (1879), the Court held that death by shooting did not constitute cruel and unusual punishment. The Court emphasized, however, that torturous methods of execution, such as burning a live offender, would violate the Eighth Amendment. In re Kemmler, 136 U.S. 436 (1890), provided the Court with its second opportunity to review methods of carrying out a death penalty. That case involved a constitutional challenge to New York's use of electrocution. Although the Court did not apply the Eighth Amendment to state action, it did conclude that electrocution would not deprive the petitioner of due process of law. See also Louisiana ex rel. Francis v. Resweber, 329 U.S. 459, 464 (1947).

B

The scope of the Cruel and Unusual Punishments Clause extends not only to barbarous methods of punishment, but also to punishments that are grossly disproportionate. Disproportionality analysis measures the relationship between the nature and number of offenses committed and the severity of the punishment inflicted upon the offender. The inquiry focuses on whether a person deserves such punishment, not simply on whether punishment would serve a utilitarian goal. A statute that levied a mandatory life sentence for overtime parking might well deter vehicular lawlessness, but it would offend our felt sense of justice. The Court concedes today that the principle of disproportionality plays a role in the review of sentences imposing the death penalty, but suggests that the principle may be less applicable when a noncapital sentence is challenged. Such a limitation finds no support in the history of Eighth Amendment jurisprudence.

The principle of disproportionality is rooted deeply in English constitutional law. The Magna Carta of 1215 insured that "[a] free man shall not be [fined] for a trivial offence, except in accordance with the degree of the offence; and for a serious offence he shall be [fined] according to its gravity." By 1400, the English common law had embraced the principle, not always followed in practice, that punishment should not be excessive either in severity or length. One commentator's survey of English law demonstrates that the "cruel and unusual punishments" clause of the English Bill of Rights of 1689 "was first, an objection to the imposition of punishments which were unauthorized by statute and outside the jurisdiction of the sentencing court, and second, a reiteration of the English policy against disproportionate penalties." Granucci, supra, at 860.

In Weems v. United States (1910), a public official convicted for falsifying a public record claimed that he suffered cruel and unusual punishment when he was sentenced to serve 15 years' imprisonment in hard labor with chains.[1] The sentence also subjected Weems to loss of civil rights and perpetual surveillance after his release. This Court agreed that the punishment was cruel and unusual. The Court was attentive to the methods of the punishment, but its conclusion did not rest solely upon the nature of punishment. The Court relied explicitly upon the relationship between the crime committed and the punishment imposed:

1. The principle that grossly disproportionate sentences violate the Eighth Amendment was first enunciated in this Court by Mr. Justice Field in O'Neil v. Vermont, 144 U.S. 323 (1892). In that case, a defendant convicted of 307 offenses for selling alcoholic beverages in Vermont had been sentenced to more than 54 years in prison. The Court did not reach the question whether the sentence violated the Eighth Amendment because the issue had not been raised properly, and because the Eighth Amendment had yet to be applied against the States. But Mr. Justice Field dissented, asserting that the "cruel and unusual punishment" Clause was directed "against all punishments which by their excessive length or severity are greatly disproportioned to the offences charged."

"Such penalties for such offenses amaze those who have formed their conception of the relation of a state to even its offending citizens from the practice of the American commonwealths, and believe that it is a precept of justice that punishment for crime should be graduated and proportioned to offense."

In both capital and noncapital cases this Court has recognized that the decision in Weems v. United States "proscribes punishment grossly disproportionate to the severity of the crime."

In order to resolve the constitutional issue, the *Weems* Court measured the relationship between the punishment and the offense. The Court noted that Weems had been punished more severely than persons in the same jurisdiction who committed more serious crimes, or persons who committed a similar crime in other American jurisdictions.

Robinson v. California (1962), established that the Cruel and Unusual Punishments Clause applies to the States through the operation of the Fourteenth Amendment. The Court held that imprisonment for the crime of being a drug addict was cruel and unusual. The Court based its holding not upon the method of punishment, but on the nature of the "crime." Because drug addition is an illness which may be contracted involuntarily, the Court said that "imprisonment for ninety days is not, in the abstract, a punishment which is either cruel or unusual. But the question cannot be considered in the abstract. Even one day in prison would be a cruel and unusual punishment for the 'crime' of having a common cold."

In Furman v. Georgia (1972), the Court held that the death penalty may constitute cruel and unusual punishment in some circumstances. The special relevance of *Furman* to this case lies in the general acceptance by Members of the Court of two basic principles. First, the Eighth Amendment prohibits grossly excessive punishment. Second, the scope of the Eighth Amendment is to be measured by "evolving standards of decency."

* * *

In sum, a few basic principles emerge from the history of the Eighth Amendment. Both barbarous forms of punishment and grossly excessive punishments are cruel and unusual. A sentence may be excessive if it serves no acceptable social purpose, or is grossly disproportionate to the seriousness of the crime. The principle of disproportionality has been acknowledged to apply to both capital and noncapital sentences.

* * *

III

* * *

IV

The Eighth Amendment commands this Court to enforce the constitutional limitation of the Cruel and Unusual Punishments Clause. In discharging this responsibility, we should minimize the risk of constitutionalizing the personal predilections of federal judges by relying upon certain objective factors. Among these are (i) the nature of the offense; (ii) the sentence imposed for commission of the same crime in other jurisdictions; and (iii) the sentence imposed upon other criminals in the same jurisdiction.

A

Each of the crimes that underlies the petitioner's conviction as a habitual offender involves the use of fraud to obtain small sums of money ranging from $28.36 to $120.75. In total, the three crimes involved slightly less than $230. None of the crimes involved injury to one's person, threat of injury to one's person, violence, the threat of violence, or the use of a weapon. Nor does the commission of any such crimes ordinarily involve a threat of violent action against another person or his property. It is difficult to imagine felonies that pose less danger to the peace and good order of a civilized society than the three crimes committed by the petitioner. Indeed, the state legislature's recodification of its criminal law supports this conclusion. Since the petitioner was convicted as a habitual offender, the State has reclassified his third offense, theft by false pretext, as a misdemeanor.

B

Apparently, only 12 States have ever enacted habitual offender statutes imposing a mandatory life sentence for the commission of two or three nonviolent felonies and only 3, Texas, Washington, and West Virginia, have retained such a statute. Thus, three-fourths of the States that experimented with the Texas scheme appear to have decided that the imposition of a mandatory life sentence upon some persons who have committed three felonies represents excess punishment. Kentucky, for example, replaced the mandatory life sentence with a more flexible scheme "because of a judgment that under some circumstances life imprisonment for an habitual criminal is not justified. An example would be an offender who has committed three Class D felonies, none involving injury to person." Commentary following Criminal Law of Kentucky Annotated, Penal Code § 532.080, p. 790 (1978). The State of Kansas abolished its statute mandating a life sentence for the commission of three felonies after a state legislative commission concluded that "[t]he legislative policy as expressed in the habitual criminal law bears no particular resemblance to the enforcement policy of prosecutors and judges." Kansas Legislative Council, The Operation of the Kansas Habitual Criminal Law, Pub. No. 47, p. 4 (1936). In the eight years following enactment of the Kansas statute, only 96 of the 733 defendants who committed their third felony were sentenced to life imprisonment. This statistic strongly supports the belief that prosecutors and judges thought the habitual offender statute too severe. In Washington, which retains the Texas rule, the State Supreme Court has suggested that application of its statute to persons like the petitioner might constitute cruel and unusual punishment.

More than three-quarters of American jurisdictions have never adopted a habitual offender statute that would commit the petitioner to mandatory life imprisonment. The jurisdictions that currently employ habitual offender statutes either (i) require the commission of more than three offenses, (ii) require the commission of at least one violent crime, (iii) limit a mandatory penalty to less than life, or (iv) grant discretion to the sentencing authority. In none of the jurisdictions could the petitioner have received a mandatory life sentence merely upon the showing that he committed three nonviolent property-related offenses.

The federal habitual offender statute also differs materially from the Texas statute. Title 18 U.S.C. § 3575 provides increased sentences for "dangerous special offenders" who have been convicted of a felony. A defendant is a "dangerous special offender" if he has committed two or more previous felonies, one of them within the last five years, if the current felony arose from a pattern of conduct "which constituted a substantial source of his income, and in which he manifested special skill or expertise," or if the felony involved a criminal conspiracy in which the defendant played a supervisory role. Federal courts may sentence such persons "to imprisonment for an appropriate term not to exceed twenty-five years and not disproportionate in severity to the maximum term otherwise authorized by law for such felony." Thus, Congress and an overwhelming number of state legislatures have not adopted the Texas scheme. These legislative decisions lend credence to the view that a mandatory life sentence for the commission of three nonviolent felonies is unconstitutionally disproportionate.[2]

* * *

C

* * *

2. The American Law Institute proposes that a felon be sentenced to an extended term of punishment only if he is a persistent offender, professional criminal, dangerous mentally abnormal person whose extended commitment is necessary for the protection of the public, or "a multiple offender whose criminality was so extensive that a sentence of imprisonment for an extended term is warranted." ALI, Model Penal Code § 7.03 (Prop.Off.Draft 1962). The term for a multiple offender may not exceed the longest sentences of imprisonment authorized for each of the offender's crimes if they ran consecutively.

Under this proposal the petitioner could have been sentenced up to 25 years.

The American Bar Association has proposed that habitual offenders be sentenced to no more than 25 years and that "[a]ny increased term which can be imposed because of prior criminality should be related in severity to the sentence otherwise provided for the new offense." The choice of sentence would be left to the discretion of the sentencing court. ABA Project on Standards for Criminal Justice, Sentencing Alternatives and Procedures § 3.3 (App. Draft 1968).

V

The Court today agrees with the State's arguments that a decision in petitioner's favor would violate principles of federalism and, because of difficulty in formulating standards to guide the decision of the federal courts, would lead to excessive interference with state sentencing decisions. Neither contention is convincing.

Each State has sovereign responsibilities to promulgate and enforce its criminal law. In our federal system we should never forget that the Constitution "recognizes and preserves the autonomy and independence of the States—independence in their legislative and independence in their judicial departments." But even as the Constitution recognizes a sphere of state activity free from federal interference, it explicitly compels the States to follow certain constitutional commands. When we apply the Cruel and Unusual Punishments Clause against the States, we merely enforce an obligation that the Constitution has created. As Mr. Justice Rehnquist has stated, "[c]ourts are exercising no more than the judicial function conferred upon them by Art. III of the Constitution when they assess, in a case before them, whether or not a particular legislative enactment is within the authority granted by the Constitution to the enacting body, and whether it runs afoul of some limitation placed by the Constitution on the authority of that body."

Because the State believes that the federal courts can formulate no practicable standard to identify grossly disproportionate sentences, it fears that the courts would intervene into state criminal justice systems at will. Such a "floodgates" argument can be easy to make and difficult to rebut. But in this case we can identify and apply objective criteria that reflect constitutional standards of punishment and minimize the risk of judicial subjectivity. Moreover, we can rely upon the experience of the United States Court of Appeals for the Fourth Circuit in applying criteria similar to those that I believe should govern this case.

In 1974, the Fourth Circuit considered the claim of a West Virginia prisoner who alleged that the imposition of a mandatory life sentence for three nonviolent crimes violated the Eighth Amendment. In Hart v. Coiner, 483 F.2d 136 (1973), cert. denied, 415 U.S. 983 (1974), the court held that the mandatory sentence was unconstitutional as applied to the prisoner. The court noted that none of the offenses involved violence or the danger of violence, that only a few States would apply such a sentence, and that West Virginia gave less severe sentences to first- and second-time offenders who committed more serious offenses. The holding in Hart v. Coiner is the holding that the State contends will undercut the ability of the States to exercise independent sentencing authority. Yet the Fourth Circuit subsequently has found only twice that noncapital sentences violate the Eighth Amendment. In Davis v. Davis, 601 F.2d 153 (1979) (en banc), the court held that a 40–

year sentence for possession and distribution of less than nine ounces of marihuana was cruel and unusual. In Roberts v. Collins, 544 F.2d 168 (1976), the court held that a person could not receive a longer sentence for a lesser included offense (assault) than he could have received for the greater offense (assault with intent to murder).

More significant are those cases in which the Fourth Circuit held that the principles of Hart v. Coiner were inapplicable. In a case decided the same day as Hart v. Coiner, the Court of Appeals held that a 10–year sentence given for two obscene telephone calls did not violate the Cruel and Unusual Punishments Clause. The court stated that "[w]hatever may be our subjective view of the matter, we fail to discern here objective factors establishing disproportionality in violation of the eighth amendment." Wood v. South Carolina, 483 F.2d 149, 150 (1973). In Griffin v. Warden, 517 F.2d 756 (1975), the court refused to hold that the West Virginia statute was unconstitutionally applied to a person who had been convicted of breaking and entering a gasoline and grocery store, burglary of a residence, and grand larceny. The court distinguished Hart v. Coiner on the ground that Griffin's offenses "clearly involve the potentiality of violence and danger to life as well as property." Similarly, the Fourth Circuit turned aside an Eighth Amendment challenge to the imposition of a 10– to 20–year sentence for statutory rape of a 13–year–old female. Hall v. McKenzie, 537 F.2d 1232, 1235–1236 (1976). The court emphasized that the sentence was less severe than a mandatory life sentence, that the petitioner would have received a similar sentence in 17 other American jurisdictions, and that the crime involved violation of personal integrity and the potential of physical injury. The Fourth Circuit also has rejected Eighth Amendment challenges brought by persons sentenced to 12 years for possession and distribution of heroin, United States v. Atkinson, 513 F.2d 38, 42 (1975), 2 years for unlawful possession of a firearm, United States v. Wooten, 503 F.2d 65, 67 (1974), 15 years for assault with intent to commit murder, Robinson v. Warden, 455 F.2d 1172 (1972), and 40 years for kidnaping, United States v. Martell, 335 F.2d 764 (1964).

I do not suggest that each of the decisions in which the Court of Appeals for the Fourth Circuit applied Hart v. Coiner is necessarily correct. But I do believe that the body of Eighth Amendment law that has developed in that Circuit constitutes impressive empirical evidence that the federal courts are capable of applying the Eighth Amendment to disproportionate noncapital sentences with a high degree of sensitivity to principles of federalism and state autonomy.

VI

I recognize that the difference between the petitioner's grossly disproportionate sentence and other prisoners' constitutionally valid sentences is not separated by the clear distinction that separates capital from noncapital punishment. "But the fact that a line has to be drawn somewhere does not justify its being drawn anywhere." The Court has, in my view, chosen the easiest line rather than the best.

* * *

We are construing a living Constitution. The sentence imposed upon the petitioner would be viewed as grossly unjust by virtually every layman and lawyer. In my view, objective criteria clearly establish that a mandatory life sentence for defrauding persons of about $230 crosses any rationally drawn line separating punishment that lawfully may be imposed from that which is proscribed by the Eighth Amendment. I would reverse the decision of the Court of Appeals.

NOTES

1. In Hutto v. Davis, 454 U.S. 370, 102 S.Ct. 703, 70 L.Ed.2d 556 (1982) (per curiam), the Court upheld, on the basis of *Rummel,* a 40–year sentence for two marijuana convictions. Yet, in Helm v. Solem, 684 F.2d 582 (8th Cir.1982), the U.S. Court of Appeals for the Eighth Circuit did not feel *Rummel* and Hutto v. Davis precluded a "disproportionality" inquiry in the sentence imposed by a state court. Helm, an alcoholic, had a record of several non-violent felonies, including third-degree burglary, drunk driving, grand larceny, and obtaining money under false pretenses. When he pleaded guilty to the offense of uttering a "no account" check, he was sentenced to life imprisonment under the habitual offender statute. At the time he was sentenced, state law provided that a life sentence was coupled with ineligibility for parole. The federal appeals court found that the life sentence, without the possibility of parole, constituted cruel and unusual punishment. Compare the latter case with Terrebonne v. Blackburn, 646 F.2d 997 (5th Cir.1981) and United States v. Valenzuela, 646 F.2d 352 (9th Cir.1980), upholding life sentences without parole for drug convictions not involving actual violence.

2. Is it cruel and unusual punishment for a court to impose a sentence of 999 years in a murder conviction? E.g., Jones v. State, 504 S.W.2d 906 (Tex. Crim.App.1974). Can an inmate in a penitentiary successfully bring an action contending that deprivation of heterosexual contact while in prison constitutes cruel and unusual punishment, considering that the federal courts have held that food, medication, and hygiene were matters of federal concern in the treatment of state prisoners?

3. Would giving a convicted rapist a choice between surgical castration and a lengthy prison sentence be constitutional? In State v. Brown, 284 S.C. 407, 326 S.E.2d 410 (1985), the South Carolina Supreme Court ruled that castration of convicted rapists would be cruel and unusual punishment.

4. In Ingraham v. Wright, 430 U.S. 651, 97 S.Ct. 1401, 51 L.Ed.2d 711 (1977), a civil case, the Court had to deal with the issue of corporal punishment of children in public schools. In a 5–4 decision, the Court concluded that such punishment, which dates back to the colonial period and which has survived the transformation of early private instruction to our present system of compulsory education, is not cruel and unusual punishment.

5. Article 3 of the European Convention on Human Rights provides, "No one shall be subjected to torture or to inhuman or degrading treatment or punishment." To what type of official sanctions might this apply?

Part II

CRIMES

Chapter 5

HOMICIDE

A. MURDER

1. THE MALICE FACTOR

COMMONWEALTH v. WEBSTER

Supreme Judicial Court of Massachusetts, 1850.
59 Mass. (5 Cush.) 295, 386.

The defendant, professor of chemistry, in the medical college, in Boston, attached to the university at Cambridge, was indicted in the municipal court at the January term, 1850, for the murder of Dr. George Parkman, at Boston, on the 23d of November, 1849. . . .

The government introduced evidence, that George Parkman, quite peculiar in person and manners, and very well known to most persons in the city of Boston, left his home in Walnut Street in Boston in the forenoon of the 23d of November, 1849, in good health and spirits; and that he was traced through various streets of the city until about a quarter before two o'clock of that day, when he was seen going towards and about to enter the medical college: That he did not return to his home: That on the next day a very active, particular, and extended search was commenced in Boston and the neighboring towns and cities, and continued until the 30th of November; and that large rewards were offered for information about Dr. Parkman: That on the 30th of November certain parts of a human body were discovered, in and about the defendant's laboratory in the medical college; and a great number of fragments of human bones and certain blocks of mineral teeth, imbedded in slag and cinders, together with small quantities of gold, which had been melted, were found in an assay furnace of the laboratory: That in consequence of some of these discoveries the defendant was arrested on the evening of the 30th of November: That the parts of a human body so found resembled in every respect the corresponding portions of the body of Dr. Parkman, and that among them all there were no duplicate parts; and that they were not the remains of a body

438

which had been dissected: That the artificial teeth found in the furnace were made for Dr. Parkman by a dentist in Boston in 1846, and refitted in his mouth by the same dentist a fortnight before his disappearance: That the defendant was indebted to Dr. Parkman on certain notes, and was pressed by him for payment; that the defendant has said that on the 23d of November, about nine o'clock in the morning, he left word at Dr. Parkman's house, that if he would come to the medical college at half past one o'clock on that day, he would pay him; and that, as he said, he accordingly had an interview with Dr. Parkman at half past one o'clock on that day, at his laboratory in the medical college: That the defendant then had no means of paying, and that the notes were afterwards found in his possession. . . .

[The defendant was tried before the Chief Justice, and Justices Wilde, Dewey and Metcalf. The opinion of the court on the law of the case was given in the charge to the jury as follows:]

SHAW, C. J. Homicide, of which murder is the highest and most criminal species, is of various degrees, according to circumstances. The term, in its largest sense, is generic, embracing every mode by which the life of one man is taken by the act of another. Homicide may be lawful or unlawful; it is lawful when done in lawful war upon an enemy in battle, it is lawful when done by an officer in the execution of justice upon a criminal, pursuant to a proper warrant. It may also be justifiable, and of course lawful, in necessary self-defence. But it is not necessary to dwell on these distinctions; it will be sufficient to ask attention to the two species of criminal homicide, familiarly known as murder and manslaughter.

In seeking for the sources of our law upon this subject, it is proper to say, that whilst the statute law of the commonwealth declares that "Every person who shall commit the crime of murder shall suffer the punishment of death for the same;" yet it nowhere defines the crimes of murder or manslaughter, with all their minute and carefully-considered distinctions and qualifications. For these, we resort to that great repository of rules, principles, and forms, the common law. This we commonly designate as the common law of England; but it might now be properly called the common law of Massachusetts. It was adopted when our ancestors first settled here, by general consent. It was adopted and confirmed by an early act of the provincial government, and was formally confirmed by the provision of the constitution declaring that all the laws which had theretofore been adopted, used, and approved, in the province or state of Massachusetts bay, and usually practiced on in the courts of law, should still remain and be in full force until altered or repealed by the legislature. So far, therefore, as the rules and principles of the common law are applicable to the administration of criminal law, and have not been altered and modified by acts of the colonial or provincial government or by the state legislature, they have the same force and effect as laws formally enacted.

By the existing law, as adopted and practiced on, unlawful homicide is distinguished into murder and manslaughter.

Murder, in the sense in which it is now understood, is the killing of any person in the peace of the commonwealth, with *malice afore-thought,* either express or implied by law. Malice in this definition, is used in a technical sense, including not only anger, hatred, and revenge, but every other unlawful and unjustifiable motive. It is not confined to ill-will towards one or more individual persons, but is intended to denote an action flowing from any wicked and corrupt motive, a thing done *malo animo,* where the fact has been attended with such circumstances as carry in them the plain indications of a heart regardless of social duty, and fatally bent on mischief. And therefore malice is implied from any deliberate or cruel act against another, however sudden.

Manslaughter is the unlawful killing of another without malice; and may be either voluntary, as when the act is committed with a real design and purpose to kill, but through the violence of sudden passion, occasioned by some great provocation, which in tenderness for the frailty of human nature the law considers sufficient to paliate the criminality of the offence; or involuntary, as when the death of another is caused by some unlawful act not accompanied by any intention to take life.

From these two definitions, it will be at once perceived, that the characteristic distinction between murder and manslaughter is malice, express or implied. It therefore becomes necessary, in every case of homicide proved, and in order to an intelligent inquiry into the legal character of the act, to ascertain with some precision the nature of legal malice, and what evidence is requisite to establish its existence.

Upon this subject, the rule as deduced from the authorities is, that the implication of malice arises in every case of international homicide; and, the fact of killing being first proved, all the circumstances of accident, necessity, or infirmity, are to be satisfactorily established by the party charged, unless they arise out of the evidence produced against him to prove the homicide, and the circumstances attending it. If there are, in fact, circumstances of justification, excuse, or palliation, such proof will naturally indicate them. But where the fact of killing is proved by satisfactory evidence, and there are no circumstances disclosed, tending to show justification or excuse, there is nothing to rebut the natural presumption of malice. This rule is founded on the plain and obvious principle, that a person must be presumed to intend to do that which he voluntarily and willfully does in fact do, and that he must intend all the natural, probable, and usual consequences of his own acts. Therefore, when one person assails another violently with a dangerous weapon likely to kill and which does in fact destroy the life of the party assailed, the natural presumption is, that he intended death or other great bodily harm; and, as there can be no presumption of any proper motive or legal excuse for such a cruel act, the consequence follows, that, in the absence of all proof to the contrary, there is nothing to rebut the presumption of malice. On the other hand, if death, though wilfully intended, was inflicted immediately after provocation given by the deceased, supposing that such provocation consisted of a blow or an assault, or other provocation on his part, which the law deems adequate to excite sudden and angry passion and create heat of blood, this fact rebuts the presumption of malice; but still, the homicide being unlawful, because a man is bound to curb his passions, is criminal, and is manslaughter.

In considering what is regarded as such adequate provocation, it is a settled rule of law, that no provocation by words only, however opprobrious, will mitigate an intentional homicide, so as to reduce it to manslaughter. Therefore, if, upon provoking language given, the party immediately revenges himself by the use of a dangerous and deadly weapon likely to cause death, such as a pistol discharged at the person, a heavy bludgeon, an axe, or a knife; if death ensues, it is a homicide not mitigated to manslaughter by the circumstances, and so is homicide by malice aforethought, within the true definition of murder. It is not the less malice aforethought, within the meaning of the law, because the act is done suddenly after the intention to commit the homicide is formed; it is sufficient that the malicious intention precedes and accompanies the act of homicide. It is manifest, therefore, that the words "malice aforethought," in the description of murder, do not imply deliberation, or the lapse of considerable time between the malicious intent to take life and the actual execution of that intent, but rather denote purpose and design, in contradistinction to accident and mischance.

In speaking of the use of a dangerous weapon, and the mode of using it upon the person of another, I have spoken of it as indicating an intention to kill him, or do him great bodily harm. The reason is this. Where a man, without justification or excuse, causes the death of another by the intentional use of a dangerous weapon likely to destroy life, he is responsible for the consequences, upon the principle already stated, that he is liable for the natural and probable consequences of his act. Suppose, therefore, for the purpose of revenge, one fires a pistol at another, regardless of consequences, intending to kill, maim, or grievously wound him, as the case may be, without any definite intention to take his life; yet, if that is the result, the law attributes the same consequences to homicide so committed, as if done under an actual and declared purpose to take the life of the party assailed. . . .

The true nature of manslaughter is, that it is homicide mitigated out of tenderness to the frailty of human nature. Every man, when assailed with violence or great rudeness, is inspired with a sudden impulse of anger, which puts him upon resistance before time for cool reflection; and if, during that period, he attacks his assailant with a weapon likely to endanger life, and death ensues, it is regarded as done through heat of blood or violence of anger, and not through malice, or that cold-blooded desire of revenge which more properly constitutes the feeling, emotion or passion of malice.

The same rule applies to homicide in mutual combat, which is attributed to sudden and violent anger occasioned by the combat, and not to malice. When two meet, not intending to quarrel, and angry words suddenly arise, and a conflict springs up in which blows are given on both sides, without much regard to who is the assailant, it is mutual combat. And if no unfair advantage is taken in the outset, and the occasion is not sought for the purpose of gratifying malice, and one seizes a weapon and strikes a deadly blow, it is regarded as homicide in heat of blood; and though not excusable, because a man is bound to control his angry passions, yet it is not the higher offence of murder.

We have stated these distinctions, not because there is much evidence in the present case which calls for their application, but that the jury may have a clear and distinct view of the leading principles in the law of homicide. There seems to have been little evidence in the present case that the parties had a contest. There is some evidence tending to show the previous existence of angry feelings; but unless these feelings resulted in angry words, and words were followed by blows, there would be no proof of heat of blood in mutual combat, or under provocation of an assault, on the one side or the other; and the proof of the defendant's declarations, as to the circumstances under which the parties met and parted, as far as they go, repel the supposition of such a contest.

With these views of the law of homicide, we will proceed to the further consideration of the present case. The prisoner at the bar is charged with the wilful murder of Dr. George Parkman. This charge divides itself into two principal questions, to be resolved by the proof: first, whether the party alleged to have been murdered came to his death by an act of violence inflicted by any person; and if so, secondly, whether the act was committed by the accused. . . .

This case is to be proved, if proved at all, by circumstantial evidence; because it is not suggested that any direct evidence can be given, or that any witness can be called to give direct testimony, upon the main fact of the killing. It becomes important, therefore, to state what circumstantial evidence is; to point out the distinction between that and positive or direct evidence.

The distinction, then, between direct and circumstantial evidence, is this. Direct or positive evidence is when a witness can be called to testify to the precise fact which is the subject of the issue on trial; that is, in a case of homicide, that the party accused did cause the death of the deceased. Whatever may be the kind of force of the evidence, that is the fact to be proved. But suppose no person was present on the occasion of the death, and of course that no one can be called to testify to it; is it wholly unsusceptible of legal proof? Experience has shown that circumstantial evidence may be offered in such a case; that is, that a body of facts may be proved of so conclusive a character, as to warrant a firm belief of the fact, quite as strong and certain as that on which discreet men are accustomed to act, in relation to their most important concerns. It would be injurious to the best interests of society, if such proof could not avail in judicial proceedings. If it was necessary always to have positive evidence how many criminal acts committed in the community, destructive of its peace and subversive of its order and security, would go wholly undetected and unpunished?

The necessity, therefore, of resorting to circumstantial evidence, if it is a safe and reliable proceeding, is obvious and absolute. Crimes are secret. Most men, conscious of criminal purposes, and about the execution of criminal acts, seek the security of secrecy and darkness. It is therefore necessary to use all modes of evidence besides that of direct testimony, provided such proofs may be relied on as leading to safe and satisfactory conclusions; and, thanks to a beneficent providence, the laws of nature and the relations of things to each other are so linked and combined together, that a medium of proof is often thereby furnished, leading to inferences and conclusions as strong as those arising from direct testimony. . . . The evidence must establish the *corpus delicti*, as it is termed, or the offence committed as charged; and, in case of homicide, must not only prove a death by violence, but must, to a reasonable extent, exclude the hypothesis of suicide, and a death by the act of any other person. This is to be proved beyond reasonable doubt.

Then, what is reasonable doubt? It is a term often used, probably pretty well understood, but not easily defined. It is not mere possible doubt; because every thing relating to human affairs, and depending on moral evidence, is open to some possible or imaginary doubt. It is that state of the case, which, after the entire comparison and consideration of all the evidence, leaves the minds of the jurors in that condition and they cannot say they feel an abiding conviction, to a moral certainty, of the truth of the charge. The burden of proof is upon the prosecutor. All the presumptions of law independent of evidence are in favor of innocence; and every person is presumed to be innocent until he is proved guilty. If upon such proof there is reasonable doubt remaining, the accused is entitled to the benefit of it by an acquittal. For it is not sufficient to establish a probability, though a strong one arising from the doctrine of chances, that the fact charged is more likely to be true than the contrary; but the evidence must establish the truth of the fact to a reasonable and moral certainty; a certainty that convinces and directs the understanding, and satisfies the reason and judgment of those who are bound to act conscientiously upon it. This we take to be proof beyond reasonable doubt; because if the law, which mostly depends upon considerations of a moral nature, should go further than this, and require absolute certainty, it would exclude circumstantial evidence altogether. . . .

[The jury returned a verdict of guilty, and the defendant's sentence of death by hanging was sustained by the Supreme Judicial Court of Massachusetts. Subsequently, Dr. Webster confessed:

"On Tuesday the 20th of November, I sent the note to Dr. Parkman. . . . It was to ask Dr. Parkman to call at my rooms on Friday the 23d, after my lecture. . . . My purpose was, if he should accede to the proposed interview, to state to him my embarrassments and utter inability to pay him at present, to apologize for those things in my conduct which had offended him, to throw myself upon his mercy, to beg for further time and indulgence for the sake of my family, if not for my own, and to make as good promises to him as I could have any hope of keeping. . . .

"Dr. Parkman agreed to call on me as I proposed.

"He came, accordingly, between half-past one and two. . . . He immediately addressed me with great energy: 'Are you ready for me, sir? Have you got the money?' I replied, 'No, Dr. Parkman'; and was then beginning to state my condition and make my appeal to him. He would not listen to me, but interrupted me with much vehemence. He called me 'scoundrel' and 'liar', and went on heaping upon me the most bitter taunts and opprobrious epithets. . . . I cannot tell how long the torrent of threats and invectives continued, and I can now recall to memory but a small portion of what he said. At first I kept interposing, trying to pacify him, so that I might obtain the object for which I had sought the interview. But I could not stop him, and soon my own temper was up. I forgot everything. I felt nothing but the sting of his words. I was excited to the highest degree of passion; and while he was speaking and gesticulating in the most violent and menacing manner, thrusting the letter and his fist into my face, in my fury I seized whatever was the handiest,—it was a stick of wood,—and dealt him an instantaneous blow with all the force that passion could give it. I did not know, nor think, nor care where I should hit him, nor how hard nor what the effect would be. It was on the side of his head, and there was nothing to break the force of the blow. He fell instantly upon the pavement. . . . Perhaps I spent ten minutes in attempts to resuscitate him; but I found that he was absolutely dead. . . .

"My next move was to get the body into the sink which stands in the small private room. By setting the body partially erect against the corner, and getting up into the sink myself, I succeeded in drawing it up. There it was entirely dismembered. . . .

"There was a fire burning in the furnace of the lower laboratory. . . . The head and viscera were put into that furnace that day. . . .

"When the body had been thus all disposed of, I cleared away all traces of what had been done. I took up the stick with which the fatal blow had been struck. It proved to be the stump of a large grape vine, say two inches in diameter, and two feet long. . . . I had carried it in from Cambridge . . . for the purpose of showing the effect of certain chemical fluids in coloring wood. . . . I put it into the fire. . . ."

The full confession appears in Bemis, Report of the Case of John W. Webster, pp. 564–71 (1850).

Had the above story been told at the trial, and believed, should the jury, in light of the judge's charge, have convicted Dr. Webster of murder or manslaughter?]*

NOTES

Malice Aforethought

1. As Chief Justice Shaw noted in his charge to the jury in the Webster case, supra, "[T]he characteristic distinction between murder and manslaughter is malice, express or implied."

"Malice aforethought" is the mental state required for murder. Is this the equivalent of specific intent? Or is it general intent? Refer to materials on "mental states" in Chapter 2, supra.

With respect to the meaning and significance of the term "malice," consider the following:

"The meaning of 'malice aforethought', which is the distinguishing criterion of murder, is certainly not beyond the range of controversy. The first thing that must be said about it is that neither of the two words is used in its ordinary sense. . . . 'It is now only an arbitrary symbol. For the "malice" may have in it nothing really malicious; and need never be really "afore-thought", except in the sense that every desire must necessarily come before— though perhaps only an instant before—the act which is desired. The word "aforethought", in the definition, has thus become either false or else superfluous. The word "malice" is neither; but it is apt to be misleading, for it is not employed in its original (and its popular) meaning.' 'Malice aforethought' is simply a comprehensive name for a number of different mental attitudes which have been variously defined at different stages in the development of the law, the presence of any one of which in the accused has been held by the courts to render a homicide particularly heinous and therefore to make it murder. . . . As Stephen put it '. . . when a particular state of mind came under their notice the Judges called it malice or not according to their view of the propriety of hanging particular people. . . .'." Report of the Royal Commission on Capital Punishment, 26–28 (1953).

2. Consider, with respect to the present English concept, the case of Hyam v. Director of Public Prosecutions, 2 All E.R. 41 (1974), the defendant was a woman who had been abandoned by her lover in favor of another woman. She set fire to the house where her rival lived, supposedly to frighten her into

---

* For an interesting account of the trial of Dr. Webster, see the article by Justice Robert Sullivan, "The Murder Trial of Dr. Webster, Boston, 1850", in 51 Mass.L.Q. 367 (1966) and 52 ibid., 67 (1967). Also see the same author's book "The Disappearance of Dr. Parkman" (1971), in which he states that the "charge to the jury" by Justice Shaw was not the one actually de-livered, but rather an extensively rewritten and moderated third draft, partly composed after Webster's execution. See also, Borowitz, The Janitor's Story: An Ethical Dilemma in the Harvard Murder Case, 66 A.B.A.J. 1540 (1980), suggesting that the confession was a "hoax" and was viewed by the press as a last-ditch effort by Webster to save his life.

leaving town, but the fire killed two of the occupant's infants. The jury was instructed that it could convict if it found that "when the accused set fire to the house she knew that it was highly probable that this would cause . . . serious bodily harm." The House of Lords ultimately affirmed the conviction by a three to two vote. The various opinions of the Lords deserve careful analysis for any extensive discussion of the effect of the mental state on the concept of malice in murder.

The statement was made in the *Hyam* case that despite the wording of the English Homicide Act of 1957 which abolished "constructive malice," "malice aforethought" was retained without declaring what it meant. The conclusion was reached that the law actually remained the same as it was before. (Sec. p. 87 of the case report.)

3. The following definition of "malice aforethought" is deserving of consideration: "an unjustifiable, inexcusable and unmitigated man-endangering-state-of-mind." Perkins, Criminal Law (1957) 40.

A good example within Professor Perkins' definition is the early case of Banks v. State, 85 Tex.Cr.R. 165, 211 S.W. 217 (1919), which involved the firing of shots into a moving train and resulted in the death of one of the crew, and where the court said:

"One who deliberately used a deadly weapon in such reckless manner as to evince a heart regardless of social duty and fatally bent on mischief, as is shown by firing into a moving train upon which human beings necessarily are, cannot shield himself from the consequences of his acts by disclaiming malice. Malice may be toward a group of persons as well as toward an individual. It may exist without former grudges or antecedent menaces. The intentional doing of any wrongful act in such manner and under such circumstances as that the death of a human being may result therefrom is malice."

Another example is Commonwealth v. Ashburn, 459 Pa. 625, 331 A.2d 167 (1975), where the defendant was convicted of murder for killing a friend in a game of Russian Roulette. Only one chamber of the revolver had been loaded with live ammunition. When defendant argued there was only one chance in six that the victim would be killed and that such odds do not make it highly foreseeable that death would result, the Pennsylvania Supreme Court stated that the finding of malice does not depend on any precise mathematical calculation of the probable consequences of defendant's acts. A somewhat similar case is Commonwealth v. Malone, 354 Pa. 180, 47 A.2d 445 (1946), in which the defendant's conviction for murder was affirmed when it was shown he had placed a gun against the decedent and pulled the trigger three times. He erroneously believed that he had placed the bullet in such a manner that the gun would not fire.

For other Russian Roulette cases see infra the materials on involuntary manslaughter.

4. Consider the following interesting definition of malice in the California Penal Code, Title 8, § 188 (which provision was enacted in 1872): "Malice may be express or implied. It is express when there is manifested a deliberate intention unlawfully to take away the life of a fellow creature. It is implied, when no considerable provocation appears, or when the circumstances attending the killing show an abandoned and malignant heart."

In 1981, the California legislature added a new paragraph to the statute: "When it is shown that the killing resulted from the intentional doing of an act with express or implied malice as defined above, no other mental state need be shown to establish the mental state of malice aforethought. Neither an awareness of the obligation to act within the general body of laws regulating society nor acting despite such awareness is included within the definition of malice."

Also consider Kasieta v. State, 62 Wis.2d 564, 215 N.W.2d 412 (1974), in which the defendant was convicted of the murder of his girl friend whom he had discovered in bed with another man. The victim had Hodgkins' disease, a condition of which the defendant was aware. He had hit the victim and caused several bruises about her face as well as a superficial wound over the left eye, a wound on the scalp, and a fractured nose which caused bleeding. The doctor testified that due to the Hodgkins' disease, as well as some other factors such as intoxication by alcohol and drugs, she had been unable to cough up or expel the blood as a result of which the blood filled her diseased lungs. The Supreme Court of Wisconsin held that the jury could find that the striking of someone in the nose, while not imminently dangerous in ordinary cases, was dangerous in the instant case because of the fact the victim was seriously ill, and that the blows struck by defendant under such circumstances evinced a depraved mind regardless of human life.

At the common law there were no degrees of murder. Any homicide, committed with malice aforethought, express or implied, constituted murder. The penalty for murder under the common law was death.

In order to lessen the penalty attaching to certain forms of murder not thought to warrant the punishment of death, many states have statutorily divided the crime of murder into various degrees, with a sliding scale of penalties deemed appropriate to the various degrees.

MIDGETT v. STATE

Supreme Court of Arkansas, 1987.
292 Ark. 278, 729 S.W.2d 410.

NEWBERN, JUSTICE.

This child abuse case resulted in the appellant's conviction of first degree murder. The sole issue on appeal is whether the state's evidence was sufficient to sustain the conviction. We hold there was no evidence of the ". . . premeditated and deliberated purpose of causing the death of another person . . ." required for conviction of first degree murder by Ark.Stat.Ann. § 41–1502(1)(b) (Repl.1977). However, we find the evidence was sufficient to sustain a conviction of second degree murder, described in Ark.Stat.Ann. § 41–1503(1)(c) (Repl.1977), as the appellant was shown to have caused his son's death by delivering a blow to his abdomen or chest ". . . with the purpose of causing serious physical injury. . . ." The conviction is thus modified from one of first degree murder to one of second degree murder and affirmed.

The facts of this case are as heart-rending as any we are likely to see. The appellant is six feet two inches tall and weighs 300 pounds.

His son, Ronnie Midgett, Jr., was eight years old and weighed between thirty-eight and forty-five pounds. The evidence showed that Ronnie Jr. had been abused by brutal beating over a substantial period of time. Typically, as in other child abuse cases, the bruises had been noticed by school personnel, and a school counselor as well as a SCAN worker had gone to the Midgett home to inquire. Ronnie Jr. would not say how he had obtained the bruises or why he was so lethargic at school except to blame it all, vaguely, on a rough playing little brother. He did not even complain to his siblings about the treatment he was receiving from the appellant. His mother, the wife of the appellant, was not living in the home. The other children apparently were not being physically abused by the appellant.

Ronnie Jr.'s sister, Sherry, aged ten, testified that on the Saturday preceding the Wednesday of Ronnie Jr.'s death their father, the appellant, was drinking whiskey (two to three quarts that day) and beating on Ronnie Jr. She testified that the appellant would "bundle up his fist" and hit Ronnie Jr. in the stomach and in the back. On direct examination she said that she had not previously seen the appellant beat Ronnie Jr., but she had seen the appellant choke him for no particular reason on Sunday nights after she and Ronnie Jr. returned from church. On cross-examination, Sherry testified that Ronnie Jr. had lied and her father was, on that Saturday, trying to get him to tell the truth. She said the bruises on Ronnie Jr.'s body noticed over the preceding six months had been caused by the appellant. She said the beating administered on the Saturday in question consisted of four blows, two to the stomach and two to the back.

On the Wednesday Ronnie Jr. died, the appellant appeared at a hospital carrying the body. He told hospital personnel something was wrong with the child. An autopsy was performed, and it showed Ronnie Jr. was a very poorly nourished and under-developed eight-year-old. There were recently caused bruises on the lips, center of the chest plate, and forehead as well as on the back part of the lateral chest wall, the soft tissue near the spine, and the buttocks. There was discloration of the abdominal wall and prominent bruising on the palms of the hands. Older bruises were found on the right temple, under the chin, and on the left mandible. Recent as well as older, healed, rib fractures were found.

The conclusion of the medical examiner who performed the autopsy was that Ronnie Jr. died as the result of intra-abdominal hemorrhage caused by a blunt force trauma consistent with having been delivered by a human fist. The appellant argues that in spite of all this evidence of child abuse, there is no evidence that he killed Ronnie Jr. having premeditated and deliberated causing his death. We must agree.

It is true that premeditation and deliberation may be found on the basis of circumstantial evidence. That was the holding in House v. State, 230 Ark. 622, 324 S.W.2d 112 (1959), where the evidence showed a twenty-four-year-old man killed a nineteen-year-old woman with whom he was attempting to have sexual intercourse. The evidence showed a protracted fight after which the appellant dumped the body in a water-filled ditch not knowing, according to House's testimony, whether she was dead or alive. Although it is not spelled out, presumably the rationale of the opinion was that House had time to premeditate during the fight and there was substantial evidence he intended the death of the victim when he left her in the water. Our only citation of authority on the point of showing premeditation and deliberation by circumstantial evidence in that case was Weldon v. State, 168 Ark. 534, 270 S.W. 968 (1925), where we said:

> The very manner in which the deadly weapons were used was sufficient to justify the jury in finding that whoever killed Jones used the weapons with a deliberate purpose to kill. Jones' body was perforated three times through the center with bullets from a pistol or rifle, and was also horribly mutilated with a knife. The manner, therefore, in which these deadly weapons were used tended to show that the death of Jones was the result of premeditation and deliberation.

While a fist may be a deadly weapon, the evidence of the use of the fist in this case is not comparable to the evidence in *House v. State*, supra, and *Weldon v. State*, supra, where there was some substantial evidence consisting of other circumstances that the appellant who dumped the apparently immobile body in the water and walked away and the appellant who wielded the deadly weapons intended and premeditated that death occur. Nor do we have in this case evidence of any remark made or other demonstration that the appellant was abusing his son in the hope that he eventually would die.

The annotation at 89 A.L.R.2d 396 (1963) deals with the subject of crimes resulting from excessive punishment of children. While some of the cases cited are ones in which a parent or stepparent flew into a one-time rage and killed the child, others are plain child abuse syndrome cases like the one before us now. None of them, with one exception, resulted in affirmance of a first degree murder conviction. Several were decisions in which first degree murder convictions were set aside for lack of evidence of premeditation and deliberation. See, e.g., People v. Ingraham, 232 N.Y. 245, 133 N.E. 575 (1921); Pannill v. Commonwealth, 185 Va. 244, 38 S.W.2d 457 (1946). The case cited in the annotation in which a first degree murder conviction was affirmed is Morris v. State, 270 Ind. 245, 384 N.E.2d 1022 (1979). There the appellant was left alone for about fifteen minutes with his five-month-old baby. When the child's mother returned to their home she found the baby had been burned severely on one side. About a month later, the appellant and his wife were engaged in an argument when the baby began to whine. The appellant laid the baby on the floor, began hitting the baby in the face and then hit the baby's head on the floor, causing the baby's death. At the time of the offense, the Indiana law required malice, purpose, and premeditation to convict of first degree murder. In discussing the premeditation requirement, the court said only:

Premeditation which also may be inferred from the facts and circumstances surrounding the killing, need not long be deliberated upon, but may occur merely an instant before the act. [Citation omitted.] It is clear from the facts adduced at trial regarding the burning and beating of the child that the jury could well have inferred that his killing was perpetrated purposely and with premeditated malice.

No explanation is given for the quantum leap from "the facts," horrible as they were, to the inference of premeditation. We made the same error in Burnett v. State, 287 Ark. 158, 697 S.W.2d 95 (1985), another child abuse case in which the facts were particularly repugnant, where we said:

Premeditation, deliberation and intent may be inferred from the circumstances of the case, such as the weapon used and the nature, extent and location of the wounds inflicted. . . . [T]he weapon used was a fist which struck the abdomen with such force as to rupture the colon. The child sustained fingernail scratches, four broken ribs, and other internal damage, as well as numerous bruises due to blows with a fist all over his body. The required mental state for first degree murder can be inferred from the evidence of abuse, which is substantial.

The problem with these cases is that they give no reason, like the reasons found in *House v. State,* supra, and *Weldon v. State,* supra, to make the inference of premeditation and deliberation.

. . . The appellant argues, and we must agree, that in a case of child abuse of long duration the jury could well infer that the perpetrator comes not to expect death of the child from his action, but rather that the child will live so that the abuse may be administered again and again. Had the appellant planned his son's death, he could have accomplished it in a previous beating.

In this case the evidence might possibly support the inference that the blows which proved fatal to Ronnie Jr. could have been struck with the intent to cause his death developed in a drunken, misguided, and overheated attempt at disciplining him for not having told the truth. Even if we were to conclude there was substantial evidence from which the jury could fairly have found the appellant intended to cause Ronnie Jr.'s death in a drunken disciplinary beating on that Saturday, there would still be no evidence whatever of a premeditated and deliberated killing.

In Ford v. State, 276 Ark. 98, 633 S.W.2d 3, cert. den. 459 U.S. 1022, 103 S.Ct. 389, 74 L.Ed.2d 519 (1980), we held that to show the appellant acted with a premeditated and deliberated purpose, the state must prove that he (1) had the conscious object to cause death, (2) formed that intention before acting, and (3) weighed in his mind the consequences of a course of conduct, as distinguished from acting upon sudden impulse without the exercise of reasoning power. Viewing the evidence most favorable to the appellee, the circumstances of this case are not substantial evidence the appellant did (2) and (3), as opposed to acting on impulse or with no conscious object of causing death. The jury was thus forced to resort to speculation on these important elements.

A clear exposition of the premeditation and deliberation requirement which separates first degree from second degree murder is found in 2 W. LaFave and A. Scott, Jr., Substantive Criminal Law § 7.7 (1986):

> Almost all American jurisdictions which divide murder into degrees include the following two murder situations in the category of first degree murder: (1) intent-to-kill murder where there exists (in addition to the intent to kill) the elements of premeditation and deliberation, and (2) felony murder where the felony in question is one of five or six listed felonies, generally including rape, robbery, kidnapping, arson and burglary. Some states instead or in addition have other kinds of first degree murder.

> (a) Premeditated, Deliberate, Intentional Killing. To be guilty of this form of first degree murder the defendant must not only intend to kill but in addition he must premeditate the killing and deliberate about it. It is not easy to give a meaningful definition of the words "premeditate" and "deliberate" as they are used in connection with first degree murder. Perhaps the best that can be said of "deliberation" is that it requires a cool mind that is capable of reflection, and of "premeditation" that it requires that the one with the cool mind did in fact reflect, at least for a short period of time before his act of killing.

> It is often said that premeditation and deliberation require only a "brief moment of thought" or a "matter of seconds," and convictions for first degree murder have frequently been affirmed where such short periods of time were involved. The better view, however, is that to "speak of premeditation and deliberation which are instantaneous, or which take no appreciable time, . . . destroys the statutory distinction between first and second degree murder," and (in much the same fashion that the felony-murder rule is being increasingly limited) this view is growing in popularity. This is not to say, however, that premeditation and deliberation cannot exist when the act of killing follows immediately after the formation of the intent. The intention may be finally formed only as a conclusion of prior premeditation and deliberation, while in other cases the intention may be formed without prior thought so that premeditation and deliberation occurs only with the passage of additional time for "further thought, and a turning over in the mind." [Footnotes omitted.]

The evidence in this case supports only the conclusion that the appellant intended not to kill his son but to further abuse him or that his intent, if it was to kill the child, was developed in a drunken, heated, rage while disciplining the child. Neither of those supports a finding of premeditation or deliberation.

Perhaps because they wish to punish more severely child abusers who kill their children, other states' legislatures have created laws permitting them to go beyond second degree murder. For example, Illinois has made aggravated battery one of the felonies qualifying for "felony murder," and a child abuser can be convicted of murder if the child dies as a result of aggravated battery. See People v. Ray, 80 Ill. App.3d 151, 35 Ill.Dec. 688, 399 N.E.2d 977 (1979). Georgia makes "cruelty to children" a felony, and homicide in the course of cruelty to children is "felony murder." See Bethea v. State, 251 Ga. 328, 304 S.E.2d 713 (1983). Idaho has made murder by torture a first degree offense, regardless of intent of the perpetrator to kill the victim, and the offense is punishable by the death penalty. See State v. Stuart, 110 Idaho 163, 715 P.2d 833 (1985). California has also adopted a murder by torture statute making the offense murder in the first degree without regard to the intent to kill. See People v. Demond, 59 Cal.App. 3d 574, 130 Cal.Rptr. 590 (1976). Cf. People v. Steger, 16 Cal.3d 539, 128 Cal.Rptr. 161, 546 P.2d 665 (1976), in which the California Supreme Court held that the person accused of torture murder in the first degree must be shown to have had a premeditated intent to inflict extreme and prolonged pain in order to be convicted.

All of this goes to show that there remains a difference between first and second degree murder, not only under our statute, but generally. Unless our law is changed to permit conviction of first degree murder for something like child abuse or torture resulting in death, our duty is to give those accused of first degree murder the benefit of the requirement that they be shown by substantial evidence to have premeditated and deliberated the killing, no matter how heinous the facts may otherwise be. We understand and appreciate the state's citation of *Burnett v. State*, supra, but, to the extent it is inconsistent with this opinion, we must overrule it.

The dissenting opinion begins by stating the majority concludes that one who starves and beats a child to death cannot be convicted of murder. That is not so, as we are affirming the conviction of murder; we are, however, reducing it to second degree murder. The dissenting opinion's conclusion that the appellant starved Ronnie Jr., must be based solely on the child's underdeveloped condition which could, presumably, have been caused by any number of physical malfunctions. There is no evidence the appellant starved the child. The dissenting opinion says it is for the jury to determine the degree of murder of which the appellant is guilty. That is true so long as there is substantial evidence to support the jury's choice. The point of this opinion is to note that there was no evidence of premeditation or deliberation which are required elements of the crime of first degree murder. . . .

In this case we have no difficulty with reducing the sentence to the maximum for second degree murder. Dixon v. State, 260 Ark. 857, 545 S.W.2d 606 (1977). The jury gave the appellant a sentence of forty years imprisonment which was the maximum for first degree murder, and we reduce that to twenty years which is the maximum imprisonment for second degree murder. Just as walking away from the victim in the water-filled ditch in *House v. State,* supra, after a protracted fight, and the "overkill" and mutilation of the body in *Weldon v. State,* supra, were circumstances creating substantial evidence of premeditation and deliberation, the obvious effect the beatings were having on Ronnie Jr. and his emaciated condition when the final beating occurred are circumstances constituting substantial evidence that the appellant's purpose was to cause serious physical injury, and that he caused his death in the process. That is second degree murder, § 41–1503(1)(c). Therefore, we reduce the appellant's sentence to imprisonment for twenty years.

Affirmed as modified.

HICKMAN, HAYS and GLAZE, JJ., dissent.

HICKMAN, JUSTICE, dissenting.

Simply put, if a parent deliberately starves and beats a child to death, he cannot be convicted of the child's murder. In reaching this decision, the majority overrules a previous unanimous decision and substitutes its judgment for that of the jury. The majority has decided it cannot come to grips with the question of the battered child who dies as a result of deliberate, methodical, intentional and severe abuse. A death caused by such acts is murder by any legal standard, and that fact cannot be changed—not even by the majority. The degree of murder committed is for the jury to decide—not us.

Convictions for murder resulting from child abuse have become more common in our courts. That is probably because such cases are being reported more often and prosecutors are more apt to seek retribution.

The decision of what charge to file in a homicide case rests with the prosecuting attorney. He has the duty to prove the charge. The decision of whether the state has proved the crime rests with the jury. Our role is only to determine if substantial evidence exists to support the verdict.

Sometimes the facts may warrant a charge of second degree murder. We have affirmed convictions for second degree murder in two such cases.

Whether the particular acts of child abuse amount to first degree murder depend on the particular facts and circumstances in each case. Just as in any other murder case, the state must prove each element of the crime. For a first degree murder conviction, the state must prove premeditation and deliberation.

We have never held motive relevant to murder, nor do we even try to look into the warped minds that commit murder to make their acts rational. Consequently, circumstantial evidence usually plays a strong part in determining intent in any murder case.

In this case the majority, with clairvoyance, decides that this parent did not intend to kill his child, but rather to keep him alive for further abuse. This is not a child neglect case. The state proved Midgett starved the boy, choked him, and struck him several times in the stomach and back. The jury could easily conclude that such repeated treatment was intended to kill the child.

In *Burnett v. State,* supra, the state chose to seek a first degree murder conviction. The child was killed in an extremely horrible way. He was malnourished and dehydrated, bruises on his face and upper and lower extremeties, four broken ribs, a ruptured colon, and abrasions. His life was made intolerable and insufferable until at last a blow killed him. The parents, who could not have been unaware or innocent, were found guilty of killing him, which they did. We unanimously upheld that jury verdict. It was no "quantum leap" on our part (whatever that means), just a decision based on the facts and the law. The majority unanimously joined in the *Burnett* decision.

The facts in this case are substantial to support a first degree murder conviction. The defendant was in charge of three small children. The victim was eight years old and had been starved; he weighed only 38 pounds at the time of his death. He had multiple bruises and abrasions. The cause of death was an internal hemorrhage due to blunt force trauma. His body was black and blue from repeated blows. The victim's sister testified she saw the defendant, a 30 year old man, 6'2" tall, weighing 300 pounds, repeatedly strike the victim in the stomach and back with his fist. One time he choked the child.

The majority is saying that as a matter of law a parent cannot be guilty of intentionally killing a child by such deliberate acts. Why not? Is it because it is inconceivable to rational people that a parent would intend to kill his own child? Evidently, this is the majority's conclusion, because they hold the intention of Midgett was to keep him alive for further abuse, not to kill him. How does the majority know that? How do we ever know the actual or subliminal intent of a defendant? "If the *act* appellant intended was criminal, then the law holds him accountable, even though such *result* was not intended." Hankins v. State, 206 Ark. 881, 178 S.W.2d 56 (1944). There is no difference so far as the law is concerned in this case than in any other murder case. It is simply a question of proof. This parent killed his own child, and the majority cannot accept the fact that he intended to do just that.

Undoubtedly, the majority could accept it if the child were murdered with a bullet or a knife; but they cannot accept the fact, and it is a fact, that this defendant beat and starved his own child to death. His course of conduct could not have been negligent or unintentional.

Other states have not hesitated to uphold a conviction for first degree murder in such cases. The fact that some states (California and Idaho) have passed a murder by torture statute is irrelevant. Those statutes may make it easier to prosecute child murderers, but they do not replace or intend to replace the law of murder. Whether murder exists is a question of the facts—not the method. The majority spends a good deal of effort laboring over the words "premeditation and deliberation," ignoring what the defendant did. Oliver Wendell Holmes said: "We must think things not words . . ." Holmes, "Law in Science and Science in Law," Collected Legal Papers, p. 238 (1921). If what Midgett did was deliberate and intentional, and that is not disputed, and he killed the child, a jury can find first degree murder.

I cannot fathom how this father could have done what he did; but it is not my place to sit in judgment of his mental state, nor allow my human feelings to color my judgment of his accountability to the law. The law has an objective standard of accountability for all who take human life. If one does certain acts and the result is murder, one must pay. The jury found Midgett guilty and, according to the law, there is substantial evidence to support that verdict. That should end the matter for us. He is guilty of first degree murder in the eyes of the law. His moral crime as a father is another matter, and it is not for us to speculate why he did it.

I would affirm the judgment.

HAYS and GLAZE, JJ., join in the dissent.

NOTES

1. Consider, in the light of the dissent's statement that motive is not relevant to murder, the article by Professor Samuel H. Pillsbury, titled "Evil and the Law of Murder," 24 U.C.Davis L.Rev. 437, 447 (1990), who states that "Anglo–American criminal law, with its emphasis upon mental states, clearly concerns itself with the 'why' of criminal acts and so makes a basic inquiry into moral disposition." He adds that "where culpability distinctions are of great importance, as in murder, motivation analysis provides a critical means of judging culpability. There is no substitute."

2. Under one modern type of statute, the common law definition of murder is retained. However, certain types of common law murder are denominated as being capital murder (punishable by death or imprisonment for life) or of the first degree, with all other kinds classified as murder in the second degree. Illustrative of the latter are the Code of Virginia provisions which read as follows:

§ 18.2–31. **Capital murder defined; punishment.**—The following offenses shall constitute capital murder, punishable as a Class 1 felony:

1. The willful, deliberate, and premeditated killing of any person in the commission of abduction, as defined in § 18.2–48, when such

abduction was committed with the intent to extort money or a pecuniary benefit;

2. The willful, deliberate, and premeditated killing of any person by another for hire;

3. The willful, deliberate, and premeditated killing of any person by a prisoner confined in a state or local correctional facility as defined in § 53.1–1, or while in the custody of an employee thereof;

4. The willful, deliberate, and premeditated killing of any person in the commission of robbery or attempted robbery while armed with a deadly weapon;

5. The willful, deliberate, and premeditated killing of any person in the commission of, or subsequent to, rape or attempted rape;

6. The willful, deliberate, and premeditated killing of a law-enforcement officer as defined in § 9–169(9) when such killing is for the purpose of interfering with the performance of his official duties;

7. The willful, deliberate, and premeditated killing of more than one person as a part of the same act or transaction;

8. The willful, deliberate, and premeditated killing of a child under the age of twelve years in the commission of abduction as defined in § 18.2–48 when such abduction was committed with the intent to extort money or a pecuniary benefit, or with the intent to defile the victim of such abduction; and

9. The willful, deliberate, and premeditated killing of any person in the commission of or attempted commission of a violation of § 18.2–248, involving a Schedule I or II controlled substance, when such killing is for the purpose of furthering the commission or attempted commission of such violation.

If any one or more subsections, sentences, or parts of this section shall be judged unconstitutional or invalid, such adjudication shall not affect, impair, or invalidate the remaining provisions thereof but shall be confined in its operation to the specific provisions so held unconstitutional or invalid.

§ 18.2–32. **First and second degree murder defined; punishment.**—Murder, other than capital murder, by poison, lying in wait, imprisonment, starving, or by any willful, deliberate, and premeditated killing, or in the commission of, or attempt to commit, arson, rape, forcible sodomy, inanimate object sexual penetration, robbery, burglary or abduction, except as provided in § 18.2–31, is murder of the first degree, punishable as a Class 2 felony.

All murder other than capital murder and murder in the first degree is murder of the second degree and is punishable as a Class 3 felony.

3. Contrast the approach of the Virginia General Assembly in dividing common law murders into capital murder, first degree murder, and second degree murder, with the approach taken by the Illinois legislature. Illinois, prior to 1987, divided criminal homicides into murder (no degrees), voluntary manslaughter, involuntary manslaughter, and reckless homicide. In 1987, Illinois began using degrees of murder, calling what was previously known as

"murder," now "murder in the first degree." The offense of voluntary manslaughter was redefined as "murder in the second degree."

The offense of first degree murder does not use the term "malice aforethought," but instead defines, in § 9–1(a) of the Criminal Code, the required mental state, and in subsection (b) lists the first degree murders for which the death penalty may be imposed:

§ 9–1 (a) A person who kills an individual without lawful justification commits first degree murder if, in performing the acts which cause the death:

(1) He either intends to kill or do great bodily harm to that individual or another, or knows that such acts will cause death to that individual or another; or

(2) He knows that such acts create a strong probability of death or great bodily harm to that individual or another; or

(3) He is attempting or committing a forcible felony other than second degree murder.

(b) Aggravating Factors. A defendant who at the time of the commission of the offense has attained the age of 18 or more and who has been found guilty of first degree murder may be sentenced to death if:

1. the murdered individual was a peace officer or fireman killed in the course of performing his official duties and the defendant knew or should have known that the murdered individual was a peace officer or fireman; or

2. the murdered individual was an employee of an institution or facility of the Department of Corrections, or any similar local correctional agency, killed in the course of performing his official duties, or the murdered individual was an inmate at such institution or facility and was killed on the grounds thereof, or the murdered individual was otherwise present in such institution or facility with the knowledge and approval of the chief administrative officer thereof; or

3. the defendant has been convicted of murdering two or more individuals under subsection (a) of this Section or under any law of the United States or of any state which is substantially similar to subsection (a) of this Section regardless of whether the deaths occurred as the result of the same act or of several related or unrelated acts so long as the deaths were the result of either an intent to kill more than one person or of separate acts which the defendant knew would cause death or create a strong probability of death or great bodily harm to the murdered individual or another; or

4. the murdered individual was killed as a result of the hijacking of an airplane, train, ship, bus or other public conveyance; or

5. the defendant committed the murder pursuant to a contract, agreement or understanding by which he was to receive money or anything of value in return for committing the murder or procured another to commit the murder for money or anything of value; or

CRIMES

Pt. 2

6. the murdered individual was killed in the course of another felony if:

(a) the murdered individual:

(i) was actually killed by the defendant, or

(ii) received physical injuries personally inflicted by the defendant substantially contemporaneously with physical injuries caused by one or more persons for whose conduct the defendant is legally accountable under Section 5–2 of this Code, and the physical injuries inflicted by either the defendant or the other person or persons for whose conduct he is legally accountable caused the death of the murdered individual; and

(b) in performing the acts which caused the death of the murdered individual or which resulted in physical injuries personally inflicted by the defendant on the murdered individual under the circumstances of subdivision (ii) of subparagraph (a) of paragraph (6) of subsection (b) of this Section, the defendant acted with the intent to kill the murdered individual or with the knowledge that his acts created a strong probability of death or great bodily harm to the murdered individual or another; and

(c) the other felony was one of the following: armed robbery, robbery, aggravated criminal sexual assault, aggravated kidnapping, forcible detention, arson, aggravated arson, burglary, home invasion, or the attempt to commit any of the felonies listed in this subsection (c); or

7. the murdered individual was under 12 years of age and the death resulted from exceptionally brutal or heinous behavior indicative of wanton cruelty; or

8. the defendant committed the murder with intent to prevent the murdered individual from testifying in any criminal prosecution or giving material assistance to the State in any investigation or prosecution, either against the defendant or another; or the defendant committed the murder because the murdered individual was a witness in any prosecution or gave material assistance to the State in any investigation or prosecution, either against the defendant or another.

* * *

Considering "Aggravating Factor # 7" of the above statute, do the words "exceptionally brutal or heinous behavior indicative of wanton cruelty" give fair warning as to what type of conduct is intended? Or is that provision unconstitutionally vague?

4. The words "deliberation and premeditation" are commonly found in statutory provisions concerning first degree murder. Clear as the meaning of these terms may appear to be, courts have disagreed as to how they should be construed. Consider the following decisions and their bearing upon (1) the distinction between first and second degree murder, and (2) the usefulness of the degree device as a means of graduating the severity of punishment for different kinds of murder:

In Bullock v. United States, 74 App.D.C. 220, 122 F.2d 213 (1941), the trial court instructed the jury that "deliberate and premeditated malice" required that the killer turn over in his mind the intention to kill, but that "it does not take any appreciable time to turn a thought of that kind over in your mind."

In disapproving the instruction, the Court of Appeals for the District of Columbia stated: "To speak of premeditation and deliberation which are instantaneous, or which take no appreciable time, is a contradiction in terms. It deprives the statutory requirement of all meaning and destroys the statutory distinction between first and second degree murder. At common law there were no degrees of murder. If the accused had no overwhelming provocation to kill, he was equally guilty whether he carried out his murderous intent at once or after mature reflection. Statutes like ours, which distinguish deliberate and premeditated murder from other murder, reflect a belief that one who meditates an intent to kill and then deliberately executes it is more dangerous, more culpable or less capable of reformation than one who kills on sudden impulse; or that the prospect of the death penalty is more likely to deter men from deliberate than from impulsive murder. The deliberate killer is guilty of first degree murder; the impulsive killer is not."

In Wooten v. State, 104 Fla. 597, 140 So. 474 (1932), the court stated: "The record shows that the deceased was riding on a running board of a car in which the accused and others were also riding; that the driver of the car . . . caused the car to brush against the top of a tree which had fallen across the road, and McCray, the deceased, exclaimed to the driver, 'That's right; wreck it, wreck it,' evidently in criticism of the manner of the driver. Wooten, the accused, thereupon got a pistol from the pocket of the car and said 'I'll kill you,' and thereupon shot and killed McCray.

"It would be rather puzzling to conceive more definite proof of premeditated design than that shown by the statement of the accused just before he shot the deceased.

"A 'premeditated design' is not required to exist in the mind of the perpetrator of a homicide for any particular length of time to constitute such homicide murder in the first degree. If the accused is shown to have arrived at a definitely formed purpose to effect the death of the person assaulted in the manner and by the means in and with which the homicide is committed, and under such conditions that such homicide will neither be justifiable nor excusable, nor under such conditions as to reduce the crime to manslaughter or murder in the third degree, the homicide will constitute murder in the first degree, although the design and intent to commit such homicide was formed by the accused immediately before the act is actually committed." See also Jones v. United States, 175 F.2d 544 (9th Cir.1949).

With respect to the terms "deliberate and premeditated," Mr. Justice Benjamin Cardozo has stated the following:

". . . A long series of decisions, beginning many years ago, has given to these words a meaning that differs to some extent from the one revealed upon the surface. To deliberate and premeditate within the meaning of the statute, one does not have to plan the murder days or hours or even minutes in advance, as where one lies in wait for one's enemy or places poison in his food and drink. The law does not say that any particular length of time must intervene between the volition and the act. The human brain, we are reminded, acts at times with extraordinary celerity. All that the statute requires is that the act must not be the result of immediate or spontaneous impulse. . . . One may say indeed in a rough way that an intent to kill is always deliberate and premeditated within the meaning of the law unless the mind is so blinded by pain or rage as to make the act little more than an automatic or spontaneous reaction to the environment—not strictly automatic or spontaneous, for there could then be no intent, and yet a near approach thereto. . . .

"I think the distinction is much too vague to be continued in our law. There can be no intent unless there is a choice, yet by the hypothesis, the choice without more is enough to justify the inference that the intent was deliberate and premeditated. The presence of a sudden impulse is said to mark the dividing line, but how can an impulse be anything but sudden when the time for its formation is measured by the lapse of seconds? Yet the decisions are to the effect that seconds may be enough. . . . What we have is merely a privilege offered to the jury to find the lesser degree when the suddenness of the intent, the vehemence of the passion, seems to call irresistibly for the exercise of mercy. I have no objection to giving them this dispensing power, but it should be given to them directly and not in a mystifying cloud of words. The present distinction is so obscure that no jury hearing it for the first time can fairly be expected to assimilate and understand it. I am not at all sure that I understand it myself after trying to apply it for many years and after diligent study of what has been written in the books. Upon the basis of this fine distinction with its obscure and mystifying psychology, scores of men have gone to their death." [1]

For a thorough consideration of the problems presented by statutes on first degree murder, see Brenner, The Impulsive Murder and the Degree Device, 22 Fordham L.Rev. 274 (1953).

5. Can the mens rea needed for proof of first degree murder be affected by terror and panic? In a case of first impression in its state, the Pennsylvania Supreme Court, in Commonwealth v. Stewart, 461 Pa. 274, 336 A.2d 282 (1975), stated: "Although our research on this issue reveals no Pennsylvania case specifically holding that terror stricken panic may negate the mens rea element of murder in the first degree, we are convinced that it may do so. Strong emotions have previously been found to prevent the formulation of the intent required for first degree murder. . . . We hold that in excluding evidence of gang activity in appellant's neighborhood, the trial court withheld from the jury evidence of vital probative value to a determination of the defendant's state of mind. . . . In the context of gang violence, the violent nature not only of the deceased, but also of the gang of which he was a member may be relevant to the inquiry into the defendant's state of mind, for his state of mind is related to the threat presented by group violence."

LANGFORD v. STATE
Supreme Court of Alabama, 1977.
354 So.2d 313.

JONES, JUSTICE.

* * *

On June 24, 1975, Heflin Mack Langford, Petitioner, was involved in an automobile collision which resulted in the death of sixteen-year-old Randall Holt. Langford's automobile struck a mileage marker on the right side of a four-lane highway in Montgomery County, swerved

1. Cardozo, What Medicine Can Do for Law, an address before the New York Academy of Medicine, 1928, reprinted in Cardozo, Law and Literature and Other Essays, 96–101 (1931).

to the left and crossed the median. It collided with Holt's automobile which was traveling in the opposite direction, and killed Holt instantly.

The extent to which Langford had been drinking was in dispute. Several witnesses stated that alcohol could be smelled on his breath; and it was shown that his blood-alcohol level was 0.25 per cent. Furthermore, witnesses testified that they had seen Langford's car traveling in excess of 90 miles per hour immediately preceding the collision.

In response to this evidence, Langford stated that he had consumed only "two beers" and was not intoxicated. He stated that mechanical steering problems had caused his loss of control of the vehicle.

The jury was charged as to the law involved, and no exceptions or objections were taken, except for an adverse ruling to Langford's motion for directed verdict at the close of the evidence. The jury found Langford guilty of murder in the first degree and he was sentenced to life imprisonment. It was in this posture, then, that the Court of Criminal Appeals addressed the merits of the defendant's contention that the evidence was insufficient to support a conviction of murder in the first degree. That Court affirmed, holding:

> "Although a case of first impression, and while a very close question of whether Langford's gross and wanton misconduct rises to the degree necessary to show universal malice by evidencing a 'depraved mind regardless of human life,' . . . the evidence was sufficient to present a jury question in that regard."

Our grant of the petition for writ of certiorari was limited to a review of that holding.

Langford contends that an individual cannot be convicted of murder in the first degree where the facts show only that he determined to, and did, drive an automobile which was involved in a collision which caused the death of an individual, even though the driver had knowledge of his own intoxication. . . .

The applicable statute, Tit. 14, § 314, Code, provides:

> Every homicide, perpetrated by poison lying in wait, or any other kind of wilful deliberate, malicious and premeditated killing; or committed in the perpetration of, or the attempt to perpetrate, any arson, rape, robbery, or burglary; or perpetrated from a premeditated design unlawfully and maliciously to effect the death of any human being other than him who is killed; *or perpetrated by any act greatly dangerous to the lives of others, and evidencing a depraved mind regardless of human life, although without any preconceived purpose to deprive any particular person of life, is murder in the first degree* . . . (Emphasis added.)

Langford was charged and convicted of the fourth type of first-degree murder (the emphasized segment).

It is settled that, in appropriate circumstances, a homicide committed by an intoxicated driver of an automobile may be murder. This, however, does not satisfy the inquiry before us; and this for the reason that this State has two degrees of murder, and a determination that a conviction of murder may be appropriate does not necessarily assure the appropriateness of a conviction of murder in the first degree.

Justice Stone, in Mitchell v. State, 60 Ala. 26 (1877), stated:

" . . . the legislature, in this [fourth] clause, intended to raise to the high grade of murder in the first degree those homicides which are the result of what is called 'universal malice.' By universal malice we do not mean a malicious purpose to take the life of all persons. It is that depravity of the human heart which *determines* to take life upon slight or insufficient provocation, without knowing or caring who may be the victim." (Emphasis added.)

The word "determines" presupposes that some mental operation has taken place; the reasoning faculty must be called into play. State v. Massey, 20 Ala.App. 56, 100 So. 625 (1924).

"If one *knowingly* and *consciously* drives a high-powered automobile . . . at an excessive rate of speed into a railroad train moving over a street crossing, *knowing* that the train is moving over the crossing, and *that the automobile will strike the train,* and that death will probably result to one or more occupants of the car, although without any preconceived purpose to deprive any particular person of life, but with a reckless disregard of human life, and death results from such act, the driver of the automobile may be guilty of murder in the first degree under the fourth division . . . If he *did not know that he was driving the automobile into the train and he did not determine to drive it into the train regardless of consequences,* but if the act of so driving it was purely accidental, but while in the commission of an unlawful act, such as driving along a public highway at a reckless rate of speed, or exceeding the speed limit, the offense would be manslaughter." (Emphasis added.)

As Langford has correctly pointed out, in the instant case, the defendant *determined* only to drive upon the highway after drinking. There is no showing that he *determined* to have a collision; nor is there any evidence that he realized the likelihood of a collision; and the consequent taking of human life, and proceeded in the face of such probabilities.

The State has cited various cases where an intoxicated driver was found guilty of murder. It should be noted, however, that no case has been cited, or found, wherein an intoxicated automobile driver was found guilty of murder in the first degree.

The classic examples of universal malice include shooting into an occupied house, and driving an automobile into a crowd. While these examples are not exhaustive, they do illustrate the parameter of the type factual situation wherein such malice may be found or implied. We do not believe that the facts before us are within the ambit of the degree of malice exemplified by the above-stated circumstances.

We hold that the trial court erred in not granting the motion for directed verdict as to the charge of murder in the first degree. As to all lesser included offenses, however, the evidence was sufficient for submission to the jury. The judgment of the Court of Criminal Appeals is reversed with instructions to remand the cause for a new trial not inconsistent with this opinion.

Reversed and remanded.

TORBERT, C. J., and BLOODWORTH, FAULKNER, ALMON, SHORES and EMBRY, JJ., concur.

MADDOX and BEATTY, JJ., dissent.

MADDOX, JUSTICE (dissenting).

I think the Court of Criminal Appeals was absolutely correct in this case by upholding a *jury's determination* that the defendant was guilty of murder in the first degree. As Judge Bookout points out in his special concurrence, there have been several cases where drivers of automobiles have been indicted for murder in the first degree and the *jury* has convicted for *second degree,* but this is the first time that this Court has held as a *matter of law,* that a jury could not find a person guilty of murder in the first degree when he had done what Langford did here. I think the majority has erred.

The law of this case is contained in Reed v. State, 25 Ala.App. 18, 142 So. 441 (1932), certiorari denied, 225 Ala. 219, 142 So. 442 (1932). Reed was indicted for *first degree* murder. The jury found him guilty of *second degree* murder. From the opinion is the following:

"The court delivered an able and explicit charge to the jury covering every phase of the law applicable to this case. No exception was reserved to this charge, nor was it subject to objection and exception. Among other things, the court charged the jury: '* * * If a person driving an automobile along the public highway knew that he was intoxicated, and, with that knowledge and the knowledge of other persons present on the highway, should proceed to drive the car in a highly reckless manner and operate the car in such manner as to be greatly dangerous to the lives of others and thus evidencing a depraved mind and regardless of human life, then you might consider that fact in determining whether or not the operator of the car was guilty of murder.' * * * "

In Nixon v. State, 268 Ala. 101, 105 So.2d 349 (1958), this Court, commenting on the earlier *Reed* case, stated:

"The earliest case which we have found in this jurisdiction in which a conviction for murder in the second degree caused by an automobile was affirmed is Reed v. State, 25 Ala.App. 18,

142 So. 441, 442, certiorari denied, 225 Ala. 219, 142 So. 442. The indictment was for murder in the first degree. As to the oral charge of the trial court in that case, the Court of Appeals said:

> " 'The court delivered an able and explicit charge to the jury covering every phase of the law applicable to this case. No exception was reserved to this charge, nor was it subject to objection and exception. * * *'
>
> "While the charge in the *Reed* case does not comply strictly with the statutory definition in that the charge characterizes the act as having been done without intention to deprive 'the deceased' of life, where the statute employs the term 'any particular person,' *both charge and statute declare that the facts hypothesized constitute murder in the first, not in the second, degree.*"

The jury here was sufficiently charged on the fourth class of murder in the first degree. It was a *jury question* whether Langford drove an automobile along a public highway knowing he was highly intoxicated—the evidence was conflicting. It was a *jury question* whether he knew other persons were present on the highway. It was a *jury question* whether he proceeded to drive the car in a highly reckless manner and operated it in such a manner as to be greatly dangerous to the lives of others. It was a *jury question* whether he had a depraved mind and did this without regard to human life.

The majority has substituted its determination of the facts for that of the jury by holding as a *matter of law* that first degree murder was not proved. Consequently, I dissent.

BEATTY, J., concurs.

NOTES

1. As in the *Langford* case, the defendant in Essex v. Commonwealth, 228 Va. 273, 322 S.E.2d 216 (1984), was driving an automobile while under the influence of alcohol, and caused a collision as a result of which three people died. He was charged and convicted of three counts of second-degree murder. The Virginia Supreme Court reversed, holding that if the killing resulted from negligence, however gross or culpable, and the killing was contrary to the defendant's intention, malice cannot be implied. The court continued:

> "In order to elevate the crime to second-degree murder, the defendant must be shown to have willfully or purposefully, rather than negligently, embarked upon a course of wrongful conduct likely to cause death or great bodily harm.
>
> "A motor vehicle, wrongfully used, can be a weapon as deadly as a gun or a knife. . . . [T]he premeditated use of an automobile to kill can be first-degree murder. . . . A killing in sudden heat of passion, upon reasonable provocation, by the use of a motor vehicle, could be voluntary manslaughter. Killings caused by the grossly negligent operation of motor vehicles, showing a reckless disregard of human

life, have frequently resulted in convictions of involuntary manslaughter.

"We have not, heretofore, had occasion to review a second-degree murder conviction based upon the use of an automobile, but the governing principles are the same as those which apply to any other kind of second-degree murder: the victim must be shown to have died as a result of the defendant's conduct, and the defendant's conduct must be shown to be malicious. In the absence of express malice, this element may only be implied from conduct likely to cause death or great bodily harm, wilfully or purposefully undertaken. Thus, for example, one who deliberately drives a car into a crowd of people at high speed, not intending to kill or injure any particular person, but rather seeking the perverse thrill of terrifying them and causing them to scatter, might be convicted of second-degree murder if death results. *One who accomplishes the same result inadvertently, because of grossly negligent driving, causing him to lose control of his car, could be convicted only of involuntary manslaughter.*" [Emphasis supplied.]

2. For a contrary view, see Pears v. State, 672 P.2d 903 (Alaska App.1983), affirming a two-count conviction of second degree murder of a driver involved in an accident which caused two deaths. The court opined that under the Alaska statutes, "where a driver's recklessness manifests an extreme indifference to human life he can be charged with murder even though the instrument by which he causes death is an automobile." But see the concurring opinion of two judges, viewing the result as a "rare" vehicular homicide case that qualifies for treatment as murder because the defendant had been warned by a companion and a police officer that he was too drunk to drive. See also the Alaska Supreme Court's remand by a divided court. 698 P.2d 1198 (1985).

See also, People v. Watson, 30 Cal.3d 290, 179 Cal.Rptr. 43, 637 P.2d 279 (1981), wherein a majority of the California Supreme Court upheld a second degree murder conviction of the culpable driver in a fatal accident, finding "implied malice" in the evidence of defendant's presumed knowledge that he would be driving his car while intoxicated, his high rate of speed, his near collision with another car followed by a resumption of excessive speed, and his belated braking at the time of the fatal accident. This finding of implied malice was strongly disputed in the dissenting opinions.

---

2. EUTHANASIA—"MERCY KILLINGS"

Malice may be present even though the motive for a killing is of the highest order. Thus, a "mercy killing" is usually murder, inasmuch as it constitutes an intentional taking of life without provocation or other mitigation, and without legal justification or excuse. The present state of the law concerning euthanasia is well summarized in the following excerpt from Williams, The Sanctity of Life and the Criminal Law, 318–26 (1957):

"Under the present law, voluntary euthanasia would, except in certain narrow circumstances, be regarded as suicide, in the patient who consents and murder in the doctor who administers; even on a lenient view, most lawyers would say that it could not be less than manslaughter in the doctor, the punishment for which, according to the jurisdiction and the degree of manslaughter, can be anything up to imprisonment for life.

"More specifically, the following principles may be stated:

"(a) If the doctor gives the patient a fatal injection with the intention of killing him, and the patient dies in consequence, the doctor is a common murderer because it is his hand that caused the death. Neither the consent of the patient, nor the extremity of his suffering, nor the imminence of death by natural causes, nor all of these factors taken together, is a defence. . . .

"(b) If the doctor furnishes poison (for example, an overdose of sleeping tablets) for the purpose of enabling the patient to commit suicide, and the patient takes it accordingly and dies, this is suicide and a kind of self-murder in the patient, and the doctor, as an abettor, again becomes guilty of murder. So, at any rate, is it in strict legal theory. . . .

"(c) A case that may be thought to be distinguishable from both of those already considered is that of the administration of a fatal dose of a drug where this dose is in fact the minimum necessary to deaden pain. Where a patient is suffering from an incurable and agonizing disease, and ordinary quantities of a drug fail to render the pain tolerable, many doctors will give the minimum dose necessary to kill the pain, knowing that this minimum is at the same time an amount that is likely to kill the patient. In other words, with the choice of either doing nothing, or killing both the pain and the patient, the doctor chooses the latter course. . . . Thus a point is reached at which, proceeding upon the same principles as he has followed heretofore, and which have so far been lawful, the doctor is led to give what he knows is likely to be an immediately fatal dose. It would be extremely artificial to say that this last dose, which is administered upon the same principle as all the previous ones, is alone unlawful. . . . [The physician's] legal excuse . . . rests upon the doctrine of necessity, there being at this junction no way of relieving pain without ending life. In this limited form the excuse of necessity would be likely to be accepted by a judge, and to this extent it may be held that euthanasia is permitted under the existing law. . . .

"(d) We come, finally, to the problem of killing by inaction. 'Mercy-killing' by omission to use medical means to prolong life is probably lawful. Although a physician is normally under a duty to use reasonable care to conserve his patient's life, he is probably exempted from that duty if life has become a burden to the patient."

NOTES

1. Administration of the law in this area reflects a contemporary conflict between the thought that euthanasia is less reprehensible than other forms of

murder, and the idea that, morally, such homicide cannot be condoned. Consider the following histories of several cases of euthanasia:

(a) Louis Rapouille filed a petition for naturalization on September 22, 1944, and the federal district court entered an order granting the petition. The federal district attorney appealed on the ground that the petitioner had not established the fact of "good moral character" for the five-year period preceding his petition in that it was alleged and proved at the district court hearing that the petitioner had, during that period, deliberately put to death his thirteen-year-old son. The Court of Appeals for the Second Circuit reversed the order of the district court and dismissed Rapouille's petition, but without prejudice to the filing of a second petition. Rapouille v. United States, 165 F.2d 152 (1947). In rendering the court's decision, Judge Learned Hand stated:

"His reason for this tragic deed was that the child had 'suffered from birth from a brain injury which destined him to be an idiot and a physical monstrosity malformed in all four limbs. The child was blind, mute, and deformed. He had to be fed; the movements of his bladder and bowels were involuntary, and his entire life was spent in a small crib'. Rapouille had four other children at the time, towards whom he has always been a dutiful and responsible parent; it may be assumed that his act was to help him in their nurture, which was being compromised by the burden imposed upon him in the care of the fifth. The family was altogether dependent upon his industry for its support. He was indicted for manslaughter in the first degree; but the jury brought in a verdict of manslaughter in the second degree with a recommendation of the 'utmost clemency'; and the judge sentenced him to not less than five years or more than ten, execution to be stayed, and the defendant to be placed on probation, from which he was discharged in December, 1945. Concededly, except for this act he conducted himself as a person of 'good moral character' during the five years before he filed his petition. Indeed, if he had waited before filing his petition from September 22, to October 14, 1944, he would have had a clear record for the necessary period, and would have been admitted without question. . . .

"It is reasonably clear that the jury which tried Rapouille did not feel any moral repulsion at his crime. Although it was inescapably murder in the first degree, not only did they bring in a verdict that was flatly in the face of the facts and utterly absurd—for manslaughter in the second degree presupposes that the killing has not been deliberate—but they coupled even that with a recommendation which showed that in substance they wished to exculpate the offender. Moreover, it is also plain, from the sentence which he imposed, that the judge could not have seriously disagreed with their recommendation.

"One might be tempted to seize upon all this as a reliable measure of current morals; and no doubt it should have its place in the scale; but we should hesitate to accept it as decisive, when, for example, we compare it with the fate of a similar offender in Massachusetts, who, although he was not executed, was imprisoned for life. Left at large as we are, without means of verifying our conclusion, and without authority to substitute our individual beliefs, the outcome must needs be tentative; and not much is gained by discussion. We can say no more than that, quite independently of what may be the current moral feeling as to legally administered euthanasia, we feel reasonably secure in holding that only a minority of virtuous persons would deem the practice morally justifiable, while it remains in private hands, even when the provocation is as overwhelming as it was in this instance."

(b) The Massachusetts case referred to by the Court in the preceding paragraph was Commonwealth v. Noxon, 319 Mass. 495, 66 N.E.2d 814 (1946). The history of the *Noxon* case, particularly that portion of it occurring after the above decision on the *Rapouille* petition, sheds light on the many factors which affect the ultimate outcome of such cases. The following brief history is taken from the January 17, 1949, issue of Newsweek Magazine:

"When John F. Noxon was charged in 1943 with electrocuting his incurably Mongoloid 6-month-old son Larry, the newspapers labeled the case a 'mercy killing.' Noxon pleaded innocent. He insisted that the death had been accidental—that it was only by chance the boy had come in contact with a metal tray that touched a short-circuited radio wire.

"The wealthy Pittsfield, Mass., lawyer's trial became much more than a simple attempt to arrive at facts. In a heavily Catholic state, the idea of mercy killing was anathema. Noxon's social position and his personality—dour and uncommunicative—lost him much sympathy among those who might have supported him. After a sensational trial, he was found guilty and sentenced to the electric chair.

"But Noxon's lawyer, ex-Gov. Joseph B. Ely, did not give up. When the State Supreme Court rejected his appeal, Ely turned to Gov. Maurice J. Tobin. His argument: Noxon, half-crippled by infantile paralysis, would be punished enough if his sentence was commuted to life imprisonment. Although a Catholic, Tobin agreed and won the approval of his nine-man Executive Council. Noxon was moved from the condemned row in the state prison at Charleston to the Norfolk prison colony where thenceforth he served as prison librarian.

"Last month Gov. Robert F. Bradford, Ely's onetime law partner, who was defeated for reelection in November, asked the Pardon and Parole Committee of his council to consider a further reduction of Noxon's sentence—from life to six-years-to-life, making parole possible at once. This time, Tobin, now Secretary of Labor, advised against further leniency. More sensationally, District Attorney William J. Foley openly charged that Bradford was deliberately turning loose murderers in the last days of his administration and hinted at corruption.

"In the midst of the hullabaloo, Bradford's committee, headed by Lt. Gov. Arthur Coolidge, approved the governor's recommendation. Then the full council, by a 6-to-3 vote, granted the reduction in sentence. Last week the State Parole Board closed the books on the controversial case by releasing Noxon. On Friday, Jan. 7, 1949, he walked out of the Norfolk prison colony."

Another unusual case history is discussed in Note, 34 Notre Dame Law 460 (1959).

(c) An interesting "mercy killing" case occurred in Belgium in 1962. A child was born very badly malformed as a result of the mother having taken thalidomide while pregnant. The parents and a doctor arranged for killing the child 8 days old, by placing barbiturates with honey in a bottle of milk.

Following are portions of a news report (Chicago Daily News, Nov. 12, 1962) of the public reaction to the acquittal:

"When the verdict was announced yesterday, spectators in the courtroom, who earlier in the day had applauded the defense and hissed the prosecutor, cheered, stamped, jumped in the air, and shout-ed, 'Bravo!'

"A woman in the crowds suffered a broken leg."

2. Present attitudes regarding legislative change in the law concerning euthanasia include (1) the view that the status quo has sufficient flexibility, through such factors as the jury system and the pardoning power, to afford just treatment in each case according to its merits; (2) the position that the penalty for a killing motivated by mercy should be reduced; and (3) the view that euthanasia should be legalized within certain narrow bounds and placed under state supervision and control. These positions are ably discussed and evaluated in Silving, Euthanasia: A Study in Comparative Criminal Law, 103 U.Pa.L.Rev. 350 (1954). See also, Kamisar, Some Non-Religious Views Against Proposed "Mercy-Killing" Legislation, 42 Minn.L.Rev. 969 (1958), and Williams, "Mercy-Killing" Legislation—A Rejoinder, 43 Minn.L.Rev. 1 (1958). Also see Levin-sohn, Voluntary Mercy Deaths, 8 J.For.Med. 57 (1961), and Sanders, Euthana-sia: None Dare Call It Murder, 60 J.Crim.L., C. & P.S. 351 (1969); Survey, Euthanasia: Criminal, Tort, Constitutional and Legislative Considerations, 48 Notre Dame L. 1202 (1973); Russell, Moral and Legal Aspects of Euthanasia, 34 Humanist 22 (1974).

3. DESTRUCTION OF THE UNBORN CHILD

Since the common law of homicide refers to the killing of a "human being," the courts in this country have generally not considered the aborting of an unborn child to be a homicide. The child must be shown to have achieved an independent circulation. See, in this regard, the materials in the section on "When Does Life Begin" in Chapter 3, supra.

NOTES

1. In State v. Gyles, 313 So.2d 799 (La.1975), the Supreme Court of Louisiana observed that "The common law crime of murder   .   .   .   contem-plates only the killing of those human beings who have been born alive and who thus have an existence independent of their mothers at the time of their death. The crime does not punish conduct which causes the death of a fetus not born alive due to an assault on the mother, in the absence of a statute expressly changing the common law definition of the crime. The uniform authority in all American jurisdictions is to this effect." A dissenting judge would have defined a child in the mother's womb at eight months of pregnancy a human being. For a view critical of the common law concept, see People v. Chavez, 77 Cal.App.2d 621, 176 P.2d 92 (1947).

2. Once the fetus has emerged totally and the breathing process started, it is not needed that the umbilical cord be severed; it achieves the status of a "human being". Jackson v. Commonwealth, 265 Ky. 295, 96 S.W.2d 1014 (1936). But see, Morgan v. State, 148 Tenn. 417, 256 S.W. 433 (1923), sug-gesting that an independent circulation cannot be established until after the umbilical cord is severed.

3. The infliction of injuries upon an unborn child who dies after having been born alive may be considered homicide. In Abrams v. Foshee, 3 Iowa 274 (1856), the court held that if a child is born alive and subsequently dies as a result of potions or bruises while still in the womb, the person administering

the potions or bruises with intent to produce a miscarriage could be convicted of murder. And in State v. Anderson, 135 N.J.Super. 423, 343 A.2d 505 (1975), a mother seven months pregnant with twin fetuses, received a gunshot wound and was delivered of the fetuses after the injury by Caesarian section. After the operation both fetuses were alive, but they died shortly thereafter. One of the fetuses was said to have died of a bullet wound across the back as the missile passed through the mother, the other was not struck by the bullet and death was said to be immaturity. The court held that "fetuses which are the victim of a criminal blow or wound upon their mother and are subsequently born alive, and thereafter die by reason of a chain of circumstances precipitated by such blow or wound, may be the victims of murder" and would be considered "persons" within the meaning of the state's homicide statutes.

In People v. Bolar, 109 Ill.App.3d 384, 64 Ill.Dec. 919, 440 N.E.2d 639 (1982), the majority of the court held that even though the medical evidence showed there may not have been any brain activity, testimony that there were a few heartbeats during rescussitation was sufficient to support the fact determination that the baby was born alive.

4. In State v. Amaro, 448 A.2d 1257 (R.I.1982), a nine-month pregnant woman was taken to the hospital after a traffic accident. She delivered a stillborn female fetus. The Rhode Island Supreme Court held that the information for vehicular homicide of defendant should have been dismissed, upholding the common law rule.

If a person intentionally kills a 28–30-week old fetus being carried by his wife, by forcing his hand into her vagina against her will, as a result of which a physician subsequently delivered the dead fetus by abdominal incision, can the defendant be convicted of murder? See, Hollis v. Commonwealth, 652 S.W.2d 61 (Ky.1983), continuing the common law rule that limits criminal homicide to killing of a child after it has first been born alive.

On the other hand, a majority of the Massachusetts Supreme Judicial Court held, in Commonwealth v. Cass, 392 Mass. 799, 467 N.E.2d 1324 (1984), that for the purposes of the state's vehicular homicide statute, a viable fetus is a "person" and is therefore capable of being the victim of a homicide. (The ruling was held to have prospective application only.) See, Criminal Liability for the Death of a Viable Fetus Under the Massachusetts Vehicular Homicide Statute, 21 New Engl.L.Rev. 147 (1985–1986). Accord, State v. Horne, 282 S.C. 444, 319 S.E.2d 703 (1984), also holding that an unborn child is a "person" within the statutory definition of murder contained in the South Carolina Code; accordingly, a defendant can be charged with homicide for the death of a viable unborn fetus, but, like in Cass, the "law of feticide" is given prospective application only.

Following the California decision in Keeler v. Superior Court, 2 Cal.3d 619, 87 Cal.Rptr. 481, 470 P.2d 617 (1970), holding that the destruction of a fetus caused by a criminally inflicted blow to its mother was not a homicide because it was not a "human being," the legislature declared that murder included the "killing of a fetus" with "malice aforethought." Exceptions were made, of course, as regards authorized abortions. Cal. Penal Code, Title 8, Ch. 1, § 187.

5. In the precedent setting abortion decision of Roe v. Wade, supra Chapter 4–c, "Right of Privacy," the United States Supreme Court carefully avoided the issue of when does life begin. From time to time, legislators have introduced bills in Congress to declare that life begins at conception but, so far, no such law has been enacted. See also, Anno. 40 A.L.R.3d 444, Homicide

Based on Killing of Unborn Child; and Anno. 65 A.L.R.3d 413, Proof of Live Birth in Prosecution for Killing Newborn Child.

6. Because it is sometimes very difficult to establish that the issue was born alive, which proof is needed to support a prosecution for murder or manslaughter, some states have specially provided that concealment of an infant death is a misdemeanor. For example, the Illinois Criminal Code (§ 9-4) provides as follows:

(a) A person commits the offense of concealing the death of a bastard when that person conceals the death of any issue of a human body which if born alive would be a bastard.

(b) Nothing herein contained shall be so construed as to prevent any person from being indicted for the first degree, second degree murder or involuntary manslaughter of such bastard child.

In Williams v. People, 114 Colo. 207, 158 P.2d 447 (1945), the court affirmed a conviction of murder and of concealing the death of a bastard, but a strong dissent suggested there was no proof the child was ever born alive. The dissenting opinion analyzed in great detail the requirement of the corpus delicti in infanticides and reviewed the case law in other states on the issue.

4. THE "CORPUS DELICTI"

R. v. ONUFREJCZYK
Court of Criminal Appeals.
[1955] 1 All Eng.R. 247.

[The evidence was that the defendant and one Sykut had a farm which was a financial failure. The defendant was trying, unsuccessfully, to borrow money to buy out Sykut's interest, in order to avoid a sale of the farm by auction. On or about December 14th, Sykut disappeared. On December 18th, defendant told a sheriff's officer that Sykut had gone to another city to see a doctor. Later, however, he said that three men had forced Sykut into a car at gun point and driven him away from the farm. He also wrote letters suggesting that Sykut had returned to Poland. Sykut's wife, who lived in Poland, had not heard from him, however, well after the time it would have taken him to reach Poland. The defendant was still trying to borrow money, and he tried to persuade a friend to go to a solicitor with him and impersonate Sykut. He was also arranging for a woman to draft some supposed agreements and forge Sykut's signature to them. In addition, he tried to get a blacksmith to say that Sykut had fetched a horse at the blacksmith's on December 17th, when Sykut had actually called for the horse on the 14th.]

LORD GODDARD, C. J., delivered the judgment of the court: The appellant, who is a Pole and who has been in this country since 1947, was convicted of the murder of another Pole, Sykut, his partner.

The principal question that has been argued, is whether there was proof of what the law calls a corpus delicti. In this case the remarkable fact, which has remained remarkable and unexplained, is that the body of this man, who was last seen so far as anybody knows on Dec. 14,

1953, has completely disappeared and there is no trace whatever either of him, or of his clothes, or of his ashes. It has been submitted to us that the law is that, unless the body can be found or an account can be given of the death, there is no proof of a corpus delicti. Corpus delicti means, first, that a crime has been committed, that is to say that the man is dead, and that his death has been caused by a crime.

There is, apparently, no reported case in English law where a man has been convicted of murder and there has been no trace of the body at all. But it is, we think, clear that the fact of death can be proved, like any other fact can be proved, by circumstantial evidence, that is to say, by evidence of facts which lead to one conclusion, provided the jury are satisfied and are warned that the evidence must lead to one conclusion only. . . .

. . . The case for the prosecution was:—This man has disappeared. He has completely gone from the ken of mankind. It is impossible to believe that he is alive now. I suppose it would have been possible for him to have got out of the country and become immured behind what is sometimes called the Iron Curtain; but here you have facts which point irresistably towards the appellant being the person who knows and who disposed of that man in one form or another. It may be that it would be desirable to emphasise to the jury that the first thing to which they must apply their mind is: Was a murder committed? Speaking for myself, I think that the way the learned judge put it in the two passages which I have read did sufficiently direct the attention of the jury to the fact that they had to be satisfied of that, and, if they were satisfied of the death, and the violent death, of this man, they need not go any further. It is, no doubt, true that the prosecution relied considerably on certain minute spots of blood which were found in the kitchen when it was scientifically examined, spots so small that they might easily have escaped the attention of somebody who was trying to wash or wipe up blood. The appellant did not deny that the blood that was found, although it was a minute quantity, on the wall of the kitchen, and, I think, on the ceiling of the kitchen, was the blood of his partner. He said that its presence there was due to the fact that his partner had cut his hand in the field with, I think, one of the tractors, and on coming in must have shaken his hand and shaken off some blood. That, of course, was a possibility and it was put to the jury. It was also a possibility that Sykut was disposed of in the kitchen, but there is no evidence that he was and, a matter which has been very properly stressed by counsel for the appellant, there is no evidence here how Sykut met his death. This court is of the opinion, however, that there was evidence on which the jury could infer that he met his death, that he was dead; and, if he was dead, the circumstances of the case point to the fact that his death was not a natural death. Then, if that establishes, as it would, a corpus delicti, the evidence was such that the jury were entitled to find that the appellant murdered his partner. . . .

We have come to the conclusion that there was evidence on which the jury were entitled to find that the appellant's partner was murdered and that the appellant was the murderer. Accordingly, this appeal is dismissed.

NOTES

1. For other murder cases in which the corpus delicti was established by circumstantial evidence alone, consider the following:

(a) In People v. Scott, 176 Cal.App.2d 458, 1 Cal.Rptr. 600 (1959), the defendant's wife, a woman in excellent health, disappeared. Although her glasses and dentures were found in a trash pile, no traces of her body were ever found. Before his arrest the defendant had told his friends a number of conflicting stories and lies by way of trying to explain his wife's disappearance. He also forged her name on checks and had obtained large sums of her money. The affirmance of his murder conviction was disapproved in 34 Tul.L.Rev. 820 (1960).

(b) In Commonwealth v. Burns, 409 Pa. 619, 187 A.2d 552 (1963), the Supreme Court of Pennsylvania held that circumstantial evidence, which included proof of complete, sudden termination of a long-established, consistent pattern of living of the alleged victim, a healthy, 49-year old woman, who was last seen lying on the floor in defendant's presence in an apparently helpless condition with blood on her head, was sufficient to prove the corpus delicti.

(c) In King v. Horry, [1952] N.Z.L.R. 111, the defendant, George Horry, in 1942, while using an alias, married one Eileen Turner, in New Zealand. He had told her and her parents a number of fine things about himself; however, he concealed the fact that he was an ex-convict. After marriage Eileen converted all of her assets, about 1,000 pounds, into cash to take on their honeymoon. The day after the marriage, and while at a sea resort, she and George talked to her attorney about her finances. They also visited some friends to whom they told of plans to leave New Zealand the next day. George told them that a secret military mission precluded his giving them any further details about their trip. This was the last time Eileen was seen. The next day George, alone, was back in the town where he and Eileen had been married. (It was later established that he had never left New Zealand.) He opened a bank account in an amount of 767 pounds. Five months later he married another woman.

Shortly after Eileen's disappearance her parents received a letter, postmarked "Australia" and signed "George and Eileen," in which it was stated that they were leaving Australia for England. George said Eileen was busy visiting someone else. (It was later established that George, while still in New Zealand, had arranged for another person in Australia to mail the letter from there.) Thereafter George called on Eileen's parents and told them that he and Eileen had left Australia for England on the "Empress of India", and that the ship had been torpedoed and that he last saw Eileen in a life boat. He said he had been picked up by a British warship. In fact, no "Empress of India" ever existed.

Nine years after Eileen's disappearance George was prosecuted for murder and his conviction was sustained on appeal. See comment on the case in Morris, Corpus Delicti and Circumstantial Evidence, 68 L.Q.R. 391 (1952).

(d) In Epperly v. Commonwealth, 224 Va. 214, 294 S.E.2d 882 (1982), a coed disappeared after going to a dance. She had left the dance with the defendant. Her body was never found. Citing the *Onufrejczyk* case with approval, defendant's conviction was affirmed by the Virginia Supreme Court upon the circumstantial evidence given by forensic scientists who testified as to hairs, fibers, and bloodstain examinations.

(e) Among the numerous crimes and atrocities of which Charles Manson was convicted in California was the murder of one person whose body was never found. In upholding the conviction, the court said: "The fact that Shea's body was never recovered would justify an inference by the jury that death was caused by a criminal agency. It is highly unlikely that a person who dies from natural causes will successfully dispose of his own body. Although such a result may be a theoretical possibility, it is contrary to the normal course of human affairs." People v. Manson, 71 Cal.App.3d 1, 139 Cal.Rptr. 275 (1977), certiorari denied 435 U.S. 953, 98 S.Ct. 1582 (1978).

Also, for an account of case convictions for murders where no killings had ever occurred, see Borchand, Convicting the Innocent (1932). For another case involving the corpus delicti issue, see Commonwealth v. Burns, 409 Pa. 619, 187 A.2d 552 (1963).

2. In the United States, there is disagreement among the courts as to what constitutes the corpus delicti. Some courts require only that the particular loss or injury involved in the case be proved. Other courts—probably a majority—also require proof that the loss or injury was caused by a criminal act. Some courts go even further and require a third element—proof that the accused himself committed the crime involved.

Wigmore favored the first of these views, commenting about the view of the courts in the second category that it "makes the rule much more difficult for the jury to apply amid a complex mass of evidence, and tends to reduce the rule to a juggling formula." 7 Wigmore Evidence, § 2072 (3d ed. 1940). A different opinion is expressed in Note, The Corpus Delicti—Confession Problem, 43 J.Crim.L., C. & P.S. 214, 215 (1952), where it is stated that the second view "demands the proof of a crime and no more or less. The first view, however, can be criticized for requiring proof of less than an actual crime and thereby failing to provide adequate protection from unwarranted prosecution." As for the view held by the courts in the third category, Wigmore asserted it is "too absurd to be argued with."

The courts are also in disagreement as to what degree of proof is required to establish the elements which comprise the corpus delicti. A majority of the courts hold that the corpus delicti need not be proven beyond a reasonable doubt. But see, e.g., Smith v. Commonwealth, 62 Va. (21 Gratt.) 809, 820 (1871): "(T)he fact of the death must be established by clear and unequivocal proof, either by direct testimony or by presumptive evidence of the most cogent and irresistible kind." On the other hand, in State v. Kelley, 308 A.2d 877 (Me. 1973), the court said the corpus delicti should be proved by "credible evidence which, if believed, would create in the mind of a reasonable man, not a mere surmise or suspicion but rather a really substantial belief" that the crime has occurred. Does "a really substantial belief" require a greater or a lesser quantum of proof than "evidence of the most cogent and irresistible kind."?

Compare also People v. Rife, 382 Ill. 588, 48 N.E.2d 367 (1943) and People v. Franklin, 415 Ill. 514, 114 N.E.2d 661 (1953).

3. When the evidence as to the corpus delicti is entirely circumstantial, there is a tendency to require a greater quantum of proof. In Trowell v. State, 288 So.2d 506 (Fla.App.1973), a manslaughter prosecution, the only testimony about the victim came from the pathologist who had done the autopsy, but who did not know of his own knowledge the identity of the individual upon whom he performed the autopsy. In reversing, the court said that the corpus delicti required (1) proof of the fact of death; (2) the criminal agency of another person as the cause thereof; and (3) the identity of the deceased person. With respect to how the corpus delicti might have been proved, the court said:

> Since we are not confronted in the case sub judice with a situation where the body was unknown, mutilated, decomposed or lost, which might justify a lesser degree of proof, we are bound by the rule as stated in Lee, supra, that is, the corpus delicti must be proved beyond a reasonable doubt.

> It would have been manifestly easy for the State in its zeal to prove beyond a reasonable doubt that Raymond Jones was dead and to identify his dead body:

> 1. There could have been the testimony of a relative or friend who saw his dead body as late as the funeral service;

> 2. The funeral director, if he knew him personally;

> 3. Any person who saw his corpse at the hospital who knew him personally;

> 4. A photograph could have been taken of the cadaver which was autopsied which could later at trial have been identified by any person who knew him in his lifetime;

> 5. A picture properly identified as Raymond Jones when alive could have been identified at trial as the person upon whom Doctor Klein performed the autopsy;

> 6. Since allegedly death occurred sometime after the incident at the Santa Fe Bar, a certified copy of the death certificate could have been proffered;

> 7. Circumstantial evidence, such as the contents of the body's billfold, rings and other personal effects, garments, etc., could have been utilized;

> 8. Scientific evidence, such as fingerprints, identification of teeth, hair, etc., tending to establish identity, may have been available to the State; and finally

> 9. The prosecution could have at least proffered the hospital records where presumably Raymond Jones died, as well as the bullet which caused the death of the person whose body was somehow delivered to the autopsy room of the Alachua General Hospital on July 3, 1972.

> We belabor and detail these elementary procedures so that hopefully never again will this Court have to reverse a conviction because the State failed to prove the alleged victim dead and his identity.

4. A majority of courts hold that the corpus delicti cannot be established solely by the extra-judicial confession of an accused. Some independent corroboration is required. Opper v. United States, 348 U.S. 84, 75 S.Ct. 158 (1954). People v. Holmes, 38 Ill.App.3d 122, 347 N.E.2d 407 (1976), contains a thorough

analysis of the corpus delicti problem but it was reversed by the Illinois Supreme Court that had determined that the corpus delicti had been independently established. 67 Ill.2d 236, 10 Ill.Dec. 210, 367 N.E.2d 663 (1977). In People v. Furby, 138 Ill.2d 434, 447, 150 Ill.Dec. 534, 537, 563 N.E.2d 421 (1990), however, the validity of the rule was questioned, but since the state did not contend that the rule ought to be relaxed, the court had no occasion to reexamine its requirement.

The reason for requiring such corroboration is said to be the judicial distrust for the reliability of extrajudicial confessions. This reason, according to one appellate court, "may now be dissipating because of the greater reliability that may be attributed to confessions as a result of the application of recent decisions such as Miranda v. Arizona [a decision by the United States Supreme Court holding that an arrestee is entitled to be warned of his right to remain silent, that anything he says may be used against him in court, that he has the right to consult with a lawyer prior to or during questioning, and that if he cannot afford a lawyer the court will appoint one for him] . . . ." Self v. State, 513 S.W.2d 832 (Tex.Crim.App.1974).

5. Contrary to a prevailing misconception, proof of corpus delicti is a requirement of all criminal cases and not merely in homicide cases. In Commonwealth v. Leslie, 424 Pa. 331, 227 A.2d 900 (1967), the defendant confessed that he had started the fire which destroyed a summer cottage. While the police had suspected as much, they could not uncover any evidence that the fire had been started deliberately. In reversing the conviction, the Supreme Court of Pennsylvania, while recognizing that the corpus delicti could be proved by circumstantial evidence, found that the state had relied on the confession alone to prove the corpus delicti and held that this was insufficient. Proof of corpus delicti is one of the most difficult tasks facing the prosecution in arson cases. See Comment, 45 J.Crim.L., C. & P.S. 185 (1954). For corpus delicti issues in other crimes, see People v. Call, 176 Ill.App.3d 571, 126 Ill.Dec. 156, 531 N.E.2d 451 (1988) [Driving under the influence of alcohol or drugs].

5. FELONY MURDER

COMMONWEALTH v. ALMEIDA
Supreme Court of Pennsylvania, 1949.
362 Pa. 596, 68 A.2d 595.

[During an exchange of shots between robbers and police, Ingling, a police officer, was killed. The prosecution claimed that one of the felons killed Ingling; the defense, on the other hand, contended that Ingling was shot by a fellow officer. The defendant was convicted of first degree murder committed in the course of the robbery and sentenced to death.]

MAXEY, CHIEF JUSTICE. . . . The defendant's thirteenth point for charge which the trial judge correctly rejected was in effect a request that the court instruct the jury that in order to convict the defendant of the death of Officer Ingling, the jury would have to find that the fatal shot was fired by one of the three robbers. . . .

. . . The *legal* question presented [is] . . . when men who are feloniously shot at by robbers return their fire in self-defense and a third person is killed by a shot fired by the defenders, are the robbers whose felonious action caused the shooting guilty of murder? . . .

[In] the instant case, we have a band of robbers engaged in an exchange of shots with city policemen *whose duty it is to subdue the bandits if possible.* In the course of the exchange of deadly bullets Officer Ingling is slain. The policemen cannot be charged with any wrongdoing because their participation in the exchange of bullets with the bandits was both in justifiable self-defense and *in the performance of their duty.* The felonious acts of the robbers in firing shots at the policemen, well knowing that their fire would be returned, as it should have been, was the proximate cause of Officer Ingling's death. . . .

. . . Their acts were "the cause of the cause" of the murder. They "set in motion the physical power" which resulted in Ingling's death and they are criminally responsible for that result. Whether the fatal bullet was fired by one of the bandits or by one of the policemen who were performing their duty in repelling the bandit's assault and defending themselves and endeavoring to prevent the escape of the felons is immaterial. Whoever fired the fatal shot, the killing of Officer Ingling had its genesis in the robbing by the defendant and his confederates . . . and in their firing upon the police officers who in the performance of their duty were attempting to take them into custody. . . .

There can be no doubt about the "justice" of holding that felon guilty of murder in the first degree who engages in a robbery or burglary and thereby inevitably calls into action defensive forces against him, the activity of which forces result in the death of a human being. Neither can there be any doubt about the "general utility" of a ruling which holds this defendant Almeida guilty of the murder of Officer Ingling, even if it had been established that the bullet which killed that officer was fired by one of the police officers who were returning the fire of Almeida and his confederates and were attempting to prevent their escape. . . .

A knave who feloniously and maliciously starts "a chain reaction" of acts dangerous to human life must be held responsible for the natural fatal results of such acts. This is the doctrine enunciated by the textbook writers on criminal law, and which has been applied by the courts.

When men engaged in a scheme of robbery arm themselves with loaded revolvers they show that they expect to encounter forcible opposition and that to overcome it they are prepared to kill anyone who stands in their way. If in the course of their felonious enterprise they open deadly fire upon policemen or others and if in self-defense and to vindicate the law the fire is returned and someone is killed by a bullet fired in the exchange of shots, who can challenge the conclusion that the *proximate cause* of the killing was the malicious criminal action of the felons? No *other* genesis can justly be assigned to the homicide.

The felons should be adjudged guilty of murder in the perpetration of a robbery, that is, murder in the first degree. . . .

The judgment is affirmed and the record is remitted to the court below so that the sentence imposed may be carried out. * * *

JONES, JUSTICE (dissenting). I would reverse the judgment and remand the case for a retrial because of fundamental error in the trial court's charge to the jury. The case was submitted on the felony murder theory, yet, the trial judge charged in effect that, even though the fatal shot was not fired by one of the felons but by someone attempting to frustrate the robbery, all the jury would need find in order to hold the defendant guilty of murder was that he was engaged in a robbery at the time of the killing. That instruction inadequately stated the law applicable to the circumstances.

On proof of no more than the perpetration of a felony and an incidental killing, liability for murder can be visited upon the participating felons *only* where the causation of the homicide is direct, i.e., where one of the felons or one acting in furtherance of the felonious design inflicted the fatal wound . . . [E]ven though a felon or one acting in his aid does not fire the fatal bullet, his conduct may have initiated such a causative chain of events as to render him legally chargeable with having been the causa causans of the homicide. . . . In such circumstances, the felony murder theory supplies the malice necessary to make the killing murder while the proximate (although indirect) causation of the death is capable of fastening on the felon responsibility for the homicide. Sufficiency of the evidence to support a finding of the "chain of events" is, of course, a question of law for a court, but whether the "chain of events" existed unbroken and was the proximate cause of the homicide are questions of fact that only *a jury* can properly resolve. . . . Those important factual inquiries were not submitted in the instant case. Causation was assumed by the learned trial judge and all that was left to the jury to determine, in order to hold the defendant guilty of murder, was that he was engaged in a "holdup" at the time of the killing notwithstanding there was evidence that someone other than the felons had fired the fatal bullet. . . .

. . . Whether the acts of Almeida and his confederates *were sufficient* to constitute the proximate cause of the killing was a question of law but whether they *did constitute* the proximate cause was a question of fact for the jury. . . .

The jury should have been instructed that, in order to find the defendant guilty of murder, it was not only necessary for them to find the killing to have been coincidental with the perpetration of a felony in which the defendant was at the time participating but that they would also have to find that the fatal shot was fired by one of the felons or, if not fired by one of them, that the conduct of the defendant or his accomplices set in motion a chain of events among whose reasonably foreseeable consequences was a killing such as actually occurred. The only way that the question of the defendant's guilt can any longer be properly adjudicated upon adequate instructions to the jury is by the medium of a new trial. . . .

NOTES

1.   Subsequent to the *Almeida* case the Pennsylvania Supreme Court was required to rule on the following fact situation, in Commonwealth v. Thomas, 382 Pa. 639, 117 A.2d 204 (1955): Thomas and a confederate committed a robbery.   While fleeing from the scene, the confederate was shot and killed by the store owner.   Thomas was indicted for murder of his co-felon.   However, the trial court sustained Thomas' demurrer to the commonwealth's evidence and the decision was appealed.   The Supreme Court, with three justices dissenting, reversed the judgment of the lower court.   In so doing, the court stated:

"The sole question is whether defendant can be convicted of murder under this state of facts.   That is, can a co-felon be found guilty of murder where the victim of an armed robbery justifiably kills the other felon as they flee from the scene of the crime?   . . . If the defendant sets in motion the physical power of another, he is liable for its result. . . .   Commonwealth v. Almeida. . . . . As has been said many times, such a rule is equally consistent with reason and sound public policy, and is essential to the protection of human life.   The felon's robbery set in motion a chain of events which were or should have been within his contemplation when the motion was initiated.   He therefore should be held responsible for *any death* which by direct and almost inevitable sequence results from the initial criminal act. . . .   We can see no sound reason for distinction merely because the one killed was a co-felon."

Following the above action of the Supreme Court in the *Thomas* case, the District Attorney of Philadelphia moved the trial court for entry of a *nolle prosequi* on the murder indictment, and the court approved the motion.   At the same time, Thomas pleaded guilty to an indictment charging him with armed robbery and was sentenced to the penitentiary.   The Pennsylvania penalty for armed robbery is a fine not exceeding ten thousand dollars, or imprisonment in solitary confinement at labor for not exceeding twenty years, or both.

2.   A few years later, the Pennsylvania Supreme Court again found it necessary to struggle with the felony-murder concept.   The occasion was the case of Commonwealth v. Redline, 391 Pa. 486, 137 A.2d 472 (1958), where the defendant and his accomplice perpetrated a robbery and, while fleeing from the scene, engaged in a gun battle with the police.   The accomplice was killed by a policeman, and defendant was indicted for and convicted of the murder of the accomplice.   Here, the Supreme Court changed its mind and overruled *Thomas,* holding that felony-murder applies only if the killing is done by one of the felons, and not if the killing is done by a police officer or a bystander.   The court did not overrule *Almeida,* although it expressed its dissatisfaction with that case, because the two cases could be distinguished on the basis that in *Almeida* the victim of the killing was a police officer, while in *Redline,* the victim was one of the felons.

3.   On the same day that the Supreme Court of Pennsylvania decided the *Redline* case, it handed down a decision in Commonwealth v. Bolish, 391 Pa. 550, 138 A.2d 447 (1958).   Bolish and one Flynn planned an arson, and in carrying out the plan Flynn was fatally injured by an explosion which occurred when he placed a jar of gasoline on an electric hot plate.   Bolish was convicted

of first degree murder and sentenced to life imprisonment. The judgment was affirmed on appeal, the court rejecting the defendant's contention that the felony-murder doctrine does not apply to the death of an accomplice resulting from the accomplice's own act. The court stated that the defendant "was actively participating in the felony which resulted in death. The element of malice, present in the design of defendant, necessarily must be imputed to the resulting killing, and made him responsible for the death. . . . The fact that the victim was an accomplice does not alter the situation, since his own act which caused his death was in furtherance of the felony." Two justices dissented.

Is the *Bolish* case distinguishable from *Redline?*

Was the majority holding in *Bolish* correct in view of the wording of the Pennsylvania statute which provides, in part, as follows: "All murder which shall be . . . committed in the perpetration of . . . arson . . . shall be murder in the first degree"?

4. The conviction in the *Almeida* case was set aside by a federal district court, upon a habeas corpus hearing because of the fact that the prosecution had suppressed evidence establishing that the fatal bullet was actually fired by a police officer and not by one of the felons. 104 F.Supp. 321 (E.D.Pa.1951), affirmed 195 F.2d 815 (3d Cir.1952). Almeida was retried. He pled guilty and received a life sentence.

After the court's decision in *Redline,* Almeida appealed on the basis that under the new (Redline) rule he was not guilty of murder. The Pennsylvania Supreme Court held that the *Redline* decision was not relevant because the legality of Almeida's conviction must be governed by the law as it existed at that time. Commonwealth ex rel. Almeida v. Rundle, 409 Pa. 460, 187 A.2d 266 (1963). To the same effect see United States ex rel. Almeida v. Rundle, 383 F.2d 421 (3d Cir.1967).

COMMONWEALTH EX REL. SMITH v. MYERS

Supreme Court of Pennsylvania, 1970.
438 Pa. 218, 261 A.2d 550.

O'BRIEN, JUSTICE. This is an appeal from the order of the Court of Common Pleas of Philadelphia County, denying James Smith's petition for a writ of habeas corpus. The facts upon which the convictions of appellant and his co-felons, Almeida and Hough, rest are well known to this Court and to the federal courts. In addition to vexing the courts, these cases have perplexed a generation of law students, both within and without the Commonwealth, and along with their progeny, have spawned reams of critical commentary.[1]

Briefly, the facts of the crime are these. On January 30, 1947, Smith, along with Edward Hough and David Almeida, engaged in an armed robbery of a supermarket in the City of Philadelphia. An off-duty policeman, who happened to be in the area, was shot and killed

---

1. It would be virtually impossible to catalogue all of the articles on these cases which have been published in the learned journals. Some of the more enlightening include Morris, The Felon's Responsibility for the Lethal Acts of Others, 105 U.Pa.L. Rev. 50 (1956); Ludwig, Foreseeable Death in Felony Murder, 18 U.Pitt.L.Rev. 51 (1956); and Case Notes, 71 Harv.L.Rev. 1565 (1958), and 106 U.Pa.L.Rev. 1176 (1958).

while attempting to thwart the escape of the felons. Although the evidence as to who fired the fatal shot was conflicting in appellant's 1948 trial, the court charged the jury that it was irrelevant who fired the fatal bullet:

> "Even if you should find from the evidence that Ingling was killed by a bullet from the gun of one of the policemen, that policeman having shot at the felons in an attempt to prevent the robbery or the escape of the robbers, or to protect Ingling, the felons would be guilty of murder, or if they did that in returning the fire of the felons that was directed toward them."

To this part of the charge appellant took a specific exception.

The jury convicted Smith of first degree murder, with punishment fixed at life imprisonment. He filed no post-trial motions, and took no appeal. Nor did Smith initiate any post-conviction proceedings until the instant case, despite the litigious propensities of his co-felons.

On February 4, 1966, appellant filed the present petition for a writ of habeas corpus. * * *

. . . The court below held that appellant had knowingly waived his right to appeal, and although the opinion does not discuss the question, the denial of relief necessarily manifested a belief by the court below that appellant was aware of his right to counsel on appeal. The other issues raised by appellant were not mentioned by the court, apparently of the view that they were cognizable only if it appeared that appellant had been denied his right to appeal, and was entitled to an appeal nunc pro tunc.

We reverse, grant the writ, allow an appeal nunc pro tunc, and grant a new trial. * * *

Appellant urges that he was denied due process by virtue of the trial court's charge that it was irrelevant who fired the fatal bullet. Such a charge was consistent with the dictum of this Court in Commonwealth v. Moyer and Byron, 357 Pa. 181, 53 A.2d 736 (1947), and with the holding shortly thereafter in the appeal of appellant's co-felon, David Almeida, in Commonwealth v. Almeida, . . . (1949). In the latter case, by a stretch of the felony-murder rule, we held that Almeida could indeed be found guilty of murder even though the fatal bullet was fired by another officer acting in opposition to the felony. We adopted a proximate cause theory of murder: "[H]e whose felonious act is the *proximate* cause of another's death is *criminally* responsible for that death and must answer to society for it exactly as he who is *negligently* the *proximate cause* of another's death is civilly responsible for that death and must answer in damages for it. . . ."

The proximate cause theory was taken a millimeter further by this Court in Commonwealth v. Thomas, . . . (1955). In that case the victim of an armed robbery shot and killed one of the felons, Jackson; the other felon, Thomas, was convicted of the murder.

Thomas was repudiated by this Court in Commonwealth v. Redline, . . . (1958). The facts there were virtually identical to those of *Thomas;* a policeman shot one fleeing felon and the other was convicted of murder. In a famous opinion by the late Chief Justice Charles Alvin Jones, this Court interred *Thomas* and dealt a fatal blow to *Almeida.* At the outset of this Court's opinion in *Redline,* we stated: "The decision in the Almeida case was a radical departure from common law criminal jurisprudence." The thorough documentation which followed in this lengthy opinion proved beyond a shadow of a doubt that *Almeida* and *Thomas* constituted aberrations in the annals of Anglo–American adjudicature.

Redline began with a rather general review of the entire felony-murder theory. If we may presume to elaborate a bit on that review, we should point out that the felony-murder rule really has two separate branches in Pennsylvania. The first, and the easier concept, is statutory. The Act of June 24, 1939 provides, *inter alia:* "All murder which shall ＊ ＊ ＊ be committed in the perpetration of, or attempting to perpetrate any arson, rape, robbery, burglary, or kidnapping, shall be murder in the first degree. All other kinds of murder shall be murder in the second degree." Clearly this statutory felony-murder rule merely serves to raise the degree of certain murders to first degree; it gives no aid to the determination of what constitutes murder in the first place. *Redline,* pointing out that except for one isolated situation there is no statutory crime of murder, directed us to the common law for a determination of what constitutes murder. It is here that the other branch of the felony-murder rule, the common law branch, comes into play. Citing Commonwealth v. Drum, 58 Pa. 9 (1868), the early leading case on murder in the Commonwealth, and Blackstone, Commentaries, *Redline* reaffirmed that the distinguishing criterion of murder is malice. The common law felony-murder rule is a means of imputing malice where it may not exist expressly. Under this rule, the malice necessary to make a killing, even an accidental one, murder, is constructively inferred from the malice incident to the perpetration of the initial felony.

The common law felony-murder rule as thus explicated has been subjected to some harsh criticism, most of it thoroughly warranted. ＊   ＊   ＊

In fact, not only is the felony-murder rule non-essential, but it is very doubtful that it has the deterrent effect its proponents assert.[2] On

---

2. See, e.g. the dissenting opinion of Justice (now Chief Justice) Bell in Commonwealth v. Redline, supra, where he stated: "The brutal crime wave which is sweeping and appalling our Country can be halted only if the Courts stop coddling, and stop freeing murderers, communists and criminals on technicalities made of straw." To similar effect is the statement in Commonwealth v. Kelly, 333 Pa. 280, 287, 4 A.2d 805 (1939): "To this Commonwealth one must answer as a malicious criminal for any fatal injury he here causes a human being by anything done by him intentionally or unintentionally during the commission or attempted commission of any of the specified felonies, for malice is the mainspring of his outlawed enterprise and his every act within the latter's ambit is imputable to that base quality. *Such a rule is essential to the protection of human life.*" (Emphasis added).

the contrary, it appears that juries rebel against convictions, adopting a homemade rule against fortuities, where a conviction must result in life imprisonment. . . .　　To similar effect, Justice Oliver Wendell Holmes, in The Common Law, argued that the wise policy is not to punish the fortuity, but rather to impose severe penalties on those types of criminal activity which experience has demonstrated carry a high degree of risk to human life. . . .

We have gone into this lengthy discussion of the felony-murder rule not for the purpose of hereby abolishing it.　That is hardly necessary in the instant case.　But we do want to make clear how shaky are the basic premises on which it rests.　With so weak a foundation, it behooves us not to extend it further and indeed, to restrain it within the bounds it has always known.　As stated above, *Redline* . . . demolished the extension to the felony-murder rule made in *Almeida:* "In adjudging a felony-murder, it is to be remembered at all times that the thing which is imputed to a felon for a killing incidental to his felony is *malice* and *not the act of killing.* . . . 'The malice of the initial* offense attaches to whatever else the *criminal* may do in connection therewith.' ＊　＊　＊ And so, until the decision of this court in Commonwealth v. Almeida, supra, in 1949, the rule which was uniformly followed, whether by express statement or by implication, was that in order to convict for felony-murder, *the killing must have been done by the defendant or by an accomplice or confederate or by one acting in furtherance of the felonious undertaking.* [citing a long line of cases.]

"Until the Almeida case there was no reported instance in this State of a jury ever having been instructed on the trial of an indictment for murder for a killing occurring contemporaneously with the perpetration of a felony that the defendant was guilty of murder regardless of the fact that the fatal shot was fired by a third person acting in hostility and resistance to the felon and in deliberate opposition to the success of the felon's criminal undertaking." (Emphasis in original).

Redline proceeded to discuss the cases, both within and without Pennsylvania, which establish the rule that murder is not present where the fatal shot is fired by a third person acting in opposition to the felon. . . .

We then proceeded to distinguish the cases relied upon in *Almeida.* Chief among those cases was Commonwealth v. Moyer and Byron, . . . We referred to the statement in that case to the effect that a felon can be convicted of murder if the shot is fired by the intended victim as "a palpable gratuity," since the court below had charged that the defendant was entitled to an acquittal unless the Commonwealth proved beyond a reasonable doubt that one of the felons had fired the fatal bullet.　We further distinguished the cases, cited in *Almeida,* in which the death-dealing act was committed by one participating in the initial felony. . . .

Finally, we distinguished the *express* malice cases. These included the so-called "shield" cases, where a felon used the interposition of the body of an innocent person to escape harm in flight from the scene of the crime. . . . These cases were not based on the felony-murder rule and imputed malice, but on the express malice found in the use of an innocent person as a shield or breastwork against hostile bullets. . . .

This lengthy review of *Redline* should have made it clear that the cases on which *Almeida* was based did not support the result reached therein, nor do the later cases. However, *Redline,* was not limited merely to a factual explication of the cases on which *Almeida* relied. *Redline,* . . . rejected the proximate cause tort analogy which Almeida found so appealing: "As we have already seen, the 'causation' requirement for responsibility in a felony-murder is that the homicide stem from the commission of the felony. Obviously, the assumed analogy between that concept and the tort-liability requirement of proximate cause is not conclusive. If it were, then the doctrine of supervening cause, which, for centuries courts have recognized and rendered operative on questions of proximate cause, would have to be considered and passed upon by the jury. But, that qualification, the Almeida case entirely disregarded."

The issue of the application of tort proximate cause principles to homicide prosecutions again arose a few years after *Redline* in Commonwealth v. Root [infra p. 263] (1961). In that case the defendant was engaged in a drag race on a public highway with another person who swerved to the left side of the road, crashed head-on into an on-coming truck, and was killed. This Court reversed Root's conviction for involuntary manslaughter, and rejected utterly the tort concept of proximate cause in criminal homicide prosecutions:

"While precedent is to be found for application of the tort law concept of 'proximate cause' in fixing responsibility for criminal homicide, the want of any rational basis for its use in determining criminal liability can no longer be properly disregarded. When proximate cause was first borrowed from the field of tort law and applied to homicide prosecutions in Pennsylvania, the concept connoted a much more direct causal relation in producing the alleged culpable result than it does today. Proximate cause, as an essential element of a tort founded in negligence, has undergone in recent times, and is still undergoing, a marked extension. More specifically, this area of civil law has been progressively liberalized in favor of claims for damages for personal injuries to which careless conduct of others can in some way be associated. To persist in applying the tort liability concept of proximate cause to prosecutions for criminal homicide after the marked expansion of *civil* liability of defendants in tort actions for negligence would be to extend possible *criminal* liability to persons chargeable with unlawful or reckless conduct in circumstances not generally considered to present the likelihood of a resultant death." * * *

After this review of *Redline,* the uninitiated might be surprised to learn that *Redline* did not specifically overrule *Almeida.* This Court did overrule *Thomas,* holding that no conviction was possible for a *justifiable* homicide where a policeman shot a felon, but "distinguished" *Almeida* on the ground that the homicide there, where an innocent third party was killed by a policeman, was only *excusable.*

The "distinction" *Redline* half-heartedly tries to draw has not escaped criticism from the commentators. While the result reached in *Redline* and most of its reasoning have met with almost unanimous approval, the *deus ex machina* ending has been condemned. One learned journal has commented:

"It seems, however, that Almeida cannot validly be distinguished from [Redline]. The probability that a felon will be killed seems at least as great as the probability that the victim will be an innocent bystander. Any distinction based on the fact that the killing of a felon by a policeman is sanctioned by the law and therefore justifiable, while the killing of an innocent bystander is merely excusable, seems unwarranted. No criminal sanctions now attach to either in other areas of criminal law, and any distinction here would seem anomalous. Indeed, to make the result hinge on the character of the victim is, in many instances, to make it hinge on the marksmanship of resisters. Any attempt to distinguish between the cases on the theory that the cofelon assumes the risk of being killed would also be improper since this tort doctrine has no place in the criminal law in which the wrong to be redressed is a public one—a killing with the victim's consent is nevertheless murder. It is very doubtful that public desire for vengeance should alone justify a conviction of felony murder for the death of an innocent bystander when no criminal responsibility will attach for the death of a cofelon." * * *

Appellant is therefore in no way precluded from asserting his claim that *Almeida* should be overruled. We thus give *Almeida* burial, taking it out of its limbo, and plunging it downward into the bowels of the earth.[3]

The order of the court below is reversed, an appeal is allowed *nunc pro tunc,* and a new trial is granted.

EAGEN, J., concurs in the result.

BELL, C.J., files a dissenting opinion.

This is the age of Crime and Criminals, and the peace-loving citizen is the forgotten man. Murder, robbery and rape are rampant, and this tidal wave of ruthless crime, violence and widespread lawlessness which too often goes unpunished is due in considerable part to recent

3. See fn # 14, . . . of the Dissenting Opinion in *Redline,* where Justice (now Chief Justice) Bell laments: "In the majority opinion, Commonwealth v. Almeida, like Mohammed's coffin, is suspended between Heaven and earth. However, unlike Mohammed's coffin, which is headed upward toward Heaven, the coffin containing Commonwealth v. Almeida is pointed downward in preparation for a speedy flight into the bowels of the earth."

procriminal decisions of the highest Courts in our State and Country.
No matter how guilty a convicted criminal undoubtedly is, no matter
how terrible his crime was, or how many crimes he has previously
committed, the highest Courts of our Country (1) have in recent years
extended and continue to *expand* the so-called rights of criminals, and
(2) are completely oblivious of the rights, the security, the safety and
the welfare of the law-abiding public. * * *

The Majority specifically hold that if a killing occurs during the
commission or attempted perpetration of robbery or other major felony,
or during the attempted escape of one of the robbers or any of the
dangerous co-felons, none of the robbers and *none of the co-felons is
guilty of murder—if the fatal shot was fired by the holdup victim or by
a policeman* or other law enforcement officer, or by a person attempting
to prevent the robbery or the robber's (or felon's) escape, *or by anyone
except one of the robbers or a co-felon.* This decision, which is so
disastrous to Society, is reached by unrealistic, and at times far-fetched
reasoning which together with its predecessor, Commonwealth v. Redline, . . . which it expands, will produce the most harmful damage to
law-abiding citizens ever inflicted sua sponte by the Supreme Court of
Pennsylvania. * * *

For ages, it has been the well-settled and wisely-established law
that when a person intentionally commits or joins or conspires with
another to commit a felonious act, or sets or joins another in setting in
motion a chain of circumstances the natural and probable or reasonably foreseeable result of which will be death or serious bodily harm to
some person, he and his co-felons are guilty of the crime which was a
product or result of the aforesaid criminal act or chain of circumstances. If the felon or co-felons possessed legal malice, and death
resulted, all the felons who participated in the felonious act or in the
aforesaid chain of circumstances would be guilty of murder.

In the leading case of Commonwealth v. Moyer and Commonwealth
v. Byron, 357 Pa. 181, 53 A.2d 736, the Court unanimously held that
every person who committed or attempted to commit a felony such as
robbery, or feloniously participated therein, was guilty of murder in the
first degree, even though the fatal bullet is fired by the intended victim
in repelling the robbery. Chief Justice Maxey, speaking for a unanimous Court, relevantly and wisely said (pages 190–191, 53 A.2d page
741–742):

"The doctrine that when malice is the mainspring of a criminal act
the actor will be held responsible for any consequence of his act though
it was not the one intended was recognized centuries ago when it was
held that, quoting from Blackstone, Book IV, page 1599, Sec. 201, 'if one
shoots at A and misses him, but kills B, this is murder, because of the
previous felonious intent, *which the law transfers from one to the other.*'
(Italics supplied.) It is equally consistent with reason and sound public
policy to hold that when a felon's attempt to commit robbery or
burglary sets in motion a chain of events which were or should have

been within his contemplation when the motion was initiated, he should be held responsible for any death which by direct and almost inevitable sequence results from the initial criminal act. For any individual forcibly to defend himself or his family or his property from criminal aggression is a primal human instinct. It is the right and duty of both individuals and nations to meet criminal aggression with effective countermeasures. Every robber or burglar knows when he attempts to commit his crime that he is inviting dangerous resistance. Any robber or burglar who carries deadly weapons (as most of them do and as these robbers did) thereby reveals that he expects to meet and overcome forcible opposition. . . . Every robber or burglar knows that a likely later act in the chain of events he inaugurates will be the use of deadly force against him on the part of the selected victim. For whatever results follow from that natural and legal use of retaliating force, the felon must be held responsible. For Earl Shank, the proprietor of a gas station in Ridley Township, Delaware County, which at 11 P.M. on July 13, 1946, was being attacked by armed robbers, to return the fire of these robbers with a pistol which he had at hand was as proper and as inevitable as it was for the American forces at Pearl Harbor on the morning of December 7, 1941, to return the fire of the Japanese invaders. The Japanese felonious invasion of the Hawaiian Islands on that date was in law and morals the proximate cause of all the resultant fatalities. The Moyer–Byron felonious invasion of the Shank gas station on July 13, 1946, was likewise the proximate cause of the resultant fatality. . . ."

In Commonwealth v. Lowry, . . . we held that the driver of the alleged get-away car was guilty of first-degree murder, and in an unanimous Opinion said: "Where a killing occurs in the course of a robbery, all who participate in the robbery including the driver of the get-away car are equally guilty of murder in the first degree even though someone other than the defendant fired the fatal shot. . . .

In Commonwealth v. Robb, the defendant was indicted and convicted of murder. He was a lookout and had nothing to do with the burglary or the murder. The Court said: "If defendants 'combine to commit a felony or make an assault, and, in carrying out the common purpose, another is killed, the one who enters into the combination but does not personally commit the wrongful act is equally responsible for the homicide with the one who directly causes it.' " . . .

MR. JUSTICE CARDOZO in "the Nature of the Judicial Process," wisely said: "When they [judges] are called upon to say how far existing rules are to be extended or restricted, they must let the welfare of society fix the path, its direction and its distance ∗ ∗ ∗ The final cause of law is the welfare of society. ∗ ∗ ∗ "

Blackstone, . . .: "If a man, however, does such an act of which the probable consequences may be, and eventually is, death; such killing may be murder, although no stroke be struck by himself and no killing primarily intended."

All of the aforesaid cases were actually or in practical effect overruled when there was a change of personnel in the Supreme Court of Pennsylvania, at which time they ignored all the reasoning and the principles and the prior decisions of this Court and changed the law and decided Commonwealth v. Redline, 391 Pa. 486, 137 A.2d 472. This was until today, I repeat, the most damaging blow to the protection and safety of Society ever delivered by the Supreme Court of Pennsylvania.

For all of the reasons hereinabove mentioned, I very vigorously dissent.

The decision of the Majority giving Smith a new trial—Smith never took any kind of appeal or any post-conviction petition until the present appeal—is inexcusably unfair and unjust to Almeida and Hough, whose repeated petitions for a new trial and their appeals from the judgment of sentence of murder were rejected and dismissed by this Court.

It has often been said that "Justice is blind," meaning thereby that Justice is absolutely fair to each and every one and is not subject to any outside influence whatsoever. In this case, Justice is certainly blind, but its blindness is real and realistic and not figurative blindness, and what it erroneously terms "Justice" is "gross injustice."

NOTES

1. The *Redline* rationale was adopted in People v. Morris, 1 Ill.App.3d 566, 274 N.E.2d 898 (1971), holding that the felony-murder doctrine is not applicable to convict the surviving felon when his accomplice was justifiably killed during the commission of a forcible felony. However, in People v. Hickman, 59 Ill.2d 89, 319 N.E.2d 511 (1974), the Illinois Supreme Court specifically rejected the approach of *Redline* and Commonwealth ex rel. Smith v. Myers as well as that reached in Taylor v. Superior Court of Alameda County (infra Note 3), and held that a felony murder conviction is possible for fleeing perpetrators of a forcible felony when a pursuing police officer is shot by a fellow officer. In discussing the cases cited above, the court stated, "Our statutory and case law, however, dictate a different, and we believe preferable, result."

Among the state courts holding that their felony-murder statutes should apply only when an innocent person is killed, and not when the deceased is one of the felons, are: State v. Williams, 254 So.2d 548 (Fla.App.1971). Other similar holdings noted include: People v. Austin, 370 Mich. 12, 120 N.W.2d 766 (1963); People v. Wood, 8 N.Y.2d 48, 201 N.Y.S.2d 328, 167 N.E.2d 736 (1960); State v. Schwensen, 237 Or. 506, 392 P.2d 328 (1964).

2. In People v. Washington, 62 Cal.2d 777, 44 Cal.Rptr. 442, 402 P.2d 130 (1965), the defendant was convicted of murder for participating in a robbery in which his accomplice was killed by the victim of the robbery. Upon his appeal he urged the court to confine a felon's homicide responsibility to situations where the victim was an *innocent* person. Here, of course, the person killed was one of the felons. Although ultimately reversing the defendant's conviction the majority of the California Supreme Court (per Chief Justice Traynor) expressed the view that a distinction based upon a consideration of the person killed would make the defendant's criminal liability turn upon the marksmanship of the police and the victims of the felony during which the killing

occurred. The court preferred to face up to the basic issue as to whether a felon can be convicted of murder for the killing of *any* person by another who is resisting the robbery; and it held that there could be no conviction in such instances. It interpreted the language of the California felony-murder statute to mean that for a killing to occur in the "perpetration", or in an "attempt to perpetrate" a felony, it had to be done by one of the felons; in other words, in furtherance of the felony. The court rejected the causation theory upon which the opposite result would have been reached. Also, as regards the prosecution's contention that responsibility for any death would serve to prevent dangerous felonies, the court said:

"Neither the common-law rationale of the rule nor the Penal Code supports this contention. In every robbery there is a possibility that the victim will resist and kill. The robber has little control over such a killing once the robbery is undertaken as this case demonstrates. To impose an additional penalty for the killing would discriminate between robbers, not on the basis of any difference in their own conduct, but solely on the basis of the response by others that the robber's conduct happened to induce. An additional penalty for a homicide committed by the victim would deter robbery haphazardly at best."

Two justices dissented; they expressed the view that the rule adopted by the court contained the following implicit advice to would-be felons:

"Henceforth in committing certain crimes, including robbery, rape and burglary, you are free to arm yourselves with a gun and brandish it in the faces of your victims without fear of a murder conviction unless you or your accomplice pulls the trigger. If the menacing effect of your gun causes a victim or policeman to fire and kill an innocent person or a cofelon, you are absolved of responsibility for such killing unless you shoot first."

They added:

"Obviously this advance judicial absolution removes one of the most meaningful deterrents to the commission of armed felonies."

3. On the other hand, in Taylor v. Superior Court, 3 Cal.3d 578, 91 Cal. Rptr. 275, 477 P.2d 131 (1970), a sharply divided California Supreme Court upheld the conviction of murder of the driver of a getaway car where one of his accomplices, who were engaged in a robbery and assault with a deadly weapon, was shot and killed by the robbery victim. The court cited with approval the following language from its earlier case of People v. Gilbert:

When the defendant or his accomplice, with a conscious disregard for life, intentionally commits an act that is likely to cause death, and his victim or a police officer kills in reasonable response to such act, the defendant is guilty of murder. In such a case, the killing is attributable, not merely to the commission of a felony, but to the intentional act of the defendant or his accomplice committed with conscious disregard for life.

4. Where an offender seizes hostages to be used as shields, and one of the hostages is killed by a policeman or other victim of the crime, the felony-murder rule applies. Thus, in Johnson v. State, 252 Ark. 1113, 482 S.W.2d 600 (1972), a burglar who had been discovered seized the daughter of the householder as a shield. A struggle ensued in the course of which the householder shot his daughter. The murder conviction was upheld because the defendant had placed the deceased in the perilous position.

5. The 1978 California voters initiative resulted in the reenactment of the death penalty or life imprisonment without the possibility of parole, for a murder committed "while the defendant was engaged in or was an accomplice in the commission" of a list of nine felonies, robbery among them. In Carlos v. Superior Court, 35 Cal.3d 131, 197 Cal.Rptr. 79, 672 P.2d 862 (1983), a majority of the California Supreme Court construed this statute to match punishment with culpability and held that a defendant convicted of felony murder may not be sentenced to death or life imprisonment without parole unless he is found to have intended to kill or aid in a killing.

6. Need the prosecution in a felony-murder case prove that the underlying felony in which defendant was engaged proximately caused the death? Holding that it did not, the court in Wade v. State, 581 P.2d 914 (Okl.Crim.App.1978), said that "under the Felony–Murder Doctrine, the malice or premeditated intent involved in the perpetration or attempted perpetration of the felony is 'transferred' or 'imputed' to the commission of the homicide so that the accused can be found guilty of murder even though the killing is unintentional."

The court continued, "The application of this Doctrine is subject to the limitation that there must be a nexus between the underlying felony and the death of the victim. The felony must be inherently or potentially dangerous to human life, . . ."

7. What felonies are "inherently or potentially dangerous to human life"?

Some states list or define, in their statutes, the felonies which trigger the applicability of the felony-murder rule. The California Penal Code, in § 189, includes among its first degree murders killings occurring during the commission or attempted commission of "arson, rape, robbery, burglary, mayhem, or any act punishable under Section 288 [lewd or lascivious acts, willfully and lewdly committed upon children under 14]." Pennsylvania, on the other hand, views felony-murder in a broader context and considers such acts essentially murders in the second degree. Purdon's Penn.Consol.Stats.Ann. 18, § 2502, in subsection (b), provides: "(b) Murder of the second degree.—A criminal homicide constitutes murder of the second degree when it is committed while defendant was engaged as a principal or an accomplice in the perpetration of a felony."

In Illinois, first degree murder encompasses a killing during the attempt or commission of a "forcible felony other than second degree murder" (ch. 38, § 9–1(a)(3)). Elsewhere, in § 2–8, forcible felony "means treason, first degree murder, second degree murder, aggravated criminal sexual assault, criminal sexual assault, robbery, burglary, arson, aggravated kidnapping, kidnapping, aggravated battery and any other felony which involves the use or threat of physical force or violence against any individual."

Virginia, apart from its first degree murder statute (a Class 2 felony), which incorporates specific felonies, also has a separate Class 3 felony offense called Felony Homicide, which is defined as, "The killing of one accidentally, contrary to the intention of the parties, while in the prosecution of some felonious act other than those specified in §§ 18.2–31 [capital murders] and 18.2–32 [first degree murders]." Va.Code § 18.2–33.

8. If defendant sells drugs to a user who then dies from an overdose, can defendant be convicted of felony-murder?

See Sheriff, Clark County v. Morris, 99 Nev. 109, 659 P.2d 852 (1983), wherein a majority of the Nevada Supreme Court held that a drug dealer could be convicted of second-degree felony-murder where he is involved in helping the recipient consume the drugs or is present when he does so. The court was careful to point out that it did not intend to hold that all deaths resulting from sales of dangerous drugs would be felony murder, but only when there is a direct and causal relationship between the defendant's act and the decedent's death.

On the other hand, in Heacock v. Commonwealth, 228 Va. 397, 323 S.E.2d 90 (1984), the Virginia Supreme Court applied the felony homicide statute mentioned in Note 7, supra, to the supplier of cocaine when his victim died as a result of an overdose. The court said it was immaterial that the defendant did not administer the drug himself. In an earlier case, Wooden v. Commonwealth, the court had chosen to follow the *Redline* case (Casebook p. 479, Note 2), refusing to extend felony murder punishment for a co-felon's death, but that rule was not applicable to the Heacock, who died from the overdose, said the court. She was not a co-felon, but a victim.

In People v. Phillips, 42 Cal.Rptr. 868 (Cal.App.1965), the California District Court of Appeal refused to extend what it called the "archaic and much criticized" felony-murder doctrine to non-dangerous felonies. Here a chiropractor falsely induced the parents of a child who had cancer of the eye to forego surgery and accept his "treatments" for a considerable fee. The child died and defendant was found guilty of murder in the second degree. Defendant's conviction was reversed because of the error of giving a felony-murder instruction. The California Supreme Court vacated that opinion, but because of prejudicial instructions to the jury. 51 Cal.Rptr. 225 (1966).

Similarly, the felony of possession of a concealed firearm by a felon was deemed not in itself to be a felony inherently dangerous to human life. It was therefore deemed improper to dispense with the requirement of proof of malice for murder. People v. Satchell, 6 Cal.3d 28, 98 Cal.Rptr. 33, 489 P.2d 1361 (1971). The felony of escape from a county jail was another offense which was deemed incapable of serving as a basis for the imputation of malice aforethought in a murder prosecution. People v. Lopez, 6 Cal.3d 45, 98 Cal.Rptr. 44, 489 P.2d 1372 (1971). Selling liquor, under circumstances amounting to a felony, to a purchaser who became drunk and died from exposure, was found not to be an act in itself directly and naturally dangerous to life sufficient to support a murder conviction. People v. Pavlic, 227 Mich. 562, 199 N.W. 373 (1924).

9. Inasmuch as some cases have suggested that the felony murder rule provides a conclusive presumption of "malice aforethought," the culpable mental state required for murder, whenever an unintended death occurs in the commission of another felony, does the rule run afoul of *Sandstrom v. Montana?* See, Roth & Sundby, "The Felony–Murder Rule: A Doctrine At Constitutional Crossroads," 70 Cornell L.Rev. 446 (1985).

PEOPLE v. SALAS

Supreme Court of California, 1972.
7 Cal.3d 812, 103 Cal.Rptr. 431, 500 P.2d 7.

WRIGHT, CHIEF JUSTICE.

* * *

On the morning of June 7, 1968, five or ten minutes after midnight, defendant entered the Hub Bar in Sacramento and asked the bartender, George Finnegan, for a six-pack of beer. After Finnegan reached into the cooler for the beer he saw that defendant was pointing a pistol directly at him. David Wright, a customer, and Richard Schwab, an insurance salesman who entered the bar at this moment, were ordered to lie down on the floor at the back of the barroom. Defendant then ordered Finnegan to deliver all the money in the bar's cash register.

The cash register had two drawers and after Finnegan had emptied the contents of one of them (amounting to about $150) into a cloth bank bag, defendant asked, "How about the other drawer on the register?" Upon being satisfied that the second drawer was empty defendant took the bank bag, ordered Finnegan to lie down near the other men, told them not to move or he would shoot them and backed out of the front door.

Defendant had been driven to the bar by Arlin Damion, a friend who remained in the car during the robbery. When defendant emerged from the bar and entered the vehicle on the passenger's side of the front seat, Damion drove away.

Shortly after midnight Deputy Sheriff George O'Neal received a radio broadcast advising that the Hub Bar had just been robbed. He immediately drove his patrol car three-tenths of a mile to an intersection 1.2 miles from the bar. He knew that this intersection was on a route frequently used by robbers in making escapes from the general area. Just as he reached the intersection he saw an approaching car with two men who appeared to be of Mexican descent. The car approached from the direction of the bar and was the only vehicle in sight. The deputy followed the car and was then advised by radio that the suspect was a "male Mexican." After further radio communication the deputy activated the red light and siren of the police vehicle and the suspects eventually stopped their vehicle.

The deputy halted his patrol car about 15 to 18 feet behind the suspects' car, stepped out and shouted to the two men to put their hands out of the car windows. Neither suspect responded to the demand; the deputy thereupon reached for his shotgun. Damion opened the door on the driver's side of his car and fled on foot into an open field. Defendant, however, did not respond to the officer's further demands.

A second deputy sheriff, Kenneth B. Royal, arrived in his patrol car. Royal drew his service revolver and walked toward the suspects' car on the driver's side. O'Neal heard shots fired and saw Royal fall to the ground. Defendant emerged from the car on the passenger's side with a gun in his hand. O'Neal fired his shotgun at defendant. Defendant fell to the ground and then arose. Royal fired his revolver, and O'Neal fired his shotgun a second time. Defendant again fell to the ground, but once more got up and continued down the road away from the deputies. Defendant fell to the ground again and was then apprehended by another officer who had arrived at the scene. Royal died of a single gunshot wound in the neck.

* * *

We deal next with defendant's contention that, as a matter of law, the robbery had been completed prior to the time of and at a different place than the killing; that the homicide therefore could not have been committed in the course of the robbery within the felony-murder rule and that the trial court erred in instructing the jury on such rule. Defendant further contends that, even assuming that instructions on the felony-murder rule were appropriate, it was error for the court to refuse to define the term "scrambling possession" as applied to the proceeds of the robbery when requested to do so by the jury.

Section 189, which establishes the limits of the felony-first-degree-murder rule, provides that all "murder . . . which is committed in the perpetration of, or attempt to perpetrate . . . robbery . . . is murder of the first degree. . . ." Our particular concern is whether the killing of the deputy after defendant had been stopped while fleeing from the scene of the robbery, was a killing in the "perpetration" of the robbery. The trial court gave four instructions which we have numbered and set forth in the margin concerning the time within which a robbery is still in progress for purposes of application of the felony-murder rule.[1]

After retiring to deliberate, the jury returned to the court requesting further instructions on . . . the law applying to "zone of danger," that is, how long a felony continues in progress. Included in the instructions read by the court pursuant to the request were the four instructions heretofore quoted. Some of them, after questions by the jurors, were read more than once. Two jurors requested that the court

1. (1) "A robbery is still in commission while the perpetrator is being pursued immediately after the commission of the act of taking the property of another by force or fear with the fruits of the crime in his possession so long as the culprit has not won his way even momentarily to a place of temporary safety and the possession of the plunder is nothing more than a scrambling possession."

(2) "A robbery is still in commission during the continuous, integrated attempt to successfully leave with the loot."

(3) "If the robbery has been completed and terminated prior to the killing, then the robbery may not be used to find the defendant guilty of murder of the first degree. Whether the killing was committed during the perpetration of the robbery must be decided by the jury.

"A robbery is still being committed, no matter how far from the scene of the robbery, nor how long afterward, if the robber has not won his way even momentarily to a place of temporary safety and the possession of the plunder is nothing more than a scrambling possession." (This instruction was given at defendant's request.)

(4) "If the robbery has been completed and terminated prior to the killing then the robbery may not be used to find the defendant guilty of the murder of the first degree. On the other hand, the unlawful killing of a human being which is committed in the perpetration or attempt to perpetrate robbery, the commission of which crime itself must be proved beyond a reasonable doubt, is murder of the first degree whether the killing was intentional, unintentional or even accidental.

"Whether the killing was committed during the perpetration of robbery must be decided by the jury.

"A robbery is still being committed no matter how far from the scene of the robbery nor how long afterward if the robber has not won his way, even momentarily, to a place of temporary safety. That is to say, that a robbery is not completed at the moment the robber obtains possession of the stolen property, but is still in progress during the robber's attempt to escape with the loot. In other words, the escape of the robbers with the loot is a part of the robbery itself." (This instruction was given at the request of the prosecution.)

define "scrambling." The court, after saying that the dictionary definition would not help and that the jurors should consider the word in the context of a person fleeing from the scene of a robbery with the plunder. Approximately two hours later, the jury again returned and a juror asked the court to reread the instructions in connection with whether the robbery was in progress. The court read the instructions designated as (1) through (4) in footnote [1] several times enabling the jurors to write them down. The jury deliberated for a little more than an hour before retiring for the night and returned its verdict shortly after reconvening the following morning.

Instructions (1) and (3) appear to require that the jury find *both* that the robber did not win his way to a "place of temporary safety" *and* that his possession of the plunder was no more than a "scrambling possession" before it could find that the robbery was still in progress. Instruction (1) further requires pursuit "immediately" after the physical taking of the property. Instructions (2) and (4), on the other hand, appear to require that the jury find only that the robber did not win his way to a "place of temporary safety"—that is, that the robber was still attempting to escape—to find that the robbery was still in progress.

The phrases "place of temporary safety" and "scrambling possession" are derived from the landmark case of People v. Boss (1930) 210 Cal. 245, 290 P. 881. In that case two defendants robbed a store and ran into the street; an employee immediately pursued them and was shot by Boss a moment later when the furthermost defendant was no more than 125 feet from the store. We held that the trial court properly instructed the jury as to first degree felony murder as the homicide was committed in the perpetration of a robbery and we stated: "It is a sound principle of law which inheres in common reason that where two or more persons engaged in a conspiracy to commit robbery and an officer or citizen is murdered while in immediate pursuit of one of their number who is fleeing from the scene of the crime with the fruits thereof in his possession, or in the possession of a coconspirator, the crime is not complete in the purview of the law, inasmuch as said conspirators have not won their way even momentarily to a place of temporary safety and the possession of the plunder is nothing more than a scrambling possession. In such a case the continuation of the use of arms which was necessary to aid the felon in reducing the property to possession is necessary to protect him in its possession and in making good his escape. Robbery, unlike burglary, is not confined to a fixed *locus,* but is frequently spread over considerable distance and varying periods of time. The escape of the robbers with the loot, by means of arms, necessarily is as important to the execution of the plan as gaining possession of the property. Without revolvers to terrify, or, if occasion requires, to kill any person, who attempts to apprehend them at the time of or immediately upon gaining possession of said property, their plan would be childlike. The defense of felonious possession which is challenged immediately upon the forcible taking is a part of the plan of robbery, or, as the books express it, it is *res gestae* of the crime."

* * *

The great majority of felony-murder rule cases involving robbery as the underlying felony decided by this court since *Boss* involve fact situations with both elements, continuous flight (lack of a "place of temporary safety") and continuous challenging pursuit ("scrambling possession") and generally set forth the language of *Boss* without further analysis. Thus these cases do little to clarify the question whether *both* elements are required for a robbery to be considered continuing for purposes of the felony-murder rule.

In People v. Kendrick (1961) 56 Cal.2d 71, 14 Cal.Rptr. 13, 363 P.2d 13, however, the element of "scrambling possession" was clearly missing. It was nevertheless held in that case that instructions on the felony-murder rule were properly given when the killing occurred about 48 minutes after the robbery victim had first been accosted by the defendant and when the police officer who was fatally shot by the defendant had apparently stopped him for a traffic violation and had no information about the robbery. We ignored the language in *Boss* concerning "place of temporary safety" and "scrambling possession" and quoted that part of *Boss* which stresses the importance of "[t]he escape . . . with the loot . . . to the execution of the plan," . . . Although not expressly so described, the "rule" as applied in *Kendrick* required only the element of the defendant's failure to have reached a "place of temporary safety."

People v. Ketchel (1963) 59 Cal.2d 503, 30 Cal.Rptr. 538, 381 P.2d 394 involved a fact situation with both elements present: "place of temporary safety" and "scrambling possession." Defendants attempted to bring themselves within *Boss* and relied upon the language in that case which spoke of both "a place of temporary safety" and "scrambling possession." In rejecting their contention we relied only upon facts which established that the defendants had not reached a place of temporary safety and ignored the element of scrambling possession. That case like *Kendrick* must stand for the proposition that a fleeing robber's failure to reach a place of temporary safety is alone sufficient to establish the continuity of the robbery within the felony-murder rule.

In the present case as in *Ketchel,* the homicide was committed before defendant had reached a place of safety while he "was in hot flight with the stolen property and in the belief that the officer was about to arrest him for the robbery." Deputy O'Neal commenced to follow defendant's vehicle within three minutes of the time defendant left the bar and the killing occurred within six or seven minutes of that time. Thus the robbery was still in the escape stage, as conceded by defendant at trial. Defendant testified not only that he was caught while attempting to escape with the loot, but also that he did not know whether he would split the loot with Damion as they had had no opportunity to make that determination.

Under the circumstances here present and even if the killing were accidental or unintentional as contended by defendant, it occurred while the robbery continued in progress and constituted first degree murder under the felony-murder rule. Although the introduction in the instructions to the jury of concepts of immediate pursuit together with scrambling possession and the court's refusal to define "scrambling possession" may have been erroneous, no prejudice resulted to defendant as in any event the jurors were compelled to find that the homicide was committed before defendant had reached a place of safety. The introduction of the pursuit and scrambling concepts did in fact confer benefits to which defendant was not entitled. . . .

The judgment, insofar as it provides for the penalty of death, is modified to provide in place of the death penalty a punishment of life imprisonment and as so modified is affirmed in all other respects.

TOBRINER, MOSK, BURKE, and SULLIVAN, JJ., concur.

PETERS, J., dissenting.

I dissent.

The majority have extended the felony-murder rule and repudiated in part the landmark decision in People v. Boss (1930) 210 Cal. 245, 290 P. 881. I would adhere to the decision in *Boss,* and when this is done, it is clear that prejudicial error occurred in instructing the jury on the felony-murder doctrine thus requiring reversal of the judgment.

Section 189 of the Penal Code, which establishes the felony-first-degree-murder rule, provides that all "murder . . . which is committed in the perpetration of, or attempt to perpetrate . . . robbery . . . is murder of the first degree; . . ."

Section 211 of the Penal Code defines robbery as "the felonious taking of personal property in the possession of another, from his person or immediate presence, and against his will, accomplished by means of force or fear."

A literal reading of the sections, in light of the requirement of commission in the perpetration of the robbery and in light of the definition of robbery, would mean that the homicide must occur during the taking of the property and prior to the termination of the force and fear by which the taking was accomplished.

However, this court rejected a literal construction of the two statutes in People v. Boss, supra, and established a broader rule for determining whether a homicide occurred in the perpetration of the robbery or after its termination. In expanding the operation of the felony-murder rule in the robbery situation, the court in *Boss* established two limitations on the continuation of the robbery. Today, the majority repudiate one of the limitations and to that extent overrule *Boss.* I cannot agree with the further expansion of the felony-murder doctrine.

* * *

The court [in *Boss*] thus established two requirements to establish that the robbery was not complete. First, there must be "immediate pursuit" which means that the possession is merely a "scrambling possession." This limitation finds some support in the language of the robbery statute because, so long as there is "immediate pursuit" and a mere "scrambling possession," it can be argued that the "taking" of the property is not complete because it is being physically disputed. Second, the robbers must not have reached "a place of temporary safety."

The majority today recognize but repudiate the first limitation, holding that the sole test is a place of temporary safety. In doing so, the majority rely upon People v. Ketchel, 59 Cal.2d 503, 30 Cal.Rptr. 538, 381 P.2d 394, and People v. Kendrick, 56 Cal.2d 71, 14 Cal.Rptr. 13, 363 P.2d 13. *Ketchel,* however, on its facts involved a homicide which occurred within both limitations. There was immediate pursuit with the resulting mere scrambling possession, and the robbers had not reached a place of temporary safety. Although the court spoke only of the failure to reach a place of temporary safety in connection with the defendants' contention, this was because the defendants' contention was based on the temporary-safety language in *Boss.* There was no intent to depart from the immediate pursuit and scrambling possession limitation; the court in fact quoted that limitation from *Boss.*

It is true that in *Kendrick* there was no immediate pursuit or scrambling possession and that the court, although citing and relying upon *Boss,* merely relied upon the failure of the robber to reach a point of temporary safety in upholding instructions on the felony-murder rule. However, I do not believe that *Kendrick* may be viewed as substantial authority warranting repudiation of the limitation of immediate pursuit and scrambling possession and of *Boss* and the numerous cases which have followed it. The defendant in that case urged that the homicide was too distant in time and place to classify it as having occurred during perpetration of the robbery. So far as appears, the defendant did not rely on the limitation of immediate pursuit and scrambling possession, and in answering the specific contention of defendant, it was proper to point out that *Boss* had established a rule which meant that it was not determinative that the homicide occurred some distance from the robbery and sometime later. Under the circumstances, it seems improper to hold that the court intended to repudiate one of the requirements of *Boss,* the case which was quoted from and principally relied upon.

Apart from their reliance on *Ketchel* and *Kendrick,* the majority give no reason to repudiate the first limitation of *Boss,* and in my view, those cases provide a weak foundation for the majority's action. . . .

The felony-murder doctrine ascribes malice aforethought to the felon who kills in the perpetration of an inherently dangerous felony and classifies the offense as murder of the first degree in homicides which are the direct result of those six felonies enumerated in section 189 of the Penal Code. . . .

"The felony-murder rule has been criticized on the grounds that in almost all cases in which it is applied it is unnecessary and that it erodes the relation between criminal liability and moral culpability." The rule has been abolished in England where it had its origin (English Homicide Act, § 1, 1957, 5 & 6 Eliz. II, ch. 11.) We have recently pointed out that the rule "expresses a highly artificial concept that deserves no extension beyond its required application." (People v. Phillips, 64 Cal.2d 574, 582, 51 Cal.Rptr. 225, 232, 414 P.2d 353, 360.) Although the rule remains the law in this state, I do not believe we should extend its applicability by broadly defining the term robbery; instead in furtherance of the policy to equate criminal liability with culpability we should strictly limit the meaning of the term robbery as used in section 189.

To extend the felony-murder rule until the robber has reached a place of temporary safety, without regard to whether the decedent is a victim or witness of the crime and without regard to whether there has been a break in the pursuit, would mean that the death of victims of automobile collisions or of pedestrians occurring accidentally during an escape may constitute first degree murder. In the absence of a direct pursuit by victims or witnesses, such a broad application of the first degree felony-murder rule to accidental killings is not in accord with the purpose of the rule or the language of the statutes.

Once we depart from the literal definition of robbery in section 211 of the Penal Code, any test that might be used to determine whether a robbery is complete for purposes of the felony-murder rule is necessarily arbitrary. The place of temporary safety, or continuous flight, test is not directly related either to the increased foreseeable danger caused by the robbery or to the robber's motive in seeking to escape detection. The increased risk of a killing occurring due to the commission of the robbery continues long after the robber reaches a place of temporary safety for he will continue to have the motive to kill to escape apprehension. In other words, the risk of injury or death to investigating officers seeking to apprehend the criminal may relate to whether the robber has the loot, is armed, or anticipates conviction, but it bears little relationship to whether the robber has reached a place of temporary safety.

A test based solely on place of temporary safety makes the *length* of the escape route the decisive consideration. If the robber leaves the scene of the robbery and reaches his hideout or home near the scene, the felony-murder rule is inapplicable under the place-of-temporary-safety test whether he is armed or still in possession of the loot, but if he must cross the city to his hideout and the homicide occurs prior to his doing so, the test would make the felony-murder rule applicable although the robber was not armed, he had lost or disposed of the loot, a pedestrian was killed, and the homicide occurred a substantial time after the taking of the property and the termination of the force and fear incident to it. . . .

On the other hand, the limitation to immediate pursuit and scrambling possession, as we have seen, finds some support in the definition of robbery in section 211 of the Penal Code. Although this court may refuse to adhere to the literal wording of the statute as was done in *Boss* and the case following it, we should not ignore the terms of the statute entirely. Where there is immediate pursuit by victims or witnesses of the taking or of the force and fear used in the robbery, the risk of injury or death is greatly increased, and it is not the same risk as exists with regard to apprehension occurring subsequent to the taking.

* * *

Accordingly, I would not repudiate either of the limitations established in *Boss* and the cases which have followed it.

As the majority point out, the evidence in the instant case is sufficient to warrant a finding of first degree murder on a theory of premeditation. . . . The felony-murder instructions, however, permitted a finding of first degree murder even if the shooting was inadvertent or unintentional, and in view of the jury's express concern with the felony-murder instructions, the error must be held prejudicial.

I would reverse the judgment.

NOTES

1.   Compare the principal case with Commonwealth v. Doris, 287 Pa. 547, 135 A. 313 (1926). Doris and three companions robbed the occupants of a bank car transporting funds. In the course of the robbery, Doris was captured; however, his companions fled from the scene. In the chase that followed, one of the pursuing policemen was shot and killed by the felons, who were captured a short time thereafter. Doris was separately tried, convicted of first degree murder committed "in the perpetration of . . . robbery", and sentenced to death. The Pennsylvania Supreme Court affirmed. "The proof of the common purpose to take, by force, the money of the bank, carrying it away, and make a safe escape, may be inferred from the attending circumstances. Whether such a criminal intent existed was a question for the jury, and the evidence warranted their conclusion. . . . It is urged that the escape and flight are not to be considered as part of the perpetration of the robbery, which, it is claimed, had been completed . . . and thereafter no responsibility attached to any individual for the act of the other. . . . Whether the act of departing is a continuous part of the attempted or accomplished crime is for the jury."

2.   The felony-murder doctrine was applied in Commonwealth v. De Moss, 401 Pa. 395, 165 A.2d 14 (1960) to convict for murder a robbery conspirator who was in another state at the time of the robbery-murder.

3.   For a general discussion of the subject matter in the foregoing cases, see "What Constitutes Termination of Felony for Purpose of the Felony–Murder Rule," 58 A.L.R.3d 851.

4.   The issue of whether the intent to commit a felony arose before or after the fatal injury was interestingly presented and disposed of in Commonwealth

v. Hart, 403 Pa. 652, 170 A.2d 850 (1961).   Following are the case facts and the relevant portion of the opinion of the Pennsylvania Supreme Court:

"Defendant and Patricia K. lived together.   He rented her out as a prostitute.   Querey, the deceased victim, after his mother's death, came from North Carolina to Pennsylvania to collect her life insurance.   He collected the insurance and on his way home engaged Patricia through a cab driver for purposes of intercourse.   The price was $50.   He paid her the $50 and also bought her some presents.   Patricia remained some time and after it was over went back to the Naples Restaurant to meet defendant.   She gave defendant $50.   He became very angry because his price was $50 an hour and she had stayed three hours.   Defendant shouted at her and said "You are going out and see that man with me."   He said the man was trying to get something for nothing.   Patricia was afraid to tell defendant that Querey had bought her presents because he had told her that if she ever let anybody buy her anything he would beat her—which he had already done on a prior occasion.   Defendant and Patricia, at his insistence, went to the Airport to see Querey to get the additional money to which he claimed he was entitled. They knocked on Querey's door and telephoned repeatedly but unsuccessfully. Defendant insisted they try once again and after defendant banged very loudly on Querey's door he forced Patricia to call Querey once more.   Querey then opened the door slightly.   Defendant pushed the door open and pushed Patricia inside.   Then Querey asked: "What's this all about?"   Defendant answered "I think you owe this girl some money."   Querey denied knowing Patricia and told defendant to get out.   Patricia begged defendant to leave the room, but defendant replied *he wanted that money.*   Querey threatened to call the police.   He went to the phone and defendant followed him.   They began struggling over the telephone.   Patricia begged defendant to leave Querey alone.   Querey started to put his leg in his trousers and at that point defendant, who was 6 feet 4 inches tall and weighed 170 pounds, started hitting Querey in the face with his fists.   Patricia screamed at defendant, who repeatedly told her to be quiet and threatened to hit her too if she were not.   Querey, who was about 5 feet 8 inches tall and weighed 150 pounds and was further handicapped by putting on his trousers, just stood there while defendant beat him until he fell to the floor.   While he lay there defendant kicked him in the back of the head—which was later proved to be the cause of death.   Then defendant bent down, and while Querey was unconscious, took the wallet out of Querey's pocket, removed four (or more) $50 bills from the wallet, and threw the wallet between Querey's legs.   *   *   *

"Defendant's highly technical argument amounts to this: Unless the Commonwealth proves that the intention to commit a robbery was formed before the beginning of the fatal assault, the evidence cannot amount to a murder which was committed in the perpetration of a robbery.   In other words, defendant would require a televised stop-watch in every robbery or felony-killing to prove that the felonious intent existed before the attack.   It is rare, we repeat, that a criminal telephones or telegraphs his criminal intent and consequently such intent can be properly found by the jury from the facts and circumstances in a particular case.   In the instant case the facts and circumstances, particularly defendant's belligerently expressed intent to get the money (to which he said he was entitled) out of Querey, followed by his use of force to obtain it, were amply sufficient to justify a jury in finding the necessary criminal intent beyond a reasonable doubt. . . ."

5. Can a defendant, who is charged with burglary and with felony-murder (occurring during the burglary) be acquitted of burglary and convicted of felony-murder? See People v. Mitchell, 64 A.D.2d 119, 408 N.Y.S.2d 513 (1978).

THE LINDBERGH–HAUPTMANN CASE

"During the evening of March 1, 1932, between the hours of eight and ten o'clock, little Charles A. Lindbergh, Jr., disappeared from the home of his parents at East Amwell, New Jersey. In the baby's room was left a letter, demanding $50,000 in ransom, and stating that later instructions as to the method of payment and the return of the child would be forthcoming. Immediately negotiations were begun by the child's father, through one Dr. J.F. Condon, with supposed agents of the child's abductors, during the course of which the baby's sleeping suit was sent by mail to Condon as evidence that the family was 'dealing with the right parties.' Subsequently, on April 2, the ransom was paid, in marked money, to a man who met Condon in a cemetery in the Bronx, New York. The baby was never returned. On May 12 his body was found in the adjoining county of Mercer, several miles from the home of his parents. An autopsy disclosed that the child had suffered three violent fractures of the skull, and that death had been instantaneous.

"As a result of investigations covering many months, the defendant was arrested on October 8, 1934, and indicted for first-degree murder. The indictment charged the killing of a human being during the commission of a burglary. On this charge he was convicted and sentenced to death. Held: on appeal, affirmed. There was adequate evidence to establish common-law burglary and a killing resulting therefrom: State v. Hauptmann, 115 N.J.L. 412, 180 A. 809 (1935)" [1]

The burglary with which the defendant was charged in the indictment was breaking and entering the Lindbergh home, in the nighttime, with intent to steal *the sleeping suit of the child*. Legally, Hauptmann was electrocuted because he caused the death of a child in the course of stealing its sleeping suit.

Why did the result in the Hauptmann case rest upon such a technicality? Although any child kidnapping case attracts a great deal of public attention, there was an added factor here: the victim was the son of the famous Charles A. Lindbergh, the first person to fly the Atlantic Ocean alone, and his flight was only six years old in the public memory. Accordingly, the public demanded a death penalty. In this regard, however, the prosecution was faced with several difficulties. Kidnapping itself was only a "high misdemeanor" in New Jersey and not punishable with death. The death penalty could be awarded only for premeditated murder, common law felony murder, and statutory felony murder—the killing of another during the commission of (or attempt to commit) arson, burglary, rape, robbery or sodomy. Since

---

1. The foregoing statement of facts is taken from a student comment on this case which appeared in 26 J.Crim.L. & C. 759 (1935).

the state had no evidence that Hauptmann had a preconceived intent to kill the child, and accordingly could not proceed on the theory of premeditated murder, the prosecution was forced to seek a conviction of felony murder, either at common law or under the statute. Since kidnapping was not among the crimes enumerated in the felony murder statute, and inasmuch as it was not a felony under the common law, a killing arising out of a kidnapping would not sustain a death penalty sentence. Accordingly, the prosecution's only possible course lay in charging that the killing occurred during the commission of a burglary, although the only thing which Hauptmann took in addition to the child (who, under the common law, could not be a subject of larceny) was the sleeping suit it wore.

The defense contended that the evidence did not show the commission of a burglary. It was argued that there was no evidence of the required intent to steal the sleeping garment, since it was surrendered by the defendant of his own volition. It was held, however, that the evidence showed the commission of a burglary, in that the jury could find that the defendant took the sleeping suit for his own advantage in furthering the plan of extortion, and that he would not have returned the sleeping suit had the preliminaries of the extortion been unsuccessful.

Thus the felony murder doctrine, possibly stretched to the utmost limits of application, was employed to obtain the result desired by the prosecution and demanded by public sentiment. The case affords an interesting study of the effect a heinous offense may have upon judicial reasoning and the criminal law generally.

NOTES

1. Modern kidnaping statutes typically are felonies, thereby avoiding the dilemma created for the prosecution in the *Hauptmann* case.

2. An interesting sequel to the *Hauptmann* case developed almost fifty years after his trial and execution. In 1982, his widow filed a $100,000,000 suit against the State of New Jersey based upon her claim that he was innocent of any involvement in the crime.

Prior to the filing of the suit, but after legal action had been taken to obtain access to the New Jersey State Police files, a lengthy article appeared in the press of October 10, 1981, under the title: "Lindbergh Case Still on Trial in Many Minds," written by Stephen Salisbury. Among the papers that carried it was the Chicago Tribune, in which the distinct impression was created that Hauptmann was innocent. A similar impression appeared in another lengthy feature article published after the $100,000,000 suit had been filed. It was carried in the Chicago Tribune of August 29, 1982. Authored by Cheryl Lavin, it bore the title, "Widow's Mission: Clearing Husband in Lindbergh Case."

The foregoing articles correctly stated that the newspaper reporters and photographers covering the trial made the New Jersey courtroom like a circus, and the ransom intermediary's behind-the-wall identification of Hauptmann's voice lacks credibility, but there were the following facts establishing Hauptmann's guilt: on a board in a dark closet of Hauptmann's home there was the name and telephone number of the ransom intermediary, for which Hauptmann offered no explanation; as regards the substantial amount of the marked ransom money that was found buried in Hauptmann's garage, he said he was holding it for a friend, Isadore Fisch, whose whereabouts Hauptmann did not know; parts of the kidnap ladder matched exactly with sawed off boards in Hauptmann's attic; hand-plane markings on the crudely constructed kidnap ladder matched perfectly with marks left on wood samples planed with Hauptmann's plane; and the photographically illustrated testimony of eight of the country's top professional document examiners established positively that the ransom notes were written by Hauptmann. The scientific evidence that was used against Hauptmann is described in: Sellers, The Handwriting Evidence Against Hauptmann, 27 J.Crim.L. & C. 874 (1937); and, Koehler, Technique Used in Tracing the Lindbergh Kidnapping Ladder, 27 J.Crim.L. & C. 712 (1937).

3. For an excellent analysis of the case, see Fisher, The Lindbergh Case (1987).

PEOPLE v. AARON
Supreme Court of Michigan, 1980.
409 Mich. 672, 299 N.W.2d 304.

FITZGERALD, JUSTICE. The existence and scope of the felony murder doctrine have perplexed generations of law students, commentators and jurists in the United States and England, and have split our own Court of Appeals. In these cases, we must decide whether Michigan has a felony murder rule which allows the element of malice required for murder to be satisfied by the intent to commit the underlying felony or whether malice must be otherwise found by the trier of fact. We must also determine what is the *mens rea* required to support a conviction under Michigan's first-degree murder statute.

I. FACTS

In [People v. Thompson, 81 Mich.App. 348, 265 N.W.2d 632 (1978)], defendant was convicted by a jury of first-degree felony murder as the result of a death which occurred during an armed robbery. The trial judge instructed the jury that it was not necessary for the prosecution to prove malice, as a finding of intent to rob was all that was necessary for the homicide to constitute first-degree murder.[1] The Court of

1. "In other words, if you believe the evidence beyond a reasonable doubt, that the defendant, Robert Thompson, killed the decedent, Mary Emma Hendry, that at the time of such homicide the said defendant was perpetrating or attempting to perpetrate said assult upon the deceased, Mary Emma Hendry, with intent to rob, then it is not necessary for the state to prove a premeditated design or intent. And you should find the defendant, Mr. Thompson, guilty of murder in the first degree, under count two of the information.

"Now, what I'm saying, members of the jury, is that then there may be with [sic] the intent to commit a robbery but without the intent of injuring anyone. If in this frame of mind he enters a place, and in committing or attempting to commit the robbery he kills a person, that killing would be murder under the law even though there was no ill will, hatred or malevolence toward the person killed. Because the evil intent to commit the robbery carries over to make that crime murder in the first degree under the law in this state."

Appeals held that reversible error resulted from the trial court's failure to instruct the jury on the element of malice in the felony-murder charge.

In [People v. Wright, 80 Mich.App. 172, 262 N.W.2d 917 (1977)], defendant was convicted by a jury of two counts of first-degree felony murder for setting fire to a dwelling causing the death of two people. The trial court instructed the jury that proof that the killings occurred during the perpetration of arson was sufficient to establish first-degree murder. The Court of Appeals reversed the convictions, holding that it was error to remove the element of malice from the jury's consideration.

Defendant Aaron was convicted of first-degree felony murder as a result of a homicide committed during the perpetration of an armed robbery. The jury was instructed that they could convict defendant of first-degree murder if they found that defendant killed the victim during the commission or attempted commission of an armed robbery. The trial court refused defendant's request to instruct on lesser included offenses. The Court of Appeals affirmed and we remanded the case to the trial court for entry of a judgment of conviction of the lesser included offense of second-degree murder and for resentencing. Defendant subsequently filed an application for reconsideration with this Court.

In *Thompson* and *Wright* we granted leave to appeal limited to the question: "Whether the Court of Appeals erred in reversing the murder conviction in this case because of the lack of an instruction on a requirement for finding malice in a felony murder situation."

In *Aaron,* we granted leave to appeal to consider whether defendant's conviction of first-degree murder could be reduced to second-degree murder where the jury was instructed only on felony-murder.

II. HISTORY OF THE FELONY MURDER DOCTRINE

Felony murder has never been a static, well-defined rule at common law, but throughout its history has been characterized by judicial reinterpretation to limit the harshness of the application of the rule. Historians and commentators have concluded that the rule is of questionable origin and that the reasons for the rule no longer exist, making it an anachronistic remnant, "a historic survivor for which there is no logical or practical basis for existence in modern law."

The first formal statement of the doctrine is often said to be *Lord Dacres'* case, Moore 86; 72 Eng.Rep. 458 (KB, 1535). Lord Dacres and some companions agreed to enter a park without permission to hunt, an unlawful act, *and to kill anyone who might resist them.* While Lord Dacres was a quarter of a mile away, one member of his group killed a gamekeeper who confronted him in the park. Although Lord Dacres was not present when the killing occurred, he, along with the rest of his companions, was convicted of murder and was hanged. Contrary to the construction placed on this case by those who see it as a source of the felony-murder rule, the holding was not that Lord Dacres and his companions were guilty of murder because they had joined in an unlawful hunt in the course of which a person was killed, but rather that those not present physically at the killing were held liable as principals on the theory of constructive presence. Moreover, because they had agreed previously to kill anyone who might resist them, all the members of the group shared in the *mens rea* of the crime. Thus, because *Lord Dacres'* case involved express malice, no doctrine finding malice from the intention to commit an unlawful act was necessary or in fact utilized.

Another early case which has been cited for the origin of the felony-murder doctrine was decided after *Lord Dacres'* case. In *Mansell & Herbert's* case, 2 Dyer 128b; 73 Eng.Rep. 279 (KB, 1558), Herbert and a group of more than 40 followers had gone to Sir Richard Mansfield's house "with force to seize goods under pretence of lawful authority". One of Herbert's servants threw a stone at a person in the gateway which instead hit and killed an unarmed woman coming out of Mansfield's house. . . . Although the court divided, the majority held that if one deliberately performed an act of violence to third parties, and a person not intended died, it was murder regardless of any mistake or misapplication of force. The minority would have held it to be manslaughter because the violent act was not directed against the woman who died. Thus, *Herbert's* case involved a *deliberate act of violence* against a person, which resulted in an unintended person being the recipient of the violent act.

Some commentators suggest that an incorrect version of *Dacres'* case, which was repeated by Crompton, formed the basis of Lord Coke's statement of the felony-murder rule:

> "If the act be unlawful it is murder. As if A. meaning to steale a deere in the park of B., shooteth at the deer, and by the glance of the arrow killeth a boy that is hidden in a bush: this is murder, for that the act was unlawfull, although A. had no intent to hurt the boy, nor knew not of him. But if B. the owner of the park had shot at his own deer, and without any ill intent had killed the boy by the glance of his arrow, this had been homicide by misadventure, and no felony.

> "So if one shooteth at any wild fowle upon a tree, and the arrow killeth any reasonable creature afar off, without any evill intent in him, this is *per infortunium* [misadventure]: for it was not unlawful to shoot at the wilde fowle: but if he had shot at a cock or hen, or any tame fowle of another mans, and the arrow by mischance had killed a man, this had been murder, for the act was unlawfull." [2]

The above excerpt from Coke is, along with *Lord Dacres'* and *Herbert's* cases, most often cited as the origin of the felony-murder

2. Coke, Third Institutes (1797), p. 56.

doctrine.[3] Unfortunately, Coke's statement has been criticized as completely lacking in authority. "A telling historical comment on the essential non-logic of the rule is made by those who see its genesis as a blunder by Coke in the translation and interpretation of a passage from Bracton." The passage from Bracton is as follows:

"But here it is to be distinguished whether a person is employed upon a *lawful* or *unlawful work,* as if a person has projected a stone towards a place across which men are accustomed to pass, or whilst a person pursues a horse or an ox, and some one has been struck by the horse or the ox, and such like, this is imputed to his account. But if he was employed in a lawful work, as if a master is flogging his scholar for the sake of discipline, or if when a person was casting down hay from a cart, or cutting into a tree and such like, if he had taken as diligent care as he could, by looking out and by calling out, * * * or the master not exceeding moderation in flogging his scholar, blame is not imputable to him." (Emphasis added.)

This authority, however, does not support Coke's unwarranted extension which Stephen termed "astonishing" and "monstrous". . . .

In addition to his citation to Bracton, Coke cites three cases to support his statement of the felony-murder rule. Yet Stephen, "upon careful search into Coke's authority", concludes that Coke's statement of the rule is "entirely unwarranted by the authorities which he quotes". Another early writer, commenting on the harsh doctrine propounded by Coke, states, " 'This is not distinguished by any statute but is the common law only of Sir Edward Coke'."

At early common law, the felony-murder rule went unchallenged because at that time practically all felonies were punishable by death.[4]

---

3. Professors Moreland and Perkins also give explanations for the origin of the felony-murder rule. Moreland sees the felony-murder rule as an extension of the doctrine of malice aforethought. For this proposition he cites Lambard, who states:

"'And therefore if a thief do kill a man whom he never saw before and whom he intended to rob only, it is murder in the judgment of law, which implyeth a former malicious disposition in him rather to kill the man than not to have his money from him.'" 3 Stephen, fn. 23 supra, pp. 50–51.

Moreland observes that this was an attempt to justify the rule as an inference of fact in order to satisfy the definition of malice aforethought prevailing at that time. But, in Moreland's opinion, it does not carry conviction as such. Moreland, Law of Homicide (Indianapolis: Bobbs–Merrill, 1952), p. 14. . . .

Perkins contends that the primary purpose of the felony-murder rule was to deal with homicides committed during unsuccessful attempted felonies. An attempt to commit a felony was only a misdemeanor at common law. The felony-murder rule placed the defendant in the position he would have been in had the felony been successful without the homicide, for in either case it would be a capital crime. Perkins, Criminal Law (2d ed.), p. 44.

4. By a practice known as "benefit of clergy" a defendant could avoid the death penalty. At early law, members of the clergy could be tried only by an ecclesiastical court. The test for determining entitlement to the benefit was the ability to read. The effect of the benefit was to shield from the death penalty those who qualified for its protection since a court of the Church could not pronounce a judgment of blood. However, a series of statutes in the late Fifteenth and early Sixteenth Centuries

It was, therefore, "of no particular moment whether the condemned was hanged for the initial felony or for the death accidentally resulting from the felony." . . .

Chief Justice Holt, writing in Rex v. Keate, 90 Eng.Rep. 557 (KB, 1697), said that Coke's statement was a very exaggerated proposition of law and that for unintentional homicides to constitute murder there must be an intent to commit a felony or a design to do mischief toward a person.

Foster stated that an unintentional killing resulting from an unlawful act would amount to murder only if done "in the prosecution of a felonious intention".[5] . . .

Case law of Nineteenth–Century England reflects the efforts of the English courts to limit the application of the felony-murder doctrine. See, e.g., Regina v. Greenwood, 7 Cox, Crim.Cas. 404 (1857); Regina v. Horsey, 3 F & F 287, 176 Eng.Rep. 129 (1862), culminating in Regina v. Serne, 16 Cox, Crim.Cas. 311 (1887). In the latter case, involving a death resulting from arson, Judge Stephen instructed the jury as follows:

> "[I]nstead of saying that any act done with intent to commit a felony and which causes death amounts to murder, it should be reasonable to say that any act known to be dangerous to life and likely in itself to cause death, done for the purpose of committing a felony which causes death, should be murder."

In this century, the felony-murder doctrine was comparatively rarely invoked in England and in 1957 England abolished the felony-murder rule. Section 1 of England's Homicide Act, 1957, 5 & 6 Eliz. 2, c. 11, § 1, provides that a killing occurring in a felony-murder situation will not amount to murder unless done with the same malice aforethought as is required for all other murder.

Thus, an examination of the felony-murder rule indicates that the doctrine is of doubtful origin. Derived from the misinterpretation of case law, it went unchallenged because of circumstances which no longer exist. The doctrine was continuously modified and restricted in England, the country of its birth, until its ultimate rejection by Parliament in 1957.

removed the more culpable homicides from the protection of the benefit of clergy. 12 Hen. 7, c. 7 (1496); 4 Hen. 8, c. 2 (1512); 23 Hen. 8, c. 1, §§ 3, 4 (1531); 1 Edw. 6, c. 12, § 10 (1547). Anachronism Retained, fn. 15 supra, pp. 428–429; Perkins, A Re-examination of Malice Aforethought, 43 Yale L.J. 537, 542–543 (1934); Moesel, fn. 23 supra, p. 455.

5. Foster, Crown Law (2d ed., 1791), p. 258. See also 3 Stephen, fn. 23 supra, p. 75.

III. LIMITATION OF THE FELONY MURDER DOCTRINE
IN THE UNITED STATES

While only a few states have followed the lead of Great Britain in abolishing felony murder, various legislative and judicial limitations on the doctrine have effectively narrowed the scope of the rule in the United States. . . .

The draftsmen of the Model Penal Code have summarized the limitations imposed by American courts as follows:

(1) "The felonious act must be dangerous to life."

(2) and (3). "The homicide must be a natural and probable consequence of the felonious act." "Death must be 'proximately' caused." Courts have also required that the killing be the result of an act done in the furtherance of the felonious purpose and not merely coincidental to the perpetration of a felony. These cases often make distinctions based on the identity of the victim (i.e., whether the decedent was the victim of the felony or whether he was someone else, e.g., a policeman or one of the felons) and the identity of the person causing the death.

(4) "The felony must be *malum in se.*"

(5) "The act must be a common-law felony."

(6) "The period during which the felony is in the process of commission must be narrowly construed."

(7) "The underlying felony must be 'independent' of the homicide."

Some courts, recognizing the questionable wisdom of the rule, have refused to extend it beyond what is required. . . .   "We have thus recognized that the felony-murder doctrine expresses a highly artificial concept that deserves no extension beyond its required application. Indeed, the rule itself has been abandoned by the courts of England, where it had its inception. It has been subjected to severe and sweeping criticism." People v. Phillips, 51 Cal.Rptr. 225, 414 P.2d 353, 360 (1966).

Other courts have required a finding of a separate *mens rea* connected with the killing in addition to the intent associated with the felony. In State v. Millette, 112 N.H. 458, 462, 299 A.2d 150, 153 (1972), the Court stated:

> "Neither the legislature nor our court ever adopted a presumption of malice from the commission of an unlawful act whether felony or misdemeanor. While language in our cases defining murder may be construed to presume malice from a homicide occurring during the commission of the named inherently dangerous felonies [citations omitted] malice remains an indispensable element in the crime of murder. 'Malice is not an inference of law from the mere act of killing; but like any other fact in issue, it must be found by the jury upon competent evidence'."

This Court has held, at least with killings occurring during commission of non-enumerated felonies, that malice may be inferred but the nature of the felonious act must be considered. Similarly, New Mexico has declared that where a non-first-degree felony (this category would include many of Michigan's enumerated felonies) is involved, the presumption that the defendant has the requisite *mens rea* to commit first-degree murder "is a legal fiction we no longer can support".

The Iowa Supreme Court has recently ruled that the issue of malice aforethought necessary for murder must be submitted to the jury and that it may not be satisfied by proof of intent to commit the underlying felony.

Many state legislatures have also been active in restricting the scope of felony murder by imposing additional limitations.

Kentucky[6] and Hawaii[7] have specifically abolished the felony-murder doctrine. The commentary to Hawaii's murder statute is instructive as to that state's reasoning in abolishing the doctrine:

> "Even in its limited formulation the felony murder rule is still objectionable. It is not sound principle to convert an accidental, negligent, or reckless homicide into a murder simply because, without more, the killing was in furtherance of a criminal objective of some defined class. Engaging in certain penally-prohibited behavior may, of course, evidence a recklessness sufficient to establish manslaughter, or a practical certainty or intent, with respect to causing death, sufficient to establish murder, but such a finding is an independent determination which must rest on the facts of each case.
>
> * * *
>
> "In recognition of the trend toward, and the substantial body of criticism supporting, the abolition of the felony-murder rule, and because of the extremely questionable results which the rule has worked in other jurisdictions, the Code has eliminated from our law the felony-murder rule."[8]

Ohio[9] has effectively abolished the felony-murder rule. It defines as *involuntary manslaughter* the death of another proximately resulting from the offender's commission or attempt to commit a felony.[10]

Seven states have downgraded the offense and consequently reduced the punishment. Alaska, Louisiana, New York, Pennsylvania and Utah have reduced it to second-degree murder.[11] Minnesota classifies felony murder as third-degree murder (with the exception of a

6. Ky.Rev.Stat., § 507.020.

7. Hawaii Rev.Stat., § 707–701.

8. 7A Hawaii Rev.Stat., § 707–701, Commentary, p. 347.

9. Ohio Rev.Code Ann. § 2903.04 (Page).

10. Manslaughter by definition does not require malice. As the primary purpose of the felony-murder rule is to supply malice from the underlying felony, the rule has no usefulness as such in Ohio.

11. Alaska Stat., §§ 11.41.110, 11.41.115; La.Rev.Stat.Ann., § 14:30.1; N.Y. Penal Law, § 125.25 (McKinney); Pa. Cons.Stat.Ann., tit. 18, § 2502 (Purdon); Utah Code Ann., § 76–5–203(1).

killing in the course of criminal sexual conduct in the first or second degree committed with force or violence, which is punished as first-degree murder) which involves a sentence of not more than 25 years.[12] Wisconsin makes felony murder a class B felony which is punishable by imprisonment not to exceed 20 years.[13]

Three states require a demonstration of *mens rea* beyond the intent to cause the felony. The Arkansas statute states that the defendant must cause the death "under circumstances manifesting extreme indifference to the value of human life." [14] Delaware's first-degree murder statute requires that the defendant cause death recklessly in the course of a felony or with at least criminal negligence in the course of one of the enumerated felonies.[15] It defines as second-degree murder death caused with criminal negligence in the course of nonenumerated felonies. New Hampshire's capital and first-degree murder statutes require that death be caused knowingly in connection with certain enumerated felonies while its second-degree murder statute requires that death be caused "recklessly under circumstances manifesting an extreme indifference to the value of human life." [16]

Some of the limitations on the felony-murder doctrine which have been imposed by the courts, as mentioned above, have been codified by statute. These limitations include restrictions on the underlying felony, requiring that it be forcible, violent or clearly dangerous to human life, that death be proximately caused, that death be a natural or probable consequence or a reasonably foreseeable consequence of the commission or attempted commission of the felony, that the felon must have caused the death, and that the victim must not be one of the felons.

Other restrictions of the common-law rule include the enumeration of felonies which are to be included within the felony-murder category, and the reduction to manslaughter of killings in the course of non-enumerated felonies. . . .

Finally, a limitation of relatively recent origin is the availability of affirmative defenses where a defendant is not the only participant in the commission of the underlying felony. The New York statute provides, as do similar statutes of nine other states, an affirmative defense to the defendant when he:

"(a) Did not commit the homicidal act or in any way solicit, request, command, importune, cause or aid the commission thereof; and

"(b) Was not armed with a deadly weapon, or any instrument, article or substance readily capable of causing death or

12. Minn.Stat.Ann., §§ 609.185, 609.195.

13. Wis.Stat.Ann. §§ 940.02(2), 939.50(3)(b).

14. Ark.Stat.Ann., § 41.1502.

15. Del.Code, tit. 11, § 636.

16. N.H.Rev.Stat.Ann., §§ 630:1, 630:1–a, 630:1–b.

serious physical injury and of a sort not ordinarily carried in public places by law-abiding persons; and

"(c) Had no reasonable ground to believe that any other participant was armed with such a weapon, instrument, article or substance; and

"(d) Had no reasonable ground to believe that any other participant intended to engage in conduct likely to result in death or serious physical injury."

The commentary to the New York statute states that the provision is premised "upon the theory that the felony murder doctrine, in its rigid automatic envelopment of all participants in the underlying felony, may be unduly harsh * * *." The comment acknowledges that there may be some cases where it would be "just and desirable to allow a non-killer defendant of relatively minor culpability a chance of extricating himself from liability for murder, though not, of course, from liability for the underlying felony."

The numerous modifications and restrictions placed upon the common-law felony-murder doctrine by courts and legislatures reflect dissatisfaction with the harshness and injustice of the rule. Even though the felony murder doctrine survives in this country, it bears increasingly less resemblance to the traditional felony-murder concept. To the extent that these modifications reduce the scope and significance of the common law doctrine, they also call into question the continued existence of the doctrine itself.

IV. THE REQUIREMENT OF INDIVIDUAL CULPABILITY FOR CRIMINAL RESPONSIBILITY

"If one had to choose the most basic principle of the criminal law in general * * * it would be that criminal liability for causing a particular result is not justified in the absence of some culpable mental state in respect to that result * * *."

The most fundamental characteristic of the felony-murder rule violates this basic principle in that it punishes all homicides committed in the perpetration or attempted perpetration of proscribed felonies whether intentional, unintentional or accidental, without the necessity of proving the relation between the homicide and the perpetrator's state of mind. This is most evident when a killing is done by one of a group of co-felons. The felony-murder rule completely ignores the concept of determination of guilt on the basis of individual misconduct. The felony-murder rule thus "erodes the relation between criminal liability and moral culpability." People v. Washington, 44 Cal.Rptr. 442, 402 P.2d 130 (1965).

The felony-murder rule's most egregious violation of basic rules of culpability occurs where felony murder is categorized as first-degree murder. All other murders carrying equal punishment require a showing of premeditation, deliberation and willfulness while felony murder only requires a showing of intent to do the underlying felony. Although the purpose of our degree statutes is to punish more severely the more culpable forms of murder, People v. Garcia, 398 Mich. 250, 258, 247 N.W.2d 547 (1976), an accidental killing occurring during the perpetration of a felony would be punished more severely than a second-degree murder requiring intent to kill, intent to cause great bodily harm or wantonness and willfulness. Furthermore, a defendant charged with felony murder is permitted to raise defenses only to the mental element of the felony, thus precluding certain defenses available to a defendant charged with premeditated murder who may raise defenses to the mental element of murder (e.g., self-defense, accident). Certainly, felony murder is no more reprehensible than premeditated murder.

LaFave and Scott explain the felony-murder doctrine's failure to account for a defendant's moral culpability as follows:

> "The rationale of the doctrine is that one who commits a felony is a bad person with a bad state of mind, and he has caused a bad result, so that we should not worry too much about the fact that the fatal result he accomplished was quite different and a good deal worse than the bad result he intended. Yet it is a general principle of criminal law that one is not ordinarily criminally liable for bad results which differ greatly from intended results." [17]

* * *

While it is understandable that little compassion may be felt for the criminal whose innocent victim dies, this does not justify ignoring the principles underlying our system of criminal law. As Professor Hall argues in his treatise on criminal law:

> "The underlying rationale of the felony-murder doctrine— that the offender has shown himself to be a 'bad actor,' and that this is enough to exclude the niceties bearing on the gravity of the harm actually committed—might have been defensible in early law. The survival of the felony-murder doctrine is a tribute to the tenacity of legal conceptions rooted in simple moral attitudes. For as long ago as 1771 the doctrine was severely criticized by Eden [Baron Auckland], who felt that it 'may be reconciled to the philosophy of slaves; but it is surely repugnant to that noble, and active confidence, which a free people ought to possess in the laws of their constitution, the rule of their actions'." [18]

* * *

The failure of the felony-murder rule to consider the defendant's moral culpability is explained by examining the state of the law at the

17. LaFave & Scott, fn. 34 supra, p. 560.   18. Hall, General Principles of Criminal Law (Indianapolis: Bobbs–Merrill, 1947), p. 455.

time of the rule's inception. The concept of culpability was not an element of homicide at early common law. The early definition of malice aforethought was vague. The concept meant little more than intentional wrongdoing with no other emphasis on intention except to exclude homicides that were committed by misadventure or in some otherwise pardonable manner. Thus, under this early definition of malice aforethought, an intent to commit the felony would in itself constitute malice. Furthermore, as all felonies were punished alike, it made little difference whether the felon was hanged for the felony or for the death.

Thus, the felony-murder rule did not broaden the concept of murder at the time of its origin because proof of the intention to commit a felony met the test of culpability based on the vague definition of malice aforethought governing at that time. Today, however, malice is a term of art. It does not include the nebulous definition of intentional wrongdoing. Thus, although the felony-murder rule did not broaden the definition of murder at early common law, it does so today. We find this enlargement of the scope of murder unacceptable, . . .

V. The Felony–Murder Doctrine in Michigan

A. Murder and Malice Defined

In order to understand the operation of any state's felony-murder doctrine, initially it is essential to understand how that state defines murder and malice.

In Michigan, murder is not statutorily defined. This Court early defined the term as follows:

> "Murder is where a person of sound memory and discretion unlawfully kills any reasonable creature in being, in the peace of the state, with malice prepense or aforethought, either express or implied."

Thus, malice aforethought is the "grand criterion" which elevates a homicide, which may be innocent or criminal, to murder. However, "[t]he nature of malice aforethought is the source of much of the confusion that attends the law of homicide." People v. Morrin, 31 Mich.App. 301, 310–311, 187 N.W.2d 434 (1971), lv. den. 385 Mich. 775 (1971). See, also, Moreland, Law of Homicide (Indianapolis: Bobbs–Merrill, 1952), pp. 205–206. Overbroad and ill-considered instructions on malice have plagued appellate courts for decades.

We agree with the following analysis of murder and malice aforethought presented by LaFave & Scott:

> "Though murder is frequently defined as the unlawful killing of another 'living human being' with 'malice aforethought', in modern times the latter phrase does not even approximate its literal meaning. Hence it is preferable not to rely upon that misleading expression for an understanding of murder but rather to consider the various types of murder

(typed according to the mental element) which the common law came to recognize and which exist today in most jurisdictions:

"(1) intent-to-kill murder;

"(2) intent-to-do-serious-bodily-injury murder;

"(3) depraved-heart murder [wanton and willful disregard that the natural tendency of the defendant's behavior is to cause death or great bodily harm]; and

"(4) felony murder." [19]

Under the common law, which we refer to in defining murder in this state, each of the four types of murder noted above has its own mental element which independently satisfies the requirement of malice aforethought. It is, therefore, not necessary for the law to imply or for the jury to infer the intention to kill once the finder of fact determines the existence of any of the other three mental states because each one, by itself, constitutes the element of malice aforethought.

Our focus in this opinion is upon the last category of murder, i.e., felony murder. We do not believe the felony-murder doctrine, as some courts and commentators would suggest, abolishes the requirement of malice, nor do we believe that it equates the *mens rea* of the felony with the *mens rea* required for a non-felony murder. We construe the felony-murder doctrine as providing a separate definition of malice, thereby establishing a fourth category of murder. The effect of the doctrine is to recognize the intent to commit the underlying felony, in itself, as a sufficient *mens rea* for murder. This analysis of the felony-murder doctrine is consistent with the historical development of the doctrine.

The question we address today is whether Michigan recognizes the felony-murder doctrine and, accordingly, the category of malice arising from the underlying felony. The relevant inquiry is first whether Michigan has a statutory felony-murder doctrine. If it does not, it must then be determined whether Michigan has or should have a common-law felony-murder doctrine.

B. Statutory Felony Murder

Michigan does not have a statutory felony-murder doctrine which designates as murder any *death* occurring in the course of a felony without regard to whether it was the result of accident, negligence, recklessness or willfulness. Rather, Michigan has a statute which

---

19. LaFave & Scott, Criminal Law, p. 528. In this opinion, we continue to use the term, "malice" for the sake of convenience. However, we will narrowly define the term to avoid making it the "misleading expression" referred to by LaFave & Scott. We see no reason why trial judges, in instructing on the mental element required for first-degree murder committed in the course of an enumerated felony, need specifically refer to the term "malice." Juries may simply be instructed that they must find one of the three elements described later in this opinion.

makes a *murder* occurring in the course of one of the enumerated felonies a first-degree murder.

> "Murder which is perpetrated by means of poison, lying in wait, or other wilful, deliberate, and premeditated killing, or which is committed in the perpetration, or attempt to perpetrate arson, criminal sexual conduct in the first or third degree, robbery, breaking and entering of a dwelling, larceny of any kind, extortion, or kidnapping, is murder of the first degree, and shall be punished by imprisonment for life." M.C.L. § 750.316; M.S.A. § 28.548.

* * *

Michigan case law also makes it clear that the purpose of our first-degree murder statute is to graduate punishment and that the statute only serves to raise an already established *murder* to the first-degree level, not to transform a death, without more, into a murder.

> "The statute does not undertake to define the crime of murder, but only to distinguish it into two degrees, for the purpose of graduating the punishment."

> "It speaks of the offense *as one already ascertained* and defined, and divides it into degrees * * *." People v. Potter, (1858) (emphasis added).

> "Neither murder nor manslaughter is defined in our statutes. The [first-degree murder statute] simply classifies a *murder* perpetrated in a particular manner as murder in the first degree. *It has no application until a murder has been established.*" People v. Charles Austin, (1923) (emphasis added).

* * *

Professor Perkins is in accord:

> "Such a statute, let it be emphasized, makes no attempt to define murder. 'It has no application until a murder has been established.' If the homicide meets the requirements of murder in general, and is shown to have been committed in any of these ways, then the statute applies and makes the killing murder in the first degree. If the death would not otherwise be murder at all this statute does not make it first degree murder, because it speaks of all 'murder' so perpetrated—not all 'homicide.'" Perkins, Criminal Law (2d ed.), p. 90.

Thus, we conclude that Michigan has not codified the common-law felony-murder rule. The use of the term "murder" in the first-degree statute requires that a murder must first be established before the statute is applied to elevate the degree.

C. Common–Law Felony–Murder in Michigan

The prosecution argues that even if Michigan does not have a statutory codification of the felony-murder rule, the common-law definition of murder included a homicide in the course of a felony. Thus, the argument continues, once a homicide in the course of a felony is proven, under the common-law felony-murder rule a murder has been established and the first-degree murder statute then becomes applicable. This Court has ruled that the term murder as used in the first-degree murder statute includes all types of murder at common law. People v. Samuel Scott, supra, 292–293. Hence, we must determine whether Michigan in fact has a common-law felony-murder rule.

Our research has uncovered no Michigan cases, nor do the parties refer us to any, which have expressly considered whether Michigan has or should continue to have a common-law felony-murder doctrine. While there are some cases containing language which may be construed as assuming the existence of such a rule in Michigan, the language is clearly dictum as the question was neither at issue nor expressly considered. * * *

However, our finding that Michigan has never specifically adopted the doctrine which defines malice to include the intent to commit the underlying felony is not the end of our inquiry. In Michigan, the general rule is that the common law prevails except as abrogated by the Constitution, the Legislature or this Court. Const.1963, art. 3, § 7.

This Court has not been faced previously with a decision as to whether it should abolish the felony-murder doctrine. Thus, the common-law doctrine remains the law in Michigan. Moreover, the assumption by appellate decisions that the doctrine exists, combined with the fact that Michigan trial courts have applied the doctrine in numerous cases resulting in convictions of first-degree felony-murder, requires us to address the common-law felony-murder issue. The cases before us today squarely present us with the opportunity to review the doctrine and to consider its continued existence in Michigan. Although there are no Michigan cases which specifically abrogate the felony-murder rule, there exists a number of decisions of this Court which have significantly restricted the doctrine in Michigan and which lead us to conclude that the rule should be abolished.

* * *

[After considering a number of earlier Michigan decisions in detail, the opinion continues:]

Our review of Michigan case law persuades us that we should abolish the rule which defines malice as the intent to commit the underlying felony. Abrogation of the felony-murder rule is not a drastic move in light of the significant restrictions this Court has already imposed. Further, it is a logical extension of our decisions as discussed above.

We believe that it is no longer acceptable to equate the intent to commit a felony with the intent to kill, intent to do great bodily harm, or wanton and willful disregard of the likelihood that the natural tendency of a person's behavior is to cause death or great bodily harm. In People v. Hansen, 368 Mich. 344, 350, 118 N.W.2d 422 (1962), this

Court said that "[m]alice requires an intent to cause the very harm that results or some harm of the same general nature, or an act done in wanton or wilful disregard of the plaintiff and strong likelihood that such harm will result." In a charge of felony murder, it is the murder which is the harm which is being punished. A defendant who only intends to commit the felony does not intend to commit the harm that results and may or may not be guilty of perpetrating an act done in wanton or wilful disregard of the plain and strong likelihood that such harm will result. Although the circumstances surrounding the commission of the felony may evidence a greater intent beyond the intent to commit the felony, or a wanton and wilful act in disregard of the possible consequence of death or serious injury, the intent to commit the felony, of itself, does not connote a "man-endangering-state-of-mind". Hence, we do not believe that it constitutes a sufficient *mens rea* to establish the crime of murder.

Accordingly, we hold today that malice is the intention to kill, the intention to do great bodily harm, or the wanton and wilful disregard of the likelihood that the natural tendency of defendant's behavior is to cause death or great bodily harm. We further hold that malice is an essential element of any murder, as that term is judicially defined, whether the murder occurs in the course of a felony or otherwise. The facts and circumstances involved in the perpetration of a felony may evidence an intent to kill, an intent to cause great bodily harm, or a wanton and wilful disregard of the likelihood that the natural tendency of defendant's behavior is to cause death or great bodily harm; however, the conclusion must be left to the jury to infer from all the evidence. Otherwise, "juries might be required to find the fact of malice where they were satisfied from the whole evidence it did not exist".

VI. PRACTICAL EFFECT OF ABROGATION OF THE COMMON–LAW FELONY–MURDER DOCTRINE

From a practical standpoint, the abolition of the category of malice arising from the intent to commit the underlying felony should have little effect on the result of the majority of cases. In many cases where felony murder has been applied, the use of the doctrine was unnecessary because the other types of malice could have been inferred from the evidence.

Abrogation of this rule does not make irrelevant the fact that a death occurred in the course of a felony. A jury can properly *infer* malice from evidence that a defendant intentionally set in motion a force likely to cause death or great bodily harm. Thus, whenever a killing occurs in the perpetration or attempted perpetration of an inherently dangerous felony, in order to establish malice the jury may consider the "nature of the underlying felony and the circumstances surrounding its commission", People v. Fountain, 71 Mich.App. 491, 506, 248 N.W.2d 589 (1976). If the jury concludes that malice existed, they can find murder and, if they determine that the murder occurred in the perpetration or attempted perpetration of one of the enumerated felonies, by statute the murder would become first-degree murder.

The difference is that the jury may not find malice from the intent to commit the underlying felony alone. The defendant will be permitted to assert any of the applicable defenses relating to *mens rea* which he would be allowed to assert if charged with premeditated murder. The latter result is reasonable in light of the fact that felony murder is certainly no more heinous than premeditated murder. The prosecution will still be able to prove first-degree murder without proof of premeditation when a homicide is committed with malice, as we have defined it, and the perpetration or attempted perpetration of an enumerated felony is established. Hence, our first-degree murder statute continues to elevate to first-degree murder a *murder* which is committed in the perpetration or attempted perpetration of one of the enumerated felonies.

As previously noted, in many circumstances the commission of a felony, particularly one involving violence or the use of force, will indicate an intention to kill, an intention to cause great bodily harm, or wanton or willful disregard of the likelihood that the natural tendency of defendant's behavior is to cause death or great bodily harm. Thus, the felony-murder rule is not necessary to establish *mens rea* in these cases.

In the past, the felony-murder rule has been employed where unforeseen or accidental deaths occur and where the state seeks to prove vicarious liability of co-felons. In situations involving the vicarious liability of co-felons, the individual liability of each felon must be shown. It is fundamentally unfair and in violation of basic principles of individual criminal culpability to hold one felon liable for the unforeseen and unagreed-to results of another felon. In cases where the felons are acting intentionally or recklessly in pursuit of a common plan, the felony-murder rule is unnecessary because liability may be established on agency principles.

Finally, in cases where the death was purely accidental, application of the felony-murder doctrine is unjust and should be precluded. The underlying felony, of course, will still be subject to punishment. The draftsmen of the Model Penal Code report that juries are not disposed to accept unfounded claims of accident in Ohio where all first-degree murder requires a purpose to kill.

Thus, in the three situations in which the felony-murder doctrine typically has applied, the rule is either unnecessary or contrary to fundamental principles of our criminal law. * * *

The Pennsylvania Supreme Court has called the felony-murder rule "nonessential",[20] and the commentators to the Hawaii statute abolishing felony murder concluded that "[t]he rule certainly is not an

---

20. Commonwealth ex rel. Smith v. Myers, fn. 51 supra, 438 Pa. 226, 261 A.2d 550.

indispensable ingredient in a system of criminal justice." [21] The penal code of India has done away with felony murder and the doctrine is also unknown as such in continental Europe. England, the birthplace of the felony-murder doctrine, has been without the rule for over 20 years and "its passing apparently has not been mourned". One writer suggests that the experience in England demonstrates that its demise would have little effect on the rate of convictions for murders occurring in the perpetration of felonies.

* * *

VII. CONCLUSION

Whatever reasons can be gleaned from the dubious origin of the felony-murder rule to explain its existence, those reasons no longer exist today. Indeed, most states, including our own, have recognized the harshness and inequity of the rule as is evidenced by the numerous restrictions placed on it. The felony-murder doctrine is unnecessary and in many cases unjust in that it violates the basic premise of individual moral culpability upon which our criminal law is based.

We conclude that Michigan has no statutory felony-murder rule which allows the mental element of murder to be satisfied by proof of the intention to commit the underlying felony. Today we exercise our role in the development of the common law by abrogating the common-law felony-murder rule. We hold that in order to convict a defendant of murder, as that term is defined by Michigan case law, it must be shown that he acted with intent to kill or to inflict great bodily harm or with a wanton and willful disregard of the likelihood that the natural tendency of his behavior is to cause death or great bodily harm. We further hold that the issue of malice must always be submitted to the jury.

The first-degree murder statute will continue to operate in that all *murder* committed in the perpetration or attempted perpetration of the enumerated felonies will be elevated to first-degree murder.

This decision shall apply to all trials in progress and those occurring after the date of this opinion.

In *Aaron,* the judgment of conviction of second-degree murder is reversed and this case is remanded to the trial court for a new trial. In *Thompson* and in *Wright,* the decisions of the Court of Appeals are affirmed and both cases are remanded to the trial court for new trial.

COLEMAN, C.J., and MOODY, LEVIN and KAVANAGH, JJ., concur.

RYAN, JUSTICE (concurring in part, dissenting in part).

I concur in the results reached by Justice Fitzgerald in these cases but write separately to express my disagreement with the reasoning employed in his opinion.

21. 7A Hawaii Rev.Stat. § 707–701, Commentary, p. 346.

I

* * *

Proper resolution of the stated issues requires us to determine what the terms "murder" and "malice" mean in our jurisprudence, and to determine what the common-law felony-murder rule is, and how it operates.

II

A. Murder

I agree with the definition of murder which appears in Justice Fitzgerald's opinion and repeat it here for the reader's convenience:

> "Murder is where a person of sound memory and discretion unlawfully kills any reasonable creature in being, in the peace of the state, with malice prepense or aforethought, either express or implied.

The common-law offense of murder, which is incorporated into our murder statutes, includes at a minimum two essential or ultimate factual elements: (1) a homicide, (2) committed with malice, express or implied. . . .

I am also in agreement with Justice Fitzgerald that our murder statutes operate not to define murder, but rather to declare differing penalties for the different statutory degrees of murder as defined at common law: . . .

Thus it is clear that under Michigan law the substantive offense of murder, that is, a homicide with malice, express or implied, must be proven before the punishment-grading statutory provisions come into operation.

B. Malice

I also agree with the definition of malice which is contained in Justice, then Judge, Levin's opinion in People v. Morrin, 31 Mich.App. 310–311, 187 N.W.2d 434:

> "A person who kills another is guilty of the crime of murder if the homicide is committed with malice aforethought. Malice aforethought is the intention to kill, actual or implied, under circumstances which do not constitute excuse or justification or mitigate the degree of the offense to manslaughter. The intent to kill may be implied where the actor actually intends to inflict great bodily harm or the natural tendency of his behavior is to cause death or great bodily harm."

Our jurisprudence contains no common-law definition of malice as the intent to commit an inherently dangerous felony.

C. The Felony–Murder Rule

In *Morrin,* directly following the definition of malice, Justice, then Judge, Levin noted parenthetically that "[t]he common-law felony-murder rule is an example of implied intent or implied malice afore-thought". This parenthetical language suggests that the felony-murder rule is a method of proof which establishes a "conclusive implication", or an "imputation (as a matter of law)", or a "conclusive presumption" of the implied intent to *kill* out of factual proof of an intent to commit a *felony.*

Under the felony-murder rule, as it is generally understood then, evidence establishing the intent to commit a felony, by operation of law, irrebuttably satisfies the prosecution's burden of proving the necessary factual element of the intent to kill. Stated otherwise, upon proof of the intent to commit a *felony,* the felony-murder rule operates to relieve the prosecution of its burden of proving *at all,* much less beyond a reasonable doubt, the factual element of malice; that is, the intent to kill, the intent to inflict great bodily harm, or wanton and willful disregard of the likelihood that the natural tendency of one's behavior is to cause death or great bodily harm.

The result then is that under the felony-murder rule the defen-dant's state of mind *with respect to the killing* is irrelevant. The only *mens rea* involved pertains solely to the underlying felony. Because malice, correctly understood, is a characterization of a particular state of mind *with respect to a killing,* it follows that the common-law offense of felony-murder does not require malice. Yet, historically, acceptance of this reality, has, in general, been resisted by many courts and commentators who insist, erroneously in my view, that felony-murder requires malice. Their theory begins with the proposition that felony-murder, like all murder, requires malice and ends with the proposition that malice is imputed, as a matter of law, from the intent to commit the underlying felony. This is a useless fiction at best. The offense of felony-murder requires only (1) the commission or attempt to commit a felony and (2) a killing causally connected with the commission or attempt.

Survival of the fiction that felony-murder requires malice but that malice is imputed is undoubtedly attributable to unreasoned allegiance to the axiom that murder requires malice, express or implied. Because malice is the *sine qua non* of murder, courts, when confronted with the crime of felony murder which does not require malice, have resorted to conceptualizing felony murder in a way that professes obedience to the "murder requires malice" commandment. As a result, a fourth type of mental state has been created by some courts and commentators and included under the heading of malice, so that malice is said to include:

(1) An intent to kill;

(2) An intent to inflict great bodily harm;

(3) Wanton and willful disregard of the likelihood that the natural tendency of one's behavior is to cause death or great bodily harm; *and*

(4) *An intent to perpetrate a (dangerous) felony.*

Thus, with disingenuously circular reasoning, obeisance is mistakenly paid to the axiom that murder requires malice by including within the definition of malice a case in which it is not an element. The price paid is continuing confusion in the law of homicide. Consequently, I disagree with the following statement by my Brother Fitzgerald: "We construe the felony-murder doctrine as providing a separate definition of malice * * **." Malice has nothing to do with common-law felony-murder; it is not an element of the crime, and is not properly considered by the jury. Except for its name, felony-murder bears little if any resemblance to the offense of murder. It is a mistaken analysis, therefore, that permits one to deem the intent to commit a felony a kind of malice, and felony-murder a kind of common-law murder.

III

Perhaps for reasons relating to a failure to fully grasp the nature of the relationship between felony-murder and murder, felony-murder has led a dubious and enigmatic existence in the jurisprudence of this state. I fully agree with Justice Fitzgerald's observation that this Court has "never specifically adopted" the common-law crime of felony-murder, nor ever "expressly considered whether Michigan has or should continue to have a common-law felony-murder doctrine". Although there is language in *Michigan Reports* that ostensibly adverts to felony-murder, the discussion is invariably superficial, tangential, opaque, and, as my brother Fitzgerald notes, almost always "clearly dictum." . . .

IV

That we differ greatly in how we understand the concept of felony-murder and its relationship to murder should not obscure the fact that Justice Fitzgerald and I are in agreement on the principal issue: the merits of the felony-murder rule.

Part IV of his opinion correctly outlines, in my view, the injudicious and unprincipled premises on which the common-law doctrine of felony-murder rests. The basic infirmity of felony-murder lies in its failure to correlate, to any degree, criminal liability with moral culpability. It permits one to be punished for a killing, usually with the most severe penalty in the law, without requiring proof of *any* mental state with respect to the killing. This incongruity is simply more than we are willing to permit our criminal jurisprudence to bear.

For these reasons I concur in today's holding and the disposition of these consolidated cases.

V

The effect of this decision is not, as my brother suggests, to redefine malice or murder. Those terms will mean what they have always meant in this state: murder is a killing accompanied by malice; malice is the intent to kill, the intent to inflict great bodily harm, or wanton and willful disregard of the likelihood that the natural tendency of one's behavior is to cause death or great bodily harm. Moreover, malice is and always has been a question of fact for the trier of fact and, as all questions of fact, may be established by direct evidence, circumstantial evidence, or both. These principles are unaffected by this case.

Today we simply declare that the offense popularly known as felony-murder, which, properly understood, has nothing to do with malice and is not a species of common-law murder, shall no longer exist in Michigan, if indeed it ever did.

WILLIAMS, JUSTICE (concurring in part).

I concur in the result reached by my brothers Fitzgerald and Ryan. I agree with my brother Fitzgerald's and my brother Ryan's opinions as to their definitions of murder and as to definitions of malice in People v. Morrin (1971).

In my opinion, it is the language of the statute that determines whether there need be proof of malice in a so-called felony-murder case. M.C.L. § 750.316; M.S.A. § 28.548, until its amendment this year, read as follows:

> "*All murder which* shall be perpetrated by means of poison, or lying in wait, or any other kind of wilful, deliberate and premeditated killing, or which shall be committed in the perpetration, or attempt to perpetrate any arson, rape, robbery, burglary, larceny of any kind, extortion or kidnapping, *shall be murder of the first degree * * *.*" (Emphasis supplied.)

What is critical in the statutory language is that the section begins "All murder which" and ends "shall be murder of the first degree". In other words, what becomes murder of the first degree is not any *homicide which* is in connection with a poisoning, for example, or certain named felonies but a *murder which* is in connection with a poisoning or certain named felonies. The proof of malice is not essential to all forms of *homicide,* but it is essential to all forms of *murder.* Hence, proof of a so-called felony murder under M.C.L. § 750.316 requires proof of malice as does any other murder. . . .

NOTE

Much of the casebook's material has been devoted to a discussion of decisions that limit the common law felony murder rule. Some opinions have been critical of the rule, like *Aaron,* and condemn it as an anachronistic and unnecessary part of the criminal law. Yet, most legislatures that have amended criminal statutes have chosen to retain the rule in the face of scorn and criticism heaped upon the felony murder doctrine by scholars and some courts. This raises the question whether there are legitimate contemporary purposes served by a retention of the concept of punishing as murder conduct that does not exhibit the "malice" blameworthiness traditionally associated with that crime.

For a thought-provoking article that bucks the trend of scholarly comment, and in the process also characterizes the *Aaron* decision as "superficial," see Crump & Crump, In Defense Of The Felony Murder Doctrine, 8 Harv.J.Law & Public Policy 359 (1985). The authors conclude that there are substantial arguments to be made in favor of the doctrine, though it is possible to disagree with the applicability of some stated policies to the precise issue.

B. VOLUNTARY MANSLAUGHTER

STATE v. FLORY

Supreme Court of Wyoming, 1929.
40 Wyo. 184, 276 P. 458.

BLUME, C.J. The defendant was convicted of murder in the second degree for killing E.T. Ostrum on January 16, 1928, and he appeals.

The deceased, aged between 65 to 70 years, was the father of Daisy Flory, the wife of defendant, who is about 21 years of age, and who married defendant in 1923. The mother and father of Daisy were, it seems, divorced, for a number of years prior to the homicide in question in this case. The father apparently was not well acquainted with his daughter and paid little attention to her, although he sent her some small presents when her two children, age 3 years and 1 year, respectively, were born. At the time of the homicide and for some time prior thereto, the deceased lived on a farm in Campbell county, Wyo., the defendant on a farm in Montana; the distance, by road, between the two places being about 50 miles. The deceased was engaged in farming and in performing common labor. The defendant was a "dry farmer" in the summer and a trapper in the winter. Deceased wrote to his daughter in the summer of 1927, wanting to visit her, and she and her husband invited him to come. He arrived on the day after Thanksgiving, during the absence of the defendant, who came home on November 30th. The visit between the deceased and defendant was pleasant, and it was agreed, in fact, upon suggestion of the deceased, that the latter might somewhat later, move over to defendant's place, build himself a house, and in the meantime occupy the "bunkhouse" on defendant's place. He was invited to continue his visit at that time until after Christmas, which he agreed to do. Defendant left home, to go trapping, about the middle of December, and returned, as was expected, on the afternoon of December 23d. He claims that during this time the deceased made indecent proposals to Daisy Flory, defendant's wife, and raped her and committed incest upon her on the morning of December 23d. According to the testimony, defendant was not told thereof until later, although she immediately indicated to him that she did not want her father to stay longer and did not want him to move as had been planned. Deceased left on December 26th, first to visit at another place and then to go home. On January 3, 1928, defendant had occasion to go to Ostrum's place to get some poison for coyotes and to tell him not to move. During this time the deceased mentioned to defendant that he had discussed with Daisy the subject of not having any more children, and he gave defendant a package containing a silk sponge and three rubbers, used for prevention of conception, stating that while at Sheridan, a few days previously he had bought nine of them. Defendant had never discussed the subject with his wife, and when he arrived home and showed her the package, she was perturbed, exclaimed, "O, God!" and from that time to the morning of January 15th she gradually told him of the details of the indecent advances and rape above mentioned, telling the final scenes on the morning of the date last mentioned, and that deceased had said: "Don't be foolish and say anything about this." The defendant thereupon took his gun, as he was accustomed to do when going on trips, with the intention, as he testified, of going to deceased's home and getting an explanation of the latter's conduct. He stopped overnight at the house of Mr. Hudsonpillar, and the next morning went to the house of deceased, arriving there about 11 o'clock in the forenoon, finding the deceased at home. The house is nearly 24 feet square, entered by a door in the south into a large room occupying the whole of the south 13 feet. The north side of the house is divided between a kitchen, about 9×10 feet in area, in the northwest corner, and a storeroom in the northeast corner, each being connected with the large room by a door. No one else was there, and the only living witness to the tragedy is the defendant himself. He testified at length, and his testimony, condensed, is about as follows:

"I took the gun along in because I knew he was stouter than I and I knew he could handle me. I had no intentions when I went in of killing the man at all. He says 'Hello' to me, and I walked towards him, and I said 'What made you rape Daisy.' And he came right straight towards me. I looked at both hands, but he didn't have anything in them, and he says to me 'Let's talk it over,' and I says to him, 'Don't come any closer,' and he turned around and walked back, and I walked after him—to see what he was going to do, and when he got to the stove (in the northwest corner of the kitchen) he says 'Let's talk it over.' He was facing me in a stooped-over position and I says to him 'Charley, do you know you just about ruined my home?' And he says, 'I will keep the girl,' and when he said that, I says 'You are a pretty son of a bitch to keep your daughter.' I was thinking of some of the things he had done, was pretty nervous, and that man he just sprang after me, and when he did I jerked the rifle back, and just then I heard the report of the gun, and I saw him fall, and I turned around and went out. At no time did he deny he didn't rape his daughter. When I jerked the rifle back, I have no recollection of pulling the trigger with my finger. I didn't intend to shoot him when I jerked the rifle back, and it surprised me, and I turned around and went out. I had fear when he came at me. He had the meanest look in his face of any man I ever saw, and I knew he could handle me, if he got hold of me. I was giddy when I went out."

On cross-examination he testified, among other things:

"I was mad on my way over there and when I got there, but not any madder than any one else under the circumstances. I didn't tell Hudsonpillar I was going to Ostrum's. I didn't want to talk to him about it. I can't say that I was mad when I got to Hudsonpillar's. The gun was cocked when I took it out of the scabbard; I didn't examine it, but usually carry it with the safety on. I didn't rap when I went in. As I was opening the door, on the south, he showed up in the kitchen. I went right in; had the gun in the right hand. I walked towards the deceased; deceased was in the kitchen; I walked close to the kitchen door, keeping my eyes on deceased; I pointed the gun at him, when he came toward me the first time, and shouted at him 'Don't come any closer,' and he went back into the kitchen. I went next to the door. He had nothing in his hands, but when he sprang for me, I don't think so. I saw nothing in them. When he said 'I can keep the girl' it made me mad. I didn't take my eyes off Ostrum. I must have taken the safety off the gun when he rushed at me the first time. It looked like to me he was rushing for the rifle, and when he rushed towards me, I jerked the rifle, and that was when the shot was fired. I didn't intent to shoot him. The gun went off accidentally. I didn't intend to shoot him, and it got me so I couldn't stay there and look at him, I was intending to get away from him as he came toward me. I jerked the gun back and went backwards, and the gun went off. I was standing right in the door (leading to the kitchen). I knew he was dead the way he fell. I later gave myself up at Sheridan."

On re-examination he testified that he wept twice while going to Ostrum's. . . .

The defendant contends that the information given him by his wife as to the rape and incest committed upon her by the decedent so aroused his passions and deprived him of such self-control that his act cannot be held to be murder. The incest and rape, if true, could not justify the killing of the deceased. . . . But the evidence may be admissible for the purpose of mitigation and to reduce the crime to manslaughter. . . . The state contends that the testimony was not admissible in this case, because ample time—at least a day and probably longer—had elapsed after the defendant had been informed of the acts of decedent; further, that defendant's own testimony shows that when he was at Hudsonpillar's during the evening and night of January 15, 1928, his blood had cooled and he was no longer perturbed. Counsel for the defendant say that when he, on the morning of January 16th, met the deceased, and the latter did not deny the rape and said that he would keep his daughter, this was heaping insult upon injury and vividly recalled to defendant's mind what had been told him on the previous days. There is other testimony which shows to some extent at least that defendant's mind was perturbed on his way to Ostrum's. We are inclined to agree with defendant's contention. The crime of deceased, if true, was most heinous and was calculated to create a most violent passion in the mind of the defendant, and it is hardly to be expected that it would, as a matter of law, subside within so short a time, especially when, as testified, a situation arose by which past facts were clearly recalled. Courts are not altogether agreed as to whether the question of cooling time is one of law or one for the jury. Some hold it to be a question of law and that 24 hours is sufficient for the mind to cool. . . . We think, however, that the weight of authority is that, in cases like that at bar, the question of cooling time depends on the circumstances and is ordinarily one for the jury. . . .

In [State v. Thomas, 169 Iowa 591, 151 N.W. 842] it is said: "Where the want of provocation is so clear as to admit of no reasonable doubt that the alleged provocation could not have had any tendency to produce such state of mind in ordinary men, the evidence thereof should be excluded; but if there be a reasonable doubt as to whether the alleged provocation had such tendency, it is the safer rule to let the issue go to the jury under proper instructions. Of course, the reasonableness or adequacy of the provocation must depend on the facts of each particular case. In some cases, the courts declare that only actual personal knowledge of the wife's infidelity will extenuate the crime of killing by the husband to manslaughter.

. . . But others with better reason hold that information of the recent liaison of the wife with a paramour, reaching the husband for the first time, may be shown as likely to have thrown him into ungovernable passion. . . . The circumstances of each case necessarily must determine the admissibility of the evidence as well as its bearing on the different issues presented. Again, it is to be remarked that there is no definite time within which the passions when aroused by such a wrong may be said to have so far subsided and reason to have resumed its sway to such an extent as that thereafter the killing may be denounced as in vengeance alone. The question is one of reasonable time and dependent on all the facts of the case. While the time may be so long as to exclude all doubt on the subject and exact the exclusion of the evidence in so far as offered in extenuation, more frequently it should be submitted to the jury under proper instructions. . . ."

The court, in fact, permitted the defendant to show that the wife of the defendant told him of the commission of the rape and incest, but excluded all details, and collateral facts tending to show the state of the defendant's mind. In this we think there was error. While no cases discuss the point directly . . ., courts seem to have admitted the details told a defendant as a matter of course, and the reasons for that are plain. In the first place, a bare statement of the ultimate fact might give the jury the impression that it is fabricated, while a detailed statement might add credibility to the witness. Again, the pertinent inquiry is as to what was the condition of the defendant's mind as the result of what has been told him. In order to determine that, the jury must, mentally, be placed as near as possible in the position of the defendant, in order to be able to judge properly. Details of an atrocious character would be more apt to affect the mind of the defendant, just as details are more apt to affect the mind of any one else. . . . It is true of course, as argued, that the details might prejudice and inflame the minds of the jury; if so, the same details would be apt to inflame the mind of the defendant, and that is the very point that was to be determined by the jury. . . .

We have a case here, accordingly, in which we find that there is no error in the case, except as to the refusal to admit evidence which, if admitted, might have induced the jury to find the degree of the crime to be no greater than that of manslaughter. . . . [T]he state may elect by writing, filed in this case within 30 days, to take a new trial, in which event the judgment will be reversed and the cause remanded for a new trial. Unless that is done, the judgment will stand reversed as to murder in the second degree and affirmed for manslaughter, and the case will be remanded to the district court with direction to cause the prisoner to be brought before it to be resentenced for that crime, taking into consideration the time already served by the defendant, and to make all other necessary orders not inconsistent herewith.

Remanded, with directions.

BEDDER v. DIRECTOR OF PUBLIC PROSECUTIONS

House of Lords, 1954.
2 All Eng.R. 801.

LORD SIMONDS, L.C.: My Lords, this appeal raises once more a question of importance in the criminal law. Your Lordships, I think, agree with me that, on examination, the question appears to be amply covered by the highest authority, but the answer can usefully be restated.

The appellant, a youth of eighteen years, was convicted on May 27, 1954, at Leicester Assizes of the murder of Doreen Mary Redding, a prostitute. He appealed to the Court of Criminal Appeal on the substantial ground of misdirection, claiming that the learned judge who tried the case had wrongly directed the jury on the test of provocation and that, had they been rightly directed, they might have found him guilty not of murder but of manslaughter only. The Court of Criminal Appeal dismissed his appeal, holding that the jury had been rightly directed.

The relevant facts, so far as they bear on the question of provocation, can be shortly stated. The appellant has the misfortune to be sexually impotent, a fact which he naturally well knew and, according to his own evidence had allowed to prey on his mind. On the night of the crime he saw the prostitute with another man, and when they had parted, went and spoke to her and was led by her to a quiet court off a street in Leicester. There he attempted in vain to have intercourse with her whereupon—and I summarise the evidence in the way most favourable to him—she jeered at him and attempted to get away. He tried still to hold her and then she slapped him in the face and punched him in the stomach: he grabbed her shoulders and pushed her back from him whereat (I use his words),

"She kicked me in the privates. Whether it was her knee or foot, I do not know. After that I do not know what happened till she fell".

She fell, because he had taken a knife from his pocket and stabbed her with it twice, the second blow inflicting a mortal injury. It was in these circumstances that the appellant pleaded that there had been such provocation by the deceased as to reduce the crime from murder to manslaughter, and the question is whether the learned judge rightly directed the jury on this issue. In my opinion, the summing-up of the learned judge was impeccable. Adapting the language used in this House in the cases of Mancini v. Public Prosecutions Director, [1941] 3 All E.R. 272; and Holmes v. Public Prosecutions Director, [1946] 2 All E.R. 124 . . ., he thus directed the jury:

"Provocation would arise if the conduct of the deceased woman, Mrs. Redding, to the prisoner was such as would cause a reasonable person, and actually caused the person to lose his self-control suddenly and to drive him into such a passion and lack of self-control that he might use violence of the degree and nature which the prisoner used here. The provocation must be such as would reasonably justify the violence used, the use of a knife", . . . and a little later he addressed them thus:

"The reasonable person, the ordinary person, is the person you must consider when you are considering the effect which any acts, any conduct, any words, might have to justify the steps which were taken in response thereto, so that an unusually excitable or pugnacious individual, or a drunken one or a man who is sexually impotent is not entitled to rely on provocation which would not have led an ordinary person to have acted in the way which was in fact carried out. There may be, members of the jury, infirmity of mind and instability of character, but if it does not amount to insanity, it is no defence. Likewise infirmity of body or affliction of the mind of the assailant is not material in testing whether there has been provocation by the deceased to justify the violence used so as to reduce the act of killing to manslaughter. They must be tested throughout this by the reactions of a reasonable man to the acts, or series of acts, done by the deceased woman". . . .

My Lords, . . . I am at a loss to know what other direction than that which he gave could properly have been given by the learned judge to the jury in this case. The argument, as I understood it, for the appellant was that the jury, in considering the reaction of the hypothetical reasonable man to the acts of provocation, must not only place him in the circumstances in which the accused was placed, but must also invest him with the personal physical peculiarities of the accused. Learned counsel, who argued the case for the appellant with great ability, did not, I think, venture to say that he should be invested with mental or temperamental qualities which distinguished him from the reasonable man: for this would have been directly in conflict with . . . the recent decision of the House in Mancini's case which I have cited. But he urged that the reasonable man should be invested with the peculiar physical qualities of the accused, as in the present case with the characteristic of impotence, and the question should be asked: what would be the reaction of the impotent reasonable man in the circumstances? For that proposition I know of no authority: nor can I see any reason in it. It would be plainly illogical not to recognise an unusually excitable or pugnacious temperament in the accused as a matter to be taken into account but yet to recognise for that purpose some unusual physical characteristic, be it impotence or another. Moreover, the proposed distinction appears to me to ignore the fundamental fact that the temper of a man which leads him to react in such and such a way to provocation is, or may be, itself conditioned by some physical defect. It is too subtle a refinement for my mind or, I think, for that of a jury to grasp that the temper may be ignored but the physical defect taken into account.

It was urged on your Lordships that the hypothetical reasonable man must be confronted with all the same circumstances as the accused, and that this could not be fairly done unless he was also invested with the peculiar characteristics of the accused. But this makes nonsense of the test. Its purpose is to invite the jury to consider the act of the accused by reference to a certain standard or norm of conduct and with this object the "reasonable" or the "average" or the "normal" man is invoked. If the reasonable man is then deprived in whole or in part of his reason, or the normal man endowed with abnormal characteristics, the test ceases to have any value. This is precisely the consideration which led this House in Mancini's case to say that an unusually excitable or pugnacious person is not entitled to rely on provocation which would not have led an ordinary person to act as he did. In my opinion, then, the Court of Criminal Appeal was right in approving the direction given to the jury by the learned judge and this appeal must fail.

NOTES

1. While voluntary manslaughter has traditionally been defined as a "heat of passion" killing, the courts also recognize, as voluntary manslaughter, those killings which result from mutual quarrel or combat, as well as those which occur when a defendant kills the victim while unreasonably believing he is using justifiable deadly force. See, infra, Part C of this chapter.

In 1987, Illinois did away with its offense of voluntary manslaughter and renamed it murder in the second degree. For an extensive analysis of what prompted the change and the anticipated difficulties flowing from it, see Haddad, Second Degree Murder Replaces Voluntary Manslaughter in Illinois: Problems Solved, Problems Created, 19 Loyola U.L.J. 995 (1988).

2. The "Reasonable Person"

Compare the approach of the Lords in the *Bedder* case with the comments regarding provocation contained in the 1953 Report of the Royal Commission on Capital Punishment, pp. 51–53.

"[The proposal has been put before us that], in considering whether there is provocation sufficient to reduce the crime to manslaughter, the sole test should be whether the accused was in fact deprived of self-control and that the jury should not be required to consider also whether a 'reasonable man' would have been so deprived. . . .

"[The suggestion is] prompted by the feeling that objective tests of provocation are unsatisfactory and inequitable, and that the question whether a crime is murder or manslaughter ought to depend only on whether the accused did in fact commit it in ungovernable passion caused by sudden provocation, of whatever kind. . . .

"[The argument suggesting] that this test of the 'reasonable man' should be abolished . . . was simple and direct. This test, it is said, is inequitable. . . . As Mr. Nield put it, 'the jury should be permitted to determine the effect of the provocation on this particular man whom they have seen and may have heard and whose circumstances have probably been described to them.'

"This proposal was strongly opposed by the Judges who gave evidence before us. . . . Lord Cooper observed that if the existing rule was changed, 'there might be circumstances in which a bad-tempered man would be acquitted and a good-tempered man would be hanged, which, of course, is neither law nor sense.'

"We recognize the force of the Judge's objections. . . . We think that this argument is in principle sound, at least so far as minor abnormalities of character are concerned. . . .

"Nevertheless we feel sympathy with the view which prompted the proposal that provocation should be judged by the standard of the accused. The objections of the Judges take no account of that fundamental difference between the law of murder and the law applicable to all other crimes. . . . In the case of the other crimes the court can and does take account of extenuating circumstances in assessing the sentence; in the case of murder alone the sentence is fixed and automatic. Provocation is in essence only an extenuating circumstance. . . . The rule of law that provocation may, within narrow bounds, reduce murder to manslaughter, represents an attempt by the courts to reconcile the preservation of the fixed penalty for murder with a limited concession to natural human weakness, but it suffers from the common defects of a compromise. . . .

"We have indeed no doubt that if the criterion of the 'reasonable man' was strictly applied by the courts and the sentence of death was carried out in cases where it was so applied, it would be too harsh in its operation. In practice, however, the courts not infrequently give weight to factors personal to the prisoner in considering a plea of provocation, and where there is a conviction of murder such factors are taken into account by the Home Secretary and may often lead to commutation of the sentence. The application of the test does not therefore lead to any eventual miscarriage of justice. At the same time, as we have seen, there are serious objections of principle to its abrogation. In these circumstances we do not feel justified in recommending any change in the existing law."

For a provocative and thoughtful exploration of the topic, see Dressler, Rethinking Heat of Passion: A Defense In Search of a Rationale, 73 J.Crim.L. & Criminology 421 (1982).

3. Provocation

In situations where a homicide is committed in the heat of passion brought on by provoking circumstances, several types of provocation have traditionally been recognized as legally sufficient to reduce the grade of the homicide from murder to voluntary manslaughter.

(a) *Assault and Battery.* The law takes account of the possibility that an assault and battery may so provoke a "reasonable man" that he may lose his powers of reason and judgment and kill as a consequence. The states are not uniform, however, in their treatment of this type of provocation.

Some jurisdictions follow a flexible rule and regard assault alone as legally adequate provocation where the particular circumstances appear sufficient to excite the passions of a reasonable man. Thus, in Beasley v. State, 64 Miss. 518, 8 So. 234 (1886), adequate provocation was held to exist where the defendant shot the deceased after the latter had first fired at the defendant and then turned to run.

Other jurisdictions, notably Missouri, require an actual battery, as a matter of law, before sufficient provocation is deemed to exist. Under this rule, it was held, for example, that where the deceased had chased the defendant with an axe and then broke into the latter's house, threatening to kill him, the defendant, who shot the deceased, had no right to an instruction on voluntary manslaughter, since there had been no actual battery. State v. Kizer, 360 Mo. 744, 230 S.W.2d 690 (1950).

Ordinarily, a battery that is no more than "technical" is regarded as too slight to qualify as legal incitement to homicide. Commonwealth v. Cisneros, 381 Pa. 447, 113 A.2d 293 (1955). Moreover, a battery that is somewhat more than "technical" may occasionally be held insufficient as a matter of law where the court concludes that the provocation was insufficient under the circumstances to cause a reasonable person to kill. In Commonwealth v. Webb, 252 Pa. 187, 97 A. 189 (1916), the defendant's wife (5' 7"; 200+ lbs.) hit the defendant (6'; 165 lbs.) with a fifteen inch poker. He retaliated with five mortal razor slashes. The Supreme Court of Pennsylvania, after discussing the comparative sizes of defendant and his wife, and noting that the defendant was not left with a mark on his head from the blow he received, concluded that there was not adequate provocation for the homicide. Normally such considerations would probably be left to the jury; the court apparently felt, however, that the defendant's brutality was out of all proportion to the nature of the provocation.

(b) *Adultery.* Adultery, under common law principles, constituted sufficient provocation where a husband discovered his wife in the act of intercourse and kills either her or her paramour. Sheppard v. State, 243 Ala. 498, 10 So.2d 822 (1942). It had also been held that adequate provocation exists where a mistake of fact could lead to the homicide, as in the case of the husband finding his wife in suspicious circumstances and having a reasonable belief that she has committed adultery. State v. Yanz, 74 Conn. 177, 50 A. 37 (1901).

In marked contrast to the common law, under which paramour killings are manslaughter at least, several states had statutes, now repealed, which provided that such killings were *justifiable.* The following provision was contained in the Texas Penal Code (Vernon's Ann.P.C. art. 1220):

> Homicide is justifiable when committed by the husband upon one taken in the act of adultery with the wife, provided the killing takes place before the parties to the act have separated. Such circumstances cannot justify a homicide when it appears that there has been on the part of the husband, any connivance in or assent to the adulterous connection.

As interpreted in Price v. State, 18 Tex.App. 474 (1885), the above statement "taken in the act of adultery" did not mean that the husband must be an actual eyewitness to the physical act. "It is sufficient if he sees them in bed together, or leaving that position, or in such a position as indicates with reasonable certainty to a rational mind that they have just then committed the adulterous act, or were then about to commit it."

Although a husband in Texas, under this earlier law, was justified in killing his wife's paramour, there was no privilege to use a razor merely to maim and torture. Sensobaugh v. State, 92 Tex.Crim.R. 417, 244 S.W. 379 (App.1922). Also see Shaw v. State, 510 S.W.2d 926 (Tex.Crim.App.1974). Similar statutes were in effect in New Mexico and Utah, but they, along with the Texas statute, have been repealed.

Apart from other considerations behind the repeal of such adultery killing statutes, it will be observed that they accorded such "open season" privileges only to the husband; the wife was not accorded the same privilege as regards her adulterous husband. Clearly, this blatantly sexist approach, once so pervasive in the development of the criminal law, has no place in modern jurisprudence.

In today's society, ought the partial "heat of passion" defense, which reduces an intentional killing from murder to voluntary manslaughter upon reasonable provocation, also be extended to cover infidelity in connection with a long-standing romantic relationship in which the parties are not married? Equivocating on the issue, without resolving it, see People v. McCarthy, 132 Ill. 2d 331, 341, 138 Ill.Dec. 292, 302, 547 N.E.2d 459 (1989).

(c) *Trespass.* By one view, trespass constitutes legally sufficient provocation for a homicide committed in the heat of passion. Pearce v. State, 154 Fla. 656, 18 So.2d 754 (1944). Under another view, however, trespass is regarded as too minor an incident to qualify as legal incitement. People v. Free, 37 Ill.App. 3d 1050, 347 N.E.2d 505 (1976).

(d) *Acts Against Third Persons.* It is generally held that certain acts committed by one against a close relative of the slayer constitute sufficient provocation. See, e.g., People v. Rice, 351 Ill. 604, 184 N.E. 894 (1933) (murder or felonious injury); State v. Flory, 40 Wyo. 184, 276 P. 458 (1929) (rape); Toler v. State, 152 Tenn. 1, 260 S.W. 134 (1924) (seduction); State v. Burnett, 354 Mo. 45, 188 S.W.2d 51 (1945) (illegal arrest). In Commonwealth v. Paese, 220 Pa. 371, 69 A. 891 (1908), a severe beating of a friend was held to be insufficient as a matter of law, inasmuch as there was no family relationship between the slayer and the victim of the beating.

(e) *Words and Gestures.* Strongly entrenched in the United States is the almost uniform rule that words or gestures, alone, are never sufficient provocation for an intentional homicide. A few legislatures have altered this doctrine. See, e.g., People v. Valentine, 28 Cal.2d 121, 169 P.2d 1 (1946), and Elsmore v. State, 132 Tex.Crim.R. 261, 104 S.W.2d 493 (App.1937), interpreting legislative omission of former codification of the rule as abolishing it. For the most part, however, the states have firmly adhered to the rule, and the courts have rigidly applied it, often with harsh results. See, e.g., Freddo v. State, 127 Tenn. 376, 155 S.W. 170 (1913) (deceased intentionally and continuously used epithets which he knew were highly upsetting to the defendant); Commonwealth v. Cisneros, 381 Pa. 447, 113 A.2d 293 (1955) (deceased, defendant's estranged wife, refused reconciliation, explaining in strongly insulting terms that she would not live with or have children by one who was half-Mexican and half-Puerto Rican). Occasionally sufficient provocation is held to exist where the words or gestures are accompanied by a technical battery or other minor incident. See Lamp v. State, 38 Ga.App. 36, 142 S.E. 202 (1928); State v. Davis, 34 S.W.2d 133 (Mo.1930). Such additional aggravations, however, are not always permitted to alter the rule. See Commonwealth v. Cisneros, 381 Pa. 447, 113 A.2d 293 (1955).

Under one view, informational language, as opposed to words which in themselves constitute the incitement, may qualify as adequate provocation where the fact communicated would be sufficient, and where the slayer has not previously known of the matter revealed. See Commonwealth v. Berry, 461 Pa. 233, 336 A.2d 262 (1975); People v. Rice, 351 Ill. 604, 184 N.E. 894 (1933). Another view, however, does not admit of this exception. See Humphreys v. State, 175 Ga. 705, 165 S.E. 733 (1932).

Contemporary appraisal of the law concerning words as provocation indicates dissatisfaction with the inflexibility of a rule which fails to grant legal recognition to the inciting character of language which may be regarded as highly provoking by the general community. The 1953 Report of the Royal Commission on Capital Punishment, pp. 53–56, contains the following remarks on this subject:

"The suggestion is not new that the ancient rule excluding words and gestures from the scope of 'reasonable provocation' is itself unreasonable. . . . [I]t would appear that provocation by words is . . . admissible in most of the [countries of the Commonwealth]. We understand too that provocation, whether by assault or by words, would be regarded in most countries of Western Europe as a mitigating circumstance which might justify reduction of the maximum penalty for homicide. On the other hand we were informed that in the United States . . . it is the almost universal rule that words, no matter how opprobrious, will not constitute sufficient provocation.

"The witnesses in favour of admitting provocation based on words alone . . . thought it beyond doubt that words might constitute provocation as gross as blows, even to a reasonable man, and considered that the right course was to leave it to the jury to decide whether in any particular case the provocation was sufficient to reduce the crime to manslaughter. . . .

"We have no doubt that cases from time to time occur where words are grossly provocative and ought to be accepted as provocation sufficient to reduce murder to manslaughter. . . .

"Our conclusion is as follows: Where the jury is satisfied that the accused killed the deceased upon provocation, that he was deprived of his self-control as a result of that provocation and that a reasonable man might have been so deprived, the nature (as distinct from the degree) of the provocation should be immaterial and it should be open to them to return a verdict of manslaughter. . . . We fully recognise that words alone will seldom constitute adequate provocation to a reasonable man, but we agree with those witnesses who considered that the question whether such provocation was given is essentially one for the determination of the jury. We think that if the issue is left to the jury and they are allowed to consider each case on its merits, irrespective of whether the alleged provocation was by word or deed, they can be trusted to arrive at a just and reasonable decision and will not hesitate to convict the accused of murder where he has acted on only slight provocation, whether by words or otherwise."

Compare the Commission's conclusion with the provisions of Section 3 of the English Homicide Act of 1957, which provided as follows:

Provocation. Where on a charge of murder there is evidence on which the jury can find that the person charged was provoked (whether by things done or by things said or both together) to lose his self-control, the question whether the provocation was enough to make a reasonable man do as he did shall be left to be determined by the jury; and in determining that question the jury shall take into account everything both done and said according to the effect which, in their opinion, it would have on a reasonable man.

(This provision is unaffected by the 1965 act to be discussed subsequently.)

4. Cooling of Blood

Consider the following comments of the court in Ex parte Fraley, 3 Okl. Crim. 719, 109 P. 295 (1910), and compare them with the statements of the court on this subject in State v. Flory, supra, p. 512:

"[I]t was stated by counsel for the petitioner . . . that the deceased, some nine or ten months previously, had shot and killed the son of the petitioner . . . and it is urged here that when the petitioner saw the deceased . . . the recollection of that event must have engendered in him a passion which overcame him; that the killing was committed in the heat of such passion, was without premeditation, and therefore was not murder. To this we cannot assent. . . . In Ragland v. State . . ., four hours intervening between the provocation and the killing was held as a matter of law to be sufficient cooling time to preclude the reduction of a homicide to manslaughter. Perry v. State . . . and Rockmore v. State . . . each hold three days as a matter of law sufficient cooling time. Commonwealth v. Aiello . . . holds from one to two hours sufficient, and State v. Williams . . . holds fifteen minutes sufficient. And the authorities are all agreed that the question is not alone whether the defendant's passion in fact cooled, but also was there sufficient time in which the passion of a reasonable man would cool. If in fact the defendant's passion did cool, which may be shown by circumstances, such as the transaction of other business in the meantime, rational conversations upon other subjects, evidence of preparation for the killing, etc., then the length of time intervening is immaterial. But if in fact it did not cool yet if such time intervened between the provocation and the killing that the passion of the average man would have cooled and his reason have resumed its sway, then still there is not reduction of the homicide to manslaughter. . . . If the fatal wound be inflicted immediately following a sufficient provocation given, then the question as to whether the defendant's passion thereby aroused had in fact cooled, or as to whether or not such time had elapsed that the passion of a reasonable man would have cooled, is a question of fact to be determined upon a consideration of all the facts and circumstances in evidence; but when an unreasonable period of time has elapsed between the provocation and the killing, then the court is authorized to say as a matter of law that the cooling time was sufficient."

Also see Farr v. State, 54 Ala.App. 80, 304 So.2d 898 (1974).

With regard to the application of the "reasonable man" test in this area, compare the following statement of the court in State v. Hazlett, 16 N.D. 426, 113 N.W. 374 (1907):

"Where the evidence shows that a homicide was committed, in the heat of passion and with provocation, we think the jury, in determining whether there was sufficient cooling time for the passion to subside and reason to resume its sway, should be governed, not by the standard of an ideal, reasonable man, but they should determine such question from the standpoint of the defendant in the light of all the facts and circumstances disclosed by the evidence. . . . We are aware that some courts have held to the contrary, but we are convinced that the rule as above announced is the more reasonable and just one."

C. JUSTIFIABLE USE OF DEADLY FORCE

1. SELF DEFENSE

PEOPLE v. GOETZ

Court of Appeals of New York, 1986.
68 N.Y.2d 96, 506 N.Y.S.2d 18, 497 N.E.2d 41.

CHIEF JUDGE WACHTLER.

A Grand Jury has indicted defendant on attempted murder, assault, and other charges for having shot and wounded four youths on a New York City subway train after one or two of the youths approached him and asked for $5. The lower courts, concluding that the prosecutor's charge to the Grand Jury on the defense of justification was erroneous, have dismissed the attempted murder, assault and weapons possession charges. We now reverse and reinstate all counts of the indictment.

I.

The precise circumstances of the incident giving rise to the charges against defendant are disputed, and ultimately it will be for a trial jury to determine what occurred. We feel it necessary, however, to provide some factual background to properly frame the legal issues before us. Accordingly, we have summarized the facts as they appear from the evidence before the Grand Jury. We stress, however, that we do not purport to reach any conclusions or holding as to exactly what transpired or whether defendant is blameworthy. The credibility of witnesses and the reasonableness of defendant's conduct are to be resolved by the trial jury.

On Saturday afternoon, December 22, 1984, Troy Canty, Darryl Cabey, James Ramseur, and Barry Allen boarded an IRT express subway train in The Bronx and headed south toward lower Manhattan.

The four youths rode together in the rear portion of the seventh car of the train. Two of the four, Ramseur and Cabey, had screwdrivers inside their coats, which they said were to be used to break into the coin boxes of video machines.

Defendant Bernhard Goetz boarded this subway train at 14th Street in Manhattan and sat down on a bench towards the rear section of the same car occupied by the four youths. Goetz was carrying an unlicensed .38 caliber pistol loaded with five rounds of ammunition in a waistband holster. The train left the 14th Street station and headed towards Chambers Street.

It appears from the evidence before the Grand Jury that Canty approached Goetz, possibly with Allen beside him, and stated "give me five dollars". Neither Canty nor any of the other youths displayed a weapon. Goetz responded by standing up, pulling out his handgun and firing four shots in rapid succession. The first shot hit Canty in the chest; the second struck Allen in the back; the third went through Ramseur's arm and into his left side; the fourth was fired at Cabey, who apparently was then standing in the corner of the car, but missed, deflecting instead off of a wall of the conductor's cab. After Goetz briefly surveyed the scene around him, he fired another shot at Cabey, who then was sitting on the end bench of the car. The bullet entered the rear of Cabey's side and severed his spinal cord.

All but two of the other passengers fled the car when, or immediately after, the shots were fired. The conductor, who had been in the next car, heard the shots and instructed the motorman to radio for emergency assistance. The conductor then went into the car where the shooting occurred and saw Goetz sitting on a bench, the injured youths lying on the floor or slumped against a seat, and two women who had apparently taken cover, also lying on the floor. Goetz told the conductor that the four youths had tried to rob him.

While the conductor was aiding the youths, Goetz headed towards the front of the car. The train had stopped just before the Chambers Street station and Goetz went between two of the cars, jumped onto the tracks and fled. Police and ambulance crews arrived at the scene shortly thereafter. Ramseur and Canty, initially listed in critical condition, have fully recovered. Cabey remains paralyzed, and has suffered some degree of brain damage.

On December 31, 1984, Goetz surrendered to police in Concord, New Hampshire, identifying himself as the gunman being sought for the subway shootings in New York nine days earlier. Later that day, after receiving *Miranda* warnings, he made two lengthy statements, both of which were tape recorded with his permission. In the statements, which are substantially similar, Goetz admitted that he had been illegally carrying a handgun in New York City for three years. He stated that he had first purchased a gun in 1981 after he had been injured in a mugging. Goetz also revealed that twice between 1981 and

1984 he had successfully warded off assailants simply by displaying the pistol.

According to Goetz's statement, the first contact he had with the four youths came when Canty, sitting or lying on the bench across from him, asked "how are you," to which he replied "fine". Shortly thereafter, Canty, followed by one of the other youths, walked over to the defendant and stood to his left, while the other two youths remained to his right, in the corner of the subway car. Canty then said "give me five dollars". Goetz stated that he knew from the smile on Canty's face that they wanted to "play with me". Although he was certain that none of the youths had a gun, he had a fear, based on prior experiences, of being "maimed".

Goetz then established "a pattern of fire," deciding specifically to fire from left to right. His stated intention at that point was to "murder [the four youths], to hurt them, to make them suffer as much as possible". When Canty again requested money, Goetz stood up, drew his weapon, and began firing, aiming for the center of the body of each of the four. Goetz recalled that the first two he shot "tried to run through the crowd [but] they had nowhere to run". Goetz then turned to his right to "go after the other two". One of these two "tried to run through the wall of the train, but * * * he had nowhere to go". The other youth (Cabey) "tried pretending that he wasn't with [the others]" by standing still, holding on to one of the subway hand straps, and not looking at Goetz. Goetz nonetheless fired his fourth shot at him. He then ran back to the first two youths to make sure they had been "taken care of". Seeing that they had both been shot, he spun back to check on the latter two. Goetz noticed that the youth who had been standing still was now sitting on a bench and seemed unhurt. As Goetz told the police, "I said '[y]ou seem to be all right, here's another' ", and he then fired the shot which severed Cabey's spinal cord. Goetz added that "if I was a little more under self-control * * * I would have put the barrel against his forehead and fired." He also admitted that "if I had had more [bullets], I would have shot them again, and again, and again."

II.

After waiving extradition, Goetz was brought back to New York and arraigned on a felony complaint charging him with attempted murder and criminal possession of a weapon. The matter was presented to a Grand Jury in January 1985, with the prosecutor seeking an indictment for attempted murder, assault, reckless endangerment, and criminal possession of a weapon. Neither the defendant nor any of the wounded youths testified before this Grand Jury. On January 25, 1985, the Grand Jury indicted defendant on one count of criminal possession of a weapon in the third degree (Penal Law § 265.02), for possessing the gun used in the subway shootings, and two counts of criminal possession of a weapon in the fourth degree (Penal Law § 265.01), for possessing two other guns in his apartment building. It dismissed, however, the attempted murder and other charges stemming from the shootings themselves.

Several weeks after the Grand Jury's action, the People, asserting that they had newly available evidence, moved for an order authorizing them to resubmit the dismissed charges to a second Grand Jury. . . . Presentation of the case to the second Grand Jury began on March 14, 1985. Two of the four youths, Canty and Ramseur, testified. Among the other witnesses were four passengers from the seventh car of the subway who had seen some portions of the incident. Goetz again chose not to testify, though the tapes of his two statements were played for the grand jurors, as had been done with the first Grand Jury.

On March 27, 1985, the second Grand Jury filed a 10–count indictment, containing four charges of attempted murder, four charges of assault in the first degree, one charge of reckless endangerment in the first degree, and one charge of criminal possession of a weapon in the second degree [possession of loaded firearm with intent to use it unlawfully against another]. . . .

On October 14, 1985, Goetz moved to dismiss the charges contained in the second indictment. . . .

On November 25, 1985, while the motion to dismiss was pending before Criminal Term, a column appeared in the New York Daily News containing an interview which the columnist had conducted with Darryl Cabey the previous day in Cabey's hospital room. The columnist claimed that Cabey had told him in this interview that the other three youths had all approached Goetz with the intention of robbing him. The day after the column was published, a New York City police officer informed the prosecutor that he had been one of the first police officers to enter the subway car after the shootings, and that Canty had said to him "we were going to rob [Goetz]". The prosecutor immediately disclosed this information to the court and to defense counsel, adding that this was the first time his office had been told of this alleged statement and that none of the police reports filed on the incident contained any such information. . . .

In an order dated January 21, 1986, Criminal Term granted Goetz's motion to the extent that it dismissed all counts of the second indictment, other than the reckless endangerment charge, . . .

* * *

On appeal by the People, a divided Appellate Division affirmed Criminal Term's dismissal of the charges. . . .

* * *

Justice Asch granted the People leave to appeal to this court. . . .

III.

Penal Law article 35 recognizes the defense of justification, which "permits the use of force under certain circumstances". One such set of circumstances pertains to the use of force in defense of a person, encompassing both self-defense and defense of a third person (Penal Law § 35.15). Penal Law § 35.15(1) sets forth the general principles governing all such uses of force: "[a] person may * * * use physical force upon another person when and to the extent he *reasonably believes* such to be necessary to defend himself or a third person from what he *reasonably believes* to be the use or imminent use of unlawful physical force by such other person" (emphasis added).

Section 35.15(2) sets forth further limitations on these general principles with respect to the use of "deadly physical force": "A person may not use deadly physical force upon another person under circumstances specified in subdivision one unless (a) He *reasonably believes* that such other person is using or about to use deadly physical force * * * or (b) He *reasonably believes* that such other person is committing or attempting to commit a kidnapping, forcible rape, forcible sodomy or robbery" (emphasis added).

Thus, consistent with most justification provisions, Penal Law § 35.15 permits the use of deadly physical force only where requirements as to triggering conditions and the necessity of a particular response are met. As to the triggering conditions, the statute requires that the actor "reasonably believes" that another person either is using or about to use deadly physical force or is committing or attempting to commit one of certain enumerated felonies, including robbery. As to the need for the use of deadly physical force as a response, the statute requires that the actor "reasonably believes" that such force is necessary to avert the perceived threat.

Because the evidence before the second Grand Jury included statements by Goetz that he acted to protect himself from being maimed or to avert a robbery, the prosecutor correctly chose to charge the justification defense in section 35.15 to the Grand Jury. The prosecutor properly instructed the grand jurors to consider whether the use of deadly physical force was justified to prevent either serious physical injury or a robbery, and, in doing so, to separately analyze the defense with respect to each of the charges. He elaborated upon the prerequisites for the use of deadly physical force essentially by reading or paraphrasing the language in Penal Law § 35.15. The defense does not contend that he committed any error in this portion of the charge.

When the prosecutor had completed his charge, one of the grand jurors asked for clarification of the term "reasonably believes". The prosecutor responded by instructing the grand jurors that they were to consider the circumstances of the incident and determine "whether the defendant's conduct was that of a reasonable man in the defendant's situation". It is this response by the prosecutor—and specifically his use of "a reasonable man"—which is the basis for the dismissal of the charges by the lower courts. As expressed repeatedly in the Appellate Division's plurality opinion, because section 35.15 uses the term "*he reasonably believes*", the appropriate test, according to that court, is whether a defendant's beliefs and reactions were "reasonable to *him*". Under that reading of the statute, a jury which believed a defendant's testimony that he felt that his own actions were warranted and were reasonable would have to acquit him, regardless of what anyone else in defendant's situation might have concluded. Such an interpretation defies the ordinary meaning and significance of the term "reasonably" in a statute, and misconstrues the clear intent of the Legislature, in enacting section 35.15, to retain an objective element as part of any provision authorizing the use of deadly physical force.

Penal statutes in New York have long codified the right recognized at common law to use deadly physical force, under appropriate circumstances, in self-defense. These provisions have never required that an actor's belief as to the intention of another person to inflict serious injury be correct in order for the use of deadly force to be justified, but they have uniformly required that the belief comport with an objective notion of reasonableness. The 1829 statute, using language which was followed almost in its entirety until the 1965 recodification of the Penal Law, provided that the use of deadly force was justified in self-defense or in the defense of specified third persons "when there shall be a reasonable ground to apprehend a design to commit a felony, or to do some great personal injury, and there shall be imminent danger of such design being accomplished".

In Shorter v. People, 2 N.Y. 193, we emphasized that deadly force could be justified under the statute even if the actor's beliefs as to the intentions of another turned out to be wrong, but noted there had to be a reasonable basis, viewed objectively, for the beliefs. We explicitly rejected the position that the defendant's own belief that the use of deadly force was necessary sufficed to justify such force regardless of the reasonableness of the beliefs.

In 1881, New York reexamined the many criminal provisions set forth in the revised statutes and enacted, for the first time, a separate Penal Code (see generally, 1937 Report of NY Law Rev Commn, Communication to Legislature Relating to Homicide, at 525, 529 [hereafter cited as Communication Relating to Homicide]). The provision in the 1881 Penal Code for the use of deadly force in self-defense or to defend a third person was virtually a reenactment of the language in the 1829 statutes, and the "reasonable ground" requirement was maintained.

The 1909 Penal Law replaced the 1881 Penal Code. The language of section 205 of the 1881 code pertaining to the use of deadly force in self-defense or in defense of a third person was reenacted, verbatim, as part of section 1055 of the new Penal Law. Several cases from this court interpreting the 1909 provision demonstrate unmistakably that an objective element of reasonableness was a vital part of any claim of self-defense. . . .

Accordingly, the Law Revision Commission, in a 1937 Report to the Legislature on the Law of Homicide in New York, summarized the self-defense statute as requiring a "reasonable belief in the imminence of danger", and stated that the standard to be followed by a jury in determining whether a belief was reasonable "is that of a man of ordinary courage in the circumstances surrounding the defendant at the time of the killing" (Communication Relating to Homicide, op. cit., at 814). The Report added that New York did not follow the view, adopted in a few States, that "the jury is required to adopt the subjective view and judge from the standpoint of the very defendant concerned."

In 1961 the Legislature established a Commission to undertake a complete revision of the Penal Law and the Criminal Code. The impetus for the decision to update the Penal Law came in part from the drafting of the Model Penal Code by the American Law Institute, as well as from the fact that the existing law was poorly organized and in many aspects antiquated. Following the submission by the Commission of several reports and proposals, the Legislature approved the present Penal Law in 1965 (L.1965, ch. 1030), and it became effective on September 1, 1967. The drafting of the general provisions of the new Penal Law, including the article on justification, was particularly influenced by the Model Penal Code. While using the Model Penal Code provisions on justification as general guidelines, however, the drafters of the new Penal Law did not simply adopt them verbatim.

The provisions of the Model Penal Code with respect to the use of deadly force in self-defense reflect the position of its drafters that any culpability which arises from a mistaken belief in the need to use such force should be no greater than the culpability such a mistake would give rise to if it were made with respect to an element of a crime (see, ALI, Model Penal Code and Commentaries, part I, at 32, 34 [hereafter cited as MPC Commentaries]. Accordingly, under Model Penal Code § 3.04(2)(b), a defendant charged with murder (or attempted murder) need only show that he "*believe[d]* that [the use of deadly force] was necessary to protect himself against death, serious bodily injury, kidnapping or [forcible] sexual intercourse" to prevail on a self-defense claim (emphasis added). If the defendant's belief was wrong, and was recklessly, or negligently formed, however, he may be convicted of the type of homicide charge requiring only a reckless or negligent, as the case may be, criminal intent (see, Model Penal Code § 3.09[2]; MPC Commentaries, op. cit., part I, at 32, 150).

The drafters of the Model Penal Code recognized that the wholly subjective test set forth in section 3.04 differed from the existing law in most States by its omission of any requirement of reasonableness (see, MPC Commentaries, op. cit., part I, at 35; LaFave & Scott, Criminal Law § 53, at 393–394). The drafters were also keenly aware that requiring that the actor have a "reasonable belief" rather than just a "belief" would alter the wholly subjective test (MPC Commentaries, op. cit., part I, at 35–36). This basic distinction was recognized years earlier by the New York Law Revision Commission and continues to be noted by the commentators. Note, Justification: The Impact of the Model Penal Code on Statutory Reform, 75 Colum L Rev 914, 918–920).

New York did not follow the Model Penal Code's equation of a mistake as to the need to use deadly force with a mistake negating an element of a crime, choosing instead to use a single statutory section which would provide either a complete defense or no defense at all to a defendant charged with any crime involving the use of deadly force. The drafters of the new Penal Law adopted in large part the structure and content of Model Penal Code § 3.04, but, crucially, inserted the word "reasonably" before "believes".

The plurality below agreed with defendant's argument that the change in the statutory language from "reasonable ground," used prior to 1965, to "he reasonably believes" in Penal Law § 35.15 evinced a legislative intent to conform to the subjective standard contained in Model Penal Code § 3.04. This argument, however, ignores the plain significance of the insertion of "reasonably". Had the drafters of section 35.15 wanted to adopt a subjective standard, they could have simply used the language of section 3.04. "Believes" by itself requires an honest or genuine belief by a defendant as to the need to use deadly force. Interpreting the statute to require only that the defendant's belief was "reasonable to *him*," as done by the plurality below, would hardly be different from requiring only a genuine belief; in either case, the defendant's own perceptions could completely exonerate him from any criminal liability.

We cannot lightly impute to the Legislature an intent to fundamentally alter the principles of justification to allow the perpetrator of a serious crime to go free simply because that person believed his actions were reasonable and necessary to prevent some perceived harm. To completely exonerate such an individual, no matter how aberrational or bizarre his thought patterns, would allow citizens to set their own standards for the permissible use of force. It would also allow a legally competent defendant suffering from delusions to kill or perform acts of violence with impunity, contrary to fundamental principles of justice and criminal law.

We can only conclude that the Legislature retained a reasonableness requirement to avoid giving a license for such actions. The plurality's interpretation, as the dissenters below recognized, excises the impact of the word "reasonably". . . .

The change from "reasonable ground" to "reasonably believes" is better explained by the fact that the drafters of section 35.15 were proposing a single section which, for the first time, would govern both the use of ordinary force and deadly force in self-defense or defense of another. Under the 1909 Penal Law and its predecessors, the use of ordinary force was governed by separate sections which, at least by their literal terms, required that the defendant was *in fact* responding to an unlawful assault, and not just that he had a reasonable ground for believing that such an assault was occurring. Following the example of the Model Penal Code, the drafters of section 35.15 eliminated this sharp dichotomy between the use of ordinary force and deadly force in defense of a person. Not surprisingly then, the integrated section reflects the wording of Model Penal Code § 3.04, with the addition of "reasonably" to incorporate the long-standing requirement of "reasonable ground" for the use of deadly force and apply it to the use of ordinary force as well.

The conclusion that section 35.15 retains an objective element to justify the use of deadly force is buttressed by the statements of its drafters. The executive director and counsel to the Commission which revised the Penal Law have stated that the provisions of the statute with respect to the use of deadly physical force largely conformed with the prior law, with the only changes they noted not being relevant here (Denzer & McQuillan, Practice Commentary, McKinney's Cons.Laws of N.Y., Book 39, Penal Law § 35.15, p. 63 [1967]). Nowhere in the legislative history is there any indication that "reasonably believes" was designed to change the law on the use of deadly force or establish a subjective standard. To the contrary, the Commission, in the staff comment governing arrests by police officers, specifically equated "[he] reasonably believes" with having a reasonable ground for believing (Penal Law § 35.30; Fourth Interim Report of the Temporary State Commission on Revision of the Penal Law and Criminal Code at 17–18, 1965 NY Legis Doc No. 25).

Statutes or rules of law requiring a person to act "reasonably" or to have a "reasonable belief" uniformly prescribe conduct meeting an objective standard measured with reference to how "a reasonable person" could have acted . . .

In People v. Collice, 41 N.Y.2d 906, 394 N.Y.S.2d 615, 363 N.E.2d 340, we rejected the position that section 35.15 contains a wholly subjective standard. The defendant in *Collice* asserted, on appeal, that the trial court had erred in refusing to charge the justification defense. We upheld the trial court's action because we concluded that, even if the defendant had actually believed that he was threatened with the imminent use of deadly physical force, the evidence clearly indicated that "his reactions were not those of a reasonable man acting in self-defense". Numerous decisions from other States interpreting "reasonably believes" in justification statutes enacted subsequent to the drafting of the Model Penal Code are consistent with *Collice,* as they hold that such language refers to what a reasonable person could have believed under the same circumstances.

The defense contends that our memorandum in *Collice* is inconsistent with our prior opinion in People v. Miller, 39 N.Y.2d 543, 384 N.Y.S.2d 741, 349 N.E.2d 841. In *Miller,* we held that a defendant charged with homicide could introduce, in support of a claim of self-defense, evidence of prior acts of violence committed by the deceased of which the defendant had knowledge. The defense, as well as the plurality below, place great emphasis on the statement in *Miller* that "the crucial fact at issue [is] the state of mind of the defendant". This language, however, in no way indicates that a wholly subjective test is appropriate. To begin, it is undisputed that section 35.15 does contain a subjective element, namely that the defendant believed that deadly force was necessary to avert the imminent use of deadly force or the commission of certain felonies. Evidence that the defendant knew of prior acts of violence by the deceased could help establish his requisite beliefs. Moreover, such knowledge would also be relevant on the issue of reasonableness, as the jury must consider the circumstances a defendant found himself in, which would include any relevant knowledge of the nature of persons confronting him. Finally, in *Miller,* we specifically recognized that there had to be "reasonable grounds" for the defendant's belief.

* * *

Goetz also argues that the introduction of an objective element will preclude a jury from considering factors such as the prior experiences of a given actor and thus, require it to make a determination of "reasonableness" without regard to the actual circumstances of a particular incident. This argument, however, falsely presupposes that an objective standard means that the background and other relevant characteristics of a particular actor must be ignored. To the contrary, we have frequently noted that a determination of reasonableness must be based on the "circumstances" facing a defendant or his "situation". Such terms encompass more than the physical movements of the potential assailant. As just discussed, these terms include any relevant knowledge the defendant had about that person. They also necessarily bring in the physical attributes of all persons involved, including the defendant. Furthermore, the defendant's circumstances encompass any prior experiences he had which could provide a reasonable basis for a belief that another person's intentions were to injure or rob him or that the use of deadly force was necessary under the circumstances.

Accordingly, a jury should be instructed to consider this type of evidence in weighing the defendant's actions. The jury must first determine whether the defendant had the requisite beliefs under section 35.15, that is, whether he believed deadly force was necessary to avert the imminent use of deadly force or the commission of one of the felonies enumerated therein. If the People do not prove beyond a reasonable doubt that he did not have such beliefs, then the jury must also consider whether these beliefs were reasonable. The jury would have to determine, in light of all the "circumstances", as explicated above, if a reasonable person could have had these beliefs.

The prosecutor's instruction to the second Grand Jury that it had to determine whether, under the circumstances, Goetz's conduct was that of a reasonable man in his situation was thus essentially an accurate charge. It is true that the prosecutor did not elaborate on the meaning of "circumstances" or "situation" and inform the grand jurors that they could consider, for example, the prior experiences Goetz related in his statement to the police. We have held, however, that a Grand Jury need not be instructed on the law with the same degree of precision as the petit jury. This lesser standard is premised upon the different functions of the Grand Jury and the petit jury: the former determines whether sufficient evidence exists to accuse a person of a crime and thereby subject him to criminal prosecution; the latter ultimately determines the guilt or innocence of the accused, and may convict only where the People have proven his guilt beyond a reasonable doubt.

* * *

IV.

Criminal Term's second ground for dismissal of the charges, premised upon the *Daily News* column and the police officer's statement to the prosecutor, can be rejected more summarily. The court relied upon People v. Pelchat, 62 N.Y.2d 97, 476 N.Y.S.2d 79, 464 N.E.2d 447, supra, the facts of which, however, are markedly different from those here. In *Pelchat,* the defendant was one of 21 persons arrested in a house to which police officers had seen marihuana delivered. The only evidence before the Grand Jury showing that defendant had anything to do with the marihuana was the testimony of a police officer listing defendant as one of 21 persons he had observed transporting the drug. After defendant was indicted, this same police officer told the prosecutor that he had misunderstood his question when testifying before the Grand Jury and that he had not seen defendant engage in any criminal activity. Although the prosecutor knew that there was no other evidence before the Grand Jury to establish the defendant's guilt, he did not disclose the police officer's admission, and instead, accepted a guilty plea from the defendant. We reversed the conviction and dismissed the indictment, holding that the prosecutor should not have allowed the proceedings against defendant to continue when he knew that the only evidence against him before the Grand Jury was false, and thus, knew that there was not legally sufficient evidence to support the indictment.

Here, in contrast, Canty and Ramseur have not recanted any of their Grand Jury testimony or told the prosecutor that they misunderstood any questions. Instead, all that has come to light is hearsay evidence that conflicts with part of Canty's testimony. There is no statute or controlling case law requiring dismissal of an indictment merely because, months later, the prosecutor becomes aware of some information which may lead to the defendant's acquittal. There was no basis for the Criminal Term Justice to speculate as to whether Canty's and Ramseur's testimony was perjurious, and his conclusion that the testimony "strongly appeared" to be perjured is particularly inappropriate given the nature of the "evidence" he relied upon to reach such a conclusion and that he was not in the Grand Jury room when the two youths testified.

Moreover, unlike *Pelchat*, the testimony of Canty and Ramseur was not the only evidence before the Grand Jury establishing that the offenses submitted to that body were committed by Goetz. Goetz's own statements, together with the testimony of the passengers, clearly support the elements of the crimes charged, and provide ample basis for concluding that a trial of this matter is needed to determine whether Goetz could have reasonably believed that he was about to be robbed or seriously injured and whether it was reasonably necessary for him to shoot four youths to avert any such threat.

Accordingly, the order of the Appellate Division should be reversed, and the dismissed counts of the indictment reinstated.

MEYER, SIMONS, KAYE, ALEXANDER, TITONE and HANCOCK, JJ., concur.

Order reversed, etc.

NOTES

1. For a comment on the principal case, see, Note, The Proper Standard for Self–Defense In New York: Should People v. Goetz Be Viewed As Judicial Legislation or Judicial Restraint?", 39 Syracuse L.Rev. 845 (1988).

2. The use of force to defend one's self is an undisputed right. It is only with respect to the manner in which he does it, or the circumstances under which it occurs, that there are differences and uncertainties in the law. For instance, when a person who is free from fault is faced with a threat of great bodily danger, may he stand his ground and kill his assailant, or is he under an obligation to retreat?

The American Law Institute, in its Model Penal Code provides (in § 3.04 of its Tentative Draft No. 8) that:

> The use of deadly force is not justifiable . . . if the actor knows . . . that he can avoid the necessity of using such force with complete safety by retreating or by surrendering possession of a thing to a person asserting a claim of right thereto or by complying with a demand that he abstain from any action which he has no duty to take, except that:
>
> (1) the actor is not obliged to retreat from his dwelling or place of work, unless he was the initial aggressor . . .

In adopting the "retreat to the wall" doctrine the drafters of the code, in their commentary, offer the following justification (ibid. p. 23):

"There is a sense in which a duty to retreat may be regarded as a logical derivative of the underlying justifying principle of self-defense, belief in the necessity of the protective action; the actor who knows he can retreat with safety also knows that the necessity can be avoided in that way. The logic of this position never has been accepted when moderate force is used in self-defense; here all agree that the actor may stand his ground and estimate necessity upon that basis. When the resort is to deadly force, however, Beale argued that the common law was otherwise, that the law of homicide demanded that the estimation of necessity take account of the possibility of safe retreat. . . . Perkins has challenged this conclusion in the case of actors free from fault in bringing on the struggle, urging that it was only true with respect to aggressors or cases of mutual combat. . . . American jurisdictions have divided on the question, no less in crime than tort, with the preponderant position favoring the right to stand one's ground. . . . In a famous opinion Justice Holmes advanced what seems to be a median position: 'Rationally the failure to retreat is a circumstance to be considered with all the others in order to determine whether the defendant went farther than he was justified in doing; not a categorical proof of guilt.' . . . This would apparently remit the issue to the jury, without a legal mandate on the point. . . .

"The Institute has deemed considerations of this kind decisive with respect to torts and it is clear that they apply with equal force to penal law."

In rejecting the rationale of the retreat rule, Mr. Justice Holmes said this is an early case:

"Rationally, the failure to retreat is a circumstance to be considered with all the others in order to determine whether the defendant went farther than he was justified in doing; not a categorical proof of guilt. The law has grown, and even if historical mistakes have contributed to its growth, it has tended in the direction of rules consistent with human nature. Many respectable writers agree that if a man reasonably believes that he is in immediate danger of death or grievous bodily harm from his assailant, he may stand his ground, and that if he kills him, he has not exceeded the bounds of lawful self-defense. That has been the decision of this court. . . . Detached reflection cannot be demanded in the presence of an uplifted knife. Therefore, in this court, at least, it is not a condition of immunity that one in that situation should pause to consider whether a reasonable man might not think it possible to fly with safety, or to disable his assailant rather than to kill him." [1]

The majority of states permit one to stand his own ground and meet force with force, as long as the defender is not the original aggressor.[2]

Even in those jurisdictions following the so-called "true man" rule that permits a self-defender to stand his ground, a person who "brings on the difficulty" will find that his self-defense right becomes an "imperfect" one. He may then be required to retreat before he can excusably kill, even though he used non-deadly force at the outset; and under some circumstances he is completely foreclosed and must settle, as a minimum, for a manslaughter conviction.[3]

3. What if a defendant acted with an "imperfect" self defense? That is, she acted under a subjective belief that the use of deadly force was necessary to prevent death or great bodily harm from occurring, but that belief was not objectively reasonable?

In Faulkner v. State, 54 Md.App. 113, 458 A.2d 81 (1983), it was said that this defense "requires no more than a subjective honest belief on the part of the killer that his actions were necessary for his safety, even though, on an objective appraisal by a reasonable man, they would not be found to be so. If established, the killer remains culpable and his actions are excused only to the

1. Brown v. United States, 256 U.S. 335, 343, 41 S.Ct. 501, 502 (1921).

2. LaFave & Scott, Criminal Law, 1972, at 395.

The early history of the "retreat to the wall" concept is traced in Inbau, Firearms and Legal Doctrine, 7 Tulane L.Rev. 529 (1933) at pp. 531–536.

3. For a general discussion of the "perfect" as well as the "imperfect" right to self-defense, consult Perkins, Self–Defense Re–Examined, 1 U.C.L.A.L.Rev. 133, 154–159 (1954).

extent that mitigation is invoked. The mitigating effect of imperfect self defense is to negate malice. It therefore serves not only to reduce murder to manslaughter in the case of a felonious homicide but applies also to the felony of assault with intent to murder." In dissent, Judge Lowe concluded that "The criminal law as an instrument of societal control cannot allow violence to be excused solely upon the whims of the perpetrator."

In a carefully reasoned opinion, and after examining all of the cases and statutes of other jurisdictions, the Maryland Court of Appeals came to the same conclusion as did the majority of the Court of Special Appeals, permitting the imperfect self defense to be used as a defense to murder to achieve, as the result, a conviction of manslaughter instead. See, State v. Faulkner, 301 Md. 482, 483 A.2d 759 (1984).

WERNER v. STATE
Court of Criminal Appeals of Texas, 1986.
711 S.W.2d 639.

Before the court en banc.

OPINION ON APPELLANT'S PETITION FOR DISCRETIONARY REVIEW

ONION, PRESIDING JUDGE.

A jury found appellant guilty of murder and assessed punishment at 10 years' confinement in the Department of Corrections.

The evidence showed that appellant shot and killed Tarbell Griffin Travis, after Travis allegedly damaged an automobile owned by appellant's friend, Kenneth Netterville.

On appeal the appellant raised four grounds of error, the second of which contended the trial court erred in refusing to allow him to introduce certain evidence on the condition of his mind "at the time of the offense" by virtue of the testimony of two police officers and a psychiatrist. The Court of Appeals found the excluded evidence was not relevant to any issue and overruled ground of error number two. Likewise the Court of Appeals rejected the other grounds of error and affirmed the conviction. We granted appellant's petition to determine whether the Court of Appeals was correct in overruling the second ground of error relating to the Holocaust syndrome.

The facts form the necessary backdrop for a discussion of appellant's contention. The 21–year–old appellant left work about 10:45 p.m. on April 1, 1982. He bought a six pack of beer and about 11 p.m. went to the Netterville residence on Stillbrooke in Houston to see Kenneth Netterville. Approximately 45 minutes later while he was on the porch with Kenneth's sister, Carole, appellant saw a car driven by the deceased, Tarbell Travis, speeding onto Stillbrooke from Greenwillow. The car swerved to miss a parked car and collided with Netterville's vehicle on the opposite side of the street. The car backed into Greenwillow and took off at a high rate of speed. Kenneth Netterville came out of the house and gave appellant a pistol stating "Let's go get him" and instructing appellant to go "that way."

Appellant found the vehicle on Spellman Street where the deceased Travis and his passenger, John Christensen, had gotten out to inspect the damage to the vehicle in which they were riding. Appellant parked his car parallel to the other vehicle and got out carrying a flashlight in one hand and the pistol in the other hand. Christensen testified appellant said, "What the hell do you think you're doing? You hit my friend's car. I ought to shoot you." Christensen recalled the deceased responded, "Well, then, why don't you?" At this time appellant shot the deceased in the chest from which wound he expired.

Appellant testified that he pursued the deceased's vehicle "to hold whoever hit my friend's car for the police." After he found the vehicle he stated he "yelled at him to get up against the car," and the deceased replied, "You're just going to have to shoot me, you son of a bitch." Appellant testified the deceased made a "shrugging" motion with his shoulders and took a step towards him. With the flashlight he saw the deceased's face and the deceased "looked crazy." He couldn't see the deceased's hands and didn't know whether the deceased was armed. Appellant stated he was in fear of his life, and to protect himself he shot the deceased in the chest.

Appellant did not know the deceased and apparently had not seen the deceased before the occasion in question. At no time during his testimony was he asked or did he state that he was a son or grandson of survivors of the Holocaust, or that stories about the Holocaust had any influence upon his state of mind at the time of the offense.

The excluded testimony was preserved for review by informal bills of exception. It appears from the record that an hour and a half after the officers arrived at the scene of the shooting two officers took the appellant in a patrol car to the police station. It was the conversation in the patrol car that the appellant sought to introduce before the jury.

Officer N.K. McErlane testified he drove the car on the occasion in question and heard a conversation with the appellant about the Holocaust, but that there was no interrogation of appellant. He did not consider it significant, did not include it in any offense report and did not relay the information to anyone connected with the prosecution of the case. McErlane stated the conversation had not been called to his attention until shortly before he testified. He remembered the appellant had stated appellant's father was a survivor of the Holocaust, had been "in some camp . . . during the forties" and that the father still had memories of those events which bothered him (the father). McErlane didn't see any relationship between the Holocaust and the shooting. All he could recall of the conversation was that the father was involved in the Holocaust.

Officer Duane Hartman was also in the patrol car when appellant was transported to the police station. He testified that for 10 or 15 minutes appellant voluntarily talked about his family, that his father and grandparents were in the Holocaust, that his father had come from Poland and had been raised in a certain manner, and tried to raise him (appellant) in the same manner. He thought appellant had mentioned appellant's father had been in a Nazi concentration camp and had witnessed people going without argument to the gas chambers, and the father had told appellant about these things as he grew up. When asked if the appellant had related what his father had told him about the concentration camps, the record reflects:

"A. Basically what he related to me is his sorrow for his father having to see this situation after having seen what he had seen when he was at the Holocaust.

"Q. Basically, he expressed sadness for what his dad had gone through?

"A. Not what his dad had gone through, but what at that time he was putting his father through for the incident, the situation he was in.

"Q. Because of the shooting?

"A. The fact that he was ashamed for putting his father through that again."

Officer Hartman also related appellant stated he knew how Jews felt during the Holocaust as a result of his being handcuffed in the back of the patrol car and being "taken away."

When asked if appellant had said that in growing up he had decided because of his father's experiences to be able to defend himself if he felt threatened, Officer Hartman answered:

"Not exactly like that. We discussed guns and he was very knowledgeable on that. He reflected through *that,* that's how he planned to protect himself. . . . that he would be ready if the time ever arose." (Emphasis added.)

Hartman testified he gave no significance to the statements, did not mention the same in any offense report, and did not relate the information to the prosecutor until that very day of the trial. When asked why, Officer Hartman replied, "As a result of becoming aware that was what he was going to use a defense on the basis of the Holocaust.

Appellant also proffered the testimony of Dr. Rudolph Roden, a board-certified psychiatrist, who received a degree in Russian Literature from Charles University in Prague, Czechoslovakia in 1948, a medical degree from Queen's University in Kingston, Ontario in 1955, and a Ph.D. from the University of Montreal in 1965. It was stated Dr. Roden had come to this country three years before from Canada; was board-certified in psychiatry; that Dr. Roden's particular interest was research into the area of survivors and children of survivors of Nazi concentration camps; that the doctor himself was incarcerated in concentration camps from 1940 to 1945. It was also offered that Dr. Roden had lectured and written articles in the field of his specialty. He had conducted seminars in pre-Freudian and Freud, Freud's general psychological theory, male chauvinism, survivor syndrome, and survival.

It was proffered that Dr. Roden would testify that beginning in August, 1982, four months after the alleged offense, he began to see the appellant as a patient, and saw him some 18 or 19 times. Dr. Roden learned that the appellant's paternal grandmother was Jewish, his paternal grandfather was Protestant, and after the grandfather's death in 1941 or 1942 appellant's grandmother and his half-Jewish father and other members of the family were placed in concentration camps, that the father and grandmother survived, the other members of the family did not. Dr. Roden also learned the appellant grew up with stories of concentration camps told to him by his father and grandmother, who related seeing people beaten to death who did not fight back. Dr. Roden determined appellant showed "some" of the characteristics of an individual who has the syndrome associated with children of survivors of Nazi concentration camps.

It was also stated Dr. Roden would testify that the appellant told him of the events that occurred on the night in question. Dr. Roden related that appellant told him the moment he (appellant) pulled the trigger that he wasn't thinking about anything except protecting himself. Dr. Roden would testify, however, "that one does not need to be thinking of an event for another event in one's life to have an effect, a subconscious effect on him;" that the appellant disliked injustice, and one of the greatest injustices was the Holocaust, and that his knowledge thereof shaped his view of self-defense, that the act of the deceased in "running into a car and leaving the scene was an unjust act in the appellant's view, and he sought to right the wrong by detaining the deceased for the police." Dr. Roden would testify that appellant's background caused him to make the decision to protect himself if his life was threatened, and though at the moment the alleged offense occurred he was not thinking of the Holocaust, it "was his state of mind to defend himself because he comes from a family that did not."

The State objected to the proffered testimony of Dr. Roden on the ground of relevancy, that if self-defense is urged the "test to be made by the jury in applying the standard of an ordinary and prudent person in the Defendant's position at the time of the offense."

The appellant disclaimed there was any issue of insanity at the time of the commission of the offense, but urged "the law which requires that the jury be given all the facts and circumstances bearing on the state of mind of the Defendant."

The court overruled the proffer of Dr. Roden's testimony stating:

"THE COURT: In light of the Defendant's testimony, the fact that there is no legal authority at all for such testimony coming before the jury, and because there are no two people alike, everybody is different, everybody comes from a different background, different things happen in the past, because there is no special breed of people that should be treated differently, all must come within the standard of law that we have in the state of Texas, and although the Holocaust is an example of man's inhumane acts towards their fellow man, the Court is going to sustain the objection at this time."

Later the officers' testimony developed earlier in the hearing on the motion in limine was offered by agreement as part of the bill of exception. This, too, was not permitted to be introduced before the jury on the grounds of relevancy.

There is no claim that the testimony of the appellant in his own behalf was limited or restricted in any way. He simply did not testify that he was suffering from a Holocaust syndrome, or that it had any effect on his actions that night. It was not mentioned at all. What appellant does assert is that it was error to exclude his oral statements to the officers and the opinion testimony of a psychiatrist. An examination of the officers' testimony shows appellant referred to the Holocaust during the conversation in the patrol car, but Officer Hartman described it basically as an expression of sorrow that his father had been through the Holocaust and would now be confronted with appellant's arrest. Appellant made no claim to the officers that he acted in self-defense because of the Holocaust syndrome. Dr. Roden stated appellant told him he was not thinking of the Holocaust at the time of the event in question, that appellant showed "some" of the characteristics of a child of a survivor of the Holocaust, that in his opinion he could have had a subconscious effect on him.

* * *

Be that as it may, even if the self-defense issue was validly before the jury the proffered testimony was still immaterial. The police officers related appellant spoke of the Holocaust, but his misgivings about the shooting and the effect upon his father were future oriented and did not necessarily explain appellant's state of mind at the time of the offense. Dr. Roden's testimony was that, although appellant continued to disclaim he was not thinking of the Holocaust at the time of the offense, he showed "some" characteristics of the syndrome associated with children of the survivors of the Holocaust, and the same might have had a subconscious effect on him. All that can be inferred from this evidence is that appellant may have been more susceptible to actions in self-defense. It did not establish that appellant did in fact act under the influence of the Holocaust on the night of the offense. The self-defense statutes permit the use of force only when and to the degree a person "reasonably believes" it immediately necessary. . . .

The evidence excluded only tended to show that possibly appellant was not an ordinary and prudent man with respect to self-defense. This did not entitle appellant to an enlargement of the statutory defense on account of his psychological peculiarities. . . .

The judgment of the Court of Appeals is affirmed.

CLINTON, J., dissents.

TEAGUE, JUDGE, dissenting.

Because the majority opinion's interpretation of V.T.C.A., Penal Code, Section 19.06, is clearly and totally erroneous, I dissent. In light of the way the majority opinion interprets Section 19.06, to me at least, it closely resembles something that Piscasso might have painted when he was a very young child.

Section 19.06 is clearly written and provides as follows:

In all prosecutions for murder or voluntary manslaughter, the state or defendant shall be permitted to offer testimony as to all relevant facts and circumstances surrounding the killing and the previous relationship existing between the accused and the deceased, *together with all relevant facts and circumstances going to show the condition of the mind of the accused at the time of the offense.* (My emphasis.)

This statute has been a part of our law at least since 1927, and is evidence that the Legislature recognized that the state of mind of the slayer was to be considered by the trier of fact. The Legislature placed no restrictions or limitations on the admissibility of such evidence, save and except that such evidence must go to the condition of the mind of the accused at the time of the offense, and the majority opinion errs in holding that it did otherwise. The fact that this Court might have erroneously interpreted the statute in the past is no justification for this Court to continue to compound the error of interpretation.

In interpreting this statute, and holding that the proffered testimony that Peter Alan Werner, hereinafter referred to as the appellant, wanted admitted into evidence was inadmissible evidence, the majority opinion appears to subscribe to the rule that because we cannot directly see, hear, or feel the state of another person's mind, testimony going to another person's state of mind is based on mere conjecture and therefore has an inadequate data base for its admissibility. Dean Wigmore made short shrift of such foolish thinking when he stated the following: "This argument is finical enough; and it proves too much, for if valid it would forbid the jury to find a verdict upon the supposed state of a person's mind. If they are required and allowed to find such a fact, it is not too much to hear such testimony from a witness who has observed the person exhibiting in his conduct the operations of his mind." 2 J. Wigmore, Wigmore on Evidence, Sec. 661 at 773–74 (3rd ed. 1940).

Because Section 19.06 is so unmistakenly clearly written, this court has no business trying to rewrite it so that it will read as some members of this Court might desire it to read. It is not the function of this Court to rewrite Section 19.06; it is the function of this Court to interpret the statute as it is written, and, in this instance, because the statute is written in unambiguous language, it is subject to only one interpretation. This Court should give the statute the broad meaning that the Legislature obviously intended it to have when it enacted the statute.

Under Section 19.06, supra, *any* relevant facts and circumstances going to show the condition of the mind of the accused at the time of the offense is admissible evidence. So saith our Legislature. However, by the statute's very terms, before evidence is admissible on the issue of the defendant's state or condition of his mind at the time of the offense, such evidence must be relevant. What this means to me is that any evidence going to the defendant's state of mind at the time the offense was committed is admissible; the statute merely restricts the proof of the state of mind to relevant facts and circumstances going to the state of mind of the defendant at the time the offense is committed. So saith our Legislature.

* * *

My understanding of the appellant's proffer of proof regarding Dr. Roden is that Dr. Roden would not have testified to any ultimate factual issue that had to be resolved by the jury, but, instead, would have merely supplied the jury with background data on the state of mind that the appellant had at the time in question in order to aid the jury in finding what the appellant's state or condition of his mind was at the time of the fatal shooting; thus, he would have explained to them that because the appellant was suffering from the effects of "The Holocaust Syndrome" this affected his state or condition of his mind at the time of the fatal shooting.

The relevant question, therefore, is whether Dr. Roden's methodology had the required general acceptance—not whether there was, in addition, a general acceptance of the Holocaust syndrome derived from that methodology.

The proffered testimony of Dr. Roden on "The Holocaust Syndrome", and how it affected the condition of the appellant's mind at the time he shot the deceased, should make it obvious to anyone that it comes within the rule that expert opinion testimony on issues to be decided by the jury is admissible where the conclusion of the expert is one which jurors would not ordinarily be able to draw for themselves. . . .

The subject "The Holocaust Syndrome" appears to be a new type of syndrome in psychiatric circles. Excluding a reference to one book entitled Adolescent Psychiatry: Developmental and Clinical Studies, at p. 66 (1982), all other references that counsel for the appellant directs us to are articles found in three newspapers. My independent research has yet to find a single reported court case which has discussed this syndrome.[1]

---

1. My independent research also reveals that the following articles have been written on the subject: Kestenberg, "Psychoanalyses of Children of Survivors From the Nazi Persecution: The Continuing Struggle of Survivor Parents," 5 Victimology 368–373 (Spr–Fall 1980); Danieli, "Countertransference in the Treatment and Study of Nazi Holocaust Survivors and Their Children," 5 Victimology 355–367 (Spr–Fall 1980); Ammon, "Symposium on the Psychodynamics of the Holocaust—Psychiatric and Psychohistorical Aspects," 17 Dynamische Psychiatrie (1984); Nadler, Kav–Venaki, Gleitman, "Transgenerational Effects of the Holocaust: Externalization of Aggression in Second Generation of Holocaust Survivors," 53 Journal of Con-

Although there appears to be a paucity of case law regarding "The Holocaust Syndrome," this in itself should not have been reason for the trial judge to have excluded Dr. Roden's testimony; to the contrary, this is probably the best reason why such testimony should have been admitted in this case. Dr. Roden's testimony was highly relevant on the issue of the condition of the appellant's state of mind at the time he fired the fatal shot, and would have aided the jury, all of whom were probably totally unfamiliar with this type syndrome, in better deciding what the appellant's state or condition of his mind was when he shot the deceased, and how his suffering from "The Holocaust Syndrome" affected the condition of his mind at that time.

*   *   *

Although I would prefer to have this record more complete on the subject of "The Holocaust Syndrome," nevertheless, I find that all of the requisites for the admissibility of Dr. Roden's testimony have been satisfied. See *Holloway v. State,* supra, which discusses the topic, the requisites for admissibility of an expert witness' testimony. Also see *Hopkins v. State,* supra.

When a relatively large number of persons, having the same symptoms, exhibit a combination or variation of functional psychiatric disorders that leads to purely emotional stress that causes intense mental anguish or emotional trauma, i.e., trauma having no direct physical effect upon the body, psychiatrists put those persons under one or more labels. Today, we have the following labels: "The Battered Wife Syndrome;" (see post); "The Battered Woman Syndrome;" The Battered Child Syndrome;" The Battered Husband Syndrome," (see Steinmetz, "The Battered Husband Syndrome, Victimology," An International Journal (1977–1978); Gelles, "The Myth of Battered Husbands—And Other Facts About Sanity Violence," Ms. (Oct., 1979); Schultz, "The Wife Assaulter," 6 J. Soc. Therapy 103 (1960);" "The Battered Parent Syndrome;" "The Familial Child Sexual Abuse Syndrome," (see State v. Middleton, 294 Or. 427, 657 P.2d 1215 (1983); "The Rape Trauma Syndrome," (see "Admissibility, at Criminal Prosecution, of Expert Testimony on Rape Trauma Syndrome," 42 A.L.R.4th, commencing at page 879); "The Battle Fatigue Syndrome;" "The Viet Nam Post–Traumatic Stress Syndrome," (see Miller v. State, 338 N.W.2d 673, 678 (S.D.1983) (Henderson, J., dissenting opinion); State v. Felde, 422 So.2d 370 (La.1982); "The Policeman's Syndrome," see

sulting & Clinical Psychology 365–369 (1985); Krell, "Holocaust Survivors and Their Children: Comments on Psychiatric Consequences and Psychiatric Terminology," 25 Comprehensive Psychiatry 521–528 (1984); Virag, "Children of the Holocaust and Their Children's Children: Working Through Current Trauma in the Psychotherapeutic Process," 2 Dynamic Psychotherapy 47–60 (Spr–Sum 1984); Schmolling, "Human Reactions to the Nazi Concentration Camps: A Summing Up," 10 Journal of Human Stress 108–120 (Fall, 1984); Roden, "Children of Holocaust Survivors," 10 Adolescent Psychiatry 66–72 (1982); Steinitz, "Psychological–Social Effects of the Holocaust on Aging Survivors and Their Families," 4 Journal of Gerontological Social Work 145–152 (Spr–Sum, 1982); Ornstein, "The Effects of the Holocaust on Life–Cycle Experiences: The Creation and Recreation of Families," 14 Journal of Geriatric Psychiatry 135–154 (1981).

Binder, Psychiatry in the Everyday Practice of Law (2nd ed. 1982);" "The Post–Concussive Syndrome," (Id.); "The Whiplash Syndrome;" "The Low–Back Syndrome;" "The Lover's Syndrome;" "The Love Fear Syndrome," (People v. Terry, 2 Cal.3d 362, 85 Cal.Rptr. 409, 466 P.2d 961 (1970); "The Organic Delusional Syndrome;" "The Chronic Brain Syndrome," (Illinois v. Reed, 8 Ill.App.3d 977, 290 N.E.2d 612 (1972); and "The Holocaust Syndrome." Tomorrow, there will probably be additions to the list, such as "The Appellate Court Judge Syndrome."

In this instance, there is no challenge by the State to Dr. Roden's qualifications to testify on the subject "The Holocaust Syndrome." From his impressive list of credentials, as well as his study of the subject, Dr. Roden appears to possess special knowledge upon the specific matter about which his expertise was sought.

If scientific, technical, or other specialized knowledge will assist the trier of fact to better understand the evidence or determine a fact in issue, a witness is qualified as an expert by knowledge, skill, experience, training, or education, and he should be able to testify in the form of opinion evidence.

In this instance, I find that the subject "The Holocaust Syndrome" was beyond the ken of the average lay person. The jury was entitled to know that when the appellant fired the fatal shot he believed that because of his past experiences, if his life was ever threatened, he would act to protect himself, and that is why he acted in the manner in which he did, i.e., that his state of mind at the time was affected, not only by that which he visually saw on the night in question, but also because of his belief that it was necessary for him to defend himself because he comes from a family who did not defend themselves, thus causing them to perish in the Holocaust. Dr. Roden's proffered testimony as to what effect being a descendant of a survivor of "The Holocaust" had upon the appellant, as to his reasonable belief of danger, was not only relevant and material as to his state of mind, but it was also relevant and material on his defense of self-defense, on which the jury was instructed.

* * *

Today, the majority opinion rules out evidence concerning "The Holocaust Syndrome." In light of this opinion, what will tomorrow bring?

Although there are obvious differences between the syndrome now known as "The Battered Wife Syndrome" and the syndrome now known as "The Holocaust Syndrome," in principle they have much in common. Today, it is not unusual for our more enlightened trial courts to admit testimony of expert witnesses on "The Battered Wife Syndrome," as relevant to explain the legitimacy of a wife's reactions to threats of danger from her spouse, and to counteract prosecutorial claims that the wife's continued presence in the home means that the homicide was not necessary. It should be obvious to almost anyone that without such testimony it would be difficult, if not impossible, for persons unfamiliar with how "The Battered Wife Syndrome" manifests itself to understand what effect the actions of the former spouse had on the state or condition of the wife's mind when she shot and killed her former spouse. In any event, it simply cannot be logically argued that such testimony would not be of assistance to the trier of fact in determining what the condition of the defendant's mind might have been when the offense was committed. See Robinson, 2 Criminal Law Defenses, Section 131(a), footnote 4.

All courts are not in agreement that expert testimony in "The Battered Woman Syndrome" type case is always admissible. Some courts have held that such testimony is relevant to the issue of self-defense and therefore admissible, see State v. Allery, 101 Wash.2d 591, 682 P.2d 312 (1984); State v. Kelly, 97 N.J. 178, 478 A.2d 364 (1984); State v. Leidholm, 334 N.W.2d 811 (N.D.1983); State v. Anaya, 438 A.2d 892 (Me.1981); Smith v. State, 247 Ga. 580, 277 S.E.2d 687 (1981), on remand, 159 Ga.App. 183, 283 S.E.2d 98 (1982); Hawthorne v. State, 408 So.2d 801 (Fla.Dis.Ct.App.1982); State v. Middleton, 294 Or. 427, 657 P.2d 1215 (1983); Ibn–Tamas v. United States, 407 A.2d 626 (D.C.1979), appeal after remand, 455 A.2d 893 (D.C.1983), other courts have held that such testimony is admissible for reasons other than self-defense, see People v. Minnis, 118 Ill.App.3d 345, 74 Ill.Dec. 179, 455 N.E.2d 209 (1983); State v. Baker, 120 N.H. 773, 424 A.2d 171 (1980); State v. Kelly, 102 Wash.2d 188, 685 P.2d 564 (1984); Buhrle v. State, 627 P.2d 1374 (Wyo.1981); Fultz v. State, 439 N.E.2d 659 (Ind.App. 1982); Commonwealth v. McCusker, 448 Pa. 382, 292 A.2d 286 (1972), while other courts hold that such testimony is absolutely inadmissible, see State v. Thomas, 66 Ohio St.2d 518, 423 N.E.2d 137 (1981); People v. White, 90 Ill.App.3d 1067, 46 Ill.Dec. 474, 414 N.E.2d 196 (1980). Also see the annotation entitled "Admissibility of Expert or Opinion Testimony on Battered Wife or Battered Woman Syndrome," 18 A.L.R.4th, commencing at page 1153; Criminal Law Defenses, supra; Thar, "The Admissibility of Expert Testimony on Battered Wife Syndrome . . . An Evidentiary Analysis," 77 Northwestern Law Review 348 (1982); Jones, "When Battered Women Fight Back," 9 Barrister 12 (Fall, 1982); "The Battered Wife's Dilemma: To Kill or to be Killed," 32 Hastings Law Journal 895 (1981); Cross, "The Expert as Educator: A Proposed Approach to the Use of Battered Woman Syndrome Expert Testimony," 35 Vanderbilt Law Review 741 (1982); Giannelli, "The Admissibility of Novel Scientific Evidence: Frye v. United States, A Half–Century Later," 80 Colum. Law Review 1197 (1980); Comment, "Expert Testimony Based Upon Novel Scientific Technique: Admissibility Under Federal Rules of Evidence," 48 George Washington Law Review 774 (1980); Graham, "Lay Witness Opinion Testimony; Opinion on Ultimate Issue By Lay or Expert Witness," Criminal Law Bulletin, (March–April 1986), commencing at page 144.

* * *

How testimony going to the defendant's state of mind can ever be inadmissible under Section 19.06, in making the determination of what the state or condition of his mind might have been at the time in question, clearly escapes me, and the majority opinion does not truly explain how, under the express provisions of Section 19.06, the testimony of Dr. Roden was inadmissible to show the appellant's state or condition of his mind at the time he fired the fatal shot. For this reason, if no other, the majority opinion is simply dead wrong in holding that the trial court did not err in excluding the proffered testimony of Dr. Roden.

For the above and foregoing reasons, I respectfully dissent.

NOTES

1. That the problem of domestic violence is a serious one seems well established. In 1978, a California Commission on Family Law studying domestic violence reported that the yearly number of women beaten by their husbands or lovers exceeds one million.

Most women who kill their husbands or lovers are charged with second degree murder or voluntary manslaughter, although first degree murder charges and involuntary manslaughter are not unheard of. The defenses of self-defense, not guilty by reason of mental disease or defect (insanity), and heat of passion mitigation are most frequently used. Because of the conditioning through which a battered woman goes as a result of repetitive beatings to which she may have been subjected over an extended period of time, all three approaches to defense or mitigation may be used where a woman is diagnosed as suffering from the battered woman syndrome. To properly present the issues to the court, however, it is ordinarily necessary to use expert testimony to explain the nature of the condition and its progression in a particular case that culminated in a killing.

2. While ordinarily the admissibility of expert testimony is left to the discretion of the trial judge, there are some criteria the courts use in admitting opinion testimony based on novel scientific theories or discoveries. See, e.g., Moenssens, et al., Scientific Evidence in Criminal Cases, Third Edition, 1986, Chapter 1 on Expert Testimony. In connection with the admissibility of battered woman syndrome opinion testimony, the early courts were reluctant to admit the evidence on the ground that its scientific or medical acceptability was still not widespread. See, e.g., Buhrle v. State, 627 P.2d 1374 (Wyo.1981); State v. Thomas, 66 Ohio St.2d 518, 423 N.E.2d 137 (1981); State v. Griffiths, 101 Idaho 163, 610 P.2d 522 (1980). Other courts, however, have acknowledged the scientific acceptability of the battered woman syndrome and the reliability of the methodology used by practitioners in the fields of psychiatry and psychology. See, e.g., Ibn–Tamas v. United States, 407 A.2d 626 (D.C.App.1979) [but see the decision on remand, 455 A.2d 893 (D.C.App.1983)]; State v. Anaya, 438 A.2d 892 (Me.1981); Smith v. State, 247 Ga. 612, 277 S.E.2d 678 (1981); State v. Allery, 101 Wash.2d 591, 682 P.2d 312 (1984); State v. Kelly, 97 N.J. 178, 478 A.2d 364 (1984); People v. Torres, 128 Misc.2d 129, 488 N.Y.S.2d 358 (1985); Hawthorne v. State, 408 So.2d 801 (Fla.App.1982), review denied 415 So.2d 1361 (Fla.); State v. Hill, 287 S.C. 398, 339 S.E.2d 121 (1986).

3. In State v. Hodges, 239 Kan. 63, 716 P.2d 563 (1986), the defendant was convicted of the voluntary manslaughter of her husband and contended on appeal that the trial court erred in refusing to allow expert testimony on the

battered woman syndrome. The proffered testimony of the clinical psychologist on the syndrome was to this effect:

"Dr. Bristow explained the battered woman syndrome is a post-traumatic stress disorder with the particular stressor being wife abuse. Symptoms manifested by a woman suffering from the syndrome include an attempt to minimize the violence and to live for the positive aspects of the relationship. She lives in a highly fearful state, becoming very sensitive to when the situation is becoming more violent and to those things that precede argument. The batterer isolates the woman and will not allow her to go places, and she becomes more and more withdrawn. Few women will discuss their problems even with close family members because of their feeling that there is nothing that can be done about the situation. They have a 'learned helplessness'; the more the repeated trauma occurs, the more the woman learns she has no control."

In holding that it was error to exclude the evidence, the Kansas Supreme Court said that such evidence is admissible, where self defense is asserted, to prove the reasonableness of defendant's belief that she was in imminent danger. The court said:

"Expert testimony on the battered woman syndrome would help dispel the ordinary lay person's perception that a woman in a battering relationship is free to leave at any time. The expert evidence would counter any 'common sense' conclusions by the jury that if the beatings were really bad the woman would have left her husband much earlier. Popular misconceptions about battered women would be put to rest, including the beliefs the women are masochistic and enjoy the beatings and that they intentionally provoke their husbands into fits of rage."

In addressing the issue of whether the belief in the imminency of danger to herself would have to be an objectively or subjectively reasonable one, the court said:

". . . [W]e hold where the battered woman syndrome is in issue, the proper standard to determine whether the accused's belief in asserting self defense was reasonable is a subjective standard. The jury must determine, from the viewpoint of the defendant's mental state, whether the defendant's belief in the need to defend herself was reasonable."

The court stressed that the battered woman's syndrome was not a defense to murder; it is used only to help the jury understand why a battered woman is psychologically unable to leave the battering relationship and why she lives in a high anxiety of fear from the batterer. The jury is aided by this evidence in determining whether her fear and her claim of self defense are reasonable.

4. See also the following penetrating comments on the battered spouses syndrome defense: Rosen, The Execuse of Self–Defense: Correcting a Historical Accident On Behalf Of Battered Women Who Kill, 36 Am.U.L.Rev. 11 (1986); Ewing, Psychological Self–Defense—A Proposed Justification for Battered Women Who Kill, 14 Law & Human Behav. 579 (1990)—suggesting that traditional self defense concepts rarely apply comfortably to battered spouses but arguing that current law be expanded; Morse, The Misbegotten Marriage of Soft Psychology and Bad Law: Psychological Self–Defense as a Justification for Homicide, 14 Law & Hum. Behav. 595 (1990)—arguing that a recognition of a battered spouses defense rests on an insecure scientific foundation, that an

expansion of self defense would create substantial administrative problems and would facilitate adoption or expansion of related undesirable doctrines. See further, Reece, Mothers Who Kill: Postpartum Disorders and Criminal Infanticide, 38 U.C.L.A. L.Rev. 699 (1991), and, Note, Postpartum Depression Defense: Are Mothers Getting Away with Murder?, 24 New Eng.L.Rev. 953 (1990).

5. Applying an analogous issue of self defense by a battered child, defending a patricide, see Jahnke v. State, 682 P.2d 991 (Wyo.1984), where a defendant charged with the first degree murder of his father sought to show, through expert testimony that he was a battered child who believed that he was in imminent danger of his life when he shot his father. The proffered expert testimony was excluded and the defendant was convicted of voluntary manslaughter. In upholding the conviction, the majority of the Wyoming Supreme Court, over vigorous dissent, said, in part: "Although many people, and the public media, seem to be prepared to espouse the notion that a victim of abuse is entitled to kill the abuser, that special justification defense is antithetical to the mores of modern civilized society. . . ." See also: State v. Mapp, 45 N.C. App. 574, 264 S.E.2d 348 (1980). See, Note, Links Between the Battered Woman Syndrome and the Battered Child Syndrome: An Argument For Consistent Standards in the Admissibility of Expert Testimony in Family Abuse Cases, 36 Wayne L.Rev. 1619 (1990).

2. DEFENSE OF OTHERS

The law recognizes the right of a person to kill in defense of not only his own life but also that of another. Two doctrines bear upon this privilege to defend others: (1) the rule that one may defend a close relative, and (2) the rule that one may take life if necessary to prevent a dangerous or forcible felony. In application to specific situations, these principles are frequently cumulative. Thus, if one kills the assailant of a near relative, he may invoke his specific right to defend a member of his family, as well as his general privilege to interfere to prevent a felonious assault.

Cases involving defense of a party who, at the time of the killing, was engaged in an affray brought on by his own misconduct have resulted in disagreement among the courts as to whether the "assistant" must "stand in the shoes" of the wrongdoer, or instead be judged according to the reasonableness of his own conduct in interfering to protect one whose life seemed to be unlawfully endangered.

It is a matter of speculation as to which view is the more socially tolerable. In other words, will a person who sees a close relative in great and immediate danger pause to determine whether the relative was himself free from fault?

PEOPLE v. YOUNG
Court of Appeals of New York, 1962.
11 N.Y.2d 274, 229 N.Y.S.2d 1, 183 N.E.2d 319.

PER CURIAM. Whether one, who in good faith aggressively intervenes in a struggle between another person and a police officer in civilian dress attempting to effect the lawful arrest of the third person, may be properly convicted of assault in the third degree is a question of law of first impression here.

The opinions in the court below [the Appellate Division of the Supreme Court] in the absence of precedents in this State carefully expound the opposing views found in other jurisdictions. The majority in the Appellate Division have adopted the minority rule in the other States that one who intervenes in a struggle between strangers under the mistaken but reasonable belief that he is protecting another who he assumes is being unlawfully beaten is thereby exonerated from criminal liability . . . The weight of authority holds with the dissenters below that one who goes to the aid of a third person does so at his own peril. . . .

While the doctrine espoused by the majority of the court below may have support in some States, we feel that such a policy would not be conducive to an orderly society. We agree with the settled policy of law in most jurisdictions that the right of a person to defend another ordinarily should not be greater than such person's right to defend himself. Subdivision 3 of section 246 of the Penal Law, Consol.Laws, c. 40, does not apply as no offense was being committed on the person of the one resisting the lawful arrest. Whatever may be the public policy where the felony charged requires proof of a specific intent and the issue is justifiable homicide . . . ., it is not relevant in a prosecution for assault in the third degree where it is only necessary to show that the defendant knowingly struck a blow.

In this case there can be no doubt that the defendant intended to assault the police officer in civilian dress. The resulting assault was forceful. Hence motive or mistake of fact is of no significance as the defendant was not charged with a crime requiring such intent or knowledge. To be guilty of third degree assault "It is sufficient that the defendant voluntarily intended to commit the unlawful act of touching". . . . Since in these circumstances the aggression was inexcusable the defendant was properly convicted.

Accordingly, the order of the Appellate Division should be reversed and the information reinstated.

FROESSEL, JUDGE (dissenting). [Concurrence by VAN VOORHIS, J.] The law is clear that one may kill in defense of another when there is reasonable, though mistaken, ground for believing that the person slain is about to commit a felony or to do some great personal injury to the apparent victim . . .; yet the majority now hold, for the first time, that in the event of a simple assault under similar circumstances, the mistaken belief, no matter how reasonable, is no defense.

Briefly, the relevant facts are these: On a Friday afternoon at about 3:40, Detectives, Driscoll and Murphy, not in uniform, observed an argument taking place between a motorist and one McGriff in the street in front of premises 64 West 54th Street, in midtown Manhattan. Driscoll attempted to chase McGriff out of the roadway in order to allow traffic to pass, but McGriff refused to move back; his actions caused a crowd to collect. After identifying himself to McGriff, Driscoll placed him under arrest. As McGriff resisted, defendant "came out of the crowd" from Driscoll's rear and struck Murphy about the head with his fist. In the ensuing struggle Driscoll's right kneecap was injured when defendant fell on top of him. At the station house, defendant said he had not known or thought Driscoll and Murphy were police officers.

Defendant testified that while he was proceeding on 54th Street he observed two white men, who appeared to be 45 or 50 years old, pulling on a "colored boy" (McGriff), who appeared to be a lad about 18, whom he did not know. The men had nearly pulled McGriff's pants off, and he was crying. Defendant admitted he knew nothing of what had transpired between the officers and McGriff, and made no inquiry of anyone; he just came there and pulled the officer away from McGriff.

Defendant was convicted of assault third degree. In reversing upon the law and dismissing the information, the Appellate Division held that one is not "criminally liable for assault in the third degree if he goes to the aid of another who he mistakenly, but *reasonably*, believes is being unlawfully beaten, and thereby injures one of the apparent assaulters" (emphasis supplied). While in my opinion the majority below correctly stated the law, I would reverse here and remit so that the Appellate Division may pass on the question of whether or not defendant's conduct was reasonable in light of the circumstances presented at the trial . . .

As the majority below pointed out, assault is a crime derived from the common law. Basic to the imposition of criminal liability both at common law and under our statutory law is the existence in the one who committed the prohibited act of what has been variously termed a guilty mind, a *mens rea* or a criminal intent . . .

Criminal intent requires an awareness of wrongdoing. When conduct is based upon mistake of fact reasonably entertained, there can be no such awareness and, therefore, no criminal culpability. In People ex rel. Hegeman v. Corrigan, 195 N.Y. 1, 12, 87 N.E. 792, 796, we stated: "it is very apparent that the innocence or criminality of the intent in a particular act generally depends on the knowledge or belief of the actor at the time. An honest and *reasonable* belief in the existence of circumstances which, if true, would make the act for which the defendant is prosecuted innocent, would be a good defense." (Emphasis supplied.)

It is undisputed that defendant did not know that Driscoll and Murphy were detectives in plain clothes engaged in lawfully apprehending an alleged disorderly person. If, therefore, defendant *reasonably* believed he was lawfully assisting another, he would not have been guilty of a crime. Subdivision 3 of section 246 of the Penal Law provides that it is not unlawful to use force "When committed either by the party about to be injured or *by another person in his aid or defense, in preventing or attempting to prevent an offense against his person,*

* * * if the force or violence used is not more than sufficient to prevent such offense" (emphasis supplied). The law is thus clear that if defendant entertained an "honest and reasonable belief" . . ., that the facts were as he perceived them to be, he would be exonerated from criminal liability.

By ignoring one of the most basic principles of criminal law—that crimes *mala in se* require proof of at least general criminal intent—the majority now hold that the defense of mistake of fact is "of no significance". We are not here dealing with one of "a narrow class of exceptions" . . . where the Legislature has created crimes which do not depend on *criminal* intent but which are complete on the mere intentional doing of an act *malum prohibitum* . . .

There is no need, in my opinion, to consider the law of other States, for New York policy clearly supports the view that one may act on appearances reasonably ascertained, as does New Jersey . . . Our Penal Law (§ 1055), to which I have already alluded, is a statement of that policy. The same policy was expressed by this court in People v. Maine, . . . There, the defendant observed his brother fighting in the street with two other men; he stepped in and stabbed to death one of the latter. The defense was justifiable homicide under the predecessor of section 1055. The court held it reversible error to admit into evidence the declarations of the defendant's brother, made before defendant happened upon the scene, which tended to show that the brother was the aggressor. We said: "Of course, the acts and conduct of the defendant must be judged solely with reference to the situation as it was when he first and afterwards saw it." Mistake of relevant fact, reasonably entertained, is thus a defense to homicide under section 1055 . . . and one who kills in defense of another and proffers this defense of justification is to be judged according to the circumstances as they appeared to him.

The mistaken belief, however, must be one which is reasonably entertained and the question of reasonableness is for the trier of the facts . . . "The question is not, merely, what did the accused believe? but also, what did he have the right to believe?" . . .

Although the majority of our courts are now purporting to fashion a policy "conducive to an orderly society", by their decision they have defeated their avowed purpose. What public interest is promoted by a principle which would deter one from coming to the aid of a fellow citizen who he has reasonable ground to apprehend is in imminent danger of personal injury at the hands of assailants? Is it reasonable to denominate, as justifiable homicide, a slaying committed under a mistaken but reasonably held belief, and deny this same defense of justification to one using less force? Logic, as well as historical background and related precedent, dictates that the rule and policy expressed by our Legislature in the case of homicide, which is an assault resulting in death, should likewise be applicable to a much less serious assault not resulting in death.

I would reverse the order appealed from and remit the case to the Appellate Division pursuant to section 543–b of the Code of Criminal Procedure "for determination upon the questions of fact raised in that court".

NOTES

1. Consider the following from State v. Westlund, 13 Wash.App. 460, 536 P.2d 20 (1975):

"We hold that a bystander may not come to the aid of one being lawfully or unlawfully arrested by a uniformed police officer or one known or who should have been known to the bystander to be a police officer unless the arrestee was in actual danger of serious physical injury. Several elements, therefore, must be present before such a third person's assault of a police officer can be justified on the basis of defense of another. First, a third party may never intervene when the only threat to the arrestee is deprivation of his liberty by an arrest which has no legal justification. Aid is justified only if serious physical injury or death is threatened or inflicted. Second, the serious physical danger threatened or inflicted must be actual. A reasonable but mistaken belief that the arrestee was about to be seriously injured or that the arrestee was entitled to protect himself from such danger is insufficient. The third party acts at his own peril and if it is subsequently determined that the arrestee was not about to be seriously injured, the third party's assault is not justifiable. Third, the physical injury must be serious, the police actions of the type which shock the conscience. Fourth, only force reasonable and necessary to protect the arrestee may be used against the officer."

2. Nebraska enacted a statute which read in part as follows: "No person in this state shall be placed in legal jeopardy of any kind whatsoever for protecting, by any means necessary, himself, his family, or his real or personal property, or when coming to the aid of another who is in imminent danger of or the victim of aggravated assault, armed robbery, holdup, rape, murder, or other heinous crime." It was held unconstitutional on the ground that the legislature could not delegate to private citizens the power to fix and execute punishment. State v. Goodseal, 186 Neb. 359, 183 N.W.2d 258 (1971).

3. DEFENSE OF HABITATION

PEOPLE v. GUENTHER

Supreme Court of Colorado, 1987.
740 P.2d 971.

QUINN, CHIEF JUSTICE.

The People appeal from a judgment dismissing charges of second degree murder, first degree assault, and the commission of a crime of violence filed against the defendant, David Alan Guenther. The district court dismissed the charges pursuant to section 18–1–704.5(3), 8B C.R.S. (1986), which provides that under certain circumstances an occupant of a dwelling using any degree of physical force against an intruder, including deadly physical force, shall be immune from criminal prosecution. We construe section 18–1–704.5(3) to authorize a district court to dismiss a pending criminal charge prior to trial when the defendant establishes the statutory conditions for immunity by a preponderance of the evidence. In this case, however, the district court erroneously imposed upon the prosecution the burden of proving beyond a reasonable doubt that the defendant's conduct did not satisfy the statutory conditions for immunity. We accordingly reverse the judgment of dismissal and remand the case to the district court for further proceedings.

I.

A.

The defendant was charged in a four-count information with the following crimes allegedly committed on April 20, 1986, at or near the defendant's home in Northglenn, Colorado: second degree murder committed against Josslyn Volosin, § 18–3–103(1)(a), 8B C.R.S. (1986); two counts of first degree assault committed against Michael Volosin and Robbie Alan Wardwell, § 18–3–202(1)(a), 8B C.R.S. (1986); and one count of the commission of a crime of violence, § 16–11–309, 8A C.R.S. (1986). After these charges were filed, the defendant filed a motion to dismiss and to enjoin further prosecution. It was the defendant's contention that since he fired the shots only after an unlawful entry had been made into his house and after it appeared that his wife was being harmed, he was immune from prosecution under section 18–1–704.5(3), 8B C.R.S. (1986). . . . We summarize the facts from the evidence relied on by the district court.

During the evening of April 19 and the early morning hours of April 20, 1986, a small group of people were drinking and playing pool at the home of Michael and Josslyn Volosin, which was located across the street and two houses to the north of David and Pam Guenther's home. Late in the evening three of the men left the party and went to the Guenthers'. One of the men began banging on the Guenthers' car, shouting obscenities, and challenging David Guenther to come out of the house. The men left after Pam Guenther told them her husband was not at home and she was going to call the police. The police arrived, discussed the incident with Pam Guenther, went to the Volosins' home and talked to Josslyn Volosin, and then left.

The events that followed constituted the basis for the criminal charges against the defendant and for the district court's subsequent dismissal of those charges. The witnesses' versions of these events, however, are in substantial conflict with one another. Michael Volosin stated that shortly after the police left he heard a loud noise at his front door. When he saw no one at his door, he ran to the Guenthers' house and knocked on the front door, whereupon Pam Guenther opened the door, grabbed him, threw him out onto the grass, and had him on the ground when her husband came out of the house shooting. Volosin's version was corroborated by Bonnie Smith, a neighbor who had observed the incident from her window. Smith testified that she had seen Pam Guenther standing over a figure lying next to the

Guenthers' porch, shouting obscenities and trying to pick the person up off the ground.

In contrast to the account given by Michael Volosin and Bonnie Smith, Pam Guenther testified that when she went to the front door and opened it, Michael Volosin grabbed her, pulled her out the door, threw her against the wall, and began to beat her up. Pam Guenther stated that as she and Michael began struggling, she screamed for her husband to get the gun. It was her further testimony that Josslyn Volosin had appeared and was trying to break up the fight when the sound of gunshots was heard. After Pam Guenther screamed for help, the defendant came to the front door of his house and, from the doorway, fired four shots from a Smith and Wesson .357 Magnum six-inch revolver. The defendant's account of the events was substantially the same as his wife's.

One shot hit and wounded Michael Volosin, who was lying on the ground next to the Guenthers' porch. Robbie Alan Wardwell, a guest of the Volosins, was wounded by a second shot as he was walking across the Guenthers' front yard to help Josslyn Volosin break up the fight. A third shot killed Josslyn Volosin. There was conflicting evidence as to whether she was hit while standing near the Guenthers' front porch or in the street as she was running away.

The district court found that Michael Volosin had made an unlawful entry into the Guenthers' residence and that the defendant had a reasonable belief that Volosin was committing a crime against Pam Guenther and was using physical force against her. The court concluded as follows: that section 18–1–704.5(3) does not simply provide an affirmative defense to criminal charges, but grants immunity from prosecution for the crimes charged; that this statute does not impermissibly interfere with the prosecutor's executive function in determining whether to file criminal charges in a given case; that the statutory immunity applied to charges based on force directed not only against an actual intruder into the Guenthers' home but also to charges based on force directed against other persons involved in the incident who did not enter the Guenther home; that it was the prosecution's burden to disprove beyond a reasonable doubt the facts constituting the basis for the application of the statutory immunity; and that the prosecution had failed to meet its burden. The court accordingly dismissed all the charges against the defendant.

B.

The issues raised on appeal center on section 18–1–704.5, 8B C.R.S. (1986), which became effective on June 6, 1985, and provides as follows:

(1) The general assembly hereby recognizes that the citizens of Colorado have a right to expect absolute safety within their own homes.

(2) Notwithstanding the provisions of section 18–1–704,[1] any occupant of a dwelling is justified in using any degree of physical force, including deadly physical force, against another person when that other person has made an unlawful entry into the dwelling, and when the occupant has a reasonable belief that such other person has committed a crime in the dwelling in addition to the uninvited entry, or is committing or intends to commit a crime against a person or property in addition to the uninvited entry, and when the occupant reasonably believes that such other person might use any physical force, no matter how slight, against any occupant.

(3) Any occupant of a dwelling using physical force, including deadly physical force, in accordance with the provisions of subsection (2) of this section shall be immune from criminal prosecution for the use of such force.

(4) Any occupant of a dwelling using physical force, including deadly physical force, in accordance with the provisions of subsection (2) of this section shall be immune from any civil liability for injuries or death resulting from the use of such force.

The People raise alternative arguments in urging a reversal of the district court's order of dismissal. . . .

*   *   *

II.

We initially address whether section 18–1–704.5(3) confers jurisdiction on a court to dismiss a criminal action at the pretrial stage of the case or merely creates an affirmative defense to be adjudicated at trial. We conclude that section 18–1–704.5(3) was intended to and indeed does authorize a court to dismiss a criminal prosecution at the pretrial stage of the case when the conditions of the statute have been satisfied.

Our primary task in construing a statute is to ascertain and give effect to the intent of the General Assembly. To discern that intent, we look first to the language of the statute itself, giving the statutory terms their commonly accepted and understood meaning. Section 18–

---

1. Section 18–1–704, 8B C.R.S. (1986), dealing with the use of physical force in defense of a person, provides that a person may use "a degree of force which he reasonably believes to be necessary" for the purpose of defending himself or a third person, but that:

(2) Deadly physical force may be used only if a person reasonably believes a lesser degree of force is inadequate and:

(a) The actor has reasonable ground to believe, and does believe, that he or another person is in imminent danger of being killed or of receiving great bodily injury; or

(b) The other person is using or reasonably appears about to use physical force against an occupant of a dwelling or business establishment while committing or attempting to commit burglary as defined in section 18–4–202 to 18–4–204; or

(c) The other person is committing or reasonably appears about to commit kidnapping as defined in section 18–3–301 or 18–3–302, robbery as defined in section 18–4–301 or 18–4–302, sexual assault as set forth in section 18–3–402 or 18–3–403, or assault as defined in sections 18–3–202 and 18–3–203.

1–704.5(3) states that any occupant of a dwelling who uses physical force in accordance with the provisions of subsection (2) of the statute *"shall be immune from criminal prosecution* for the use of such force" (emphasis added). In our view, this language is susceptible of only one interpretation. The word "shall," when used in a statute, involves a "mandatory connotation" and hence is the antithesis of discretion or choice. "Immunity" means "freedom from duty or penalty." Black's Law Dictionary 676 (5th ed. 1979). The word "prosecution" is defined as "a proceeding instituted and carried on by due process of law, before a competent tribunal, for the purpose of determining the guilt or innocence of a person charged with crime." Black's Law Dictionary (1099). In accordance with the plain meaning of these terms, the phrase "shall be immune from criminal prosecution" can only be construed to mean that the statute was intended to bar criminal proceedings against a person for the use of force under the circumstances set forth in subsection (2) of section 18–1–704.5.

Although the People would have us read section 18–1–704.5(3) as creating an affirmative defense, . . . we do not believe that the People's proposed construction can be reconciled with the plain language of the statute. . . .

*   *   *

We find further support for our construction of the statute in its legislative history. In explaining the need for the proposed legislation, the co-sponsor of the statute, Senator Brandon, stated at a legislative committee hearing on the bill that under current Colorado law a homeowner might not be convicted in the situation addressed by the bill, but would in any event be required to hire an attorney and perhaps "put his home on the block" in order to avoid a jail sentence. This statement clearly suggests that the bill was intended to spare a homeowner the financial burden of a trial. . . .

*   *   *

III.

*   *   *

IV.

Having concluded that a criminally accused is entitled to a pretrial determination of his immunity claim under section 18–1–704.5(3), and having further determined that the immunity statute does not violate the constitutional separation of powers, we next consider the scope of the statutory immunity, the allocation of the burden of proof and the standard of proof applicable to a pretrial motion for dismissal on the basis of statutory immunity, and the effect of a court's denial of a pretrial motion for statutory immunity on the trial of the case.

A.

We first address the scope of the statutory immunity created by section 18–1–704.5. In resolving this issue we look to the plain terms of the statute.

Subsection (2) of the statute states that an occupant of a dwelling is justified in using physical force "against *another person* when *that other person* has made an unlawful entry into the dwelling" (emphasis added) and when the additional statutory requirements are met. Subsection (3) provides immunity from criminal prosecution for an occupant using physical force "in accordance with the provisions of subsection (2) of this section." . . .

Since there is no ambiguity in this statutory language, we need not resort to other rules of statutory construction. Rather, we must give effect to the plain language of the statutory text. In accordance with the explicit terms of the statute, we hold that section 18–1–704.5 provides the home occupant with immunity from prosecution only for force used against one who has made an unlawful entry into the dwelling, and that this immunity does not extend to force used against non-entrants.

B.

The district court construed section 18–1–704.5 to require that once the accused has established a prima facie case of the conditions for statutory immunity, the prosecution must then disprove those conditions beyond a reasonable doubt. We reject the district court's apportionment of proof on the immunity issue.

* * *

There is a constitutionally significant difference in kind between requiring a defendant, on the one hand, to bear the burden of proving a claim of pretrial entitlement to immunity from prosecution and, on the other, to carry the burden of proof at trial on an affirmative defense to criminal charges. Section 18–1–704.5(3) creates a benefit to a defendant far greater than an affirmative defense. If the statute is found to apply to the facts of the case, it will completely prohibit any further prosecution of charges for which, but for the statute, the defendant would otherwise be required to stand trial. Although the wisdom of such legislation is not for us to decide, it cannot be disputed that the immunity created by section 18–1–704.5(3) is an extraordinary protection which, so far as we know, has no analogue in Colorado statutory or decisional law.

Since section 18–1–704.5(3) contemplates that an accused should be permitted to claim an entitlement to immunity at the pretrial stage of a criminal prosecution, we believe it reasonable to require the accused to prove his entitlement to an order of dismissal on the basis of statutory immunity. A hearing to determine the applicability of section 18–1–704.5(3) to pending criminal charges is not a criminal trial, but, rather, is an ancillary proceeding in the nature of a motion to dismiss a pending criminal prosecution on the basis of a statutory bar. We have often imposed on a criminally accused the burden of establishing his entitlement to dismissal of criminal charges at the pretrial stage of the case, and we find it appropriate to impose that same burden on the defendant in connection with a pretrial claim for statutory immunity under section 18–1–704.5(3). Furthermore, the accused presumably has a greater knowledge of the existence or nonexistence of the facts which would call into play the protective shield of the statute and, under these circumstances, should be in a better position than the prosecution to establish the existence of those statutory conditions which entitle him to immunity.

While we conclude that the burden of proof should be placed on the defendant, we decline to require that the defendant prove his entitlement to immunity beyond a reasonable doubt. We believe that the "preponderance of the evidence" is the appropriate standard of proof applicable to a defendant's pretrial motion to dismiss pursuant to section 18–1–704.5(3). . . .

We thus hold that when section 18–1–704.5(3) is invoked prior to trial as a bar to a criminal prosecution, the burden is on the defendant seeking the benefit of the statutory immunity to establish by a preponderance of evidence that: (1) another person made an unlawful entry into the defendant's dwelling; (2) the defendant had a reasonable belief that such other person had committed a crime in the dwelling in addition to the uninvited entry, or was committing or intended to commit a crime against a person or property in addition to the uninvited entry; (3) the defendant reasonably believed that such other person might use physical force, no matter now slight, against any occupant of the dwelling; and (4) the defendant used force against the person who actually made the unlawful entry into the dwelling.

C.

We turn then to the effect of the court's ruling on a pretrial claim of immunity on the trial of the case. If, of course, a court finds that the defendant seeking immunity has met the appropriate burden of proof, then the court must grant immunity from prosecution and dismiss the charges to which the immunity bar applies. If, on the other hand, the court determines that the defendant has not met his burden of proof and denies the motion to dismiss the charges, there is nothing in section 18–1–704.5 to suggest that the defendant should somehow be precluded from raising the same statutory conditions for immunity as an affirmative defense to the charges at trial. Since the legislature clearly intended section 18–1–704.5 to operate as a complete immunity to criminal charges when an occupant of a dwelling used physical force against an intruder under the conditions set forth in the statute, it cannot plausibly be argued that the legislature thereby intended to deprive an accused of the lesser benefit of an affirmative defense at trial when those same statutory conditions are established under appropriate standards of proof applicable to the trial of a criminal case.

Thus, if the pretrial motion to dismiss on grounds of statutory immunity is denied, the defendant may nonetheless raise at trial, as an affirmative defense to criminal charges arising out of the defendant's use of physical force against an intruder into his home, the statutory conditions set forth in section 18–1–704.5(2). In such an instance, the burden of proof generally applicable to affirmative defenses would apply to the defense created by section 18–1–704.5(2). The defendant would be required to present some credible evidence supporting the applicability of section 18–1–704.5(2); and, if such evidence is presented, the prosecution would then bear the burden of proving beyond a reasonable doubt the guilt of the defendant as to the issue raised by the affirmative defense as well as all other elements of the offense charged. § 18–1–407, 8B C.R.S. (1986).

V.

In light of these aforementioned guidelines, we consider the district court's judgment of dismissal in this case. The defendant sought to invoke the protections of section 18–1–704.5(3) by filing a motion to dismiss after criminal charges were filed against him. Section 18–1–704.5(3) contemplates such a motion by a person claiming immunity from criminal prosecution by reason of the existence of those conditions on which a grant of statutory immunity may properly be based. The district court clearly had jurisdiction to hear the defendant's motion prior to trial and to rule on the applicability of section 18–1–704.5(3) to the pending charges.

The district court erred, however, in concluding that the defendant was entitled to a dismissal of the charges because the prosecution had failed to disprove beyond a reasonable doubt the statutory conditions for immunity outlined in section 18–1–704.5(2). In so ruling, the court incorrectly allocated the burden of proof and applied an erroneous standard of proof. Under the correct standard, the defendant would be entitled to immunity only if he established by a preponderance of the evidence those statutory conditions of immunity set forth in section 18–1–704.5(2).

The district court also erred in concluding that section 18–1–704.5(3) immunizes from criminal prosecution an occupant of a dwelling who uses force against persons who did not actually enter the dwelling. If on remand the district court concludes that the immunity criteria of section 18–1–704.5(2) are established, then the defendant would be entitled to immunity from prosecution for any force used against any person or persons who actually entered his dwelling, but would not be immune from prosecution for any force used against non-entrants.

We reverse the district court's order of dismissal, and we remand the case for further proceedings not inconsistent with the views herein expressed.

NOTES

1. The leading case interprets Colorado's so-called "make my day" statute (a reference to a movie wherein Clint Eastwood taunts a thug to make threatening moves toward him so that he will be legally justified in killing the thug. The statute, and similar ones like it enacted in a few other states, were passed because of some celebrated civil cases in which homeowners who shot— but failed to kill—intruders then lost their home and all their belongings in defending damage suits brought by the intruders. In some cases, homeowners were convicted of manslaughter for killings under circumstances where the threats were not deemed serious enough to permit the use of deadly force. Make-my-day statutes do not represent the general view in the United States.

2. Defense of the habitation against a dangerous intruder is a right which stems from the law's early view that a man's home is his "fortress" or "castle." This privilege permits one to take the life of an intending trespasser, if the dweller reasonably believes that the threatened entry is for the purpose of committing a felony or inflicting great bodily harm upon an occupant of the house.[1] The rule is even broader in some jurisdictions, allowing the occupant to prevent an intrusion the apparent purpose of which is an assault or other violence non-felonious in nature.[2] The right to defend the habitation permits one to use non-deadly force to prevent a mere civil trespass, although it does not countenance the use of deadly force for that purpose.[3] Where deadly force is inflicted upon a trespasser, however, aggravating circumstances of the trespass may constitute such provocation as to make the killing manslaughter, rather than murder.[4]

The rule allows defense of the habitation by guests or servants of the household, where the occupant himself would be justified in making a defense.[5] It has also been held to encompass the protection of one's place of business, in addition to his dwelling.[6]

One is not bound to retreat from his own house, even if he may do so with safety, in order to avoid taking the life of an assailant. He may stand his ground and kill the aggressor if it becomes necessary.[7]

1. 52 A.L.R.2d 1458.

2. See, e.g., Hayner v. People, 213 Ill. 142, 72 N.E. 792 (1904), and also § 7-2 of the 1961 Illinois Criminal Code which permits the use of deadly force if the entry into a dwelling is made in a "violent, riotous, or tumultuous manner, and he reasonably believes that such force is necessary to prevent an assault upon, or offer personal violence to him or another then in the dwelling. . . ." See also Rex v. Hussey, 18 Cr.App.R. 160 (1924), criticized in 2 Cambridge L.Q. 231 (1925), as carrying the defense of one in his home to an "extreme limit."

3. State v. Hibler, 79 S.C. 170, 60 S.E. 438 (1907).

4. State v. Welch, 37 N.M. 549, 25 P.2d 211 (1933); State v. Adams, 78 Iowa 292, 43 N.W. 194 (1889).

5. Davis v. Commonwealth, 252 S.W.2d 9 (Ky.1952).

6. Suell v. Derricott, 161 Ala. 259, 49 So. 895 (1909). Commonwealth v. Johnston, 438 Pa. 485, 263 A.2d 376 (1970). See, also, 41 A.L.R.3d 584.

7. Jones v. State, 76 Ala. 8 (1884).

But see, Cooper v. United States, 512 A.2d 1002 (D.C.App.1986), holding that a defendant who sought to prove that he acted in self-defense in killing his brother in their home was not entitled to a jury instruction that he had no duty whatsoever to retreat in his own home. The "castle doctrine" does not apply where a defendant claims self defense in response to an attack in his home by a co-occupant.

The use of spring guns or traps for the protection of property or dwellings, resulting in the death of an intruder, may expose the owner of the property to liability for homicide,[8] although some cases have suggested that where the landowner would have been entitled to use similar force if he had been present, the use of the device was lawful.[9]

4. DEFENSE OF PROPERTY OTHER THAN DWELLING

Ordinarily, deadly force cannot be used to protect property or to preserve a lawful right of possession. Use of such force, to be justified, must be sanctioned under a different principle, such as that of self defense, defense of dwelling, or preventing a felony.

Consider the following provision of the Illinois Criminal Code (S.H.A. ch. 38):

§ 7–3.   Use of Force in Defense of Other Property.

A person is justified in the use of force against another when and to the extent that he reasonably believes that such conduct is necessary to prevent or terminate such other's trespass on or other tortious or criminal interference with either real property (other than a dwelling) or personal property, lawfully in his possession or in the possession of another who is a member of his immediate family or household or of a person whose property he has a legal duty to protect. However, he is justified in the use of force which is intended or likely to cause death or great bodily harm only if he reasonably believes that such force is necessary to prevent the commission of a forcible felony.

5. PREVENTION OF A FELONY AND APPREHENSION OF DANGEROUS FELONS

The right to take life to prevent the commission of a felony is confined to the prevention of a *dangerous* felony. A corollary of this principle is the rule that homicide is not justifiable when committed for the protection of mere property rights or interests, although the punishment for such killings is usually of the manslaughter grade rather than murder.[1]

8. State v. Childers, 133 Ohio St. 508, 14 N.E.2d 767 (1938); Pierce v. Commonwealth, 135 Va. 635, 115 S.E. 686 (1923); Katko v. Briney, 183 N.W.2d 657 (Iowa 1971); People v. Ceballos, 12 Cal.3d 470, 116 Cal.Rptr. 233, 526 P.2d 241 (1974).

9. State v. Beckham, 306 Mo. 566, 267 S.W. 817 (1924); State v. Barr, 11 Wash. 481, 39 P. 1080 (1895). However, in State v. Marfaudille, 48 Wash. 117, 92 P. 939 (1907), the court indicated that use of a device could be sanctioned only to prevent atrocious and violent felonies creating danger to human life.

1. See State v. Green, 118 S.C. 279, 110 S.E. 145, 19 A.L.R. 1431 (1921) ("spring gun" killing). Thus a burglar or robber—but not a larcenist or trespasser—may be killed, if such a measure reasonably seems necessary to frustrate the criminal. In Commonwealth v. Beverly, 237 Ky. 35, 34 S.W.2d 941 (1931), which involved the shooting of chicken thieves, the court said: "The law does not justify the taking of human life to prevent a mere trespass without felonious intention, nor to prevent a felony not involving the security of the person or the home or in which violence is not a constituent part."

6. DEADLY FORCE BY POLICE OFFICERS

TENNESSEE v. GARNER

Supreme Court of United States, 1985.
471 U.S. 1, 105 S.Ct. 1694.

JUSTICE WHITE delivered the opinion of the Court.

* * *

I

At about 10:45 p.m. on October 3, 1974, Memphis Police Officers Elton Hymon and Leslie Wright were dispatched to answer a "prowler inside call." Upon arriving at the scene they saw a woman standing on her porch and gesturing toward the adjacent house. She told them she had heard glass breaking and that "they" or "someone" was breaking in next door. While Wright radioed the dispatcher to say that they were on the scene, Hymon went behind the house. He heard a door slam and saw someone run across the backyard. The fleeing suspect, who was appellee-respondent's decedent, Edward Garner, stopped at a 6–feet–high chain link fence at the edge of the yard. With the aid of a flashlight, Hymon was able to see Garner's face and hands. He saw no sign of a weapon, and, though not certain, was "reasonably sure" and "figured" that Garner was unarmed. He thought Garner was 17 or 18 years old and about 5'5" or 5'7" tall. While Garner was crouched at the base of the fence, Hymon called out "police, halt" and took a few steps toward him. Garner then began to climb over the fence. Convinced that if Garner made it over the fence he would elude capture, Hymon shot him. The bullet hit Garner in the back of the head. Garner was taken by ambulance to a hospital, where he died on the operating table. Ten dollars and a purse taken from the house were found on his body.

In using deadly force to prevent the escape, Hymon was acting under the authority of a Tennessee statute and pursuant to Police Department policy. The statute provides that "[i]f, after notice of the intention to arrest the defendant, he either flee or forcibly resist, the officer may use all the necessary means to effect the arrest." Tenn.

The right to kill to prevent a felony applies at any stage prior to completion of the crime. In Vilibovghi v. State, 45 Ariz. 275, 291, 43 P.2d 210, 217 (1935), the court stated: ". . . the owner of the premises burglarized may, at any stage of a burglary, kill the burglar if it be reasonably necessary to prevent the final completion of his felonious purpose, regardless at what stage of the crime the shooting occurs. He may, even after the burglary has been completed, and the burglar is withdrawing from the scene of his crime, if the latter attempts to resist or flee from arrest, use such force as is reasonably necessary for the apprehension of the offender, even to the taking of life."

An individual not only has a right but also an obligation to prevent the commission of a felony in his presence. "According to the common law, it is the duty of everyone, seeing any felony attempted by force to prevent it, if need be, by the extinguishment of the felon's existence. This is a public duty, and the discharge of it is regarded as promotive of justice. Any one who fails to discharge it is guilty of an indictable misdemeanor, called misprision of felony." Carpenter v. State, 62 Ark. 286, 308, 36 S.W. 900, 906 (1896).

Code Ann. § 40–7–108 (1982). The Department policy was slightly more restrictive than the statute, but still allowed the use of deadly force in cases of burglary. The incident was reviewed by the Memphis Police Firearm's Review Board and presented to a grand jury. Neither took any action.

Garner's father then brought this action in the Federal District Court for the Western District of Tennessee, seeking damages under 42 U.S.C. § 1983 for asserted violations of Garner's constitutional rights. . . . [T]he District Court entered judgment for all defendants. It dismissed the claims against the Mayor and the Director for lack of evidence. . . .

* * *

. . . The Court of Appeals reversed and remanded. It reasoned that the killing of a fleeing suspect is a "seizure" under the Fourth Amendment, and is therefore constitutional only if "reasonable." . . . The State of Tennessee, which had intervened to defend the statute, appealed to this Court. . . .

II

Whenever an officer restrains the freedom of a person to walk away, he has seized that person. While it is not always clear just when minimal police interference becomes a seizure, there can be no question that apprehension by the use of deadly force is a seizure subject to the reasonableness requirement of the Fourth Amendment.

A police officer may arrest a person if he has probable cause to believe that person has committed a crime. Petitioners and appellant argue that if this requirement is satisfied the Fourth Amendment has nothing to say about *how* that seizure is made. This submission ignores the many cases in which this Court, by balancing the extent of the intrusion against the need for it, has examined the reasonableness of the manner in which a search and seizure is conducted. . . . We have described the balancing of competing interests as the key principle of the Fourth Amendment. Because one of the factors is the extent of the intrusion, it is plain that reasonableness depends on not only when a seizure is made, but also how it is carried out.

* * *

The same balancing process applied in the cases cited above demonstrates that, notwithstanding probable cause to seize a suspect, an officer may not always do so by killing him. The intrusiveness of a seizure by means of deadly force is unmatched. The suspect's fundamental interest in his own life need not be elaborated upon. The use of deadly force also frustrates the interests of the individual, and of society, in judicial determination of guilt and punishment. Against these interests are ranged governmental interests in effective law enforcement. It is argued that overall violence will be reduced by encouraging the peaceful submission of suspects who know that they may be shot if they flee. Effectiveness in making arrests requires the resort to deadly force, or at least the meaningful threat thereof. . . .

Without in any way disparaging the importance of these goals, we are not convinced that the use of deadly force is a sufficiently productive means of accomplishing them to justify the killing of nonviolent suspects. The use of deadly force is a self-defeating way of apprehending a suspect and so setting the criminal justice mechanism in motion. If successful, it guarantees that that mechanism will not be set in motion. And while the meaningful threat of deadly force might be thought to lead to the arrest of more live suspects by discouraging escape attempts, the presently available evidence does not support this thesis. The fact is that a majority of police departments in this country have forbidden the use of deadly force against nonviolent suspects. If those charged with the enforcement of the criminal law have adjured the use of deadly force in arresting nondangerous felons, there is a substantial basis for doubting that the use of such force is an essential attribute of the arrest power in all felony cases. Petitioners and appellant have not persuaded us that shooting nondangerous fleeing suspects is so vital as to outweigh the suspect's interest in his own life.

The use of deadly force to prevent the escape of all felony suspects, whatever the circumstances, is constitutionally unreasonable. It is not better that all felony suspects die than that they escape. Where the suspect poses no immediate threat to the officer and no threat to others, the harm resulting from failing to apprehend him does not justify the use of deadly force to do so. It is no doubt unfortunate when a suspect who is in sight escapes, but the fact that the police arrive a little late or are a little slower afoot does not always justify killing the suspect. A police officer may not seize an unarmed, nondangerous suspect by shooting him dead. The Tennessee statute is unconstitutional insofar as it authorizes the use of deadly force against such fleeing suspects.

It is not, however, unconstitutional on its face. Where the officer has probable cause to believe that the suspect poses a threat of serious physical harm, either to the officer or to others, it is not constitutionally unreasonable to prevent escape by using deadly force. Thus, if the suspect threatens the officer with a weapon or there is probable cause to believe that he has committed a crime involving the infliction or threatened infliction of serious physical harm, deadly force may be used if necessary to prevent escape, and if, where feasible, some warning has been given. . . .

III

It is insisted that the Fourth Amendment must be construed in light of the common-law rule, which allowed the use of whatever force was necessary to effect the arrest of a fleeing felon, though not a misdemeanant. . . .

The State and city argue that because this was the prevailing rule at the time of the adoption of the Fourth Amendment and for some time thereafter, and is still in force in some States, use of deadly force against a fleeing felon must be "reasonable." It is true that this Court has often looked to the common law in evaluating the reasonableness, for Fourth Amendment purposes, of police activity. On the other hand, it has not simply frozen into constitutional law those law enforcement practices that existed at the time of the Fourth Amendment's passage. Because of sweeping change in the legal and technological context, reliance on the common-law rule in this case would be a mistaken literalism that ignores the purposes of an historical inquiry.

It has been pointed out many times that the common-law rule is best understood in light of the fact that it arose at a time when virtually all felonies were punishable by death. "Though effected without the protections and formalities of an orderly trial and conviction, the killing of a resisting or fleeing felon resulted in no greater consequences than those authorized for punishment of the felony of which the individual was charged or suspected." American Law Institute, Model Penal Code § 3.07, Comment 3, p. 56 (Tentative Draft No. 8, 1958) (hereinafter Model Penal Code Comment). Courts have also justified the common-law rule by emphasizing the relative dangerousness of felons.

Neither of these justifications makes sense today. Almost all crimes formerly punishable by death no longer are or can be. And while in earlier times "the gulf between the felonies and the minor offences was broad and deep," today the distinction is minor and often arbitrary. Many crimes classified as misdemeanors, or nonexistent, at common law are now felonies. These changes have undermined the concept, which was questionable to begin with, that use of deadly force against a fleeing felon is merely a speedier execution of someone who has already forfeited his life. They have also made the assumption that a "felon" is more dangerous than a misdemeanant untenable. Indeed, numerous misdemeanors involve conduct more dangerous than many felonies.

There is an additional reason why the common-law rule cannot be directly translated to the present day. The common-law rule developed at a time when weapons were rudimentary. Deadly force could be inflicted almost solely in a hand-to-hand struggle during which, necessarily, the safety of the arresting officer was at risk. Handguns were not carried by police officers until the latter half of the last century. Only then did it become possible to use deadly force from a distance as a means of apprehension. As a practical matter, the use of deadly force under the standard articulation of the common-law rule has an altogether different meaning—and harsher consequences—now than in past centuries.

One other aspect of the common-law rule bears emphasis. It forbids the use of deadly force to apprehend a misdemeanant, condemning such action as disproportionately severe.

In short, though the common law pedigree of Tennessee's rule is pure on its face, changes in the legal and technological context mean the rule is distorted almost beyond recognition when literally applied.

In evaluating the reasonableness of police procedures under the Fourth Amendment, we have also looked to prevailing rules in individual jurisdictions. The rules in the States are varied. Some 19 States have codified the common-law rule,[1] though in two of these the courts have significantly limited the statute.[2] Four States, though without a relevant statute, apparently retain the common-law rule.[3] Two States have adopted the Model Penal Code's provision verbatim.[4] Eighteen others allow, in slightly varying language, the use of deadly force only if the suspect has committed a felony involving the use or threat of physical or deadly force, or is escaping with a deadly weapon, or is likely to endanger life or inflict serious physical injury if not arrested.[5]

1. Ala.Code § 13A–3–27 (1982); Ark. Stat.Ann. § 41–510 (1977); Cal.Penal Code Ann. § 196 (West 1970); Conn.Gen.Stat. § 53a–22 (1972); Fla.Stat. § 776.05 (1983); Idaho Code § 19–610 (1979); Ind.Code § 35–41–3–3 (1982); Kan.Stat.Ann. § 21–3215 (1981); Miss.Code Ann. § 97–3–15(d) (Supp.1984); Mo.Rev.Stat. § 563.046 (1979); Nev.Rev.Stat. § 200.140 (1983); N.M.Stat. Ann. § 30–2–6 (1984); Okla.Stat., Tit. 21, § 732 (1981); R.I.Gen.Laws § 12–7–9 (1981); S.D.Codified Laws §§ 22–16–32, –33 (1979); Tenn.Code Ann. § 40–7–108 (1982); Wash.Rev.Code § 9A.16.040(3) (1977). Oregon limits use of deadly force to violent felons, but also allows its use against any felon if "necessary." Ore.Rev.Stat. § 161.239 (1983). Wisconsin's statute is ambiguous, but should probably be added to this list. Wis.Stat. § 939.45(4) (1981–1982) (officer may use force necessary for "a reasonable accomplishment of a lawful arrest").

2. In California, the police may use deadly force to arrest only if the crime for which the arrest is sought was "a forcible and atrocious one which threatens death or serious bodily harm," or there is a substantial risk that the person whose arrest is sought will cause death or serious bodily harm if apprehension is delayed. Kortum v. Alkire, 69 Cal.App.3d 325, 333, 138 Cal. Rptr. 26, 30–31 (1977). See also Long Beach Police Officers Assn. v. Long Beach, 61 Cal.App.3d 364, 373–374, 132 Cal.Rptr. 348, 353–354 (1976). In Indiana, deadly force may be used only to prevent injury, the imminent danger of injury or force, or the threat of force. It is not permitted

simply to prevent escape. Rose v. State, 431 N.E.2d 521 (Ind.App.1982).

3. These are Michigan, Ohio, Virginia, and West Virginia. Werner v. Hartfelder, 113 Mich.App. 747, 318 N.W.2d 825 (1982); State v. Foster, 60 Ohio Misc. 46, 59–66, 396 N.E.2d 246, 255–258 (Com.Pl.1979) (citing cases); Berry v. Hamman, 203 Va. 596, 125 S.E.2d 851 (1962); Thompson v. Norfolk & W.R. Co., 116 W.Va. 705, 711–712, 182 S.E. 880, 883–884 (1935).

4. Haw.Rev.Stat. § 703–307 (1976); Neb.Rev.Stat. § 28–1412 (1979). Massachusetts probably belongs in this category. Though it once rejected distinctions between felonies, Uraneck v. Lima, 359 Mass. 749, 750, 269 N.E.2d 670, 671 (1971), it has since adopted the Model Penal Code limitations with regard to private citizens, Commonwealth v. Klein, 372 Mass. 823, 363 N.E.2d 1313 (1977), and seems to have extended that decision to police officers, Julian v. Randazzo, 380 Mass. 391, 403 N.E.2d 931 (1980).

5. Alaska Stat.Ann. § 11.81.370(a) (1983); Ariz.Rev.Stat.Ann. § 13–410 (1978); Colo.Rev.Stat. § 18–1–707 (1978); Del.Code Ann., Tit. 11, § 467 (1979) (felony involving physical force *and* a substantial risk that the suspect will cause death or serious bodily injury *or* will never be recaptured); Ga.Code § 16–3–21(a) (1984); Ill.Rev.Stat., ch. 38, § 7–5 (1984); Iowa Code § 804.8 (1983) (suspect has used or threatened deadly force in commission of a felony, or would use deadly force if not caught); Ky. Rev.Stat. § 503.090 (1984) (suspect committed felony involving use or threat of physical force likely to cause death or serious

M., I. & B. Cs. Crim.Law 5th Ed. UCB—14

Louisiana and Vermont, though without statutes or case-law on point, do forbid the use of deadly force to prevent any but violent felonies.[6] The remaining States either have no relevant statute or case-law, or have positions that are unclear.[7]

It cannot be said that there is a constant or overwhelming trend away from the common-law rule. In recent years, some States have reviewed their laws and expressly rejected abandonment of the common-law rule.[8] Nonetheless, the long-term movement has been away from the rule that deadly force may be used against any fleeing felon, and that remains the rule in less than half the States.

This trend is more evident and impressive when viewed in light of the policies adopted by the police departments themselves. Overwhelmingly, these are more restrictive than the common-law rule. The Federal Bureau of Investigation and the New York City Police Department, for example, both forbid the use of firearms except when necessary to prevent death or grievous bodily harm. For accreditation by the Commission on Accreditation for Law Enforcement Agencies, a department must restrict the use of deadly force to situations where "the officer reasonably believes that the action is in defense of human life . . . or in defense of any person in immediate danger of serious physical injury." . . . Overall, only 7.5% of departmental and municipal policies explicitly permit the use of deadly force against any felon; 86.8% explicitly do not. In light of the rules adopted by those who must actually administer them, the older and fading common-law view is a dubious indicium of the constitutionality of the Tennessee statute now before us.

Actual departmental policies are important for an additional reason. We would hesitate to declare a police practice of longstanding "unreasonable" if doing so would severely hamper effective law enforce-

---

injury, *and* is likely to endanger life unless apprehended without delay); Me.Rev.Stat. Ann., Tit. 17–A, § 107 (1983) (commentary notes that deadly force may be used only "where the person to be arrested poses a threat to human life"); Minn.Stat. § 609.066 (1984); N.H.Rev.Stat.Ann. § 627:5(II) (Supp.1983); N.J.Stat.Ann. § 2C–3–7 (West 1982); N.Y.Penal Law § 35.30 (McKinney Supp. 1984–1985); N.C. Gen.Stat. § 15A–401 (1983); N.D.Cent. Code § 12.1–05–07.2.d (1976); Pa.Stat. Ann., Tit. 18, § 508 (Purdon); Tex.Penal Code Ann. § 9.51(c) (1974); Utah Code Ann. § 76–2–404 (1978).

6. See La.Rev.Stat.Ann. § 14:20(2) (West 1974); Vt.Stat.Ann., Tit. 13, § 2305 (1974 and Supp.1984). A Federal District Court has interpreted the Louisiana statute to limit the use of deadly force against fleeing suspects to situations where "life itself is endangered or great bodily harm is threatened." Sauls v. Hutto, 304 F.Supp. 124, 132 (ED La.1969).

7. These are Maryland, Montana, South Carolina, and Wyoming. A Maryland appellate court has indicated, however, that deadly force may not be used against a felon who "was in the process of fleeing and, at the time, presented no immediate danger to . . . anyone. . . ." Giant Food, Inc. v. Scherry, 51 Md.App. 586, 589, 596, 444 A.2d 483, 486, 489 (1982).

8. In adopting its current statute in 1979, for example, Alabama expressly chose the common-law rule over more restrictive provisions. Ala.Code §§ 67–68 (1982). Missouri likewise considered but rejected a proposal akin to the Model Penal Code rule. See Mattis v. Schnarr, 547 F.2d 1007, 1022 (CA8 1976) (Gibson, C.J., dissenting), vacated as moot sub nom. Ashcroft v. Mattis, 431 U.S. 171, 97 S.Ct. 1739, 52 L.Ed.2d 219 (1977). Idaho, whose current statute codifies the common-law rule, adopted the Model Penal Code in 1971, but abandoned it in 1972.

ment. But the indications are to the contrary. There has been no suggestion that crime has worsened in any way in jurisdictions that have adopted, by legislation or departmental policy, rules similar to that announced today. *Amici* noted that "[a]fter extensive research and consideration, [they] have concluded that laws permitting police officers to use deadly force to apprehend unarmed, non-violent fleeing felony suspects actually do not protect citizens or law enforcement officers, do not deter crime or alleviate problems caused by crime, and do not improve the crime-fighting ability of law enforcement agencies." The submission is that the obvious state interests in apprehension are not sufficiently served to warrant the use of lethal weapons against all fleeing felons.

*   *   *

V

. . . We hold that the statute is invalid insofar as it purported to give Hymon the authority to act as he did. As for the policy of the Police Department, the absence of any discussion of this issue by the courts below, and the uncertain state of the record, preclude any consideration of its validity.

The judgment of the Court of Appeals is affirmed, and the case is remanded for further proceedings consistent with this opinion.

So ordered.

JUSTICE O'CONNOR, with whom THE CHIEF JUSTICE, and JUSTICE REHNQUIST join, dissenting.

The Court today holds that the Fourth Amendment prohibits a police officer from using deadly force as a last resort to apprehend a criminal suspect who refuses to halt when fleeing the scene of a nighttime burglary. This conclusion rests on the majority's balancing of the interests of the suspect and the public interest in effective law enforcement. Notwithstanding the venerable common-law rule authorizing the use of deadly force if necessary to apprehend a fleeing felon, and continued acceptance of this rule by nearly half the States, the majority concludes that Tennessee's statute is unconstitutional inasmuch as it allows the use of such force to apprehend a burglary suspect who is not obviously armed or otherwise dangerous. Although the circumstances of this case are unquestionably tragic and unfortunate, our constitutional holdings must be sensitive both to the history of the Fourth Amendment and to the general implications of the Court's reasoning. By disregarding the serious and dangerous nature of residential burglaries and the longstanding practice of many States, the Court effectively creates a Fourth Amendment right allowing a burglary suspect to flee unimpeded from a police officer who has probable cause to arrest, who has ordered the suspect to halt, and who has no means short of firing his weapon to prevent escape. I do not believe that the Fourth Amendment supports such a right, and I accordingly dissent.

I

The facts below warrant brief review because they highlight the difficult, split-second decisions police officers must make in these circumstances. Memphis Police Officers Elton Hymon and Leslie Wright responded to a late-night call that a burglary was in progress at a private residence. When the officers arrived at the scene, the caller said that "they" were breaking into the house next door. The officers found the residence had been forcibly entered through a window and saw lights on inside the house. Officer Hymon testified that when he saw the broken window he realized "that something was wrong inside," but that he could not determine whether anyone—either a burglar or a member of the household—was within the residence. As Officer Hymon walked behind the house, he heard a door slam. He saw Edward Eugene Garner run away from the house through the dark and cluttered backyard. Garner crouched next to a 6–foot–high fence. Officer Hymon thought Garner was an adult and was unsure whether Garner was armed because Hymon "had no idea what was in the hand [that he could not see] or what he might have had on his person." In fact, Garner was 15 years old and unarmed. Hymon also did not know whether accomplices remained inside the house. The officer identified himself as a police officer and ordered Garner to halt. Garner paused briefly and then sprang to the top of the fence. Believing that Garner would escape if he climbed over the fence, Hymon fired his revolver and mortally wounded the suspected burglar.

* * *

The Court affirms on the ground that application of the Tennessee statute to authorize Officer Hymon's use of deadly force constituted an unreasonable seizure in violation of the Fourth Amendment. The precise issue before the Court deserves emphasis, because both the decision below and the majority obscure what must be decided in this case. The issue is not the constitutional validity of the Tennessee statute on its face or as applied to some hypothetical set of facts. Instead, the issue is whether the use of deadly force by Officer Hymon under the circumstances of this case violated Garner's constitutional rights. . . . The question we must address is whether the Constitution allows the use of such force to apprehend a suspect who resists arrest by attempting to flee the scene of a nighttime burglary of a residence.

II

For purposes of Fourth Amendment analysis, I agree with the Court that Officer Hymon "seized" Garner by shooting him. Whether that seizure was reasonable and therefore permitted by the Fourth Amendment requires a careful balancing of the important public interest in crime prevention and detection and the nature and quality of the intrusion upon legitimate interests of the individual. . . .

The public interest involved in the use of deadly force as a last resort to apprehend a fleeing burglary suspect relates primarily to the serious nature of the crime. Household burglaries represent not only the illegal entry into a person's home, but also "pos[e] real risk of serious harm to others." . . . According to recent Department of Justice statistics, "[t]hree-fifths of all rapes in the home, three-fifths of all home robberies, and about a third of home aggravated and simple assaults are committed by burglars." During the period 1973–1982, 2.8 million such violent crimes were committed in the course of burglaries. Victims of a forcible intrusion into their home by a nighttime prowler will find little consolation in the majority's confident assertion that "burglaries only rarely involve physical violence." Moreover, even if a particular burglary, when viewed in retrospect, does not involve physical harm to others, the "harsh potentialities for violence" inherent in the forced entry into a home preclude characterization of the crime as "innocuous, inconsequential, minor, or 'nonviolent.' " . . .

Because burglary is a serious and dangerous felony, the public interest in the prevention and detection of the crime is of compelling importance. Where a police officer has probable cause to arrest a suspected burglar, the use of deadly force as a last resort might well be the only means of apprehending the suspect. With respect to a particular burglary, subsequent investigation simply cannot represent a substitute for immediate apprehension of the criminal suspect at the scene. Indeed, the Captain of the Memphis Police Department testified that in his city, if apprehension is not immediate, it is likely that the suspect will not be caught. Although some law enforcement agencies may choose to assume the risk that a criminal will remain at large, the Tennessee statute reflects a legislative determination that the use of deadly force in prescribed circumstances will serve generally to protect the public. Such statutes assist the police in apprehending suspected perpetrators of serious crimes and provide notice that a lawful police order to stop and submit to arrest may not be ignored with impunity.

The Court unconvincingly dismisses the general deterrence effects by stating that "the presently available evidence does not support [the] thesis" that the threat of force discourages escape and that "there is a substantial basis for doubting that the use of such force is an essential attribute to the arrest power in all felony cases." There is no question that the effectiveness of police use of deadly force is arguable and that many States or individual police departments have decided not to authorize it in circumstances similar to those presented here. But it should go without saying that the effectiveness or popularity of a particular police practice does not determine its constitutionality. . . . Moreover, the fact that police conduct pursuant to a state statute is challenged on constitutional grounds does not impose a burden on the State to produce social science statistics or to dispel any possible doubts about the necessity of the conduct. This observation, I believe, has particular force where the challenged practice both predates enactment of the Bill of Rights and continues to be accepted by a substantial number of the States.

Against the strong public interests justifying the conduct at issue here must be weighed the individual interests implicated in the use of deadly force by police officers. The majority declares that "[t]he suspect's fundamental interest in his own life need not be elaborated upon." This blithe assertion hardly provides an adequate substitute for the majority's failure to acknowledge the distinctive manner in which the suspect's interest in his life is even exposed to risk. For purposes of this case, we must recall that the police officer, in the course of investigating a nighttime burglary, had reasonable cause to arrest the suspect and ordered him to halt. The officer's use of force resulted because the suspected burglar refused to heed this command and the officer reasonably believed that there was no means short of firing his weapon to apprehend the suspect. Without questioning the importance of a person's interest in his life, I do not think this interest encompasses a right to flee unimpeded from the scene of a burglary. . . . The legitimate interests of the suspect in these circumstances are adequately accommodated by the Tennessee statute: to avoid the use of deadly force and the consequent risk to his life, the suspect need merely obey the valid order to halt.

A proper balancing of the interests involved suggests that use of deadly force as a last resort to apprehend a criminal suspect fleeing from the scene of a nighttime burglary is not unreasonable within the meaning of the Fourth Amendment. . . .

* * *

III

Even if I agreed that the Fourth Amendment was violated under the circumstances of this case, I would be unable to join the Court's opinion. The Court holds that deadly force may be used only if the suspect "threatens the officer with a weapon or there is probable cause to believe that he has committed a crime involving the infliction or threatened infliction of serious physical harm." The Court ignores the more general implications of its reasoning. Relying on the Fourth Amendment, the majority asserts that it is constitutionally unreasonable to *use* deadly force against fleeing criminal suspects who do not appear to pose a threat of serious physical harm to others. By declining to limit its holding to the use of firearms, the Court unnecessarily implies that the Fourth Amendment constrains the use of any police practice that is potentially lethal, no matter how remote the risk.

Although it is unclear from the language of the opinion, I assume that the majority intends the word "use" to include only those circumstances in which the suspect is actually apprehended. Absent apprehension of the suspect, there is no "seizure" for Fourth Amendment purposes. I doubt that the Court intends to allow criminal suspects who successfully escape to return later with § 1983 claims against officers who used, albeit unsuccessfully, deadly force in their futile attempt to capture the fleeing suspect. The Court's opinion, despite its broad language, actually decides only that the shooting of a fleeing burglary suspect who was in fact neither armed nor dangerous can support a § 1983 action.

The Court's silence on critical factors in the decision to use deadly force simply invites second-guessing of difficult police decisions that must be made quickly in the most trying of circumstances. Police are given no guidance for determining which objects, among an array of potentially lethal weapons ranging from guns to knives to baseball bats to rope, will justify the use of deadly force. The Court also declines to outline the additional factors necessary to provide "probable cause" for believing that a suspect "poses a significant threat of death or serious physical injury," when the officer has probable cause to arrest and the suspect refuses to obey an order to halt. But even if it were appropriate in this case to limit the use of deadly force to that ambiguous class of suspects, I believe the class should include nighttime residential burglars who resist arrest by attempting to flee the scene of the crime. We can expect an escalating volume of litigation as the lower courts struggle to determine if a police officer's split-second decision to shoot was justified by the danger posed by a particular object and other facts related to the crime.

IV

The Court's opinion sweeps broadly to adopt an entirely new standard for the constitutionality of the use of deadly force to apprehend fleeing felons. Thus, the Court lightly brushe[s] aside a long-standing police practice that predates the Fourth Amendment and continues to receive the approval of nearly half of the state legislatures. I cannot accept the majority's creation of a constitutional right to flight for burglary suspects seeking to avoid capture at the scene of the crime. Whatever the constitutional limits on police use of deadly force in order to apprehend a fleeing felon, I do not believe they are exceeded in a case in which a police officer has probable cause to arrest a suspect at the scene of a residential burglary, orders the suspect to halt, and then fires his weapon as a last resort to prevent the suspect's escape into the night. I respectfully dissent.

NOTES

1. With respect to the listing of Illinois among the various states in footnote 6, consider the wording of the following Illinois Criminal Code provision, Ch. 38, of the Illinois Revised Statutes, § 7–5, and particularly (a)(2):

7–5.   § 7–5 Peace Officer's Use of Force in Making Arrest. (a) A peace officer, or any person whom he has summoned or directed to assist him, need not retreat or desist from efforts to make a lawful arrest because of resistance or threatened resistance to the arrest. He is justified in the use of any force which he reasonably believes to be necessary to effect the arrest and of any force which he reasonably believes to be necessary to defend himself or another from bodily harm while making the arrest. However, he is justified in using force likely to cause death or great bodily harm only when he reasonably believes that such force is necessary to prevent death or great bodily harm to himself or such other person, or when he reasonably believes both that:

(1) Such force is necessary to prevent the arrest from being defeated by resistance or escape; and

(2) The person to be arrested has committed or attempted a forcible felony or is attempting to escape by use of a deadly weapon, or otherwise indicates that he will endanger human life or inflict great bodily harm unless arrested without delay.

(b) A peace officer making an arrest pursuant to an invalid warrant is justified in the use of any force which he would be justified in using if the warrant were valid, unless he knows that the warrant is invalid.

2. Pursuant to a grant from the National Institute of Justice (United States Department of Justice), the International Association of Chiefs of Police conducted an eighteen month study of police homicides from 1970 through 1979 in the nation's fifty-seven largest municipal police agencies. The report was published in 1981 under the title of A Balance of Forces: A Study of Justifiable Homicide by the Police. A brief summary of the report appears in the IACP Newsletter of December, 1981. The summary reads as follows:

"The authority to use deadly force is the most critical responsibility that will ever be placed on a police officer. No other single person has the right and the immediate means to lawfully take another's life.

"The consequences of a decision to use deadly force are irreversible after the fact—it is a final action. No court of competent jurisdiction, administrative tribunal, or Presidential grant of clemency can ever reverse the decision. Similarly, a decision not to use deadly force can also mean finality. A hesitation, or conscious decision on the part of the police officer could very well result in the death of the officer or another person the officer is sworn to safeguard. These are decisions unlike any other which are required by our society.

"The control of deadly force through the development of policy is also an awesome responsibility for the police administrator. The police administrator must promulgate use of deadly force policy that will provide sufficient protection to his officers; provide officers with guidance yet allow for a realistic exercise of discretion; provide all citizens with an assurance of safety; and provide all persons with the guarantees granted to them by the Constitution of the United States. Policy statements which meet these criteria can only be set forth after extensive research.

"The object of this study was to provide the police administrator with sufficient research data from which to:

- Identify factors of law enforcement that underlie and determine the frequency of use of deadly force by police officers.

- Gain an understanding of the interrelationships of these factors and their causal role in homicides by police officers.

- Develop 'model' policy and procedure designed to reduce police homicides while preserving the officer's ability to fulfill his law enforcement duties and protect himself from death or personal harm.

"This study primarily addresses those justifiable homicides which *may* be preventable through the adoption of new policy, training, equipment, and operational techniques.

"On the premise that a significant number of law enforcement-related homicides occur within urban areas, this study is focused on the 57 police agencies operating in urban areas having a population of 250,000 or more.

"The study included both empirical research and analytical review of factors considered to be associated with the use of deadly force by the police. The format of the final report includes:

- An introduction of the issues

- A legal review of the deadly force issues

- A statistical review which compares crime to justifiable homicide

- A survey and analysis of deadly force factors in 54 law enforcement agencies (three did not respond)

- A content analysis of deadly force policy in 53 law enforcement agencies (four did not respond)

- Recommended 'deadly force' policy guidelines

*   *   *

Statistical Comparison of Crime to Justifiable Homicide

"Various authors have indicated that there may be a serious flaw in the statistical reporting of justifiable homicides by the police. Other criminal justice authorities who recognized the limitations have called for mandatory reporting of justifiable homicides. Despite the known limitations, it is felt that a careful analysis of justifiable homicide data would yield significant information. Accordingly, it was possible to secure from the FBI Uniform Crime Reports unpublished data regarding justifiable homicide for the years 1970 through 1979. For the 57 cities, the justifiable homicide totals were 291 in 1970, 388 in 1971, 314 in 1972, 317 in 1973, 356 in 1974, 360 in 1975, 268 in 1976, 262 in 1977, 249 in 1978 and 289 in 1979.

"For the years 1975–79, this data was verified with the reporting police agencies. Although the data was not always immediately parallel, it was ultimately possible to resolve any discrepancies that existed between the FBI data and the data submitted directly to IACP.

"Using the justifiable homicide totals as the common denominator, a comparison was made of the totals of selected crimes and justifiable homicide from the same cities. The following were found to be significantly related to justifiable homicide by the police:

- robbery offenses

- police officer murdered

- justifiable homicide by civilian

- total community homicide

Next, a comparison was made of *each* individual city's justifiable homicides by the police to selected crimes and justifiable homicide. This comparison was made by using a five-year average of justifiable homicide with the five-year average of crime. The significant correlations were:

- homicide

- violent crime

- robbery
- justifiable homicide by civilian
- police officers murdered

These correlations constitute the central research findings of this report. The findings imply that the use of deadly force by the police is concentrated within an environment of community violence in general.

The Issue of Race

"It has been known that blacks are overrepresented among victims of justifiable homicide by the police. But never has the issue been presented in such a manner as in recent years. For example:

'Police have one trigger finger for whites and another for blacks.' (Dr. Paul Takagi, University of California researcher, in a speech before United Methodist Clergy and Laity, April 1979.)

'In the absence of more conclusive evidence, the demonstrably higher rates of police homicide of blacks strongly suggest racial discrimination on a national basis.' (Lawrence W. Sherman, Execution Without Trial: Police Homicide and the Constitution, Vanderbilt Law Review, January 1981, p. 97.)

'While we meet here, some police officer somewhere in America is shooting a civilian. And if today's case is typical, that civilian will be a black or a Hispanic person. If that incident follows the averages, it is likely the victim is a young person. It is likely that the incident involved a non-felony offense. It is possible the victim was unarmed. It is possible that the shooting could have been avoided. And it is certain that no punitive action will be taken against the policeman doing the shooting.' (Vernon E. Jordan, Jr., President, National Urban League, National Consultation on Safety and Force Summary Report, U.S. Department of Justice, Dec. '79, p. 7.)

"Like other researchers before us, this study found that blacks are overrepresented (59.6) as victims of police use of deadly force. However, our findings show that blacks are also overrepresented in other areas of violence:

- Justifiable homicide by police (59.6)
- Victims of justifiable homicide by civilians (73.1)
- Persons arrested for robbery (71.0)
- Persons arrested for violent crimes (63.7)
- Persons arrested for weapon violations (57.9)

"Concerning the shooters, 15.7 percent of all police officers who shoot civilians are black, 58.3 percent are white, 25.1 percent are of unreported race, and 0.9 percent are of 'other' races.

"These research findings do not statistically prove or disprove the existence of police discrimination. What the data are consistent with is that the disproportionate rate of black victims of police justifiable homicide is in proportion to the level of police exposure to blacks as represented by blacks arrested for crime.

Survey and Analyses of Potential Deadly Force Factors

"Using the number of justifiable homicides identified (1975–79) and the number of police officers, a Justifiable Homicide Rate (JHR) was established for each city. The rate ranged from a low of .04 justifiable homicides per 100 officers per year to a high of .77 with the mean being .28.

"A survey instrument consisting of more than 300 data points was developed and mailed to 57 major police agencies (fifty-four agencies completed the survey). The instrument was designed to identify pertinent data relative to each agency's personnel practices, training, firearms equipment, organizational units, policy, and procedure which could lead to answers as to why police agencies use deadly force in differing frequencies. Responses to the survey were statistically compared to the JHR in each city. One or more statistical tests were used to test hypotheses concerning the independent variables represented by the survey responses and the dependent variable represented by the JHR.

"The results of this analysis showed the following variables to be associated with high justifiable homicide rates:

1. A high supervisory/officer ratio
2. The use of semi-automatic handguns by SWAT [Special Weapons and Tactics] units
3. In-service SWAT unit training
4. The absence of policy for the management of stake-out units
5. The absence of policy for the management of decoy units
6. Patrol command response to the scene of deadly force incidents
7. Police chief and district attorney review of deadly force incidents
8. In-service crisis intervention training
9. Exertion type of pre-service firearms training
10. Exertion and stress in-service firearms training
11. The awarding of incentives for firearms marksmanship
12. In-service officer survival training
13. The issuance of on-duty firearms larger than .38 caliber
14. The issuance of shotguns

"These findings should be interpreted with caution since it was not always possible to clearly establish a cause/effect relationship using this research approach. For example, patrol command, police chief and district attorney response to deadly force may be the effect of a high JHR rather than the cause; likewise, the emphasis on training may have come about as a result of a high justifiable homicide rate.

Policy Content Analysis

"Selected national deadly force policy recommendations were reviewed in an effort to obtain a 'feel' for the community desires. Such reviews included policy, resolutions, or recommendations offered by: (1) the American Law Institute, (2) Federal Bureau of Investigation, (3) International Association of Chiefs of Police, (4) the President's Commission on Law Enforcement and Administration of Justice, (5) the Wisconsin Institute of Government Affairs, (6) the American Bar Association, (7) the National Organization of Black Law Enforcement Executives, (8) the United Nations, and (9) the American Civil Liberties Union. These recommendations were found to be inconsistent, vague, and generally less than comprehensive.

"Next a cursory analysis of a limited number of deadly force directives submitted by federal law enforcement agencies was conducted. This analysis shed only a little light on the issue of municipal police use of deadly force. Their statements are more general in nature than are the guidelines issued by municipal agencies. The differences in federal law enforcement missions was evident in the directives.

"A similar analysis was undertaken of state police and state patrol agencies. Their deadly force directives were found to be generally consistent with state law but not more restrictive than law.

"Fifty-three municipal police agencies responded to our request for a copy of their deadly force directives. These directives (policy, general order, operating procedure, training bulletin) were evaluated in relationship to each agency's justifiable homicide rate in an effort to determine if any relationships existed.

Recommended Policy Guidelines

"The research report is concluded with a chapter which details 'model' use of deadly force policy and procedural guidelines which are designed to aid the police chief executive in determining specific agency directives. These 'model' guidelines are based on the report's (1) legal findings, (2) statistical testing of 40 hypotheses which took into account more than 300 management and operational factors which were considered as possible influences on the rate of justifiable homicide, (3) analysis and statistical testing of 53 agencies' written directives which deal with the use of deadly force issue, and (4) the thorough review of findings from other deadly force research efforts.

"The 'model' guidelines specifically address the policy, procedural, and equipment issues related to defense of life, reasonable danger, imminent threat, prevention of felonies, fleeing felons, juveniles, moving vehicles, warning shots, shooting of animals, on-duty firearms, off-duty firearms, secondary firearms, control of all firearms, type and frequency of certification training, post-shooting legal services, post-shooting psychological services, the shooting investigation, and the shooting review process.

"Deadly force policy decisions are not easily made by the chief executive, nor is the ultimate decision to shoot an easy one for the law enforcement officer. The consequences of deadly force policy and action decisions are far-reaching. It is, however, far better that most of the decision considerations be critically researched and developed from within a calm, rational atmosphere of the administrator's office than from the explosive, irrational, and unpredictable 'office' (the street) of the police officer.

"Consequently, each police chief executive must promulgate and continuously update use of deadly force directives. The executive is encouraged to use the 'model' guidelines and supporting research as a framework to develop local deadly force training standards, equipment standards, and policy and procedural directives."

3. In a 1982 article by Professor James J. Fyfe, Blind Justice: Police Shootings in Memphis, 73 J.Crim.L. & C. 707 (1982), he reports the following conclusion:

"Police shootings are a consequence of violence in the community and the number of times members of various population subgroups expose themselves to the danger of being shot at by police; but levels of police shootings are also greatly affected by organizational variables. Thus, analysis of the circumstances under which shootings occur can point the way to police administrative action to reduce elective shootings. It may also suggest broader social action to change the conditions which spawn the nonelective shootings over which police chiefs and police officers have very limited direct control.

"Administrative action to reduce elective shootings in Memphis has occurred since the end of the period studied in this report. In 1979, for example, that department instituted a more stringent shooting policy and incident review procedure than had existed. It has also recently initiated an 'officer survival' training program designed to help police more safely respond to the potentially violent situations which often precipitate nonelective shootings. In short, apparently the Memphis Police Department has acted responsibly to address major problems in the use of deadly force by its officers."

See, also, Geller, Deadly Force, What We Know, 10 J.Police Sci. & Adm. 151 (1982).

D. INVOLUNTARY MANSLAUGHTER

STATE v. HORTON

Supreme Court of North Carolina, 1905.
139 N.C. 588, 51 S.E. 945.

[The defendant, Horton, in violation of a statute, was hunting turkeys on the land of another without the written consent of the owner of the land or his lawful agent. While hunting, Horton unintentionally killed one Hunt, mistaking him for a wild turkey. Horton was indicted for manslaughter, convicted and sentenced to four months in the county jail. Thereupon, the defendant appealed.]

HOKE, JUSTICE. It will be noted that the finding of the jury declares that the act of the defendant was not in itself dangerous to human life, and excludes every element of criminal negligence, and rests the guilt or innocence of the defendant on the fact alone that at the time of the homicide the defendant was hunting on another's land without written permission from the owner. The act . . . makes the conduct a misdemeanor, and imposes a punishment on conviction of not less than $5 nor more than $10. The statement sometimes appears in works of approved excellence to the effect that an unintentional homicide is a criminal offense when occasioned by a person engaged at the time in an unlawful act. In nearly every instance, however, will be found the qualification that if the act in question is free from negligence, and not in itself of dangerous tendency, and the criminality must arise, if at all, entirely from the fact that it is unlawful, in such case, the unlawful act must be one that is "malum in se," and not merely "malum prohibitum," and this we hold to be the correct doctrine. . . .

. . . Bishop, in his work entitled New Criminal Law (volume 1, § 332), treats of the matter as follows: "In these cases of an unintended evil result, the intent whence the act accidentally sprang must probably be, if specific, to do a thing which is malum in se, and not merely malum prohibitum." Thus Archbold says: "When a man in the execution of one act, by misfortune or chance, and not designedly, does another act, for which, if he had willfully committed it, he would be liable to be punished, in that case, if the act he were doing were lawful, or merely malum prohibitum, he shall not be punishable for the act arising from misfortune or chance; but, if it be malum in se, it is otherwise. To illustrate: Since it is malum prohibitum, not malum in se, for an unauthorized person to kill game in England contrary to the statutes, if, in unlawfully shooting at game, he accidentally kills a man, it is no more criminal in him than if he were authorized. But to shoot at another's fowls, wantonly or in sport, an act which is malum in se, though a civil trespass, and thereby accidentally to kill a human being, is manslaughter. If the intent in the shooting were to commit larceny of the fowls, we have seen that it would be murder." To same effect is Estell v. State, 51 N.J.L. 182, 17 A. 118; Com. v. Adams, 114 Mass. 323, 19 Am.Rep. 362. An offense malum in se is properly defined as one which is naturally evil as adjudged by the sense of a civilized community, whereas an act malum prohibitum is wrong only because made so by statute. For the reason that acts malum in se have, as a rule, become criminal offenses by the course and development of the common law, an impression has sometimes obtained that only acts can be so classified which the common law makes criminal; but this is not at all the test. An act can be, and frequently is, malum in se, when it amounts only to a civil trespass, provided it has a malicious element or manifests an evil nature or wrongful disposition to harm or injure another in his person or property. The distinction between the two classes of acts is well stated in 19 Am. & Eng.Enc. (2d Ed.), at page 705: "An offense malum in se is one which is naturally evil, as murder, theft, and the like. Offenses at common law are generally malum in se. An offense malum prohibitum, on the contrary, is not naturally an evil, but becomes so in consequence of being forbidden."

We do not hesitate to declare that the offense of the defendant in hunting on the land without written permission of the owner was malum prohibitum, and, the special verdict having found that the act in which the defendant was engaged was not in itself dangerous to human life and negatived all idea of negligence, we hold that the case is one of excusable homicide, and the defendant should be declared not guilty. . . .

. . . [I]t has been called to our attention that courts of the highest authority have declared that the distinction between malum prohibitum and malum in se is unsound, and has now entirely disappeared. Our own court so held in Sharp v. Farmer, 20 N.C. 255, and decisions to the same effect have been made several times since. Said Ruffin, C.J., in Sharp v. Farmer: "The distinction between an act malum in se and one malum prohibitum was never sound, and is entirely disregarded; for the law would be false to itself if it allowed a party through its tribunals to derive advantage from a contract made against the intent and express provisions of the law." It will be noted that this decision was on a case involving the validity of a contract, and the principle there established is undoubtedly correct. The fact, however, that the judge who delivered the opinion uses the words "was never sound," and that other opinions to the same effect use the words "has disappeared," shows that the distinction has existed; and it existed, too, at a time when this feature in the law of homicide was established. And we are well assured that because the courts, in administering the law on the civil side of the docket, have come to the conclusion that a principle once established is unsound and should be rejected, this should not have the effect of changing the character of an act from innocence to guilt, which had its status fixed when the distinction was recognized and enforced. . . .

There was error in holding the defendant guilty, and, on the facts declared, a verdict of not guilty should be directed, and the defendant discharged.

Reversed.

NOTE

Compare the following statement of the court in State v. Brown, 205 S.C. 514, 519, 32 S.E.2d 825, 827 (1945):

"The responsibility for a death is sometimes made to depend on whether the unlawful act is malum in se or malum prohibitum. The authorities agree, however, without regard to this distinction, that if the act is a violation of a statute intended and designated to prevent injury to the person, and is itself dangerous, and death ensues, the person violating the statute is guilty of manslaughter at least."

PEOPLE v. MARSHALL

Supreme Court of Michigan, 1961.
362 Mich. 170, 106 N.W.2d 842.

SMITH, JUSTICE. At approximately 3:00 a.m. on the morning of February 4, 1958, a car driven by Neal McClary, traveling in the wrong direction on the Edsel Ford Expressway, crashed head-on into another vehicle driven by James Coldiron. The drivers of both cars were killed. Defendant William Marshall has been found guilty of involuntary manslaughter of Coldiron. At the time that the fatal accident took place, he, the defendant William Marshall, was in bed at his place of residence. His connection with it was that he owned the car driven by McClary, and as the evidence tended to prove, he voluntarily gave his keys to the car to McClary, with knowledge that McClary was drunk.

The principal issue in the case is whether, upon these facts, the defendant may be found guilty of involuntary manslaughter. It is axiomatic that "criminal guilt under our law is personal fault." . . . As Sayre . . . puts the doctrine "it is of the very essence of our deeprooted notions of criminal liability that guilt be personal and individual." This was not always true in our law, nor is it universally true in all countries even today, but for us it is settled doctrine.

The State relies on a case, Story v. United States, . . . in which the owner, driving with a drunk, permitted him to take the wheel, and was held liable for aiding and abetting him "in his criminal negligence." The owner, said the court, sat by his side and permitted him "without protest so recklessly and negligently to operate the car as to cause the death of another." . . . If defendant Marshall had been by McClary's side an entirely different case would be presented, but on the facts before us Marshall, as we noted, was at home in bed. The State also points out that although it is only a misdemeanor to drive while drunk, yet convictions for manslaughter arising out of drunk driving have often been sustained. It argues from these cases that although it was only a misdemeanor for an owner to turn his keys over to a drunk driver, nevertheless a conviction for manslaughter may be sustained if such driver kills another. This does not follow from such cases as Story, supra. In the case before us death resulted from the misconduct of driver. The accountability of the owner must rest as a matter of general principle, upon his complicity in such misconduct. In turning his keys over, he was guilty of a specific offense, for which he incurred a specific penalty. Upon these facts he cannot be held a principal with respect to the fatal accident: the killing of Coldiron was not counselled by him, accomplished by another acting jointly with him, nor did it occur in the attempted achievement of some common enterprise.

This is not to say that defendant is guilty of nothing. He was properly found guilty of violation of paragraph (b) of section 625 of the Michigan vehicle code which makes it punishable for the owner of an automobile knowingly to permit it to be driven by a person "who is under the influence of intoxicating liquor." The State urges that this is not enough, that its manslaughter theory, above outlined, "was born of necessity," and that the urgency of the drunk-driver problem "has made it incumbent upon responsible and concerned law enforcement officials to seek new approaches to a new problem within the limits of our law." What the State actually seeks from us is an interpretation that the manslaughter statute imposes an open-end criminal liability. That is to say, whether the owner may ultimately go to prison for manslaughter or some lesser offense will depend upon whatever unlawful act the driver commits while in the car. Such a theory may be defensible as a matter of civil liability but [in his American Rights, 85, 86] Gellhorn's language in another criminal context is equally applicable here: "It is a basic proposition in a constitutional society that crimes should be defined in advance, and not after action has been taken." We are not unaware of the magnitude of the problem presented, but the new approaches demanded for its solution rest with the legislature, not the courts.

The view we have taken of the case renders it unnecessary to pass upon other allegations of error. The verdict and sentence on that count of the information dealing with involuntary manslaughter are set aside and the case remanded to the circuit court for sentencing on the verdict of the jury respecting the violation, as charged, of section 625(b) of the Michigan Vehicle Code, discussed hereinabove.

COMMONWEALTH v. FEINBERG

Superior Court of Pennsylvania, 1967.
211 Pa.Super. 100, 234 A.2d 913.
Affirmed 433 Pa. 558, 253 A.2d 636 (1969).

MONTGOMERY, JUDGE. These appeals are from judgments of sentence imposed following appellant's conviction on five charges of involuntary manslaughter. They arose by reason of the deaths of five individuals from methyl alcohol (methanol) poisoning due to their consumption of Sterno, a jelly-like substance prepared and intended for heating purposes. It is solidified alcohol popularly called "canned heat" but has additives specified by the United States government to render it unfit for drinking purposes.

Appellant Max Feinberg was the owner of a cigar store handling tobacco, candy, etc., in the skid-row section of Philadelphia and sold to residents of that area Sterno in two types of containers, one for home use and one for institutional use. Such sales were made under circumstances from which it could be reasonably concluded that appellant knew the purchasers were intending to use it for drinking purposes by diluting it with water or other beverages, and not for its intended use. Prior to December, 1963, there had been no known fatal consequences resulting from this practice, presumably for the reason that the product then sold by appellant contained only four per cent methyl alcohol (methanol). However, on December 21, 1963 appellant bought from the Richter Paper Company ten additional cases of institutional Sterno containing seventy-two cans each, unaware that it contained fifty-four per cent methanol, although the lid of each container was marked "Institutional Sterno. Danger. Poison; Not for home use. For commercial and industrial use only", and had a skull and crossbones imprinted thereon. Nevertheless appellant ignored this warning and sold part of this supply in the same manner he had previously dispensed his other supply of the product. The containers of the regular Sterno and the institutional type previously sold contained no such warning and were merely marked "Caution. Flammable. For use only as a fuel." The only difference in the containers previously sold was that the institutional type was so marked but had no wrap-around label as was affixed to the container intended for regular use. Both containers were the same size, as were the containers sold after December 21st which did not contain wrap-around labels. Between December 23 and December 30, 1963, thirty-one persons died in this area as a result of methyl alcohol poisoning. After hearing of their deaths, appellant, on December 28, 1963 returned to the Richter Paper Company four cases and forty-two cans which remained unsold from the ten cases he had purchased on December 21, 1963, at which time he remarked about the change in markings on the cans. Appellant was the only purchaser in the Philadelphia area of this new institutional product from the Richter Company. The methanol content of institutional Sterno had been increased by the manufacturer from four per cent to fifty-four per cent in September, 1963 but the new product was not marketed until December, 1963. Richter received the first shipment of it on December 11, and another on December 17, 1963. The chemical contents of the new institutional product were not stated on the container; nor was the appellant informed otherwise of any change in the contents of that product except by the notice of its dangerous contents for home use, as previously recited.

It is the contention of the appellant that his convictions on the charges of involuntary manslaughter cannot be sustained . . . as a result of any criminal negligence on his part. * * *

There remains the question of whether the Commonwealth has established that the deaths under consideration were due to the criminal negligence of the appellant. Involuntary manslaughter consists of the killing of another person without malice and unintentionally, but in doing some unlawful act not amounting to a felony, or in doing some lawful act in an unlawful way. Where the act in itself is not unlawful, to make it criminal the negligence must be of such a departure from prudent conduct as to evidence a disregard of human life or an indifference to consequences. . . .

We are satisfied that the record clearly establishes that appellant, in the operation of his small store with part-time help, knew that he was selling Sterno in substantial quantities to a clientele that was misusing it; that in order to profit more from such sales he induced Richter Paper Company to procure for him a supply of the institutional product because the cost of same was less than the regular type with labels; that he was aware of the "poison" notice and warning of harmful effects of the new shipment received on December 21, 1963 but nevertheless placed it in stock for general sale by himself and his employees; and thereafter sold several hundred cans of it; and that he dispensed it without warning his purchasers of the harmful effect it would have if misused for drinking purposes, and without directing their attention to the warning on the containers.

If the deaths of these five persons were the result of appellant's actions, it justifies his conviction for involuntary manslaughter. Although a more culpable degree of negligence is required to establish a criminal homicide than is required in a civil action for damages, we find the appellant's actions as fully meeting the definition and requirement of proof set forth in Commonwealth v. Aurick, 342 Pa. 282, 19 A.2d 920 (1941). In the light of the recognized weaknesses of the purchasers of the product, the appellant's greater concern for profit than with the results of his actions, he was grossly negligent and demonstrated a wanton and reckless disregard for the welfare of those whom he might reasonably have expected to use the product for drinking purposes. * * *

We find no merit in appellant's argument that there is no evidence to prove he ever sold a can of the new institutional Sterno. The evidence clearly shows that he was in full charge of the operation of the store when the bulk of the new product was sold. Harold was only a part-time employe coming in after school and on Saturdays, and during this period appellant's wife and family were in Florida, which left appellant as the one who made the bulk of the sales.

Nor do we find any merit in his argument that he was unaware of the warning on the cans. He must have handled many of them during the course of events when almost four hundred cans were sold. The circumstances established by the evidence sufficiently supports a finding that he did know of the change in markings but disregarded it. As far as instructing anyone else to sell the product, the fact that it was available for sale in an opened carton under the counter is sufficient to indicate an implied authorization.

The facts in this case do not indicate the prosecution of a person for acts done by another without his knowledge or consent. Appellant was the active participant with full knowledge. He, personally, and through his part-time employe, acting under his orders, committed the crimes. . . .

The judgments of sentence, therefore, are affirmed in the cases of Lynwood Scott; John Streich; James Newsome; and Juanita Williams; and the judgment is reversed and appellant discharged in the case of Edward Harrell.

HOFFMAN, J., files a dissenting opinion.

* * *

NOTES

1. When death is caused through an overdose of drugs or excessive use of liquor, the courts generally require that the person furnishing the drugs or liquor be shown to have unlawfully furnished the substances. Also, it must be established that the unlawful furnishing is the proximate cause of the death. In People v. Cruciani, 70 Misc.2d 528, 334 N.Y.S.2d 515 (Suffolk County Ct. 1972), an indictment of criminally negligent homicide was sustained when it was shown to be predicated upon the defendant having injected a 19–year old girl with a hypodermic syringe containing heroin. The court held it was proper for the jury to determine whether the defendant's administering of the heroin created a substantial and unjustifiable risk of death.

Depending upon the degree of foreseeability of death under the circumstances of a case, the charge could properly be murder. In Ureta v. Superior Court, 199 Cal.App.2d 672, 18 Cal.Rptr. 873 (1962), a murder prosecution for a death produced by morphine poisoning, the court stated it made no difference whether the decedent or the defendant who furnished the drug actually injected it. See also cases cited in Note 8, supra on p. 149.

2. If, during a legal abortion, a doctor fails to take steps to keep an aborted fetus alive, can the doctor be convicted of involuntary manslaughter? A Massachusetts jury answered affirmatively in the 1975 trial of Dr. Kenneth C. Edelin, chief resident in surgery in a Boston hospital, who aborted a fetus during a legal hysterotomy performed on a woman between 22 and 24 weeks pregnant. Superior Court Judge James P. McGuire sentenced Dr. Edelin to one year's probation, but stayed the sentence pending an appeal. The Massachusetts Supreme Judicial Court reversed the conviction and ordered that a judgment of acquittal be entered. Commonwealth v. Edelin, 371 Mass. 497, 359 N.E.2d 4 (1976). See also Commonwealth v. Cass, 392 Mass. 799, 467 N.E.2d 1324 (1984).

3. In People v. Nelson, 309 N.Y. 231, 128 N.E.2d 391 (1955), the owner of an apartment building which was in violation of the New York Multiple Dwelling Law and constituted a fire hazard was convicted of manslaughter when two tenants died in a fire. The court held that failure to comply with various building codes regarding fire safety constituted conduct of such a nature that human life was endangered.

4. In State v. Strobel, 130 Mont. 442, 304 P.2d 606 (1956), the defendant, while driving to the left of the centerline of the highway, collided with a gasoline truck driven by one Little. The truck overturned and exploded causing Little's death. The defendant was convicted of manslaughter and appealed. In reversing the judgment and ordering a new trial, the court stated:

"Instruction No. 7, submitting the question of driving on the wrong side of the road in violation of the statutes, was apparently intended to present to the jury the issue of defendant's guilt in the unlawful killing of a human being 'in the commission of an unlawful act, not amounting to felony.' . . .

"The driving of an automobile to the left of the centerline of the highway appears to be an act merely *malum prohibitum*. . . . In some jurisdictions it is held that when one commits an act expressly prohibited by law which results in the death of a human being he is thereby guilty of manslaughter and that in such a case an instruction on criminal negligence is neither necessary nor proper. . . . [That] rule . . . has not been followed in Montana. . . . This court has committed itself to the rule that the unlawful killing of a human being, 'in the commission of an unlawful act, not amounting to felony,' does not constitute involuntary manslaughter unless the element of criminal negligence is also present. . . .

"It is not incumbent upon us to go further and determine the character of the unlawful act, *aside from such criminal negligence*, which makes a person guilty of manslaughter should death ensue. Irrespective of the character of the unlawful act, whether *malum in se* or merely *malum prohibitum*, the criminality of the act resulting in death is established if that act was done negligently in such a manner as to evince a disregard for human life or an indifference to consequences. Negligence of this character is culpable in itself. Hence it is wholly unnecessary in involuntary manslaughter cases to superimpose upon the requirement of the element of criminal negligence the further requirement that a determination must be made as to whether the act resulting in death might ordinarily be classified as *malum in se* or *malum prohibitum*, for, if that act is done in a manner which is criminally negligent, it thereby becomes *malum in se* and thereby includes the element of *mens rea*. . . .

"Applying the foregoing discussion to the case at bar, we hold that Instruction No. 7 . . . was erroneous in advising that jury that they might find the defendant guilty if she was driving on the wrong side of the road in violation of the statutes and if she thereby caused the death of Gerald Little. . . ."

5. In State v. Pankow, 134 Mont. 519, 333 P.2d 1017 (1958), an involuntary manslaughter prosecution against a motorist arising out of the deaths of his three passengers when his automobile passed two preceding automobiles near a curve and skidded and ran over the left edge of the road and tumbled to its side in a creek below, the court had this to say about *Strobel:*

"Much confusion has been caused . . . by this court's discussion of criminal negligence in an involuntary manslaughter case in State v. Strobel. Insofar as that case would seem to add the requirement of a willful or evil intent as an element of involuntary manslaughter, we hereby overrule the holding on that point in that case."

6. Deaths resulting from traffic offenses are viewed as possible involuntary manslaughter offenses if the degree of foreseeability of death was fairly high, but not if the causal connection is less obvious. Thus, in Beck v. Commonwealth, 216 Va. 1, 216 S.E.2d 8 (1975), the court affirmed a conviction of involuntary manslaughter where the defendant had consumed "around seven beers" in a very short period of time, was unsteady on his feet and had difficulty closing his car door, failed to see seven young men with his lights on and after striking something in "a blur" was reported by other witnesses to have departed at high speed. The finding of driving while intoxicated was deemed to be the proximate cause of the resulting homicide which occurred during the performance of an unlawful act. On the other hand, in King v. Commonwealth, 217 Va. 601, 231 S.E.2d 312 (1977), the defendant was operating a motor vehicle without headlights at night, in violation of a state statute, as a result of which a death occurred and she was convicted of involuntary manslaughter. The Virginia Supreme Court reversed, stating that the operation of an automobile without headlights in violation of law amounted only to ordinary negligence and was therefore an insufficient predicate for a conviction of involuntary manslaughter. The court said: "In the operation of motor vehicles violation of a safety statute amounting to mere negligence proximately causing an accidental death is not sufficient to support a conviction of involuntary manslaughter. Likewise, the improper performance of a lawful act proximately causing an accidental killing is also insufficient unless that improper performance constitutes criminal negligence."

Chapter 6

SEX OFFENSES AND RELATED PROBLEMS

A. CRIMINAL SEXUAL ASSAULT

---

1. "BY FORCE AND WITHOUT CONSENT"

COMMONWEALTH v. BURKE

Supreme Judicial Court of Massachusetts, 1870.
105 Mass. 376.

GRAY, J. The defendant has been indicted and convicted for aiding and assisting Dennis Green in committing a rape upon Joanna Caton. The single exception taken at the trial was to the refusal of the presiding judge to rule that the evidence introduced was not sufficient to warrant a verdict of guilty. The instructions given were not objected to, and are not reported in the bill of exceptions. The only question before us therefore is, whether, under any instructions applicable to the case, the evidence would support a conviction.

That evidence, which it is unnecessary to state in detail, was sufficient to authorize the jury to find that Green, with the aid and assistance of this defendant, had carnal intercourse with Mrs. Caton, without her previous assent, and while she was, as Green and the defendant both knew, so drunk as to be utterly senseless and incapable of consenting, and with such force as was necessary to effect the purpose.

All the statutes of England and of Massachusetts, and all the text books of authority, which have undertaken to define the crime of rape, have defined it as the having carnal knowledge of a woman by force and against her will. The crime consists in the enforcement of a woman without her consent. The simple question, expressed in the briefest form, is, Was the woman willing or unwilling? The earlier and more weighty authorities show that the words "against her will," in the standard definitions, mean exactly the same thing as "without her consent;" and that the distinction between these phrases, as applied to this crime, which has been suggested in some modern books, is unfounded.

* * *

Coke treats the two phrases as equivalent; for he says: "Rape is felony by the common law declared by parliament, for the unlawful and carnal knowledge and abuse of any woman above the age of ten years against her will, or of a woman child under the age of ten years with her will or against her will;" although in the latter case the words of the St. of Westm. I. (as we have already seen) were "neither by her own consent, nor without her consent." 3 Inst. 60. Coke elsewhere repeatedly defines rape as "the carnal knowledge of a woman by force and against her will." Co.Lit. 123 b. 2 Inst. 180. A similar definition is given by Hale, Hawkins, Comyn, Blackstone, East and Starkie, who wrote while the Statutes of Westminster were in force; as well as by the text writers of most reputation since the St. of 9 Geo. IV, c. 31, repealed the earlier statutes, and assuming the definition of the crime to be well established, provided simply that "every person convicted of the crime of rape shall suffer death as a felon." . . .

In the leading modern English case of The Queen v. Camplin, the great majority of the English judges held that a man who gave intoxicating liquor to a girl of thirteen, for the purpose, as the jury found, "of exciting her, not with the intention of rendering her insensible, and then having sexual connection with her," and made her quite drunk, and, while she was in a state of insensibility, took advantage of it, and ravished her, was guilty of rape. It appears indeed by the judgment delivered by Patteson, J., in passing sentence, as reported in 1 Cox Crim.Cas. 220, and 1 C. & K. 746, as well by the contemporaneous notes of Parke, B., printed in a note to 1 Denison, 92, and of Alderson, B., as read by him in The Queen v. Page, 2 Cox Crim.Cas. 133, that the decision was influenced by its having been proved at the trial that, before the girl became insensible the man had attempted to procure her consent, and had failed. But it further appears by those notes that Lord Denman, C.J., Parke, B., and Patteson, J., thought that the violation of any woman without her consent, while she was in a state of insensibility and had no power over her will, by a man knowing at the time that she was in that state, was a rape, whether such state was caused by him or not; for example, as Alderson, B., adds, "in the case of a woman insensibly drunk in the streets, not made so by the prisoner." And in the course of the argument this able judge himself said that it might be considered against the general presumable will of a woman that a man should have unlawful connection with her. The later decisions have established the rule in England that unlawful and forcible connection with a woman in a state of unconsciousness at the time, whether that state has been produced by the act of the prisoner or not, is presumed to be without her consent, and is rape. . . .

* * *

We are therefore unanimously of opinion that the crime, which the evidence in this case tended to prove, of a man's having carnal intercourse with a woman, without her consent, while she was, as he knew, wholly insensible so as to be incapable of consenting, and with such force as was necessary to accomplish the purpose, was rape. If it were otherwise, any woman in a state of utter stupefaction, whether caused by drunkenness, sudden disease, the blow of a third person, or drugs which she had been persuaded to take even by the defendant himself, would be unprotected from personal dishonor. The law is not open to such a reproach.

STATE v. RUSK

Court of Appeals of Maryland, 1981.
289 Md. 230, 424 A.2d 720.

MURPHY, CHIEF JUDGE.

Edward Rusk was found guilty by a jury in the Criminal Court of Baltimore (Karwacki, J. presiding) of second degree rape in violation of Maryland Code (1957, 1976 Repl.Vol., 1980 Cum.Supp.), Art. 27, § 463(a)(1), which provides in pertinent part:

"A person is guilty of rape in the second degree if the person engages in vaginal intercourse with another person:

(1) By force or threat of force against the will and without the consent of the other person; . . . ."

On appeal, the Court of Special Appeals, sitting en banc, reversed the conviction; it concluded by an 8–5 majority that in view of the prevailing law as set forth in Hazel v. State, 221 Md. 464, 157 A.2d 922 (1960), insufficient evidence of Rusk's guilt had been adduced at the trial to permit the case to go to the jury. We granted certiorari to consider whether the Court of Special Appeals properly applied the principles of Hazel in determining that insufficient evidence had been produced to support Rusk's conviction.

At the trial, the 21–year–old prosecuting witness, Pat, testified that on the evening of September 21, 1977, she attended a high school alumnae meeting where she met a girl friend, Terry. After the meeting, Terry and Pat agreed to drive in their respective cars to Fells Point to have a few drinks. On the way, Pat stopped to telephone her mother, who was baby sitting for Pat's two-year-old son; she told her mother that she was going with Terry to Fells Point and would not be late in arriving home.

The women arrived in Fells Point about 9:45 p.m. They went to a bar where each had one drink. After staying approximately one hour, Pat and Terry walked several blocks to a second bar, where each of them had another drink. After about thirty minutes, they walked two blocks to a third bar known as E.J. Buggs. The bar was crowded and a band was playing in the back. Pat ordered another drink and as she and Terry were leaning against the wall, Rusk approached and said "hello" to Terry. Terry, who was then conversing with another individual, momentarily interrupted her conversation and said "Hi, Eddie." Rusk then began talking with Pat and during their conversation both of them acknowledged being separated from their respective spouses and having a child. Pat told Rusk that she had to go home because it was a week-night and she had to wake up with her baby early in the morning.

Rusk asked Pat the direction in which she was driving and after she responded, Rusk requested a ride to his apartment. Although Pat did not know Rusk, she thought that Terry knew him. She thereafter agreed to give him a ride. Pat cautioned Rusk on the way to the car that "I'm just giving a ride home, you know, as a friend, not anything to be, you know, thought of other than a ride;'" and he said, "'Oh, okay.'" They left the bar between 12:00 and 12:20 a.m.

Pat testified that on the way to Rusk's apartment, they continued the general conversation that they had started in the bar. After a twenty-minute drive, they arrived at Rusk's apartment in the 3100 block of Guilford Avenue. Pat testified that she was totally unfamiliar with the neighborhood. She parked the car at the curb on the opposite side of the street from Rusk's apartment but left the engine running. Rusk asked Pat to come in, but she refused. He invited her again, and she again declined. She told Rusk that she could not go into his apartment even if she wanted to because she was separated from her husband and a detective could be observing her movements. Pat said that Rusk was fully aware that she did not want to accompany him to his room. Notwithstanding her repeated refusals, Pat testified that Rusk reached over and turned off the ignition to her car and took her car keys. He got out of the car, walked over to her side, opened the door and said, "'Now, will you come up?'" Pat explained her subsequent actions:

> "At that point, because I was scared, because he had my car keys. I didn't know what to do. I was someplace I didn't even know where I was. It was in the city. I didn't know whether to run. I really didn't think at that point, what to do.
>
> "Now, I know that I should have blown the horn. I should have run. There were a million things I could have done. I was scared, at that point, and I didn't do any of them."

Pat testified that at this moment she feared that Rusk would rape her. She said: "[I]t was the way he looked at me, and said 'Come on up, come on up;' and when he took the keys, I knew that was wrong."

It was then about 1 a.m. Pat accompanied Rusk across the street into a totally dark house. She followed him up two flights of stairs. She neither saw nor heard anyone in the building. Once they ascended the stairs, Rusk unlocked the door to his one-room apartment, and turned on the light. According to Pat, he told her to sit down. She sat in a chair beside the bed. Rusk sat on the bed. After Rusk talked for a few minutes, he left the room for about one to five minutes. Pat remained seated in the chair. She made no noise and did not attempt to leave. She said that she did not notice a telephone in the room. When Rusk returned, he turned off the light and sat down on the bed. Pat asked if she could leave; she told him that she wanted to go home and "didn't want to come up." She said, "'Now, [that] I came up, can I go?'" Rusk, who was still in possession of her car keys, said he wanted her to stay.

Rusk then asked Pat to get on the bed with him. He pulled her by the arms to the bed and began to undress her, removing her blouse and bra. He unzipped her slacks and she took them off after he told her to do so. Pat removed the rest of her clothing, and then removed Rusk's pants because "he asked me to do it." After they were both undressed Rusk started kissing Pat as she was lying on her back. Pat explained what happened next:

> "I was still begging him to please let, you know, let me leave. I said, 'you can get a lot of other girls down there, for what you want,' and he just kept saying, 'no'; and then I was really scared, because I can't describe, you know, what was said. It was more the look in his eyes; and I said, at that point—I didn't know what to say; and I said, 'If I do what you want, will you let me go without killing me?' Because I didn't know, at that point, what he was going to do; and I started to cry; and when I did, he put his hands on my throat, and started lightly to choke me; and I said, 'If I do what you want, will you let me go?' And he said, yes, and at that time, I proceeded to do what he wanted me to."

Pat testified that Rusk made her perform oral sex and then vaginal intercourse.

Immediately after the intercourse, Pat asked if she could leave. She testified that Rusk said, " 'Yes,' " after which she got up and got dressed and Rusk returned her car keys. She said that Rusk then "walked me to my car, and asked if he could see me again; and I said, 'Yes;' and he asked me for my telephone number; and I said, 'No, I'll see you down Fells Point sometime,' just so I could leave." Pat testified that she "had no intention of meeting him again." She asked him for directions out of the neighborhood and left.

On her way home, Pat stopped at a gas station, went to the ladies room, and then drove "pretty much straight home and pulled up and parked the car." At first she was not going to say anything about the incident. She explained her initial reaction not to report the incident: "I didn't want to go through what I'm going through now [at the trial]." As she sat in her car reflecting on the incident, Pat said she began to "wonder what would happen if I hadn't of done what he wanted me to do. So I thought the right thing to do was to go report it, and I went from there to Hillendale to find a police car." She reported the incident to the police at about 3:15 a.m. Subsequently, Pat took the police to Rusk's apartment, which she located without any great difficulty.

Pat's girlfriend Terry corroborated her testimony concerning the events which occurred up to the time that Pat left the bar with Rusk. Questioned about Pat's alcohol consumption, Terry said she was drinking screwdrivers that night but normally did not finish a drink. Terry testified about her acquaintanceship with Rusk: "I knew his face, and his first name, but I honestly couldn't tell you—apparently I ran into him sometime before. I couldn't tell you how I know him. I don't know him very well at all."

Officer Hammett of the Baltimore City Police Department acknowledged receiving Pat's rape complaint at 3:15 a.m. on September 22, 1977. He accompanied her to the 3100 block of Guilford Avenue where it took Pat several minutes to locate Rusk's apartment. Officer Hammett entered Rusk's multi-dwelling apartment house, which contained at least six apartments, and arrested Rusk in a room on the second floor.

Hammett testified that Pat was sober, and she was taken to City Hospital for an examination. The examination disclosed that seminal fluid and spermatozoa were detected in Pat's vagina, on her underpants, and on the bed sheets recovered from Rusk's bed.

At the close of the State's case-in-chief, Rusk moved for a judgment of acquittal. In denying the motion, the trial court said:

> "There is evidence that there is a taking of automobile keys forcibly, a request that the prosecuting witness accompany the Defendant to the upstairs apartment. She described a look in his eye which put her in fear.

> "Now, you are absolutely correct that there was no weapon, no physical threatening testified to. However, while she was seated on a chair next to the bed, the Defendant excused himself, and came back in five minutes; and then she testifies, he pulled her on to the bed by reaching over and grabbing her wrists, and/or had her or requested, that she disrobe, and assist him in disrobing.

> "Again, she said she was scared, and then she testified to something to the effect that she said to him, she was begging him to let her leave. She was scared. She started to cry. He started to strangle her softly she said. She asked the Defendant, that if she'd submit, would he not kill her, at which point he indicated that he would not; and she performed oral sex on him, and then had intercourse."

Rusk and two of his friends, Michael Trimp and David Carroll, testified on his behalf. According to Trimp, they went in Carroll's car to Buggs' bar to dance, drink and "tr[y] to pick up some ladies." Rusk stayed at the bar, while the others went to get something to eat.

Trimp and Carroll next saw Rusk walking down the street arm-in-arm with a lady whom Trimp was unable to identify. Trimp asked Rusk if he needed a ride home. Rusk responded that the woman he was with was going to drive him home. Trimp testified that at about 2:00–2:30 a.m. he returned to the room he rented with Rusk on Guilford Avenue and found Rusk to be the only person present. Trimp said that as many as twelve people lived in the entire building and that the room he rented with Rusk was referred to as their "pit stop." Both Rusk and Trimp actually resided at places other than the Guilford Avenue room. Trimp testified that there was a telephone in the apartment.

Carroll's testimony corroborated Trimp's. He saw Rusk walking down the street arm-in-arm with a woman. He said "[s]he was kind of like, you know, snuggling up to him like. . . . She was hanging all over him then." Carroll was fairly certain that Pat was the woman who was with Rusk.

Rusk, the 31–year–old defendant, testified that he was in the Buggs Tavern for about thirty minutes when he noticed Pat standing at the bar. Rusk said: "She looked at me, and she smiled. I walked over and said, hi, and started talking to her." He did not remember either knowing or speaking to Terry. When Pat mentioned that she was about to leave, Rusk asked her if she wanted to go home with him. In response, Pat said that she would like to, but could not because she had her car. Rusk then suggested that they take her car. Pat agreed and they left the bar arm-in-arm.

Rusk testified that during the drive to her apartment, he discussed with Pat their similar marital situations and talked about their children. He said that Pat asked him if he was going to rape her. When he inquired why she was asking, Pat said that she had been raped once before. Rusk expressed his sympathy for her. Pat then asked him if he planned to beat her. He inquired why she was asking and Pat explained that her husband used to beat her. Rusk again expressed his sympathy. He testified that at no time did Pat express a fear that she was being followed by her separated husband.

According to Rusk, when they arrived in front of his apartment Pat parked the car and turned the engine off. They sat for several minutes "petting each other." Rusk denied switching off the ignition and removing the keys. He said that they walked to the apartment house and proceeded up the stairs to his room. Rusk testified that Pat came willingly to his room and that at no time did he make threatening facial expressions. Once inside his room, Rusk left Pat alone for several minutes while he used the bathroom down the hall. Upon his return, he switched the light on but immediately turned it off because Pat, who was seated in the dark in a chair next to the bed, complained it was too bright. Rusk said that he sat on the bed across from Pat and reached out

> "and started to put my arms around her, and started kissing her; and we fell back into the bed, and she—we were petting, kissing, and she stuck her hand down in my pants and started playing with me; and I undid her blouse, and took off her bra; and then I sat up and I said 'Let's take our clothes off;' and she said, 'Okay;' and I took my clothes off, and she took her clothes off; and then we proceeded to have intercourse."

Rusk explained that after the intercourse, Pat "got uptight."

"Well, she started to cry. She said that—she said, 'You guys are all alike,' she says, 'just out for,' you know, 'one thing.'

"She started talking about—I don't know, she was crying and all. I tried to calm her down and all; and I said, 'What's the matter?' And she said, that she just wanted to leave; and I said, 'Well, okay;' and she walked out to the car. I walked out to the car. She got in the car and left."

Rusk denied placing his hands on Pat's throat or attempting to strangle her. He also denied using force or threats of force to get Pat to have intercourse with him.

In reversing Rusk's second degree rape conviction, the Court of Special Appeals, quoting from *Hazel*, noted that:

> "Force is an essential element of the crime [of rape] and to justify a conviction, the evidence must warrant a conclusion either that the victim resisted and her resistance was overcome by force or that she was prevented from resisting by threats to her safety."

Writing for the majority, Judge Thompson said:

> "In all of the victim's testimony we have been unable to see any resistance on her part to the sex acts and certainly can we see no fear as would overcome her attempt to resist or escape as required by *Hazel*. Possession of the keys by the accused may have deterred her vehicular escape but hardly a departure seeking help in the rooming house or in the street. We must say that 'the way he looked' fails utterly to support the fear required by *Hazel*."

The Court of Special Appeals interpreted *Hazel* as requiring a showing of a reasonable apprehension of fear in instances where the prosecutrix did not resist. It concluded:

> "we find the evidence legally insufficient to warrant a conclusion that appellant's words or actions created in the mind of the victim a reasonable fear that if she resisted, he would have harmed her, or that faced with such resistance, he would have used force to overcome it. The prosecutrix stated that she was afraid, and submitted because of 'the look in his eyes.' After both were undressed and in the bed, and she pleaded to him that she wanted to leave, he started to lightly choke her. At oral argument it was brought out that the 'lightly choking' could have been a heavy caress. We do not believe that 'lightly choking' along with all the facts and circumstances in the case, were sufficient to cause a reasonable fear which overcame her ability to resist. In the absence of any other evidence showing force used by appellant, we find that the evidence was insufficient to convict appellant of rape." Id. at 484, 406 A.2d 624.

In argument before us on the merits of the case, the parties agreed that the issue was whether, in light of the principles of *Hazel*, there was evidence before the jury legally sufficient to prove beyond a reasonable doubt that the intercourse was "[b]y force or threat of force against the will and without the consent" of the victim in violation of Art. 27,

§ 463(a)(1). Of course, due process requirements mandate that a criminal conviction not be obtained if the evidence does not reasonably support a finding of guilt beyond a reasonable doubt. However, as the Supreme Court made clear in Jackson v. Virginia, 443 U.S. 307, 99 S.Ct. 2781, 61 L.Ed.2d 560 (1979), the reviewing court does not ask itself whether *it* believes that the evidence established guilt beyond a reasonable doubt; rather, the applicable standard is "whether, after viewing the evidence in the light most favorable to the prosecution, *any* rational trier of fact could have found the essential elements of the crime beyond a reasonable doubt." (emphasis in original).

The vaginal intercourse once being established, the remaining elements of rape in the second degree under § 463(a)(1) are, as in a prosecution for common law rape (1) force—actual or constructive, and (2) lack of consent. The terms in § 463(a)(1)—"force," "threat of force," "against the will" and "without the consent"—are not defined in the statute, but are to be afforded their "judicially determined meaning" as applied in cases involving common law rape. In this regard, it is well settled that the terms "against the will" and "without the consent" are synonymous in the law of rape.

Hazel, which was decided in 1960, long before the enactment of § 463(a)(1), involved a prosecution for common law rape, there defined as "the act of a man having unlawful carnal knowledge of a female over the age of ten years by force without the consent and against the will of the victim." The evidence in that case disclosed that Hazel followed the prosecutrix into her home while she was unloading groceries from her car. He put his arm around her neck, said he had a gun, and threatened to shoot her baby if she moved. Although the prosecutrix never saw a gun, Hazel kept one hand in his pocket and repeatedly stated that he had a gun. He robbed the prosecutrix, tied her hands, gagged her, and took her into the cellar. The prosecutrix complied with Hazel's commands to lie on the floor and to raise her legs. Hazel proceeded to have intercourse with her while her hands were still tied. The victim testified that she did not struggle because she was afraid for her life. There was evidence that she told the police that Hazel did not use force at any time and was extremely gentle. Hazel claimed that the intercourse was consensual and that he never made any threats. The Court said that the issue before it was whether "the evidence was insufficient to sustain the conviction of rape because the conduct of the prosecutrix was such as to render her failure to resist consent in law." It was in the context of this evidentiary background that the Court set forth the principles of law which controlled the disposition of the case. It recognized that force and lack of consent are distinct elements of the crime of rape. It said:

> "Force is an essential element of the crime and to justify a conviction, the evidence must warrant a conclusion either that the victim resisted and her resistance was overcome by force or that she was prevented from resisting by threats to her safety. But no particular amount of force, either actual or construc-

tive, is required to constitute rape. Necessarily, that fact must depend upon the prevailing circumstances. As in this case force may exist without violence. If the acts and threats of the defendant were reasonably calculated to create in the mind of the victim—having regard to the circumstances in which she was placed—a real apprehension, due to fear, of imminent bodily harm, serious enough to impair or overcome her will to resist, then such acts and threats are the equivalent of force."

As to the element of lack of consent, the Court said in *Hazel:*

"[I]t is true, of course, that however reluctantly given, consent to the act at any time prior to penetration deprives the subsequent intercourse of its criminal character. There is, however, a wide difference between consent and a submission to the act. Consent may involve submission, but submission does not necessarily imply consent. Furthermore, submission to a compelling force, or as a result of being put in fear, is not consent."

The Court noted that lack of consent is generally established through proof of resistance or by proof that the victim failed to resist because of fear. The degree of fear necessary to obviate the need to prove resistance, and thereby establish lack of consent, was defined in the following manner:

"The kind of fear which would render resistance by a woman unnecessary to support a conviction of rape includes, but is not necessarily limited to, a fear of death or serious bodily harm, or a fear so extreme as to preclude resistance, or a fear which would well nigh render her mind incapable of continuing to resist, or a fear that so overpowers her that she does not dare resist."

Hazel thus made it clear that lack of consent could be established through proof that the victim submitted as a result of fear of imminent death or serious bodily harm. In addition, if the actions and conduct of the defendant were reasonably calculated to induce this fear in the victim's mind, then the element of force is present. *Hazel* recognized, therefore, that the same kind of evidence may be used in establishing both force and non-consent, particularly when a threat rather than actual force is involved.

The Court noted in *Hazel* that the judges who heard the evidence, and who sat as the trier of fact in Hazel's non-jury case, had concluded that, in light of the defendant's acts of violence and threats of serious harm, there existed a genuine and continuing fear of such harm on the victim's part, so that the ensuing act of sexual intercourse under this fear " 'amounted to a felonious and forcible act of the defendant against the will and consent of the prosecuting witness.' " In finding the evidence sufficient to sustain the conviction, the Court observed that "[t]he issue of whether the intercourse was accomplished by force and against the will and consent of the victim was one of credibility, properly to be resolved by the trial court."

Hazel did not expressly determine whether the victim's fear must be "reasonable." Its only reference to reasonableness related to whether "the acts and threats of the defendant were reasonably calculated to create in the mind of the victim . . . a real apprehension, due to fear, of imminent bodily harm. . . ." Manifestly, the Court was there referring to the calculations of the accused, not to the fear of the victim. While *Hazel* made it clear that the victim's fear had to be genuine, it did not pass upon whether a real but unreasonable fear of imminent death or serious bodily harm would suffice. The vast majority of jurisdictions have required that the victim's fear be reasonably grounded in order to obviate the need for either proof of actual force on the part of the assailant or physical resistance on the part of the victim.[1] We think that, generally, this is the correct standard.

As earlier indicated, the Court of Special Appeals held that a showing of a reasonable apprehension of fear was essential under *Hazel* to establish the elements of the offense where the victim did not resist. The Court did not believe, however, that the evidence was legally sufficient to demonstrate the existence of "a reasonable fear" which overcame Pat's ability to resist. In support of the Court's conclusion, Rusk maintains that the evidence showed that Pat voluntarily entered his apartment without being subjected to a "single threat nor a scintilla of force"; that she made no effort to run away nor did she scream for help; that she never exhibited a will to resist; and that her subjective reaction of fear to the situation in which she had voluntarily placed herself was unreasonable and exaggerated. Rusk claims that his acts were not reasonably calculated to overcome a will to resist; that Pat's verbal resistance was not resistance within the contemplation of *Hazel;* that his alleged menacing look did not constitute a threat of force; and that even had he pulled Pat to the bed, and lightly choked her, as she claimed, these actions, viewed in the context of the entire incident—no prior threats having been made—would be insufficient to constitute force or a threat of force or render the intercourse non-consensual.

---

1. See State v. Reinhold, 123 Ariz. 50, 597 P.2d 532 (1979); People v. Hunt, 72 Cal.App.3d 190, 139 Cal.Rptr. 675 (1977); State v. Dill, 3 Terry 533, 42 Del. 533, 40 A.2d 443 (1944); Arnold v. United States, 358 A.2d 335 (D.C.App.1976); Doyle v. State, 39 Fla. 155, 22 So. 272 (1897); Curtis v. State, 236 Ga. 362, 223 S.E.2d 721 (1976); People v. Murphy, 124 Ill.App.2d 71, 260 N.E.2d 386 (1970); Carroll v. State, 263 Ind. 86, 324 N.E.2d 809 (1975); Fields v. State, 293 So.2d 430 (Miss.1974); State v. Beck, 368 S.W.2d 490 (Mo.1963); Cascio v. State, 147 Neb. 1075, 25 N.W.2d 897 (1947); State v. Burns, 287 N.C. 102, 214 S.E.2d 56, cert. denied, 423 U.S. 933, 96 S.Ct. 288, 46 L.Ed.2d 264 (1975); State v. Verdone, 114 R.I. 613, 337 A.2d 804 (1975); Brown v. State, 576 S.W.2d 820 (Tex.Cr.App.1979); Jones v. Com., 219 Va. 983, 252 S.E.2d 370 (1979); State v. Baker, 30 Wash.2d 601, 192 P.2d 839 (1948); Brown v. State, 581 P.2d 189 (Wyo.1978).

Some jurisdictions do not require that the victim's fear be reasonably grounded. See Struggs v. State, 372 So.2d 49 (Ala.Cr. App.), cert. denied, 444 U.S. 936, 100 S.Ct. 285, 62 L.Ed.2d 195 (1979); Kirby v.State, 5 Ala.App. 128, 59 So. 374 (1912); Dinkens v. State, 92 Nev. 74, 546 P.2d 228 (1976); citing Hazel v. State, supra; State v. Herfel, 49 Wis.2d 513, 182 N.W.2d 232 (1971). See also Salsman v. Com., 565 S.W.2d 638 (Ky.App.1978); State v. Havens, 264 N.W.2d 918 (S.D.1978).

We think the reversal of Rusk's conviction by the Court of Special Appeals was in error for the fundamental reason so well expressed in the dissenting opinion by Judge Wilner when he observed that the majority had "trampled upon the first principle of appellate restraint . . . [because it had] substituted [its] own view of the evidence (and the inferences that may fairly be drawn from it) for that of the judge and jury . . . [and had thereby] improperly invaded the province allotted to those tribunals." In view of the evidence adduced at the trial, the reasonableness of Pat's apprehension of fear was plainly a question of fact for the jury to determine. . . . Quite obviously, the jury disbelieved Rusk and believed Pat's testimony. From her testimony, the jury could have reasonably concluded that the taking of her car keys was intended by Rusk to immobilize her alone, late at night, in a neighborhood with which she was not familiar; that after Pat had repeatedly refused to enter his apartment, Rusk commanded in firm tones that she do so; that Pat was badly frightened and feared that Rusk intended to rape her; that unable to think clearly and believing that she had no other choice in the circumstances, Pat entered Rusk's apartment; that once inside Pat asked permission to leave but Rusk told her to stay; that he then pulled Pat by the arms to the bed and undressed her; that Pat was afraid that Rusk would kill her unless she submitted; that she began to cry and Rusk then put his hands on her throat and began " 'lightly to choke' " her; that Pat asked him if he would let her go without killing her if she complied with his demands; that Rusk gave an affirmative response, after which she finally submitted.

Just where persuasion ends and force begins in cases like the present is essentially a factual issue, to be resolved in light of the controlling legal precepts. That threats of force need not be made in any particular manner in order to put a person in fear of bodily harm is well established. Indeed, conduct, rather than words, may convey the threat. That a victim did not scream out for help or attempt to escape, while bearing on the question of consent, is unnecessary where she is restrained by fear of violence.

Considering all of the evidence in the case, with particular focus upon the actual force applied by Rusk to Pat's neck, we conclude that the jury could rationally find that the essential elements of second degree rape had been established and that Rusk was guilty of that offense beyond a reasonable doubt.

Judgment of the Court of Special Appeals reversed; case remanded to that court with directions that it affirm the judgment of the Criminal Court of Baltimore; costs to be paid by the appellee.

SMITH, DIGGES and COLE, JJ., dissent.

COLE, JUDGE, dissenting.

I agree with the Court of Special Appeals that the evidence adduced at the trial of Edward Salvatore Rusk was insufficient to convict him of rape. I, therefore, respectfully dissent.

The standard of appellate review in deciding a question of sufficiency, as the majority correctly notes, is whether, after viewing the evidence in the light most favorable to the prosecution, *any* rational trier of fact could have found the essential elements of the crime beyond a reasonable doubt. However, it is equally well settled that when one of the essential elements of a crime is not sustained by the evidence, the conviction of the defendant cannot stand as a matter of law.

The majority, in applying this standard, concludes that "[i]n view of the evidence adduced at the trial, the reasonableness of Pat's apprehension of fear was plainly a question of fact for the jury to determine." In so concluding, the majority has skipped over the crucial issue. It seems to me that whether the prosecutrix's fear is reasonable becomes a question only after the court determines that the defendant's conduct under the circumstances was reasonably calculated to give rise to a fear on her part to the extent that she was unable to resist. In other words, the fear must stem from his articulable conduct, and equally, if not more importantly, cannot be inconsistent with her own contemporaneous reaction to that conduct. The conduct of the defendant, in and of itself, must clearly indicate force or the threat of force such as to overpower the prosecutrix's ability to resist or will to resist. In my view, there is no evidence to support the majority's conclusion that the prosecutrix was forced to submit to sexual intercourse, certainly not fellatio.

This Court defined rape in Hazel v. State, 221 Md. 464, 468–69, 157 A.2d 922 (1960), as "the act of a man having unlawful carnal knowledge of a female over the age of ten years by force without the consent and against the will of the victim." . . .

* * *

By way of illustration, we cited certain cases. In State v. Thompson, 227 N.C. 19, 40 S.E.2d 620 (1946), the victim and her friend, Straughan, were riding in a car which stalled and could not be started again even with the help of the defendants, who were strangers. One of the defendants persuaded Straughan to accompany him down the road to get a chain for the purpose of towing the car. After Straughan and one defendant left, the other three forcibly took the victim from her car into an unfinished house, a block away, and each had intercourse with her. The victim did not object to intercourse with the three defendants because she was frightened and afraid they would kill her. In addition, it was plainly a jury question whether the prosecutrix was "[i]n such place and position that resistance would have been useless." (quoting Mills v. United States, 164 U.S. 644, 649, 17 S.Ct. 210, 41 L.Ed. 584 (1879)).

* * *

In State v. Hoffman, 228 Wis. 235, 280 N.W. 357 (1938), the complaining witness entered the defendant's car under friendly circumstances and was driven out into the country without protest. When the defendant made his advances she shouted she was going home, pulled

away from him and ran. He caught up with her and there was a
tussle; she fell and tried to kick him. Again she ran and he caught her
and said "if you run again I will choke you and throw you in the
ditch. . . ." After that she walked with him back to the car. He did
not order her to get in, but begged her. No force was used thereafter.
Finally, she consented and acquiesced in the events which followed. At
trial the complainant testified she was terribly frightened. Nevertheless the court concluded:

> Suffice it to say that we have painstakingly read and re-read
> her testimony with the result that in our opinion it falls far
> short of proving that resistance which our law requires, unless
> her failure to resist was excused because of a fear of death or of
> great bodily harm or unless she was so terrified as to be unable
> to resist the defendant. It is apparently conceded by the State
> that her resistance was insufficient to prove the crime of rape
> unless her acquiescence or submission to the defendant was the
> result of that fear which our settled rules require. From the
> testimony of the complaining witness, it appears that she was
> fully cognizant of everything that was going on, fully able to
> relate every detail thereof and that she was in no reasonable
> sense dominated by that fear which excused the "utmost resis-
> tance" within her power.

> While the evidence is well calculated to arouse keen indigna-
> tion against the defendant who so persistently and importu-
> nately pursued the complaining witness, who at that time was
> a virgin, it falls short, in our opinion, of proving a case of rape.

> * * *

* * *

In Kidd v. State, 97 Okl.Cr. 415, 266 P.2d 992 (1953), the rape took
place in a car in an isolated spot. One assailant in that case told the
victim that if she did not shut up he would kill her with a beer bottle.
"By the time [the defendant] took over," the court concluded, "this
victim was whipped down and demoralized."

These cases make plain that *Hazel* intended to require clear and
cognizable evidence of force or the threat of force sufficient to overcome
or prevent resistance by the female before there would arise a jury
question of whether the prosecutrix had a reasonable apprehension of
harm. The majority today departs from this requirement and places its
imprimatur on the female's conclusory statements that she was in fear,
as sufficient to support a conviction of rape.

It is significant to note that in each of the fourteen reported rape
cases decided since *Hazel,* in which sufficiency of the evidence was the
issue, the appellate courts of this State have adhered to the requirement that evidence of force or the threat of force overcoming or
preventing resistance by the female must be demonstrated on the
record to sustain a conviction. In two of those cases the convictions
were reversed by the Court of Special Appeals. Goldberg [v. State, 41

Md.App. 58, 395 A.2d 1213 (1979)] concerned a student, professing to be a talent agent, who lured a young woman to an apartment upon the pretext of offering her a modeling job. She freely accompanied him, and though she protested verbally, she did not physically resist his advances. The Court of Special Appeals held:

> The prosecutrix swore that the reasons for her fear of being killed if she did not accede to appellant's advances were twofold: 1) she was alone with the appellant in a house with no buildings close by and no one to help her if she resisted, and 2) the appellant was much larger than she was. In the complete absence of any threatening words or actions by the appellant, these two factors, as a matter of law, are simply not enough to have created a reasonable fear of harm so as to preclude resistance and be "the equivalent of force". Without proof of force, actual or constructive, evidenced by words or conduct of the defendant or those acting in consort with him, sexual intercourse is not rape.

* * *

Of the other twelve cases, four from this Court, not one contains the paucity of evidence regarding force or threat of force which exists in the case *sub judice*. In Johnson v. State, 232 Md. 199, 192 A.2d 506 (1963), the court stated that although there was some evidence tending to indicate consent, which, standing alone, might have justified a judgment of acquittal, there was also evidence of violent acts and verbal threats on the part of the appellant, which, if believed, would have been the equivalent of such force as was reasonably calculated to create the apprehension of imminent bodily harm which could have impaired or overcome the victim's will to resist. . . .

* * *

In each of the above 12 cases there was either physical violence or specific threatening words or conduct which were calculated to create a very real and specific fear of *immediate* physical injury to the victim if she did not comply, coupled with the apparent power to execute those threats in the event of non-submission.

While courts no longer require a female to resist to the utmost or to resist where resistance would be foolhardy, they do require her acquiescence in the act of intercourse to stem from fear generated by something of substance. She may not simply say, "I was really scared," and thereby transform consent or mere unwillingness into submission by force. These words do not transform a seducer into a rapist. She must follow the natural instinct of every proud female to resist, by more than mere words, the violation of her person by a stranger or an unwelcomed friend. She must make it plain that she regards such sexual acts as abhorrent and repugnant to her natural sense of pride. She must resist unless the defendant has objectively manifested his intent to use physical force to accomplish his purpose. The law regards rape as a crime of violence. The majority today attenuates this proposition. It declares the innocence of an at best distraught young woman. It does not demonstrate the defendant's guilt of the crime of rape.

My examination of the evidence in a light most favorable to the State reveals no conduct by the defendant reasonably calculated to cause the prosecutrix to be so fearful that she should fail to resist and thus, the element of force is lacking in the State's proof.

Here we have a full grown married woman who meets the defendant in a bar under friendly circumstances. They drink and talk together. She agrees to give him a ride home in her car. When they arrive at his house, located in an area with which she was unfamiliar but which was certainly not isolated, he invites her to come up to his apartment and she refuses. According to her testimony he takes her keys, walks around to her side of the car, and says "Now will you come up?" She answers, "yes." The majority suggests that "from her testimony the jury could have reasonably concluded that the taking of her keys was intended by Rusk to immobilize her alone, late at night, in a neighborhood with which she was unfamiliar. . . ." But on what facts does the majority so conclude? There is no evidence descriptive of the tone of his voice; her testimony indicates only the bare statement quoted above. How can the majority extract from this conduct a threat reasonably calculated to create a fear of imminent bodily harm? There was no weapon, no threat to inflict physical injury.

She also testified that she was afraid of "the way he looked," and afraid of his statement, "come on up, come on up." But what can the majority conclude from this statement coupled with a "look" that remained undescribed? There is no evidence whatsoever to suggest that this was anything other than a pattern of conduct consistent with the ordinary seduction of a female acquaintance who at first suggests her disinclination.

After reaching the room she described what occurred as follows:

> I was still begging him to please let, you know, let me leave. I said, "you can get a lot of other girls down there, for what you want," and he just kept saying, "no," and then I was really scared, because I can't describe, you know, what was said. It was more the look in his eyes; and I said, at that point—I didn't know what to say; and I said, "If I do what you want, will you let me go without killing me?" Because I didn't know, at that point, what he was going to do; and I started to cry; and when I did, he put his hands on my throat and started lightly to choke me; and I said "If I do what you want, will you let me go?" And he said, yes, and at that time. I proceeded to do what he wanted me to.

The majority relies on the trial court's statement that the defendant responded affirmatively to her question "If I do what you want, will you let me go without killing me?" The majority further suggests that the jury could infer the defendant's affirmative response. The facts belie such inference since by the prosecutrix's own testimony the defendant made *no* response. *He said nothing!*

She then testified that she started to cry and he "started lightly to choke" her, whatever that means. Obviously, the choking was not of any persuasive significance. During this "choking" she was able to talk. She said "If I do what you want will you let me go?" It was at this point that the defendant said yes.

I find it incredible for the majority to conclude that on these facts, without more, a woman was *forced* to commit oral sex upon the defendant and then to engage in vaginal intercourse. In the absence of any verbal threat to do her grievous bodily harm or the display of any weapon and threat to use it, I find it difficult to understand how a victim could participate in these sexual activities and not be willing.

What was the nature and extent of her fear anyhow? She herself testified she was "fearful that maybe I had someone following me." She was afraid because she didn't know him and she was afraid he was going to "rape" her. But there are no acts or conduct on the part of the defendant to suggest that these fears were created by the defendant or that he made any objective, identifiable threats to her which would give rise to this woman's failure to flee, summon help, scream, or make physical resistance.

As the defendant well knew, this was not a child. This was a married woman with children, a woman familiar with the social setting in which these two actors met. It was an ordinary city street, not an isolated spot. He had not forced his way into her car; he had not taken advantage of a difference in years or any state of intoxication or mental or physical incapacity on her part. He did not grapple with her. She got out of the car, *walked with him* across the street and *followed* him up the stairs to his room. She certainly had to realize that they were not going upstairs to play *Scrabble*.

Once in the room she waited while he went to the bathroom where he stayed for five minutes. In his absence, the room was lighted but she did not seek a means of escape. She did not even "try the door" to determine if it was locked. She waited.

Upon his return, he turned off the lights and pulled her on the bed. There is no suggestion or inference to be drawn from her testimony that he yanked her on the bed or in any manner physically abused her by this conduct. As a matter of fact there is no suggestion by her that he bruised or hurt her in any manner, or that the "choking" was intended to be disabling.

He then proceeded to unbutton her blouse and her bra. He did not rip her clothes off or use any greater force than was necessary to unfasten her garments. He did not even complete this procedure but requested that she do it, which she did "because he asked me to." However, she not only removed her clothing but took his clothes off, too.

Then for a while they lay together on the bed kissing, though she says she did not return his kisses. However, without protest she then proceeded to perform oral sex and later submitted to vaginal intercourse. After these activities were completed, she asked to leave. They dressed and he walked her to her car and asked to see her again. She indicated that perhaps they might meet at Fells Point. He gave her directions home and returned to his apartment where the police found him later that morning.

The record does not disclose the basis for this young woman's misgivings about her experience with the defendant. The only substantive fear she had was that she would be late arriving home. The objective facts make it inherently improbable that the defendant's conduct generated any fear for her physical well-being.

In my judgment the State failed to prove the essential element of force beyond a reasonable doubt and, therefore, the judgment of conviction should be reversed.

Judges Smith and Digges have authorized me to state that they concur in the views expressed herein.

APPENDIX

In the following cases rape convictions were overturned because the requirement of force necessary to affirmatively demonstrate lack of consent was not strictly complied with, or the facts were so sketchy or inherently improbable that this element could not be established, as a matter of law, beyond a reasonable doubt.

In Zamora v. State, 449 S.W.2d 43 (Tex.Cr.App.1969), it was held that the evidence was insufficient to sustain a conviction of rape by force and threats where the sixteen-year-old prosecutrix, who had been engaging in sexual relations with the defendant stepfather for about six years, went to his bedroom to take him coffee, did not try to leave, took off part of her clothes at his request, made no outcry, and did not resist in any way, even though she knew what was going to happen when she sat on the bed. On appeal reference was made to certain threats which, if sufficient, would have excused the complainant's failure to resist. The defendant threatened to put the girl in a juvenile home and to whip her younger brother and sisters if she told her mother. But the court explained, "the threats that were made occurred after the alleged act and were *not made to cause the prosecutrix to yield,* but to prevent her from informing her mother." The conviction was reversed.

In People v. Bales, 74 Cal.App.2d 732, 169 P.2d 262 (1946), the complaining witness testified that she met the appellant in a bar and later he physically forced her into his car and drove off. (The evidence in this respect was sufficient to sustain a charge of kidnapping.) Appellant next drove the woman down the highway and stopped the car off the road. He "came around to her side, and made a remark to the effect that he would then find out what kind of woman she was."

She testified "that she was 'afraid of the threat.' " The court concluded:

> There is an entire absence of evidence that she voiced any
> objection, made any appeal for help or tried to fight or strug-
> gle.   There is no evidence of any force or threat by the
> appellant at that time, and no substantial evidence of any
> apprehension of immediate bodily harm accompanied by appar-
> ent power of execution.   The evidence material to his charge
> fails to show either any reasonable resistance or any reasona-
> ble excuse for its absence.   The old rule that there must be
> resistance to the utmost has been relaxed, but not to the extent
> of doing away with the need of showing some resistance or, in
> proper cases, showing facts which fairly indicate some good
> reason for not resisting.

In Farrar v. United States, 275 F.2d 868 (D.C.Cir.1959), opinion
amended (1960), the words of Chief Judge Prettyman, speaking for the
court, are better left to speak for themselves:

> As I understand the law of rape, if no force is used and the
> girl in fact acquiesces, the acquiescence may nevertheless be
> deemed to be non-consent if it is induced by fear; but the fear,
> to be sufficient for this purpose, must be based upon something
> of substance; and furthermore the fear must be of death or
> severe bodily harm.   A girl cannot simply say, "I was scared,"
> and thus transform an apparent consent into a legal non-
> consent which makes the man's act a capital offense.   She
> must have a reasonable apprehension, as I understand the law,
> of something real; her fear must be not fanciful but substan-
> tial.

> In the case at bar there was an apparent acquiescence on
> the girl's part.   She said she took off all her clothes, lay down
> on the bed, and had intercourse twice, some forty-five minutes
> apart.   But she said she did this because she was scared.   And
> she was quite clear, emphatic and insistent upon the cause of
> her fear; the man had a knife in his hand.   The reason for her
> fear was tangible and definite.   It was a knife, and it was in his
> hand.   She so testified repeatedly.

> But she never saw any knife.   Now it is perfectly apparent
> that, if this man had had a knife in his hand while he was
> doing all the things she said he did over this two or three hour
> period, she must have seen it.   He could not have had a knife
> and have done all these things, with her watching him as she
> said she did, without her seeing the knife.   As a matter of fact,
> at the close of the Government's testimony the trial judge
> struck from the record all the testimony concerning the knife,
> "leaving her testimony in that it was something that felt sharp
> and felt like a knife."   The judge said if there had been a knife
> the girl would have seen it.

Upon the foregoing facts and circumstances, when the knife disappeared from the record as a possible fact, the charge of rape disappeared, as I view the matter. The only basis for fear advanced by the prosecutrix was the knife; she suggested no alternative cause for fear. The only factual substance to any of the intangible threats allegedly made by him to her was the knife. There was no force or violence and no threat or fear of force or violence except for the knife. The charge of rape rested upon the presence of the knife. The Government failed to prove a case of rape.

In Gonzales v. State, 516 P.2d 592 (Wyo.1973), the complaining witness was 33 years old and the divorced mother of three children. She was working in a bar and defendant, someone she knew, came in shortly before closing and had been drinking. He asked her for a ride home and she refused, but he followed her and got into her car anyway. She testified she was nervous and scared at the time and made no further protest nor signalled with her horn. On a side road "[h]e asked her to stop 'to go to the bathroom' and took the keys out of the ignition, telling her she would not drive off and leave him. She stayed in the car. . . ."

When he returned he told her he was going to rape her and she kept trying to talk him out of it. He told her he was getting mad at her and then put his fist against her face and said, "I'm going to do it. You can have it one way or the other."

There were no other threats. The witness testified she knew defendant's temper and was scared of him. She related several previous incidents to sustain her knowledge of his temper. The court concluded, "This is not a firm basis upon which to sketch a man of violence and one who would inspire fear." It should be noted that although the conviction was reversed on other grounds, the court concluded that:

[i]nasmuch as the case must be retried in conformity with these principles [having quoted from Farrar and cited *Winegan v. State* (1970)] we do not deem it amiss to state it is not entirely fair to a trial court or to the defendant to rely on the sketchy showing and lack of detail presented at this trial.

There are a number of other cases in which the threats relied upon were found insufficient. In State v. Horne, 12 Utah 2d 162, 364 P.2d 109 (1961), the prosecutrix was a 21–year–old married woman with two young children. They lived in a trailer. The defendant and she were acquainted, and he had visited her on previous occasions. On this particular night he entered her trailer uninvited and stated he was going to make love to her. She protested, she struggled, and her little girl, who had been asleep in her mother's bed, awoke and began crying. Finally he let her go to the bathroom and she refused to come out. He came and got her and they struggled some more. Eventually she gave in. She testified she was afraid for her children.

The court set forth the rule to be applied and applied it to the facts:

The old rule of "resistance to the utmost" is obsolete. The law does not require that the woman shall do more than her age, strength, the surrounding facts, and all attending circumstances make reasonable for her to do in order to manifest her opposition. However, in determining the sufficiency of the evidence, there must be considered the ease of assertion of the forcible accomplishment of the sexual act, with impossibility of defense except by direct denial, or of the proneness of the woman, when she finds the fact of her disgrace discovered or likely of discovery to minimize her fault by asserting force or violence, which had led courts to hold to a very strict rule of proof in such cases.

. . .

The prosecutrix did not attempt to leave the trailer to seek help, although she had ample opportunity. When she went to the bathroom the defendant, according to her testimony, had already removed his pants and had made indecent proposals and advances. Yet, she did not avail herself of the opportunity to seek help. It is the natural impulse of every honest and virtuous female to flee from threatened outrage. Her explanation that she did not want to leave the children alone with the defendant is a rather weak one, to say the least. It would have taken less than a minute to rouse her neighbors. Furthermore, she left the defendant with the children for 10 to 15 minutes while she was in the bathroom.

. . .

There was no evidence of any threats made to either the prosecutrix or her children.

We have carefully evaluated the testimony of the prosecutrix and conclude that it is so inherently improbable as to be unworthy of belief and that, upon objective analysis, it appears that reasonable minds could not believe beyond a reasonable doubt that the defendant was guilty. The jury's verdict cannot stand.

In Johnson v. State, 118 So.2d 806 (Fla.Dist.Ct.App.1960), the evidence was insufficient to sustain a jury finding that the prosecutrix was forced against her will to have intercourse with defendant or that her fear was sufficient for the jury to find that defendant was guilty of rape through fear. In this case an eighteen-year-old high school student accepted a ride home from an acquaintance, which eventually led to her seduction. At no time did the defendant threaten her with any weapon. She screamed, but did not resist in any other way, nor attempt to flee. Quoting from State v. Remley, 237 S.W. 489, 492 (Mo. 1922), the Florida court stated:

The statements of plaintiff as to this occurrence must be viewed in the light of all the surrounding facts and circumstances. If the physical facts and all the circumstances appearing in evidence, together with the surrounding conditions, absolutely negative and destroy the force of such statements, then, in contemplation of law, such statements do not amount to any substantial evidence of the facts to which they relate. We do not mean by this fact that the prosecutrix must be corroborated, for such is not the law of this State. State v. Marcks, 140 Mo. 656, [41 S.W. 973, 43 S.W. 1095]. But we do hold that statements made by a witness that are not only in conflict with the experience of common life and of the ordinary instincts and promptings of human nature, but negatived as well by the conduct of the witness, and the conditions and circumstances surrounding the occurrence to which they have application, are not sufficient to support the grave and serious charge of rape, and this is true whether the charge is made in either a civil or criminal proceeding. [118 So.2d at 815–16.]

And in People v. Blevins, 98 Ill.App.2d 172, 240 N.E.2d 434 (1968), the evidence was insufficient where there were unexplained inconsistencies in the prosecution's case and the defendant was found peacefully asleep at the scene of the "crime" when arrested.

Even in the closest cases which have been upheld by other jurisdictions there existed more evidence of threat-induced fear of imminent bodily harm than existed in the present case.

In Brown v. State, 59 Wis.2d 200, 207 N.W.2d 602 (1973), the defendant threatened his victim with a water pistol. She had reason to believe it was real, and reason to believe he would shoot her if she did not comply.

In Johnson v. United States, 426 F.2d 651, 654 (D.C.Cir.1970), the victim's failure to resist "was based on a *general fear of her assailant* who had dragged her from her car, kept his arm around her neck when they stopped for gas, drove her to a deserted location and told her it would be useless for her to scream because no one would hear." (Emphasis in original.)

In Brown v. State, 581 P.2d 189 (Wyo.1978), the victim was treated very roughly and bruised. She didn't resist because she was three or four months pregnant (which the defendant knew) and because she was afraid for both her own and her baby's lives.

In Tryon v. State, 567 P.2d 290 (Wyo.1970), the victim did not resist out of fear. Although he did not threaten her, the conviction was sustained. The court explained:

> We find here a child afraid of the dark alone with this defendant several miles from her home, very late at night—and with a man whom she knew had been drinking and quarreling with the woman for whom she had been babysitting. We cannot help but suggest that all of these elements could totally terrify a child of tender years or that the jury could have so reasonably inferred.

. . .

Although the defendant did not express threats, wielded no weapons, and did not strike the victim, the force applied when considered in light of the facts previously related is sufficient to support the jury's finding of non-consent. [567 P.2d at 292–93.]

NOTES

1. In the seminal article by Prof. Susan Estrich on sexism in the legal treatment of rape in the United States, the author begins her analysis of criminal sexual assaults against women by stating: "The history of rape, as the law has been enforced in this country, is a history of both racism and sexism." Her exhaustive study represents an important contribution to the process of debunking myths and misconceptions upon which the earlier development of rape laws rests. Estrich, Rape, 95 Yale L.J. 1087 (1986). The author states, at 1090–1091:

To examine rape within the criminal law tradition is to expose fully the sexism of the law. Much that is striking about the crime of rape—and revealing of the sexism of the system—emerges only when rape is examined relative to other crimes, which the feminist literature by and large does not do. For example, rape is most assuredly not the only crime in which consent is a defense; but it is the only crime that has required the victim to resist physically in order to establish nonconsent. Nor is rape the only crime where prior relationship is taken into account by prosecutors in screening cases; yet we have not asked whether considering prior relationship in rape cases is different, and less justifiable, than considering it in cases of assault.

Sexism in the law of rape is no matter of mere historical interest; it endures, even where some of the most blatant testaments to that sexism have disappeared. Corroboration requirements unique to rape may have been repealed, but they continue to be enforced as a matter of practice in many jurisdictions. The victim of rape may not be required to resist to the utmost as a matter of statutory law in any jurisdiction, but the definitions accorded to force and consent may render "reasonable" resistance both a practical and a legal necessity. In the law of rape, supposedly dead horses continue to run.

The study of rape as an illustration of sexism in the criminal law also raises broader questions about the way conceptions of gender and the different backgrounds and perspectives of men and women should be encompassed within the criminal law. In one of his most celebrated essays, Oliver Wendell Holmes explained that the law does not exist to tell the good man what to do, but to tell the bad man what not to do. Holmes was interested in the distinction between the good and bad man; I cannot help noticing that both are men. Most of the time, a criminal law that reflects male views and male standards imposes its judgment on men who have injured other men. It is "boys' rules" applied to a boys' fight. In rape, the male standard defines a crime committed against women, and male standards are used not only to judge men, but also to judge the conduct of women victims. Moreover, because the crime involves sex itself, the law of rape inevitably treads on the explosive ground of sex roles, of male aggression and female passivity, of our understandings of sexuality—areas where differences between a male and a female perspective may be most pronounced.

* * *

2. While until fairly recently statutory law was modeled closely on the common law principles that are deemed outmoded, a number of states have revised their statutes to conform to currently prevailing concepts about sex offenders.

For instance, Illinois, in Ch. 38, Sec. 12–13 of the Criminal Code, states:

§ 12–13. Criminal Sexual Assault. (a) The accused commits criminal sexual assault if he or she:

(1) commits an act of sexual penetration by the use of force or threat of force; or

(2) commits an act of sexual penetration and the accused knew that the victim was unable to understand the nature of the act or was unable to give knowing consent; or

(3) commits an act of sexual penetration with a victim who was under 18 years of age when the act was committed and the accused was a family member; or

(4) commits an act of sexual penetration with a victim who was at least 13 years of age but under 18 years of age when the act was committed and the accused was 17 years of age or over and held a position of trust, authority or supervision in relation to the victim.

(b) Sentence. Criminal sexual assault is a Class 1 felony. A second or subsequent conviction for a violation of this Section or under any similar statute of this State or any other state for any offense involving criminal sexual assault that is substantially equivalent to or more serious than the sexual assault prohibited under this Section is a Class X felony. When a person has any such prior conviction, the information or indictment charging that person shall state such prior conviction so as to give notice of the State's intention to treat the charge as a Class X felony. The fact of such prior conviction is not an element of the offense and may not be disclosed to the jury during trial unless otherwise permitted by issues properly raised during such trial.

§ 12–14. Aggravated Criminal Sexual Assault. (a) The accused commits aggravated criminal sexual assault if he or she commits criminal sexual assault and any of the following aggravating circumstances existed during the commission of the offense:

(1) the accused displayed, threatened to use, or used a dangerous weapon or any object fashioned or utilized in such a manner as to lead the victim under the circumstances reasonably to believe it to be a dangerous weapon; or

(2) the accused caused bodily harm to the victim; or

(3) the accused acted in such a manner as to threaten or endanger the life of the victim or any other person; or

(4) the criminal sexual assault was perpetrated during the course of the commission or attempted commission of any other felony by the accused; or

(5) the victim was 60 years of age or over when the offense was committed.

(b) The accused commits aggravated criminal sexual assault if:

(1) the accused was 17 years of age or over and commits an act of sexual penetration, with a victim who was under 13 years of age when the act was committed; or

(2) the accused was under 17 years of age and (i) commits an act of sexual penetration, with a victim who was under 9 years of age when the act was committed; or (ii) commits an act of sexual penetration with a victim who was at least 9 years of age but under 13 years of age when the act was committed and the accused used force or threat of force to commit the act.

(c) The accused commits aggravated criminal sexual assault if he or she commits an act of sexual penetration with a victim who was an institutionalized severely or profoundly mentally retarded person at the time the act was committed.

3. Considerable older case law of the common law courts refers to the need of the victim to resist "to the utmost," unless it is clearly demonstrated that resistance poses a danger to the victim and she has clearly indicated a lack of consent. Is the fact that a woman is alone in a home, and is confronted by a man who is larger than she is, sufficiently fearful to her so that resistance may be dispensed with? In Goldberg v. State, 41 Md.App. 58, 395 A.2d 1213 (1979), the court said:

"In the complete absence of any threatening words or actions by the [defendant], these two factors, as a matter of law, are simply not enough to have created a reasonable fear of harm so as to preclude resistance and be 'the equivalent of force.' . . . Without proof of force, actual or constructive, evidenced by words or conduct of the defendant or those acting in consort with him, sexual intercourse is not rape. This is so even though the intercourse may have occurred without the actual consent and against the will of the alleged victim. . . ."

A 1980 amendment to the California rape statute dropped all references to the need of a victim to resist her attacker. As a result, the California Supreme Court held, in People v. Barnes, 42 Cal.3d 284, 228 Cal.Rptr. 228, 721 P.2d 110 (1986), that a rape victim's failure to resist, because she believed that if she did so the attacker would become physically violent and psychotic, does not invalidate defendant's conviction. The court referred to studies that demonstrate that while some women respond to rape with active resistance, others show "psychological infantilism," a condition that resembles "freezing" and can resemble cooperative behavior. Thus, the victim may smile, can appear calm, and may even initiate acts while at the same time being in a state of terror. The legislature, so the court recognized, has demonstrated its unwillingness to dictate that only one response to sexual assault is legally recognized, by removing the reference to resistance from the law.

4. Is sexual intercourse with a sleeping woman intercourse "by force and against her will," or is it intercourse with a "physically helpless" person?

North Carolina punishes, as second degree rape (Gen.Stat. 14–27.3(a)) vaginal intercourse with another person:

(1) By force and against the will of the other person; or

(2) Who is . . . physically helpless, and the person performing the act knows or should reasonably know the other person is . . . physically helpless.

In State v. Moorman, 82 N.C.App. 594, 347 S.E.2d 857 (1986), the opinion gave this account of the evidence presented:

"On the evening of 31 August 1984, the prosecutrix dated a friend from Charlotte and met with friends. During the evening she consumed two beers. She returned to her room at approximately 1:00 a.m. on the morning of 1 September 1984. She entered her room, closed the door, and turned on the radio to a low volume. She then fell asleep on her bed fully clothed. The next thing she remembered was that she dreamed she was having sexual intercourse. She awoke in a darkened room to find a male on top of her engaging in sexual intercourse. She tried to sit up, but the male grabbed her by the neck and pushed her back down causing multiple scratches about the neck. Afraid that the male might injure her, she offered no further resistance. After ejaculating in her vagina, the male engaged in anal intercourse with the prosecutrix, causing a one-half inch tear or fissure in her anus. She did not resist due to the pain and fear that the male might strangle her. After the male stopped, she went to the door and turned on the light. She recognized the face of the male, but could not remember his name. The male told her not to call the police, that he was her roommate's friend Percy, that he thought she was the roommate, and that he would not have done what he did if he had known she was not the roommate."

Under the above facts, is defendant guilty of violating subsection (a)(1) or (a)(2)?

The Court of Appeals of North Carolina held that a person who is asleep is "physically helpless" within the meaning of the statute. "Physically helpless" is defined in General Statute 14–27.1(3) as: (i) a victim who is unconscious; or (ii) a victim who is physically unable to resist an act of vaginal intercourse or a sexual act or communicate unwillingness to submit to an act of vaginal intercourse or a sexual act." Where the indictment is for the rape of one who is asleep, the prosecutor must proceed on the theory that the victim was "physically helpless". Since defendant was charged in the indictment with engaging in intercourse by force and against the will of another person, there was a fatal variance between the offense charged and the evidence produced.

On further appeal, however, the Supreme Court of North Carolina, 320 N.C. 387, 358 S.E.2d 502 (1987), said the Court of Appeals erred in that defendant was also charged with second degree sexual offense which requires (1) a sexual act, (2) against the will and without the consent of the victim, (3) using force sufficient to overcome any resistance of the victim. (General Statute 14–27.5(a)(1). In that regard, the court said:

"Defendant in his testimony admits engaging in anal intercourse with the prosecutrix. The only remaining question is whether there is sufficient evidence that such intercourse was by force and against the will of the prosecutrix. The State's evidence indicates that upon awakening and prior to the anal intercourse, the prosecutrix attempted to sit up but defendant grabbed the prosecutrix by the neck and pushed her back down onto the bed with enough force to cause multiple scratches and bruising about the neck. After this use of force, the prosecutrix was scared that defendant might injure her further, and thus offered no other resistance. As a result of the anal intercourse, the prosecutrix received a one-half inch tear or fissure in the anus.

We find this evidence constitutes substantial evidence of all material elements of second degree sexual offense and is thus sufficient to withstand a motion to dismiss."

For a student Note surveying the law of other jurisdictions, see *State v. Moorman:* Can Sex With a Sleeping Woman Constitute Forcible Rape?, 65 N.C.L.Rev. 1246 (1987). See also Woodward v. Commonwealth, 12 Va.App. 118, 402 S.E.2d 244 (1991).

5. At common law, in order to be guilty of rape, the offender must be at least 14 years of age. This early concept, still retained in most jurisdictions, is not based on considerations of physical capacity, but rather on a belief that sexual intercourse by one below that age should not be punished as rape. Accordingly, in Foster v. Commonwealth, 96 Va. 306, 31 S.E. 503 (1898), it was held that a boy under 14 years of age is conclusively presumed to be incapable of committing the crime of rape, or of attempting to commit it, whatever may be the real facts. Therefore, evidence to rebut the presumption is inadmissible. (However, the court added that where the boy assists another in an attempted rape, he may be convicted as a principal in the second degree, and punished the same as the principal in the first degree.)

6. The principal cases deal with "forcible rape", as distinguished from "statutory rape"—an offense based solely upon the age of the female and without reference to force, consent or chastity. The usual age below which the act is rape is 16. Some states combine rape and statutory rape crimes in one statutory section. See, for example, Virginia Code Sec. 18.2–61, which provides:

"If any person has sexual intercourse with a female or causes a female to engage in sexual intercourse with any person and such act is accomplished (i) against her will, by force, threat or intimidation, or (ii) through the use of the female's mental incapacity or physical helplessness, or (iii) with a female child under age thirteen as the victim, he or she shall, in the discretion of the court or jury, be punished with confinement in the penitentiary for life or for any term not less than five years."

Does the foregoing statutory provision, identifying the defendant as any *person,* permit indictment of a woman for rape?

Does the statutory rape law, punishing only males for the act of sexual intercourse, and not females, violate the constitutional right to equal protection under the laws? See the case of Michael M. v. Superior Court of Sonoma County, 450 U.S. 464, 101 S.Ct. 1200 (1981), in Chapter 4–c, supra.

2. DEMONSTRATING THE TRAUMA OF RAPE

PEOPLE v. NELSON

Illinois Appellate Court, 1990.
203 Ill.App.3d 1038, 149 Ill.Dec. 161, 561 N.E.2d 439.

JUSTICE RARICK delivered the opinion of the court:

Defendant, Art Nelson, was found guilty after a jury trial of aggravated criminal sexual assault and aggravated criminal sexual abuse. . . . Defendant appeals his conviction, arguing the court improperly allowed the testimony of the State's expert to be presented to the jury. We affirm.

According to the evidence presented at trial, the victim first became acquainted with defendant when he was in the third grade. The victim, his father, and defendant would all go fishing together. By the time the victim was in the fifth grade, he was allowed to go fishing alone with defendant. Defendant would buy him snack cakes for such trips and often stopped at a Dairy Queen for ice cream afterwards. Often defendant would allow the victim to drive the car if the victim sat on defendant's lap while so doing. Eventually the victim noticed defendant frequently encouraged him to go to the bathroom and would try to get close to him while he was urinating. In the summer between the fifth and sixth grades, defendant's encouragement culminated in touching the victim's penis with both his hands and mouth. The last incident occurred sometime in February of 1987 while the victim was in sixth grade. The victim refused to go on any other fishing trips with defendant after the assault in February but did not tell anyone about defendant's activities. Sometime in April, the victim's mother, after hearing some rumors, questioned the victim about defendant and whether he ever had done anything "bad" to the victim. The victim eventually revealed the nature of the activities to his mother and a caseworker from the Department of Children and Family Services. The victim's mother further testified the victim no longer wanted to go fishing wih anyone, his grades in school had dropped and he often was afraid, sleeping on the floor of his parents' bedroom. Defendant denied any abuse had occurred. He believed the accusations arose from ill-feelings between the two families. He further testified he had worked the first three Saturdays in February and on the fourth Saturday went fishing with some friends at another lake than where the alleged abuse occurred. The jury, however, chose to believe the victim.

Defendant argues on appeal he was denied a fair trial through the rebuttal testimony of the State's expert, Dr. Hoffman, a psychologist. According to defendant, Dr. Hoffman, in relating to the jury the victim's behavior and attitude not only was allowed to testify to hearsay statements of the victim, but also was allowed to place the weight of her opinion behind the credibility of the victim. More importantly, she was permitted to explain to the jury the "child sexual abuse syndrome" and how the victim's behavior coincided with such a syndrome when the field of psychology, according to defendant's expert, has not recognized the term. In ruling on his post-trial motion, the trial court apparently agreed with defendant that the expert's testimony pertaining to the child sexual abuse syndrome was improper but amounted to nothing more than harmless error in this instance. Defendant takes exception with this finding, arguing that when the only evidence against him came from the victim, the expert went too far in diagnosing the victim as suffering from the syndrome, being the equivalent of an assertion by a professional that the victim was being truthful when admittedly much of the victim's behavior could have been caused by other factors.

We, like many other jurisdictions, are increasingly faced with cases of sexual abuse of children. And, like many other jurisdictions, we are now required to decide whether certain types of expert testimony pertaining to such abuse, particularly the child sexual abuse syndrome, are admissible to aid the prosecution in presenting its case. Given the nature of the crime and perceived inherent weaknesses of such cases, a young, often traumatized child pitted against a seemingly respectable adult, this is not a surprising development. (See generally Gardner, Prosecutors Should Think Twice Before Using Experts in Child Abuse Cases, 3 Crim.Just. 12, 12 (1988); Roe, Expert Testimony in child Sexual Abuse Cases, 40 U. Miami L.Rev. 97, 97 (1985); Comment, The Admissibility of Expert Testimony in Intrafamily Child Sexual Abuse Cases, 34 U.C.L.A. L.Rev. 175, 175–76 (1986) (hereinafter cited as Intrafamily Child Sexual Abuse).) With this opinion, we choose to join the ranks of those jurisdictions which, in limited circumstances, allow expert testimony pertaining to the child sexual abuse syndrome.

In general, "syndrome" refers to a concurrence of symptoms or a group of signs tending to indicate a particular condition. (See Note, The Syndrome Syndrome: Problems Concerning the Admissibility of Expert Testimony on Psychological Profiles, 37 U.Fla.L.Rev. 1035, 1036 (1985); Comment, Syndrome Testimony in Child Abuse Prosecutions: The Wave of the Future?, 8 St. Louis U.Pub.L.Rev. 207, 208 (1989).) The child sexual abuse syndrome, also known as the child sexual abuse accommodation syndrome, then refers to that group of symptoms or behavior patterns typically manifested by young victims of sexual abuse. (See Summit, The Child Sexual Abuse Accommodation Syndrome, 7 Int'l J. Child Abuse & Neglect 177 (1983).) One scholar, Dr. Ronald Summit, lists five such typical reactions or stages under the label of child sexual abuse accommodation syndrome, these being: (1) secrecy; (2) helplessness; (3) entrapment and accommodation; (4) delayed, conflicted, and unconvincing disclosure; and (5) retraction. (Summit, 7 Int'l J. Child Abuse & Neglect at 181–88.) Other researchers, on the other hand, believe the number of possible symptom constellations is infinite because of the various degrees of abuse committed upon children from various backgrounds and ages. (See McCord, Expert Psychological Testimony About Child Complaints in Sexual Abuse Prosecutions: A Foray into the Admissibility of Novel Psychological Evidence, 77 J.Crim.L. & Criminology 1, 18–24 (1986); Comment, The Admissibility of Expert Psychological Testimony in Cases Involving the Sexual Misuse of a Child, 42 U. Miami L.Rev. 1033, 1048–50 (1988) (hereinafter cited as Expert Psychological Testimony).) What is certain, however, is that children who have been sexually abused behave differently from children who have not been abused. Explaining such differences is the critical element, not what label may be selected to aid in the explanations.

We are not unfamiliar with syndrome testimony in general. Our courts have previously found admissible evidence of rape trauma syndrome, battered child syndrome and battered woman syndrome. We have even gone so far as to allow experts to explain or testify with respect to the behavior of child victims being consistent with certain models for victims of child sexual assault under the guise of the rape trauma syndrome or under the label of post-traumatic stress syndrome. The clear trend in Illinois is toward the admission of expert testimony pertaining to psychological syndromes where such evidence aids the trier of fact. Generally speaking, expert testimony will be admitted if the expert has some knowledge or experience, not common to the world, which will aid the finder of fact in arriving at a determination on the question or issue. Behavioral and psychological characteristics of child sexual abuse victims are proper subjects for expert testimony. Few jurors have sufficient familiarity with child sexual abuse to understand the dynamics of a sexually abusive relationship. Additionally, the behavior exhibited by sexually abused children is often contrary to what most adults would expect. We therefore see no reason to withhold expert testimony from the jury explaining a child victim's "unusual" behavior merely because the expert chooses to describe such behavior under a certain label.

Defendant argues, however, literature in the field of psychology does not recognize "child sexual abuse syndrome." Our own research does not bear out defendant's contention. It is true the syndrome is not listed in the Diagnostic and Statistical Manual of Mental Health III (D.S.M. III). This, however, is but one factor to consider in balancing the probative value of the testimony against possible prejudice to the defendant or confusion for the jury. Indeed, very few concepts are generally accepted by all behavioral scientists. Similarly, the reality that many of the symptoms may be caused by factors other than sexual abuse goes only to the weight to be accorded such testimony, not its admissibility. The question really is not whether such testimony is admissible at all, but rather how much of it can be admitted and under what circumstances.

Turning to other jurisdictions' handling of this question, from our research of the issue we note several approaches. At one extreme is the stand taken by Hawaii, which permits a psychologist to testify as to the credibility of the child victim's testimony, if adequately supported by comprehensible testimony which a jury could evaluate itself, pertaining to the occurrence of the abuse and the identity of the offender. (See State v. Kim (1982), 64 Hawaii 598, 607–10, 645 P.2d 1330, 1338–39. Contra State v. Moran (1986), 151 Ariz. 378, 382–83, 728 P.2d 248, 252–53; People v. Ortega (Colo.App.1983), 672 P.2d 215, 218; State v. Lash (1985), 237 Kan. 384, 386, 699 P.2d 49, 51; State v. Keen (1983), 309 N.C. 158, 162–64, 305 S.E.2d 535, 537–38.) Other jurisdictions permit the expert to testify regarding the results of a psychological evaluation of the child and to determine whether the results of such an examination are consistent with those expected for a child victim subjected to sexual abuse. (See Kruse v. State (Fla.App.1986), 483 So.2d 1383, 1387–88; Myers, 359 N.W.2d at 609–10; In re Nicole V. (1987), 123 A.D.2d 97, 106–09, 510 N.Y.S.2d 567, 573–74, aff'd (1987), 71 N.Y.2d

112, 518 N.E.2d 914, 524 N.Y.S.2d 19; State v. Middleton (1983), 294 Or.
427, 432–38, 657 P.2d 1215, 1217–21. See also Allison v. Georgia (1987),
256 Ga. 851, 353 S.E.2d 805; State v. Snapp (1986), 110 Idaho 269, 715
P.2d 939; People v. Beckley (1987), 161 Mich.App. 120, 409 N.W.2d 759,
aff'd (1990), 434 Mich. 691, 456 N.W.2d 391; State v. Maule (1983), 35
Wash.App. 287, 667 P.2d 96.) Still other approaches permit experts
who have not evaluated the particular victim to present testimony
pertaining to general behavior patterns and psychological symptoms
associated with sexual abuse and then to apply such knowledge to
either hypothetical facts presented or to facts admitted into evidence.
Others restrict the expert's testimony to a discussion of general principles only, thereby leaving the application of these principles to the trier
of fact. (See State v. Moran (1986), 151 Ariz. 378, 384–86, 728 P.2d 248,
254–56; People v. Gray (1986), 187 Cal.App.3d 213, 217–20, 231 Cal.
Rptr. 658, 660–62; People v. Roscoe (1985), 168 Cal.App.3d 1093, 1099–
1100, 215 Cal.Rptr. 45, 49–50; Commonwealth v. Baldwin (1985), 348
Pa.Super. 368, 373–79, 502 A.2d 253, 255–57, disapproved of in part by
Commonwealth v. Davis (1988), 518 Pa. 77, 541 A.2d 315 (error for
expert to give opinion regarding credibility of child sexual abuse
victims).) Many of these same jurisdictions also allow the expert to
refer specifically to the term "child sexual abuse syndrome" or one of
its variants in their testimony to the jury. (See People v. Gray (1986),
187 Cal.App.3d 213, 231 Cal.Rptr. 658; Wheat v. State (Del.1987), 527
A.2d 269; Allison v. State (1987), 256 Ga. 851, 353 S.E.2d 805; State v.
Snapp (1986), 110 Idaho 269, 715 P.2d 939; State v. Carlson (Minn.App.
1985), 360 N.W.2d 442; People v. Grady (1986), 133 Misc.2d 211, 506
N.Y.S.2d 922.) Those jurisdictions, on the other hand, which do not
allow the use of child sexual abuse syndrome testimony include Kentucky (see Bussey v. Commonwealth (Ky.1985), 697 S.W.2d 139 (syndrome testimony immaterial to establishing defendant's guilt)), Mississippi (see Hosford v. State (Miss.1990), 560 So.2d 163 (syndrome
testimony not sanctioned but general testimony admissible especially
when elicited in direct response to assault on credibility of victim)),
Ohio (see State v. Davis (Ohio Ct.App. Dec. 29, 1989), No. CA88–09–017
(available on Westlaw 1989 W.L. 157206) (syndrome testimony impermissible because it has no scientific reliability and improperly bolsters
uncorroborated victim's testimony)) and Tennessee (see State v.
Schimpf (Tenn.Crim.App.1989), 782 S.W.2d 186 (syndrome testimony
invades jury's province as to credibility of victim)). (See also State v.
Rimmasch (Utah 1989), 775 P.2d 388 (testimony concerning typical
child abuse profile inherently unreliable).) This lack of uniformity
among the various jurisdictions is not surprising; attempts to expand
testimony into new fields often result in judicial confusion and inconsistency. We should not, however, be unduly prejudiced against the
introduction of expert testimony based upon a theory in its relative
infancy.[1] We therefore choose to follow the reasoning of the majority

---

1. One commentator also notes that an expert testifying as to general facts ob- tained through the application of tradition- al research methods is not applying new

of the jurisdictions which fall in the middle of the extremes of absolute rejection as represented by Ohio and absolute acceptance to the point of vouching for the credibility of the victim as represented by Hawaii. This middle position ensures that the trier of fact will be informed as to the general characteristics exhibited by victims of child abuse, which often are inexplicable or conflicting, but at the same time will not invade the province of that same trier of fact in weighing the credibility of witnesses. The mere fact an expert's testimony, if believed, tends to bolster the victim's credibility does not make such evidence inadmissible. The testimony of one witness often corroborates or enhances that of another. The jury, however, is still free to disregard such evidence. Nor should we hold expert testimony inadmissible merely because it may include an ultimate issue to be decided by the trier of fact, i.e., whether the victim had indeed been abused. Medical experts traditionally have been allowed to testify on numerous issues ultimately to be decided by a jury. We also do not believe that by allowing such testimony we are encouraging a battle of experts any different than those commonly found in any case involving expert testimony. Again, the jury ultimately must choose which group of experts to believe. This does not mean, however, we are wholeheartedly accepting child sexual abuse syndrome testimony under all circumstances. At this time, we choose to limit the admissibility of such testimony to rebuttal after the victim's credibility has first been attacked. Under such circumstances, defendant's own actions have necessitated the use of syndrome testimony, especially when defense counsel emphasizes some unusual aspect of the victim's behavior such as recantation or delayed reporting. (See People v. Dunnahoo (1984), 152 Cal.App.3d 561, 577, 199 Cal.Rptr. 796, 804; People v. Benjamin R. (1984), 103 A.D.2d 663, 669, 481 N.Y.S.2d 827, 832. See also *Hosford,* 560 So.2d at 166 (even though syndrome testimony in general not allowed, expert allowed to explain victim's behavior in response to assault on credibility). Cf. People v. Bergschneider (1989), 211 Cal.App.3d 144, 158–60, 259 Cal. Rptr. 219, 226–28 (prosecutor not limited to introducing expert testimony on rebuttal if misconceptions targeted during case in chief).) To prohibit syndrome testimony in these instances would, in effect, for example in the situation of recantation, allow powerful impeachment evidence to remain unrebutted when a plausible reason exists why the jury should not give such impeachment the same weight as most prior inconsistent statements. At the same time, however, admission of syndrome testimony on rebuttal, even if believed, would not be dispositive of the case, thereby ensuring defendant a fair trial.

Turning back to the specifics of this case, we initially note section 115–7.2 of the Code of Criminal Procedure of 1963 (Ill.Rev.Stat.1987, ch. 38, par. 115–7.2) provides:

scientific techniques but rather is testifying as to facts within either personal knowledge or contained in learned treatises reasonably relied upon by experts in the field. See Expert Psychological Testimony, 42 U. Miami L.Rev. at 1060. See also People v. Beckley (1990), 434 Mich. 691, 717–21, 456 N.W.2d 391, 402–04.

"In a prosecution for an illegal sexual act perpetrated upon a victim, including but not limited to prosecutions for violations of Sections 12–13 through 12–16 of the Criminal Code of 1961, expert testimony by a behavioral psychologist, psychiatrist or physician relating to any recognized and accepted form of post-traumatic stress syndrome shall be admissible as evidence."

Effective January 1, 1989, the legislature amended this same section to allow testimony from persons other than those in the medical field. (See Ill.Rev.Stat.1989, ch. 38, par. 115–7.2.) Such an amendment reiterates the legislature's intention to grant the trial court broad discretion in the admission of evidence of post-traumatic syndromes from a qualified source. We believe such discretion is broad enough to include child sexual abuse syndrome testimony under the general label of post-traumatic stress syndrome.

Here, Dr. Hoffman, a psychologist and expert in the field of child abuse, was called to testify only in rebuttal for a very limited purpose after the victim's credibility already had been attacked by defendant. She explained how children act when they have been sexually abused, how offenders act when they are trying to lure children into a situation where they may be sexually abused and how the characteristics displayed by this particular victim were consistent with those which could be expected to be displayed by a victim of sexual abuse. She made no reference on direct examination to the person who may have abused the victim, nor did she testify the victim was sexually abused or that the victim was telling the truth. She also did not include descriptions of the actual acts related to her by the victim. Any limited references to the victim's description of the offense were properly offered to explain the reason for the victim's behavior. She did not attempt to inform the jury whose credibility was paramount nor did she try to bolster the victim's testimony. Moreover, she herself pointed out the lack of recognition of child sexual abuse syndrome in D.S.M. III. She further informed the jury of the possibility that the "unusual" behaviors she observed in the victim could have been triggered by factors other than sexual abuse. Finally, at the conclusion of her testimony, the court admonished the jury that her testimony was admitted "for the limited purpose of giving testimony regarding child sexual abuse syndrome." In addition, the jury heard testimony by defendant's expert disputing Dr. Hoffman's knowledge and testimony concerning child sexual abuse syndrome. Under such circumstances, we cannot say the court abused its discretion in allowing the testimony of Dr. Hoffman, even though the court, upon reflection, later indicated perhaps such testimony should not have been allowed.

Defendant argues, however, the expert went too far by diagnosing the victim as suffering from child sexual abuse syndrome. Defendant misses the point. While in general it may be true that it is not proper medically to diagnose the existence of a syndrome, any possible confusion or error here was prompted by defendant himself. On cross-examination, defendant specifically asked Dr. Hoffman if she had diagnosed the victim as having the characteristics of a sexually abused child. Any "vouching" for the credibility of the victim therefore resulted from defendant's own trial tactics. Under such circumstances, defendant cannot be heard to complain on appeal with respect to any error he created or caused.

In light of all the testimony and evidence on the record before us, we believe the verdict of the jury was not so improbable that it had no reasonable basis. Even though there were minor inconsistencies in the victim's testimony, that testimony was certain regarding the offense and the manner in which it occurred.

Affirmed.

NOTES

1. In Commonwealth v. Gallagher, 519 Pa. 291, 547 A.2d 355 (1988) the court held it was error to present expert testimony concerning the effects of "rape trauma" on the victim's failure to identify the assailant two weeks after the attack, even though she did identify the defendant four years later. In describing the rape trauma syndrome, the court said:

> "Burgess first described RTS as occurring in two phases. The first is the acute phase, lasting days or weeks, during which the victim is emotionally overwhelmed and has difficulty performing ordinary functions; this is followed by a long term reorganization phase, lasting months or years, during which the victim deals with symptoms specific to the rape which must be integrated into the victim's psychological experience to enable her to function at a precrisis level. Burgess then elaborated on how these symptoms could affect the victim's ability to identify the rapist:

> Q And, what about the phobia about repetition of seeing the face? Could you describe that and explain that to us?

> A The—right. She had an opportunity to see the assailant's face, and, so, that imprinted, if you will, in her mind, and that is a flashback. That keeps coming back.

> In fact, right after the assault, she described how this would happen, where suddenly thinking she saw someone, again a common reaction that she also had, feeling that he is everywhere, because the assault was still so new, still so fresh.

> Q How is that integrated, that phobia?

> A . . . .

> It's a gradual process.

> Q Is a five-year time period a telling time period for this gradual integration process?

> A Our study of our victims showed four to six years later we had still twenty-five percent that were still very symptomatic. We had others, of course, who had recovered, but five years you still have a very—in certain areas you can have specific symptoms in the phobic area, because that's more or less the definition of a phobia. It wards off into a particular area of symptoms.

Q   And, would that account for her flood of emotions still to this day about the material?

A   Yes. What seems to happen in the research we have been looking at is traumatic events are what is called actively stored in the mind, and when a certain, if you will, button is pressed: i.e., seeing someone, or whatever, all of that emotion and everything can just come flooding back, and that's the phenomenon of a flashback out of the past.

An event comes back, because there has been some triggering in the environment that the person is in, and it just kind of brings it all back.

Q   By bringing it all back, does it also bring the phase back of the original assailant? Is that the kind of thing that would flash right back before your eyes?

* * *

The crux of the testimony appears to be that the victim's failure to identify the appellant two weeks after the rape is unremarkable, as she was in the acute phase of RTS in which a victim has difficulty performing even normal functions, and the in-court identification five years later is particularly credible, as it results from a flashback, with the mind operating like a computer. It is clear that the only purpose of the expert testimony was to *enhance the credibility* of the victim.

* * *

We therefore hold that expert testimony on rape trauma syndrome should not have been admitted in the trial of this case. Accordingly, we reverse the order of Superior Court and remand for a new trial.

Order reversed and case remanded.

It should be noted there were two dissenting opinions in this case.

In Commonwealth v. Garcia, 403 Pa.Super. 280, 588 A.2d 951 (1990) [No. 01076, decided June 4, 1990] the Pennsylvania Superior Court held that to admit expert testimony that it is not uncommon for young sexual assault victims to delay reporting the abuse is error, because it improperly bolsters the credibility of complainants and invites the jurors to abdicate their responsibility in assessing the credibility of victim-witnesses. The court reversed the earlier decision in Commonwealth v. Baldwin, 348 Pa.Super. 368, 502 A.2d 253 (1985), wherein the court had approved the admission of expert testimony on the behavior patterns of incest victims. The *Baldwin* case had been eroded by later cases holding that even indirect comment, through testimony about the behavior of the victim, on the veracity of the witness, invaded the jury's fact finding province.

2. In People v. Bledsoe, 36 Cal.3d 236, 203 Cal.Rptr. 450, 681 P.2d 291 (1984), the Supreme Court of California held that evidence of rape trauma syndrome is not admissible to prove that a rape had in fact occurred. Rather than seeking to use the evidence to rebut misconceptions about the popularly presumed behavior of rape victims, the prosecutor sought to use the evidence as a means of establishing that the legal requirements of rape were satisfied. The court said that "because the literature does not even purport to claim that the syndrome is a scientifically reliable means of proving that a rape has occurred, we conclude that it may not properly be used for that purpose in a criminal trial."

Is it admissible for the stated purpose in a civil trial? Assume that D and a friend take a woman to a bar and, after she allegedly has become unconscious from excessive drinking, awakens to find herself in circumstances where she is being touched "in what was a clearly sexual manner." The woman thereupon reports D to SCWAR, a nonprofit corporation organized to assist and counsel women who have been the victims of sexual abuse, which organization then publishes, in its periodic newsletter, the name, address, physical description, place of employment, and a statement that D has forced himself upon the woman. The notice appears in the bulletin under the heading "Assault and Attempted Rape." D brings an action for libel, invasion of privacy, and intentional infliction of emotional distress against SCWAR. Should SCWAR be permitted to use, at trial, lay and expert testimony to show that the woman's behavior was consistent with rape trauma syndrome? See, Carney v. SCWAR, 221 Cal.App.3d 1009, 271 Cal.Rptr. 30 (1990).

3. For a perceptive analysis of the legal issues, see Massaro, "Experts, Psychology, Credibility, and Rape: The Rape Trauma Syndrome Issue and its Implications for Expert Psychological Testimony," 69 Minn.L.Rev. 395 (1985). Professor Massaro concludes her extensive survey of the law by predicting that:

"As the law of sexual assault and the attitudes toward the crime and its victims change, the role of mental health experts in sexual assault cases also will change. For example, public education about sexual assault eventually may reduce the need for education of the fact finder about the psychological aftermath of a nonstereotypical assault. When the myths about the crime of rape and its victims are dispelled, then the need for experts to combat those myths ideally well disappear as well. . . ." Considering these words were written in 1984, have we reached the point where RTS expert testimony is no longer necessary?

For writings on RTS other than those cited in the case in chief and above, see, e.g.: Burgess & Holmstrom, "Rape Trauma Syndrome," 131 Am.J.Psychiatry 981 (1974), coining the term "rape trauma syndrome" for the first time; Note, "The Unreliability of Expert Testimony on the Typical Characteristics of Sexual Abuse Victims," 74 Geo.L.J. 429 (1985); Coleman & Clancy, "False Allegations of Child Sexual Abuse—Why is it happening? What can we do?" Criminal Justice p. 14 (Fall, 1990); Comment, "Expert Testimony on Rape Trauma Syndrome: Admissibility and Effective Use in Criminal Rape Prosecution," 33 American U.L.Rev. 417 (1984); Comment, "Checking the Allure of Increased Conviction Rates: The Admissibility of Expert Testimony on Rape Trauma Syndrome in Criminal Proceedings," 70 Va.L.Rev. 1657 (1984); Ross, "The Overlooked Expert in Rape Prosecutions," 14 U.Tol.L.Rev. 707 (1983); Donohue, "Another Door Closed: Rape Trauma Syndrome," 23 Gonz.L.Rev. 1 (1987); Note, "Rape Trauma Syndrome and the Admissibility of Statements Made by Rape Victims," 64 N.C.L.Rev. 1364 (1986); Comment, " 'Rape Trauma Syndrome' and Inconsistent Rulings on its Admissibility Around the Nation," 24 Willamette L.Rev. 1011 (1988); Comment, "Psychological Expert Testimony on a Child's Veracity in Child Sexual Abuse Prosecutions," 50 Louisiana L.Rev. 1039 (1990).

4. Knowledge about RTS can help juries understand incongruities in the victim's story or behavior, such as delayed reporting, inability to recall some but not all the facts surrounding the attack, as well as seemingly inappropriate reactions of some victims. The Minnesota Supreme Court held that RTS evidence of that type was information within common knowledge and therefore expert testimony on it was not needed or helpful in the jury's assessment of

witness credibility or whether a rape had occurred. State v. Saldana, 324 N.W.2d 227 (Minn.1982). On August 19, 1986, the Minnesota Court of Appeals followed the *Saldana* decision and reversed a conviction for the rape of a 14–year–old babysitter because RTS evidence had been introduced. State v. Hall, 392 N.W.2d 285 (Minn.App.1986). On the very same day, a different panel of the same appellate court allowed an expert on child abuse to testify regarding the characteristics of sexual abuse victims and upheld the connection for the rape of a 13 year old girl. State v. Sandberg, 392 N.W.2d 298 (Minn.App.1986). However, the *Hall* case was reversed by the Minnesota Supreme Court. It distinguished its earlier decision in *Saldana* on the ground of the youthfulness of the victim in the present one. Expert testimony, said the court, was within the sound discretion of the trial court, but it cautioned that, even if expert testimony is helpful, "its probative value must be balanced against the danger of unfair prejudice, confusion, or misleading the jury," and that "if its probative value is substantially outweighed by any of these considerations, it may be excluded." State v. Hall, 406 N.W.2d 503 (Minn.1987).

Both the Montana and North Carolina Supreme Courts have ruled that RTS experts may not testify as to their opinion that the victim had in fact been raped or their opinion on the victim's credibility. See State v. Heath, 316 N.C. 337, 341 S.E.2d 565 (1986) and State v. Brodniak, 221 Mont. 212, 718 P.2d 322 (1986). The Court of Appeals for the Eighth Circuit held similarly in United States v. Azure, 801 F.2d 336 (8th Cir.1986) where the prosecutor had elicited testimony from its witness, a pediatrician and expert on child abuse, that he could see no reason why the alleged victim of child abuse was not telling the truth. The court said that expert testimony on the credibility of other witnesses is generally inadmissible as invading the province of the jury because "the jury is the lie detector in the courtroom." The court rejected the prosecution's argument that child abuse cases or rape represent special circumstances where ordinary jurors need help in assessing the credibility of a child witness:

> ". . . [P]utting an impressively qualified expert's stamp of truthfulness on a witness' story goes too far . . . [The expert] might have aided the jurors without usurping their exclusive function by generally testifying about a child's ability to separate truth from fantasy, by summarizing the medical evidence and expressing his opinion as to whether it was consistent with [the victim's] story that she was sexually abused. . . ."

By going farther, said the court, the expert essentially told the jury the victim was truthful when she accused the defendant, something the expert cannot assert, because no reliable test for truthfulness exists.

5. Would a social worker's testimony that the behavior of a sexually abused child was consistent with "sexual abuse accommodation syndrome" be admissible? The Kentucky Supreme Court said that admitting such testimony constituted reversible error because there was no evidence in the record that the so-called "sexual abuse accommodation syndrome" has attained a scientific acceptance or credibility among clinical psychologists or psychiatrists. But the court went farther and said, "Even should it become accepted by the scientific community that a child who has been sexually abused is likely to develop certain symptoms or personality traits, there would remain the question of whether other children who had not been similarly abused might also develop the same symptoms or traits. If so, the development of those symptoms . . . would not suffice, per se, to prove the fact of sexual abuse." Lantrip v. Commonwealth, 713 S.W.2d 816 (Ky.1986).

6.   In State v. Allewalt, 308 Md. 89, 517 A.2d 741 (1986), a majority of the Maryland Court of Appeals, reversing the contrary decision of the state's intermediate appellate court, held that where consent is in issue, a trial judge did not abuse his discretion in permitting a psychiatric expert to testify for the state that the complainant suffered from a condition known as "post traumatic stress disorder" (PTSD), and that, in his opinion, the cause of the disorder was the rape.   Calling it "significant" that the expert never used the term "rape trauma syndrome," which some courts have condemned, and did not attempt to express a personal opinion on the victim's credibility, the court said that the probative value of the evidence outweighed its potential prejudice.

3.   THE CORROBORATION REQUIREMENT

STATE v. WHEELER

Supreme Judicial Court of Maine, 1954.
150 Me. 332, 110 A.2d 578.

TAPLEY, JUSTICE. . . . . The respondent was indicted for the crime of rape.   The case was tried at the October Term, 1953, of the Superior Court for the County of Sagadahoc and State of Maine before a jury. Jury found respondent guilty.   Respondent excepted to rulings as to the admissibility of evidence and to the refusal of the presiding Justice to direct a verdict of not guilty at the conclusion of the testimony.

The indictment charged the respondent with rape of a female of the age of sixteen years.   The act was alleged to have occurred on September 28, 1953 at Bowdoinham, Maine.   The prosecutrix resided in the Town of South Freeport, Maine and on the twenty-seventh day of September, 1953, she went to the Town of Richmond where she was accustomed to spending considerable time.   There is much testimony in the record relating to her activities with three boys with whom she was acquainted.   It appears that during the evening of September 27th she went to ride with these boys for a distance of one or two miles from Richmond and that during this ride she was submitted to physical violence by being slapped on the face and having her arm twisted in an attempt to remove a portion of her clothing; that she was forcibly ejected from the car and later made her way back to Richmond; that following her return to Richmond she was again approached by the same boys, caused to re-enter the car and then taken to a point outside of Richmond where the car was stopped and an attempt made by one of them to rape her.   During this attempt, a car passing the parked car of the boys was stopped by one of them.   This car was operated by the respondent.   The prosecutrix was transferred from the boys car to that of the respondent.   He drove some distance, stopped his automobile on a side road and there committed the act complained of, for which he was indicted, tried and found guilty.

The State must prove beyond a reasonable doubt that the respondent carnally knew the prosecutrix by force, without her consent or against her will. . . . .   The element of force and the act against her will are inconsistent with consent. It is obvious, of course, if the prosecutrix willingly consented to the act, there would be no rape.

During the course of the trial the State presented a witness in the person of one Donald Shields, a boy of sixteen years of age, who testified in direct examination that he was a passenger in the back seat of the respondent's car and was present at the time of the alleged rape. The substance of his testimony was that no act of intercourse occurred between the respondent and the prosecutrix. After completion of his direct testimony there was no cross-examination by the defense. Later he was called to the stand by the State and at that time testified that his testimony in direct was false and that he so testified because he was requested and urged to do so by the respondent.

The State's case was predicated on the testimony of the prosecutrix with very little, if any, corroboration. There is no statute in Maine requiring corroboration on the part of the prosecutrix in cases of this nature and it is well settled that a verdict based on the uncorroborated testimony of a complainant will not be disturbed on the mere fact of lack of corroboration. State v. Newcomb, 146 Me. 173, at page 181, 78 A.2d 787. Corroboration, if there is corroboration, must come from sources other than the prosecutrix. Although corroboration is not necessary, it is well for the purpose of this case to analyze the record to determine what corroboration, if any, there is present. The cases hold that where corroboration to any reasonable degree is lacking, it becomes necessary to scrutinize and analyze the testimony of the prosecutrix with great care. Her testimony as to the acts complained of must be such they would be within the realms of probability and credibility.

C.J.S. Rape, § 78, page 560:

> "At common law, and in the absence of a statute requiring corroboration, it is generally held that the unsupported testimony of the prosecutrix, if not contradictory *or incredible, or inherently improbable,* if believed by the jury, is sufficient to sustain a conviction of rape. . . ." (Italics ours.)

The prosecutrix testified that soon after the alleged act occurred she complained to her mother. The mother did not appear as a witness in corroboration of the complainant. There was medical testimony resulting from the examination of the girl but this did not disclose in any way that she had been raped by the defendant.

There is evidence that the complainant suffered some injury to her jaw and she complained of a soreness in the vicinity of her ribs. This condition, according to her own testimony, resulted from the violent physical treatment that she received from the three boys. This fact is further established by the testimony of the boys. The prosecutrix furnishes the only testimony of the actual act of rape.

The testimony of the prosecutrix is of such sordid nature that a detailed account will serve no good purpose. It is suffice to say that the prosecutrix' narration of the rape is inherently improbable and incredible and does not meet the test of common sense. . . .

Reversed.

NOTES

1. For another application of the "implausibility" rule enunciated in the principal case, see Penn v. State, 237 Ind. 374, 146 N.E.2d 240 (1957), in which the defendant was prosecuted for the statutory rape of a "baby sitter," aged 16, who testified that she became pregnant as a result of intercourse with the defendant, Penn. She testified that "when Mr. and Mrs. Penn would return from the evening out, [Penn] would usually go to bed, but that prosecutrix and Mrs. Penn would usually stay up late—popping corn, talking and watching television. They were friends. That, on prior occasions, prosecutrix slept on the davenport in the living room, but that beginning in October she slept in [Penn's] bed with Penn and his wife. Prosecutrix testified that on these occasions the accused would there have intercourse first with one and then the other, with knowledge of both. . . . Both Penn and his wife flatly denied the entire story of any sexual relations between prosecutrix and appellant." In reversing the defendant's conviction, the Supreme Court of Indiana said:

"Ordinarily reasonable men know that a wife will not knowingly and willingly share the sex life of her husband. Experience teaches that where another woman enters the sex life of her husband a wife does not remain on good terms with the other woman. She does not thereafter invite the other woman to her home to visit, pop corn, and watch television. Especially, she will not share her husband and aid and abet the act by inviting the other woman to her home and accompanying her to the bed of her husband. . . . We conclude therefore that in this case the uncorroborated testimony of the prosecutrix was so improbable and incredible that no reasonable man could say that the appellant's guilt had been proved beyond a reasonable doubt." [1]

1. As another example of a member of an appellate court drawing on human experience in order to deal with cases in this area, consider the majority opinion of Pearson, C.J., in State v. Neely, 74 N.C. 425 (1876), where the defendant was convicted of assault with intent to commit rape:

"A majority of the Court are of the opinion that there was evidence to be left to the jury as to the intent charged. For my own part, I think the evidence plenary, and had I been on the jury would not have hesitated one moment.

"I see a chicken-cock drop his wings and take after a hen; my experience and observation assure me that his purpose is sexual intercourse; no other evidence is needed.

"Whether the cock supposes that the hen is running by female instinct to increase the estimate of her favor and excite passion, or whether the cock intends to carry his purpose by force and against her will, is a question about which there

may be some doubt: as for instance, if she is a setting hen and 'makes flight', not merely amorous resistance. There may be evidence from experience and observation of the nature of the animals and of male and female instincts fit to be left to the jury, upon all of the circumstances and surroundings of the case, was the pursuit made with the expectation that he would be gratified voluntarily, or was it made with the intent to have his will against her will and by force? Upon the case of the cock and the hen, can any one seriously insist that a jury has no right to call to their assistance their own experience and observation of the nature of animals and of male and female instincts. . . .

"The prisoner had some intent when he pursued the woman. There is no evidence tending to show that his intent was to kill her or to rob her; so that intent must have been to have sexual intercourse. . . ."

In People v. Taylor, 48 Ill.2d 91, 268 N.E.2d 865 (1971), a conviction was reversed where the record showed that the complaining witness had testified that as she was getting out of the defendant's car, where the alleged forcible rape occurred, she kissed him goodbye. For another interesting case situation, see Lewis v. State, 440 N.E.2d 1125 (Ind.1982).

2. British and American courts have frequently quoted with approval in sex offense cases the ancient admonition of Sir Matthew Hale that ". . . it is an accusation easily made and hard to be proved, and harder to be defended by the party accused, though ever so innocent; . . ." It is necessary, Hale continued, to "be the more cautious upon trials of offenses of this nature wherein the court and jury may with so much ease be imposed upon without great care and vigilance; the heinousness of the offense many times transporting the judge and jury with so much indignation that they are over hastily carried to the conviction of the person accused thereof by the confident testimony, sometimes of malicious and false witnesses". 1 Hale, Pleas of the Crown, 635, 636. Undoubtedly, concern over convicting the innocent, on the one hand, and indignation produced by this species of crime, on the other, have strongly influenced both the substantive doctrines and the evidentiary rules in this area.

In the past, most jurisdictions permitted the giving of a jury instruction that a rape charge is easily made and difficult to defend against. Some jurisdictions made such an instruction mandatory. In recent years, however, a strong trend away from the Sir Matthew Hale language has been noted in the courts. In People v. Rincon–Pineda, 14 Cal.3d 864, 123 Cal.Rptr. 119, 538 P.2d 247 (1975), the California Supreme Court found the giving of the cautionary instruction which originated in the 17th century as reflecting adversely on the credibility of the rape victim. The court intimated that a woman can be believed or disbelieved as a witness in rape cases without the giving of the ancient cautionary instruction and disapproved of any further use of such instruction, even though it had been mandatory in some cases previously. Accord, State v. Smoot, 99 Idaho 855, 590 P.2d 1001 (1978).

3. As illustrated by the Wheeler case, supra, the courts in many states have held that, in the absence of statute, the testimony of the prosecutrix need not be supported by other corroborative evidence. In Fogg v. Commonwealth, 208 Va. 541, 159 S.E.2d 616 (1968), the court said that the prosecutrix's testimony alone is sufficient, if it is credible and the jury believes the accused to be guilty beyond a reasonable doubt. Some courts, however, have indicated that the judge may be under a duty to caution the jury in placing reliance on such uncorroborated testimony, and other modifications and qualifications have been introduced.

4. Consider, as regards protection against false accusations in sex cases, the following cases involving the issue of psychiatric examinations of complaining witnesses in sex cases:

Burton v. State, 232 Ind. 246, 111 N.E.2d 892 (1953). This was a sodomy case involving a prosecutrix who was ten years old. The court said: "This record is wholly silent that the state took any steps whatever to determine the prosecutrix was not a fantast, or was not under the compelling domination of her mother. . . . With such a record before us we fail to find any evidence that would convince us beyond a reasonable doubt of the appellant's guilt. . . . By this decision we do not hold that in every case where a sexual offense is charged there should be a psychiatric examination of the prosecutrix.

There are many cases where the facts and circumstances leave no doubt of the guilt of the accused, but the record here does not present such a case."

In a dissenting opinion, Draper, J., commented as follows: ". . . No objection was made to the testimony of this child because she had not been cleared by a psychiatrist. None such could be made. Our legislature has not seen fit to require such as a condition precedent to the right to testify in court, and I do not believe this court has any right to impose it. . . . To say that a woman may not testify against a man in a sex case unless she first submits to a psychiatric examination covering, perhaps, a period of many months, in the absence of legislation requiring it, seems to me to be an unwarranted arrogation of authority which this court does not have. . . ."

The Supreme Court of California has expressed the following viewpoint, in Ballard v. Superior Court of San Diego County, 64 Cal.2d 159, 49 Cal.Rptr. 302, 410 P.2d 838 (1966):

". . . a general rule requiring a psychiatric examination of complaining witnesses in every sex case or, as an alternative, in any such case that rests upon the uncorroborated testimony of the complaining witness would, in many instances, not be necessary or appropriate. Moreover, victims of sex crimes might be deterred by such an absolute requirement from disclosing such offenses.

"Rather than formulate a fixed rule in this matter we believe that discretion should repose in the trial judge to order a psychiatric examination of the complaining witness in a case involving a sex violation if the defendant presents a compelling reason for such an examination. . . .

"We therefore believe that the trial judge should be authorized to order the prosecutrix to submit to a psychiatric examination if the circumstances indicate a necessity for an examination. Such necessity would generally arise only if little or no corroboration supported the charge and if the defense raised the issue of the effect of the complaining witness' mental or emotional condition upon her veracity. Thus, in rejecting the polar extremes of an absolute prohibition and an absolute requirement that the prosecutrix submit to a psychiatric examination, we have accepted a middle ground, placing the matter in the discretion of the trial judge.

"The complaining witness should not, and realistically cannot, be forced to submit to a psychiatric examination or to cooperate with a psychiatrist. In the event that the witness thus refuses to cooperate, however, a comment on that refusal should be permitted."

For a law review comment upon the general subject, consult 64 J.Crim.L. & Criminology 71 (1973).

4. PROTECTING THE VICTIM

WINFIELD v. COMMONWEALTH

Supreme Court of Virginia, 1983.
225 Va. 211, 301 S.E.2d 15.

RUSSELL, J., delivered the opinion of the Court.

In this case of first impression involving a prosecution for sexual assault, we must examine the admissibility of evidence of the complaining witness's specific acts of sexual conduct with persons other than the accused, in light of the "rape shield" provision of Code § 18.2–67.7.[1]

Herbert Winfield, Jr., was indicted for the forcible rape and forcible sodomy of Sandra Nelson. Prior to the trial, Winfield gave written notice to the Commonwealth, pursuant to Code § 18.2–67.7(B), that he wished to offer the following evidence as to Sandra's prior sexual conduct with others:

(1) Testimony of Leon Moore that Sandra Nelson agreed to have sexual intercourse with him on the condition he pay her twenty dollars; that he had sexual intercourse with Sandra Nelson; that he did not pay her the twenty dollars; that Sandra Nelson stated that if he did not pay her the twenty dollars that she would tell his wife; that he paid her twenty dollars; that Sandra Nelson has a reputation in the community for being unchaste and immoral.

(2) Testimony of Lawrence Winfield that Sandra Nelson asked him if she should have sexual intercourse with Leon Moore for money; that Sandra Nelson stated to him that she

1. § 18.2–67.7 Admission of evidence.—A. In prosecutions under this article, general reputation or opinion evidence of the complaining witness's unchaste character or prior sexual conduct shall not be admitted. Unless the complaining witness voluntarily agrees otherwise, evidence of specific instances of his or her prior sexual conduct shall be admitted only if it is relevant and is:

1. Evidence offered to provide an alternative explanation for physical evidence of the offense charged which is introduced by the prosecution, limited to evidence designed to explain the presence of semen, pregnancy, disease, or physical injury to the complaining witness's intimate parts; or

2. Evidence of sexual conduct between the complaining witness and the accused offered to support a contention that the alleged offense was not accomplished by force, threat or intimidation or through the use of the complaining witness's mental incapacity or physical helplessness, provided that the sexual conduct occurred within a period of time reasonably proximate to the offense charged under the circumstances of this case; or

3. Evidence offered to rebut evidence of the complaining witness's prior sexual conduct introduced by the prosecution.

B. Nothing contained in this section shall prohibit the accused from presenting evidence relevant to show that the complaining witness had a motive to fabricate the charge against the accused. If such evidence relates to the past sexual conduct of the complaining witness with a person other than the accused, it shall not be admitted and may not be referred to at any preliminary hearing or trial unless the party offering same files a written notice generally describing the evidence prior to the introduction of any evidence, or the opening statement of either counsel, whichever first occurs, at the preliminary hearing or trial at which the admission of the evidence may be sought.

C. Evidence described in subsections A and B of this section shall not be admitted and may not be referred to at any preliminary hearing or trial until the court first determines the admissibility of that evidence at an evidentiary hearing to be held before the evidence is introduced at such preliminary hearing or trial. The court shall exclude from the evidentiary hearing all persons except the accused, the complaining witness, other necessary witnesses, and required court personnel. If the court determines that the evidence meets the requirements of subsections A and B of this section, it shall be admissible before the judge or jury trying the case in the ordinary course of the preliminary hearing or trial. If the court initially determines that the evidence is inadmissible, but new information is discovered during the course of the preliminary hearing or trial which may make such evidence admissible, the court shall determine in an evidentiary hearing whether such evidence is admissible. (1981, c. 397.)

needed the money so she would have sexual intercourse with Leon Moore; that Lawrence Winfield has had sexual intercourse with Sandra Nelson; that he paid her ten dollars after having sexual intercourse with her; that Sandra Nelson has a reputation in the community for being unchaste and immoral.

(3) Testimony of Denise Daniels that Sandra Nelson has stated to her that a man was going to give Sandra Nelson $100.00 if she would go to bed with him and she decided not to do it but that she allowed him to feel her breasts for $25.00; that Sandra Nelson has a bad reputation in the community.

(4) Testimony of Towana Parham that Sandra Nelson has stated to her on three different occasions that Sandra Nelson has been to bed with different men; that Sandra Nelson stated to her Sandra Nelson was pregnant but did not know who the father of the child was; that Sandra Nelson has a bad reputation in the community.

(5) Testimony of Anthony Branch that Sandra Nelson has an unchaste and immoral reputation in the community; that Sandra Nelson has on several occasions had sexual intercourse with various men and then told the man's wife or girl friend of the incident in an effort to create trouble between the man and his wife or girl friend.

(6) Testimony of Carol Jackson that Sandra Nelson has an unchaste and immoral reputation in the community; that he has had sexual intercourse with Sandra Nelson; that he had a friend tell him he paid Sandra Nelson $150.00 to have sexual intercourse with her; that Sandra Nelson has had sexual intercourse with a man and then told the man's girl friend about the incident in an effort to create trouble between the man and his girl friend.

The matter was set for hearing in advance of trial for a determination of the admissibility of the proffered evidence. For the purposes of the hearing, the Commonwealth stipulated that the six witnesses would testify as indicated in the notice quoted above. Accordingly, their actual testimony was dispensed with, and the parties submitted the question of admissibility to the court as a matter of law. The court determined that the evidence was "inadmissible . . . as evidence relevant to show that the complaining witness had a motive to fabricate the charge against the accused." This ruling presents the dispositive question on appeal.

At Winfield's subsequent jury trial, the Commonwealth's evidence showed that Sandra, nineteen years of age, and Winfield, thirty-two, lived in the same apartment development in Chesterfield County and were on friendly terms. On the afternoon of July 24, 1981, Sandra asked Winfield to give her a ride in his car to a "night spot" in

Petersburg that night. She testified that long after dark, he picked her up and drove her to a rural area in Dinwiddie County and frightened her by telling her they were in an area where the "KKK" met and that she would be caught by the "KKK" if she attempted to leave the car. He then stopped the car, threatened to hurt her if she resisted, forcibly removed her clothing, pinned her hands behind her and forcibly subjected her to rape and sodomy. She testified that she cried and attempted to push him away but "just didn't have the strength." Afterwards, driving back toward Petersburg, the defendant stopped at a service station and went inside to buy cigarettes. At this point, Sandra testified, she jumped out of the car and ran to three strangers in a truck, offering them all the money in her purse if they would take her home. When she arrived home, she told a friend that Winfield had raped her and called the police.

A state trooper interviewed her at her apartment at about 2:00 a.m. on July 25th, within thirty minutes of her call. He found her upset, nervous, and crying. He saw no signs of physical injury. She accompanied him to Dinwiddie County and pointed out the area in which she said the offenses had occurred. Sandra and the trooper were the only witnesses called by the Commonwealth.

Winfield testified that he had known Sandra for six months and that they had frequent discussions concerning sex. On the afternoon of July 24, 1981, he said that she asked him if he thought she should spend the night with another man who had offered her $150.00. Winfield responded that that was up to her, but that he would give her $50.00 for sexual favors. She agreed. About 11:00 p.m. that night, she came to his apartment and said she was ready to go with him. He drove her down Interstate 95 and she suggested that they stop at a motel. He told her that he could not afford a motel room and drove her to the end of a country road. He testified that they then engaged in sexual intercourse with Sandra's consent and willing participation. On the way home, Sandra asked him for the promised $50.00. He told her that he had it at home, but not with him. She became angry and said that she was going to have him arrested. When he stopped at a service station to buy $2.00 worth of gas and some cigarettes, she got into a car with somebody he didn't know and left. He returned home and went to bed. Later, he said, he was awakened by Sandra's boyfriend who asked him about the money and threatened him with jail. Soon thereafter the police took him to the Dinwiddie County jail on a rape charge.

Winfield's testimony was partially corroborated by three defense witnesses. William Swann testified that he had been present during the afternoon conversation between Sandra and Winfield and had heard Sandra agree to accept $50.00 for sexual favors. Sandra admitted on cross-examination that Swann had been present, along with another man, when she had an afternoon conversation with Winfield. Clifford Coles, a cousin of Sandra's, testified that she later told him that she had had sexual intercourse with Winfield, that she "wished he had given her $50.00," and that she was "going to make sure he gets some time." James Harris, who knew both parties, testified that he saw them sitting together in Winfield's parked car late on the evening of July 24th and that Sandra was sitting close against Winfield, who had his arm over the seat. Harris stopped to talk, but Sandra seemed to be in a hurry, saying: "Ah, come on, let's go." Harris left, and heard of Winfield's arrest for rape the next day.

The jury found Winfield guilty under both indictments and fixed his punishment at five years confinement in each case. The court overruled his post-trial motions and imposed the two sentences to run consecutively.

We first consider Winfield's principal assignment of error: that the trial court erred in ruling, as a matter of law, that the evidence of the six witnesses proffered in his notice was not relevant to show a motive to fabricate the charge against him.

Prior to July 1, 1981, Virginia followed the well-settled rules of the common law that the accused in a rape case, asserting the defense of consent, might introduce evidence of the previously unchaste character of his accuser. This could only be shown by proof of general reputation of the complaining witness in the community for unchastity or prostitution. . . .

* * *

This rule has been subjected to increasing criticism in recent years. Commentators observed, first, that there is no logical connection between a woman's wilingness to submit to the defendant accused of raping her, and her willingness to share intimacies with another man with whom she might have had a special relationship. This is particularly true since the law always permitted the defendant to show that he personally had a prior sexual relationship with the complaining witness. Second, proof of general reputation in the community has very little probative weight. In a transient urban society, it often boils down to the uninformed opinion of a character witness. Finally, such reputation evidence was extremely prejudicial to the rape victim. It tended to turn the trial into an inquiry as to her chastity, rather than the guilt of the accused. Defense counsel was enabled to focus the trial so effectively upon her prior life that she was understandably reluctant to testify. The result was that many sexual assaults went unreported because of fear of the traumatic effects of prosecuting them. See Kneedler, Sexual Assault Law Reform in Virginia—A Legislative History, 68 Va.L.Rev. 459 (1982); Berger, Man's Trial, Woman's Tribulation: Rape Cases in the Courtroom, 77 Colum.L.Rev. 1 (1977); Tanford and Bocchino, Rape Victim Shield Laws and the Sixth Amendment, 128 U.Pa.L.Rev. 544 (1980).

The legislative response was a series of "rape shield" laws, adopted by forty-seven states and by the Congress. Most of these limit or prohibit the admission of general reputation evidence as to the prior unchastity of the complaining witness, but some, like ours, permit the introduction of evidence of specific acts of sexual conduct between the

complaining witness and third persons in carefully limited circumstances.

The application of these laws has presented the courts with the
concomitant problem that no legislation, however salutary its purpose,
can be so construed as to deprive a criminal defendant of his Sixth
Amendment right to confront and cross-examine his accuser and to call
witnesses in his defense. . . .   Some jurisdictions have held such laws
unconstitutional where they purport to preclude the defendant from
showing the prior sexual conduct of the complaining witness.   Others
have, in order to give the statute a constitutional interpretation,
implied an exception where the trial court, in an *in camera* hearing,
makes a preliminary determination that the proffered evidence would
be relevant and probative on the issue of consent.

Instructed by the experience of other jurisdictions, and with the
evident purpose of steering a safe course through these shoals, the
Virginia General Assembly enacted Code § 18.2–67.7 as a part of a
sweeping revision of the general laws pertaining to criminal sexual
assault, effective July 1, 1981.   Kneedler's analysis suggests that the
specific sanction given by Code § 18.2–67.7 to evidence of the victim's
prior sexual conduct, for strictly limited purposes, will accommodate
most of the foreseeable constitutional claims which a defendant might
legitimately raise.   While the constitutional problems are instructive in
determining the legislative intent as to the scope of the exceptions
contained in the statute, no constitutional challenge is raised in this
case.   Indeed, the parties here debate only whether the proffered
evidence meets the requirements of the statute—that is, was it *relevant*
to show that the complaining witness had a "motive to fabricate" the
charge against the accused.

Winfield argues that his defense was "contract and consent;" that
Sandra, having no other way to enforce collection of her agreed fee,
threatened a rape prosecution to "blackmail the appellant into payment, to obtain revenge for non-payment and to maintain her standing
in her 'business community'."   This, he says, was her "motive to
fabricate."   He argues that the excluded evidence shows a pattern of
such past sexual conduct on her part, and that it is thus relevant to
show her "motive to fabricate" the charge.   The Commonwealth re-
sponds that the evidence amounts to nothing more than a generalized
assault on the character of the complaining witness, tending to attack
her credibility but not showing any particular motive to fabricate.
Evidence of specific prior sexual conduct with third persons as a
general attack on credibility was, the Commonwealth argues, prohibited at common law and is still prohibited under the "rape shield" law.

On the limited record before us, consisting only of the terse
representations contained in the notice quoted above, it is impossible
for us to determine the entire form and extent of the proffered evidence, but certain conclusions may be drawn.   In our view, the General
Assembly intended to preclude evidence of general reputation or opin-

ion of the unchaste character of the complaining witness in all circumstances. This view arises not only from the criticisms of this kind of
evidence, mentioned above, which underlay the legislative reforms of
1981, but also from the fact that the new law gives a defendant access
for the first time to far more probative evidence: specific prior sexual
conduct with third persons, if it is relevant for the purposes set forth in
Code § 18.2–67.7. All six of the proffered witnesses would testify to
Sandra's bad reputation, and that part of their testimony was properly
excluded.

We agree with Winfield, however, that evidence tending to show
that Sandra had a distinctive pattern of past sexual conduct, involving
the extortion of money by threat after acts of prostitution, of which her
alleged conduct in this case was but an example, is relevant, probative,
and admissible in his defense. The proffered testimony of Leon Moore
appears to contain elements of this kind. If, upon an evidentiary
hearing conducted pursuant to Code § 18.2–67.7(C), it tends to show
such a pattern, and otherwise meets the rules of evidence, it should be
admitted. Its exclusion as a matter of law, based only upon the
description contained in the notice, is error requiring reversal.

Evidence of past sexual conduct, to be admissible under the "motive to fabricate" provisions of Code § 18.2–67.7(B), however, must show
a pattern of behavior which directly relates to the conduct charged
against the complaining witness in the case on trial. Thus there is a
sufficient nexus between Sandra's alleged efforts to extort money by
threats from others, after acts of prostitution, and Winfield's version of
her conduct in the present case, to render such evidence relevant and
probative of a motive to fabricate. On the other hand, the proffered
evidence of most of the witnesses to the effect that Sandra had engaged
in sexual acts with others for money, is a mere attack on her character,
related only indirectly to the theory of the defense. It attempts to show
her reputation, by specific acts, as a prostitute, but it does not directly
establish a motive to fabricate any charge against the accused.[2] Such
evidence was inadmissible at common law and the new statutory
scheme does not open the door to its admission.

Finally, any evidence of prior sexual conduct by the complaining
witness must comply with the usual rules of evidence as well as the
requirements of the "rape shield" law. Since general reputation or
opinion evidence as to unchaste character is to be excluded, it appears
probable from the defendant's notice that at least three of the proffered
witnesses would relate nothing more than inadmissible hearsay. We
cannot make this determination on the record before us. In an evidentiary hearing conducted pursuant to Code § 18.2–67.7(C), the trial court
should ascertain whether the evidence is presented in a form which
meets an exception to the hearsay rule, and is otherwise admissible.

---

2. This is not to say that evidence showing that the complaining witness had acted
as a prostitute would never be admissible.
In certain circumstances it might be directly relevant to the defense, as showing a
motive to fabricate the charge. See, e.g.,
State v. Blue, 225 Kan. 576, 592 P.2d 897
(1979).

*   *   *

For the reasons earlier stated, the judgments appealed from will be reversed, and the cases remanded to the trial court for such further proceedings as the Commonwealth may be advised, not inconsistent with this opinion.

Reversed and remanded.

THOMPSON, J., dissenting in part.

As I construe the majority opinion, the only evidence in the proffer that would be admissible is (1) involving Leon Moore.

*   *   *

The majority pays due respect to the analysis of the statute by Dean Kneedler, but omits his explication of the "motive-to-fabricate" provision:

> [The provision] was intended to be quite narrow in scope, limited to instances in which evidence of the victim's prior sexual conduct creates an inference that the victim had an ulterior motive to charge the defendant with sexual assault.
>
>   .   .   .
>
>   . . . Properly interpreted, therefore, the provision operates only where the motive to fabricate arises directly from the past sexual conduct. . . .

The victim's relationship with a third person may suggest a motive to fabricate the charge apart from evidence of the victim's past sexual conduct with that person. In such cases, evidence of the victim's past sexual conduct with that person should be excluded. For example, if a man finds his fiancee in bed with his best friend, and his fiancee then accuses the best friend of rape, how much evidence of the relationship between the man and his fiancee should be admitted to support the defense that the fiancee fabricated the charge? Obviously, the best friend would be permitted to introduce evidence of the victim's relationship with her fiancee as evidence that she had a motive to fabricate the charge. The provision, however, does not permit the admission of evidence of the sexual relationship between the victim and her fiancee unless it is the sexual relationship that gave rise to the motive to fabricate. On the facts of this hypothetical, unless it could be shown that the victim's past sexual conduct with her fiancee gave rise to the motive to fabricate, evidence of that conduct would not be probative of a motive to fabricate and should, therefore, be excluded. An even clearer case would arise if the accused attempted to show that the victim had had prior sexual relations with third persons with whom the victim had no current relationship. Such evidence clearly would be irrelevant to the existence of a motive to fabricate. Its only use would be either to show that the victim had a general propensity to engage in consensual sexual acts or to impeach the victim's general credibility, both of which are prohibited under the new sexual assault law.

In sum, a sexual relationship may be relevant to demonstrate a motive to fabricate, but it will not be relevant in every case. Thus, under the motive-to-fabricate provision, the trial judge must consider carefully whether there is a sufficiently direct link between the past sexual conduct and the motive to fabricate to warrant admission of that conduct.

Kneedler, Sexual Assault Law Reform in Virginia—A Legislative History, 68 Va.L.Rev. 459, 494, 495–496 (1982).

These isolated episodes have two common ingredients: (1) sexual intercourse; and (2) the client's unwillingness to pay for the services rendered. In the first instance, compliance was effected after a threat to expose the client's conduct to his spouse; in this case, it was alleged that the collection method was an accusation of rape. The majority states there is a nexus or common link between the two. I disagree.

In the Leon Moore liaison, there was no falsehood, no motive to fabricate. Yet from this can the fact finder logically infer the motive to fabricate the charges against Winfield? Is a threat to expose the truth the same as a motive to fabricate? I do not perceive a common thread in such dissimilar conduct.

In my opinion, the Leon Moore incident is not admissible. A threat to extort money is not the legal equivalent of a motive to fabricate, and I dissent to that extent.

NOTES

1. At a hearing on a motion under the statute cites in the *Winfield* case, defendant offers to introduce evidence of an act of sexual intercourse between defendant and the prosecutrix on an unspecified date eight or nine months before the alleged rape, and that the prosecutrix had told him that if he wanted more sex in the future it would be for money. Does such testimony come within the statute? See, League v. Commonwealth, 9 Va.App. 199, 385 S.E.2d 232 (1989).

Is testimony admissible under the same statute where a defendant is charged with several counts of rape and aggravated sexual assault involving three victims, and defendant wants to present evidence that two of the victims were involved in a lesbian relationship and fabricated charges against him to keep him from breaking up their relationship? See, Johnson v. Commonwealth, 9 Va.App. 176, 385 S.E.2d 223 (1989).

2. When the issue is consent, may defense counsel, while cross-examining the complaining witness, ask her whether or not she had, prior to the present case, made accusations that other men have raped her, and if so how many times. In Commonwealth v. Bohannon, 376 Mass. 90, 378 N.E.2d 987 (1978) the court held that while ordinarily evidence of prior bad acts may not be used to impeach a witness' credibility, there are exceptions and there are cases in which such evidence would be competent. The court said that, "in this case the possibility that this evidence might have had a significant impact on the issue of credibility is enhanced by the facts that the complainant's testimony was

inconsistent and confused. . . . In the circumstances of this case, we therefore think the exclusion of the defendant's proposed questions violated his right to present his defense fully." It must be pointed out, however, that defense counsel had made an offer of proof which indicated there was a factual basis from independent third party records that such prior allegations had in fact been made.

3. In 1979, Gary Dotson, after steadfastly protesting his innocence, was sentenced to 25 to 50 years for the rape and mutilation of a 16–year–old girl. In March of 1985, the victim, Cathleen Crowell Webb, accompanied by her husband, at a press conference stated that her story of rape and abduction had been a lie. She stated for the television news cameras that she had never met or seen Gary Dotson and that the physical evidence—torn clothes, bruises, cuts on her vagina and abdomen—was all self-inflicted; the rape complaint, she explained, was her panicked reaction to a fear that she was pregnant. Dotson's lawyer immediately filed a motion for a hearing to vacate the conviction, and when the trial judge scheduled such a hearing to validate the "victim's" recantation, public outcry in the media demanded that Dotson be released immediately. After two days of hearings, however, the judge decided that the "victim's" exoneration of Dotson was not credible and that Dotson was to be remanded to the penitentiary. While her television appearance had seemed sincere, on cross-examination during the hearings the judge characterized her as "evasive, combative and prone to selective memory." According to a commentator, the "firestorm of news media and public pressure" compelled Illinois Governor James R. Thompson [a co-author of previous editions of this text] "to conduct an extraordinary expanded clemency hearing," at the conclusion of which he "agreed with the judge's ruling but nonetheless freed Dotson 'under the circumstances.'" See Black, "Why Judge Samuels Sent Gary Dotson Back to Prison," 71 ABA Jl. p. 56 (Sept. 1985).

4. Congress, on October 28, 1978, amended Section 2(a), Article IV of the Federal Rules of Evidence by adding to it the following new rule:

"Rule 412. Rape Cases; Relevance of Victim's Past Behavior

"(a) Notwithstanding any other provision of law, in a criminal case in which a person is accused of rape or of assault with intent to commit rape, reputation or opinion evidence of the past sexual behavior of an alleged victim of such rape or assault is not admissible.

"(b) Notwithstanding any other provision of law, in a criminal case in which a person is accused of rape or of assault with intent to commit rape, evidence of a victim's past sexual behavior other than reputation or opinion evidence is also not admissible, unless such evidence other than reputation or opinion evidence is—

"(1) admitted in accordance with subdivisions (c)(1) and (c)(2) and is constitutionally required to be admitted; or

"(2) admitted in accordance with subdivision (c) and is evidence of—

"(A) past sexual behavior with persons other than the accused, offered by the accused upon the issue of whether the accused was or was not, with respect to the alleged victim, the source of semen or injury; or

"(B) past sexual behavior with the accused and is offered by the accused upon the issue of whether the alleged victim consented to the sexual behavior with respect to which rape or assault is alleged.

"(c)(1) If the person accused of committing rape or assault with intent to commit rape intends to offer under subdivision (b) evidence of specific instances of the alleged victim's past sexual behavior, the accused shall make a written motion to offer such evidence not later than fifteen days before the date on which the trial in which such evidence is to be offered is scheduled to begin, except that the court may allow the motion to be made at a later date, including during trial, if the court determines either that the evidence is newly discovered and could not have been obtained earlier through the exercise of due diligence or that the issue to which such evidence relates has newly arisen in the case. Any motion made under this paragraph shall be served on all other parties and on the alleged victim.

"(2) The motion described in paragraph (1) shall be accompanied by a written offer of proof. If the court determines that the offer of proof contains evidence described in subdivision (b), the court shall order a hearing in chambers to determine if such evidence is admissible. At such hearing the parties may call witnesses, including the alleged victim, and offer relevant evidence. Notwithstanding subdivision (b) of rule 104, if the relevancy of the evidence which the accused seeks to offer in the trial depends upon the fulfillment of a condition of fact, the court, at the hearing in chambers or at a subsequent hearing in chambers scheduled for such purpose, shall accept evidence on the issue of whether such condition of fact is fulfilled and shall determine such issue.

"(3) If the court determines on the basis of the hearing described in paragraph (2) that the evidence which the accused seeks to offer is relevant and that the probative value of such evidence outweighs the danger of unfair prejudice, such evidence shall be admissible in the trial to the extent an order made by the court specifies evidence which may be offered and areas with respect to which the alleged victim may be examined or cross-examined.

"(d) For purposes of this rule, the term 'past sexual behavior' means sexual behavior other than the sexual behavior with respect to which rape or assault with intent to commit rape is alleged."   *   *   *

Is Fed.R.Evid. 412(b)(2)(A) triggered by proof that the complainant's hymen is no longer intact? See Gamble v. State, 257 Ga. 325, 357 S.E.2d 792 (1987).

5. Consider Mosley v. Commonwealth, 420 S.W.2d 679 (Ky.1967):

"Appellant was convicted of the crime of rape and sentenced to ten years' servitude in the state penitentiary. The sole ground for reversal of the conviction is that the trial court erred in excluding the testimony of James Gay a psychologist, concerning the mental condition of the prosecuting witness at the time of the alleged rape.

"The record reflects that for several months prior to May 11, 1966, the date of the alleged offense, Geraldine Eden, the prosecuting witness, had been staying in the home of Elihu Asher where she was employed as a fulltime babysitter. Geraldine who is 27 years of age, testified that during the evening of May 11, 1966, the Ashers had left their residence to go bowling. Appellant, an acquaintance of Geraldine and a relative of Asher entered the Asher home for the purpose of staying overnight. Geraldine stated that after the Asher children went to bed, appellant tried to make love to her and when she resisted his amorous advances he forcibly tied her hands behind her back, pushed her down on a couch, removed her underclothing and raped her.

"Appellant, age 54, testified that upon his arrival at the Asher residence Geraldine informed him that she wanted to talk with him before he retired. He had waited only a short time when Geraldine came over and sat beside him on a couch where they immediately began making love and Geraldine voluntarily submitted to sexual intercourse with him as she had on several previous occasions. He stated that following the intercourse they went to the kitchen and Geraldine prepared a snack for them. When they were later questioned that night as to their conduct, appellant stated that much to his surprise Geraldine claimed he had raped her.

"Appellant urges that the court erred in refusing to permit the jury to consider, for the purpose of impeaching Geraldine's credibility, the testimony of Doctor Gay concerning Geraldine's mental condition. Doctor Gay has obtained a Ph.D. degree in psychology and has been licensed by the state of Kentucky as a clinical psychologist. (KRS 319.010 defines the practice of clinical psychology to include the administration of tests for the purpose of psychological diagnosis, classification and evaluation and recognizes services involving the reeducation, guidance or readjustment of the patient.) He is a member of the American and Kentucky Psychological Associations and is presently the psychologist in charge of the Fayette County Program, a special program at Eastern State Hospital for out-patient treatment.

"Doctor Gay, who is in charge of the treatment of Geraldine's mental disorder, testified, by way of avowal out of the presence of the jury, that Geraldine had entered a state hospital for mental treatment during October 1961. At that time she was complaining that her father and brothers had molested her sexually during her adolescence. She was discharged from the hospital in January 1962 and readmitted for treatment on a voluntary basis during 1964. She has been treated by Doctor Gay since September 1965.

"While Doctor Gay believed that Geraldine was in a state of remission at the time of the alleged rape, it was his opinion that she is schizophrenic and is an immature individual. She could not tolerate frustration, was easily disturbed and had a guilt complex. Doctor Gay stated that schizophrenia is a complex phenomenon, that it is a disturbance of behavioral effect and thinking which has not been found to be caused or related to any physical or organic condition, but it has a psychiatric origin, i.e. an emotional basis. He further stated that one of the manifestations of schizophrenic reaction is fantasies and when asked whether Geraldine's fantasies extend to the area of sex, he answered, 'In this particular case I think it does.'

"Since the Commonwealth relied upon the uncorroborated testimony of Geraldine to establish its case against appellant, the principal question at issue had reference to the credit to be given to the testimony of Geraldine. Therefore, Doctor Gay's testimony may have had an important impact on the jury as it tended to impeach Geraldine's credibility.

"It is our opinion that the proffered testimony of Dr. Gay was relevant and competent and should have been received, not in extenuation of rape, but for its bearing upon the question of the weight to be accorded Geraldine's testimony. For this reason the court should admonish the jury that the expert testimony should be considered by it only for the purpose of affecting the credibility of this witness, if it does so." * * *

6. The Polygraph ("Lie–Detector") Technique has been of great value in sex offense investigations, and particularly as a safeguard against false accusations. See Reid & Inbau, Truth and Deception: The Polygraph ("Lie–Detector")

Technique (2d ed. 1977). See also Moenssens et al., Scientific Evidence in Criminal Cases (Ch. 14 on the Polygraph) (3d ed. 1986).

7. Should the victim of a sexual assault be permitted to learn whether his or her assailant has AIDS? Consider, in this regard, the statute passed by the Virginia General Assembly in 1990:

§ 18.2–62. Testing of certain persons for human immunodeficiency virus.—A. As soon as practicable following arrest, the attorney for the Commonwealth may request, after consultation with any victim, that any person charged with any crime involving sexual assault pursuant to this article or any offenses against children . . . be requested to submit to testing for infection with human immunodeficiency virus. The person so charged shall be counseled about the meaning of the test, about acquired immunodeficiency syndrome, and about the transmission and prevention of infection with human immunodeficiency virus.

In the event the person so charged refuses to submit to the test, a hearing shall be conducted in camera before the circuit court to determine probable cause by a preponderance of the evidence that the individual has committed the crime with which he is charged. Upon a finding of probable cause, the court shall order the accused to undergo testing for infection with human immunodeficiency virus.

B. Upon conviction of any crime involving sexual assault pursuant to this article or any offenses against children . . . the attorney for the Commonwealth may request, after consultation with any victim, and the court shall order the defendant to submit to testing for infection with human immunodeficiency virus. Any test conducted following conviction shall be in addition to such tests as may have been conducted following arrest pursuant to subsection A.

C. Confirmatory tests shall be conducted before any test result shall be determined to be positive. The results of the tests for infection with human immunodeficiency virus shall be confidential as provided in § 32.1–36.1; however, the Department of Health shall also disclose the results to any victim. The Department shall conduct surveillance and investigation in accordance with § 32.1–39 of this Code.

The results of such tests shall not be admissible as evidence in any criminal proceeding.

The cost of such tests shall be paid by the Commonwealth and taxed as part of the cost of such criminal proceedings.

5. MARITAL RAPE

WARREN v. STATE

Supreme Court of Georgia, 1985.
255 Ga. 151, 336 S.E.2d 221.

SMITH, JUSTICE.

"When a woman says I do, does she give up her right to say I won't?" [1] This question does not pose the real question, because rape [2] and aggravated sodomy are not sexual acts of an ardent husband performed upon an initially apathetic wife, they are acts of violence that are accompanied with physical and mental abuse and often leave the victim with physical and psychological damage that is almost always long lasting.   Thus we find the more appropriate question: When a woman says "I do" in Georgia does she give up her right to State protection from the violent acts of rape and aggravated sodomy performed by her husband.   The answer is no.   We affirm.

The appellant, Daniel Steven Warren, was indicted by a Fulton County Grand Jury for the rape and aggravated sodomy of his wife. They were living together as husband and wife at the time.   The appellant filed a pre-trial general demurrer and motion to dismiss the indictment.   After a hearing, the motions were denied.   The appellant sought and was issued a certificate of immediate review and filed an application for an interlocutory appeal which was granted by this court.

1.   The appellant asserts that there exists within the rape statute an implicit marital exclusion that makes it legally impossible for a husband to be guilty of raping his wife.

1. Griffin, In 44 States, It's Legal to Rape Your Wife, 21 Student Lawyer. Another question posed is: "But if you can't rape your wife, who[m] can you rape?" Freeman, "But If You Can't Rape Your Wife, Who[m] Can You Rape?": The Marital Rape Exemption Re-examined.   15 Family Law Quarterly (1981).

2. "As one author has observed, people have 'trouble with rape' because: [T]he mention of rape makes us all uneasy—for different reasons depending on who we are. It makes men uneasiest of all perhaps, and usually brings forth an initial response of nervous laughter or guffaw-evoking jokes. After all, as far as the normal, but uninformed, man knows, rape is something he might suddenly do himself some night if life becomes too dull.   It isn't, of course, but he knows too little about it to realize that.

On the other hand, the thoughtful normal man, after hearing the details of a forcible rape, finds it difficult to believe. . . .   He knows that all thoughts

of sex—which he equates with fun, romance, and mutual admiration—would leave him if the woman were *really* struggling to get free. . . . He does not realize that, to the rapist, the act is not 'love,' nor ardor, and usually not even passion; it is a way of debasing and degrading a woman. . . .   This gives rise to the commonly held view that: 'There is no such thing as rape.'   . . . To most women, [rape] is almost as unreal as it is to most men because they themselves have not experienced it, and few people who have done so are in the habit of talking about it. . . .

At the same time, an occasional newspaper story about a particularly brutal rape-murder makes all women shudder.   They wonder if it could possibly happen to them, and if it did, how would they react. . . ." (Emphasis in original.)   Massaro, Experts, Psychology, Credibility, and Rape: The Rape Trauma Syndrome Issue and Its Implications for Expert Psychological Testimony, 69 Minn.L.R. 395, 399 n. 27 (1985).

Until the late 1970's there was no real examination of this apparently widely held belief. Within the last few years several jurisdictions have been faced with similar issues and they have decided that under certain circumstances a husband can be held criminally liable for raping his wife.

What is behind the theory and belief that a husband could not be guilty of raping his wife? There are various explanations for the rule and all of them flow from the common law attitude toward women, the status of women and marriage.

Perhaps the most often used basis for the marital rape exemption is the view set out by Lord Hale[3] in 1 Hale P.C. 629. It is known as Lord Hale's contractual theory. The statement attributed to Lord Hale used to support the theory is: "but a husband cannot be guilty of a rape committed by himself upon his lawful wife, for by their mutual matrimonial consent and contract the wife hath given up herself in this kind unto her husband which she cannot retreat."

There is some thought that the foundation of his theory might well have been the subsequent marriage doctrine of English law, wherein the perpetrator could, by marrying his victim, avoid rape charges. It was thus argued as a corollary, rape within the marital relationship would result in the same immunity.

Another theory stemming from medieval times is that of a wife being the husband's chattel or property. Since a married woman was part of her husband's property, nothing more than a chattel, rape was nothing more than a man making use of his own property.

A third theory is the unity in marriage or unity of person theory that held the very being or legal existence of a woman was suspended during marriage, or at least was incorporated and consolidated into that of her husband. In view of the fact that there was only one legal being, the husband, he could not be convicted of raping himself.

These three theories have been used to support the marital rape exemption. Others have tried to fill the chasm between these three theories with justifications for continuing the exemption in the face of changes in the recognition of women, their status, and the status of marriage. Some of the justifications include: Prevention of fabricated charges; Preventing wives from using rape charges for revenge; Preventing state intervention into marriage so that possible reconciliation will not be thwarted. A closer examination of the theories and justifi-

---

3. Hale was Chief Justice of the Court of King's Bench from 1671 until 1675 when he resigned at age 66, one year before his death. A book based on his manuscripts was published in 1736, and the first American edition of the book was published in America in 1847, 1 M. Hale, Pleas of the Crown. Although we could not find a Georgia case that cited Hale's implied consent theory, we found a case that gives us a glimpse into Hale's world of more than three hundred years ago. "In 2 P.C. 290, this great judge and illustrious author says, 'But of all difficulties in evidence, there are two sorts of crimes that give the greatest difficulty, namely, rapes and witchcraft, ...' " Smith v. State, 77 Ga. 705, 712 (1886).

cations indicates that they are no longer valid, if they ever had any validity.

Hale's implied consent theory was created [4] at a time when marriages were irrevocable and when all wives promised to "love, honor, and obey" and all husbands promised to "love, cherish, and protect until death do us part." Wives were subservient to their husbands, her identity was merged into his, her property became his property, and she took his name for her own.

There have been dramatic changes in women's rights and the status of women and marriage. Today our State Constitution provides that, "no person shall be deprived of life, *liberty,* or property except by due process," (Emphasis supplied.) Art. I, § I, Par. I, and "protection to *person* and property is the paramount duty of government and shall be impartial and complete. No person shall be denied the equal protection of the laws." (Emphasis supplied.) Art. I, § I, Par. II. Our State Constitution also provides that each spouse has a right to retain his or her own property. Art. I, § I, Par. XXVII. Our statutory laws provide that, "[t]he rights of citizens include, *without limitation,* the following: (1) The right of *personal security,* [and] (2) The right of *personal liberty* . . . ." (Emphasis supplied.) OCGA § 1-2-6. Women in Georgia "are entitled to the privilege of the elective franchise and have the right to hold any civil office or perform any civil function as fully and completely as do male citizens." OCGA § 1-2-7. Couples who contemplate marriage today may choose either spouse's surname or a combination of both names for their married surname, OCGA § 19-3-33.1. No longer is a wife's domicile presumed to be that of her husband, OCGA § 19-2-3 and no longer is the husband head of the family with the wife subject to him. OCGA § 19-3-8. Marriages are revocable without fault by either party, OCGA § 19-5-3(13); either party, not just the husband, can be required to pay alimony upon divorce, OCGA § 19-6-1; and both parties have a joint and several duty to provide for the maintenance, protection, and education of their children, OCGA § 19-7-2. Couples may write antenuptial agreements in which they are able to decide, prior to marriage, future settlements, OCGA § 19-3-62; and our legislature has recognized that there can be violence in modern family life and it has enacted special laws to protect family members who live in the same household from one another's violent acts, Ga.L. 1981, 880; OCGA § 19-13-1 et seq.

Today, many couples write their own marriage vows in which they specifically decide the terms of their marriage contract. Certainly no normal woman who falls in love and wishes " 'to marry, establish a home and bring up children' . . . a central part of the *liberty* protect-

---

4. Hale cited no legal authority for his proposition, "[t]hus the marital exemption rule expressly adopted by many of our sister states has its [ORIGIN] in a bare, extrajudicial declaration made some 300 years ago. Such a declaration cannot itself be considered a definitive and binding statement of the common law, although legal commentators have often restated the rule since the time of Hale without evaluating its merits, [cits.]" State v. Smith, 85 N.J. 193, 426 A.2d 38, 41 (1981).

ed by the Due Process Clause, [Cits.]" (Emphasis supplied.) Zablocki v. Redhail, 434 U.S. 374, 384, 98 S.Ct. 673, 679, 54 L.Ed.2d 618 (1978), would knowingly include an irrevocable term to her revocable marriage contract that would allow her husband to rape her. Rape "is highly reprehensible, both in a moral sense and in its almost total contempt for the personal integrity and autonomy of the female victim. . . . Short of homicide, it is the 'ultimate violation of self.' " Coker v. Georgia, 433 U.S. 584, 599, 97 S.Ct. 2861, 2869, 53 L.Ed.2d 982 (1977). It is incredible to think that any state would sanction such behavior by adding an implied consent term *to all marriage contracts* that would leave *all* wives with no protection under the law from the "ultimate violation of self," *Coker*, supra, 97 S.Ct. at 2869, simply because they choose to enter into a relationship that is respected and protected by the law. The implied consent theory to spousal rape is without logical meaning, and *obviously conflicts* with our Constitutional and statutory laws and our regard for all citizens of this State.

One would be hard pressed to argue that a husband can rape his wife because she is his chattel. Even in the darkest days of slavery when slaves were also considered chattel, rape was defined as "the carnal knowledge of a female whether free or slave, forcibly and against her will." Georgia Code, § 4248, p. 824 (1863). Both the chattel and unity of identity rationales have been cast aside. "Nowhere in the common-law world—[or] in any modern society—is a woman regarded as chattel or demeaned by denial of a separate legal identity and the dignity associated with recognition as a whole human being." Trammel v. United States, 445 U.S. 40, 52, 100 S.Ct. 906, 913, 63 L.Ed.2d 186 (1980).

We find that none of the theories have any validity. The justifications likewise are without efficacy. There is no other crime we can think of in which *all of the victims are denied protection* simply because someone might fabricate a charge; there is no evidence that wives have flooded the district attorneys with revenge filled trumped-up charges, and once a marital relationship is at the point where a husband rapes his wife, state intervention is needed for the wife's protection.

There never has been an expressly stated marital exemption included in the Georgia rape statute. Furthermore, our statute never included the word "unlawful" which has been widely recognized as signifying the incorporation of the common law spousal exclusion. A reading of the statute indicates that there is no marital exclusion. "A person commits the offense of rape when he has carnal knowledge of a female forcibly and against her will." OCGA § 16–6–1. We need not decide whether or not a common law marital exemption became part of our old statutory rape law, because the rape statute that was similar to the common law definition was specifically repealed in 1968, Ga.L.1968, p. 1338, and our new broader statute, OCGA § 16–6–1, was enacted in its place which plainly on its face includes a husband.

2. The appellant contends that there is an implicit marital exclusion within the aggravated sodomy statute that makes it legally impossible for a husband to be guilty of an offense of aggravated sodomy performed upon his wife.

Sodomy was originally defined as "the carnal knowledge and connection against the order of nature by man with man, or in the same unnatural manner with woman." Laws 1833, Cobb's 1851 Digest, p. 787. The punishment for sodomy was "imprisonment at labor in the penitentiary for and during the natural life of the person convicted of this detestable crime." Laws 1833, Id.

Under the original rape and sodomy statutes, a man accused of rape could defend by alleging that the victim consented. If the consent could be proven, he could not be guilty of rape, because the third element of the offense "against her will" would be missing. One accused of sodomy could not defend by alleging consent, as lack of consent was not an element of the offense, and "[w]here a man and a woman voluntarily have carnal knowledge and connection against the order of nature with each other, they are both guilty of sodomy, . . ." Comer v. State, 21 Ga.App. 306, 94 S.E. 314 (1917). Thus an allegation of consent would only go to show the other party's guilt. "One who voluntarily participates in an unnatural act of sexual intercourse with another is also guilty of sodomy. One who does not so participate is not guilty." Perryman v. State, 63 Ga.App. 819, 823, 12 S.E.2d 388 (1940).

In 1968 the sodomy statute was specifically repealed, Ga.L.1968, p. 1338, and two new offenses were enacted, sodomy and aggravated sodomy, Ga.L.1968, 1299. There can be no common law marital exemption under the aggravated sodomy statute based on "implied consent," when the statute was enacted in 1968 and when there clearly was no marital exemption for sodomy based on "consent" under the original sodomy statute.

3. The appellant contends that if we find no marital exemptions under the rape and aggravated sodomy statutes it would be a new interpretation of the criminal law, and to apply the statutes to him would deprive him of his due process rights.

"All the Due Process Clause requires is that the law give sufficient warning that men may conduct themselves so as to avoid that which is forbidden. [Cit.]" *Rose v. Locke,* (1975). Both the rape and aggravated sodomy statutes are broadly written and they are plain on their face. This is a first application of these statutes to this particular set of facts, this is not an unforeseeable judicial enlargement of criminal statutes that are narrowly drawn.

*   *   *

Judgment affirmed.

All the Justices concur.

NOTES

1. In Kizer v. Commonwealth, 228 Va. 256, 321 S.E.2d 291 (1984), the majority of the Virginia Supreme Court said that to prove the offense of marital rape, the prosecution must establish, in addition to a violation of the general rape statute, that the wife (1) has lived separate and apart from the husband; (2) has refrained from voluntary sexual intercourse with her husband; and (3) in light of the circumstances has conducted herself in a manner that establishes a *de facto* end to the marriage.

Thereafter, the legislature incorporated into Virginia Code Sec. 18.2–61 (the rape statute), special marital rape provisions:

§ 18.2–61. Rape.—* * *

B. If any person has sexual intercourse with his or her spouse and such act is accomplished against the spouse's will by force, threat or intimidation of or against the spouse or another, he or she shall be guilty of rape.

However, no person shall be found guilty under this subsection unless, at the time of the alleged offense, (i) the spouses were living separate and apart, or (ii) the defendant caused serious physical injury to the spouse by the use of force or violence.

Additionally, there shall be no prosecution under this subsection unless the spouse or someone acting on the spouse's behalf reports the violation to a law-enforcement agency within ten days of the commission of the alleged offense. However, the ten-day limitation shall not apply while the spouse is physically unable to make such report or is restrained or otherwise prevented from reporting the violation.

C. A violation of this section shall be punishable, in the discretion of the court or jury, by confinement in a state correctional facility for life or for any term not less than five years. In any case deemed appropriate by the court, all or part of any sentence imposed for a violation of subsection B may be suspended upon the defendant's completion of counseling or therapy, if not already provided, in the manner prescribed under § 19.2–218.1 if, after consideration of the views of the complaining witness and such other evidence as may be relevant, the court finds such action will promote maintenance of the family unit and will be in the best interest of the complaining witness.

D. Upon a finding of guilt under subsection B in any case tried by the court without a jury, the court, without entering a judgment of guilt, upon motion of the defendant and with the consent of the complaining witness and the attorney for the Commonwealth, may defer further proceedings and place the defendant on probation pending completion of counseling or therapy, if not already provided, in the manner prescribed under § 19.2–218.1. If the defendant fails to so complete such counseling or therapy, the court may make final disposition of the case and proceed as otherwise provided. If such counseling is completed as prescribed under § 19.2–218.1, the court may discharge the defendant and dismiss the proceedings against him if, after consideration of the views of the complaining witness and such other evidence as may be relevant, the court finds such action will promote maintenance of the family unit and be in the best interest of the complaining witness.

2. For a commentary on the leading case, see, Abrogation of a Common Law Sanctuary for Husband Rapists: Warren v. State, 2 Detroit Coll.L.Rev. 599 (1986). See also, Buckborough, Family Law: Recent Developments in the Law of Marital Rape, 1989 Annual Survey of American Law 343 (1989); Comment, Spousal Exemption to Rape, 65 Marquette L.Rev. 120 (1980); Comment, Sexism and the Common Law: Spousal Rape in Virginia, 8 GMU L.Rev. 369 (1986).

3. In People v. Liberta, 64 N.Y.2d 152, 485 N.Y.S.2d 207, 474 N.E.2d 567 (1984), the New York Court of Appeals struck down, on equal protection grounds, the marital exemptions of both the rape and sodomy statutes as it redefined the two crimes in gender-neutral terms. While the court recognized that over forty states still retain some form of marital exemption for rape, the court examined the traditional reasons advanced for such distinctions, but found classifications based upon marital status to be lacking in justification.

In *Liberta,* the defendant was living separate and apart from his wife. In State v. Rider, 449 So.2d 903 (Fla.App.1984), however, the court ruled that a husband could be convicted under the rape statute even if the couple's marriage was ongoing and no separation or divorce proceedings had been instituted.

For a Note on *Liberta,* see, New York Court Abrogates Marital Rape Exemption as a Violation of Equal Protection, 19 Suffolk U.L.Rev. 1039 (1985).

4. In a state following the common law, can a man be convicted of the rape of his own wife by assisting or procuring another male to have intercourse with her? Can a woman be charged with rape of another woman in a common law state, by aiding and abetting a man in the commission of the rape?

B. "DEVIATE" SEXUAL BEHAVIOR

Under the term "deviate" sexual behavior we classify conduct that, at common law, was variously referred to as, sodomy, the "crime against nature," or the "abominable and detestable crime against nature." For a discussion on the scope of such offenses, refer to Rose v. Locke, discussed supra in Chapter 4–B.

With regard to the extent to which the law should attempt to control unconventional sexual conduct, consider the following excerpts from Kinsey, Pomeroy and Martin, Sexual Behavior in the Human Male (1948):

A. *"Mouth-genital Contact.* Mouth-genital contacts of some sort, with the subject as either the active or the passive member in the relationship, occur at some time in the histories of nearly 60 per cent of all males. . . ." (Page 371)

B. *"Animal Contacts.* In the total population only one male in twelve or fourteen (estimated at about 8%) ever has sexual experience with animals. . . . Frequencies of animal contact are similarly low taken as a whole. For most individuals, they do not occur more than once or twice, or a few times in a lifetime." (Page 670)

C. *"Homosexuality.* 37 per cent of the total male population has at least some overt homosexual experience to the point of orgasm between adolescence and old age. This accounts for nearly 2 males out of every 5 that one may meet.

"50 per cent of the males who remain single until age 35 have had overt homosexual experience to the point of orgasm, since the onset of adolescence." (Page 650)

For the incidence of comparable sexual conduct among females see Kinsey, Pomeroy, Martin and Gebhard, Sexual Behavior in the Human Female (1953), in which, on page 485, the authors state that "Both the incidences and frequencies of homosexual activity among females are actually much lower than among males."

Among the other studies of human sexual behavior, see Masters and Johnson, The Pleasure Bond (1970).

In consideration of the realities of human sexual behavior, the American Law Institute, in its Model Penal Code, does not proscribe unconventional sexual conduct between consenting adults, either heterosexual or homosexual. Its relevant provisions are as follows:

§ 213.2 Deviate Sexual Intercourse by Force or Imposition

(1) *By Force or Its Equivalent.* A person who engages in deviate sexual intercourse with another person, or who causes another to engage in deviate sexual intercourse, commits a felony of the second degree if:

(a) he compels the other person to participate by force or by threat of imminent death, serious bodily injury, extreme pain or kidnapping, to be inflicted on anyone; or

(b) he has substantially impaired the other person's power to appraise or control his conduct, by administering or employing without the knowledge of the other person drugs, intoxicants or other means for the purpose of preventing resistance; or

(c) the other person is unconscious; or

(d) the other person is less than 10 years old.

(2) *By Other Imposition.* A person who engages in deviate sexual intercourse with another person, or who causes another to engage in deviate sexual intercourse, commits a felony of the third degree if:

(a) he compels the other person to participate by any threat that would prevent resistance by a person of ordinary resolution; or

(b) he knows that the other person suffers from a mental disease or defect which renders him incapable of appraising the nature of his conduct; or

(c) he knows that the other person submits because he is unaware that a sexual act is being committed upon him.

§ 213.3 Corruption of Minors and Seduction

(1) *Offense Defined.* A male who has sexual intercourse with a female not his wife, or any person who engages in deviate sexual intercourse or causes another to engage in deviate sexual intercourse, is guilty of an offense if:

(a) the other person is less than [16] years old and the actor is at least [4] years older than the other person; or

(b) the other person is less than 21 years old and the actor is his guardian or otherwise responsible for general supervision of his welfare; or

(c) the other person is in custody of law or detained in a hospital or other institution and the actor has supervisory or disciplinary authority over him; or

(d) the other person is a female who is induced to participate by a promise of marriage which the actor does not mean to perform.

(2) *Grading.* An offense under paragraph (a) of Subsection (1) is a felony of the third degree. Otherwise an offense under this section is a misdemeanor.

C. FORNICATION AND ADULTERY

DOE v. DULING

United States Court of Appeals, Fourth Circuit, 1986.
782 F.2d 1202.

WILKINSON, CIRCUIT JUDGE.

Plaintiffs brought suit under the pseudonyms Jane Doe and James Doe challenging the constitutionality of Virginia statutes prohibiting fornication and cohabitation. Va. Code §§ 18.2–344, 18.2–345 (1982). The district court granted both injunctive and declaratory relief on the grounds that these statutes violated plaintiffs' right to privacy. Plaintiffs, however failed to show even a remote chance that they are threatened with prosecution under these provisions. To adjudge this fanciful dispute would undermine the proper role of federal courts in our system of government and usurp the position of state courts and legislatures as primary arbiters of state law. We therefore vacate the judgment of the court below and remand with directions to dismiss for want of a justiciable case or controversy. We express no view on the merits of the constitutional questions addressed by the district court.

I.

Plaintiffs (appellees in this action) are unmarried adults who maintain separate residences in the City of Richmond. In depositions, affidavits, and stipulations of fact, they state that they have engaged in sexual intercourse in the city with unmarried members of the opposite sex. Jane Doe further alleges that she has engaged in unlawful cohabitation. The Does believe that fornication and cohabitation are "common forms of conduct in society generally and in the City of Richmond in particular" and that an arrest for such activity could cause them "considerable personal embarrassment" and affect professional standing. Though neither has ever been arrested or threatened with arrest for violation of these statutes, the Does maintain that each has abstained from sexual intercourse and cohabitation since they learned of the laws in question for fear of prosecution. Finally, each expresses a desire to engage in private, consensual heterosexual activity free from government intrusion.

Virginia has prohibited fornication since at least 1819. The current code provides that "[a]ny person, not being married, who voluntarily shall have sexual intercourse with any other person shall be guilty of fornication." The last reported conviction for fornication in Virginia was in 1849.

Cohabitation is prohibited under § 18.2–345 of the current code: "If any persons, not married to each other, lewdly and lasciviously associate and cohabit together, or whether married or not, be guilty of open and gross lewdness and lasciviousness, each of them shall be guilty of a . . . misdemeanor." This section contains two distinct prohibitions, the second of which involves open and conspicuous lewd behavior. The cohabitation offense presumably requires no such openness. Virginia has maintained its statutory prohibition on cohabitation for well over 100 years. The last recorded conviction for private, consensual cohabitation occurred in 1883.

The Does introduced depositions of police officers and arrest records that purportedly reveal a pattern of current enforcement on which their fears of prosecution are grounded. Four current or former members of the Richmond vice division testified in general terms that all laws are enforced and specifically stated that they would investigate complaints of fornication and cohabitation if time and personnel limitations allowed. None of the officers however, recalled any arrests for fornication in a private, consensual setting except for those involving prostitution. Lieutenant John Carlson, for example, was head of the vice division during the depositions and testified that all fornication arrests he recalled in the last five years were prostitution-related. Officer William C. Bailey, involved in more than thirty fornication arrests, stated that nearly all were prostitution-related and none involved activity in a private home. None of the officers recalled a cohabitation arrest since 1976. Carlson stated his belief that cohabitation had to involve open sexual conduct before it fell within the prohibitions of the statute.

The arrest records entered into evidence bear this testimony out. The parties stipulated that none of these arrests involved fornication in a private residence. To the extent the record discloses the circumstances of these arrests, it shows that all involved public conduct. Two arrests, for example, were of individuals in a car; three arrests occurred in a public park.

The district court first considered the question of justiciability. The court found that the Does had standing because the challenged statutes apply expressly to them. Recognizing that there must be "a threat of prosecution sufficient to make this controversy ripe for review," the court held that the general policy of enforcing criminal laws, coupled with recent enforcement of the challenged statutes, established a credible threat, making the case ripe for review. On the merits, the court found that "the constitutional right to privacy extends to a single adult's decision whether to engage in sexual intercourse." Finding no compelling state interest, it struck down the fornication statute and that portion of § 18.2–345 prohibiting cohabitation. It found the prohibition in § 18.2–345 of "open and gross lewdness and lasciviousness" within the state's proper sphere of regulation.

II.

* * *

The record in this case establishes that the Does face only the most theoretical threat of prosecution. As noted by the district court, plaintiffs seek to determine "whether the State, consistent with the Constitution, may restrict the non-prostitutional, heterosexual activities of two unmarried, consenting adults when such activities occur in the privacy of one's home." Recorded cases reveal that the application of the statutes to such activity is, at most, a matter of historical curiosity. Attempts to update that history by showing recent arrest records were equally unavailing, for not one arrest has been shown to involve the behavior at issue in this case. Arrests for fornication and cohabitation arose instead from prostitutional or non-private behavior, not at issue here. The parties in fact stipulated that no arrests in evidence related to activity in a private residence, though the Does recognize that this conduct is common in society. The total absence of prosecutions in this context establishes that appellees have "no fears of prosecution except those that are imaginary or speculative."

The Does maintain, however, that they are fearful of cohabiting or engaging in sexual intercourse since they have learned of the statutes in question. Such subjective fear of prosecution does not establish an objective threat. There are, of course, occasions when the chilling effect of a statute is so powerful and the rights it inhibits so important that the mere existence of the statute may warrant judicial intervention. These cases, however, must be rare, for otherwise the case or controversy requirement would be set at naught. Every criminal law, by its very existence, may have some chilling effect on personal behavior. That was the reason for its passage. A subjective chill, however, is "not an adequate substitute for a claim of specific present objective harm or a threat of specific future harm," save in rare cases involving core First Amendment rights. Even in the area of First Amendment disputes, the Supreme Court has generally required a credible threat of prosecution before a federal court may review a state statute. . . .

The Does would have us overlook this deficiency and opine in the abstract on the validity of state enactments. Their argument is essentially that the mischief in these antique statutes justifies whatever arrogation of authority is needed to invalidate them. Authority, however, achieves acceptance through scrupulous exercise. The Constitution delegates to the legislative and executive branches, not to federal courts, the establishment of broad social agendas and the expression of ideals of public morality. Absent threatened injury, such as prosecution, review of criminal laws is, in effect, an appropriation of power by the federal judiciary. Such an exercise would leave "the federal courts as virtually continuing monitors of the wisdom and soundness of Executive [and Legislative] action." Federal judges would come to operate as second vetoes, through whom laws must pass for approval before they could be enforced. . . .

There is no better example of the need for judicial circumspection than the instant case. In the absence of a threat of prosecution, this action represents no more than an abstract debate, albeit a volatile one. Here, two plaintiffs disagree with a state statute and desire a federal court to declare it unconstitutional. Their views undoubtedly deserve consideration. The proper forum for their presentation is not, however, a federal court. The briefs before this court present instead the clash of argument in the abstract that would be better suited to a campaign for public office or a legislative hearing.

We are not concerned that this unenforced statute may escape the attention of the political process. Nor are we persuaded by the argument that if quaint statutes are never enforced, then defendants' constitutional rights will never be tested, and the Does lack any meaningful remedy. The absence of a "remedy" works no injustice on those who have never suffered so much as the threat of an injury. Furthermore, statutes whose status may be largely symbolic are appropriate subjects for political debate.

The instant case well illustrates this point. To many, the Virginia statutes here compromise the sacred component of privacy in sexual expression. They represent the potential intrusion of the state into the sanctity of the home or apartment, the potential for police action on nothing more than pretext and suspicion, and the imposition of antiquated attitudes about sex that bear little relevance to the diversity of individual lifestyles in a contemporary world. To others, these statutes express the value society places upon the life of the family and the institution of marriage, upon the realization of love through the encouragement of sexual fidelity, and upon the prevention of sexually transmitted diseases brought on by promiscuity. They discern in old laws renewed relevance as traditional values come under siege.

Each view has its adherents, and the pendulum of social conscience will doubtless swing between the two indefinitely. It is, however, for state legislatures, not federal courts, to face that political choice. States still bear primary responsibility in our system for the protection of public health, welfare, safety, and morals. Many states, moreover, have modified statutes similar to those at issue here. . . . To undertake our own updating would preempt the role of elective politics in the revision of public morality. It may well be that the Virginia legislature will not repeal these statutes tomorrow or the day thereafter. We cannot, however, take for our mandate the fact that democratic reform, like the proverbial mule, is often stubborn and slow.

* * *

Our resolution of this matter does not mean that federal review of these statutes is to be forever foreclosed. Should individual rights be implicated by actual or threatened enforcement of the statutes, the federal courts may assume an appropriate reviewing role under Article III. Federal courts may, for example, consider the validity of these statutes if the state undertakes bad faith enforcement of them, or if other extraordinary circumstances demonstrate irreparable injury. Even after state prosecution, of course, federal courts may have the opportunity to review these statutes on direct Supreme Court review or in collateral proceedings. Each of these is more consonant with the structure of government established by the Constitution and set forth by the Supreme Court than the abstract gesture we are asked to make here.

Without a case or controversy, we are essentially invited to make a symbolic pronouncement endorsing one of many possible visions of social governance and sexual morality. This responsibility, however, has been delegated to others in our system of government. Federal courts, of course, stand ready to protect individual rights whenever such rights are tangibly threatened by the operation of suspect laws. But the timing of our role is crucial; the prospect that our word may sometimes be the final one suggests it need not always be the first.

III.

For the reasons herein stated, the decision of the district court is hereby vacated, and this action is remanded with directions to dismiss for want of a case or controversy.

NOTES

1. Compare and appraise the following state statutory provisions:

Wisconsin Criminal Code

§ 944.15 *Fornication.* Whoever has sexual intercourse with a person not his or her spouse [may be fined not to exceed $10,000 or imprisonment not to exceed 9 months, or both].

§ 944.16 *Adultery.* Whoever does either of the following [may be fined not to exceed $10,000 or imprisonment not to exceed 2 years, or both]:

(1) A married person who has sexual intercourse with a person not his spouse; or

(2) A person who has sexual intercourse with a person who is married to another.

Illinois Criminal Code

§ 11–7.

(a) Any person who cohabits or has sexual intercourse with another not his spouse commits adultery, if the behavior is open and notorious, and

(1) The person is married and the other person involved in such intercourse is not his spouse; or

(2) The person is not married and knows that the other person involved in such intercourse is married.

A person shall be exempt from prosecution under this section if his liability is based solely on evidence he has given in order to comply with the requirements of Section 4–1.7 of the Illinois Public Aid Code [a section that deals with the enforcement of parental support].

* * *

[Adultery is a Class A misdemeanor, punishable for any term up to one year.]

§ 11–8.

(a) Any person who cohabits or has sexual intercourse with another not his spouse commits fornication if the behavior is open and notorious.

A person shall be exempt from prosecution under this section if his liability is based solely on evidence he has given in order to comply with the requirements of Section 4–1.7 of the Illinois Public Aid Code [a section that deals with the enforcement of parental support].

* * *

[Fornication is a Class B misdemeanor, punishable up to 6 months.]

2. It is of interest to observe that although Illinois followed the recommendation of the American Law Institute with respect to deviate sexual conduct, Illinois' Criminal Code, in the foregoing Sections 11–7 and 11–8, perpetuated the proscription on fornication and adultery, contrary to the position of ALI Model Penal Code. The Illinois provisions do contain the qualification, however, that the "behavior" of fornication and adultery must be "open and notorious." As to the meaning of that phrase, consider the following comment of the drafters of the Illinois Code:

Since it is the scandalousness, the affront to public decency and the marital institution that is of pivotal concern in this crime, notoriety must extend not only to the sexual intercourse of cohabitation, but must also extend to the fact of the absence of the marital relationship between parties engaging in such behavior.

The explanation for the ALI viewpoint is expressed in the 1980 commentary, at pp. 436–7:

The principal reason for punishing fornication and adultery is that they contravene community notions of ethical behavior. The Model Code regards this fact as an insufficient basis for imposition of penal sanctions. In a variety of aspects, societal ethics set standards of behavior more demanding than the law can expediently enforce.

Also consider the recommendation of the Louisiana Penal Code Advisory Committee regarding the omission of fornication and adultery (as quoted on page 435 of the 1980 ALI Model Penal Code Commentaries): ". . . to make such conduct a crime will do more harm than good, in that it will not prevent illicit and promiscuous relations by faithless husbands or wives, and the prosecutions will rarely occur except in blackmail or semi-blackmail situations."

D. PROSTITUTION

Review here the case of Caminetti v. United States, discussed earlier in Chapter 3–A–(2), supra. Observe particularly footnote 1 on p. 166.

NOTES

1. William Seagle, in his article, The Twilight of the Mann Act, 55 A.B. A.J. 641, 642 (1969), dispells the notion that the *Caminetti* case involved as innocent an episode of private interstate sex as the opinion seems to suggest:

> It has been the habit of commentators to pretend that the *Caminetti* case involved a mere interstate weekend on which two men took their mistresses. Actually the affair was more serious. The interstate weekend was the culmination of the seduction of two girls of Sacramento, California, ages respectively 19 and 20, by two married men who apparently had concealed their matrimonial state, as well as their fatherhood, from the objects of their passion. The seducers were Drew Caminetti, who was the son of Anthony Caminetti, then Commissioner of Immigration (a circumstance that was undoubtedly part of the explanation for the excited national interest in the case), and Maury Diggs, a boon companion. When the girls discovered the truth of the situation and indignation in Sacramento began to mount, Drew Caminetti and Maury Diggs decided it was time to get out of town. To induce the girls to run away with them to Reno, Nevada, they told them that their wives would hale them before the juvenile court and have them put away in a reformatory.

2. Consider Cleveland v. United States, 329 U.S. 14, 67 S.Ct. 13 (1946), a 6 to 3 decision sustaining Mann Act convictions of fundamentalist Utah Mormon adherents of polygamy who transported one or more of their "celestial" wives across state lines. Also see critical comment on the Caminetti and Cleveland decisions in 56 Yale L.J. 718, 727 (1947).

See also the Note, "The White Slave Traffic Act: The Historical Impact of a Criminal Law Policy on Women," 72 Georgetown L.J. 1111 (1984), tracing what it calls "the transformation of the Mann Act from its original formulation as a weapon against commercial vice to its eventual use as a federal morals law."

For another holding relying upon the principal case, see United States v. Reginelli, 133 F.2d 595 (3d Cir.1943), certiorari denied 318 U.S. 783, 63 S.Ct. 856. (Defendant went from his home in New Jersey to Miami, Florida for a visit. Enroute, as well as after arrival, he repeatedly telegraphed and telephoned a woman friend in New Jersey urging her to come to Miami. Pursuant to his requests, the woman, at defendant's expense, flew to Miami and there shared a hotel room with defendant for a period of ten days. During that time, they occupied the same bed and had sexual relations. Defendant was convicted of violating the Mann Act, and his conviction was affirmed.) See also Batsell v. United States, 217 F.2d 257 (8th Cir.1954) (Defendant, in an attempt to procure work for a woman in a house of prostitution, drove her from Minneapolis, Minnesota, to Duluth, Minnesota, passing briefly through a portion of Wisconsin in order to avoid road difficulties. In upholding his conviction, the Court of Appeals stated: "While it had been first intended that they would cross no state lines . . ., exigencies of the situation made it necessary for them to cross into Wisconsin . . . and return again into Minnesota. This, in the opinion of the Court, constituted interstate commerce and established a violation of the act").

3. The following excerpts from a 1971 federal appeals court opinion in a Mann Act case, United States v. Jenkins, 442 F.2d 429 (5th Cir.1971), present an interesting point of law entwined in an almost incredible series of events:

"Bell, Circuit Judge:

"This is a Mann Act case. Appellant, a practicing lawyer in St. Petersburg, Florida, was tried before a jury and convicted on a one count indictment charging a violation of [the Mann Act]. He was sentenced to four years imprisonment and fined $5,000. The trial consumed approximately six weeks and was a vigorous contest throughout. One indicia of this vigor is seen in the fact that appellant now urges fifty assignments of error. Upon consideration of the record and all assignments of error, and after extended oral argument, we find no error and accordingly affirm the judgment of the district court.

"The indictment charged that Jenkins induced Diane Feldman to go from Atlanta, Georgia to St. Petersburg, Florida, via a common carrier in interstate commerce, for the purpose of prostitution and debauchery in violation of the statute. The essence of Jenkins' defense was that his conduct, whatever it may have been, was not the moving force in the inducement of Feldman to travel as charged. * * *

"On November 11, 1966 Jenkins accompanied members of the St. Petersburg Quarterback Club to Atlanta, Georgia for a weekend of football games. The members of the club stayed at the Atlanta Biltmore Hotel. Upon arrival Jenkins was assigned to a suite with another member on the fifth floor.

"That evening, through the efforts of some of the members and various other persons, several prostitutes came to the hotel and began successfully plying their trade. Diane Feldman, a professional prostitute accompanied three of the members to a room in the hotel. After completing her business in their room she left and went to the elevator. There she met another member of the St. Petersburg group who invited her to a party then in progress in Jenkins' suite.

"She was introduced to Jenkins and had sexual intercourse with him and others in the group who were attending the party. During the course of the evening Jenkins told her that he recognized her and recalled that he had seen a warrant for her arrest in St. Petersburg. She was charged in the warrant with grand larceny. He told her that she could get in serious trouble if she did not return and that he could handle her case and get her off. He urged her to return to the Biltmore the following night when he would introduce her to the judge (a committing magistrate), who had signed the warrant, and they could discuss it.

"On the following night, Saturday, Feldman returned to Jenkins' hotel suite. She again participated in acts of sexual intercourse with various persons in the room as did several other prostitutes who were there. While there she met Justice of the Peace Dadswell. They discussed her case and he urged her to return to Florida, stating that Jenkins was a fine lawyer and that he could handle things so that she would not have to go to jail.

"She talked further with Jenkins about the charges at which time he told her that the offense of grand larceny was a serious one and that she could be extradited and held without bond. He again offered to represent her in the case. The fee was to be that she would have to furnish her services as a prostitute to Jenkins and his law partner one time. He also assured her that she could find plenty of work as a prostitute in St. Petersburg and that he would help her find a job as a go-go dancer. He then stated that he wanted her to ride back to St. Petersburg on the train with him and that he would pay her way. She declined this offer to return on the train.

"On Sunday Feldman talked with her husband who was then in Florida. After relating the incident with Jenkins, he told her that she should return if she thought Jenkins could clear up the charges against her. Feldman also called the St. Petersburg Police Department and verified that there was an outstanding grand larceny warrant against her. She then called Jenkins at his hotel to accept his offer, but he had already checked out. Later that night she took a plane to St. Petersburg.

"On Monday she contacted Jenkins and went to his office. He arranged for a bondsman, and agreed to represent her for the previously discussed fee.

"On November 16, 1966 she appeared in Justice of the Peace Court for a preliminary hearing on the grand larceny charge. She was transported to court in a black cadillac owned by Jenkins from the hotel where she was staying at the direction of Jenkins. Jenkins, his partner Abernathy, Estes the bondsman, and a law clerk were all in the vehicle.

"She was represented at the hearing by Jenkins and Abernathy. During the hearing, argument became quite heated. The judge and counsel retired to chambers. Jenkins came out and told Feldman that something was wrong because a different judge from the one he expected was presiding and that she would have to go to bed with the judge and the prosecutor in order to get the charges dismissed. She agreed. The case was dismissed.

"That evening or the next, she was taken to the Gulf Winds Motel where she engaged in sexual relations with seven men, according to her testimony, which was corroborated by some of the participants. Included in the group were Jenkins, Abernathy, the state's attorney who had prosecuted her that afternoon, Estes the bondsman, and Manderscheid, the owner of the motel. The trial judge was not involved.

"Jenkins continued his association with Feldman during the next several days. . . .

"On November 22, 1966, Feldman appeared before Judge Richard Carr, a Justice of the Peace, on a traffic ticket charge and was again represented by Jenkins and Abernathy. Jenkins again reminded her that she could get into serious trouble. She agreed with Jenkins to have sexual relations with Jenkins, Abernathy, and the judge in return for their services. There is no evidence that Feldman responded immediately following this court appearance.

"Several days later Jenkins arranged for Feldman to contact Jemison, one of his clients or friends. Jemison had customers who were arriving in Florida. For a negotiated price of $100.00, Feldman spent a night with one of these customers at the Happy Dolphin Inn.

* * *

"On December 9, 1966, Feldman made a third court appearance, this time appearing only with Abernathy. That evening, at the instruction of Jenkins, she met Judge Carr at the Office Lounge. They went from there to the Venice Motel where she engaged in sexual relations with Carr. She testified that Jenkins told her to do this.

* * *

"She later phoned Carr and Estes and asked them for money. Estes directed her to come to his office where she was met by Abernathy and Jenkins. After refusing her demands for money, she testified that they threatened to harm her for having 'talked'. She also testified that Abernathy threatened her by waving a letter opener or a knife in her face and advised her to keep quiet and leave town.

"It developed that Feldman had previously related her story to the vice squad of the St. Petersburg police force. The police advised her to leave town. She also tried to sell her story without success to a local newspaper. The newspaper referred her to the county sheriff who listened to her story and then referred her to the FBI. This prosecution followed.

"One group of appellant's contentions turns on the notion that judgment for acquittal should have been granted because the evidence allegedly shows that Jenkins was not the moving inducement for Feldman's travel in interstate commerce. This argument is based on what appellant characterizes as a rejection of his illicit offer to return to St. Petersburg on the train with the Quarterback Club. . . . [But] she only temporarily rejected his offer. [She] was unable to contact appellant at his hotel prior to his departure.

"The interstate transportation here by United Airlines, a common carrier, was not disputed. The fact of prostitution and debauchery in St. Petersburg was clearly established by direct evidence. There was also direct evidence of inducement on the part of Jenkins. This meets the test of Nunnally v. United States, (5 Cir., 1961) 291 F.2d 205, and makes a question for the jury. . . .

"Nunnally v. United States, supra, also forecloses the claim that the evidence was insufficient as to prostitution because Feldman and Jenkins had another purpose in mind, i.e., having the warrant dismissed. *Nunnally* teaches that there can be dual purposes under this statute—prostitution need only be one of the principal purposes. *Nun-*

nally also destroys the argument that Jenkins did not know an inter-state carrier would be employed in the trip to St. Petersburg. It is sufficient as here that a common carrier in interstate commerce would likely be and was utilized. * * *"

E. "SEXUALLY DANGEROUS PERSONS" LEGISLATION

Over the period of many years, approximately thirty states, and the District of Columbia, have enacted legislation designed to institutional-ize potentially dangerous sex offenders "for treatment and cure". One such statute, that of the District of Columbia (as appearing in its 1970 Code), reads as follows:

§ 22–3503. Definitions

For the purposes of sections 22–3503 to 22–3511—

(1) The term "sexual psychopath" means a person, not insane, who by a course of repeated misconduct in sexual matters has evidenced such lack of power to control his sexual impulses as to be dangerous to other persons because he is likely to attack or otherwise inflict injury, loss, pain, or other evil on the objects of his desire.

(2) The term "court" means a court in the District of Columbia having jurisdiction of criminal offenses or delinquent acts.

(3) The term "patient" means a person with respect to whom there has been filed with the clerk of any court a statement in writing setting forth facts tending to show that such person is a sexual psychopath.

(4) The term "criminal proceeding" means a proceeding in any court against a person for a criminal offense, and includes all stages of such a proceeding from (A) the time the person is indicted, charged by an information, or charged with a delinquent act, to (B) the entry of judgment, or, if the person is granted probation, the completion of the period of probation.

§ 22–3504. Filing of Statement

(a) Whenever it shall appear to the United States attorney for the District of Columbia that any person within the District of Columbia, other than a defendant in a criminal proceeding, is a sexual psycho-path, such attorney may file with the clerk of the Superior Court of the District Court of District of Columbia a statement in writing setting forth the facts tending to show that such a person is a sexual psycho-path.

(b) Whenever it shall appear to the United States attorney for the District of Columbia that any defendant in any criminal proceeding prosecuted by such attorney or any of his assistants is a sexual psychopath, such attorney may file with the clerk of the court in which such proceeding is pending a statement in writing setting forth the facts tending to show that such defendant is a sexual psychopath.

(c) Whenever it shall appear to any court that any defendant in any criminal proceeding pending in such court is a sexual psychopath, the court may, if it deems such procedure advisable, direct the officer prosecuting the defendant to file with the clerk of such court a statement in writing setting forth the facts tending to show that such defendant is a sexual psychopath.

(d) Any statement filed in a criminal proceeding pursuant to subsection (b) or (c) may be filed only (1) before trial, (2) after conviction or plea of guilty but before sentencing, or (3) after conviction or plea of guilty but before the completion of probation.

(e) This section shall not apply to an individual in a criminal proceeding who is charged with rape or assault with intent to rape.

§ 22–3505. Right to Counsel

A patient shall have the assistance of counsel at every stage of the proceeding under sections 22–3503 to 22–3511. Before the court appoints psychiatrists pursuant to section 22–3506 it shall advise the patient of his right to counsel and shall assign counsel to represent him unless the patient is able to obtain counsel or elects to proceed without counsel.

§ 22–3506. Examination by Psychiatrists

(a) When a statement has been filed with the clerk of any court pursuant to section 22–3504, such court shall appoint two qualified psychiatrists to make a personal examination of the patient. The patient shall be required to answer questions asked by the psychiatrists under penalty of contempt of court. Each psychiatrist shall file a written report of the examination, which shall include a statement of his conclusion as to whether the patient is a sexual psychopath.

(b) The counsel for the patient shall have the right to inspect the reports of the examination of the patient. No such report and no evidence resulting from the personal examination of the patient shall be admissible against him in any judicial proceeding except a proceeding under sections 22–3503 to 22–3511 to determine whether the patient is a sexual psychopath.

§ 22–3507. When Hearing Is Required

If, in their reports filed pursuant to section 22–3506, both psychiatrists state that the patient is a sexual psychopath, or if both state that they are unable to reach any conclusion by reason of the partial or complete refusal of the patient to submit to thorough examination, or if one states that the patient is a sexual psychopath and the other states that he is unable to reach any conclusion by reason of the partial or complete refusal of the patient to submit to thorough examination, then the court shall conduct a hearing in the manner provided in section 22–3508 to determine whether the patient is a sexual psychopath. If, on the basis of the reports filed, the court is not required to conduct such a hearing, the court shall enter an order dismissing the proceeding under sections 22–3503 to 22–3511 to determine whether the patient is a sexual psychopath.

§ 22–3508. Hearing—Commitment to Saint Elizabeths Hospital

Upon the evidence introduced at a hearing held for that purpose, the court shall determine whether or not the patient is a sexual psychopath. Such hearing shall be conducted without a jury unless, before such hearing and within fifteen days after the date on which the second report is filed pursuant to section 22–3506, a jury is demanded by the patient or by the officer filing the statement. The rules of evidence applicable in judicial proceedings in the court shall be applicable to hearings pursuant to this section; but, notwithstanding any such rule, evidence of conviction of any number of crimes the commission of which tends to show that the patient is a sexual psychopath and of the punishment inflicted therefor shall be admissible at any such hearing. The patient shall be entitled to an appeal as in other cases. If the patient is determined to be a sexual psychopath, the court shall commit him to Saint Elizabeths Hospital to be confined there until released in accordance with section 22–3509.

§ 22–3509. Parole—Discharge

Any person committed under sections 22–3503 to 22–3511 may be released from confinement when the Superintendent of Saint Elizabeths Hospital finds that he has sufficiently recovered so as to not be dangerous to other persons, provided if the person to be released be one charged with crime or undergoing sentence therefor, the Superintendent of the hospital shall give notice thereof to the judge of the criminal court and deliver him to the court in obedience to proper precept.

§ 22–3510. Stay of Criminal Proceedings

Any statement filed in a criminal proceeding pursuant to subsection (b) or (c) of section 22–3504 shall stay such criminal proceeding until whichever of the following first occurs:

(1) The proceeding under sections 22–3503 to 22–3511 to determine whether the patient is a sexual psychopath is dismissed pursuant to section 22–3507 or withdrawn;

(2) It is determined pursuant to section 22–3508 that the patient is not a sexual psychopath; or

(3) The patient is discharged from Saint Elizabeths Hospital pursuant to section 22–3509.

§ 22–3511. Criminal Law Unchanged

Nothing in sections 22–3503 to 22–3511 shall alter in any respect the tests of mental capacity applied in criminal prosecutions under the laws of the District of Columbia.

A number of constitutional problems have arisen in cases involving "sexually dangerous persons" statutes, including the one created by incarceration in an institution where there is a total lack or inadequate treatment of the committed person.[1] But the real issue with respect to such legislation is whether it has any basic validity. Concluding that such validity is lacking, and that the problem of the sexually dangerous person can be handled more effectively by other methods and procedures, several states, among them being California and Michigan, have repealed their statutes.[2] Total repeal of "sexually dangerous persons" legislation, or, at the least, considerable modification is recommended in a "reference document" submitted to the President's Commission on Law Enforcement and Administration of Justice, by Roger Craig, under the title of Sexual Psychopath Legislation (1967). It makes the following recommendations:

"(A) The most constructive step would begin with repeal of the sexual psychopath statutes. The observation that 'on the whole, very few authorities have called for repeal of these laws on the ground that the underlying assumptions are incorrect' is invalid. In fact, the underlying assumptions of the statutes have been attacked time and time again and repeal is frequently advocated.

"There exists no reason why the ordinary processes of criminal and civil commitment cannot handle the problem of the dangerous sex offender adequately, something the sexual psychopath statutes fail to do. Three collateral changes should or may accompany the repeal of sexual psychopath legislation, however.

"First, a comprehensive review of all underlying sex crimes should be undertaken. The dimensions of such a review are outside the scope of this paper, but it is clear that many of our criminal laws making illegal conduct which is participated in between consenting individuals and which harms no third party are of extremely dubious validity. On the other hand, a comprehensive review should also consider stepping up the potential punishment for certain kinds of sex crimes. If society considers exhibitionism a serious crime—particularly when a very

1. Commonwealth v. Page, 339 Mass. 313, 159 N.E.2d 82 (1959) ("[T]o be sustained as a non-penal statute . . ., it is necessary that the remedial aspect of confinement thereunder have foundation in fact. It is not sufficient that the Legislature announce a remedial purpose if the consequences to the individual are penal. . . . [C]onfinement in a prison which is undifferentiated from the incarceration of convicted criminals is not remedial so as to escape constitutional requirements of due process."). See also Miller v. Overholser, 206 F.2d 415 (D.C.Cir.1953).

2. West's Ann.Cal.Welfare and Institutions Code, §§ 5500–5515, with repeal effective July 1, 1969; Mich.Comp.Laws Ann. § 767.27, with repeal effective August 1, 1968.

young 'victim' is involved—it should deal with the problem directly, by authorizing maximum sentences of several years instead of several months.

"Second, disturbed sex offenders who are committed criminally, sex offenders found not-guilty by reason of insanity and thereafter committed, and insane sex offenders who are committed civilly all have a right to receive treatment. As the sexual psychopath statutes are repealed, whatever resources had previously been used for treating sexual psychopaths should be made available generally to needy individuals in prisons and mental hospitals. All jurisdictions undoubtedly need to improve their facilities for treating the mental disabilities of those committed to state institutions.

"Finally, thought should be given to adopting a special statute, applicable to all dangerous offenders, which might result in increased periods of incarceration, given certain attitudes and behavior patterns on the part of the offender. In particular, such a statute might enable society to deal more effectively with dangerous recidivists. Legislators might begin their thinking by considering the provisions of the Model Sentencing Act drafted by the Advisory Counsel of Judges of the National Council on Crime and Delinquency.

"(B) Short of repeal, the following recommendations necessarily center on making the statutes work more fairly:

"(1) If the sexual psychopath statutes continue to involve substantially longer period of confinement than the criminal law permits, statutory definitions of sexual psychopathy must be re-written in more exacting language. The key to confinement must be dangerousness, not perversion. Moreover, it must be made clear that the issue of dangerousness is one to be decided by the court—or preferably by a jury if desired by the alleged psychopath—on the basis of all relevant testimony, not one to be decided in effect by a psychiatrist on the basis of his examination alone.

"(2) Treatment facilities for committed sexual psychopaths and for all other needy individuals in state prisons and mental hospitals must be expanded.

"(3) Prior conviction for a sex crime must be a prerequisite for a finding of sexual psychopathy. Such a requirement would guarantee that proper procedures are followed in proving at least one example of aberrant sexual conduct before such conduct is relied upon to justify commitment.

"(4) Recognizing that a finding of sexual psychopathy is very important to the individual involved—even at the post-conviction stage—legislators and, in their silence, judges should see that appropriate rights to a hearing, to counsel, to silence, to jury trial, etc., are elaborated and enforced.

"(5) Some limitation should be placed upon the time which the committed sexual psychopath can be forced to serve. (The Model

Sentencing Act contains a thirty year maximum, except for the crime of murder.) The most desirable limitation—given the general failure of the laws to single out only the most dangerous offenders—would be to do as the New Jersey statute does, i.e., to limit incarceration to the maximum term under the relevant criminal statute. So limited, the sexual psychopath statute could truly become a method of insuring better treatment for mentally disturbed offenders, and nothing more.

"(6) Release procedures should be improved. Periodical review— by psychiatrists, by a parole board, and by the committing court— should put the state to the test of proving from time to time that the individual continues to be dangerous. The committed sexual psychopath or someone interested in him should be able to initiate review proceedings, and the state should take steps to insure that his rights are adequately protected in the process. In addition, outpatient care, work release and parole opportunities should be multiplied so that the restriction on the committed sexual psychopath's liberty will be as small as possible."

Consider the following views of two highly respected writers upon the subject of sex offenses—Manfred Guttmacher, M.D., a psychiatrist, and Henry Weihofen, a law professor:

"Three widely held misconceptions have been responsible for most of the defects in the so-called sexual psychopathic laws. In the first place, sex offenders are treated as if they comprised a separate and homogenous group of criminals. The reverse is true. There is as much difference between the average exhibitionist and the average rapist as there is between the shoplifter and the safe cracker. Secondly, it is believed that sex offenders regularly progress from minor offenses such as exhibitionism to major offenses like forced rape. Such a graduation is almost unknown. The exhibitionist is acting out an intra-psychic conflict, he has adopted this method of relieving an intolerable state of anxiety and tension. Paradoxically this has worked satisfactorily for him and he could not be induced to try a substitute. Then, there is the widespread belief that sex offenses are today rampant—that there has been a sudden alarming increase in their incidence. All of the careful investigations made recently have failed to demonstrate any persistent trend in that direction. A fourth major source of error is the belief that all sex offenders tend to be recidivists. . . .

* * *

"Probably the most constructive measures for combatting sex criminality are informal community-level educational programs, aimed at seeking out and treating deviational characteristics among children; particularly the excessively aggressive or passive children in the schools—getting teachers to realize, for example, that the boy who is *too* quiet and *too* good may be as much a problem child, and as likely to grow into a dangerous criminal, as the boy who is obviously bad.

"Psychiatrists and educators have developed some sensible rules of child rearing which, if properly applied, would doubtless decrease the incidence of sex crime. Parental over-protection and parental rejection account in large measure for the great number of emotionally immature and dependent persons that we have in our society. And many of them are incapable of achieving mature sexuality. A far greater number of parents than we imagine seduce their children psychologically, binding them with chains from which they attempt to free themselves by abnormal, and sometimes violent sexual behavior. . . .

"Freud's significant statement on the role of parental relations should be heeded in any campaign to reduce abnormal sexuality: 'Quarrels between parents and unhappy marital relations between them, determine the severest predispositions for disturbed sexual development or neurotic disease in children.'

"Realistic sex education has been a part of the high school curriculum in Sweden since 1935. There is reason to believe that this would be an important step in the progress of prevention. It will take continued educational efforts and publicity to convince the public that it is a sound investment to expend money in preventive work, rather than to wait until a sensational sex murder shocks us into enacting legislation by which we undertake to support for life individuals whom we have unconcernedly permitted to become incurably dangerous."[3]

In Allen v. Illinois, 478 U.S. 364, 106 S.Ct. 2988, 92 L.Ed.2d 296 (1986), the United States Supreme Court, in a 5–to–4 decision, held that proceedings under the Illinois Sexually Dangerous Persons Act (Ill.Rev. Stat., ch. 38, Sec. 105–1.01 et seq. [1985]) were civil in nature, and not criminal. The Court concluded that the Fifth Amendment's guarantee against compulsory self-incrimination was therefore not applicable to such proceedings, and a defendant could be compelled to answer questions posed by court appointed psychiatrists upon which the latter would base their opinions on whether the defendant had been suffering from a mental disorder and had propensities to commit sex offenses.

3. Guttmacher and Weihofen, Sex Offenses, 43 J.Crim.L., C. & P.S. 153 (1952); also as Chapter 6, in the same authors' book, Psychiatry and the Law (1952).

Chapter 7

MISAPPROPRIATION AND RELATED PROPERTY OFFENSES

A. LARCENY

Larceny, generally speaking, is the crime of stealing. Technically, it consists of several specific elements, namely

a. a taking and

b. a carrying away

c. of the personal property

d. of another

e. with intent to steal

An act which lacks any one of these elements cannot be larceny.

To understand why the law of larceny is so technical as to require these elements, reference must be made to the history of the offense.

First, larceny was the only form of theft criminally punished under the early common law. The offense was narrowly construed, inasmuch as many forms of deception were not commonly regarded as criminal. The social and economic community lacked the complexity of modern times, and it was thought that with the exercise of ordinary prudence one could protect himself from most sorts of deception. For example, it was held in 1761 that it was not a crime to "make a fool of another" by deliberately delivering fewer goods than were ordered.[1] The civil law was relied upon to correct such a deception; the criminal law would intervene only if the fraud was one which common care could not prevent, such as the use of false weights and measures. As commerce increased, the criminal law expanded to punish new forms of theft; however, the law of larceny had become so fixed that gaps were filled by the addition of new crimes, such as embezzlement and false pretenses, rather than by redefining larceny.

Second, the technicalities surrounding the law of larceny derive to some extent from the fact that grand larceny (larceny of goods having a certain minimum value) was a capital offense. Gradually, as attitudes toward the death penalty changed, the bench became reluctant to award the death penalty to thieves, especially since the amount which divided grand and petit larceny was very low. Thus, judges would frequently rely upon technicalities to acquit in larceny cases.[2]

---

1. Rex v. Wheatly, 97 E.R. 746 (1761).

2. A definitive treatment of the development of the law of larceny and the of-fenses related thereto is found in Hall, Theft, Law and Society 3–109 (2d ed. 1952).

679

The complex nature of the law of theft has little justification today. Some efforts have been made to simplify the law in this area. Notably, several states have abolished the separate offenses of larceny, embezzlement, etc., and combined them in a new crime called "theft." [3] Until such time, however, as reform in this area is general, it will be necessary for the lawyer to understand the complexities of the law of larceny, as well as the offenses that have been developed to supplement larceny in the field of theft.

1. THE ELEMENTS OF LARCENY

(a) TAKING

Under the early common law, the "taking" required for larceny had to be by force or stealth, and as a consequence the principle developed that the taking had to be trespassory. It was said that the taking had to be such as would give rise to a civil action of trespass *de bonis asportatis.*[4] The requirement of a trespass still exists. It is customarily stated that this requirement means that the taking must be without the consent of the owner of the goods.[5]

In one case the court reversed a larceny conviction where the victim of a scheme paid the money over to the defendant at the urging of the police. The court said that "Larceny is not committed if the owner consents to the taking of his goods even though the consent is given solely for the purpose of apprehending the taker in the commission of the act".[6]

It should be stressed at the outset that the "taking" refers to a taking of *possession* of the personal goods of another. Thus, one can take possession of goods over which he has mere *custody,* and such a taking amounts to larceny if the other requirements are present.[7] However, if actual possession is never acquired by the thief, or by one acting at his direction or instigation, larceny has not been committed.[8] Moreover, there is no taking unless the object is first in someone else's possession, either actual or constructive.[9]

---

3. See, e.g., West's Ann.Cal.Pen.Code § 484 (1955); Wis.Stats. § 943.20 (1955); Ill.Rev.Stats., ch. 38, Arts. 16 and 17.

4. Reg. v. Smith, 2 Den.C.C. 449, 5 Cox C.C. 533, 16 Eng.Rep. 567 (1852).

5. People v. Johnson, 136 Cal.App.2d 665, 673, 289 P.2d 90, 94 (1955).

6. State v. Durham, 196 N.W.2d 428 (Iowa 1972).

7. One's servant, for example, has mere custody of money which his master has given him to mail. If the servant converts the money to his own use, he has committed larceny. Rex v. Paradice, 2 East P.C. 565 (1766).

8. In Thompson v. State, 94 Ala. 535, 10 So. 520 (1891), the defendant had jostled the arm of another to make him drop some money in his hand. The defendant, however, was unable to find the money dropped; consequently, it was held that he was not guilty of larceny, since he had not obtained possession of the money.

9. Abandoned property is therefore not the subject of larceny, inasmuch as it is not in anyone's possession, either actual or constructive. Such property is cast aside, the owner intending to have no further interest therein. See Commonwealth v. Metcalfe, 184 Ky. 540, 543, 212 S.W. 434, 436 (1919).

The taking can be effected by the hands of the thief, by a mechanical device, or even by an animal trained for that purpose, or by an innocent human being acting under the thief's direction. A "lifting up" of an object by any one of these means is a "taking." [10]

PEOPLE v. OLIVO

PEOPLE v. GASPARIK

PEOPLE v. SPATZIER

New York Court of Appeals, 1981.
52 N.Y.2d 309, 438 N.Y.S.2d 242, 420 N.E.2d 40.

COOKE, CHIEF JUDGE. These cases present a recurring question in this era of the self-service store which has never been resolved by this court: may a person be convicted of larceny for shoplifting if the person is caught with goods while still inside the store? For reasons outlined below, it is concluded that a larceny conviction may be sustained, in certain situations, even though the shoplifter was apprehended before leaving the store.

I

In People v. Olivo, defendant was observed by a security guard in the hardware area of a department store. Initially conversing with another person, defendant began to look around furtively when his acquaintance departed. The security agent continued to observe and saw defendant assume a crouching position, take a set of wrenches and secret it in his clothes. After again looking around, defendant began walking toward an exit, passing a number of cash registers en route. When defendant did not stop to pay for the merchandise, the officer accosted him a few feet from the exit. In response to the guard's inquiry, denied having the wrenches, but as he proceeded to the security office, defendant removed the wrenches and placed them under his jacket. At trial, defendant testified that he had placed the tools under his arm and was in line at a cashier when apprehended. The jury returned a verdict of guilty on the charge of petit larceny. The conviction was affirmed by Appellate Term.

II

In People v. Gasparik, defendant was in a department store trying on a leather jacket. Two store detectives observed him tear off the price tag and remove a "sensormatic" device designed to set off an

---

10. For instance, where a thief puts his hand into another person's pocket and lifts up a pocket book, this constitutes a "taking" even though the owner prevents a removal of the wallet from his pocket.

Are larceny statutes effective in the conviction of pickpockets? For an opinion that they are not, and for suggestions with respect to other types of statutes which may be relied upon (e.g., vagrancy, known-thief laws, disorderly conduct, criminal registration ordinances), see Pickpocketing: A Survey of the Crime and its Control, 104 U.Pa.L.Rev. 408 (1955).

alarm if the jacket were carried through a detection machine. There was at least one such machine at the exit of each floor. Defendant placed the tag and the device in the pocket of another jacket on the merchandise rack. He took his own jacket, which he had been carrying with him, and placed it on a table. Leaving his own jacket, defendant put on the leather jacket and walked through the store, still on the same floor, by passing several cash registers. When he headed for the exit from that floor, in the direction of the main floor, he was apprehended by security personnel. At trial, defendant denied removing the price tag and the sensormatic device from the jacket, and testified that he was looking for a cashier without a long line when he was stopped. The court, sitting without a jury, convicted defendant of petit larceny. Appellate Term affirmed. . . . .

III

In People v. Spatzier, defendant entered a bookstore on Fulton Street in Hempstead carrying an attaché case. The two co-owners of the store observed the defendant in a ceiling mirror as he browsed through the store. They watched defendant remove a book from the shelf, look up and down the aisle, and place the book in his case. He then placed the case at his feet and continued to browse. One of the owners approached defendant and accused him of stealing the book. An altercation ensued and when defendant allegedly struck the owner with the attaché case, the case opened and the book fell out. At trial, defendant denied secreting the book in his case and claimed that the owner had suddenly and unjustifiably accused him of stealing. The jury found defendant guilty of petit larceny, and the conviction was affirmed by the Appellate Term.

IV

The primary issue in each case is whether the evidence, viewed in the light most favorable to the prosecution, was sufficient to establish the elements of larceny as defined by the Penal Law. To resolve this common question, the development of the common-law crime of larceny and its evolution into modern statutory form must be briefly traced.

Larceny at common law was defined as a trespassory taking and carrying away of the property of another with intent to steal it. The early common-law courts apparently viewed larceny as defending society against breach of the peace, rather than protecting individual property rights, and therefore placed heavy emphasis upon the requirement of a *trespassory taking* (e.g., Fletcher, Metamorphosis of Larceny, 89 Harv.L.Rev. 469). Thus, a person such as a bailee who had rightfully obtained possession of property from its owner could not be guilty of larceny. The result was that the crime of larceny was quite narrow in scope.

Gradually, the courts began to expand the reach of the offense, initially by subtle alterations in the common-law concept of possession.

Thus, for instance, it became a general rule that goods entrusted to an employee were not deemed to be in his possession, but were only considered to be in his custody, so long as he remained on the employer's premises (e.g., 3 Holdsworth, A History of English Law [3d ed, 1923], at p. 365. And, in the case of *Chisser* (Raym.Sir.T. 275, 83 Eng. Rep. 142), it was held that a shop owner retained legal possession of merchandise being examined by a prospective customer until the actual sale was made. In these situations, the employee and the customer would not have been guilty of larceny if they had first obtained lawful possession of the property from the owner. By holding that they had not acquired possession, but merely custody, the court was able to sustain a larceny conviction.

As the reach of larceny expanded, the intent element of the crime became of increasing importance, while the requirement of a trespassory taking became less significant. As a result, the bar against convicting a person who had initially obtained lawful possession of property faded. In King v. Pear (1 Leach 212, 168 Eng.Rep. 208), for instance, a defendant who had lied about his address and ultimate destination when renting a horse was found guilty of larceny for later converting the horse. Because of the fraudulent misrepresentation, the court reasoned, the defendant had never obtained legal possession (id., see King v. Semple, 1 Leach, 420, 421–424, 168 Eng.Rep. 312, 313; 1 Hawkins, Pleas of the Crown [Leach 6th ed], 135, n. 1). Thus, "larceny by trick" was born (see Hall, Theft, Law and Society [2d ed], at p. 40).

Later cases went even further, often ignoring the fact that a defendant had initially obtained possession lawfully, and instead focused upon his later intent (e.g., Queen v. Middleton, LR 2 Cr.Cas.Res. 38 [1873]; Queen v. Ashwell, 16 QBD 190 [1885]). The crime of larceny then encompassed, not only situations where the defendant initially obtained property by a trespassory taking, but many situations where an individual, possessing the requisite intent, exercised control over property inconsistent with the continued rights of the owner. During this evolutionary process, the purpose served by the crime of larceny obviously shifted from protecting society's peace to general protection of property rights.

Modern penal statutes generally have incorporated these developments under a unified definition of larceny (see e.g., American Law Institute, Model Penal Code [Tent. Draft No. 1], § 206.1 [theft is appropriation of property of another, which includes unauthorized exercise of control]). Case law, too, now tends to focus upon the actor's intent and the exercise of dominion and control over the property. Indeed, this court has recognized in construing the New York Penal Law,[1] that the "*ancient* common-law concepts of larceny" no longer

---

1. Section 155.05 of the Penal Law defines larceny: "1. A person steals property and commits larceny when, with intent to deprive another of property or to appropriate the same to himself or to a third person, he wrongfully takes, obtains, or withholds such property from an owner thereof. 2. Larceny includes a wrongful taking, obtaining or withholding of another's property, with the intent prescribed in subdivi-

strictly apply (People v. Alamo, supra, 34 N.Y.2d at p. 459, 358 N.Y.S.2d 375, 315 N.E.2d 446 [emphasis added]).

This evolution is particularly relevant to thefts occurring in modern self-service stores. In stores of that type, customers are impliedly invited to examine, try on, and carry about the merchandise on display. Thus in a sense, the owner has consented to the customer's possession of the goods for a limited purpose. That the owner has consented to that possession does not, however, preclude a conviction for larceny. If the customer exercises dominion and control wholly inconsistent with the continued rights of the owner, and the other elements of the crime are present, a larceny has occurred. Such conduct on the part of a customer satisfies the "taking" element of the crime.

It is this element that forms the core of the controversy in these cases. The defendants argue, in essence, that the crime is not established, as a matter of law, unless there is evidence that the customer departed the shop without paying for the merchandise.

Although this court has not addressed the issue, case law from other jurisdictions seems unanimous in holding that a shoplifter need not leave the store to be guilty of larceny (e.g., State v. Grant, 135 Vt. 222, 373 A.2d 847; Groomes v. United States, 155 A.2d 73 [D.C.Mun. App.], supra; People v. Baker, 365 Ill. 328, 6 N.E.2d 665; People v. Bradovich, 305 Mich. 329, 9 N.W.2d 560; accord People v. Britto, 93 Misc.2d 151, 402 N.Y.S.2d 546, supra). This is because a shopper may treat merchandise in a manner inconsistent with the owner's continued rights—and in a manner not in accord with that of prospective purchaser—without actually walking out of the store. Indeed, depending upon the circumstances of each case, a variety of conduct may be sufficient to allow the trier of fact to find a taking. It would be well-nigh impossible, and unwise, to attempt to delineate all the situations which would establish a taking. But it is possible to identify some of the factors used in determining whether the evidence is sufficient to be submitted to the fact finder.

In many cases, it will be particularly relevant that defendant concealed the goods under clothing or in a container (see, e.g., People v. Baker, 365 Ill. 328, 6 N.E.2d 665, supra; People v. Bradovich, 305 Mich. 329, 9 N.W.2d 560, supra). Such conduct is not generally expected in a self-service store and may in a proper case be deemed an exercise of dominion and control inconsistent with the store's continued rights. Other furtive or unusual behavior on the part of the defendant should also be weighed. Thus, if the defendant surveys the area while secreting the merchandise or abandoned his or her own property in exchange for the concealed goods, this may evince larcenous rather than innocent behavior. Relevant too is the customer's proximity to or movement towards one of the store's exits. Certainly it is highly probative of guilt

sion one of this section, committed in any of the following ways: (a) By conduct heretofore defined or known as common law larceny by trick, embezzlement, or obtaining property by false pretenses."

that the customer was in possession of secreted goods just a few short steps from the door or moving in that direction. Finally, possession of a known shoplifting device actually used to conceal merchandise, such as a specially designed outer garment or false bottomed carrying case, would be all but decisive.

Of course, in a particular case, any one or any combination of these factors may take on special significance. And there may be other considerations, not now identified, which should be examined. So long as it bears upon the principal issue—whether the shopper exercised control wholly inconsistent with the owner's continued rights—any attending circumstance is relevant and may be taken into account.

V

Under these principles, there was ample evidence in each case to raise a factual question as to the defendants' guilt. In *People v. Olivo*, defendant not only concealed goods in his clothing, but he did so in a particularly suspicious manner. And, when defendant was stopped, he was moving towards the door, just three feet short of exiting the store. It cannot be said as a matter of law that these circumstances failed to establish a taking.[2]

In People v. Gasparik, defendant removed the price tag and sensor device from a jacket, abandoned his own garment, put the jacket on and ultimately headed for the main floor of the store. Removal of the price tag and sensor device, and careful concealment of those items, is highly unusual and suspicious conduct for a shopper. Coupled with defendant's abandonment of his own coat and his attempt to leave the floor, those factors were sufficient to make out a prima facie case of a taking.

In People v. Spatzier, defendant concealed a book in an attaché case. Unaware that he was being observed in an overhead mirror, defendant looked furtively up and down an aisle before secreting the book. In these circumstances, given the manner in which defendant concealed the book and his suspicious behavior, the evidence was not insufficient as a matter of law.

* * *

VII

In sum, in view of the modern definition of the crime of larceny, and its purpose of protecting individual property rights, a taking of property in the self-service store context can be established by evidence that a customer exercised control over merchandise wholly inconsistent with the store's continued rights. Quite simply, a customer who crosses the line between the limited right he or she has to deal with merchan-

2. As discussed, the same evidence which establishes dominion and control in these circumstances will often establish movement of the property. And, the requisite intent generally may be inferred from all the surrounding circumstances. It would be the rare case indeed in which the evidence establishes all the other elements of the crime but would be insufficient to give rise to an inference of intent (cf. People v. Licitra, 47 N.Y.2d 554, 558–559, 419 N.Y.S.2d 461, 393 N.E.2d 456).

dise and the store owner's rights may be subject to prosecution for larceny. Such a rule should foster the legitimate interests and continued operation of self-service shops, a convenience which most members of the society enjoy.

Accordingly, in each case, the order of the Appellate Term should be affirmed.

JASEN, GABRIELLI, JONES, WACHTLER, FUCHSBERG and MEYER, JJ., concur.

In each case: Order affirmed.

(1) *Finding of Lost Goods*

PEOPLE v. BETTS

Supreme Court of Illinois, 1937.
367 Ill. 499, 11 N.E.2d 942.

JONES, JUSTICE. Plaintiff in error, Everett Betts, was convicted in the circuit court of Pike county of the larceny of three heifers, and the cause is here for a review.

Charles Williams was the owner of the heifers. They were kept in his pasture, which was about a half mile wide north and south and extended west to the Mississippi river. The pasture was inclosed by a barbed wire fence consisting of three wires; the lowest wire was one foot from the ground, the highest about four feet, and the other wire halfway between them. The fence had been repaired during the latter part of July or August. The defendant's farm, also on the Mississippi river, was about three miles away, being separated from the Williams farm by another large farm. Williams and his wife testified that they saw the heifers in their pasture about the last part of August or the first of September and that they did not go to the pasture again until October 16, at which time the heifers were gone. Defendant testified that he first saw the heifers in his pasture sometime in August; that he did not know whose they were, and that he always waited for the owners to come after stray cattle, instead of inquiring for the owner. Several other people kept their cattle in defendant's pasture for hire. One of them was Guy Crowder, who, with his son Carl, was previously tried and acquitted on a charge of larceny of the same heifers. Williams and his wife testified that they asked defendant, about a day or two after they missed the heifers, if he had seen three heifers and that he said he had not. Mrs. Williams referred to them as "stray heifers" and testified that she told defendant that if he saw them wandering around to let them know. Defendant denied that Mrs. Williams asked him about the heifers at all, and said that Williams asked him, after the heifers had been disposed of in October, if he had seen "any cow" and defendant told him he had not, not thinking about these three heifers.

The evidence is conflicting as to the disposal of the heifers. Defendant testified that Guy Crowder owed him $50 pasture rent after deducting a $10 difference in threshing accounts; that Crowder asked if he could take the heifers to St. Louis and sell them to get the money with which to pay defendant; that he told Crowder they did not belong to him, but were "strays" and that he would have nothing to do with it. Crowder and his son Carl testified that defendant sold the heifers to Guy without saying anything about the ownership. The Crowders hauled the heifers away from defendant's farm on Saturday, October 5. They took them to the farm of Tony Arth, near Collinsville, arriving about 3 a.m. Sunday. On that day they sold them to Arth for $66 and a few days later paid defendant $50. The uncontradicted testimony of eight witnesses shows defendant's good reputation for truth and honesty.

One of the numerous errors assigned is that the evidence is not sufficient to sustain a conviction of larceny. It was incumbent on the People to prove the corpus delicti, one element of which was that the heifers were lost to the owner through a felonious stealing.　.　.　. While the corpus delicti may be proved by circumstantial evidence, the fact that the heifers were in defendant's pasture soon after they disappeared from the Williams pasture is not of itself, enough to prove they had been stolen, or that defendant had any connection with it. The exclusive, unexplained possession of recently stolen property may raise an inference of guilt sufficient to authorize a conviction for larceny in the absence of other evidence raising a reasonable doubt of guilt.　.　.　. The rule is not applicable to this case. In the first place, it was not proved that the heifers were stolen from the Williams pasture. There is no evidence as to how they got out of there. While the testimony shows the fence had been repaired in July or August, there is no testimony to show that it was in good repair when the heifers left the pasture, or that they could not reasonably have escaped or that defendant's fence would prevent the entry of estrays. The record shows that cattle frequently strayed in that vicinity. The testimony of both Williams and his wife refers to them as "stray heifers," indicating they realized that they might have escaped from the pasture unaided.

The People claim that, even if a taking from the owner's pasture was not proved, still defendant was guilty of larceny by his subsequent conversion of the heifers to his own benefit. It is the general rule of law, in the case of lost goods, that if the finder, at the time of finding, intends to deprive the owner permanently of his property, and if he knows or has a reasonable clue as to who the owner is, he is guilty of larceny.　.　.　. Tested by this rule defendant has not been proved guilty of larceny. There is no proof that he knew who the owner was, that he ever visited the Williams farm, or ever saw their cattle. The People stress the fact that one heifer had a stub horn and another a peaked face. While that would make description or identification of the heifers easier, yet, without a showing that defendant know Williams had heifers of that description, it does not tend to prove his guilt. Defendant was under no duty to advertise or to make inquiry for the owner as far as the crime of larceny is concerned. Although the elder Crowder claims that he purchased the heifers from the defendant, the surrounding facts and circumstances indicate the truth of defendant's testimony that he permitted the Crowders to take the heifers and sell them in order that they might pay him for pasture rent. The alleged sale does not bear the earmarks of an ordinary transaction. It would be quite unusual for a poor tenant to make a sale of livestock to someone else and receive no down payment or some evidence of an indebtedness. The stock was sold by Crowder and the $50 he sent by his son was not delivered for some days after the father returned from the East St. Louis stockyards.

In order to constitute larceny by conversion of goods found or of stray animals, there must be, at the time of the finding, an intent to deprive the owner of his property. The evidence does not show such intent here. Defendant allowed the heifers to remain openly in his pasture for some 30 to 40 days where a number of other people were pasturing their cattle. The evidence tends to show he had no intent to convert them to his own benefit, at least up to the time they were taken away by the Crowders. Assuming that he later sold them and that the sale showed such an intent formed subsequent to the finding of the animals in his pasture, such an intent will not relate back to the finding so as to constitute the crime of larceny. . . . The testimony shows defendant's good reputation for truth and honesty. However poor his judgment may have been in failing to make inquiry to learn the name of the owner of the property, the proof is not sufficient to support a conviction for larceny.

The judgment is reversed, and the cause is remanded.

FARTHING, C. J., and SHAW, J., dissenting.

NOTES

1. In Brooks v. State, 35 Ohio St. 46 (1878), the defendant, a street cleaner, found a roll of money; without notifying his fellow workers nearby, he picked up the money and put it in his pocket. A few minutes later, the defendant quit his job and shortly thereafter began to make various purchases with the money. Newton, who had lost the money about a month before the defendant found it, advertised his loss in several local newspapers, but there was no evidence that the defendant had seen any of the notices.

In affirming the defendant's conviction of larceny, the Supreme Court of Ohio stated:

"Larceny may be committed of property that is casually lost as well as of that which is not. The title to the property, and its constructive possession, still remains in the owner; and the finder if he takes possession of it for his own use, and not for the benefit of the owner, would be guilty of trespass, unless the circumstances were such to show that it had been abandoned by the owner. . . . In Baker v. The State, 29 Ohio St. 184, . . . it was . . . laid down, that 'when a person finds goods that have actually been lost, and takes possession with intent to appropriate them to his own use, really believing, at the time, or having good ground to believe, that the owner can be found, it is larceny.'

"It must not be understood from the rule, as thus stated, that the finder is bound to use diligence or take pains in making search for the owner. His belief, or grounds of belief, in regard to finding the owner, is not to be determined by the degree of diligence that he might be able to use to accomplish that purpose, but by the circumstances apparent to him at the time of finding the property. If the property has not been abandoned by the owner, it is the subject of larceny by the finder, when, at the time he finds it, he had reasonable ground to believe, from the nature of the property or the circumstances under which it is found, that if he does not conceal but deals honestly with it, the owner will appear or be ascertained. But before the finder can be guilty of larceny, the intent to steal the property must have existed at the time he took it into his possession. . . .

"The case was fairly submitted to the jury; and from an examination of the evidence, we find no ground for interfering with the action of the court below in refusing a new trial."

Okey, J., dissented in an opinion in which Gilmore, C. J., concurred. The dissent stated:

"I do not think the plaintiff was properly convicted. . . . [The money] had lain there several weeks, and the owner had ceased to make search for it. The evidence fails to show that the plaintiff [in error] had any information of a loss previous to the finding, and in his testimony he denied such notice. There was no mark on the money to indicate the owner, nor was there any thing in the attending circumstances pointing to one owner more than another. . . . .

2. Compare State v. Dean, 49 Iowa 73 (1878). In that case, the defendant, following a flood in which large stocks of merchandise were swept away, found certain items of clothing on the banks of a nearby creek. He took the clothing home and had his wife wash it. While the items were drying on a clothes-line outside defendant's house, they were discovered and the defendant was indicted and convicted of larceny. In reversing his conviction, the Supreme Court of Iowa stated:

" . . . There was no evidence tending to show that the defendant knew who owned the . . . property, and as to a part of it the ownership does not seem to have been ascertained yet.

"The defendant asked the court to give an instruction in these words: 'If you find from the evidence that said goods were lost; that the same were found by the defendant; that at the time he found the same he did not know who owned them; that there were no marks upon or about the goods showing to whom they belonged, so that defendant could identify the owner at once—even though the defendant could afterwards have discovered the owner by honest diligence—then you must acquit the defendant.' The court refused to give this instruction, and instructed the jury as follows: 'Lost goods may be the subject of larceny, and should receive the same protection from the civil and criminal law as goods in any other situation. Where the finder knows or has the immediate means of knowing who was the owner, and, instead of returning the goods, converts them to his own use, such conversion will constitute larceny. Reasonable diligence in discovering the owner should be shown by the finding party. The intention of a party committing a larceny at first may not be felonious, but if the property is wrongfully used or converted it is larceny.' In giving these instructions and in refusing to instruct as asked, we think that the court erred. . . . The crime, if committed, must consist in the original taking. It cannot consist in a subsequent lack of diligence in attempting to find the owner, nor in a subsequent conversion. . . . .

3. Consider and compare the provisions of § 16–2 of the Illinois Criminal Code (S.H.A. Chap. 38):

A person who obtains control over lost or mislaid property commits theft when he:

(a) Knows or learns the identity of the owner or knows, or is aware of, or learns of a reasonable method of identifying the owner. and

(b) Fails to take reasonable measures to restore the property to the owner, and

(c) Intends to reprive the owner permanently of the use or benefit of the property.

4. The Model Penal Code, in § 223.5, provides: "A person who comes into control of property of another that he knows to have been lost, mislaid, or delivered under a mistake as to the nature or amount of the property or the identity of the recipient is guilty of theft if, with purpose to deprive the owner thereof, he fails to take reasonable measures to restore the property to a person entitled to have."

How does this provision differ from the rules in *Betts* and the cases in Notes 1 and 2?

(2) *Trickery*

In the Connecticut case of State v. Robington,[1] the defendant went to an automobile dealer and said that she wanted to buy a black Chrysler sedan. The dealer turned over to her the model she requested, on the assurance that she would either return the car on the following Monday or pay the sum of $3,015. The defendant failed to do either. It was found that she had not intended to pay for the car, and that the dealer had not intended to transfer the title of the car to her at the time he delivered possession. On appeal, the defendant argued that title had passed to her, and that, as a consequence, she could not be guilty of larceny. The Supreme Court of Errors of Connecticut stated: "The state was attempting to establish the crime of larceny by trick. This crime is committed when one obtains 'the possession of personal property of another by deception, artifice, fraud, or force, with the intent on the part of the person obtaining it to convert it to his own use and permanently to deprive the owner of his property.' It should be added, however, that 'if the owner intends to part with the title to the property as well as possession, whatever other crime may have been committed, it will not be theft.'" The court held that because the dealer delivered the car to the defendant on condition of either return or payment, the sale was not complete, and title had not passed. The larceny conviction of the defendant was therefore sustained.

1. 137 Conn. 140, 75 A.2d 394 (1950).

In Hawes v. State,[2] the defendant took Hudson for a ride in a Ford to demonstrate the car's performance in order to induce its purchase by Hudson. Hudson said he would buy the car and gave the defendant $100 in payment. The defendant then drove away, on the pretext that he was going to the courthouse to get the proper papers and would return shortly. He failed to return and kept both the car and the money. On these facts it was held that he could not be guilty of larceny of the money, inasmuch as he obtained title to the money at the time it was delivered by Hudson.

In Murchinson v. State,[3] the court stated: "The law is well settled that 'if the owner of money or a chattel delivers it to another with the intention not only of parting with the possession, but also of investing the person to whom it is delivered with the title to it, such person is not guilty of larceny in receiving it, although the delivery was induced by the most flagrant fraud . . . for the reason that the title having passed, there is no one other than himself in whom an indictment for larceny can lay the ownership and possession of the thing taken.' 36 C.J. p. 777, § 139."

(3) *Delivery by Mistake*

UNITED STATES v. ROGERS
United States Court of Appeals, Fourth Circuit, 1961.
289 F.2d 433.

HAYNSWORTH, CIRCUIT JUDGE. The defendant has appealed from his conviction under the "bank robbery statute," complaining that the proof did not show the commission of larceny. . . . We think the proof did support the conviction. . . .

There was testimony showing that, at the request of his brother, the defendant took a payroll check, payable to the brother in the face amount of $97.92, to a bank where the brother maintained an account. In accordance with the brother's request, he asked the teller to deposit $80 to the credit of the brother's account and to deliver to him the balance of the check in cash. The teller was inexperienced. She first inquired of another teller whether the check could be credited to an account in part and cashed in part. Having been told that this was permissible, she required the defendant's endorsement on the check, and, misreading its date (12 06 59) as the amount payable, she deducted the $80 deposit and placed $1,126.59 on the counter. There were two strapped packages, each containing $500, and $126.59 in miscellaneous bills and change. The defendant took the $1,126.59 in cash thus placed upon the counter and departed.

There was also testimony that when the day's business was done, the teller who handled the transaction was found to be short in her accounts by $1,108.67, the exact amount of the difference between the

2. 216 Ala. 151, 112 So. 761 (1927).   3. 30 Ala.App. 15, 199 So. 897 (1940).

$1,206.59, for which she had supposed the check to have been drawn, and $97.92, its actual face amount, and that her adding machine tape showed that she had accepted the check as having been drawn for $1,206.59.

There was corroboration from other witnesses of some phases of this story as told by the tellers and the bookkeeper.

The defendant agreed that he took the check to the bank for his brother, asked that $80 be credited to his brother's account, and that the excess be paid to him in cash. He stated, however, that he received in cash only the $17.92, to which he was entitled, denying that he had received the larger sum.

The case was submitted to the jury under instructions that they should find the defendant guilty if they found the much larger sum was placed upon the counter and was taken by the defendant with the intention to appropriate the overpayment, or if he thereafter formed the intention to, and did, appropriate the overpayment to his own use. . . .

We accept the defendant's premise that . . . the bank robbery act reaches only the offense of larceny as that crime has been defined by the common law. It does not encompass the crimes of embezzlement from a bank, reached by another statute, or obtaining goods by false pretense. . . .

The defendant's premise that the prosecution was required to show the commission of larceny does not lead, however, to the conclusion that he should have been acquitted. The indictment charged larceny and the evidence offered by the prosecution, if accepted by the jury, proved the commission of that crime, not false pretense, embezzlement or some other lesser offense.

An essential element of the crime of larceny, the " 'felonious taking and carrying' away the personal goods of another," is that the taking must be trespassory. It is an invasion of the other's right to possession, and therein is found the principal distinction between larceny and other related offenses.

It has long been recognized, however, that when the transferor acts under a unilateral mistake of fact, his delivery of a chattel may be ineffective to transfer title or his right to possession. If the transferee, knowing of the transferor's mistake, receives the goods with the intention of appropriating them, his receipt and removal of them is a trespass and his offense is larceny.

Such a situation was presented in Regina v. Middleton . . . [1873]. There it appeared that the defendant had a credit balance of 11 s. in a postal savings account. He obtained a warrant for the withdrawal of 10 s. which he presented to the postal clerk. The clerk mistakenly referred to the wrong letter of advice, one which had been received in connection with the prospective withdrawal of a much larger sum by another depositor. The clerk then placed upon the counter a 5 L note,

3 sovereigns, a half crown and silver and copper amounting altogether to 8 L 16 s. 10 d. The defendant gathered up the money and departed. The jury found that the defendant was aware of the clerk's mistake and took the money with intent to steal it. His conviction of larceny was affirmed by the Court of Criminal Appeals, the fifteen judges dividing eleven to four.

The majority of the judges in Middleton's case were divided among themselves as to the basis for the conclusion that there was the requisite taking. Seven of them were of the opinion that, because of the clerk's mistake as to the identity of the depositor, no legal interest in the money passed to Middleton. Three of them thought that the clerk had no authority to transfer to Middleton any interest in any money in excess of 10 s. One judge was of the opinion that the delivery was not complete when the clerk placed the money upon the counter and that Middleton's act of picking it up and removing it was a taking.

Subsequently, it appears to have become settled in England that, if the initial receipt of the chattel is innocent, its subsequent conversion cannot be larceny, but, if the recipient knows at the time he is receiving more than his due and intends to convert it to his own use, he is guilty of larceny. . . . That is the established rule of the American cases. . . .

The District Court went too far, however, when it told the jury it might convict if, though his initial receipt of the overpayment was innocent, the defendant thereafter formed the intention to, and did, convert the overpayment.

The charge as given finds support in earlier cases. . . . Subsequent cases in the United States and in England, however, have consistently held that, if there is a mutual mistake and the recipient is innocent of wrongful purpose at the time of his initial receipt of the overpayment, its subsequent conversion by him cannot be larceny.

Upon the retrial, therefore, the jury should be instructed that among the essential elements of the offense are (1) that the defendant knew when he received the money from the teller or picked it up from the counter that it was more than his due and (2) that he took it from the bank with the intention of converting it. . . .

Reversed and remanded.

NOTE

In Merry v. Green, 7 M. & W. 623, 151 Eng.Rep. 916 (1841), Merry purchased a bureau at a public auction. He later discovered a secret drawer in the bureau containing money and other valuables, which he appropriated to his own use. He was prosecuted for felony, but the magistrate discharged him, doubting whether a felony had been committed on these facts. Merry then instituted an action for trespass and false imprisonment and recovered damages; however, on appeal the case was remanded for a new trial on the ground that there was evidence on which the jury could find that Merry had committed larceny of the money and valuables. The court stated that if Merry had a reasonable ground for believing that he had purchased both the bureau and any contents, he had a colorable right to the property found in the bureau and would not be guilty of larceny. The court also stated, however: "If we assume, as the defendant's case was, that the plaintiff had express notice that he was not to have any title to the contents of the secretary if there happened to be anything in it, and indeed without such express notice if he had no ground to believe that he had bought the contents, we are all of opinion that there was evidence to make out a case of larceny. It was contended that there was a delivery of the secretary, and the money in it, to the plaintiff as his own property, which gave him a lawful possession, and that his subsequent misappropriation did not constitute a felony. But it seems to us, that though there was a delivery of the secretary, and a lawful property in it thereby vested in the plaintiff, there was no delivery so as to give a lawful possession of the purse and money. The vendor had no intention to deliver it, nor the vendee to receive it; both were ignorant of its existence; and when the plaintiff discovered that there was a secret drawer containing the purse and money, it was a simple case of finding, and the law applicable to all cases of finding applies to this. . . .

(4) Bailee Misappropriation

Illustrative of the effect which an expanding commercial community had upon the law of larceny is the 1473 "Carrier's Case."[1] There, the defendant was hired to transport some bales to Southampton. Instead, he broke open the bales and took the contents. He was convicted of "felony." It was argued on his behalf that he had lawful possession of the property, and thus he could not be guilty of taking the goods "with vi et armis [or] against the peace." The conviction, however, was sustained. Choke, J., stated: "It seems to me that where a man has goods in his possession by reason of a bailment, he cannot take them feloniously, being in possession; but again it seems to me that here there is felony, for here the things which were inside the bales were not bailed to him; only the bales as an entire thing were bailed ut supra to carry; in which case if he had given the bales or sold them etc., it is no felony, but when he broke them and took out of them what was inside he did that without warrant, as if one bailed a tun of wine to carry, if he sells the tun it is not felony nor trespass, but if he took some out it is felony; and here the twenty pounds were not bailed to him, and peradventure he knew not of them at the time of the bailment. So it is if I bail the key to my chamber to one to guard my chamber and he takes my goods from my chamber, it is felony for they are not bailed to him."

The doctrine of the Carrier's Case was later extended to cover not only "breaking bale" but also "breaking bulk." Thus, one would be guilty of larceny if he took a part of any goods delivered to him in bulk, although he would not be guilty of larceny if he took the entire mass.[2]

1. Year Book, 13 Ed. IV, 9 p. 5 (1473). For an excellent discussion of the Carrier's Case and the commercial situation which probably led to the decision, see Hall, Theft, Law and Society 3–33 (2d ed. 1952).

2. Rex v. Howell, 7 Car. & P. 325, 173 Eng.Rep. 145 (1836).

For the most part, modern statutes have abolished these distinctions, and it is larceny (or some other crime) to convert any goods entrusted to another, whether they are taken in whole or in part.

UNITED STATES v. PARKER

United States Court of Appeals, Fourth Circuit, 1975.
522 F.2d 801.

PER CURIAM: On February 15, 1974, Charles Edward Parker rented an automobile from the Avis Rent-A-Car System, Inc., while at National Airport in Washington, D. C., an area within federal jurisdiction. According to his rental agreement, the car was to be returned three days later. It was not until April 18, 1974, however, that Avis was able to recover the car. On the basis of these events, Parker was indicted and convicted under 18 U.S.C. § 13, the Federal Assimilative Crimes Statute, for violating Section 18.1–163 of the Code of Virginia.[1] He now appeals this conviction, claiming that Section 18.1–163 of the Virginia Code is unconstitutional, both on its face and as applied.

I

The first sentence of that statute clearly sets forth two elements of the conduct prohibited thereunder: (1) the actor must be a bailee of an animal, aircraft, vehicle, boat or vessel; and (2) he must fail to return such possession in accordance with the terms of the bailment agreement. Nowhere in that statute, however, is there an explicit requirement of criminal intent. Petitioner argues that such omission renders the statute fatally defective. We disagree.

At common law, criminal intent was an essential element of proof of every crime. United States v. Balint, 258 U.S. 250, 42 S.Ct. 301 (1922). It remains an essential element, today, in crimes *mala in se,* particularly ones involving the taking of another's property. Morissette v. United States, 342 U.S. 246, 72 S.Ct. 240 (1952). Undoubtedly cognizant of these principles, the Virginia Supreme Court of Appeals upheld the challenged statute as constitutional on the basis that the requirement of criminal intent would be read into it by the courts. Maye v. Commonwealth, 213 Va. 48, 189 S.E.2d 350 (1972). While the Virginia court did not consider the nature of this intent which would be required under the act, we think that when and if faced with that issue it will look to the common law elements of larceny. Our conclusion is

---

1. Va.Code § 18.1–163 states:

Failure to return such animal, aircraft, vehicle or boat. If any person comes into the possession as bailee of any animal, aircraft, vehicle, boat or vessel, and fail to return the same to the bailor, in accordance with the bailment agreement, he shall be deemed guilty of larceny thereof and receive the same punishment, according to the value of the thing stolen, prescribed for the punishment of the larceny of goods and chattels. The failure to return to the bailor such animal, aircraft, vehicle, boat or vessel, within five days from the time the bailee has agreed in writing to return the same shall be prima facie evidence of larceny by such bailee of such animal, aircraft, vehicle, boat or vessel.

[Currently this crime is codified as § 18.2–117.]

based on the label affixed by the legislature to the crime defined: larceny after bailment. Such label clearly indicates an intent to create a new statutory crime, incorporating some elements of the existing crime of larceny, defined as it was at common law.[2] Elements of common law larceny which are consistent with a taking by a bailee, such as the intent at the time of taking to permanently deprive another of his possession, would be incorporated, while elements not consistent therewith, such as a trespassory taking, would not be. Parker's contentions that the statute is void for failure to define the time and nature of the requisite criminal intent are therefore meritless. The statute attacked is not so vague as to deny to the average individual of ordinary intelligence fair notice that certain actions are proscribed.

II

Parker directs his second attack to the presumption written into the statute that the failure of a bailee to return the bailed possession within five days of the date agreed upon in writing constitutes prima facie evidence of larceny. He asserts that it is unconstitutional both on its face and as applied to the present case. We must again disagree.

Aside from the question as to whether the presumption is constitutional on its face, any harm resulting from its application to the present case was avoided by the trial court's exhaustive instructions to the jury:

> The crime charged in the case requires proof of specific intent before the defendant can be convicted.
>
> . . . Such intent may be determined from all the facts and circumstances surrounding the case. . . .
>
> . . .
>
> If you find beyond a reasonable doubt that the defendant failed to return the motor vehicle to Avis within five days from the time he had agreed in writing to do so [. . .] and such failure is not satisfactorily explained [. . .] you may find from these facts and may draw from these facts the inference [. . .] that at the time he failed to return it he did so with the intent to steal the vehicle.
>
> *This is an inference which you may but are not obliged to draw.* [Emphasis added]

These instructions were based not on the statutory presumption assailed by Parker but on standard legal principles applicable in the absence of such a presumption. As a result, the jury's verdict was not rendered infirm by the alleged invalidity of that statutory presumption.

2. Virginia has not enacted a statutory definition of larceny, looking instead to the Common Law.

III

That the vehicle allegedly stolen was returned prior to prosecution in no way undermines the jury's verdict. It does, of course, constitute relevant evidence on the issue of whether Parker originally intended to deprive Avis of the car permanently. It does not, however, constitute an absolute defense. Were we to hold otherwise, to be consistent we would have to declare that the perpetrator of a theft could escape prosecution by returning stolen items prior to institution of criminal proceedings. Such a holding would be contrary to the dictates of commonsense; moreover, it would violate well-established principles of law.

Accordingly, the judgment of the district court is

Affirmed.

(5) Continuing Trespass

In Regina v. Riley,[1] the prosecutor put some sheep into a field owned by John Clarke. The defendant subsequently put twenty-nine sheep into the same field for a night, paying Clarke for the right to do so. He took them out early the next morning and drove them to another farm to sell them. On counting the lambs, the buyer discovered there were thirty, instead of twenty-nine. The defendant offered to draw out one lamb if the buyer wished him to do so. The buyer took all thirty. The prosecutor later identified one of the thirty lambs as his. It was found that the defendant had taken the prosecutor's lamb from the field by mistake; nevertheless, the defendant was held guilty of larceny, and the conviction was upheld on appeal. Parke, B., stated: "The original taking was not lawful, but a trespass, upon which an action in that form might have been founded; but it was not felony, because there was no intention to appropriate. There was, however, a continuing trespass up to the time of appropriation, and at that time, therefore, the felony was committed."

In the 1868 Maine case of State v. Coombs,[2] the defendant was charged with the larceny of a horse, sleigh and buffalo robes. He had borrowed the horse and sleigh, representing that he intended to drive to a certain place and be gone a certain length of time. In fact, he intended to drive to a more distant place and be gone a longer time than he stated. He did not intend to steal the property at the time he borrowed it. Subsequently, however, he sold it. His conviction of larceny was sustained on appeal. The court stated: "In the case at bar, the prisoner obtained possession of the property by fraud. This negatives the idea of a contract, or that the possession of the prisoner was a lawful one, when he sold the horse. He was not the bailee of the owner, but was a wrongdoer from the beginning; and the owner had a right to reclaim his property at any time. * * * The color of

1. 6 Cox C.C. 88, 169 Eng.Rep. 674   2. 55 Me. 477 (1868).
(1853).

consent to the possession obtained by fraud, does not change the character of the offence from larceny to trespass or other wrongful act. In such case it is not necessary that the felonious intent should exist at the time of the original taking to constitute larceny, the wrongful taking being all the while continuous."

In a 1945 Virginia case, Dunlavey v. Commonwealth,[3] two men had stolen an automobile in the city of Richmond. Three days after the theft, Dunlavey met the thieves and agreed to push the stolen automobile with his own car in order to start the motor of the stolen vehicle. The three had apparently agreed that Dunlavey would purchase some parts from the stolen automobile. After they had succeeded in driving the stolen car to a secluded section of the city, they were arrested. Dunlavey was later charged with and convicted of larceny of an automobile. On appeal the Commonwealth argued that once property is stolen the trespass against the true owner is deemed to be a continuing one as long as the stolen property remains in the possession of the original thief, and when another party later intervenes to assist in the asportation he is deemed to join in with and become a party to the continuing trespass. In affirming the conviction, the Supreme Court of Appeals of Virginia stated: ". . . The part taken by the accused was one incident of a continuous transaction. He was in possession of the automobile when he started it by pushing it, even though his possession might have been a joint one. His conduct amounted to a trespass upon the constructive possession of the true owner with *animus furandi*. Larceny has been held to be a continuous offense. This seems to be the weight of authority in other jurisdictions. . . ."

For a general analysis of the "continuing trespass" doctrine, see Davies, Continuing Trespass, 58 J.Crim.L., C. & P.S. 24 (1968).

(b) CARRYING AWAY

Miss Flora May Barr checked her trunk with the Goodrich Transportation Company and took passage on a steamship belonging to that company. On arrival at her destination, she presented her check for the trunk. She received in return a trunk, other than her own, filled with waste paper. Subsequently, Miss Barr's trunk and its contents were found in the possession of the defendant and, accordingly, he was charged with and convicted of larceny. In affirming the conviction, the Supreme Court of Illinois, in the 1906 case of Aldrich v. People,[1] stated:

> [This] case comes within the rule laid down in Commonwealth v. Barry, 125 Mass. 390. [That] case, in all of its essential facts, is like the case at bar. The charge was for the larceny of a trunk, and the offense was committed by the shifting of checks, as is alleged in the case at bar. In disposing of the case the court said: 'It does not appear that the question whether there was an asportation at or before the changing of

3. 184 Va. 521, 35 S.E.2d 763 (1945).   1. 224 Ill. 622, 79 N.E. 964 (1906).

the checks was raised at the trial. An asportation at that precise time was unimportant. The real question was whether the defendant then, feloniously and with an intent to steal, set in motion an innocent agency by which the trunk and its contents were to be removed from the possession of the true owner and into the defendant's possession, and by means of such agency effected the purpose. . . . There is no occasion that the carrying away be by the hand of the party accused, for, if he procured an innocent agent to take the property, by means of which he became possessed of it, he will himself be the principal offender. 3 Chitty on Crim.Law, 925. . . .

It will thus be seen that an asportation may be effected by means of innocent human agency as well as mechanical agency, or by the offender's own hands. One may effect an asportation of personal property so as to be guilty of larceny by attaching a gas pipe to the pipes of the company and thus draw the gas into his house and consuming it without its passing through the meter. Clark & Marshall on Law of Crimes, p. 446, and cases cited in note; Woods v. People, 222 Ill. 293, 78 N.E. 607. From these cases the law appears to be well settled that, where, with the intent to steal, the wrongdoer employs or sets in motion any agency, either animate or inanimate, with the design of effecting a transfer of the possession of the goods of another to him in order that he may feloniously convert and steal them, the larceny will be complete, if, in pursuance of such agency, the goods come into the hands of the thief and he feloniously converts them to his own use, and in such case a conviction may be had upon a common-law indictment charging a felonious taking and carrying away of such goods. . . .

What if the thief fails in his attempt to carry away goods? In the case of People v. Lardner,[2] the defendant took some beaded bags from a show case and put them in the pocket of an overcoat he was carrying on his arm. When a salesman's suspicion was aroused the defendant departed from the store but left his overcoat behind, with the merchandise in it, on a counter about six feet away from the one from which he had taken the objects. This was held to be a "carrying away" within the meaning of the larceny provision of the Illinois Criminal Code then in effect.

In People v. Baker,[3] it was said: "Any change of location whereby control of the article is, with intent to steal, transferred from the true owner to the thief is sufficient. . . . The fact that possession was brief and the goods were not removed from the store is immaterial."

Carrying away, without achieving actual possession, however, is insufficient. In the early California case of People v. Myer,[4] the defendant lifted an overcoat from a store dummy and started to walk

2. 300 Ill. 264, 133 N.E. 375 (1921).   4. 75 Cal. 383, 17 P. 431 (1888).
3. 365 Ill. 328, 6 N.E.2d 665 (1937).

away with it. The coat, however, was secured to the dummy by a chain, which the defendant was unable to break. It was held that the defendant was not guilty of larceny, inasmuch as he never had actual possession of the coat.

(c) PERSONAL PROPERTY

LUND v. COMMONWEALTH

Supreme Court of Virginia, 1977.
217 Va. 688, 232 S.E.2d 745.

I'ANSON, C. J., delivered the opinion of the court.

Defendant, Charles Walter Lund, was charged in an indictment with the theft of keys, computer cards, computer print-outs and using "without authority computer operation time and services of Computer Center Personnel at Virginia Polytechnic Institute and State University [V.P.I. or University] . . . with intent to defraud, such property and services having a value of one hundred dollars or more." . . .

Defendant was a graduate student in statistics and a candidate for a Ph.D. degree at V.P.I. The preparation of his dissertation on the subject assigned to him by his faculty advisor required the use of computer operation time and services of the computer center personnel at the University. His faculty advisor neglected to arrange for defendant's use of the computer, but defendant used it without obtaining the proper authorization.

The computer used by the defendant was leased on an annual basis by V.P.I. from the IBM Corporation. The rental was paid by V.P.I. which allocates the cost of the computer center to various departments within the University by charging it to the budget of that department. This is a bookkeeping entry, and no money actually changes hands. The departments are allocated "computer credits [in dollars] back for their use [on] a proportional basis of their [budgetary] allotments." Each department manager receives a monthly statement showing the allotments used and the running balance in each account of his department.

An account is established when a duly authorized administrator or "department head" fills out a form allocating funds to a department of the University and an individual. When such form is received, the computer center assigns an account number to this allocation and provides a key to a locked post office box which is also numbered to the authorized individual and department. The account number and the post office box number are the access code which must be provided with each request before the computer will process a "deck of cards" prepared by the user and delivered to computer center personnel. The computer print-outs are usually returned to the locked post office box. When the product is too large for the box, a "check" is placed in the box, and it is used to receive the print-outs at the "computer center main window."

Defendant came under surveillance on October 12, 1974, because of complaints from various departments that unauthorized charges were being made to one or more of their accounts. When confronted by the University's investigator, defendant initially denied that he had used the computer service, but later admitted that he had. He gave to the investigator seven keys for boxes assigned to other persons. One of these keys was secreted in his sock. He told the investigating officer he had been given the keys by another student. A large number of computer cards and print-outs were taken from defendant's apartment.

The director of the computer center testified that the unauthorized sum spent out of the accounts associated with the seven post office box keys, amounted to $5,065. He estimated that on the basis of the computer cards and print-outs obtained from the defendant, as much as $26,384.16 in unauthorized computer time had been used by the defendant. He said, however, that the value of the cards and print-outs obtained from the defendant was "whatever scrap paper is worth."

Defendant testified that he used the computer without specific authority. He stated that he knew he was a large computer user, but, because he was doing work on his doctoral dissertation, he did not consider this use excessive or that "he was doing anything wrong."

Four faculty members testified in defendant's behalf. They all agreed that computer time "probably would have been" or "would have been" assigned to defendant if properly requested. . . .

* * *

The defendant contends that his conviction of grand larceny of the keys, computer cards, and computer print-outs cannot be upheld under the provisions of Code § 18.1–100 because (1) there was no evidence that the articles were stolen, or that they had a value of $100 or more, and (2) computer time and services are not the subject of larceny under the provisions of Code §§ 18.1–100 or 18.1–118.

Code § 18.1–100 (now § 18.2–95) provides as follows:*

"Any person who: (1) Commits larceny from the person of another of money or other thing of value of five dollars or more, or

(2) Commits simple larceny not from the person of another of goods and chattels of the value of one hundred dollars or more, shall be deemed guilty of grand larceny . . . .."

Section 18.1–118 (now § 18.2–178) provides as follows:

"If any person obtain, by any false pretense or token, from any person, with intent to defraud, money or other property which may be the subject of larceny, he shall be deemed guilty of larceny thereof; . . . .."

The Commonwealth concedes that the defendant could not be convicted of grand larceny of the keys and computer cards because

---

* The 1980 amendment raised the value for grand larceny not from the person to $200 or more. See Virginia Code § 18.2–95. Editor.

there was no evidence that those articles were stolen and that they had a market value of $100 or more. The Commonwealth argues, however, that the evidence shows the defendant violated the provisions of § 18.1–118 when he obtained by false pretense or token, with intent to defraud, the computer print-outs which had a value of over $5,000.

Under the provisions of Code § 18.1–118, for one to be guilty of the crime of larceny by false pretense, he must make a false representation of an existing fact with knowledge of its falsity and, on that basis, obtain from another person money or other property which may be the subject of larceny, with the intent to defraud.

At common law, larceny is the taking and carrying away of the goods and chattels of another with intent to deprive the owner of the possession thereof permanently. Code § 18.1–100 defines grand larceny as a taking from the person of another money or other thing of value of five dollars or more or the taking not from the person of another goods and chattels of the value of $100 or more. The phrase "goods and chattels" cannot be interpreted to include computer time and services in light of the often repeated mandate that criminal statutes must be strictly construed.

At common law, labor or services could not be the subject of the crime of false pretense because neither time nor services may be taken and carried away. It has been generally held that, in the absence of a clearly expressed legislative intent, labor or services could not be the subject of the statutory crime of false pretense. McCray, supra; 2 Wharton, Criminal Law and Procedure § 604 at 369 (Anderson ed. 1957). Some jurisdictions have amended their criminal codes specifically to make it a crime to obtain labor or services by means of false pretense. E.g., New York Penal Code § 165.15, New Jersey Penal Code ch. 2A:111; and California Criminal Code § 322. We have no such provision in our statutes.

Furthermore, the unauthorized *use* of the computer is not the subject of larceny. Nowhere in Code § 18.1–100 or § 18.1–118 do we find the word "use." The language of the statutes connotes more than just the unauthorized use of the property of another. It refers to a taking and carrying away of a certain concrete article of personal property. See People v. Ashworth, 220 App.Div. 498, 222 N.Y.S. 24, 27 (1927). There it was held that the unauthorized *use* of machinery and spinning facilities of another to process wool did not constitute larceny under New York's false pretense statute.

We hold that labor and services and the unauthorized use of the University's computer cannot be construed to be subjects of larceny under the provisions of Code §§ 18.1–100 and 18.1–118.

* * *

For the reasons stated, the judgment of the trial court is reversed, and the indictment is quashed.

Reversed.

NOTES

1. As a result of this decision, the Virginia General Assembly, at its 1978 session, first enacted a new provision that was codified as § 18.2–98.1, making "computer time" or computer services or data processing services "personal property" within the meaning of the larceny, embezzlement, and false pretenses statutes. In 1984, however, the legislature repealed § 18.2–98.1 as it enacted, at the same time, a comprehensive statute called the "Virginia Computer Crimes Act," codified in § 18.2–152.1 et seq. In its definitions section (18.2–152.2), the statute considers as "property" both tangibles and intangibles, as well as computer services in the broadest sense. The comprehensive act creates a number of new statutory crimes, such as Computer fraud (§ 18.2–152.3), Computer trespass (§ 18.2–152.4), Computer invasion of privacy (§ 18.2–152.5), Theft of computer services (§ 18.2–152.6); and Personal trespass by computer (§ 18.2–152.7).

In 1990 a 24-year old Cornell University graduate student was accused of planting a computer virus that crippled 6,000 university, corporate and military computers across the nation. Is such conduct a violation of a computer fraud and abuse statute that makes it a felony to intentionally access the computer of another without authorization, even though the accused "hacker" did not take any information out of the computer nor used it for other purposes?

The difficulty encountered by the Virginia Supreme Court is obviated in states which have statutes broadly defining "property" to be "anything of value." E.g., Illinois Revised Stats., c. 38, § 15–1.

2. In State v. Jackson, 218 N.C. 373, 11 S.E.2d 149 (1940), the defendant was charged with and convicted of the common law crime of larceny, for the theft of a tombstone from a grave in a cemetery. On appeal, the Supreme Court of North Carolina reversed the conviction on the ground that "it was not larceny, at common law, to steal anything adhering to the soil." The court held that the indictment was insufficient to support a conviction under a statute making it larceny to steal a chattel real. In discussing the statute, the court stated: "The only purpose of statutes making chattels real the subject of larceny, and thus extending the common law crime, is to abrogate, so far as it affects the prosecution for larceny, the rule that things in their nature personal are or become realty while or when affixed to the soil and to abolish the subtle distinction between its severance and taking as a single and indivisible act and a severance and a taking as separate and distinct acts. 36 C.J. 736. Thus, C.S. § 4259 was enacted to eliminate a defect in the common law rule and to extend it so as to make chattels real, such as growing trees, plants, minerals, metals and fences, connected in some way with the land, the subject of larceny. The obvious intent of the act was to prevent the wilful and unlawful entry upon the land of another and the taking and carrying away of such articles as were not, at common law or by previous statute the subject of larceny. . . ."

In Stansbury v. Luttrell, 152 Md. 553, 137 A. 339 (1927), the court stated: "If the unlawful severance of the trees from the freehold and their carrying away by the trespasser had been parts of one continuous transaction, there could have been no larceny at common law, for there would have had [sic] no time between the severance and the carrying away during which it could have been said that the trees, in their new character as personalty because of the severance, had been in the actual or constructive possession of the owners; but here, after the trees were severed, they were cut into logs and remained on the place until they were carried away. The felling of the trees was on Friday and Saturday, and all the logs were not carried away until the afternoon of the last day. There was, therefore, a time when the trespasser relinquished possession of some of the trees by leaving them on the land of the owners, and thereby the owners acquired constructive, if not actual, possession of the logs in their new character of personalty and the return of the trespasser and his carrying away of the logs, with the necessary felonious intent, would have been larceny according to the modern authorities. . . ."

In Stephens v. Commonwealth, 304 Ky. 38, 199 S.W.2d 719 (1947), the court stated: "Real estate is not a subject of larceny, and, according to the common law rule, if anything savoring of or adhering to real property is severed and carried away by one continuous act it amounts merely to an act of trespass. Some courts have gone to the extreme of holding that the acts of severance and asportation must occur on separate days, while others hold that the two acts must be so separated by time as not to constitute one transaction. Annotation in 131 A.L.R. 146. There has been a tendency in more recent decisions to discard that technical rule and to adopt what we deem to be the true rule, which is stated as follows in 32 Am.Jur., Larceny, section 83: '. . . the technical requirement of even a moment's lapse of time has been superseded by decisions adopting the simpler, more modern, and assertedly better doctrine that by the very act of severance the wrongdoer converts the property into a chattel which may be the object of larceny, so that if he then removes the severed property with felonious intent to steal it he is guilty of larceny, whatever dispatch may be employed by him in such removal.' "

For a current statute incorporating this concept in somewhat archaic terminology, see Code of Virginia, § 18.2–99: "Things which savor of the realty, and are at the time they are taken part of the freehold, whether they be of the substance or produce thereof, or affixed thereto, shall be deemed goods and chattels of which larceny may be committed, although there be no interval between the severing and taking away."

3. In United States v. Carlos, 21 Philippine Rep. 553 (1911), the defendant argued that electric current could not be the subject of larceny. In holding to the contrary, the court stated: "Counsel for the appellant insists that only corporeal property can be the subject of the crime of larceny, and in support of this proposition cites several authorities for the purpose of showing that the only subjects of larceny are tangible, movable, chattels, something which could be taken in possession and carried away, and which had some, although trifling, intrinsic value. . . . The true test of what is a proper subject of larceny seems to be not whether the subject is corporeal or incorporeal, but whether it is capable of appropriation by another than the owner. It is well settled that illuminating gas may be the subject of larceny, even in the absence of a statute so providing. . . . Electricity, the same as gas, is a valuable article of merchandise, bought and sold like other personal property and is capable of appropriation by another. So no error was committed by the trial court in holding that electricity is a subject of larceny."

4. In The Case of the Peacocks, Y.B. 18 Hen. 8, f. 9, p. 11 (K.B.1526), the chancellor asked to justices of the Court of the King's Bench the question if it was a felony for a man to steal peacocks which are tame and domestic. The opinion states that two justices declared, ". . . [I]t is not felony, for they are *ferae naturae*. . . . And the law is the same as to a mastiff, a hound, or a spaniel, or a goshawk which is tamed, for they are more properly things for

pleasure than for profit. And similarly the peacock is a bird more for pleasure than for profit. . . . But FitzJames and the other justices said that peacocks are commonly of the same nature of hens or capons, geese or ducks, and that the owner has property in them. They have *animus revertendi* and they are not fowls of warren, like pheasant or partridge . . . as to which taking, even with felonious intent, is not felony. And finally all the justices agreed that the taking of peacocks was felony. . . ."

Thus developed the common law concept that animals of a base nature were not considered personalty. The theft of a dog, cat, monkey, or fox was not deemed a larceny. However, those animals of a domestic nature that were useful for the sustenance of life came under the umbrella of personalty and could therefore be the subject of a larceny. They included cows, horses, hogs, and chickens.

With respect to "Man's best friend", the Supreme Court of the United States was prompted to say, in Sentell v. New Orleans & C. R. Co., 166 U.S. 698, 701, 17 S.Ct. 693, 694 (1897): "While the higher breeds rank among the noblest representatives of the animal kingdom, and are justly esteemed for their intelligence, sagacity, fidelity, watchfulness, affection, and, above all, for their natural companionship with man, others are afflicted with such serious infirmities of temper as to be little better than a public nuisance."

Early decisions in the United States tended to follow the common law rule, but later all animals reduced to possession came to be looked upon as personal property. This change came about both by court decision and by statutes. Consider, for example, the Virginia Criminal Code which has a separate statutory provision (§ 18.2–97) for "Larceny of certain animals and poultry", which refers to the theft of a dog, horse, pony, mule, cow, steer, bull or calf, as well as poultry, sheep, swine, lamb, or goat.

(d) ANOTHER'S PROPERTY

According to the common law, one co-owner cannot be guilty of larceny from another co-owner. Thus, a partner who steals partnership property is not guilty of larceny.[1] Likewise, at common law, a spouse does not commit larceny by taking property from the other spouse.[2] In the 1859 case of Regina v. Avery,[3] the court stated: "A wife

1. Dethlefsen v. Stull, 86 Cal.App.2d 499, 195 P.2d 56 (1948).

2. 1 Hale, Pleas of the Crown 513 (1736): "The wife cannot commit felony of the goods of her husband, for they are one person in law,. . . ."

Modern statutes frequently alter the common law rules concerning larceny of the goods of a partner or spouse. The Model Penal Code, for example, provides:

§ 223.1(3). It is no defense to a charge of theft that the actor is an owner or co-owner of the property or has any other interest therein, if the person deprived also has an interest to which the actor is not entitled. . . .

§ 223.1(4). Where the property involved is that of the actor's spouse, no

prosecution for theft may be maintained unless:

(a) the parties had ceased living together as man and wife prior to the alleged theft; or

(b) the alleged theft was committed when the actor was leaving or deserting or about to leave or desert his spouse; or

(c) the actor entered into the marriage within 6 months prior to the alleged theft with the purpose of committing theft; or

(d) the property involved exceeded $500 in value exclusive of household belongings.

3. 8 Cox C.C. 184, 169 Eng.Rep. 1207 (1859).

cannot be guilty of larceny in simply taking the goods of her husband; and, if a stranger do no more than merely assist her in the taking, inasmuch as the wife, as principal, cannot be guilty of larceny, the stranger, as accessory, cannot be guilty."

It has also been held that a stranger who takes goods with the consent of the wife is not guilty of larceny.[4] Where it is clear to the stranger, however, that the husband has not consented to the taking, the rule is different.

In People v. Zinke, 76 N.Y.2d 8, 556 N.Y.S.2d 11, 555 N.E.2d 263 (1990), the sole general partner in a limited partnership misappropriated in excess of one million dollars by writing checks on the partnership's money-market account. The court held, as a matter of statutory interpretation, that a partner was a co-owner of the funds and, like at common law, "a joint or common owner of property shall not be deemed to have a right of possession thereto superior to that of any other joint or common owner thereof." This decision was reached because the New York legislature had defined, in Penal Law Section 155.05(1), "owner" as a person "who has a right to possession [of the property taken] superior to that of the taker, obtainer, or withholder." In taking that legislative position, the Court of Appeals noted, the legislature rejected the Model Penal Code provisions which, contrary to the common law, see larceny as the depriving of one of a property interest regardless of whether the actor also has an interest in the same property. The court rejected the State's argument that partners who misappropriate partnership funds ought to be treated the same as officers of a corporation who, if they misappropriate corporate funds, are guilty of larceny. Officers or agents of a corporation, unlike partners in a partnership, are not co-owners of corporate property. If the law is to be changed, the court suggested, that is a matter of legislative policy, not for judicial activism.

(e) INTENT TO STEAL

SKEETER v. COMMONWEALTH

Supreme Court of Virginia, 1977.
217 Va. 722, 232 S.E.2d 756.

HARRISON, JUSTICE.

Richard Lee Skeeter, Jr. was convicted of grand larceny in the court below under an indictment containing a count which charged that defendant, on November 7, 1975, "did steal U.S. currency . . . having a value of approximately $200 belonging to Charlie R. Mason". This appeal questions the form of the indictment and the sufficiency of the evidence to convict him.

4. Rex v. Harrison, 168 Eng.Rep. 126 (1756).

Charlie R. Mason operates an insurance agency in Portsmouth. On November 7, 1975, Skeeter entered Mason's office ostensibly to seek information regarding automobile insurance. During their conversation Skeeter inquired if Mason would "like to have three color television sets real cheap", "a hundred dollars for all three". Defendant's plan, as outlined to Mason, was that they would go to the J. M. Fields store in Portsmouth, pay $200 to a girl friend of Skeeter's who worked there and that she would go back to the credit department, run through the necessary papers and receive a pickup slip which would entitle them to receive the television sets from the store's loading ramp.

Mason said that defendant wanted him to go immediately to the J. M. Fields store, but that, being suspicious that defendant was attempting "a ripoff" or some "confidence scheme", Mason told Skeeter that he could not close his insurance office at that time and asked defendant to come back an hour later. As soon as Skeeter left the insurance office, Mason called the Portsmouth detective bureau, and arrangements were made for Mason to obtain identifiable money from a local bank and otherwise cooperate with defendant. It was understood that at the appropriate time the police would apprehend defendant and frustrate his scheme.

When Mason returned to his office, after having obtained the money, he was approached by a "girl dressed in black, trimmed in red", who asked if he was "looking for Mr. Skeeter". When Mason replied in the affirmative, she said: "Well, I am with him," Mason noticed that Skeeter was sitting in a Cadillac automobile parked near his office. Mason in his automobile, and defendant with the girl in the Cadillac, then drove to the J. M. Fields store. After parking, all three walked inside the store. Although defendant requested that Mason give him the money before the three parties entered, Mason declined, having been instructed by the police not to give Skeeter any money until they were inside the store. When the parties got about midway in the store Mason gave Skeeter two $100 bills, and defendant, in turn, gave the money to the girl. Mason testified that at this point the girl "made a left turn down the aisle and he [Skeeter] told me, . . . 'Let's wait out in the mall part here and give her a chance to get the televisions back to the loading platform and bring me the ticket back' to where we could go in the back and pick them up".

It appears that after waiting approximately five minutes Skeeter suggested that they go back to the platform where he said the girl would probably be; that when they went to the platform, no one was there; that Mason said to defendant, "Well, you and I have been ripped off."; and that Skeeter responded, "Well, let's go back to your office. Maybe she's down at your office with the receipts." Mason and Skeeter drove to a place near Mason's office known as "Bob's Hot Dog Stand", where defendant made a telephone call and told Mason, "She's [the girl] going to meet us in the parking lot of an old abandoned station at Frederick Boulevard and Turnpike Road." Mason and Skeeter then went to this location where defendant made another telephone call from a telephone booth. He then represented to Mason that, "We are supposed to go to a girl friend's apartment." When asked where the girl friend lived defendant replied: "You just go where I tell you to go." Shortly thereafter the police stopped Mason and Skeeter and arrested defendant.

Mason never received any television sets or recovered the two $100 bills which he gave defendant and which defendant handed to the girl. Between the time the three parties entered the Fields store and the time Mason and Skeeter went to the loading platform, Mason said the Cadillac automobile used by Skeeter and the girl had disappeared.
* * *

Contrary to defendant's contention, it was unnecessary that there be a specific allegation of felonious intent contained in the indictment. In Satterfield v. Commonwealth, 105 Va. 867, 870, 52 S.E. 979, 980 (1906), we held that a charge in a warrant that the accused did unlawfully take, steal and carry away the property of another is sufficient to charge larceny. * * *

Larceny has often been defined as "the wrongful or fraudulent taking of personal goods of some intrinsic value, belonging to another, without his assent, and with the intention to deprive the owner thereof permanently. The *animus furandi* must accompany the taking, but the wrongful taking of property in itself imports the *animus furandi*". . . .

We do not agree with defendant's contentions that the Commonwealth failed to establish the requisite intent on defendant's part to steal, or that the taking of Mason's money was not established to be wrongful because Mason consented to the taking.

The fact that Mason consented to surrender temporarily the possession of $200 to defendant, pursuant to instructions of the police and for the specific purpose of aiding the police in frustrating the perpetration of a fraud on either himself or on the J. M. Fields store, does not have the effect of negating the wrongful act perpetrated by defendant. Had defendant carried out his original proposal and, with the aid of an accomplice within the J. M. Fields store, delivered to Mason three color television sets for $200, he would have committed larceny from the store. Instead, the evidence discloses that larceny from the store was never in fact intended by defendant. Rather his scheme was to commit larceny of money from Mason upon the pretense of obtaining color television sets for a grossly inadequate price with the aid and cooperation of an accomplice in the store.

The criminal design originated with defendant. Mason neither suggested nor urged Skeeter on to the commission of a crime. The larceny of Mason's money was completed when defendant accepted it from Mason in the Field store with larcenous intent.

Our observations in Webb v. Commonwealth, 122 Va. 899, 904, 94 S.E. 773, 775 (1918), are pertinent here:

> "With respect to the contention that the evidence is not sufficient to sustain the verdict. It is true, and the jury were so instructed, that in order to find the accused guilty, it was essential for the Commonwealth to prove that the original taking was felonious—that is to say, that the taking was done with no intention to return the horse, but to deprive the owner thereof permanently. Yet, whether or not there was such intent was a question of fact for the determination of the jury; and, if from the whole evidence, such intent might fairly be inferred, the verdict of the jury to that effect, approved by the trial court, ought not to be disturbed by an appellate court. It has been well said that there is not one case in a hundred where the felonious intent in the original taking can be proved by direct evidence. From the nature of the case, intent, generally, must be inferred from circumstances. Booth v. Commonwealth, 4 Gratt. (45 Va.) 525."

The judgment of the lower court will be affirmed.

NOTES

1. See, however, Smith v. State, 571 S.W.2d 917 (Tex.Crim.App.1978), where the failure to allege "intent to deprive the owner of his property" was deemed to be a fundamental defect in the charge of theft.

In People v. Brown, 105 Cal. 66, 38 P. 518 (1894), the defendant, a boy 17 years old, was convicted of burglary, alleged to have been committed in entering a house with intent to commit larceny. The alleged larceny was the taking of a bicycle. The defendant testified, "I took the wheel to get even with the boy, and, of course, I didn't intend to keep it." He said that he meant to return the bicycle the next night, but that he was caught with it before he could return it. In reversing the conviction and remanding the case for a new trial, the Supreme Court of California stated: "The court told the jury that larceny may be committed, even though it was only the intent of the party taking the property to deprive the owner of it temporarily. . . . But the test of law to be applied to these circumstances for the purpose of determining the ultimate fact as to the man's guilt or innocence is, did he intend to permanently deprive the owner of his property? If he did not intend so to do, there is no felonious intent, and his acts constitute but a trespass. While the felonious intent of the party taking need not necessarily be an intention to convert the property to his own use, still it must in all cases be an intent to wholly and permanently deprive the owner thereof."

In State v. Ward, 19 Nev. 297, 10 P. 133 (1886), the defendant was convicted of grand larceny for taking some horses. He and a companion took the horses from a ranch in order to ride to the state line. They abandoned the horses near the state line, about 12 miles from the ranch. The defendant claimed that he had previously arranged with one Thomas to pick up the horses and return them to the owner. When Thomas did not appear at the appointed place, the defendant, according to his testimony, left the horses, thinking that Thomas would get them later or that the horses would find their way back to the ranch.

The horses, in fact, were found at the ranch several days later. In affirming the conviction, the Supreme Court of Nevada stated: "From [the trial court's] instructions it is urged that 'the jury might have understood that, in order to escape a verdict of guilty, it was necessary that appellant should have intended to return the horses to the possession of Gibbs, and that such is not the law.' . . . In order to find appellant guilty, the jury were bound to believe, from all the evidence, that he intended to deprive the owner permanently of his property. The jury did not believe that appellant intended to return it. Having discarded that theory, the intention had to be gathered from acts alone. Now, it may be that a person might take another's property, and carry it away, without intending to return it, but without intending a permanent deprivation. His acts, including his treatment of the property, and the circumstances surrounding the taking, might show that latter intention in the absence of the former. But since the jury, after discarding appellant's *alleged* intention, had to decide, *by acts alone,* as to his *real* intention at the time of taking; and since he is presumed to have intended the natural consequences of his acts, in the absence of an intention to return the property,—if the jury were satisfied, beyond a reasonable doubt, that he used the property in such a manner that the owner would be likely to be permanently deprived of it, the presumption is that he intended to so use it, and the burden was upon him to rebut such presumption by competent evidence. So the jury were charged by appellant's eleventh instruction, which declared the law correctly in case he did not intend to return the property."

2. In Commonwealth v. Mason, 105 Mass. 163 (1870), the defendant took a horse with the intent of concealing it until the owner should offer a reward for the horse, or until the owner could be induced to sell the horse for a price less than its value. In upholding the conviction, the court stated, "When a person takes property of another with intent to deprive the owner of a portion of the property taken, or of its value, such intent is felonious, and the taking is larceny."

In State v. Hauptmann, 115 N.J.L. 412, 180 A. 809 (1935), the defendant contended that there was no proof of an intent to steal the sleeping clothes of the kidnapped Lindbergh child. (The defendant was convicted of felony-murder, and the felony charged was breaking and entering the Lindbergh home in the nighttime with intent to commit larceny by taking the sleeping suit of the child.) (For an account of the reasons why the prosecution proceeded on this charge, see earlier discussion of the *Hauptmann* case in the Homicide chapter.) The court noted that the evidence tended to show that the defendant had the sleeping suit in his possession, and that, in the course of the ransom negotiations, he sent the sleeping suit to the negotiator for the Lindberghs in order to prove that he was the actual kidnapper. The defendant argued that the return of the suit established that there was no intent permanently to deprive the owner of the property. In rejecting this argument, the court stated: "[T]he intent to return should be unconditional; and, where there is an element of coercion or of reward, as a condition of return, larceny is inferable. . . . In the present case the evidence pointed to use of the sleeping suit to further the purposes of defendant and assist him in extorting many thousand dollars from the rightful owner. True, it was surrendered without payment; but, on the other hand, it was an initial and probably essential step in the intended extortion of money. . . . It was well within the province of the jury to infer that, if Condon had refused to go on with the preliminaries, the sleeping suit would never have been delivered. In that situation, the larceny was established."

3. Is larceny committed by one who takes property and converts it to his own use under the mistaken belief that the property is abandoned? Does his intent to take the property under such circumstances meet the requirement of felonious intent? See Morissette v. United States, 342 U.S. 246, 72 S.Ct. 240 (1952), infra in Chapter 8. Is the retaking of money lost at gambling considered larceny? See Anno. 77 A.L.R.3d 1363.

4. Because of the requirement of an intent to steal, it is often difficult to obtain larceny convictions in cases involving so-called "joyriding." See, e.g., People v. Pastel, 306 Ill. 565, 138 N.E. 194 (1923). Where an automobile is taken with the intent to use it for a few hours and then return it to the place where taken, or to leave it in a place where the owner will be likely to recover it, all of the elements of larceny are usually present except for the intent to steal. As a consequence, most states have enacted special legislation concerning this offense. Section 206.6 of the Model Penal Code, for example, provides: "A person who takes the vehicle of another without his consent, under circumstances not amounting to theft, commits a petty misdemeanor."

5. In Butts v. Commonwealth, 145 Va. 800, 133 S.E. 764 (1926), the Virginia Supreme Court, in reflecting the common law, stated that if A in good faith takes an item of property believing it belongs to him, although the taking is trespassory, yet he is not guilty of larceny because there was no criminal intent to deprive another of his property. Whether or not a defendant acts in good faith is ordinarily a jury question.

6. In shoplifting situations, many merchants are under the impression that the offense is not completed until the goods are taken out of the store, for until then the "intent to steal" cannot be established. But the intent to steal is provable by other factors, such as the carrying of goods from one floor to another. See People v. Baker, 365 Ill. 328, 6 N.E.2d 665 (1937). In other words, conduct on the part of the accused that is clearly inconsistent with the ordinary behavior of customers can be used as evidence of intent to steal. According to this test, therefore, a person should not be arrested while he is carrying an unconcealed piece of merchandise in the direction of clerks whom he could conceivably be approaching for an inquiry about the merchandise or where it conceivably appears that he is taking it to a better lighted place for closer inspection. In such instances the accused could reasonably offer such explanations as evidence of no intent to steal. On the other hand, the taking of an object from a counter, placing it in a bag or purse, and walking away from the counter without paying for it, is conduct unbecoming a customer and may reasonably be taken as evidence of intent to steal. See also the case of People v. Olivo, supra p. 681.

In the earlier principal case in the section on the "taking" element the New York Court of Appeals had no difficulty finding the requisite specific intent.

7. In a number of jurisdictions, the courts have held that the unexplained possession of recently stolen property gives rise to a presumption or an inference that the possessor is either the thief or the receiver of stolen property. Frequently the jury is so instructed. A discussion of the constitutionality of these presumptions is best reserved until after study of the case of United States v. Barnes, infra, under "Receiving Stolen Property."

2. GRADES OF LARCENY

STATE v. JACQUITH
Supreme Court of South Dakota, 1978.
272 N.W.2d 90.

MORGAN, JUSTICE.

* * *

Appellant, Norman Jacquith, Jr., was arrested at the scene by members of the Vermillion Police Department on June 22, 1977, for breaking into a van and stealing a pair of prescription sunglasses. He was charged by a two-count information with burglary in the third degree and with grand larceny. Trial was held before a jury on August 1, 1977, and appellant was found guilty of grand larceny and fourth-degree burglary. Appellant now appeals the grand larceny conviction.

Appellant contends that the trial court erred in refusing to accept and give to the jury his proposed instruction which defines "value" as referring to fair market value for the purpose of determining whether or not appellant committed grand larceny.

Appellant was found guilty by the jury of violating SDCL 22–37–1 and 22–37–2.[1] The former statute defines the crime of larceny and the latter statute differentiates between petit and grand larceny. It is well settled that when a statute delineates a specific dollar amount as the differentiation between petit and grand larceny, proof of the value of the item(s) stolen in excess of the statutory amount is an essential element of the crime of grand larceny. Proof of value in excess of the requisite amount is as essential to the prosecution for grand larceny as is the proof of the elements of specific intent, fraud or stealth, and the actual taking of another's property, and the burden is fully upon the State to prove said value beyond a reasonable doubt.

It is also well settled that the determination of said value is strictly within the province of the jury. . . .

To aid the jury in determining value, the courts have offered various tests for the determination of value as used in statutes distinguishing between petit and grand larceny and other similar statutes involving theft of property. The most widely accepted test is the "fair market value" test. This test provides that the value to be proved is the fair market value at the time and place of the theft.

Appellant submitted, and the trial court rejected, a proposed jury instruction which stated, in essence, the "fair market value" test. Appellant contends that the trial court's rejection of the proposed instruction was error. The State's proposed instruction on value, using

1. SDCL 22–37–2 provides:

Grand larceny is larceny committed in any of the following cases:

(1) When the property taken is of a value exceeding fifty dollars;

(2) When such property, although not a value exceeding fifty dollars, is taken from the person of another;

(3) When such property is livestock. Larceny in other cases is petit larceny.

the "replacement value" test as the proper test, was also rejected by the court. The State, on appeal, contends that there is "no market" for prescription sunglasses and thus a fair market value cannot be ascertained and a different test should be used. In looking to the case law of other jurisdictions that use the "fair market value" test, it is apparent that they do indeed, upon a showing that there is no market for a particular item of stolen property, allowed another test to be used. However, the burden is upon the prosecution to affirmatively prove that there is "no market" for the item(s) as a prerequisite to allowing the use of any other test. The prosecution in this case neither alleged nor submitted evidence that no market existed for used prescription sunglasses.

The jury's determination of whether or not the value of the sunglasses stolen exceeded $50.00 is crucial. The maximum sentence for grand larceny is ten years in the state penitentiary, while the maximum sentence for petit larceny is thirty days in the county jail. The former is a felony, the latter is a misdemeanor. It cannot be said that the determination of value in this case is of little consequence. Since the jury was given separate instructions on petit larceny and grand larceny, it is only reasonable that they be given some guidance in determining the distinction between the two crimes.

This court has not had previous occasion to decide which test shall be used for determining "value" in theft or larceny cases such as this, but we find the decisions of those courts that have adopted the "fair market value" test to be sound and well reasoned. Therefore, we adopt the "fair market value" test as herein stated for use in the courts of this state. Further, when it is contended that a stolen item has no fair market value because no market exists for that item, the burden shall be upon the prosecution to affirmatively prove that no market exists and that a different test should be used. If it is determined that no market exists from which a fair market value could be ascertained, then the jury may properly use the "replacement value less depreciation" test.

The evidence in the record pertaining to the value of the sunglasses is minimal. The glasses were prescription glasses which had been converted to sunglasses by the addition of colored coating after use in their original condition for about a year and a half. They had various pits or chips in the lenses from a burning torch. The owner of the sunglasses stated that his personal feeling was that they were worth $70.00 or $80.00 and an optometrist called by the state testified that the current replacement cost would be "in the neighborhood of $75.00," but the optometrist further testified that considering their condition it was questionable whether they would meet OSHA industrial safety standards. It is certainly conceivable that the jury would have concluded, under proper instruction, that the value of the sunglasses was below $50.00. Accordingly, we reverse the conviction and remand for new trial.

* * *

All the Justices concur.

NOTES

1. Determining the value of stolen property is usually a function of the jury. Where the evidence is in conflict, the jury's determination will not be disturbed. In a larceny prosecution for the theft of dogs alleged to be worth $100 each, the defendant introduced evidence that they had no commercial value whatever. The court said that the verdict of guilty of grand larceny settled this conflict against the defendant. Blankenship v. Commonwealth, 133 Va. 638, 112 S.E. 622 (1922). Where there is no market value of an article that has been stolen, the better rule is that its actual value should be proved. See Lund v. Commonwealth, 217 Va. 688, 232 S.E.2d 745 (1977).

2. Suppose that the division between grand and petit larceny is $50 and a person steals an automobile owner's license plates for which he paid $60, but the cost to the owner for having them replaced is $5. Is the thief guilty of grand or petit larceny? For an interesting case of this nature see Cowan v. State, 171 Ark. 1018, 287 S.W. 201 (1926).

3. In People v. Fognini, 374 Ill. 161, 28 N.E.2d 95 (1940), the defendants were charged with the larceny of two suits of clothes. The jury returned a verdict of guilty and found the value of the property stolen to be the sum of $30. In reversing the decision and remanding the cause for a new trial, the Supreme Court of Illinois stated:

"It is argued, as one of the reasons for reversal, that the proof failed to show the fair, cash market value of these suits on the date of the larceny.

"Three witnesses testified as to this matter and the evidence offered by them is substantially alike. It appears from the testimony that the two suits in question were old stock and had been on the shelves of the company three and one-half years. . . . One of the witnesses said he thought the suits had cost $18.50 and that they were worth $20 apiece.

"Over repeated objections and motions to strike, the witnesses were all questioned by the assistant State's attorney as to the 'fair, cash value' of the merchandise omitting the word 'market' from the question. . . . It is clear from the evidence that these suits had proved unmarketable over a period of three and one-half years by any usual retail methods. . . . Whether or not there was a market through some cut rate or special sale means, was not proved or touched upon by the evidence. The verdict of the jury that the suits were worth $15 each is not supported by any evidence.

"In those types of larceny where the value of the property is material, that value must be alleged and proved, and the proof must show the fair, cash market value at the time and place of the theft. . . ."

Defendant, a turnstile maintainer in the New York subway system, was tried for the theft of fares deposited by subway passengers in the station turnstiles. The first larceny involved approximately $1,500, alleged to have been taken over a period of 11 months, while the second charge involved the theft of more than $370 over a period of 10 months. The defendant was convicted of grand larceny, although he had contended at the trial that since the takings occurred over a period of time and in no one instance exceeded $100 (the jurisdiction's statutory dividing line between grand and petty larceny), he was guilty only of a number of petty larcenies. In affirming the defendant's conviction, the New York Court of Appeals, in People v. Cox, 286 N.Y. 137, 36 N.E.2d 84 (1941), said:

"There is evidence sufficient in the case at bar to sustain the verdict of the jury that the entire taking was governed by a single intent and a general illegal design. This total sum stolen by defendant . . . under the two counts of the indictment was stolen pursuant to this general fraudulent design which was created before the misappropriations began and continued throughout the entire period. If the jury did not find such to be the fact, they were instructed to acquit the defendant. It is submitted that the record supports the above finding of the jury rather than that there were a number of isolated transactions or distinct larcenies coincident solely in method, place or time. . . . Here there was a continuing larceny by a thief operating under a single purpose to carry out a general fraudulent plan. We have first the formulation of a plan for systemized thievery, then the adoption of the plan by persons able to make it effective, and lastly its subsequent realization, together with the taking of the necessary steps to preserve a continuing operation unmolested. . . . Logic and reason join . . . in holding that the People may prosecute for a single crime a defendant who, pursuant to a single intent and one general fraudulent plan, steals in the aggregate as a felon and not as a petty thief. If this were not so, a crime of grand larceny would go unpunished and a felon escape because the law classified him only as a petty thief."

4. Compare Camp v. State, 7 Okl.Crim.R. 531, 124 P. 331 (1912). In that case, the defendant was tried and convicted of grand larceny based on the theft of various items of clothing from a dry goods store over a period of several months. In reversing the defendant's conviction, the Criminal Court of Appeals of Oklahoma stated:

"We have examined the record carefully, and fail to find any testimony that the value of the property taken at any one time exceeded $20 [the statutory dividing line between grand and petit larceny]. Counsel for appellant made this point in their brief, and insisted that, under the evidence, appellant should not have been convicted for more than petit larceny. It was therefore the duty of the attorney for the state, if there was any evidence in the record showing that goods had ben taken at any one time worth exceeding $20, to call our attention to it. As he has not done so, and as we have been unable to find such testimony, we feel that we should sustain the contention of counsel for appellant, and hold that the testimony in this case does not support a verdict for grand larceny."

The cases dealing with this aspect of prosecutions for larceny are collected in 37 A.L.R.3d 1407 (1971).

5. In United States v. Bryant, 454 F.2d 248 (4th Cir. 1972), the court stated that proof of value was required when a defendant was charged with grand larceny (property worth over $100). But where the evidence failed to establish such value, a new trial was not required since the defendant would stand convicted of the lesser included misdemeanor offense of larceny of property having a value not exceeding $100.

6. Many states make special provisions for certain types of larceny usually called "compound" or "aggravated" larceny. It is common, for example, to provide special penalties for "larceny from a building" and "larceny from the person," to supplement the crimes of burglary and robbery, respectively.

B. EMBEZZLEMENT

WARREN v. STATE
Supreme Court of Indiana, 1945.
223 Ind. 552, 62 N.E.2d 624.

RICHMAN, CHIEF JUSTICE. Waiving a jury appellant was tried and convicted of larceny of four cans of Prestone. The only question presented is whether the finding is contrary to law. The evidence leaves no doubt that for more than six months he continued to take property of his employer and convert it to his own use, but he contends that his employment was such as to make his crime embezzlement rather than larceny.

He was employed as a member of a maintenance crew under a foreman in Plant No. 2 of the Allison Division of General Motors Corporation. The plant contained tanks for reception and storage of gasoline, oil and Prestone. To a storage building housing Prestone both the foreman and appellant had keys. "The Chief Engineer . . . had exclusive control in Plant No. 2 of this Prestone." Appellant was not authorized to remove Prestone from the building except on requisition from some other person in authority. One of appellant's duties was to receive gasoline. A confederate (who pleaded guilty to the same affidavit upon which appellant was tried) was employed by a trucking company to deliver gasoline to the plant and thus obtained ingress. His truck was used to take away Prestone abstracted by appellant from the storage building. The Prestone was sold and the proceeds divided by appellant and the truck driver. A statement signed by appellant, and admitted in evidence, related numerous such transactions from June through August, 1943. In November they "took out some 30 to 35 drums of Prestone," each containing 55 gallons and sold them for $83 per drum. Appellant's employer became suspicious and early in January, 1944, investigators observed appellant surreptitiously placing four cans in the truck. It was followed away from the plant and the cans, containing Prestone, were recovered. No contention is made by appellant that he had a requisition when he took this Prestone. There was other testimony more favorable to appellant's theory, but upon appeal we look only to the evidence tending to support the finding.

The facts related bring the case within the rule of Colip v. State [1899] . . . and cases from other jurisdictions cited in a note in 125 A.L.R. at p. 368, holding that an employe who has "mere custody of personal property, as distinguished from legal possession" and with animo furandi converts same to his own use is guilty of larceny. Here there was no "relation of special trust in regard to the article appropriated" which this court in Colip v. State, supra, said was necessary to an embezzlement. Appellant had access to the storage building but the Prestone therein was in the possession of the employer. We see no essential difference between this case and the hypothetical case of the watchman referred to in the following quotation from Vinnedge v. State [1906]:

"Where there is at most but a naked possession or control—that is, a bare charge—or where the access consists of a mere physical propinquity as an incident of the employment, the felonious appropriation should be regarded as larceny. The reference in the embezzlement statute to officers, agents, attorneys, clerks, servants, and employés is plainly indicative of the intent to limit the denouncement of the statute to cases in which such persons have, as an element of their employment, a special trust concerning the money, article, or thing of value that involves an actual possession thereof or a special right of access to or control over the same. This requirement would not be satisfied, as we may indicate by way of illustration, by the mere control or possession, or physical opportunity of access, which a watchman in charge of a store might have. As before indicated, the relationship contemplated by the statute is one of special trust and confidence; a relationship in which there inheres, either for the particular transaction or for all purposes, a special right of access to, or control or possession of, the money, article, or thing of value which is appropriated."

Usually a watchman carries a key. Appellant's key made access easier but did not give him possession. We regard as immaterial the fact that he was bonded against embezzlement. It perhaps was a circumstance which the court might have taken into consideration in determining the relationship of the parties, but it was in no sense controlling. Appellant's contention that animus furandi was not proved is controverted by the evidence showing that the crime was preceded by similar consummated thefts over a period of many months. Similar transactions may be shown to prove felonious intent, knowledge and other similar states of mind. . . .

The cases relied upon by appellant belong to another category. Davis v. State [1925] recognizes the principle quoted from Colip v. State, supra, but holds that the facts establish the crime of embezzlement. The appellant therein received money as treasurer of an association and later converted it to his own use. He had exclusive possession and control of the fund under a trust to account to his employer. In Jones v. State [1877] a merchant gave his employe some money in an unsealed envelope, directing him to deliver it to other merchants as the purchase price of a load of flour. On the day he succumbed to temptation and fled with the money to another state. State v. Wingo [1883] had similar facts. Each employe was given exclusive possession of the property under a special trust and later formed the felonious intent. . . .

Judgment affirmed.

NOTES

1. There is little or no justification today for the distinction between larceny and embezzlement. The Virginia Criminal Code, for example, in § 18.2–111, provides that "If any person wrongfully and fraudulently use,

dispose of, conceal or embezzle any money, bill, note, check, order, draft, bond, receipt, bill of lading or any other personal property, tangible or intangible, which he shall have received for another or for his employer, principal or bailor, or by virtue of his office, trust, or employment, or which shall have been entrusted or delivered to him by another or by any court, corporation or company, *he shall be deemed guilty of larceny thereof,* . . . and proof of embezzlement under this section shall be sufficient to sustain the charge. . . ." (Emphasis supplied.)

Both the offenses of larceny and embezzlement, as well as many related ones, can be adequately covered under a general statutory offense of "Theft". See, for example, Article 16 of the Illinois Criminal Code, Ill.Rev.Stats. ch. 38.

2. In view of the fact that in many instances thefts by employees from their employers are never reported to the law enforcement authorities because of restitution being made by the employee, or someone on his behalf, attorneys should be mindful of the offense known as "compounding a felony" or as "misprision of felony". Consider, for instance, the following provision in the Illinois Criminal Code (S.H.A. ch. 38, § 32–1):

A person compounds a crime when he receives or offers to another any consideration for a promise not to prosecute or aid in the prosecution of an offender.

The United States Code (18 U.S.C.A.) contains the following provision:

§ 4. Misprision of felony

Whoever, having knowledge of the actual commission of a felony cognizable by a court of the United States, conceals and does not as soon as possible make known the same to some judge or other person in civil or military authority under the United States, shall be fined not more than $500 or imprisoned not more than three years, or both.

Under the foregoing federal statute, there must be an affirmative act of concealment; mere failure to report an offense does not constitute a violation. United States v. Daddano, 432 F.2d 1119 (7th Cir. 1970), cert. denied 402 U.S. 905, 91 S.Ct. 1391 (1971); United States v. Johnson, 546 F.2d 1225 (5th Cir. 1977).

The offense of misprision of felony is discussed further in Chapter 8 under "Parties to Crime."

3. The mayor of a town asks a repair shop whether they can repair a jeep which belonged to the city pest control department. After the repairs are completed, the shop sends a bill for $816.05 to the town. The town clerk, recognizing that the bill was not an obligation of the town, took it to the mayor who told the clerk he would "take care of it." Sometime later, the mayor asks the man in charge of the pest control department to sign the repair bill submitted by the shop. The bill for repairs to the jeep is not submitted to the town for payment by either the mayor or anyone else at the time the mayor is indicted for attempted embezzlement of $816.05. Did the mayor commit an overt act in an attempt to commit the crime of embezzlement? See, e.g. Bucklew v. State, 206 So.2d 200 (Miss.1968).

C. FALSE PRETENSES—DECEPTIVE PRACTICES

HUBBARD v. COMMONWEALTH

Supreme Court of Virginia, 1959.
201 Va. 61, 109 S.E.2d 100.

EGGLESTON, C. J., delivered the opinion of the court.

Samuel R. Hubbard, Jr., herein referred to as the defendant, was charged in a three-count indictment with (1) making and drawing a check for the payment of money in the sum of $3,150 upon a named bank, payable to the order of Reynolds Pontiac, with intent to defraud, knowing at the time of the making and drawing of such check that he did not have sufficient funds in, or credit with the bank for the payment of the instrument; (2) uttering and delivering the check to Reynolds Pontiac, with intent to defraud, knowing at the time of such uttering and delivery that he did not have sufficient funds in, or credit with, the bank for the payment of the instrument; and (3) larceny of a 1957 Pontiac automobile of the value of $3,150, the property of Reynolds Pontiac.

Upon arraignment and a plea of not guilty the defendant waived a trial by a jury and with the concurrence of the Commonwealth's attorney and of the court entered of record, was tried by the court. In its bill of particulars the Commonwealth charged that the first two counts were based upon the violation of Code, § 6–129, and the third upon the violation of Code, § 18–180. After hearing the evidence the court found the defendant guilty on all three counts, as charged in the indictment, and sentenced him to confinement in the penitentiary for one year on each count.

The matter is now before us on a writ of error granted the defendant who claims that the evidence is insufficient to sustain his conviction on the three counts, or any of them.

The undisputed facts are these: On Wednesday, September 18, 1957, the defendant, who was then engaged in the business of selling used cars in the city of Richmond telephoned Chester A. Reynolds, Jr., general manager of Reynolds Pontiac at Orange, Virginia, relative to purchasing two Pontaic station wagons. Reynolds agreed to sell the defendant two such cars, one of which was owned by Reynolds Pontiac and the other by Earl Lonergan, one of its customers, and left with it for sale. About 2:00 p.m. on the same day the defendant went to Orange for the purpose of consummating the purchase of the two cars. He told Reynolds that in the conduct of his used-car business he always kept approximately twenty late model cars on his lot, that he frequently bought new cars, and that he needed "a couple of new Pontiacs." As Reynolds said, "He [Hubbard] said his condition of business was very, very good, he gave me a very good picture of his business."

Since, the defendant said, considerable capital was required for him to carry on his business, he had made arrangements with the Savings

Bank & Trust Company of Richmond for a "$20,000 floor plan," that is, a line of credit in that amount secured by liens on cars. The defendant gave Reynolds a check bearing the date of the transaction, September 18 payable to the order of Reynolds Pontiac, drawn on the Savings Bank & Trust Company, signed by him (the defendant), in the sum of $3,150, that being the agreed price of the Pontiac station wagon which he was buying from Reynolds Pontiac. He told Reynolds that he must have the title certificate to the car in order that he might use it as collateral in consummating his "floor plan" with the bank, and that from the proceeds of such arrangement with the bank "the check would be good by the time it got to Richmond." Relying upon these representations, Reynolds accepted the check and delivered the car and the title certificate thereto to the defendant. At the same time and for the same reason Reynolds delivered to the defendant the Lonergan car and the title certificate thereto.

On the next day, Thursday, September 19, the defendant telephoned Reynolds that his "floor plan" with the bank had not been completed and asked him to "hold the check." He made the same request a day or two later. On Monday, September 23, Reynolds, whose suspicions had been aroused, deposited the check in his firm's account at Orange. The check was presented to the drawee bank on September 24, and returned with the notation that the account had been closed. Reynolds then called upon the defendant at his place of business and was told, "Don't worry! I am going to get the money for you." However the check was never paid.

An officer of the bank testified that on or about September 13, the bank had agreed to let the defendant have a $20,000 line of credit to be secured by liens on cars, provided the titles and cars were acceptable to the bank. It was further shown that on September 19, the day following that on which the defendant had obtained possession of the Reynolds car, he had obtained a loan of $5,500 from the Savings Bank & Trust Company on that car and the Lonergan car which he had also purchased through Reynolds Pontiac. While the proceeds of this loan were deposited to the defendant's credit in that bank, they were exhausted by checks presented on the same day. At the request of the bank the account was closed on September 23, the day before the check with which we are here concerned was presented.

It was also developed from the Commonwealth's evidence that during the period from July to September 13, 1957, the defendant had engaged in the same type of transaction with four other automobile dealers within a radius of 100 miles of Richmond. Under similar circumstances each of these dealers, in return for a worthless check, gave the defendant possession of a car or cars and the certificate or certificates of title therefor. In a similar fashion, the defendant obtained loans on these cars which precluded the dealers from recovering possession of them.

[Discussion of the first two counts of the indictment is omitted.]

* * *

The pertinent portion of Code, § 18–180, under which the third count of the indictment is laid, reads thus: "If any person obtain, by any false pretense or token from any person, with intent to defraud, money or other property which may be the subject of larceny, he shall be deemed guilty of larceny thereof; * * *."

As this court has previously pointed out, to constitute the offense described in the statute four things must concur: (1) There must be an intent to defraud; (2) there must be an actual fraud committed; (3) false pretenses must be used for the purpose of perpetrating the fraud; and (4) the fraud must be accomplished by means of the false pretenses made use of for the purpose, that is, they must be in some degree the cause, if not the controlling and decisive cause, which induced the owner to part with his property.

A criminal false pretense has been defined to be "the false representation of a past or existing fact, whether by oral or written words or conduct, which is calculated to deceive, intended to deceive, and does in fact deceive, and by means of which one person obtains value from another without compensation." C.J.S. False Pretenses § 1, p. 636. According to the definition, the false pretense must be a representation as to an existing fact or past event. False representations amounting to mere promises or statements of intention have reference to future events and are not criminal within the statute, even though they induce the party defrauded to part with his property. 22 Am.Jur., False Pretenses, § 14, p. 452; C.J.S., False Pretenses, § 8, p. 646. But if false representations are made, some of which refer to existing facts or past events, while others refer solely to future events, a conviction may be had if it is shown that any of the representations as to existing facts induced the complaining witness to part with his property.

Tested by these principles, we hold that the evidence on behalf of the Commonwealth is sufficient to sustain a conviction under this statute on which the third count is based. The evidence shows the intent to defraud, the commission of an actual fraud, and the use of false pretenses for the purpose of perpetrating a fraud, which induced the prosecuting witness to part with his property.

The false representations were not, as the defendant claims, merely promissory in nature. Just before the sale of the car was consummated the defendant represented to Reynolds that the condition of his business was "very, very good." He also represented to this witness that he had arranged for a $20,000 "floor plan" with the Savings Bank & Trust Company of Richmond, and that as the result of such plan he would have in bank sufficient funds to meet the check when it was presented for payment. Both of these representations were false because the evidence clearly shows that his business was not in sound condition, nor had he in fact consummated the necessary arrangements with the bank in order to insure the payment of the check which he gave Reynolds. Indeed, the records of the bank show that he had overdrawn his account on September 17, the day before he purchased the car from Reynolds. When he obtained from the bank a loan on the two cars which he had purchased from or through Reynolds, and deposited the proceeds, the fund was immediately exhausted by checks which he had previously drawn and which were presented to the bank before his check to Reynolds reached there. He is bound to have known this condition. * * *

The judgment under review will be modified by finding the defendant not guilty as charged in counts 1 and 2 of the indictment and setting aside the sentences imposed pursuant to convictions under these counts. The judgment finding the defendant guilty as charged in the third count of the indictment . . . is affirmed.

Modified and affirmed.

NOTES

1. Consider the viewpoint expressed in the A.L.I. Model Penal Code, which provides, in its official Commentary, (1980) on § 223.3:

Theft by Deception

(1) *General.* A person commits theft if he obtains property of another by means of deception. A person deceives if he purposely:

(a) creates or reinforces an impression which is false and which he does not believe to be true; or

(b) prevents another from acquiring information which the actor knows would influence the other party in the transaction; or

(c) fails to disclose a lien, adverse claim, or other legal impediment to the enjoyment of property being sold or otherwise transferred or encumbered, regardless of the legal validity of the impediment and regardless of any official record disclosing its existence;

(d) fails to correct a false impression previously created or reinforced by him; or

(e) fails to correct a false impression which he knows to be influencing another to whom he stands in a relationship of special trust and confidence.

(2) *Value, Law, Opinion, Intention; False Promises.* Deception may relate to value, law, opinion, intention or other state of mind. A promise which creates the impression that the promisor intends that the promise shall be performed is deception if he does not have that intention at the time of the promise; but the nonexistence of that intention shall not be inferred from the fact alone that the promise was not performed.

(3) *Puffing Excepted.* Exaggerated commendation of wares in communications addressed to the public or to a class or group shall not be deemed deceptive if:

(a) it would be unlikely to mislead the ordinary person of the class or group addressed; and

(b) there is no deception other than as to the actor's belief in the commendation; and

(c) the actor was not in a position of special trust and confidence in relation to the misled party.

"Commendation of wares" includes representation that the price asked is low.

(4) *Non-pecuniary Deception Excepted.* A person does not commit theft by deception where, in a business transaction, the only deception is as to matters having no pecuniary significance.

2. The Illinois Criminal Code (Ill.Rev.Stats. ch. 38) provides, in § 16–1(a)(3), that a person commits theft when he knowingly "obtains by deception control over property of the owner", and, in § 15–4(e), that "deception" means to knowingly "promise performance which the offender does not intend to perform or knows will not be performed". "Failure to perform", however, "standing alone is not evidence that the offender did not intend to perform" (§ 15–4(e)).

3. With regard to overdrawn checks or checks on defunct or non-existing bank accounts, see Williams v. United States, infra, in subsection H: The Terminology of Theft—Problems of Construction, for a recent United States Supreme Court opinion on the subject of "check kiting." Can there be a misappropriation by one partner giving another partner a "bad check" for a partnership settlement of a dispute? See, Payne v. Commonwealth, 222 Va. 485, 281 S.E.2d 873 (1981).

4. In People v. Vinnola, 177 Colo. 405, 494 P.2d 826 (1972), the Colorado Supreme Court struck down the state's bad-check statute as unconstitutional. Several reasons were given: (1) The statutory definition of "insufficient funds"—"that the drawer has no legal right to require drawee to pay the check in accordance with the ordinary course of the banking business",—was unconstitutionally vague, because the terms "legal right" and "ordinary course of banking business" were terms open to conjecture; (2) the provision that guilt was established when a person "utters a check knowing or having reasonable cause to know at the time of uttering that it will not be paid, and is not paid because of insufficient funds" omitted a requirement of criminal intent; and (3) the provision that guilt would be presumed if the maker does not redeem the check within fifteen days after presentment and refusal, without requiring proof of an intent to defraud, turned the statute into a collection statute imposing imprisonment for debts.

5. In order to obtain a conviction for false pretenses or misrepresentation, is it necessary that the person to whom the misrepresentation be made be the victim? See Mosteller v. Commonwealth, 222 Va. 143, 279 S.E.2d 380 (1981), where a manufacturer's representative assisted vendors of his company's product to prepare inflated bids to the State of Virginia for furniture.

Comprehensive Theft Statutes

Several states, following the pioneering proposals of the American Law Institute have enacted general theft statutes which have abolished the separate offenses of larceny, embezzlement, and false pretenses. See Wisconsin Criminal Code, W.S.A. 943.20, and Illinois Criminal Code (S.H.A. ch. 38), Art. 16.

1. Consider the Illinois Criminal Code section on deceptive practices. It reads in relevant part as follows (Ill.Rev.Stats., ch. 38, § 17):

§ 17–1. Deceptive practices.

(A) As used in this Section:

(i) A financial institution means any bank, savings and loan association, credit union, or other depository of money, or medium of savings and collective investment.

(ii) An account holder is any person, having a checking account or savings account in a financial institution.

(iii) To act with the "intent to defraud" means to act wilfully, and with the specific intent to deceive or cheat, for the purpose of causing financial loss to another, or to bring some financial gain to oneself. It is not necessary to establish that any person was actually defrauded or deceived.

(B) General Deception

A person commits a deceptive practice when, with intent to defraud:

(a) He causes another, by deception or threat to execute a document disposing of property or a document by which a pecuniary obligation is incurred, or

(b) Being an officer, manager or other person participating in the direction of a financial institution, he knowingly receives or permits the receipt of a deposit or other investment, knowing that the institution is insolvent, or

(c) He knowingly makes or directs another to make a false or deceptive statement addressed to the public for the purpose of promoting the sale of property or services, or

(d) With intent to obtain control over property or to pay for property, labor or services of another, or in satisfaction of an obligation for payment of tax under the Retailers' Occupation Tax Act or any other tax due to the State of Illinois, he issues or delivers a check or other order upon a real or fictitious depository for the payment of money, knowing that it will not be paid by the depository. Failure to have sufficient funds or credit with the depository when the check or other order is issued or delivered, or when such check or other order is presented for payment and dishonored on each of 2 occasions at least 7 days apart, is prima facie evidence that the offender knows that it will not be paid by the depository, and that he has the intent to defraud.

(e) He issues or delivers a check or other order upon a real or fictitious depository in an amount exceeding $150 in payment of an amount owed on any credit transaction for property, labor or services, or in payment of the entire amount owed on any credit transaction for property, labor or services knowing that it will not be paid by the depository, and thereafter fails to provide funds or credit with the depository in the face amount of the check or order within seven days of receiving actual notice from the depository or payee of the dishonor of the check or order.

Sentence.

A person convicted of deceptive practice under paragraphs (a) through (d) of this subsection (B), except as otherwise provided by this Section, is guilty of a Class A misdemeanor.

A person convicted of a deceptive practice in violation of paragraph (d) a second or subsequent time shall be guilty of a Class 4 felony.

A person convicted of deceptive practices in violation of paragraph (d), when the value of the property so obtained, in a single transaction, or in separate transactions within a 90 day period, exceeds $150, shall be guilty of a Class 4 felony. In the case of a prosecution for separate transactions totalling more than $150 within a 90 day period, such separate transactions shall be alleged in a single charge and provided in a single prosecution.

(C) Deception on a Bank or Other Financial Institution: False Statements

(1) Any person who, with the intent to defraud, makes or causes to be made, any false statement in writing in order to obtain an account with a bank or other financial institution, or to obtain credit from a bank or other financial institution, knowing such writing to be false, and with the intent that it be relied upon, is guilty of a Class A misdemeanor.

For purposes of this subsection (C), a false statement shall mean any false statement representing identity, address, or employment, or the identity, address or employment of any person, firm or corporation.

Possession of Stolen or Fraudulently Obtained Checks

(2) Any person who possesses, with the intent to defraud, any check or order for the payment of money, upon a real or fictitious account, without the consent of the account holder, or the issuing financial institution, is guilty of a Class A misdemeanor.

Any person who, within any 12 month period, violates this Section with respect to 3 or more checks or orders for the payment of money at the same time or consecutively, each the property of a different account holder or financial institution, is guilty of a Class 4 felony.

(3) Possession of Implements of Check Fraud. Any person who possesses, with the intent to defraud, and without the authority of the account holder or financial institution any check imprinter, signature imprinter, or "certified" stamp is guilty of a Class A misdemeanor.

A person who within any 12 month period violates this subsection (C) as to possession of 3 or more such devices at the same time or consecutively, is guilty of a Class 4 felony.

Possession of Identification Card

(4) Any person, who with the intent to defraud, possesses any check guarantee card or key card or identification card for cash dispensing machines without the authority of the account holder or financial institution, is guilty of a Class A misdemeanor.

A person who, within any 12 month period, violates this Section at the same time or consecutively with respect to 3 or more cards, each the property of different account holders, is guilty of a Class 4 felony.

A person convicted under this Section, when the value of property so obtained, in a single transaction, or in separate transactions within any 90 day period, exceeds $150 shall be guilty of a Class 4 felony.

2. The difficult legal problems presented by improper credit card use and impermissible credit transactions were given considerable attention by the Illinois legislature, which resulted in the adoption of several comprehensive credit card statutes, the latest of which went into effect in 1985 and is known as the Illinois Credit Card and Debit Card Act. See Ill.Rev.Stats., ch. 17, § 5915.1 et seq.

3. The question whether federal authorities have jurisdiction to deal with the criminal use of credit cards has been raised in complex and controversial litigation. Prosecutions have been initiated under the mail fraud statute (18 U.S.C.A. § 1341) and the statute punishing interstate transportation of stolen securities or things used in forging or falsely making a security (18 U.S.C.A. §§ 2311, 2314). In prosecutions under the latter statute, the theory is that credit cards, while not "securities" themselves, are "things" which can be used to forge or falsely make securities, i.e., the sales slips signed by the credit card purchaser. Prosecutions under the mail fraud statute are undertaken on the theory that the mailing by the retailer of signed sales slips to the organization extending the credit by issuing the card furnishes the nexus between the actions of the defendant and the loss to the victim. The validity of these theories is discussed in Merrill v. United States, 338 F.2d 763 (5th Cir. 1964); Beam v. United States, 364 F.2d 756 (6th Cir. 1966) (securities); Adams v. United States, 312 F.2d 137 (5th Cir. 1963) and Kloian v. United States, 349 F.2d 291 (5th Cir. 1965) (mail fraud). See also Katz, Federal Prosecution For The Interstate Transportation Of Stolen Credit Cards, 38 U.Colo.L.Rev. 323 (1966); Comment, Credit Cards, 57 Nw.U.L.Rev. 207 (1962).

4. Specific efforts by legislatures and courts to reach "commercial bribery" schemes, e.g., secret profits, kickbacks, and other conflicts of interest, have increased in recent years, even in jurisdictions such as Illinois which have already enacted comprehensive theft provisions. In this connection, consider the following case:

> A is the purchasing agent of the Acme company, a manufacturer of radio and television sets. B is the president of a company which supplies wooden cabinets to Acme. In return for the purchase of B's cabinets by Acme, B, through a third party, "kicked-back" a secret commission of $1.00 for each cabinet to A. B was the only bidder for the contract to supply cabinets. A's superiors at Acme thought the price per cabinet was reasonable, and B's profit margin was within the 10% limit allowed by Acme. Acme has a company policy which prohibits suppliers from giving gratuities to its purchasing agents and both A and B were aware of this policy.

Do these facts make out an offense by B under the following provision of the comprehensive Illinois theft law, § 16–3 of the Illinois Criminal Code:

> A person commits theft when he obtains temporary use of . . . services of another which are available only for hire, by means of . . . deception or knowing that such use is without the consent of the person providing the . . . services.

Under another section of the Code, § 15–4, "deception" includes knowingly to "prevent another from acquiring information pertinent to the disposition of the property involved" or "create or confirm another's impression which is false and which the offender does not believe to be true" or "fail to correct a false impression which the offender previously has created or confirmed".

Do the facts of the Acme company case constitute a violation by *B* of Section 17–1(a) Illinois Criminal Code which provides:

"A person commits a deceptive practice when, with intent to defraud, . . . he causes another, by deception or threat to execute a document disposing of property or a document by which a pecuniary obligation is incurred."

Perhaps the Illinois legislature felt that such conduct did not fit comfortably within the reach of even its modern, comprehensive theft provisions, for another section (§ 29A–1) provides:

"A person commits commercial bribery when he confers, or offers or agrees to confer, any benefit upon any employee, agent or fiduciary without the consent of the latter's employer or principal, with intent to influence his conduct in relation to his employer's or principal's affairs".

Compare the treatment of the same foregoing case facts by the Court of Appeals for the Seventh Circuit in United States v. George, 477 F.2d 508 (1973):

Cummings, Circuit Judge.

The three defendants were indicted for mail fraud in violation of 18 U.S.C.A. § 1341 and for aiding and abetting that fraud under 18 U.S.C.A. § 2. The indictment was ultimately in 18 counts. The only variance in counts was that the last 17 involved additional mailing dates.

The indictment described defendant Peter K. Yonan as a cabinet buyer in the Purchasing Department of Zenith Radio Corporation. Defendant Andrew George was said to do business as A & G Woodworking Co. The other defendant Irving H. Greensphan, was specified as president of Accurate Box Corporation, which supplied cabinets to Zenith.

The grand jury charged that from June 1967 through January 1971, the three friends devised a scheme to defraud Zenith whereby Yonan received kickbacks on Accurate Box Corporation's sales of cabinets to Zenith. To accomplish this, George allegedly submitted fictitious "commission" invoices of A & G Woodworking Co. to Greensphan's company. After these invoices were paid, George supposedly paid part of the proceeds to Yonan. The kickbacks were of course not disclosed to Zenith. The indictment alleged that the scheme deprived Zenith of its lawful money and property and of the honest and faithful performance of its employee Yonan's duties. The mailings mentioned in the indictment covered checks sent by Zenith to Greensphan's cabinet company before the latter was billed by George's company. . . .

The evidence brought forward at the trial disclosed a novel scheme. Yonan went to work for Zenith in 1961 and was a buyer in the cabinet division of Zenith's Purchasing Department. He had "primary responsibility" for negotiating with cabinet vendors, and, in the words of his immediate supervisor, that meant "his responsibility was to send out the blueprints and gather in quotations, and where the price was too high, to try to negotiate it down to a proper level." Of course, the quotations Yonan negotiated were reviewed by his superiors and by other departments of Zenith. In 1966, Yonan was given the responsibility for finding and negotiating with a supplier of cabinets for Zenith's newly conceived "Circle of Sound" product. His responsibility also included arranging for delivery and monitoring the quality of the cabinets. His friend since the mid-fifties, defendant Greensphan, the owner of Accurate Box Corporation ("Accurate"), was tapped as the supplier. During the indictment years, Accurate was the sole bidder on and supplier of these cabinets. Yonan's supervisor thought Accurate's prices to be fair and reasonable, but in the absence of other bidders, could not conclude they were competitive. Zenith normally allowed its suppliers a maximum of 10% profit, and Accurate's prices reflected that profit margin. The Circle of Sound product proved to be a tremendous financial success. The Zenith checks listed in the indictment were received by Accurate in payment of the cabinets sold to Zenith.

Without recounting any actual threat by Yonan, Greensphan testified that he agreed to pay Yonan $1 per cabinet kickback on the model 565 Circle of Sound unit and later per cabinet kickbacks on other models because he was afraid he was otherwise going to lose Zenith's business. Yonan assertedly told him that "everybody and their uncle would like to get into this to manufacture this unit." He stated that Yonan's request for such payments originated in October 1967. When he asked Yonan how the kickbacks were to be paid, Greensphan was told to pay A & G Woodworking Co.'s commission invoices. Greensphan never related these events to anyone at Zenith. He had known defendant George since 1960. He denied inflating any quotations to cover monies paid to Yonan.

Commencing in December 1967, Accurate received commission invoices from defendant George's A & G Woodworking Co. even though neither George nor A & G Woodworking Co. provided any services to Accurate. Accurate paid these invoices on the basis of a commission per unit on the types of models it shipped to Zenith. Greensphan also cashed a $3,000 Accurate check payable to himself and gave the proceeds to George because he was fearful of losing Zenith's business. To conceal the set fee per unit commission on the cabinets shipped, Accurate's records showed the payments to George's company as 3.4% on monies Accurate received from Zenith rather than as fixed sums on each cabinet. However, on these records the total prices of the cabinets shipped to Zenith were not correct, but were altered to make the commissions correspond to 3.4% thereof. From December 1967 until December 1970, Accurate paid George's company in excess of $300,000 in commissions. During the period in which Greensphan's company was paying the commission invoices of George's company, the latter paid Yonan kickbacks in excess of $100,000 through checks made out by George.

The Government's theory, credited by the jury, was that the kickbacks to Yonan were accomplished by Greensphan's payments of George's company's fictitious commission invoices, with George then acting as a kickback conduit to Yonan. In this connection, it should be noted that in 1969 or 1970, Yonan asked Greensphan's company's controller for a report of the total commission payments then made by that company to George. Shipping quantities on at least one A & G invoice were confirmed to Yonan by Accurate's plant superintendent.

Zenith had a conflict-of-interest policy providing that no gratuities of any nature were to be bestowed on its Purchasing Department employees by suppliers. Yonan twice signed documents embodying that policy, which was annually brought to the attention of all suppliers of Zenith through letters sent out to them. Greensphan admitted receiving these letters during the period of time he was channeling the payments to Yonan.

A number of Zenith's employees testified that Yonan did not request preferential treatment for Greensphan and his company and that they had no knowledge of Yonan providing such treatment for them. It appears Yonan was insistent on quality and efficiency from Accurate.

Evidentiary Sufficiency of a Scheme to Defraud

The mail fraud statute [1] delineates two essential elements constituting the crime: a scheme to defraud and use of the mails in furtherance of the scheme. There is no dispute as to the sufficiency of the evidence to establish use of the mails, nor could there be. Defendants contend that the evidence was insufficient to satisfy the first element—the existence of a scheme to defraud. Reduced to its essential distillation, their argument is that because the kickbacks were never shown to come out of Zenith's pockets, as opposed to Greensphan's, because Yonan was never shown to provide or secure any special services for Greensphan and his company, and because Zenith was never shown to be dissatisfied with Accurate's cabinets or prices, no fraud within the contemplation of the statute can have occurred. We reject this argument, in part because it misses the point in two respects and in part because the particular scheme shown by the evidence to defraud Zenith is, from every defendant's point of view, within the reach of the mail fraud statute.

Since the gravamen of the offense is a "scheme to defraud," it is unnecessary that the Government allege or prove that the victim of the scheme was actually defrauded or suffered a loss. . . . If there was intent on the part of a schemer to deprive Zenith of Yonan's honest and loyal services in the form of his giving Greensphan preferential treatment, it is simply beside the point that Yonan may not have had to (or had occasion to) exert special influence in favor of Greensphan or that Zenith was satisfied with Accurate's product and prices. And it is of no moment whether or not the kickback money actually came from Zenith. Thus the district court correctly charged

---

1. 18 U.S.C.A. § 1341 provides:

"Whoever, having devised or intending to devise any scheme or artifice to defraud, or for obtaining money or property by means of false or fraudulent pretenses, representations, or promises, or to sell, dispose of, loan, exchange, alter, give away, distribute, supply, or furnish or procure for unlawful use any counterfeit or spurious coin, obligation, security, or other article, or anything represented to be or intimated or held out to be such counterfeit or spurious article, for the purpose of executing such scheme or artifice or attempting so to do, places in any post office or authorized depository for mail matter, any matter or thing whatever to be sent or delivered by the Post Office Department, or takes or receives therefrom, any such matter or thing, or knowingly causes to be delivered by mail according to the direction thereon, or at the place at which it is directed to be delivered by the person to whom it is addressed, any such matter or thing, shall be fined not more than $1,000 or imprisoned not more than five years, or both."

the jury that it was unnecessary for the Government to prove "that anyone actually be defrauded." Contrary to defendants' contentions, the evidence hardly shows that it was impossible for Yonan to exercise favoritism toward Greensphan. As the Court noted in Shushan v. United States, 117 F.2d 110, 115 (5th Cir. 1941): "The fact that the official who is bribed is only one of several and could not award the contract by himself does not change the character of the scheme where he is expected to have influence enough to secure the end in view." In our view the evidence shows that Yonan did have opportunities to give Greensphan preferential treatment, particularly by avoiding the solicitation of potential competitors. Of course, the actual exercise of any such opportunity by a person in Yonan's position may be practically undetectable.

Furthermore, even if Yonan never intended to give Greensphan preferential treatment, and the Government does not argue that the evidence was sufficient to support a conclusion that he did, the defendants' argument still misses the mark. The evidence shows Yonan actually defrauded Zenith. We need not accept the Government's far-ranging argument that anytime an agent secretly profits from his agency he has committed criminal fraud.[2] Not every breach of every fiduciary duty works a criminal fraud.[3] But here Yonan's duty was to negotiate the best price possible for Zenith or at least to apprise Zenith that Greensphan was willing to sell his cabinets for substantially less money. Not only did Yonan secretly earn a profit from his agency but also he deprived Zenith of material knowledge that Greensphan would accept less profit. There was a very real and tangible harm to Zenith in losing the discount or losing the opportunity to bargain with a most relevant fact before it. As Judge Learned Hand stated in a related context:

"A man is none the less cheated out of his property, when he is induced to part with it by fraud, because he gets a quid pro quo of equal value. It may be impossible to measure his loss by the gross scales available to a court, but he has suffered a wrong; he has lost his chance to bargain with the facts before him. That is the evil against

---

2. See United States v. Faser, 303 F.Supp. 380, 383–384 (E.D.La.1969); United States v. Hoffa, 205 F.Supp. 710, 716 (S.D.Fla.1962).

3. See Epstein v. United States, 174 F.2d 754 (6th Cir. 1949). In that case, heavily relied on by defendants, two of the defendants had directorates in both breweries and brewery supply companies, and the Government argued that because the breweries bought from these suppliers and the defendants did not disclose their conflict-of-interest positions, the defendants were guilty of mail fraud. The Court held such conduct was "constructive" and not "active" fraud and outside the purview of the mail fraud statute absent a showing that the supply companies' prices were unfair. Its rationale was that under applicable civil law, directors, on behalf of their corporations, could contract with themselves or corporations in which they were interested, and such contracts were completely valid so long as they were advantageous and made in good faith. Under these circumstances mere non-disclosure did not generate a profit at the corporation's expense. However, those defendants did not have a duty to make their profit— the return on their investment in the supply companies—available to the breweries, whereas Yonan did have a duty to make his profit—an assumedly unmerited kickback—available to Zenith. There was no reason to believe disclosure by the defendants in *Epstein* would have, under the particular circumstances, there, made any bargaining difference to the breweries, but Yonan's disclosure, in addition to making the scheme impossible, would have enabled Zenith to realize a substantial discount.

which the statute is directed." United States v. Rowe, 56 F.2d 747, 749 (2d Cir. 1932).

Here the fraud consisted in Yonan's holding himself out to be a loyal employee, acting in Zenith's best interests, but actually not giving his honest and faithful services, to Zenith's real detriment.

No refuge can be taken in Zenith's policy "normally" to allow suppliers a 10% profit and in Accurate's prices being within that margin. Nothing would have prevented Zenith from bargaining with Accurate for a lesser profit margin, and it would be unrealistic to presume that Zenith would consider the fact of better than $100,000 in actual kickbacks to its buyer—over $300,000 in agreed-to-kickbacks—to be immaterial in its dealings with Greensphan. It is preposterous to claim that Zenith would have spurned such a discount if offered.

In this case, whether Zenith was to be deprived of Yonan's honest and faithful performance of his duties to the extent of his secretly profiting from his agency and concealing knowledge of the availability of that material sum from Zenith, or to the further extent of his meriting the payments which he received, a fraud within the reach of the mail fraud statute would be present.[4] The statute requires the existence of a scheme to perpetrate this fraud, and the question of evidentiary sufficiency boils down to whether the Government has proven that the defendants contemplated that Zenith suffer the loss of Yonan's honest and loyal services.

Indubitably the evidence showed a "scheme." The critical element is fraudulent intent. Each of the defendants asserts that there was insufficient evidence as to his intent to defraud Zenith of Yonan's loyalty and honesty, but we conclude to the contrary.

Does the rationale of *George* apply to undisclosed conflicts of interest by public officers? Assume that *A*, an alderman, holds an interest in land which is subject to back taxes and assessments levied by the city. *A*, after having carried on correspondence by mail with interested parties, then introduces an ordinance in the city council, and votes in favor of its passage, which compromises the city's claims at 10% of the taxes and assessments without disclosing his ownership of the property. Previous settlements by the council with other owners of encumbered property have ranged from 10% to 30%. Does such conduct violate the mail fraud statute? Compare United States v. Isaacs, 347 F.Supp. 743 (N.D.Ill.1972).

4. The court properly charged the jury as follows:

"Now, to knowingly tamper or interfere with an employer-employee relationship for the purpose of and with the intent of depriving the employer of the employee's honest and faithful performance of his duties for the employer may constitute a fraud within the meaning of the mail fraud statute." See United States v. Procter & Gamble Co., 47 F.Supp. 676, 678 (D.Mass.1942).

D.   RECEIVING STOLEN PROPERTY—THE
PRESUMPTION FACTOR

PEOPLE v. RIFE

Supreme Court of Illinois, 1943.
382 Ill. 588, 48 N.E.2d 367.

THOMPSON, JUSTICE.   Plaintiff in error, Noah D. Rife, and his wife, Mabel, operators of a junk yard in the city of Danville, were jointly indicted at the January term, 1941, of the circuit court of Vermilion county, charged in three counts with receiving, buying and aiding in concealing 132 pounds of engine brass and 167 pounds of journal brass, and in a fourth count with receiving, buying and aiding in concealing 299 pounds of brass, all of the property of and stolen from Benjamin Wham, trustee of the Chicago and Eastern Illinois Railway Company, a corporation.   Each of the counts charged that defendant knew that said brass had been stolen.   Defendants pleaded not guilty and were tried by a jury.   Plaintiff in error was found guilty and the value of the property received was found to be $9.35.   His wife, the other defendant, was found not guilty.   Motion for a new trial was denied and plaintiff in error was sentenced to the Illinois State Penal Farm at Vandalia for one year and fined $1,000. . . .

The roundhouse foreman in the Chicago and Eastern Illinois railway yards at Chicago, in October, 1940, supervised the replacing of brass on engines 3643 and 1908.   The old brass taken off these engines was loaded in two freight cars, sealed and shipped to the railroad shops or roundhouse at Danville.   One of these cars arrived on October 22, 1940, and was unloaded and put in the bins at the Danville shops on October 22 and 23.   The other car came in November 2, 1940, and from that time until it was unloaded on November 8, stood upon the company's track at the storeroom in the Danville yards of the C. & E. I. On November 5, 1940, plaintiff in error bought 187 pounds of railroad brass from [a boy named Henry Brandon].   On the day previous he had also bought brass from Brandon.   On November 5, 1940, W. B. Sloan, the chief of police of the railway company, Theodore Alberts, general foreman of the company, and Robert Meade, a deputy sheriff, went to the junk yard of plaintiff in error, where they recovered 132 pounds of railway-engine brass and 167 pounds of journal brass.   This brass was positively identified by Mr. Alberts from the engine numbers, 3643 and 1908, and the patent number A–D 830 stamped on the various pieces.

The contention is made that the evidence is not sufficient to prove beyond a reasonable doubt that the brass described in the indictment was ever stolen, and also that the evidence is not sufficient to prove beyond a reasonable doubt that plaintiff in error knew the brass had been stolen at the time he purchased it from Henry Brandon.   Before there can be a conviction for receiving stolen property the evidence must show beyond a reasonable doubt, first, that the property has, in fact, been stolen by a person other than the one charged with receiving the property; second, that the one charged with receiving it has actually received it or aided in concealing it; third, that the person so receiving the stolen property knew that it was stolen at the time of receiving it; and, fourth, that he received the property for his own gain or to prevent the owner from again possessing it. . . . But while it is true that these four propositions must all be proved beyond a reasonable doubt, it is also true that neither is required to be established by direct evidence. Circumstantial evidence may be resorted to for the purpose of proving the corpus delicti as well as for the purpose of connecting the accused with the crime. . . . There is no invariable rule as to the quantum of proof necessary to establish the corpus delicti. Each case must depend, in a measure, upon its own particular circumstances. . . . Circumstantial evidence is legal evidence and there is no legal distinction between direct and circumstantial evidence so far as weight and effect are concerned. . . . It is not necessary that someone testify, in so many words, to the theft of this brass and that plaintiff in error had knowledge of such theft at the time he purchased the brass from Henry Brandon, but such facts may be shown by circumstantial evidence. The brass found in the Rife junk yard was positively identified as brass which had been removed from the Chicago and Eastern Illinois engines in Chicago and shipped to Danville, within twenty days at the most, previous to that time. It was conclusively proved by the evidence that this brass shipped from Chicago to Danville for use in the railroad shops there, and received at the C. & E. I. shops at Danville, where it was in the exclusive possession of the railway company on its own private premises. It then disappeared. It must have been taken by somebody. The only conclusion that can follow, under all the circumstances, is that a larceny had been committed. There was no contention by the plaintiff in error on the trial that the brass was not stolen. Indeed, his wife testified that he had told her that Henry Brandon had stolen it. In the case of People v. Feeley . . . where department-store merchandise, including shirts, ties, socks, and other wearing apparel, was discovered in an automobile, this court held that the fact that none of the articles had been wrapped in packages by the stores, but had been stuffed in large quantities in cardboard boxes, and the finding of the shoplifters' boxes in the automobile, were circumstances sufficiently proving the theft of such merchandise. In the Feeley case, supra, there was no evidence that the merchandise had been missed or was known to be stolen before found in the automobile. It is not necessary in the instant case, to warrant the jury in finding that a larceny of the brass had been committed, for the evidence to show that it had been missed by the employees of the Chicago and Eastern Illinois Railway Company or that they knew that it had been stolen. . . .

Plaintiff in error testified that when Brandon sold him the brass, he told him that the brass was not stolen, that he had found it, that it was all right for plaintiff in error to buy it, and that if any one inquired he could say that he had bought it from Brandon. He also testified that the possession of a large amount of heavy brass by [a boy] who claimed to have found it did not arouse his suspicions. . . . .

There was no direct evidence that plaintiff in error purchased the brass in question knowing it to have been stolen. The People relied upon circumstantial evidence for such proof, but this does not militate against the prosecution.. . . . Knowledge that property was stolen is seldom susceptible of direct proof, but may be inferred from all the surrounding facts and circumstances. . . . Circumstances which will induce a belief in the mind of a reasonable person that property has been stolen are sufficient proof of such guilty knowledge. . . . The knowledge need not be that actual or positive knowledge which one acquires from personal observation of the fact, but it is sufficient if the circumstances accompanying the transaction be such as to make the accused believe the goods had been stolen. This knowledge of the accused is an essential element of the offense and must be found by the jury as a fact. In determining whether the fact existed, the jury will be justified in presuming that the accused acted rationally and that whatever would convey knowledge or induce belief in the mind of a reasonable person, would, in the absence of countervailing evidence, be sufficient to apprise him of the like fact, or induce in his mind the like impression and belief. . . .

In the instant case plaintiff in error, after recent and repeated warnings to be on the alert for stolen railroad brass and to notify the sheriff's office of any suspicious circumstances, failed to report the circumstance to the officers when [a boy] offered him a large amount of such brass with no explanation other than that he had found it and had not stolen it. Plaintiff in error made no inquiry into the details of the [boy's] improbable story of his acquisition of such a large amount of brass. The story of plaintiff in error, of his purchase of this brass in good faith and innocence, is not supported either by any direct or circumstantial evidence. On the contrary, all the evidence points conclusively to, and is sufficient to warrant the jury in believing, beyond a reasonable doubt, that plaintiff in error knew when he purchased this brass that he was handling stolen property. . . . All of the evidence, and facts and circumstances in evidence, in the instant case, when considered together, cannot consistently be reconciled with any theory other than that of the guilt of the accused. Upon a review of the record in a criminal case, it is the duty of this court to consider the evidence, and if it does not establish guilt beyond a reasonable doubt, the conviction must be reversed. We have carefully considered all of the evidence, both that of the People and that of plaintiff in error, and we cannot say that it is not amply sufficient to justify the jury in believing beyond a reasonable doubt that the plaintiff in error is guilty of the crime with which he is charged. . . .

The judgment will therefore be affirmed.

Judgment affirmed.

BARNES v. UNITED STATES

Supreme Court of the United States, 1973.
412 U.S. 837, 93 S.Ct. 2357.

MR. JUSTICE POWELL delivered the opinion of the Court.

Petitioner Barnes was convicted in United States District Court on two counts of possessing United State Treasury checks stolen from the mails, knowing them to be stolen, two counts of forging the checks, and two counts of uttering the checks, knowing the endorsements to be forged. The trial court instructed the jury that ordinarily it would be justified in inferring from unexplained possession of recently stolen mail that the defendant possessed the mail with knowledge that it was stolen. We granted certiorari to consider whether this instruction comports with due process. 409 U.S. 1037, 93 S.Ct. 544 (1972).

The evidence at petitioner's trial established that on June 2, 1971, he opened a checking account using the pseudonym "Clarence Smith." On July 1, and July 3, 1971, the United States Disbursing Office at San Francisco mailed four Government checks in the amounts of $269.02, $154.70, $184, and $268.80 to Nettie Lewis, Albert Young, Arthur Salazar, and Mary Hernandez, respectively. On July 8, 1971, petitioner deposited these four checks into the "Smith" account. Each check bore the apparent endorsement of the payee and a second endorsement by "Clarence Smith."

At petitioner's trial the four payees testified that they had never received, endorsed, or authorized endorsement of the checks. A Government handwriting expert testified that petitioner had made the "Clarence Smith" endorsement on all four checks and that he had signed the payees' names on the Lewis and Hernandez checks. Although petitioner did not take the stand, a postal inspector testified to certain statements made by petitioner at a post-arrest interview. Petitioner explained to the inspector that he received the checks in question from people who sold furniture for him door to door and that the checks had been signed in the payees' names when he received them. Petitioner further stated that he could not name or identify any of the salespeople. Nor could he substantiate the existence of any furniture orders because the salespeople allegedly wrote their orders on scratch paper that had not been retained. Petitioner admitted that he executed the Clarence Smith endorsements and deposited the checks but denied making the payees' endorsements.

The District Court instructed the jury that "[p]ossession of recently stolen property, if not satisfactorily explained, is ordinarily a circumstance from which you may reasonably draw the inference and find, in the light of the surrounding circumstances shown by the evidence in the case, that the person in possession knew the property had been stolen."[1]

The jury brought in guilty verdicts on all six counts, and the District Court sentenced petitioner to concurrent three-year prison terms. The Court of Appeals for the Ninth Circuit affirmed, finding no lack of "rational connection" between unexplained possession of recently stolen property and knowledge that the propety was stolen. Because petitioner received identical concurrent sentences on all six counts, the court declined to consider his challenges to conviction on the forgery and uttering counts. We affirm.

I.

We begin our consideration of the challenged jury instruction with a review of four recent decisions which have considered the validity under the Due Process Clause of criminal law presumptions and inferences. Turner v. United States, 396 U.S. 398, 90 S.Ct. 642 (1970); Leary v. United States, 395 U.S. 6, 89 S.Ct. 1532 (1969); United States v. Romano, 382 U.S. 136, 86 S.Ct. 279 (1965); United States v. Gainey, 380 U.S. 63, 85 S.Ct. 754 (1965).

In United States v. Gainey, supra, the Court sustained the constitutionality of an instruction tracking a statute which authorized the jury to infer from defendant's unexplained presence at an illegal still that he was carrying on "the business of a distiller or rectifier without having given bond as required by law." Relying on the holding of Tot v. United States, 319 U.S. 463, 467, 63 S.Ct. 1241, 1245 (1943), that

---

1. The full instruction on the inference arising from possession of stolen property stated:

"Possession of recently stolen property, if not satisfactorily explained, is ordinarily a circumstance from which you may reasonably draw the inference and find, in the light of the surrounding circumstances shown by the evidence in the case, that the person in possession knew the property had been stolen.

"However, you are never required to make this inference. It is the exclusive province of the jury to determine whether the facts and circumstances shown by the evidence in this case warrant any inference which the law permits the jury to draw from the possession of recently stolen property.

"The term 'recently' is a relative term, and has no fixed meaning. Whether property may be considered as recently stolen depends upon the nature of the property, and all the facts and circumstances shown by the evidence in the case. The longer the period of time since the theft the more doubtful becomes the inference which may reasonably be drawn from unexplained possession.

"If you should find beyond a reasonable doubt from the evidence in the case that the mail described in the indictment was stolen, and that while recently stolen the contents of said mail here, the four United States Treasury checks, were in the possession of the defendant you would ordinarily be justified in drawing from those facts the inference that the contents were possessed by the accused with knowledge that it was stolen property, unless such possession is explained by facts and circumstances in this case which are in some way consistent with the defendant's innocence.

"In considering whether possession of recently stolen property has been satisfactorily explained, you are reminded that in the exercise of constitutional rights the accused need not take the witness stand and testify.

"Possession may be satisfactorily explained through other circumstances, other evidence, independent of any testimony of the accused." Tr. 123–124.

there must be a "rational connection between the fact proved and the ultimate fact presumed," the Court upheld the inference on the basis of the comprehensive nature of the "carrying on" offense and the common knowledge that illegal stills are secluded, secret operations. The following Term the Court determined, however, that presence at an illegal still could not support the inference that the defendant was in possession, custody, or control of the still, a narrower offense. "Presence is relevant and admissible evidence in a trial on a possession charge; but absent some showing of the defendant's function at the still, its connection with possession is too tenuous to permit a reasonable inference of guilt—'the inference of the one from proof of the other is arbitrary . . . .' Tot v. United States, 319 U.S. 463, 467, 63 S.Ct. 1241, 1245." United States v. Romano, supra, at 141, 86 S.Ct. at 282.

Three and one-half years after *Romano*, the Court in Leary v. United States, supra, considered a challenge to a statutory inference that possession of marihuana, unless satisfactorily explained, was sufficient to prove that the defendant knew that the marihuana had been illegally imported into the United States. The Court concluded that in view of the significant possibility that any given marihuana was domestically grown and the improbability that a marihuana user would know whether his marihuana was of domestic or imported origin, the inference did not meet the standards set by *Tot*, *Gainey*, and *Romano*. Referring to these three cases, the *Leary* Court stated that an inference is " 'irrational' or 'arbitrary,' and hence unconstitutional, unless it can at least be said with substantial assurance that the presumed fact is more likely than not to flow from the proved fact on which it is made to depend." In a footnote the Court stated that since the challenged inference failed to satisfy the more-likely-than-not standard, it did not have to "reach the question whether a criminal presumption which passes muster when so judged must also satisfy the criminal 'reasonable doubt' standard if proof of the crime charged or an essential element thereof depends upon its use."

Finally, in Turner v. United States, supra, decided the year following *Leary*, the Court considered the constitutionality of instructing the jury that it may infer from possession of heroin and cocaine that the defendant knew these drugs had been illegally imported. The Court noted that *Leary* reserved the question of whether the more-likely-than-not or the reasonable-doubt standard controlled in criminal cases, but it likewise found no need to resolve that question. It held that the inference with regard to heroin was valid judged by either standard. With regard to cocaine, the inference failed to satisfy even the more-likely-than-not standard.

The teaching of the foregoing cases is not altogether clear. To the extent that the "rational connection," "more likely than not," and "reasonable doubt" standards bear ambiguous relationships to one another, the ambiguity is traceable in large part to variations in language and focus rather than to differences of substance. What has been established by the cases, however, is at least this: that if a statutory inference submitted to the jury as sufficient to support conviction satisfies the reasonable-doubt standard (that is, the evidence necessary to invoke the inference is sufficient for a rational juror to find the inferred fact beyond a reasonable doubt) as well as the more-likely-than-not standard, then it clearly accords with due process.

In the present case we deal with a traditional common-law inference deeply rooted in our law. For centuries courts have instructed juries that an inference of guilty knowledge may be drawn from the fact of unexplained possession of stolen goods. James Thayer, writing in his Preliminary Treatise on Evidence (1898), cited this inference as the descendant of a presumption "running through a dozen centuries." Early American cases consistently upheld instructions permitting conviction upon such an inference, and the courts of appeals on numerous occasions have approved instructions essentially identical to the instruction given in this case. This longstanding and consistent judicial approval of the instruction, reflecting accumulated common experience, provides strong indication that the instruction comports with due process.

This impressive historical basis, however, is not in itself sufficient to establish the instruction's constitutionality. Common-law inferences, like their statutory counterparts, must satisfy due process standards in light of present-day experience. In the present case the challenged instruction only permitted the inference of guilt from *unexplained* possession of recently stolen property. The evidence established that petitioner possessed recently stolen Treasury checks payable to persons he did not know, and it provided no plausible explanation for such possession consistent with innocence. On the basis of this evidence alone common sense and experience tell us that petitioner must have known or been aware of the high probability that the checks were stolen. Such evidence was clearly sufficient to enable the jury to find beyond a reasonable doubt that petitioner knew the checks were stolen. Since the inference thus satisfies the reasonable-doubt standard, the most stringent standard the Court has applied in judging permissive criminal law inferences, we conclude that it satisfies the requirements of due process.[2]

2. It is true that the practical effect of instructing the jury on the inference arising from unexplained possession of recently stolen property is to shift the burden of going forward with evidence to the defendant. If the Government proves possession and nothing more, this evidence remains unexplained unless the defendant introduces evidence, since ordinarily the Government's evidence will not provide an explanation of his possession consistent with innocence. In Tot v. United States, 319 U.S. 463, 63 S.Ct. 1241 (1943), the Court stated that the burden of going forward may not be freely shifted to the defendant. See also Leary v. United States, 395 U.S. 6, 44–45, 89 S.Ct. 1532, 1552 (1969). *Tot* held, however, that where there is a "rational connection" between the facts proved and the fact presumed or inferred, it is permissible to shift the burden of going forward to the defendant. Where an inference satisfies the reasonable-doubt standard, as in the present case, there will certainly be a rational connection between the fact presumed or inferred (in this case, knowledge) and the facts the Government must prove in order to shift the burden of going forward (possession of recently stolen property).

Petitioner also argues that the permissive inference in question infringes his privilege against self-incrimination. The Court has twice rejected this argument, and we find no reason to re-examine the issue at length. The trial court specifically instructed the jury that petitioner had a constitutional right not to take the witness stand and that possession could be satisfactorily explained by evidence independent of petitioner's testimony. Introduction of any evidence, direct or circumstantial, tending to implicate the defendant in the alleged crime increases the pressure on him to testify. The mere massing of evidence against a defendant cannot be regarded as a violation of his privilege against self-incrimination.

Petitioner further challenges his conviction on the ground that there was insufficient evidence that he knew the checks were stolen *from the mails.* He contends that 18 U.S.C.A. § 1708 requires knowledge not only that the checks were stolen, but specifically that they were stolen from the mails. The legislative history of the statute conclusively refutes this argument and the courts of appeals that have addressed the issue have uniformly interpreted the statute to require only knowledge that the property was stolen.

Since we find that the statute was correctly interpreted and that the trial court's instructions on the inference to be drawn from unexplained possession of stolen property were fully consistent with petitioner's constitutional rights, it is unnecessary to consider petitioner's challenges to his conviction on the forging and uttering counts.

Affirmed.

MR. JUSTICE DOUGLAS, dissenting.

Possession of stolen property is traditionally under our federal system a local law question. It becomes a federal concern in the present case only if the "mail" was implicated. The indictment, insofar as the unlawful possession counts are concerned, charges that the items had been *"stolen from the mail."* While there was evidence that these items had gone through the mail petitioner did not take the stand, nor was there any evidence that petitioner knew that the items had been "stolen from the mail." As to the possession counts in the indictment the District Court charged the jury that "three essential elements" were required to prove the possession offenses:

"FIRST: The act or acts of unlawfully having in one's possession the contents of a letter, namely, the United States Treasury checks as alleged;

"SECOND: That the contents of the letter, namely, the United States Treasury checks as alleged, were stolen from the mail; and

"THIRD: That the defendant James Edward Barnes knew the contents had been stolen."

We not decide today whether a judge-formulated inference of less antiquity or authority may properly be emphasized by a jury instruction.

The District Court also charged the jury:

> "If you should find beyond a reasonable doubt from the evidence in the case that the mail described in the indictment was stolen, and that while recently stolen the contents of said mail here, the four United States Treasury checks, were in the possession of the defendant you would ordinarily be justified in drawing from those facts the inference that the contents were possessed by the accused with knowledge that it was stolen property, unless such possession is explained by facts and circumstances in this case which are in some way consistent with the defendant's."

As noted by the Court, the Act, which originally required proof of possession of articles stolen from the mail "knowing the same to have been so stolen," 18 U.S.C.A. § 317 (1934 ed.), was changed by eliminating the word "so" before "stolen." And the Act under which petitioner was charged and convicted does not require as an ingredient of the offense that petitioner knew the property had been stolen from the mails.

That, however, is the beginning, not the end of the problem. For without a nexus with the "mails" there is no federal offense. How can we rationally say that "possession" of a stolen check allows a judge or jury to conclude that the accused knew the check was *stolen from the mails?* We held in Tot v. United States, 319 U.S. 463, 63 S.Ct. 1241, that where a federal Act made it unlawful for any convicted person to possess a firearm that had been shipped in interstate or foreign commerce, it was unconstitutional to presume that a firearm possessed by such person had been received in interstate or foreign commerce. The decision was unanimous. The vice in *Tot* was that the burden is on the government in a criminal case to prove guilt beyond a reasonable doubt and that use of the presumption shifts that burden. We said: "[I]t is not permissible thus to shift the burden by arbitrarily making one fact, which has no relevance to guilt of the offense, the occasion of casting on the defendant the obligation of exculpation." The use of presumptions and inferences to prove an element of the crime is indeed treacherous, for it allows men to go to jail without any evidence on one essential ingredient of the offense. It thus implicates the integrity of the judicial system. We held in In re Winship, 397 U.S. 358, 364, 90 S.Ct. 1068, 1073, that the Due Process Clause requires "proof beyond a reasonable doubt of every fact necessary to constitute the crime. . . ." Some evidence of wrongdoing is basic and essential in the judicial system, unless the way of prosecutors be made easy by dispensing with the requirement of presumption of innocence, which is the effect of what the Court does today. In practical effect the use of these presumptions often means that the great barriers to the protection of procedural due process contained in the Bill of Rights are subtly diluted.

May Congress constitutionally enact a law that says juries can convict a defendant without any evidence at all from which an inference of guilt could be drawn? If Thompson v. Louisville, 362 U.S. 199, 80 S.Ct. 624, means anything, the answer is in the negative. The Congress is as unwarranted in telling courts what evidence is enough to convict an accused as we would be to tell Congress what criminal laws should be enacted. That seems inescapably plain by the regime of separation of powers under which we live.

In Leary v. United States, 395 U.S. 6, 89 S.Ct. 1532, we held that it was constitutionally impermissible to presume that one who possessed marihuana would be presumed to know of its unlawful importation. We said it would be sheer "speculation" to conclude that even a majority of the users of the plant knew the source of it. The overall test, we said, was whether it can be said "with substantial assurance that the presumed fact is more likely than not to flow from the proved fact on which it is made to depend."

In that case there were some statistics as to the quantity of marihuana grown here and the amount grown abroad that enters the country. There was evidence of the characteristics of local and foreign marihuana, and the like.

Stolen checks may be the product of local burglaries of private homes or offices.

Stolen checks may come from purses snatched or purloined.

Stolen checks may involve any one of numerous artifices or tricks.

In other words, there are various sources of stolen checks which in no way implicate federal jurisdiction.

Checks stolen from national banks, checks stolen from federal agencies, checks lifted from the mails are other sources.

But, unlike *Leary*, we have no evidence whatsoever showing what amount of stolen property, let alone stolen checks, *implicates the mails*. Without some evidence or statistics of that nature we have no way of assessing the likelihood that this petitioner knew that these checks were *stolen from the mails*. We can take judicial notice that checks are stolen from the mails. But it would take a large degree of assumed omniscience to say with "substantial assurance" that this petitioner more likely than not knew from the realities of the underworld that this stolen propety came *from the mails*. But without evidence of that knowledge there would be no federal offense of the kind charged.

The step we take today will be applauded by prosecutors, as it makes their way easy. But the Bill of Rights was designed to make the job of the prosecutor difficult. There is a presumption of innocence. Proof beyond a reasonable doubt is necessary. The jury, not the court, is the factfinder. These basic principles make the use of these easy presumptions dangerous. What we do today is, I think extremely disrespectful of the constitutional regime that controls the dispensation of criminal justice.

MR. JUSTICE BRENNAN, with whom MR. JUSTICE MARSHALL joins, dissenting.

Petitioner was charged in two counts of a six-count indictment with possession of United States Treasury checks stolen from the mails, knowing them to be stolen. The essential elements of such an offense are (1) that the defendant was in possession of the checks, (2) that the checks were stolen from the mails, and (3) that the defendant knew that the checks were stolen. The Government proved that petitioner had been in possession of the checks and that the checks had been stolen from the mails; and, in addition, the Government introduced some evidence intended to show that petitioner knew or should have known that the checks were stolen. But rather than leaving the jury to determine the element of "knowledge" on the basis of that evidence, the trial court instructed it that it was free to infer the essential element of "knowledge" from petitioner's unexplained possession of the checks. In my view, that instruction violated the Due Process Clause of the Fifth Amendment because it permitted the jury to convict even though the actual evidence bearing on "knowledge" may have been insufficient to establish guilt beyond a reasonable doubt. I therefore dissent.

We held in In re Winship, 397 U.S. 358, 364, 90 S.Ct. 1068, 1073 (1970), that the Due Process Clause requires "proof beyond a reasonable doubt of every fact necessary to constitute the crime . . .." Thus, in Turner v. United States, 396 U.S. 398, 417, 90 S.Ct. 642, 653 (1970), we approved the inference of "knowledge" from the fact of possessing smuggled heroin because " '[c]ommon sense' . . . tells us that those who traffic in heroin will *inevitably* become aware that the product they deal in is smuggled . . .." (Emphasis added.) The basis of that "common sense" judgment was, of course, the indisputable fact that all or virtually all heroin in this country is necessarily smuggled. Here, however, it cannot be said that all or virtually all endorsed United States Treasury checks have been stolen. Indeed, it is neither unlawful nor unusual for people to use such checks as direct payment for goods and services. Thus, unlike *Turner,* "common sense" simply will not permit the inference that the possessor of stolen Treasury checks *"inevitably"* knew that the checks were stolen. Cf. Leary v. United States, 395 U.S. 6, 89 S.Ct. 1532 (1969).

In short, the practical effect of the challenged instruction was to permit the jury to convict petitioner even if it found insufficient or disbelieved all of the Government's evidence bearing directly on the issue of "knowledge." By authorizing the jury to rely exclusively on the inference in determining the element of "knowledge," the instruction relieved the Government of the burden of proving that element beyond a reasonable doubt. The instruction thereby violated the principle of *Winship* that every essential element of the crime must be proved beyond a reasonable doubt.

NOTES

1. As already indicated, the presumption of guilt which the jury is allowed to draw in many jurisdictions is far reaching. In the majority of jurisdictions, the presumption might be used to infer the possessor was a criminal receiver. In other jurisdictions, however, the presumption permits a finding that the defendant was the thief. In Ferrell v. Commonwealth, 11 Va.App. 380, 399 S.E.2d 614 (1990), the court said that where the evidence shows a breaking and entering followed by the theft of goods, and the evidence warrants the inference that the breaking and entering and the theft were committed at the same time by the same person as part of the same transaction then the conscious assertion of exclusive possession of the stolen goods shortly thereafter gives rise to the inference that the possessor is guilty of breaking and entering.

In People v. Baxa, 50 Ill.2d 111, 277 N.E.2d 876 (1971), the defendant was arrested while he was riding as a passenger in a car which contained merchandise stolen the night before. The Illinois Supreme Court said, "That presumption, when its basic facts have been established, has been held sufficient in itself to permit conviction of larceny. [Citations omitted.] The defendant in this case however, was charged with having 'knowingly obtained unauthorized control of stolen property.' While possession is an element of this offense, knowledge that the property was stolen is also an essential element. Both elements must be proved in order to establish guilt. [Citations omitted.] Knowledge may be established by proof of circumstances that would cause a reasonable man to believe that the property had been stolen. But possession alone, even if exclusive, is insufficient to establish that a defendant knew that the property was stolen when he received it. . . ." Does the Illinois court say that conviction or larceny (theft) is permitted by use of the presumption, but not conviction of receiving stolen property? What is the essential difference in the use of the presumption for the one, but not for the other crime?

In Best v. Commonwealth, 222 Va. 387, 282 S.E.2d 16 (1981), the court said that the defendant can be in exclusive possession of recently stolen property when he jointly possesses it with another person. But the presumption does not arise, said the court, when the evidence merely reveals that the stolen property was found in a place to which several people, including the accused, had access.

2. In the light of Sandstrom v. Montana, supra in Chapter 2, which was decided subsequent to the *Barnes* case, is the latter case still good law? In Williamson v. State, 248 Ga. 47, 281 S.E.2d 512 (1981), the Georgia Supreme Court held that *Sandstrom* precludes proof of a material element of a crime by way of a mandatory presumption, but does not affect a permissive inference of guilt from the "recent unexplained" possession of stolen goods, which does not relieve the prosecution of its burden of proof nor require the defense to prove the contrary by any quantum of proof.

3. The giving of an instruction to the effect that exclusive possession of stolen property "if not explained to the satisfaction of the jury, may raise an inference that the person in possession of such stolen property is guilty of the theft or burglary" was deemed to be reversible error in Abel v. State, 165 Ind. App. 664, 333 N.E.2d 848 (1975). The court said that the "language of the instruction that said that an inference of guilt may arise from possession of the goods 'coupled with the absence of a satisfactory explanation' should be construed as nothing more than a comment on defendant's failure to testify, and

such comment by the court is strictly forbidden. . . ." Is that legal conclusion consistent with Mr. Justice Powell's opinion in United States v. Barnes?

In State v. Trowbridge, 97 Idaho 93, 540 P.2d 278 (1975), the court said: "There is insufficient connection between the proved fact of possession or recently stolen property and the ultimate fact of guilty knowledge or belief—or of felonious intent to deprive of ownership—to justify a jury instruction . . . that a presumption of guilt arises from the unsatisfactorily explained possession of recently stolen property." The court nevertheless permitted the jury to be instructed that "unsatisfactorily explained possession of recently stolen property is a circumstance tending to infer knowledge of the unlawful character of the property, and that circumstance taken together with a necessary quantum of evidence, may be used by the jury to reach a verdict, in light of their collective common experience, and the circumstances surrounding the case."

4. Some states, although not operating under a comprehensive theft statute, treat receiving stolen property as larceny. Gunter v. Peyton, 287 F.Supp. 928 (W.D.Va.1968). In Cabbler v. Commonwealth, 212 Va. 520, 184 S.E.2d 781 (1971), it was stated that larceny by receiving stolen goods is a lesser offense which is included in the major one of larceny. If the prosecution elects to charge the greater offense under the general larceny statutes, the defendant could nevertheless be found guilty of receiving stolen property.

E. EXTORTION

STATE v. HARRINGTON
Supreme Court of Vermont, 1969.
128 Vt. 242, 260 A.2d 692.

HOLDEN, CHIEF JUSTICE. The respondent John B. Harrington has been tried and found guilty of the offense of threatening to accuse Armand Morin of Littleton, New Hampshire, of the crime of adultery. The indictment charges that the threat was maliciously made with the intent to extort $175,000 and to compel Morin to do an act against his will in violation of 13 V.S.A. § 1701.

* * *

At the time of the alleged offense the respondent was engaged in the general practice of law in a firm with offices in Burlington, Vermont. Early in March, 1968, he was consulted by Mrs. Norma Morin, the wife of the alleged victim, Armand E. Morin. Mrs. Morin had separated from her husband because of his recent and severe physical abuse. Prior to their separation they owned and operated the Continental 93 Motel in Littleton, New Hampshire, where the Morins maintained a residential apartment. The respondent learned the marital estate of the parties had a net value of approximately $500,000. Mrs. Morin reported to the respondent that her husband had also been guilty of numerous marital infidelities with different women at the motel. Mrs. Morin also disclosed that she had been guilty of marital misconduct which apparently had been condoned.

During the first conference the respondent advised Mrs. Morin that, because of her residence in New Hampshire, she could not undertake divorce proceedings in Vermont for at least six months and for her to obtain a divorce in New Hampshire it would be necessary that she obtain counsel from that state. Mrs. Morin indicated she wished to retain Mr. Harrington to represent her.

On one of the subsequent conferences a friend of Mrs. Morin's, who accompanied her to the respondent's office, suggested that an effort should be made to procure corroborative evidence of Mr. Morin's marital misconduct. To this end, the floor plan of the motel was discussed and a diagram prepared. At this time a scheme was designed to procure the services of a girl who would visit the motel in an effort to obtain corroborative evidence of Morin's infidelity.

After some screening, a Mrs. Mazza, who had been suggested by the respondent, was selected to carry out the assignment. The respondent explained to Mrs. Mazza the purpose of her employment and the results she was expected to accomplish and provided her with a "cover story" to explain her registration and presence as a guest at the Continental 93 Motel. Warning Mrs. Mazza against enticement and entrapment, the respondent instructed the employee to be "receptive and available," but not aggressive. The agreement with Mrs. Mazza was that she would be paid one hundred dollars at the time she undertook the assignment and one hundred dollars when her mission was completed.

Mrs. Morin was without funds at the time. A contingent fee agreement was signed by Mrs. Morin and the firm of Harrington and Jackson, by the respondent. The agreement was dated March 5, 1968 and provided that in the event a satisfactory property settlement was obtained, the respondent's firm was to receive twelve and a half percent of the settlement, in addition to reimbursement for expenses advanced by counsel. Electronic listening and recording equipment was ordered and delivered by air.

On the afternoon of March 6 the respondent and two office associates traveled to St. Johnfhbury in two vehicles. Mrs. Mazza continued on to Littleton unaccompanied. She registered on arrival at the Continental 93 Motel under the name of Jeanne Raeder. She called the respondent at St. Johnfhbury from a public telephone and informed him of her room number and location. Mrs. Mazza later delivered the key to her room to the respondent to enable him to procure a duplicate. The respondent, representing that he was a book salesman, registered at the motel and procured a room directly above that occupied by Mrs. Mazza. He was accompanied by a junior associate and an investigator,—both employed by the respondent's law firm.

During the next day Mrs. Mazza attracted Mr. Morin's attention. The sequence of events which followed led to an invitation by Morin for her to join him at his apartment for a cocktail. Mrs. Mazza accepted. Later she suggested that they go to her room because Mr. Morin's young son was asleep in his quarters. Morin went to Mrs. Mazza's room about midnight. Soon after the appointed hour the respondent and his associates entered the room. With one or more cameras, several photographs were taken of Morin and Mrs. Mazza in bed and unclothed. Morin grabbed for one camera and broke it.

During the time of her stay at the motel Mrs. Mazza carried an electronic transmitter in her handbag. By means of this device, her conversations with Morin were monitored by the respondent and his associates.

The respondent and his companions checked out of the motel at about one in the morning. Before doing so, there was a brief confrontation with Morin. According to Morin's testimony, the respondent demanded $125,000. Morin testified—"at that time I made him an offer of $25,000 to return everything he had, and in a second breath I retracted the offer."

The following day the respondent conferred with Mrs. Morin and reported the events of the trip to New Hampshire. He asked Mrs. Morin to consider reconciliation over the weekend. On March 11, 1968, Mrs. Morin informed the respondent she decided it was too late for reconciliation. With this decision, the respondent dictated, in the presence of Mrs. Morin, a letter which was received in evidence as State's Exhibit 1. The letter was addressed to Armand Morin at Littleton, New Hampshire, and was placed in the United States mail at Burlington the same day.

The communication is designated personal and confidential. The following excerpts are taken from the full text:

"—Basically, your wife desires a divorce, and if it can be equitably arranged, she would prefer that the divorce be as quiet and as undamaging as possible.

This letter is being written in your wife's presence and has been completely authorized by your wife. The offer of settlement contained herein is made in the process of negotiation and is, of course, made without prejudice to your wife's rights.

It is the writer's thinking that for the children's sake, for your sake, and for Mrs. Morin's sake, that neither the courts in New Hampshire nor in Vermont, should become involved in this potentially explosive divorce. If a suitable 'stipulation or separation agreement' can be worked out, the writer would recommend a Mexican, Stipulation-Divorce. This divorce would be based upon the catch-all grounds 'Incompatability'. . . .

Mrs. Morin is willing to give up the following:

1. All of her marital rights, including her rights to share in your estate.

2. All of her right, title and interest, jointly or by reason of marital status, that she has in and to, any or all property of the marriage, including the Continental 93 Motel, the three (3) farms in Vermont, the capital stock that you own, the house in

Lindenville, the joint venture in land in East Burke, all personal property except as is specifically hereinafter mentioned and in short, all rights that she may now have or might acquire in the future, as your wife. Furthermore, any such settlement would include the return to you of all tape recordings, all negatives, all photographs and copies of photographs that might in any way, bring discredit upon yourself. Finally, there would be an absolute undertaking on the part of your wife not to divulge any information of any kind or nature which might be embarrassing to you in your business life, your personal life, your financial life, of your life as it might be affected by the Internal Revenue Service, the United States Customs Service, or any other governmental agency.—"

The letter goes on to specify the terms of settlement required by Mrs. Morin, concerning custody of the minor child, her retention of an automobile and the disposition of certain designated personal effects. It further provides:

"5. Mrs. Morin would waive all alimony upon receipt of One Hundred Seventy Five Thousand Dollars ($175,000)—."

The sum of $25,000 is specified to be paid at the signing of the separation agreement, with the balance due according to a schedule of payments over the period of eighteen months.

The letter continues:

"—At the present time Mrs. Morin is almost without funds. . . . Because of her shortage of money, and, because she is badly missing David, and finally, because she cannot continue for any substantial period of time to live in the present vacuum, the writer must require prompt communication from you with respect to the proposed settlement contained herein. . . . Unless the writer has heard from you on or before March 22, we will have no alternative but to withdraw the offer and bring immediate divorce proceedings in Grafton County. This will, of course, require the participation by the writer's correspondent attorneys in New Hampshire. If we were to proceed under New Hampshire laws, without any stipulation, it would be necessary to allege, in detail, all of the grounds that Mrs. Morin has in seeking the divorce. The writer is, at present, undecided as to advising Mrs. Morin whether or not to file for 'informer fees' with respect to the Internal Revenue Service and the United States Customs Service. In any event, we would file, alleging adultery, including affidavits, alleging extreme cruelty and beatings, and asking for a court order enjoining you from disposing of any property, including your stock interests, during the pendency of the proceeding.

The thought has been expressed that you might, under certain circumstances, decide to liquidate what you could and abscond to Canada or elsewhere. The writer would advise you that this would in no way impede Mrs. Morin's action. You would be served by publication and under those circumstances, I am very certain that all property in New Hampshire and in Vermont, would be awarded, beyond any question, to Mrs. Morin.

With absolutely no other purpose than to prove to you that we have all of the proof necessary to prove adultery beyond a reasonable doubt, we are enclosing a photograph taken by one of my investigators on the early morning of March 8. The purpose of enclosing the photograph as previously stated, is simply to show you that cameras and equipment were in full operating order.—"

It was stipulated that the letter was received by Morin in Littleton, New Hampshire "in the due course of the mail."

Such is the evidence upon which the respondent was found guilty. . . .

*   *   *

Turning to the other grounds advanced in the motion for acquittal, the respondent maintains his letter (State's Exhibit 1) does not constitute a threat to accuse Morin of the crime of adultery. He argues the implicit threats contained in the communication were "not to accuse of the CRIME of adultery but to bring an embarassing, reputation-running divorce proceeding in Mr. Morin's county of residence unless a stipulation could be negotiated." . . .

In dealing with a parallel contention in State v. Louanis, 79 Vt. 463, 467, 65 A. 532, 533, the Court answered the argument in an opinion by Chief Judge Rowell. "The statute is aimed at blackmailing, and a threat of any public accusation is as much within the reason of the statute as a threat of a formal complaint, and is much easier made, and may be quite as likely to accomplish its purpose. There is nothing in the statute that requires such a restricted meaning of the word 'accuse'; and to restrict it thus, would well nigh destroy the efficacy of the act."

The letter, marked "personal and confidential," makes a private accusation of adultery in support of a demand for a cash settlement. An incriminating photograph was enclosed for the avowed purpose of demonstrating "we have all of the proof necessary to prove adultery beyond a reasonable doubt." According to the writing itself, cost of refusal will be public exposure of incriminating conduct in the courts of New Hampshire where the event took place.

In further support of motion for acquittal, the respondent urges that the totality of the evidence does not exclude the inference that he acted merely as an attorney, attempting to secure a divorce for his client on the most favorable terms possible. This of course, was the theory of the defense.

The case presented by the State did not require the court to accept the hypothesis of innocence claimed by the respondent. The acts which he performed and the words that he wrote are established by direct and documentary evidence that is not contradicted. The doctrine . . . advanced by the defense to the effect that the evidence must exclude every reasonable hypothesis except that the respondent is guilty, does not avail him. The rule applies only where the evidence is entirely circumstantial.

The law affords him a presumption of innocence which attends him until the jury returns its verdict. As in all criminal causes, consistent with the right to trial by jury, it was within the province of the triers of the fact to accept the defendant's claim of innocence. After weighing all the evidence in the area of reasonable doubt, the jury might have been persuaded to infer that the accused acted without malicious intent. But the evidence contains the requisite proof to convince the jury to a contrary conclusion.

At the time of the writing, the respondent was undecided whether to advise his client to seek "informer fees." One of the advantages tendered to Morin for a "quiet" and "undamaging" divorce is an "absolute undertaking" on the part of the respondent's client not to inform against him in any way. The Internal Revenue Service, the United States Customs Service and other governmental agencies are suggested as being interested in such information. Quite clearly, these veiled threats exceeded the limits of the respondent's representation of his client in the divorce action. Although these matters were not specified in the indictment, they have a competent bearing on the question of intent.

Apart from this, the advancement of his client's claim to the marital property, however well founded, does not afford legal cause for the trial court to direct a verdict of acquittal in the background and context of his letter to Morin. A demand for settlement of a civil action, accompanied by a malicious threat to expose the wrongdoer's criminal conduct, if made with intent to extort payment, against his will, constitutes the crime alleged in the indictment.

The evidence at hand establishes beyond dispute the respondent's participation was done with preconceived design. The incriminating evidence which his letter threatens to expose was wilfully contrived and procured by a temptress hired for that purpose. These factors in the proof are sufficient to sustain a finding that the respondent acted maliciously and without just cause, within the meaning of our criminal statutes. The sum of the evidence supports the further inference that the act was done with intent to extort a substantial contingent fee to the respondent's personal advantage.

The pronouncement of the jury, in resolving guilt against innocence, does not result from pyramiding inference on inference. Whether the letter threatened to accuse Morin of a crime must be determined from its text. The question of malicious intent similarly depends on the language of the letter. It can also be referred to extraneous facts and circumstances which occurred prior to the writing.

* * *

The record sustains the court's jurisdiction to try the offense. The evidence of guilt is ample to support the verdict and the trial was free from errors in law.

Judgment affirmed.

F. ROBBERY *

1. THE GENERAL LAW

PEOPLE v. PATTON
Supreme Court of Illinois, 1979.
76 Ill.2d 45, 27 Ill.Dec. 766, 389 N.E.2d 1174.

MR. JUSTICE WARD delivered the opinion of the court:

Verdicts of guilty were returned against defendant, Ray Patton, on both counts of an indictment charging robbery (Ill.Rev.Stat.1975, ch. 38, par. 18–1) and theft from the person (Ill.Rev.Stat.1975, ch. 38, par. 16–1) arising out of a single incident of "purse snatching." The trial court did not enter judgment on the theft verdict, but entered judgment on the verdict of robbery and sentenced the defendant to a term of 1 year to 6 years. On the defendant's appeal the appellate court, with one justice dissenting, reversed the judgment and remanded the cause . . . with directions to enter a judgment of conviction for the less serious offense of theft from the person. We granted the People's petition for leave to appeal.

On June 27, 1976, Rita Alexander, her husband and their four young children were hurrying along a sidewalk toward a church in Peoria Heights, so as not to be late for a 5:30 p.m. service. A few other persons in the immediate vicinity were likewise walking swiftly toward the church entrance. Mrs. Alexander was carrying her purse "[i]n the fingertips of my left hand down at my side." She noticed the defendant cross the street in front of the Alexanders and thought that perhaps he too was going to the service. Instead, the defendant changed direction and walked toward the Alexander family. As he came abreast of Mrs. Alexander, he "swift[ly] grab[bed]" her purse, throwing her arm back "a little bit," she said, and fled. She testified that the purse was gone before she realized what had happened. Once she overcame her momentary shock, Mrs. Alexander screamed and Mr. Alexander unsuccessfully chased the defendant. He was subsequently apprehended through the tracing of a license plate number on an automobile which

---

* Robbery is traditionally classified as a crime against the person; however, since the ultimate purpose of the crime is the misappropriation of property, it is included in this section.

witnesses had observed him enter. There was no other evidence offered bearing on the questions of use of force, threat of the imminent use of force, and resistance by or injury to Mrs. Alexander.

The question we consider is whether the simple taking or "snatching" of a purse from the fingertips of its unsuspecting possessor in itself constitutes a sufficient use of force, or threat of the imminent use of force, to warrant a conviction of robbery. It is the People's contention that any amount of physical force whatsoever, employed to overcome the force exerted by the person to maintain control over the object in hand, is sufficient to bring the act of taking within the robbery statute. Robbery is a Class 2 felony. The defendant contends that his behavior, without more, amounted only to theft from the person, which is a Class 3 felony, a lesser offense.

Our statute defines robbery:

> "A person commits robbery when he takes property from the person or presence of another by the use of force or by threatening the imminent use of force." (Ill.Rev.Stat.1975, ch. 38, par. 18–1.)

Thus, if no force or threat of imminent force is used in the taking, there is no robbery, although the act may constitute a theft. Mrs. Alexander did not realize what was happening until after the defendant had begun his flight, and it is clear there was no robbery through the "threatening [of] the imminent use of force." The People maintain that the defendant's act of grabbing was a "use of force" such as is contemplated by the robbery statute, and that no minimum amount of force need be shown to constitute robbery under the statute.

In most jurisdictions where the question has been considered it has been held that a simple snatching or sudden taking of property from the person of another does not of itself involve sufficient force to constitute robbery, though the act may be robbery where a struggle ensues, the victim is injured in the taking, or the property is so attached to the victim's person or clothing as to create resistance to the taking. . . . This view is of long standing. In 1839, the (English) Fourth Report of the Commissioners on Criminal Law, lxviii, stated that there was not sufficient "violence" in the "snatching or taking of property unawares from the person without some actual injury to the person" to constitute robbery; but the "stealing is by violence whensoever it is effected by doing any the least injury to the person, or whensoever the act of taking is accompanied by any degree of force employed to overcome resistance to such taking." (Michael & Wechsler, Criminal Law and Its Administration, 383, n.2 (1940).) Thus, in the English case of King v. Lapier (1784), 1 Leach (3d ed.) 321, 168 Eng.Rep. 263, there was sufficient violence where a lady's ear was "torn entirely through" in an endeavor by the prisoner to snatch her earring. And in Rex v. Mason (1820), Russ. & Ry. 420, 168 Eng.Rep. 876, enough "actual force" existed where the prisoner jerked and broke a steel watch chain around the victim's neck. The decisions in this jurisdiction considering the question of force in the taking of property have corresponded with the above statements.

To illustrate, in Hall v. People, 171 Ill. 540, 49 N.E. 495 (1898), this court held that it was not robbery where the defendant unbuttoned his inebriated drinking companion's vest, "possibly by pulling at it, and took the pocket-book from his inside vest pocket." In distinguishing between private stealing from the person of another and robbery, the court said that "where it appeared that the article was taken without any sensible or material violence to the person, as snatching a hat from the head or a cane or umbrella from the hand of the wearer,—rather by sleight of hand and adroitness than by open violence, and without any struggle on his part,—it is merely larceny from the person." The court further observed that if the facts of the case were held to constitute robbery, "then no practical distinction between that crime and larceny from the person exists. The two crimes approach each other so closely that cases may arise where it may be doubtful upon which side of the line they should fall. Still it is the duty of courts, as well as of juries, to resolve such doubts in favor of the accused."

The court in Klein v. People (1885), 113 Ill. 596, affirmed a conviction of robbery where the evidence established that the defendant was one of two men who grabbed a handbag "with such force," the prosecuting witness testified, "that it bruised my arm, and it was lame for several days."

Robbery convictions were affirmed in People v. Campbell (1908), 234 Ill. 391, where the defendants had scuffled with their victim over possession of a diamond stud fastened in his shirt front. The court stated: "In the absence of active opposition, if the article is so attached to the person or clothes as to create resistance, however slight, or if there be a struggle to keep it, the taking is robbery."

One year later in People v. Ryan (1909), 239 Ill. 410, this court reversed a conviction for assault with intent to commit robbery. The defendant there by "stealth and adroitness" had placed a newspaper under the chin of his intended victim while tugging on his diamond tie stud. The victim grabbed the defendant's hand, and the defendant fled. It was said: "If the taking is by actual violence causing a substantial injury to the person, such as grabbing a hand-bag from a lady's arm with such force that the arm is bruised and lame for several days, it will be robbery." Because there was no injury to the victim, no violence or struggle, and no intent to obtain or retain the stud by force, the evidence was held to be sufficient only to show an assault with intent to steal from the person.

In People v. Jones (1919), 290 Ill. 603, the evidence was held insufficient to support a robbery conviction where the defendant had stealthily removed a pocket-book from his intoxicated victim's pocket and transferred it to his own. When the victim, who had observed the transfer, said, "You have my pocket-book," the defendant "hit him over the eye and 'knocked him out.'" The court concluded there was no evidence of a struggle to retain possession, but only an accusation after the theft occurred "which the plaintiff in error resented by assaulting the accuser." His actions were therefore "those of a pick-pocket and not of a highwayman."

Robbery convictions of defendants who had grabbed a pocket-book from the hand of their victim were reversed in People v. O'Connor (1923), 310 Ill. 403, for lack of evidence that force or intimidation was used. Although some testimony of violence and threats by the defendants was offered at trial by the complaining witness, the court concluded it appeared to be the "vague remembrance of impressions received while strongly under the influence of alcoholic liquor." And in People v. Chambliss (1966), 69 Ill.App.2d 459, the court sustained a robbery conviction where the necessary force was held to have occurred during the course of a struggle for possession of a wallet immediately after the victim's pocket had been picked.

We consider that our cases show that where an article is taken, as it was put in Hall v. People, 171 Ill. 540, 542–43, 49 N.E. 495, 496 (1898), "without any sensible or material violence to the person, as snatching a hat from the head or a cane or umbrella from the hand" the offense will be held to be theft from the person rather than robbery.

There has been no action by the legislature evincing an intention to change the law as to the nature and elements of robbery. To the contrary the legislative design, it has been said, has been to leave the nature of the crime unchanged. The committee comments to Section 18–1 state: "This section codifies the law in Illinois on robbery and retains the same penalty. No change is intended. * * * [T]he taking by force or threat of force is the gist of the offense * * *." Ill.Ann.Stat. ch. 38, par. 18–1, Committee Comments, at 213 (Smith-Hurd 1970).

We have noted that Mrs. Alexander testified her arm was thrown back "a little bit," but "[w]here it is doubtful under the facts whether the accused is guilty of robbery or larceny from the person, it is the duty of the court and the jury to resolve that doubt in favor of the lesser offense." (People v. Williams, 23 Ill.2d 295, 301, 178 N.E.2d 372, 376 (1961).) For the reasons, given, the judgment of the appellate court is affirmed.

NOTES

1. Compare Brown v. Commonwealth, 135 Ky. 635, 117 S.W. 281 (1909), from which the following quotation is taken:

". . . Pearl Wiggins asked Roberts for a dime to buy a bucket of beer. Evidently intending to comply with her request, Roberts drew some money from his pocket, and after he did so the . . . man with Pearl Wiggins suddenly, and with force and violence, snatched or wrenched the money from Roberts' hand, and with equal suddenness swiftly fled and escaped with it. . . . The arrest of the . . . appellants speedily followed. . . . The evidence clearly shows that force was required and used to deprive Roberts of his money, and to constitute robbery the person robbed must be deprived of his property by force, or by putting him in fear. In Davis v. Commonwealth, . . . it was held the fact that the defendant snatched money from the hand of another was evidence of actual violence, which entitled the prosecution to an instruction to the jury to convict if the money was taken against the owner's will, by actual force. And in Jones v. Commonwealth, . . . it was also held that, where defendant snatched a pocketbook from the hand of another so quickly that he had no chance to actively resist, there was such a taking by violence as authorized a conviction under an indictment for robbery.

"The trial court did not err in failing to give an instruction under which the jury might have found appellants guilty of larceny. There was indeed no proof of larceny; and it was wholly and altogether to the effect that Roberts' money was taken from him by force and with such violence and suddenness as gave him no opportunity to resist the robbers. The crime was therefore robbery, and the instruction authorizing the jury to find appellants guilty of robbery . . . gave the jury all the law of the case."

In Commonwealth v. Jones, 362 Mass. 83, 283 N.E.2d 840 (1972), the Massachusetts court, in a case of first impression, decided that the snatching, without additional use of force, can satisfy the requisite element of force to permit a jury verdict of robbery to stand. See also 42 A.L.R.3d 1381, Purse Snatching as Robbery or Theft. Nevertheless, it appears to be the general view among American jurisdictions that the sudden taking or snatching of property from another person does not involve that amount of force or violence which is needed to constitute a robbery. See 42 A.L.R.3d 1381 (1972).

2. The common law typically required that the taking be from the person or a person's presence. Are these requirements met when a bank teller receives a call from the defendant, who threatens to set off a bomb at the teller's home unless a large sum of money be delivered to a hidden location designated by the caller? Compare People v. Smith, 78 Ill.2d 298, 35 Ill.Dec. 761, 399 N.E.2d 1289 (1980) and Brinkley v. United States, 560 F.2d 871 (8th Cir. 1977), cert. denied 434 U.S. 941, 98 S.Ct. 435, with United States v. Culbert, 548 F.2d 1355 (9th Cir. 1977), reversed on other grounds 435 U.S. 371, 98 S.Ct. 1112, and People v. Moore, 184 Colo. 110, 518 P.2d 944 (1974).

Under the common law, obtaining money by a threat to destroy one's home, or by a threat to accuse one of sodomy (whether true or not) constituted robbery. Regina v. Astley, 2 East P.C. 729 (1792).

3. In Pierce v. Commonwealth, 205 Va. 528, 138 S.E.2d 28 (1964), the court, in following the general common law concept, stated that the crime of robbery includes all of the elements of the crime of larceny. There must be *animus furandi*, an intent to steal. See, however, People v. Smith, supra, where the court said that, "Specific intent is not however, an element of robbery."

In People v. Moseley, 193 Colo. 256, 566 P.2d 331 (1977), the court specifically held that statutory robbery requires no specific intent to permanently deprive the owner of the use or benefit of his property, and the decision expressly overruled prior case decisions to the contrary. See also, State v. Gordon, 321 A.2d 352 (Me.1974). *Pierce*, however, appears to represent the majority view in the United States.

Is the issue easier to resolve where a statute defines robbery as larceny committed through force, violence, or fear, as in old Fla.Stat.Sec. 812.12? What if the statute is later amended to change "larceny" to "theft"? (See,

Fla.Stat.Sec. 812.13.) Is an intent to temporarily deprive the owner of his property sufficient for robbery? See Daniels v. State, 570 So.2d 319 (Fla.App.1990).

Proof that the defendant in good faith believed he was acting under a claim of right, as where he seeks to enforce payment of a debt, negates the existence of the required mental state even though the taking be accompanied by violence or putting in fear. Contrary to larceny, however, a prosecution for robbery does not require a distinct proof of the specific value of the property taken. As long as the stolen property is described sufficiently so that it may be shown to have some value, a conviction can be sustained. Pierce v. Commonwealth, supra. See also, People v. Karasek, 63 Mich.App. 706, 234 N.W.2d 761 (1975). Cf. Luckey v. State, 529 P.2d 994 (Okl.Crim.App.1974).

4. Defendant, after losing a gambling bet, uses force to regain possession of his lost money. Does this constitute robbery? See People v. Rosen, 11 Cal.2d 147, 78 P.2d 727 (1938), and compare Livingston v. State, 214 S.W.2d 119 (Tex. Crim.App.1948). In such cases, of what significance is the fact that a state statute permits (or even compels) the loser (or someone on his behalf) to sue for a recovery of the lost money? See People v. Henry, 202 Mich. 450, 168 N.W. 534 (1918). Consult also 41 J.Crim.L. & C. 467 (1950), and Anno., 75 A.L.R.3d 1000.

5. In Carey v. United States, 296 F.2d 422 (D.C.Cir. 1961), appellant sought to have his robbery conviction set aside, arguing that, assuming the intent to take the victim's money did not occur until after she was dead, he could not be guilty of robbery when he removed the money from the victim's blouse. "In other words," said the Court, "he argues that unless the necessary mens rea antedates or at least coincides with, the death of the victim, robbery is legally impossible, a corpse not being a 'person' as that term is understood in the robbery statute." The Court of Appeals rejected the contention, holding that, at the time her money was taken, in the particular circumstances of the case, the victim, "dead or not, was still a 'person' " within the robbery statute of the jurisdiction. "The time interval between the stabbing of [the victim] and the taking of her money was so short that it can hardly be said as a matter of law that the act of asportation was not performed upon a 'person.' . . . It is well to note also that appellant himself testified that when he removed [the victim's] money he was under the impression that she was only unconscious, not dead."

In Grigsby v. State, 260 Ark. 499, 542 S.W.2d 275 (1976), the court felt that stealing from a dead body as an afterthought would not constitute a capital felony as armed robbery would be. But, the court emphasized, the jury was not required to believe defendant's testimony. "The sequence of events is unimportant and the killing may precede, coincide with or follow the robbery and still be committed in its perpetration. . . . It has been aptly said that from the very nature of things it is often impossible for the state to know at just what instant a killing was committed—whether in the commission of a felony, or in attempting to commit a felony, or while withdrawing from the scene of a felony." See also, People. v. Pack, 34 Ill.App.3d 894, 341 N.E.2d 4 (1976).

6. Considering that robbery is viewed as an offense against the person, is an indictment charging the defendant with robbing a bank properly alleging commission of a robbery? In Crawford v. Commonwealth, 217 Va. 595, 231 S.E.2d 309 (1977), the court said that a corporation could act only through persons—its agents, servants, employees and officers, and that when the indict-

ment read that the defendant robbed The Southland Corporation of $256.39 "it in effect charged that he committed robbery by putting the agents of the corporation in fear and taking its money from their personal protection and in their presence." The court distinguished an earlier decision, Falden v. Commonwealth, 167 Va. 542, 189 S.E. 326 (1937), where it had reversed a judgment convicting the defendant on an indictment which charged conspiracy "to rob a certain United States mail truck," stating that robbery is a crime against the person.

2. ARMED ROBBERY

A sizeable number of jurisdictions provide, by statute, for an aggravated form of robbery, usually called "armed robbery", for which a greater penalty is provided. Typically, some statutes provide that an armed robbery requires the commission of a robbery "while armed with a dangerous weapon".[1] The Supreme Judicial Court of Massachusetts has stated that the gist of the offense of armed robbery is the commission of an offense while armed and it is not necessary to show the use of a dangerous weapon in proving the offense.[2] All that need be shown is that the defendant carried a weapon on his person while he committed the robbery.[3]

NOTES

1. Is an unloaded gun a "dangerous weapon"? Most courts seem to hold that any unloaded firearm that can be used as a bludgeon is a dangerous weapon. See 79 A.L.R.2d 1426, and 81 A.L.R.3d 1006. In People v. Roden, 21 N.Y.2d 810, 288 N.Y.S.2d 638, 235 N.E.2d 776 (1968), the Court of Appeals of New York held that an unloaded gun was a dangerous weapon within the meaning of the former Penal Law under which the appellant was charged, even though there was no evidence that the gun had been used as a bludgeon. But see, cf., People v. Richards, 28 Ill.App.3d 505, 328 N.E.2d 692 (1975), and People v. Santucci, 48 A.D.2d 909, 369 N.Y.S.2d 490 (1975).

Where a statute provides that a person charged with exhibiting a pistol during the course of a robbery is guilty in the first degree, unless he shows, as an affirmative defense, that it was not loaded, is the defendant's Fifth Amendment self-incrimination right violated by compelling him to take the stand if he wishes to escape a first degree robbery charge? People v. Felder, 39 A.D.2d 373, 334 N.Y.S.2d 992 (1972), held that there was no violation of right against self-incrimination.

2. Can toy guns be dangerous weapons? It was stated in Johnson v. Commonwealth, 209 Va. 291, 163 S.E.2d 570 (1968), that the use of a pistol with a blocked barrel, capable of firing blank cartridges only, would sustain a charge of robbery with firearms. This seems to be in line with the majority view, although there are a number of jurisdictions holding differently. See 81 A.L.R.3d 1006. In State v. Dye, 14 Ohio App.2d 7, 235 N.E.2d 250 (1968), the Court of Appeals of Ohio suggested that the gravamen of the crime was the fear

1. For example, Ill.Rev.Stats., Ch. 38, § 18–2.

2. Commonwealth v. Blackburn, 354 Mass. 200, 237 N.E.2d 35 (1968).

3. People v. Magby, 37 Ill.2d 197, 226 N.E.2d 33 (1967).

induced in the victim and this jury instruction had been given: "Even though you find that one of the revolvers used was a toy cap pistol it would make no difference. If those who were held up had reasonable cause to believe that it was a loaded revolver and such put him or them in fear, then you will say the cap pistol becomes a dangerous weapon." It must be pointed out, however, that the toy pistol used in the case and admitted in evidence was described as "so natural in appearance as to be accepted as real. It was of such weight and size that it could, if used as a blackjack or bludgeon, cause severe harm to the head or face of a victim". Would the same reasoning support a conviction for armed robbery where the toy gun used was a plastic one which, though appearing real, was very light in weight?

In People v. Skelton, 83 Ill.2d 58, 46 Ill.Dec. 571, 414 N.E.2d 455 (1980), the Illinois Supreme Court adopted a fact-oriented test to determine whether a weapon that had been used in a robbery is a "dangerous weapon" within the meaning of the armed robbery statute:

> [M]any objects, including guns, can be dangerous and cause serious injury, even when used in a fashion for which they were not intended. Most, if not all, unloaded real guns and many toy guns, because of their size and weight, could be used in deadly fashion as bludgeons. Since the robbery victim could be quite badly hurt or even killed by such weapons if used in that fashion, it seems to us they can properly be classified as dangerous weapons although they were not in fact used in that manner during the commission of the particular offense. It suffices that the potential for such use is present; the victim need not provoke its actual use in such manner. In the great majority of cases it becomes a question for the fact finder whether the particular object was sufficiently susceptible to use in manner likely to cause serious injury to qualify as a dangerous weapon. Where, however, the character of the weapon is such as to admit of only one conclusion, the question becomes one of law for the court. . . . The toy gun in this case, in our judgment, falls into the latter category. It does not fire blank shells or give off a flash as did the starter pistols in [an earlier case] . . .; it is entirely too small and light in weight to be effectively used as a bludgeon . . .; it fires no pellets as did the gas pellet pistol [in another case]; and, except that it could, conceivably, be used to poke the victim in the eye (and a finger could be used for the purpose), it is harmless. It simply is not, in our opinion, the type of weapon which can be used to cause the additional violence and harm which the greater penalty attached to armed robbery was designed to deter.

3. Some states distinguish robberies in first-degree and second-degree offenses, the first-degree offense being the equivalent of armed robbery. New Jersey has such a statute, N.J.S.A. 2C:15–1(b) which provided that it will be first-degree robbery "if in the course of committing the theft the actor attempts to kill anyone or purposely inflicts or attempts to inflict serious bodily harm, or is armed with or uses or *threatens the immediate use of a deadly weapon.*" (Emphasis supplied.) In State v. Butler, 89 N.J. 220, 445 A.2d 399 (1982), a majority of the New Jersey Supreme Court ruled that it is the objective prospect of harm, rather than the victim's subjective perception of danger, which divides robbery into offenses of two different degrees. Therefore, an offender who simulates a weapon by placing a hand in his coat pocket to create the impression he is concealing a handgun—an impression believed by the

victim—is not guilty of first degree robbery, unless he actually used a dangerous weapon. As the majority noted, the legislature, as of 1982, has expanded the definition of "deadly weapons" so as to include objects of simulations reasonably believed by the victim to be deadly weapons. The dissent noted, "it is simply not true that a robbery committed with a simulated weapon is necessarily less serious than one committed with an actual gun. The victim experiences as much fear whether or not a deadly weapon is used, and either way the robbery is as likely to provoke a violent response."

4. Treating the use of a firearm in the commission of a robbery as a separate crime is the Virginia Code § 18.2–53.1, which provides:

> It shall be unlawful for any person to use or attempt to use any pistol, shotgun, rifle, or other firearm or display such weapon in a threatening manner while committing or attempting to commit murder, rape, robbery, burglary, malicious wounding . . ., or abduction. Violation of this section shall constitute a separate and distinct felony and any person found guilty thereof shall be sentenced to a term of imprisonment of two years for a first conviction, and for a term of four years for a second or subsequent conviction under the provisions of this section. Notwithstanding any other provision of law, the sentence prescribed for a violation of the provisions of this section shall not be suspended in whole or in part, nor shall anyone convicted hereunder be placed on probation. Such punishment shall be separate and apart from, and shall be made to run consecutively with, any punishment received for the commission of the primary felony. (As amended, 1982.)

If an individual engages in concerted criminal activity with others, he incurs vicarious criminal responsibility under this statute for the use of a firearm in the commission of a felony by one of his co-actors, even where the individual neither used the firearm nor even knew that his co-actor possessed it, a majority of the Virginia Supreme Court held in Carter v. Commonwealth, 232 Va. 122, 348 S.E.2d 265 (1986). Four men acting in concert had robbed another man; one of them shot the victim. Under these facts, said the majority, "each co-actor is criminally responsible for the shooting, even those who did not intend it or anticipate that it would occur. . . ."

5. A man and woman drove into a gasoline station and directed the attendant to "fill it up all the way." "While the attendant was hanging up the gasoline hose, after filling the tank with gasoline, Richard Hermann [one of the defendants] got out of the car and walked partly around the same. The station attendant then walked near him to inform him as to how much gasoline he had placed in the tank and what the price of the same was. The attendant testified that during that time 'the woman in the car [the other defendant] slipped over under the wheel.' Richard Hermann opened the car door, and was standing with his head inside of the car in a stooping position, and then 'took a step back and just wheeled with this rifle pointed at my stomach.' Hermann then stated to the attendant, 'Don't try anything,' and when the attendant saw him wheel with the rifle on him, he raised his arms and hands automatically. The attendant testified 'he didn't tell me to throw my hands up, but they just automatically went up.' . . . Richard Hermann then got into the car and 'the woman drove the car away.'"

In affirming the conviction of defendants for armed robbery, the Supreme Court of Mississippi, in Hermann v. State, 239 Miss. 523, 123 So.2d 846 (1960), stated:

> It will be seen from the foregoing that the crime of stealthily obtaining the gasoline was completed before Richard Hermann pointed the rifle at [the attendant], with the exception that there had been no asportation of the gasoline from the place of business . . . at that time. The appellants were able to make their getaway with the gasoline by placing the gasoline station attendant in fear by the exhibition of the deadly weapon, telling him not to start anything, and that 'if you try to follow me, I will hurt you.' The car was driven away while the gasoline station attendant was still standing with his arms and hands raised in the air."

> The appellants rely almost entirely on Register v. State, decided by this Court on November 18, 1957 . . . .. The decision in that case followed the general rule at to what was necessary to constitute the crime of armed robbery, this being the offense of which the appellants were convicted in the case at bar. But that which distinguishes the Register case from the case at bar is the fact that in the instant case it was clearly shown, according to the testimony on behalf of the State, that there was no asportation of the gasoline until after the appellant, Richard Hermann, had drawn the deadly weapon on the gasoline station attendant and put him in fear whereas in the Register case there was no proof at all as to whether the intruder in the room of Miss June Flowers took her money out of her billfold prior or subsequent to the time that he choked her and put her in fear. * * *

6. Can a dog be a dangerous weapon within the meaning of the armed robbery statutes? In Commonwealth v. Tarrant, 367 Mass. 411, 326 N.E.2d 710 (1975), the court concluded "that the Commonwealth, in order to prove the crime of armed robbery . . . was not actually required to have affirmatively demonstrated that the dog was actually dangerous . . . or was in fact used in a harm-inflicting manner, since the proper inquiry is whether the instrumentality is such as to present an objective threat of danger to a person of reasonable and average sensibility." Further, the court said, "[Here] the dog entered the victim's bedroom with the defendant who was carrying a knife; roamed about the room while the defendant searched for goods, moving within close proximity to the victim; and answered to the defendant's orders. A German shepherd is a relatively large and well known breed with the physical capability of inflicting harm. . . ." See also an Annotation on the subject at 7 A.L.R.4th 607.

For a case holding that a trained German shepherd may be a "dangerous instrument" within the meaning of that phrase as used in a robbery statute, but not a "dangerous weapon" as defined in another statutory provision, see, People v. Torrez, 86 Misc.2d 369, 382 N.Y.S.2d 233 (1976).

G. BURGLARY *

UNITED STATES v. MELTON, JR.

United States Court of Appeals, District of Columbia Circuit, 1973.
491 F.2d 45.

BAZELON, CHIEF JUDGE:

* * *

I.

Appellant was charged with first degree burglary—the unlawful breaking and entering into the dwelling of another while a person was present therein with the intent to commit a criminal offense—in this case, larceny. At the close of the government's case, defense counsel moved for a directed verdict of acquittal for a failure of proof on the question of ultimate criminal intent. The trial judge agreed that there had been *no* evidence introduced demonstrating the intent to commit a crime after entry.

> I find that he entered and that there was an unlawful entry, no question about it, but I don't find any evidence here of intent to steal; unlawful entry just isn't [inconsistent] with intending to enter for some other purpose.

Nonetheless, after reviewing points and authorities for both sides, the trial judge concluded that mere unlawful entry into another's house supports an inference that the interloper was there to steal. Accordingly, he denied the defense motion for acquittal and submitted the charge of burglary to the jury. On this appeal, we concern ourselves only with the discrete legal issue of whether that ruling was premised on an erroneous interpretation of law.

II.

The trial judge erred in submitting a burglary charge to the jury where he found a complete absence of any evidence of an intent to commit a crime after the unlawful entry. By doing so, the trial judge invited the jury "to conjecture merely, or to conclude upon pure speculation or from passion, prejudice or sympathy," rather than any factual predicate, why appellant entered the dwelling.

In addition, the trial court's ruling conflicts with the statutory scheme of property offenses. Unlawful entry carries a maximum penalty of six months' imprisonment. First degree burglary carries a penalty of not less than five or more than thirty years. The element that distinguishes burglary from unlawful entry is the intent to commit a crime once unlawful entry has been accomplished. To allow proof of

---

* The common law crime of burglary which is treated in this section, is a crime against the habitation; under modern leg- islation, however, it has, as here, been grouped with the property offenses.

unlawful entry, *ipso facto*, to support a burglary charge is, in effect, to increase sixty-fold the statutory penalty for unlawful entry.

III.

The trial judge relied on three cases to sustain his ruling on the motion for acquittal—Cady v. United States, 54 App.D.C. 10, 293 F. 829 (1923); Washington v. United States, 105 U.S.App.D.C. 58, 263 F.2d 742 (1958), cert. denied, 359 U.S. 1002, 79 S.Ct. 1142 (1959); and United States v. Thomas, 144 U.S.App.D.C. 44, 444 F.2d 919 (1971). These decisions do not control the case before us. In *Washington*, there was evidence that, after gaining entry, the defendant attacked and assaulted two of the occupants, as an indication of his ultimate criminal intent. In *Cady*, there was evidence of flight. . . .

*   *   *

In each of the cases on which the trial judge relied in making his ruling, some circumstantial evidence of the requisite intent to commit a crime on the premises was either shown or noted—flight upon discovery, carrying or trying to conceal stolen goods, an assault upon a resident. Here, as the trial judge noted, there does not appear to be any circumstantial evidence of an ulterior criminal purpose other than the unlawful entry itself. Appellant did not attack Mrs. Vessels after she had discovered his presence. Despite a readily accessible means of escape provided by the nearby opened window, appellant did not escape during the several minutes between his discovery and his apprehension. Appellant had no stolen goods, weapons, or burglary tools with him when apprehended. He could not have been concealed, since the arresting officers saw him immediately upon peering through the door into the sunroom, nor did he resist arrest.

Nor should the fact that the unlawful entry occurred in the nighttime support the inference of intent to steal. An element of common law burglary was that it occurred at night; nighttime entry was seen as more likely to pose a threat to occupants. Congress abolished the "nighttime" requirement and focused instead on the specific consideration—the danger to occupants of a home. First degree burglary requires entrance into a dwelling while someone is present; second degree burglary, to which lesser penalties attach, requires neither that the building be a dwelling nor that it be occupied. The "common law" nighttime element, clearly abandoned by Congress, should not be resurrected by judicial fiat to make an act proscribed by Congress as a breaking and entering into a first degree burglary. . . .

IV.

Appellant's burglary conviction is therefore reversed. . . .

MacKINNON, CIRCUIT JUDGE, dissenting:

In an unprecedented opinion in the criminal law of the United States reversing this conviction for first degree burglary without even a remand, the majority rests its reversal on what it asserts to be an absence of "any evidence of an intent to commit a crime after the unlawful entry." Quite to the contrary, it must be concluded under well settled principles of criminal law in this jurisdiction and elsewhere that the record contains ample evidence to support the trial judge's decision to submit the issue of intent to steal to the jury. Hence the following dissent.

Stating the facts in the light most favorable to the Government as should be done, the evidence indicates that around 10 P.M. on January 29, 1971, appellant broke into Mrs. Vessels' two-story house by prying open and breaking the lock to the window of the sun room. Appellant had first attempted to gain entrance through the back door where he cut open the screen door, but had failed to penetrate the locked door. The sun room was used as an unheated storage room by Mrs. Vessels, and while in this room appellant next tried to gain further entrance into the interior of the house through some French doors. However, as appellant opened these French doors, he knocked over "nine pieces of half-inch thick 2 x 4 plywood" which had been "stacked" against the doors. This noise awakened Mrs. Vessels, who, after noticing the disturbed plywood, the open window and the screen-cut on the back door, quickly had called the police from her neighbor's house. Two policemen arrived within two to five minutes. They went into the house, and saw appellant "on the floor by the window," i.e., in the sun room next to the open window. After commanding him "don't move," the officers "walked over" to him, "he rose up" and they arrested him.

The majority opinion states, *inter alia, "Nothing of value in the house had been moved so as to indicate an attempt to steal."* (Emphasis added.) This statement is erroneous as the transcript discloses:

Q. Now when you [Mrs. Vessels] came down and after you went back in the house, when the police came, did you find anything else [other than the plywood disturbed in the house?

A. *Yes, there were things disturbed in the sunroom.*

Q. What?

A. Well, there were things which were broken in there because there were things stored there. There was a *clock which was broken, a lamp, some paintings in frames*, which were there, and there were some pieces of gill [*sic*] which had been bent because they were on the floor. (Emphasis added.)

The clock, the lamp and the pictures were clearly "items of value," and there is no evidentiary support in the record for the gratuitous conclusion of the majority opinion that these items of value had *not* "been moved so as to indicate an attempt to steal." There was no specific testimony as to why the goods had been moved, but they had been disturbed by the appellant and the conclusion as to what such acts indicated as to appellant's intent was within the province of the jury. The jury would have been perfectly justified in concluding that such acts by appellant indicated an "attempt" or more importantly, an *intent* "to steal" on his part; and on this appeal the record must be read in the light most favorable to the jury's verdict. Thus, the inference in this respect which is drawn by the majority opinion is impermissible.

* * *

As to the additional facts which support a finding that appellant entered the house with intent to steal, there are a number of facts here from which the jury could infer that appellant entered the house with an intent to steal, and thus place the jury verdict beyond one based on conjecture or speculation.

First, and most important, is the fact that the entry was made in the nighttime. The law is clear in this circuit that a jury may infer an intent to steal from a breaking and entering of an occupied dwelling place in the nighttime, where the defendant can offer no other explanation for his presence. [Citations omitted.] This is *not* a required inference which the jury must make when there is a breaking and entering in the nighttime, but it is almost universally held that the jury may draw this inference based *solely* upon such an entry in the nighttime, in the absence of evidence suggesting another explanation for the unlawful entry. [Citations omitted.] And where there is additional evidence tending to show intent to steal, as there is here, it is universally recognized that forcible entry in the *nighttime* is strong circumstantial evidence indicating the entrant had such an intent. [Citations omitted.]

The majority opinion . . . asserts that the " 'common law' nighttime element [was] abandoned by Congress." This is incorrect, the "nightime" provision was retained and additional features were *added* thereto which broadened the crime. In attempting to make its point in this respect the majority opinion gets mixed up over what is involved and completely misses the mark, i.e., that we are not relying upon the provisions of a statute but upon an evidentiary inference that, while it may have been recognized at common law, really rests on common sense and is just as valid today as heretofore. In fact, the long line of unbroken authorities, quoted above, indicate it is the applicable law in the United States, including this court, in all decisions except the preceding majority opinion. The cases cited above are based on the common sense rationale that a person who breaks into and enters a dwelling or building in the nighttime, if no other motive is apparent, generally has the purpose of stealing something. Were the law otherwise, every unsuccessful nighttime burglar, caught before he could steal anything, would be guilty only of unlawful entry, but as the above cited cases show, the law has universally been held to be to the contrary for more than a century. Certainly there are situations where a person may break into a dwelling or building in the nighttime with an innocent intent. However, the cases cited above recognize such an innocent intent might occur, and they hold only that where a defendant completely fails to explain his presence or there is a lack of another explanation, then the jury *may* infer an intent to steal.

Despite this large body of case law, some of which is in this circuit, the majority opinion suggests that there is no controlling authority contrary to the position it takes. It is submitted that Washington v. United States and Cady v. United States, directly control this factual situation and require affirmance. . . .

* * *

Were this the only evidence—that appellant had broken into and entered this house in the nighttime and offered no explanation for his presence, *Cady* and *Washington* would both require affirmance. Yet the majority opinion fails to mention additional evidence which supports the jury's conclusion that appellant had an intent to steal and which makes affirmance all the more compelling. The record establishes that there was evidence of (1) a forcible entry, (2) an attempt to gain further access into the interior of the house, (3) disturbance of various personal property in the sun room (4) concealment of the individual, and finally (5) appellant's suggestion that he resisted arrest was not negated. Any one of these acts is evidence of criminal intent sufficient to support a finding of intent to steal. However, the majority would have it believed that appellent's presence in this house was wholly innocent, subtly suggesting that he was merely attempting to get out of the cold and went to sleep on Mrs. Vessels' floor. These are mere assertions and have no factual support in the evidence. Thus, the majority notes only that Mrs. Vessels noticed that the sun room window had been opened, but fails to add that closer inspection revealed that the lock had been broken because it had been pried open. The majority attempts to negate any concealment by appellant by describing his position as "lying on the floor" when found by the police, suggesting appellant was only resting. Yet, there is *no* evidence that he was "lying." The evidence is that he was "on the floor by the window."

The majority further attempts to support its interpretation of the innocent nature of appellant's forcible midnight entry by noting that he failed to attack Mrs. Vessels when she discovered his presence. The record, however, indicates that Mrs. Vessels never directly saw appellant, but only suspected he was still in the sun room and the plywood which had been knocked over when appellant attempted to open the French doors presented some obstacle to easy entry from the sun room to the dining room. Further, it finds significantly exculpatory the fact that appellant did not escape during the several minutes between discovery of his presence and his apprehension, even though there was an open window nearby. There is no evidence that appellant could have escaped had he attempted to do so. The policemen were undoubtedly armed and with armed policemen in close proximity, an open window is no guarantee of escape—so a refusal to attempt to so escape is not any indication of the absence of criminal intent. The point the majority opinion attempts to make in this respect is merely another example of where it is straining at gnats and thus indicating the weakness of its entire conclusion.

* * *

It should also be noted that appellant had not been stationary in the room, as the majority implies. He had attempted to gain access to the dining room, he had disturbed a number of articles in the sun room, and he had finally moved back on the floor below the window he had entered. All this activity proves he was not just seeking sanctuary from the "pleasant night" in January.

Finally, the unsupported statement by the majority "that nothing of value in the house had been moved so as to indicate an attempt to steal" merits further discussion. While the record does not disclose the value of the personal property in the sun room, Mrs. Vessels testified that upon inspecting that room she discovered that a clock had been broken, and a lamp, some paintings in frames, and some pieces of "gill" had been disturbed. As mentioned previously, the record is unclear whether these items were disturbed by appellant before his arrest, or whether this occurred during his arrest. If before his arrest, the jury could have concluded that appellant was rummaging around for something to steal. If they were disturbed during his arrest, then the jury might well have reasoned that appellant was resisting his arrest. Either interpretation supports a conclusion by the jury that appellant possessed criminal intent from which an intent to steal could be inferred.

What has happened here is that not only has the majority misread controlling precedent in this circuit and the general law of the land on the subject, but it has taken a defendant-slanted selective view of the evidence to support reversal, when the law requires that the evidence should be viewed in the light most favorable to the jury's verdict. To do otherwise, and particularly to state facts which have no support in the transcript, is to violate one of the best established rules of appellate procedure.

* * *

For the majority of this panel to take this convicted burglar with a 20-year narcotics problem who has a self-admitted compulsion to commit larceny when he is using drugs and, contrary to all the law for over a century, turn him loose to prowl and prey further upon the citizens of the District of Columbia is in my considered opinion worse than the offense the appellant committed. . . . Of all the sad cases that have gone through our court, turning this man loose, under such circumstances, is the saddest and one of the most gross miscarriages of justice that I have encountered.

* * *

On Appellee's Petition for Rehearing and/or Suggestion for Rehearing En Banc

Before: BAZELON, CHIEF JUDGE; and WRIGHT and MACKINNON, CIRCUIT JUDGES.

ORDER

On consideration of the petition of the United States for rehearing and its suggestion for rehearing en banc, it is ordered by the Court that the petition for rehearing is granted for the limited purpose of modifying the Court's original opinion and judgment by amending Part IV of the opinion to read as follows:

Appellant's burglary conviction is reversed. However, in convicting appellant of burglary, the jury necessarily found the facts required for conviction of the lesser included offense of unlawful entry, and there is no question that the evidence was sufficient to support this determination. We therefore exercise our power under 28 U.S.C. § 2106 (1970) to remand the case with instructions either to enter, if the Government consents, a judgment of conviction of unlawful entry or, if the court believes it in the interest of justice, to grant a new trial on the lesser offense.

* * *

Reversed and Remanded.

Per Curiam.

MACKINNON, CIRCUIT JUDGE, dissenting:

My vote is cast for rehearing *en banc*. A majority of the court—for differently stated reasons has denied the suggestion of the United States for rehearing *en banc*. On rehearing the panel has improved its original disposition which would have completely reversed the conviction and freed appellant of all offenses. But the alteration in the disposition of this case will not correct the major decisional error in the majority opinion nor will it respond adequately to appellant's cry for help in his pitiful situation. . . .

STATE v. HOWE

STATE v. JENSEN

STATE v. WALSH

Supreme Court of Washington, 1991.
116 Wash.2d 466, 805 P.2d 806.

UTTER, JUSTICE.

The juvenile defendants in these three consolidated cases were each convicted of burglarizing their parents' homes. Each case raises the same central issue: When is a parental order to a juvenile to stay away from the parental home sufficient to establish the lack of privilege element of a burglary charge? We hold that a burglary conviction can only be sustained where the parent (1) expressly and unequivocally ordered the child out of the parental home, and (2) provided some alternative means of assuring that the parents' statutory duty of care is met.

I

Former RCW 9A.52.030(1) provides:

A person is guilty of burglary in the second degree if, with intent to commit a crime against a person or property therein, he enters or remains unlawfully in a building other than a vehicle.

The State must prove both intent to commit a crime and unlawful entry in order to prove second degree burglary. A person unlawfully enters a building when he is not then licensed, invited, or otherwise privileged to enter or remain. If a person is privileged to enter the building, then he cannot be convicted of burglary. The juveniles in each of these cases assert that they were privileged to enter their parents' homes by virtue of their parents' obligation to provide for their dependent children.

Parents have a statutory duty to provide for their dependent children. RCW 26.20.035(1)(a), (b) provides:

(1) Any person who is able to provide support, or has the ability to earn the means to provide support, and who:

(a) Wilfully omits to provide necessary food, clothing, shelter, or medical attendance to a child dependent upon him or her . . .

(b) . . . is guilty of the crime of family nonsupport.

The duty of the parent to provide for the child results in the child having a privilege to enter the family home. Therefore, the State can only prove burglary if the child's privilege to enter the home has been revoked.

This holding is supported by our decision in *State v. Steinbach,* . . . In *Steinbach,* a juvenile petitioned the court for alternative residential placement (hereinafter ARP) under the provisions of RCW ch. 13.32A. Approximately 2 weeks after the court entered the ARP order, the juvenile entered her mother's home without permission and removed several items. The trial court found that the juvenile entered the home with the intent to commit a crime and entered a judgment convicting her of second degree burglary. This court overturned the conviction. We held that the juvenile's entry into her mother's home was privileged, and therefore could not be unlawful. In so holding, we noted that the ARP did not revoke the juvenile's privilege to enter the parental home unless it contained a specific provision doing so. We declined, however, to decide whether a conviction for burglary is appropriate where either the ARP or the parent expressly prohibits the child from returning home. That is the question before us in these consolidated cases.

The focal issue here is whether a parent can revoke the child's privilege to enter the parental home, and under what conditions is that revocation effective?

The statutory parental obligation to provide for a dependent child is limited. The "necessary" care mandated by statute is the minimum standard of the quality and quantity of food, clothing, shelter and medical care that a parent is required by law to furnish. The parent does not have to provide that care directly, as long as he or she assures that such care is provided to the child. Thus, a parent fulfills her statutory duty when she provides alternative means for taking care of her child's necessities. Since the child's privilege to enter the parental home rises out of the parent's duty to provide for the child, once the parent fulfills that duty in some manner that does not require the child to have access to the home, the parent may revoke the child's privilege to enter. This revocation does not require a formal court proceeding, but it must be clearly and unequivocally conveyed to the child. The revocation can only be effective if the parent has first met his or her statutory duty to provide the necessary care for the child.

II

State v. Howe

In August 1986, John Howe III moved to Shelton to live with his father. Prior to that, John lived with his mother in Alaska. Shortly after arriving in Shelton, John and his father began having difficulties. These difficulties eventually led John to move out of his father's house and into the house of his aunt and uncle, the Ackermans.

Police subsequently arrested John for taking the Ackermans' car without their permission. John was placed in juvenile detention, and while in detention, John's father told John he was no longer welcome in his father's home. After his release from detention, John moved into a foster home. His father again told John that he could not return home until such time as he could exhibit law-abiding behavior.

While in foster care, John entered his father's home through an unlocked door and took his father's car, boat, canteen and some gas. John was subsequently arrested and found guilty of burglary and several other crimes not relevant to this appeal.

Division Two of the Court of Appeals reversed the burglary conviction. Judge Alexander, writing for the majority, interpreted *State v. Steinbach,* supra, as recognizing that a child has a "right" to enter the parental home. The majority then concluded that a parent cannot unilaterally terminate that right, and that John's entry into his father's home was, therefore, lawful. We disagree.

The Court of Appeals correctly concluded that the privilege the child has to enter the parental home derives from a parent's duty to provide for the care of minor children. As noted above, the parent's statutory duty is set out in RCW 26.20.035(1)(a). John's father met that statutory duty. He informed the State that John could not return home, and he took John to a state-appointed shelter. By doing so, John's father fulfilled his statutory duty. John was placed in foster care, and he was at no time without the necessities the statute requires. John's father also explicitly told John that he could not return to his house. The trial court found that John's father clearly indicated to John that he was no longer welcome in his father's home, and that John knew and understood his father's communications. That fact distinguishes this case from *Steinbach*.

Since John's father fulfilled his obligations under RCW 26.20.035(1), he had the power to revoke John's privilege to enter the house. This revocation is not a "unilateral termination" of the child's rights. The revocation can only be done after the parent insures that the child's rights are protected. John's father made the revocation effective by expressly and unequivocally telling John that he could not return to the house. Since his father revoked that privilege, John's entry into the house was unlawful. We therefore reverse the Court of Appeals and affirm the juvenile court's finding of guilt.

State v. Walsh

In early October 1987, Lucille Walsh left her 16–year–old son Michael home alone when she went out of town on business. While she was away, Michael had a keg party at the family home. An estimated 50–150 people attended the party. The police were called to the party, and one child was taken away in an ambulance. Some of Lucille Walsh's furniture was smashed.

Over the course of the next few weeks Michael's behavior grew out of control. On October 20th, Ms. Walsh came home early and found Michael at home with some of his friends. At the time Michael was supposed to be at school. Ms. Walsh asked Michael to leave, but he refused and she went back to work. When she returned home that night Michael was gone. The next morning Ms. Walsh had the door locks changed. Michael had not come home the night of the 20th, and there is nothing in the record to indicate Ms. Walsh knew where he was. She did not give him any money or suggest any alternative living arrangement. Ms. Walsh simply locked Michael out of the house. At the time Michael had no other relatives in the area.

When Ms. Walsh returned home on the 21st, the day the locks were changed, she discovered someone had entered the house through a window in Michael's bedroom. She concluded that Michael was the intruder because his dirty clothes were on the floor, the shower had been used, and Michael's toothbrush was wet. She did not notice anything missing from the house.

On the 22nd, Ms. Walsh returned from work and again discovered that someone had been in the house. As before, Michael's dirty clothes were on the floor and his toothbrush was wet. She also discovered that 10 $1 bills were missing from a stack of 25 bills that she kept in a dresser drawer. Several silver and commemorative coins were missing from the same drawer. That night Michael returned home and asked to spend the night. Ms. Walsh gave him a sleeping bag and told him to sleep on the porch. She did not ask him about the missing money.

On October 23rd, a neighbor called police and reported a break-in at the Walsh home. Police discovered Michael and some friends in the house and arrested them for burglary. During a search incident to the arrest, police found several silver coins in Michael's possession. Ms. Walsh later identified the coins as the ones taken from her drawer on the 22nd.

On October 30th, Ms. Walsh opened her monthly bank statement. She discovered a cancelled check that she had not written. Michael later admitted that he and some friends had taken the check and used it to buy pizza.

Following a fact-finding hearing, the juvenile court found Michael guilty of burglary for the October 22nd break-in. Division One of the Court of Appeals reversed the burglary conviction.

Judge Pekelis, writing for the majority, recognized the competing societal interests inherent in these cases. As she noted:

> Parents undeniably have an interest in preserving the security and tranquility of the family home from destructive, out-of-control teenagers. However, society has a comparable interest in ensuring that children are provided with basic needs, such as food, shelter and clothing.

That societal interest is reflected in RCW 26.20.035(1)(a). The State argued that society's interest in the child's welfare can be met by allowing the child to raise a necessity defense to the burglary charge. We agree with Judge Pekelis, however, that such a solution would saddle the courts with the difficult task of evaluating the competing interests on a case-by-case basis. We therefore reject the State's argument.

Judge Pekelis also correctly concluded that a parent cannot unilaterally revoke the child's right to enter the parental home unless the parent has met his or her statutory duty to provide for the child's necessities. While we agree with her reasoning, we disagree with her resolution of the problem. Judge Pekelis would require parents to provide some alternative means for their child's care by obtaining a formal court order. We believe society's competing interests are better served by allowing the parents to make the initial choice of how to provide the statutorily required care for their children. If the parents make adequate arrangements for their child's care without the necessity of an ARP, we see no reason for the courts to interfere with those arrangements.

We stress that our holding should not be taken as an abdication of the court's responsibility for protecting the rights of children. Our holding simply reflects our belief that, where the needs of the child are adequately provided for, the parents should make the initial decision of how to provide for their children. Until the Legislature clearly indicates that such decisions should be made by the courts, we believe it is wiser to leave the initial decision to the parents.

Although we disagree with the Court of Appeals resolution of the issue, we affirm its reversal of Michael Walsh's conviction. Ms. Walsh did not meet her statutory duty to provide for Michael's care. She locked him out of the house without arranging for a place for him to stay. She did not give him any money or food. All of his personal belongings, including his clothes, were still in the house. Ms. Walsh knew that Michael did not have a job and had no relatives he could turn to for shelter. Since she failed to fulfill her statutory duty to provide for Michael, she could not revoke his privilege to enter the family home. Therefore, his entry was lawful, and his conviction is reversed.

State v. Jensen

In the Spring of 1988, Michael Jensen's parents placed him in a temporary home through the Department of Social and Health Services. They did this because they could not deal with Michael's drug problem. Some time after that Michael left the temporary home and began living in a trailer parked in front of the family home. His parents allowed him into the home to eat and to shower, but Michael did not have a key to the house. The juvenile court found that his parents explicitly told Michael he could not enter the house unless one of his parents was there.

On June 10, 1988, Michael broke into his parents' house by smashing the back door. He stole 40 ounces of his father's silver. A juvenile court found him guilty of burglary. Division One of the Court of Appeals affirmed the conviction. We affirm.

The Jensens met their statutory duty of care for Michael. As Judge Swanson found, they provided Michael with alternative living quarters and there was no evidence that they failed to meet their statutory duty. Additionally, the Jensens clearly told Michael he could not enter the home unless one of his parents was present. Thus, they met both of the requirements for revoking Michael's privilege to enter the house. They told him explicitly that he could not enter and they met their statutory duty of care. Therefore, we affirm his conviction.

Our holdings in these cases are supported by cases from other jurisdictions. In In re G.L., 73 Ill.App.3d 467, 29 Ill.Dec. 425, 391 N.E.2d 1108 (1979), the trial court found a 15–year–old guilty of burglarizing his parents' home. At the time of the burglary, G.L. was committed to a drug rehabilitation program. In affirming the conviction, the court of appeals emphasized that G.L.'s parents had expressly forbidden him to enter their home. The court also noted that the director of the drug rehabilitation agency, and not G.L.'s parents, had legal custody of G.L. Thus, the court concluded that the parents' duty to provide for G.L. was reduced to a financial duty. The court then held that the parents had a superior right of possession to the family home, and that G.L.'s entry was unlawful. This holding comports with our decision. G.L.'s parents explicitly told him he could not enter their house, and G.L.'s needs were taken care of by his placement in the drug rehabilitation program.

In In re Richard M., 205 Cal.App.3d 7, 252 Cal.Rptr. 36 (1988), the juvenile was committed to a youth facility as a ward of the court. He escaped from the facility and broke into the apartment of his father and stepmother. He took several items belonging to his stepmother, and a trial court subsequently found him guilty of burglary. The court of appeals affirmed the conviction and rejected Richard M.'s claim that his parents' obligation to support him gave him the right to enter their apartment. The court held that the parental obligation to provide for necessities does not imply a possessory right in the parental residence. Again, this holding comports with our decision. Richard M.'s stepmother expressly told him he could not enter her home, and his needs were taken care of by his placement in the youth facility.

In conclusion, we hold that a juvenile can only be convicted of burglary of his family home if his privilege to enter the home is revoked. A juvenile's parents can only revoke his or her privilege to enter if they (1) do so expressly and unequivocally, and (2) provide some alternative means of assuring that the parents' statutory duty of care is met. We therefore affirm the Court of Appeals in *State v. Jensen,* supra; affirm the Court of Appeals as modified in *State v. Walsh,* supra; and reverse the Court of Appeals in *State v. Howe,* supra.

DORE, C.J., BRACHTENBACH, DOLLIVER, DURHAM, ANDERSEN, SMITH and GUY, JJ., and CALLOW, J. Pro Tem., concur.

NOTES

A Summary of the Common Law and Modern Legislation on Burglary

1. *The Common Law on Burglary*

At common law the offense of burglary consisted of a *breaking* and *entering* of the *dwelling house* of another, in the *nighttime,* with *intent* to commit a felony. The problems which have arisen over the years with respect to each of these elements are perhaps as complex as those concerning the elements of larceny. Fortunately, many of the early troublesome issues have been obviated by statute. Familiarity with some of the major common law rules is nevertheless helpful to an understanding of the legislation in this area.

a. *Breaking.* The requirement of a "breaking" or "breach" means that the burglar must make a trespassory entry involving the creation of an opening into the dwelling. In State v. Boon, 35 N.C. 244, 246 (1852), the court stated: "Passing an imaginary line is a 'breaking of the close,' and will sustain an action of trespass *quare clausum fregit.* In burglary more is required—there must be a breaking, moving or putting aside of something material, which constitutes a part of the dwelling-house, and is relied on as a security against intrusion."

The breaking may be into any part of a building and need not be a breaking in from the outside. Opening the door of an inner room is therefore sufficient. Davidson v. State, 86 Tex.Crim.R. 243, 216 S.W. 624 (1919). See Anno., 43 A.L.R.3d 1147 and 70 A.L.R.3d 881.

Constructive breaking occurs under certain circumstances where no force is used to make a way for the entry. The use of a trick or an artifice to gain entry is one type of constructive breaking. In Nichols v. State, 68 Wis. 416, 32 N.W. 543 (1887), for example, the burglar gained entry by concealing himself in a box. In Le Mott's Case, 84 Eng.Rep. 1073 (1650), the burglars merely told a maid that they wanted to speak to the master, and when she opened the door for them they entered and robbed him. Another type of constructive breaking occurs when one who has access to the dwelling, such as a servant, conspires to let another into the house. See Regina v. Johnson, Car. & M. 218, 174 Eng.Rep. 479 (1841).

Entering a dwelling which one has a right to enter at the time entry is made does not constitute a breaking because there is no trespass. Thus, using a key to enter a building which one has an unrestricted right to enter is not a breaking. People v. Kelley, 253 App.Div. 430, 3 N.Y.S.2d 46 (1938); Davis v. Commonwealth, 132 Va. 521, 110 S.E. 356 (1922). However, if the entry by use of a key is made at an unauthorized time, a trespass exists and a breaking occurs. State v. Corcoran, 82 Wash. 44, 143 Pac. 453 (1914). Is it a "breaking" to enter through a partly opened door or window? See cases collected at Anno., 70 A.L.R.3d 881.

State v. Hicks, 421 So.2d 510 (Fla.1982), treats "consent to enter [as] an affirmative defense to, rather than an essential element of, [statutory] burglary. Thus, the absence of consent need not be alleged in a burglary indictment.

b. *Entering.* An entry is made if any part of the body is inside the dwelling, even if only a hand or finger intrudes for the purpose of the breaking. State v. Whitaker, 275 S.W.2d 316 (Mo.1955); Regina v. O'Brien, 4 Cox C.C. 400 (1850); Franco v. State, 42 Tex. 276 (1875). An entry may also be made by inserting an object into the dwelling; however, the object must be inserted for the purpose of carrying out the felonious design, and it is insufficient if the instrument is used only to effect the breach. Walker v. State, 63 Ala. 49 (1879); Rex v. Rust, 1 Mood.C.C. 183 (1828); People v. Williams, 28 Ill.App.3d 402, 328 N.E.2d 682 (1975). The entry must be "consequent upon the breaking," so that if one enters a dwelling through an open door and then opens an inner door but does not go through it, the requirement of entry is lacking. Regina v. Davis, 6 Cox C.C. 369 (1854).

c. *The Dwelling House of Another.* (1) A dwelling house, under the rules of common law burglary, is a building habitually used as a place to sleep. Rex v. Stock, Russ. & R. 185, 2 Leach C.C. 1015, 7 Taunt. 339 (1810). It may be a store or other place of business, if someone regularly sleeps there, State v. Outlaw, 72 N.C. 598 (1875); but the fact that someone may sleep there from time to time is insufficient, State v. Jenkins, 50 N.C. 430 (1858). If a building is regularly used as a residence during a certain time of the year, for example a summer home, it qualifies as a dwelling house even during the period when it is not occupied. State v. Bair, 112 W.Va. 655, 166 S.E. 369 (1932). The test is whether the occupant intends to return. State v. Meerchouse, 34 Mo. 344 (1864). A building that no one has yet moved into is not considered a dwelling house for purposes of burglary. Woods v. State, 186 Miss. 463, 191 So. 283

(1939); Jones v. State, 532 S.W.2d 596 (Tex.Crim.App.1976), overruled on other grounds in Moss v. State, 574 S.W.2d 542 (Tex.Crim.App.1978).

Rooms in an inn, hotel, or apartment building are the dwellings of the occupants, unless the occupants are merely transients. People v. Carr, 255 Ill. 203, 99 N.E. 357 (1912). Where the rooms are occupied by transients, however, the rooms are considered the dwelling house of the landlord, whether or not the landlord lives in the building. See Rodgers v. People, 86 N.Y. 360 (1881).

The dwelling house is considered to include not only the dwelling itself but also buildings which are "within the curtilage." The purpose of including buildings used in connection with the dwelling is to protect against the dangers resulting from the likelihood that a dweller who hears a prowler in the nighttime will go forth to protect his family and property. Thus a garage is considered part of the dwelling house where it is in reasonable proximity to the house. Harris v. State, 41 Okl.Crim. 121, 271 P. 957 (1928). A cellar is also within the "curtilage" even though it has no entrance from the dwelling itself and must be entered from the outside. Mitchell v. Commonwealth, 88 Ky. 349, 11 S.W. 209 (1889).

The dwelling house must be that "of another," in the sense that it must be occupied by another. It need not be owned by victim, inasmuch as burglary at common law is a crime against the habitation and not against property. One may therefore burglarize a building leased to, and occupied by, someone else. Smith v. People, 115 Ill. 17, 3 N.E. 733 (1885). The dweller, however, cannot burglarize his own dwelling, even though it has other occupants. Clarke v. Commonwealth, 66 Va. 908 (25 Grat) (1874).

d. *Nighttime.* As an element of burglary, nighttime is the period of time between sunset and sunrise, and it is not considered night if there is enough natural daylight so that one can discern the countenance of another man's face. People v. Griffin, 19 Cal. 578 (1862). State v. Billings, 242 N.W.2d 726 (Iowa 1976). Both the breaking and entering must occur during the nighttime, but they need not occur on the same night. Rex v. Smith, Russ. & Ry. 417, 168 Eng.Rep. 874 (1820).

e. *With Intent to Commit a Felony.* Although burglary is commonly thought of as an offense committed with intent to steal, the required intent actually includes the intent to commit any felony. It is not necessary that the felony in fact be committed, Wilson v. State, 24 Conn. 57 (1855); however, both the breaking and entering must be made with the necessary intent. Colbert v. State, 91 Ga. 705, 17 S.E. 840 (1893). As noted in the section on larceny, supra at page 551, at common law both grand and petit larceny are felonies. Petit larceny is now frequently made a misdemeanor by statute; however, it is also commonly provided that burglarious intent exists where there is an intent to commit a felony "or to steal."

2. *Modern Legislation on Burglary*

a. Modern legislation on burglary has made a number of changes in the common law, generally broadening the scope of the offense. Following are the various changes, as revealed in an excellent summary of the modern law of burglary in Note, A Rationale of the Law of Burglary, 57 Colum.L.Rev. 1009 (1951):

(1) All jurisdictions now include virtually all buildings in the scope of the crime, although most jurisdictions attach a more severe penalty to the offense where a dwelling is involved.

(2) A few jurisdictions dispense with the requirement of "entry."

(3) A few jurisdictions dispense with the requirement of "breaking," but some of these require a trespass instead. Others provide a higher penalty where a "breaking" occurs. Where breaking is retained, some jurisdictions provide that absent a "breaking in," a "breaking out" will suffice.

(4) All jurisdictions recognize daytime burglaries, although some provide a more severe penalty for burglaries committed at night.

(5) The jurisdictions define burglarious intent in four principal ways: (a) intent to commit a felony; (b) intent to commit a felony or larceny; (c) intent to commit any crime (with respect to one or more degrees or forms of burglary); and (d) intent to commit certain specified crimes. A few jurisdictions dispense entirely with the requirement of an intent to commit another crime for the lowest degree or form of burglary.

(6) Many jurisdictions have added new elements to the common law crime of burglary. For example, some make special provisions for armed burglary and burglary involving the use of (or attempt or intent to use) explosives, and some require for the offense of first degree burglary that someone be in the building at the time of the offense.

b. For a modern code provision covering the offense of burglary, consider the following from the Illinois Criminal Code (S.H.A. ch. 38):

§ 19–1. Burglary

(a) A person commits burglary when without authority he knowingly enters or without authority remains within a building, housetrailer, watercraft, aircraft, motor vehicle (as defined in the Illinois Motor Vehicle Law) railroad car, or any part thereof, with intent to commit therein a felony or theft. . . .

Modern statutes on "housebreaking," the day-time burglary of a dwelling offense, still require interpretation on what constitutes a dwelling. In Holtman v. State, 12 Md.App. 168, 278 A.2d 82 (1971) a conviction for daytime housebreaking was reversed upon a showing that the defendant had broken into a church. Though it may be the "mansion house of God", the court did not consider it a dwelling within the meaning of the burglary law. On the other hand, an Illinois court construed a "car wash" to be a building falling within the modern Illinois burglary statute above. People v. Blair, 1 Ill.App.3d 6, 272 N.E.2d 404 (1971).

c. Since burglary is a specific intent crime, the prosecution must prove that the defendant entered with the intent to commit larceny or one of the other felonies specified in the statute. This is sometimes difficult. Consider the following hypothetical case:

Defendant is first perceived by the victim when she wakes up and sees him standing next to her bed. He says, "Don't scream," and when she attempts to jump out of the bed on the opposite side, he grabs her and they struggle briefly. The defendant then steps back, strikes the victim about the face several times, and walks out.

Can he be convicted of (a) common law burglary or (b) breaking and entering with intent to commit larceny, or (c) breaking and entering with intent to commit rape? See State v. Keaton, 27 N.C.App. 84, 217 S.E.2d 749 (1975).

H. MISAPPROPRIATION TERMINOLOGY: PROBLEMS
OF CONSTRUCTION

UNITED STATES v. TURLEY
Supreme Court of the United States, 1957.
352 U.S. 407, 77 S.Ct. 397.

MR. JUSTICE BURTON delivered the opinion of the Court.

This case concerns the meaning of the word "stolen" in the following provision of the National Motor Vehicle Theft Act, commonly known as the Dyer Act:

"Whoever transports in interstate or foreign commerce a motor vehicle or aircraft, knowing the same to have been stolen, shall be fined not more than $5,000 or imprisoned not more than five years, or both."

The issue before us is whether the meaning of the word "stolen," as used in this provision, is limited to a taking which amounts to common-law larceny, or whether it includes an embezzlement or other felonious taking with intent to deprive the owner of the rights and benefits of ownership. For the reasons hereafter stated, we accept the broader interpretation.

In 1956, an information based on this section was filed against James Vernon Turley in the United States District Court for the District of Maryland. It charged that Turley, in South Carolina, lawfully obtained possession of an automobile from its owner for the purpose of driving certain of their friends to the homes of the latter in South Carolina, but that, without permission of the owner and with intent to steal the automobile, Turley converted it to his own use and unlawfully transported it in interstate commerce to Baltimore, Maryland, where he sold it without permission of the owner. The information thus charged Turley with transporting the automobile in interstate commerce knowing it to have been obtained by embezzlement rather than by common-law larceny.

Counsel appointed for Turley moved to dismiss the information on the ground that it did not state facts sufficient to constitute an offense against the United States. He contended that the word "stolen" as used in the Act referred only to takings which constitute common-law larceny and that the acts charged did not. The District Court agreed and dismissed the information. . . . The United States concedes that the facts alleged in the information do not constitute common-law larceny, but disputes the holding that a motor vehicle obtained by embezzlement is not "stolen" within the meaning of the Act. . . .

Decisions involving the meaning of "stolen" as used in the National Motor Vehicle Theft Act did not arise frequently until comparatively recently. Two of the earlier cases interpreted "stolen" as meaning statutory larceny as defined by the State in which the taking occurred.

The later decisions rejected that interpretation but divided on whether to give "stolen" a uniformly narrow meaning restricted to common-law larceny, or a uniformly broader meaning inclusive of embezzlement and other felonious takings with intent to deprive the owner of the rights and benefits of ownership. The Fifth, Eighth and Tenth Circuits favored the narrow definition while the Fourth, Sixth and Ninth Circuits favored the broader one. We agree that in the absence of a plain indication of an intent to incorporate diverse state laws into a federal criminal statute, the meaning of the federal statute should not be dependent on state law. . . .

We recognize that where a federal criminal statute uses a common-law term of established meaning without otherwise defining it, the general practice is to give that term its common-law meaning. But "stolen" (or "stealing") has no accepted common-law meaning. On this point the Court of Appeals for the Fourth Circuit recently said:

> "But while 'stolen' is constantly identified with larceny, the term was never at common law equated or exclusively dedicated to larceny. 'Steal' (originally 'stale') at first denoted in general usage a taking through secrecy, as implied in 'stealth,' or through stratagem, according to the Oxford English Dictionary. Expanded through the years, it became the generic designation for dishonest acquisition, but it never lost its initial connotation. Nor in law is 'steal' or 'stolen' a word of art. Blackstone does not mention 'steal' in defining larceny—'the felonious taking and carrying away of the personal goods of another'—or in expounding its several elements. . . ."

Webster's New International Dictionary (2d ed., 1953) likewise defines "stolen" as "Obtained or accomplished by theft, stealth, or craft . . . ." Black's Law Dictionary (4th ed., 1951) states that "steal" "may denote the criminal taking of personal property either by larceny, embezzlement, or false pretenses." Furthermore, "stolen" and "steal" have been used in federal criminal statutes, and the courts interpreting those words have declared that they do not have a necessary common-law meaning coterminous with larceny and exclusive of other theft crimes. Freed from a common-law meaning, we should give "stolen" the meaning consistent with the context in which it appears.

> "That criminal statutes are to be construed strictly is a proposition which calls for the citation of no authority. But this does not mean that every criminal statute must be given the narrowest possible meaning in complete disregard of the purpose of the legislature." . . .

It is, therefore, appropriate to consider the purpose of the Act and to gain what light we can from its legislative history.

By 1919, the law of most States against local theft had developed so as to include not only common-law larceny but embezzlement, false pretenses, larceny by trick, and other types of wrongful taking. The advent of the automobile, however, created a new problem with which the States found it difficult to deal. The automobile was uniquely suited to felonious taking whether by larceny, embezzlement or false pretenses. It was a valuable, salable article which itself supplied the means for speedy escape. "The automobile [became] the perfect chattel for modern large-scale theft." This challenge could be best met through use of the Federal Government's jurisdiction over interstate commerce. The need for federal action increased with the number, distribution and speed of the motor vehicles until, by 1919, it became a necessity. The result was the National Motor Vehicle Theft Act.

This background was reflected in the Committee Report on the bill presented by its author and sponsor, Representative Dyer. . . . This report, entitled "Theft of Automobiles," pointed to the increasing number of automobile thefts, the resulting financial losses, and the increasing cost of automobile theft insurance. It asserted that state laws were inadequate to cope with the problem because the offenders evaded state officers by transporting the automobiles across state lines where associates received and sold them. Throughout the legislative history Congress used the word "stolen" as synonymous with "theft," a term generally considered to be broader than "common-law larceny." To be sure, the discussion referred to "larceny" but nothing was said about excluding other forms of "theft." The report stated the object of the Act in broad terms, primarily emphasizing the need for the exercise of federal powers. No mention is made of a purpose to distinguish between different forms of theft, as would be expected if the distinction had been intended.

"Larceny" is also mentioned in Brooks v. United States, 1925, . . . This reference however, carries no necessary implication excluding the taking of automobiles by embezzlement or false pretenses. Public and private rights are violated to a comparable degree whatever label is attached to the felonious taking. A typical example of common-law larceny is the taking of an unattended automobile. But an automobile is no less "stolen" because it is rented, transported interstate, and sold without the permission of the owner (embezzlement). The same is true where an automobile is purchased with a worthless check, transported interstate, and sold (false pretenses). Professional thieves resort to innumerable forms of theft and Congress presumably sought to meet the need for federal action effectively rather than to leave loopholes for wholesale evasion.

We conclude that the Act requires an interpretation of "stolen" which does not limit it to situations which at common law would be considered larceny. The refinements of that crime are not related to the primary congressional purpose of eliminating the interstate traffic in unlawfully obtained motor vehicles. The Government's interpretation is neither unclear nor vague. "Stolen" as used in 18 U.S.C. § 2312, . . . includes all felonious takings of motor vehicles with intent to deprive the owner of the rights and benefits of ownership, regardless of whether or not the theft constitutes common-law larceny.

Reversed and remanded.

MR. JUSTICE FRANKFURTER, whom MR. JUSTICE BLACK and MR. JUSTICE DOUGLAS join, dissenting.

If Congress desires to make cheating, in all its myriad varieties, a federal offense when employed to obtain an automobile that is then taken across a state line, it should express itself with less ambiguity than by language that leads three Courts of Appeals to decide that it has not said so and three that it has. If "stealing" (describing a thing as "stolen") be not a term of art, it must be deemed a colloquial, everyday term. As such, it would hardly be used, even loosely, by the man in the street to cover "cheating." Legislative drafting is dependent on treacherous words to convey, as often as not, complicated ideas, and courts should not be pedantically exacting in construing legislation. But to sweep into the jurisdiction of the federal courts the transportation of cars obtained not only by theft but also by trickery does not present a problem so complicated that the Court should search for hints to find a command. When Congress has wanted to deal with many different ways of despoiling another of his property and not merely with larceny, it has found it easy enough to do so, as a number of federal enactments attest. . . . No doubt, penal legislation should not be artificially restricted so as to allow escape for those for whom it was with fair intendment designed. But the principle of lenity which should guide construction of criminal statutes, . . . precludes extending the term "stolen" to include every form of dishonest acquisition. This conclusion is encouraged not only by the general consideration governing the construction of penal laws; it also has regard for not bringing to the federal courts a mass of minor offenses that are local in origin until Congress expresses, if not an explicit, at least an unequivocal, desire to do so.

I would affirm the judgment.

TAYLOR v. UNITED STATES

Supreme Court of the United States, 1990.
____ U.S. ____, 110 S.Ct. 2143.

JUSTICE BLACKMUN delivered the opinion of the Court.

In this case we are called upon to determine the meaning of the word "burglary" as it is used in § 1402 of Subtitle I (the Career Criminals Amendment Act of 1986) of the Anti–Drug Abuse Act of 1986, 18 U.S.C. § 924(e). This statute provides a sentence enhancement for a defendant who is convicted under 18 U.S.C. § 922(g) (unlawful possession of a firearm) and who has three prior convictions for specified types of offenses, including "burglary."

I

Under 18 U.S.C. § 922(g)(1), it is unlawful for a person who has been convicted previously for a felony to possess a firearm. A defendant convicted for a violation of § 922(g)(1) is subject to the sentence-enhancement provision at issue, § 924(e):

"(1) In the case of a person who violates section 922(g) of this title and has three previous convictions by any court . . . for a violent felony or a serious drug offense, or both . . . such person shall be fined not more than $25,000 and imprisoned not less than fifteen years. . . .

"(2) As used in this subsection—

. . . .

"(B) The term 'violent felony' means any crime punishable by imprisonment for a term exceeding one year . . . that—

"(i) has as an element the use, attempted use, or threatened use of physical force against the person of another; or

"(ii) is burglary, arson, or extortion, involves use of explosives, or otherwise involves conduct that presents a serious potential risk of physical injury to another."

In January 1988, in the United States District Court for the Eastern District of Missouri, petitioner Arthur Lajuane Taylor pleaded guilty to one count of possession of a firearm by a convicted felon, in violation of 18 U.S.C. § 922(g)(1). At the time of his plea, Taylor had four prior convictions. One was for robbery, one was for assault, and the other two were for second-degree burglary under Missouri law.

The Government sought sentence enhancement under § 924(e). Taylor conceded that his robbery and assault convictions properly could be counted as two of the three prior convictions required for enhancement, because they involved the use of physical force against persons, under § 924(e)(2)(B)(i). Taylor contended, however, that his burglary convictions should not count for enhancement, because they did not involve "conduct that presents a serious potential risk of physical injury to another," under § 924(e)(2)(B)(ii). His guilty plea was conditioned on the right to appeal this issue. The District Court, pursuant to § 924(e)(1), sentenced Taylor to 15 years' imprisonment without possibility of parole.

The United States Court of Appeals for the Eighth Circuit, by a divided vote, affirmed Taylor's sentence. . . .

The word "burglary" has not been given a single accepted meaning by the state courts; the criminal codes of the States define burglary in many different ways. See United States v. Hill, 863 F.2d 1575, 1582, and n. 5 (CA11 1989) (surveying a number of burglary statutes). On the face of the federal enhancement provision, it is not readily apparent whether Congress intended "burglary" to mean whatever the State of the defendant's prior conviction defines as burglary, or whether it intended that some uniform definition of burglary be applied to all cases in which the Government seeks a § 924(e) enhancement. And if Congress intended that a uniform definition of burglary be applied, was that definition to be the traditional common-law definition, or one of the broader "generic" definitions articulated in the Model Penal Code and in a predecessor statute to § 924(e), or some other definition specifically tailored to the purposes of the enhancement statute?

II

Before examining these possibilities, we think it helpful to review the background of § 924(e). Six years ago, Congress enacted the first version of the sentence-enhancement provision. Under the Armed Career Criminal Act of 1984, Pub.L. 98–473, ch. 18, 98 Stat. 2185, 18 U.S.C.App. § 1202(a) (1982 ed. Supp. III) (repealed in 1986 by Pub.L. 99–308, § 104(b), 100 Stat. 459), any convicted felon found guilty of possession of a firearm, who had three previous convictions "for robbery or burglary," was to receive a mandatory minimum sentence of imprisonment for 15 years. Burglary was defined in the statute itself as "any felony consisting of entering or remaining surreptitiously within a building that is property of another with intent to engage in conduct constituting a Federal or State offense." § 1202(c)(9).

The Act was intended to supplement the States' law-enforcement efforts against "career" criminals. The House Report accompanying the Act explained that a "large percentage" of crimes of theft and violence "are committed by a very small percentage of repeat offenders," and that robbery and burglary are the crimes most frequently committed by these career criminals. The House Report quoted the sponsor of the legislation, Sen. Specter, who found burglary one of the "most damaging crimes to society" because it involves "invasion of [victims'] homes or workplaces, violation of their privacy, and loss of their most personal and valued possessions." Similarly, the Senate Report stated that burglary was included because it is one of "the most common violent street crimes," and "[w]hile burglary is sometimes viewed as a non-violent crime, its character can change rapidly, depending on the fortuitous presence of the occupants of the home when the burglar enters, or their arrival while he is still on the premises."

The only explanation of why Congress chose the specific definition of burglary included in § 1202 appears in the Senate Report:

"Because of the wide variation among states and localities in the ways that offenses are labeled, the absence of definitions raised the possibility that culpable offenders might escape punishment on a technicality. For instance, the common law definition of burglary includes a requirement that the offense be committed during the nighttime and with respect to a dwelling. However, for purposes of this Act, such limitations are not appropriate. Furthermore, in terms of fundamental fairness, the Act should ensure, to the extent that it is consistent with the prerogatives of the States in defining their own offenses, that the same type of conduct is punishable on the Federal level in all cases." S.Rep., at 20.

In 1986, § 1202 was recodified as 18 U.S.C. § 924(e) by the Firearms Owners' Protection Act, Pub.L. 99–308, § 104, 100 Stat. 458. The definition of burglary was amended slightly, by replacing the words "any felony" with "any crime punishable by a term of imprisonment exceeding one year and. . . . ."

Only five months later, § 924(e) again was amended, into its present form, by § 1402 of Subtitle I (the Career Criminals Amendment Act) of the Anti–Drug Abuse Act of 1986, 100 Stat. 3207–39. This amendment effected three changes that, taken together, give rise to the problem presented in this case. It expanded the predicate offenses triggering the sentence enhancement from "robbery or burglary" to "a violent felony or a serious drug offense"; it defined the term "violent felony" to include "burglary"; and it deleted the pre-existing definition of burglary.

The legislative history is silent as to Congress' reason for deleting the definition of burglary. It does reveal, however, the general purpose and approach of the Career Criminals Amendment Act of 1986. Two bills were proposed; from these the current statutory language emerged as a compromise. The first bill, introduced in the Senate by Sen. Specter and in the House by Rep. Wyden, provided that any "crime of violence" would count towards the three prior convictions required for a sentence enhancement, and defined "crime of violence" as "an offense that has as an element the use, attempted use, or threatened use of physical force against the person or property of another," or any felony "that, by its nature, involves a substantial risk that physical force against the person or property of another may be used in the course of committing the offense." S. 2312, 99th Cong., 2d Sess. (1986); H.R. 4639, 99th Cong., 2d Sess. (1986). The second bill, introduced in the House by Reps. Hughes and McCollum, took a narrower approach, restricting the crimes that would count towards enhancement to "any State or Federal felony that has as an element the use, attempted use, or threatened use of physical force against the person of another."

When Sen. Specter introduced S. 2312 in the Senate, he stated that since the enhancement provision had been in effect for a year and a half, and "has been successful with the basic classification of robberies and burglaries as the definition for 'career criminal,' the time has come to broaden that definition so that we may have a greater sweep and more effective use of this important statute." 132 Cong.Rec. 7697 (1986). Similarly, during the House and Senate hearings on the bills, the witnesses reiterated the concerns that prompted the original enactment of the enhancement provision in 1984: the large proportion of crimes committed by a small number of career offenders, and the inadequacy of state prosecutorial resources to address this problem.

The issue under consideration was uniformly referred to as "expanding" the range of predicate offenses. House Hearing, at 8 ("all of us want to see the legislation expanded to other violent offenders and career drug dealers") (statement of Rep. Wyden); id., at 11 ("I think we can all agree that we should expand the predicate offenses") (statement of Rep. Hughes); id., at 14 (statement of Deputy Assistant Attorney General James Knapp); id., at 32–33 (statement of Bruce Lyons, President-elect of National Association of Criminal Defense Lawyers); id., at 44 (statement of Sen. Specter); Senate Hearing, at 1 ("The time seems ripe in many quarters, including the Department of Justice, to expand the armed career criminal bill to include other offenses") (statement of Sen. Specter); id., at 15 (statement of United States Attorney Edward S.G. Dennis, Jr.); id., at 20 (statement of David Dart Queen of the Department of the Treasury); id., at 49 and 55 (statement of Ronald D. Castille, District Attorney, Philadelphia).

Witnesses criticized the narrower bill, H.R. 4768, for excluding property crimes, pointing out that some such crimes present a serious risk of harm to persons, and that the career offenders at whom the enhancement provision is aimed often specialize in property crimes, especially burglary. See House Hearing, at 9 and 12 ("I would hope . . . that at least some violent felonies against property could be included"; "people . . . make a full-time career and commit hundreds of burglaries") (statements of Rep. Wyden); id., at 49–53 (statement of Mr. Castille). The testimony of Mr. Knapp focused specifically on whether the enhancement provision should include burglary as a predicate offense. He criticized H.R. 4768 for excluding "such serious felonies against property as most burglary offenses" and thus "inadvertently narrow[ing] the scope of the present Armed Career Criminal Act," and went on to say:

> "Now the question has been raised, well, what crimes against property should be included? We think burglary, of course; arson; extortion; and various explosives offenses. . . .

> The one problem I see in using a specific generic term like burglary or arson—that's fine for those statutes—but a lot of these newer explosives offenses don't have a single generic term that covers them, and that is something that the committee may want to be very careful about in coming up with the final statutory language.

> It is these crimes against property—which are inherently dangerous—that we think should be considered as predicate offenses."

In response to a question by Rep. Hughes as to the justification for retaining burglary as a predicate offense, Mr. Knapp explained that "your typical career criminal is most likely to be a burglar," and that "even though injury is not an element of the offense, it is a potentially very dangerous offense, because when you take your very typical residential burglary or even your professional commercial burglary, there is a very serious danger to people who might be inadvertently found on the premises." He qualified his remarks, however, by saying: "Obviously, we would not consider, as prior convictions, what I would call misdemeanor burglaries, or your technical burglaries, or anything like that."

Rep. Hughes put the same question to the next witness, Mr. Lyons. The witness replied:

"When you use burglary, burglary is going back to really what the original legislative history and intent was, to get a hold of the profit motive and to the recidivist armed career criminal. The NACDL really has no problem with burglary as a predicate offense."

In his prepared statement for the Subcommittee, the witness had noted that H.R. 4768 "would not appear to encompass . . . burglary," and that "[i]f the Subcommittee concludes that it can accept no retreat from current law, we would suggest that the preservation of burglary as a prior offense be accomplished simply by retaining 'burglary' . . . rather than by substituting for it the all-inclusive 'crime of violence' definition proposed in H.R. 4639."

H.R. 4639, on the other hand, was seen as too broad. See id., at 11 ("it is important to prioritize offenses") (statement of Rep. Hughes); ("the answer probably lies somewhere between the two bills") (statement of Mr. Knapp). The hearing concluded with a statement by Rep. Hughes, a sponsor of the narrower bill, H.R. 4768:

"Frankly, I think on the question of burglaries, I can see the arguments both ways. We have already included burglaries.

My leanings would be to leave it alone; it is in the existing law; it was the existing statute. We can still be specific enough. We are talking about burglaries that probably are being carried out by an armed criminal, because the triggering mechanism is that they possess a weapon. . . . So we are not talking about the average run-of-the-mill burglar necessarily, we are talking about somebody who also illegally possesses or has been transferred a firearm."

After the House hearing, the Subcommittee drafted a compromise bill, H.R. 4885. This bill included "violent felony" as a predicate offense, and provided that

"the term 'violent felony' means any crime punishable by imprisonment for a term exceeding one year that—

(i) has as an element the use, attempted use, or threatened use of force against the person of another; or

(ii) involves conduct that presents a serious potential risk of physical injury to another."

H.R. 4885 was favorably reported by the House Committee on the Judiciary. H.R.Rep. No. 99–849 (1986). The Report explained:

"The Subcommittee on Crime held a hearing . . . to consider whether it should expand the predicate offenses (robbery and burglary) in existing law in order to add to its effectiveness. At this hearing a consensus developed in support of an expansion of the predicate offenses to include serious drug trafficking offenses . . . and violent felonies, generally. This concept was encompassed in H.R. 4885 by deleting the specific predicate offenses for robbery and burglary and adding as predicate offenses [certain drug offenses] and violent felonies. . . .

"The other major question involved in these hearings was as to what violent felonies involving physical force against *property* should be included in the definition of 'violent' felony. The Subcommittee agreed to add the crimes punishable for a term exceeding one year that involve conduct that presents a serious potential risk of physical injury to others. This will add State and Federal crimes against property such as burglary, arson, extortion, use of explosives and similar crimes as predicate offenses where the conduct involved presents a serious risk of injury to a person" (emphasis in original).

The provision as finally enacted, however, added to the above-quoted subsection (ii) the phrase that is critical in this case: ". . . *is burglary, arson, or extortion, involves use of explosives, or otherwise* involves conduct that presents a serious potential risk of physical injury to another." 18 U.S.C. § 924(e)(2)(B)(ii).

Some useful observations may be drawn. First, throughout the history of the enhancement provision, Congress focused its efforts on career offenders—those who commit a large number of fairly serious crimes as their means of livelihood, and who, because they possess weapons, present at least a potential threat of harm to persons. This concern was not limited to offenders who had actually been convicted of crimes of violence against persons. (Only H.R. 4768, rejected by the House Subcommittee, would have restricted the predicate offenses to crimes actually involving violence against persons.)

The legislative history also indicates that Congress singled out burglary (as opposed to other frequently committed property crimes such as larceny and auto theft) for inclusion as a predicate offense, both in 1984 and in 1986, because of its inherent potential for harm to persons. The fact that an offender enters a building to commit a crime often creates the possibility of a violent confrontation between the offender and an occupant, caretaker, or some other person who comes to investigate. And the offender's own awareness of this possibility may mean that he is prepared to use violence if necessary to carry out his plans or to escape. Congress apparently thought that all burglaries serious enough to be punishable by imprisonment for more than a year constituted a category of crimes that shared this potential for violence, and that were likely to be committed by career criminals. There never was any proposal to limit the predicate offense to some special subclass of burglaries that might be especially dangerous, such as those where the offender is armed, or the building is occupied, or the crime occurs at night.

Second, the enhancement provision always has embodied a categorical approach to the designation of predicate offenses. In the 1984 statute, "robbery" and "burglary" were defined in the statute itself, not left to the vagaries of state law. See 18 U.S.C.App. §§ 1202(c)(8) and (9) (1982 ed. Supp. III). Thus, Congress intended that the enhancement provision be triggered by crimes having certain specified elements, not by crimes that happened to be labeled "robbery" or "burglary" by the laws of the State of conviction. Each of the proposed versions of the 1986 amendment carried forward this categorical approach, extending the range of predicate offenses to all crimes having certain common characteristics—the use or threatened use of force, or the risk that force would be used—regardless of how they were labeled by state law.

Third, the 1984 definition of burglary shows that Congress, at least at that time, had in mind a modern "generic" view of burglary, roughly corresponding to the definitions of burglary in a majority of the States' criminal codes. In adopting this definition, Congress both prevented offenders from invoking the arcane technicalities of the common-law definition of burglary to evade the sentence-enhancement provision, and protected offenders from the unfairness of having enhancement depend upon the label employed by the State of conviction.

Nothing in the legislative history of the 1986 amendment shows that Congress was dissatisfied with the 1984 definition. All the testimony and reports read as if the meaning of burglary was undisputed. The debate at the 1986 hearings centered upon whether any property crimes should be included as predicate offenses, and if so, which ones. At the House hearing, the Subcommittee reached a consensus that at least some property crimes, including burglary, should be included, but again there was no debate over the proper definition of burglary. The compromise bill, H.R. 4885, apparently was intended to include burglary, among other serious property offenses, by implication, as a crime that "involves conduct that presents a serious potential risk of physical injury to another." The language added to H.R. 4885 before its enactment seemingly was meant simply to make explicit the provision's implied coverage of crimes such as burglary.

The legislative history as a whole suggests that the deletion of the 1984 definition of burglary may have been an inadvertent casualty of a complex drafting process. In any event, there is nothing in the history to show that Congress intended in 1986 to replace the 1984 "generic" definition of burglary with something entirely different. Although the omission of a preexisting definition of a term often indicates Congress' intent to reject that definition, we draw no such inference here.

Nor is there any indication that Congress ever abandoned its general approach, in designating predicate offenses, of using uniform, categorical definitions to capture all offenses of a certain level of seriousness that involve violence or an inherent risk thereof, and that are likely to be committed by career offenders, regardless of technical definitions and labels under state law.

III

These observations about the purpose and general approach of the enhancement provision enable us to narrow the range of possible meanings of the term "burglary."

A

First, we are led to reject the view of the Court of Appeals in this case. It seems to us to be implausible that Congress intended the meaning of "burglary" for purposes of § 924(e) to depend on the definition adopted by the State of conviction. That would mean that a person convicted of unlawful possession of a firearm would, or would not, receive a sentence enhancement based on exactly the same conduct, depending on whether the State of his prior conviction happened to call that conduct "burglary."

For example, Michigan has no offense formally labeled "burglary." It classifies burglaries into several grades of "breaking and entering." See Mich.Comp.Laws § 750.110 (1979). In contrast, California defines "burglary" so broadly as to include shoplifting and theft of goods from a "locked" but unoccupied automobile. See Cal.Penal Code Ann. § 459 (West Supp.1990); United States v. Chatman, 869 F.2d 525, 528–529, and n. 2 (CA9 1989) (entry through unsecured window of an unoccupied auto, and entry of a store open to the public with intent to commit theft, are "burglary" under California law); see also Tex.Penal Code Ann. §§ 30.01–30.05 (1989 and Supp.1990) (defining burglary to include theft from coin-operated vending machine or automobile); United States v. Leonard, 868 F.2d 1393, 1395, n. 2 (CA5 1989), cert. pending, No. 88–1885.

Thus, a person imprudent enough to shoplift or steal from an automobile in California would be found, under the Ninth Circuit's view, to have committed a burglary constituting a "violent felony" for enhancement purposes—yet a person who did so in Michigan might not. Without a clear indication that with the 1986 amendment Congress intended to abandon its general approach of using uniform categorical definitions to identify predicate offenses, we do not interpret Congress' omission of a definition of "burglary" in a way that leads to odd results of this kind. . . .

This Court's response to the similar problem of interpreting the term "extortion" in the Travel Act, 18 U.S.C. § 1952, is instructive:

> "Appellees argue that Congress' decision not to define extortion combined with its decision to prohibit only extortion in violation of state law compels the conclusion that peculiar

variations of state terminology are controlling. . . . The fallacy of this contention lies in its assumption that, by defining extortion with reference to state law, Congress also incorporated state labels for particular offenses. Congress' intent was to aid local law enforcement officials, not to eradicate only those extortionate activities which any given State denominated extortion. . . . Giving controlling effect to state classifications would result in coverage under § 1952 if appellees' activities were centered in Massachusetts, Michigan, or Oregon, but would deny coverage in Indiana, Kansas, Minnesota, or Wisconsin although each of these States prohibits identical criminal activities."

We think that "burglary" in § 924(e) must have some uniform definition independent of the labels employed by the various States' criminal codes.

B

Some Courts of Appeals have ruled that § 924(e) incorporates the common-law definition of burglary, relying on the maxim that a statutory term is generally presumed to have its common-law meaning. See *Morissette v. United States* (1952). This view has some appeal, in that common-law burglary is the core, or common denominator, of the contemporary usage of the term. Almost all States include a breaking and entering of a dwelling at night, with intent to commit a felony, among their definitions of burglary. Whatever else the Members of Congress might have been thinking of, they presumably had in mind at least the "classic" common-law definition when they considered the inclusion of burglary as a predicate offense.

The problem with this view is that the contemporary understanding of "burglary" has diverged a long way from its common-law roots. Only a few States retain the common-law definition, or something closely resembling it. Most other States have expanded this definition to include entry without a "breaking," structures other than dwellings, offenses committed in the daytime, entry with intent to commit a crime other than a felony, etc. This statutory development, "when viewed in totality, has resulted in a modern crime which has little in common with its common-law ancestor except for the title of burglary."

Also, interpreting "burglary" in § 924(e) to mean common-law burglary would not comport with the purposes of the enhancement statute. The arcane distinctions embedded in the common-law definition have little relevance to modern law enforcement concerns. It seems unlikely that the Members of Congress, immersed in the intensely practical concerns of controlling violent crime, would have decided to abandon their modern, generic 1984 definition of burglary and revert to a definition developed in the ancient English law—a definition mentioned nowhere in the legislative history. Moreover, construing "burglary" to mean common-law burglary would come close to nullifying that term's effect in the statute, because few of the crimes now generally recognized as burglaries would fall within the common-law definition.

It could be argued, of course, that common-law burglary, by and large, involves a greater "potential risk of physical injury to another." § 924(e)(2)(B)(ii). But, even assuming that Congress intended to restrict the predicate offense to some especially dangerous subclass of burglaries, restricting it to common-law burglary would not be a rational way of doing so. The common-law definition does not require that the offender be armed, or that the dwelling be occupied at the time of the crime. An armed burglary of an occupied commercial building, in the daytime, would seem to pose a far greater risk of harm to persons than an unarmed nocturnal breaking and entering of an unoccupied house. It seems unlikely that Congress would have considered the latter, but not the former, to be a "violent felony" counting towards a sentence enhancement. In the absence of any specific indication that Congress meant to incorporate the common-law meaning of burglary, we shall not read into the statute a definition of "burglary" so obviously ill-suited to its purposes.

This Court has declined to follow any rule that a statutory term is to be given its common-law meaning, when that meaning is obsolete or inconsistent with the statute's purpose.

* * *

Petitioner argues that the narrow common-law definition of burglary would comport with the rule of lenity—that criminal statutes, including sentencing provisions, are to be construed in favor of the accused. This maxim of statutory construction, however, cannot dictate an implausible interpretation of a statute, nor one at odds with the generally accepted contemporary meaning of a term.

C

Petitioner suggests another narrowing construction of the term "burglary," more suited to the purpose of the enhancement statute:

"Burglary is any crime punishable by a term of imprisonment exceeding one year and consisting of entering or remaining within a building that is the property of another with intent to engage in conduct constituting a Federal or State offense that has as an element necessary for conviction conduct that presents a serious risk of physical injury to another."

As examples of burglary statutes that would fit this definition, petitioner points to first-degree or aggravated-burglary statutes having elements such as entering an occupied building; being armed with a deadly weapon; or causing or threatening physical injury to a person. See n. 4, supra. This definition has some appeal, because it avoids the arbitrariness of the state-law approach, by restricting the predicate offense in a manner congruent with the general purpose of the enhancement statute.

We do not accept petitioner's proposal, however, for two reasons. First, it is not supported by the language of the statute or the legislative history. Petitioner essentially asserts that Congress meant to include as predicate offenses only a subclass of burglaries whose elements include "conduct that presents a serious risk of physical injury to another," over and above the risk inherent in ordinary burglaries. But if this were Congress' intent, there would have been no reason to add the word "burglary" to § 924(e)(2)(B)(ii), since that provision already includes *any* crime that "involves conduct that presents a serious potential risk of physical injury to another." We must assume that Congress had a purpose in adding the word "burglary" to H.R. 4885 before enacting it into law. The most likely explanation, in view of the legislative history, is that Congress thought that certain general categories of property crimes—namely burglary, arson, extortion, and use of explosives—so often presented a risk of injury to persons, or were so often committed by career criminals, that they should be included in the enhancement statute even though, considered solely in terms of their statutory elements, they do not necessarily involve the use or threat of force against a person.

Second, if Congress had meant to include only an especially dangerous subclass of burglaries as predicate offenses, it is unlikely that it would have used the unqualified language "*is* burglary . . . or otherwise involves conduct that presents a serious potential risk" in § 924(e)(2)(B)(ii). Congress presumably realized that the word "burglary" is commonly understood to include not only aggravated burglaries, but also run-of-the-mill burglaries involving an unarmed offender, an unoccupied building, and no use or threat of force. This choice of language indicates that Congress thought ordinary burglaries, as well as burglaries involving some element making them especially dangerous, presented a sufficiently "serious potential risk" to count towards enhancement.

D

We therefore reject petitioner's view that Congress meant to include only a special subclass of burglaries, either those that would have been burglaries at common law, or those that involve especially dangerous conduct. These limiting constructions are not dictated by the rule of lenity. We believe that Congress meant, by "burglary," the generic sense in which the term is now used in the criminal codes of most States.

Although the exact formulations vary, the generic, contemporary meaning of burglary contains at least the following elements: an unlawful or unprivileged entry into or remaining in a building or other structure, with intent to commit a crime.

This generic meaning, of course, is practically identical to the 1984 definition that, in 1986, was omitted from the enhancement provision. The 1984 definition, however, was not explicitly replaced with a different or narrower one; the legislative history discloses that no alternative definition of burglary was ever discussed. As we have seen, there simply is no plausible alternative that Congress could have had in mind. The omission of a definition of burglary in the 1986 Act therefore implies, at most, that Congress did not wish to specify an exact formulation that an offense must meet in order to count as "burglary" for enhancement purposes.

We conclude that a person has been convicted of burglary for purposes of a § 924(e) enhancement if he is convicted of any crime, regardless of its exact definition or label, having the basic elements of unlawful or unprivileged entry into, or remaining in, a building or structure, with intent to commit a crime.

IV

There remains the problem of applying this conclusion to cases in which the state statute under which a defendant is convicted varies from the generic definition of "burglary." If the state statute is narrower than the generic view, e.g., in cases of burglary convictions in common-law States or convictions of first-degree or aggravated burglary, there is no problem, because the conviction necessarily implies that the defendant has been found guilty of all the elements of generic burglary. And if the defendant was convicted of burglary in a State where the generic definition has been adopted, with minor variations in terminology, then the trial court need find only that the state statute corresponds in substance to the generic meaning of burglary.

A few States' burglary statutes, however, as has been noted above, define burglary more broadly, e.g., by eliminating the requirement that the entry be unlawful, or by including places, such as automobiles and vending machines, other than buildings. One of Missouri's second-degree burglary statutes in effect at the times of petitioner Taylor's convictions included breaking and entering "any booth or tent, or any boat or vessel, or railroad car." Mo.Rev.Stat. § 560.070 (1969) (repealed). Also, there may be offenses under some States' laws that, while not called "burglary," correspond in substantial part to generic burglary. We therefore must address the question whether, in the case of a defendant who has been convicted under a nongeneric-burglary statute, the Government may seek enhancement on the grounds that he actually committed a generic burglary.

This question requires us to address a more general issue—whether the sentencing court in applying § 924(e) must look only to the statutory definitions of the prior offenses, or whether the court may consider other evidence concerning the defendant's prior crimes. The Courts of Appeals uniformly have held that § 924(e) mandates a formal categorical approach, looking only to the statutory definitions of the prior offenses, and not to the particular facts underlying those convictions. We find the reasoning of these cases persuasive.

First, the language of § 924(e) generally supports the inference that Congress intended the sentencing court to look only to the fact that the defendant had been convicted of crimes falling within certain categories, and not to the facts underlying the prior convictions. Section 924(e)(1) refers to "a person who . . . has three previous convictions" for—not a person who has committed—three previous violent felonies or drug offenses. Section 924(e)(2)(B)(i) defines "violent felony" as any crime punishable by imprisonment for more than a year that "has as an element"—not any crime that, in a particular case, involves—the use or threat of force. Read in this context, the phrase "is burglary" in § 924(e)(2)(B)(ii) most likely refers to the elements of the statute of conviction, not to the facts of each defendant's conduct.

Second, as we have said, the legislative history of the enhancement statute shows that Congress generally took a categorical approach to predicate offenses. There was considerable debate over what kinds of offenses to include and how to define them, but no one suggested that a particular crime might sometimes count towards enhancement and sometimes not, depending on the facts of the case. If Congress had meant to adopt an approach that would require the sentencing court to engage in an elaborate fact finding process regarding the defendant's prior offenses, surely this would have been mentioned somewhere in the legislative history.

Third, the practical difficulties and potential unfairness of a factual approach are daunting. In all cases where the Government alleges that the defendant's actual conduct would fit the generic definition of burglary, the trial court would have to determine what that conduct was. In some cases, the indictment or other charging paper might reveal the theory or theories of the case presented to the jury. In other cases, however, only the Government's actual proof at trial would indicate whether the defendant's conduct constituted generic burglary. Would the Government be permitted to introduce the trial transcript before the sentencing court, or if no transcript is available, present the testimony of witnesses? Could the defense present witnesses of its own, and argue that the jury might have returned a guilty verdict on some theory that did not require a finding that the defendant committed generic burglary? If the sentencing court were to conclude, from its own review of the record, that the defendant actually committed a generic burglary, could the defendant challenge this conclusion as abridging his right to a jury trial? Also, in cases where the defendant pleaded guilty, there often is no record of the underlying facts. Even if the Government were able to prove those facts, if a guilty plea to a lesser, nonburglary offense was the result of a plea bargain, it would seem unfair to impose a sentence enhancement as if the defendant had pleaded guilty to burglary.

We think the only plausible interpretation of § 924(e)(2)(B)(ii) is that, like the rest of the enhancement statute, it generally requires the trial court to look only to the fact of conviction and the statutory definition of the prior offense. This categorical approach, however, may permit the sentencing court to go beyond the mere fact of conviction in a narrow range of cases where a jury was actually required to find all the elements of generic burglary. For example, in a State whose burglary statutes include entry of an automobile as well as a building, if the indictment or information and jury instructions show that the defendant was charged only with a burglary of a building, and that the jury necessarily had to find an entry of a building to convict, then the Government should be allowed to use the conviction for enhancement.

We therefore hold that an offense constitutes "burglary" for purposes of a § 924(e) sentence enhancement if either its statutory definition substantially corresponds to "generic" burglary, or the charging paper and jury instructions actually required the jury to find all the elements of generic burglary in order to convict the defendant.

In Taylor's case, most but not all the former Missouri statutes defining second-degree burglary include all the elements of generic burglary. See n. 1, supra. Despite the Government's argument to the contrary, it is not apparent to us from the sparse record before us which of those statutes were the bases for Taylor's prior convictions. We therefore vacate the judgment of the Court of Appeals and remand the case for further proceedings consistent with this opinion.

It is so ordered.

[JUSTICE SCALIA's concurring opinion is omitted.]

NOTE

In Bell v. United States, 462 U.S. 356, 103 S.Ct. 2398, 76 L.Ed.2d 638 (1983), the United States Supreme Court held that the federal bank robbery act was not limited to common law larceny, but also proscribed the crime of obtaining money under false pretenses.

The defendant was charged with violating the Bank Robbery Act, 18 U.S.C.A. § 2113(b), which provides, in part: "Whoever takes and carries away, with intent to steal or purloin, any property or money or any other thing of value exceeding $100 belonging to, or in the care, custody, control, management, or possession of any bank, credit union, or any savings and loan association, shall be fined not more than $5,000 or imprisoned not more than ten years, or both. . . ." The question before the Supreme Court was whether this statute embraces all felonious takings—including obtaining money by false pretenses, or is it limited to those acts which at common law would have been larceny? The Court opted for a broad reading, stating, in part:

". . . We cannot believe that Congress wished to limit the scope of the amended Act's coverage, and thus its remedial purpose, on the basis of an arcane and artificial distinction more suited to the social conditions of 18th century England than the need of 20th Century America. . . ."

Chapter 8

UNCOMPLETED CRIMINAL CONDUCT AND CRIMINAL COMBINATIONS

A. UNCOMPLETED CRIMINAL CONDUCT

1. ATTEMPT

(a) THE ACT

PEOPLE v. PALUCH

Appellate Court of Illinois, Second District, 1966.
78 Ill.App.2d 356, 222 N.E.2d 508.

DAVIS, JUSTICE. The defendant, Michael Paluch, was charged, in the Circuit Court of the 18th Judicial Circuit, DuPage County, with attempting to practice barbering without a certificate of registration as a barber in violation of Ill.Rev.Stat.1965, ch. 16¾, par. 14.92(b)(1). The case was tried before the court without a jury and the defendant was found guilty as charged and a fine in the sum of $25 was imposed. The defendant contends that the evidence was not sufficient to sustain the judgment.

On November 5, 1965, Ernie Pinkston, an agent of the barber's union, went to a barber shop located in Glen Ellyn. It was 9:00 A.M. and the shop was not yet open. He then saw the defendant unlock the rear door and enter the shop. Shortly thereafter, he went to the front door and asked the defendant if the shop was open. The defendant unlocked the door, admitted Pinkston, walked over to the barber chair, put on his smock and offered the chair to Pinkston. The defendant had his own barber tools—clipping shears, razors and combs.

Pinkston then showed the defendant his business card and asked to see his license. The defendant twice motioned to a particular license which, in fact, was not his. No one else was in the shop at the time. When later asked if he worked at the shop, the defendant answered "yes" and admitted that he had no license.

794

Both the defendant and the State refer to the Criminal Code of 1961, . . . with reference to the elements necessary to establish the offense of an "attempt," which provides:

"A person commits an attempt when, with intent to commit a specific offense, he does any act which constitutes a substantial step toward the commission of that offense."

Two elements must be present to constitute an attempt: (1) an intent to commit a specific offense, and (2) an act which is a substantial step towards its commission. The defendant contends that all that can be shown by the record in this case is a mere preparation to do something, but that no act constituting a substantial step toward barbering was committed. . . .

As pointed out in the Committee Comments to par. 8–4 of the Criminal Code . . . the determination of when the preparation to commit an offense ceases and the perpetration of the offense begins, is a troublesome problem. The distinction between the preparation and the attempt is largely a matter of degree, and whether certain given conduct constitutes an actual attempt is a question unique to each particular case.

In order to constitute an attempt, it is not requisite that the act of the defendant is necessarily the last deed immediately preceding that which would render the substantive crime complete. . . . In Commonwealth v. Peaslee . . . [1901], Mr. Justice Holmes, as Chief Justice of the Supreme Judicial Court of Massachusetts, discussed the considerations necessary in determining whether there were sufficient acts to constitute an attempt to commit an offense under circumstances where further acts were required to perpetrate the offense. He there noted that the acts may then be nothing more than preparation to commit an offense which is not punishable, but also stated that given preparations may constitute an attempt, the determining factor being a matter of degree. As illustrative of this comment, his opinion states:

"If the preparation comes very near to the accomplishment of the act, the intent to complete it renders the crime so probable that the act will be a misdemeanor, although there is still a locus poenitentiae, in the need of a further exertion of the will to complete the crime. As was observed in a recent case, the degree of proximity held sufficient may vary with circumstances, including, among other things, the apprehension which the particular crime is calculated to excite."

The crux of the determination of whether the acts are sufficient to constitute an attempt really is whether, when given the specific intent to commit an offense, the acts taken in furtherance thereof are such that there is a dangerous proximity to success in carrying out the intent. In Hyde v. United States . . . (1911), Mr. Justice Holmes, in his dissenting opinion, . . . adequately delineates the distinction between the mere preparation to commit an offense and an attempt to perpetrate the offense, in these words:

"But combination, intention, and overt act may all be present without amounting to a criminal attempt,—as if all that were done should be an agreement to murder a man 50 miles away, and the purchase of a pistol for the purpose. There must be dangerous proximity to success. But when that exists the overt act is the essence of the offense."

The language of par. 8–4 of the Criminal Code, stating that there must be a substantial step toward the commission of the offense indicates that it is not necessary for an "attempt" that the last proximate act to the completion of the offense be done. In addition, the Illinois Supreme Court has likewise considered this problem. In People v. Woods, . . . it stated:

"Mere preparation to commit a crime, of course, does not constitute an attempt to commit it. We feel however that an attempt does exist where a person, with intent to commit a specific offense, performs acts which constitute substantial steps toward the commission of that offense."

The defendant, who conceded that he worked at the barber shop, was the only person there. He had a key and unlocked the shop. He had barber tools. He had a fraudulent license which was posted near the barber chair. He admitted Pinkston to the shop, put on his smock—as it was referred to by the witness—and motioned him to the chair. At this point the defendant was precluded from barbering without a certification of registration, only by the fact that the witness showed the defendant his business card and did not get into the chair. These facts are sufficient to establish the defendant's attempt to violate the statute, as charged.

The defendant argues that barber tools need not be used exclusively for barbering, and that there is nothing to establish that he had a specific intent to practice barbering. In view of the foregoing facts, we find it unbelievable that the defendant had any intent other than to barber and to use the barbering tools, chair and shop for that purpose.

The acts of the defendant were not of such serious character and consequence that he could be expected to feel genuinely apprehensive about what he was doing. The degree of proximity to the actual commission of a crime necessary for there to be an attempt is, in part, determined by the apprehension which the particular crime is calculated to excite. The greater the apprehension, the greater the likelihood that a would-be offender will not follow through with his intended plans. Inasmuch as the offense involved was only a misdemeanor and the penalty inconsequential, there was no cause for serious apprehension on the part of the defendant in connection with the commission of this particular offense, and it was inconceivable that at this late moment he would repent and alter his course of conduct out of fear or concern. He had then taken substantial steps toward the commission of the act of barbering without a certificate of registration. His intention and overt acts resulted in conduct in the very close proximity to the commission of the offense and constituted an attempt. . . .

Judgment affirmed.

MORAN, PRESIDING JUSTICE (dissenting).

I agree with the majority opinion up to the point where it holds that the defendant was guilty of certain acts which constituted a substantial step toward the commission of the offense charged. It is this facet of the case alone with which I disagree.

While it is true that the distinction between the preparation and the substantial step toward the commission of an act, is one of degree, and must be determined by the circumstances of each case; nevertheless, I believe the facts in the case at bar are insufficient to establish the act which constitutes a substantial step toward the commission of the offense.

The majority opinion relies upon, among others, People v. Woods . . . (1962); however, in that case the defendant commenced toward performance of the act by giving the complaining witness a sedative, although not taken by her, nevertheless it was directed toward her. There was, in addition, the fact that the defendant had received a fee for services to be rendered; the fact that instruments needed to perform the operation were in a pan on the stove; and the fact that the complaining witness stated she was ready and began to remove her clothing.

In the case at bar, while there is no doubt that the necessary intent was present, still there is no evidence that the defendant took a "first step" toward commission of the intended crime against Pinkston, the complaining witness. Pinkston, the only one present other than the defendant at the time of the alleged "act", testified that the defendant unlocked the barbershop door, walked back to the barber chair and put on his smock. He further testified that he, Pinkston, walked over and set his briefcase down and the defendant "offered me to get into the chair; at that, I handed him my business card." Thereafter, Pinkston looked around to see where his license was but did not see it. In addition, the defendant had his own barber tools present.

This is the only evidence offered to establish the act which together with the intent is a necessary element to constitute the offense of an "attempt." I would concede that if Pinkston had sat in the barber chair, as offered, and an over-garment placed upon him, then it could be said that a substantial step toward the commission of the offense charged had taken place—even though not one hair was clipped from his head. However, this is not the evidence. The best that can be said of the evidence adduced in this case toward the charge of attempting to practice barbering without a certificate of registration as a barber, is that the defendant started preparing himself but never got to the point of preparing the person against whom the attempt was to have been made. Therefore, I must, and do, dissent from my learned colleagues.

NOTES

1. In Martin v. Commonwealth, 195 Va. 1107, 81 S.E.2d 574 (1954), defendant was charged with attempt to commit pandering by feloniously placing a female in his dwelling house for the purpose of causing her "to cohabit" with male persons. It appeared that after taking the girl to his apartment, the defendant solicited three young men to have sexual intercourse with the girl upon payment of money to him. He took the boys to his room, where the girl was lying in bed nude. One of the boys said he would go get the necessary money, but when he returned shortly thereafter the defendant had already been arrested by the police. The question arose whether the attempt to commit pandering had occurred when the girl had not yet commenced any preparation to have sexual relations with the boys nor had the defendant received the money. In that regard, the court stated:

> It is well settled in this jurisdiction that in criminal law an attempt is an unfinished crime, and is compounded of two elements, the intent to commit the crime and the doing of some direct act towards its consummation, but falling short of the execution of the ultimate design; that it need not be the last proximate act towards the consummation of the crime in contemplation, but is sufficient if it be an act apparently adopted to produce the result intended; mere preparation is not sufficient. . . .

> The defendant contends that the acts charged amounted to nothing more than a mere preparation to commit a crime, and that the allegations do not show any overt act towards its accomplishment. . . .

> The undisputed evidence shows that the defendant did everything but receive money in the pursuance of his plans. He placed the female in his room, exhibited her lying in bed nude to three male persons, and solicited money from those persons for the purpose of causing her to have sexual intercourse with them. One of the males went to get the money to be paid to Martin, but the intervention of the police prevented payment and the final consummation of the intended crime. This was not due to any fault or change of plans on Martin's part. He performed direct ineffectual acts towards the commission of the offense of pandering, and when he did this, the attempt to commit the offense was complete. . . .

2. In People v. Rizzo, 246 N.Y. 334, 158 N.E. 888 (1927), the defendant and others planned to hold up a man carrying money for a payroll from the bank to a company. Armed with firearms, they started out in an automobile looking for the carrier of the money, whom Rizzo claimed to be able to identify. They drove from the bank to the company and back in an attempt to spot the carrier, but failed to find him. Meanwhile they were watched and followed by police officers who moved in and arrested the defendant and his cohorts. In reversing the conviction of attempt to commit robbery the court held that the acts of the defendant and his friends had not progressed to the point of nearness to commission of the act as is required for a conviction for attempt. They were looking for the man who was transporting the money, but they had not seen nor discovered him at the time they were arrested. The court said: "In a word, these defendants had planned to commit a crime, and were looking around the city for an opportunity to commit it, but the opportunity fortunately never

came. Men would not be guilty of an attempt at burglary if they had planned to break into a building and were arrested while they were hunting about the streets for the building not knowing where it was. Neither would a man be guilty of an attempt to commit murder if he armed himself and started out to find the person whom he had planned to kill but could not find him."

(b) THE SPECIFIC INTENT

PEOPLE v. MIGLIORE
Appellate Court of Illinois, 1988.
170 Ill.App.3d 581, 121 Ill.Dec. 376, 525 N.E.2d 182.

JUSTICE REINHARD delivered the opinion of the court:

Defendant, Michael Migliore, was found guilty in a bench trial in the circuit court of Winnebago County of the offense of attempted murder (Ill.Rev.Stat.1985, ch. 38, par. 8–4) and was sentenced to a 10–year term of imprisonment.

On appeal, defendant contends that (1) the evidence failed to prove that his actions constituted an attempt to kill, (2) the State failed to prove its theory of transferred intent, (3) the evidence was insufficient to prove him guilty beyond a reasonable doubt of attempted murder, and (4) the trial court abused its sentencing discretion in imposing a 10–year term of imprisonment.

Defendant and a codefendant, David Krueger, were charged in an indictment with committing the offense of attempted murder of Dominic Iasparro on September 11, 1986. The codefendants were tried separately. At defendant's trial, the State adduced evidence that, on the evening of September 11, 1986, defendant, Krueger, and Krueger's wife, Christine, were at Tom's Tap in Rockford at 9 p.m. during a lunch break on Christine's work shift at Amerock Corporation. Christine related that during their conversation, defendant stated that Bill Knight said something that day about burying him and his Cadillac with his two Budweiser cans. After leaving the tavern, defendant and Krueger dropped Christine off at work and drove off in her car.

Bill Knight, an attorney in Rockford, represented a client who was previously injured in an automobile accident with defendant. Defendant had been charged with leaving the scene of an accident involving personal injury or death. At the preliminary hearing on that charge, held on September 11, 1986, Knight attended and gave defendant and his attorney Knight's professional card and introduced himself. Knight testified that there was no other conversation and that he sat next to defendant for awhile during the hearing. Becky Knight, the former wife of attorney Knight, who worked as an investigator and photographer for attorney Knight, was also present at the preliminary hearing and sat next to defendant at some point. She tried to take defendant's photograph outside the courtroom, and defendant was pushed away by his father and friends to avoid being photographed. She had no conversation with defendant. Attorney Knight lives at 1205 Lundvall Avenue in Rockford.

Dominic Iasparro lives at 1311 Lundvall Avenue, which is about one block from attorney Knight's house. He is a police officer for the City of Rockford and was not acquainted personally or professionally with defendant or David Krueger. At approximately 10 p.m. on September 11, 1986, Iasparro was at home watching television in the front living room with his wife when he heard a car with loud mufflers pass his house two or three times. He thought the car slowed down the last time, and he went to the front door. He looked out a window in the top of the door and observed a car containing two males parked near the curb. The person on the passenger side, later identified by Iasparro as Krueger, left the car and walked up Iasparro's front lawn to his front porch. Iasparro turned on the porch light and opened the door. Krueger turned and ran back to the car, which was driven off at a high rate of speed with its lights off. A neighbor of Iasparro's testified that he observed the car stop in front of Iasparro's house and saw a person get out of the car, approach the house, and return to the car. He heard the person say "That's the fellow" or "That's the guy" when he returned to the car.

Other evidence established that, on September 11, 1986, at between 10 p.m. and 10:30 p.m., defendant and Krueger went to the Surf Lounge in Rockford. Each consumed several beers. They were loud and having a good time. They left the bar at about 11:15 p.m.

At approximately 11:40 p.m., Iasparro was still watching television in his front living room. As he was walking back to the couch, after changing the stations on the television set, he heard what sounded like the same car with the loud mufflers that he had heard earlier. At that time, he was in front of the front window with his back turned to the window. He heard one gunshot and then he heard a rapid series of six to eight gunshots, some of which hit his house. No one was injured, and Iasparro did not see the car or anyone who had done the shooting.

Testimony established that eight slugs hit Iasparro's house. An impact slug was found in the driveway, which was located to the west of the picture window. A slug had hit the house just to the west of the railing on the front porch and two others hit the steps of the front porch. A fifth bullet was found lodged in the upper portion of the wooden front door. Another hit the lower portion of the master bedroom window which is located directly to the east of the front door, and three others impacted the house to the east of the bedroom window. The front picture window is located immediately to the west edge of the front porch and is set in several feet from the front door. A fairly large bush, between 4 and 4½ feet high, stands in front of Iasparro's home and blocked a portion of the picture window.

At about 12:13 a.m. on September 12, 1986, a Winnebago County sheriff's deputy was dispatched to the 400 block of Marquette Street in Machesney Park, adjacent to Rockford, for a possible burglary in progress. As the deputy turned onto Marquette Road, he noticed a vehicle with its lights off, moving slowly, which he stopped. The passenger, defendant, got out of the car and walked around to the rear. Defendant was repeatedly told to remain in the car, but he got nasty and began yelling profanities. The driver, Krueger, was told to step out of the car. The deputy then noticed a shotgun in two or three pieces on the rear seat of the vehicle. The deputy removed several open and several sealed cans of beer from the car as well as the dismantled shotgun. He also noticed that defendant's breath smelled of alcohol.

Another sheriff's deputy, who assisted in the arrest of the two individuals, searched the vehicle and recovered, among other things, two spent nine-millimeter "Para Geco" casings from the floorboard of the rear seat.

At approximately 1 a.m. on September 12, 1986, Iasparro was summoned to the Machesney Park location. He stated that the car, which had been started, sounded like the same car that was in front of his residence around 10 p.m. and, again, at 11:40 p.m. Further, the car appeared to be the same size and color as the one he had seen. At that time, Iasparro also recognized Krueger to be the man who had come to his door at 10 p.m. that night.

Six nine-millimeter Para Geco shell casings were recovered on the street in front of Iasparro's house. Three or four bullet slugs or fragments were recovered from the area in front of Iasparro's home, including one that had been taken from the front door of the home. A search of defendant's home revealed another 11 nine-millimeter Para Geco shells.

The owner of Madison's Gun Shop, located in nearby Loves Park, Illinois, stated that his records indicated that he had sold a nine-millimeter pistol to defendant on January 26, 1986. Terrence Dahm, a Rockford city police officer assigned to the identification unit, testified that, on September 12, 1986, he and his partner were directed to proceed to an address at 36 Marquette Road in Machesney Park, Illinois, near the location of defendant's arrest, where they uncovered various packages that had been buried under approximately six inches of dirt. These packages were sent directly to the State Crime Laboratory in Joliet, Illinois, in that condition. Walter Sherk, a firearms and tool marks expert with the Illinois State Police Department at the State Crime Lab Facility in Joliet, Illinois, testified that he ran ballistics examinations of various cartridge cases recovered from the vicinity of the Iasparro home, in addition to those recovered in the car in which defendant was seated when stopped, and determined that they all had been fired from the same weapon. Sherk also performed ballistics examinations on the nine-millimeter semiautomatic pistol and magazine clip that he received in the various unwrapped packages and certain of the bullets recovered by police during the course of their earlier investigation and determined that they had been fired from that pistol.

Defendant presented no evidence on his own behalf, and, following closing arguments, the trial court found defendant guilty of attempted murder.

Defendant first contends that the evidence was insufficient to prove that his actions constituted an intent to kill. He maintains that this argument is supported by the evidence which shows that (1) the gunshots, which never entered Iasparro's home or struck anyone, were fired from the street by an occupant of a moving car who obviously did not aim the weapon, (2) the pattern of the bullet marks on the house indicates that the person standing in the picture window was not targeted for killing, the closest bullet impact being around the front door and not the picture window, (3) no person tried to forcibly enter Iasparro's house, and (4) the internal illumination of the house was insufficient to identify clearly any person standing behind the front picture window.

The State contends that intent can rarely be based on direct evidence and may be shown through surrounding circumstances, such as the character of the assault and the use of a deadly weapon. The State points to the fact that defendant fired nine shots from a nine-millimeter semiautomatic weapon, eight of which hit Iasparro's home, that the shooting began when Iasparro was standing three to five feet from his front window, and that the shots were fired at a level calculated to kill, not scare, someone. The State asserts further that the accuracy of defendant's aim is irrelevant and that Christine Krueger's testimony and other evidence regarding attorney Knight's interaction with defendant at the preliminary hearing earlier on the day of the shooting was indicative of defendant's intent prior to the shooting.

In order to sustain a conviction for attempted murder, the prosecution must prove that defendant had the intent to kill the victim. The specific intent to kill, if not admitted, may be shown by surrounding circumstances, including the character of the assault, the use of a deadly weapon, and other circumstances. Such intent may be inferred if one wilfully does an act, the direct and natural tendency of which is to destroy another's life. It is the function of the trier of fact to determine the existence of the requisite intent, and that determination will not be disturbed on review unless it clearly appears that there exists a reasonable doubt as to the defendant's guilt.

We consider the remarks of the trial judge, in rendering his decision, to be particularly instructive regarding his finding of the intent to kill. The judge stated, in pertinent part, as follows:

> "I conclude from the evidence that the Defendant and one Krueger drove by the residence of Iasparro on the night in question and one or both of them using the Defendant's weapon fired that weapon from a moving vehicle in the direction of the Iasparro house. How that came about is the next inquiry.

It was obviously no accident. With what intention was this done we don't—we don't have a statement from any of the participants as to the intentions in the mind of either occupant of that car. We must infer those things that are not specifically before the Court in the way of physical testimony and evidence from that testimony and evidence.

I have come to the conclusion that there are two hypothesis [*sic*] in this case and one is that the Defendant and Krueger drove back to that location with the gun loaded and aimed for the picture window silhouetted in the light intending to kill that person but missed through inaccuracy occasioned by either the nature of the gun, a semi-automatic, the fact that they were in a moving car or diminished ability of the operator of the gun to aim it because of drinking or otherwise. The other hypothesis is that the Defendant and Krueger were driving by in their car, never intended to aim at the picture window at the silhouette.

From the evidence it appears to me that the occupant of the house, the complaining witness here was already on his feet when the car approached. The occupants of the car knew from previous experience that very same evening that without any more stimulus than the car driving by with a muffler, a loud muffler, the occupant of that house had left whatever he was doing and had come to the door and flashed the light on. Noting that that occupant had done with only that stimulus earlier in the evening I hypothesize that the Defendant and his companion expected the individual they saw already on his feet in that living room which was a few short steps from the front door to come to the front door in response to the same stimulus, the loud muffler and that they, indeed, fired this weapon at the front door and it appears clear to me from the evidence that not only were the cluster of bullets where they struck bracketing the front door upward and downward and on either side but that the bullets were at levels that would be calculated to kill somebody who came to the front door, both the bullets to the right of the door and the bullets that clipped off the ledge on the bedroom to the left of the door.

I also am mindful of the fact that many of these photographs do not show the perspective that those operating a motor vehicle driving by would have had and it appears to me from the evidence that from the time the occupants of a motor vehicle was [*sic*] somewhat west of the premises until they were somewhat east of the premises they would have had a good view of the entire front of the house with the exception of that shrubbery immediately in front of the house which, however, was not high enough to conceal either the picture window, the door or the bedroom window to any extent.

Again the fact that the bullets did not enter the front door at mid-level can easily be attributed to the inaccuracy of that kind of a gun, the fact it was fired from a moving vehicle and again the condition of the occupants of the car. Under either hypothesis I have no doubt from the evidence that the Defendant intended to kill the occupant, whoever that occupant was, and it is a matter of no moment to me that the occupant was Iasparro and not Knight nor is it essential to the decision in this case. Accordingly having considered all the evidence and the arguments of counsel the Court finds the Defendant guilty of the crime charged."

We agree with the trial court's analysis of the evidence and conclude that the State proved the requisite state of mind to sustain the attempted murder conviction. In addition to the trial judge's comments on the evidence, the record discloses that Krueger said "[t]hat's the guy," after the first incident at the home at 10 p.m. This fact, coupled with the earlier events that day involving attorney Knight in court, Knight's former wife's attempt to take defendant's photograph, and the return of defendant and Krueger to perform the shooting, further show their intent to do deadly violence to someone whom they apparently believed was acting against defendant in the criminal prosecution pending against him. The shots were fired either at the door where Iasparro had previously appeared or at both the door and the nearby picture window, albeit slightly inaccurately at the window, where Iasparro was silhouetted. We are satisfied on this record that the intent to kill was shown by the surrounding circumstances of this assault.

* * *

Where a defendant is charged with attempted murder, it must be proved that he acted with intent to kill the victim and that he took a substantial step toward the commission of the crime. A conviction for attempted murder must be based on a charge and upon evidence that defendant had the intent to take a life.

As discussed earlier, the proofs here were sufficient to show an intent to kill Iasparro, and the material allegations of the indictment were proved beyond a reasonable doubt. While it is possible that defendant may have intended to kill attorney Knight, as there was no known reason that Iasparro could attribute to defendant's and Krueger's assault on him, any mistaken identity situation does not negative the intent to kill. Even if the attempted murder of Iasparro was a mistake, defendant intended to kill the person he aimed at, namely Iasparro. Mistaken identity does not negative an intent to kill, as pointed out by Professors La Fave and Scott in their works entitled Substantive Criminal Law, as follows:

"The situation, discussed above, concerning the unintended victim of an intentional crime—which we have referred to for short as the bad-aim situation—is to be distinguished from an entirely different unintended-victim case—the mistaken-identity situation—which is governed by a quite separate set of legal rules. Thus in the semi-darkness *A* shoots, with intent to kill, at a vague form he supposes to be his enemy *B* but who is actually another person *C;* his well-aimed bullet kills *C*. Here too *A* is guilty of murdering *C*, to the same extent he would have been guilty of murdering *B* had he made no mistake. *A* intended to kill the person at whom he aimed, so there is even less difficulty in holding him guilty than in the bad-aim situation. And of course *A* 's conceivable argument that his mistake of fact (as to the victim's identity) somehow negatives his guilt of murder would be unavailing: his mistake does not negative his intent to kill; and on the facts as he supposes them to be *A* is just as guilty of murder as he is on the facts which actually exist." 1 W. La Fave & A. Scott, Jr., Substantive Criminal Law § 3.12, at 402 (1986).

For the foregoing reasons, we reject defendant's contentions that the State failed to prove an intent to kill Iasparro.

* * *

Affirmed.

LINDBERG, P.J., and UNVERZAGT, J., concur.

NOTES

1. In People v. Frysig, 628 P.2d 1004 (Colo.1981), the court had to interpret the effect upon the elements of the crime of attempt of the legislative change of 1977 which deleted "intentionally" from the criminal attempt statute. Did this mean that the legislature wished to eliminate the requirement that any type of intent accompany the substantial step? The court did not read the revision in that manner:

> One purpose of the general revision was to change certain crimes from specific intent crimes to general intent crimes so that intoxication could not be used to negate the existence of the intent which is an element of the crime charged. * * * We are persuaded that the legislature amended the criminal attempt statute for such a purpose but did not intend thereby to depart from the tradition of the criminal law in Colorado and elsewhere that an essential element of criminal attempt is the intent "to do an act or to bring about certain consequences which would in law amount to a crime." . . .

However, in 1985, the court rejected a reading of *Frysig* that would require proof of specific intent in a prosecution for attempted aggravated robbery. "[C]ulpability for criminal attempt rests primarily upon the actor's purpose to cause harmful consequences," said the Colorado Supreme Court in People v. Krovarz, 697 P.2d 378 (Colo.1985), holding that proof of the culpable mental state of "knowledge" was sufficient for an attempt conviction.

2. What is the status of one who intends to commit a crime and takes certain steps toward its perpetration but who voluntarily abandons the project prior to its completion? It seems clear that if the requisite elements of an attempt are present, abandonment due to some extrinsic cause, such as the unexpected arrival of police officers or the intended victim, will be of no effect.

In People v. Dillon, 34 Cal.3d 441, 194 Cal.Rptr. 390, 668 P.2d 697 (1983), the court refused to carve out a defense of voluntary abandonment, once the requisite intent and overt act was proved. The court said, "The armed robber who feels a pang of conscience or chill of fear and bolts from the bank moments before the teller can hand over the loot has nevertheless endangered the lives of innocent people."

On the other hand, consider this language from People v. Kimball, 109 Mich.App. 273, 311 N.W.2d 343 (1981) [remanded for further fact findings, 412 Mich. 890, 313 N.W.2d 285 (1981)]:

> "We are persuaded by the trend of modern authority and hold that voluntary abandonment is an affirmative defense to a prosecution for criminal attempt. The burden is on the defendant to establish by a preponderance of the evidence that he or she has voluntarily and completely abandoned his or her criminal purpose. Abandonment is not 'voluntary' when the defendant fails to complete the attempted crime because of unanticipated difficulties, unexpected resistance, or circumstances which increase the probability of detention or apprehension. Nor is the abandonment 'voluntary' when the defendant fails to consummate the attempted offense after deciding to postpone the criminal conduct until another time or to substitute another victim or another but similar objective."

If the plans of a would-be offender are abandoned before the "act is put in process of final execution", is this really a defense of abandonment, or should we rather say that the offense of attempt had not yet been committed because the defendant's act, though preparation for an offense, had not yet reached the stage of a "substantial step" needed to constitute the offense of attempt? See, e.g., People v. Myers, 85 Ill.2d 281, 55 Ill.Dec. 389, 426 N.E.2d 535 (1981).

3. The Model Penal Code, Proposed Official Draft (1962), in Section 5.01, has the following language on "Renunciation of Criminal Purpose":

> 4. . . . (d) Renunciation of Criminal Purpose. When the actor's conduct would otherwise constitute an attempt under Subsection (1)(b) or (1)(c) of this Section, it is an affirmative defense that he abandoned his effort to commit the crime or otherwise prevented its commission, under circumstances manifesting a complete and voluntary renunciation of his criminal purpose. The establishment of such a defense does not, however, affect the liability of an accomplice who did not join in such abandonment or prevention.

(c) INTEGRATING ACT AND INTENT

UNITED STATES v. BUFFINGTON

United States Court of Appeals, Ninth Circuit, 1987.
815 F.2d 1292.

POOLE, CIRCUIT JUDGE:

Appellants William Buffington, Ceariaco Cabrellis and Booker T. Cook appeal their convictions of conspiracy to commit bank robbery, attempted bank robbery, use of a firearm in commission of a federal felony and being felons in possession of a firearm. They raise a series of objections to pretrial proceedings as well as events at trial. For reasons set forth below, we affirm in part and reverse in part.

FACTS

An informant told the Sacramento Police Department that appellants Buffington, Ceariaco Cabrellis, and Jimmy Cabrellis planned to rob a bank in the shopping center at Florin Road and Franklin Boulevard, and that appellant Cabrellis would be dressed as a woman. On December 17, 1982, a police officer observed two vehicles driving slowly around the Farmers Bank. He believed one of the drivers to be appellant Cabrellis, to whom one of the vehicles was determined in fact to be registered. Five days later on December 22, about 4:20 p.m., two men, later identified as Buffington and Cook, and a third person appearing to be a woman, later identified as appellant Cabrellis, driving a white Pontiac, entered the shopping center.

The Pontiac proceeded down one aisle of parking and slowly went past Bay View Federal Savings, toward which the occupants of the vehicle seemed to be looking. They then drove out of the parking area, onto an adjacent street behind the bank. After a U-turn, the car slowly returned down another aisle of parking past the bank, and the occupants again looked toward Bay View Federal. The driver, Buffington, parked the vehicle about one hundred fifty feet from a Payless Store, which was about the same distance from the bank. Buffington left the car, entered Payless, and walked to a window which overlooked Bay View Federal. He did not purchase, inspect goods, or shop, but after three minutes, walked over and stood in a cashier line.

About two minutes after Buffington left the vehicle, Cook also emerged and stood by the car door. He wore a large peacoat, a hat, and a long scarf. The government concedes that the Sacramento weather on that December day was "inclement." The person dressed in women's clothes, Cabrellis, also exited the car and stood by the door. Both persons were facing Bay View.

By sheer coincidence, a major power outage then occurred affecting the shopping center area. Shortly afterwards, Margaret Morningstar, a Bay View Federal teller, walked to the front door of the bank and locked the door, at which time she noticed Cook wrapping the scarf over his face so that only his glasses showed. She mentioned to a security guard that the man would be unable to rob the bank because she had just locked the door. Buffington, meanwhile, returned to the car, which he, Cabrellis and Cook reentered. Buffington drove out of the parking area, passing Police Officer Torres, who identified the female as Cabrellis from a photograph. Police officers then stopped the vehicle, ordered the appellants to exit the car at gunpoint, and forced them to lie face down on the pavement. Police found a revolver on Cook's person and a revolver on the left rear floorboard of the vehicle.

Appellants were then arrested. Officers later discovered that Cook was wearing four to five coats or jackets.

Appellants were subsequently indicted by a United States grand jury on four counts. . . . Count II charged attempted unarmed bank robbery. 18 U.S.C. § 2113(a).

[We only consider, here, defendants' contention on appeal that the evidence was insufficient to support their convictions for attempted bank robbery.]

II. *Sufficiency of the Evidence*

We must next determine whether the evidence, exclusive of any reliance upon the communications supplied by the informant, was sufficient to sustain their convictions for the charges of . . . attempted federal bank robbery, . . . In reviewing these issues, we inquire whether, viewing the evidence in the light most favorable to prosecution and to the verdicts, any rational trier of fact could have found the essential elements of the crime to have been proved beyond a reasonable doubt.

A conviction for attempt requires the government to prove (1) culpable intent, and (2) conduct constituting a substantial step toward commission of the crime that is in pursuit of that intent. A substantial step consists of conduct that is strongly corroborative of the firmness of a defendant's criminal intent. Mere preparation does not constitute a substantial step. The issue then is whether the evidence presented at trial was sufficient of itself to prove intent and a substantial step toward bank robbery.

The government contends that appellant's intent to rob Bay View Federal may be inferred from the following circumstantial evidence:

> (1) the assemblage and possession of materials necessary to commit the crime—two handguns, female clothing and a makeup disguise for Cabrellis, and a multi-layered clothing disguise for Cook;

> (2) the two visits to the location of the crime, Cabrellis' on Dec. 17 and all three appellants' presence on Dec. 22; and

> (3) certain actions allegedly taken to effectuate the plan, namely, twice driving slowly by the bank while staring into it, driving to the rear of the bank, Buffington's behavior in the Payless Store, and the fact that Cook and Cabrellis were armed when they exited the vehicle and stood with their attention directed toward the bank.

The above constitutes little more than a summary of the evidence; it does not answer the question whether the rquisite elements of the offense were shown to exist beyond a reasonable doubt. If the prosecution could bring to these bare allegations the light shed by the informant, a reasonable jury could find at least the substantially unequivocal intent to rob someone or some institution. But the government's solemn commitment to avoid that light, and the trial court's ruling that it must be avoided, forbids resolving the ambiguities with that help. Thus unaided, the circumstances fall short of showing the intent to rob a federal bank. If intent to rob existed at all, it could easily have been directed against the Payless market, or the nearby state bank.

Of course, circumstantial evidence is fully admissible in criminal cases, including bank robbery cases. It is permissible to infer intent from a defendant's conduct and the surrounding circumstances. For example, in Rumfelt v. United States, 445 F.2d 134 (7th Cir.), cert. denied, 404 U.S. 853, 92 S.Ct. 92, 30 L.Ed.2d 94 (1971), the Seventh Circuit sustained a conviction of attempted bank robbery where intent to rob was shown by circumstantial evidence. In *Rumfelt,* the court noted that actual entry into the bank was not required to find that an attempt occurred. The defendant's presence in front of a bank while wearing a ski mask, and his use of a rifle to intimidate a passerby into trying to open the door to the bank for him were sufficient to infer an intent to steal. Id. at 137. That is not comparable to this case.

Other cases that have permitted the inference of an intent to rob a bank have involved testimony by informants or co-conspirators.

Evidence of the defendants' intent here has no such background upon which to rely. There was no admissible testimony concerning defendants' intent by an informant or co-conspirator. No defendant came within 50 yards of the bank. The suggestion that they were "casing" something could be true, but is supported by little more than speculation. The evidence is focused no more on Bay View than on other nearby institutions. Even viewing the evidence in as favorable a light to the government as we may, the evidence presented to the jury could reasonably generate no more than suspicion, and is certainly not sufficient for a rational trier of fact to find intent to commit bank robbery beyond a reasonable doubt.

Moreover, even if sufficient intent to rob were shown, the conduct fell short of constituting a substantial step toward the commission of a robbery. For conduct to be "strongly corroborative of the firmness of the defendant's criminal intent," [p]reparation alone is not enough, there must be some appreciable fragment of the crime committed, it must be in such progress that it will be consummated unless interrupted by circumstances independent of the will of the attempter, and the act must not be equivocal in nature. Thus, while conduct need not be incompatible with innocence to be punishable as an attempt, the conduct must be necessary to the consummation of the crime and of such nature that a reasonable observer, viewing it in context, could conclude beyond a reasonable doubt that it was undertaken in accordance with a design to violate the statute.

Knowing all that we have learned—which the jury did not have before it—we could well believe that the defendants intended to do what the informant claimed they had planned; but their actual conduct did not cross the boundary between preparation and attempt. Appellants were afterwards found to be armed and may have appeared to be reconnoitering Bay View Federal, but none made any move toward the bank. The situation is therefore distinguishable from United States v. Stallworth, 543 F.2d 1038 (2d Cir.1976), where the *testimony* of an informant established the defendant's intent. The defendant was armed, had stolen materials for disguises, had reconnoitered the bank and moved toward it; all of this confirmed in a taped conversation in which he had discussed the plan of attack.

The government argues the generality that movement toward a bank is not required to show attempt, citing United States v. Snell, 627 F.2d 186 (9th Cir.1980), cert. denied, 450 U.S. 957, 101 S.Ct. 1416, 67 L.Ed.2d 382 (1981). But that case is distinguishable upon several grounds. In *Snell,* the defendants planned to kidnap a bank manager and his wife, and to hold her hostage while forcing the manager to go to the bank to obtain money. They went to the house and knocked on the door, but the plan was frustrated when the wife came to the door accompanied by a Great Dane. One of the co-conspirators later revealed the plan to the police. Snell was convicted of attempted robbery of a federal bank. The court observed that Snell's entry into the home was "factually precedent but so far as the total scheme is concerned is analytically little different than entry into the bank itself." Id. at 188. There is no comparable entry, nor movement toward the bank in this case. The conduct in *Snell* was unequivocal; that here is entirely tentative and unfocused. Fortified by their information from the informant, the police concluded that, standing by their car 150 feet away, the defendants were "casing" the bank; but resort to that knowledge cannot be utilized because the prosecution had eschewed its use. Not only did appellants not take a single step toward the bank, they displayed no weapons and no indication that they were about to make an entry. Standing alone, their conduct did not constitute that requisite "appreciable fragment" of a bank robbery, nor a step toward commission of the crime of such substantiality that, unless frustrated, the crime would have occurred.

* * *

We reverse the convictions of appellants on Counts I, II and III of the indictment.

(d) IMPOSSIBILITY OF COMPLETION

PEOPLE v. DLUGASH

Court of Appeals of New York, 1977.
41 N.Y.2d 725, 395 N.Y.S.2d 419, 363 N.E.2d 1155.

JASEN, JUDGE. The criminal law is of ancient origin, but criminal liability for attempt to commit a crime is comparatively recent. At the root of the concept of attempt liability are the very aims and purposes of penal law. The ultimate issue is whether an individual's intentions and actions, though failing to achieve a manifest and malevolent criminal purpose, constitute a danger to organized society of sufficient magnitude to warrant the imposition of criminal sanctions. Difficulties in theoretical analysis and concomitant debate over very pragmatic questions of blameworthiness appear dramatically in reference to situations where the criminal attempt failed to achieve its purpose solely because the factual or legal context in which the individual acted was not as the actor supposed them to be. Phrased somewhat differently, the concern centers on whether an individual should be liable for an attempt to commit a crime when, unknown to him, it was impossible to successfully complete the crime attempted. For years, serious studies have been made on the subject in an effort to resolve the continuing controversy when, if at all, the impossibility of successfully completing the criminal act should preclude liability for even making the futile attempt. The 1967 revision of the Penal Law approached the impossibility defense to the inchoate crime of attempt in a novel fashion. The statute provides that, if a person engages in conduct which would otherwise constitute an attempt to commit a crime, "it is no defense to a prosecution for such attempt that the crime charged to have been attempted was, under the attendant circumstances, factually or legally impossible of commission, if such crime could have been committed had the attendant circumstances been as such person believed them to be." (Penal Law, § 110.10.) This appeal presents to us, for the first time, a case involving the application of the modern statute. We hold that, under the proof presented by the People at trial, defendant Melvin Dlugash may be held for attempted murder, though the target of the attempt may have already been slain, by the hand of another, when Dlugash made his felonious attempt.

On December 22, 1973, Michael Geller, 25 years old, was found shot to death in the bedroom of his Brooklyn apartment. The body, which had literally been riddled by bullets, was found lying face up on the floor. An autopsy revealed that the victim had been shot in the face and head no less than seven times. Powder burns on the face indicated that the shots had been fired from within one foot of the victim. Four small caliber bullets were recovered from the victim's skull. The victim had also been critically wounded in the chest. One heavy caliber bullet passed through the left lung, penetrated the heart chamber, pierced the left ventricle of the heart upon entrance and again upon exit, and lodged in the victim's torso. A second bullet entered the left lung and passed, through to the chest, but without reaching the heart area. Although the second bullet was damaged beyond identification, the bullet tracks indicated that these wounds were also inflicted by a bullet of heavy caliber. A tenth bullet, of unknown caliber, passed through the thumb of the victim's left hand. The autopsy report listed the cause of death as "[m]ultiple bullet wounds of head and chest with brain injury and massive bilateral hemothorax with penetration of [the] heart." Subsequent ballistics examination established that the four bullets recovered from the victim's head were .25 caliber bullets and that the heart-piercing bullet was of .38 caliber.

Detective Joseph Carrasquillo of the New York City Police Department was assigned to investigate the homicide. On December 27, 1973, five days after the discovery of the body, Detective Carrasquillo and a fellow officer went to the defendant's residence in an effort to locate him. The officers arrived at approximately 6:00 p.m. The defendant answered the door and, when informed that the officers were investigating the death of Michael Geller, a friend of his, defendant invited the officers into the house. Detective Carrasquillo informed defendant that the officers desired any information defendant might have regarding the death of Geller and, since defendant was regarded as a suspect, administered the standard preinterrogation warnings. The defendant told the officers that he and another friend, Joe Bush, had just returned from a four- or five-day trip "upstate someplace" and learned of Geller's death only upon his return. Since Bush was also a suspect in the case and defendant admitted knowing Bush, defendant agreed to accompany the officers to the station house for the purposes of identifying photographs of Bush and of lending assistance to the investigation. Upon arrival at the police station, Detective Carrasquillo and the defendant went directly into an interview room. Carrasquillo advised the defendant that he had witnesses and information to the effect that as late as 7:00 p.m. on the day before the body was found, defendant had been observed carrying a .25 caliber pistol. Once again, Carrasquillo administered the standard preinterrogation statement of rights. The defendant then proceeded to relate his version of the events which culminated in the death of Geller. Defendant stated that, on the night of December 21, 1973, he, Bush and Geller had been out drinking. Bush had been staying at Geller's apartment and, during the course of the evening, Geller several times demanded that Bush pay $100 towards the rent on the apartment. According to defendant, Bush rejected these demands, telling Geller that "you better shut up or you're going to get a bullet". All three returned to Geller's apartment at approximately midnight, took seats in the bedroom, and continued to drink until sometime between 3:00 and 3:30 in the morning. When Geller again pressed his demand for rent money, Bush drew his .38 caliber pistol, aimed it at Geller and fired three times. Geller fell to the floor. After the passage of a few minutes, perhaps two, perhaps as much as five, defendant walked over to the fallen Geller, drew his .25 caliber pistol, and fired approximately five shots in the victim's head and face. Defendant contended that, by the time he fired the shots, "it looked like Mike Geller was already dead". After the shots were fired, defendant and Bush walked to the apartment of a female acquaintance. Bush removed his shirt, wrapped the two guns and a knife in it, and left the apartment, telling Dlugash that he intended to dispose of the weapons. Bush returned 10 or 15 minutes later and stated that he had thrown the weapons down a sewer two or three blocks away.

After Carrasquillo had taken the bulk of the statement, he asked the defendant why he would do such a thing. According to Carrasquillo, the defendant said, "gee, I really don't know". Carrasquillo repeated the question 10 minutes later, but received the same response. After a while, Carrasquillo asked the question for a third time and defendant replied, "well gee, I guess it must have been because I was afraid of Joe Bush."

* * *

Defendant was indicted by the Grand Jury of Kings County on a single count of murder in that, acting in concert with another person actually present, he intentionally caused the death of Michael Geller. . . .

* * *

The trial court declined to charge the jury, as requested by the prosecution, that defendant could be guilty of murder on the theory that he had aided and abetted the killing of Geller by Bush. Instead, the court submitted only two theories to the jury: that defendant had either intentionally murdered Geller or had attempted to murder Geller.

The jury found the defendant guilty of murder. The defendant then moved to set the verdict aside. He submitted an affidavit in which he contended that he "was absolutely, unequivocally and positively certain that Michael Geller was dead before [he] shot him." Further, the defendant averred that he was in fear for his life when he shot Geller. "This fear stemmed from the fact that Joseph Bush, the admitted killer of Geller, was holding a gun on me and telling me, in no uncertain terms, that if I didn't shoot the dead body I, too would be killed." This motion was denied.

On appeal, the Appellate Division reversed the judgment of conviction on the law and dismissed the indictment. The court ruled that "the People failed to prove beyond a reasonable doubt that Geller had been alive at the time he was shot by defendant; defendant's conviction of murder thus cannot stand." Further, the court held that the judgment could not be modified to reflect a conviction for attempted murder because "the uncontradicted evidence is that the defendant, at the time that he fired the five shots into the body of the decedent, believed him to be dead, and * * * there is not a scintilla of evidence to contradict his assertion in that regard".

Preliminarily, we state our agreement with the Appellate Division that the evidence did not establish, beyond a reasonable doubt, that Geller was alive at the time defendant fired into his body. To sustain a homicide conviction, it must be established, beyond a reasonable doubt, that the defendant caused the death of another person. The People were required to establish that the shots fired by defendant Dlugash were a sufficiently direct cause of Geller's death. While the defendant admitted firing five shots at the victim approximately two to five minutes after Bush had fired three times, all three medical expert witnesses testified that they could not, with any degree of medical certainty, state whether the victim had been alive at the time the latter shots were fired by the defendant. Thus, the People failed to prove beyond a reasonable doubt that the victim had been alive at the time he was shot by the defendant. Whatever else it may be, it is not murder to shoot a dead body. Man dies but once.

* * *

The procedural context of this matter, a nonappealable but erroneous dismissal of the issue of accessorial conduct, contributes to the unique nature of the attempt issue presented here. Where two or more persons have combined to murder, proof of the relationship between perpetrators is sufficient to hold all for the same degree of homicide, notwithstanding the absence of proof as to which specific act of which individual was the immediate cause of the victim's death. On the other hand, it is quite unlikely and improbable that two persons, unknown and unconnected to each other, would attempt to kill the same third person at the same time and place. Thus, it is rare for criminal liability for homicide to turn on which of several attempts actually succeeded. In the case of coconspirators, it is not necessary to do so and the case of truly independent actors is unlikely. However, procedural developments make this case the unlikely one and we must now decide whether, under the evidence presented, the defendant may be held for attempted murder, though someone else perhaps succeeded in killing the victim.

The concept that there could be criminal liability for an attempt, even if ultimately unsuccessful, to commit a crime is comparatively recent. The modern concept of attempt has been said to date from Rex v. Scofield (Cald 397), decided in 1784. (Sayre, Criminal Attempts, 41 Harv.L.Rev. 821, 834.) In that case, Lord Mansfield stated that "[t]he intent may make an act, innocent in itself, criminal; nor is the completion of an act, criminal in itself, necessary to constitute criminality. Is it no offence to set fire to a train of gunpowder with intent to burn a house, because by accident, or the interposition of another, the mischief is prevented?" The Revised Penal Law now provides that a person is guilty of an attempt to commit a crime when, with intent to commit a crime, he engages in conduct which tends to effect the commission of such crime. The revised statute clarified confusion in the former provision which, on its face, seemed to state that an attempt was not punishable as an attempt unless it was unsuccessful.

The most intriguing attempt cases are those where the attempt to commit a crime was unsuccessful due to mistakes of fact or law on the part of the would-be criminal. A general rule developed in most American jurisdictions that legal impossibility is a good defense but factual impossibility is not. Thus, for example, it was held that defendants who shot at a stuffed deer did not attempt to take a deer out of season, even though they believed the dummy to be a live animal. The court stated that there was no criminal attempt because it was no crime to "take" a stuffed deer, and it is no crime to attempt to do that which is legal. State v. Taylor, 345 Mo. 325, 133 S.W.2d 336 [no liability for attempt to bribe a juror where person bribed was not, in fact, a juror].) These cases are illustrative of legal impossibility. A further example is Francis Wharton's classic hypothetical involving Lady Eldon and her French lace. Lady Eldon, traveling in Europe, purchased a quantity of French lace at a high price, intending to smuggle it into England without payment of the duty. When discovered in a customs search, the lace turned out to be of English origin, of little value and not subject to duty. The traditional view is that Lady Eldon is not liable for an attempt to smuggle. (1 Wharton, Criminal Law [12th ed.], § 225, p. 304, n. 9; for variations on the hypothetical see Hughes, One Further Footnote on Attempting the Impossible, 42 N.Y. U.L.Rev. 1005.)

On the other hand, factual impossibility was no defense. For example, a man was held liable for attempted murder when he shot into the room in which his target usually slept and, fortuitously, the target was sleeping elsewhere in the house that night. (State v. Mitchell, 170 Mo. 633, 71 S.W. 175.) Although one bullet struck the target's customary pillow, attainment of the criminal objective was factually impossible. State v. Moretti, 52 N.J. 182, 244 A.2d 499, cert. den. 393 U.S. 952, 89 S.Ct. 376, 21 L.Ed.2d 363, presents a similar instance of factual impossibility. The defendant agreed to perform an abortion, then a criminal act, upon a female undercover police investigator who was not, in fact, pregnant. The court sustained the conviction, ruling that "when the consequences sought by a defendant are forbidden by the law as criminal, it is no defense that the defendant could not succeed in reaching his goal because of circumstances unknown to him." On the same view, it was held that men who had sexual intercourse with a woman, with the belief that she was alive and did not consent to the intercourse, could be charged for attempted rape when the woman had, in fact, died from an unrelated ailment prior to the acts of intercourse.

The New York cases can be parsed out along similar lines. One of the leading cases on legal impossibility is People v. Jaffe, 185 N.Y. 497, 78 N.E. 169, in which we held that there was no liability for the attempted receipt of stolen property when the property received by the defendant in the belief that it was stolen was, in fact under the control of the true owner. Similarly, in People v. Teal, 196 N.Y. 372, 89 N.E. 1086, a conviction for attempted subornation of perjury was overturned on the theory that the testimony attempted to be suborned was irrelevant to the merits of the case. Since it was not subornation of perjury to solicit false, but irrelevant, testimony, "the person through whose procuration the testimony is given cannot be guilty of subornation of perjury and, by the same rule, an unsuccessful attempt to that which is not a crime when effectuated, cannot be held to be an attempt to commit the crime specified." Factual impossibility, however, was no defense. Thus, a man could be held for attempted grand larceny when he picked an empty pocket.

As can be seen from even this abbreviated discussion, the distinction between "factual" and "legal" impossibility was a nice one indeed and the courts tended to place a greater value on legal form than on any substantive danger the defendant's actions posed for society. The approach of the draftsmen of the Model Penal Code was to eliminate the defense of impossibility in virtually all situations. Under the code provision, to constitute an attempt, it is still necessary that the result intended or desired by the actor constitute a crime. However, the code suggested a fundamental change to shift the locus of analysis to the actor's mental frame of reference and away from undue dependence upon external considerations. The basic premise of the code provision is that what was in the actor's own mind should be the standard for determining his dangerousness to society and, hence, his liability for attempted criminal conduct.

In the belief that neither of the two branches of the traditional impossibility arguments detracts from the offender's moral culpability, the Legislature substantially carried the code's treatment of impossibility into the 1967 revision of the Penal Law. Thus, a person is guilty of an attempt when, with intent to commit a crime, he engages in conduct which tends to effect the commission of such crime. It is no defense that, under the attendant circumstances, the crime was factually or legally impossible of commission, "if such crime could have been committed had the attendant circumstances been as such person believed them to be." Thus, if defendant believed the victim to be alive at the time of the shooting, it is no defense to the charge of attempted murder that the victim may have been dead.

Turning to the facts of the case before us, we believe that there is sufficient evidence in the record from which the jury could conclude that the defendant believed Geller to be alive at the time defendant fired shots into Geller's head. Defendant admitted firing five shots at a most vital part of the victim's anatomy from virtually point blank range. Although defendant contended that the victim had already been grievously wounded by another, from the defendant's admitted actions, the jury could conclude that the defendant's purpose and intention was to administer the coup de grace. The jury never learned of defendant's subsequent allegation that Bush had a gun on him and directed defendant to fire at Geller on the pain of his own life. Defendant did not testify and this statement of duress was made only in a postverdict affidavit, which obviously was never placed before the jury. In his admissions that were related to the jury, defendant never made such a claim. Nor did he offer any explanation for his conduct, except for an offhand aside made casually to Detective Carrasquillo. Any remaining doubt as to the question of duress is dispelled by defendant's earlier statement that he and Joe Bush had peacefully spent a few days together on vacation in the country. Moreover, defendant admitted to freely assisting Bush in disposing of the weapons after the murder and, once the weapons were out of the picture, defendant made no effort at all to flee from Bush. Indeed, not only did defendant not come forward with his story immediately, but when the police arrived at his house, he related a false version designed to conceal his and Bush's complicity in the murder. All of these facts indicate a consciousness of guilt which defendant would not have had if he had truly believed that Geller was dead when he shot him.

Defendant argues that the jury was bound to accept, at face value, the indications in his admissions that he believed Geller dead. Certainly, it is true that the defendant was entitled to have the entirety of the admissions, both the inculpatory and the exculpatory portions, placed in evidence before the trier of facts. However, the jury was not required to automatically credit the exculpatory portions of the admissions. The general rule is, of course, that the credibility of witnesses is a question of fact and the jury may choose to believe some, but not all, of a witness' testimony. The general rule applies with equal force to proof of admissions. Thus, it has been stated that "where that part of the declaration which discharges the party making it is in itself highly improbable or is discredited by other evidence the [jury] may believe one part of the admission and reject the other." (People ex rel. Perkins v. Moss, 187 N.Y. 410, 428, 80 N.E. 383, 389.) In People v. Miller, 247 App.Div. 489, 493, 286 N.Y.S. 702, 706, relied upon by defendant, Justice Lewis (later Chief Judge) concluded that the damaging aspects of an admission should not be accepted and the exculpatory portion rejected *"unless the latter is disputed by other evidence in the case, or is so improbable as to be unworthy of belief"* (emphasis added). In this case, there is ample other evidence to contradict the defendant's assertion that he believed Geller dead. There were five bullet wounds inflicted with stunning accuracy in a vital part of the victim's anatomy. The medical testimony indicated that Geller may have been alive at the time defendant fired at him. The defendant voluntarily left the jurisdiction immediately after the crime with his coperpetrator. Defendant did not report the crime to the police when left on his own by Bush. Instead, he attempted to conceal his and Bush's involvement with the homicide. In addition, the other portions of defendant's admissions make his contended belief that Geller was dead extremely improbable. Defendant, without a word of instruction from Bush, voluntarily got up from his seat after the passage of just a few minutes and fired five times point blank into the victim's face, snuffing out any remaining chance of life that Geller possessed. Certainly, this alone indicates a callous indifference to the taking of a human life. His admissions are barren of any claim of duress [1] and reflect, instead, an unstinting cooperation in efforts to dispose of vital incriminating evidence. Indeed, defendant maintained a false version of the occurrence until such time as the police informed him that they had evidence that he lately possessed a gun of the same caliber as one of the weapons involved in the shooting. From all of this, the jury was certainly warranted in concluding that the defendant acted in the belief that Geller was yet alive when shot by defendant.

---

1. Notwithstanding the Appellate Division's implication to the contrary, the record indicates that defendant told the Assistant District Attorney that Bush, after shooting Geller, kept his gun aimed at Geller, and not at Dlugash. As defendant stated, "this was after Joe had his .38 on him, I started shooting on him."

The jury convicted the defendant of murder. Necessarily, they found that defendant intended to kill a live human being. Subsumed within this finding is the conclusion that defendant acted in the belief that Geller was alive. Thus, there is no need for additional fact findings by a jury. Although it was not established beyond a reasonable doubt that Geller was, in fact, alive, such is no defense to attempted murder since a murder would have been committed "had the attendant circumstances been as [defendant] believe them to be." The jury necessarily found that defendant believed Geller to be alive when defendant shot at him.

The Appellate Division erred in not modifying the judgment to reflect a conviction for the lesser included offense of attempted murder. An attempt to commit a murder is a lesser included offense of murder and the Appellate Division has the authority, where the trial evidence is not legally sufficient to establish the offense of which the defendant was convicted, to modify the judgment to one of conviction for a lesser included offense which is legally established by the evidence. Thus, the Appellate Division, by dismissing the indictment, failed to take the appropriate corrective action. Further, questions of law were erroneously determined in favor of the appellant at the Appellate Division. While we affirm the order of the Appellate Division to the extent that the order reflects that the judgment of conviction for murder cannot stand, a modification of the order and a remittal for further proceedings is necessary.

Accordingly, the order of the Appellate Division should be modified and the case remitted to the Appellate Division for its review of the facts pursuant to CPL § 470.15 and for further proceedings with respect to the sentence (see CPL § 470.20, subd. 4) in the event that the facts are found favorably to the People. As so modified, the order of the Appellate Division should be affirmed.

BREITEL, C. J., and GABRIELLI, JONES, WACHTLER, FUCHSBERG and COOKE, JJ., concur.

Order modified and the case remitted to the Appellate Division, Second Department, for further proceedings in accordance with the opinion herein and, as so modified, affirmed.

ADAMS v. MURPHY

Supreme Court of Florida, 1981.
394 So.2d 411.

BOYD, JUSTICE. This cause is before the Court on the certificate of the United States Court of Appeals for the Fifth Circuit that a question of Florida law upon which there is no controlling precedent is determinative of the instant appeal pending in that court. We have authority to answer the certified question by written opinion.

Adams was charged with the crime of perjury in violation of section 837.02, Florida Statutes (1973). It was alleged that he had lied to a grand jury. At trial, Adams' attorney requested that the court instruct the jury on the crime of attempt to commit perjury. The court gave the requested instruction and the jury returned a verdict finding Adams guilty of attempted perjury.

On appeal, the judgment of conviction of attempted perjury was affirmed, per curiam, without opinion. Adams then sought review in this Court. The Court initially issued the writ of certiorari but later determined that it lacked jurisdiction. The writ was discharged. A subsequent petition for writ of habeas corpus, filed in this Court, was denied.

The case is pending in the Fifth Circuit on appeal from an order of the United States District Court for the Middle District of Florida, which granted Adams relief on his petition for writ of habeas corpus. The district court ruled that the Florida trial court's instruction on and judgment of conviction of the nonexistent offense of attempted perjury denied due process. The United States Court of Appeals has certified the following question: "Is attempted perjury in an official proceeding a criminal offense under the laws of Florida?"

Section 837.02, Florida Statutes (1973), provides:

> Whoever being lawfully required to depose the truth in any proceeding in a court of justice, commits perjury, shall, if the perjury is committed on the trial of an indictment for a capital crime, be guilty of a felony of the first degree, punishable as provided in § 775.082, § 775.083, or § 775.084; and if committed in any other case, guilty of a felony of the second degree, punishable as provided in § 775.082 or § 775.083.

Thus the statute forbids, but does not fully define, the crime of perjury. In such circumstances, it is appropriate to look to the common law for the definition of the crime.

In the decisional law of Florida, perjury is defined as the willful giving of false testimony under lawful oath on a material matter in a judicial proceeding.

Appellees-respondents, officials of the State of Florida, argue that there is such a crime as attempted perjury. They suggest that the existence of such a crime is logically plausible for the following reasons. An attempt consists of a specific criminal intent to commit the crime and an overt act beyond preparation toward that end. Therefore, one who intentionally testifies falsely under oath, unaware that the testimony is not material or that the person administering the oath has no authority to do so or that the proceeding is not an official judicial proceeding, commits the crime of attempted perjury.

Appellees-respondents correctly state that an attempt to commit crime consists of two essential elements: a specific intent to commit the crime and an overt act, beyond mere preparation, done towards its commission. The intent and the act must be such that they would have resulted, except for the interference of some cause preventing the carrying out of the intent, in the completed commission of the crime.

The State of Florida has incorporated this definition in its general attempt statute:

> Whoever attempts to commit an offense prohibited by law and in such attempt does any act toward the commission of such an offense, but fails in the perpetration, or is intercepted or prevented in the execution of the same, shall, when no express provision is made by law for the punishment of such attempt, be punished as follows:

Thus the state officials' argument is that where the intent and the overt act of falsely testifying are shown, but the crime is not completed because one of the other elements is lacking, then the facts establish the crime of attempted perjury.

Even though we have a broadly applicable general attempt statute in Florida, there are some crimes of which it can be said that the attempt thereof simply does not exist as an offense. See, e.g., State v. Thomas, 362 So.2d 1348 (Fla.1978) (attempted possession of burglary tools is not a crime); King v. State, 317 So.2d 852 (Fla. 1st DCA 1975) (attempted uttering of a forged instrument is not a crime).

In King v. State, the defendant was charged with uttering a forged instrument. At trial, he asked that the jury be charged on attempt pursuant to Florida Rule of Criminal Procedure 3.510. The court refused. The defendant was convicted and on appeal assigned the refusal to instruct as error. The appellate court said: "If a crime is itself an attempt to do an act or accomplish a result, there can be no attempt to commit that crime." Applying this principle, the court held that under Florida law there is no offense of attempted uttering of a forged instrument, and therefore the refusal to charge on attempt was proper.

This view of the nature of criminal attempts was also expressed in Hutchinson v. State, 315 So.2d 546 (Fla.2d DCA 1975), where the state prosecuted a solicitation as an "attempted conspiracy." The court analyzed the general attempt statute. The court prefaced its analysis as follows:

> In construing a criminal statutory provision, the primary function of the court is to give effect to the intent of the legislature; and in so doing, each section of the criminal code should be considered in making this determination. But it is also axiomatic that statutes creating and defining crimes cannot be extended by construction or interpretation to punish an act, however wrongful, unless clearly within the intent and terms of the statute.

The court then observed that the general attempt statute by its terms can apply to any offense, but went on to explain why conspiracy is an exception:

> We note that § 776.04 purports to prohibit an attempt to commit any offense prohibited by law. Since there is no

express limiting language as to what crimes may or may not be criminally attempted, the statute would appear to prohibit attempted conspiracy if it were not for the remaining language of the statute, and the history and judicial construction of the crime of attempt. Construing the words "and in such an attempt does any act toward commission of such an offense but fails in the perpetration, or is intercepted or prevented in the execution of the same," we think the legislature intended to limit attempts to physical acts carried beyond preparation toward proximate accomplishment of what would be a complete crime. In this respect, solicitation and conspiracy are more remote from the actual perpetration of the intended crime than is an attempt to commit it. This conclusion is supported by Florida courts that have interpreted an attempt to consist of two essential elements: 1) a specific intent to commit the crime; and 2) a separate overt ineffectual act done toward its commission.

The Florida case that is perhaps most closely analogous to the problem we are presented with now is Silvestri v. State, 332 So.2d 351 (Fla. 4th DCA 1976). There the appellant was charged with, among other things, making a false report of a crime. She was convicted of an attempt to make such a false report. The court compared the problem to that of uttering a forged instrument, discussed above:

Just as the crime of uttering a forged instrument may be proven merely by an *attempt* to negotiate one, so it would seem, the offense of making a false report is fully proven by demonstrating an attempt to convey false information to a police officer. Thus, the holding of the First District in King v. State, 317 So.2d 852 (Fla.App. 1st 1975) which we followed in Jackson v. State, 328 So.2d 457 (Fla.App. 4th 1976) that there is no offense in Florida of attempted uttering of a forged instrument because "there can be no attempt to commit . . . ." a crime which "is itself an attempt to do an act or accomplish a result" . . . directly applies. See People v. Schmidt, 76 Misc.2d 976, 352 N.Y.S.2d 399, 403 (Crim.Ct.1974) (no offense of "attempted 'interference with governmental administration' ").

We find this reasoning to be directly applicable to the question of whether there can be an attempt to violate section 837.02, Florida Statutes (1973).

We are not persuaded by the argument that the crime of attempt can be extended to cover attempted perjury. The argument is based on the hypothetical where the intention to perjure is frustrated by the absence of an element extraneous to the offender's actions, such as the authority of the person administering the oath. In the typical case of a criminal attempt, the factor distinguishing the attempt from the completed crime is that the intended criminal result, an element of the completed crime, was not achieved. In a case, for example, of murder, or robbery, or arson, there is an interference or intervention preventing the consummation of the criminal intent: the victim did not die, or the robber did not get away with any money, or the fire went out without causing damage. The absence of the element of a criminal result is different from the absence of an element extraneous to the offender's conduct, such as the element of the authority of the person administering the oath.

The lack of such elements of the crime of perjury as the materiality of the testimony, the lawfulness of the oath, or the official judicial nature of the proceeding is not, we think, what is contemplated by the common law and statutory concepts of failure, intervention, interception or prevention. When the elements of materiality, lawful oath, and official judicial proceeding are established, the crime of perjury is fully proven by an "attempt" to commit perjury. That is, it is fully proven by the overt act of a willful false statement. That the false statement be believed is not an element of the crime of perjury. Thus no criminal result such as a miscarriage of justice need be proved to establish the crime. As in *Silvestri*, the crime is fully proven by showing an "attempt" to commit the crime. We conclude that there can be no crime of attempted perjury.

We answer the certified question in the negative.

SUNDBERG, C. J., and ADKINS, J., concur. OVERTON, J., concurs in part and dissents in part with an opinion. ALDERMAN, J., dissents with an opinion, with which ENGLAND and McDONALD, JJ., concur.

OVERTON, JUSTICE, concurring in part, dissenting in part.

I concur in the finding that attempted perjury is not a crime, but, under the facts of this case, I would advise the Fifth Circuit Court of Appeals that this cause must be remanded for a new trial and that the defendant should not be discharged.

By his counsel, the defendant in this cause directly induced the trial court to include attempted perjury as a lesser included offense. He now contends he is entitled to a discharge because the judge granted this request and the government failed to object. Our criminal justice system will reach a new height in ridiculousness if a defendant through his counsel can cause erroneous verdict choices or alternatives to be presented to the jury and then walk free because of the problem he created. This is not justice and should not be allowed under any circumstances. At most, the defendant is entitled to a new trial.

ALDERMAN, JUSTICE, dissenting.

Where there is an intent to commit perjury and there is an overt act of falsely testifying but the crime is not completed because one of the essential elements of the crime of perjury, such as materiality, is lacking, the facts establish attempted perjury. The majority explains the elements of perjury and the definition of attempt, yet, inconsistently with its definitions, concludes that the crime of perjury is fully proven by an attempt to commit the crime of perjury and that, therefore, there is no such crime of attempted perjury. This cannot be true because if materiality or the authority of the person administering the oath is lacking, then there can be no crime of perjury. However, if any one of these particular elements is lacking, yet defendant has formulated an intention to commit perjury during an official proceeding and has done a physical act intended to accomplish the commission of the crime other than mere preparation to commit the offense but has failed in the actual commission of the offense, then he has committed attempted perjury. I would, therefore, answer the certified question in the affirmative.

ENGLAND and McDONALD, JJ., concur.

CHARLTON v. WAINWRIGHT

United States Court of Appeals, Fifth Circuit, 1979.
588 F.2d 162.

PER CURIAM: This is an appeal from the district court's denial of habeas corpus relief to petitioner Karle Charlton, a prisoner of the State of Florida. Charlton claims that he was convicted of attempted manslaughter by culpable negligence, a crime that did not exist; or, alternatively, that the jury was asked to choose between a legally valid and invalid theory for conviction, and may have chosen the latter. Finding no error in the denial of habeas relief below, we affirm.

The facts of this case are not in dispute. On October 29, 1974, Charlton was employed by Big Daddy's Lounge in Naples, Florida. On that evening he and two other employees attempted to evict an intoxicated patron from the lounge and an argument ensued. The patron fell down a flight of stairs, suffered head injuries, and died several days later. Petitioner was charged with manslaughter in a single count Information. The Information, tracking the language of Fla.Stat. § 782.07, charged him with murder by act, procurement, or culpable negligence.

At trial the evidence about petitioner's state of mind when he evicted the patron was in conflict. The trial court instructed the jury on manslaughter, and on attempt, although the appellant had waived the latter instruction. Without objection, the court also instructed the jury that it could render a verdict of not guilty, guilty of attempted manslaughter, or guilty of manslaughter. The jury found the petitioner guilty of attempted manslaughter.

On direct appeal, his conviction was affirmed without a written opinion. The Florida Supreme Court denied certiorari. After a hearing, the federal district court denied habeas relief under 28 U.S.C. § 2254.

The petitioner concedes that if he had been convicted of attempted manslaughter by either "act" or "procurement," his conviction would be valid. He observes, however, that the verdict of "guilty of attempted manslaughter" may have been based on attempted manslaughter "by culpable negligence" as well. He contends that such a crime is a logical absurdity, since it involves the intent to commit a negligent (involuntary) act; and that it had never before been recognized as a crime in Florida.

Charlton's argument fails because Florida cases have clearly defined "culpable negligence" to require proof of something more than a purely involuntary act.

Florida courts have long recognized the crimes of assault with intent to commit manslaughter and accessory before the fact to manslaughter. Both of these crimes, assault with intent and accessory before the fact, involve specific intent. The Florida Supreme Court has stated that assault with intent to commit manslaughter is a crime where the mode of assault constitutes "culpable negligence."

In addition to recognizing that a person can have the specific intent to commit manslaughter, Florida courts have implicitly recognized the crime of attempted manslaughter. Devoe v. Tucker, 113 Fla. 805, 152 So. 624, 626 (1934).

Florida courts have given a special definition to "culpable negligence." Instead of construing it to emphasize involuntary and unintentional behavior, they have construed it to emphasize culpability which rests on intentional, or quasi-intentional, behavior:

> 'Culpable negligence' as used in the manslaughter statute means negligence of a gross and flagrant character evincing a reckless disregard of human life or the safety of persons exposed to its dangerous effects, or that entire want of care which would raise the presumption of indifference to consequences; or which shows such wantonness or recklessness, or a grossly careless disregard of the safety and welfare of the public, or that reckless indifference to the rights of others which is equivalent to an *intentional* violation of them.

In sum, Florida has defined culpable negligence to involve a state of mind so wanton or reckless that the behavior it produces may be regarded as intentional. As a result, Florida manslaughter convictions based on cuplable negligence, like those based on act or procurement, demand proof of a level of intent greater than that of ordinary negligence. Since each of these three ways of committing manslaughter requires that intent predominate over accident or chance, petitioner's attack on the logic of attempted manslaughter by culpable negligence must fail.

Petitioner's contention, therefore, that the conviction was based on the jury's choice between a valid and invalid theory cannot stand. In this case, no such choice was presented. The jury chose between attempted manslaughter by act, attempted manslaughter by procurement, and attempted manslaughter by culpable negligence. We do not know which of these theories the jury applied in reaching its verdict of "guilty of attempted manslaughter," but we are confident that each is legally sound under Florida law.

Relying on their own jurisprudence and statutes, other courts have reached results different from Florida.[1] This result does not validate a conviction for the attempt to perform an involuntary act or an act involving ordinary negligence.

A Florida conviction for attempted manslaughter by culpable negligence is valid under the law of that State, and does not offend the United States Constitution.

Affirmed.

<h2 style="text-align:center">NOTES</h2>

1. After learning he was infected with the deadly disease, AIDS, defendant attempted to cut short what was left of his life by slashing his wrists. When his attempt to commit suicide is thwarted by police and paramedics, the defendant, enraged, turns on his rescuers and attempts to bite, spit, and spray blood toward the police officer, yelling he would "show everyone else what it was like to have the disease and die." Assuming defendant is convicted of attempted murder upon the policeman, should the conviction be sustained? See, State v. Haines, 545 N.E.2d 834 (Ind.App.1989).

See also, Deadly and Dangerous Weapons and AIDS: The *Moore* Analysis is Likely to be Dangerous, 74 Iowa L.Rev. 951 (1989); Comment, The Real Fatal Attraction: Civil and Criminal Liability for the Sexual Transmission of AIDS, 37 Drake L.Rev. 657 (1987–1988).

2. In Darr v. People, 193 Colo. 445, 568 P.2d 32 (1977), two policemen sold jewelry to the defendant, representing it as being stolen though it had not been stolen. In holding that a conviction for attempted receiving stolen goods would lie, the Colorado Supreme Court said, "It is irrelevant whether the goods are recovered stolen goods or have never been stolen. The intent and acts of the defendant, not the surrounding circumstances, are the crucial elements of the attempt offense, as the statutory provision prohibiting the defense of impossibility for attempt crimes makes clear."

Construing the state statute on criminal attempts as following the modern trend to abolish legal impossibility as a defense to inchoate crimes, see Commonwealth v. Henley, 504 Pa. 408, 474 A.2d 1115 (1984). A jewelry store proprietor agreed to buy gold chains from an undercover policeman believing them to be stolen. His conviction of attempted theft was affirmed. For a provocative and comprehensive article on the subject, see Robbins, "Attempting the Impossible: The Emerging Consensus," 23 Harv.J.Legisl. 377 (1986).

3. Consider Waters v. State, 2 Md.App. 216, 234 A.2d 147 (1967), in which an 80 year old man was convicted of assault with intent to commit rape. He contended that physical inability to engage in "sexual activity" precluded a conviction of an offense based upon "intent to rape". In affirming defendant's conviction the court said: "While there can be no attempt in a case involving legal impossibility, as attempting to do what is not a crime is not attempting to commit a crime, factual impossibility of success does not prevent the attempt from being made. Physical incapacity to commit a crime does not affect the capacity of one to be guilty of an attempt. Thus a man who is physically impotent may be guilty of an attempt to commit rape."

1. See, e.g., Commonwealth v. Hebert, 368 N.E.2d 1204 (Mass.1977); People v. Weeks, 86 Ill.App.2d 480, 230 N.E.2d 12 (1967).

In State v. Ray, 63 Wash.2d 224, 386 P.2d 423 (1963), it was held that in a prosecution for attempted rape, the fact that the defendant's "zipper stuck" was no defense.

Since at common law an accused under the age of fourteen is conclusively presumed to be incapable of committing the crime of rape, whatever the real facts may be, "it logically follows, as a plain legal deduction, that he was also incapable in law of an attempt to commit it. . . ." Foster v. Commonwealth, 96 Va. 306, 31 S.E. 503 (1898). But in Preddy v. Commonwealth, 184 Va. 765, 36 S.E.2d 549 (1946), the court held that a 67-year old man was properly convicted of attempting to rape a ten-year old girl even though the defendant might have been impotent. See, in this connection, the excellent note on impossibility of consummation of substantive crime as a defense to conspiracy or attempt prosecutions at 37 A.L.R.3d 375 (1971).

4. Is there such a crime as attempted felony murder? See People v. Hassin, 48 A.D.2d 705, 368 N.Y.S.2d 253 (1975). Is there a crime of attempted possession of burglary tools? See Vogel v. State, 365 So.2d 1079 (Fla.App.1979). There is no crime of attempt to incite a riot, the court held in State v. Eames, 365 So.2d 1361 (La.1978). Why not?

B. SOLICITATION

PEOPLE v. LUBOW
Court of Appeals of New York, 1971.
29 N.Y.2d 58, 323 N.Y.S.2d 829, 272 N.E.2d 331.

BERGAN, JUDGE.

The revised Penal Law creates a new kind of offense, simpler in structure than an attempt or a conspiracy, and resting solely on communication without need for any resulting action (art. 100, Criminal Solicitation, part of tit. G, Anticipatory Offenses, L.1965, ch. 1030) Consol.Laws, c. 40. Attempts to commit crimes and conspiracies are continued with some changes as crimes and these, too, are grouped within title G as "Anticipatory Offenses" (art. 105, Conspiracies; art. 110, Attempts).

The basic statutory definition of criminal solicitation is that with intent that another person shall "engage in conduct constituting a crime" the accused "solicits, requests, commands, importunes or otherwise attempts to cause such other person to engage in such conduct". This basic definitory language is continued through three grades of solicitation, the gravity depending on what crime the conduct sought to be induced would effectuate.

If the conduct would be "a crime" it is criminal solicitation in the third degree, a "violation" (§ 100.00); if the conduct would be "a felony" it is criminal solicitation in the second degree, a class A misdemeanor (§ 100.05); and if the conduct would be murder or kidnapping in the first degree it is criminal solicitation in the first degree, a class D felony (§ 100.10).

As it has been noted, nothing need be done under the statute in furtherance of the communication ("solicits, commands, importunes") to constitute the offense. The communication itself with intent the other person engage in the unlawful conduct is enough. It needs no corroboration.

And an attempt at communication which fails to reach the other person may also constitute the offense for the concluding clause "or otherwise attempts to cause such other person to engage in such conduct" would seem literally to embrace as an attempt an undelivered letter or message initiated with the necessary intent.

Appellants have been convicted after a trial by a three-Judge panel in the Criminal Court of the City of New York of violation of section 100.05 which describes solicitation to commit a felony. The information on which the prosecution is based is made by complainant Max Silverman. It describes the charge as criminal solicitation and states that "defendants attempted to cause deponent to commit the crime of grand larceny" in that they "attempted to induce the deponent to obtain precious stones on partial credit with a view towards appropriating the property to their own use and not paying the creditors, said conduct constituting the crime of larceny by false promise".

Although the Penal Law section number is not stated in the information, it was clearly stated in court before the opening of the trial that the charge was a violation of section 100.05 and the facts alleged that the inducement was to commit grand larceny, a felony, which gave adequate notice of the nature of the offense involved.

The proof in support of the charge, if factually accepted by the trial court, as it was by a majority of the Judges (one dissenting), was sufficient to warrant conviction. The Appellate Term affirmed unanimously.

The evidence showed that complainant Silverman and both defendants were engaged in the jewelry business. It could be found that defendant Lubow owed Silverman $30,000 for diamonds on notes which were unpaid; that Lubow had told Silverman he was associated with a big operator interested in buying diamonds and introduced him to defendant Gissinger.

It could also be found that in October, 1967, Silverman met the two defendants together at their office, demanded his money, and said that because of the amount owed him he was being forced into bankruptcy.

Silverman testified in response to this Lubow said "Well, let's make it a big one, a big bankruptcy", and Gissinger said this was a good idea. When Silverman asked "how it is done" he testified that Lubow, with Gissinger participating, outlined a method by which diamonds would be purchased partly on credit, sold for less than cost, with the proceeds pyramided to boost Silverman's credit rating until very substantial amounts came in, when there was to be a bankruptcy with Silverman explaining that he had lost the cash gambling in Puerto Rico and Las Vegas. The cash would be divided among the three men. The gambling explanation for the disappearance of cash would be made to seem believable by producing credit cards for Puerto Rico and Las Vegas.

Silverman testified that Lubow said "we would eventually wind up with a quarter of a million dollars each" and that Gissinger said "maybe millions".

Silverman reported this proposal to the District Attorney in October, 1967 and the following month a police detective equipped Silverman with a tape recorder concealed on his person which was in operation during conversations with defendants on November 16 and which tends to substantiate the charge. The reel was received in evidence on concession that it was taken from the machine Silverman wore November 16.

A police detective testified as an expert that a "bust out operation" is a "pyramiding of credit by rapid purchasing of merchandise, and the rapid selling of the same merchandise sometimes 10 and 20 per cent the cost of the merchandise itself, and they keep selling and buying until they establish such a credit rating that they are able to purchase a large order at the end of their operation, and at this time they go into bankruptcy or they just leave".

There thus seems sufficient evidence in the record to find that defendants intended Silverman to engage in conduct constituting a felony by defrauding creditors of amounts making out grand larceny and that they importuned Silverman to engage in such conduct. Thus the proof meets the actual terms of the statute.

The statute itself is a valid exercise of legislative power. Commentators closely associated with the drafting of the Model Penal Code of the American Law Institute, from which the New York solicitation statute stems, have observed: "Purposeful solicitation presents dangers calling for preventive intervention and is sufficiently indicative of a disposition towards criminal activity to call for liability. Moreover, the fortuity that the person solicited does not agree to commit or attempt to commit the incited crime plainly should not relieve the solicitor of liability, when otherwise he would be a conspirator or an accomplice."

Solicitation to commit a felony was a misdemeanor at common law. Summarizing this historical fact Judge Cardozo observed: "So at common law, incitement to a felony, when it did not reach the stage of an attempt, was itself a separate crime, and like conspiracy, which it resembled, was a misdemeanor, not a felony" (People v. Werblow, 241 N.Y. 55, 66, 148 N.E. 786, 791, citing Higgins and Rex v. Gregory, L.R. 1 C.C.R. 77).

But . . . the solicitation in early New York cases was treated as closely related to an attempt. [In People v. Bush, 4 Hill 133] defendant asked another to burn a barn and gave him a match for that purpose. This principle was followed to some extent (e.g., People v. Bloom, 149 App.Div. 295, 296–299, 133 N.Y.S. 708, 709–711) but there were fundamental difficulties with it under the concept of attempt and it seems not to have been followed after *Bloom*.

Although this Penal Law provision is the first statutory enactment in New York, there have been statutes aimed at criminal solicitation in some other States, notably California.

In commenting on the criminal solicitation enactment of article 100, two lawyers who were active in the work of the State Commission on Revision of the Penal Law and Criminal Code which prepared the present statute observed that article 100 "closes that gap" for those who believe, as apparently the commission and the American Law Institute did, that "solicitation to commit a crime involves sufficient culpability to warrant criminal sanctions".

There are, however, potential difficulties inherent in this penal provision which should be looked at, even though all of them are not decisive in this present case. One, of course, is the absence of any need for corroboration. The tape recording here tends to give some independent support to the testimony of Silverman, but there are types of criminal conduct which might be solicited where there would be a heavy thrust placed on the credibility of a single witness testifying to a conversation. Extraordinary care might be required in deciding when to prosecute; in determining the truth; and in appellate review of the factual decision.

One example would be the suggestion of one person to another that he commit a sexual offense; another is the suggestion that he commit perjury. The Model Penal Code did not require corroboration; but aside from the need for corroboration which is traditional in some sexual offenses, there are dangers in the misinterpretation of innuendos or remarks which could be taken as invitations to commit sexual offenses. . . .

In two opinions for the California Supreme Court, Justice Traynor has analyzed that State's criminal solicitations statute (Penal Code, § 653f; Benson v. Superior Ct. of Los Angeles County, 57 Cal.2d 240, 18 Cal.Rptr. 516, 368 P.2d 116 [1962], and People v. Burt, 45 Cal.2d 311, 288 P.2d 503 [1955]).

The first case was for solicitation to commit perjury and the second for solicitation to commit extortion.

The California statute is based on a specific list of serious crimes to which criminal solicitation expressly applies; but as to all of them the statute requires that the offense "must be proved by the testimony of two witnesses, or of one witness and corroborating circumstances".

The basic public justification for legislative enactment is, however, very similar to New York's and was developed in the *Burt* opinion: "Legislative concern with the proscribed soliciting is demonstrated not only by the gravity of the crimes specified but by the fact that the crime, unlike conspiracy, does not require the commission of any overt act. It is complete when the solicitation is made, and it is immaterial that the object of the solicitation is never consummated, or that no steps are taken toward its consummation." The California Legislature was concerned "not only with the prevention of the harm that would result should the inducements prove successful, but with protecting inhabitants of this state from being exposed to inducements to commit or join in the commission of the crimes specified"

Another potential problem with the statute is that it includes an attempt to commit unlawful solicitation, i.e., solicits, etc., "or otherwise attempts to cause" the conduct. This has the same effect as the Model Penal Code, but the language there is different. The code spells the purpose out more specifically that: "It is immaterial * * * that the actor fails to communicate with the person he solicits to commit a crime if his conduct was designed to effect such communication" (Model Penal Code, § 5.02, subd. [2], Tent. Draft No. 10). This could be an attempt in the classic sense and might be committed by a telephone message initiated but never delivered. The present Penal Law, stated in different language, has the same effect.

Appellants raise a point based on the reduplicative overplay of section 100.00 which is a "violation" and section 100.05, of which they have been convicted, a "class A misdemeanor".

Literally, the same act could fall within either section; and specifically the acts charged to appellants could come within either.

Section 100.00 relates to solicitation of another person to "engage in conduct constituting a crime" and section 100.05 to "engage in conduct constituting a felony".

Since a felony is a crime, whenever a charge is made based on solicitation to commit felony, it would come within both sections. It is not entirely clear why the statute was drawn this way. The commentators Denzer and McQuillan observe that although section 100.00 "embraces solicitation to commit any crime from a class B misdemeanor up to a class A felony, its principal application would normally be to those solicitation offenses not covered by the higher degrees".

Whatever may be said of the abstract merits of a choice of prosecution based on the same act between a higher or lesser degree of crime, it seems to have been decided that prosecution for the higher degree is permissible.

* * *

The judgment should be affirmed.

FULD, C.J., and SCILEPPI, BREITEL, JASEN and GIBSON, JJ., concur with BERGAN, J.

BURKE, J., concurs in result only.

NOTES

1. Illustrative of solicitation statutes are the following:

West's Ann.California Pen.Code, § 653f:

(a) Every person who solicits another to offer or accept or join in the offer or acceptance of a bribe, or to commit or join in the commission of robbery, burglary, grand theft, receiving stolen property, extortion, perjury, subornation of perjury, forgery, kidnapping, arson or assault with a deadly weapon or instrument or by means of force likely to produce great bodily injury, or, by the use of force or a threat of force, to prevent or dissuade any person who is or may become a witness from attending upon, or testifying at, any trial, proceeding, or inquiry authorized by law, is punishable by imprisonment in the county jail not more than one year or in the state prison, or by fine of not more than ten thousand dollars ($10,000), or the amount which could have been assessed for commission of the offense itself, whichever is greater, or by both such fine and imprisonment.

(b) Every person who solicits another to commit or join in the commission of murder is punishable by imprisonment in the state prison for two, four, or six years.

(c) Every person who solicits another to commit rape by force or violence, sodomy by force or violence, oral copulation by force or violence, or any violation of Section 264.1, 288 or 289, is punishable by imprisonment in a state prison for two, three or four years.

(d) An offense charged in violation of subdivision (a), (b) or (c) must be proved by the testimony of two witnesses, or of one witness and corroborating circumstances.

Section 8–1.1, Illinois Criminal Code (S.H.A. ch. 38): A person commits solicitation when, with intent that an offense other than first degree murder be committed, he commands, encourages or requests another to commit that offense.

2. In Dickerson v. Richmond, 2 Va.App. 473, 346 S.E.2d 333 (1986), defendant was arrested when officers in an unmarked patrolcar observed him dressed in female attire and approaching vehicles with male occupants only late at night. He was charged with "loitering for the purpose of soliciting or engaging in prostitution or other lewd, lascivious or indecent act," in violation of the Richmond City Code. Upon his conviction, the Virginia Court of Appeals reversed. Treating the case as a "solicitation" prosecution, the court stated that proof of specific intent was required:

"That Dickerson appeared to be dressed in female attire . . . and seemed to be drawn only to those vehicles with male occupants create a suspicion that his loitering was sexual in nature. . . . The City was not required to prove prostitution or attempted prostitution because solicitation may be completed before an attempt is made to commit the solicited act. The evidence, however, must prove that Dickerson's specific intent was . . . to solicit or engage in any other lewd, lascivious or indecent act."

The court concluded that the evidence creates a strong suspicion of guilt, but fell short of proof beyond a reasonable doubt on the specific intent to solicit.

C. CONSPIRACY

_____

1. BASIC ELEMENTS AND THE "OVERT ACT"

COMMONWEALTH v. DYER
Supreme Judicial Court of Massachusetts, 1923.
243 Mass. 472, 138 N.E. 296.

RUGG, C. J.   The first two counts of this indictment are framed on the common law.   Numerous defendants therein are charged, with conspiracy to create a monopoly in fresh fish, to fix, regulate, control, and to enhance exorbitantly and unreasonably the price of fresh fish, and thus to cheat and defraud the public. . . .

The principles by which to determine the elements essential to conspiracy as a common-law crime are settled in this commonwealth. The subject was discussed at large by Chief Justice Shaw in Commonwealth v. Hunt, 4 Metc. 111, where at page 123 (38 Am.Dec. 346), it was said:

"A conspiracy must be a combination of two or more persons by some concerted action to accomplish some criminal or unlawful purpose, or to accomplish some purpose not in itself criminal or unlawful by criminal or unlawful means.   We use the terms criminal or unlawful, because it is manifest that many acts are unlawful, which are not punishable by indictment or other public prosecution; and yet there is no doubt, we think, that a combination by numbers to do them would be an unlawful conspiracy, and punishable by indictment.   Of this character was a conspiracy to cheat by false pretenses, without false tokens, when a cheat by false pretenses only, by a single person, was not a punishable offense.   Commonwealth v. Boynton, 3 Law Reporter, 295, 296. . . .   So a combination to destroy the reputation of an individual, by verbal calumny which is not indictable.   So a conspiracy to induce and persuade a young female, by false representations, to leave the protection of her parent's house, with a view to facilitate her prostitution.   Rex v. Lord Grey, 3 Hargrave's State Trials, 519.   But yet it is clear, that it is not every combination to do unlawful acts, to the prejudice of another by a concerted action, which is punishable as conspiracy. . . ."   . . .

The principles thus declared were affirmed in Commonwealth v. Waterman, 122 Mass. 43, where it was said, at page 57:

"It is not always essential that the acts contemplated should constitute a criminal offense, for which, without the element of conspiracy, one alone could be indicted. . . .   It is said to be sufficient if the end proposed, or the means to be employed, are by reason of the power of the combination, particularly dangerous to the public interests, or

particularly injurious to some individual, although not criminal."
. . .

The law has never declared otherwise than by the decision of specific cases as they arise the unlawful but not criminal acts which when made the object of cooperative design between two or more persons constitute criminal conspiracy. Manifestly the instances given by Chief Justice Shaw . . . were intended to be illustrative only and not exhaustive.

The great weight of authority in other jurisdictions is in harmony with the principle declared in Commonwealth v. Hunt, [supra]. That decision has been followed in many of the states of the Union. It is the consensus of opinion that conspiracy as a criminal offense is established when the object of the combination is either a crime, or if not a crime, is unlawful, or when the means contemplated are either criminal, or if not criminal, are illegal, provided that, where no crime is contemplated either as the end or the means, the illegal but noncriminal element involves prejudice to the general welfare or oppression of the individual of sufficient gravity to be injurious to the public interest. . . .

Referring first to the common-law counts—they conform to the principles of criminal conspiracy. The intent of the combination is alleged to be the oppression and injury of the public through the unreasonable enhancement of the price of a foodstuff of prime necessity for the people during the exigency created by the great war. The means by which it is alleged that the purpose was designed to be achieved are in some particulars unlawful and in others criminal under our law. . . .

NOTES

1. For some interesting cases pertinent to the subject matter of the principal case, see People v. Tilton, 357 Ill. 47, 191 N.E. 257 (1934); People v. Balkan, 351 Ill.App. 95, 113 N.E.2d 813 (1953); and People v. Dorman, 415 Ill. 385, 114 N.E.2d 404 (1953). All three cases, however, were decided prior to the new Illinois Criminal Code (S.H.A. ch. 38). The Code (§ 8–2), as does the A.L.I. Model Penal Code (Tent.Draft #10, 5.03), confines conspiracy prosecutions to cases where the conspiratorial objective is itself a crime.

2. Some states create substantive conspiracy statutes to reach conduct of the type described by the court in *Dyer.* See, e.g., Virginia Code § 18.2–499, which provides:

"(a) Any two or more persons who shall combine, associate, agree, mutually undertake or concert together for the purpose of willfully and maliciously injuring another in his reputation, trade, business or profession by any means whatever, or for the purpose of wilfully and maliciously compelling another to do or perform any act against his will, or preventing or hindering another from doing or performing any lawful act, shall be jointly and severally guilty of a Class 3 misdemeanor. . . .

    "* * *"

The section of the code following the foregoing one affords injured parties civil relief in the way of treble damages, including lost profits, attorney's fees, as well as injunctive relief.

3. The fact that the object of the conspiracy, e.g., murder, was committed in one state does not prevent another [Rhode Island] from prosecution of the conspiracy. "The common law crime of conspiracy involves a combination of two or more persons to commit some unlawful act or to do some lawful act for an unlawful purpose. . . . The gravamen of the crime is entry into an unlawful agreement and once that occurs the offense is complete. Rhode Island continues to adhere to the common law definition of this crime and, unlike other jurisdictions, it does not require that any overt acts have been committed in execution of the unlawful agreement. . . ." State v. LaPlume, 118 R.I. 670, 375 A.2d 938 (1977).

4. In Albernaz v. United States, 450 U.S. 333, 101 S.Ct. 1137 (1981), the United States Supreme Court held that a single agreement can support convictions for violation of more than one conspiracy statute. The defendant had conspired to import and distribute marijuana. He was found guilty of violating 21 U.S.C.A. § 963 and 21 U.S.C.A. § 846. The two sections contain identical language, but are found in different subchapters of the Comprehensive Drug Abuse Prevention and Control Act of 1970. The Court held the multiple sections evidenced Congressional intent to impose multiple punishments for a single conspiracy and the convictions were therefore in conformance with statutory and constitutional law.

COMMONWEALTH v. BENESCH
Supreme Judicial Court of Massachusetts, 1935.
290 Mass. 125, 194 N.E. 905.

QUA, JUSTICE. These two indictments are now before this court on the exceptions of the defendants, Benesch, Davison, and Tibbetts. . . . The second indictment charges the [defendants] with conspiring to have registered brokers or salesmen sell securities in accordance with an instalment or partial payment contract which was not approved by the Public Utilities Commission. G.L. c. 110A, § 8, as amended by St.1924, c. 487, § 4. . . .

. . . It is not disputed that the instalment plan contracts had not been approved by the Public Utilities Commission. Under this indictment, in order to hold any one defendant, it was necessary for the commonwealth to show as to that defendant that he entered into a combination with others for the purpose of doing the illegal act of selling securities on an instalment plan contract which had not been approved by the commission. In the case of conspiracy, as with other common law crimes, it is necessary that criminal intent be shown. Speaking in general terms, there must be an intent to do wrong. Selling the shares on instalments was not in itself wrong. It need involve no deceit or other element detrimental to the individual purchaser or to the public interest. So long as the contracts had not been approved, sale of the shares was malum prohibitum because of the statute, and nothing more. While no decision in this commonwealth directly in point has been called to our attention, it has been held by excellent authority in other jurisdictions that in order to sustain an indictment for conspiracy to commit an offence which, like that here involved, is malum prohibitum only, belonging to a general type of offences which has been greatly extended by modern legislation in many fields, it must appear that the defendant knew of the illegal element involved in that which the combination was intended to accomplish. . . . We believe this is sound law, where the charge is conspiracy. We do not imply that proof of criminal intent is required to sustain a complaint or indictment for the substantive offence prohibited by the statute.

To constitute the criminal intent necessary to establish a conspiracy there must be both knowledge of the existence of the law and knowledge of its actual or intended violation. The trial judge charged the jury in accordance with these principles, but he left it for the jury to say whether all three of the defendants now before the court had a criminal intent with respect to this second indictment. We think this was error. Perhaps as to Benesch alone there was evidence of the necessary intent. . . . But one cannot be a conspirator alone. We are of opinion that the evidence is insufficient to support a verdict that any of the other alleged conspirators had the knowledge both of the existence of the prohibition and of its violation which is necessary to prove affirmatively a criminal intent. There is no evidence that any of them knew that the contracts had not been approved or that any of them occupied such a position in the Trust that such knowledge could be inferred. There is at most no more than a scintilla of evidence that any of the alleged co-conspirators with Benesch consciously and intentionally joined in a conspiracy to sell shares for instalments on unapproved contracts. . . .

It follows . . . that the exceptions of all three defendants in the second case are sustained.

So ordered.

NOTES

1. "The judge rightly declined to rule as requested by the defendants in substance that in order to prove the intent necessary for a criminal conspiracy there must be evidence that the defendants had knowledge of the law which they conspired to violate. The ruling requested involved a misapplication of the principle discussed in Commonwealth v. Benesch. . . . That principle is a narrow one. It has no application where there is anything inherently wrong or inimical to the public interest in that which the defendants have combined to do. The making and use of false nomination papers is in its very nature wrongful and detrimental to the public interest. The doing of these acts can almost never be consistent with an innocent purpose. . . . One who joins in a conspiracy to that end may be found to entertain a criminal intent regardless of his knowledge of the statutes. . . ." Commonwealth v. O'Rourke, 311 Mass. 213, 221–222, 40 N.E.2d 883, 887 (1942).

2. In Davidson v. United States, 61 F.2d 250 (8th Cir. 1932), defendants were convicted of conspiracy to violate the National Motor Vehicle Theft Act.

In reversing their conviction, the court stated: "If this verdict on the first count charging conspiracy is to be sustained, it must not only appear that the car in question constituted interstate commerce, but also that these defendants, when they received the car, had knowledge of the interstate character of the transaction. In other words, it must appear that they knew where this car came from, in order to warrant a conclusion that by receiving and selling the car, they participated in the furtherance of a conspiracy as alleged in count 1 of this indictment." For a criticism of the requirement of anti-federal intent, see Comment, Developments in the Law of Criminal Conspiracy, 72 Harv.L.Rev. 920, 937–39 (1959).

UNITED STATES v. FEOLA

Supreme Court of the United States, 1975.
420 U.S. 671, 95 S.Ct. 1255.

MR. JUSTICE BLACKMUN delivered the opinion of the Court.

This case presents the issue whether knowledge that the intended victim is a federal officer is a requisite for the crime of conspiracy, under 18 U.S.C. § 371, to commit an offense violative of 18 U.S.C. § 111, that is, an assault upon a federal officer while engaged in the performance of his official duties.

Respondent Feola and three others (Alsondo, Rosa, and Farr) were indicted for violations of §§ 371 and 111. A jury found all four defendants guilty of both charges. Feola received a sentence of four years for the conspiracy and one of three years, plus a $3,000 fine, for the assault. The three-year sentence, however, was suspended and he was given three years' probation "to commence at the expiration of confinement" for the conspiracy. The respective appeals of Feola, Alsondo, and Rosa were considered by the United States Court of Appeals for the Second Circuit in a single opinion. After an initial ruling partially to the contrary, that court affirmed the judgment of conviction on the substantive charges, but reversed the conspiracy convictions. United States v. Alsondo, 486 F.2d 1339, 1346 (1973). Because of a conflict among the federal Circuits on the scienter issue with respect to a conspiracy charge, we granted the Government's petition for a writ of certiorari in Feola's case.

I

The facts reveal a classic narcotics "rip-off." The details are not particularly important for our present purposes. We need note only that the evidence shows that Feola and his confederates arranged for a sale of heroin to buyers who turned out to be undercover agents for the Bureau of Narcotics and Dangerous Drugs. The group planned to palm off on the purchasers, for a substantial sum, a form of sugar in place of heroin and, should that ruse fail, simply to surprise their unwitting buyers and relieve them of the cash they had brought along for payment. The plan failed when one agent, his suspicions being aroused, drew his revolver in time to counter an assault upon another agent from the rear. Instead of enjoying the rich benefits of a successful swindle, Feola and his associates found themselves charged, to their undoubted surprise, with conspiring to assault, and with assaulting, federal officers.

At the trial, the District Court, without objection from the defense, charged the jurors that, in order to find any of the defendants guilty on either the conspiracy count or the substantive one, they were not required to conclude that the defendants were aware that their quarry were federal officers.

The Court of Appeals reversed the conspiracy convictions on a ground not advanced by any of the defendants. Although it approved the trial court's instructions to the jury on the substantive charge of assaulting a federal officer, it nonetheless concluded that the failure to charge that knowledge of the victim's official identity must be proved in order to convict on the conspiracy charge amounted to plain error. The court perceived itself bound by a line of cases, commencing with Judge Learned Hand's opinion in United States v. Crimmins, 123 F.2d 271 (CA2 1941), all holding that scienter of a factual element that confers federal jurisdiction, while unnecessary for conviction of the substantive offense, is required in order to sustain a conviction for conspiracy to commit the substantive offense. . . .

II

The Government's plea is for symmetry. It urges that since criminal liability for the offense described in 18 U.S.C. § 111 does not depend on whether the assailant harbored the specific intent to assault a federal officer, no greater scienter requirement can be engrafted upon the conspiracy offense, which is merely an agreement to commit the act proscribed by § 111. Consideration of the Government's contention requires us preliminarily to pass upon its premise, the proposition that responsibility for assault upon a federal officer does not depend upon whether the assailant was aware of the official identity of his victim at the time he acted.

That the "federal officer" requirement is anything other than jurisdictional is not seriously urged upon us; indeed, both Feola and the Court of Appeals, concede that scienter is not a necessary element of the substantive offense under § 111. . . . Nevertheless, we are not always guided by concessions of the parties, and the very considerations of symmetry urged by the Government suggest that we first turn our attention to the substantive offense.

The Court has considered § 111 before. In Ladner v. United States, 358 U.S. 169, 79 S.Ct. 209 (1958), the issue was whether a single shotgun blast which wounded two federal agents effected multiple assaults, within the meaning of 18 U.S.C. § 254 (1940 ed.), one of the statutory predecessors to the present § 111. The Government urged that § 254 had been intended not only to deter interference with federal law enforcement activities but, as well, to forestall injury to individual officers, as "wards" of the United States. Given the latter formulation of legislative intent, argued the Government, a single blast wounding two officers would constitute two offenses. The Court disagreed because it found an equally plausible reading of the legislative intent to be that "the congressional aim was to prevent hindrance to the execution of official duty . . . and was not to protect federal officers except as incident to that aim." Under that view of legislative purpose, to have punishment depend upon the number of officers impeded would be incongruous. With no clear choice between these alternative formulations of congressional intent, in light of the statutory language and sparse legislative history, the Court applied a policy of lenity and, for purposes of the case, adopted the less harsh reading. It therefore held that the single discharge of a shotgun constituted only a single violation of § 254.

In the present case, we see again the possible consequences of an interpretation of § 111 that focuses on only one of the statute's apparent aims. If the primary purpose is to protect federal law enforcement personnel, that purpose could well be frustrated by the imposition of a strict scienter requirement. On the other hand, if § 111 is seen primarily as an anti-obstruction statute, it is likely that Congress intended criminal liability to be imposed only when a person acted with the specific intent to impede enforcement activities. Otherwise, it has been said: "Were knowledge not required in obstruction of justice offenses described by these terms, wholly innocent (or even socially desirable) behavior could be transformed into a felony by the wholly fortuitous circumstance of the concealed identity of the person resisted." Although we adhere to the conclusion in *Ladner* that either view of legislative intent is "plausible," we think it plain that Congress intended to protect *both* federal officers and federal functions, and that, indeed, furtherance of the one policy advances the other. The rejection of a strict scienter requirement is consistent with both purposes.

Section 111 has its origin in § 2 of the Act of May 18, 1934, c. 299, 48 Stat. 781. Section 1 of that Act, in which the present 18 U.S.C. § 1114 has its roots, made it a federal crime to kill certain federal law enforcement personnel while engaged in, or on account of, the performance of official duties, and § 2 forbade forcible resistance or interference with, or assault upon, any officer designated in § 1 while so engaged. The history of the 1934 Act, though scanty, offers insight into its multiple purposes. The pertinent committee reports consist, almost in their entirety, of a letter dated January 3, 1934, from Attorney General Cummings urging the passage of the legislation. In that letter the Attorney General states that this was needed "for the protection of Federal officers and employees." Compelled reliance upon state courts, "however respectable and well disposed, for the protection of [federal] investigative and law-enforcement personnel" was inadequate, and there was need for resort to a federal forum.

Although the letter refers only to the need to protect federal personnel, Congress clearly was concerned with the safety of federal officers insofar as it was tied to the efficacy of law enforcement activities. This concern is implicit in the decision to list those officers protected rather than merely to forbid assault on any federal employee. Indeed, the statute as originally formulated would have prohibited attack on "any civil official, inspector, agent, or other officer or employee of the United States." The House rejected this and insisted on the version that was ultimately enacted. Although the reason for the insistence is unexplained, it is fair to assume that the House was of the view that the bill as originally drafted strayed too far from the purpose of insuring the integrity of law enforcement pursuits.

In resolving the question whether Congress intended to condition responsibility for violation of § 111 on the actor's awareness of the identity of his victim, we give weight to both purposes of the statute, but here again, as in *Ladner,* we need not make a choice between them. Rather, regardless of which purpose we would emphasize, we must take note of the means Congress chose for its achievement.

*   *   *

We conclude, from all this, that in order to effectuate the congressional purpose of according maximum protection to federal officers by making prosecution for assaults upon them cognizable in the federal courts, § 111 cannot be construed as embodying an unexpressed requirement that an assailant be aware that his victim is a federal officer. All the statute requires is an intent to assault, not an intent to assault a federal officer. A contrary conclusion would give insufficient protection to the agent enforcing an unpopular law, and none to the agent acting under cover.

This interpretation poses no risk of unfairness to defendants. It is no snare for the unsuspecting. Although the perpetrator of a narcotics "rip-off," such as the one involved here, may be surprised to find that his intended victim is a federal officer in civilian apparel, he nonetheless knows from the very outset that his planned course of conduct is wrongful. The situation is not one where legitimate conduct becomes unlawful solely because of the identity of the individual or agency affected. In a case of this kind the offender takes his victim as he finds him. The concept of criminal intent does not extend so far as to require that the actor understand not only the nature of his act but also its consequence for the choice of a judicial forum.

We are not to be understood as implying that the defendant's state of knowledge is never a relevant consideration under § 111. The statute does require a criminal intent, and there may well be circumstances in which ignorance of the official status of the person assaulted or resisted negates the very existence of *mens rea*. For example, where an officer fails to identify himself or his purpose, his conduct in certain circumstances might reasonably be interpreted as the unlawful use of force directed either at the defendant or his property. In a situation of that kind, one might be justified in exerting an element of resistance, and an honest mistake of fact would not be consistent with criminal intent. We hold, therefore, that in order to incur criminal liability under § 111 an actor must entertain merely the criminal intent to do the acts therein specified. We now consider whether the rule should be different where persons conspire to commit those acts.

III

Our decisions establish that in order to sustain a judgment of conviction on a charge of conspiracy to violate a federal statute, the Government must prove at least the degree of criminal intent necessary for the substantive offense itself. Respondent Feola urges upon us the proposition that the Government must show a degree of criminal intent in the conspiracy count greater than is necessary to convict for the substantive offense; he urges that even though it is not necessary to show that he was aware of the official identity of his assaulted victims in order to find him guilty of assaulting federal officers, in violation of 18 U.S.C. § 111, the Government nonetheless must show that he was aware that his intended victims were undercover agents, if it is successfully to prosecute him for conspiring to assault federal agents. And the Court of Appeals held that the trial court's failure to charge the jury to this effect constituted plain error.

The general conspiracy statute, 18 U.S.C. § 371, offers no textual support for the proposition that to be guilty of conspiracy a defendant in effect must have known that his conduct violated federal law. The statute makes it unlawful simply to "conspire . . . to commit any offense against the United States." A natural reading of these words would be that since one can violate a criminal statute simply by engaging in the forbidden conduct, a conspiracy to commit that offense is nothing more than an agreement to engage in the prohibited conduct. Then where, as here, the substantive statute does not require that an assailant know the official status of his victim, there is nothing on the face of the conspiracy statute that would seem to require that those agreeing to the assault have a greater degree of knowledge.

We have been unable to find any decision of this Court that lends support to the respondent. . . .

* * *

With no support on the face of the general conspiracy statute or in this court's decisions, respondent relies solely on the line of cases commencing with United States v. Crimmins, 123 F.2d 271 (CA2 1941), for the principle that the Government must prove "antifederal" intent in order to establish liability under § 371. In *Crimmins,* the defendant had been found guilty of conspiring to receive stolen bonds that had been transported in interstate commerce. Upon review, the Court of Appeals pointed out that the evidence failed to establish that Crimmins actually knew the stolen bonds had moved into the State. Accepting for the sake of argument the assumption that such knowledge was not necessary to sustain a conviction on the substantive offense, Judge Learned Hand nevertheless concluded that to permit conspiratorial liability where the conspirators were ignorant of the federal implications of their acts would be to enlarge their agreement beyond its terms as they understood them. He capsulized the distinction in what has become well known as his "traffic light" analogy:

> "While one may, for instance, be guilty of running past a traffic light of whose existence one is ignorant, one cannot be guilty of conspiring to run past such a light, for one cannot agree to run past a light unless one supposes that there is a light to run past."

Judge Hand's attractive, but perhaps seductive, analogy has received a mixed reception in the Courts of Appeals. The Second Circuit, of course, has followed it; others have rejected it. It appears that most have avoided it by the simple expedient of inferring the requisite knowledge from the scope of the conspiratorial venture. We conclude that the analogy, though effective prose, is, as applied to the facts before us, bad law.

The question posed by the traffic light analogy is not before us, just as it was not before the Second Circuit in *Crimmins*. Criminal liability, of course, may be imposed on one who runs a traffic light regardless of whether he harbored the "evil intent" of disobeying the light's command; whether he drove so recklessly as to be unable to perceive the light; whether, thinking he was observing all traffic rules, he simply failed to notice the light; or whether, having been reared elsewhere, he thought that the light was only an ornament. Traffic violations generally fall into that category of offenses that dispense with a *mens rea* requirement. . . .

But this case does not call upon us to answer this question, and we decline to do so, just as we have once before. We note in passing, however, that the analogy comes close to stating what has been known as the "*Powell* doctrine," originating in People v. Powell, 63 N.Y. 88 (1875), to the effect that a conspiracy, to be criminal, must be animated by a corrupt motive or a motive to do wrong. Under this principle, such a motive could be easily demonstrated if the underlying offense involved an act clearly wrongful in itself; but it had to be independently demonstrated if the acts agreed to were wrongful solely because of statutory proscription. See Note, Developments in the Law—Criminal Conspiracy, 72 Harv.L.Rev. 920, 936–937 (1959). Interestingly, Judge Hand himself was one of the more severe critics of the *Powell* doctrine.

That Judge Hand should reject the *Powell* doctrine and then create the *Crimmins* doctrine seems curious enough. Fatal to the latter, however, is the fact that it was announced in a case to which it could not have been meant to apply. In *Crimmins*, the substantive offense, namely, the receipt of stolen securities that had been in interstate commerce, proscribed clearly wrongful conduct. Such conduct could not be engaged in without an intent to accomplish the forbidden result. So, too, it is with assault, the conduct forbidden by the substantive statute, § 111, presently before us. One may run a traffic light "of whose existence one is ignorant," but assaulting another "of whose existence one is ignorant," probably would require unearthly intervention. Thus, the traffic light analogy, even if it were a correct statement of the law, is inapt, for the conduct proscribed by the substantive offense, here assault, is not of the type outlawed without regard to the intent of the actor to accomplish the result that is made criminal. If the analogy has any vitality at all, it is to conduct of the latter variety; that, however, is a question we save for another day. We hold here only that where a substantive offense embodies only a requirement of *mens rea* as to each of its elements, the general federal conspiracy statute requires no more.

The *Crimmins* rule rests upon another foundation: that it is improper to find conspiratorial liability where the parties to the illicit agreement were not aware of the fact giving rise to federal jurisdiction, because the essence of conspiracy is agreement and persons cannot be punished for acts beyond the scope of their agreement. This "reason" states little more than a conclusion, for it is clear that one may be guilty as a conspirator for acts the precise details of which one does not know at the time of the agreement. . . . The question is not merely whether the official status of an assaulted victim was known to the parties at the time of their agreement, but whether the acts contemplated by the conspirators are to be deemed legally different from those actually performed solely because of the official identity of the victim. Put another way, does the identity of the proposed victim alter the legal character of the acts agreed to, or is it no more germane to the nature of those acts than the color of the victim's hair?

Our analysis of the substantive offense in Part II, supra, is sufficient to convince us that for the purpose of individual guilt or innocence, awareness of the official identity of the assault victim is irrelevant. We would expect the same to obtain with respect to the conspiracy offense unless one of the policies behind the imposition of conspiratorial liability is not served where the parties to the agreement are unaware that the intended target is a federal law enforcement official.

It is well settled that the law of conspiracy serves ends different from, and complementary to, those served by criminal prohibitions of the substantive offense. Because of this, consecutive sentences may be imposed for the conspiracy and for the underlying crime. Our decisions have identified two independent values served by the law of conspiracy. The first is protection of society from the dangers of concerted criminal activity,. . . . That individuals know that their planned joint venture violates federal as well as state law seems totally irrelevant to that purpose of conspiracy law which seeks to protect society from the dangers of concerted criminal activity. Given the level of criminal intent necessary to sustain conviction for the substantive offense, the act of agreement to commit the crime is no less opprobrious and no less dangerous because of the absence of knowledge of a fact unnecessary to the formation of criminal intent. Indeed, unless imposition of an "anti-federal" knowledge requirement serves social purposes external to the law of conspiracy of which we are unaware, its imposition here would serve only to make it more difficult to obtain convictions on charges of conspiracy, a policy with no apparent purpose.

The second aspect is that conspiracy is an inchoate crime. This is to say, that, although the law generally makes criminal only antisocial conduct, at some point in the continuum between preparation and consummation, the likelihood of a commission of an act is sufficiently great and the criminal intent sufficiently well formed to justify the intervention of the criminal law. The law of conspiracy identifies the agreement to engage in a criminal venture as an event of sufficient threat to social order to permit the imposition of criminal sanctions for the agreement alone, plus an overt act in pursuit of it, regardless of whether the crime agreed upon actually is committed. Criminal intent has crystallized, and the likelihood of actual, fulfilled commission warrants preventive action.

. . . Given the level of intent needed to carry out the substantive offense, we fail to see how the agreement is any less blameworthy or constitutes less of a danger to society solely because the participants are unaware which body of law they intend to violate. Therefore, we again conclude that imposition of a requirement of knowledge of those facts that serve only to establish federal jurisdiction would render it more difficult to serve the policy behind the law of conspiracy without serving any other apparent social policy.

* * *

Again we point out, however, that the state of knowledge of the parties to an agreement is not always irrelevant in a proceeding charging a violation of conspiracy law. First, the knowledge of the parties is relevant to the same issues and to the same extent as it may be for conviction of the substantive offense. Second, whether conspirators knew the official identity of their quarry may be important, in some cases, in establishing the existence of federal jurisdiction. The jurisdictional requirement is satisfied by the existence of facts tying the proscribed conduct to the area of federal concern delineated by the statute. Federal jurisdiction always exists where the substantive offense is committed in the manner therein described, that is, when a federal officer is attacked. Where, however, there is an unfulfilled agreement to assault, it must be established whether the agreement, standing alone, constituted a sufficient threat to the safety of a federal officer so as to give rise to federal jurisdiction. If the agreement calls for an attack on an individual specifically identified, either by name or by some unique characteristic, as the putative buyers in the present case, and that specifically identified individual is in fact a federal officer, the agreement may be fairly characterized as one calling for an assault upon a federal officer, even though the parties were unaware of the victim's actual identity and even though they would not have agreed to the assault had they known that identity. Where the object of the intended attack is not identified with sufficient specificity so as to give rise to the conclusion that had the attack been carried out the victim would have been a federal officer, it is impossible to assert that the mere act of agreement to assault poses a sufficient threat to federal personnel and functions so as to give rise to federal jurisdiction.

To summarize, with the exception of the infrequent situation in which reference to the knowledge of the parties to an illegal agreement is necessary to establish the existence of federal jurisdiction, we hold that where knowledge of the facts giving rise to federal jurisdiction is not necessary for conviction of a substantive offense embodying a *mens rea* requirement, such knowledge is equally irrelevant to questions of responsibility for conspiracy to commit that offense.

The judgment of the Court of Appeals with respect to the respondent's conspiracy conviction is reversed.

It is so ordered.

MR. JUSTICE STEWART, with whom MR. JUSTICE DOUGLAS joins, dissenting.

Does an assault on a federal officer violate 18 U.S.C. § 111 even when the assailant is unaware, and has no reason to know, that the victim is other than a private citizen or, indeed, a confederate in crime? . . . This question was not contained in the petition for certiorari in the present case, and has not been addressed in either the briefs or oral arguments. The parties have merely assumed the answer to the question, and directed their attention to the separate question whether scienter is an element of *conspiring* to violate § 111. Nevertheless the Court sets out *sua sponte* to decide the basic question . . . without the benefit of either briefing or oral argument by counsel.

This conspicuous disregard of the most basic principle of our adversary system of justice seems to me indefensible. . . .

The Court recognizes that "[t]he question . . . is not whether the ['federal officer'] requirement is jurisdictional, but whether it is jurisdictional only." Put otherwise, the question is whether Congress intended to write an aggravated assault statute, analogous to the many state statutes which protect the persons and functions of state officers against assault, or whether Congress intended merely to federalize every assault which happens to have a federal officer as its victim. The Court chooses the latter interpretation, reading the federal-officer requirement to be jurisdictional only. This conclusion is inconsistent with the pertinent legislative history, the verbal structure of § 111, accepted canons of statutory construction, and the dictates of common sense.

Many States provide an aggravated penalty for assaults upon state law enforcement officers; typically the victim-status element transforms the assault from a misdemeanor to a felony. These statutes have a twofold purpose: to reflect the societal gravity associated with assaulting a public officer and, by providing an enhanced deterrent against such assault, to accord to public officers and their functions a protection greater than that which the law of assault otherwise provides to private citizens and their private activities. Consonant with these purposes, the accused's knowledge that his victim had an official status or function is invariably recognized by the States as an essential element of the aggravated offense. Where an assailant had no such knowledge, he could not of course be deterred by the statutory threat of enhanced punishment, and it makes no sense to regard the unknowing assault as being any more reprehensible, in a moral or retributive sense, than if the victim had been, as the assailant supposed, a private citizen.

The state statutes protect only state officers. I would read § 111 as filling the gap and supplying analogous protection for federal officers and their functions. An aggravated penalty should apply only where an assailant knew, or had reason to know, that his victim had some official status or function. It is immaterial whether the assailant knew the victim was employed by the federal, as opposed to a state or local, government. That *is* a matter of "jurisdiction only," for it does not affect the moral gravity of the act. If the victim was a federal officer, § 111 applies; if he was a state or local officer, an analogous state statute or local ordinance will generally apply. But where the assailant reasonably thought his victim a common citizen or, indeed, a confederate in crime, aggravation is simply out of place, and the case should be tried in the appropriate forum under the general law of assault, as are unknowing assaults on state officers.

The history of § 111 permits no doubt that this is an aggravated assault statute, requiring proof of scienter.   *   *   *

Rummaging through the spare legislative history of the 1934 law, the Court manages to persuade itself that Congress intended to reach unknowing assaults on federal officers. But if that was the congressional intention, which I seriously doubt, it found no expression in the legislative product. *The fact is that the 1934 statute expressly required scienter for an assault conviction.* An assault on a federal officer was proscribed only if perpetrated "*on account of* the performance of his official duties." That is, it was necessary not only that the assailant have notice that his victim possessed official status or duties but also that the assailant's *motive* be retaliation against the exercise of those duties.

It was not until the *1948 recodification* that the proscription was expanded to cover assaults on federal officers "while engaged in," as well as "on account of," the performance of official duties. This was, as the Reviser observed, a technical alteration; it produced no instructive legislative history. As presently written, the statute does clearly reach knowing assaults regardless of motive. But to suggest that it also reaches wholly unknowing assaults is to

convert the 1948 alteration into one of major substantive importance, which it concededly was not.

* * *

   While the legislative history of the 1934 law is "scant," Ladner v.
United States, it is sufficient to locate a congressional purpose consistent only with implication of a scienter requirement. As the Court said
in *Ladner:* "[T]he congressional aim was to prevent hindrance to the
execution of official duty, and thus to assure the carrying out of federal
purposes and interests, and was not to protect federal officers except as
incident to that aim." This purpose is, of course, exactly analogous to
the purposes supporting the state statutes which provide enhanced
punishment for assault on state officers. A statute proscribing interference with official duty does not "prevent hindrance" with that duty
where the assailant thinks his victim is a mere private citizen, or
indeed, a confederate in his criminal activity.

   To avoid this self-evident proposition, the Court effectively overrules *Ladner* and concludes that the assault statute aims as much at
protecting individual officers as it does at protecting the functions they
execute. If the *Ladner* Court had shared this opinion, it would not
have held, as it did, that a single shotgun blast wounding two federal
agents was to be considered a single assault. But in any event, even
today's revisionist treatment of *Ladner* does not succeed in getting the
Court where it wants to go. So far as the scienter requirement is
concerned, it makes no difference whether the statute aims to protect
individuals, or functions, or both. The Court appears to think that
extending § 111 to unknowing assaults will deter such assaults—will
"give . . . protection . . . to the agent acting under cover." This, of
course, is nonsense. The federal statute "protects" an officer from
assault only when the assailant knows that the victim is an officer. . . .

* * *

   The implication of scienter here is as necessary and proper as it
was in Morissette v. United States, 342 U.S. 246, 72 S.Ct. 240. The
Court there read a scienter requirement into a federal larceny statute
over the Government's objection that the need for scienter should not
be implied for a federal offense when the statute that created the
offense was silent on the subject. * * * The same principle applies
here. The terms and purposes of § 111 flow from well-defined and
familiar law proscribing obstructions of justice, and the provision com-
plements a pattern of state aggravated assault statutes which are
uniform and unambiguous in requiring scienter.

   We see today the unfortunate consequences of deciding an important question without the benefit of the adversary process. In
this rush to judgment, settled precedents, such as Ladner v. United
States, supra, and Pettibone v. United States, supra, are subverted.
Legislative history is ignored or imaginatively reconstructed. Statutory terms are broken from their context and given unnatural
readings. On top of it all, the Court disregards two firmly estab-

lished canons of statutory construction—"two wise principles this Court has long followed":

> "First, as we have recently reaffirmed, 'ambiguity concerning the ambit of criminal statutes should be resolved in favor of lenity.

*   *   *

> ". . . [S]econd . . .: unless Congress conveys its purpose clearly, it will not be deemed to have significantly changed the federal-state balance. . . . In traditionally sensitive areas, such as legislation affecting the federal balance, the requirement of clear statement assures that the legislature has in fact faced, and intended to bring into issue, the critical matters involved in the judicial decision."

If the Congress desires to sweep all assaults upon federal employees into the federal courts, a suitable statute could be easily enacted. I should hope that in so doing the Congress, like every State which has dealt with the matter, would make a distinction in penalty between an assailant who knows the official identity of the victim and one who does not. That result would have a double advantage over the result reached by the Court today. It would be a fair law, and it would be the product of the law-making branch of our Government.

For the reasons stated, I believe that before there can be a violation of 18 U.S.C. § 111, an assailant must know or have reason to know that the person he assaults is an officer. It follows *a fortiori* that there can be no criminal conspiracy to violate the statute in the absence of at least equivalent knowledge. Accordingly, I respectfully dissent from the opinion and judgment of the Court.

UNITED STATES v. FALCONE

Supreme Court of the United States, 1940.
311 U.S. 205, 61 S.Ct. 204.

MR. JUSTICE STONE delivered the opinion of the Court.

The question presented by this record is whether one who sells materials with knowledge that they are intended for use or will be used in the production of illicit distilled spirits may be convicted as a coconspirator with a distiller who conspired with others to distill the spirits in violation of the revenue laws.

Respondents were indicted with sixty-three others in the Northern District of New York for conspiring to violate the revenue laws by the operation of twenty-two illicit stills in the vicinity of Utica, New York. The case was submitted to the jury as to twenty-four defendants, of whom the five respondents and sixteen operators of stills were convicted. The Court of Appeals for the Second Circuit reversed the conviction of the five respondents on the ground that as there was no evidence that respondents were themselves conspirators, the sale by them of materials, knowing that they would be used by others in illicit distilling, was not sufficient to establish that respondents were guilty of the conspiracy charged. . . .

All of the respondents were jobbers or distributors who, during the period in question, sold sugar, yeast or cans, some of which found their way into the possession and use of some of the distiller defendants. The indictment while charging generally that all the defendants were parties to the conspiracy did not allege specifically that any of respondents had knowledge of the conspiracy, but it did allege that respondents Alberico and Nole brothers sold the materials mentioned knowing that they were to be used in illicit distilling. The Court of Appeals reviewing the evidence thought, in the case of some of the respondents, that the jury might take it that they were knowingly supplying the distillers. As to Nicholas Nole, whose case it considered most doubtful, it thought that his equivocal conduct "was as likely to have come from a belief that it was a crime to sell the yeast and the cans to distillers as from being in fact any further involved in their business". But it assumed for purposes of decision that all furnished supplies which they knew ultimately reached and were used by some of the distillers. Upon this assumption it said, "In the light of all this, it is apparent that the first question is whether the seller of goods, in themselves innocent, becomes a conspirator with—or, what is in substance the same thing, an abettor of—the buyer because he knows that the buyer means to use the goods to commit a crime." And it concluded that merely because respondent did not forego a "normally lawful activity, of the fruits of which he [knew] that others [were making] an unlawful use" he is not guilty of a conspiracy.

The Government does not argue here the point which seems to be implicit in the question raised by its petition for certiorari, that conviction of conspiracy can rest on proof alone of knowingly supplying an illicit distiller, who is not conspiring with others. In such a case, as the Government concedes, the act of supplying or some other proof must import an agreement or concert of action between buyer and seller, which admittedly is not present here. But the Government does contend that one who with knowledge of a conspiracy to distill illicit spirits sells materials to a conspirator knowing that they will be used in the distilling, is himself guilty of the conspiracy. It is said that he is, either because his knowledge combined with his action makes him a participant in the agreement which is the conspiracy, or what is the same thing he is a principal in the conspiracy as an aider or abettor by virtue of § 332 of the Criminal Code, 18 U.S.C. § 550, 18 U.S.C.A. § 550, which provides: "Whoever directly commits any act constituting an offense defined in any law of the United States, or aids, abets, counsels, commands, induces, or procures its commission, is a principal."

The argument, the merits of which we do not consider, overlooks the fact that the opinion below proceeded on the assumption that the evidence showed only that respondents or some of them knew that the materials sold would be used in the distillation of illicit spirits, and fell short of showing respondents' participation in the conspiracy or that they knew of it. We did not bring the case here to review the evidence, but we are satisfied that the evidence on which the Government relies does not do more than show knowledge by respondents that the materials would be used for illicit distilling if it does as much in the case of some.[1] In the case of Alberico, as in the case of Nicholas Nole, the jury could have found that he knew that one of their customers who is an unconvicted defendant was using the purchased material in illicit distilling. But it could not be inferred from that or from the casual and unexplained meetings of some of respondents with others who were convicted as conspirators that respondents knew of the conspiracy.

1. The two Falcones who were in business as sugar jobbers were shown to have sold sugar to three wholesale grocers who in turn were shown to have sold some of the sugar to distillers. To establish guilty knowledge the Government relies upon evidence showing that the volume of their sales was materially larger during the periods of activity of the illicit stills; that Joseph Falcone was shown on two occasions, at one of which Salvatore Falcone was present, to have been in conversation with one of the conspirators who was a distiller, and on one occasion with another distiller conspirator who was his brother-in-law; that Joseph Falcone had been seen at the Venezia Restaurant which was patronized by some of the conspirators and knew its proprietor; and on two occasions Salvatore Falcone had visited the restaurant, on one to collect funds for the Red Cross and on another for a monument to Marconi.

Respondent Alberico was a member of a firm of wholesale grocers who dealt in sugar and five-gallon tin cans among other things. They sold sugar to wholesale grocers and jobbers. To establish Alberico's guilty knowledge the Government relies on evidence that his total purchases of sugar materially increased during the period when the illicit stills were shown to be in operation; that some of his sugar purchases from a local wholesaler were at higher prices than he was then paying others; that on the premises of one of the distillers there were found fifty-five cardboard cartons, each suitable for containing one dozen five-gallon cans, on one of which was stencilled the name of Alberico's firm; that on eight to ten occasions Alberico sold sugar and cans in unnamed amounts to Morreale, one of the defendant distillers who was not convicted, and on one occasion was overheard to say, in refusing credit to Morreale, "I could not trust you because your business is too risky."

Respondent Nicholas Nole was shown to be proprietor of Acme Yeast Company and also the Utica Freight Forwarding Company, to which one and one-half tons of K & M yeast was consigned by the seller. Wrappers bearing the distinctive marks of the Acme Yeast Company and K & M yeast, quantity not stated, were found at one of the stills; and a K & M yeast container was found at another. To show guilty knowledge of Nicholas Nole the Government relies on the circumstance that he registered the Acme Yeast Company in the county clerk's office in the name of a cousin; that the order for the consignment of K & M yeast was placed in the name of an unidentified person; that Nole had been seen in conversation with some of the convicted distillers at a time when some of the illicit stills were in operation, and that on one occasion during that period he sold and delivered fifteen five-gallon cans of illicit alcohol from a source not stated.

Respondent John Nole was shown to be a distributor for the National Grain Yeast Company in Utica during the period in question. Yeast wrappers bearing the National labels were found at three of the stills. To show guilty knowledge of John Nole the Government relies on evidence that he had assisted his brother Nicholas in unloading yeast at the Utica Freight Forwarding Co.; that he was a patron of the Venezia Restaurant; that on one occasion he was seen talking with Morreale, the unconvicted distiller, in the vicinity of a store in Utica, whose store it does not appear. On three occasions Morreale and another convicted defendant procured yeast in cartons and some in kegs at the store and on one occasion John Nole told the person in charge of the store to let them have the yeast; that John Noles' information return required by the Government of all sales of yeast in excess of five pounds to one person did not show in February or March, 1938, any sale of yeast to Morreale or any sale of keg yeast.

The evidence respecting the volume of sales to any known to be distillers is too vague and inconclusive to support a jury finding that respondents knew of a conspiracy from the size of the purchases even though we were to assume what we do not decide that the knowledge would make them conspirators or aiders or abettors of the conspiracy. Respondents are not charged with aiding and abetting illicit distilling, and they cannot be brought within the sweep of the Government's conspiracy dragnet if they had no knowledge that there was a conspiracy.

The gist of the offense of conspiracy as defined by § 37 of the Criminal Code, 18 U.S.C. § 88, 18 U.S.C.A. § 88, is agreement among the conspirators to commit an offense attended by an act of one or more of the conspirators to effect the object of the conspiracy. Those having no knowledge of the conspiracy are not conspirators; and one who without more furnishes supplies to an illicit distiller is not guilty of conspiracy even though his sale may have furthered the object of a conspiracy to which the distiller was a party but of which the supplier had no knowledge. On this record we have no occasion to decide any other question.

Affirmed.

NOTES

1. See, however, Direct Sales Co. v. United States, 319 U.S. 703, 63 S.Ct. 1265, 87 L.Ed. 1674 (1943), where a wholesaler of drugs was convicted of conspiracy to violate the federal narcotic laws by selling drugs in quantity to a codefendant physician who was supplying them to addicts. The conviction was affirmed on a showing that he had actively promoted the sale of morphine sulfate in quantity and had sold to the defendant, a small-town physician from South Carolina, more than 300 times his normal requirements of the drug. In contrasting *Falcone,* the Court said: "All articles of commerce may be put to illegal ends. But all do not have inherently the same susceptibility to harmful and illegal use. . . . This difference is important for two purposes. One is for making certain that the seller knows the buyer's intended illegal use. The other is to show that by the sale he intends to further, promote and cooperate in it. This intent, when given effect by overt act, is the gist of conspiracy. While it is not identical with mere knowledge that another purposes unlawful action, it is not unrelated to such knowledge. . . ."

2. In United States v. United States Gypsum Company, 438 U.S. 422, 98 S.Ct. 2864, 57 L.Ed.2d 854 (1978), the defendants, manufacturers or producers of gypsum board, were charged with violating the Sherman Anti–Trust Act by consulting with one another on prices charged to particular customers. The Government posited that if defendants knew that the consultations would have an effect on price fixing, then guilt was established, regardless of what there actual intent was. Defendants had argued that the price verifications were undertaken in good faith to comply with the Robinson–Patman [prevention of unfair competition] Act, and that no evidence of criminal intent was shown. The jury was instructed that if it found interseller verification had the effect of raising, fixing, maintaining or stabilizing the price of gypsum board, then such verification could be considered as evidence of an agreement to so affect prices,

and were further told that "if the effect of the exchanges of pricing information was to raise, fix, maintain, and stabilize prices, then the parties to them are presumed, as a matter of law, to have intended that result.

After concluding that intent was a necessary element of a criminal antitrust violation, the Court had to decide what level of intent would support a conviction under the Act:

> The ALI Model Penal Code is one source of guidance upon which the Court has relied to illuminate questions of this type.

> . . . Recognizing that "mens rea is not a unitary concept," the Code enumerates four possible levels of intent—purpose, knowledge, recklessness and negligence. In dealing with the kinds of business decisions upon which the antitrust laws focus, the concepts of recklessness and negligence have no place. Our question instead is whether a criminal violation of the antitrust laws requires, in addition to proof of anticompetitive effects, a demonstration that the disputed conduct was undertaken with the "conscious object" of producing such effects or whether it is sufficient that the conduct is shown to have been undertaken with knowledge that the proscribed effects would most likely follow. While the difference between these formulations is a narrow one, see ALI Model Penal Code § 2.02, comment, at 125 (Tent. Draft 4 1955), we conclude that action undertaken with knowledge of its probable consequences and having the requisite anticompetitive effects can be a sufficient predicate for a finding of criminal liability under the antitrust laws.

> Several considerations fortify this conclusion. The element of intent in the criminal law has traditionally been viewed as a bifurcated concept embracing either the specific requirement of purpose or the more general one of knowledge or awareness.

>> "[I]t is now generally accepted that a person who acts (or omits to act) intends a result of his act (or omission) under two quite different circumstances: (1) when he consciously desires that result, whatever the likelihood of that result happening from his conduct; and (2) when he knew that the result is practically certain to follow from his conduct, whatever his desire may be as to that result."

> LaFave & Scott, Criminal Law 196 (1972).

> Generally this limited distinction between knowledge and purpose has not been considered important since "there is good reason for imposing liability whether the defendant desired or merely knew of the practical certainty of the result." LaFave & Scott, supra, at 197. See also ALI Model Penal Code, § 2.02 comments, at 125 (Tent. Draft 4, 1955). In either circumstance, the defendants are consciously behaving in a way the law prohibits, and such conduct is a fitting object of criminal punishment. See Working Papers of the National Commission on Reform of Federal Criminal Laws, Vol. I, 124 (1970).

> Nothing in our analysis of the Sherman Act persuades us that this general understanding of intent should not be applied to criminal antitrust violations such as charged here. The business behavior which is likely to give rise to criminal antitrust charges is conscious behavior normally undertaken only after a full consideration of the desired results and a weighing of the costs, benefits and risks. A

requirement of proof not only of this knowledge of likely effects, but also of a conscious desire to bring them to fruition or to violate the law would seem, particularly in such a context, both unnecessarily cumulative and unduly burdensome. Where carefully planned and calculated conduct is being scrutinized in the context of a criminal prosecution, the perpetrator's knowledge of the anticipated consequences is a sufficient predicate for a finding of criminal intent.

When viewed in terms of this standard, the jury instructions on the price-fixing charge cannot be sustained. "A conclusive presumption [of intent], which testimony could not overthrow would effectively eliminate intent as an ingredient of the offense." The challenged jury instruction, as we read it, had precisely this effect; the jury was told that the requisite intent followed, *as a matter of law,* from a finding that the exchange of price information had an impact on prices. Although an effect on prices may well support an inference that the defendant had knowledge of the probability of such a consequence at the time he acted, the jury must remain free to consider additional evidence before accepting or rejecting the inference. Therefore, although it would be correct to instruct the jury that it may infer intent from an effect on prices, ultimately the decision on the issue of intent must be left to the trier of fact alone. The instruction given invaded this factfinding function. * * *

3. In People v. Lauria, 251 Cal.App.2d 471, 59 Cal.Rptr. 628 (1967), Lauria's telephone answering service was used by three prostitutes to book "appointments" for their business. When an undercover policewoman obtained a job at the telephone answering service, she was told by the office manager, who hinted that she was a prostitute concerned with the secrecy of her activities, that the operation of the service was discreet and "about as safe as you can get." Lauria admits knowing that some of his customers are prostitutes. The prosecution maintains that continuing to furnish his prostitute-clients with telephone answering service makes him a co-conspirator with his clients. Is Lauria guilty of conspiracy to commit prostitution? How valid is the prosecution's argument that since Lauria knew his customers were using his service for illegal purposes, and continued furnishing those services, he must have intended to assist them in carrying out their illegal activities? How much proof of an intent to facilitate the business of prostitution must there be?

In exploring that issue, and after discussing the *Falcone* and the *Direct Sales* cases, Associate Justice Fleming said:

In examining precedents in this field we find that sometimes, but not always, the criminal intent of the supplier may be inferred from his knowledge of the unlawful use made of the product he supplies. Some consideration of characteristic patterns may be helpful.

1. Intent may be inferred from knowledge, when the purveyor of legal goods for illegal use has acquired a stake in the venture. (United States v. Falcone, 2 Cir., 109 F.2d 579, 581.) For example, in Regina v. Thomas, (1957), 2 All.E.R. 181, 342, a prosecution for living off the earnings of prostitution, the evidence showed that the accused, knowing the woman to be a convicted prostitute, agreed to let her have the use of his room between the hours of 9 p.m. and 2 a.m. for a charge of £3 a night. The Court of Criminal Appeal refused an appeal from the conviction, holding that when the accused rented a room at a grossly

inflated rent to a prostitute for the purpose of carrying on her trade, a jury could find he was living on the earnings of prostitution.

In the present case, no proof was offered of inflated charges for the telephone answering services furnished the codefendants.

2. Intent may be inferred from knowledge, when no legitimate use for the goods or services exists. The leading California case is People v. McLaughlin, 111 Cal.App.2d 781, 245 P.2d 1076, in which the court upheld a conviction of the suppliers of horse-racing information by wire for conspiracy to promote bookmaking, when it had been established that wireservice information had no other use than to supply information needed by bookmakers to conduct illegal gambling operations.

* * *

In Shaw v. Director of Public Prosecutions, [1962] A.C. 220, the defendant was convicted of conspiracy to corrupt public morals and of living on the earnings of prostitution, when he published a directory consisting almost entirely of advertisements of the names, addresses, and specialized talents of prostitutes. Publication of such a directory, said the court, could have no legitimate use and serve no other purpose than to advertise the professional services of the prostitutes whose advertisements appeared in the directory. The publisher could be deemed a participant in the profits from the business activities of his principal advertisers.

Other services of a comparable nature came to mind: the manufacturer of crooked dice and marked cards who sells his product to gambling casinos; the tipster who furnishes information on the movement of law enforcement officers to known lawbreakers. . . .

However, there is nothing in the furnishing of telephone answering service which would necessarily imply assistance in the performance of illegal activities. Nor is any inference to be derived from the use of an answering service by women, either in any particular volume of calls, or outside normal working hours. Night-club entertainers, registered nurses, faith healers, public stenographers, photographic models, and free lance substitute employees, provide examples of women in legitimate occupations whose employment might cause them to receive a volume of telephone calls at irregular hours.

3. Intent may be inferred from knowledge, when the volume of business with the buyer is grossly disproportionate to any legitimate demand, or when sales for illegal use amount to a high proportion of the seller's total business. In such cases an intent to participate in the illegal enterprise may be inferred from the quantity of the business done. For example, in *Direct Sales,* supra, the sale of narcotics to a rural physician in quantities 300 times greater than he would have normal use for provided potent evidence of an intent to further the illegal activity. . . .

No evidence of any unusual volume of business with prostitutes was presented by the prosecution against Lauria.

* * *

Yet there are cases in which it cannot reasonably be said that the supplier has a stake in the venture or has acquired a special interest in the enterprise, but in which he has been held liable as a participant on the basis of knowledge alone. * * * In Regina v. Bainbridge (1959), 3 W.L.R. 656 (CCA 6), a supplier of oxygen-cutting equipment to one known to intend to use it to break into a bank was convicted as an accessory to the crime. In Sykes v. Director of Public Prosecutions [1962] A.C. 528, one having knowledge of the theft of 100 pistols, 4 submachine guns, and 1960 rounds of ammunition was convicted of misprision of felony for failure to disclose the theft to the public authorities. It seems apparent from these cases that a supplier who furnishes equipment which he *knows* will be used to commit a serious crime may be deemed from that knowledge alone to have intended to produce the result. Such proof may justify an inference that the furnisher intended to aid the execution of the crime and that he thereby became a participant. For instance, we think the operator of a telephone answering service with positive knowledge that his service was being used to facilitate the extortion of ransom, the distribution of heroin, or the passing of counterfeit money who continued to furnish the service with knowledge of its use, might be chargeable on knowledge alone with participation in a scheme to extort money, to distribute narcotics, or to pass counterfeit money. The same result would follow the seller of gasoline who knew the buyer was using his product to make Molotov cocktails for terroristic use.

Logically, the same reasoning could be extended to crimes of every description. Yet we do not believe an inference of intent drawn from knowledge of criminal use properly applies to the less serious crimes classified as misdemeanors. The duty to take positive action to dissociate oneself from activities helpful to violations of the criminal law as far stronger and more compelling for felonies than it is for misdemeanors or petty offenses. In this respect, as in others, the distinction between felonies and misdemeanors, between more serious and less serious crime, retains continuing vitality. * * *

With respect to misdemeanors, we conclude that positive knowledge of the supplier that his products or services are being used for criminal purposes does not, without more, establish an intent of the supplier to participate in the misdemeanors. With respect to felonies, we do not decide the converse, viz. that in all cases of felony knowledge of criminal use alone may justify an inference of the supplier's intent to participate in the crime. The implications of Falcone make the matter uncertain with respect to those felonies which are merely prohibited wrongs. . . .

From this analysis of precedent we deduce the following rule: the intent of a supplier who knows of the criminal use to which his supplies are put to participate in the criminal activity connected with the use of his supplies may be established by (1) direct evidence that he intends to participate, or (2) through an inference that he intends to participate based on, (a) his special interest in the activity, or (b) the aggravated nature of the crime itself.

* * *

In the context of these principles, how should they be applied to Lauria's situation?

2. THE CRIMINAL PURPOSE AND RICO PROSECUTIONS

UNITED STATES v. TURKETTE

Supreme Court of the United States, 1981.
452 U.S. 576, 101 S.Ct. 2524.

JUSTICE WHITE delivered the opinion of the Court.

Chapter 96 of Title 18 of the United States Code, 18 U.S.C. §§ 1961–1968, entitled Racketeer Influenced and Corrupt Organizations (RICO), was added to Title 18 by Title IX of the Organized Crime Control Act of 1970, Pub.L. 91–452, 84 Stat. 941. The question in this case is whether the term "enterprise" as used in RICO encompasses both legitimate and illegitimate enterprises or is limited in application to the former. The Court of Appeals for the First Circuit held that Congress did not intend to include within the definition of "enterprise" those organizations with are exclusively criminal. This position is contrary to that adopted by every other circuit that has addressed the issue. We granted certiorari to resolve this conflict.

I

Count Nine of a nine-count indictment charged respondent and 12 others with conspiracy to conduct and participate in the affairs of an enterprise engaged in interstate commerce through a pattern of racketeering activities, in violation of 18 U.S.C. § 1962(d). The indictment described the enterprise as "a group of individuals associated in fact for the purpose of illegally trafficking in narcotics and other dangerous drugs, committing arsons, utilizing the United States mails to defraud insurance companies, bribing and attempting to bribe local police officers, and corruptly influencing and attempting to corruptly influence the outcome of state court proceedings. . . ." The other eight counts of the indictment charged the commission of various substantive criminal acts by those engaged in and associated with the criminal enterprise, including possession with intent to distribute and distribution of controlled substances, and several counts of insurance fraud by arson and other means. The common thread to all counts was respondent's alleged leadership of this criminal organization through which he orchestrated and participated in the commission of the various crimes delineated in the RICO count or charged in the eight preceding counts.

After a 6-week jury trial, in which the evidence focused upon both the professional nature of this organization and the execution of a number of distinct criminal acts, respondent was convicted on all nine counts. He was sentenced to a term of 20 years on the substantive counts, as well as a 2-year special parole term on the drug count. On the RICO conspiracy count he was sentenced to a 20-year concurrent term and fined $20,000.

On appeal, respondent argued that RICO was intended solely to protect legitimate business enterprises from infiltration by racketeers and that RICO does not make criminal the participation in an association which performs only illegal acts and which has not infiltrated or attempted to infiltrate a legitimate enterprise. The Court of Appeals agreed. We reverse.

II

In determining the scope of a statute, we look first to its language. If the statutory language is unambiguous, in the absence of "a clearly expressed legislative intent to the contrary, that language must ordinarily be regarded as conclusive." Of course, there is no errorless test for identifying or recognizing "plain" or "unambiguous" language. Also, authoritative administrative constructions should be given the deference to which they are entitled, absurd results are to be avoided and internal inconsistencies in the statute must be dealt with. We nevertheless begin with the language of the statute.

Section 1962(c) makes it unlawful "for any person employed by or associated with any enterprise engaged in, or the activities of which affect, interstate or foreign commerce, to conduct or participate, directly or indirectly, in the conduct of such enterprise's affairs through a pattern of racketeering activity or collection of unlawful debt." The term "enterprise" is defined as including "any individual, partnership, corporation, association, or other legal entity, and any union or group of individuals associated in fact although not a legal entity." There is no restriction upon the associations embraced by the definition: an enterprise includes any union or group of individuals associated in fact. On its face, the definition appears to include both legitimate and illegitimate enterprises within its scope; it no more excludes criminal enterprises than it does legitimate ones. Had Congress not intended to reach criminal associations, it could easily have narrowed the sweep of the definition by inserting a single word, "legitimate." But it did nothing to indicate that an enterprise consisting of a group of individuals was not covered by RICO if the purpose of the enterprise was exclusively criminal.

The Court of Appeals, however, clearly departed from and limited the statutory language. It gave several reasons for doing so, none of which is adequate. First, it relied in part on the rule of *ejusdem generis* as an aid to statutory construction problems suggesting that where general words follow a specific enumeration of persons or things, the general words should be limited to persons or things similar to those specifically enumerated. The Court of Appeals ruled that because each of the specific enterprises enumerated in § 1961(4) is a "legitimate" one, the final catch-all phrase—"any union or group of individuals associated in fact"—should also be limited to legitimate enterprises. There are at least two flaws in this reasoning. The rule of *ejusdem generis* is no more than an aid to construction and comes into play only when there is some uncertainty as to the meaning of a particular clause in a statute. Considering the language and structure of § 1961(4), however, we not only perceive no uncertainty in the meaning to be attributed to the phrase, "any union or group of individuals associated in fact" but we are convinced for another reason that *ejusdem generis* is wholly inapplicable in this context.

Section 1961(4) describes two categories of associations that come within the purview of the "enterprise" definition. The first encompasses organizations such as corporations and partnerships, and other "legal entities." The second covers "any union or group of individuals associated in fact although not a legal entity." The Court of Appeals assumed that the second category was merely a more general description of the first. Having made that assumption, the court concluded that the more generalized description in the second category should be limited by the specific examples enumerated in the first. But that assumption is untenable. Each category describes a separate type of enterprise to be covered by the statute—those that are recognized as legal entities and those that are not. The latter is not a more general description of the former. The second category itself not containing any specific enumeration that is followed by a general description, *ejusdem generis* has no bearing on the meaning to be attributed to that part of § 1961(4).

A second reason offered by the Court of Appeals in support of its judgment was that giving the definition of "enterprise" its ordinary meaning would create several internal inconsistencies in the Act. With respect to § 1962(c), it was said that:

> "If 'a pattern of racketeering' can itself be an 'enterprise' for purposes of section 1962(c), then the two phrases 'employed by or associated with any enterprise' and 'the conduct of such enterprise's affairs through [a pattern of racketeering activity]' add nothing to the meaning of the section. The words are coherent and logical only if they are read as applying to legitimate enterprises."

This conclusion is based on a faulty premise. That a wholly criminal enterprise comes within the ambit of the statute does not mean that a "pattern of racketeering activity" is an "enterprise." In order to secure a conviction under RICO, the Government must prove both the existence of an "enterprise" and the connected "pattern of racketeering activity." The enterprise is an entity, for present purposes a group of persons associated together for a common purpose of engaging in a course of conduct. The pattern of racketeering activity is, on the other hand, a series of criminal acts as defined by the statute. The former is proved by evidence of an ongoing organization, formal or informal, and by evidence that the various associates function as a continuing unit. The latter is proved by evidence of the requisite number of acts of racketeering committed by the participants in the enterprise. While the proof used to establish these separate elements may in particular cases coalesce, proof of one does not necessarily establish the other. The "enterprise" is not the "pattern of racketeering activity"; it is an entity separate and apart from the pattern of activity in which it engages. The existence of an enterprise at all times remains a separate element which must be proved by the Government.

Apart from § 1962(c)'s proscription against participating in an enterprise through a pattern of racketeering activities, RICO also proscribes the investment of income derived from racketeering activity in an enterprise engaged in or which affects interstate commerce as well as the acquisition of an interest in or control or any such enterprise through a pattern of racketeering activity. 18 U.S.C. § 1962(a) and (b).[1] The Court of Appeals concluded that these provisions of RICO should be interpreted so as to apply only to legitimate enterprises. If these two sections are so limited, the Court of Appeals held that the proscription in § 1962(c), at issue here, must be similarly limited. Again, we do not accept the premise from which the Court of Appeals derived its conclusion. It is obvious that § 1962(a) and (b) address the infiltration by organized crime of legitimate businesses, but we cannot agree that these sections were not also aimed at preventing racketeers from investing or reinvesting in wholly illegal enterprises and from acquiring through a pattern of racketeering activity wholly illegitimate enterprises such as an illegal gambling business or a loan-sharking operation. There is no inconsistency or anamoly in recognizing that § 1962 applies to both legitimate and illegitimate enterprise. Certainly the language of the statute does not warrant the Court of Appeals' conclusion to the contrary.

Similarly, the Court of Appeals noted that various civil remedies were provided by § 1964,[2] including devestiture, dissolution, reorganiza-

1. Title 18 U.S.C. § 1962(a) and (b) provide:

(a) "It shall be unlawful for any person who has received any income derived, directly or indirectly, from a pattern of racketeering activity or through collection of an unlawful debt in which such person has participated as a principal within the meaning of section 2, title 18, United States Code, to use or invest, directly or indirectly, any part of such income, or the proceeds of such income, in acquisition of any interest in, or the establishment or operation of, any enterprise which is engaged in, or the activities of which affect, interstate or foreign commerce. A purchase of securities on the open market for purposes of investment, and without the intention of controlling or participating in the control of the issuer, or of assisting another to do so, shall not be unlawful under this subsection if the securities of the issuer held by the purchaser, the members of his immediate family, and his or their ac-

complices in any pattern or racketeering activity or the collection of an unlawful debt after such purchase do not amount in the aggregate to one percent of the outstanding securities of any one class, and do not confer, either in law or in fact, the power to elect one or more directors of the issuer.

(b) "It shall be unlawful for any person through a pattern of racketeering activity or through collection of an unlawful debt to acquire or maintain, directly or indirectly, any interest in or control of any enterprise which is engaged in, or of the activities of which affect, interstate or foreign commerce."

2. Title 18 U.S.C. § 1964(a) and (c) provide:

(a) "The district courts of the United States shall have jurisdiction to prevent and restrain violations of section 1962 of this chapter by issuing appropriate orders, including, but not limited to: ordering any person to divest himself of any

tion, restrictions on future activities by violators of RICO and treble damages. These remedies it thought would have utility only with respect to legitimate enterprises. As a general proposition, however, the civil remedies could be useful in eradicating organized crime from the social fabric, whether the enterprise be ostensibly legitimate or admittedly criminal. The aim is to divest the association of the fruits of its ill-gotten gains. Even if one or more of the civil remedies might be inapplicable to a particular illegitimate enterprise, this fact would not serve to limit the enterprise concept. Congress has provided civil remedies for use when the circumstances so warrant. It is untenable to argue that their existence limits the scope of the criminal provisions.

Finally, it is urged that the interpretation of RICO to include both legitimate and illegitimate enterprises will substantially alter the balance between federal and state enforcement of criminal law. This is particularly true, so the argument goes, since included within the definition of racketeering activity are a significant number of acts made criminal under state law. 18 U.S.C. § 1961(1). But even assuming that the more inclusive definition of enterprise will have the effect suggested, the language of the statute and its legislative history indicate that Congress was well aware that it was entering a new domain of federal involvement through the enactment of this measure. Indeed, the very purpose of the Organized Crime Control Act of 1970 was to enable the Federal Government to address a large and seemingly neglected problem. The view was that existing law, state and federal, was not adequate to address the problem, which was of national dimensions. That Congress included within the definition of racketeering activities a number of state crimes strongly indicates that RICO criminalized conduct that was also criminal under state law, at least when the requisite elements of a RICO offense are present. As the hearings and legislative debates reveal, Congress was well aware of the fear that RICO would "move large substantive areas formerly totally within the police power of the State into the Federal realm." 116 Cong.Rec. 35217 (remarks of Rep. Eckhardt). See also id., at 35205 (remarks of Rep. Mikva); id., at 35213 (comments of the American Civil Liberties Union); Hearings on Organized Crime Control before Subcommittee No. 5 of the House Committee on the Judiciary, 91st Cong., 2d Sess., 329, 370 (statement of Sheldon H. Eisen on behalf of the Association of the Bar of the City of New York). In the face of these objections, Congress nonetheless proceeded to enact the measure, knowing that it

interest, direct or indirect, in any enterprise; imposing reasonable restrictions on the future activities or investments of any person, including, but not limited to, prohibiting any person from engaging in the same type of endeavor as the enterprise engaged in, the activities of which affect interstate or foreign commerce; or ordering dissolution or reorganization of any enterprise, making due provision for the rights of innocent persons.

. . .

(c) "Any person injured in his business or property by reason of a violation of section 1962 of this chapter may sue therefore in any appropriate United States district court and shall recover threefold the damages he sustains and the cost of the suit, including a reasonable attorney's fee."

would alter somewhat the role of the Federal Government in the war against organized crime and that the alteration would entail prosecutions involving acts of racketeering that are also crimes under state law. There is no argument that Congress acted beyond its power in so doing. That being the case, the courts are without authority to restrict the application of the statute.

Contrary to the judgment below, neither the language nor structure of RICO limits its application to legitimate "enterprises." Applying it also to criminal organizations does not render any portion of the statute superfluous nor does it create any structural incongruities within the framework of the Act. The result is neither absurd nor surprising. On the contrary, insulating the wholly criminal enterprise from prosecution under RICO is the more incongruous position.

Section 904(a) of RICO, 84 Stat. 947, directs that "the provisions of this Title shall be liberally construed to effectuate its remedial purposes." With or without this admonition, we could not agree with the Court of Appeals that legitimate enterprises should be excluded from coverage. We are also quite sure that nothing in the legislative history of RICO requires a contrary conclusion.

III

The statement of findings that prefaces the Organized Crime Control Act of 1970 reveals the pervasiveness of the problem that Congress was addressing by this enactment:

"The Congress finds that (1) organized crime in the United States is a highly sophisticated, diversified, and widespread activity that annually drains billions of dollars from America's economy by unlawful conduct and the illegal use of force, fraud, and corruption; (2) organized crime derives a major portion of its power through money obtained from such illegal endeavors as syndicated gambling, loan sharking, the theft and fencing of property, the importation and distribution of narcotics and other dangerous drugs, and other forms of social exploitation; (3) this money and power are increasingly used to infiltrate and corrupt legitimate business and labor unions and to subvert and corrupt our democratic processes; (4) organized crime activities in the United States weaken the stability of the Nation's economic system, harm innocent investors and competing organizations, interfere with free competition, seriously burden interstate and foreign commerce, threaten the domestic security, and undermine the general welfare of the Nation and its citizens; and (5) organized crime continues to grow because of defects in the evidence-gathering process of the law inhibiting the development of the legally admissible evidence necessary to bring criminal and other sanctions or remedies to bear on the unlawful activities of those engaged in organized crime and because the sanctions and remedies available to the Government are unnecessarily limited in scope and impact."

In light of the above findings, it was the declared purpose of Congress, "to seek the eradication of organized crime in the United States by strengthening the legal tools in the evidence-gathering process, by establishing new penal prohibitions, and by providing enhanced sanctions and new remedies to deal with the unlawful activities of those engaged in organized crime." [3] The various titles of the Act provide the tools through which this goal is to be accomplished. Only three of those titles create substantive offenses, Title VIII, which is directed at illegal gambling operations, Title IX, at issue here, and Title XI, which addresses the importation, distribution and storage of explosive materials. The other titles provide various procedural and remedial devices to aid in the prosecution and incarceration of persons involved in organized crime.

Considering this statement of the Act's broad purposes, the construction of RICO suggested by respondent and the court below is unacceptable. Whole areas of organized criminal activity would be placed beyond the substantive reach of the enactment. For example, associations of persons engaged solely in "loan sharking, the theft and fencing of property, the importation and distribution of narcotics and other dangerous drugs," would be immune from prosecution under RICO so long as the association did not deviate from the criminal path. Yet these are among the very crimes that Congress specifically found to be typical of the crimes committed by persons involved in organized crime, and as a major source of revenue and power for such organizations.

This is not to gainsay that the legislative history forcefully supports the view that the major purpose of Title IX is to address the infiltration of legitimate business by organized crime. The point is made time and again during the debates and in the hearings before the House and Senate. But none of these statements requires the negative inference that Title IX did not reach the activities of enterprises organized and existing for criminal purposes.

On the contrary, these statements are in full accord with the proposition that RICO is equally applicable to a criminal enterprise that has no legitimate dimension or has yet to acquire one. Accepting that the primary purpose of RICO is to cope with the infiltration of legitimate businesses, applying the statute in accordance with its terms, so as to reach criminal enterprises, would seek to deal with the problem at its very source. Supporters of the bill recognized that organized crime uses its primary sources of revenue and power—illegal gambling,

---

3. See also 116 Cong.Rec. 602 (1970) (remarks of Sen. Yarborough) ("a full scale attack on organized crime"); id., at 819 (remarks of Sen. Scott) ("purpose is to eradicate organized crime in the United States"); id., at 35199 (remarks of Rep. Rodino) ("a truly full-scale commitment to destroy the insidious power of organized crime groups"); id., at 35300 (remarks of Rep. Mayne) (organized crime "must be sternly and irrevocably eradicated").

loan-sharking and illicit drug distribution—as a springboard into the sphere of legitimate enterprise. * * *

As a measure to deal with the infiltration of legitimate businesses by organized crime, RICO was both preventive and remedial. Respondent's view would ignore the preventive function of the statute. If Congress had intended the more circumscribed approach espoused by the Court of Appeals, there would have been some positive sign that the law was not to reach organized criminal activities that give rise to the concerns about infiltration. The language of the statute, however,—the most reliable evidence of its intent—reveals that Congress opted for a far broader definition of the word "enterprise," and we are unconvinced by anything in the legislative history that this definition should be given less than its full effect.

The judgment of the Court of Appeals is accordingly

Reversed.

JUSTICE STEWART agrees with the reasoning and conclusion of the Court of Appeals as to the meaning of the term "enterprise" in this statute. See United States v. Turkette, 1 Cir., 632 F.2d 896. Accordingly, he respectfully dissents.

NOTES

1. The Racketeer Influenced And Corrupt Organizations (RICO) Act (18 U.S.C.A. § 1961 et seq.) provides, in part:

§ 1962. Prohibited activities

(a) It shall be unlawful for any person who has received any income derived, directly or indirectly, from a pattern of racketeering activity or through collection of an unlawful debt in which such person has participated as a principal within the meaning of section 2, title 18, United States Code, to use or invest, directly or indirectly, any part of such income, or the proceeds of such income, in acquisition of any interest in, or the establishment or operation of, any enterprise which is engaged in, or the activities of which affect, interstate or foreign commerce. A purchase of securities on the open market for purposes of investment, and without the intention of controlling or participating in the control of the issuer, or of assisting another to do so, shall not be unlawful under this subsection if the securities of the issuer held by the purchaser, the members of his immediate family, and his or their accomplices in any pattern of racketeering activity or the collection of an unlawful debt after such purchase do not amount in the aggregate to one percent of the outstanding securities of any one class, and do not confer, either in law or in fact, the power to elect one or more directors of the issuer.

(b) It shall be unlawful for any person through a pattern of racketeering activity or through collection of an unlawful debt to acquire or maintain, directly or indirectly, any interest in or control of any enterprise which is engaged in, or the activities of which affect, interstate or foreign commerce.

(c) It shall be unlawful for any person employed by or associated with any enterprise engaged in, or the activities of which affect, interstate or foreign commerce, to conduct or participate, directly or indirectly, in the conduct of such enterprise's affairs through a pattern of racketeering activity or collection of unlawful debt.

(d) It shall be unlawful for any person to conspire to violate any of the provisions of subsections (a), (b), or (c) of this section.

§ 1963. Criminal penalties

(a) Whoever violates any provision of section 1962 of this chapter shall be fined not more than $25,000 or imprisoned not more than twenty years, or both, and shall forfeit to the United States, irrespective of any provision of State law—

(1) any interest the person has acquired or maintained in violation of section 1962;

(2) any—

(A) interest in;

(B) security of;

(C) claim against; or

(D) property or contractual right of any kind affording a source of influence over;

any enterprise which the person has established, operated, controlled, conducted, or participated in the conduct of in violation of section 1962; and

(3) any property constituting, or derived from, any proceeds which the person obtained, directly or indirectly, from racketeering activity or unlawful debt collection in violation of section 1962.

The court, in imposing sentence on such person shall order, in addition to any other sentence imposed pursuant to this section, that the person forfeit to the United States all property described in this subsection. In lieu of a fine otherwise authorized by this section, a defendant who derives profits or other proceeds from an offense may be fined not more than twice the gross profits or other proceeds.

(b) Property subject to criminal forfeiture under this section includes—

(1) real property, including things growing on, affixed to, and found in land; and

(2) tangible and intangible personal property, including rights, privileges, interests, claims and securities.

(c) All right, title, and interest in property described in subsection (a) vests in the United States upon the commission of the act giving rise to forfeiture under this section. Any such property that is subsequently transferred to a person other than the defendant may be the subject of a special verdict of forfeiture and thereafter shall be ordered forfeited to the United States, unless the transferee establishes in a hearing pursuant to subsection (m) that he is a bona fide purchaser for value of such property who at the time of purchase was reasonably without cause to believe that the property was subject to forfeiture under this section.

* * *

§ 1964. Civil remedies

(a) The district courts of the United States shall have jurisdiction to prevent and restrain violations of section 1962 of this chapter by issuing appropriate orders, including, but not limited to: ordering any person to divest himself of any interest, direct or indirect, in any enterprise; imposing reasonable restrictions on the future activities or investments of any person, including, but not limited to, prohibiting any person from engaging in the same type of endeavor as the enterprise engaged in, the activities of which affect interstate or foreign commerce; or ordering dissolution or reorganization of any enterprise, making due provision for the rights of innocent persons.

(b) The Attorney General may institute proceedings under this section. Pending final determination thereof, the court may at any time enter such restraining orders or prohibitions, or take such other actions, including the acceptance of satisfactory performance bonds, as it shall deem proper.

(c) Any person injured in his business or property by reason of a violation of section 1962 of this chapter may sue therefor in any appropriate United States district court and shall recover threefold the damages he sustains and the cost of the suit, including a reasonable attorney's fee.

(d) A final judgment or decree rendered in favor of the United States in any criminal proceeding brought by the United States under this chapter shall estop the defendant from denying the essential allegations of the criminal offense in any subsequent civil proceeding brought by the United States.

2. In § 1962 of the RICO statute, the act refers, in subsections (a), (b), and (c) to "a pattern of racketeering activity." While the act does explain what racketeering activity consists of, it is less clear on how many acts must be proved in order for a "pattern" to exist. In § 1961(5) it states that a "pattern" requires at least two acts of racketeering activity, one of which occurred after the effective date of the law and the last of which occurred within ten years of the commission of a prior act of prohibited activity. Does this mean that proof of two acts within a ten-year period is sufficient for conviction?

In H.J. Inc. v. Northwestern Bell Telephone Co., 492 U.S. 229, 109 S.Ct. 2893, 106 L.Ed.2d 195 (1989), Justice Brennan wrote that a "pattern" means more than just two predicate acts, it also requires "continuity plus relationship." He stated that to "prove a pattern of racketeering activity a plaintiff or prosecutor must show that the racketeering predicates are related, *and* that they amount to or pose a threat of continued criminal activity." A law review note termed this case "Another Contribution To RICO Confusion." See, 50 La.L.Rev. 1219 (1990). See also the RICO Symposium, containing four leading articles, in 35 Villanova L.Rev. [Number 5] (1990).

3. Can RICO be applied to international terrorism, such as acts of the hijackers of the *Achille Lauro* cruise ship in the Mediterranean, or the intentional causing of massive oil spills in the Arabian Gulf or the willful destruction of the oil fields in Kuwait by Iraq's Saddam Hussein? Arguing that

RICO is "a potentially powerful weapon available to the federal government in the war on terrorism," see the Comment at 58 Fordham L.Rev. 1071 (1990).

3. THE AGREEMENT

UNITED STATES v. DEGE

Supreme Court of the United States, 1960.
364 U.S. 51, 80 S.Ct. 1589.

MR. JUSTICE FRANKFURTER delivered the opinion of the Court.

This is an indictment charging husband and wife with conspiring to commit an offense against the United States . . . in that they sought illicitly to bring goods into the United States with intent to defraud it. On authority of controlling decisions of its Circuit, . . . the District Court dismissed the indictment on the ground that it did not state an offense, to wit, a husband and wife are legally incapable of conspiring. . . . The construction . . . by the Court of Appeals for the Ninth Circuit has been explicitly rejected by the Court of Appeals for the District of Columbia Circuit . . . and by the Court of Appeals for the Fifth Circuit, . . .

The question raised by these conflicting views is clear-cut and uncomplicated. The claim that husband and wife are outside the scope of an enactment of Congress in 1948, making it an offense for two persons to conspire, must be given short shrift once we heed the admonition of this Court that "we free our minds from the notion that criminal statutes must be construed by some artificial and conventional rule," . . ., and therefore do not allow ourselves to be obfuscated by medieval views regarding the legal status of woman and the common law's reflection of them. Considering that legitimate business enterprises between husband and wife have long been commonplace in our time, it would enthrone an unreality into a rule of law to suggest that man and wife are legally incapable of engaging in illicit enterprises and therefore, forsooth, do not engage in them.

None of the considerations of policy touching the law's encouragement or discouragement of domestic felicities on the basis of which this Court determined appropriate rules for testimonial compulsion as between spouses . . . are relevant to yielding to the claim that an unqualified interdiction by Congress against a conspiracy between two persons precludes a husband and wife from being two persons. Such an immunity to husband and wife as a pair of conspirators would have to attribute to Congress one of two assumptions: either that responsibility of husband and wife for joint participation in a criminal enterprise would make for marital disharmony, or that a wife must be presumed to act under the coercive influence of her husband and, therefore, cannot be a willing participant. The former assumption is unnourished by sense; the latter implies a view of American womanhood offensive to the ethos of our society.

The fact of the matter is that we are asked to write into law a doctrine that parrot-like has been repeated in decisions and texts from what was given its authoritative expression by Hawkins early in the eighteenth century. He wrote:

> "It plainly appears from the Words of the Statute, That one Person alone cannot be guilty of Conspiracy within the Purport of it; from whence it follows, * * * That no such Prosecution is maintainable against a Husband and Wife only, because they are esteemed but as one Person in Law, and are presumed to have but one Will." . . .

The pronouncement of Hawkins apparently rests on a case in a Year Book of 38 Edward III, decided in 1365. The learning invoked for this ancient doctrine has been questioned by modern scholarship. . . . But in any event the answer to Hawkins with his Year Book authority, as a basis for a decision by the Supreme Court of the United States in 1960 construing a statute enacted in 1948, was definitively made long ago by Mr. Justice Holmes:

> "It is revolting to have no better reason for a rule of law than that so it was laid down in the time of Henry IV. It is still more revolting if the grounds upon which it was laid down have vanished long since, and the rule simply persists from blind imitation of the past."

For this Court now to act on Hawkins's formulation of the medieval view that husband and wife "are esteemed but as one Person in Law, and are presumed to have but one Will" would indeed be "blind imitation of the past." It would require us to disregard the vast changes in the status of woman—the extension of her rights and correlative duties—whereby a wife's legal submission to her husband has been wholly wiped out, not only in the English-speaking world generally but emphatically so in this country. . . .

. . . Suffice it to say that we cannot infuse into the conspiracy statute a fictitious attribution to Congress of regard for the medieval notion of woman's submissiveness to the benevolent coercive powers of a husband in order to relieve her of her obligation of obedience to an unqualifiedly expressed Act of Congress by regarding her as a person whose legal personality is merged in that of her husband making the two one.

Reversed.

Mr. Chief Justice Warren, with whom Mr. Justice Black and Mr. Justice Whittaker join, dissenting.

If the Court's opinion reflects all that there is to this case, it is astonishing that it has taken so many years for the federal judiciary to loose itself from the medieval chains of the husband-wife conspiracy doctrine. The problem, as the Court sees it, is almost absurdly uncomplicated: The basis for the notion that husband and wife are not subject to a conspiracy charge is that man and wife are one; but we know that man and wife are two, not one; therefore, there is no basis for the notion that husband and wife are not subject to a conspiracy charge. I submit that this simplistic an approach will not do.

The Court apparently does not assert that if the husband-wife conspiracy doctrine was widely accepted when the conspiracy statute was passed in 1867, 14 Stat. 484, and therefore was presumably within Congress' understanding of the reach of that statute, nonetheless this Court should now reject the rule because it finds it nonsensical. Instead the Court's position is that

"It would be an idle parade of learning to document the statement that these common-law disabilities [of women] were extensively swept away in our different state of society, both by legislation and adjudication, long before the originating conspiracy Act of 1867 was passed."

But, however rapidly nineteenth century jurisprudence moved toward a recognition of the individuality of women in other areas, it is wholly inaccurate to imply that the law of conspiracy changed apace. In fact, the earliest case repudiating the husband-wife doctrine which the Government has been able to cite is Dalton v. People, 68 Colo. 44, 189 P. 37, which was decided, as the Government puts it, "[a]s early as 1920." And if the doctrine is an anachronism today, as the Court says, its unusual hardiness is demonstrated by the fact that the decision of the Court represents a departure from the general rule which prevails today in the English-speaking world. As recently as 1957, the Privy Council approved the husband-wife doctrine, and other Commonwealth courts are in accord. . . .

Thus it seems clear that if the 1867 statute is to be construed to reflect Congress' intent as it was in 1867, the Court's decision is erroneous. And I believe that we must focus upon that intent, inasmuch as there is no indication that Congress meant to change the law by the 1948 legislation which re-enacted without material variation the old conspiracy statute. Surely when a rule of law is well established in the common law and is part of the legislative purpose when a relevant statute is passed, that rule should not be rejected by this Court in the absence of an explicit subsequent repudiation of it by Congress. Consequently, I would be compelled to dissent whether or not I believed the rule to be supported by reason.

But more, I cannot agree that the rule is without justification. Inasmuch as Mr. Justice Holmes' observation that it is "revolting" to follow a doctrine only "from blind imitation of the past" is hardly novel, the tenacious adherence of the judiciary to the husband-wife conspiracy doctrine indicates to me that the rule may be predicated upon underlying policies unconnected with problems of women's suffrage or capacity to sue. The "definitive answer" to the question posed by this case is not to be found in a breezy aphorism from the collected papers of Mr. Justice Holmes, for "[g]eneral propositions do not decide concrete cases."

It is not necessary to be wedded to fictions to approve the husband-wife conspiracy doctrine, for one of the dangers which that doctrine averts is the prosecution and conviction of persons for "conspiracies" which Congress never meant to be included within the statute. A wife, simply by virtue of the intimate life she shares with her husband, might easily perform acts that would technically be sufficient to involve her in a criminal conspiracy with him, but which might be far removed from the arm's-length agreement typical of that crime. It is not a medieval mental quirk or an attitude "unnourished by sense" to believe that husbands and wives should not be subjected to such a risk, or that such a possibility should not be permitted to endanger the confidentiality of the marriage relationship. While it is easy enough to ridicule Hawkins' pronouncement in Pleas of the Crown from a metaphysical point of view, the concept of the "oneness" of a married couple may reflect an abiding belief that the communion between husband and wife is such that their actions are not always to be regarded by the criminal law as if there were no marriage.

By making inroads in the name of law enforcement into the protection which Congress has afforded to the marriage relationship, the Court today continues in the path charted by the recent decision in Wyatt v. United States, 362 U.S. 525, 80 S.Ct. 901, where the Court held that, under the circumstances of that case, a wife could be compelled to testify against her husband over her objection. One need not waver in his belief in virile law enforcement to insist that there are other things in American life which are also of great importance, and to which even law enforcement must accommodate itself. One of these is the solidarity and the confidential relationship of marriage. The Court's opinion dogmatically asserts that the husband-wife conspiracy doctrine does not in fact protect this relationship, and that hence the doctrine "en-throne[s] an unreality into a rule of law." I am not easily persuaded that a rule accepted by so many people for so many centuries can be so lightly dismissed. But in any event, I submit that the power to depose belongs to Congress, not to this Court. I dissent.

PEOPLE v. FOSTER

Supreme Court of Illinois, 1983.
99 Ill.2d 48, 75 Ill.Dec. 411, 457 N.E.2d 405.

UNDERWOOD, JUSTICE:

Following a jury trial in the circuit court of McLean County the defendant, James Foster, was convicted of conspiracy to commit robbery, and sentenced to an extended term of six years' imprisonment. Based upon its interpretation of the Illinois conspiracy statute the appellate court reversed . . .. We granted the State's petition for leave to appeal.

On September 28, 1981, defendant initiated his plan to commit a robbery when he approached John Ragsdale in a Rantoul bar and asked Ragsdale if he was "interested in making some money." Defendant told Ragsdale of an elderly man, A.O. Hedrick, who kept many valuables in his possession. Although Ragsdale stated that he was interested in making money he did not believe defendant was serious until defendant returned to the bar the next day and discussed in detail his plan to rob Hedrick. In an effort to gather additional information, Ragsdale decided to feign agreement to defendant's plan but did not contact the police.

On October 1, defendant went to Ragsdale's residence to find out if Ragsdale was "ready to go." Since Ragsdale had not yet contacted the police he told defendant that he would not be ready until he found someone else to help them. Ragsdale informed the police of the planned robbery on October 3. Defendant and Ragsdale were met at Hedrick's residence the following day and arrested.

The appellate court determined that the conspiracy statute (Ill.Rev.Stat.1981, ch. 38, par. 8–2) required actual agreement between at least two persons to support a conspiracy conviction. Reasoning that Ragsdale never intended to agree to defendant's plan but merely feigned agreement, the court reversed defendant's conviction.

On appeal to this court the State argues that under the conspiracy statute it suffices if only one of the participants to the alleged conspiracy actually intends to agree to commit an offense. Alternatively, the State contends that there was sufficient evidence to convict defendant even under the appellate court's interpretation of the statute.

The question is whether the Illinois legislature, in amending the conspiracy statute in 1961, intended to adopt the unilateral theory of conspiracy. To support a conspiracy conviction under the unilateral theory only one of the alleged conspirators need intend to agree to the commission of an offense. (See Burgman, Unilateral Conspiracy: Three Critical Perspectives, 29 DePaul L.Rev. 75 (1979).) Prior to the 1961 amendment the statute clearly encompassed the traditional, bilateral theory, requiring the actual agreement of at least two participants. The relevant portion of the former statute is as follows:

> "If any *two or more persons* conspire or *agree together* . . . to do any illegal act . . . they shall be deemed guilty of a conspiracy." (Emphasis added.) (Ill.Rev.Stat.1961, ch. 38, par. 139.)

The amended version of the statute provides:

> "*A person* commits conspiracy when, with intent that an offense be committed, *he agrees* with another to the commission of that offense." (Emphasis added.) Ill.Rev.Stat.1981, ch. 38, par. 8–2(a).

Since the statute is presently worded in terms of "a person" rather than "two or more persons" it is urged by the State that only one person need intend to agree to the commission of an offense. In support of its position the State compares the Illinois statute with the Model Penal Code conspiracy provision and the commentary thereto.

The Model Penal Code provision is similar to section 8–2(a) in that it is also worded in terms of "a person":

> "*A person* is guilty of conspiracy with another person or persons to commit a crime if with the purpose of promoting or facilitating its commission *he:*
>
> (a) *agrees* with such other person or persons that they or one or more of them will engage in conduct which constitutes such crime or an attempt or solicitation to commit such crime . . . ." (Emphasis added.) Model Penal Code sec. 5.03 (Tent.Draft No. 10, 1960).

The commentary following section 5.03 expressly indicates the drafters' intent to adopt the unilateral theory of conspiracy. More importantly, the comments specify the drafters' reason for abandoning the traditional language "two or more persons":

> "The definition of the Draft departs from the traditional view of conspiracy as an entirely bilateral or multilateral relationship, the view inherent in the standard formulation cast in terms of 'two or more persons' . . . ."

There is no question that the drafters of section 8–2(a) were aware of this provision since several references were made to the Model Penal Code in the committee comments to section 8–2. Consequently, the State reasons that the drafters would not have deleted the words "two or more persons" if they had intended to retain the bilateral theory. Similar reasoning was employed in State v. Marian (1980), 62 Ohio St.2d 250, 405 N.E.2d 267, and State v. St. Christopher (1975), 305 Minn. 226, 232 N.W.2d 798, where the courts were asked to interpret statutory provisions analogous to section 8–2(a). In each of those decisions it was determined that deletion of the words "two or more persons" from the State's conspiracy statute reflected a legislative intent to abandon the bilateral theory. The Ohio court, however, also relied to a considerable degree upon the absence from Ohio criminal law of a statute making solicitation to commit a crime an offense. Illinois does have such a statute.

While impressed with the logic of the State's interpretation of section 8–2(a), we are troubled by the committee's failure to explain the reason for deleting the words "two or more persons" from the statute. The committee comments to section 8–2 detail the several changes in the law of conspiracy that were intended by the 1961 amendment. The comments simply do not address the unilateral/bilateral issue. The State suggests that the new language was so clear on its face that it did not warrant additional discussion. We doubt, however, that the drafters could have intended what represents a rather profound change in the law of conspiracy without mentioning it in the comments to section 8–2. Nor do we regard the reasoning of the Indiana Supreme Court in Garcia v. State (1979), 271 Ind. 510, 394 N.E.2d 106, cited by the State, as applicable here. Moreover, the precedential value of the Indiana, Ohio and Minnesota decisions is diminished when compared to other foreign decisions which, despite statutes which speak in terms of "a person," require actual agreement between at least two persons to support a conspiracy conviction.

As earlier noted, Illinois does have a solicitation statute which embraces virtually every situation in which one could be convicted of conspiracy under the unilateral theory. Moreover, the penalties for solicitation and conspiracy are substantially similar. There would appear to have been little need for the legislature to adopt the unilateral theory of conspiracy in light of the existence of the solicitation statute. Even though the Model Penal Code also contains a separate solicitation offense (Model Penal Code sec. 5.02 (Tent.Draft No. 10, 1960)) and still provides for the unilateral theory, its commentary makes explicit its intent to do so. The absence of similar comments upon our statute seems difficult to explain if the intent was the same.

We cannot agree with the State's argument that section 8–2(b) of the statute supports a unilateral interpretation of section 8–2(a). Section 8–2(b) provides:

> "It shall not be a defense to conspiracy that the person or persons with whom the accused is alleged to have conspired:

> *   *   *   *   *   *   *   *   *

> (4) Has been acquitted, or

> (5) Lacked the capacity to commit an offense."

The State argues that subsections (4) and (5) focus on the culpability of only one of the conspirators and are therefore consistent with a legislative intent to adopt the unilateral theory. However, the committee comments clearly indicate that the limited purpose of those subsections is to avoid the recurrent problems inherent in conducting separate trials:

> "Previously, acquittal of all other conspirators absolved the remaining one, since, theoretically, there must be at least two guilty parties to a conspiracy. [Citation.] However, this rationale was rejected as being too technical and overlooking the realities of trials which involve differences in juries, contingent availability of witnesses, the varying ability of different prosecutors and defense attorneys, etc."

Additionally, if the drafters had intended to adopt the unilateral theory in section 8–2(a), it would have been unnecessary to include section 8–2(b) in the statute, since the provisions of section 8–2(b) are encompassed by the unilateral theory.

It is also not without significance that two appellate court panels have construed section 8–2(a) as encompassing the bilateral theory of conspiracy (People v. Hill (1982), 108 Ill.App.3d 716, 64 Ill.Dec. 298, 439 N.E.2d 549, and People v. Ambrose (1975), 28 Ill.App.3d 627, 329 N.E.2d 11) since its amendment in 1961. While it is true that a legislature's failure to amend a statute after judicial interpretation is not conclusive evidence of the correctness of that interpretation, such inaction is suggestive of legislative agreement. We agree with defendant that, here, the legislature's failure to act after the decisions in *Ambrose* and *Hill* lends considerable support to the conclusion that a bilateral theory of conspiracy was intended, particularly since *Ambrose* was a 1975 decision. We are also mindful of the rule of construction in Illinois which requires us to resolve statutory ambiguities in favor of criminal defendants.

For the above reasons we conclude that section 8–2(a) encompasses the bilateral theory of conspiracy.

Our conclusion requires consideration of the State's argument that there was sufficient evidence to convict defendant even under the bilateral theory of conspiracy. We find no basis for this assertion and agree with the appellate court that at best the jury could have found beyond a reasonable doubt only that Ragsdale considered defendant's offer before going to the police.

The judgment of the appellate court is therefore affirmed.

Judgment affirmed.

NOTE

For an argument in favor of the unilateral view, see People v. Lanni, 95 Misc.2d 4, 406 N.Y.S.2d 1011 (1978). The court said, in part:

If the ultimate goal is essentially crime prevention, then should not the danger to society be measured by the individual criminal disposition, rather than by reference to the effect or result such would-be criminal may have after others are recruited by or voluntarily join him in a criminal combine? Additionally, the perceived danger is that, if the efforts of the criminally intentioned to conspire with others are not aborted and the conspirator is not isolated, the guilty will continue to find solace in the law's inability to appropriately deal with him. There is sure logic in the view that the law should "focus inquiry on the culpability of the actor whose liability is in issue, rather than the group of which he is alleged to be a part." (Wechsler, Jones and Korn, Treatment of Inchoate Crimes in the Model Penal Code of the American Law Institute: Attempt, Solicitation, and Conspiracy, 61 Col.L.Rev. 957, 963.)

Experience has demonstrated that when conviction of any one defendant in conspiracy prosecutions requires a mutual agreement and a common intent by two or more, societal goals of crime prevention have been and would continue to be frustrated in many cases. Logic and experience dictate a new approach . . .

(a) "Necessary Parties" and the Wharton Rule

GEBARDI v. UNITED STATES

Supreme Court of the United States, 1932.
287 U.S. 112, 53 S.Ct. 35.

Mr. Justice Stone delivered the opinion of the Court.

. . . Petitioners, a man and a woman, not then husband and wife, were indicted in the District Court for Northern Illinois, for conspiring together, and with others not named, to transport the woman from one state to another for the purpose of engaging in sexual intercourse with the man. At the trial without a jury there was evidence from which the court could have found that the petitioners had engaged in illicit sexual relations in the course of each of the journeys alleged; that the man purchased the railway tickets for both petitioners for at least one journey; and that in each instance the woman, in advance of the purchase of the tickets, consented to go on the journey and did go on it voluntarily for the specified immoral purpose. There was no evidence supporting the allegation that any other person had conspired. The trial court . . . gave judgment of conviction, which the Court of Appeals for the Seventh Circuit affirmed, on the authority of United States v. Holte, 236 U.S. 140, 35 S.Ct. 271.

The only question which we need consider here is whether, within the principles announced in that case, the evidence was sufficient to support the conviction. There the defendants, a man and a woman, were indicted for conspiring together that the man should transport the woman from one state to another for purposes of prostitution. In holding the indictment sufficient, the court said: "As the defendant is the woman, the district court sustained a demurrer on the ground that although the offense could not be committed without her, she was no party to it, but only the victim. The single question is whether that ruling is right. We do not have to consider what would be necessary to constitute the substantive crime under the act of 1910 [the Mann Act], or what evidence would be required to convict a woman under an indictment like this; but only to decide whether it is impossible for the transported woman to be guilty of a crime in conspiring as alleged." The court assumed that there might be a degree of co-operation which would fall short of the commission of any crime, as in the case of the purchaser of liquor illegally sold. But it declined to hold that a woman could not under some circumstances not precisely defined, be guilty of a violation of the Mann Act and of a conspiracy to violate it as well. Light is thrown upon the intended scope of this conclusion by the supposititious case which the court put: "Suppose, for instance, that a professional prostitute, as well able to look out for herself as was the man, should suggest and carry out a journey within the act of 1910 in the hope of blackmailing the man, and should buy the railroad tickets, or should pay the fare from Jersey City to New York,—she would be within the letter of the act of 1910 and we see no reason why the act should not be held to apply. We see equally little reason for not treating the preliminary agreement as a conspiracy that the law can reach, if we abandon the illusion that the woman always is the victim."

In the present case we must apply the law to the evidence; the very inquiry which was said to be unnecessary to decision in United States v. Holte, supra.

First. Those exceptional circumstances envisaged in United States v. Holte, supra, as possible instances in which the woman might violate the act itself, are clearly not present here. There is no evidence that she purchased the railroad tickets or that hers was the active or moving spirit in conceiving or carrying out the transportation. The proof shows no more than that she went willingly upon the journeys for the purposes alleged.

Section 2 of the Mann Act (18 U.S.C. § 398 [18 USCA § 398]), violation of which is charged by the indictment here as the object of the conspiracy, imposes the penalty upon "any person who shall knowingly transport or cause to be transported, or aid or assist in obtaining transportation for, or in transporting, in interstate or foreign commerce * * * any woman or girl for the purpose of prostitution or debauchery, or for any other immoral purpose. * * *" Transportation of a woman or girl whether with or without her consent, or causing or aiding it, or furthering it in any of the specified ways, are the acts punished, when done with a purpose which is immoral within the meaning of the law.

The act does not punish the woman for transporting herself; it contemplates two persons—one to transport and the woman or girl to be transported. For the woman to fall within the ban of the statute she must, at the least, "aid or assist" some one else in transporting or in procuring transportation for herself. But such aid and assistance must, as in the case supposed in United States v. Holte, supra, be more active than mere agreement on her part to the transportation and its immoral purpose. For the statute is drawn to include those cases in which the woman consents to her own transportation. Yet it does not specifically impose any penalty upon her, although it deals in detail with the person by whom she is transported. In applying this criminal statute we cannot infer that the mere acquiescence of the woman transported was intended to be condemned by the general language punishing those who aid and assist the transporter, any more than it has been inferred that the purchaser of liquor was to be regarded as an abettor of the illegal sale. The penalties of the statute are too clearly directed against the acts of the transporter as distinguished from the consent of the subject of the transportation. So it was intimated in United States v. Holte, supra, and this conclusion is not disputed by the government here, which contends only that the conspiracy charge will lie though the woman could not commit the substantive offense.

Second. We come thus to the main question in the case, whether, admitting that the woman by consenting, has not violated the Mann Act, she may be convicted of a conspiracy with the man to violate it. Section 37 of the Criminal Code (18 U.S.C. § 88 [18 USCA § 88]), punishes a conspiracy by two or more persons "to commit any offense against the United States." The offense which she is charged with conspiring to commit is that perpetrated by the man, for it is not questioned that in transporting her he contravened section 2 of the Mann Act. Hence we must decide whether her concurrence, which was not criminal before the Mann Act, nor punished by it, may, without more, support a conviction under the conspiracy section, enacted many years before.

As was said in the Holte Case an agreement to commit an offense may be criminal, though its purpose is to do what some of the conspirators may be free to do alone. Incapacity of one to commit the substantive offense does not necessarily imply that he may with impunity conspire with others who are able to commit it. For it is the collective planning of criminal conduct at which the statute aims. The plan is itself a wrong which, if any act be done to effect its object, the state has elected to treat as criminal. And one may plan that others shall do what he cannot do himself.

But in this case we are concerned with something more than an agreement between two persons for one of them to commit an offense which the other cannot commit. There is the added element that the offense planned, the criminal object of the conspiracy, involves the agreement of the woman to her transportation by the man, which is the very conspiracy charged.

Congress set out in the Mann Act to deal with cases which frequently, if not normally, involve consent and agreement on the part of the woman to the forbidden transportation. In every case in which she is not intimidated or forced into the transportation, the statute necessarily contemplates her acquiescence. Yet this acquiescence, though an incident of a type of transportation specifically dealt with by the statute, was not made a crime under the Mann Act itself. Of this class of cases we say that the substantive offense contemplated by the statute itself involves the same combination or community of purpose of two persons only which is prosecuted here as conspiracy. If this were the only case covered by the act, it would be within those decisions which hold, consistently with the theory upon which conspiracies are punished, that where it is impossible under any circumstances to commit the substantive offense without co-operative action, the preliminary agreement between the same parties to commit the offense is not an indictable conspiracy either at common law, or under the federal statute.* But criminal transportation under the Mann Act may be

---

* The rule was applied in United States v. New York Cent. & H. R. R. Co. (C.C.) 146 F. 298; United States v. Sager (C.C.A.) 49 F.(2d) 725. In the following cases it was recognized and held inapplicable for the reason that the substantive crime could be committed by a single individual: Chadwick v. United States (C.C.A.) 141 F. 225;

effected without the woman's consent as in cases of intimidation or force (with which we are not now concerned). We assume, therefore for present purposes, as was suggested in the Holte Case, supra, that the decisions last mentioned do not in all strictness apply. We do not rest our decision upon the theory of those cases, nor upon the related one that the attempt is to prosecute as conspiracy acts identical with the substantive offense. We place it rather upon the ground that we perceive in the failure of the Mann Act to condemn the woman's participation in those transportations which are effected with her mere consent, evidence of an affirmative legislative policy to leave her acquiescence unpunished. We think it a necessary implication of that policy that when the Mann Act and the conspiracy statute came to be construed together, as they necessarily would be, the same participation which the former contemplates as an inseparable incident of all cases in which the woman is a voluntary agent at all, but does not punish, was not automatically to be made punishable under the latter. It would contravene that policy to hold that the very passage of the Mann Act effected a withdrawal by the conspiracy statute of that immunity which the Mann Act itself confers.

It is not to be supposed that the consent of an unmarried person to adultery with a married person, where the latter alone is guilty of the substantive offense, would render the former an abettor or a conspirator, or that the acquiescence of a woman under the age of consent would make her a co-conspirator with the man to commit statutory rape upon herself. The principle, determinative of this case, is the same.

On the evidence before us the woman petitioner has not violated the Mann Act and, we hold, is not guilty of a conspiracy to do so. As there is no proof that the man conspired with anyone else to bring about the transportation, the convictions of both petitioners must be

Reversed.

MR. JUSTICE CARDOZO concurs in the result.

IANNELLI v. UNITED STATES

Supreme Court of the United States, 1975.
420 U.S. 770, 95 S.Ct. 1284.

MR. JUSTICE POWELL delivered the opinion of the Court.

This case requires the Court to consider Wharton's Rule, a doctrine of criminal law enunciating an exception to the general principle that a

Laughter v. United States (C.C.A.) 259 F. 94; Lisansky v. United States (C.C.A.) 31 F.(2d) 846, 67 A.L.R. 67, certiorari denied 279 U.S. 873, 49 S.Ct. 514, 74 L.Ed. 1008. The conspiracy was also deemed criminal where it contemplated the co-operation of a greater number of parties than were necessary to the commission of the principal offense, as in Thomas v. United States (C.C.A.) 156 F. 897, 17 L.R.A. (N.S.) 720; McKnight v. United States (C.C.A.) 252 F. 687. Cf. Vannata v. United States (C.C.A.) 289 F. 424; Ex parte O'Leary (C.C.A.) 53 F.(2d) 956. Compare Queen v. Whitchurch, 24 Q.B.D. 420.

conspiracy and the substantive offense that is its immediate end are discrete crimes for which separate sanctions may be imposed.

I

Petitioners were tried under a six-count indictment alleging a variety of federal gambling offense. Each of the eight petitioners, along with seven unindicted coconspirators and six codefendants, was charged with conspiring to violate and violating 18 U.S.C.A. § 1955, a federal gambling statute making it a crime for five or more persons to conduct, finance, manage, supervise, direct, or own a gambling business prohibited by state law. Each petitioner was convicted of both offenses, and each was sentenced under both counts. The Court of Appeals for the Third Circuit affirmed, finding that a recognized exception to Wharton's Rule permitted prosecution and punishment for both offenses. We granted certiorari to resolve the conflicts caused by the federal courts' disparate approaches to the application of Wharton's Rule to conspiracies to violate § 1955. For the reasons now to be stated, we affirm.

II

Wharton's Rule owes its name to Francis Wharton, whose treatise on criminal law identified the doctrine and its fundamental rationale:

> "When to the idea of an offense plurality of agents is logically necessary, conspiracy, which assumes the voluntary accession of a person to a crime of such a character that it is aggravated by a plurality of agents, cannot be maintained. . . . In other words, when the law says, 'a combination between two persons to effect a particular end shall be called, if the end be effected, by a certain name,' it is not lawful for the prosecution to call it by some other name; and when the law says, such an offense—e.g., adultery—shall have a certain punishment, it is not lawful for the prosecution to evade this limitation by indicting the offense as conspiracy." 2 F. Wharton, Criminal Law § 1604, p. 1862 (12th ed. 1932).

The Rule has been applied by numerous courts, state[1] and federal[2] alike. It also has been recognized by this Court, although we have had no previous occasion carefully to analyze its justification and proper role in federal law.

* * *

1. See, e.g., People v. Wettengel, 98 Colo. 193, 198, 58 P.2d 279, 281 (1935); People v. Purcell, 304 Ill.App. 215, 217, 26 N.E.2d 153, 154 (1940); Robinson v. State, 184 A.2d 814, 820 (Md.Ct.App.1962).

2. See, e.g., United States v. New York C. & H. R. R. Co., 146 F. 298, 303–305 (C.C. S.D.N.Y.1906), aff'd, 212 U.S. 481, 29 S.Ct. 304 (1909); United States v. Zeuli, 137 F.2d 845 (C.A.2 1943); United States v. Dietrich, 126 F. 659, 667 (C.C.Neb.1904); United States v. Sager, 49 F.2d 725, 727 (C.A.2 1931).

III

A

Traditionally the law has considered conspiracy and the completed substantive offense to be separate crimes. Conspiracy is an inchoate offense, the essence of which is an agreement to commit an unlawful act. Unlike some crimes that arise in a single transaction, . . . the conspiracy to commit an offense and the subsequent commission of that crime normally do not merge into a single punishable act. Thus, it is well recognized that in most cases separate sentences can be imposed for the conspiracy to do an act and for the subsequent accomplishment of that end. Indeed, the Court has even held that the conspiracy can be punished more harshly than the accomplishment of its purpose.

The consistent rationale of this long line of decisions rests on the very nature of the crime of conspiracy. This Court repeatedly has recognized that a conspiracy poses distinct dangers quite apart from those of the substantive offense.

*   *   *

B

The historical difference between the conspiracy and its end has led this Court consistently to attribute to Congress "a tacit purpose—in the absence of any inconsistent expression—to maintain a long-established distinction between offenses essentially different; a distinction whose practical importance in the criminal law is not easily overestimated." Wharton's Rule announces an exception to this general principle.

The Rule traces its origin to the decision of the Pennsylvania Supreme Court in Shannon v. Commonwealth, 14 Pa. 226 (1850), a case in which the court ordered dismissal of an indictment alleging conspiracy to commit adultery that was brought after the State had failed to obtain conviction for the substantive offense. Prominent among the concerns voiced in the *Shannon* opinion is the possibility that the State could force the defendant to undergo subsequent prosecution for a lesser offense after failing to prove the greater. The *Shannon* court's holding reflects this concern, stating that "where concert is a constituent part of the act to be done, as it is in fornication and adultery, *a party acquitted of the major cannot be indicted of the minor.*"

*   *   *

This Court's previous discussions of Wharton's Rule have not elaborated upon its precise role in federal law. In most instances, the Court simply has identified the Rule and described it in terms similar to those used in Wharton's treatise. But in United States v. Holte, 236 U.S. 140 (1915), the sole case in which the Court felt compelled specifically to consider the applicability of Wharton's Rule, it declined to adopt an expansive definition of its parameters. In that case,

Wharton's Rule was advanced as a bar to prosecution of a female for conspiracy to violate the Mann Act. Rejecting that contention, the Court adopted a narrow construction of the Rule that focuses on the statutory requirements of the substantive offense rather than the evidence offered to prove those elements at trial:

> "The substantive offense might be committed without the woman's consent, for instance, if she were drugged or taken by force. Therefore the decisions that it is impossible to turn the concurrence necessary to effect certain crimes such as bigamy or duelling into a conspiracy to commit them do not apply."

Wharton's Rule first emerged at a time when the contours of the law of conspiracy were in the process of active formulation. The general question whether the conspiracy merged into the completed felony offense remained for some time a matter of uncertain resolution. That issue is now settled, however, and the Rule currently stands as an exception to the general principle that a conspiracy and the substantive offense that is its immediate end do not merge upon proof of the latter. See Pinkerton v. United States, 328 U.S. 640 (1946). If the Rule is to serve a rational purpose in the context of the modern law of conspiracy, its role must be more precisely identified.

C

This Court's prior decisions indicate that the broadly formulated Wharton's Rule does not rest on principles of double jeopardy. Instead, it has current vitality only as a judicial presumption, to be applied in the absence of legislative intent to the contrary. The classic Wharton's Rule offenses—adultery, incest, bigamy, duelling—are crimes that are characterized by the general congruence of the agreement and the completed substantive offense. The parties to the agreement are the only persons who participate in commission of the substantive offense, and the immediate consequences of the crime rest on the parties themselves rather than on society at large. Finally, the agreement that attends the substantive offense does not appear likely to pose the distinct kinds of threats to society that the law of conspiracy seeks to avert. It cannot, for example, readily be assumed that an agreement to commit an offense of this nature will produce agreements to engage in a more general pattern of criminal conduct.

The conduct proscribed by § 1955 is significantly different from the offenses to which the Rule traditionally has been applied. Unlike the consequences of the classic Wharton's Rule offenses, the harm attendant upon the commission of the substantive offense is not restricted to the parties to the agreement. Large-scale gambling activities seek to elicit the participation of additional persons—the bettors—who are parties neither to the conspiracy nor to the substantive offense that results from it. Moreover, the parties prosecuted for the conspiracy need not be the same persons who are prosecuted for commission of the substantive offense. An endeavor as complex as a large-scale gambling enterprise might involve persons who have played appreciably different roles, and whose level of culpability varies significantly. It might, therefore, be appropriate to prosecute the owners and organizers of large-scale gambling operations both for the conspiracy and for the substantive offense but to prosecute the lesser participants only for the substantive offense. Nor can it fairly be maintained that agreements to enter into large-scale gambling activities are not likely to generate additional agreements to engage in other criminal endeavors. As shown in Part IV hereof, the legislative history of § 1955 provides documented testimony to the contrary.

Wharton's Rule applies only to offenses that *require* concerted criminal activity, a plurality of criminal agents. In such cases, a closer relationship exists between the conspiracy and the substantive offense because *both* require collective criminal activity. The substantive offense therefore presents some of the same threats that the law of conspiracy normally is thought to guard against, and it cannot automatically be assumed that the Legislature intended the conspiracy and the substantive offense to remain as discrete crimes upon consummation of the latter. Thus, absent legislative intent to the contrary, the Rule supports a presumption that the two merge when the substantive offense is proved.

But a legal principle commands less respect when extended beyond the logic that supports it. In this case, the significant differences in characteristics and consequences of the kinds of offenses that gave rise to Wharton's Rule and the activities proscribed by § 1955 counsel against attributing significant weight to the presumption the Rule erects. More important, as the Rule is essentially an aid to the determination of legislative intent, it must defer to a discernible legislative judgment. We turn now to that inquiry.

IV

The basic purpose of the Organized Crime Control Act of 1970, was "to seek the eradication of organized crime in the United States by strengthening the legal tools in the evidence-gathering process, by establishing new penal prohibitions, and by providing enhanced sanctions and new remedies to deal with the unlawful activities of those engaged in organized crime." The content of the Act reflects the dedication with which the Legislature pursued this purpose. In addition to enacting provisions to facilitate the discovery and proof of organized criminal activities, Congress passed a number of relatively severe penalty provisions. For example, Title X, codified in 18 U.S.C.A. §§ 3575–3578, identifies for harsher sentencing treatment certain "dangerous special offenders," among them persons who initiate, direct, or supervise patterns of criminal conduct or conspiracies to engage in such conduct, and persons who derive substantial portions of their income from those activities.

Major gambling activities were a principal focus of congressional concern. Large-scale gambling enterprises were seen to be both a substantive evil and a source of funds for other criminal conduct. Title VIII thus was enacted "to give the Federal Government a new substantive weapon, a weapon which will strike at organized crime's principal source of revenue: illegal gambling." In addition to declaring that certain gambling activities violate federal as well as state law, Title VIII provides new penalties for conspiracies to obstruct state law enforcement efforts for the purpose of facilitating the conduct of these activities.

In drafting the Organized Crime Control Act of 1970, Congress manifested its clear awareness of the distinct nature of a conspiracy and the substantive offenses that might constitute its immediate end. The identification of "special offenders" in Title X speaks both to persons who commit specific felonies during the course of a pattern of criminal activity and to those who enter into conspiracies to engage in patterns of criminal conduct. And Congress specifically utilized the law of conspiracy to discourage organized crime's corruption of state and local officials for the purpose of facilitating gambling enterprises.

But the § 1955 definition of "gambling activities" pointedly avoids reference to conspiracy or to agreement, the essential element of conspiracy. Moreover, the limited § 1955 definition is repeated in identifying the reach of § 1511, a provision that specifically prohibits conspiracies. Viewed in this context, and in light of the numerous references to conspiracies throughout the extensive consideration of the Organized Crime Control Act, we think that the limited congressional definition of "gambling activities" in § 1955 is significant. The Act is a carefully crafted piece of legislation. Had Congress intended to foreclose the possibility of prosecuting conspiracy offenses under § 371 by merging them into prosecutions under § 1955, we think it would have so indicated explicitly. It chose instead to define the substantive offense punished by § 1955 in a manner that fails specifically to invoke the concerns which underlie the law of conspiracy.

Nor do we find merit to the argument that the congressional requirement of participation of "five or more persons" as an element of the substantive offense under § 1955 represents a legislative attempt to merge the conspiracy and the substantive offense into a single crime. The history of the Act instead reveals that this requirement was designed to restrict federal intervention to cases in which federal interests are substantially implicated. The findings accompanying Title VIII would appear to support the assertion of federal jurisdiction over all illegal gambling activities. Congress did not, however, choose to exercise its power to the fullest. Recognizing that gambling activities normally are matters of state concern, Congress indicated a desire to extend federal criminal jurisdiction to reach only "those who are engaged in an illicit gambling business of major proportions." It accordingly conditioned the application of § 1955 on a finding that the gambling activities involve five or more persons and that they remain substantially in operation in excess of 30 days or attain gross revenues of $2,000 in a single day. Thus the requirement of "concerted activity" in § 1955 reflects no more than a concern to avoid federal prosecution of small-scale gambling activities which pose a limited threat to federal interests and normally can be combated effectively by local law enforcement efforts.

Viewed in the context of this legislation there simply is no basis for relying on a presumption to reach a result so plainly at odds with congressional intent. We think it evident that Congress intended to retain each offense as an "independent curb" available for use in the strategy against organized crime. We conclude, therefore, that the history and structure of the Organized Crime Control Act of 1970 manifest a clear and unmistakable legislative judgment that more than outweighs any presumption of merger between the conspiracy to violate § 1955 and the consummation of that substantive offense.

V

In expressing these conclusions we do not imply that the distinct nature of the crimes of conspiracy to violate and violation of § 1955 should prompt prosecutors to seek separate convictions in every case, or judges necessarily to sentence in a manner that imposes an additional sanction for conspiracy to violate § 1955 and the consummation of that end. Those decisions fall within the sound discretion of each, and should be rendered in accordance with the facts and circumstances of a particular case. We conclude only that Congress intended to retain these traditional options. Neither Wharton's Rule nor the history and structure of the Organized Crime Control Act of 1970 persuade us to the contrary.

Affirmed.

[The dissenting opinion of Mr. Justice Douglas, in which Justices Stewart and Marshall joined, and the dissenting opinion of Mr. Justice Brennan are omitted.]

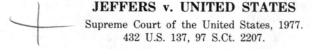

JEFFERS v. UNITED STATES
Supreme Court of the United States, 1977.
432 U.S. 137, 97 S.Ct. 2207.

MR. JUSTICE BLACKMUN announced the judgment of the Court and an opinion in which THE CHIEF JUSTICE, MR. JUSTICE POWELL, and MR. JUSTICE REHNQUIST join.

This case involves the extent of the protection against multiple prosecutions afforded by the Double Jeopardy Clause of the Fifth Amendment, under circumstances in which the defendant *opposes* the Government's efforts to try charges under 21 U.S.C.A. §§ 846 and 848 in one proceeding. It also raises the question whether § 846 is a lesser included offense of § 848. Finally, it requires further explication of the Court's decision in Iannelli v. United States.

I

A. According to evidence presented at trial, petitioner Garland Jeffers was the head of a highly sophisticated narcotics distribution network that operated in Gary, Ind., from January 1972 to March 1974. The "Family," as the organization was known, originally was formed by Jeffers and five others and was designed to control the local drug traffic in the city of Gary. Petitioner soon became the dominant figure in the organization. He exercised ultimate authority over the substantial revenues derived from the Family's drug sales, extortionate practices, and robberies. He disbursed funds to pay salaries of Family members, commissions of street workers, and incidental expenditures for items such as apartment rental fees, bail bond fees, and automobiles for certain members. Finally, he maintained a strict and ruthless discipline within the group, beating and shooting members on occasion. The Family typically distributed daily between 1,000 and 2,000 capsules of heroin. This resulted in net daily receipts of about $5,000, exclusive of street commissions. According to what the Court of Appeals stated was "an extremely conservative estimate," petitioner's personal share from the operations exceeded a million dollars over the two-year period.

On March 18, 1974, a federal grand jury for the Northern District of Indiana returned two indictments against petitioner in connection with his role in the Family's operations. The first charged petitioner and nine others with an offense under 21 U.S.C.A. § 846, by conspiring to distribute both heroin and cocaine during the period between November 1, 1971, and the date of the indictment in violation of 21 U.S. C.A. § 841(a)(1). The indictment specified, among other things, that the conspiracy was to be accomplished by petitioner's assumption of leadership of the Family organization, by distribution of controlled substances, and by acquisition of substantial sums of money through the distribution of the controlled substances. The second indictment charged petitioner alone with a violation of 21 U.S.C.A. § 848, which prohibits conducting a continuing criminal enterprise to violate the drug laws. Like the first or conspiracy, indictment, this second indictment charged that petitioner had distributed and possessed with intent to distribute both heroin and cocaine, in violation of § 841(a)(1), again between November 1, 1971, and the date of the indictment. As required by the statute, the indictment alleged that petitioner had undertaken the distribution "in concert with five or more other people with respect to whom he occupied a position of organizer, supervisor and manager," and that as a result of the distribution and other activity he had obtained substantial income.

Shortly after the indictments were returned, the Government filed a motion for trial together, requesting that the continuing criminal enterprise charge be tried with the general conspiracy charges against petitioner and his nine codefendants. . . .

The defendants in the § 846 case filed a joint objection to the government's motion . . . on May 7, the court denied the Government's motion for trial together and thereby set the stage for petitioner's first trial on the conspiracy charges.

B. The trial on the § 846 indictment took place in June 1974. A jury found petitioner and six of his codefendants guilty. Petitioner received the maximum punishment applicable to him under the statute—15 years in prison, a fine of $25,000, and a three-year special parole term. . . .

While the conspiracy trial and appeal were proceeding, petitioner was filing a series of pretrial motions in the pending criminal enterprise case. When it appeared that trial was imminent, petitioner filed a motion to dismiss the indictment on the ground that in the conspiracy trial he already had been placed in jeopardy once for the same offense. He argued both that the two indictments arose out of the same transaction, and therefore the second trial should be barred under that theory of double jeopardy, and that the "same evidence" rule of Blockburger v. United States, 284 U.S. 299, 52 S.Ct. 180 (1932), should bar the second prosecution, since a § 846 conspiracy was a lesser included offense of a § 848 continuing criminal enterprise. To forestall the Government's anticipated waiver argument, petitioner asserted that waiver was impossible, since his objection to trying the two counts together was based on his Sixth Amendment right to a fair trial, and his opposition to the § 848 trial was based on his Fifth Amendment double jeopardy right. A finding of waiver, according to his argument, would amount to penalizing the exercise of one constitutional right by denying another.

The government, in its response to the motion to dismiss, asserted that §§ 846 and 848 were separate offenses, and for this reason petitioner would not be placed twice in jeopardy by the second trial. The District Court agreed with this analysis and denied petitioner's motion shortly before the second trial began.

At the second trial, the jury found petitioner guilty of engaging in a continuing criminal enterprise. Again, he received the maximum sentence for a first offender: life imprisonment and a fine of $100,000. The judgment specified that the prison sentence and the fine were "to run consecutive with sentence imposed in [the conspiracy case]." Thus, at the conclusion of the second trial, petitioner found himself with a life sentence without possibility of probation, parole, or suspension of sentence, and with fines totalling $125,000. . . .

On appeal, the conviction and sentence were upheld. The Court of Appeals concluded that § 846 was a lesser included offense of § 848, since the continuing criminal enterprise statute expressly required proof that the accused had acted in concert with five or more other persons. In the court's view, this requirement was tantamount to a proof of conspiracy requirement. . . . Although the court stated that ordinarily conviction of a lesser included offense would bar a subsequent prosecution for the greater offense, it read Iannelli v. United States to create a new double jeopardy rule applicable only to complex statutory crimes.

The two statutes at issue in *Iannelli* were 18 U.S.C.A. § 371, the general federal conspiracy statute, and 18 U.S.C.A. § 1955, the statute prohibiting illegal gambling businesses involving five or more persons. Despite language in *Iannelli* seemingly to the contrary, the Court of Appeals stated that § 371 is a lesser included offense of § 1955. The court attached no significance to the fact that § 1955 contains no requirement of action "in concert." It believed that *Iannelli* held that greater and lesser offenses could be punished separately if Congress so intended, and it adopted the same approach to the multiple prosecution question before it. Finding that Congress, in enacting § 848, was interested in punishing severely those who made a substantial living from drug dealing, and that Congress intended to make § 848 an independent crime, the court concluded that §§ 846 and 848 were not the "same offense" for double jeopardy purposes. It therefore held that the conviction on the first indictment did not bar the prosecution on the second.

In his petition for certiorari, petitioner challenged the Court of Appeals' reading of *Iannelli* and suggested again that § 846 was a lesser included offense of § 848. He also contended that the Double Jeopardy Clause was violated by the prosecution on the greater offense after conviction for the lesser. Finally, he argued that he had not waived the double jeopardy issue. In addition to these issues, it appears that cumulative fines were imposed on petitioner, which creates a multiple punishment problem. We granted certiorari. We consider first the multiple prosecution, lesser included offense, and waiver points, and then we address the multiple punishment problem.

II

A. The Government's principal argument for affirming the judgment of the Court of Appeals is that *Iannelli* controls this case. Like the conspiracy and gambling statutes at issue in *Iannelli,* the conspiracy and continuing criminal enterprise statutes at issue here, in the Government's view, create two separate offenses under the "same evidence" test of *Blockburger.* The Government's position is premised on its contention that agreement is not an essential element of the § 848 offense, despite the presence in § 848(b)(2)(A) of the phrase "in concert with." If five "innocent dupes" each separately acted "in concert with" the ringleader of the continuing criminal enterprise, the Government asserts, the statutory requirement would be satisfied.

If the Government's position were right, this would be a simple case. In our opinion, however, it is not so easy to transfer the *Iannelli* result, reached in the context of two other and different statutes, to this case. In *Iannelli,* the Court specifically noted: "Wharton's Rule applies only to offenses that *require* concerted criminal activity, a plurality of criminal agents." (emphasis in original). Elaborating on that point, the Court stated: "The essence of the crime of conspiracy is agreement, . . . an element not contained in the statutory definition of the § 1955 offense." Because of the silence of § 1955 with regard to the necessity of concerted activity, the Court felt constrained to construe the statute to permit the possibility that the five persons "involved" in the gambling operation might not be acting together.

The same flexibility does not exist with respect to the continuing criminal enterprise statute. Section 848(b)(2)(A) restricts the definition of the crime to a continuing series of violations undertaken by the accused "in concert with five or more other persons." Clearly, then, a conviction would be impossible unless concerted activity were present. The express "in concert" language in the statutory definition quite plausibly may be read to provide the necessary element of "agreement" found wanting in § 1955. Even if § 848 were read to require individual agreements between the leader of the enterprise and each of the other five necessary participants, enough would be shown to prove a conspiracy. It would be unreasonable to assume that Congress did not mean anything at all when it inserted these critical words in § 848. In the absence of any indication from the legislative history or elsewhere to the contrary, the far more likely explanation is that Congress intended the word "concert" to have its common meaning of agreement in a design or plan. For the purposes of this case, therefore, we assume, *arguendo,* that § 848 does require proof of an agreement among the persons involved in the continuing criminal enterprise. So construed, § 846 is a lesser included offense of § 848, because § 848 requires proof of every fact necessary to show a violation under § 846 as well as proof of several addition elements.

B. Brown v. Ohio, 432 U.S. 161, 97 S.Ct. 2221 decided today, establishes the general rule that the Double Jeopardy Clause prohibits a State or the Federal Government from trying a defendant for a greater offense after it has convicted him of a lesser included offense. What lies at the heart of the Double Jeopardy Clause is the prohibition against multiple prosecutions for "the same offense." *Brown* reaffirms the rule that one convicted of the greater offense may not be subjected to a second prosecution on the lesser offense, since that would be the equivalent of two trials for "the same offense." Because two offenses are "the same" for double jeopardy purposes unless each requires proof of an additional fact that the other does not, it follows that the sequence of the two trials for the greater and the lesser offense is immaterial and trial on a greater offense after conviction on a lesser ordinarily is just as objectionable under the Double Jeopardy Clause as the reverse order of proceedings. Contrary to the suggestion of the Court of Appeals, *Iannelli* created no exception to these general jeopardy principles for complex statutory crimes.

The rule established in *Brown,* however, does have some exceptions. One commonly recognized exception is when all the events necessary to the greater crime have not taken place at the time the prosecution for the lesser is begun. This exception may also apply when the facts necessary to the greater were not discovered despite the exercise of due diligence before the first trial.

If the defendant expressly asks for separate trials on the greater and the lesser offenses, or, in connection with his opposition to trial together, fails to raise the issue that one offense might be a lesser included offense of the other, another exception to the *Brown* rule emerges. This situation is no different from others in which a defendant enjoys protection under the Double Jeopardy Clause, but for one reason or another retrial is not barred. Thus, for example, in the case of a retrial after a successful appeal from a conviction, the concept of continuing jeopardy on the offense for which the defendant was convicted applies, thereby making retrial on that offense permissible.

* * *

C. In this case, trial together of the conspiracy and continuing criminal enterprise charges could have taken place without undue prejudice to petitioner's Sixth Amendment right to a fair trial. If the two charges had been tried in one proceeding, it appears that petitioner would have been entitled to a lesser included offense instruction. If such an instruction had been denied on the ground that § 846 was not a lesser included offense of § 848, petitioner could have preserved his point by proper objection. Nevertheless, petitioner did not adopt that course. Instead, he was solely responsible for the successive prosecutions for the conspiracy offense and the continuing criminal enterprise offense. Under the circumstances, we hold that his action deprived him of any right that he might have had against consecutive trials. It follows, therefore, that the Government was entitled to prosecute petitioner for the § 848 offense, and the only issue remaining is that of cumulative punishments upon such prosecution and conviction.

III

Although both parties, throughout the proceedings, appear to have assumed that no cumulative punishment problem is present in this case, the imposition of the separate fines seems squarely to contradict that assumption. Fines, of course, are treated in the same way as prison sentences for purposes of double jeopardy and multiple punishment analysis. In this case, since petitioner received the maximum fine applicable to him under § 848, it is necessary to decide whether cumulative punishments are permissible for violations of §§ 846 and 848.

The critical inquiry is whether Congress intended to punish each statutory violation separately. In Iannelli v. United States, supra, the Court concluded that Congress did intend to punish violations of § 1955 separately from § 371 conspiracy violations. Since the two offenses were different, there was no need to go further. If some possibility exists that the two statutory offenses are the "same offense" for double jeopardy purposes, however, it is necessary to examine the problem closely, in order to avoid constitutional multiple punishment difficulties.

As petitioner concedes, the first issue to be considered is whether Congress intended to allow cumulative punishment for violations of §§ 846 and 848. We have concluded that it did not, and this again makes it unnecessary to reach the lesser included offense issue.
* * *

. . . The policy reasons usually offered to justify separate punishment of conspiracies and underlying substantive offenses, however, are inapplicable to §§ 846 and 848. In Callanan v. United States, 364 U.S., at 593–594, 81 S.Ct., at 325, the Court summarized these reasons:

> "[C]ollective criminal agreement—partnership in crime—presents a greater potential threat to the public than individual delicts. Concerted action both increases the likelihood that the criminal object will be successfully attained and decreases the probability that the individuals involved will depart from their path of criminality. Group association for criminal purposes often, if not normally, makes possible the attainment of ends more complex than those which one criminal could accomplish. Nor is the danger of a conspiratorial group limited to the particular end toward which it has embarked. Combination in crime makes more likely the commission of crimes unrelated to the original purpose for which the group was formed. In sum, the danger which a conspiracy generates is not confined to the substantive offense which is the immediate aim of the enterprise."

As this discussion makes clear, the reason for separate penalties for conspiracies lies in the additional dangers posed by concerted activity. Section 848, however, already expressly prohibits this kind of conduct. Thus, there is little legislative need to further this admittedly important interest by authorizing consecutive penalties from the conspiracy statute.

Our conclusion that Congress did not intend to impose cumulative penalties under §§ 846 and 848 is of minor significance in this particular case. Since the Government had the right to try petitioner on the § 848 indictment, the court had the power to sentence him to whatever penalty was authorized by that statute. It had no power, however, to impose on him a fine greater than the maximum permitted by § 848. Thus, if petitioner received a total of $125,000 in fines on the two convictions, as the record indicates, he is entitled to have the fine imposed at the second trial reduced so that the two fines together do not exceed $100,000.

The judgment of the Court of Appeals, accordingly, is affirmed in part and vacated in part, and the case is remanded for further proceedings consistent with this opinion.

It is so ordered.

MR. JUSTICE WHITE, concurring in part in the judgment and dissenting in part.

Because I agree with the United States that Iannelli v. United States, 420 U.S. 770, 95 S.Ct. 1284 (1975), controls this case, I for that reason concur in the judgment of the Court with respect to petitioner's conviction. For the same reason and because the conspiracy proved was not used to establish the continuing criminal enterprise charged, I dissent from the Court's judgment with respect to the fines and from Part III of its opinion.

MR. JUSTICE STEVENS, with whom MR. JUSTICE BRENNAN, MR. JUSTICE STEWART, and MR. JUSTICE MARSHALL join, dissenting.

There is nothing novel about the rule that a defendant may not be tried for a greater offense after conviction of a lesser included offense. It can be traced back to Blackstone, and "has been this Court's understanding of the Double Jeopardy Clause at least since In re Nielsen [131 U.S. 176, 9 S.Ct. 672] was decided in 1889." I would not permit the prosecutor to claim ignorance of this ancient rule, or to evade it by arguing that the defendant failed to advise him of its existence or its applicability.

The defendant surely cannot be held responsible for the fact that two separate indictments were returned, or for the fact that other defendants were named in the earlier indictment, or for the fact that the Government elected to proceed to trial first on the lesser charge. The other defendants had valid objections to the Government's motion to consolidate the two cases for trial. Most trial lawyers will be startled to learn that a rather routine joint opposition to that motion to consolidate has resulted in the loss of what this Court used to regard as "a vital safeguard in our society, one that was dearly won and one that should continue to be highly valued."

It is ironic that, while the State's duty to give advice to an accused is contracting, see, e.g., Oregon v. Mathiason, 429 U.S. 492, 97 S.Ct. 711, a new requirement is emerging that the accused, in order to preserve a constitutional right, must inform the prosecution about the legal consequences of its acts. Even the desirability of extending Mr. Jeffers' incarceration does not justify this unique decision.

While I concur in the judgment to the extent that it vacates the cumulative fines, I respectfully dissent from the affirmance of the conviction.

4. SCOPE AND DURATION OF CONSPIRACY

BRAVERMAN v. UNITED STATES

Supreme Court of the United States, 1942.
317 U.S. 49, 63 S.Ct. 99, 87 L.Ed. 23.

MR. CHIEF JUSTICE STONE delivered the opinion of the Court.

The questions for decision are: (1) Whether a conviction upon the several counts of an indictment, each charging conspiracy to violate a different provision of the Internal Revenue laws, where the jury's verdict is supported by evidence of but a single conspiracy, will sustain a sentence of more than two years' imprisonment, the maximum penalty for a single violation of the conspiracy statute, and (2) whether the six-year period of limitation prescribed by § 3748(a) of the Internal Revenue Code, 26 U.S.C.A. Int.Rev.Code § 3748(a), is applicable to offenses arising under § 37 of the Criminal Code, 18 U.S.C. 88, 18 U.S.C.A. § 88 (the conspiracy statute), where the object of the conspiracy is to evade or defeat the payment of a federal tax.

Petitioners were indicted, with others, on seven counts, each charging a conspiracy to violate a separate and distinct internal revenue law of the United States. On the trial there was evidence from which the jury could have found that for a considerable period of time petitioners, with others, collaborated in the illicit manufacture, transportation, and distribution of distilled spirits involving the violations of statute mentioned in the several counts of the indictment. At the close of the trial petitioners renewed a motion which they had made at its beginning to require the Government to elect one of the seven counts of the indictment upon which to proceed, contending that the proof could not and did not establish more than one agreement. In response the Government's attorney took the position that the seven counts of the indictment charged as distinct offenses the several illegal objects of one continuing conspiracy, that if the jury found such a conspiracy it might find the defendants guilty of as many offenses as it had illegal objects, and that for each such offense the two-year statutory penalty could be imposed.

The trial judge submitted the case to the jury on that theory. The jury returned a general verdict finding petitioners "guilty as charged", and the court sentenced each to eight years' imprisonment. On appeal the Court of Appeals for the Sixth Circuit affirmed, . . . It found that "From the evidence may be readily deduced a common design of appellants and others, followed by concerted action" to commit the several unlawful acts specified in the several counts of the indictment. It concluded that the fact that the conspiracy was "a general one to violate all laws repressive of its consummation does not gainsay the separate identity of each of the seven conspiracies". We granted certiorari, to resolve an asserted conflict of decisions. The Government, in its argument here, submitted the case for our decision with the suggestion that the decision below is erroneous.

Both courts below recognized that a single agreement to commit an offense does not become several conspiracies because it continues over a period of time, and that there may be such a single continuing agreement to commit several offenses. But they thought that in the latter case each contemplated offense renders the agreement punishable as a separate conspiracy.

The question whether a single agreement to commit acts in violation of several penal statutes is to be punished as one or several conspiracies is raised on the present record, not by the construction of the indictment, but by the Government's concession at the trial and here, reflected in the charge to the jury, that only a single agreement to commit the offenses alleged was proven. Where each of the counts of an indictment alleges a conspiracy to violate a different penal statute it may be proper to conclude, in the absence of a bill of exceptions bringing up the evidence, that several conspiracies are charged rather than one, and that the conviction is for each. But it is a different matter to hold, as the court below appears to have done in this case . . . that even though a single agreement is entered into, the conspirators are guilty of as many offenses as the agreement has criminal objects.

The gist of the crime of conspiracy as defined by the statute is the agreement or confederation of the conspirators to commit one or more unlawful acts where "one or more of such parties do any act to effect the object of the conspiracy". The overt act, without proof of which a charge of conspiracy cannot be submitted to the jury, may be that of only a single one of the conspirators and need not be itself a crime. But it is unimportant, for present purposes, whether we regard the overt act as a part of the crime which the statute defines and makes punishable, or as something apart from it, either an indispensable mode of corroborating the existence of the conspiracy or a device for affording a locus poenitentiae.

For when a single agreement to commit one or more substantive crimes is evidenced by an overt act, as the statute requires, the precise nature and extent of the conspiracy must be determined by reference to the agreement which embraces and defines its objects. Whether the object of a single agreement is to commit one or many crimes, it is in either case that agreement which constitutes the conspiracy which the statute punishes. The one agreement cannot be taken to be several agreements and hence several conspiracies because it envisages the violation of several statutes rather than one.

The allegation in a single count of a conspiracy to commit several crimes is not duplicitous, for "The conspiracy is the crime, and that is one, however diverse its objects". A conspiracy is not the commission of the crime which it contemplates, and neither violates nor "arises under" the statute whose violation is its object. Since the single continuing agreement, which is the conspiracy here, thus embraces its criminal objects, it differs from successive acts which violate a single penal statute and from a single act which violates two statutes. The single agreement is the prohibited conspiracy, and however diverse its objects it violates but a single statute, § 37 of the Criminal Code. For such a violation only the single penalty prescribed by the statute can be imposed.

Petitioner Wainer contends that his prosecution was barred by the three-year statute of limitations, since he withdrew from the conspiracy more than three although not more than six years before his indictment. This Court, in United States v. McElvain, 272 U.S. 633, 638, 47 S.Ct. 219, 220, 71 L.Ed. 451, and United States v. Scharton, 285 U.S. 518, 52 S.Ct. 416, 76 L.Ed. 917, held that the three-year statute of limitations applicable generally to criminal offenses barred prosecution for a conspiracy to violate the Revenue Acts, since it was not within the exception created by the Act of November 17, 1921, 42 Stat. 220, now § 3748(a)(1) of the Internal Revenue Code, 26 U.S.C.A. Int.Rev.Code § 3748(a)(1), which provided a six-year statute of limitations "for offenses involving the defrauding or attempting to defraud the United States or any agency thereof, whether by conspiracy or not". To overcome the effect of these decisions, that Act was amended, Revenue Act of 1932, 47 Stat. 169, 288, 26 U.S.C.A. Int.Rev.Code § 3748(a) by the addition of a second exception, which provided a six-year statute of limitations "for the offense of willfully attempting in any manner to evade or defeat any tax or the payment thereof", and by the addition of a new paragraph, reading as follows:

> "For offenses arising under section 37 of the Criminal Code, * * * where the object of the conspiracy is to attempt in any manner to evade or defeat any tax or the payment thereof, the period of limitation shall also be six years."

To be within this last paragraph it is not necessary that the conspiracy have as its object the commission of an offense in which defrauding or attempting to defraud the United States is an element. It is enough that the conspiracy involves an attempt to evade or defeat the payment of federal taxes, which was among the objects of the conspiracy of which petitioner was convicted. Enlargement, to six years, of the time for prosecution of such conspiracies was the expressed purpose of the amendment.

We do not pass upon petitioner Wainer's argument that his plea of former jeopardy should have been sustained, since the earlier indictment to which he pleaded guilty and which he insists charged the same offense as that of which he has now been convicted, is not a part of the record.

The judgment of conviction will be reversed and the cause remanded to the district court where the petitioners will be resentenced in conformity to this opinion.

Reversed.

NOTES

1. In Pinkerton v. United States, 328 U.S. 640, 66 S.Ct. 1180, 90 L.Ed. 1489 (1946), it was held that each member of a continuing conspiracy is criminally liable for any substantive offenses committed by coconspirators during the course of and in furtherance of the conspiracy. If A and B, after having agreed that they will carry no weapons, agree to sell narcotics to C, and A kills C when C argues with A over the purity of the narcotics, is B guilty of the murder upon C, assuming he had no knowledge that A would carry a gun in violation of their agreement? If you believe that B ought to be liable for the

homicide, would your view be different if B was not present when the killing occurred?

Consider United States v. Alvarez, 755 F.2d 830 (11th Cir.1985), and United States v. Diaz, 864 F.2d 544 (7th Cir.1988). See also, Shellow, et al., *Pinkerton v. United States* and Vicarious Criminal Liability, 36 Mercer L.Rev. 1079 (1985).

2. Significant problems arise in determining whether the relationships that exist between a great number of individuals involve all of them in one single conspiracy, or whether several distinct conspiracies exist involving a smaller number of individuals—different ones for each offense charged. In solving the problems thus encountered, courts and legal commentators have referred to the "rimless wheel" and the "chain" relationships. In a "wheel" relationship, a central individual, who is at the "hub" of the wheel, has criminal dealings with different individuals, each one of whom might be symbolized by a spoke of the wheel. There is a different conspiracy in existence between the hub and each spoke of the wheel, but there is no conspiracy between the spokes themselves, unless there were a rim on the wheel that, independently, would connect all of the spokes.

See, in this regard, Kotteakos v. United States, 328 U.S. 750, 66 S.Ct. 1239, 90 L.Ed. 1557 (1946), where the "hub" was a broker who procured loans for 32 different individuals (the spokes) by false and fraudulent applications to the Federal Housing Administration. The government charged all individuals as members of a single conspiracy to obtain fraudulent loans. The Supreme Court reversed.

In a "chain" relationship, a single conspiracy exists that links a number of individuals together. See, e.g., Blumenthal v. United States, 332 U.S. 539, 68 S.Ct. 248, 92 L.Ed. 154 (1947), where A and B agreed to sell C's product and A knew that C existed but was unaware of who he was. The Court said that A, B and C were "links" in a criminal chain, rather than "spokes" in a wheel.

3. In People v. Manson, 61 Cal.App.3d 102, 132 Cal.Rptr. 265 (1976), Charles Manson (of "Helter Skelter" fame), along with Patricia Krenwinkel, Susan Atkins, and Leslie Van Houten, members of Manson's commune who were known as the "Family" even though none were related by blood or marriage, were charged with and convicted of several counts of murder and one count of conspiracy to commit murder in the killings at the Sharon Tate Polanski home. The court said that the existence of a conspiracy can ordinarily only be proved by circumstantial evidence—the actions of the parties as they bear upon the common design. In the related case of People v. Van Houten, 113 Cal.App.3d 280, 170 Cal.Rptr. 189 (1980) that involved the La Bianca killings, termed by the court as "grotesque, gruesome, horrendous affairs, involving in most instances a great deal of cutting and hacking as per the instruction of Charles Manson," the court applied the established doctrine that a defendant can also be convicted of crimes committed by other coconspirators prior to the defendant joining the conspiracy.

5. IMPOSSIBILITY

STATE v. MORETTI

STATE v. SCHMIDT

Superior Court of New Jersey, Appellate Division, 1967.
97 N.J.Super. 418, 235 A.2d 226.

SULLIVAN, S. J. A. D.   Defendants John J. Moretti and Marietta
Schmidt appeal from a conviction of unlawful conspiracy to commit the
statutory crime of abortion of one Sylvia Swidler,   . . .   Lawrence
Gianettino was also convicted under the same charge but died shortly
after the trial.

The State's case may be summarized as follows.

Sylvia Swidler, a special investigator employed in the Essex County
Prosecutor's office, was used as a decoy to arrange through defendants
Schmidt and Moretti to have an abortion to terminate an allegedly
unwanted pregnancy.   The abortion was to have been performed by
defendant Gianettino, an inspector for the New Jersey State Board of
Barber Examiners.   Gianettino, by appointment, arrived at Mrs. Swidler's home with a bag of instruments to perform the abortion.   As soon
as Mrs. Swidler paid him $600 in marked money, detectives who were
secreted in and about the house arrested him.

The State concedes, and Mrs. Swidler testified, that she was not
actually pregnant at the time.

A principal argument made by both defendants on this appeal is
that there cannot be a criminal conspiracy where attainment of the
unlawful object thereof is inherently impossible.   It is pointed out that
in this State an essential element of the crime of abortion is the
pregnancy of the woman.   Since Mrs. Swidler was not pregnant and
could not have been aborted, defendants argue that it was legally
impossible for defendants to have conspired to commit such act.

We conclude that Mrs. Swidler's nonpregnancy was not a defense
to the charge of conspiracy herein.   She could have been pregnant, as
defendants manifestly thought she was, so that attainment of the
unlawful object was not inherently impossible.   The essential elements
of the statutory crime of conspiracy are the criminal agreement and
overt act in furtherance thereof.   Defendants' corrupt plan and overt
acts towards its accomplishment were no less anti-social, even though
Mrs. Swidler was not *enceinte*. . . .

Affirmed.

LEONARD, J. A. D. (dissenting).

I disagree with the conclusion of the majority.   I cannot concur
with the premise that because defendants manifestly thought the
prosecutor's investigator was pregnant, "the attainment of the unlawful

object was not inherently impossible" and consequently "there was no legal impossibility to commit the substantive act."

Defendants were convicted of the statutory crime of conspiring to commit abortion. . . . In this State pregnancy of the woman is an essential element of the crime of abortion and proof thereof is required for conviction. It is conceded that the investigator was not pregnant. Thus it could not have been legally possible to convict defendants of the substantive crime.

I therefore conclude that the impossibility here present is not factual, but to the contrary, legal and inherent in the very nature of the crime charged. This conclusion mandates a reversal of defendants' convictions. . . .

The distinction between legal and factual impossibility is recognized in State v. Meisch, 86 N.J.Super. 279, 281, 206 A.2d 763 (App.Div. 1965). . . .

As the court said in Ventimiglia v. United States, [242 F.2d 620 (4th Cir. 1957)],

"The furtiveness with which the defendants acted does not convert into a crime what Congress has not made criminal. Whatever opinion one may have as to the moral quality of what was done, it must be said it is not what the statute forbade."

I would reverse defendants' convictions.

NOTES

1. In Eyman v. Deutsch, 92 Ariz. 82, 373 P.2d 716 (1962), the defendant pleaded guilty to an indictment for conspiracy (with one Crosby Holden) to commit "grand theft". Prior thereto his alleged co-conspirator (Holden) stood trial and was found not guilty. The Arizona Supreme Court held, in accordance with the "weight of authority" that if one of two alleged co-conspirators is acquitted the conviction of the other one cannot stand. Two dissenting justices commented:

". . . It is true that in the case of two defendants, if they are tried jointly, the acquittal of one is the acquittal of the other and, if separate trials, the acquittal of one will generally *bar further proceedings against the other.* But the principle applied in those cases should not be extended to discharge a defendant on the facts of this case. Here, petitioner, Deutsch, pleaded guilty *after* his co-conspirator was found not guilty. He was represented, as the record shows, by able counsel at each stage of the proceedings. The record also reflects from the dismissal of five more serious counts, three of grand theft and two of presenting false claims, that the prosecution was satisfied with somewhat less than a pound of flesh from around the heart.

"This particular petitioner does not deserve sympathy. Having made a bargain with the prosecution of the court, he refuses to abide by it. There is no reason for this Court to enfold him in the cloak of benevolent paternalism."

In Commonwealth v. Campbell, 257 Pa.Super. 160, 390 A.2d 761 (1978), the court reaffirms that where the only other conspirator was acquitted, the conviction of the defendant as a conspirator is precluded. Even though the new state criminal code was patterned after the Model Penal Code (which would permit the later conviction of the second conspirator), the court said it would "not presume a change in a well-established principle of our law merely on the basis of Model Penal Code commentary, the import of which is in no way reflected in the statute as adopted."

2. For a legislative rejection of the "consistency" rule, consider the following provision in the 1961 Illinois Criminal Code (§ 8–2(b)):

It shall not be a defense to conspiracy that the person or persons with whom the accused is alleged to have conspired:

    (1) Has not been prosecuted or convicted, or

    (2) Has been convicted of a different offense, or

    (3) Is not amenable to justice, or

    (4) Has been acquitted, or

    (5) Lacked the capacity to commit an offense.

See also Smith v. State, 250 Ga. 264, 297 S.E.2d 273 (1982): "In a joint trial of co-conspirators, a failure of proof as to one co-conspirator would amount to a failure of proof as to both, the evidence presented being identical. Co-conspirators, alleged to be the only two parties to the conspiracy, may not receive different verdicts when they are tried together. With two trials, the issue before the court in each case is the guilt or innocence of that particular defendant, which must be proved beyond a reasonable doubt. When the jury returns a verdict of guilty, it indicates that as to this defendant the burden of proving the conspiracy and the defendant's participation has been met. Where the trials are severed, it is highly possible that co-conspirators could receive different verdicts without those verdicts being fatally inconsistent. In the first trial the evidence may be properly presented, the burden of proving X guilty of conspiracy may be met, and the jury can properly return a verdict of guilty. In the subsequent trial of conspirator Y, however, the death or unavailability of certain witnesses, the failure of the prosecution to present all available evidence, the ineffectiveness of the prosecution in presenting its case, or the difference in jury composition could all affect the verdict. The failure of the prosecution to prove all elements of the conspiracy in the subsequent case would justify a directed verdict of acquittal, as happened in this case, without being inconsistent with the earlier conviction."

3. With regard to the risks of possible injustices in conspiracy prosecutions, consider the following comments of Jackson, J., in his concurring opinion in Krulewitch v. United States, 336 U.S. 440, 445, 69 S.Ct. 716, 719 (1949):

"This case illustrates a present drift in the federal law of conspiracy which warrants some further comment because it is characteristic of the long evolution of that elastic, sprawling and pervasive offense. Its history exemplifies the 'tendency of a principle to expand itself to the limit of its logic.' The unavailing protest of courts against the growing habit to indict for conspiracy in lieu of prosecuting for the substantive offense itself, or in addition thereto, suggests that loose practice as to this offense constitutes a serious threat to fairness in our administration of justice.

"The modern crime of conspiracy is so vague that it almost defies definition. Despite certain elementary and essential elements, it also, chameleon-like, takes on a special coloration from each of the many independent offenses on which it may be overlaid. It is always 'predominantly mental in composition' because it consists primarily of a meeting of minds and an intent.

"The crime comes down to us wrapped in vague but unpleasant connotations. It sounds historical undertones of treachery, secret plotting and violence on a scale that menaces social stability and the security of the state itself. 'Privy conspiracy' ranks with sedition and rebellion in the Litany's prayer for deliverance. Conspirational movements do indeed lie back of the political assassination, the *coup d'etat,* the *putsch,* the revolution and seizures of power in modern times, as they have in all history.

"But the conspiracy concept also is superimposed upon many concerted crimes having no political motivation. It is not intended to question that the basic conspiracy principle has some place in modern criminal law, because to unite, back of a criminal purpose, the strength, opportunities and resources of many is obviously more dangerous and more difficult to police than the efforts of a lone wrongdoer. . . .

"Conspiracy in federal law aggravates the degree of crime over that of unconcerted offending. The act of confederating to commit a misdemeanor, followed by even an innocent overt act in its execution is a felony and is such even if the misdemeanor is never consummated. The more radical proposition also is well-established that at common law and under some statutes a combination may be a criminal conspiracy even if it contemplates only acts which are not crimes at all when perpetrated by an individual or by many acting severally.

"Thus the conspiracy doctrine will incriminate persons on the fringe of offending who would not be guilty of aiding and abetting or of becoming an accessory, for those charges only lie when an act which is a crime has actually been committed.

"Attribution of criminality to a confederation which contemplates no act that would be criminal if carried out by any one of the conspirators is a practice peculiar to Anglo-American law. 'There can be little doubt that this wide definition of the crime of conspiracy originates in the criminal equity administered in the Star Chamber.' In fact, we are advised that 'The modern law of conspiracy is almost entirely the result of the manner in which conspiracy was treated by the Court of the Star Chamber.' The doctrine does not commend itself to jurists of civil-law countries, despite universal recognition that an organized society must have legal weapons for combatting organized criminality. Most other countries have devised what they consider more discriminating principles upon which to prosecute criminal gangs, secret associations and subversive syndicates. . . .

"Of course, it is for prosecutors rather than courts to determine when to use a scatter gun to bring down the defendant, but there are procedural advantages from using it which add to the danger of unguarded extension of the concept.

"An accused, under the Sixth Amendment, has the right to trial 'by an impartial jury of the State and district wherein the crime shall have been committed.' The leverage of a conspiracy charge lifts this limitation from the prosecution and reduces its protection to a phantom, for the crime is considered so vagrant as to have been committed in any district where any one of the conspirators did any one of the acts, however innocent, intended to accomplish its object. The Government may, and often does, compel one to defend at a great distance from any place he ever did any act because some accused confederate did some trivial and by itself innocent act in the chosen district. Circumstances may even enable the prosecution to fix the place of trial in Washington, D. C., where a defendant may lawfully be put to trial before a jury partly or even wholly made up of employees of the Government that accuses him. . . .

"When the trial starts, the accused feels the full impact of the conspiracy strategy. Strictly, the prosecution should first establish *prima facie* the conspiracy and identify the conspirators, after which evidence of acts and declarations of each in the course of its execution are admissible against all. But the order of proof of so sprawling a charge is difficult for a judge to control. As a practical matter, the accused often is confronted with a hodgepodge of acts and statements by others which he may never have authorized or intended or even known about, but which help to persuade the jury of existence of the conspiracy itself. In other words, a conspiracy often is proved by evidence that is admissible only upon assumption that conspiracy existed. The naive assumption that prejudicial effects can be overcome by instructions to the jury . . ., all practicing lawyers know to be unmitigated fiction. . . .

"The trial of a conspiracy charge doubtless imposes a heavy burden on the prosecution, but it is an especially difficult situation for the defendant. The hazard from loose application of rules of evidence is aggravated where the Government institutes mass trials. Moreover, in federal practice there is no rule preventing conviction on uncorroborated testimony of accomplices, as there are in many jurisdictions, and the most comfort a defendant can expect is that the court can be induced to follow the 'better practice' and caution the jury against 'too much reliance upon the testimony of accomplices.' . . .

"A co-defendant in a conspiracy trial occupies an uneasy seat. There generally will be evidence of wrongdoing by somebody. It is difficult for the individual to make his own case stand on its own merits in the minds of jurors who are ready to believe that birds of a feather are flocked together. If he is silent, he is taken to admit it and if, as often happens, co-defendants can be prodded into accusing or contradicting each other, they convict each other. There are many practical difficulties in defending against a charge of conspiracy which I will not enumerate."

Also see, Wessel, Procedural Safeguards for the Mass Conspiracy Trial, 48 A.B.A.J. 628 (1962).

D. PARTIES TO CRIME

Normally, criminal liability is predicated upon the doing of an act, usually by the defendant. Early in the development of the common law, however, the courts recognized that criminal liability could be predicated upon conduct done by a party other than the defendant, for whose conduct the defendant would be held responsible. Consider, in this connection, the following excerpt from Usselton v. People, 149 Ill. 612, 36 N.E. 952 (1894):

"By the ancient common law, existing prior to the reign of Henry IV,—the latter part of the fourteenth and beginning of the fifteenth centuries,—those persons only were considered principals who committed the overt act, while those who were present, aiding and abetting, were deemed accessories at the fact, and those who, not being present had advised or encouraged the perpetration of the crime, were deemed accessories before the fact. During that reign it seems to have been settled as the law that he who was present, aiding and abetting in the perpetration of the crime, was to be considered as a principal, the courts holding that all who were actually or constsructively present, but not actively participating in the crime, were principals of the second degree. (1 Russell on Crimes, (Greenl. ed.) 26; 1 Bishop on Crim.Law, 648.) And this continued to be the common law as it was adopted in this State.

"An accessory before the fact, at common law, is defined by Sir Mathew Hale to be 'one who, being absent at the time of the commission of the offense, doth yet procure, counsel or command another to commit it.' And absence, it is said, is indispensably necessary to constitute one an accessory, for if he be actually or constructively present when the felony is committed, he is an aider and abettor, and not an accessory before the fact, (1 Hale's P.C. 615; 4 Blackstone's Com. 36, 37; 1 Archbold on Crim.Pl. and Pr. 14;) or, as defined by Bishop, (1 Crim.Law, 673): 'An accessory before the fact is one whose will contributes to another's felonious act, committed while too far himself from the act to be a principal.' No distinction was made in the punishment of a principal and of an accessory before the fact by the common law, the principle that what one does by the agency of another he does by himself, applying equally in criminal and civil cases. Broom's Legal Maxims, (2d ed.) 643. At common law, an accessory before the fact, without his consent, could only be tried after the conviction of the principal. While the principal remained amenable to indictment and conviction, the accessory had the right to insist upon the conviction of the principal offender before he was put upon trial, for, as said by Blackstone, (book 4, 323), "*non constitit* whether any felony was committed or no, till the principal was attainted, and it might so happen that the accessory be convicted one day and the principal acquitted the next, which would be absurd.' And this absurdity might happen wherever the trial of the principal might occur subsequently to that of the accessory. This was subject to the exception, that where the accessory was indicted with the principal he might waive the right, and thereupon they might be put upon trial jointly.

"It seems that the distinction between accessories before the fact and principals, up to a late date, at least, has been retained in England. By Statute 7, Geo. IV, chap. 64, sec. 9, it is provided that persons who shall counsel, procure or command any other person to commit a felony shall be deemed guilty of a felony, and may be indicted and convicted, either as accessory before the fact to the principal felony, together with the principal felon, or after his conviction, or may be indicted and convicted of a substantive felony, whether the principal felon shall have been convicted or not, etc. (See 11 and 12 Vic. 46, sec. 1.) And such seems to be the rule in some of the States which have adopted, in substance, Statute 7, Geo. IV. In this State, however, the distinction between accessories before the fact and principals has been abolished.

By section 2, division 2, of the Criminal Code, (par. 331, Starr & Curtis,) it is provided: 'An accessory is he who stands by and aids, abets or assists, or who, not being present aiding, abetting or assisting, hath advised, encouraged, aided or abetted the perpetration of the crime. He who thus aids, abets, assists, advises or encourages shall be considered as principal, and punished accordingly.' It is to be observed that in the definition of accessories are included those who were principals in the second degree at common law,—that is, those standing by, aiding and abetting,—as well as those who, not being present, had advised and encouraged the perpretration of the crime, and it is expressly provided that all persons who are thus defined to be accessories shall be deemed principals, and punished accordingly. It necessarily follows, that none of the rights of the defendant incident to the prosecution of the defendant as an accessory,—such as, that he may insist upon the conviction of the principal before his arraignment and trial,—can inhere, for the reason that he is himself to be considered and regarded as a principal in the crime charged. All stand before the law as principals in the perpetration of the crime. By the express provision of the succeeding section of the Code, every person falling within the definition of an accessory thus given may be put upon trial with the principal actor in the perpetration of the crime, or before or after the latter's conviction, or whether he is amenable to justice or not, and 'punished as principal.'

"It is observable, that the advising or encouraging of another to commit a felony is not created into a substantive felony, of itself, but is made to so connect the offender with the principal felony that he becomes a principal in its commission. There is, in the nature of things, no difference in the degree of moral turpitude between the man whose will has procured the commission of a crime, and the one who willfully carries out his malignant purpose. . . ."

In defining the relationships and responsibilities of the parties to criminal offenses, modern statutory treatment has obliterated the common law distinctions between "principals" and "accessories before the fact".* The Illinois statutory scheme, together with the comments of the Code draftees are set out hereafter, as representative of the modern approach to the question of accountability for the acts of another in the criminal law:

ARTICLE 5.   PARTIES TO CRIME

§ 5–1. **Accountability for Conduct of Another.**   A person is responsible for conduct which is an element of an offense if the conduct is either that of the person himself, or

---

* For a complete historical survey of the common law of accountability, see Perkins, Parties To Crime, 89 U.Pa.L.Rev. 581 (1941); I Wharton's Criminal Law and Procedure, §§ 102–116 (1957); Clark and Marshall, Crimes, Ch. 8 (6th ed. 1958).

that of another and he is legally accountable for such conduct as provided in Section 5–2, or both.

Committee Comments

Revised by Charles H. Bowman

Section 5–1 states the general principle that criminal liability is based on conduct and that the conduct may be that of another person. Section 5–2 states the circumstances in which a person is legally accountable for the conduct of another. Subsection 5–2(a) states the universally accepted principle, most frequently encountered as liability based on the acts of an "innocent agent". Thus, if a defendant induces a child below the age of criminal capacity or an insane person to commit an act, the former is guilty precisely in the same way as he would be had he himself committed the act. (See e.g., People v. Mutchler, 309 Ill. 207, 140 N.E. 820 (1923), where a fraudulent check was cashed by an innocent agent.) . . .

§ 5–2. **When Accountability Exists.** A person is legally accountable for the conduct of another when:

(a) Having a mental state described by the statute defining the offense, he causes another to perform the conduct, and the other person in fact or by reason of legal incapacity lacks such a mental state; or

(b) The statute defining the offense makes him so accountable; or

(c) Either before or during the commission of an offense, and with the intent to promote or facilitate such commission, he solicits, aids, abets, agrees or attempts to aid, such other person in the planning or commission of the offense. However, a person is not so accountable, unless the statute defining the offense provides otherwise, if:

(1) He is a victim of the offense committed; or

(2) The offense is so defined that his conduct was inevitably incident to its commission; or

(3) Before the commission of the offense, he terminates his effort to promote or facilitate such commission, and does one of the following: wholly deprives his prior efforts of effectiveness in such commission, or gives timely warning to the proper law enforcement authorities, or otherwise makes proper effort to prevent the commission of the offense.

Committee Comments

Revised by Charles H. Bowman

Section 5–2 is a statement of principles of accessoryship although that term is not employed in the Code. It provides a much fuller statement of applicable law in this important field and, in some respects, alters and modifies the former law.

The prior statutory provisions . . . had as their primary purpose the fundamental modification of the elaborate common law distinctions between principals in the first degree, in the second degree, and accessories before the fact. Persons who at common law would be principals in the second degree or accessories before the fact were to be punished as principals in the first degree. . . . Certain procedural consequences of the common law distinctions were eliminated . . . . Section 5–2(a) accepts the approach of the former law and endeavors to develop it in a full and systematic fashion. (The draft is derived from Model Penal Code comment at 19–21 (Tent. Draft No. 4, 1955).)

Subsection 5–2(b) makes clear that there may be situations in which a person may be held legally accountable in circumstances not otherwise included in Section 5–2, where the particular statute under which he is prosecuted so provides. In such case the particular provision, of course, prevails. An example of such a statute might be one imposing vicarious criminal liability on a tavern owner for the act of an employee resulting in sale of liquor to a minor.

Subsection 5–2(c) is a comprehensive statement of liability based on counseling, aiding and abetting and the like, which includes those situations that, at common law, involve the liability of principals in the second degree and accessories before the fact. It will be observed that liability under this subsection requires proof of an "intent to promote or facilitate . . . commission" of the substantive offense. Moreover, "conspiracy" between the actor and defendant is not of itself made the basis of accountability for the actor's conduct although the acts of conspiring may in many cases satisfy the particular requirements of this subsection. (See, e.g., Pinkerton v. United States, 328 U.S. 640, 66 S.Ct. 1180, 90 L.Ed. 1489 (1946) and Model Penal Code comment at 20–26 (Tent. Draft No. 1, 1953).)

Subsections (c)(1), (2) and (3) state certain principles for relieving a person from accountability for the conduct of another who would otherwise fall under the prior provisions of subsection (c). Subsection (c)(1) states that the person who is a "victim" of the criminal act does not, unless the particular statute so states, share the guilt of the actor. This is true even though the person is a "willing" victim and counseled commission of the crime. Thus, a victim of a blackmail plot who pays over money, even though he "aids" the commission of the crime, or the girl under age of consent in "statutory rape," even though she solicited the criminal act, are not deemed guilty of the substantive offense. The same principle is extended in subsection (c)(2) to situations in which the person does not fit comfortably in the category of victim. The Model Penal Code suggests such examples as these: Should a man accepting a prostitute's solicitation be guilty of prostitution? Should a woman upon whom a miscarriage is produced be guilty of abortion? Should a bribe-taker be guilty of bribery? (Model Penal Code comment at 35 (Tent. Draft No. 1, 1953).)   . . .

Subsection (c)(3) poses the question: What can a person do who has aided and abetted, under the prior provisions of subsection (c), to relieve himself of liability for the substantive crime? It appears desirable to provide some escape route, if for no other reason than to provide an inducement for disclosure of crimes before they occur and efforts to prevent commission of crimes. The problem here should be distinguished from the question in the law of conspiracy as to what actions are required for a person to dissociate himself from a conspiratorial agreement.

To obtain this release from liability the person must, of course, terminate his affirmative efforts to facilitate commission of the crime. In addition, it is provided that he may be relieved if he is able wholly to deprive *his* contributions to the commission of an offense of their effectiveness. Thus, suppose that defendant, learning that A plans to kill B, unknown to A, sends a telegram to C asking the latter to prevent B from getting word of A's intentions. Later the defendant is able to prevent delivery of the telegram to C. In such case the defendant may be relieved of criminal liability even though A succeeds in killing B. (Cf. State ex rel. Attorney General v. Tally, Judge, 102 Ala. 25, 15 So. 722 (1894).) Also, if a timely warning is given the police, the person should be relieved even if through negligence or act of God the police fail to prevent the crime. Finally, a general clause "otherwise makes proper effort to prevent commission to the offense" is included. This will, of course, require interpretation, but judicial interpretation will be furthered by the manifest purposes of the subsection.

§ 5–3. Separate Conviction of Person Accountable.

A person who is legally accountable for the conduct of another which is an element of an offense may be convicted upon proof that the offense was committed and that he was so accountable, although the other person claimed to have committed the offense has not been prosecuted or convicted, or has been convicted of a different offense or degree of offense, or is not amenable to justice, or has been acquitted.

Committee Comments

Revised by Charles H. Bowman

Section 5–3 completes the task of eliminating the common-law consequences of categorizing accomplices into accessories before the fact and principals in the second degree. In most respects this had already been accomplished in Illinois law . . .. One major change is that of making it possible to convict a person who at common law would be an accessory, even though the person who at common law would be the principal, is tried and acquitted. (People v. Wyherk, 347 Ill. 28, 178 N.E. 890 (1931).) To be sure, inconsistent verdicts of juries produce a problem. It is clear, however, that at common law if two persons, both principals in the first degree, are tried separately and one is acquitted, the state is not precluded from proceeding to trial and obtaining a conviction of the second. Since the effort of the Code is to eliminate the common-law distinctions between the various persons who may be guilty of the substantive offense, the provision in Section 5–3 seems clearly required. (See especially, Sears, "Principals and Accessories— Some Modern Problems," 25 Ill.L.Rev. 845 (1931).)

The so-called accessory after the fact presents an entirely different range of problems. He does not share in the substantive liability of the person he aids. Consequently, his act is basically a distinct offense against public authority. Provisions relating to this matter are included in Section 31–5 of the Code.

1. THE EVIDENCE OF ACCESSORYSHIP

UNITED STATES v. GARGUILO
United States Court of Appeals, Second Circuit, 1962.
310 F.2d 249.

Ralph Garguilo and Joseph Macchia appeal from judgments of the District Court for the Southern District of New York, convicting them after a verdict under a single count indictment which charged the making of a likeness of a $10 bill in violation of 18 U.S.C. § 474. Because of a serious question raised by Macchia as to the sufficiency of the evidence against him, it is necessary to recount the testimony in some detail.

The Government's principal witnesses were Mario Villari, owner of Graphic Printing Company, a co-defendant who pleaded guilty, and Albert Della Monica, a photographer and long-time friend of the Garguilo family, whose innocence was not questioned. Villari first met Garguilo in Magistrate's Court on August 17, 1960, while both were waiting to pay traffic fines; Villari told Garguilo he was in the printing business and gave Garguilo his card. About a month later Garguilo came to Villari's shop on West 53rd Street in Manhattan. Joseph Macchia was with him. According to Villari, Garguilo introduced Macchia as "Tony", saying "that he is buddy-buddy, that they do everything together as a group." Garguilo took Villari "on the side", approximately 25 feet away from Macchia, and, placing his arm around Villari's shoulder, asked Villari to join him in a counterfeiting endeavor; Villari said he was not interested and the two visitors left about ten minutes after they had arrived. There is no evidence that Macchia talked about counterfeiting or anything else.

Some time during the summer of 1961, Garguilo came to Della Monica's photography studio in Brooklyn and asked to be taught how to develop a picture and make a copy. He came "several times," "about a week or so". He had Macchia with him "only once or two" of these times. Garguilo introduced Macchia to Della Monica as "my friend, Joe". After Garguilo had learned how to develop pictures, he "started to practice himself" and apparently did so regularly at Della Monica's studio; Macchia was there "two or three times" in all, never alone but always with Garguilo. Garguilo borrowed a camera and other photographic equipment from Della Monica, explaining that he was going into the advertising business and needed the camera to make copies. Inquiries by Della Monica as to Garguilo's progress produced no satisfactory response. There was no evidence that Macchia witnessed the loan of the equipment or participated in its use.

In July, 1961, Garguilo returned to Villari's printing shop. The record is not altogether plain whether there were two or three visits during July, but it is clear that Garguilo was alone on each of them. Assuming that there were three, the first was devoted to a general request for help, which Villari declined, as he had a year before; on the second, Garguilo asked Villari to check his negatives of $10 bills, which Villari again refused to do; on the third, Villari "succumbed", looked at the negatives, which Garguilo carried in a newspaper, through a "view box" and pronounced them too dark, whereupon Garguilo destroyed them.

Garguilo again came to Villari's shop in early August, 1961. This time Macchia accompanied him. Garguilo had brought some more negatives which Villari viewed and found "pretty good"—good enough so that he "burnt in" a plate. This was done with Macchia two or three feet away, "very close". The plate being blurred and inadequate, Garguilo erased it, whereupon he and Macchia "went away. They took the negatives with them and went away." Who carried the negatives is not clear. Villari testified this was the last he saw of Macchia.

Garguilo came to Villari's shop a few days later with some more negatives. Again a plate was "burnt in", found inadequate, and destroyed.

One of Garguilo's visits to the printing shop was witnessed by Secret Service Agent Motto. He testified that on August 11, 1961, he saw Garguilo and another man drive up in an automobile. Garguilo got out, carrying a newspaper wrapped tightly under his arm, and went into the building where Villari's shop was located. He remained for approximately one hour. Then he and Villari came out, got in the car in which the other man was seated, and drove off. Motto could not identify the man who stayed in the car; he did estimate the man's age, height and weight, but there is nothing to tell whether these estimates bear any correspondence with Macchia or whether the unidentified man was the driver. Toward the end of August, Secret Service Agents searched Villari's shop and found the erased plate of early August, which bore Garguilo's fingerprints.

The only other evidence against Macchia was that, when brought before an Assistant United States Attorney for questioning, he admitted that he knew Garguilo, that on several occasions he accompanied Garguilo to the photographer in Brooklyn, and that several times he went to a printing place with him. He claimed, however, "that he never went up to the printer's establishment but merely sat on the stoop." Macchia also admitted that he knew what was in the newspaper taken out of the car by Garguilo, but refused to say what this was.

* * *

Macchia claims that the evidence was insufficient to warrant submission to the jury of the case against him as an aider or abettor. Insofar as his claim relates to alleged lack of knowledge of the crime in which Garguilo was engaged, it is baseless—an inference of such knowledge would be not only permissible but virtually inescapable if the jury credited the testimony that Macchia was "very close" to Garguilo and Villari when the telltale plate was made, and that Macchia had admitted knowing what was in the newspaper that Garguilo had removed from the car. But knowledge that a crime is being committed, even when coupled with presence at the scene, is generally not enough to constitute aiding and abetting. . . .

It is true, as the Government urges, that evidence of an act of relatively slight moment may warrant a jury's finding participation in a crime. Thus it would have been enough here if the Government adduced evidence from which the jury could find, in addition to guilty knowledge, that Macchia had carried the negatives or driven the car. Perhaps the evidence is, in fact, susceptible of exactly such a construction. Villari testified that on the first unsuccessful plate burning "They took the negatives with them and went away." And Motto's testimony, coupled with the evidence as to Macchia's admission of knowing what was in the paper that Garguilo took out of the car, would be consistent with Macchia's having been the driver on August 11, although if this was Garguilo's final visit, a finding of Macchia's presence on that occasion would run counter to Villari's testimony that the penultimate visit was the last time he saw Macchia. It is true also that participation may be proved by circumstantial evidence, as in United States v. Lefkowitz, 284 F.2d 310, 315–316 (2 Cir. 1960), where we held that defendant Dryja's fingerprints on stolen cartons, together with evidence tending to negate the possibility of his having had access to them at the point of origin, permitted an inference that he had handled them after the theft, and, since other evidence tended to show guilty knowledge, that submission to the jury was proper. There may even be instances where the mere presence of a defendant at the scene of a crime he knows is being committed will permit a jury to be convinced beyond a reasonable doubt that the defendant sought "by his action to make it succeed"—for example, the attendance of a 250-pound bruiser at a shake-down as a companion to the extortionist, or the maintenance at the scene of crime of someone useful as a lookout. Here presence in the car on August 11 might be thought to have been for the latter purpose. Again, it is enough if the presence of the alleged aider and abettor has stimulated others to help the perpetrator, as, for example, if Macchia rather than Garguilo had been the friend of Della Monica, or perhaps simply on the sole basis that it is proved to have positively encouraged the perpetrator himself, see State v. Hargett, 255 N.C. 412, 415, 121 S.E.2d 589, 592 (1961) (dictum). Yet, even in an age when solitude is so detested and "togetherness" so valued, a jury could hardly be permitted to find that the mere furnishing of company to a person engaged in crime renders the companion an aider or abettor. Here, on every occasion that was the subject of testimony, Garguilo was the actor, often he was alone, and when he first propositioned Villari, he left Macchia to one side; any inference that Macchia had some role beyond that of a companion rested on the rather equivocal evidence just discussed and on the repetitive instances of his presence, all colored by Garguilo's unusual introduction of Macchia to Villari on their first visit to the print shop.

If the evidence against Macchia passed the test of sufficiency applicable in a criminal case, it did so, as was said in United States v. Lefkowitz, supra, 284 F.2d at 315, "only by a hair's breadth". We are not here required to make so fine a judgment, since we believe reversal for a new trial to be called for in any event. If the evidence was insufficient it came near enough to the line to entitle the Government, if it desires, to an opportunity to put it across on a new trial. . . . On the other hand, we would still be disposed to direct a new trial even though the evidence was sufficient. The closeness of the issue against Macchia imposed an obligation on the trial judge to instruct the jury with extreme precision, as he realized, and on us to review the charge with what, in a less doubtful case, would be undue meticulousness. . . . Reading the entire charge, we cannot overcome a fear that the judge, quite unwittingly and simply by emphasis, may have led the jury to believe that a finding of presence and knowledge on the part of Macchia was enough for conviction. True, there is much in the charge that would argue against this. Turning to the case against Macchia the judge began by stating the law as to aiding and abetting with entire correctness. However, when he came to apply these principles to the facts, very nearly the whole of his comment, and a vivid illustration that he used, related solely to the issue of "conscious, intelligent awareness of what was going on.[1] The jury evidenced its concern over

---

1. The judge stated:

"Now let us take it from there, making those basic assumptions [that the jury believed Villari and Della Monica]. Was Macchia [sic.] close enough to the transactions, to the conversations, to the general atmosphere of the transactions to know what was going on? Did he have an intelligent, conscious awareness of what was going on? And if he did have

that conscious intelligent awareness of what was going on, was it sufficient to constitute an aiding or abetting within the terms of the definition I gave you?"

He then gave as an illustration the case of a man in the back seat of a car "who was fast asleep and all rolled up in a rug or with his overcoat over his head," who, even though introduced by the principal defendant as "my pal, my partner, and my

the case against Macchia by a request for further instructions as to what constituted aiding or abetting; although what the judge said would have been adequate, indeed excellent, in the usual trial, the contrasting hypothetical cases which he put to the jury turned on the issue of knowledge,[2] whereas his instructions with respect to purposive participation, although correct, were rather abstract. Never were the jurors told in plain words that mere presence and guilty knowledge on the part of Macchia would not suffice unless they were also convinced beyond a reasonable doubt that Macchia was doing something to forward the crime—that he was a participant rather than merely a knowing spectator. In the usual case we should not think of finding reversible error in such a charge when there was no objection, or perhaps even if there had been. However, in the exceptional circumstances here presented, and in the light of our powers under 28 U.S. C.A. § 2106 and F.R.Crim.Proc. 52(b), we believe that the interests of justice as between the Government and Macchia will be best served by reversal and remand for a new trial.

. . .

The judgment of conviction . . . of Macchia is reversed and remanded for a new trial.

LUMBARD, CHIEF JUDGE (concurring and dissenting).

As I believe that the jury may well have thought that knowledge of Macchia of what was afoot was sufficient to convict, I concur in the result which permits a retrial of the case against him. But I disagree with my brethren insofar as Judge Friendly's opinion implies that there was not enough evidence from which the jury could conclude that Macchia was guilty as an aider and abettor in the sense of wishing to see Garguilo succeed and assisting him by his actions. I think there was sufficient evidence to support a verdict of guilty upon a proper charge from the court.

There can be little doubt that when Macchia, together with Garguilo, visited Villari at his printing shop at 537 West 53rd Street, Manhattan and Della Monica at his photography shop on New Utrecht Avenue in Brooklyn, they must have thought that Macchia was interested in Garguilo's business. Each of them saw him at least twice. The presence of a friend is not only an encouragement to the one who is accompanied but it may also be of assistance in persuading others to be of help. From these four or five visits which Macchia made with Garguilo to the business places of Villari and Della Monica, and from all the surrounding circumstances, and the admissions of Macchia, it seems to me that it was a question for the jury as to whether Macchia's

coconspirator," would not be an aider or abettor.

2. These cases concerned a taxi driver who drove a narcotics smuggler to an illegal appointment with special celerity and made a telephone call for him, without knowing that he was dealing with a narcotics smuggler, and another who performed the same acts with knowledge of the illegality of the venture.

accompanying Garguilo did not contribute to the likelihood of the success of Garguilo's efforts.

In Hicks v. United States . . . (1893), the Supreme Court recognized that presence without action may constitute aiding and abetting if there is evidence that the defendant had a purpose to aid but did not act only because action proved to be unnecessary and it is shown that the presence was pursuant to an understanding. Here there was enough evidence for the jury to infer that Macchia was going along to be of help. There was also enough evidence to infer an agreement between Macchia and Garguilo to commit the counterfeiting offense. In short, there was evidence of purpose and conspiracy which, if the jury had been properly charged, would require an affirmance.

As Judge Friendly says, if Macchia had said one single word of encouragement to Villari or Della Monica, it would have been enough. I think the jury could construe his mere presence on these occasions as tantamount to such encouragement. It seems to me naive to suppose that the kind of company and moral (or immoral) support which Macchia gave to Garguilo by being with him was not of the kind which would help Garguilo in his business with Villari and Della Monica. While there is nothing to show that Macchia might have been a hoodlum or bodyguard, his presence certainly rendered it less likely that Villari or Della Monica might report the matter to the police. Moreover, Macchia's presence gave Garguilo an ally and at least a possible witness if any dispute had arisen. It is precisely because two persons together are more formidable that [than] two persons acting separately in carrying out any illegal design that conspiracy has been made a crime even though it may not succeed.

In my opinion there was enough evidence to permit the jury to decide on a proper charge whether or not Macchia was guilty as an aider and abettor.

NOTES

1. In State v. Scott, 289 N.C. 712, 224 S.E.2d 185 (1976), the court said (at 190–191): "The case against Scott then comes to this: he was a friend of the actual perpetrator and was present at the time and place the crime was committed. . . . Where, . . ., as here, presence is proved only by inference and there is no direct evidence of the crime scene itself it would be unreasonable to infer also such knowledge of the bystander from the mere fact of his presence."

2. Once some aiding of another is shown, knowing of the criminal undertaking which is afoot, it has been held that "an aider and abettor need only have knowledge of the criminal purpose of the perpetrator and criminal intent . . . and need not have the specific intent to commit the target crime." People v. Germany, 42 Cal.App.3d 414, 116 Cal.Rptr. 841 (1974). But see, United States v. Barclay, 560 F.2d 812 (7th Cir. 1977).

3. Can a friend of the robber, who arrives as the robbery is ending, be convicted as an aider and abettor if he gives the robber a ride away from the

crime scene? Consider People v. Valerio, 64 A.D.2d 516, 406 N.Y.S.2d 481 (1978).

4. What is the criminal liability of an "instigator" of a crime? See, e.g., McGhee v. Commonwealth, 221 Va. 422, 270 S.E.2d 729 (1980).

2. THE EXTENT OF ACCESSORYSHIP

UNITED STATES v. PEONI

United States Court of Appeals, Second Circuit, 1938.
100 F.2d 401.

L. HAND, CIRCUIT JUDGE. Peoni was indicted in the Eastern District of New York upon three counts for possessing counterfeit money . . .. The jury convicted him on all counts, and the only question we need consider is whether the evidence was enough to sustain the verdict. It was this. In the Borough of the Bronx Peoni sold counterfeit bills to one, Regno; and Regno sold the same bills to one, Dorsey, also in the Bronx. All three knew that the bills were counterfeit, and Dorsey was arrested while trying to pass them in the Borough of Brooklyn. The question is whether Peoni was guilty as an accessory to Dorsey's possession . . . whether he was party to a conspiracy by which Dorsey should possess the bills.

The prosecution's argument is that, as Peoni put the bills in circulation and knew that Regno would be likely, not to pass them himself, but to sell them to another guilty possessor, the possession of the second buyer was a natural consequence of Peoni's original act, with which he might be charged. If this were a civil case, that would be true; an innocent buyer from Dorsey could sue Peoni and get judgment against him for his loss. But the rule of criminal liability is not the same; since Dorsey's possession was not de facto Peoni's, and since Dorsey was not Peoni's agent, Peoni can be liable only as an accessory to Dorsey's act of possession. The test of that must be found in the appropriate federal statute . . .

It will be observed that all these [common law] definitions have nothing whatever to do with the probability that the forbidden result would follow upon the accessory's conduct; and that they all demand that he in some sort associate himself with the venture, that he participate in it as in something that he wishes to bring about, that he seek by his action to make it succeed. All the words used—even the most colorless, "abet"—carry an implication of purposive attitude towards it. So understood, Peoni was not an accessory to Dorsey's possession; his connection with the business ended when he got his money from Regno, who might dispose of the bills as he chose; it was of no moment to him whether Regno passed them himself, and so ended the possibility of further guilty possession, or whether he sold them to a second possible passer. His utterance of the bills was indeed a step in the causal chain which ended in Dorsey's possession, but that was all. Perhaps he was Regno's accessory. Rudner v. United States, 6 Cir., 281

F. 516, and Anstess v. United States, 7 Cir., 22 F.2d 594, do indeed hold that a seller, knowing the buyer's criminal purpose, is a conspirator with him. On the other hand in Rex v. Lomas, 22 Cox's Cr.Cas. 765, the court acquitted the accused who had given back to a burglar a jimmy which the burglar had lent him, though he knew the burglar would use it to commit the crime; Lord Reading saying that in such cases "advice or procuring" was a necessary element. Moreover, the law is at least unsettled whether action for the price will not lie, though the seller knows that the buyer means to use the goods to commit a crime, Williston, § 1754, and in perhaps the leading case, Graves v. Johnson, 179 Mass. 53, 60 N.E. 383, 88 Am.St.Rep. 355 the seller recovered. Be that as it may nobody, so far as we can find, has ever held that a contract is criminal, because the seller has reason to know, not that the buyer will use the goods unlawfully, but that some one further down the line may do so. Nor is it at all desirable that the seller should be held indefinitely. The real gravamen of the charge against him is his utterance of the bills; and he ought not to be tried for that wherever the prosecution may pick up any guilty possessor— perhaps thousands of miles away. The oppression against which the Sixth Amendment is directed could be easily compassed by this device, because if the seller be a real accessory he may be removed to the place of the crime. Hoss v. United States, 8 Cir., 232 F. 328, 335; United States v. Littleton, D.C., 1 F.2d 751. * * *

Conviction reversed; accused discharged.

NOTE

In Enmund v. Florida, 458 U.S. 782, 102 S.Ct. 3368, 73 L.Ed.2d 1140 (1982), the Court held that while an accomplice to a first degree murderer could also be found guilty of first degree murder on an accountability theory, the imposition of the death penalty upon a person who neither took life, attempted to take life, nor intended to take life, is inconsistent with the constitutional prohibition against cruel and unusual punishment. See this case, supra, in Chapter 4–D, under 2, The Death Penalty.

For a similar statutory limitation upon accomplice liability, see Virginia Code S 18.2–18: "In the case of every felony, every principal in the second degree and every accessory before the fact may be indicted, tried, convicted and punished in all respects as if a principal in the first degree, provided, however, that *except in the case of a killing for hire under the provisions of [the capital murder statute] an accessory before the fact or principal in the second degree to a capital murder shall be indicted, tried, convicted and punished as though the offense were murder in the first degree.* [Emphasis supplied.]" Virginia punishes first degree murders by imprisonment for life or a term not less than twenty years.

STANDEFER v. UNITED STATES
Supreme Court of the United States, 1980.
447 U.S. 10, 100 S.Ct. 1999, 64 L.Ed.2d 689.

MR. CHIEF JUSTICE BURGER delivered the opinion of the Court.

We granted certiorari in this case to decide whether a defendant accused of aiding and abetting in the commission of a federal offense may be convicted after the named principal has been acquitted of that offense.

I

In June 1977, petitioner Standefer was indicted on four counts of making gifts to a public official, in violation of 18 U.S.C. § 201(f), and on five counts of aiding and abetting a revenue official in accepting compensation in addition to that authorized by law, in violation of 26 U.S.C. § 7214(a)(2) and 18 U.S.C. § 2. The indictment charged that petitioner, as head of Gulf Oil Company's tax department, had authorized payments for five vacation trips to Cyril Niederberger, who then was the Internal Revenue Service agent in charge of the audits of Gulf's federal income tax returns. Specifically, the indictment alleged that Gulf, on petitioner's authorization, had paid for vacations for Niederberger in Pompano Beach (July 1971), Miami (January 1973), Absecon (August-September 1973), Pebble Beach (April 1974), and Las Vegas (June 1974). The four counts under 18 U.S.C. § 201(f) related to the Miami, Absecon, Pebble Beach, and Las Vegas vacations; the five counts under 26 U.S.C. § 7214(a)(2) and 18 U.S.C. § 2 were one for each vacation.

Prior to the filing of this indictment, Niederberger was separately charged in a 10-count indictment—two counts for each of the five vacations—with violating 18 U.S.C. § 201(g) and 26 U.S.C. § 7214(a)(2). In February 1977, Niederberger was tried on these charges. He was convicted on four counts of violating § 201(g) in connection with the vacations in Miami, Absecon, Pebble Beach, and Las Vegas and of two counts of violating § 7214(a)(2) for the Pebble Beach and Las Vegas trips. He was acquitted on the § 201(g) count involving the Pompano Beach trip and on the three counts under § 7214(a)(2) charging him with accepting payments from Gulf for trips to Pompano Beach, Miami, and Absecon.

In July 1977, following Niederberger's trial and before the trial in his own case commenced, petitioner moved to dismiss the counts under § 7214(a)(2) and 18 U.S.C. § 2 which charged him with aiding and abetting Niederberger in connection with the Pompano Beach, Miami, and Absecon vacations. . . .

Petitioner's case then proceeded to trial on all nine counts. At trial, petitioner admitted authorizing payment for all five vacation trips, but testified that the trips were purely social and not designed to influence Niederberger in the performance of his official duties. The jury returned guilty verdicts on all nine counts. Petitioner was sentenced to concurrent terms of six months' imprisonment followed by two years' probation; he was fined a total of $18,000—$2,000 on each count.

Petitioner appealed his convictions to the Court of Appeals for the Third Circuit claiming, *inter alia,* that he could not be convicted of aiding and abetting a principal, Niederberger, when that principal had been acquitted of the charged offense. By a divided vote, the Court of Appeals, sitting en banc, rejected that contention. It concluded that "the outcome of Niederberger's prosecution has no effect on [petitioner's] convictions."

Because the question presented is one of importance to the administration of criminal justice on which the Courts of Appeals are in conflict, we granted certiorari. We affirm.

II

Petitioner makes two main arguments: first, that Congress in enacting 18 U.S.C. § 2 did not intend to authorize prosecution of an aider and abettor after the principal has been acquitted of the offense charged; second, that, even if § 2 permits such a prosecution, the government should be barred from relitigating the issue of whether Niederberger accepted unlawful compensation in connection with the Pompano Beach, Miami, and Absecon vacations. The first contention relies largely on the common law as it prevailed before the enactment of 18 U.S.C. § 2. The second rests on the contemporary doctrine of nonmutual collateral estoppel.

A

At common law, the subject of principals and accessories was riddled with "intricate" distinctions. 2 J. Stephen, History of the Criminal Law of England 231 (1883). In felony cases, parties to a crime were divided into four distinct categories: (1) principals in the first degree who actually perpetrated the offense; (2) principals in the second degree who were actually or constructively present at the scene of the crime and aided or abetted its commission; (3) accessories before the fact who aided or abetted the crime, but were not present at its commission; and (4) accessories after the fact who rendered assistance after the crime was complete. By contrast, misdemeanor cases "d[id] not admit of accessaries [sic either before or after the fact," United States v. Hartwell, 26 F.Cas. No. 15, 318 p. 196, 199 (1869); instead, all parties to a misdemeanor, whatever their roles, were principals.

Because at early common law all parties to a felony received the death penalty, certain procedural rules developed tending to shield accessories from punishment. Among them was one of special relevance to this case: the rule that an accessory could not be convicted without the prior conviction of the principal offender. Under this rule, the principal's flight, death, or acquittal barred prosecution of the accessory. And if the principal were pardoned or his conviction reversed on appeal, the accessory's conviction could not stand. In every way "an accessory follow[ed], like a shadow, his principal." 1 J.Bishop, Criminal Law § 666 (8th ed. 1892).

This procedural bar applied only to the prosecution of accessories in felony cases. In misdemeanor cases, where all participants were deemed principals, a prior acquittal of the actual perpetrator did not prevent the subsequent conviction of a person who rendered assistance. And in felony cases a principal in the second degree could be convicted notwithstanding the prior acquittal of the first-degree principal. Not surprisingly, considerable effort was expended in defining the categories—in determining, for instance, when a person was "constructively present" so as to be a second-degree principal. In the process, justice all too frequently was defeated.

To overcome these judge-made rules, statutes were enacted in England and in the United States. In 1848 the Parliament enacted a statute providing that an accessory before the fact could be "indicted, tried, convicted, and punished in all respects *as if he were a principal felon.*" As interpreted, the statute permitted an accessory to be convicted "although the principal be acquitted." R. v. Hughes, Bell's Crown Cases 242, 248 (1860). Several state legislatures followed suit.[1]

1. By 1909, when § 2 was enacted, 13 states had enacted legislation providing that the acquittal of the actual perpetrator was not a bar to the conviction of one charged with giving him aid. See Cal.Stat. ch 99, §§ 11–12 (1850) (see People v. Bearss, 10 Cal. 68–70 (1858)); Del.Laws (Rev.Code) §§ 2919–2921 (1852); Iowa Rev. Code § 4314 (1882) (see State v. Lee, 91 Iowa 499, 501–502, 60 N.W. 119, 120 (1894)); Kan.Gen.Stat. § 5180 (1889) (see State v. Bogue, 52 Kan. 79, 86–87, 34 P. 410, 412 (1893)); Ky.Stat. § 1128 (1903) (see Commonwealth v. Hicks, 118 Ky. 637, 642, 82 S.W. 265, 266 (1904); Miss.Code § 1026 (1906) (see Fleming v. State, 142 Miss. 872, 880–881, 108 So. 143, 144–145 (1926)); Mont.Codes Ann. (Penal Code) § 1854 (1895); N.Y. Penal Code § 29 (1895) (see People v. Kief, 126 N.Y. 661, 663–664, 27 N.E. 556, 557 (1891)); N.D.Rev.Codes § 8060 (1895); Okla.Stat. § 5523 (1890); S.D.Ann.Stat. § 8520 (1899); Utah Comp. Laws § 4752 (1907); Wash.Code of Proc. § 1189 (1891) (see State v. Gifford, 19 Wash. 464, 467–468, 53 P. 709, 710 (1898).

Since then, at least 21 other states have enacted legislation with that effect. See 1977 Ala.Laws, Act. No. 607, § 425; Ariz. Rev.Stat.Ann. § 13–304(1) (1978); Ark. Stat.Ann. § 41–304 (1977); Colo.Rev.Stat. § 18–1–605 (1973) (see Robert v. People, 103 Colo. 250, 87 P.2d 251 (1938)); Conn.Gen.Stat. § 53a–9 (1979); Fla.Stat. § 777.011 (1976) (see Butts v. State, Fla. App., 286 So.2d 28 (1973)); Ga.Code § 26–802 (1978); Ill.Rev.Stat. ch. 38 § 5–3 (1972); Ind.Code § 35–41–2–4 (1979); La.Rev.Stat. Ann. § 14:24 (West) (1974) (see State v. McAllister, La., 366 So.2d 1340 (1978));

Me.Rev.Stat.Ann., Tit. 17–A § 57; Mich. Comp.Laws § 767.39 (1968) (People v. Smith, 271 Mich. 553, 260 N.W. 911 (1935)); Mo.Rev.Stat. § 562.046 (1978); Neb.Rev.Stat. § 28–206 (Cum.Supp.1978) (State v. Rice, 188 Neb.R. 728, 199 N.W.2d 480 (1972)); N.H.Rev.Stat.Ann. § 626:8 (1974); N.J.Stat.Ann. § 2C:2–6 (West 1979); N.M.Stat.Ann. § 30–1–13 (1978); Penn. Cons.Stat. 18 § 306 (Cum.Supp.1979); S.C. Code § 16–1–50 (State v. Massey, 267 S.C. 432, 229 S.E.2d 332 (1976)); Tex.Penal Code § 7.03 (1974); Wis.Stat. § 39.05 (1958).

Eleven other states have enacted statutes that modify the common-law rule; these statutes have not been authoritatively construed on whether an accessory can be prosecuted after his principal's acquittal. See Haw.Rev.Stat. § 702–225 (1976); Idaho Code § 19–1431 (1979); Mass.Gen. Laws Ann. ch. 274 § 3 (1970); Minn.Stat. § 609.05 (1964); Nev.Rev.Stat. § 195.040 (1979); Ohio Rev.Code Ann. § 2923.03 (1979); Okla.Stat., Tit. 21 § 172 (1971); Ore.Rev.Stat. § 161.160 (1979); Vt.Stat. Ann., Tit. 13 § 3 (1974); Va.Code § 18.2–21 (1975); W.Va.Code § 61–11–7 (1977); Wyo. Stat. § 6–1–7114 (1977).

Only four states—Maryland, North Carolina, Rhode Island, and Tennessee—clearly retain the common-law bar. See State v. Ward, 284 Md. 189, 396 A.2d 1041 (1978); State v. Jones, 101 N.C. 719, 8 S.E. 147 (1888) (interpreting N.C.Gen.Stat. § 14–15 (1969)); R.I.Gen.Laws § 11–1–3 (1956); Pierce v. State, 130 Tenn. 24, 168 S.W. 851 (1914).

In 1899, Congress joined this growing reform movement with the enactment of a general penal code for Alaska which "abrogated" the common-law distinctions and provided that "all persons concerned in the commission of a felony . . . must be indicted, tried, and punished as principals, *as in the case of a misdemeanor.* Act of Mar. 3, 1899, ch. 429, §§ 184–187, 30 Stat. 1282 (emphasis added). In 1901 Congress enacted a similar provision for the District of Columbia.

The enactment of 18 U.S.C. § 2 in 1909 was part and parcel of this same reform movement. The language of the statute, as enacted, unmistakably demonstrates the point:

> "Whoever directly commits any act constituting an offense defined in any law of the United States, or aids, abets, counsels, commands, induces or procures its commission, *is a principal."* Act of March 4, 1909, ch. 321, 35 Stat. 1152 (emphasis added).

The statute "abolishe[d] the distinction between principals and accessories and [made] them all principals." Hammer v. United States, 271 U.S. 620, 628, 46 S.Ct. 603, 604 (1926). Read against its common-law background, the provision evinces a clear intent to permit the conviction of accessories to federal criminal offenses despite the prior acquittal of the actual perpetrator of the offense. It gives general effect to what had always been the rule for second-degree principals and for all misdemeanants.

The legislative history of § 2 confirms this understanding. The provision was recommended by the Commission to Revise and Codify the Criminal and Penal Laws of the United States as "in accordance with the policy of recent legislation" by which "those whose relations to a crime would be that of accessories before the fact according to the common law are made principals." Final Report of the Commission to Revise and Codify the Laws of the United States 118–119 (1906). The Commission's recommendation was adopted without change. The House and Senate Committee reports, in identical language, stated its intended effect:

> "The committee has deemed it wise to make those who are accessories before the fact at common-law principal offenders, thereby permitting their indictment and conviction for a substantive offense. At common law an accessory can not be tried without his consent before the conviction or outlawry of the principal except where the principal and accessory are tried together; if the principal could not be found or if he had been indicted and refused to plea, had been pardoned or died before conviction, the accessory could not be tried at all. This change of the existing law renders these obstacles to justice impossi-

---

The Model Penal code provides that an accomplice may be convicted "though the person claimed to have committed the of- fense . . . has been acquitted." § 2.06(7) and see comments Tentative Draft No. 1, May 1953, at 38–39.

ble." S.Rep. No. 10, 60th Cong., 1st Sess., Pt. 1, at 13 (1908); H.R.Rep. No. 2, 6th Cong., 1st Sess., at 13 (1908). * * *

This history plainly rebuts petitioner's contention that § 2 was not intended to authorize conviction of an aider and abettor after the principal had been acquitted of the offense charged. With the enactment of that section, all participants in conduct violating a federal criminal statute are "principals." As such, they are punishable for their criminal conduct; the fate of other participants is irrelevant.[2]

[The portion of the opinion in which the Court rejects defendant's arguments based on the doctrine of nonmutual collateral estoppel is omitted.]

III

In denying preclusive effect to Niederberger's acquittal, we do not deviate from the sound teaching that "justice must satisfy the appearance of justice." Offutt v. United States, 348 U.S. 11, 14, 75 S.Ct. 11, 13 (1954). This case does no more than manifest the simple, if discomforting, reality that "different juries may reach different results under any criminal statute. That is one of the consequences we accept under our jury system." While symmetry of results may be intellectually satisfying, it is not required.

Here, petitioner received a fair trial at which the Government bore the burden of proving beyond reasonable doubt that Niederberger violated 26 U.S.C. § 7214(a)(2) and that petitioner aided and abetted him in that venture. He was entitled to no less—and to no more.

The judgment of the Court of Appeals is

Affirmed.

NOTES

1. Can a participant in a criminal undertaking withdraw from it before the criminal purpose has been accomplished and thus escape accountability for it? The problem has already been discussed briefly in connection with conspiracy offenses and withdrawal from a conspiracy. Consider, in this connection, language quoted in Blevins v. Commonwealth, 209 Va. 622, 166 S.E.2d 325 (1969):

> " * * * Where the perpetration of a felony has been entered on, one who has aided and encouraged its commission may nevertheless, before its completion, withdraw all his aid and encouragement and escape criminal liability for the completed felony; but his withdrawal

2. Nothing in Shuttlesworth v. Birmingham, 373 U.S. 262, 83 S.Ct. 1130 (1963), relied on by petitioner, is to the contrary. There, petitioner had been convicted of aiding and abetting others to violate a city trespass ordinance which subsequently was declared constitutionally invalid. See Gober v. Birmingham, 373 U.S. 374, 83 S.Ct. 1311 (1963). Shuttlesworth's case merely applied the rule that "there can be no conviction for aiding and abetting someone to do an innocent act." Id., 373 U.S., at 265, 83 S.Ct., at 1132. Here, by contrast, the government proved in petitioner's case that Niederberger had violated § 7214(a)(2) in connection with each of the five trips.

must be evidenced by acts or words showing to his confederates that he disapproves or opposes the contemplated crime. Moreover, it is essential that he withdraw in due time, that the one seeking to avoid liability do everything practicable to detach himself from the criminal enterprise and to prevent the consummation of the crime, and that, if committed, it be imputable to some independent cause. . . ."

2. Some participants in criminal activities are not held accountable for the criminal activities of their confederates. This concept was discussed earlier in Section C, in the comments on the Illinois accountability statute. Thus, in State v. Goff, 86 S.D. 354, 195 N.W.2d 521 (1972), the court held that the prosecutrix in an incest case, a girl 11 years of age, was not legally capable of giving consent and therefore was a "victim" rather than an "accomplice" to the crime of incest. For a similar holding involving a seventeen year old girl who had engaged in sexual intercourse and an alleged perverted practice with her father, see Lusby v. State, 217 Md. 191, 141 A.2d 893 (1958).

3. In People v. Trumbley, 252 Ill. 29, 96 N.E. 573 (1911), the court held that while a woman could not commit the crime of rape as a principal actor, she could nevertheless be punished as an accessory before the fact for aiding and abetting in the commission of the crime of rape. The court said, ". . . Undoubtedly, a woman may be punished for aiding and abetting in the commission of the crime and rape, and as our statute has abolished all distinction between the principal actor and one who is an accessory before or at the fact, the accessory is to be considered as a principal and indicted accordingly."

Agreeing with the foregoing concept, the court in People v. Evans, 58 A.D.2d 919, 396 N.Y.S.2d 727 (1977), held that a female can be found guilty of rape in aiding and abetting her male codefendant to have sexual intercourse with the female victim, or by beating and holding the victim during the act.

3. ACCESSORY AFTER THE FACT—MISPRISION OF FELONY—COMPOUNDING A CRIME

(a) THE ACCESSORY AFTER THE FACT

PEOPLE v. ZIERLION
Supreme Court of Illinois, 1959.
16 Ill.2d 217, 157 N.E.2d 72.

KLINGBIEL, JUSTICE. After a trial in the criminal court of Cook County before the judge sitting without a jury, Richard Zierlion was convicted of the crime of burglary. He was sentenced to imprisonment in the penitentiary for a term of not less than one nor more than four years. He brings the case to this court for review by writ of error, contending that the evidence is insufficient to prove him guilty of the crime charged.

The evidence shows that on the night of February 4, 1958, four men, namely Tony Gallas, Tom Hills, Paul Petropulos and Ronald Utterbach, entered the office-warehouse of Martin Oil Service, Inc., in Chicago. They pushed a safe belonging to the company out of a second floor window into the yard of the premises. It proved to be too heavy to move, so the four men left for help. In the meantime they had been observed by an employee of the company who came to work at about 11:45 P.M. The police were notified, arrived at the scene, and waited there until about 2:15 A.M. At that time two automobiles appeared, a Cadillac and a Ford, each containing three men. The Cadillac backed up to the safe with the trunk open whereupon the police called to the men. The men fled and the police fired shots killing one and wounding the defendant Zierlion. It further appears that after the original four men left to get assistance they met defendant and one Mike Rudis, the deceased, in a tavern; and that the six of them thereafter went to the yard of the Martin Oil Service to get the safe. There is no evidence that the defendant participated in the affair prior to being called upon to aid in moving the safe.

Defendant argues that to warrant a conviction for burglary it must be shown that the accused entered a building with intent to commit a felony, and that since the evidence fails to show such conduct on the part of defendant the present conviction cannot stand. The contention has merit. Evidence that he was guilty of assisting the burglars after the safe had been removed from the building cannot make him a principal in the crime charged. Proof that a person is an accessory after the fact is proof of an independent offense.

The evidence is insufficient to sustain the judgment, which is accordingly hereby reversed.

Judgment reversed.

DAVIS, JUSTICE. I dissent from the conclusions of the court that to warrant a conviction for burglary it must be shown that the accused entered a building with intent to commit a felony, and that evidence that he was assisting the burglars, after the safe had been removed from the building, cannot make him a principal in the crime charged.

Burglary consists of willfully and maliciously entering any dwelling or other building, with or without force, with intent to commit murder, robbery, rape, mayhem, or other felony or larceny. An accessory is defined as "he who stands by, and aids, abets or assists, or who not being present, aiding, abetting, or assisting, hath advised, encouraged, aided or abetted the perpetration of the crime." One who thus "aids, abets, assists, advises or encourages shall be considered as principal, and punished accordingly." Ill.Rev.Stat.1957, chap. 38, par. 582.

While the gist of the offense of burglary is the entering with felonious intent . . ., it does not follow that only those who actually enter the building may be convicted and punished as principals. Thus, one who in furtherance of a common design, stands outside as lookout or waits outside in an automobile, while his confederates enter, is equally guilty with them of the crime of burglary. . . .

The opinion erroneously assumes that the burglary had been completed prior to defendant's participation in efforts to remove the safe from the company premises. While we have held that a burglary is

complete upon the breaking and entering with intent to steal . . .,
this does not preclude the crime from being a continuing one as long as
the participants are still in the process of committing larceny of the
property. . . .

It is a general rule of law that "one who withdraws from a criminal
enterprise is not responsible for the act of another subsequently committed in furtherance of the enterprise, provided the fact of withdrawal
is communicated to the other conspirators." Conversely, one who joins
and participates in completing a criminal enterprise should be responsible for both the prior and subsequent acts committed in furtherance of
such venture.

The evidence establishes that the entry of the building had been
accomplished, but the intent to steal the safe had been thwarted at the
time the defendant joined the burglars and aided, abetted and participated in furtherance of the original intent to commit larceny of the
safe, the purpose of the burglary. Consequently, he is liable as principal even though he did not enter the building. I would affirm the
criminal court of Cook County.

NOTE

The foregoing case was decided shortly before the enactment of the 1961
Illinois Criminal Code. In the drafters' commentary regarding the section of
the code dealing with "accountability for the conduct of another" (Section 5),
the statement is made that the crime of accessory after the fact . . . is
basically a distinct offense against public authority." The provision relating to
that conduct appears in Section 31–5 of the Code (Ill.Rev.Stats., Ch. 38), which
reads as follows:

> Concealing or Aiding a Fugitive. Every person not standing in the
> relation of husband, wife, parent, child, brother or sister to the offend-
> er, who, with intent to prevent the apprehension of the offender,
> conceals his knowledge that an offense has been committed or harbors,
> aids or conceals the offender, commits a Class 4 felony.

This section of the Illinois Criminal Code has been interpreted so that
"concealing" means more than a mere failure to come forward with information; there must be an affirmative act toward concealment. People v. Donel-
son, 45 Ill.App.3d 609, 4 Ill.Dec. 273, 359 N.E.2d 1225 (1977); People v.
Bradford, 71 Ill.App.3d 731, 27 Ill.Dec. 572, 389 N.E.2d 636 (1979).

(b) MISPRISION OF FELONY

HOLLAND v. STATE
Florida Appellate Court, 1974.
302 So.2d 806.

McNULTY, CHIEF JUDGE. Petitioner seeks review by common law
certiorari of an order of the Circuit Court of Pinellas County, sitting in
its appellate capacity, which reversed the county court's dismissal of an

indictment charging petitioner with the crime of "misprision of felony." We grant certiorari and reinstate the order quashing the indictment.

As far as we know or are able to determine, this is the first case in Florida involving the crime of misprision of felony. Such offense is not proscribed by the statutes of Florida, but was a crime at common law. The circuit court order now under review, as did the county court order before it, recognized it as such common law offense and held it to be a "crime under the laws of the State of Florida" pursuant to the provisions of § 775.01, F.S.1971, which declares common law crimes to be of full force in this state in the absence of a specific statute on the subject. We disagree on this fundamental finding and therefore deem it unnecessary to discuss the factual issues which the circuit court considered viable and upon which he predicated his reversal of the county court's dismissal of the indictment.

Before continuing further, and to assist in lighting the path we take, we briefly define the offense as it existed at common law. We will more fully discuss it, infra; but for now, let it be said that it was the bare failure of a person with knowledge of the commission of a felony to bring the crime to the attention of the proper authorities.[1]

Now the facts. Petitioner was, at the times material herein, City Manager of the City of Pinellas Park, Florida. On or about the critical date herein, to wit: August 2, 1973, he was attempting to contact his assistant city manager, one Rutherford, and had been unable to do so by telephone. He drove to Rutherford's residence but though Rutherford's car was parked in front he was unable to raise him. He went around to the rear of the house looking for him and, at that time, noticed several plants growing in the rear yard which he suspected to be marijuana. He picked two leaves from two different plants and returned to his office. He contacted one T. W. Kelley, Captain of the Pinellas Park Police Department, to whom he related his findings. The two men then caused the plant samples to be chemically analyzed and their suspicions were confirmed.

Subsequently, Captain Kelley accompanied appellant back to Rutherford's house where they confronted Mr. Rutherford and accused him of the offense of which they suspected he was guilty. After some equivocation Rutherford finally indicated to them his guilt. In Mr. Rutherford's presence, then, appellant and Kelley uprooted a sufficient number of the aforesaid plants to constitute an aggregate of more than five grams of marijuana thus establishing the offense as *felony* possession of marijuana.

1. See I Bishop, New Criminal Law § 699 (8th ed. 1892); I Chitty, A Practical Treatise on the Criminal Law 3 (1819); 20 The American and English Encyclopedia of Law 803–04 (2d ed. 1902).

We note here that misprision of felony does exist by statute under Federal law. 18 U.S.C.A. § 4. However, this statutory crime of misprision includes the added element of a positive act of concealment. Neal v. United States, 102 F.2d 643 (8th Cir. 1939); Bratton v. United States, 73 F.2d 795 (CCA 10th 1934). In Florida, this type of behavior is proscribed by §§ 776.03 and 843.14, F.S.1971, which respectively condemn such conduct as "accessory after the fact" or "compounding a felony."

Thereafter, appellant requested Rutherford's resignation as assistant city manager, which Rutherford submitted, and then both appellant and Captain Kelley contacted Pinellas Park Police Chief Ernest Van Horn to whom they related all of the foregoing. The decision was then made by appellant, and concurred in by Chief Van Horn and Captain Kelley, that the matter would be handled administratively as an internal affair, that they would avoid unfavorable publicity and dishonor to the City of Pinellas Park and that, to preclude further dishonor and disgrace to Rutherford and his family, no criminal prosecution would ensue.

Within several days thereafter appellant related the entire incident, together with a full disclosure of the decision aforesaid, to three city councilmen, the city clerk, six high level city officials, four lower level city officials, one newspaper editor, one newspaper reporter and one prominent clergyman of the city. Each of these seventeen persons filed an identical affidavit herein in which he acknowledges his full and complete knowledge of the matter and each of whom made the following sworn statement:

> "Douglas J. Holland . . . advised me what action was taken in this matter, at which time I told him in effect that I felt he had taken the appropriate steps and agreed that this was good so as to avoid unfavorable publicity and dishonor to the City of Pinellas Park and to further avoid any dishonor to Rutherford's career and disgrace and serious harm to his family. I certainly felt that we should not proceed to cause the arrest of Mr. Rutherford."

As hereinabove noted, we chose to decide this case on the fundamental issue of whether misprision of felony is a crime in Florida. We parenthetically insert here, however, that had we not so chosen it is difficult to conclude from the foregoing facts, which are not in dispute, that appellant Holland failed to bring knowledge of the commission of a felony to the "proper authorities" or was guilty of concealing such knowledge in any respect.

In any case, we now get on to the merits of the question we decide today. We begin by pointing out that almost every state in the United States has adopted the Common Law of England to some extent. Many of these states have done so by constitutional or statutory provisions similar to ours. But the nearly universal interpretation of such provisions is that they adopt the common law of England only to the extent that such laws are consistent with the existing physical and social conditions in the country or in the given state.

To some degree Florida courts have discussed this principle in other contexts. In Duval v. Thomas, for example, our Supreme Court said:

> "[W]hen grave doubt exists of a true common law doctrine . . . we may, as was written in Ripley v. Ewell, [Fla.1952, 61 So.2d 420] exercise a 'broad discretion' taking 'into account the

changes in our social and economic customs and present day
conceptions of right and justice.' It is, to repeat, only when the
common law is plain that we must observe it."

Moreover, our courts have not hesitated in other respects to reject
anachronistic common law concepts.

Consonant with this, therefore, we think that the legislature in
enacting § 775.01, supra, recognized this judicial precept and intended
to grant our courts the discretion necessary to prevent blind adherence
to those portions of the common law which are not suited to our present
conditions, our public policy, our traditions or our sense of right and
justice.

With the foregoing as a predicate, we now consider the history of
the crime of misprision of felony and whether the reasons therefor have
ceased to exist, if indeed they ever did exist, in this country. The origin
of the crime is well described in 8 U. of Chi.L.Rev. 338, as follows:

> "[M]isprision of felony as defined by Blackstone is merely one
> phase of the system of communal responsibility for the appre-
> hension of criminals which received its original impetus from
> William I, under pressure of the need to protect the invading
> Normans in hostile country, and which endured up to the
> Seventeenth Century in England. In order to secure vigilant
> prosecution of criminal conduct, the vill or hundred in which
> such conduct occurred was subject to fine, as was the tithing to
> which the criminal belonged, and every person who knew of
> the felony and failed to make report thereof was subject to
> punishment for misprision of felony. Compulsory membership
> in the tithing group, the obligation to pursue criminals when
> the hue and cry was raised, broad powers of private arrest, and
> the periodic visitations of the General Eyre for the purpose of
> penalizing laxity in regard to crime, are all suggestive of the
> administrative background against which misprision of felony
> developed. With the appearance of specialized and paid law
> enforcement officers, such as constables and justices of the
> peace in the Seventeenth Century, there was a movement
> away from strict communal responsibility, and a growing ten-
> dency to rely on professional police . . .."

In short, the initial reason for the existence of misprision of felony as a
crime at common law was to aid an alien, dictorial sovereign in his
forcible subjugation of England's inhabitants. Enforcement of the
crime was summary, harsh and oppressive; and commentators note
that most prosecutors in this country long ago recognized the inapplicability or obsolescence of the law and its harshness in their contemporary society by simply not charging people with that crime. This very
case, in fact, serves well to illustrate the potential mischief of the
charge and the possible discriminatory, oppressive or absurd results
thereof. For example, should not Captain Kelley have been indicted
too? Or Chief Van Horn? And if not why only Holland? Or, perhaps,

should not the three city councilmen have been indicted? Or the city clerk? Or the other city officials, the newspaper people or the clergyman in their turn? Should there be fully nineteen indictments herein, or any given lesser number, when for aught we know the principal felon hasn't even been charged?

Many courts faced with this issue have also found, though with varying degrees of clarity that the reasons for the proscription of this crime do not exist. Moreover, as early as 1822 in this country Chief Justice John Marshall stated in Marbury v. Brooks.

"It may be the duty of a citizen to accuse every offender, and to proclaim every offense which comes to his knowledge; but the law which would punish him in every case, for not performing this duty, is too harsh for man."

In Michigan, whose constitution contains a provision incorporating common law crimes in a fashion similar to our Florida Statute § 775.01, supra, the Supreme Court of that state resolved a situation analogous to ours by the following holding:

"The old-time common-law offense of misprision of felony, short of an accessory after the fact . . ., is not now a substantive offense and not adopted by the Constitution, because wholly unsuited to American criminal law and procedure as used in this State."

The Supreme Judicial Court of Massachusetts, without actually reaching the point of whether misprision was a part of Massachusetts law, nevertheless stated that:

"[N]ot every principle of the English common law became part of the common law of Massachusetts. Some doctrines were judged inapplicable to the 'new state and condition' of the settlers in this country. . . ."

The court then suggested that if squarely faced with the question they would either declare misprision to be such an inapplicable doctrine or else interpret into that crime the element of evil motive, as was done by the Vermont court. . . .

We agree with Chief Justice Marshall and with the above cases and commentaries that the crime of misprision of felony is wholly unsuited to American criminal law. We are unable to agree with the course followed in [Vermont], because we think we should not alter the elements of common law misprision merely to make it coalesce with Florida law. Rather, we meet the question head-on. While it may be desirable, even essential, that we encourage citizens to "get involved" to help reduce crime, they ought not be adjudicated criminals themselves if they don't. The fear of such a consequence is a fear from which our traditional concepts of peace and quietude guarantee freedom. We cherish the right to mind our own business when our own best interests dictate. Accordingly we hold that misprision of felony has not been adopted into, and is not a part of, Florida substantive law.

Certiorari is granted, the decision of the circuit court is hereby quashed, and the cause is remanded with directions that the petitioner be ordered discharged.

HOBSON and GRIMES, JJ., concur.

NOTES

1. Professor Shannonhouse III, in his article, Misprision of a Federal Felony: Dangerous Relic or Scourge of Malfeasance, 4 U. Baltimore L.Rev. 59 (1974), stated of the misprision of felony class of crime, that while it has been "on the books" since 1790, it is discussed in "less than two dozen cases."

2. In Pope v. State, 38 Md.App. 520, 382 A.2d 880 (1978), the court held that misprision of a felony was a crime at common law, carried forward into Maryland law by the state constitution, and therefore an indictable offense. Early in 1979, however, the Maryland Court of Appeals said that since the crime had not been included in the state criminal code, it could not exist except as a common law crime. Commenting on the infrequency with which such a charge has been made, the court concluded, "If the legislature finds it advisable that the people be obligated under peril of criminal penalty to disclose knowledge of criminal acts, it is, of course, free to create an offense to that end, within constitutional limits, and, hopefully, with adequate safeguards. We believe that the common law offense is not acceptable by today's standards, and we are not free to usurp the power of the General Assembly by attempting to fashion one that would be. We hold that misprision of felony is not a chargeable offense in Maryland." Pope v. State, 284 Md. 309, 396 A.2d 1054 (1979).

3. The United States Code (18 U.S.C.A.) contains the following provision:

§ 4. Misprision of felony

Whoever, having knowledge of the actual commission of a felony cognizable by a court of the United States, conceals and does not as soon as possible make known the same to some judge or other person in civil or military authority under the United States, shall be fined not more than $500 or imprisoned not more than three years, or both.

No violation of the statute occurs merely because of the possession of information that another person has committed a federal felony; there must be an *affirmative act* of concealment. See United States v. Johnson, 546 F.2d 1225 (5th Cir. 1977), and the other cases cited therein.

4. In a 1948 English case, R. v. Aberg, 32 Crim.App.Reps. 144, Lord Chief Justice Goddard said that "misprision of felony is an offense which is described in the books, but which has been generally regarded nowadays as obsolete or fallen into desuetude". But thirteen years later the House of Lords declared that the offense of misprision of felony still existed in all its vigor. Sykes v. Director of Public Prosecution, [1961] 3 All.Eng.L.R. 33, held that if one knows that a felony has been committed and fails to report it, he is guilty of misprision of felony. Concealment, it was held, need not involve a positive act; mere omission is sufficient. Exempted, apparently, were persons within a privileged relationship with the felon (e.g., lawyers, clergymen), for the court in the Sykes case referred to "a claim of right made in good faith". In 1967, however, Parliament, in its Criminal Law Act of that year, abolished the crime of misprision of felony, except for

treason. It substituted, as will be discussed in the next section C, the offense of "compounding a crime."

(c) COMPOUNDING A CRIME

As a modern day substitution for the old common law crime of misprision of felony, some statutes have created the offense of "compounding a crime." An example is Section 32–1 of the Illinois Criminal Code (Ill.Rev.Stats., Ch. 38). It reads as follows:

> *Compounding a Crime.* (a) A person compounds a crime when he receives or offers to another any consideration for a promise not to prosecute or aid in the prosecution of an offender. (b) Compounding a crime is a petty offense [punishable by fine up to $500].

This offense is most likely to occur in embezzlement case situations where the employer (or his insurer) may seek to recoup a loss, or part of it, in return for withholding a criminal charge.

The 1967 English Criminal Law Act, in Part I, Section 5, contains the following provision on compounding a crime:

> Where a person has committed an arrestable offence, any other person who, knowing or believing that the offence or some other arrestable offence has been committed, and that he has information which might be of material assistance in securing the prosecution or conviction of an offender for it, accepts or agrees to accept for not disclosing that information any consideration other than the making good of loss or injury caused by the offence, or the making of reasonable compensation for that loss or injury, shall be liable on conviction on indictment to imprisonment for not more than two years.

4. LIABILITY OF CORPORATIONS

COMMONWEALTH v. McILWAIN SCHOOL BUS LINES, INC.

Superior Court of Pennsylvania, 1980.
283 Pa.Super. 1, 423 A.2d 413.

SPAETH, JUDGE. This is an appeal by the Commonwealth from an order quashing an information. The principal issue is whether a private corporation may be held criminally liable for homicide by vehicle. On April 3, 1978, a school bus owned by the McIlwain School Bus Lines, Inc. [hereinafter, the corporation] and operated by one of its employes, ran over and killed 6 year old Lori Sharp; she had just gotten off the bus and was walking in front of it when she was run over. On May 26, 1978, the corporation was charged with homicide by vehicle. The corporation waived its right to a preliminary hearing, but subsequently filed a motion to quash the information against it. . . .

* * *

The criminal law has not always regarded a corporation as subject to criminal liability.[1] Indeed, it was once widely accepted that a corporation was incapable of committing a criminal offense:

> This doctrine of nonliability for crime arose from the theory that a corporation, being an intangible entity, could neither commit a crime nor be subjected to punishment, because any illegal act of a corporate agent was done without authority of the corporation and ultra vires.

> Today, however, it is generally recognized that a corporation may be held criminally liable for criminal acts performed by its agents on its behalf. [Citations from many jurisdictions omitted.]

As early as the 1860's Pennsylvania courts have recognized that a corporation may be subject to criminal liability. Corporations in Pennsylvania have been indicted or convicted of maintaining public nuisances, unlawful manufacture or possession of intoxicating liquors, violation of Sunday laws, and violation of the Unlawful Collection Agency Practices Act. For a time, the Pennsylvania courts were unwilling to extend corporate criminal liability to crimes involving specific intent or homicide. In Commonwealth v. Punxsutawney, (1900), the court of common pleas of Jefferson County refused to hold a street railway company criminally liable for the crime of assault in ejecting a passenger. . . .

And in Commonwealth v. Peoples Natural Gas Co., (1954), the court of common pleas of Allegheny County granted a corporation's motion to quash an indictment charging involuntary manslaughter, then the common law offense; the court reasoned that the phrase, "the killing of another," implied that the killer had to be of the same nature as the killed ("another"). Courts in other jurisdictions, however, have abandoned this limitation.

For example, the Supreme Court of New Jersey has held that a corporation may be held criminally liable for involuntary manslaughter. In State v. Lehigh Valley R. Co., 90 N.J.L. 372, 103 A. 685 (1917), in denying a corporation's motion to quash an indictment for involuntary manslaughter, the court said:

> It has long been settled in this state that a corporation aggregate may in a proper case be held criminally for acts of malfeasance as well as for nonfeasance. So well settled is the general rule that in the later cases it has not even been questioned.

The court went on to say that "[w]e can think of no reason why it [the corporation] should not be held for the criminal consequences of

---

1. See generally, Lee, Corporate Criminal Liability, 28 Columbia L.Rev. 1, 181 (1928); Edgerton, Corporate Criminal Responsibility, 36 Yale L.J. 827 (1927); Frances, Criminal Responsibility of the Corporation, 18 Ill.L.Rev. 385 (1924); Canfield, Corporate Responsibility for Crime, 14 Columbia L.Rev. 469 (1914); Note, 23 University of Pittsburgh L.Rev. 172 (1961).

its negligence or its nonfeasance." In United States v. Van Schaick et al., 134 F. 592 (C.C.S.D.N.Y.1904), the court held that a corporate owner of a steam vessel could be guilty of manslaughter for "fraud, connivance, misconduct or violation of the law" resulting in loss of life. The charge was that as owner, the corporation had failed to equip the vessel with life preservers and fire fighting equipment. In People v. Ebasco Services, Incorporated et al. (1974), the Supreme Court of New York (Queens County) held that a corporation could be guilty of negligent homicide. The court held that although the statute's use of the word "person" in referring to the victim of a homicide naturally meant a human being, the statute did not require that the "person" committing the act of homicide also be a human being:

> There is, however, no manifest impropriety in applying the broader definition of "person" to a corporation in regard to the commission of a homicide particularly in view of the statement by the Court of Appeals in People v. Rochester Railway & Light Co. (supra) [2] that the Legislature is empowered to impose criminal liability upon a corporation for a homicide. Accordingly, the court concludes that although a corporation cannot be the victim of a homicide, it may commit that offense and be held to answer therefor.

The law of Pennsylvania has developed in a manner consistent with these New Jersey and New York decisions. With the enactment of the Crimes Code, Act of Dec. 6, 1972, the criminal liability of corporations was codified, as follows:

(a) Corporations Generally. A corporation may be convicted of the commission of an offense if:

> (1) the offense is a summary offense or the offense is defined by a statute other than this title in which a legislative purpose to impose liability on corporations plainly appears and the conduct is performed by an agent of the corporation acting in behalf of the corporation within the scope of his office or employment, except that if the law defining the offense designates the agents for whose conduct the corporation is accountable or the cir-

---

2. In People v. Rochester Railway & Light Co., 195 N.Y. 102, 107, 88 N.E. 22, 24 (1909), the New York Court of Appeals held that there was insufficient evidence of the legislature's intent to impose corporate criminal liability under a particular state statute. However, the court added:

Within the principles thus and elsewhere declared, we have no doubt that a definition of certain forms of manslaughter might have been formulated which would be applicable to a corporation, and make it criminally liable for various acts of misfeasance and nonfeasance when resulting in death, and amongst which very probably might have been included conduct in its substance similar to that here charged against the respondent. Id.

cumstances under which it is accountable, such provisions shall apply;

(2) the offense consists of an omission to discharge a specific duty of affirmative performance imposed on corporations by law; or

(3) the commission of the offense was authorized, requested, commanded, performed or recklessly tolerated by the board of directors or by a high managerial agent acting in behalf of the corporation within the scope of his office or employment.

(b) Corporations, Absolute Liability. When absolute liability is imposed for the commission of an offense, a legislative purpose to impose liability on a corporation shall be assumed, unless the contrary plainly appears.

We recently had occasion to apply this provision, in Commonwealth v. J. P. Mascaro and Sons, Inc., 266 Pa.Super. 8, 402 A.2d 1050 (1979), where we held that under subsection (a)(3) of section 307, a corporation could be convicted of theft by deception, deceptive business practices, and unsworn falsification to authorities arising out of false reports pertaining to rubbish hauled pursuant to a contract between the corporation and a county. Cases such as Commonwealth v. Punxsutawney, supra, and Commonwealth v. Peoples Natural Gas Co., supra, therefore no longer have any precedential value.

When section 307 of the Crimes Code is applied to the present case, it is apparent that the critical words are that "[a] corporation may be convicted of the commission of an offense if: (1) the offense is . . . defined by a statute other than this title in which a legislative purpose to impose liability on corporations plainly appears . . .." 18 Pa.C.S. A. § 307(a)(1). Here, the offense—homicide by vehicle—is "defined by a statute other than [the Crimes Code]"; it is defined by the Vehicle Code, Act of June 17, 1976, P.L. 162, No. 81, § 1, eff. July 1, 1977, 75 Pa.C.S.A. § 3732. The question that we must decide, therefore, is whether from that definition "a legislative purpose to impose liability on corporations plainly appears."

The statute provides that homicide by vehicle may be committed by "[a]ny person who unintentionally causes the death of another person while engaged in the violation of . . .. [etc.." (Emphasis added.) Section 102 of the Vehicle Code defines "person" as "[a] natural person, firm, co-partnership, association or corporation." 75 Pa.C.S.A. § 102. It therefore "plainly appears" that homicide by vehicle may be committed by a corporation.

This conclusion is made even more plain by the opening paragraph of Section 102, which provides:

Subject to additional definitions contained in subsequent provisions of this title which are applicable to specific provisions of this title, the following words and phrases when used in this title shall have, unless the content clearly indicates otherwise, the meanings given to them in this section[.]

"Person" is one of the "following words" thus referred to. There are no "additional definitions" of "person" in Section 3732, defining homicide by vehicle. Therefore, "unless the content [of Section 3732] *clearly indicates otherwise* [emphasis added]," the meaning given "person" in Section 3732 shall be the meaning given it in Section 102, i.e., as including a corporation.

The lower court acknowledged that Section 102 defined "person" as including a corporation, but held, nevertheless, that as used in Section 3732, "person" did not include a corporation. Said the court:

> If "person" was to include a corporation, Section 3732 semantically and gramatically should have read "any person who or <u>which</u> unintentionally causes the death. . . . .." In modern usage <u>who</u> refers to <u>actual persons</u> (human beings). <u>Which</u> refers to the unnatural, artificial or inanimate as a corporation.
>
> (Webster's Collegiate 5th Edition Dictionary).
>
> The Latin "qui" means <u>who</u> referring to the natural or human, and "quod" means <u>which</u> referring to the unnatural, artificial or inanimate. (The New Century Dictionary Foreign Words and Phrases) (Court's underscoring.)

We are not persuaded by this reasoning. Initially, it may be noted that the argument from Latin is not persuasive, for reference to another language would have shown that the word for "who" and the word for "which" may be the same. Nor is the argument from grammar persuasive; indeed, it cuts just the other way. The phrase, "any person who or which," is not only extremely awkward but sounds wrong, for in ordinary usage, "person" refers only to a natural person and therefore takes only "who," not "which." Accordingly, no legislative draftsman wants to resort to the phrase, "any person who or which." Instead, the draftsman will make a choice. One choice is to avoid definitions. With respect to the Vehicle Code, that would mean that throughout the statute there would appear the phrase, "Any natural person, firm, copartnership, association or corporation who or which . . . [does one of the many acts proscribed by the Code]." This is clear but cumbersome. A second choice, therefore, is to avoid being cumbersome by using one word instead of many, and still be clear by giving that one word a definition that includes the many. This is the choice usually made when the statute in question is long and divided into many sections.[3] Here, the draftsman of the Vehicle Code made this second choice. Having done so, he wished to be grammatical, and

---

3. See, e.g., the Uniform Commercial Code:

"Person" includes an individual or an organization (Section 1–102).

12A § 1–201(30).

In this act [Uniform Commercial Code] unless the context otherwise requires

(a) words in the singular number include the plural, and in the plural include the singular;

not offend the reader with an awkward phrase. He therefore said, "Any person who . . .," knowing that by reference to the definitions in Section 102, the reader could learn what "person" referred to, and did not say, "Any person who or which . . .," which would not only be awkward and sound wrong, but because of Section 102, was unnecessary.

Other jurisdictions have similarly applied criminal statutes defining the word "person" as including corporation. For example, in Vulcan Last Co. v. State, 194 Wis. 636, 217 N.W. 412 (1928), the Supreme Court of Wisconsin held that a corporation is liable to prosecution under a statute prohibiting any "person" from attempting to influence a voter, where the statute provided that "person" included a corporation. In State v. Workers' Socialist Pub. Co., 150 Minn. 406, 185 N.W. 931 (1921), the Supreme Court of Minnesota held that a corporation was criminally liable under a statute prohibiting "any person" from advocating violence to gain political ends, where the statute provided that the word "person" included a corporation. . . .

The lower court also gave the following reasons for its decision:

> The Homicide by Vehicle Section 3732 nowhere contains the word corporation: no Pennsylvania courts have applied this section to corporations; the penalty of the section providing jail is not corporately oriented; the revocation of one's license is not corporately applicable; and the section (as with the entire Vehicle Code Serious Offense Section 3731 to 3734, inclusive) is strictly natural person solely operational driver oriented.

It is true that Section 3732 does not use the word "corporation." However, given the definition of the word "person", there is no need for it to do so. It is also true—at least so far as we know—that no court in Pennsylvania has applied Section 3732 to a corporation; the present case appears to be of first impression. However, given the fact that the section did not become effective until July 1, 1977, the fact that no case other than this one has been brought against a corporation for homicide by vehicle is hardly conclusive proof that the section may not be so applied. Neither are we persuaded by the next two reasons of the lower court that since a corporation cannot be put in jail or have its license revoked, Section 3732 does not apply to corporations.

The offense of homicide by vehicle is a misdemeanor of the first degree. 75 Pa.C.S.A. § 3732. It is true that one of the punishments

---

(b) words of the masculine gender include the feminine and the neuter, and when the sense so indicates words of the neuter gender may refer to any gender.

12A § 1–102(5).

and the Uniform Partnership Act:

"Person" includes individuals, partnerships, corporations, and other associations.

59 P.S. § 2.

that may be imposed [under 18 Pa.C.S.A. § 1104] for committing a misdemeanor of the first degree is a term of imprisonment:

> A person who has been convicted of a misdemeanor may be sentenced to imprisonment for a definite term which shall be fixed by the court and shall be not more than:
>
> > (1) Five years in the case of a misdemeanor of the first degree.

It is also true that another possible punishment for homicide by vehicle is the revocation of one's driving license:

> The department shall revoke the operating privilege of any driver for one year upon receiving a certified record of the driver's conviction of any of the following offenses:
>
> > . . . Section 3732 (relating to homicide by vehicle).
>
> 75 Pa.C.S. § 1532(a)(3).

However, a third possible punishment [under 18 Pa.C.S.A. § 1101] is the imposition of a fine:

> A person who has been convicted of any offense may be sentenced to pay a fine not exceeding: . . .
>
> > (3) $10,000, when the conviction is of a misdemeanor of the first degree.

Where alternate punishments are provided for a crime, the court may in appropriate circumstances impose the fine only [under 18 Pa.C.S. § 1326(a)]:

> *Fine only.*—The court may, as authorized by law, sentence the defendant only to pay a fine, when, having regard to the nature and circumstances of the crime and to the history and character of the defendant, it is of the opinion that the fine alone suffices.

In United States v. Hougland Barge Line, Inc., 387 F.Supp. 1110 (W.D.Pa.1974), the court held that a statute requiring any "person in charge" of a vessel to notify the United States Coast Guard of oil discharges from the vessel applied to corporations as well as individuals, and that when applied to a corporation, only a fine may be imposed:

> The defendant also argues that as a corporation it cannot be imprisoned, and therefore, this would indicate that it [the statute in question] was not intended to apply to corporations. Innumerable federal penal statutes prohibit certain activities, including business entities, and provide penalties for violation of such prohibited acts. Both individuals and corporations are penalized even though a corporation may not be imprisoned. Thus, as illustrated by antitrust cases and Internal Revenue cases, where a statute calls for imprisonment, when imposed against a defendant corporation, only the fine portion of the penalty may be imposed.

Courts in other jurisdictions have similarly applied this principle, recognizing that to do otherwise would in effect confer upon the corporation immunity for its criminal acts. Thus, the Supreme Court of Illinois has said [in People v. Duncan, 363 Ill. 495, 2 N.E.2d 705 (1936)]:

> Where the statutory penalty is both fine and imprisonment, the corporate offender can be punished by imposing a fine, inasmuch as the two penalties are independent. The theory is that a court shall apply the appropriate penalty in such instances as far as possible, in order that the corporate defendant shall not escape all punishment.

The Supreme Court of North Carolina has said [in State v. Ice & Fuel Co., 166 N.C. 366, 369, 81 S.E. 737, 738 (1914)]:

> It is true that, when the statute imposes a penalty of a fine or imprisonment, only the fine can be placed upon a corporation. But this is no reason why that should not be imposed. The corporation should not be wholly exempted from punishment, because it cannot be imprisoned . . .

And in United States v. Van Schaick et al., supra, the Circuit Court for the Southern District of New York reached a similar conclusion:

> But it is said that no punishment can follow conviction. This is an oversight in the statute. Is it to be concluded, simply because the given punishment cannot be enforced, that Congress intended to allow corporate carriers by sea to kill their passengers through misconduct that would be a punishable offense if done by a natural person?

> A corporation can be guilty of causing death by its wrongful act. It can with equal propriety be punished in a civil or criminal action. It seems a more reasonable alternative that Congress inadvertently omitted to provide suitable punishment for the offense when committed by a corporation, than it intended to give the wrongdoer impunity simply because it happened to be a corporation.

Finally, we are unable to accept the lower court's conclusion that Section 3732 "is strictly natural person solely operational driver oriented." For the reasons we have given, it appears to us equally to include corporations.

Reversed.

VAN DER VOORT, J., notes his dissent.

NOTES

1. In 1909, the United States Supreme Court in New York Central & Hudson River Railroad Co. v. United States, 212 U.S. 481, 29 S.Ct. 304 (1909),

rejected, in the following language, the claim of immunity a corporate defendant had asserted:

"It is true that there are some crimes which in their nature cannot be committed by corporations. But there is a large class of offenses . . . wherein the crime consists in purposely doing the things prohibited by statute. In that class of crimes we see no good reason why corporations may not be held responsible for and charged with the knowledge and purposes of their agents, acting within the authority conferred upon them. . . ."

In affirming the conviction, the Supreme Court encouraged legislatures and courts to expand the field of corporate liability beyond the typical strict liability regulatory offenses.

See also, Commonwealth v. Beneficial Finance Co., 360 Mass. 188, 275 N.E.2d 33 (1971).

On September 13, 1978, an Elkhart County, Indiana, grand jury returned an indictment against the Ford Motor Company of reckless homicide in connection with an incident wherein a 1973 Ford Pinto automobile caught fire when it was involved in a rear-end collision which caused the Pinto's gas tank to explode, engulfing the car in flames and killing its occupants. In extensive pre-trial litigation, the trial court rejected defendant's contentions that a corporation could not be held liable for negligent homicide, but the jury ultimately returned verdicts of not guilty. State v. Ford Motor Co., Elkhart Superior Court, Cause No. 5324.

See, on the issue of corporate liability for unintentional homicides, Maakestad, "A Historical Survey of Corporate Homicide In The United States: Could It Be Prosecuted In Illinois?", Illinois Bar Journal, August 1981, p. 772.

2. If a corporation solely owns a second corporation, which in turn commits criminal acts, is the parent corporation liable criminally for the wrongs committed by the other? In connection with the oil spill caused when Exxon Shipping Company's tanker Exxon Valdez ran aground a reef, discharging more than 11 million gallons of crude oil into Prince William Sound near Valdez, Alaska, can the parent company, Exxon Corporation, be held criminally liable for wrongs allegedly committed by its subsidiary's employees? See, Oil-Spill Indictment, ABAJ, July 1990, p. 28.

3. The Racketeering Influenced and Corrupt Organizations Act (RICO)— see, supra, United States v. Turkette in the Section on Conspiracy—has as its primary purpose to eradicate organized crime and corruption. Under 18 U.S. C.A. Sec. 1962(c) the government must prove: (1) the existence of an enterprise which affects interstate or foreign commerce; (2) that the defendant is "associated with" the enterprise; (3) that the defendant participated in the conduct of the enterprise's affairs; and (4) that the participation was through a pattern of racketeering activity. Can a corporation satisfy the "enterprise" requirement of RICO and simultaneously also be a conspirator with its own officers, agents and employees in violation of the criminal conspiracy statute? See United States v. Hartley, 678 F.2d 961 (11th Cir. 1982).

See also, Welling, "Intracorporate Plurality in Criminal Conspiracy Law," 33 Hastings L.J. 1155 (1982); Brickey, Corporate Criminal Liability: A Primer for Corporate Counsel, 40 The Business Lawyer 129 (1984); Fisse, Sentencing Options against Corporations, 1 Crim.L.Forum 211 (1990).

Part III

SPECIAL DEFENSES TO CRIMINAL PROSECUTIONS

Chapter 9

ENTRAPMENT

UNITED STATES v. RUSSELL

Supreme Court of the United States, 1973.
411 U.S. 423, 93 S.Ct. 1637.

MR. JUSTICE REHNQUIST delivered the opinion of the Court. . . .

There is little dispute concerning the essential facts in this case. On December 7, 1969, Joe Shapiro, an undercover agent for the Federal Bureau of Narcotics and Dangerous Drugs, went to respondent's home on Whidbey Island in the State of Washington where he met with respondent and his two codefendants, John and Patrick Connolly. Shapiro's assignment was to locate a laboratory where it was believed that methamphetamine was being manufactured illicitly. He told the respondent and the Connollys that he represented an organization in the Pacific Northwest that was interested in controlling the manufacture and distribution of methamphetamine. He then made an offer to supply the defendants with the chemical phenyl-2-propanone, an essential ingredient in the manufacture of methamphetamine, in return for one-half of the drug produced. This offer was made on the condition that Agent Shapiro be shown a sample of the drug which they were making and the laboratory where it was being produced.

During the conversation, Patrick Connolly revealed that he had been making the drug since May 1969 and since then had produced three pounds of it. John Connolly gave the agent a bag containing a quantity of methamphetamine that he represented as being from "the last batch that we made." Shortly thereafter, Shapiro and Patrick Connolly left respondent's house to view the laboratory which was located in the Connolly house on Whidbey Island. At the house, Shapiro observed an empty bottle bearing the chemical label phenyl-2-propanone.

By prearrangement, Shapiro returned to the Connolly house on December 9, 1969, to supply 100 grams of propanone and observe the manufacturing process. When he arrived he observed Patrick Connolly and the respondent cutting up pieces of aluminum foil and placing them in a large flask. There was testimony that some of the foil pieces

934

accidentally fell on the floor and were picked up by the respondent and Shapiro and put into the flask. Thereafter, Patrick Connolly added all of the necessary chemicals, including the propanone brought by Shapiro, to make two batches of methamphetamine. The manufacturing process having been completed the following morning, Shapiro was given one-half of the drug and respondent kept the remainder. Shapiro offered to buy, and the respondent agreed to sell, part of the remainder for $60.

About a month later, Shapiro returned to the Connolly house and met with Patrick Connolly to ask if he was still interested in their "business arrangement." Connolly replied that he was interested but that he had recently obtained two additional bottles of phenyl-2-propanone and would not be finished with them for a couple of days. He provided some additional methamphetamine to Shapiro at that time. Three days later Shapiro returned to the Connolly house with a search warrant and, among other items, seized an empty 500-gram bottle of propanone and a 100-gram bottle, not the one he had provided, that was partially filled with the chemical.

There was testimony at the trial of respondent and Patrick Connolly that phenyl-2-propanone was generally difficult to obtain. At the request of the Bureau of Narcotics and Dangerous Drugs, some chemical supply firms had voluntarily ceased selling the chemical.

At the close of the evidence, and after receiving the District Judge's standard entrapment instruction,[1] the jury found the respondent guilty on all counts charged. On appeal, the respondent conceded that the jury could have found him predisposed to commit the offenses, . . . but argued that on the facts presented there was entrapment as a matter of law. The Court of Appeals agreed, although it did not find the District Court had misconstrued or misapplied the traditional standards governing the entrapment defense. Rather, the court in effect expanded the traditional notion of entrapment, which focuses on the predisposition of the defendant, to mandate dismissal of a criminal prosecution whenever the court determines that there has been "an intolerable degree of governmental participation in the criminal enterprise." In this case the court decided that the conduct of the agent in supplying a scarce ingredient essential for the manufacture of a controlled substance established that defense.

This new defense was held to rest on either of two alternative theories. One theory is based on two lower court decisions which have found entrapment, regardless of predisposition, whenever the government supplies contraband to the defendants. United States v. Bueno,

1. The District Judge stated the governing law on entrapment as follows: "Where a person already has the willingness and the readiness to break the law, the mere fact that the government agent provides what appears to be a favorable opportunity is not entrapment." He then instructed the jury to acquit respondent if it had a "reasonable doubt whether the defendant had the previous intent or purpose to commit the offense . . . and did so only because he was induced or persuaded by some officer or agent of the government." No exception was taken by respondent to this instruction.

447 F.2d 903 (CA5 1971); United States v. Chisum, 312 F.Supp. 1307 (CD Cal.1970). The second theory, a nonentrapment rationale, is based on a recent Ninth Circuit decision that reversed a conviction because a government investigator was so enmeshed in the criminal activity that the prosecution of the defendants was held to be repugnant to the American criminal justice system, Greene v. United States, 454 F.2d 783 (CA9 1971). The court below held that these two rationales constitute the same defense, and that only the label distinguishes them. In any event, it held that "[b]oth theories are premised on fundamental concepts of due process and evince the reluctance of the judiciary to countenance 'overzealous law enforcement.'" . . .

This Court first recognized and applied the entrapment defense in Sorrells v. United States, 287 U.S. 435 (1932). In *Sorrells,* a federal prohibition agent visited the defendant while posing as a tourist and engaged him in conversation about their common war experiences. After gaining the defendant's confidence, the agent asked for some liquor, was twice refused, but upon asking a third time the defendant finally capitulated, and was subsequently prosecuted for violating the National Prohibition Act.

Mr. Chief Justice Hughes, speaking for the Court, held that as a matter of statutory construction the defense of entrapment should have been available to the defendant. Under the theory propounded by the Chief Justice, the entrapment defense prohibits law enforcement officers from instigating a criminal act by persons "otherwise innocent in order to lure them to its commission and to punish them." . . . Thus, the thrust of the entrapment defense was held to focus on the intent or predisposition of the defendant to commit the crime. "[I]f the defendant seeks acquittal by reason of entrapment he cannot complain of an appropriate and searching inquiry into his own conduct and predisposition as bearing upon that issue." . . .

Mr. Justice Roberts concurred but was of the view "that courts must be closed to the trial of a crime instigated by the government's own agents." . . . The difference in the view of the majority and the concurring opinions is that in the former the inquiry focuses on the predisposition of the defendant, whereas in the latter the inquiry focuses on whether the government "instigated the crime."

In 1958 the Court again considered the theory underlying the entrapment defense and expressly reaffirmed the view expressed by the *Sorrells* majority. Sherman v. United States [356 U.S. 360]. In *Sherman* the defendant was convicted of selling narcotics to a Government informer. As in *Sorrells,* it appears that the Government agent gained the confidence of the defendant and, despite initial reluctance, the defendant finally acceded to the repeated importunings of the agent to commit the criminal act. On the basis of *Sorrells,* this Court reversed the affirmance of the defendant's conviction.

In affirming the theory underlying *Sorrells,* Mr. Chief Justice Warren for the Court, held that "[t]o determine whether entrapment has been established, a line must be drawn between the trap for the unwary innocent and the trap for the unwary criminal." . . .

In the instant case, respondent asks us to reconsider the theory of the entrapment defense as it is set forth in the majority opinions in *Sorrells* and *Sherman*. His principal contention is that the defense should rest on constitutional grounds. He argues that the level of Shapiro's involvement in the manufacture of the methamphetamine was so high that a criminal prosecution for the drug's manufacture violates the fundamental principles of due process. The respondent contends that the same factors that led this Court to apply the exclusionary rule to illegal searches and seizures, . . . and confessions, . . . should be considered here. But he would have the Court go further in deterring undesirable official conduct by requiring that any prosecution be barred absolutely because of the police involvement in criminal activity. The analogy is imperfect in any event, for the principal reason behind the adoption of the exclusionary rule was the Government's "failure to observe its own laws." . . . Unlike the situations giving rise to the holdings in *Mapp* and *Miranda,* the Government's conduct here violated no independent constitutional right of the respondent. Nor did Shapiro violate any federal statute or rule or commit any crime in infiltrating the respondent's drug enterprise.

Respondent would overcome this basic weakness in his analogy to the exclusionary rule cases by having the Court adopt a rigid constitutional rule that would preclude any prosecution when it is shown that the criminal conduct would not have been possible had not an undercover agent "supplied an indispensable means to the commission of the crime that could not have been obtained otherwise, through legal or illegal channels." Even if we were to surmount the difficulties attending the notion that due process of law can be embodied in fixed rules, and those attending respondent's particular formulation, the rule he proposes would not appear to be of significant benefit to him. For, on the record presented, it appears that he cannot fit within the terms of the very rule he proposes.

The record discloses that although the propanone was difficult to obtain, it was by no means impossible. The defendants admitted making the drug both before and after those batches made with the propanone supplied by Shapiro. Shapiro testified that he saw an empty bottle labeled phenyl-2-propanone on his first visit to the laboratory on December 7, 1969. And when the laboratory was searched pursuant to a search warrant on January 10, 1970, two additional bottles labeled phenyl-2-propanone were seized. Thus, the facts in the record amply demonstrate that the propanone used in the illicit manufacture of methamphetamine not only *could* have been obtained without the intervention of Shapiro but was in fact obtained by these defendants.

While we may some day be presented with a situation in which the conduct of law enforcement agents is so outrageous that due process principles would absolutely bar the government from invoking judicial processes to obtain a conviction, cf. Rochin v. California, 342 U.S. 165 (1952), the instant case is distinctly not of that breed. Shapiro's contribution of propanone to the criminal enterprise already in process was scarcely objectionable. The chemical is by itself a harmless substance and its possession is legal. While the Government may have been seeking to make it more difficult for drug rings, such as that of which respondent was a member, to obtain the chemical, the evidence described above shows that it nonetheless was obtainable. The law enforcement conduct here stops far short of violating that "fundamental fairness, shocking to the universal sense of justice," mandated by the Due Process Clause of the Fifth Amendment. Kinsella v. United States ex rel. Singleton, 361 U.S. 234, 246 (1960).

The illicit manufacture of drugs is not a sporadic, isolated criminal incident, but a continuing, though illegal, business enterprise. In order to obtain convictions for illegally manufacturing drugs, the gathering of evidence of past unlawful conduct frequently proves to be an all but impossible task. Thus in drug-related offenses law enforcement personnel have turned to one of the only practicable means of detection; the infiltration of drug rings and a limited participation in their unlawful present practices. Such infiltration is a recognized and permissible means of investigation; if that be so, then the supply of some item of value that the drug ring requires must, as a general rule, also be permissible. For an agent will not be taken into the confidence of the illegal entrepreneurs unless he has something of value to offer them. Law enforcement tactics such as this can hardly be said to violate "fundamental fairness" or "shocking to the universal sense of justice," *Kinsella*, supra.

Respondent also urges, as an alternative to his constitutional argument, that we broaden the nonconstitutional defense of entrapment in order to sustain the judgment of the Court of Appeals. This Court's opinions in Sorrells v. United States, supra, and Sherman v. United States, supra, held that the principal element in the defense of entrapment was the defendant's predisposition to commit the crime. Respondent conceded in the Court of Appeals, as well he might, "that he may have harbored a predisposition to commit the charged offenses." . . .   Yet he argues that the jury's refusal to find entrapment under the charge submitted to it by the trial court should be overturned and the views of Justices Roberts and Frankfurter, in *Sorrells* and *Sherman,* respectively, which made the essential element of the defense turn on the type and degree of governmental conduct, be adopted as the law.

We decline to overrule these cases. *Sorrells* is a precedent of long standing that has already been once re-examined in *Sherman* and implicitly there reaffirmed. Since the defense is not of a constitutional dimension, Congress may address itself to the question and adopt any substantive definition of the defense that it may find desirable.

Critics of the rule laid down in *Sorrells* and *Sherman* have suggested that its basis in the implied intent of Congress is largely fictitious, and have pointed to what they conceive to be the anomalous difference between the treatment of a defendant who is solicited by a private individual and one who is entrapped by a government agent. Questions have been likewise raised as to whether "predisposition" can be factually established with the requisite degree of certainty. Arguments such as these, while not devoid of appeal, have been twice previously made to this Court, and twice rejected by it, first in *Sorrells* and then in *Sherman.*

We believe that at least equally cogent criticism has been made of the concurring views in these cases. Commenting in *Sherman* on Mr. Justice Roberts' position in *Sorrells* that "although the defendant could claim that the Government had induced him to commit the crime, the Government could not reply by showing that the defendant's criminal conduct was due to his own readiness and not to the persuasion of government agents," Sherman v. United States, 356 U.S., at 376–377, Mr. Chief Justice Warren quoted the observation of Judge Learned Hand in an earlier stage of that proceeding:

> " 'Indeed, it would seem probable that, if there were no reply [to the claim of inducement], it would be impossible ever to secure convictions of any offences which consist of transactions that are carried on in secret.' United States v. Sherman, 200 F.2d 880, 882." Sherman v. United States, 356 U.S., at 377 n. 7.

Nor does it seem particularly desirable for the law to grant complete immunity from prosecution to one who himself planned to commit a crime, and then committed it, simply because government undercover agents subjected him to inducements which might have seduced a hypothetical individual who was not so predisposed. We are content to leave the matter where it was left by the Court in *Sherman:* . . . .

Several decisions of the United States district courts and courts of appeals have undoubtedly gone beyond this Court's opinions in *Sorrells* and *Sherman* in order to bar prosecutions because of what they thought to be, for want of a better term, "overzealous law enforcement." But the defense of entrapment enunciated in those opinions was not intended to give the federal judiciary a "chancellor's foot" veto over law enforcement practices of which it did not approve. The execution of the federal laws under our Constitution is confined primarily to the Executive Branch of the Government, subject to applicable constitutional and statutory limitations and to judicially fashioned rules to enforce those limitations. We think that the decision of the Court of Appeals in this case quite unnecessarily introduces an unmanageably subjective standard which is contrary to the holdings of this Court in *Sorrells* and *Sherman.*

Those cases establish that entrapment is a relatively limited defense. It is rooted, not in any authority of the Judicial Branch to dismiss prosecutions for what it feels to have been "overzealous law enforcement," but instead in the notion that Congress could not have intended criminal punishment for a defendant who has committed all the elements of a proscribed offense, but was induced to commit them by the Government.

Sorrells and *Sherman* both recognize "that the fact that officers or employees of the Government merely afford opportunities or facilities for the commission of the offense does not defeat the prosecution," 287 U.S., at 441; 356 U.S., at 372. Nor will the mere fact of deceit defeat a prosecution, . . . for there are circumstances when the use of deceit is the only practicable law enforcement technique available. It is only when the Government's deception actually implants the criminal design in the mind of the defendant that the defense of entrapment comes into play.

Respondent's concession in the Court of Appeals that the jury finding as to predisposition was supported by the evidence is, therefore, fatal to his claim of entrapment. He was an active participant in an illegal drug manufacturing enterprise which began before the Government agent appeared on the scene, and continued after the Government agent had left the scene. He was, in the words of *Sherman*, supra, not an "unwary innocent" but an "unwary criminal." The Court of Appeals was wrong, we believe, when it sought to broaden the principle laid down in *Sorrells* and *Sherman*. Its judgment is therefore

Reversed.

MR. JUSTICE DOUGLAS, with whom MR. JUSTICE BRENNAN concurs, dissenting.

A federal agent supplied the accused with one chemical ingredient of the drug known as methamphetamine ("speed") which the accused manufactured and for which act he was sentenced to prison. His defense was entrapment, which the Court of Appeals sustained and which the Court today disallows. Since I have an opposed view of entrapment, I dissent.

. . .

In my view, the fact that the chemical ingredient supplied by the federal agent might have been obtained from other sources is quite irrelevant. Supplying the chemical ingredient used in the manufacture of this batch of "speed" made the United States an active participant in the unlawful activity. . . .

Mr. Justice Roberts in *Sorrells* put the idea in the following words:

"The applicable principle is that courts must be closed to the trial of a crime instigated by the government's own agents. No other issue, no comparison of equities as between the guilty official and the guilty defendant, has any place in the enforcement of this overruling principle of public policy." 287 U.S., at 459.

May the federal agent supply the counterfeiter with the kind of paper or ink that he needs in order to get a quick and easy arrest? The Court of Appeals in Greene v. United States, 454 F.2d 783, speaking through Judges Hamley and Hufstedler, said "no" in a case where the federal agent treated the suspects "as partners" with him, offered to supply them with a still, a still site, still equipment, and an operator and supplied them with sugar. . . .

The Court of Appeals in the instant case relied upon this line of decisions in sustaining the defense of entrapment, 459 F.2d 671. In doing so it took the view that the "prostitution of the criminal law," as Mr. Justice Roberts described it in Sorrells, 287 U.S., at 457, was the evil at which the defense of entrapment is aimed.

Federal agents play a debased role when they become the instigators of the crime, or partners in its commission, or the creative brain behind the illegal scheme. That is what the federal agent did here when he furnished the accused with one of the chemical ingredients needed to manufacture the unlawful drug.

MR. JUSTICE STEWART, with whom MR. JUSTICE BRENNAN and MR. JUSTICE MARSHALL join, dissenting.

It is common ground that "[t]he conduct with which the defense of entrapment is concerned is the *manufacturing* of crime by law enforcement officials and their agents." Lopez v. United States, 373 U.S. 427, 434 (1963). For the Government cannot be permitted to instigate the commission of a criminal offense in order to prosecute someone for committing it. Sherman v. United States, 356 U.S. 369, 372 (1958). As Mr. Justice Brandeis put it, the Government "may not provoke or create a crime and then punish the criminal, its creature." Casey v. United States, 276 U.S. 413, 423 (1928) (dissenting opinion). It is to prevent this situation from occurring in the administration of federal criminal justice that the defense of entrapment exists. Sorrells v. United States, 287 U.S. 435 (1932); Sherman v. United States, supra. Cf. Masciale v. United States, 356 U.S. 386 (1958); Lopez v. United States, supra. But the Court has been sharply divided as to the proper basis, scope, and focus of the entrapment defense, and as to whether, in the absence of a conclusive showing, the issue of entrapment is for the judge or the jury to determine.

I

In Sorrells v. United States, supra, and Sherman v. United States, supra, the Court took what might be called a "subjective" approach to the defense of entrapment. In that view, the defense is predicated on an unexpressed intent of Congress to exclude from its criminal statutes the prosecution and conviction of persons, "otherwise innocent," who have been lured to the commission of the prohibited act through the Government's instigation. . . . ["] The key phrase in this formulation is "otherwise innocent," for the entrapment defense is available under this approach only to those who would not have committed the crime but for the Government's inducements. Thus, the subjective approach focuses on the conduct and propensities of the particular defendant in each individual case: if he is "otherwise innocent," he may avail himself of the defense; but if he had the "predisposition" to commit the crime, or if the "criminal design" originated with him, then—regardless of the nature and extent of the Government's participation—there has been no entrapment. . . .

The concurring opinion of Mr. Justice Roberts, joined by Justices Brandeis and Stone, in the *Sorrells* case, and that of Mr. Justice Frankfurter, joined by Justices Douglas, Harlan, and Brennan, in the *Sherman* case, took a different view of the entrapment defense. In their concept, the defense is not grounded on some unexpressed intent of Congress to exclude from punishment under its statutes those otherwise innocent persons tempted into crime by the Government, but rather on the belief that "the methods employed on behalf of the Government to bring about conviction cannot be countenanced." . . . Thus, the focus of this approach is not on the propensities and predisposition of a specific defendant, but on "whether the police conduct revealed in the particular case falls below standards, to which common feelings respond, for the proper use of governmental power." Id., at 382. Phrased another way, the question is whether—regardless of the predisposition to crime of the particular defendant involved—the governmental agents have acted in such a way as is likely to instigate or create a criminal offense. Under this approach, the determination of the lawfulness of the Government's conduct must be made—as it is on all questions involving the legality of law enforcement methods—by the trial judge, not the jury.

In my view, this objective approach to entrapment advanced by the Roberts opinion in *Sorrells* and the Frankfurter opinion in *Sherman* is the only one truly consistent with the underlying rationale of the defense. Indeed, the very basis of the entrapment defense itself demands adherence to an approach that focuses on the conduct of the governmental agents, rather than on whether the defendant was "predisposed" or "otherwise innocent." I find it impossible to believe that the purpose of the defense is to effectuate some unexpressed congressional intent to exclude from its criminal statutes persons who committed a prohibited act, but would not have done so except for the Government's inducements. For, as Mr. Justice Frankfurter put it, "the only legislative intention that can with any show of reason be extracted from the statute is the intention to make criminal precisely the conduct in which the defendant has engaged." Sherman v. United States, supra, at 379. See also Sorrells v. United States, supra, at 456 (Roberts, J., concurring). Since, by definition, the entrapment defense cannot arise unless the defendant actually committed the proscribed act, that defendant is manifestly covered by the terms of the criminal statute involved.

Furthermore, to say that such a defendant is "otherwise innocent" or not "predisposed" to commit the crime is misleading, at best. The very fact that he has committed an act that Congress has determined to be illegal demonstrates conclusively that he is not innocent of the offense. He may not have originated the precise plan or the precise details, but he was "predisposed" in the sense that he has proved to be quite capable of committing the crime. That he was induced, provoked, or tempted to do so by government agents does not make him any more innocent or any less predisposed than he would be if he had been induced, provoked, or tempted by a private person—which, of course, would not entitle him to cry "entrapment." Since the only difference between these situations is the identity of the tempter, it follows that the significant focus must be on the conduct of the government agents, and not on the predisposition of the defendant.

The purpose of the entrapment defense, then, cannot be to protect persons who are "otherwise innocent." Rather, it must be to prohibit unlawful governmental activity in instigating crime. As Mr. Justice Brandeis stated in Casey v. United States, supra, at 425: "This prosecution should be stopped, not because some right of Casey's has been denied, but in order to protect the Government. To protect it from illegal conduct of its officers. To preserve the purity of its courts." . . . If that is so, then whether the particular defendant was "predisposed" or "otherwise innocent" is irrelevant; and the important question becomes whether the Government's conduct in inducing the crime was beyond judicial toleration.

Moreover, a test that makes the entrapment defense depend on whether the defendant had the requisite predisposition permits the introduction into evidence of all kinds of hearsay, suspicion, and rumor—all of which would be inadmissible in any other context—in order to prove the defendant's predisposition. It allows the prosecution, in offering such proof, to rely on the defendant's bad reputation or past criminal activities, including even rumored activities of which the prosecution may have insufficient evidence to obtain an indictment, and to present the agent's suspicions as to why they chose to tempt this defendant. This sort of evidence is not only unreliable, as the hearsay rule recognizes; but it is also highly prejudicial, especially if the matter is submitted to the jury, for, despite instructions to the contrary, the jury may well consider such evidence as probative not simply of the defendant's predisposition, but of his guilt of the offense with which he stands charged.

More fundamentally, focusing on the defendant's innocence or predisposition has the direct effect of making what is permissible or impermissible police conduct depend upon the past record and propensities of the particular defendant involved. Stated another way, this subjective test means that the Government is permitted to entrap a person with a criminal record or bad reputation, and then to prosecute him for the manufactured crime, confident that his record or reputation itself will be enough to show that he was predisposed to commit the offense anyway. . . .

This does not mean, of course, that the Government's use of undercover activity, strategy, or deception is necessarily unlawful. . . . Indeed, many crimes, especially so-called victimless crimes, could not otherwise be detected. Thus, government agents may engage in conduct that is likely, when objectively considered, to afford a person ready and willing to commit the crime an opportunity to do so. Osborn v. United States, 385 U.S. 323, 331–332 (1966). . . .

But when the agents' involvement in criminal activities goes beyond the mere offering of such an opportunity, and when their conduct is of a kind that could induce or instigate the commission of a crime by one not ready and willing to commit it, then—regardless of the character or propensities of the particular person induced—I think entrapment has occurred. For in that situation, the Government has engaged in the impermissible manufacturing of crime, and the federal courts should bar the prosecution in order to preserve the institutional integrity of the system of federal criminal justice.

II

In the case before us, I think that the District Court erred in submitting the issue of entrapment to the jury, with instructions to acquit only if it had a reasonable doubt as to the respondent's predisposition to committing the crime. Since, under the objective test of entrapment, predisposition is irrelevant and the issue is to be decided by the trial judge, the Court of Appeals, I believe, would have been justified in reversing the conviction on this basis alone. But since the appellate court did not remand for consideration of the issue by the District Judge under an objective standard, but rather found entrapment as a matter of law and directed that the indictment be dismissed, we must reach the merits of the respondent's entrapment defense. . . .

It is undisputed that phenyl-2-propanone is an essential ingredient in the manufacture of methamphetamine; that it is not used for any other purpose; and that, while its sale is not illegal, it is difficult to obtain, because a manufacturer's license is needed to purchase it, and because many suppliers, at the request of the Federal Bureau of Narcotics and Dangerous Drugs, do not sell it at all. It is also undisputed that the methamphetamine which the respondent was prosecuted for manufacturing and selling was all produced on December 10, 1969, and that all the phenyl-2-propanone used in the manufacture of that batch of the drug was provided by the government agent. In these circumstances, the agent's undertaking to supply this ingredient to the respondent, thus making it possible for the Government to prosecute him for manufacturing an illicit drug with it, was, I think, precisely the type of governmental conduct that the entrapment defense is meant to prevent.

Although the Court of Appeals found that the phenyl-2-propanone could not have been obtained without the agent's intervention—that "there could not have been the manufacture, delivery, or sale of the illicit drug had it not been for the Government's supply of one of the essential ingredients," . . . the Court today rejects this finding as contradicted by the facts revealed at trial. The record, as the Court states, discloses that one of the respondent's accomplices, though not the respondent himself, had obtained phenyl-2-propanone from independent sources both before and after receiving the agent's supply, and had used it in the production of methamphetamine. This demonstrates, it is said, that the chemical was obtainable other than through the government agent; and hence the agent's furnishing it for the production of the methamphetamine involved in this prosecution did no more than afford an opportunity for its production to one ready and willing to produce it. . . . Thus, the argument seems to be, there was no entrapment here, any more than there would have been if the agent had furnished common table salt, had that been necessary to the drug's production.

It cannot be doubted that if phenyl-2-propanone had been wholly unobtainable from other sources, the agent's undercover offer to supply it to the respondent in return for part of the illicit methamphetamine produced therewith—an offer initiated and carried out by the agent for the purpose of prosecuting the respondent for producing methamphetamine—would be precisely the type of governmental conduct that constitutes entrapment under any definition. For the agent's conduct in that situation would make possible the commission of an otherwise totally impossible crime, and, I should suppose, would thus be a textbook example of instigating the commission of a criminal offense in order to prosecute someone for committing it.

But assuming in this case that the phenyl-2-propanone was obtainable through independent sources, the fact remains that that used for the particular batch of methamphetamine involved in all three counts of the indictment with which the respondent was charged—i.e., that produced on December 10, 1969—was supplied by the Government. This essential ingredient was indisputably difficult to obtain, and yet what was used in committing the offenses of which the respondent was convicted was offered to the respondent by the Government agent, on the agent's own initiative, and was readily supplied to the respondent in needed amounts. If the chemical was so easily available elsewhere, then why did not the agent simply wait until the respondent had himself obtained the ingredients and produced the drug, and then buy it from him? The very fact that the agent felt it incumbent upon him to offer to supply phenyl-2-propanone in return for the drug casts considerable doubt on the theory that the chemical could easily have been procured without the agent's intervention, and that therefore the agent merely afforded an opportunity for the commission of a criminal offense.

. . .

It is the Government's duty to prevent crime, not to promote it. Here, the Government's agent asked that the illegal drug be produced for him, solved his quarry's practical problems with the assurance that he could provide the one essential ingredient that was difficult to obtain, furnished that element as he had promised, and bought the finished product from the respondent—all so that the respondent could be prosecuted for producing and selling the very drug for which the agent had asked and for which he had provided the necessary component. . . .

I would affirm the judgment of the Court of Appeals.

HAMPTON v. UNITED STATES

Supreme Court of the United States, 1976.
425 U.S. 484, 96 S.Ct. 1646.

Mr. Justice Rehnquist announced the judgment of the Court in an opinion in which The Chief Justice and Mr. Justice White join.

This case presents the question of whether a defendant may be convicted for the sale of contraband which he procured from a government informer or agent. The Court of Appeals for the Eighth Circuit held he could be, and we agree.

I

Petitioner was convicted of two counts of distributing heroin in violation of 21 U.S.C. § 841(a)(1) in the United States District Court for the Eastern District of Missouri and sentenced to concurrent terms of five years' imprisonment (suspended). The case arose from two sales of heroin by petitioner to agents of the Federal Drug Enforcement Administration (DEA) in St. Louis on February 25 and 26, 1974. The sales were arranged by one Hutton, who was a pool-playing acquaintance of petitioner at the Pud bar in St. Louis and also a DEA informant.

According to the Government's witnesses, in late February 1974, Hutton and petitioner were shooting pool at the Pud when petitioner, after observing "track" (needle) marks on Hutton's arms told Hutton that he needed money and knew where he could get some heroin. Hutton responded that he could find a buyer and petitioner suggested that he "get in touch with those people." Hutton then called DEA agent Terry Sawyer and arranged a sale for 10 p.m. on February 25.

At the appointed time, Hutton and petitioner went to a prearranged meetingplace and were met by Agent Sawyer and DEA Agent McDowell, posing as narcotics dealers. Petitioner produced a tinfoil packet from his cap and turned it over to the agents who tested it, pronounced it "okay," and negotiated a price of $145 which was paid to petitioner. Before they parted, petitioner told Sawyer that he could obtain larger quantities of heroin and gave Sawyer a phone number where he could be reached.

The next day Sawyer called petitioner and arranged for another "buy" that afternoon. Petitioner got Hutton to go along and they met the agents again near where they had been the previous night.

They all entered the agents' car, and petitioner again produced a tinfoil packet from his cap. The agents again field-tested it and pronounced it satisfactory. Petitioner then asked for $500 which Agent Sawyer said he would get from the trunk. Sawyer got out and opened the trunk which was a signal to other agents to move in and arrest petitioner, which they did.

Petitioner's version of events was quite different. According to him, in response to petitioner's statement that he was short of cash, Hutton said that he had a friend who was a pharmacist who could produce a non-narcotic counterfeit drug which would give the same reaction as heroin. Hutton proposed selling this drug to gullible acquaintances who would be led to believe they were buying heroin. Petitioner testified that they successfully duped one buyer with this fake drug and that the sales which led to the arrest was solicited by petitioner in an effort to profit further from this ploy.

Petitioner contended that he neither intended to sell, nor knew that he was dealing in heroin and that all of the drugs he sold were supplied by Hutton. His account was at least partially disbelieved by the jury which was instructed that in order to convict petitioner they had to find that the Government proved "that the defendant knowingly did an act which the law forbids, purposely intending to violate the law." Thus the guilty verdict necessarily implies that the jury rejected petitioner's claim that he did not know the substance was heroin, and petitioner himself admitted both soliciting and carrying out sales. The only relevance of his version of the facts, then, lies in his having requested an instruction embodying that version. He did not request a standard entrapment instruction but he did request the following:

> "The defendant asserts that he was the victim of entrapment as to the crimes charged in the indictment.

> "If you find that the defendant's sales of narcotics were sales of narcotics supplied to him by an informer in the employ of or acting on behalf of the government, then you must acquit the defendant because the law as a matter of policy forbids his conviction in such a case.

> "Furthermore, under this particular defense, you need not consider the predisposition of the defendant to commit the offense charged, because if the governmental involvement through its informer reached the point that I have just defined in your own minds, then the predisposition of the defendant would not matter."

The trial court refused the instruction and petitioner was found guilty. He appealed to the United States Court of Appeals for the Eighth Circuit, claiming that if the jury had believed that the drug was supplied by Hutton he should have been acquitted. The Court of Appeals rejected this argument and affirmed the conviction. . . .

II

In *Russell* we held that the statutory defense of entrapment was not available where it was conceded that a government agent supplied a necessary ingredient in the manufacture of an illicit drug. We reaffirmed the principle of Sorrells v. United States, . . . and Sherman v. United States . . ., that the entrapment defense "focus[es] on the intent or predisposition of the defendant to commit the crime," . . . rather than upon the conduct of the Government's agents. We ruled out the possibility that the defense of entrapment could ever be based upon governmental misconduct in a case, such as this one, where the predisposition of the defendant to commit the crime was established.

. . . In view of these holdings, petitioner correctly recognizes that his case does not qualify as one involving "entrapment" at all. He instead relies on the language in *Russell* that "we may some day be presented with a situation in which the conduct of law enforcement agents is so outrageous that due process principles would absolutely bar the government from invoking judicial processes to obtain a conviction. . . . ["]

In urging that this case involves a violation of his due process rights, petitioner misapprehends the meaning of the quoted language in *Russell,* supra. Admittedly petitioner's case is different from Russell's but the difference is one of degree, not of kind. In *Russell* the ingredient supplied by the Government agent was a legal drug which the defendants demonstrably could have obtained from other sources besides the Government. Here the drug which the government informant allegedly supplied to petitioner was both illegal and constituted the *corpus delicti* for the sale of which the petitioner was convicted. The Government obviously played a more significant role in enabling petitioner to sell contraband in this case than it did in *Russell.*

But in each case the Government agents were acting in concert with the defendant, and in each case either the jury found or the defendant conceded that he was predisposed to commit the crime for which he was convicted. The remedy of the criminal defendant with respect to the acts of Government agents, which, far from being resisted, are encouraged by him, lies solely in the defense of entrapment. But, as noted, petitioner's conceded predisposition rendered this defense unavailable to him.

. . .

The limitations of the Due Process Clause of the Fifth Amendment come into play only when the Government activity in question violates some protected right of the *defendant.* Here, as we have noted, the police, the Government informant, and the defendant acted in concert with one another. If the result of the governmental activity is to "implant in the mind of an innocent person the disposition to commit the alleged offense and induce its commission . . .," . . . the defendant is protected by the defense of entrapment. If the police engage in illegal activity in concert with a defendant beyond the scope of their duties the remedy lies, not in freeing the equally culpable defendant, but in prosecuting the police under the applicable provisions of state or federal law. . . . But the police conduct here no more deprived defendant of any right secured to him by the United States Constitution than did the police conduct in *Russell* deprive Russell of any rights.

Affirmed.

[The concurring opinion of Mr. Justice Powell, with whom Mr. Justice Blackmun joined, is omitted].

. . .

MR. JUSTICE BRENNAN, with whom MR. JUSTICE STEWART and MR. JUSTICE MARSHALL concur, dissenting.

I joined my Brother Stewart's dissent in United States v. Russell, . . . and Mr. Justice Frankfurter's opinion concurring in the result in Sherman v. United States. . . . Those opinions and the separate opinion of Mr. Justice Roberts in *Sorrells* . . . express the view, with which I fully agree, that "courts refuse to convict an entrapped defendant, not because his conduct falls outside the proscription of the statute, but because, even if his guilt be admitted, the methods employed on behalf of the Government to bring about conviction cannot be countenanced." . . .

In any event, I think that reversal of petitioner's conviction is also compelled for those who follow the "subjective" approach to the defense of entrapment. As Mr. Justice Rehnquist notes, the Government's role in the criminal activity involved in this case was more pervasive than the Government involvement in *Russell*. Ante, at 489. In addition, I agree with Mr. Justice Powell that *Russell* does not foreclose imposition of a bar to conviction—based upon our supervisory power or due process principles—where the conduct of law enforcement authorities is sufficiently offensive, even though the individuals entitled to invoke such a defense might be "predisposed." . . . In my view, the police activity in this case was beyond permissible limits.

Two facts significantly distinguish this case from *Russell*. First, the chemical supplied in that case was not contraband. It is legal to possess and sell phenyl-2-propanone and, although the Government there supplied an ingredient that was essential to the manufacture of methamphetamine, it did not supply the contraband itself. In contrast, petitioner claims that the very narcotic he is accused of selling was supplied by an agent of the Government. . . .

Second, the defendant in *Russell* "was an active participant in an illegal drug manufacturing enterprise which began before the Government agent appeared on the scene, and continued after the Government agent had left the scene." . . . Russell was charged with unlawfully manufacturing and processing methamphetamine, . . . and his crime was participation in an ongoing operation. In contrast, the two sales for which petitioner was convicted were allegedly instigated by Government agents and completed by the Government's purchase. The beginning and end of this crime thus coincided exactly with the Government's entry into and withdrawal from the criminal activity involved in this case, while the Government was not similarly involved in Russell's crime. . . .

. . . Where the Government's agent deliberately sets up the accused by supplying him with contraband and then bringing him to another agent as a potential purchaser, the Government's role has passed the point of toleration. . . . The Government is doing nothing less than buying contraband from itself through an intermediary and jailing the intermediary. . . . There is little, if any, law enforcement interest promoted by such conduct; plainly it is not designed to discover ongoing drug traffic. Rather, such conduct deliberately entices an individual to commit a crime. That the accused is "predisposed" cannot possibly justify the action of government officials in purposefully creating the crime. No one would suggest that the police could round up and jail all "predisposed" individuals, yet that is precisely what set-ups like the instant one are intended to accomplish. . . . Thus, this case is nothing less than an instance of "the Government . . . seeking to punish for an alleged offense which is the product of the creative activity of its own officials." . . .

. . . For the reasons stated I would at a minimum engraft the *Bueno* principle upon that defense and hold that conviction is barred as a matter of law where the subject of the criminal charge is the sale of contraband provided to the defendant by a Government agent. . . .

NOTES

1. The California Supreme Court adopted an unusual approach to entrapment defenses in People v. Barraza, 23 Cal.3d 675, 153 Cal.Rptr. 459, 591 P.2d 947 (1979):

"Mosk, J.

* * *

"The principle currently applied in California represents a hybrid position, fusing elements of both the subjective and objective theories of entrapment. In People v. Benford (1959) 53 Cal.2d 1, 9, 345 P.2d 928, this court unanimously embraced the public policy/deterrence rationale that Justices Roberts and Frankfurter had so persuasively urged. In doing so, we ruled inadmissible on the issue of entrapment the most prejudicial inquiries that are allowed under the subjective theory, i.e., evidence that the defendant 'had previously committed similar crimes or had the reputation of being engaged in the commission of such crimes or was suspected by the police of criminal activities . . ..' Despite the lessons of *Benford*, however, this court has continued to maintain that entrapment depends upon where the intent to commit the crime originated. People v. Moran (1970) 1 Cal.3d 755, 760, 83 Cal.Rptr. 411, 463 P.2d 763.

"Chief Justice Traynor, dissenting in *Moran*, in an opinion joined by two other justices of this court, recognized that in thus departing from the rationale adopted in *Benford*, we have seriously undermined the deterrent effect of the entrapment defense on impermissible police conduct. He reasoned that attempts to fix the origin of intent or determine the defendant's criminal predisposition divert the court's attention from the only proper subject of focus in the entrapment defense: the dubious police conduct which the court must deter. The success of an entrapment defense should not turn on differences among defendants; we are not concerned with who first conceived or who willingly, or reluctantly, acquiesced in a criminal project. What we do care about is how much and what manner of persuasion, pressure, and cajoling are brought to bear by law enforcement officials to induce persons to commit crimes. Even though California courts do not permit introduction of the highly prejudicial evidence of subjective predisposition allowed in jurisdictions following the federal rule, our more limited focus on the character and intent of the accused is still misplaced and impairs our courts in their task of assuring the lawfulness of law enforcement activity.

"Commentators on the subject have overwhelmingly favored judicial decision of the issue by application of a test which looks only to the nature and extent of police activity in the criminal enterprise. . . . In recent years several state courts (see Grossman v. State (Alaska 1969) 457 P.2d 226; People v. Turner (1973) 390 Mich. 7, 210 N.W.2d 336; State v. Mullen (Iowa 1974) supra, 216 N.W.2d 375) and legislatures (see N.D.Cent.Code, § 12.1–05–11 (1976); N.H.Rev.Stat.Ann., § 626:5 (1974); Pa.Const.Stat.Ann., tit. 18, § 313 (Purdon 1973); Haw. Rev.Stat., § 702–237) have recognized that such a test is more consistent with and better promotes the underlying purpose of the entrapment defense. Such support for the position no doubt derives from a developing awareness that 'entrapment is a facet of a broader problem. Along with illegal search and seizures, wiretapping, false arrest, illegal detention and the third degree, it is a type of lawless law enforcement. They all spring from common motivations. Each is a substitute for skillful and scientific investigation. Each is condoned by the sinister sophism that the end, when dealing with known criminals or the "criminal classes," justifies the employment of illegal means.' (Donnelly, Judicial Control of Informants, Spies, Stool Pigeons, and Agent Provocateurs (1951) 60 Yale L.J. 1091, 1111.)

"For all the foregoing reasons we hold that the proper test of entrapment in California is the following: was the conduct of the law enforcement agent likely to induce a normally law-abiding person to commit the offense? For the purposes of this test, we presume that such a person would normally resist the temptation to commit a crime presented by the simple opportunity to act unlawfully. Official conduct that does no more than offer that opportunity to the suspect—for example, a decoy program—is therefore permissible; but it is impermissible for the police or their agents to pressure the suspect by overbearing conduct such as badgering, cajoling, importuning, or other affirmative acts likely to induce a normally law-abiding person to commit the crime.

"Although the determination of what police conduct is impermissible must to some extent proceed on an ad hoc basis, guidance will generally be found in the application of one or both of two principles. First, if the actions of the law enforcement agent would generate in a normally law-abiding person a motive for the crime other than ordinary criminal intent, entrapment will be established. An example of such conduct would be an appeal by the police that would induce such a person to commit the act because of friendship or sympathy, instead of a desire for personal gain or other typical criminal purpose. Second, affirmative police conduct that would make commission of the crime unusually attractive to a normally law-abiding person will likewise constitute entrapment. Such conduct would include, for example, a guarantee that the act is not illegal or the offense will go undetected, an offer of exorbitant consideration or any similar enticement.

"Finally, while the inquiry must focus primarily on the conduct of the law enforcement agent, that conduct is not to be viewed in a vacuum; it should also be judged by the effect it would have on a normally law-abiding person situated in the circumstances of the case at hand. Among the circumstances that may be relevant for this purpose, for example, are the transactions preceding the offense, the suspect's response to the inducements of the officer, the gravity of the crime, and the difficulty of detecting instances of its commission. We reiterate, however, that under this test such matters as the character of the suspect, his predisposition to commit the offense, and his subjective intent are irrelevant.

"Richardson, J.

"I respectfully dissent, . . . from that portion of the majority's opinion which establishes a new test for the defense of entrapment.

"As the majority concedes, in determining the existence of an entrapment, the United States Supreme Court has consistently rejected the 'objective' ('hypothetical person') test which the majority adopts in favor of the 'subjective' ('origin of intent') test.

"In Sorrells v. United States (1932) 287 U.S. 435, 53 S.Ct. 210, Sherman v. United States (1958) 356 U.S. 369, 78 S.Ct. 819, and recently in United States v. Russell (1973) 411 U.S. 423, 93 S.Ct. 1637, the high court has approved and reapproved the 'subjective' test. Following this lead, the federal courts and the courts of the overwhelming majority of states, including California, apply the 'subjective' test, thereby keeping attention properly focused on the unique interrelationship of the police and the particular defendant who is asserting the defense of entrapment.

"The majority now proposes to ban consideration of the particular defendant and replace him with a hypothetical 'normally law-abiding person' who is described as 'a person [who] would normally resist the temptation to commit a crime presented by the simple opportunity to act unlawfully.' The briefest reflection reveals the difficulties inherent in this definition. The individual who has *never* committed a criminal act can safely be categorized as a 'normally law-abiding person' since presumably his unblemished record is proof of his ability to resist temptation. However, what of the individual who has transgressed in the past either once or several times? Is he no longer '*normally* law-abiding'? Is 'normally' synonymous with 'generally'? If it may be drawn at all, the line between 'normally law-abiding' individuals and 'others' is not so easily fixed as the majority suggests.

"The fallacy underlying the majority's thesis, of course, is that in the very real world of criminal conduct there are no hypothetical people. To attempt to judge police conduct in a vacuum is to engage in a futile and meaningless exercise in semantics. It is the recognition of this precise fact that has restrained the United States Supreme Court from discarding the subjective test whereby attention is pointed at the particular defendant rather than on some imaginary or fictitious person. The majority abandons the actual for the hypothetical. It thereby substitutes the unreal for the real, with unnecessary complications that inevitably result therefrom.

"Further, by adopting an 'objective' test, the majority does not really eliminate the 'subjective' test. Even if the jury makes a finding adverse to the defendant pursuant to the 'objective' test, the defendant may still presumably argue entrapment to the jury using the 'subjective' standard to negate intent. The question of what the defendant intended is always relevant. Indeed, in the present case defendant admitted commission of the act. He denied only the requisite intent. The majority ignores entirely this problem of the double assertion of the entrapment defense.

"The issue of entrapment is a factual matter, the determination of which is of critical importance to both parties. Regardless of any salutary effect which a trial court opinion might have on police administration, the matter is properly entrusted to the jury and should remain within its province."

2. Some crimes do not involve a victim in the traditional sense, because all are actually participants and no one sees himself as victimized. Hence, no one files a complaint with the police following the criminal offense. Examples of so-called victimless crimes include illicit narcotics transactions and dealing in non-taxed alcoholic beverages. In these kinds of cases, entrapment frequently becomes an issue. While use of a full-time government undercover agent, as in *Russell* and *Hampton*, is one answer to the difficult enforcement problem, an agent needs a long time to infiltrate the criminal world to such a degree that he is trusted. Further, the procedure is dangerous. To save time, reduce the danger to government employees, and assist undercover agents, a law enforcement agency will sometimes use an underworld person to bait the trap, thereby stimulating the unlawful conduct by the defendant. The unreliability of such character may cloud prosecutions. An underworld character's incentive to entrap an unwary person would seem to increase when a contingent arrangement motivates him to develop an unlawful narcotic or non-tax whiskey transaction. Thus, in Williamson v. United States, 311 F.2d 441 (5th Cir. 1962), the Court reversed Williamson's conviction for possession of untaxed whiskey because the government's informer was to be paid a $200 fee contingent upon his securing evidence against Williamson. In United States v. Curry, 284 F.Supp. 458 (E.D.Ill.1968), the Court granted Curry's post-trial motion for acquittal largely because the unlawful narcotic sale had been arranged by an informer who himself was a defendant in a federal narcotics complaint and had been offered a dismissal of the charge by government agents if he would develop other narcotic cases for the government.

However, not all contingent arrangements are condemned to the extent of reversing convictions. In United States v. Costner, 359 F.2d 969 (6th Cir. 1966), the Court affirmed a conviction, distinguishing the contingent fee arrangement from that in *Williamson* because Williamson was named as the object of the investigation while no one in particular was singled out in *Costner*.

In accord with *Costner*, see People v. Mills, 40 Ill.2d 4, 237 N.E.2d 697 (1968). See also United States v. Baxter, 342 F.2d 773 (6th Cir.1965), cert. denied 381 U.S. 934, 85 S.Ct. 1766.

Heard v. United States, 414 F.2d 884 (5th Cir. 1969), distinguished *Williamson* because in *Heard* the contingent fee informer was instructed to develop an unlawful narcotics sale against a person named Walker. Heard was an unexpected participant with Walker. Hence, while the contingent arrangement might have tainted a prosecution against Walker, the contingent arrangement played no part in Heard's prosecution.

In Hill v. United States, 328 F.2d 988 (5th Cir. 1964), another case dealing with possession of untaxed whiskey, the informer who induced the sale of untaxed whiskey was offered a $300 reward if Hill were caught. However, the Court refused to reverse the conviction distinguishing its own Fifth Circuit *Williamson* case from *Hill* on the basis that Hill had a past record of convictions for the same offense and the complaint of Hill's neighbors about Hill's illegal activities initiated the investigation.

See also the outstanding article by Dean Marcus, The Development of Entrapment Law, 33 Wayne L.Rev. 5 (1986). The article was adopted from the book by Marcus, The Entrapment Defense, 1986.

3. For an excellent overview of entrapment issues, see Park, The Entrapment Controversy, 60 Minn.L.Rev. 163 (1976). Professor Park has thought through the implications of alternative approaches to entrapment in various factual situations and has offered some original insights.

4. In Florida, the Supreme Court had adopted a test of entrapment that combined both subjective and objective components. See, Cruz v. State, 465 So. 2d 516 (Fla.1985). In 1987, however, the legislature passed an entrapment statute which codified the subjective (or traditional) test for the defense, and abolished *Cruz*'s objective standard. The statute also places the burden to prove entrapment on the defendant, by a preponderance of the evidence.

Query: If the criminal intent required for the commission of a crime is an element of that offense which, under Mullaney v. Wilbur [see Chapter 2–B, supra, on Burden of Proof], must be proved by the prosecution, does not the Florida entrapment statute violate due process by requiring a defendant to prove that she was *not predisposed* toward committing the offense? Is not such a provision requiring him to prove lack of criminal intent? See, Gonzalez v. State, 571 So.2d 1346 (Fla.App.1990).

MATHEWS v. UNITED STATES
Supreme Court of the United States, 1988.
485 U.S. 58, 108 S.Ct. 883.

CHIEF JUSTICE REHNQUIST delivered the opinion of the Court.

This case requires the Court to decide whether a defendant in a federal criminal prosecution who denies commission of the crime may nonetheless have the jury instructed, where the evidence warrants, on the affirmative defense of entrapment. The United States Court of Appeals for the Seventh Circuit upheld the ruling of the District Court, which had refused to instruct the jury as to entrapment because petitioner would not admit committing all of the elements of the crime of accepting a bribe. This holding conflicts with decisions of other Courts of Appeals, which have taken a variety of approaches to the question. We granted certiorari to resolve this conflict, and we now reverse.

Petitioner was employed by the Small Business Administration (SBA) in Milwaukee, Wisconsin, and was responsible for the SBA's "8A Program," which provided aid to certain small businesses. Under the program, the SBA obtained government contracts and subcontracted them to program participants. The SBA would then assist the participants in performing the contracts. Midwest Knitting Mills, whose president was James DeShazer, was one of the participants in the 8A Program. DeShazer's principal contact at the SBA was petitioner.

In October 1984, DeShazer complained to a government customer that petitioner had repeatedly asked for loans. DeShazer believed that petitioner was not providing Midwest with certain 8A Program benefits because DeShazer had not made the requested loans. In early 1985, the FBI arranged for DeShazer to assist in the investigation resulting from his complaint. Under FBI surveillance, DeShazer offered petitioner a loan that, according to DeShazer, petitioner had previously requested. Petitioner agreed to accept the loan, and two months later, DeShazer met petitioner at a restaurant and gave him the money. Petitioner was immediately arrested and charged with accepting a gratuity in exchange for an official act. 18 U.S.C. § 201(g).

Before trial petitioner filed a motion *in limine* seeking to raise an entrapment defense. The District Court denied the motion, ruling that entrapment was not available to petitioner because he would not admit all of the elements (including the requisite mental state) of the offense charged. The District Court did, however, allow petitioner to argue as his first line of defense that his acts "were procurred [sic] by the overt acts of the principle [sic] witness of the Government, Mr. DeShazer."

At trial, the Government argued that petitioner had accepted the loan in return for cooperation in SBA matters. The Government called DeShazer, who testified both that petitioner had repeatedly asked for loans and that he and petitioner had agreed that the loan at issue would result in SBA-provided benefits for Midwest. The Government also played tape recordings of conversations between DeShazer and petitioner in which they discussed the loan. Petitioner testified in his own defense that although he had accepted the loan, he believed it was a personal loan unrelated to his duties at the SBA. Petitioner stated that he and DeShazer were friends and that he had accepted a personal loan from DeShazer previously. According to petitioner, he was in dire financial straits when DeShazer broached the possibility of providing a loan. Petitioner also testified that DeShazer had stated that he needed quickly to get rid of the money that he was offering to petitioner because he had been hiding the money from his wife and was concerned that she would be upset if she discovered this secret; DeShazer had also stated at one point that if petitioner did not take the money soon, DeShazer would be tempted to spend it.

At the close of the trial, petitioner moved for a "mistrial" because of the District Court's refusal to instruct the jury as to entrapment. The District Court noted that the evidence of entrapment was "shaky at best," but rather than premise its denial of petitioner's motion on that ground, the court reaffirmed its earlier ruling that as a matter of law, petitioner was not entitled to an entrapment instruction because he would not admit committing all elements of the crime charged. The jury subsequently found petitioner guilty.

The United States Court of Appeals for the Seventh Circuit affirmed the District Court's refusal to allow petitioner to argue entrapment . . .

We granted certiorari, to consider under what circumstances a defendant is entitled to an entrapment instruction. We hold that even if the defendant denies one or more elements of the crime, he is entitled to an entrapment instruction whenever there is sufficient evidence from which a reasonable jury could find entrapment.

Because the parties agree as to the basics of the affirmative defense of entrapment as developed by this Court, there is little reason to chronicle its history in detail. Suffice it to say that the Court has consistently adhered to the view, first enunciated in *Sorrells v. United States* (1932), that a valid entrapment defense has two related elements: government inducement of the crime, and a lack of predisposition on the part of the defendant to engage in the criminal conduct. Predisposition, "the principal element in the defense of entrapment," focuses upon whether the defendant was an "unwary innocent" or instead, an "unwary criminal" who readily availed himself of the opportunity to perpetrate the crime. The question of entrapment is generally one for the jury, rather than for the court.

The Government insists that a defendant should not be allowed both to deny the offense and to rely on the affirmative defense of entrapment. Because entrapment presupposes the commission of a crime, a jury could not logically conclude that the defendant had both failed to commit the elements of the offense *and* been entrapped. According to the Government, petitioner is asking to "clai[m] the right to swear that he had no criminal intent and in the same breath to argue that he had one that did not originate with him."

As a general proposition a defendant is entitled to an instruction as to any recognized defense for which there exists evidence sufficient for a reasonable jury to find in his favor. Stevenson v. United States, 162 U.S. 313, 16 S.Ct. 839, 40 L.Ed. 980 (1896); 4 C. Torcia, Wharton's Criminal Procedure § 538, p. 11 (12th ed. 1976) (hereinafter Wharton). . . . In *Stevenson,* this Court reversed a murder conviction arising out of a gunfight in the Indian Territory. The principal holding of the Court was that the evidence was sufficient to entitle the defendant to a manslaughter instruction, but the Court also decided that the defendant was entitled as well to have the jury instructed on self-defense. The affirmative defense of self-defense is, of course, inconsistent with the claim that the defendant killed in the heat of passion.

* * *

The Government argues that allowing a defendant to rely on inconsistent defenses will encourage perjury, lead to jury confusion, and subvert the truthfinding function of the trial. These same concerns are, however, present in the civil context, yet inconsistency is expressly allowed under the Federal Rules of Civil Procedure. We do not think that allowing inconsistency necessarily sanctions perjury. Here petitioner wished to testify that he had no intent to commit the crime, and have his attorney argue to the jury that if it concluded otherwise, then it should consider whether that intent was the result of government inducement. The jury would have considered inconsistent defenses, but the petitioner would not have necessarily testified untruthfully.

We would not go so far as to say that charges on inconsistent defenses may not on occasion increase the risk of perjury, but particularly in the case of entrapment we think the practical consequences will be less burdensome than the Government fears. The Court of Appeals in United States v. Demma, 523 F.2d 981, 985 (CA9 1975) (en banc), observed:

> "Of course, it is very unlikely that the defendant will be able to prove entrapment without testifying and, in the course of testifying, without admitting that he did the acts charged. . . . When he takes the stand, the defendant forfeits his right to remain silent, subjects himself to all the rigors of cross-examination, including impeachment, and exposes himself to prosecution for perjury. Inconsistent testimony by the defendant seriously impairs and potentially destroys his credibility. While we hold that a defendant may both deny the acts and other elements necessary to constitute the crime charged and at the same time claim entrapment, the high risks to him make it unlikely as a strategic matter that he will choose to do so."

The Government finally contends that since the entrapment defense is not of "constitutional dimension," and that since it is "relatively limited," Congress would be free to make the entrapment defense available on whatever conditions and to whatever category of defendants it believed appropriate. Congress, of course, has never spoken on the subject, and so the decision is left to the courts. We are simply not persuaded by the Government's arguments that we should make the availability of an instruction on entrapment where the evidence justifies it subject to a requirement of consistency to which no other such defense is subject.

The Government contends as an alternative basis for affirming the judgment below that the evidence at trial was insufficient to support an instruction on the defense of entrapment. Of course evidence that government agents merely afforded an opportunity or facilities for the commission of the crime would be insufficient to warrant such an instruction. But this question was pretermitted by the Court of Appeals, and it will be open for consideration by that court on remand.

Reversed.

JUSTICE KENNEDY took no part in the consideration or decision of this case.

JUSTICE BRENNAN, concurring.

I join the Court's opinion. I write separately only because I have previously joined or written four opinions dissenting from this Court's holdings that the defendant's predisposition is relevant to the entrapment defense. Although some governmental misconduct might be sufficiently egregious to violate due process, my differences with the Court have been based on statutory interpretation and federal common law, not on the constitution. Were I judging on a clean slate, I would still be inclined to adopt the view that the entrapment defense should focus exclusively on the government's conduct. But I am not writing on a clean slate; the Court has spoken definitively on this point. Therefore I bow to *stare decisis,* and today join the judgment and reasoning of the Court.

JUSTICE SCALIA, concurring.

I concur in the judgment of the Court because in my view the defense of entrapment will rarely be genuinely inconsistent with the defense on the merits, and when genuine inconsistency exists its effect in destroying the defendant's credibility will suffice to protect the interests of justice.

The typical case presenting the issue before us here is one in which the defendant introduces evidence to the effect that he did not commit the unlawful acts, or did not commit them with the requisite unlawful intent, and also introduces evidence to show his lack of predisposition and inordinate government inducement. There is nothing inconsistent in these showings. The inconsistency alleged by the Government is a purely formal one, which arises only if entrapment is defined to require not only (1) inordinate government inducement to commit a crime, (2) directed at a person not predisposed to commit the crime, but also (3) causing that person to commit the crime. If the third element is added to the definition, counsel's argument to the jury cannot claim entrapment without admitting the crime. But I see no reason why the third element is essential, unless it is for the very purpose of rendering the defense unavailable without admission of the crime. Surely it does not add anything of substance to the findings the jury must make, since findings of (1) inordinate inducement plus (2) lack of predisposition will almost inevitably produce a conclusion of (3) causality. To be sure, entrapment cannot be available as a defense unless a crime by the object of the entrapment is established, since if there is no crime there is nothing to defend against; but in that sense all affirmative defenses assume commission of the crime.

My point is not that entrapment must be defined to exclude element (3). Whether it is or not, since that element seems to me unnecessary to achieve the social policy fostered by the defense I am not willing to declare the defense unavailable when it produces the formal inconsistency of the defendant's simultaneously denying the crime and asserting entrapment which assumes commission of the crime. I would not necessarily accept such formal inconsistency for other defenses, where the element contradicted is a functionally essential element of the defense.

Of course in the entrapment context, as elsewhere, the defendant's case may involve genuine, *non* formal inconsistency. The defendant might testify, for example, that he was not in the motel room where the illegal drugs changed hands, and that the drugs were pressed upon him in the motel room by agents of the Government. But that kind of genuine inconsistency here, as elsewhere, is self-penalizing. There is nothing distinctive about entrapment that justifies a special prophylactic rule.

JUSTICE WHITE, with whom JUSTICE BLACKMUN joins, dissenting.

At his criminal trial, petitioner took the stand and flatly denied accepting a loan "for or because of any official act." Petitioner later moved for a mistrial because the District Court would not permit him to rely on that testimony while he simultaneously argued that, in fact, he *had* accepted a loan for an official act, but only at the Government's instigation. Today, the Court holds that this rather sensible ruling on the part of the District Court constitutes reversible error. The reasons the Court offers for reaching this conclusion are not at all persuasive, and I respectfully dissent.

I

The Court properly recognizes that its result is not compelled by the Constitution. As the Court acknowledges, petitioner has no Fifth or Sixth Amendment right to conduct the inconsistent entrapment defense that he wished to mount at trial. And yet, if the Constitution does not compel reversal of the decision below, then what does?

Certainly not any Act of Congress, or the Federal Rules of Criminal Procedure. As the majority candidly admits, "Congress . . . has never spoken on the subject [at issue here], and so the decision is left to the courts." Moreover, the Court also frankly notes that while the Federal Rules of Civil Procedure contain a provision expressly authorizing inconsistent defenses, Federal Rule Civil Procedure 8(e)(2), the Federal Criminal Rules are without any such authorization. Indeed, the rather scant authority the majority cites in support of its view that inconsistent defenses are generally permitted in criminal trials is strongly suggestive of just how extraordinary such pleadings are in the criminal context.

Nor is the result the Court reaches urged by a predominance of authority in the lower courts. As the Court recognizes, only two Circuits have held, as the Court does today, that a criminal defendant may deny committing the elements of a crime, and then contend that the Government entrapped him into the offense. The remaining Circuits are far more restrained in their allowance of such inconsistent defenses, divided along the lines the majority discusses in its opinion.

Thus, neither the Constitution, nor a statute, nor the Criminal Rules, nor the bulk of authority compels us to reverse petitioner's conviction. Nor does the Court claim support from any of these sources for its decision. Instead, the majority rests almost exclusively on an application of the "general proposition [that] a defendant is entitled to an instruction as to any legally sufficient defense for which there exists evidence sufficient for a reasonable jury to find in his favor." There are several reasons, however, why this "general proposition" is inapposite here.

II

First, there is the unique nature of the entrapment defense. There is a valuable purpose served by having civil litigants plead alternative defenses which may be legally inconsistent. Allowing a tort defendant to claim both that he owed no duty-of-care to the plaintiff, but that if he did, he met that duty, preserves possible alternative defenses under which the defendant is entitled to relief. It prevents formalities of pleadings, or rigid application of legal doctrines, from standing in the way of the equitable resolution of a civil dispute. The same may be true for *some* criminal defenses (such as "self-defense" or "provocation") where a defendant may truthfully testify as to the facts of the crime, leaving it to his counsel to argue that these facts make out, as a matter of law, several possible defenses.

But the entrapment defense, by contrast, "is a relatively limited defense;" it is only available to "a defendant who has committed all the elements of a proscribed offense." Thus, when a defendant (as petitioner did here) testifies that he did not commit the elements of the offense he is charged with, the defense of entrapment is *not* a plausible alternate legal theory of the case; rather, it is a proper defense *only* if the accused is lying. We have rejected before the notion that a defendant has a right to lie at trial, or a right to solicit his attorney's aid in executing such a defense strategy. And there is respectable authority for concluding that no legitimate end of the criminal justice system is served by requiring a trial court to entertain such tactics, in the form of an entrapment defense which is at odds with the defendant's own testimony.

Allowing such inconsistency in defense tactics invites the scourge of an effective criminal justice system: perjury. In the past, we have taken extraordinary steps to combat perjury in criminal trials; these steps have even included permitting the admission of otherwise inadmissible evidence to prevent a defendant from procuring an acquittal via false testimony. Yet today, the Court reaches a result which it concedes "may . . . on occasion" increase the risk of perjury. This is reason enough to reject the Court's result. Worse still, the majority's prognostication may well be an understatement. Even if—as the Court suggests,—inconsistent defenses do not measurably increase the frequency of perjury in civil trials, the risk of perjury in a criminal trial is always greater than in a civil setting because the stakes are so much higher. Absent some constitutional or statutory mandate to conduct criminal trials in a particular way, we should be taking steps to minimize, not increase, the danger of perjured testimony.

* * *

Finally, even if the Court's decision does not result in increased perjury at criminal trials, it will—at the very least—result in increased confusion among criminal juries. The lower courts have rightly warned that jury confusion is likely to result from allowing a defendant to say "I did not do it" while his lawyer argues "He did it, but the government tricked him into it." Creating such confusion may enable some defendants to win acquittal on the entrapment defense, but only under the peculiar circumstances where a jury rejects the defendant's own stated view of the facts. We have not previously endorsed defense efforts to prevail at trial by playing such "shell games" with the jury; rather, we have written that "[a] defendant has no entitlement to the luck of a lawless decisionmaker." Nor, it should be added, is there any entitlement to a baffled decisionmaker.

III

Ultimately, only the petitioner knows whether he accepted a loan in exchange for an official act, or whether he obtained it as a personal favor. Today, the Court holds that petitioner has a right to take the stand and claim the latter, while having his attorney argue that he was entrapped into doing the former. Nothing counsels such a result—let alone compels it. Hence this dissent.

NOTES

1. The Supreme Courts of Florida and Arizona rejected the *Mathews* rule and decided to continue to follow earlier precedents prohibiting a defendant from interposing an entrapment defense unless she first admits commission of the crime charged. Since *Mathews* involved a non-constitutional interpretation of federal rules of criminal procedure, the state courts were not required to follow it, and both courts declined the opportunity to do so voluntarily.

In Wilson v. State, 577 So.2d 1300 (Fla.1991), the defendant was charged with sale of cocaine and possession with intent to distribute. Because he denied committing the offenses, the trial judge refused to give an entrapment instruction based on evidence that a police officer gave him $20 with which to buy, and give to her, a small piece of crack cocaine. The Supreme Court was persuaded by Justice White's dissent in *Mathews* that permitting inconsistent defenses fosters perjury, and therefore adhered to its earlier decisions refusing to allow a defendant to argue entrapment unless she admits commission of the charged offense. However, the court would permit a defendant to plead both entrapment and innocence if the two positions are not inconsistent.

In State v. Soule, ___ Ariz. ___, 811 P.2d 1071 (1991) [No. CR–90–0042–PR, decided March 21, 1991], the court's majority was satisfied to adhere to existing state precedent, which follows the traditional and prevailing view, requiring a defendant to admit all elements of an offense before he can avail himself of the defense of entrapment. The court said, "To allow a defendant to testify as to two defenses that cannot *both* be true is equivalent to sanctioning a defendant's perjury." Furthermore, said the court, the jury is likely to be confused by allowing inconsistent defenses: "What must the jury think when the defendant testifies that he had nothing to do with the sale of narcotics and then the defendant's attorney tells the jury that, yes, the defendant did commit the crime but was entrapped?"

The dissenting justices would have followed the *Mathews* rule, maintaining that the defense will not truly be inconsistent in many cases, and that where it is, the jurors will be able to handle it.

2. Even prior to *Mathews*, in California, the accused was permitted to assert entrapment and at the same time deny the acts charged. See, People v. Perez, 62 Cal.2d 769, 44 Cal.Rptr. 326, 401 P.2d 934 (1965), but the accused bears the burden of proving entrapment. People v. Moran, 1 Cal.3d 755, 83 Cal.Rptr. 411, 463 P.2d 763 (1970).

UNITED STATES v. KELLY

United States Court of Appeals, District of Columbia Circuit, 1983.
707 F.2d 1460.

PER CURIAM.

Judge MacKinnon files an opinion in Parts I, II, III(A) and IV of which Chief Judge Robinson concurs. Judge Ginsburg files an opinion in which Chief Judge Robinson concurs. Thus Parts I, II, III(A) and IV of Judge MacKinnon's opinion together with Judge Ginsburg's opinion constitute the opinion of the court. The judgment appealed from is reversed, and the case is remanded to the District Court with instructions to reinstate the indictment and the verdict of the jury, and for further proceedings.

MacKinnon, Circuit Judge.

* * *

On January 8, 1980, Congressman Richard Kelly accepted $25,000 from an agent of the FBI who was posing as a representative of two wealthy Arabs as part of the FBI's elaborate Abscam investigation. In return, Kelly agreed to use his position in Congress to assist the Arabs to become permanent residents of the United States. Unbeknownst to Kelly, the FBI recorded the entire illegal transaction on video tape.

On the basis of this and other evidence, Kelly and two other individuals, Eugene Ciuzio and Stanley Weisz, were charged with conspiracy to commit bribery, in violation of 18 U.S.C. § 371 (1976), bribery, in violation of 18 U.S.C. § 201(c) (1976), and interstate travel to commit bribery, in violation of 18 U.S.C. § 1952 (1976). A jury found each defendant guilty on all counts. However, the district court granted Kelly's motion to dismiss the indictment, entering a judgment of acquittal in his favor, because it concluded that the FBI's actions in furtherance of Abscam were so outrageous that prosecution of Kelly was barred by principles of due process.

* * *

I. FACTS

A. *The Abscam Investigation*

In the spring of 1978, the FBI's Long Island office began an undercover investigation with the initial goal of recovering stolen art and securities. The code name for this investigation was "Abscam," a name derived from Abdul Enterprises, the name of a fictitious FBI-created organization which ostensibly represented two Arabs of considerable wealth interested in "investing" in the United States. Convicted confidence man Melvin Weinberg was enlisted by the FBI to assist in the creation and operation of Abscam.[1] Weinberg played the role of financial advisor to Abdul Enterprises, while FBI agents "held" other positions in that organization. Beginning in January 1979, Anthony Amoroso, a special agent for the FBI, assumed the role of president of Abdul Enterprises.

Initially, the FBI made it known on the streets that Abdul Enterprises had money to invest and waited to be approached with proposals. Abdul Enterprises turned away individuals offering legitimate transactions, but maintained contact with those suggesting illegal activity. In November 1978 Abdul Enterprises was approached by two businessmen, William Rosenberg and William Eden, concerning the possibility of financing certain equipment to be leased to the City of Camden, New Jersey. It appeared that the transaction would require payment of a bribe to Angelo Errichetti, then Mayor of Camden. Thereafter the focus of Abscam shifted to political corruption and organized crime.[2]

---

1. From 1968 until 1976, Weinberg had operated an illegitimate business known as London Investors. Weinberg, claiming to represent wealthy investors, promised to arrange loans in exchange for "loan origination fees" *paid in advance.* Tr. at 1554–55, 1665–69. Of course, Weinburg never arranged the loans, but rather absconded with the fees.

Weinberg was arrested by the FBI in 1976 for his London Investors activities and, in 1977, pled guilty to mail and wire fraud charges brought in the United States District Court for the Western District of Pennsylvania. Tr. at 1555, 1669–71. In exchange for his cooperation in four organized crime cases, the FBI interceded on Weinberg's behalf before the district court.

As a result, Weinberg was sentenced to three years probation and permitted to return to New York to assist the FBI. Tr. at 1555–57, 1673–74, 3546–51. Thereafter, Weinberg assisted the FBI in Abscam, which was modeled after his successful London Investors scheme. Tr. at 1690–93, 3552, 3589–91. Beginning in August 1978, Weinberg received $1000 per month—raised in 1979 to $3000 per month—for his Abscam work. Tr. at 1028–30, 3546–51.

2. In December 1978 Mayor Errichetti met with the representatives of Abdul Enterprises and boasted that "he could control" Atlantic City. He later indicated that a bribe of $300,000 to $400,000 would guarantee a gambling license. Tr. at 1715, 3596–98. Errichetti ultimately *led Abscam*

On July 26, 1979, Mayor Errichetti, who had since been introduced to the Abscam agents by Eden and Rosenberg, and Howard Criden, a Philadelphia lawyer and associate of Errichetti, met with Weinberg and Amoroso on a yacht in Florida to discuss financing for a proposed casino that a client of Criden wished to build. During the day Amoroso and Errichetti discussed the problems that might face the wealthy Arabs who controlled Abdul Enterprises should an Iranian-type revolution occur in their country and they sought to come to the United States as permanent residents. Amoroso enlisted Errichetti's assistance in obtaining the "cooperation" of public officials and suggested that money would be no problem. Errichetti and Criden agreed and, on August 22, 1979, introduced the Abscam agents to Congressman Michael Myers, who accepted $50,000 in exchange for his promise to assist the wealthy Arabs. Thus was introduced the "asylum scenario"—whereby members of Congress were paid bribes to ensure that they would introduce private immigration legislation on behalf of the wealthy Arabs if and when necessary—which ultimately caught Kelly.

B. Abscam's Introduction to Kelly

On September 10, 1979, Weinberg met with Rosenberg and sought his aid in locating politicians willing to assist his Arab employers to become permanent residents of the United States. Weinberg outlined the assistance required indicating that the Arabs would pay $25,000 to a member of the House of Representatives and $50,000 to a member of the Senate for their promise of future assistance. Weinberg suggested that Amoroso would "talk one and one and make the guy safe" at the time of the payoff. In October 1979 Rosenberg related the proposal to a business associate and accountant, Stanley Weisz. Rosenberg told Weisz that the Arabs needed immigration assistance and that Weisz would receive a fee for the proper introductions.

On November 20, 1979, Weisz, while on vacation in Boynton Beach, Florida, met with his longtime business associate, Eugene Ciuzio. During their conversation, Weisz related the Arabs' need for immigration assistance to Ciuzio. Ciuzio replied that he knew a congressman who might be willing to help the Arabs and indicated he would check with him and get back to Weisz. In fact, Ciuzio had never discussed immigration matters with Kelly, having first met Kelly on October 1, 1979, in an Orlando restaurant.

Ciuzio promptly arranged to meet with Kelly at the Tampa airport on November 23, 1979. At that meeting Ciuzio told Kelly that he had some Arab clients with immigration difficulties and asked Kelly if he could help them. Kelly indicated that his office handled such matters routinely and that he would be glad to assist the Arabs, particularly

to a number of other corrupt public officials. See United States v. Myers, 692 F.2d 823 (2d Cir.1982); United States v. Jannotti, 673 F.2d 578 (3d Cir.) (en banc), cert. denied, 457 U.S. 1106, 102 S.Ct. 2906, 73 L.Ed.2d 1315 (1982). In March 1979 Abscam uncovered corruption in the Immigration and Naturalization Service. Tr. at 1252–53. See United States v. Alexandro, 675 F.2d 34 (2d Cir.), cert. denied, 459 U.S. 835, 103 S.Ct. 78, 74 L.Ed.2d 75 (1982).

since Ciuzio indicated they might invest in his district. Ciuzio informed Kelly that he—Ciuzio—would receive a large fee if Kelly helped the Arabs; Kelly told Ciuzio that the fee would cause no difficulties. Ciuzio promptly called Weisz from the Tampa airport and indicated that Kelly would be happy to help the Arabs.

In mid-December 1979 Weisz informed Rosenberg of Ciuzio's friendship with a Florida congressman who was willing to help the Arabs. On December 16, 1979, Rosenberg called Weinberg and told him that he had a "candidate" who would assist with the Arabs' immigration problems. Rosenberg indicated that the individual was a congressman from Florida, that he wanted $250,000, and that payment would have to be on "an escrow basis." Weinberg suggested that the Congressman be paid $25,000 down, with the balance paid when legisation was required. Rosenberg agreed to set up a meeting with the Congressman at Abdul Enterprises' Washington, D.C., townhouse on January 8, 1980. Rosenberg called Weisz and told him of Weinberg's positive response. Weisz gave Rosenberg Ciuzio's telephone number and agreed to call Ciuzio to ask him to contact Weinberg. On December 17, 1979, Rosenberg again called Weinberg and explained that Weinberg would be contacted by "a fellow by the name of Gino [Ciuzio] who will handle all the arrangements for you and who will give you the person."

On December 19, 1979, Amoroso and Weinberg met with Ciuzio in Hollywood, Florida, and explained the assistance that would be expected of the Congressman. *Ciuzio indicated that the individual was Congressman Richard Kelly and intimated that he and Kelly had had previous dealings of a similar nature.* Ciuzio suggested that he told Kelly of the offer and claimed that Kelly left the arrangements to him. Ciuzio opposed direct payment to Kelly and suggested that the money instead be escrowed through Weisz. Amoroso assured him that a private meeting between Amoroso and Kelly would protect the Congressman, and that the wealthy Arabs would invest in Kelly's district to provide an explanation for Kelly's assistance. Weinberg made it clear that the meeting and payment of $25,000 was to assure the Arabs that Kelly

> got the money [and] when we're ready to move that he is gonna be with us.

Ciuzio agreed to "lay out the story" for Kelly.

On December 21, 1979, Ciuzio telephoned Weinberg and suggested a January 8, 1980, meeting with Kelly. Ciuzio reiterated that he and Weisz did not want to have the money handed directly to the Congressman. Weinberg insisted that Kelly be directly involved in the transaction, but indicated that

> [a]ll he [Amoroso] wants the Congressman [to do] is to tell him what he's gonna do for him for the money.

Ciuzio agreed, but requested that they use "the right script, nice and soft."

On December 23, 1979, Ciuzio met Kelly at a restaurant in Alexandria, Virginia, and explained the proposal. Kelly *testified* that Ciuzio told him that

> there were two Arabs that were going to come into the United States and there was concern that they would have an immigration problem, and that if they did, they wanted to be assured that they would have some assistance from a person with some authority and that in this connection, a representative of these Arabs was prepared to pay a half a million dollars for this assistance. And that the arrangements would be that the two Arabs may not come into the country, but that their representatives wanted to have a meeting.

> They wanted to be sure that in the event they needed something, that they would have established a relationship, a contact that would cause this assistance to be available. And in this connection, that they would pay $25,000 just as earnest money . . . . *I would receive $25,000 just for going to the meeting,* and nothing would be expected of me, and then if at a later time there developed that there would be some need, then I would be expected to render this assistance and that *I would receive at that time an additional $100,000,* and the rest of the money was to be paid to [Ciuzio, Rosenberg and Weisz] . . . .

Ciuzio also told Kelly of the Arabs' intention of investing substantial sums in the districts of cooperative congressmen.

Kelly agreed to go to the meeting and give his assurances that he would help the Arabs, despite the fact that Ciuzio, Rosenberg, and Weisz would be paid as a result. However, Kelly testified that he refused to accept money for doing so:

> I would be glad to do it. But as far as my receiving any money for doing it, I just simply didn't want to do that. There wasn't any need to.

> There was no problem. It was a standard procedure and that I would not accept any money . . . . I said, . . . I will do that. You can depend on me, I will go to the [h]ouse and we will give these assurances to the representatives . . . .

> I am glad to do this as a favor to you. If you want to do something for me . . . I have got some real estate that I want to sell and perhaps you can help me find a buyer for that.

C. *Abscam's Payoff to Kelly*

Shortly after 10:00 p.m. on January 8, 1980, Kelly, Ciuzio, Rosenberg, and Weisz arrived at Abdul Enterprises' Washington, D.C., townhouse to meet with Weinberg and Amoroso. Initially Weinberg met with Ciuzio, who vigorously sought to dissuade Amoroso from attempting to bribe Kelly directly. The two ultimately agreed that Kelly would acknowledge that the money was in exchange for his agreement to assist the Arabs, but that Ciuzio would actually take the money from the meeting:

> WEINBERG: You can be in with him, all right?
>
> CIUZIO: Well I think I should be here to, ahh steer the f___ing thing . . .
>
> WEINBERG: Let him, let, just put the money on the table and say here, take it . . . here Congressman, here's the twenty-five thousand and that's it, you pick it up.
>
> CIUZIO: Go along with that, he knows the answers too.
>
> WEINBERG: All right, so . . .
>
> CIUZIO: I rehearsed with him.

After this conversation Kelly and Amoroso met privately. Amoroso explained the Arabs' immigration difficulties and their willingness to pay to have "friends" in Congress when required. He also indicated that the Arabs would invest in their "friends'" districts in order to protect them from pressure. Kelly's response revealed that he was aware of the purpose for the investments:

> AMOROSO: Now I realize that ahh there's a possibility that ahh if, if you were to introduce something like this, that ahh, people would ask, well why is he doing it, ya know, well what's the reason, now . . .
>
> KELLY: I've got the reason.
>
> AMOROSO: OK, what . . . would that be . . . investing?
>
> KELLY: Sure.

Kelly agreed to assist the Arabs, and, as recorded on the video tape, indicated that Amoroso's arrangement with Ciuzio was fine:

> All of this stuff that you've been talking about . . . *I don't know anything about that, I'm not involved with it* . . . Gino and these guys are my friend[s] . . . what you said makes a lot of sense to me . . . I'm gonna stick with ya . . . *and you can put me out there on the hill, and when you come back in the morning, I'll still be there* . . . . So this . . . will be helpful to me and . . . maybe . . . down the road sometime, you can do me a favor. *But in the meantime, whatever these guys are doing is all right, but I got no part in that* . . . . In other words, . . . your arrangement with these people is . . . . all fine. . . . [Y]ou have my assurance that what you have told me here, sounds like a good thing and . . . I will . . . stick by these people.

After Amoroso received a call from Assistant United States Attorney Jacobs who was monitoring the meeting and who thought Kelly was being "cute," and after Kelly conferred with Ciuzio, Amoroso sought to clarify Kelly's position. Kelly made it clear that he wanted the money given to Ciuzio:

KELLY: [Y]ou and I gotta . . . learn to talk to each other.

AMOROSO: Well I know . . .

KELLY: [D]on't stumble around, jump in there . . .

AMOROSO: Jump in there and give it to you?

KELLY: Sure.

AMOROSO: Ok. I was under the impression . . . when this thing was set up . . . that I was gonna give you something . . . tonight . . .

KELLY: Yeah.

AMOROSO: Ok, and that the rest was gonna come . . .

KELLY: Yeah.

AMOROSO: when you introduce that.

KELLY: That's right.

AMOROSO: Ok, is that, is that still . . .

KELLY: Yeah. Here's . . . what the thing is. Umm ahh just simply deal with Gino [Ciuzio] about it.

AMOROSO: Ok. You want me to give him the money . . . here?

KELLY: Sure.

However, when Amoroso indicated that all of the money was intended to go to Kelly, and that Ciuzio would be separately compensated, Kelly was confused:

I understood that what you were talking about was . . . all there was as far as Tony [sic, should be Ciuzio] was concerned and so as far as I'm concerned, he takes that . . . . [B]ut I see I didn't know . . . about this other arrangement . . . . It's . . . all right but I didn't know about that. So lets talk about it some.

Amoroso explained that he thought that giving the money directly to Kelly would avoid witnesses, thus protecting him. Kelly agreed:

AMOROSO: I thought that the best way of doing it was . . . a one on one between you and I. Now to me that sounds like . . . if you're looking for security . . . the best way of doing it.

KELLY: I think so too.

Amoroso then gave Kelly $25,000 in cash and Kelly stuffed the money into the pockets of his suit.

II. THE DISTRICT COURT DECISION

In ruling on Kelly's motion to dismiss the indictment and to set aside the verdict of the jury, the district court acknowledged the need for undercover investigative techniques to detect "diabolical criminal conduct so sophisticated as to be nearly impossible to detect," but concluded that

> as Abscam affected Kelly, it was not the type of carefully devised and supervised covert operation generally accepted by the courts. In many respects it differed sharply from traditionally accepted types of operations.

The district court complained that the asylum scenario was not triggered by any suspicion of corruption in government and that, unlike ordinary, passive sting operations, it utilized legal and illegal bait promoted by a "recruiting agent" "to persuade the Congressman to become a sting patron." The district court concluded that the sole purpose of the asylum scenario was to test the virtue of members of Congress.

The district court admitted its personal distaste for the concept of law enforcement agencies testing the virtue of congressmen, but held, assuming that such activities were proper,

> the application of the testing procedures in this case patently exceeds the outer limits of any concept of fundamental fairness.

> The litmus test—or temptation—should be one which the individual is likely to encounter in the ordinary course. To offer any other type of temptation does not serve the function of preventing crime by apprehending those who, when faced with actual opportunity, would become criminals. Instead, it creates a whole new type of crime that would not exist but for the government's actions.

> When improper proposals are rejected in these virtue-testing ventures, the guinea pig should be left alone. *In ordinary real life situations, anyone who would seek to corrupt a Congressman would certainly not continue to press in the face of a rejection for fear of being reported and arrested.* The FBI of course had no such restraints in this case.

(Emphasis added).

The district court found that Kelly rejected the bribe offer at his meeting with Ciuzio on December 23, that Ciuzio informed the Abscam agents of that fact at the townhouse on January 8, and that Kelly initially rejected the bribe in his meeting with Amoroso. Accordingly, the district court concluded

> that in the circumstances of this case, any further pursuit and pressure on the part of government agents was nothing short of outrageous . . . . If the government had no knowledge of Kelly doing anything wrong up to his rejection of illicit money, its continuing role as the third man in a fight between his conscience and temptation rises above the level of mere offensiveness to that of being "outrageous." *No concept of funda-*

mental fairness can accommodate what happened to Kelly in this case. (Emphasis added).

III. ANALYSIS

A. *The Due Process Defense*

The district court concluded that the FBI's conduct in furtherance of Abscam was so outrageous that prosecution of Kelly was barred by principles of due process.[3] The Supreme Court has recognized that there may be situations

> in which the conduct of law enforcement agents is so outrageous that due process principles would absolutely bar the government from invoking judicial processes to obtain a conviction . . . .

United States v. Russell (1973). More recently, a divided Court reaffirmed that due process principles might foreclose prosecution of a predisposed defendant if the government was excessively involved in his criminal activity. Hampton v. United States. However, Justice Powell, in his critical concurring opinion, stated:

> I emphasize that the cases, *if any,* in which proof of predisposition is not dispositive will be rare. Police over-involvement in crime would have to reach a *demonstrable level of outrageousness* before it could bar conviction. *This would be especially difficult to show with respect to* contraband *offenses, which are so difficult to detect in the absence of undercover Government involvement* . . . . [Law] [e]nforcement officials therefore must be allowed flexibility adequate to counter effectively such criminal activity.

(Emphasis added).

Our task in this case, therefore, is to assess whether the FBI's conduct in Abscam reached a "demonstrable level of outrageousness," while keeping in mind the difficulties inherent in detecting corrupt public officials. Measured against this standard, the FBI's conduct did not violate due process.

---

3. Kelly contends that the district court also held that he was entrapped as a matter of law. Although the district court did submit Kelly's entrapment defense to the jury, we do not interpret Judge Bryant's decision to hold that Kelly was entrapped as a matter of law. Rather, our review of the record reveals that the district court in fact thought that Kelly had not aggressively pursued his claim of entrapment. Judge Bryant recognized that it would be difficult for a public official such as Kelly to pursue an entrapment defense:

I know its [sic] tough for a man to come in and say, "Well, I got into a situation and I was overborne with temptation and I succumbed." I know it's tough for him to say that. This man is in public life and that kind of thing.

Furthermore, the mere fact that a judgment of acquittal was entered in Kelly's favor does not indicate that the district court ruled Kelly was entrapped as a matter of law. Kelly's own request for a judgment of acquittal on due process grounds belies any such assertion. . . .

B. *Abscam*

Abscam was indeed an elaborate hoax, involving a fictitious, FBI-created corporation purportedly representing Arabs of enormous wealth, as well as the limousines, yachts, and lavishly appointed residences necessary to make the hoax believable. Yet stripped of these trappings of wealth, Abscam was no more than an "opportunity for the commission of crime by those willing to do so." Amoroso and Weinberg let it be known that they would pay substantial sums of money to congressmen willing to promise to assist the wealthy Arabs with their immigration difficulties. Thereafter, the FBI operatives simply waited for the grapevine to work and to see who appeared to take bribes. No congressmen were targeted for investigation; rather, Abscam pursued all who were brought to the operation by the grapevine. In essence, then, Abscam was *not* significantly different from an undercover drug or fencing operation offering to buy from all who appear at its door. Instead of buying stolen goods or contraband drugs, Abscam bought corrupt official influence in Congress. Such government involvement in crime does not violate principles of due process.

We need not determine the exact limits on government involvement in crime imposed by the due process clause for it is clear that the FBI's involvement in Abscam was less than that government involvement found unobjectionable by the Supreme Court. In *Hampton,* the defendant asserted that a government informant suggested the defendant could make money by selling drugs, supplied the defendant with drugs, and provided the purchasers—who were also government agents—of those drugs. Justice Brennan characterized the government's activity as "doing nothing less than buying contraband from itself through an intermediary and jailing the intermediary." Similarly, in *Russell,* a government agent provided the defendant with a scarce chemical essential for the unlawful manufacture of methamphetamine, and purchased the illicit product.

In each of these cases the government not only provided an *opportunity* to commit a crime, but also provided the *means* to commit that crime. Nevertheless, in each case the Supreme Court concluded that the government's conduct did not violate due process. Where, as in Abscam, the government simply provides the opportunity to commit a crime, prosecution of a defendant does not violate principles of due process. This conclusion is in accord with decisions of the Second and Third Circuits upholding Abscam convictions challenged on due process grounds.

* * *

IV. Conclusion

Like the district court,

we like to think, and we hope, that our Congressmen and Senators, and indeed all public servants, are strong enough to withstand any imaginable pressure and reject any type of temptation no matter how attractive, and walk away. . . .

But in reality, the *hard fact is that our public servants* are not recruited from the seminaries and monastaries across the land and that they *are plagued by the frailties of human nature.*

(Emphasis added). Because of this fact and because dishonest public officials, responsive more to money than to their obligations to the nation, may cause grave harm to our society, we recognize the need for law enforcement efforts to detect official corruption. Furthermore, such corruption is "that type of elusive, difficult to detect, covert crime which may justify Government infiltration and undercover activities."

The Supreme Court has made it clear that "a successful due process defense must be predicated on *intolerable government conduct* which goes beyond that necessary to sustain an entrapment defense." Considering the genuine need to detect corrupt public officials, as well as the difficulties inherent in doing so, we conclude that the FBI's conduct in furtherance of its Abscam operation, insofar as it involved Kelly, simply did not reach intolerable levels. Accordingly, having carefully considered all of Kelly's claims that the government's conduct violated due process, we reverse the district court's dismissal of the indictment, as well as its entry of the judgment of acquittal, and direct the district court to reinstate the indictment and the verdict of the jury.

Judgment accordingly.

GINSBURG, CIRCUIT JUDGE:

"Abscam," as the District Court's thoughtful opinion details, was an extraordinary operation. The investigation was steered in large part by a convicted swindler; it relied upon con men to identify and attract targets, to whom legitimate as well as illegitimate inducements were offered; it proceeded without close supervision by responsible officials. The District Court allowed the jury to determine whether defendant Kelly was "predisposed" to commit the crime charged, and therefore not "entrapped" under the current definition of that defense. After the jury returned a guilty verdict, however, the District Court dismissed the indictment against Kelly on the ground that the government's conduct of the investigation was fundamentally unfair, and therefore incompatible with due process. The sole issue properly before us for review is the correctness of the due process ruling.

The District Court stated and attempted to apply an objective test to determine when government investigation exceeds tolerable limits: Was the crime-inducing conduct in which the government engaged, the temptation presented to the target, modeled on reality? This test, the District Court indicated, should apply when the government had no knowledge of prior wrongdoing by the target and no reason to believe the target was about to commit a crime; it would serve as a check against government creation (rather than apprehension) of criminals by offers or importuning that would never occur in the real world.

The real-world test, as applied by the District Court, is speculative. The District Judge assumed that a person who offers a bribe would retreat upon encountering an initial rejection and would not "have the audacity" to press on "for fear of being reported." But the first overture renders the party offering the bribe vulnerable to prosecution. "In for a calf," such a person might press on if he perceives any chance of ultimate success. Nonetheless, were the slate clean, we might be attracted to an approach similar to the District Court's, and would perhaps ask whether, in real-world circumstances, the person snared would ever encounter bait as alluring as the offer the government tendered.

However, our slate contains references that lower courts are not positioned to erase. We may not alter the contours of the entrapment defense under a due process cloak, and we lack authority, where no *specific* constitutional right of the defendant has been violated, to dismiss indictments as an exercise of supervisory power over the conduct of federal law enforcement agents. Precedent dictates that we refrain from applying the general due process constraint to bar a conviction except in the rare instance of "[p]olice overinvolvement in crime" that reaches "a demonstrable level of outrageousness."

The requisite level of outrageousness, the Supreme Court has indicated, is not established merely upon a showing of obnoxious behavior or even flagrant misconduct on the part of the police; the broad "fundamental fairness" guarantee, it appears from High Court decisions, is not transgressed absent "coercion, violence or brutality to the person." Without further Supreme Court elaboration, we have no guide to a more dynamic definition of the outrageousness concept, and no warrant, as lower court judges, to devise such a definition in advance of any signal to do so from higher authority.

The importuning of Congressman Kelly and the offers made to him, extraordinary and in excess of real-world opportunities as they appear to have been, did not involve the infliction of pain or physical or psychological coercion. We are therefore constrained to reverse, although we share the District Court's grave concern that the Abscam drama, both in its general tenor, and in "the [particular] manner in which Kelly was handled," unfolded as "an unwholesome spectacle."

NOTE

In United States v. Myers, 692 F.2d 823 (2d Cir. 1982), the court affirmed a series of Abscam-related convictions involving four congressman (Michael O. Myers of Pennsylvania, Raymond F. Lederer, also of Pennsylvania, Frank Thompson, Jr., of New Jersey, and John M. Murphy of New York), as well as former Mayor of Camden, N.J., Angelo J. Errichetti, and former City Council Member of Philadelphia, Pa., Louis Johanson, and his law partner, Howard L. Criden. Only one count of the multi-count indictments, against one of the defendants (Congressman Murphy) was reversed.

The defendants claimed, on appeal, that the convictions were obtained in violation of "an outer limit of fairness guaranteed by the Due Process Clause of the Fifth Amendment to all persons whenever the Government of the United States acts to detect and prosecute criminal activity." The court rejected the argument and said:

What is available in such circumstances is the traditional defense of entrapment, which prevents conviction of a person induced to commit a crime unless the prosecution can establish the person's predisposition to commit the crime. . . . The legal defense of entrapment is not established whenever a defendant is caught by a ruse.

Although the defense of entrapment was available to all seven applicants, none except Lederer elected to assert the defense at trial, or request a jury instruction on the issue. . . . A defendant's failure to assert an entrapment defense prevents the prosecution from responding to evidence of inducement by presenting evidence of the defendant's predisposition to commit the crime. We hold that a defendant who fails to assert entrapment as a factual defense at his trial, cannot assert it as a legal defense to his conviction.

Although Lederer, having asserted the defense of entrapment at trial, can challenge the sufficiency of the evidence of his predisposition, his claim is without merit. . . . Predisposition may be established by "the accused's ready response to the inducement." The videotape of the September 11 meeting reveals Lederer responding with alacrity. As he assured the sheik's representatives, "I'm not a Boy Scout."

The defendants' other major claim, sometimes referred to as "entrapment as a matter of law," was based on the argument that the conduct of Abscam violated standards of due process because the Government's role in the investigation was excessive and fundamentally unfair. After exhaustively considering these arguments, the court dismissed them on the authority of the two leading cases in this chapter, *Russell* and *Hampton*.

In another Abscam case, against former Philadelphia Councilmen Harry P. Jannotti and George X. Schwartz, the trial judge set aside the jury verdicts that had been returned against the defendants in United States v. Jannotti, 501 F. Supp. 1182 (E.D.Pa.1980), but on appeal the Third Circuit reinstated the verdicts. See United States v. Jannotti, 673 F.2d 578 (3d Cir. 1982) (en banc), certiorari denied 457 U.S. 1106, 102 S.Ct. 2906, 73 L.Ed.2d 1315.

UNITED STATES v. MURPHY

United States Court of Appeals for the Seventh Circuit, 1985.
768 F.2d 1518.

EASTERBROOK, CIRCUIT JUDGE.

John M. Murphy was an Associate Judge of the Circuit Court of Cook County from 1972 until 1984. He was indicted in 1983 and charged with accepting bribes to fix the outcome of hundreds of cases, from drunk driving to battery to felony theft. Some of the counts on which he was convicted grew out of contrived cases staged by the FBI and federal prosecutors as part of Operation Greylord, an investigation of the Cook County courts.

The charges spanned many years and many statutes. Part I of this opinion sets out the background. Part II addresses Murphy's challenge to Operation Greylord. Part III looks at Murphy's arguments under particular statutes, Part IV at the conduct of the trial, and Part V at the decision of the district judge not to recuse himself.

I

The evidence at trial, which we now view in the light most favorable to the prosecution, showed several categories of cases in which Murphy took bribes. We separate the evidence into several groups: traffic court, "hustling," fixed felony offenses, and the cases that were contrived as part of the investigation. We omit a great deal of the evidence and describe only enough to give the general picture. Some of the events we recount are pertinent to other Greylord cases still in litigation. Our statement of the evidence and the inferences the jury could draw about Murphy's conduct is not meant to prejudge those cases.

Traffic court. The Cook County courts are organized into divisions, and supervisory judges assign other judges to particular divisions or courtrooms. From 1972 to early 1981 Murphy was assigned to traffic court, which has courtrooms for major offenses (driving while intoxicated, leaving the scene of an accident, and so on) and minor offenses (such as running a red light). Judge Richard LeFevour was the Supervising Judge of traffic court; he had the authority to decide whether Murphy and other judges would hear major or minor cases.

Officer James LeFevour of the Chicago police, Richard LeFevour's cousin, was assigned to traffic court from 1969 through 1980. James LeFevour testified for the prosecution as part of an agreement under which the Government limited its charges against him to three tax offenses. He testified that beginning in 1975 he met regularly with Melvin Cantor, who would give him a list of his cases that day. James LeFevour would take the list to Judge Richard LeFevour; Judge LeFevour would assign Murphy to hear some of Cantor's cases. James LeFevour would present Murphy the list of Cantor's cases. Murphy then would find the defendants not guilty or sentence them to "supervision," an outcome defendants favored. Later in each day Cantor would give James LeFevour money to pass to Judge LeFevour and some for James to keep for a "tip."

Although Richard LeFevour kept the bribes for these cases, he put Murphy in a position to "earn" his own bribes. Richard LeFevour would assign to major cases, on a regular basis, only those judges who would "see" James LeFevour. Lawyers then would bribe some of the judges assigned to the major courtrooms. Murphy was in a major courtroom more often than most other judges.

Lawyers known as "miracle workers" occasionally met with James LeFevour and with Joseph Trunzo, another police officer assigned to traffic court. The lawyers would tell Office LeFevour or Officer Trunzo which defendants they represented; the officers would pass the information to Murphy; after the defendant had prevailed, the lawyer would hand an envelope to the officer with $100 per case for Murphy and another $10 or so for the officer; the officer would pass the envelope to Murphy. Prosecutors testified that although they won as many as 90% of their major traffic cases against public defenders, they almost never won a case in which the defendant was represented by one of the "miracle workers."

The testimony at the trial of this case concerned unidentified cases in traffic court. But some plays stood out, even though the players were anonymous. A prosecutor recalled one drunk driving case in which the defendant was represented by Harry Kleper, a miracle worker. The arresting police officer testified that the defendant failed the usual roadside tests of drunkenness and admitted drinking beer before driving. The defendant took the stand and did not deny imbibing; she said only that the liquor did not affect her ability to drive. Under cross-examination she admitted "feeling" the beer; the prosecutor then asked: "And don't you think it is fair to say that you were under the influence of intoxicating liquor?", to which she replied, "Yes, I guess that is a fair thing to say." Judge Murphy threw up his hands and called a recess, turning to Kleper with the remark: "Counselor, I suggest you talk to your client." As Murphy left the bench, the prosecutor heard Murphy yell down the hall to the judges' chambers: "You won't believe this. The State's Attorney just got the defendant to admit she was drunk." A few minutes later Murphy reconvened the court. Kleper asked the defendant whether she was drunk; she said no. In closing argument the prosecutor stressed the defendant's admission. Kleper did not give a closing argument. Murphy ruled: "I still have a reasonable doubt. Not guilty."

Hustlers. In 1981 Judge LeFevour became Presiding Judge for Cook County's First Municipal District court, which has a general jurisdiction. Many of the branch courts had been frequented by "hustlers." "Hustlers" are lawyers who stand outside the courtroom and solicit business from the people about to enter. Ethical rules long have prohibited such solicitation, and every appearance form in Circuit Court contains a representation that solicitation did not occur. Hustling is a profitable business nonetheless, and people find ways to pursue the profits of illegitimate enterprise with the same vigor they devote to lawful activities.

The profit in hustling comes from the bail system in Illinois. A defendant required to post bail may do so by depositing 10% of the bail in cash. If the defendant is discharged, the cash deposit (less the clerk's handling fee) is returned. This payment, called the cash bond refund (CBR), also may be assigned to the defendant's lawyer as compensation for legal services. Assignment requires the approval of the court. Hustlers make their money by persuading defendants to hire them and assign the CBR, then persuading the judge to release the CBR to them.

Judge Thaddeus L. Kowalski, who presided over the court known as Branch 29 from June 1980 to March 1981, believed that hustlers cheated their clients at the same time as they violated ethical rules. Often the hustlers appeared as counsel only when the case was bound to be dismissed anyway, as they well knew. Their "representation" of the defendants simply diverted the CBRs from the defendants to the lawyers. Judge Kowalski addressed hustling in the most effective way—by eliminating its profitability. He refused to permit the hustlers to collect the CBRs. They soon deserted Branch 29. When Richard LeFevour became the presiding judge of the first district, Judge Kowalski explained to Judge LeFevour how he had cut down on hustling. Judge LeFevour praised Judge Kowalski and promptly transferred him from Branch 29 to the East Chicago Avenue Police Court, which handles criminal cases originating in the Cabrini Green housing project. Judge LeFevour replaced Kowalski with Murphy.

Hustlers flourished under Murphy, who routinely permitted them to collect the CBRs. The hustlers showed appropriate gratitude. Every month the lawyers, collectively known as the Hustlers Club, paid James LeFevour $2500. James kept $500 and gave the rest to Richard. (The sums were reduced for some months when the hustlers' take fell. Murphy was incapacited by a broken ankle, and his replacement was apparently less compliant.) After a hustler made a certain amount, he paid an additional sum to the judge of the particular court. James LeFevour told Murphy of the Hustlers Club and Richard LeFevour's approval. Murphy told James LaFevour that he approved too.

Although Richard LeFevour kept the principal bribe, there were still rewards for Murphy. As at traffic court, Murphy was free to establish his own stable of bribe-givers. The Chicago Bar Association (CBA) maintains a Lawyer Referral Service. This service screens lawyers and assigns them to branch courtrooms to be of service to unrepresented defendants. These lawyers are potential competitors of the hustlers, and Murphy apparently cultivated them as independent sources of revenue.

Arthur Cirignani participated in the CBA's program. (The evidence at trial casts no shadows on the integrity of the CBA itself.) From June 1980 through the end of 1983 he was assigned to a courtroom three to four times a month. Whenever he was assigned to Branch 29, he paid Judge Murphy to assign cases to him rather than to continue the proceedings and allow the hustlers to claim the CBRs. For example, on June 21, 1982, Cirignani visited Murphy first thing in the morning and informed Murphy that he was there as the bar's lawyer. Murphy referred thirteen cases to Cirignani that day and allowed Cirignani to collect CBRs totalling $1,010, a return Cirignani called "excellent." On June 22 Cirignani took $200 in cash to Murphy, who accepted the money without comment. Cirignani testified that he paid Murphy then and on other occasions to ensure referrals in the future.

Fixed cases. Murphy threw business to lawyers; he also threw cases. Cirignani, who testified under an arrangement that he would not be prosecuted if he told the truth, described one such case. Cirignani represented Arthur Best, charged with felony theft. The police had seized evidence from the grounds of Best's house under authority of a warrant, and Cirignani moved to suppress the evidence. On the day of the suppression hearing Cirignani visited Murphy's chambers before court began and while they were alone told Murphy that he had a "good" motion to suppress. Murphy promised to "take a look at it." Judge Murphy later granted the motion to suppress, giving no reasons. The prosecutor then dismissed the case against Best. Before leaving the courthouse Cirignani gave Murphy an envelope containing $300. Cirignani recevied a CBR of $1800 in the case, and the client also paid $700 directly. (As it turned out, Cirignani's success was short-lived. The Appellate Court of Illinois reversed.)

Greylord cases. Most of the evidence about fixed cases was presented by witnesses who had concocted the cases for the purpose of the Greylord investigation. Terrence Hake, an agent of the FBI posing as a corrupt lawyer, would represent the defendants in ghost-written cases. Agents would file complaints and testify about made-up events.

In one case two agents of the FBI, posing as "Norman Johnson" and "John Stavros," claimed to have had a violent encounter in which Johnson injured Stavros. Hake represented Johnson, the "defendant." Wearing a tape recorder, Hake privately visited Judge Murphy's chambers on the morning the case was set for a hearing. He introduced himself as Johnson's lawyer and said he wanted a verdict of not guilty. Murphy replied: "I'll throw the fucker out the window." Hake mentioned dealings with Joseph Trunzo and suggested that Trunzo would make arrangements; Murphy said: "That's okay, everything's alright." Murphy found Johnson not guilty. But things were not well. After the trial Hake gave $300 to Officer Joseph Trunzo ($200 for Murphy, $100 for Joseph and his twin brother Jim). They did not deliver the $200 to Murphy; they apparently planned to fleece Hake (a novice at corruption) by keeping the money, leaving Hake to face an angry judge. Murphy told Hake the following week that he had not seen either Trunzo. A few days later Murphy visited traffic court, still the assignment of both Trunzos, looking for them. Joseph Trunzo then gave Murphy the $200 he had received from Hake, explaining to Murphy that "I got busy and forgot to call you." (In the other trials Joseph Trunzo kept Hake's money and Murphy did not get paid, but so far as the record shows Murphy did not know the money in these cases had been meant for him.)

Hake represented the "defendants" in several other cases fabricated by the FBI. The payoffs went more smoothly. On each occasion the "defendant" was discharged, and Hake paid Officer James LeFevour, apparently a more honest criminal than the brothers Trunzo. James LeFevour passed most of the money to Richard LeFevour and told Murphy that Judge LeFevour wanted verdicts of not guilty. Hake had some additional recorded ex parte conversations with Murphy. In one Hake conceded that his client was guilty but said he needed a verdict of not guilty; Murphy said "it'll be discharged that's all" and later acquitted the "defendant." During another meeting

Murphy produced Hake's business card—a card given to James LeFevour on which Hake had written the names of cases he wanted dismissed. David Ries, another attorney and agent of the FBI, described two other concocted cases in which he represented "defendants" and paid a bribe through yet another police officer to obtain the desired disposition. See United States v. Blackwood, 768 F.2d 131 (7th Cir. 1985), affirming that officer's conviction.

The outcome. The jury convicted Murphy on 24 of the 27 counts in the indictment. The counts involved four legal theories. Some counts charged violations of the mail fraud statute, 18 U.S.C. § 1341. The checks constituting the CBRs were mailed to the attorneys, and each mail fraud count was based on the mailing of one CBR. The "fraud" was one committed by Murphy on the people of Cook County, who lost his honest services. Some counts were based on the Hobbs Act, 18 U.S.C. § 1951(a), which prohibits extortion affecting interstate commerce. The extortion lay in the solicitation and receipt of the bribes. Some counts were based on the theory that Murphy aided and abetted others who violated the Hobbs Act. The remaining count was based on the Racketeer Influenced and Corrupt Organizations Act (RICO), 18 U.S.C. § 1962(d), which prohibits the operation of an "enterprise" in interstate commerce through a "pattern" (two or more events) of "racketeering" (the violation of specified state or federal laws). The "enterprise" here was the Cook County Circuit Court.

The district court imposed 24 concurrent sentences. The longest, ten years, are based on the RICO and Hobbs Act counts. The court did not impose a fine or a forfeiture.

II

Murphy attacks the convictions based on the Operation Greylord cases, which he depicts as frauds on the court. You cannot deprive the people of Cook County of honest services in such "cases," Murphy maintains, because they are not cases at all. The people had no right to any judicial services, honest or otherwise, in adjudicating put-up jobs, and so lost nothing from his conduct. He analogizes the situation to that of United States v. Archer, 486 F.2d 670 (2d Cir. 1973), in which the Second Circuit reversed a conviction when the Government had induced one party to place a phone call for the sole purpose of manufacturing the federal jurisdictional element of the crime.

Archer is a judicial reaction to activities the court thought overextended federal power. But this case is not *Archer*. The prosecutors did not move a state crime to a federal court by main force. Murphy's complaint is a more traditional objection to creative acts by prosecutors. He contends that there was no crime at all and that if there was a crime the prosecutors manufactured it.

These arguments can be made about any "sting" operation—indeed about any use of undercover agents. The agents who offered bribes to Members of the House and Senate in the "Abscam" sting were not trying to grease the skids for a real project or obtain an actual law. Agents who buy illegal drugs are not going to distribute them for profit. There is no "crime" in these cases, in the sense that the scheme cannot come to fruition, and the evils against which the laws are set cannot occur. Yet courts regularly sustain convictions based on these entrepreneurial efforts.

In Operation Greylord agents of the FBI took the stand in the Circuit Court of Cook County and lied about their made-up cases. Perjury is a crime, and Murphy tells us that those who commit crimes themselves cannot prosecute others' crimes. But criminal proceedings are not designed to establish the relative equities among police and defendants. In many categories of cases it is necessary for the agents to commit acts that, standing by themselves, are criminal.

Bribery, like a wholesale transaction in drugs, is a secret act. Both parties to the bribe violate the law, just as both parties to the sale of drugs violate the law. It is commonplace for agents to take one side of a transaction in drugs. Because the crime leaves no complaining witness, active participation by the agents may be necessary to establish an effective case. The agents' acts merely *appear* criminal; they are not, because they are performed without the state of mind necessary to support a conviction.

The agents who made up and testified about the Operation Greylord "cases" did so without criminal intent. They were decoys, and the Greylord cases made it easier to separate the honest judges from the dishonest ones. It may be necessary to offer bait to trap a criminal. Corrupt judges will take the bait, and honest ones will refuse. Cases are the daily work of courts, just as laws and political deals are the daily work of legislators. In the Abscam operation, the Government offered legislators an opportunity suitable to their calling, and here the opportunity was suitable to the judges' calling.

True, as Murphy emphasizes, the phantom cases had no decent place in court. But it is no more decent to make up a phantom business deal and offer to bribe a Member of Congress. In the pursuit of crime the Government is not confined to behavior suitable for the drawing room. It may use decoys, and provide the essential tools of the offense. The creation of opportunities for crime is nasty but necessary business. The Government offered Murphy opportunities to sell the powers of his office and disgrace himself. He accepted with alacrity.

The FBI and the prosecutors behaved honorably in establishing and running Operation Greylord. They assure us that they notified the Presiding Judge of the Circuit Court's Criminal Division, the State's Attorney of Cook County, the Attorney General of Illinois, and the Governor of Illinois. Such notice may not be necessary, and certainly a criminal defendant is in no position to complain of the absence of such notice (for he has no personal right to protect the dignity of the Cook County courts), but the notice dispels any argument that the federal Government has offended some principle requiring respect of the internal operations of the state courts. The Greylord cases did not interfere with the smooth operation of the local courts or diminish the rights of any third party. They were, in this respect, less offensive than "sting" operations in which the police go into business as a "fence" for stolen goods. The existence of a well-paying fence may induce people to steal goods to sell to the fence. Here no stranger was at risk. Operation Greylord harmed only the corrupt.

*   *   *

Affirmed.

NOTE

In People v. Auld, ___ P.2d ___ (Colo.App.1991), the court rejected an appeal by the state, which sought to reverse the trial court's dismissal of charges of receiving and possession of a dangerous weapon in a sting operation directed against an attorney-defendant, in the exercise of its "supervisory power in protecting judicial integrity in the face of governmental misconduct."

A drug enforcement police task force, operating on a tip that Auld might accept drugs as payment for services, induced the prosecutor to draft a false drugs and weapons complaint against an undercover agent. The prosecutor's wife notarized the complaint. When the undercover agent was first brought to court for a bond hearing, he was questioned by the judge and made false statements to the judge, who was unaware of the sting operation. The agent then sought to retain Auld as his attorney, making an initial cash payment for legal fees and offering to pay the balance by giving the lawyer drugs. Auld refused the drugs but said he might take a gun at a "black market price." The agent then gave the defendant an Uzi semi-automatic rifle. Auld's acceptance of the weapon lead to the charge of receiving stolen property and possession of a dangerous weapon. The trial court rejected Auld's motions based on alleged due process violations in targeting defendant without probable cause or reasonable suspicion, on failure to cease the sting operation when he first refused drugs, and on invasion of the attorney-client relationship. The judge granted the motion to dismiss, however, on alleged outrageous governmental conduct that had enmeshed the judiciary in law enforcement activities without its knowledge. In upholding the trial court's dismissal of the charges, the appeals court said:

"The People in effect admit that the district attorney here has perpetrated a fraud upon the court of this state by filing false documents, making false statements to a judge, and creating a counterfeit prosecution. They further concede that as a result of the district attorney's activities, the county court was duped into playing an active part in the prosecutorial function of the executive branch. . . .

*   *   *

". . . [T]he trial court [properly] exercised its supervisory power in protecting judicial integrity in the face of governmental misconduct. The trial court found, with evidentiary support, that the conduct of the district attorney, an officer of the court, and the law enforcement agencies may have violated the Colorado Criminal Code relating to perjury and false swearing.

"In addition, the district attorney may very well have violated the Code of Professional Responsibility by using perjured testimony, making false statements to the court, and by the manner in which he performed his duties as a public prosecutor. Also to be considered is ABA, Standards for Criminal Justice, Standard 3–2.8(a) (1980) which denotes as unprofessional conduct the intentional misrepresentation by a prosecutor of matters of fact or law to the court.

"The foregoing list of potential violations, which is not intended to be exhaustive, committed by the district attorney and law enforcement agencies for the purpose of duping the trial court into becoming an accomplice in their law enforcement function must be condemned by this court. * * *"

UNITED STATES v. JACOBSON

United States Court of Appeals, Eighth Circuit, 1990.
893 F.2d 999.

[Subsequent to publication of this opinion in the Advance Sheets, the court granted the Petition for Rehearing *en banc* and withdrew the opinion below from the bound volume: United States v. Jacobsen, 899 F.2d 1549 (8th Cir. 1990). The *en banc* decision had not been published when the casebook went to press.]

HEANEY, SENIOR CIRCUIT JUDGE.

Keith Jacobson was convicted of one count of receiving child pornography through the mails. On appeal, Jacobson argues that he was entrapped as a matter of law because the government failed to show that he was predisposed to commit the crime and that the government's outrageous conduct gave rise to a violation of due process. We overturn the conviction because, before instituting an undercover operation at Jacobson, the government had no evidence giving rise to a reasonable suspicion that Jacobson had committed a similar crime in the past or was likely to commit such a crime in the future.

I. BACKGROUND

Keith Jacobson is a fifty-seven year old resident of Newman Grove, Nebraska, currently living on a family farm and supporting his parents. Jacobson served in the Korean and Vietnam Wars, for which he received the Bronze Star and the Army Commendation Medal. He has no criminal history, with the exception of a conviction for driving while intoxicated in 1958.

On February 4, 1984, Jacobson ordered two magazines and a brochure from Dennis Odom, who does business as the Electric Moon in San Diego, California. On May 11, 1984, the government executed a search warrant on the Electric Moon business premises and seized the business' mailing list. Jacobson's name and address were on that mailing list.

The two magazines Jacobson ordered were "Bare Boys I" and "Bare Boys II." They were nudist magazines, the receipt of which did not violate any law. Receipts for his order were found in Blue Moon's files. Jacobson also ordered a brochure in which he failed to order any materials or contact any of the sources listed. The government had no other information at the time that Jacobson was purchasing through the mails or producing child pornography, or that he was predisposed to do either.

Nevertheless, the government made Jacobson the target of five undercover sting operations over a period of two and one-half years. Various postal inspectors surreptitiously contacted Jacobson more than eleven times. Jacobson answered a survey sent to him during the first undercover operation. In his response, he indicated a predisposition to receive through the mails sexually explicit materials depicting children. After several opportunities to purchase such materials under government observation, Jacobson ordered "Boys Who Love Boys," a magazine containing sexually explicit materials depicting minors. After sending him this publication, government agents arrested Jacobson and searched his home. No other illegal materials were found.

The government indicted Jacobson on September 14, 1987, on one count of receiving through the mails a visual depiction, the production of which involved the use of a minor engaging in sexually explicit conduct. Jacobson was tried in front of a jury consisting of nine women and three men on April 22, 1988. On April 26, 1988, the jury returned a verdict of guilty. The judge sentenced Jacobson to two years probation and 250 hours of community service.

II. DISCUSSION

Jacobson raises several arguments on appeal, but at the heart of each argument is the assertion that the government lacked a basis for making Jacobson a target of an undercover operation. In response, the government argues that, while his purchase of the two magazines from Electric Moon constituted legal conduct, the purchases evidenced a predisposition to purchase illegal child pornography. Our view is threefold: (1) the Electric Moon purchase was not evidence of predisposition and did not give rise to a reasonable suspicion based on articulable facts that Jacobson had committed a crime in the past or was likely to commit a crime in the future; (2) the government must have reasonable suspicion based on articulable facts before instituting an undercover operation directed at a person; and (3) since the undercover operation was improper, Jacobson's conviction must be set aside because there was no evidence of an intervening act which cured the government's improper conduct.

The government asserts in its brief that the Electric Moon purchase was sufficient evidence of predisposition to justify the institution of an undercover operation against Jacobson. We disagree. In our view, at the time it commenced its undercover operation, the government had no evidence giving rise to a reasonable suspicion that Jacobson had committed a crime or was about to commit one. This is simply a case where a legal act took place and the government directed an extensive undercover operation at the person who committed the legal act. When an individual engages in legal conduct and no additional or extrinsic evidence exists to give rise to a reasonable suspicion of predisposition, the government may not target that individual, no matter how distasteful the lawful conduct may be. Obviously, had the government learned, prior to targeting Jacobson, that he had purchased or had expressed a desire to purchase illegal materials or that he had otherwise engaged in illegal conduct, there would have been sufficient cause to justify the decision to offer Jacobson the opportunity to purchase illegal materials through the mail.

This case is clearly distinguishable from the cases reaching the appellate level cited by the government in its brief. First, the government had received no information that Jacobson was purchasing illegal child pornography through the mails or that he was producing illegal child pornography. Second, Jacobson had never ordered or advertised for any illegal materials. Third, the government did not inadvertently target Jacobson as a result of pre-existing investigations. Fourth, there were no independent articulable facts that gave rise to the suspicion that Jacobson had committed a crime or was likely to commit a crime.

The government argues that, even if it did not have grounds for initially targeting Jacobson, his actions in response to the targeting indicated that he was predisposed to commit the crime, and his conviction should therefore be confirmed. We cannot agree. To accept this position would be to allow government agents to target entire groups of people without specific justification, hoping to uncover some individual who is predisposed to commit a crime if given enough opportunities to do so. The government must reasonably suspect that a crime has occurred or is likely to occur before targeting an individual. Evidence tending towards a reasonable suspicion obtained during an illegal targeting operation may be used to defend against a claim of entrapment only if received independent of the illegal sting operation. No such evidence exists in this case.

The government recognized that there must be limits on its power to investigate during its review of the ABSCAM sting operation. During congressional hearings, the Federal Bureau of Investigation (FBI) made clear that it had targeted only those persons who had been identified by a reliable source as predisposed to take or offer a bribe, thus giving rise to a reasonable suspicion that the targeted individuals would commit a crime if offered the opportunity to do so. Final Report of the Select Committee to Study Undercover Activities of Components of the Department of Justice, S.Rep. No. 682, 97th Cong., 2d Sess. 13 (1982).[1]

1. In each of the ABSCAM cases, reasonable suspicion does appear from the record. United States v. Jenrette, 744 F.2d 817 (D.C.Cir.1984); United States v. Silvestri, 719 F.2d 577 (2d Cir.1983); United States v. Ciuzio, 718 F.2d 413 (D.C.Cir. 1983), cert. denied, 465 U.S. 1034, 104 S.Ct. 1305, 79 L.Ed.2d 704 (1984); United States v. Weisz, id. (Ciuzio and Weisz were tried together); United States v. Thompson, 710 F.2d 915 (2d Cir.1983), cert. denied, 464 U.S. 1039, 104 S.Ct. 702, 79 L.Ed.2d 167 (1984); United States v. Williams, 705 F.2d 603 (2d Cir.), cert. denied, 464 U.S. 1007, 104 S.Ct. 524, 78 L.Ed.2d 708 (1984); United States v. Kelly, 707 F.2d 1460 (D.C.Cir.), cert. denied, 464 U.S. 908, 104 S.Ct. 264, 78 L.Ed.2d 247 (1983); United States v. Myers, 692 F.2d 823 (2d Cir.1982), cert. denied, 461 U.S. 961, 103 S.Ct. 2437, 77 L.Ed.2d 1322 (1983); United States v. Carpentier, 689 F.2d 21 (2d Cir.1982), cert. denied, 459

In our view, reasonable suspicion based on articulable facts is a threshold limitation on the authority of government agents to target an individual for an undercover sting operation. If a particular individual's conduct gives rise to reasonable suspicion, the government may conduct any undercover operation it so desires, as long as it does not give rise to a claim of outrageousness. While the use of undercover operations is indispensible to the achievement of effective law enforcement, the potential harms of undercover operations call for the recognition that there must be some limitation on the indiscriminate use of such government targeting.[2]

At the time the government targeted Jacobson, it had no reason to believe that he was likely to commit an act which would violate federal obscenity laws. No evidence was subsequently obtained outside of the undercover operation. The evidence that Jacobson was predisposed to commit the crime for which he was convicted is tainted by the illegal targeting. We hold that Jacobson was entrapped as a matter of law. We therefore reverse his conviction and vacate his sentence.

FAGG, CIRCUIT JUDGE, dissenting.

The panel has declared war on the government's power to initiate undercover investigations. Thus, I dissent.

* * *

Instead of deciding whether the government's conduct in formulating, implementing, and enmeshing Jacobson in the investigatory scheme was fundamentally unfair, the panel has barred the government from obtaining a conviction because the undercover investigation was initiated without "reasonable suspicion based on articulable facts" that Jacobson had committed or was likely to commit a similar crime. This bar applies even when the overall character of the government's investigation "does not give rise to a claim of outrageousness." In my view, due process does not require an objectively quantified suspicion that approaches the threshold of probable cause. I believe the government can act on legitimately grounded suspicions without depriving the suspected person of any right secured by the constitution. The panel's demand for particularized suspicion runs against the grain "of the post-*Hampton* cases decided by the courts of appeals [holding] that due

U.S. 1108, 103 S.Ct. 735, 74 L.Ed.2d 957 (1983); United States v. Alexandro, 675 F.2d 34 (2d Cir.), cert. denied, 459 U.S. 835, 103 S.Ct. 78, 74 L.Ed.2d 75 (1982); United States v. Jannotti, 673 F.2d 578 (3d Cir.) (en banc), cert. denied, 457 U.S. 1106, 102 S.Ct. 2906, 73 L.Ed.2d 1315 (1982). Only three of the cases, however, dealt specifically with the requirement of reasonable suspicion. United States v. Kelly, 707 F.2d 1460, 1471 (D.C.Cir.1983) (without deciding whether reasonable suspicion is required, the court found that there was ample suspicion to justify targeting Kelly); United States v. Jannotti, 673 F.2d 578, 609 (3d

Cir.1982) (lack of reasonable suspicion does not offend due process); United States v. Myers, 635 F.2d 932, 941 (2d Cir.1980) (lack of reasonable suspicion does not offend due process or the speech or debate clause).

2. These potential harms include the creation of crime, the entrapment of innocent persons, the destruction of the reputations of innocent persons, extensive fishing expeditions among innocent citizens, the creation of an air of distrust amongst colleagues and acquaintances and the subjecting of government agents to tremendous temptations, dangers and stresses.

986 SPECIAL DEFENSES TO PROSECUTIONS Pt. 3

process grants wide leeway to law enforcement agents in their investigation of crime."

In my opinion, the panel has borrowed from the rule of probable cause to arrest, and from the rule of particularized suspicion that governs brief investigatory detentions, Terry v. Ohio, 392 U.S. 1, 16–19, 21, 88 S.Ct. 1868, 1877–1878, 1879, 20 L.Ed.2d 889 (1968), for the singular purpose of narrowing the government's power to initiate undercover investigations. Needless to say, law enforcement decisions to conduct undercover investigations are not controlled by fourth amendment doctrine. Furthermore, the terminology that functions as the backbone of the panel's rule "[is] not self-defining [and the terminology] fall[s] short of providing clear guidance dispositive of the myriad factual situations that arise" when the government invokes its investigative powers to penetrate the shadowy world of crime. At bottom, the panel's rulemaking runs squarely into "the difficulties attending the notion that due process of law can be embodied in fixed rules." *United States v. Russell,* (1973).

If the panel believes the government has violated due process by embarking on a suspicionless investigation against Jacobson, it should say so. The record, however, does not support that conclusion. Indeed, on the record presented here the government's undercover investigation fits within the terms of the very rule the panel proposes.

The government possessed well-grounded reasons to believe that an investigation aimed at Jacobson would uncover criminal behavior. Jacobson's name was found in the customer records of a reputed child pornographer. This discovery identified Jacobson as a person who had previously ordered child erotica through the mails. The customer records also disclosed that Jacobson had obtained a brochure outlining the methods of purchasing child pornography. With this information in the hands of experienced postal inspectors, I am at a loss to understand how the panel finds room to "criticize the government for reasonably pursuing available leads" concerning Jacobson's appetite for sexually explicit portrayals of children. The panel concedes that Jacobson's response to a survey mailed to him by the postal inspectors "indicated a predisposition to receive through the mails sexually explicit materials depicting children," ante at 1000, and "justif[ied] the decision to offer Jacobson the opportunity to purchase illegal materials through the mail."

It seems to me the panel is wearing blinders. This is not a case where the government was in the business of generating new crimes merely for the sake of pressing criminal charges against an individual who was "scrupulously conforming to the requirements of the law." Jacobson was not targeted in advance. To the contrary, the government had a significant amount of knowledge about Jacobson's shadowy activities, and he was targeted for investigation because of his own voluntary conduct.

What the panel has chosen to ignore in this case is the practical reality that the investigatory process does not deal with hard certainties. Law enforcement officers are entitled to draw inferences, make deductions, and arrive at common sense conclusions about human behavior based on available information and the behavioral patterns of law breakers. The accumulated information must be "seen and weighed not in terms of [judicial post mortems], but as understood by those versed in the field of law enforcement." When the whole picture known to the postal inspectors is viewed in this context, the officers clearly possessed legitimate grounds for their suspicion of Jacobson and for their belief that an undercover approachment of Jacobson would reveal criminal activity. "Here, fact on fact and clue on clue afforded a basis for the deductions and inferences that brought the officers to focus on [Jacobson]." Simply stated, the panel is unwilling to acknowledge that it is looking at reasonable police work.

Although the normal constitutional and statutory protections of criminal process have always been available to Jacobson, he necessarily wages his legal battle against the government's decision to investigate him as a question of law because the jury has rejected his entrapment defense. This court "may someday be presented with a situation in which the conduct of law enforcement agents [in initiating an undercover investigation] is so outrageous that due process principles would absolutely bar the government from invoking judicial processes to obtain a conviction, [but Jacobson's case] is distinctly not of that breed." I thus dissent from the panel's decision to overturn Jacobson's conviction.

Chapter 10

COMPULSION, INFANCY, INTOXICATION, DIMINISHED RESPONSIBILITY AND OTHER NON–CONTROLLABLE FACTORS

A. COMPULSION

---

1. DURESS

STATE v. ST. CLAIR
Supreme Court of Missouri, 1953.
262 S.W.2d 25.

HOLLINGSWORTH, JUDGE. Convicted in the Circuit Court of Jackson County of robbery in the first degree, defendant has appealed from a sentence of imprisonment in the State Penitentiary for a term of five years imposed upon him in conformity with the verdict returned by the jury. At the trial he admitted physical perpetration of the act of robbery as charged in the information but pleaded not guilty by reason of insanity and duress. The trial court submitted and instructed the jury on the issue of insanity but refused his request for an instruction submitting the issue of duress. He assigns error in the refusal of the court to so instruct. . . .

The victim of the robbery was William Rieken, who lived and operated a truck garden in or near Kansas City in Jackson County and sold the produce thereof from a roadside stand in front of his home. On the night of August 19, 1950, at about 11 o'clock and after he had retired, someone knocked at his rear bedroom door. He did not answer. The door was pushed open, a man entered and stated, "We want your money." The man held a pistol in one hand and a flashlight in the other. The flashlight enabled Rieken to see the intruder. Rieken went into another room, took $325 from his overalls and brought it to the intruder who took it and said to him, "Now you stay in there. We are going to be around here awhile, if you come out we will shoot you." When the intruder left the house, Rieken looked through a window, and saw a truck driven away with men in it. He promptly reported the matter to the police and, at the trial, identified defendant as the man who entered his home and robbed him.

On August 26, 1950, defendant and Loren Young and Calvin McNeal were arrested at defendant's home near Blue Springs in Jackson County, where were found a stolen automobile, several flashlights, numerous firearms and a large quantity of ammunition. Defendant, upon being questioned by the officers, readily admitted participation in the robbery as above detailed by Rieken, but also asserted that Young and McNeal had forced him to do so. Young and McNeal are now serving terms of imprisonment in the penitentiary. . . .

Defendant lived with his wife and son and collected and sold used automobile parts. He testified that in July, before the robbery in August, Young and McNeal first came to his home to buy an automobile part; that thereafter they made frequent visits to his home and soon began to stay there practically all of the time, in the house and yard, slept on his premises in their automobile and had his wife cook for them; that Young and McNeal there engaged in extensive target practice with firearms; that he tried to stop them but they wouldn't stop; that they shot at him and threatened him, and that he came to fear them greatly and was afraid to report them to the sheriff's office; they told him that if he did report them, they would kill both him and his wife before the officers could get them.

Defendant further testified that on the night of the robbery Young and McNeal asked him to drive his truck to Kansas City to "haul some stuff" for them; that he did not want to go, but they threatened to "punch" him; that at their direction he drove his truck with them accompanying him, to some place in Kansas City; that he did not know where they were, but one finally said, "Here is where the job is going to be", and he started to stop, but Young told him to drive on; that they went to a little town somewhere, where Young told him it was going to be a holdup of old man Rieken; that he started to argue, but they said that if he didn't do what they said to do, they were going to "blow my head out"; that they said to him, "If you get out [of Rieken's house] and run away, we are going back out and shoot your wife and boy", and he was afraid he would be shot if he did not go through with the holdup; that McNeal gave him a pistol and McNeal displayed a sawed-off shotgun. Young stayed in the truck. McNeal went with defendant to the door of Rieken's home, hammered on the door with the end of the sawed-off shotgun, and told defendant to go in and ask for the money; that he went in and held up Rieken in the manner testified by Rieken; that he then ran back to the truck preceded by McNeal, and all sped away; that McNeal took the money and the pistol from him; that Young then laughed, saying, "You robbed a man with a gun that wasn't even loaded", and showed him that the pistol which he had used in holding up Rieken had no ammunition in it.

The appellate courts of this State seem not to have dealt with duress or coercion as a defense to an otherwise criminal act. At least, we have not been cited nor have we found any such case. However, the question has been considered with some frequency in other jurisdictions. Numerous cases are cited in Wharton's Criminal Law, Vol. 1 § 384, p. 514. From these cases and others cited below it is established by the great weight of authority that although coercion does not excuse taking the life of an innocent person, yet it does excuse in all lesser crimes. But, to constitute a defense to a criminal charge, the coercion must be present, imminent, and impending and of such a nature as to induce a well grounded apprehension of death or serious bodily injury if the act is not done. Threat of future injury is not enough. Nor can one who has a reasonable opportunity to avoid doing the act without undue exposure to death or serious bodily injury invoke the doctrine as an excuse. . . .

We are convinced that the evidence in this case made a submissible issue under defendant's plea of duress. If the evidence above set forth was believed by the jury, it would have justified a finding that defendant committed the robbery not of his volition, but because of a well grounded fear of present, imminent and impending death or serious bodily injury at the hands of Young and McNeal. Furthermore, if believed by the jury, his testimony that he was under the immediate surveillance of McNeal who stood at the door with a drawn shotgun at the time he was in the Rieken home would warrant a finding that he had no reasonable opportunity to avoid committing the robbery without immediate exposure to death or great bodily injury. Under these circumstances, the court erred in refusing to instruct the jury on the issue of duress. . . .

The judgment is reversed and the cause remanded.

NOTES

1. Is the defense of duress a defense of justification, or a defense of excuse? Why should it matter?

A considerable amount of thought has been given to that issue. In his seminal article on the topic, Professor Joshua Dressler states that though at first glance the common law defense of duress looks like a justification defense, he suggests that duress excuses, rather than justifies, wrongdoing. See, Dressler, Exegesis of the Law of Duress: Justifying the Excuse and Searching for its Proper Limits, 62 So.Ca.L.Rev. 1331, 1385 (1989). He concludes his study by observing:

". . . [D]uress is at once a fascinating and very troubling excuse, for it requires us to ask ourselves what level of moral courage we have a right to demand of others through the criminal justice system. In seeking to draw the proper outer limits of the defense, we must avoid acting hypocritically or overzealously, yet we should be prepared to make moral judgments about those who were unluckily confronted with dilemmatic choices we have only faced on our nightmares. . . ."

See also Bayles, Reconceptualizing Necessity and Duress, 33 Wayne L.Rev. 1191 (1987).

2. At common law the defense of duress was not available in a murder prosecution; this view is based on the statement expressed by Blackstone, that "he ought rather to die himself than escape by the murder of an innocent." (4 Blackstone Comm. [7th ed.] 30.) This view is followed in most American jurisdictions. Why not make the defense available to murder?

Recent commentators, such as Prof. Dressler (op. cit., supra) would "allow juries to excuse persons who kill under duress." Professor Yale Kamisar, in commenting on Prof. Dressler's article, stated:

". . . I think the reason the common law doesn't recognize it, is because it never had an honest-to-God duress case. It is very easy to dismiss the defense of duress when you're convinced the guy is lying and the whole thing is a fantasy.

"But take the case where the coercer says: 'I have your wife and three kids captive and unless you agree to lure Mr. So and So to a place where my associates and I can kill him, I'm going to kill one of your kids every twenty-four hours.' The defendant does nothing. At the end of the first day the body of his oldest son is sent to him. The defendant then decides to do whatever the person holding his wife and kids wants him to do.

"I don't see why there should be any question about duress being an excuse in such a case. . . ." [Criminal law conference discussions reported at 19 Rutgers L.J. at 722–723 (1988).]

Do you agree with Prof. Kamisar?

3. Assume that the defendant in the leading case, under threat of death, had been compelled to participate in a robbery and that, during the course of the felony, the victim had been killed by one of the participants other than St. Clair, would St. Clair be permitted to invoke duress as a defense to a prosecution for felony murder? See People v. Petro, 13 Cal.App.2d 245, 56 P.2d 984 (1936). Tully v. State, 730 P.2d 1206 (Okl.Crim.1986); State v. Hunter, 241 Kan. 629, 740 P.2d 559 (1987). Compare People v. Roper, 259 N.Y. 170, 181 N.E. 88 (1932).

4. Patty Hearst, kidnaped and held confined by members of the Symbionese Liberation Army for months, participated during her "captivity" in a bank robbery. She appeared to be involved rather willingly when one viewed the bank's film tape that had been made during the commission of the crime. At her trial, the ordinary duress question was presented (threats of death), but, in addition, could not her participation in the crime be excused as coerced because of the pressures of psychological indoctrination or "brainwashing"?

See, in this regard, Delgado, Ascription of Criminal States of Mind: Toward a Defense Theory for the Coercively Persuaded ("Brainwashed") Defendant, 63 Minn.L.Rev. 1 (1978), and a further exchange of views on the article in 63 Minn.L.Rev. 335 and 361 (1979).

In Lunde & Wilson, Brainwashing as a Defense to Criminal Liability: Patty Hearst Revisited, 13 Crim.L.Bull. 341, 358 (1977), the authors state: 'a true case of coercive persuasion ['brainwashing'] cannot fit under the duress rubric. The coercive aspects of the indoctrination process may occur long before the commission of the crime for which the accused stands charged. At the time of the commission of the offense . . . the defendant may be under no immediate duress." See also, Alldridge, Brainwashing as a Criminal Defense, 1984 Crim.L.Rev. 726.

5. Consider the following excerpt from LaFave & Scott, Criminal Law, 2d ed., 1986, at 440:

"The common law rule was that, except for murder and treason, a married woman was not punishable for crime if she acted under the coercion of her husband; and, if she committed the criminal act in her husband's presence, there was a rebuttable presumption that he had coerced her. Something less in the way of pressure was required for a wife to be coerced than for an ordinary person to meet the requirements of the defense of duress; one early English case held that the husband's mere command would do."

The modern trend, however, is to do away with the presumption. In a North Carolina case its appellate court held that the "long recognized and applied" presumption had outlived its necessity and usefulness. State v. Smith, 33 N.C.App. 511, 235 S.E.2d 860 (1977). See also: Conyer v. United States, 80 F.2d 292 (6th Cir. 1935); State v. Renslow, 211 Iowa 642, 230 N.W. 316 (1930); Morton v. State, 141 Tenn. 357, 209 S.W. 644 (1919).

Consider the following provision of the Illinois Criminal Code, § 7–11 (S.H.A. ch. 38), and particularly sub. (b):

(a) A person is not guilty of an offense, other than an offense punishable with death, by reason of conduct which he performs under the compulsion of threat or menace of the imminent infliction of death or great bodily harm, if he reasonably believes death or great bodily harm will be inflicted upon him if he does not perform such conduct.

(b) A married woman is not entitled, by reason of the presence of her husband, to any presumption of compulsion, or to any defense of compulsion except that stated in Subsection (a).

2. NECESSITY

In the year 1884, a yacht was caught in a storm 1600 miles from the nearest land. Its crew of four had to abandon the vessel and put to sea in an open lifeboat which contained no water and no food except two small cans of vegetables. For three days there was no other food. On the fourth day they caught a small turtle which was their only food for the next eight days. From then on, until their twentieth day at sea, they had nothing to eat, and only a very small amount of rain water to drink. On the eighteenth day, as their boat was still drifting at sea and was still more than a thousand miles from land, one of the seamen proposed to two of the others that they kill and eat the fourth member, a boy about seventeen years of age who was then in an extremely weakened condition. Although one seaman dissented from this proposal, two days later the boy was killed. The survivors, including the one who had refused to participate in the killing, fed upon the boy's body. On the fourth day after the killing, they were rescued by a passing vessel.

Were the two seamen who killed the boy guilty of a criminal homicide? What of the third seaman? Would your answer be any different if all four members, including the boy, had drawn lots, with the boy as the loser?

Or, suppose the men in the lifeboat were in the Navy and the Captain of their vessel ordered that the youngest and weakest person in the boat be killed for this purpose. Would such a command be a defense to the men who carried out the Captain's orders?

Or, suppose the lifeboat contained both passengers and crew and that, rather than the lack of food, the difficulty had been occasioned by the unseaworthiness of the lifeboat, a condition which had been compounded by a torrential downpour. To keep the boat from sinking, the members of the crew cast fourteen male passengers overboard. Two women—sisters of one of the male victims—jumped out of the boat to join their brother in death. As a result of this human jettisoning, the boat remained afloat and the survivors were rescued a short time later. Were the members of the crew guilty of criminal homicide with respect to the male passengers who were cast overboard? With respect to the two women who jumped overboard? Would your answer be different if the crewmen, in an attempt to lighten the boat, had not thrown passengers overboard but rather had thrown overboard other members of the crew who were unnecessary to the operation of the lifeboat?

NOTES

1. With respect to the criminality concept presented in the foregoing case, consult: Regina v. Dudley, L.R. 14 Q.B.D. 273, 15 Cox CC. 624 (1884); United States v. Holmes, 1 Wall.Jr. C.C. 1, 26 Fed.Cas. 360, No. 15,383 (1842). See also, Boyer, Crime, Cannibalism and Joseph Conrad: The Influence of Regina v. Dudley and Stephens On Lord Jim, 20 Loy.L.A.L.Rev. 9 (1986).

Consider also, Fuller, The Case of the Speluncean Explorers, 62 Harv.L. Rev. 616 (1949) in which Professor Lon Fuller poses a hypothetical case in which some trapped cave explorers kill and eat one of their number in order to survive until rescue. Among the views advanced for disposing of the criminality issue the case presented, consider the follow: ". . . positive law is predicated on the possibility of men's coexistence in society. When a situation arises in which the coexistence of men becomes impossible, then the condition that underlies all of our precedents and statutes ceases to exist. When that condition disappears . . . the force of positive law disappears with it." Under such circumstances, therefore, endangered persons are not in a "state of civil society" but in a "state of nature." Id. at 620, 621. Compare Cardozo, Law and Literature, 113 (1931): "There is no rule of human jettison. . . . Who shall choose in such an hour between the victims and the saved? Who shall know when masts and sails of rescue may emerge out of the fog?"

Also see Hall, General Principles of Criminal Law 425–36 (2d ed. 1960).

2. Consider the possible disposition of the case situations presented under the following code provisions:

Illinois Criminal Code § 7–13 (S.H.A. ch. 38):

Conduct which would otherwise be an offense is justifiable by reason of necessity if the accused was without blame in occasioning or developing the situation and reasonably believed such conduct was necessary to avoid a public or private injury greater than the injury which might reasonably result from his own conduct.

Wisconsin Criminal Code 940.05 (W.S.A.):

Whoever causes the death of another human being under any of the following circumstances is guilty of a Class C felony:

* * *

Because the pressure of natural physical forces causes such person reasonably to believe that his act is the only means of preventing imminent public disaster or imminent death to himself or another.

UNITED STATES v. BAILEY

Supreme Court of the United States, 1980.
444 U.S. 394, 100 S.Ct. 624.

MR. JUSTICE REHNQUIST delivered the opinion of the Court.

In the early morning hours of August 26, 1976, respondents Clifford Bailey, James T. Cogdell, Ronald C. Cooley, and Ralph Walker, federal prisoners at the District of Columbia jail, crawled through a window from which a bar had been removed, slid down a knotted bedsheet, and escaped from custody. Federal authorities recaptured them after they had remained at large for a period of time ranging from one month to three and one-half months. Upon their apprehension, they were charged with violating 18 U.S.C. § 751 (a), which governs escape from federal custody. At their trials, each of the respondents adduced or offered to adduce evidence as to various conditions and events at the District of Columbia jail, but each was convicted by the jury. The Court of Appeals for the District of Columbia Circuit reversed the convictions by a divided vote, holding that the District Court had improperly precluded consideration by the respective juries of respondents' tendered evidence. We granted certiorari, and now reverse the judgments of the Court of Appeals.

In reaching our conclusion, we must decide the state of mind necessary for violation of § 751(a) and the elements that comprise defenses such as duress and necessity. . . .

I

* * *

The prosecution's case in chief against Bailey, Cooley, and Walker was brief. The Government introduced evidence that each of the respondents was in federal custody on August 26, 1976, that they had disappeared, apparently through a cell window, at approximately 5:35 a.m. on that date, and that they had been apprehended individually between September 27 and December 13, 1976.

Respondents' defense of duress or necessity centered on the conditions in the jail during the months of June, July, and August 1976, and on various threats and beatings directed at them during that period. In describing the conditions at the jail, they introduced evidence of frequent fires in "Northeast One," the maximum-security cellblock occupied by respondents prior to their escape. Construed in the light most favorable to them, this evidence demonstrated that the inmates of Northeast One, and on occasion the guards in that unit, set fire to trash, bedding, and other objects thrown from the cells. According to the inmates, the guards simply allowed the fires to burn until they went out. Although the fires apparently were confined to small areas and posed no substantial threat of spreading through the complex, poor ventilation caused smoke to collect and linger in the cellblock.

Respondents Cooley and Bailey also introduced testimony that the guards at the jail had subjected them to beatings and to threats of death. Walker attempted to prove that he was an epileptic and had received inadequate medical attention for his seizures.

Consistently during the trial, the District Court stressed that, to sustain their defenses, respondents would have to introduce some evidence that they attempted to surrender or engaged in equivalent conduct once they had freed themselves from the conditions they described. But the court waited for such evidence in vain. Respondent Cooley, who had eluded the authorities for one month, testified that his "people" had tried to contact the authorities, but "never got in touch with anybody." He also suggested that someone had told his sister that the FBI would kill him when he was apprehended.

Respondent Bailey, who was apprehended on November 19, 1976, told a similar story. He stated that he "had the jail officials called several times," but did not turn himself in because "I would still be under the threats of death." Like Cooley, Bailey testified that "the FBI was telling my people that they was going to shoot me."

Only respondent Walker suggested that he had attempted to negotiate a surrender. Like Cooley and Bailey, Walker testified that the FBI had told his "people" that they would kill him when they recaptured him. Nevertheless, according to Walker, he called the FBI three times and spoke with an agent whose name he could not remember. That agent allegedly assured him that the FBI would not harm him, but was unable to promise that Walker would not be returned to the D.C. jail. Walker testified that he last called the FBI in mid-October. He was finally apprehended on December 13, 1976.

At the close of all the evidence, the District Court rejected respondents' proffered instruction on duress as a defense to prison escape.[1] The court ruled that respondents had failed as a matter of law to present evidence sufficient to support such a defense because they had not turned themselves in after they had escaped the allegedly coercive conditions. After receiving instructions to disregard the evidence of the conditions in the jail, the jury convicted Bailey, Cooley, and Walker of violating § 751(a).

Two months later, respondent Cogdell came to trial before the same District Judge who had presided over the trial of his co-respon-

---

1. Respondents asked the District Court to give the following instruction:

"Coercion which would excuse the commission of a criminal act must result from:

"1) Threathening [*sic*] conduct sufficient to create in the mind of a reasonable person the fear of death or serious bodily harm;

"2) The conduct in fact caused such fear of death or serious bodily harm in the mind of the defendant;

"3) The fear or duress was operating upon the mind of the defendant at the time of the alleged act; and

"4) The defendant committed the act to avoid the threatened [*sic*] harm."

dents. When Cogdell attempted to offer testimony concerning the allegedly inhumane conditions at the D.C. jail, the District Judge inquired into Cogdell's conduct between his escape on August 26 and his apprehension on September 28. In response to Cogdell's assertion that he "may have written letters," the District Court specified that Cogdell could testify only as to "what he did . . . [n]ot what he may have done." Absent such testimony, however, the District Court ruled that Cogdell could not present evidence of conditions at the jail. Cogdell subsequently chose not to testify on his own behalf, and was convicted by the jury of violating § 751(a).

By a divided vote, the Court of Appeals reversed each respondent's conviction and remanded for new trials. The majority concluded that the District Court should have allowed the jury to consider the evidence of coercive conditions in determining whether the respondents had formulated the requisite intent to sustain a conviction under § 751(a). According to the majority, § 751(a) required the prosecution to prove that a particular defendant left federal custody voluntarily, without permission, and "with an intent to avoid confinement." 190 U.S.App. D.C., at 148, 585 F.2d, at 1093. The majority then defined the word "confinement" as encompassing only the "normal aspects" of punishment prescribed by our legal system. Thus, where a prisoner escapes in order to avoid "non-confinement" conditions such as beatings or homosexual attacks, he would not necessarily have the requisite intent to sustain a conviction under § 751(a). According to the majority:

> "When a defendant introduces evidence that he was subject to such 'non-confinement' conditions, the crucial factual determination on the intent issue is . . . whether the defendant left custody only to avoid these conditions or whether, in addition the defendant *also* intended to avoid confinement. In making this determination the jury is to be guided by the trial court's instructions pointing out those factors that are most indicative of the presence or absence of an intent to avoid confinement." (emphasis in original).

Turning to the applicability of the defense of duress or necessity, the majority assumed that escape as defined by § 751(a) was a "continuing offense" as long as the escapee was at large. Given this assumption, the majority agreed with the District Court that, under normal circumstances, an escapee must present evidence of coercion to justify his continued absence from custody as well as his initial departure. Here, however, respondents had been indicted for "flee[ing] and escap[ing]" "[o]n or about August 26, 1976," and not for "leaving *and staying away from* custody." (emphasis in original). Similarly, "[t]he trial court's instructions when read as a whole clearly give the impression that [respondents] were being tried only for leaving the jail on August 26, and not for failing to return at some later date." Under these circumstances, the majority believed that neither respondents nor the juries were acquainted with the proposition that the escapes in question were continuing offenses. This failure, according to the majority, constituted "an obvious violation of [respondents'] constitutional right to jury trial."

The dissenting judge objected to what he characterized as a revolutionary reinterpretation of criminal law by the majority. He argued that the common-law crime of escape had traditionally required only "general intent," a mental state no more sophisticated than an "intent to go beyond permitted limits." (emphasis deleted) . . .

II

Criminal liability is normally based upon the concurrence of two factors, "an evil-meaning mind [and] an evil-doing hand. . . ." Morissette v. United States. In the present case, we must examine both the mental element, or *mens rea*, required for conviction under § 751(a) and the circumstances under which the "evil-doing hand" can avoid liability under that section because coercive conditions or necessity negate a conclusion of guilt even though the necessary *mens rea* was present.

A

Few areas of criminal law pose more difficulty than the proper definition of the *mens rea* required for any particular crime. In 1970, the National Commission on Reform of Federal Criminal Laws decried the "confused and inconsistent ad hoc approach" of the federal courts to this issue and called for "a new departure." . . . Although the central focus of this and other reform movements has been the codification of workable principles for determining criminal culpability, see e.g., American Law Institute, Model Penal Code §§ 2.01–2.13 (Prop. Off. Draft 1962) (hereinafter Model Penal Code); S. 1, 94th Cong., 2d Sess. §§ 301–303 (1976), a byproduct has been a general rethinking of traditional *mens rea* analysis.

At common law, crimes generally were classified as requiring either "general intent" or "specific intent." This venerable distinction, however, has been the source of a good deal of confusion. As one treatise explained:

> "Sometimes 'general intent' is used in the same way as 'criminal intent' to mean the general notion of *mens rea*, while 'specific intent' is taken to mean the mental state required for a particular crime. Or, 'general intent' may be used to encompass all forms of the mental state requirement, while 'specific intent' is limited to the one mental state of intent. Another possibility is that 'general intent' will be used to characterize an intent to do something on an undetermined occasion, and 'specific intent' to denote an intent to do that thing at a particular time and place." W. LaFave & A. Scott, Handbook on Criminal Law § 28, pp. 201–202 (1972) (footnotes omitted) (hereinafter LaFave & Scott).

This ambiguity has led to a movement away from the traditional dichotomy of intent and toward an alternative analysis of *mens rea.* See id., at 202. This new approach, exemplified in the American Law Institute's Model Penal Code, is based on two principles. First, the ambiguous and elastic term "intent" is replaced with a hierarchy of culpable states of mind. The different levels in this hierarchy are commonly identified, in descending order of culpability, as purpose, knowledge, recklessness, and negligence. Model Penal Code § 2.02. Perhaps the most significant, and most esoteric, distinction drawn by this analysis is that between the mental states of "purpose" and "knowledge." As we pointed out in United States v. United States Gypsum Co., 438 U.S. 422, 445 (1978), a person who causes a particular result is said to act purposefully if " 'he consciously desires that result, whatever the likelihood of that result happening from his conduct,' " while he is said to act knowingly if he is aware " 'that that result is practically certain to follow from his conduct, whatever his desire may be as to that result.' "

*   *   *

In certain narrow classes of crimes, however, heightened culpability has been thought to merit special attention. Thus, the statutory and common law of homicide often distinguishes, either in setting the "degree" of the crime or in imposing punishment, between a person who knows that another person will be killed as the result of his conduct and a person who acts with the specific purpose of taking another's life. . . . Similarly, where a defendant is charged with treason, this Court has stated that the Government must demonstrate that the defendant acted with a purpose to aid the enemy. See Haupt v. United States, 330 U.S. 631, 641 (1947). Another such example is the law of inchoate offenses such as attempt and conspiracy, where a heightened mental state separates criminality itself from otherwise innocuous behavior. . . .

In a general sense, "purpose" corresponds loosely with the common-law concept of specific intent, while "knowledge" corresponds loosely with the concept of general intent. . . . Were this substitution of terms the only innovation offered by the reformers, it would hardly be dramatic. But there is another ambiguity inherent in the traditional distinction between specific intent and general intent. Generally, even time-honored common-law crimes consist of several elements, and complex statutorily defined crimes exhibit this characteristic to an even greater degree. Is the same state of mind required of the actor for each element of the crime, or may some elements require one state of mind and some another? In United States v. Feola, 420 U.S. 671 (1975), for example, . . . we concluded that Congress intended to require only "an intent to assault, not an intent to assault a federal officer." What *Feola* implied, the American Law Institute stated: "[C]lear analysis requires that the question of the kind of culpability required to establish the commission of an offense be faced separately with respect to each material element of the crime." MPC Comments 123. See also Working Papers 131; LaFave & Scott 194.

Before dissecting § 751(a) and assigning a level of culpability to each element, we believe that two observations are in order. First, in performing such analysis courts obviously must follow Congress' intent as to the required level of mental culpability for any particular offense. . . . In the case of § 751(a), however, neither the language of the statute nor the legislative history mentions the *mens rea* required for conviction.[2]

Second, while the suggested element-by-element analysis is a useful tool for making sense of an otherwise opaque concept, it is not the only principle to be considered. The administration of the federal system of criminal justice is confided to ordinary mortals, whether they be lawyers, judges, or jurors. This system could easily fall of its own weight if courts or scholars become obsessed with hair-splitting distinctions, either traditional or novel, that Congress neither stated nor implied when it made the conduct criminal.

As relevant to the charges against Bailey, Cooley, and Walker, § 751(a) required the prosecution to prove (1) that they had been in the custody of the Attorney General, (2) as the result of a conviction, and (3) that they had escaped from that custody. As for the charges against respondent Cogdell, § 751(a) required the same proof, with the exception that his confinement was based upon an arrest for a felony rather than a prior conviction. Although § 751(a) does not define the term "escape," courts and commentators are in general agreement that it means absenting oneself from custody without permission. . . .

Respondents have not challenged the District Court's instructions on the first two elements of the crime defined by § 751(a). It is undisputed that, on August 26, 1976, respondents were in the custody of the Attorney General as the result of either arrest on charges of felony or conviction. As for the element of "escape," we need not decide whether a person could be convicted on evidence of recklessness or negligence with respect to the limits on his freedom. A court may someday confront a case where an escapee did not know, but should have known, that he was exceeding the bounds of his confinement or that he was leaving without permission. Here, the District Court clearly instructed the juries that the prosecution bore the burden of proving that respondents "knowingly committed an act which the law makes a crime" and that they acted "knowingly, intentionally, and deliberately. . . ." . . . The sufficiency of the evidence to support the juries' verdicts under this charge has never seriously been questioned, nor could it be.

---

2. This omission does not mean, of course, that § 751(a) defines a "strict liability" crime for which punishment can be imposed without proof of any *mens rea* at all. As we held in Morissette v. United States, supra, at 263, "mere omission [from the statute] of any mention of intent will not be construed as eliminating that element from the crimes denounced." . . .

The majority of the Court of Appeals, however, imposed the added burden on the prosecution to prove as a part of its case in chief that respondents acted "with an intent to avoid confinement." While . . . the word "intent" is quite ambiguous, the majority left little doubt that it was requiring the Government to prove that the respondents acted with the purpose—that is, the conscious objective—of leaving the jail without authorization. . . .

We find the majority's position quite unsupportable. Nothing in the language or legislative history of § 751(a) indicates that Congress intended to require either such a heightened standard of culpability or such a narrow definition of confinement. . . . Accordingly, we hold that the prosecution fulfills its burden under § 751(a) if it demonstrates that an escapee knew his actions would result in his leaving physical confinement without permission. . . .

B

Respondents also contend that they are entitled to a new trial because they presented (or, in Cogdell's case, could have presented) sufficient evidence of duress or necessity to submit such a defense to the jury. . . .

Common law historically distinguished between the defenses of duress and necessity. Duress was said to excuse criminal conduct where the actor was under an unlawful threat of imminent death or serious bodily injury, which threat caused the actor to engage in conduct violating the literal terms of the criminal law. While the defense of duress covered the situation where the coercion had it source in the actions of other human beings, the defense of necessity, or choice of evils, traditionally covered the situation where physical forces beyond the actor's control rendered illegal conduct the lesser of two evils. Thus, where A destroyed a dike because B threatened to kill him if he did not, A would argue that he acted under duress, whereas if A destroyed the dike in order to protect more valuable property from flooding, A could claim a defense of necessity. . . .

Modern cases have tended to blur the distinction between duress and necessity. In the court below, the majority discarded the labels "duress" and "necessity," choosing instead to examine the policies underlying the traditional defenses. In particular, the majority felt that the defenses were designed to spare a person from punishment if he acted "under threats or conditions that a person of ordinary firmness would have been unable to resist," or if he reasonably believed that criminal action "was necessary to avoid a harm more serious than that sought to be prevented by the statute defining the offense." The Model Penal Code redefines the defenses along similar lines. See Model Penal Code § 2.09 (duress) and § 3.02 (choice of evils).

We need not speculate now, however, on the precise contours of whatever defenses of duress or necessity are available against charges brought under § 751(a). Under any definition of these defenses one principle remains constant: if there was a reasonable, legal alternative to violating the law, "a chance both to refuse to do the criminal act and also to avoid the threatened harm," the defenses will fail. . . . Clearly, in the context of prison escape, the escapee is not entitled to claim a defense of duress or necessity unless and until he demonstrates that, given the imminence of the threat, violation of § 751(a) was his only reasonable alternative. . . .

* * *

We need not decide whether such evidence as that submitted by respondents was sufficient to raise a jury question as to their initial departures. This is because we decline to hold that respondents' failure to return is "just one factor" for the jury to weigh in deciding whether the initial escape could be affirmatively justified. On the contrary, several considerations lead us to conclude that, in order to be entitled to an instruction on duress or necessity as a defense to the crime charged, an escapee must first offer evidence justifying his continued absence from custody as well as his initial departure and that an indispensable element of such an offer is testimony of a bona fide effort to surrender or return to custody as soon as the claimed duress or necessity had lost its coercive force.

First, we think it clear beyond peradventure that escape from federal custody as defined in § 751(a) is a continuing offense and that an escapee can be held liable for failure to return to custody as well as for his initial departure. Given the continuing threat to society posed by an escaped prisoner, "the nature of the crime involved is such that Congress must assuredly have intended that it be treated as a continuing one." Moreover, every federal court that has considered this issue has held, either explicitly or implicitly, that § 751(a) defines a continuing offense. . . .

* * *

We therefore hold that, where a criminal defendant is charged with escape and claims that he is entitled to an instruction on the theory of duress or necessity, he must proffer evidence of a bona fide effort to surrender or return to custody as soon as the claimed duress or necessity had lost its coercive force. We have reviewed the evidence examined elaborately in the majority and dissenting opinions below, and find the case not even close, even under respondents' versions of the facts, as to whether they either surrendered or offered to surrender at their earliest possible opportunity. Since we have determined that this is an indispensable element of the defense of duress or necessity, respondents were not entitled to any instruction on such a theory. Vague and necessarily self-serving statements of defendants or witnesses as to future good intentions or ambiguous conduct simply do not support a finding of this element of the defense.

* * *

This case presents a good example of the potential for wasting valuable trial resources. In general, trials for violations of § 751(a) should be simple affairs. The key elements are capable of objective demonstration; the *mens rea*, as discussed above, will usually depend upon reasonable inferences from those objective facts. Here, however, the jury in the trial of Bailey, Cooley, and Walker heard five days of testimony. It was presented with evidence of every unpleasant aspect of prison life from the amount of garbage on the cellblock floor, to the meal schedule, to the number of times the inmates were allowed to shower. Unfortunately, all this evidence was presented in a case where the defense's reach hopelessly exceeded its grasp. Were we to hold, as respondents suggest, that the jury should be subjected to this potpourri even though a critical element of the proffered defenses was concededly absent, we undoubtedly would convert every trial under § 751(a) into a hearing on the current state of the federal penal system. . . .

Because the juries below were properly instructed on the *mens rea* required by § 751(a), and because the respondents failed to introduce evidence sufficient to submit their defenses of duress and necessity to the juries, we reverse the judgments of the Court of Appeals.

Reversed.

MR. JUSTICE MARSHALL took no part in the consideration or decision of this case.

[MR. JUSTICE STEVENS' concurring opinion is omitted.]

MR. JUSTICE BLACKMUN, with whom MR. JUSTICE BRENNAN joins, dissenting.

The Court's opinion, it seems to me, is an impeccable exercise in undisputed general principles and technical legalism: The respondents were properly confined in the District of Columbia jail. They departed from that jail without authority or consent. They failed promptly to turn themselves in when, as the Court would assert by way of justification, the claimed duress or necessity "had lost its coercive force." Therefore, the Court concludes, there is no defense for a jury to weigh and consider against the respondents' prosecution for escape violative of 18 U.S.C. § 751(a).

It is with the Court's assertion that the claimed duress or necessity had lost its coercive force that I particularly disagree. The conditions that led to respondents' initial departure from the D.C. jail continue unabated. If departure was justified—and on the record before us that issue, I feel, is for the jury to resolve as a matter of fact in the light of the evidence, and not for this Court to determine as a matter of law—it seems too much to demand that respondents, in order to preserve their legal defenses, return forthwith to the hell that obviously exceeds the normal deprivations of prison life and that compelled their leaving in the first instance. The Court, however, requires that an escapee's action must amount to nothing more than a mere and temporary gesture that, it is to be hoped, just might attract attention in responsive circles. But life and health, even if convicts and accuseds, deserve better than that and are entitled to more than pious pronouncements fit for an ideal world.

The Court, in its carefully structured opinion, does reach a result that might be a proper one were we living in that ideal world, and were our American jails and penitentiaries truly places for humane and rehabilitative treatment of their inmates. Then the statutory crime of escape could not be excused by duress or necessity, by beatings, and by guard-set fires in the jails, for these would not take place, and escapees would be appropriately prosecuted and punished.

But we do not live in an ideal world "even" (to use a self-centered phrase) in America, so far as jail and prison conditions are concerned. The complaints that this Court, and every other American appellate court, receives almost daily from prisoners about conditions of incarceration, about filth, about homosexual rape, and about brutality are not always the mouthings of the purely malcontent. . . . I therefore dissent.

I

The atrocities and inhuman conditions of prison life in America are almost unbelievable; surely they are nothing less than shocking. The dissent in the *Bailey* case in the Court of Appeals acknowledged that "the circumstances of prison life are such that at least a colorable, if not credible, claim of duress or necessity can be raised with respect to virtually every escape." And the Government concedes: "In light of prison conditions that even now prevail in the United States, it would be the rare inmate who could not convince himself that continued incarceration would be harmful to his health or safety."

A youthful inmate can expect to be subjected to homosexual gang rape his first night in jail, or, it has been said, even in the van on the way to jail. Weaker inmates become the property of stronger prisoners or gangs, who sell the sexual services of the victim. Prison officials either are disinterested in stopping abuse of prisoners by other prisoners or are incapable of doing so, given the limited resources society allocates to the prison system. Prison officials often are merely indifferent to serious health and safety needs of prisoners as well.

Even more appalling is the fact that guards frequently participate in the brutalization of inmates. The classic example is the beating or other punishment in retaliation for prisoner complaints or court actions.

The evidence submitted by respondents in these cases fits that pattern exactly. Respondent Bailey presented evidence that he was continually mistreated by correctional officers during his stay at the D.C. jail. He was threatened that his testimony in the Brad King case would bring on severe retribution. Other inmates were beaten by guards as a message to Bailey. An inmate testified that on one occasion, three guards displaying a small knife told him that they were going "to get your buddy, that nigger Bailey. We're going to kill him." The threats culminated in a series of violent attacks on Bailey. Blackjacks, mace, and slapjacks (leather with a steel insert) were used in beating Bailey.

Respondent Cooley also elicited testimony from other inmates concernings beatings of Cooley by guards with slapjacks, blackjacks, and flashlights.   There was evidence that guards threatened to kill Cooley.

It is society's responsibility to protect the life and health of its prisoners.   "[W]hen a sheriff or a marshall [*sic*] takes a man from the courthouse in a prison van and transports him to confinement for two or three or ten years, *this is our act.   We* have tolled the bell for him. And whether we like it or not, we have made him our collective responsibility.   We are free to do something about him;   he is not" (emphasis in original).   Address by The Chief Justice, 25 Record of the Assn. of the Bar of the City of New York 14, 17 (Mar. 1970 Supp.). Deliberate indifference to serious and essential medical needs of prisoners constitutes "cruel and unusual" punishment violative of the Eighth Amendment.   Estelle v. Gamble, 429 U.S. 97, 104 (1976). . . .

. . . The reasons that support the Court's holding in Estelle v. Gamble lead me to conclude that failure to use reasonable measures to protect an inmate from violence inflicted by other inmates also constitutes cruel and unusual punishment.   Homosexual rape or other violence serves no penological purpose.   Such brutality is the equivalent of torture, and is offensive to any modern standard of human dignity. Prisoners must depend, and rightly so, upon the prison administrators for protection from abuse of this kind.

There can be little question that our prisons are badly overcrowded and understaffed and that this in large part is the cause of many of the shortcomings of our penal systems.   This, however, does not excuse the failure to provide a place of confinement that meets minimal standards of safety and decency.

Penal systems in other parts of the world demonstrate that vast improvement surely is not beyond our reach.   "The contrast between our indifference and the programs in some countries of Europe— Holland and the Scandinavian countries in particular—is not a happy one for us."   Address by The Chief Justice, supra, at 20. . . .   Sweden's prisons are not overcrowded, and most inmates have a private cell.   Salomon, Lessons from the Swedish Criminal Justice System: A Reappraisal, 40 Fed. Probation 40, 43 (Sept. 1976).   The prisons are small.   The largest accommodate 300–500 inmates;   most house 50– 150. . . .

II

The real question presented in this case is whether the prisoner should be punished for helping to extricate himself from a situation where society has abdicated completely its basic responsibility for providing an environment free of life-threatening conditions such as beatings, fires, lack of essential medical care, and sexual attacks.   To be sure, Congress in so many words has not enacted specific statutory duress or necessity defenses that would excuse or justify commission of an otherwise unlawful act. The concept of such a defense, however, is "anciently woven into the fabric of our culture." J. Hall, General Principles of Criminal Law 416 (2d ed. 1960), quoted in Brief for United States 21. And the Government concedes that "it has always been an accepted part of our criminal justice system that punishment is inappropriate for crimes committed under duress because the defendant in such circumstances cannot fairly be blamed for his wrongful act."

Although the Court declines to address the issue, it at least implies that it would recognize the common-law defenses of duress and necessity to the federal crime of prison escape, if the appropriate prerequisites for assertion of either defense were met. Given the universal acceptance of these defenses in the common law, I have no difficulty in concluding that Congress intended the defenses of duress and necessity to be available to persons accused of committing the federal crime of escape.

I agree with most of the Court's comments about the essential elements of the defenses. . . . I therefore agree that it is appropriate to treat unduly harsh prison conditions as an affirmative defense.

I also agree with the Court that the absence of reasonable less drastic alternatives is a prerequisite to successful assertion of a defense of necessity or duress to a charge of prison escape. One must appreciate, however, that other realistic avenues of redress seldom are open to the prisoner. Where prison officials participate in the maltreatment of an inmate, or purposefully ignore dangerous conditions or brutalities inflicted by other prisoners or guards, the inmate can do little to protect himself. Filing a complaint may well result in retribution, and appealing to the guards is a capital offense under the prisoners' code of behavior. In most instances, the question whether alternative remedies were thoroughly "exhausted" should be a matter for the jury to decide.

I, too, conclude that the jury generally should be instructed that, in order to prevail on a necessity or duress defense, the defendant must justify his continued absence from custody, as well as his initial departure. I agree with the Court that the very nature of escape makes it a continuing crime. But I cannot agree that the only way continued absence can be justified is evidence "of a bona fide effort to surrender or return to custody." The Court apparently entertains the view, naive in my estimation, that once the prisoner has escaped from a life- or health-threatening situation, he can turn himself in, secure in the faith that his escape somehow will result in improvement in those intolerable prison conditions. While it may be true in some rare circumstance that an escapee will obtain the aid of a court or of the prison administration once the escape is accomplished, the escapee, realistically, faces a high probability of being returned to the same prison and to exactly the same, or even greater, threats to life and safety.

The rationale of the necessity defense is a balancing of harms. If the harm caused by an escape is less than the harm caused by remaining in a threatening situation, the prisoner's initial departure is justified. The same rationale should apply to hesitancy and failure to return. A situation may well arise where the social balance weighs in favor of the prisoner even though he fails to return to custody. The escapee at least should be permitted to present to the jury the possibility that the harm that would result from a return to custody outweighs the harm to society from continued absence.

Even under the Court's own standard, the defendant in an escape prosecution should be permitted to submit evidence to the jury to demonstrate that surrender would result in his being placed again in a life- or health-threatening situation. The Court requires return to custody once the "claimed duress or necessity had lost its coercive force." Realistically, however, the escapee who reasonably believes that surrender will result in return to what concededly is an intolerable prison situation remains subject to the same "coercive force" that prompted his escape in the first instance. It is ironic to say that that force is automatically "lost" once the prison wall is passed.

The Court's own phrasing of its test demonstrates that it is deciding factual questions that should be presented to the jury. It states that a "bona fide" effort to surrender must be proved. Whether an effort is "bona fide" is a jury question. The Court also states that "[v]ague and necessarily self-serving statements of defendants or witnesses as to future good intentions or ambiguous conduct simply do not support a finding of this element of the defense." Traditionally, it is the function of the jury to evaluate the credibility and meaning of "necessarily self-serving statements" and "ambiguous conduct."

Finally, I of course must agree with the Court that use of the jury is to be reserved for the case in which there is sufficient evidence to support a verdict. I have no difficulty, however, in concluding that respondents here did indeed submit sufficient evidence to support a verdict of not guilty, if the jury were so inclined, based on the necessity defense. . . .

In conclusion, my major point of disagreement with the Court is whether a defendant may get his duress or necessity defense to the jury when it is supported only by "self-serving" testimony and "ambiguous conduct." It is difficult, to imagine any case, criminal or civil, in which the jury is asked to decide a factual question based on completely disinterested testimony and unambiguous actions. The very essence of a jury issue is a dispute over the credibility of testimony by interested witnesses and the meaning of ambiguous actions.

Ruling on a defense as a matter of law and preventing the jury from considering it should be a rare occurrence in criminal cases. "[I]n a criminal case the law assigns [the factfinding function] solely to the jury." . . . The jury is the conscience of society and its role in a criminal prosecution is particularly important. . . . Yet the Court here appears to place an especially strict burden of proof on defendants attempting to establish an affirmative defense to the charged crime of escape. That action is unwarranted. If respondents' allegations are true, society is grossly at fault for permitting these conditions to persist at the D.C. jail. The findings of researchers and government agencies, as well as the litigated cases, indicate that in a general sense these allegations are credible. . . . In an attempt to conserve the jury for cases it considers truly worthy of that body, the Court has ousted the jury from a role it is particularly well-suited to serve.

NOTES

1. Some other courts have taken cognizance of the fact that brutality and homosexual attacks are commonplace within some prisons and penitentiaries. In Esquibel v. State, 91 N.M. 498, 576 P.2d 1129 (1978), the court said it was not error to instruct on the defense of duress to a charge of escape when there was substantial evidence of a prolonged history of beatings and serious threats toward the defendant by certain guards and prison personnel. In People v. Harmon, 53 Mich.App. 482, 220 N.W.2d 212 (1974), affirmed 394 Mich. 625, 232 N.W.2d 187 (1975), the defendant's conviction for prison escape was reversed, holding that the evidence justified submission to the jury of the defense of duress by reason of fear of corroborated threatened homosexual attacks by other inmates. In People v. Lovercamp, 43 Cal.App.3d 823, 118 Cal.Rptr. 110 (1974), the court held that a prison escape by women prisoners induced by a threatened lesbian homosexual assault by other female inmates could be justified as a matter of necessity as long as the inmate does not resort to violence in the escape and reports to the proper authorities when he or she has reached a position of safety from the immediate threat. See, in this connection, Gardner, The Defense of Necessity and the Right to Escape from Prison—A Step Toward Incarceration Free from Sexual Assault, 49 So.Cal.L.Rev. 110 (1975). See also: State v. Reese, 272 N.W.2d 863 (Iowa 1978); Jorgensen v. State, 100 Nev. 541, 688 P.2d 308 (1984).

South Dakota's statute on the defense of "justification" requires a broader scope for the defense in escape cases than was approved in the foregoing Bailey Case. A majority of the South Dakota Supreme Court, in State v. Miller, 313 N.W.2d 460 (S.D.1981), said that the defense of necessity was properly raised "when the offered evidence, if believed by the jury, would support a finding by them that the offense of escape was justified by a reasonable fear of death or great bodily harm so imminent or emergent that, according to ordinary standards of intelligence and morality, the desirability of avoiding the injury outweighs the desirability of avoiding the public injury arising from the offense committed. . . ." See also, State v. Baker, 598 S.W.2d 540 (Mo.App.1980), holding that a post-escape effort to surrender is not an essential element for the invocation of the necessity defense; and People v. Unger, 66 Ill.2d 333, 5 Ill.Dec. 848, 362 N.E.2d 319 (1977).

2. A person may, at times, be forced to do an act other than prison escape which he knows is against the criminal laws but which he feels compelled to do under the duress of special circumstances to prevent a greater harm from occurring. The traditional example of the intentional destruction of property in order to save lives may be found in the Bible: "Then the mariners were afraid, and cried every man unto his god, and cast forth the wares that were in the ship into the sea, to lighten it of them. (Jonah, c. 1, v. 5.) With such an ancient origin, the defense of necessity has long been recognized as a justification for some crimes, although its precise limits have never been clearly defined. It is generally stated that the special circumstances which create a dangerous condition must have been occasioned by natural forces rather than by human agency. Thus, the Model Penal Code suggest these examples of the proper application of the defense of necessity: destruction of property to prevent the spread of fire; mountain climbers breaking into a house, and stealing provisions, when caught in a storm; jettisoning of cargo at sea to save the vessel; or a druggist dispensing a drug without the prescription to alleviate distress in an emergency. Yet, there are many decided cases where the circumstances that had forced a defendant to choose the lesser of two evils were in fact created solely by human agency. Thus, the defense of necessity was deemed to apply to the violation of speeding laws in an attempt to apprehend a felon in State v. Gorham, 110 Wash. 330, 188 P. 457 (1920); to a doctor performing an abortion to save the life of the mother in Rex v. Bourne, 3 All Eng.R. 615 (1938); to stopping an automobile at a place where stopping is prohibited, when caught in a traffic jam in Commonwealth v. Brooks, 99 Mass. 434 (1868), dealing with a horse and buggy antedating the advent of the horseless carriage.

3. Consider again, in this regard, the text that was presented prior to the *Bailey* case. The first paragraph of the hypothetical presents, in essence, the facts in the case of The Queen v. Dudley & Stephens, 14 Q.B.D. 273, 15 Cox C.C. 624 (1884), in which it was held that there was no justification for the killing and that the surviving crewmen were therefore guilty of murder. Accordingly, they were sentenced to death; however, their sentences were commuted to six months' imprisonment.

The fourth paragraph of the text presents, in essence, the facts of United States v. Holmes, 26 Fed.Cas. 360, No. 15383 (C.C.Pa.1842). Although most of the crew disappeared following the rescue, one of their number, Holmes, stood trial and was convicted of manslaughter. He was sentenced to six months' imprisonment.

4. What would be the result in case situations such as in The Queen v. Dudley and United States v. Holmes if they were to be decided under a criminal code containing the following provision:

> Conduct which would otherwise be an offense is justifiable by reason of necessity if the accused was without blame in occasioning or developing the situation and reasonably believed such conduct was necessary to avoid a public or private injury greater than the injury which might reasonably result from his own conduct. (Ill.Rev.Stats., Ch. 38, § 7–13.)

5. The statutory defense of "competing harms" (N.H.Rev.Stat.Ann. § 627.3) is not available in a charge of criminal trespass based on an incident where the defendant occupied the construction site of a nuclear power plant.

In State v. Dorsey, 118 N.H. 844, 395 A.2d 855 (1978), defendant argued that he believed his conduct was necessary to avoid greater harm to himself and others, which is akin to the common law defense of necessity, but the court, in rejecting the defense, stated:

> "Defendant and others who oppose nuclear power have other lawful means of protesting nuclear power; therefore, they are not justified in breaking the law. . . . The act of criminal trespass was a deliberate and calculated choice and not an act that was urgently necessary to avoid a clear and imminent danger. . . . Nothing in this opinion should be construed as favoring or not favoring nuclear power. We deal only with the law as it relates to the defense relied upon. Nor do we pass upon the motives of the defendant. Good motives are not a defense to the commission of crime, except in a case of emergency not present here."

Similarly, in State v. Warshow, 138 Vt. 22, 410 A.2d 1000 (1979) defendants were convicted of unlawful trespass when they joined a rally at a nuclear power plant known as Vermont Yankee for the purpose of prevent workers from gaining access to the plant and placing it on-line. In affirming the conviction, the majority of the court said: "There is no doubt that the defendants wished to call attention to the dangers of low-level radiation and nuclear waste, and nuclear accident. But low-level radiation and nuclear waste are not the types of imminent danger classified as an emergency sufficient to justify criminal activity. . . . Where the hazards are long term, the danger is not imminent, because the defendants have time to exercise options other than breaking the law."

6. In People v. Stiso, 93 Ill.App.3d 101, 48 Ill.Dec. 687, 416 N.E.2d 1209 (1981) the defendants entered a hospital and sought to bar access to rooms where abortions were performed. After conviction of violating the state disorderly conduct statute, they contended on appeal that they had acted to prevent the death of fetuses. The court, in affirming, found that the necessity defense was inapplicable because the alleged injury sought to be avoided—the abortions—was not a legally recognized injury.

See also, Cleveland v. Municipality of Anchorage, 631 P.2d 1073 (Alaska 1981); State v. O'Brien, 784 S.W.2d 187 (Mo.App.1989).

3. SUPERIOR ORDERS

UNITED STATES v. CALLEY

United States Court of Military Appeals, 1973.
22 USMCA 534, 48 CMR 19.

OPINION

QUINN, JUDGE: First Lieutenant Calley stands convicted of the premeditated murder of 22 infants, children, women, and old men, and of assault with intent to murder a child of about 2 years of age. All the killings and the assault took place on March 16, 1968 in the area of the village of My Lai in the Republic of South Vietnam. The Army Court of Military Review affirmed the findings of guilty and the sentence, which, as reduced by the convening authority, includes dismissal and confinement at hard labor for 20 years. The accused petitioned this Court for further review, alleging 30 assignments of error. We granted three of these assignments.

* * *

Lieutenant Calley was a platoon leader in C Company, a unit that was part of an organization known as Task Force Barker, whose mission was to subdue and drive out the enemy in an area in the Republic of Vietnam known popularly as Pinkville. Before March 16, 1968, this area, which included the village of My Lai 4, was a Viet Cong stronghold. C Company had operated in the area several times. Each time the unit had entered the area it suffered casualties by sniper fire, machine gun fire, mines, and other forms of attack. Lieutenant Calley had accompanied his platoon on some of the incursions.

On March 15, 1968, a memorial service for members of the company killed in the area during the preceding weeks was held. After the service Captain Ernest L. Medina, the commanding officer of C Company, briefed the company on a mission in the Pinkville area set for the next day. C Company was to serve as the main attack formation for Task Force Barker. In that role it would assault and neutralize My Lai 4, 5, and 6 and then mass for an assault on My Lai 1. Intelligence reports indicated that the unit would be opposed by a veteran enemy battalion, and that all civilians would be absent from the area. The objective was to destroy the enemy. Disagreement exists as to the instructions on the specifics of destruction.

Captain Medina testified that he instructed his troops that they were to destroy My Lai 4 by "burning the hootches, to kill the livestock, to close the wells and to destroy the food crops." Asked if women and children were to be killed, Medina said he replied in the negative, adding that, "You must use common sense. If they have a weapon and are trying to engage you, then you can shoot back, but you must use common sense." However, Lieutenant Calley testified that Captain Medina informed the troops they were to kill every living thing—men, women, children, and animals—and under no circumstances were they to leave any Vietnamese behind them as they passed through the villages enroute to their final objective. Other witnesses gave more or less support to both versions of the briefing.

On March 16, 1968, the operation began with interdicting fire. C Company was then brought to the area by helicopters. Lieutenant Calley's platoon was on the first lift. This platoon formed a defense perimeter until the remainder of the force was landed. The unit received no hostile fire from the village.

Calley's platoon passed the approaches to the village with his men firing heavily. Entering the village, the platoon encountered only unarmed, unresisting men, women, and children. The villagers, including infants held in their mothers' arms, were assembled and moved in separate groups to collection points. Calley testified that during this time he was radioed twice by Captain Medina, who demanded to know what was delaying the platoon. On being told that a large number of villagers had been detained, Calley said Medina ordered him to "waste them." Calley further testified that he obeyed the orders because he had been taught the doctrine of obedience throughout his military career. Medina denied that he gave any such order.

One of the collection points for the villagers was in the southern part of the village. There, Private First Class Paul D. Meadlo guarded a group of between 30 to 40 old men, women, and children. Lieutenant Calley approached Meadlo and told him, " 'You know what to do,' " and left. He returned shortly and asked Meadlo why the people were not yet dead. Meadlo replied he did not know that Calley had meant that they should be killed. Calley declared that he wanted them dead. He and Meadlo then opened fire on the group, until all but a few children fell. Calley then personally shot these children. He expended 4 or 5 magazines from his M–16 rifle in the incident.

Lieutenant Calley and Meadlo moved from this point to an irrigation ditch on the east side of My Lai 4. There, they encountered another group of civilians being held by several soldiers. Meadlo estimated that this group contained from 75 to 100 persons. Calley stated, " 'We got another job to do, Meadlo,' " and he ordered the group into the ditch. When all were in the ditch, Calley and Meadlo opened fire on them. Although ordered by Calley to shoot, Private First Class James J. Dursi refused to join in the killings, and Specialist Four Robert E. Maples refused to give his machine gun to Calley for use in the killings. Lieutenant Calley admitted that he fired into the ditch, with the muzzle of his weapon within 5 feet of people in it. He expended between 10 to 15 magazines of ammunition on this occasion.

With his radio operator, Private Charles Sledge, Calley moved to the north end of the ditch. There, he found an elderly Vietnamese monk, whom he interrogated. Calley struck the man with his rifle butt and then shot him in the head. Other testimony indicates that immediately afterwards a young child was observed running toward the village. Calley seized him by the arm, threw him into the ditch, and fired at him. Calley admitted interrogating and striking the monk, but denied shooting him. He also denied the incident involving the child.

Appellate defense counsel contend that the evidence is insufficient to establish the accused's guilt. They do not dispute Calley's participation in the homicides, but they argue that he did not act with the malice or *mens rea* essential to a conviction of murder; that the orders he received to kill everyone in the village were not palpably illegal; that he was acting in ignorance of the laws of war; that since he was told that only "the enemy" would be in the village, his honest belief that there were no innocent civilians in the village exonerates him of criminal responsibility for their deaths; and, finally, that his actions were in the heat of passion caused by reasonable provocation.

* * *

The testimony of Meadlo and others provided the court members with ample evidence from which to find that Lieutenant Calley directed and personally participated in the intentional killing of men, women, and children, who were unarmed and in the custody of armed soldiers of C Company. If the prosecution's witnesses are believed, there is also ample evidence to support a finding that the accused deliberately shot the Vietnamese monk whom he interrogated, and that he seized, threw into a ditch, and fired on a child with the intent to kill.

*   *   *

At trial, Calley's principal defense was that he acted in execution of Captain Medina's order to kill everyone in My Lai 4. Appellate defense counsel urge this defense as the most important factor in assessment of the legal sufficiency of the evidence. The argument, however, is inapplicable to whether the evidence is *legally* sufficient. Captain Medina denied that he issued any such order, either during the previous day's briefing or on the date the killings were carried out. Resolution of the conflict between his testimony and that of the accused was for the triers of the facts. United States v. Guerra, 13 USCMA 463, 32 CMR 403 (1963). The general findings of guilty, with exceptions as to the number of persons killed, does not indicate whether the court members found that Captain Medina did not issue the alleged order to kill, or whether, if he did, the court members believed that the accused knew the order was illegal. For the purpose of the legal sufficiency of the evidence, the record supports the findings of guilty.

*   *   *

We turn to the contention that the judge erred in his submission of the defense of superior orders to the court. After fairly summarizing the evidence, the judge gave the following instructions pertinent to the issue:

> The killing of resisting or fleeing enemy forces is generally recognized as a justifiable act of war, and you may consider any such killings justifiable in this case. The law attempts to protect those persons not actually engaged in warfare, however; and limits the circumstances under which their lives may be taken.
>
> Both combatants captured by and noncombatants detained by the opposing force, regardless of their loyalties, political views, or prior acts, have the right to be treated as prisoners until released, confined, or executed, in accordance with law and established procedures, by competent authority sitting in judgment of such detained or captured individuals. Summary execution of detainees or prisoners is forbidden by law. Further, it's clear under the evidence presented in this case, that hostile acts or support of the enemy North Vietnamese or Viet Cong forces by inhabitants of My Lai (4) at some time prior to 16 March 1968, would not justify the summary execution of all or a part of the occupants of My Lai (4) on 16 March, nor would hostile acts committed that day, if, following the hostility, the

belligerents surrendered or were captured by our forces. I therefore instruct you, as a matter of law, that if unresisting human beings were killed at My Lai (4) while within the effective custody and control of our military forces, their deaths cannot be considered justified, and any order to kill such people would be, as a matter of law, an illegal order. Thus, if you find that Lieutenant Calley received an order directing him to kill unresisting Vietnamese within his control or within the control of his troops, *that order would be an illegal order.*

A determination that an order is illegal does not, of itself, assign criminal responsibility to the person following the order for acts done in compliance with it. Soldiers are taught to follow orders, and special attention is given to obedience of orders on the battlefield. Military effectiveness depends upon obedience to orders. On the other hand, the obedience of a soldier is not the obedience of an automaton. A soldier is a reasoning agent, obliged to respond, not as a machine, but as a person. The law takes these factors into account in assessing criminal responsibility for acts done in compliance with illegal orders.

The acts of a subordinate done in compliance with an unlawful order given him by his superior are excused and impose no criminal liability upon him unless the superior's order is one which a man of *ordinary sense and understanding* would, under the circumstances, know to be unlawful, or if the order in question is actually known to the accused to be unlawful.

* * *

. . . In determining what orders, if any, Lieutenant Calley acted under, if you find him to have acted, you should consider all of the matters which he has testified reached him and which you can infer from other evidence that he saw and heard. Then, unless you find beyond a reasonable doubt that he was not acting under orders directing him in substance and effect to kill unresisting occupants of My Lai (4), you must determine whether Lieutenant Calley actually knew those orders to be unlawful.

. . . In determining whether or not Lieutenant Calley had knowledge of the unlawfulness of any order found by you to have been given, you may consider all relevant facts and circumstances, including Lieutenant Calley's rank; educational background; OCS schooling; other training while in the Army, including basic training, and his training in Hawaii and Vietnam; his experience on prior operations involving contact with hostile and friendly Vietnamese; his age; and any other evidence tending to prove or disprove that on 16 March 1968,

Lieutenant Calley knew the order was unlawful. If you find beyond a reasonable doubt, on the basis of all the evidence, that *Lieutenant Calley actually knew* the order under which he asserts he operated was unlawful, the fact that the order was given operates as no defense.

Unless you find beyond reasonable doubt that the accused acted with actual knowledge that the order was unlawful, you must proceed to determine whether, under the circumstances, *a man of ordinary sense and understanding would have known the order was unlawful. Your deliberations on this question do not focus on Lieutenant Calley and the manner in which he perceived the legality of the order found to have been given him. The standard is that of a man of ordinary sense and understanding under the circumstances.*

Think back to the events of 15 and 16 March 1968. . . . Then determine, in light of all the surrounding circumstances, whether the order, which to reach this point you will have found him to be operating in accordance with, is one which a man of ordinary sense and understanding would know to be unlawful. Apply this to each charged act which you have found Lieutenant Calley to have committed. Unless you are satisfied from the evidence, beyond a reasonable doubt, that a man of ordinary sense and understanding would have known the order to be unlawful, you must acquit Lieutenant Calley for committing acts done in accordance with the order. (Emphasis added.)

Appellate defense counsel contend that these instructions are prejudicially erroneous in that they require the court members to determine that Lieutenant Calley knew that an order to kill human beings in the circumstances under which he killed was illegal by the standard of whether "a man of ordinary sense and understanding" would know the order was illegal. They urge us to adopt as the governing test whether the order is so palpably or manifestly illegal that a person of "the commonest understanding" would be aware of its illegality. They maintain the standard stated by the judge is too strict and unjust; that it confronts members of the armed forces who are not persons of ordinary sense and understanding with the dilemma of choosing between the penalty of death for disobedience of an order in time of war on the one hand and the equally serious punishment for obedience on the other. Some thoughtful commentators on military law have presented much the same argument.[1]

---

1. In the words of one author: "If the standard of reasonableness continues to be applied, we run the unacceptable risk of applying serious punishment to one whose only crime is the slowness of his wit or his stupidity. The soldier, who honestly believes that he must obey an order to kill and is punished for it, is convicted not of murder but of simple negligence." Finkelstein, Duty to Obey as a Defense, March 9, 1970 (unpublished essay, Army War College). See also L. Norene, Obedience to Orders as a Defense to a Criminal Act, March 1971 (unpublished thesis presented to The Judge Advocate General's School, U.S. Army).

The "ordinary sense and understanding" standard is set forth in the present Manual for Courts-Martial, United States, 1969 (Rev) and was the standard accepted by this Court in United States v. Schultz, 18 USCMA 133, 39 CMR 133 (1969) and United States v. Keenan, 18 USCMA 108, 39 CMR 108 (1969). It appeared as early as 1917. Manual for Courts-Martial, U.S. Army, 1917, paragraph 442. Apparently, it originated in a quotation from F. Wharton, Homicide § 485 (3d ed. 1907). Wharton's authority is Riggs v. State, 3 Coldwell 85, 91 American Decisions 272, 273 (Tenn.1866), in which the court approved a charge to the jury as follows:

> "[I]n its substance being clearly illegal, so that a man of ordinary sense and understanding would know as soon as he heard the order read or given that such order was illegal, would afford a private no protection for a crime committed under such order."

* * *

In the stress of combat, a member of the armed forces cannot reasonably be expected to make a refined legal judgment and be held criminally responsible if he guesses wrong on a question as to which there may be considerable disagreement. But there is no disagreement as to the illegality of the order to kill in this case. For 100 years, it has been a settled rule of American law that even in war the summary killing of an enemy, who has submitted to, and is under, effective physical control, is murder. Appellate defense counsel acknowledge that rule of law and its continued viability, but they say that Lieutenant Calley should not be held accountable for the men, women and children he killed because the court-martial could have found that he was a person of "commonest understanding" and such a person might not know what our law provides; that his captain had ordered him to kill these unarmed and submissive people and he only carried out that order as a good disciplined soldier should.

Whether Lieutenant Calley was the most ignorant person in the United States Army in Vietnam, or the most intelligent, he must be presumed to know that he could not kill the people involved here. The United States Supreme Court has pointed out that "[t]he rule that 'ignorance of the law will not excuse' [a positive act that constitutes a crime] . . . is deep in our law." Lambert v. California, 355 U.S. 225, 228 (1957). An order to kill infants and unarmed civilians who were so demonstrably incapable of resistance to the armed might of a military force as were those killed by Lieutenant Calley is, in my opinion, so palpably illegal that whatever conceptional difference there may be between a person of "commonest understanding" and a person of "common understanding," that difference could not have had any "impact on a court of lay members receiving the respective wordings in instructions," as appellate defense counsel contend. In my judgment, there is no possibility of prejudice to Lieutenant Calley in the trial judge's reliance upon the established standard of excuse of criminal conduct, rather than the standard of "commonest understanding" presented by the defense, or by the new variable test postulated in the dissent, which, with the inclusion of such factors for consideration as grade and experience, would appear to exact a higher standard of understanding from Lieutenant Calley than that of the person of ordinary understanding.

In summary, as reflected in the record, the judge was capable and fair, and dedicated to assuring the accused a trial on the merits as provided by law; his instructions on all issues were comprehensive and correct. Lieutenant Calley was given every consideration to which he was entitled, and perhaps more. We are impressed with the absence of bias or prejudice on the part of the court members. They were instructed to determine the *truth* according to the law and this they did with due deliberation and full consideration of the evidence. Their findings of guilty represent the truth of the facts as they determined them to be and there is substantial evidence to support those findings. No mistakes of procedure cast doubt upon them.

Consequently, the decision of the Court of Military Review is affirmed.

[The concurring opinion of Duncan, Judge is omitted.]

DARDEN, CHIEF JUDGE (dissenting):

Although the charge the military judge gave on the defense of superior orders was not inconsistent with the Manual treatment of this subject, I believe the Manual provision is too strict in a combat environment. Among other things, this standard permits serious punishment of persons whose training and attitude incline them either to be enthusiastic about compliance with orders or not to challenge the authority of their superiors. The standard also permits conviction of members who are not persons of ordinary sense and understanding.

The principal opinion has accurately traced the history of the current standard. Since this Manual provision is one of substantive law rather than one relating to procedure or modes of proof, the Manual rule is not binding on this Court, which has the responsibility for determining the principles that govern justification in the law of homicide. United States v. Smith, 13 USCMA 105, 32 CMR 105 (1962). My impression is that the weight of authority, including the commentators whose articles are mentioned in the principal opinion, supports a more liberal approach to the defense of superior orders. Under this approach, superior orders should constitute a defense except "in a plain case of excess of authority, where at first blush it is apparent and palpable to the commonest understanding that the order is illegal."

While this test is phrased in language that now seems "somewhat archaic and ungrammatical," the test recognizes that the essential ingredient of discipline in any armed force is obedience to orders and that this obedience is so important it should not be penalized unless the order would be recognized as illegal, not by what some hypothetical reasonable soldier would have known, but also by "those persons at the lowest end of the scale of intelligence and experience in the services."

This is the real purpose in permitting superior orders to be a defense, and it ought not be restricted by the concept of a fictional reasonable man so that, regardless of his personal characteristics, an accused judged after the fact may find himself punished for either obedience or disobedience, depending on whether the evidence will support the finding of simple negligence on his part.

It is true that the standard of a "reasonable man" is used in other areas of military criminal law, e.g., in connection with the provocation necessary to reduce murder to voluntary manslaughter; what constitutes an honest and reasonable mistake; and, indirectly, in connection with involuntary manslaughter. But in none of these instances do we have the countervailing consideration of avoiding the subversion of obedience to discipline in combat by encouraging a member to weigh the legality of an order or whether the superior had the authority to issue it. See Martin v Mott, 25 US 19, 30 (1827).

The preservation of human life is, of course, of surpassing importance. To accomplish such preservation, members of the armed forces must be held to standards of conduct that will permit punishment of atrocities and enable this nation to follow civilized concepts of warfare. In defending the current standard, the Army Court of Military Review expressed the view that:

> Heed must be given not only to the subjective innocence-through-ignorance in the soldier, but to the consequences for his victims. Also, barbarism tends to invite reprisal to the detriment of our own force or disrepute which interferes with the achievement of war aims, even though the barbaric acts were preceded by orders for their commission. Casting the defense of obedience to orders solely in subjective terms of *mens rea* would operate practically to abrogate those objective restraints which are essential to functioning rules of war.

United States v Calley, 46 CMR 1131, 1184 (ACMR1973).

I do not disagree with these comments. But while humanitarian considerations compel us to consider the impact of actions by members of our armed forces on citizens of other nations, I am also convinced that the phrasing of the defense of superior orders should have as its principal objective fairness to the unsophisticated soldier and those of somewhat limited intellect who nonetheless are doing their best to perform their duty.

The test of palpable illegality to the commonest understanding properly balances punishment for the obedience of an obviously illegal order against protection to an accused for following his elementary duty of obeying his superiors. Such a test reinforces the need for obedience as an essential element of military discipline by broadly protecting the soldier who has been effectively trained to look to his superiors for direction. It also promotes fairness by permitting the military jury to consider the particular accused's intelligence, grade, training, and other elements directly related to the issue of whether he should have known an order was illegal. Finally, that test imputes such knowledge to an accused not as a result of simple negligence but on the much stronger circumstantial concept that almost anyone in the armed forces would have immediately recognized that the order was palpably illegal.

I would adopt this standard as the correct instruction for the jury when the defense of superior orders is in issue. Because the original case language is archaic and somewhat ungrammatical, I would rephrase it to require that the military jury be instructed that, despite his asserted defense of superior orders, an accused may be held criminally accountable for his acts, allegedly committed pursuant to such orders, if the court members are convinced beyond a reasonable doubt (1) that almost every member of the armed forces would have immediately recognized that the order was unlawful, and (2) that the accused should have recognized the order's illegality as a consequence of his age, grade, intelligence, experience, and training.

* * *

In the instant case, Lieutenant Calley's testimony placed the defense of superior orders in issue, even though he conceded that he knew prisoners were normally to be treated with respect and that the unit's normal practice was to interrogate Vietnamese villagers, release those who could account for themselves, and evacuate those suspected of being a part of the enemy forces. Although crucial parts of his testimony were sharply contested, according to Lieutenant Calley, (1) he had received a briefing before the assault in which he was instructed that every living thing in the village was to be killed, including women and children; (2) he was informed that speed was important in securing the village and moving forward; (3) he was ordered that under no circumstances were any Vietnamese to be allowed to stay behind the lines of his forces; (4) the residents of the village who were taken into custody were hindering the progress of his platoon in taking up the position it was to occupy; and (5) when he informed Captain Medina of this hindrance, he was ordered to kill the villagers and to move his platoon to a proper position.

In addition to the briefing, Lieutenant Calley's experience in the Pinkville area caused him to know that, in the past, when villagers had been left behind his unit, the unit had immediately received sniper fire from the rear as it pressed forward. Faulty intelligence apparently led him also to believe that those persons in the village were not innocent civilians but were either enemies or enemy sympathizers. For a participant in the My Lai operation, the circumstances that could have obtained there may have caused the illegality of alleged orders to kill civilians to be much less clear than they are in a hindsight review.

Since the defense of superior orders was not submitted to the military jury under what I consider to be the proper standard, I would grant Lieutenant Calley a rehearing. . . .

NOTE

Consider the contention of defense counsel in the War Crime Trials in Nürnberg, Germany following World War II. They argued that until then jurists and nations had "never even thought of incriminating statesmen, generals and economic leaders of a state using force, and still less bringing these men before an international criminal court. . . . [T]he present trial has, therefore, no legal basis in international law but is a procedure based on a new penal law; a penal law created only after the act. This is in contradiction to a legal principle that is cherished in the world. . . . This principle is the maxim: punishment is possible only if a law has been violated that was in existence at the time the act was committed and that provided punishment. . . . This principle is not a matter of opportunism but based on the knowledge that every defendant must feel treated unjustly if he is punished under a murder law created *ex post facto.*"

Professor Sheldon Glueck, in an article appearing in 59 Harv.L.Rev. 396 (1946), countered with the following argument:

". . . [T]he United Nations could have executed the Nürnberg defendants without any judicial procedure whatsoever. The 'law' of an armistice or a treaty is, in the final analysis, the will of the victor. . . . If ever there was a gang of malefactors who deserved extermination without the privilege of legal defense, it is the Nazi ringleaders. . . . It would have been poetic justice of the most appropriate kind to have dealt with the Nazi-Fascist ringleaders summarily.

"But the United Nations wished to proceed in a more civilized way. So the victors provided for indictment and trial. . . .

"It was pointed out in the argument of counsel in the Nürnberg trial . . . 'that every defendant must feel treated unjustly if he is punished under a murder law created *ex post facto*'. . . . In other words, it is brazenly claimed that because the civilized world cannot put its finger on some specific section in an international penal code which prohibits the slaughter of millions in an aggressive, unlawful and unnecessary war, such acts were *permissible* since, technically, they were not labeled 'murder' by world law at the time the killings occurred, even though by the laws of all civilized States unjustified killings are stigmatized as murders. Even to state the German lawyers' proposition is to demonstrate its melange of impudence, cynicism, and absurdity. . . .

"Surely . . . Hitler, Himmler, Goering . . . and the rest of the unholy alliance in supreme authority in Nazi Germany knew full well that murder is murder, whether wholesale or retail, whether committed in pursuance of a gigantic conspiracy . . . or of a smaller conspiracy evolved by a group of domestic murderers."

B. INFANCY

STATE v. MONAHAN
Supreme Court of New Jersey, 1954.
15 N.J. 34, 104 A.2d 21.

JACOBS, J. Prompted by mid-Twentieth Century sociological precepts, our Legislature has directed that children under 16 who commit any offenses which would be criminal if committed by adults, shall not be triable in criminal proceedings but shall be dealt with exclusively by our specialized juvenile courts. The legal issue presented to us is whether this clear statutory mandate may be judicially disregarded to enable a first degree murder trial in the County Court of a 15-year-old boy who participated in a robbery with his father during which his father killed two persons.

In April, 1953 Eugene Monahan and his 15-year-old son Michael were indicted for the murder of William Diskin and Sebastian Weilandics. Eugene Monahan has been tried, convicted and sentenced to death and his appeal is pending before this court. The State concedes that the victims were killed by the father and not the son but asserts that since the homicides occurred during a robbery in which the son participated, the son was equally triable for murder in the first degree, punishable by death unless there is a recommendation of life imprisonment. . . . A motion was made for transfer of the proceeding against the son to the Juvenile and Domestic Relations Court on the ground that under N.J.S. 2A:85–4 N.J.S.A., and N.J.S. 2A:4–14, N.J.S.A., it was cognizable exclusively in that court. The motion was denied and an appeal was taken. . . .

The principle of removing or mitigating the criminal responsibility of children has ancient origins. In the early case of State v. Aaron, . . ., Chief Justice Kirkpatrick restated the settled common law doctrine, adapted from earlier Roman law, that since a child under seven "cannot have discretion to discern between good and evil" he is incapable of committing crime; between the ages of seven and 14 he is subject to a rebuttable presumption of incapacity; and after 14 he is presumptively capable. . . . Although the common law rule precluded criminal convictions of many young offenders, there are instances in which it failed to do so, with shocking consequences. Blackstone cites cases in which children of very tender age were drastically condemned as adult criminals; he refers to the hanging of an eight-year-old for maliciously burning some barns; to the hanging of a ten-year-old who had killed one of his companions; and to the burning of a girl of 13 who had killed her mistress. . . . Similar illustrations in our own State are not lacking. In 1818 a boy of 11 was tried for murder . . ., and in 1828 a boy of 13 was hanged for an offense which he committed when he was 12. . . .. During most of the Nineteenth Century, child and adult offenders were treated alike although intermittent steps were taken towards their separate confinement. It was not until the turn of the century that modern concepts really began to take form; they embodied the upward movement in the child's age of criminal responsibility, the extended recognition of society's obligation as *parens patriae* to care for delinquent children, and the creation of independent juvenile courts. . . .

The first juvenile court in this country was established in Cook County, Illinois, by an 1899 act which provided that the child offender was to be considered a ward of the state under control of the juvenile court; proceedings were there to be conducted informally with rehabilitative supervision rather than retributive punishment in mind, and without public indictment, trial by jury and other incidents of criminal causes. Thereafter the other states adopted legislation which was comparable though specific provisions varied. Attacks on the legislation based on the absence of indictment, trial by jury and the other constitutional guarantees applicable to criminal proceedings were quickly rejected. . . . In the Fisher case [213 Pa. 48, 62 A. 200] the Supreme Court of Pennsylvania pointed out that the juvenile court proceeding is not "the trial of a child charged with a crime, but is mercifully to save it from such an ordeal with the prison or penitentiary in its wake, if the child's own good and the best interests of the state justify such salvation." In the Lindsay case [257 Ill. 328, 100 N.E. 894] the Supreme Court of Illinois noted that the "prerogative of the state, arising out of its power and duty, as *parens patriae,* to protect the interest of infants, has always been exercised by courts of chancery" and has not been questioned for generations. In the Lewis case [260 N.Y. 171, 183 N.E. 354] the New York Court of Appeals stated that there is no doubt about the power of the legislature "to say that an act done by a child shall not be a crime." And in the recent Morin case [95 N.H. 518, 68 A.2d 670] the Supreme Court of New Hampshire, in rejecting an attack on its statute relating to delinquent children, said:

> "We think it sufficiently plain that the act in question is designed to permit the exercise of the powers of the state as 'parens patriae,' for the purpose of rehabilitating minor children, and not of punishing them for the commission of a crime. 'It is generally held that the purpose of such statutes is not penal, but protective. It is not that the child shall be punished for breach of a law or regulation, but that he shall have a better chance to become a worthy citizen.' . . . Similar statutes have been universally upheld over objections based upon constitutional grounds. . . .

In In re Paniecki [N.J.1935] . . ., Vice-Chancellor Backes had occasion to deal with the issue of whether a 15-year-old boy, charged with murder, was triable in the same manner as an adult in the Court of Oyer and Terminer. The vice chancellor held that he was, expressing the sweeping view that the Legislature had no power "to vest jurisdiction in the juvenile court to try the crime of murder (or any other indictable offense) without a jury." He did not consider any of the many cases to the contrary throughout the states and if his view had ultimately prevailed it would have struck a mortal blow to the juvenile court movement in our State. . . .

Immediately after Vice-Chancellor Backes had rendered his decision in the Daniecki case holding that the 15-year-old boy before him was triable for murder in the same manner as an adult, the Legislature took affirmative steps to obviate its effects. It provided in L. 1935, c. 285, that a person under the age of 16 shall be deemed incapable of committing a crime under the common law or statute law of this State; and in L.1935, c. 284, in defining delinquency cognizable exclusively in the juvenile court, it included conduct which, if committed by any one 16 or over, would constitute a felony, high misdemeanor, misdemeanor or other offense. The statutory language was unmistakable in design. . . .

In In re Mei . . . [N.J.1937], the question was again raised as to whether a 15-year-old was triable for murder in the same manner as an adult; the court held that he was notwithstanding the express terms of L.1935, cc. 284, 285. It did not suggest that the Legislature intended to exclude murder from its comprehensive enactments; nor did it adopt the sweeping view of unconstitutionality expressed in the Daniecki case and later rejected in the Goldberg case. Instead, it rested on the unprecedented ground that since the charge of murder is "so horrible in fact and in the contemplation of society" it must remain "a crime within the purview of the Constitution, whatever name and whatever treatment may be appended to it by the Legislature." . . . Viewed strictly as a legal ground it has no supporting basis whatever since the Constitution makes no pertinent mention of murder and the guarantees, when applicable, govern murder and other indictable common law offenses with like force. Viewed strictly as an emotional ground it concededly may not be given any controlling effect.

In approximately half the states the jurisdiction of the juvenile court over children under 16 is exclusive, even where the offense would constitute murder if committed by an adult. . . . The Standard Juvenile Court Act as revised in 1949 likewise vests exclusive jurisdiction in the juvenile court over all children under 16. It also provides for jurisdiction over children from 16 to 18 but states that if the child is 16 or over and is charged "with an offense which would be a felony if committed by an adult" the juvenile court may in its discretion, certify the child for criminal proceedings. To remove any doubts, it expressly directs that "no child under sixteen years of age shall be so certified." Judicial opinions sustaining such legislation are now legion and the Mei decision stands alone in its notion that a child of seven or over, charged with murder, must be tried in the same manner as an adult regardless of what the Legislature says on the subject. Although the decision is devoid of supporting reason and authority, the suggestion is advanced that since it was rendered many years ago it should be permitted to stand until altered by the Legislature. This approach might have some merit if the Mei decision turned on a matter of statutory construction but the fact is that the court there asserted an absence of constitutional power which no amount of legislation could supply. . . . In any event, the pertinent legislative enactments after the Mei case clearly reaffirm the plain statutory purpose to vest in the juvenile court, exclusive jurisdiction over children under 16 regardless of the severity of their offenses. . . . In 1946 the Legislature, in dealing with juvenile court jurisdiction over persons between the ages of 16 and 18, expressly stated that the juvenile court may refer the matter to the prosecutor for criminal trial where the offense was of a "heinous nature." L.1946, c. 77; N.J.S. 2A:4–15, N.J.S.A. . . . No comparable provision was ever adopted with respect to children under 16, thus evidencing the legislative purpose of preserving the exclusive jurisdiction of the juvenile court in such instances. . . . When our statutes relating to civil and criminal justice were recently revised, the Legislature re-enacted its comprehensive declarations that a person under the age of 16 shall be deemed incapable of committing a crime, . . . and that juvenile delinquency shall include any act which, if committed by an adult, would constitute a felony, high misdemeanor, misdemeanor or other offense. . . .

A majority of the court is satisfied that our present legislation lawfully vests exclusive jurisdiction in the juvenile court over misconduct by children under 16 including misconduct which would constitute murder or other heinous crime if committed by an adult. Accordingly, the order entered below is set aside and the matter is remanded to the Juvenile and Domestic Relations Court of Union County for further proceedings in accordance with the governing statutes and rules of court.

Heher, J., concurring in result. [The concurring opinion of Heher, J., is omitted.] For reversal: Justices Heher, Burling, Jacobs and Brennan—4. For affirmance: Chief Justice Vanderbilt, and Justices Oliphant and Wachenfeld—3.

OLIPHANT, J. (dissenting). I find myself compelled to dissent in this case because I differ basically with the approach and reasoning of the majority opinion. . . .

The majority . . . have in effect overruled the holding in the Mei case and assert that under the *parens patriae* doctrine, both on psychological and sociological grounds, the State and the Legislature have the power to treat such a crime when committed by an infant on a psychological or sociological basis and bring it within the definition of juvenile delinquency as set forth in the statute. . . .

. . . [T]he nub of the problem here presented revolves around the statutory provision, N.J.S. 2A:85–4 N.J.S.A., which provides:

"A person under the age of 16 years is deemed incapable of committing a crime."

This provision seemingly ignores the fundamental fact of the law of nature as applied to man and facts of everyday existence which are of common knowledge and public notice.

I cannot comprehend the reasoning that suggests that marauding gangs of little hoodlums armed with guns, knives, switch knives or other lethal weapons are to be considered as a matter of law incapable of committing the crime of murder. Infants under the age of 21 years, according to statistics, perpetrate a high percentage of the heinous crimes committed throughout the country, and the situation has reached such serious proportions that it is a threat to the public welfare and safety of the law-abiding citizen. . . .

At the common law and in this State, insofar as a crime is concerned, the inability to form a criminal intent is a matter of defense. As to children under the age of seven years there is a conclusive presumption that the child was *doli incapax,* or incapable of entertaining a criminal intent, and no evidence can or should be received to show capacity in fact. Between the ages of seven and 14 the presumption is rebuttable, but the State or prosecution has the burden of showing that the infant has sufficient intelligence to distinguish between right and wrong and to understand the nature and illegality of the particular act. Over the age of 14 children were and are presumed to be *doli capax* and therefore responsible. The presumption is rebuttable but the burden of proof is upon the defendant to establish that he did not have sufficient intelligence to understand the nature and consequences of his act. These rules are consistent with the nature of man and the natural use of his faculties of intellect and will, and his freedom to acquire the necessary knowledge to make the distinction between right and wrong. They are rules to determine the ultimate fact of the ability of an individual to distinguish between right and wrong. The point in life when a person is capable of making this distinction may vary, but once it is reached that person whether it be an adult or a child, is capable of criminal intent. . . .

The views expressed here were of sufficient moment to induce the Legislatures in many states to remove the charge of murder from the field of juvenile delinquency. It is indeed a curious anomaly that in this country, where civilization in some respects has reached its highest peak insofar as the welfare and comfort of an individual is concerned and where the educational opportunities are practically unlimited for a child, we are brought face to face with a statute that in effect denied that the normal child is a rational human being insofar as the highest crime against nature is concerned. I doubt that even in the primitive state of civilization there is any society that subscribes to such a proposition. Bluntly, the statute practically says that a child, within defined age limits, is not a rational being but merely an animal without the will or mind to control its baser animal instincts. . . .

I am unable to subscribe to nor can I find support for the legal theory by which the Legislature can declare that those young in years but old in crime and depravity are incapable of committing the crime of murder. Many such are experienced criminals. A prominent jurist recently said: "The whole problem of juvenile and adolescent delinquency has become worse and is now a scandal." . . .

I would affirm the order of the court below in denying the motion for the transfer of the indictments to the Juvenile and Domestic Relations Court.

WACHENFELD, J. (dissenting).

Over the many years our present procedure in reference to these matters has worked out quite satisfactorily. No hue or cry of great injustice has been heard, nor is there a single case the disposition of which has offended the public's sense of essential fairness.

The method of disposing of these cases has now been changed, not by legislative enactment, where the power admittedly resides, but by a new judicial interpretation. In re Mei . . ., which has stood for 17 years, is overruled and is no longer the law.

Up until now, all who committed murder, whether old or young, were held strictly accountable to the law. If the offender appreciated the difference between right and wrong, he was answerable in a court of law for the highest crime known, the taking of another's life.

Today's youth is more precocious than yesterday's. His agressiveness has not been diminished and the record unfortunately shows his propensity for going out of bounds has not decreased. The child who flounts authority is becoming too prevalent, and the seriousness of these infractions is becoming increasingly grim. Juvenile delinquency is still one of our foremost problems, and its solution is being vainly sought by educator, legislator and many public agencies.

How, then, will this change in the law affect the dilemma confronting us? Will it help or hinder? Those of tender age who are likely to commit the crime involved will certainly not be additionally deterred by the knowledge that the punishment for it has practically been abolished and the worse that can befall them for committing a felony murder under the new rule is confinement in a reformatory or correctional institution for the term fixed by the trustees, not to exceed in any case a few years.

Erring youth indeed offers a fertile field for remedial effort, but I doubt if in this instance we are making much of a contribution.

The police now cannot keep track of those they have apprehended and referred to the Juvenile Court. The disposition there is confidential and secret and makes better law enforcement by those responsible for it more difficult. To the classification of the offenses so processed we now add the crime of murder. I have grave fears of its consequences.

I cannot embrace many of the expressions in Justice Oliphant's dissent, but I feel obligated to state briefly the reasons why I would adhere to the decision in In re Mei, supra, and therefore affirm the judgment below.

NOTES

1. "The common law presumption of incapacity, in the case of a child between the ages of seven and fourteen, is still very much alive in this jurisdiction [Pennsylvania]. Nothing in the Juvenile Act indicates a contrary legislative intent. In the instant case the Commonwealth made no attempt to rebut the presumption by introducing evidence of criminal capacity. In fact, the only evidence available on this issue was a neuropsychological report in the file indicating that appellant suffered from 'borderline retardation.' Counsel for the prosecution made only a cursory argument on the issue of capacity, alluding to the fact that appellant said she was going into the house to get her mother, but instead got a knife, as an indication of an awareness of guilt. This implication . . . is far from sufficient to rebut the presumption . . . ." Commonwealth v. Durham, 255 Pa.Super. 539, 389 A.2d 108 (1978). In dissent it was argued that the common law presumptions affecting the capacity of children to commit crime do not apply to juvenile proceedings to determine delinquency.

2. How strong must the evidence to rebut incompetency be? In Little v. Arkansas, 261 Ark. 859, 554 S.W.2d 312 (1977), the court said that "the burden is on the prosecution to clearly establish his capacity of appreciating the nature of his acts, but the strength of the presumption varies with the actual age of the child and decreases as the upper limit is reached."

3. The rebuttable presumption of incapacity between the ages of 7 and 14 which the common law observed must be contrasted with the conclusive presumption of incapacity under the age of 14 when the act involved is rape. In Foster v. Commonwealth, 96 Va. 306, 31 S.E. 503 (1898), the court held that a boy under 14 is conclusively presumed to be incapable of rape, whatever the real facts may be. For that reason, evidence to rebut the presumption is inadmissible.

4. In I.R. v. People, 171 Colo. 54, 464 P.2d 296 (1970), the Colorado Supreme Court rejected the argument that vehicular homicide is a violation of the traffic laws and therefore excluded from the jurisdiction of the Juvenile Court.

5. In Commonwealth v. Clark, 222 Pa.Super. 1, 292 A.2d 488 (1972), the defendant was convicted of committing sodomy upon a five-year old child. A statute provided that a person convicted of sodomy could be sentenced to twice the maximum prescribed term if a minor was involved as either principal, accomplice, accessory, or associate. In holding that the five-year old was not an "associate" within the meaning of the statute, the court held defendant could not be sentenced to the doubled term. "Associate" implies a consenting partner, the court suggested, and since a child of that age is incapable of giving consent or of being criminally responsible, the child would be treated as a victim rather than as an associate.

6. Many jurisdictions specify the minimum age for criminal responsibility by statute. A number of states give concurrent jurisdiction to juvenile courts and criminal courts over acts committed by children over the minimum age of capacity but below the age of 17 or 18.

In 1982 the Illinois legislature amended its Juvenile Court Act to provide that any minor 15 years or older who is charged with murder or other specified offenses is automatically subject to prosecution in the criminal court as though he were an adult. Ill.Rev.Stats., ch. 37, § 702–7(6)(a). In 1986, § 702–7(3) was amended to permit transfer of a juvenile 13 years or older to the criminal court for prosecution as an adult.

C. INTOXICATION

PEOPLE v. GUILLETT

Supreme Court of Michigan, 1955.
342 Mich. 1, 69 N.W.2d 140.

BUTZEL, JUSTICE. Lawrence Guillett was informed against for assault with intent to commit rape. He pleaded not guilty and was tried in circuit court where a jury found him guilty of the crime charged. Appellant *in propria persona* has appealed from his conviction on various grounds. The complainant had agreed to spend an evening with him. He, with two other friends, called for her and they visited a tavern where each of them consumed three glasses of beer. She and appellant then went to the home of the latter's parents, and later purchased a bottle of wine out of which she took one glass which she only partially consumed while he apparently finished the bottle. They sat together on a davenport and he made indecent advances which she repulsed. After she arose he then struck her, knocked her down and continued his attempt to commit rape. During a struggle she grabbed a telephone receiver and struck him so many blows on the head that he required hospitalization. She then escaped, ran across the road and the police and an ambulance were summoned. Appellant's mother testified that he had been drinking for several days and that he had come home drunk earlier that day, but she left him to go to work shortly after 3 p.m. His father said that he appeared "dozy."

In view of the testimony the trial judge in his charge to the jury stated:

"Now, there has been injected here to a great extent, the question of intoxication. I will give you an instruction on that.

"It is a well settled law in this state that voluntary drunkenness is not a defense to crime. A man who puts himself in a position to have no control over his actions must be held to intend the consequences. The safety of the community requires this rule. Intoxication is so easily counterfeited, and, when real, is so often resorted to as a means of nerving a person up to the commission of some deliberate act and withal is so inexcusable in itself that the law has never recognized it as an excuse for crime.

"In the case of an offense such as the one charged, committed during a period of intoxication, the law presumes the defendant to have intended the obscuration and perversion of his faculties which followed his voluntary intoxication. He must be held to have purposely blinded his moral perception and set his will free from the control of reason—to have suppressed the guards and invited the mutiny; and should therefore be held responsible as well for the vicious excesses of the will thus set free as for the acts done by its prompting."

Defendant has assigned error on the ground that the charge as given was incomplete and therefore misleading because it failed to state that intoxication may serve to negative the existence of the intent required for conviction of the crime charged.

We must conclude that the charge was erroneous. In Roberts v. People, 19 Mich. 401, 418, 420, the defendant was convicted of assault with intent to commit murder. On appeal, after considering the necessity for finding intent in fact, or specific intent, Justice Christiancy discussed the issue of whether drunkenness might negative the existence of that intent. He concluded:

> "In determining the question whether the assault was committed with the intent charged, it was therefore material to inquire whether the defendant's mental faculties were so far overcome by the effect of intoxication, as to render him incapable of entertaining the intent. And, for this purpose, it was the right and the duty of the jury—as upon the question of intent of which this forms a part—to take into consideration the nature and the circumstances of the assault, the actions, conduct and demeanor of the defendant, and his declaration before, at the time, and after the assault; and especially to consider the nature of the intent, and what degree of mental capacity was necessary to enable him to entertain the simple intent to kill, under the circumstances of this case—or which is the same thing, how far the mental faculties must be obscured by intoxication to render him incapable of entertaining that particular intent. . . .

> "But the Circuit Court held, in effect that no extent of intoxication could have the effect to disprove the intent; treating the intent as an inference of law for the Court, rather than a question of fact for the jury. In this we think there was error."

. . . A consideration of later Michigan authority reveals that Roberts v. People, supra, remains as the most eloquent and correct statement of law on the subject. Thus in People v. Walker, 38 Mich. 156, Judge Cooley wrote an opinion reversing a conviction of larceny stating:

> "While it is true that drunkenness cannot excuse crime, it is equally true that when a certain intent is a necessary element in a crime, the crime cannot have been committed when the intent did not exist. In larceny the crime does not consist in the wrongful taking of the property, for that might be a mere trespass; but it consists in the wrongful taking with felonious intent; and if the defendant, for any reason whatever, indulged no such intent, the crime cannot have been com-

mitted. This was fully explained by Mr. Justice Christiancy in Roberts v. People, 19 Mich. 401, and is familiar law."

. . . It is to be noted that we are here concerned with intoxication insofar as it might negative the requisite intent, as distinguished from insanity or delirium tremens brought on by intoxication, the latter, if present, being a complete excuse rather than a partial one as here. . . .

It is important in this decision to emphasize that intoxication may only negative the existence of *specific intent*. Examination of the cases reveals that where the rule was applied it was done so in cases where the crime charged also involved a specific intent. Apparently the trial judge in the instant case did not realize this. For the most part his charge was in the exact words of Justice Cooley in People v. Garbutt, 17 Mich. 9. However, it should have been noted that the crime involved in that case was murder, not a specific intent crime, or as was said in Roberts v. People, supra, 19 Mich. at page 417:

> "The correctness of the principle laid down by this Court in People v. Garbutt (17 Mich. 9–19), is not denied; that 'a man who voluntarily puts himself into a condition to have no control of his actions, must be held to intend the consequences.' But this, it is insisted, includes only the consequences which do actually ensue—the crime actually committed; and not in this case the intent charged, if the defendant was at the time incapable of entertaining it, and did not in fact entertain it."

> "We think this reasoning is entirely sound, and it is well supported by authority."

The crime of assault with intent to rape involves a specific intent. . . . The charge was therefore erroneous. . . .

The error here is one of omission. The charge is one of half-truth and misleading. The effect of the instruction given in this case was to instruct the jury that any and all evidence of intoxication had absolutely no bearing on appellant's guilt of the crime charged. It has been said that a charge stating some elements of a crime but omitting others "would have a natural tendency to cause a jury to believe that those stated were exclusive." . . . It was therefore prejudicial to the appellant. It was reversible error. . . .

NOTES

1. Reconsider here the case of Powell v. Texas, 392 U.S. 514, 88 S.Ct. 2145 (1968), discussed, supra, in Note 4 on page 377. Also consider the following case: Defendant was convicted of murder in the first degree as a result of having beaten his wife to death with a hammer. The trial court charged the jury that even though defendant had been intoxicated and hence easily provoked, the crime would not be manslaughter unless the provocation was sufficient to arouse "sudden passion" in a reasonable, sober man. In affirming

the conviction and approving the charge of the trial court, the Court of Appeals, in Bishop v. United States, 107 F.2d 297 (D.C.Cir.1939), stated:

> "It is only necessary to show that the killing was committed in 'heat of passion' upon sufficient provocation. The test of sufficiency of such provocation is that which would cause an ordinary man, a reasonable man, or an average man, to become so aroused. Such a man can only mean a 'sober man,' and the provocation must be sufficient to create 'heat of passion' in a reasonable, sober man. . . . If a defendant is intoxicated, there is no requirement that provocation for 'heat of passion' be greater than that which would arouse a reasonable, sober man to act. Certainly, if there be intoxication, a lesser provocation than that which would create 'heat of passion' in a reasonable, sober man cannot be allowed, otherwise, a premium would be granted for voluntary intoxication. The standard of provocation that may create the 'heat of passion' reducing murder to manslaughter is the same for all men, whether drunk or sober. We, therefore, conclude that the court correctly defined manslaughter and the proper standard to be applied when intoxication is pleaded as a defense."

For a case rejecting the claim that voluntary intoxication could negate the intent for voluntary manslaughter, see Commonwealth v. Bridge, 495 Pa. 568, 435 A.2d 151 (1981).

To the same effect with respect to the standard to be applied in considering a plea of self defense by one who killed another while allegedly intoxicated, see Springfield v. State, 96 Ala. 81, 11 So. 250 (1892), where the defendant's conviction of second degree murder was affirmed.

2. Some states have changed their statutes to eliminate the defense of voluntary intoxication even to rebut specific intent. See Missouri Rev.Stat. § 562.076 (As amended, 1983):

> "1. A person who is in an intoxicated or drugged condition whether from alcohol, drugs or other substance, is criminally responsible for conduct unless such condition is involuntarily produced and deprived him of the capacity to know or appreciate the nature, quality or wrongfulness of his conduct.
>
> "2. The defendant shall have the burden of injecting the issue of intoxicated or drugged condition."

Prior to 1979, Missouri followed the general rule as exemplified in the *Guillett* case. The uprooting of this long-entrenched rule was held not to be unconstitutional in Hindman v. Wyrick, 531 F.Supp. 1103 (W.D.Mo.1982), affirmed 702 F.2d 148 (8th Cir.1983).

In a state that follows the common law, evidence of intoxication is admissible to show that the defendant lacked the criminal intent required for the crime charged. Then, a statute is passed recognizing self-induced intoxication as a defense, but this statute is thereafter amended to eliminate this defense. Does this return the jurisdiction to the common law, or does it eliminate the defense of voluntary intoxication altogether? See White v. State, 290 Ark. 130, 717 S.W.2d 784 (1986).

Virginia also rejects voluntary intoxication as a defense even as to specific intent crimes, but makes an exception as to first degree murder where it appears that the accused was too drunk to be capable of the required deliberation or premeditation. Chittum v. Commonwealth, 211 Va. 12, 174 S.E.2d 779 (1970).

The view that voluntary intoxication is a defense only to specific intent crimes and not for general intent crimes, was criticized in State v. Stasio, 78 N.J. 467, 396 A.2d 1129 (1979), which rejected the intoxication defense where defendant was charged with assault with intent to rob, a specific intent crime.

3. Is voluntary defense an affirmative defense as to crimes requiring specific intent, or is it merely a way of showing that the defendant was incapable of forming the specific intent necessary for the crime charged? What is the difference, if any?

4. A number of states equate acting under the influence of drugs to intoxication, as was seen in the Missouri statute in Note 2. Consider also the following provision of the Illinois Criminal Code (S.H.A. ch. 38) § 6–3:

"A person who is in an intoxicated or drugged condition is criminally responsible for conduct unless such condition either:

"(a) Negatives the existence of a mental state which is an element of the offense; or

"(b) Is involuntarily produced and deprives him of substantial capacity either to appreciate the criminality of his conduct or to conform his conduct to the requirements of law."

For a perceptive student article on the subject, see Burke, "The Defense of Voluntary Intoxication: Now You See It, Now You Don't," 19 Indiana L.Rev. 147 (1986). On the topic generally, see also, Anno., Drug Addiction as Defense, 73 A.L.R.3d 16, at pp. 79–84; Effect of Voluntary Drug Intoxication Upon Criminal Responsibility, 73 A.L.R.3d 98.

5. Involuntary intoxication is equated frequently to mental disease, or uses at least the same standards. See Note 3, supra, dealing with the defense according to the Illinois Criminal Code. Holding that involuntary intoxication is a defense to any criminal charge, see State v. Rice, 379 A.2d 140 (Me.1977). See also, Anno., When Intoxication Deemed Involuntary So As To Constitute A Defense to Criminal Charge, 73 A.L.R.3d 195.

D.　DIMINISHED RESPONSIBILITY

FISHER v. UNITED STATES

Supreme Court of the United States, 1946.
328 U.S. 463, 66 S.Ct. 1318.

MR. JUSTICE REED delivered the opinion of the Court.

This writ of certiorari brings here for review the sentence of death imposed upon petitioner by the District Court of the United States for the District of Columbia after a verdict of guilty on the first count of an indictment which charged petitioner with killing by choking and strangling Catherine Cooper Reardon, with deliberate and premeditated malice. The United States Court of Appeals for the District of Columbia affirmed the judgment and sentence of the District Court.

The errors presented by the petition for certiorari and urged at our bar were, in substance, that the trial court refused to instruct the jurors that they should consider the evidence of the accused's psychopathic aggressive tendencies, low emotional response and borderline mental deficiency to determine whether he was guilty of murder in the first or in the second degree. The aggregate of these factors admittedly was not enough to support a finding of not guilty by reason of insanity. Deliberation and premeditation are necessary elements of first degree murder. . . .

The homicide took place in the library building on the grounds of the Cathedral of Saint Peter and Saint Paul, Washington, D.C., between eight and nine o'clock, a.m., on March 1, 1944. The victim was the librarian. She had complained to the verger a few days before about petitioner's care of the premises. The petitioner was the janitor. The verger had told him of the complaint. Miss Reardon and Fisher were alone in the library at the time of the homicide. The petitioner testified that Miss Reardon was killed by him immediately following insulting words from her over his care of the premises. After slapping her impulsively, petitioner ran up a flight of steps to reach an exit on a higher level but turned back down, after seizing a convenient stick of firewood, to stop her screaming. He struck her with the stick and when it broke choked her to silence. He then dragged her to a lavatory and left the body to clean up some spots of blood on the floor outside. While Fisher was doing this cleaning up, the victim "started hollering again." Fisher then took out his knife and stuck her in the throat. She was silent. After that he dragged her body down into an adjoining pump pit, where it was found the next morning. The above facts made up petitioner's story to the jury of the killing. . . .

The effort of the defense is to show that the murder was not deliberate and premeditated; that it was not first but second degree murder. A reading of petitioner's own testimony, summarized above, shows clearly to us that there was sufficient evidence to support a verdict of murder in the first degree, if petitioner was a normal man in his mental and emotional characteristics. . . . But the defense takes the position that the petitioner is fairly entitled to be judged as to deliberation and premeditation, not by a theoretical normality but by his own personal traits. In view of the status of the defense of partial responsibility in the District and the nation no contention is or could be made of the denial of due process. It is the contention of the defense that the mental and emotional qualities of petitioner were of such a level at the time of the crime that he was incapable of deliberation and premeditation although he was then sane in the usual legal sense. He knew right from wrong. . . . His will was capable of controlling his impulses. . . . Testimony of psychiatrists to support petitioner's contention was introduced. An instruction charging the jury to consider the personality of the petitioner in determining intent, premeditation and deliberation was sought and refused.

From the evidence of the psychiatrists for the defense, the jury might have concluded the petitioner was mentally somewhat below the average with minor stigma of mental subnormalcy. An expert testified that he was a psychopathic personality of a predominantly aggressive type. There was evidence that petitioner was unable by reason of a deranged mental condition to resist the impulse to kill Miss Reardon. All evidence offered by the defense was accepted by the trial court. The prosecution had competent evidence that petitioner was capable of understanding the nature and quality of his acts. Instructions in the usual form were given by the court submitting to the jury the issues of insanity, irresistible impulse, malice, deliberation and premeditation. Under these instructions . . . the jury could have determined from the evidence that the homicide was not the result of premeditation and deliberation. . . .

The error claimed by the petitioner is limited to the refusal of one instruction. The jury might not have reached the result it did if the theory of partial responsibility for his acts which the petitioner urges had been submitted. Petitioner sought an instruction from the trial court which would permit the jury to weigh the evidence of his mental deficiencies, which were short of insanity in the legal sense, in determining the fact of and the accused's capacity for premeditation and deliberation. . . .

Petitioner urges forcefully that mental deficiency which does not show legal irresponsibility should be declared by this Court to be a relevant factor in determining whether an accused is guilty of murder in the first or second degree, upon which an instruction should be given, as requested. It is pointed out that the courts of certain states have adopted this theory. Others have rejected it. It is urged, also, that since evidence of intoxication to a state where one guilty of the crime of murder may not be capable of deliberate premeditation requires in the District of Columbia an instruction to that effect . . . courts from this must deduce that disease and congenital defects, for which the accused may not be responsible, may also reduce the crime of murder from first to second degree. This Court reversed the Supreme Court of the Territory of Utah for failure to give a partial responsibility charge upon evidence of drunkenness in language which has been said to be broad enough to cover mental deficiency. . . . It should be noted, however, that the Territory of Utah had a statute specifically establishing such a rule.

No one doubts that there are more possible classifications of mentality than the sane and the insane. . . . Criminologists and psychologists have weighed the advantages and disadvantages of the adoption of the theory of partial responsibility as a basis of the jury's determination of the degree of crime of which a mentally deficient defendant may be guilty. Congress took a forward step in defining the degrees of murder so that only those guilty of deliberate and premeditated malice could be convicted of the first degree. It may be that psychiatry has now reached a position of certainty in its diagnosis and prognosis which will induce Congress to enact the rule of responsibility for crime for which petitioner contends. For this Court to force the District of Columbia to adopt such a requirement for criminal trials would involve a fundamental change in the common law theory of responsibility.

We express no opinion upon whether the theory for which petitioner contends should or should not be made the law of the District of Columbia. Such a radical departure from common law concepts is more properly a subject for the exercise of legislative power or at least for the discretion of the courts of the District. . . .

Affirmed.

MR. JUSTICE FRANKFURTER, dissenting.

. . . According to the more enlightened rule appellate courts may review the facts in a capital case. . . . Were such the scope of our review of death sentences, I should think it would be hard to escape what follows as the most persuasive reading of the record. . . .

The evidence in its entirety hardly provides a basis for a finding of premeditation. He struck Miss Reardon when she called him "black nigger." He kept on when her screaming frightened him. He did not know he had killed her. There is not the slightest basis for finding a motive for the killing prior to her use of the offensive phrase. Fisher, to be sure, had Miss Reardon's ring in his possession. But it came off in his hand while he was dragging her, and he put it away when he reached home to conceal its possession from his wife. He did not run away and he cleaned up the blood "because [he] did not want to leave the library dirty, leave awful spots on the floor, [he] wanted to clean them up." He treated the spots on the floor not as evidence of crime but as part of his job to keep the library clean. Fisher was curiously unconnected with the deed, unaware of what he had done. His was a very low grade mentality, unable to realize the direction of his action and its meaning. His whole behavior seems that of a man of primitive emotions reacting to the sudden stimulus of insult and proceeding from that point without purpose or design. Premeditation implies purpose and purpose is excluded by instantaneous action. Fisher's response was an instinctive response to provocation, and premeditation means nothing unless it precludes the notion of an instinctive and uncalculated reaction to stimulus. Accordingly, if existing practice authorized us to review the facts in a capital case I should be compelled to find that the ingredients of murder in the first detree were here lacking. I would have to find that the necessary premeditation and deliberation for the infliction of a death sentence were wanting, as did the New York Court of Appeals in a case of singularly striking similarity. . . .

As I have already indicated, I do not believe that the facts warrant a finding of premeditation. But, in any event, the justification for finding first-degree murder premeditation was so tenuous that the jury ought not to have been left to founder and flounder within the dark emptiness of legal jargon. The instructions to the jury on the vital issue of premeditation consisted of threadbare generalities, a jumble of empty abstractions equally suitable for any other charge of murder with none of the elements that are distinctive about this case, mingled with talk about mental disease. What the jury got was devoid of clear guidance and illumination. Inadequate direction to a jury may be as fatal as misdirection. . . .

The judgment should be reversed and a new trial granted.

MR. JUSTICE MURPHY, dissenting.

. . . The existence of general mental impairment, or partial insanity, is a scientifically established fact. There is no absolute or clear-cut dichotomous division of the inhabitants of this world into the sane and the insane. "Between the two extremes of 'sanity' and 'insanity' lies every shade of disordered or deficient mental condition, grading imperceptibly one into another." . . .

More precisely, there are persons who, while not totally insane, possess such low mental powers as to be incapable of the deliberation and premeditation requisite to statutory first degree murder. Yet under the rule adopted by the court below, the jury must either condemn such persons to death on the false premise that they possess the mental requirements of a first degree murderer or free them completely from criminal responsibility and turn them loose among society. The jury is forbidden to find them guilty of a lesser degree of murder by reason of their generally weakened or disordered intellect.

Common sense and logic recoil at such a rule. And it is difficult to marshal support for it from civilized concepts of justice or from the necessity of protecting society. When a man's life or liberty is at stake he should be adjudged according to his personal culpability as well as by the objective seriousness of his crime. That elementary principle of justice is applied to those who kill while intoxicated or in the heat of passion; if such a condition destroys their deliberation and premeditation the jury may properly consider that fact and convict them of a lesser degree of murder. No different principle should be utilized in the case of those whose mental deficiency is of a more permanent character. Society, moreover, is ill-protected by a rule which encourages a jury to acquit a partially insane person with an appealing case simply because his mental defects cannot be considered in reducing the degree of guilt.

It is undeniably difficult, as the Government points out, to determine with any high degree of certainty whether a defendant has a general mental impairment and whether such a disorder renders him incapable of the requisite deliberation and premeditation. The difficulty springs primarily from the present limited scope of medical and psychiatric knowledge of mental disease. But this knowledge is ever increasing. And juries constantly must judge the baffling psychological factors of deliberation and premeditation, Congress having entrusted the ascertainment of those factors to the good sense of juries. It seems senseless to shut the door on the assistance which medicine and psychiatry can give in regard to these matters, however inexact and incomplete that assistance may presently be. Precluding the consideration of mental deficiency only makes the jury's decision on deliberation and premeditation less intelligent and trustworthy.

It is also said that the proposed rule would require a revolutionary change in criminal procedure in the District of Columbia and that this Court should therefore leave the matter to local courts or to Congress. I cannot agree. Congress has already spoken by making the distinction between first and second degree murder turn upon the existence of deliberation and premeditation. It is the duty of the courts below to fashion rules to permit the jury to utilize all relevant evidence directed toward those factors. But when the courts below adopt rules which substantially impair the jury's function in this respect, this Court should exercise its recognized prerogative.

If, as a result, new rules of evidence or new modes of treatment for the partly defective must be devised, our system of criminal jurisprudence will be that much further enlightened. Such progress clearly outweighs any temporary dislocation of settled modes of procedure.

Only by integrating scientific advancements with our ideals of justice can law remain a part of the living fiber of our civilization.

MR. JUSTICE FRANKFURTER and MR. JUSTICE RUTLEDGE join in this dissent.

MR. JUSTICE RUTLEDGE, dissenting.

. . . Congress introduced the requirements of premeditation and deliberation into the District of Columbia Code, . . . I do not think it intended by doing so to change the preexisting law only in cases of intoxication. Hence, I cannot assent to the view that the instructions given to the jury were adequate on this phase of the case. I think the defendent was entitled to the requested instruction which was refused or one of similar import. . . .

NOTES

1. In United States v. Brawner, 471 F.2d 969 (D.C.Cir. 1972), a unanimous Court of Appeals for the District of Columbia decided to overrule its decision in Fisher v. United States, 80 U.S.App.D.C. 96, 149 F.2d 28 (1945), which the United States Supreme Court had affirmed in the preceding case. Mr. Justice Reed's opinion of the Supreme Court had suggested that the adoption of the concept of diminished responsibility was "more properly a subject for the exercise of legislative power or at least for the discretion of the courts of the District". In the *Brawner* decision, the Court of Appeals overturned the *Fisher* approach and made it clear that in trials commencing after the date of the opinion a defendant would be permitted to introduce psychiatric and other expert testimony to negative specific intent, even when there is no defense of insanity, provided "the judge determines that the testimony is grounded in sufficient scientific support, and would aid the jury in reaching a decision on the ultimate issues".

The California Supreme Court adopted the diminished responsibility concept in People v. Wolff, 61 Cal.2d 795, 40 Cal.Rptr. 271, 394 P.2d 959 (1964). But see, People v. Kitt, 83 Cal.App.3d 834, 148 Cal.Rptr. 447 (1978), the jury had rejected evidence that defendant had any substantially reduced mental capacity caused by mental illness because of epilepsy, by convicting him for murder.

For comments on the *Wolff* case, see, "Keeping Wolff From the Door: California's Diminished Capacity Concept," 60 Cal.L.Rev. 1641 (1972); "Diminished Capacity: Its Potential Effect in California," 3 Loyola L.A.L.Rev. 153 (1970).

In 1982, however, California abolished the defense of diminished capacity by statute. Cal.Pen.Code sec. 25 also now places the burden of proof of insanity on the defendant by a preponderance of the evidence. Under the new provision, evidence of diminished capacity may still be considered on the issue of disposition and sentencing. Section 25(b) overrules People v. Drew, 22 Cal.3d 333, 149 Cal.Rptr. 275, 583 P.2d 1318 (1978) which had adopted the A.L.I. test for insanity and restores the traditional M'Naghten rule to California law.

While evidence of diminished responsibility has been accepted in some states other than California, the recognition given to the defense is rather spotty and less than wholehearted. See, 22 A.L.R.3d 1228 for an extensive collection of cases of where the defense has been used in mitigation of punishment.

Also rejecting the defense of diminished capacity is Johnson v. State, 292 Md. 405, 439 A.2d 542 (1982), wherein the court stated: "We here affirm our position that the concepts of both diminished capacity and insanity involve a moral choice by the community to withhold a finding of responsibility and its consequence of punishment, and on this basis are indistinguishable. Accordingly, because the legislature, reflecting community morals, has, by its definition of criminal insanity has already determined which states of mental disorder ought to relieve one from criminal responsibility, this court is without authority to impose our views in this regard even if they differed."

2. In United States v. Cebian, 774 F.2d 446 (11th Cir.1985), the drug defendant sought to show that severe abuse by her husband had made her a victim of post-traumatic stress disorder. She sought to have the jury instructed that they should determine whether "at the time when the alleged crime was committed the Defendant was suffering from some abnormal mental or physical condition which prevented her from forming the specific intent which is the essential element of the crime with which she is charged." The trial judge refused to give the instruction. The Court of Appeals affirmed, stating that the "diminished capacity" defense based on "post traumatic stress disorder" (PTSD) is just a new way of arguing lack of specific intent. That idea was adequately conveyed, said the court, by the judge's other instruction defining specific intent.

3. In 1984, Professor Stephen Morse published an article on the subject in which he makes the point that two variants of the so-called "diminished capacity" may be observed in the cases: (1) the "mens rea variant" which is not really a defense at all but one which, through the use of evidence of a defendant's mental condition, seeks to create a reasonable doubt in the minds of the jurors as to whether the statutorily required mens rea element of the crime is present; and (2), the "true" diminished capacity, which he called the defense of "partial responsibility," where the actor commits the prohibited act with the required mental state but is adjudged guilty of a lesser crime because of mental or emotional impairment short of insanity, that quantitatively reduces his moral responsibility. Professor Morse advocates abolishing this second branch

of the diminished capacity concept. See Morse, "Undiminished Confusion in Diminished Capacity," 75 J.Crim.L. & Criminology 1 (1984).

Professor Joshua Dressler responded to this article by suggesting that his concept of justice was of a legal system "that does not lose sight of the occasional presence of mitigating psychological factor," by still expressing the condemnation of society of crime, but by also recognizing as a legitimate excuse the "partial responsibility" form of diminished capacity. See Dressler, "Reaffirming the Moral Legitimacy of the Doctrine of Diminished Capacity: A Brief Reply To Professor Morse," 75 J.Crim.L. & Criminology 953 (1984).

4. With respect to the concept of diminished responsibility, consider the following provisions of the English Homicide Act of 1957 (5 and 6 Eliz. 2, Ch. 11) (3 Halsbury's Statutes of England (3d ed. 1967) 459:

(1) Where a person kills or is a party to the killing of another, he shall not be convicted of murder if he was suffering from such abnormality of mind (whether arising from a condition of arrested or retarded development of mind or any inherent causes or induced by disease or injury) as substantially impaired his mental responsibility for his acts and omissions in doing or being a party to the killing.

(2) On a charge of murder, it shall be for the defense to prove that the person charged is by virtue of this section not liable to be convicted of murder.

(3) A person who but for this section would be liable, whether as principal or accessory, to be convicted of murder shall be liable instead to be convicted of manslaughter.

(4) The fact that one party to a killing is by virtue of this section not liable to be convicted of murder shall not affect the question whether the killing amounted to murder in the case of any other party to it.

[The foregoing portions of the 1957 Homicide Act have not been affected by the Murder Act of 1965.]

Consider the following comment on the above provision, by Hughes, The English Homicide Act of 1957, 49 J.Crim.L., C. & P.S. 521 (1959), at p. 526.

"The Homicide Act does not at all abrogate the M'Naghten Rules. The Rules are preserved, so that insanity is as much a defense as before the Act. What the Act does, however, is to introduce a *supplementary* doctrine of 'diminished responsibility.' Under this doctrine, a 'substantially impaired' mind (less than 'insanity' under the M'Naghten Rules) affords a killer a reduction of his offense from murder to manslaughter. The doctrine is professedly borrowed from Scottish law which has applied it since the middle of the nineteenth century."

In R. v. Byrne, 3 W.L.R. 440 [1960] All E.R. 734, in which the defendant was charged with murder (by strangulation and mutilation), it was held that a sexual psychopath who suffers from violent perverted sexual desires is entitled to the defense of diminished responsibility. [Compare R. v. Lloyd [1966] 1 All E.R. 107.] In commenting upon the Byrne case Professor Glanville Williams said: "If such perverted sexual aggression is covered, it seems difficult to exclude psychopathic aggression of a nonsexual character, so that the way seems now to be open for all psychopaths to be given the benefit of the section." From Medicine, Science and the Law (Oct. 1960) at p. 42. The same author has commented upon the diminished responsibility provision as follows, in 10 Howard Journal 313 (1961):

> "There are, I think, two objections to using the defence of diminished responsibility to do the work that ought to be done by the defence of insanity. In the first place, there is some danger that the defendant who is sentenced to prison on the defence of diminished responsibility is not transferred to Broadmoor or other mental hospital. Technically, the Commissioners need not transfer a prisoner unless he is found to be insane in prison.
>
> "In the second place, judges occasionally overlook the need for protection to the public, and sentence an unstable person who has already killed to a relatively short term. Even where a long term is given, it sometimes seems to be the wrong outcome where the evidence is of a confusional state amounting to insanity."

Williams reaches the following conclusion with respect to the application of the diminished responsibility provision:

> ". . . the defence of diminished responsibility has worked both badly and well. . . . It should not have been allowed to supercede the insanity defence to the extent that it has done; but it has ameliorated the law of murder where the defendant is not insane. The section has been benevolently stretched by the courts, yet its terms are not well designed to cover cases of mercy-killing and family suicide-murder. It would be an improvement if the requirement of mental abnormality were deleted from the section, leaving a discretion to reduce the conviction to manslaughter in all cases where culpability is substantially diminished."

E. OTHER NON–CONTROLLABLE FACTORS

1. XYY CHROMOSOMAL DEFECT

"The XYY chromosomal defect found in some members of the human population has recently been urged as a defense to criminal responsibility. The XYY theory is that certain individuals, due to their body chemistry, are unable to control their cognitive and/or volitional functions and, hence, should not be held responsible for their unlawful acts.

"Biologically speaking, the normal human cell is made up of 46 chromosomes, comprised of 22 pairs of autosomal chromosomes (22 Xs and 22 Ys), plus the 45th and 46th chromosomes which are either X or Y sex chromosomes. XX is female and XY is male. The X chromosome is thought by some scientists to be responsible for the passive attitude in the personality makeup, while the Y chromosome is believed to control the aggressive potential although other scientists dismiss this theory as a chauvinistic gratuity unfounded in medical science. When a male has an extra Y chromosome constituting an XYY chromosomal makeup, it is theorized that he may become intensely aggressive, display anti-social behavior, and also have a relatively low intelligence. It is also theorized he may be unable to control his behavior.

"To date, there is an absence of any reliable scientific proof that the XYY individual will develop any criminal or anti-social behavior. Research has been hindered by virtue of the fact that there is an inadequate cross-section of XYYs in the general population who are available for testing. The majority of research, thus far, has been done on prison inmates. It is possible that the XYY concept will develop to the point where it is generally accepted by the scientific community. . . ." [1]

NOTES

1. People v. Tanner, 13 Cal.App.3d 596, 91 Cal.Rptr. 656 (1970) is an example of one of the first judicial responses in this country to the problem presented by the XYY individual to traditional theories of criminal responsibility. *Tanner* held that a trial judge did not abuse his discretion in finding the evidence insufficient to establish the legal insanity of an XYY individual charged with assault with intent to murder in a state where the M'Naghten "right-wrong" test had to be met in order to establish legal insanity.

The defendant's witnesses included two geneticists who presented lengthy and complex testimony and documentary evidence concerning XYY syndrome. This evidence indicated that XYY individuals exhibit aggressive behavior as a result of their chromosomal abnormality. The court found such evidence deficient in three principal respects: First, that studies of XYY individuals were few, rudimentary in scope, and inconclusive because they indicated only that aggressive behavior may be one manifestation of XYY syndrome, but not that all XYY individuals were by nature involuntarily aggressive; *Second,* that the experts could not demonstrate a causal relationship between the assault in question and the defendant's chromosomal abnormality; and *Third,* that the experts did not testify that the possession of an extra Y chromosome results in legal insanity under the state's version of the M'Naghten rule. See also Millard v. State, 8 Md.App. 419, 261 A.2d 227 (1970); People v. Yukl, 83 Misc.2d 364, 372 N.Y.S.2d 313 (1975); and State v. Roberts, 14 Wash.App. 727, 544 P.2d 754 (1976).

2. For further discussion of criminal responsibility and the XYY syndrome see Annotation 42 A.L.R.3d 1414 (1972) and Burke, "The XYY Syndrome: Genetics, Behavior and the Law", 46 Denver L.J. 261 (1969); Farrell, "The XYY Syndrome in Criminal Law: An Introduction," 44 St. John's L.Rev. 217 (1969); Housley, "Criminal Law: The XYY Chromosome Complement and Criminal Conduct," 22 Okla.L.Rev. 287 (1969); Note, "The XYY Chromosomal Abnormality: Use and Misuse in the Legal Process," 9 Harv.J.Legis. 469 (1972).

---

1. The above description of the XYY chromosomal defect is from Moenssens & Inbau, Scientific Evidence in Criminal Cases, 2d ed. 1978, at § 3.03(6).

2. AUTOMATISM

FULCHER v. STATE

Supreme Court of Wyoming, 1981.
633 P.2d 142.

BROWN, JUSTICE. . . .

On November 17, 1979, the appellant consumed seven or eight shots of whiskey over a period of four hours in a Torrington bar, and had previously had a drink at home.

Appellant claims he got in a fight in the bar restroom, then left the bar to find a friend. According to his testimony, the last thing he remembers until awakening in jail, is going out of the door at the bar.

Appellant and his friend were found lying in the alley behind the bar by a police office who noted abrasions on their fists and faces. Appellant and his friend swore, were uncooperative, and combative. They were subsequently booked for public intoxication and disturbing the peace. During booking appellant continued to swear, and said he and his friend were jumped by a "bunch of Mexicans." Although his speech was slurred, he was able to verbally count his money, roughly $500 to $600 in increments of $20, and was able to walk to his cell without assistance.

Appellant was placed in a cell with one Martin Hernandez who was lying unconscious on the floor of the cell. After the jailer left the cell, he heard something that sounded like someone being kicked. He ran back to the cell and saw appellant standing by Hernandez. When the jailer started to leave again, the kicking sound resumed, and he observed appellant kicking and stomping on Hernandez's head. Appellant told the officer Hernandez had fallen out of bed. Hernandez was bleeding profusely and was taken to the hospital for some 52 stitches in his head and mouth. He had lost two or three teeth as a result of the kicking.

Appellant was released later in the day, November 18, 1979, and went home. He went back to Torrington on November 22, 1979, to see a doctor. Appellant testified that the doctor diagnosed he had a concussion, although there is no evidence in the record of medical treatment.

At his arraignment in district court, appellant first entered a plea of "not guilty by reason of temporary mental illness." Upon being advised by the trial judge that he would have to be committed for examination pursuant to § 7–11–304, W.S.1977, he withdrew that plea and entered a plea of not guilty.

In preparation for trial, appellant was examined by Dr. Breck LeBegue a forensic psychiatrist. The doctor reviewed the police report and conducted a number of tests.

At the trial Dr. LeBegue testified that in his expert medical opinion appellant suffered brain injury and was in a state of traumatic automatism at the time of his attack on Hernandez. Dr. LeBegue defined traumatic automatism as the state of mind in which a person does not have conscious and willful control over his actions, and lacks the ability to be aware of and to perceive his external environment. Dr. LeBegue further testified that another possible symptom is an inability to remember what occurred while in a state of traumatic automatism.

Dr. LeBegue was unable to state positively whether or not appellant had the requisite mental state for aggravated assault and battery, but thought appellant did not because of his altered state of mind. He could not state, however, that the character of an act is devoid of criminal intent because of mind alteration.

* * *

I

We hold that the trial court properly received and considered evidence of unconsciousness absent a plea of "not guilty by reason of mental illness or deficiency."

The defense of unconsciousness perhaps should be more precisely denominated as the defense of automatism. Automatism is the state of a person who, though capable of action, is not conscious of what he is doing. While in an automatistic state, an individual performs complex actions without an exercise of will. Because these actions are performed in a state of unconsciousness, they are involuntary. Automatistic behavior may be followed by complete or partial inability to recall the actions performed while unconscious. Thus, a person who acts automatically does so without intent, exercise of free will, or knowledge of the act.

Automatism may be caused by an abnormal condition of the mind capable of being designated a mental illness or deficiency. Automatism may also be manifest in a person with a perfectly healthy mind. In this opinion we are only concerned with the defense of automatism occurring in a person with a healthy mind. To further narrow the issue to be decided in this case, we are concerned with alleged automatism caused by concussion.

The defense of automatism, while not an entirely new development in the criminal law, has been discussed in relatively few decisions by American appellate courts, most of these being in California where the defense is statutory. Some courts have held that insanity and automatism are separate and distinct defenses, and that evidence of automatism may be presented under a plea of not guilty. Some states have made this distinction by statute. In other states the distinction is made by case law.

"A defense related to but different from the defense of insanity is that of unconsciousness, often referred to as automatism: one who engages in what would otherwise be criminal conduct is not guilty of a crime if he does so in a state of unconsciousness or semi-consciousness. * * * ” LaFave & Scott, Criminal Law, § 44, p. 337 (1972).

"The defenses of insanity and unconsciousness are not the same in nature, for unconsciousness at the time of the alleged criminal act need not be the result of a disease or defect of the mind. As a consequence, the two defenses are not the same in effect, for a defendant found not guilty by reason of unconsciousness, as distinct from insanity, is not subject to commitment to a hospital for the mentally ill." State v. Caddell, 287 N.C. 266, 215 S.E.2d 348, 360 (1975).

The principal reason for making a distinction between the defense of unconsciousness and insanity is that the consequences which follow an acquittal will differ. The defense of unconsciousness is usually a complete defense. That is, there are no follow-up consequences after an acquittal; all action against a defendant is concluded.

However, in the case of a finding of not guilty by reason of insanity, the defendant is ordinarily committed to a mental institution.

* * *

The mental illness or deficiency plea does not adequately cover automatic behavior. Unless the plea of automatism, separate and apart from the plea of mental illness or deficiency is allowed, certain anomalies will result. For example, if the court determines that the automatistic defendant is sane, but refuses to recognize automatism, the defendant has no defense to the crime with which he is charged. If found guilty, he faces a prison term. The rehabilitative value of imprisonment for the automatistic offender who has committed the offense unconsciously is nonexistent. The cause of the act was an uncontrollable physical disorder that may never recur and is not a moral deficiency.

If, however, the court treats automatism as insanity and then determines that the defendant is insane, he will be found not guilty. He then will be committed to a mental institution for an indefinite period. The commitment of an automatistic individual to a mental institution for rehabilitation has absolutely no value. Mental hospitals generally treat people with psychiatric or psychological problems. This form of treatment is not suited to unconscious behavior resulting from a bump on the head.

It may be argued that evidence of unconsciousness cannot be received unless a plea of not guilty by reason of mental illness or deficiency is made pursuant to Rule 15, W.R.Cr.P. We believe this approach to be illogical.

" * * * Insanity is incapacity from disease of the mind, to know the nature and quality of one's act or to distinguish between right and wrong in relation thereto. In contrast, a person who is completely unconscious when he commits an act otherwise punishable as a crime cannot know the nature and quality thereof or whether it is right or wrong. * * *"

It does not seem that the definition of "mental deficiency" in § 7–11–301(a)(iii), W.S.1977, which includes "brain damage," encompasses simple brain trauma with no permanent aftereffects. It is our view that the "brain damage" contemplated in the statute is some serious and irreversible condition having an impact upon the ability of the person to function. It is undoubtedly something far more significant than a temporary and transitory condition. The two defenses are merged, in effect, if a plea of "not guilty by reason of mental illness or deficiency" is a prerequisite for using the defense of unconsciousness.

The committee that drafted Wyoming Pattern Jury Instructions Criminal, apparently recognized mental illness or deficiency and unconsciousness as separate and distinct defenses. See § 4.301, Wyo. P.J.I. Cr. A copy is attached hereto as Appendix A. Admittedly the instructions in Wyo.P.J.I.Cr. are not authoritative, because they were not approved by the Wyoming Supreme Court, and this was a matter of design. Still they are the product of a distinguished group of legal scholars, including judges, attorneys and teachers of the law. The comment to this pattern jury instruction notes that it is limited to persons of sound mind, and the comment distinguishes persons suffering from "mental deficiency or illness." In this respect, it tracks the case law from other jurisdictions, which authorities hold that unconsciousness and insanity are completely separate grounds of exemption from criminal responsibility.

Although courts hold that unconsciousness and insanity are separate and distinct defenses, there has been some uncertainty concerning the burden of proof. We believe the better rule to be that stated in State v. Caddell, supra, 215 S.E.2d at 363:

> "We now hold that, under the law of this state, unconsciousness, or automatism, is a complete defense to the criminal charge, separate and apart from the defense of insanity; that *it is an affirmative defense; and that the burden rests upon the defendant to establish this defense, unless it arises out of the State's own evidence*, to the satisfaction of the jury." (Emphasis added.)

The rationale for this rule is that the defendant is the only person who knows his actual state of consciousness. Hill v. Baxter, 1 All E.R. 193 (1958), 1 Q.B. 277.

Our ruling on the facts of this case is that the defense of unconsciousness resulting from a concussion with no permanent brain damage is an affirmative defense and is a defense separate from the defense of not guilty by reason of mental illness or deficiency.

II

The appellant's conviction must, nevertheless, be affirmed. Dr. LeBegue was unable to state positively whether or not appellant had the requisite mental state for aggravated assault. He could not state that the character of the act was devoid of criminal intent because of the mind alteration. The presumption of mental competency was never overcome by appellant and the evidence presented formed a reasonable basis on which the trial judge could find and did find that the State had met the required burden of proof.

Further, the trial judge was not bound to follow Dr. LeBegue's opinion. The trier of the facts is not bound to accept expert opinion evidence in the face of other substantial and credible evidence to the contrary. State v. Peterson, 24 N.C.App. 404, 210 S.E.2d 883 (1975). Cf., Reilly v. State, Wyo., 496 P.2d 899 (1972), reh. denied, 498 P.2d 1236 (1972). There was an abundance of other credible evidence that appellant was not unconscious at the time of the assault and battery for which he was convicted.

Affirmed.

RAPER, JUSTICE, specially concurring, with whom ROONEY, JUSTICE, joins.

I concur only in the result reached by the majority, except to the extent I otherwise herein indicate.

The reasoning of the majority with respect to the defense of unconciousness in this case is contrary to clear legislative will and has judicially amended the statutes of this state pertaining to mental illness or deficiency excluding criminal responsibility.

I

Dr. LeBegue's testimony was inadmissible in its entirety. " 'Mental deficiency' means a defect attributable to mental retardation, *brain damage* and learning disabilities." Section 7–11–301, W.S.1977. "A person is not responsible for criminal conduct if at the time of the criminal conduct, as a result of mental illness or deficiency, he lacked substantial capacity either to appreciate the wrongfulness of his conduct or to conform his conduct to the requirements of law." Section 7–11–304(a), W.S.1977. This was appellant's defense.

Section 7–11–304(c), W.S.1977 provides that, "[e]vidence that a person is not responsible for criminal conduct by reason of mental illness or deficiency is not admissible at the trial of the defendant unless a plea of 'not guilty by reason of mental illness or deficiency' is made. * * *" No such plea was entered.

The appellant apparently does not dispute the fact that he did in fact commit the assault on his victim as charged. While the appellant argued to the trial judge by way of a written brief that the plea of unconsciousness was not mental deficiency as contemplated by § 7–11–

301 et seq., W.S.1977, the testimony of Dr. LeBegue makes it clear that appellant's condition, which he opines to have existed at the time of the crime, involved a head injury. He testified specifically:

> "In my opinion he did suffer a brain injury, in my opinion did suffer *brain damage*. He suffered a concussion which is essentially a brain bruise." (Emphasis added.)

This, according to the doctor's testimony, translated into "traumatic automatism" as well as explained the appellant's amnesia, his inability to remember kicking and stomping the victim, Hernandez. Appellant cannot avoid the effects of the statute by use of the clinical language of traumatic automatism.

* * *

I am not concerned with the fact that unconsciousness may be a defense in this case but am distressed that the procedure for taking advantage of it has been cast aside. In order to reach the conclusion of the majority that it is not necessary to plead mental deficiency as a defense in the case of unconsciousness, it is indispensable that it be pretended that § 7–11–301, supra, does not exist. The appellant's disorder, if it existed, was caused by "brain damage" according to the appellant's own testimony. That is "mental deficiency" by statutory definition. The majority has feebly attempted to jump the hurdle of a statutory definition by saying "unconsciousness" is not "insanity," but we no longer use that term. It must be pointed out that under the old statutes and before adoption of the current law pertaining to mental deficiency, "insanity" was not legislatively defined. The majority is attempting to adopt the law of an era gone by-by, rather than what the authors of the new legislation considered a more informed and modern concept.

When the legislature amends a statute, it must be presumed that some change in existing law was intended and courts should endeavor to make such amendment effective. It is not reasonable that the legislature would enact a law to declare what is already the law. The legislature will not be presumed to intend futile things. When the legislature declared that mental deficiency was a defect attributable to brain damage (§ 7–11–301), that was a definition it had never before undertaken. That was then collated by the legislature with a declaration that a person is not responsible for his criminal conduct when, because of mental deficiency (which includes brain damage), he lacked the capacity to conform his conduct to the requirements of the law (§ 7–11–304(a)). Appellant's position is that being unconscious because of a blow on the head causing brain damage rendered him not responsible for kicking his victim around. We, then, now have before us a defense of mental deficiency defined by the legislature as including brain damage, not insanity which was never defined by the legislature nor this court to either include or exclude brain damage.

* * *

It follows that damage to the brain causing a defect in its function would bring the appellant within the statute requiring conformity with all its provisions, i.e., commitment for examination and necessity of plea of "not guilty by reason of mental illness or deficiency."

* * *

I conclude that the majority opinion has no authoritative basis whatsoever; not a single case or reference cited supports their position. I would have affirmed the district court, but would not have created the new defense of unconsciousness, at least as to traumatic automatism (brain damage) clearly included as a mental deficiency by § 7–11–301(a) (iii), supra. There is no need for the court to go beyond the point. I can safely predict that defendants will disregard the plea of "not guilty by reason of mental illness or deficiency" and claim unconsciousness for many mental diseases and deficiencies which include that symptom.

[The opinion of Rooney, Justice, specially concurring, is omitted.]

NOTES

1. Prof. Michael Corrado rejects the view that automatism is properly equated with an "unconsciousness" defense. In his article, Automatism and the Theory of Action, 39 Emory L.J. 1191 (1990), he states:

"If automatism is a defense, it is not because of unconsciousness; the actors in these cases are not unconscious in any ordinary sense. It is also not because intent is lacking, or because the behavior does not amount to action . . . because the behavior in these cases is not random or accidental but purposive.

* * *

"If automatism is a defense, it is because the action involved, while conscious and purposive, is not voluntary. The action is not voluntary because, although it involves what used to be called an act of will (being purposive), the act of will is itself caused by something beyond the actor's control—a blow on the head, a sleep disorder, epilepsy, hypnotic suggestion. . . ."

2. In People v. Grant, 46 Ill.App.3d 125, 4 Ill.Dec. 696, 360 N.E.2d 809 (1977), the court held that a defendant who suffered from psychomotor epilepsy could avail himself of the defense if he could show that his actions were those of an insane person, or if he could show that his conduct consisted of the involuntary or automatic actions of a sane person. The court said, in part:

The term automatism is defined as the state of a person who though capable of action, is not conscious of what he is doing. Automatism is not insanity. In the language of section 4–1 of our Criminal Code, it is manifested by the performance of involuntary acts that can be of a simple or complex nature. Clinically, automatism has been identified in a wide variety of physical conditions including: epilepsy, organic brain disease, concussional states following head injuries, drug abuse, hypoglycemia and, less commonly in some types of schizophrenia and acute emotional disturbance. Psychomotor epileptics not only engage in automatic or fugue-like activity, but they may also suffer convulsive seizures.

In reversing the conviction for assaulting a police officer, the court said:

"On remand, the defendant will again run the risk of being convicted for the offenses of aggravated battery or obstructing a police office if the jury finds that he was not insane when he attacked Officer Vonderahe and that he either consciously committed the offense or recklessly brought about his alleged psychomotor epileptic seizure and its accompanying state of automatism. As some commentators have suggested, the jury plays an important role when the defense is raised:

> ' * * * automatism as a result of psychomotor seizures should be [a] valid criminal defense. The dearth of cases employing this defense suggests that the problem is one of proof. If one is sane immediately prior to and after the unlawful act is committed it is difficult to establish that a particular violent act occurred as a result of a psychomotor seizure.' (Barrow & Fabing, Epilepsy and the Law 92–93 (1956).)

"If the jury finds that the defendant was sane but not responsible for the attack on Officer Vonderahe, then he cannot be committed for the offenses."

The State appealed the decision of the Appellate Court to the Illinois Supreme Court. That Court reversed the appellate court and affirmed the trial court's judgment of conviction for aggravated battery. See People v. Grant, 71 Ill.2d 551, 17 Ill.Dec. 814, 377 N.E.2d 4 (1978). The court said, in part:

> "To appreciate precisely the defect to which the defendant refers, we must examine the kindred relationship between the defense of involuntary conduct and the insanity defense, as they apply to an epileptic seizure.

> "Both defenses adhere to the fundamental principle that a person is not criminally responsible for an involuntary act. Certain involuntary acts, i.e., those committed during a state of automatism, occur as bodily movements which are not controlled by the conscious mind. A person in a state of automatism lacks the volition to control or prevent the involuntary acts. Such involuntary acts may include those committed during convulsions, sleep, unconsciousness, hypnosis or seizures. (See Ill.Ann.Stat., ch. 38, par. 4–1, Committee Comments, at 250 (Smith-Hurd 1972), citing Model Penal Code § 2.01 and Comment 3, at 121 (Tent.Draft No. 4 (1955).) A cornerstone of the defense of involuntary conduct is that a person, in a state of automatism, who lacks the volition to control or prevent his conduct, cannot be criminally responsible for such involuntary acts. Similarly, the insanity defense exculpates a person whose volition is so impaired during a state of automatism that he is substantially incapable of conforming his conduct to the law. To that extent, the defense of involuntary conduct and the insanity defense are alternative theories at the disposal of a defendant whose volition to control or prevent his conduct is at issue. See Weinberg, Epilepsy and the Alternatives for a Criminal Defense, 27 Case W.Res.L.Rev. 771, 787–803 (1977); Model Penal Code § 2.01(2), Comment 3, at 121 (Tent.Draft No. 4 (1955); W. LaFave & A. Scott, Criminal Law sec. 44, at 337–41 (1972)."

3. Automatism is sometimes called the "unconsciousness" defense by courts. Recognizing this defense, see Greenfield v. Commonwealth, 214 Va. 710, 204 S.E.2d 414 (1974) habeas relief denied *sub nom.* Greenfield v. Robinson, 413 F.Supp. 1113 (W.D.Va.1976), the Supreme Court of Virginia said that unconsciousness is a complete defense if not self-induced. Unconsciousness through epilepsy was recognized as a defense in Government of the Virgin Islands v. Smith, 278 F.2d 169 (3d Cir.1960), but if a person has repeatedly suffered blackouts so as to be on notice of the possibility of recurrence, then the defense is not available. Cf. People v. Decina, 2 N.Y.2d 133, 157 N.Y.S.2d 558,

138 N.E.2d 799 (1956).   Other cases recognizing the defense of automatism include, People v. Froom, 108 Cal.App.3d 820, 166 Cal.Rptr. 786 (1980); People v. Marsh, 170 Cal.App.2d 284, 338 P.2d 495 (1959) [unconsciousness due to hypnotism]; Fain v. Commonwealth, 78 Ky. 183 (1879) [somnambulism]; State v. Caddell, 287 N.C. 266, 215 S.E.2d 348 (1975); and People v. Lisnow, 88 Cal.App.3d Supp. 21, 151 Cal.Rptr. 621 (1978) [emotional trauma].

It is generally not deemed to be a defense that a defendant was suffering from a multiple personality disorder.   State v. Grimsley, 3 Ohio App.3d 265, 444 N.E.2d 1071 (1982).   While it has been urged that the defense ought to be available where the actor was brainwashed, see Delgado, Ascription of Criminal States of Mind: Toward a Defense Theory for the Coercively Persuaded ("Brainwashed") Defendant, 63 Minn.L.Rev. 1 (1978), and also Alldridge, Brainwashing as a Criminal Defense, 1984 Crim.L.Rev. 726, that view has been strongly criticized in Dressler, Professor Delgado's "Brainwashing" Defense: Courting a Determinist Legal System, 63 Minn.L.Rev. 335 (1979).

See also, Lederman, Non-Insane and Insane Automatism: Reducing The Significance of a Problematic Distinction, 34 Int'l & Compar.L.Q. 819 (1985).

3. INVOLUNTARY "SUBLIMINAL TELEVISION INTOXICATION"

In Zamora v. State, 361 So.2d 776 (Fla.App.1978), the Court rejected arguments of defendant, charged with first degree murder and other offenses, that his involuntary subliminal television intoxication caused by exposure to an inordinate number of hours of viewing media violence should be considered a form of involuntariness that fits within the insanity defense.   Adhering to the M'Naghten Rule or "right and wrong" test, and rejecting diminished capacity, the court said the expert evidence offered was not relevant.

Ought there be a defense, independent of the insanity defense, that recognizes the influences of long exposure to television violence?   How does this defense differ from "brainwashing," previously discussed under the heading of Duress?

NOTE

The essence of the proffered defense in *Zamora* may be better understood by reading the following excerpt from the trial record, when the defense attorney, Mr. Ellis Rubin, called to the stand his expert witness, Dr. Margaret Hanratty Thomas:

Rubin: Your Honor, this witness is a Doctor of Psychology, currently the assistant Dean of Academic Affairs of Florida Technological University, Orlando, Florida.   She has a B.A. from Vanderbilt, an M.A. from Vanderbilt, a Ph.D. from Tulane.   She has fellowships and awards, several teaching positions, psychological testing and evaluation experience, and she has had published—how many papers, round figures?

Dr. Thomas: Around fifteen, I'm not sure.

Rubin: Around fifteen.

The Court: Okay. Now, that qualifies her as an expert in something. Now, what's she going to testify to?

Rubin: Well, here are some of the titles of some of the papers that she has published: "Does Media Violence Increase Children's Toleration of Real Life Aggression?" "Toleration of Real Life Aggression as a Function of Exposure to Televised Violence and Age of Subject;" Desensitization to Portrayals of Real Life Aggression as a Function of Exposure to Television Violence;" Effects of Television Violence on Expectation of Other's Aggressions."

Doctor Thomas is an expert on behavior and the social ramifications of certain types of behavior. Since 1969, she has specialized in the field of what effect, if any, does television violence have on the viewer, and, specifically, young children, adolescents, and adults. We will confine her testimony to adolescents. She is . . .

The Court: That goes beyond the scope of what the Court's instructions were at the pretrial conference.

Rubin: No, Your Honor . . .

The Court: She will have to be confined to Ronny Zamora.

Rubin: It *is* confined to Ronny Zamora, Your Honor, if I may, I would like to make this presentation.

The Court: All right. Go ahead.

Rubin: It's the heart of my defense. Your Honor, this is similar to a defense of intoxication by alcohol, intoxication by hypnosis, or any other defense. The jury has nothing to compare Ronny Zamora's conduct with, if they do not hear that there have been studies on children his age, relating what the effect of X amount of hours of violence on television has shown by experiments with children. It's the same as if I brought an expert in here, if I were defending on the grounds of not guilty by involuntary intoxication. I certainly would have a right to bring in an expert on what are the properties of alcohol, how much alcohol is required to give a 1.0 reading on the drunkometer, unless the Court wished to take judicial notice that 1.0 is drunk. Your Honor, how can the jury understand what the effect of television is on Ronny Zamora if there is no one from the defense to show, through expert experiments and testimony, what the effect has been on other youngsters his age? All that we're doing is establishing a standard. The defense of involuntary television intoxication is new, but so was insanity at one time a new defense. So was involuntary intoxication by alcohol at some stage in our civilization, a new defense. But there are expert . . .

* * *

The Court: Go ahead.

Rubin: I'm trying to make myself understood. And I realize that it may be a difficult premise.

This expert on the effects of television violence is prepared to testify, and we have others who will testify likewise, that what comes out of television on the programs that are produced by the networks and the sponsors contain an inordinate amount of violence. Young children—but especially, Your Honor, the studies will show that sociopaths and emotionally disturbed children are more affected by violence on television than any other category of human beings. And that what comes out of that television tube is not controlled by the viewer and the viewer doesn't realize that he is being desensitized to violence by seeing so much of it. Involuntarily, he is seeing all of these heroes and bad guys, the black hats and the white hats using guns, stabbing people, abnormal behavior, bizarre situations, robberies, burglaries, killings of old ladies, and this is coming to him and going into his brain and is desensitizing this child to the normal regard for violence, the normal standards of right and wrong for killing, because this boy is a classic example. And we have laid the predicate that he is an addict, that his viewing hours were more than ordinary, and his type of programs . . ..

* * *

Your Honor, what's the difference in bringing in somebody who's an expert on alcohol, a chemist, and who can testify that by experiments over the years, we find that a certain amount of alcohol will cause a loss of control? Well, that's what I want to do with television. This witness is prepared to say that television does affect the viewer, did affect Ronny Zamora. She doesn't have to interview Ronny Zamora. I have other people who have interviewed Ronny Zamora. The jury has already heard the testimony of his mother. Certainly television, if the jury believes Mrs. Zamora—and that's a jury question. Not to allow me to present an expert who will say, well, there have been so many studies, and here is what has been found, and it's uncontradicted—and she has done papers that have been accepted for publication by the scientific journals, and she has to be quizzed on those, and there has to be verification of them, and that has been done.

Your Honor, don't deny me the right to present everything to the jury that they should have for this defense, and that is this doctor who is an expert on what are the effects of television on children. Then, let the jury say does it affect Ronny Zamora—and we will have other witnesses who will so say. This is the premise for our whole defense.

* * *

Rubin: May I make the proffer, then? May I put the doctor through the testimony?

The Court: Yes.

Rubin: And then we'll see. (to Dr. Thomas) What is your name and address?

Dr. Thomas: Margaret Hanratty Thomas. (she states her address)

Q. What is your occupation or profession?

A. Psychologist and college professor.

Q. Are you prepared to say that an excessive amount of television viewing would have an effect on an emotionally disturbed fifteen-year-old male child from a middle class, poor economic background?

A. It's very possible.

Q. Very possible? Can you say it within a reasonable psychological certainty?

A. I would feel fairly confident that, given that type of background, an excessive amount of television violence would—well, it has an effect on everyone. It would be much more likely to have an unusual or extreme effect on such a child, in my opinion.

The Court: Let me ask you this. Can you state, within reasonable psychological certainty, under the set of facts that Mr. Rubin just gave you, that such an amount of television on the type of child could produce . . . a state of mind where he did not know right from wrong and could not appreciate the nature and consequence of his acts?

Dr. Thomas: Watching that much television over a long period of time, in my opinion, is at least one of the important factors as to how a person acquires a sense of right and wrong.

The Court: That's not the question. The question is can you state, with reasonable psychological certainty, in any of the tests that you've conducted, in any of the tests that you have referred to, in any of the papers that you've published—not that it could—that it has—had that effect on any individual tested, to the extent that they did not know right from wrong?

Dr. Thomas: Would studies that show that children who tend to watch a lot of violent television tend to be more approving . . .

The Court: No. Not approving. Would they be so affected that they would not know right from wrong and appreciate the nature and consequences of their act—in other words, have absolutely no idea of right or wrong, couldn't appreciate the nature and consequences of their act? In other words, are you familiar with the rule of M'Naghten's case?

Headley [Prosecutor]: Dr. Thomas, can you advise the Court of one study or one experiment or any number that have linked the viewing of television violence with insanity?

Dr. Thomas: You mean use the term "insanity"?

Headley: Yes.

Dr. Thomas: Legal insanity—of course not.

Headley: I think that's all we're resolving here, Your Honor.

The Court: That's it.

Rubin: One more chance. They're comparing apples and oranges. How can you relate, Your Honor, psychological, medical, scientific experiments of proof with the legal definition of the word "insanity"? This is not her field. Our field is the legal definition of a defense. Her field is what are the effects of television violence on children. Your Honor will instruct the jury on the law of insanity. I want to show the jury the facts that went into this child's concept of right and wrong. Your Honor, she's prepared to—I have psychiatrists who will use this testimony, subject to cross examination, who will testify as to what you asked this young doctor. She can't testify that there's ever been a case where insanity has been found to result from too much television, because they don't have the word "insanity" in her field. They don't have it even in the field of psychiatry, as you know.

The Court: I understand that.

Rubin: Let the scientists come—let the psychiatrists, Your Honor, come in. And let Your Honor voir dire the psychiatrists and say, "Has there ever been a case where too much television has caused insanity?"

And they will answer, "Yes." And the victim is Ronny Zamora. And let the jury hear that. Please.

The Court: Let me ask you this, ma'am. Let's forget the word "insanity." In any of your tests, in any scientific journal that you have read, have you ever conclusively linked any particular television program or amount of television violence directly to a homicide?

Dr. Thomas: Well, those are not scientific studies. There are cases . . .

The Court: Or any crime?

Dr. Thomas: No, because they're always after the fact. You can't . . .

The Court: Thank you. The testimony is excluded.

4. PREMENSTRUAL SYNDROME DEFENSE

A fairly novel defense which has been raised in several cases, so far unsuccessfully, has been labeled by some psychiatrists the Premenstrual Syndrome (PMS) defense.

Dr. Katherine Dalton, a British researcher of the subject for over 30 years, defined PMS as "the presence of monthly recurring symptoms in the premenstruum or early menstruation with a complete absence of symptoms after menstruation" which result in such behavioral and psychological manifestations as "irritability, anger, confusion, depression, amnesia and uncontrollable impulses resulting in violence." In 1982, the defense was raised for the first time in an American court in the unreported New York case of People v. Santos. The defendant was charged with child battering and raised PMS as a complete defense in a pretrial hearing, asserting that while she beat the child, she was unaware of what she was doing because she had blacked out and did not know what she was doing. There never was a ruling on the merits of the PMS defense, but after lengthy discussions and negotiations, the defendant pleaded guilty to a misdemeanor after the prosecutor agreed to drop the felony charges.

There were three earlier English cases in which the merits of PMS were considered and, to some extent, recognized by the courts, though not as a defense to crime, but rather in mitigation of punishment. In the case of Sandie Craddock, the 29-year-old defendant had a record of more than thirty prior convictions for violent acts and had attempted to commit suicide at least 25 times. She had been in and out of mental hospitals, but doctors were unable to diagnose a precise ailment or condition. After she was charged with murder in the stabbing to death of a barmaid, her counsel, in studying her past record, discovered that all of the offenses and suicide attempts had occurred at approximately the same time of the month. He then sought Dr. Dalton's help and Craddock was diagnosed a PMS sufferer and treated with massive doses of the hormone progesterone. Sandie's behavior altered drastically and she became more stable. The prosecution agreed to reduce the charge to manslaughter because of her "diminished responsibility." She was placed on probation on the condition she continue the progesterone treatments. See, Criminal Law—Premenstrual Syndrome: A Criminal Defense, 59 Notre Dame L.Rev. 253 (1983).

Sandie then changed her name to Sandie Smith and her probation officer was satisfied that the treatment permitted Sandie to lead a normal life. Thereafter, Dr. Dalton gradually began to reduce the dosage and the frequency of progesterone treatments, and at the time when Sandie was receiving her smallest dose of the hormone and while she was in her premenstruum, she went berserk. Wielding a knife, she twice threatened to kill a peace officer. Placed under arrest and charged, she was convicted even though she was placed on three years' probation because of the PMS evidence. On appeal, her counsel (who had also represented her in the earlier trial), asked the court of appeals to recognize PMS as a complete defense. The court refused to recognize her medical condition as a substantive defense and found it more appropriate to use PMS as a mitigating factor in sentencing.

There was a third case in England, where a woman deliberately killed her lover by pinning him against a utility pole with her car. Again, PMS was recognized as a mitigating factor, though not as a substantive defense.

NOTE

Could a defendant raise PMS as a form of insanity defense? Probably not. PMS is not a disease or defect of the mind; it is a physiological disorder and therefore no insanity can be claimed, regardless of the test for insanity that might prevail in the jurisdiction where the attempt is made.

Could a defendant raise PMS as a form of automatism? Possibly. There are some forms of automatism which are caused by mental disease or defect, but persons with a healthy mind can be just as susceptible to automatism because of such physiological disorders as somnambulism, delirium from fever or drugs, diabetic shock, and epileptic seizures.

Among the extensive recent literature on the subject, see, e.g.: Dalton, Premenstrual Syndrome and Progesterone Therapy (2d ed.), 1984; Norris, PMS: Premenstrual Syndrome, 1983; Dalton, Premenstrual Syndrome, 9 Hamline L.Rev. 143 (1986); Keye & Trunnell, Premenstrual Syndrome: A Medical Perspective, 9 Hamline L.Rev. 165 (1986); Riley, Premenstrual Syndrome As A Legal Defense, 9 Hamline L.Rev. 193 (1986); Heggestad, The Devil Made Me Do It: The Case Against Using Premenstrual Syndrome As A Defense In a Court of Law, 9 Hamline L.Rev. 155 (1986); Holtzman, Premenstrual Symptoms: No Legal Defense, 60 St. John's L.Rev. 712 (1986); Oakes, PMS: A Plea Bargain in Brooklyn Does Not A Rule of Law Make, 9 Hamline L.Rev. 203 (1986); Chait, Premenstrual Syndrome and Our Sisters in Crime: A Feminist Dilemma, 9 Women's Rts.L.Rep. 267 (1986); Pahl–Smith, Premenstrual Syndrome As A Criminal Defense: The Need For a Medico–Legal Understanding, 15 N.C.Cent. L.J. 246 (1985); Press, Premenstrual Stress Syndrome As a Defense in Criminal Cases, 1983 Duke L.J. 176 (1983).

5. OTHER CONDITIONS REDUCING RESPONSIBILITY

In recent years, there has been a proliferation of cases in which psychiatric or psychological experts have offered testimony that a defendant in a criminal case suffered from a "syndrome" or condition that affected his capacity to control his act. The opinion testimony is offered either to suggest the defendant ought to be excused for the criminal act (substantive defense) or the condition ought to be taken into account in sentencing—a form of diminished responsibility. So far, courts have been generally reluctant to recognize the "syndrome" conditions as constituting a substantive defense, though some courts have admitted such evidence for limited evidentiary purposes. In many cases, the courts have not reached the merits of a proposed defense because they hold that the syndrome testimony is based on a theory that is not generally accepted in the professional field in which it belongs. Thus, in State v. Thomas,[1] the court found that evidence that a murder defendant was a victim of the battered wife syndrome was "irrelevant and immaterial," since fitting certain statistically significant characteristics does not establish that a person's behavior necessarily was caused by it and also was inadmissible because the syndrome theory was not generally accepted as scientifically reliable.[2]

A syndrome is a set of behavioral indicators forming a very characteristic pattern of actions or emotions that tend to point to a particular condition. The existence of such a condition is most often based upon clinical psychological observations in case studies that, because of the constant presence of common events, have been statistically correlated. Expert testimony by a psychiatrist or clinical psychologist is always needed to not only testify to the existence of a particular syndrome, but also to explain how, and to what probabilistic degree, it affected a defendant's past behavior as well as to forecast how a person may act in the future.[3] Courts that are critical of such evidence often see it as disguised character testimony,[4] or question the reliability of the psychological or psychiatric opinion because it involves statistical

---

1. 66 Ohio St.2d 518, 423 N.E.2d 137 (1981).

2. On the evidentiary requirements for the admission of novel expert testimony, see Moenssens et al., Scientific Evidence in Criminal Cases, 3rd ed. 1986 (Chapter 1, Sec. 1.03 "Tests of Admissibility"). On the battered spouse syndrome generally, see the materials contained in Chapter 5, supra, under Justifiable Use of Deadly Force. The Notes also discuss the Battered Child Syndrome and the Holocaust Syndrome.

3. While "syndrome" testimony is sought to be used most frequently as a defense, prosecutors seek to make use of it also in the case of the Rape Trauma Syndrome. See Chapter 6, On Criminal Sexual Assault.

4. In United States v. Azure, 801 F.2d 336 (8th Cir. 1986), the court reversed a conviction where a prosecution expert was permitted to say he could see no reason why the alleged victim of child sex abuse was not telling the truth. The court said that the expert "might have aided the jurors without usurping their exclusive function [of determining the facts] by generally testifying about a child's ability to separate truth from fantasy . . . and expressing his opinion as to whether it was consistent with [the victim's] story that she was sexually abused." But to put the expert's stamp of approval on the victim's believability went "too far." Accord: State v. Heath, 316 N.C. 337, 341 S.E.2d 565 (1986).

A psychologist's testimony about "captivity syndrome," introduced by the govern-

probability data, the reliability or sufficiency of which cannot be adequately demonstrated.[5]

Among the "syndrome" evidence that has been presented to the courts either as a proposed defense or on the issue of the degree of responsibility, or in mitigation of punishment, other than that dealt with earlier in this casebook, we note the following:

The Battered Husband Syndrome. See, e.g., Steinmetz, The Battered Husband Syndrome, Victimology, An Int'l Journal (1977–1978); Gelles, The Myth of Battered Husbands—And Other Facts About Sanity Violence, Ms, Oct. 1979.

Vietnam Veteran Syndrome. (Sometimes also called The Battle Fatigue Syndrome.) See, e.g., Miller v. State, 338 N.W.2d 673 (S.D. 1983) (dissenting opinion); State v. Felde, 422 So.2d 370 (La.1982). See also Ford, In Defense of the Defenders: The Vietnam Vet. Syndrome, 19 Crim.L.Bull. 434 (1983); Post-Traumatic Stress Disorder—Opening Pandora's Box?, 17 New Eng.L.Rev. 91 (1981); Vietnam Veterans and the Veteran's Stress Disorder, 68 Marq.L.Rev. 647 (1985). In State v. Korell, 213 Mont. 316, 690 P.2d 992 (1984), Justice Sheehy, in the context of a classic Vietnam Veteran's Syndrome case, would have held unconstitutional Montana's abolishment of the insanity defense. The case is included herein, infra, in Chapter 11–G (last case in the book).

The Policeman's Syndrome. See Binder, Psychiatry in the Every Day Practice of Law (2d ed. 1982).

The Love Fear Syndrome. See, People v. Terry, 2 Cal.3d 362, 85 Cal.Rptr. 409, 466 P.2d 961 (1970).

The Chronic Brain Syndrome. See People v. Reed, 8 Ill.App.3d 977, 290 N.E.2d 612 (1972).

The Holocaust Syndrome. See, Werner v. State, 711 S.W.2d 639 (Tex.Crim.App.1986).

The Post Traumatic Stress Disorder. ("Characterized by the onset of affective, autonomic, and cognitive symptoms following a psychologically traumatic event . . . outside the range of usual human experience." See, Harry & Resnick, Posttraumatic Stress Disorder in Murderers, 31 J.For.Sci. 609 (1986).

The designation "post traumatic stress syndrome" is frequently used generically for many of the more specific syndromes mentioned above.

---

ment to explain why two men, allegedly held in involuntary servitude, did not try to escape when they had the chance and became "compliant," was first held properly admitted in United States v. Kozminski, 771 F.2d 125 (6th Cir. 1985), but after reargument, the court vacated its earlier opinion, and held that expert testimony on the captivity syndrome was improperly admit-

ted in that the underlying theory was not generally accepted in the scientific community. United States v. Kozminski, 821 F.2d 1186 (6th Cir. 1987).

5. Comment, The Syndrome Syndrome: Problem Concerning the Admissibility of Expert Testimony on Psychological Profiles, 37 U.Fla.L.Rev. 1035 (1985).

For a description of the symptoms of post traumatic stress disorder, see, American Psychiatric Association, Diagnostic and Statistical Manual of Mental Disorders, 3d ed. (DSM–III–R). Such disorders occur "among people who have survived traumatic events that are outside the realm of normal human experience—e.g., rape or assault, physical injury, military combat, bombings, torture, and floods or earthquakes. The afflicted person reexperiences the traumatic event through painful, intrusive recollections of nightmares. Episodes may last from several minutes to several days. During an episode, the person may behave as if he or she were reliving the event." Waldinger, Fundamentals of Psychiatry, 1986 (p. 188).

Postpartum Psychosis. Post Partum Psychosis is a psycho-medical disorder peculiar to women, asserted as a defense to infanticide. See, generally, Postpartum Psychosis as a Defense to Infant Murder, 5 Touro L.Rev. 287 (1989); Postpartum Psychosis: A Way Out For Murderous Moms?, 18 Hofstra L.Rev. 1133 (1990); Postpartum Psychosis As an Insanity Defense: Underneath a Controversial Defense Lies a Garden Variety Insanity Defense Complicated by Unique Circumstances for Recognizing Culpability in Causing, 21 Rutgers L.Rev. 669 (1990).

On the subject of syndrome defenses, also recall the discussions on the battered spouse syndrome as a justification self-defense in Chapter 5, supra, and RTS (rape trauma syndrome) evidence discussed in Chapter 6, supra. See also, generally: Postpartum Depression Defense: Are Mothers Getting Away with Murder?, 24 New.Eng.L.Rev. 953 (1990); Reece, Mothers Who Kill: Postpartum Disorders and Criminal Infanticide, 38 U.C.L.A. L.Rev. 699 (1991).

Chapter 11

INSANITY AT TIME OF THE PROHIBITED ACT AND COMPETENCY TO STAND TRIAL

A. THE M'NAGHTEN (RIGHT–WRONG) TEST

DANIEL M'NAGHTEN'S CASE
House of Lords, 1843.
10 Cl. & F. 200, 8 Eng.Reprint 718.

The prisoner had been indicted for [the murder of Edward Drummond, private secretary to Sir Robert Peel.] . . . The prisoner pleaded Not guilty.

Evidence having been given of the fact of the shooting of Mr. Drummond, and of his death in consequence thereof, witnesses were called on the part of the prisoner, to prove that he was not, at the time of committing the act, in a sound state of mind. . . .

LORD CHIEF JUSTICE TINDAL (in his charge):—The question to be determined is, whether at the time the act in question was committed, the prisoner had or had not the use of his understanding, so as to know that he was doing a wrong or wicked act. If the jurors should be of opinion that the prisoner was not sensible, at the time he committed it, that he was violating the laws both of God and man, then he would be entitled to a verdict in his favour: but if, on the contrary they were of opinion that when he committed the act he was in a sound state of mind, then their verdict must be against him.

Verdict, Not guilty, on the ground of insanity.

This verdict, and the question of the nature and extent of the unsoundness of mind which would excuse the commission of a felony of this sort, having been made the subject of debate in the House of Lords, it was determined to take the opinion of the Judges on the law governing such cases. . . .

LORD CHIEF JUSTICE TINDAL . . . The first question proposed by your Lordships is this: "What is the law respecting alleged crimes committed by persons afflicted with insane delusion in respect of one or more particular subjects or persons: as, for instance, where at the time of the commission of the alleged crime the accused knew he was acting contrary to law, but did the act complained of with a view, under the influence of insane delusion, of redressing or revenging some supposed grievance or injury, or of producing some supposed public benefit?"

In answer to which question, assuming that your Lordships inquiries are confined to those persons who labour under such partial delusions only, and are not in other respects insane, we are of opinion that, notwithstanding the party accused did the act complained of with a view, under the influence of insane delusion, of redressing or revenging some supposed grievance or injury, or of producing some public benefit he is nevertheless punishable according to the nature of the crime committed, if he knew at the time of committing such crime that he was acting contrary to law; by which expression we understand your Lordships to mean the law of the land.

Your Lordships are pleased to inquire of us, secondly, "What are the proper questions to be submitted to the jury, where a person alleged to be afflicted with insane delusion respecting one or more particular subjects or persons, is charged with the commission of a crime (murder, for example), and insanity is set up as a defence?" And, thirdly, "In what terms ought the question to be left to the jury as to the prisoner's state of mind at the time when the act was committed?" And as these two questions appear to us to be more conveniently answered together, we have to submit our opinion to be, that the jurors ought to be told in all cases that every man is to be presumed to be sane, and to possess a sufficient degree of reason to be responsible for his crimes, until the contrary be proved to their satisfaction; and that to establish a defence on the ground of insanity, it must be clearly proved that, at the time of the committing of the act, the party accused was labouring under such a defect of reason, from disease of the mind, as not to know the nature and quality of the act he was doing; or, if he did know it, that he did not know he was doing what was wrong. The mode of putting the latter part of the question to the jury on these occasions has generally been, whether the accused at the time of doing the act knew the difference between right and wrong: which mode, though rarely, if ever, leading to any mistake with the jury, is not, as we conceive, so accurate when put generally and in the abstract, as when put with reference to the party's knowledge of right and wrong in respect to the very act with which he is charged. If the question were to be put as to the knowledge of the accused solely and exclusively with reference to the law of the land, it might tend to confound the jury, by inducing them to believe that an actual knowledge of the law of the land was essential in order to lead to a conviction; whereas the law is administered upon the principle that every one must be taken conclusively to know it, without proof that he does know it. If the accused was conscious that the act was one which he ought not to do, and if that act was at the same time contrary to the law of the land, he is punishable; and the usual course therefore has been to leave the question to the jury, whether the party accused had a sufficient degree of reason to know that he was doing an act that was wrong; and this course we think is correct, accompanied with such observations and explanations as the circumstances of each particular case may require.

The fourth question which your Lordships have proposed to us is this:—"If a person under an insane delusion as to existing facts, commits an offence in consequence thereof, is he thereby excused?" To which question the answer must of course depend on the nature of the delusion: but, making the same assumption as we did before, namely, that he labours under such partial delusion only and is not in other respects insane, we think he must be considered in the same situation as to responsibility as if the facts with respect to which the delusion exists were real. For example, if under the influence of his delusion he supposes another man to be in the act of attempting to take away his life, and he kills that man, as he supposes, in self-defence, he would be exempt from punishment. If his delusion was that the deceased had inflicted a serious injury to his character and fortune, and he killed him in revenge for such supposed injury, he would be liable to punishment. . . .

NOTES

1. On the history behind the M'Naghten Rules, consider the following from the opinion of Chief Judge Biggs of the Third Circuit Court of Appeals in United States v. Currens, 290 F.2d 751 (3d Cir. 1961), at pp. 448–449:

". . . The M'Naghten Rules . . . were engendered by the excitement and fear which grew out of the aquittal of Daniel M'Naghten who had attempted to assassinate Sir Robert Peel, Prime Minister of England, but who instead shot Peel's private secretary, Drummond, because M'Naghten had mistaken Drummond for Peel. The offense against Drummond followed a series of attempted assassinations of members of the English Royal House, including Queen Victoria herself, and attacks on the Queen's ministers. Some of these were considered to have grown out of Anti-Corn-Law League plots. When M'Naghten was acquitted at his trial . . . public indignation, led by the Queen, ran so high that the Judges of England were called before the House of Lords to explain their conduct. A series of questions were propounded to them. Their answers, really an advisory opinion which were delivered by Lord Chief Justice Tindal for all fifteen Judges, save Mr. Justice Maule, constitute what are now known as the M'Naghten Rules. . . . The M'Naghten Rules, which applied primarily the test of knowing the difference between right and wrong, are set out in the ancient book, written by William Lambard of Lincolns Inn, Eirenarcha or of the Office of the Justices of Peace, reprinted at least seven times between 1582 and 1610. At 'Cap. 21.218' of this work Lambard stated: 'If a mad man or a naturall foole, or a lunatike in the time of his lunacie, or a childe y apparently hath no knowledge of good nor euil do kill a man, this is no felonious acte, nor any thing forfeited by it ＊ ＊ ＊ for they cannot be said to haue any understanding wil. But if upon examination it fal out, y they knew what they did, & y it was ill, the seemth it to be otherwise.' It will be observed that Lambard laid down as his test of criminal responsibility 'knowledge of good or evil.' The phraseology quoted is as antique and creaking as the doctrine of criminal responsibility it announces. For the words 'knowledge of good or evil,' the phrase 'knowledge of right and wrong' was substituted. This essential principle, embodied in the M'Naghten Rules, is not 118 years old. The substance of the M'Naghten Rules was set out in the Eirenarcha over 375 years ago, published in a year in which belief in witchcraft and demonology, even among well educated men, was widespread. The Eirenarcha itself contains a statute imposing severe penalties for injuries or death caused by witchcraft. The principles of law embodied in the volume were, of course, typical of the thinking of the times. . . ."

2. The name of the defendant in the principal case has been spelled several different ways. In an article in the London Times it was spelled "M'Naughten". The late Justice Frankfurter wrote to the Times and chided it for the error, whereupon the Times replied that the spelling it used was based upon a letter signed by the man himself. Justice Frankfurter, displaying (as Judge Irving R. Kaufman phrased it) "that pixy humor which delighted so many of his intimates", wrote to the editor of the Times as follows: "To what extent is a lunatic's spelling even of his own name to be deemed an authority?" (See fn. 2 of Judge Kaufman's opinion in United States v. Freeman, 357 F.2d 606, 608 (2d Cir. 1966).

3. For an article on the origin of the M'Naghten rule, see, Gambino, The Murderous Mind: Insanity v. The Law. Saturday Review, Mar. 18, 1978, at p. 10. See also, West & Walk, Daniel M'Naghten: His Trial and the Aftermath (1977).

4. See also the first in a series of five papers on the overall question of psychodynamics in insanity defense jurisprudence by Professor Michael Perlin: Perlin, Psychodynamics and the Insanity Defense: "Ordinary Common Sense" and Heuristic Reasoning, 69 Neb.L.Rev. 3 (1990).

KNIGHTS v. STATE

Supreme Court of Nebraska, 1899.
58 Neb. 225, 78 N.W. 508.

SULLIVAN, J. In the district court of Washington county, George Knights was convicted of the crime of arson, and sentenced to imprisonment in the penitentiary for a term of 12 years. . . .

In relation to the defense of insanity, upon which the prisoner relied, the court said to the jury, in the twelfth instruction: "You are instructed that the law presumes that every person is sane, and it is not necessary for the state to introduce evidence of sanity in the first instance. When, however, any evidence has been introduced tending to prove insanity of an accused, the burden is then upon the state to establish the fact of the accused's sanity, the same as any other material fact to be established by the state to warrant a conviction. If the testimony introduced in this case tending to prove that the defendant was insane at the time of the alleged burning described in the information raises in your mind a reasonable doubt of his sanity at the time of the alleged burning, then your verdict should be acquittal." It is contended that this instruction gave the jury to understand that the burden of establishing his insanity rested upon the defendant up to a certain point in the trial, and was then shifted from him to the state. . . . [T]here can be no room to doubt that the court, in the instruction now under consideration, stated the correct doctrine in unmistakable terms. In this case the jury were informed that the law presumes sanity, but that, when the defendant produced evidence tending to prove insanity, the state was charged with a burden which did not previously rest upon it. The court did not say nor imply that the burden of proving insanity was ever on the accused or that there was a shifting of the burden from him to the state. The substance of what the court did say was that, when the legal presumption of sanity encountered opposing evidence, the law then, for the first time, imposed on the state the onus of showing the prisoner's sanity by the proper measure of proof. . . .

NOTES

1. For an excellent article on the general issue, see the very perceptive view by Eule, The Presumption of Sanity: Bursting The Bubble, 25 U.C.L.A.L. Rev. 637 (1978).

2. An Oregon statute providing that the accused has the burden of proving insanity beyond a reasonable doubt has been held not to violate due process in Leland v. Oregon, 343 U.S. 790, 72 S.Ct. 1002 (1952), noted in 43 J.Crim.L., C. & P.S. 482 (1952). The same issue was raised more recently in State v. Mytych, 292 Minn. 248, 194 N.W.2d 276 (1972), where the defendant suggested that *Leland's* days were numbered. In pointing out that all jurisdictions treat the burden of proof issue as a mere rule of evidence, with the exception of Colorado, the court took cognizance of the fact that the United States Supreme Court had found no violation of the due process clause of the federal Constitution when it upheld the Oregon statute, even though the burden of proof was greater in Oregon than that required to establish the defense in other states and in the federal courts. The Minnesota Supreme Court continued:

> Defendant contends that "Leland's days are numbered". It is our view, however, that defendant was not, in fact, required to disprove one of the essential elements of the crime, and the decision in Leland, permitting states to retain latitude in establishing procedural requirements consistent with due process, is not affected. Since Leland has never been overruled and has remained the law of this land since 1952, it would seem that Leland's days are not numbered; Leland is alive and well.

> Since we hold there is no constitutional proscription against requiring a defendant to sustain the burden of proof on insanity, defendant's argument in relation to the privilege against self-incrimination evaporates. She was properly faced with a decision with respect to testifying in furtherance of her burden of proof on insanity, constitutionally permissible as imposed, or exercising her right to remain silent. . . .

Many other states have provided that insanity is an affirmative defense, with the burden of proof upon the defendant, but they differ widely as to the quantum of proof. In some, the defense must be proved "to the satisfaction of the jury", or "clearly to the reasonable satisfaction of the jury". In others the defendant must establish his irresponsibility "by a preponderance of the evidence", as was the case in the Minnesota decision. In still others the defense must raise the issue by "some evidence", which is usually interpreted to mean more than a scintilla of evidence but not as much as would be required to meet the preponderance of the evidence standard.

3. In People ex rel. Juhan v. District Court for Jefferson County, 165 Colo. 253, 439 P.2d 741 (1968), a divided Supreme Court of Colorado held unconstitutional, as violative of the "due process of law" provision of the Colorado Constitution, a state statute which required a defendant who enters a plea of not guilty by reason of insanity to establish, by a preponderance of evidence,

the fact of insanity.   In view of the *Leland* decision of the United States Supreme Court, the Colorado court could not hold the state statute repugnant to the federal Constitution, although the Colorado "due process" clause parallels that of the federal Constitution.   The majority opinion by Chief Justice Moore considered "mental state" to be one of the essential elements of crime which the prosecution had to prove beyond a reasonable doubt.   As was pointed out in the dissenting opinion of Mr. Justice McWilliams, "this is the first time that any court in a reported decision has ever held that a statute or rule of court which places on the defendant the burden of proving insanity violates due process".   Also see Washington v. People, 169 Colo. 323, 455 P.2d 656 (1969).

4.   Reconsider the case of Mullaney v. Wilbur, discussed in the *Patterson* case, supra in Ch. 2–D.

5.   Statutes have been held constitutional which require that the defense of insanity be pleaded specially, and that there shall be separate trials—one as to guilt and the other with respect to insanity.   This represents the so-called bifurcated trial concept, adopted by statute in California and Colorado.   In practice, the procedure is not much used and frequently defendants raise the defense of partial insanity in the guilt phase of the trial in an attempt to reduce a murder from first to second degree.   In Wisconsin, where the bifurcated trial was judicially adopted in State ex rel. La Follette v. Raskin, 34 Wis.2d 607, 150 N.W.2d 318 (1967), it was held that evidence concerning mental condition is not admissible during the guilt phase of the trial.   See Curl v. State, 40 Wis.2d 474, 162 N.W.2d 77 (1968).   In Commonwealth v. McCusker, 448 Pa. 382, 292 A.2d 286, 293 (1972), the court suggested that holding that "psychiatric evidence is admissible as an aid in determining whether an accused acted in the heat of passion at the time of his offense is only a natural and logical application of the orderly and authoritative development of the law of evidence in such cases".

PEOPLE v. WOOD

Court of Appeals of New York, 1962.
12 N.Y.2d 69, 236 N.Y.S.2d 44, 187 N.E.2d 116.

FROESSEL, JUDGE.   On July 4, 1960 the bodies of John Rescigno and Frederick Sess, aged 62 and about 77 respectively, were discovered in the "little house" they shared in Astoria, Queens County.   In addition to other wounds, Sess had sustained multiple skull fractures.   On Rescigno's body were about 16 wounds; his jugular vein had been severed.   Defendant, Frederick Charles Wood, aged 50, was convicted of murder first degree (two counts) and sentenced to death.

Wood was taken to custody on July 5th.   During the automobile trip to the station house, he told a detective that he had received the cut on his right thumb during a barroom altercation, but when asked the same question later at the police station, he replied that he had been cut by glass fragments while striking Rescigno with a bottle.   He thereupon admitted having killed Sess and Rescigno on June 30, 1960, and gave a particularized account of how and why he did so.   This statement, recorded in shorthand, transcribed, and signed by defendant, was admitted in evidence at trial without objection.

Defendant made no attempt to controvert the evidence which overwhelmingly established that he killed Rescigno and Sess.   His sole defense was insanity. Ordinarily, under these circumstances, we would say little more about the evidence relating to the commission of the crimes. Here, however, since it is indicative of Wood's state of mind on June 30th, we set forth in some detail his statement made to an Assistant District Attorney on July 5th.

Almost at the outset of the interrogation, Wood was asked if he had done something "wrong" in Astoria on the night of June 30th. He replied that he had, that he "knocked off those two guys", "did them in", "killed two men". Defendant then related that at about 3:00 p.m. on June 30th, while he was panhandling on Broadway, New York City, he saw John Rescigno, whom he had never met before, leaving a tavern. Wood had panhandled two dollars, but "was looking for more". He "figured" Rescigno was a "lush" and "might be good for a score". Rescigno purchased a bottle of wine. Defendant obtained an invitation from Rescigno to stay at the latter's house that night. He "figured" he "could make a score" because Rescigno "had been drinking like hell", and defendant "knew what the score was and he didn't".

During the subway ride to Astoria, Rescigno said he was a "pensioner", showed Wood his social security card, and "intimate[d] he has quite a bit of money", at which point defendant "developed an idea I would try to take [rob] him during the evening sometime". When they arrived at the house between 7:00 and 8:00 p.m., the "apartment" was dark, and Rescigno did not turn on the lights. At the time, defendant saw Sess in bed in a bedroom.

They drank some beer; Rescigno took a drink of muscatel "and he gets silly drunk", "mumbles unintelligibly", but Wood finally understood that he suggested they "go to bed together". Continuing: " * * * I don't like degenerates. I always had a distaste for them. * * * I knew right then he sealed his fate. I know I'm going to knock him off that night. Not only for his money but for the satisfaction of knocking off a degenerate." But he could not "knock him off right away because [he had] to figure out the angles". Therefore Wood went "along with the gag", gave Rescigno "a mushy kiss", suggested they take it easy, have some more drinks, and told him he was going to stay all night.

Defendant went to the kitchen to find a weapon. Because it was dark and he did not want to turn on the lights, the only weapon he could find was an empty beer bottle. He took the bottle and a package of cigarettes to Rescigno's bedroom, offered Rescigno a cigarette because "just as soon as he reached for the cigarette I had the intention of knocking his brains out, which I did". After rendering the victim unconscious, Wood severed his jugular vein with a piece of jagged glass from the broken bottle. Blood was spurting out, but Wood stood to one side in order to keep from soiling his clothes.

After taking two or three dollars from Rescigno's clothes, Wood remembered a man sleeping in the other room, whom he "figured" he "might as well finish * * * off just on the grounds he might be a degenerate also". Defendant returned to the kitchen "figuring out the best weapon to use on this guy". He found a heavy coal shovel, lifted it "to see if it had the right amount of heft", beat Sess on the head with the shovel, then "flailed him unmercifully" with a chair. Wood, in his own language, "was satisfied in my mind he couldn't recover".

Thereupon defendant went to the kitchen, where he washed, and combed his hair—"I could pass for a Sunday school teacher any place on the face of the earth". He then returned to the bedroom, searched Sess' pockets looking for money but "unfortunately" found none. Defendant did not wish to remain long because he felt that Sess' "loud [dying] noise" and the barking of a dog "would tip off the neighbors that something was *wrong*" (emphasis supplied).

Before departing, however, Wood wrote two notes which were found under a cigarette holder on a table in the kitchen. One reads: "And God bless the Parole Board. They're real intelligent people"; the other states: "Now, aren't these two murders a dirty shame. I'm so-o sorry." Wood engaged in this "little caper" to "dress the two knock offs up a bit", and because he has "a flair for the dramatics at times".

The first witness for the *defense* was the Assistant District Attorney, who had testified for the People regarding Wood's statement. He now related what Wood told him during the time the statement was being transcribed. Defendant spoke, among other things, about three murders he had committed in the past. He subsequently described them orally and in writing to the psychiatrists who examined him at Bellevue Hospital prior to trial, and who testified with reference thereto. In 1925 when he was about 15 years old, and because "he couldn't have her", Wood injected arsenic into some cream puffs which he sent to a girl, Cynthia Longo, who died as a result thereof. Thereafter, when he was about 21 years old, he bludgeoned 140 times and stabbed to death a woman he encountered one night. Having contracted syphilis and gonorrhea from another woman, thus becoming angry at women generally, he picked this stranger to kill.

In 1942 defendant murdered John Loman because the latter made a disparaging remark about Wood's girl friend. Wood caused Loman to become very drunk, attempted to asphyxiate him with gas, and when this failed to achieve the desired result, he bashed in Loman's head. With the help of his girl friend, Wood hid the body, planning to dismember it later and dispose of the parts. When arrested, he denied his guilt, and the authorities had a " 'hell of a time' " attempting to prove premeditation. Though convicted of murder second degree, defendant said he was " 'actually guilty of Murder in the First Degree' ". He was sentenced to from 20 years to life, only to be paroled less than a month before the present homicides.

Defendant further told the Assistant District Attorney that after the jury's verdict in the Loman case, but prior to sentence, he slashed his wrists in a suicide "attempt", because he did not want to spend a lot of time in prison, and felt he could obtain better treatment in a hospital. He was sent to Dannemora State Hospital, where he enjoyed himself and was allowed to play cards, but when certain privileges were withdrawn, he became dissatisfied and felt it was time to tell the psychiatrist he was not insane. Defendant boasted that "Anytime I wanted to, I knew I could get out of there because I wasn't insane"; he "could fool anybody", he was "fooling the psychiatrist all along" and "could do it anytime". He succeeded.

After the hospital released him, Wood was transferred to prison, where he determined to and did become a model prisoner as he sorely wanted to gain freedom. Paroled and assigned to Albany district, Wood obtained employment in a laundry. He was not happy there, however, knew that eventually he would begin drinking again, in which event he would lose his job and be returned to prison, and, therefore, decided to lose himself in New York City.

Although the four defense psychiatrists testified in answer to hypothetical questions that on June 30th defendant was laboring under such defect of reason as to know neither the nature nor the quality of his acts nor that they were wrong, their conclusions were largely weakened by lengthy and vigorous cross-examinations. By contrast, the People's two psychiatric experts, who testified that Wood was legally sane, were together asked but six questions on cross-examination, to two of which objections were sustained.

When the defense psychiatrists had testified, defendant, against the advice of his attorneys, took the stand, after having been duly cautioned, and stated that, although he was "very sick" while at Bellevue for examination, "at the time I committed the crime, the two murders, I knew the nature and I knew the quality of my act. I was sane then, perfectly sane, and I am perfectly sane now". He made this statement, he testified, because he had "been living on borrowed time" since 1926, and furthermore he did not "relish the prospect of going back to prison for the rest of my life or to any insane asylum". He was not cross-examined.

Defendant now merely urges that the People failed to establish beyond a reasonable doubt that he knew the acts were wrong. We now consider this contention. In substance, the expert testimony for the defense was that Wood had schizophrenic reaction, an illness from which he had suffered since about 1926, though "not probably an organic illness". In this connection, the defense psychiatrists stated that although defendant's memory was good, his sensorium clear, he was unaware of the full significance and consequences of his acts, though he knew their physical nature and quality, and that his judgment was impaired, his reasoning defective. Further, defendant told the psychiatrists at Bellevue that he considered himself to be "God's emissary" to take and to save life, and that he was presently charged with the duty of seeking out and killing those whom he believed were degenerates. Their cross-examination established beyond peradventure that Wood knew it was against the law to kill a human being.

One of the People's psychiatrists, Dr. Winkler, who first examined Wood in July, 1960 at Kings County Hospital and interviewed him in April, 1961, testified that defendant had a "highly pathological personality * * * a severe personality disorder", which manifested itself early in his life, but had not "deteriorated" since. Dr. Winkler noted that though defendant had been subjected to extensive hospital observation during the course of his lifetime, the diagnosis of schizophrenic reaction was made *for the first time* at Bellevue in the Fall of 1960. The witness further stated that Wood cannot be called "mentally ill or psychotic", and that his moral judgment was not distorted by illness or disease, but had "never developed". Another "peculiarity", Dr. Winkler testified, was defendant's "inability to control his impulses", a pathological sign but not "legal insanity". During three weeks' observation at the hospital in July, 1960, Wood had not shown any evidence of a psychotic condition.

Regarding the "God's emissary" delusion, Dr. Winkler entertained "definite doubts" that this was "a firm, fixed belief" and gave his reasons therefor. It is of some significance that Wood made this assertion for the *first* time in a psychiatric examination during the latter part of January or in February, 1961, seven months after the homicides with which he was charged, and following the administration of sodium amytal, a drug which, according to Dr. Winkler, might induce delusions. The Kings County Hospital report of July, 1960 does not contain a reference to this delusion. Most significant is the fact that Wood did not mention the delusion in his July 5th statement, but admitted he did something "wrong" on June 30th, namely, killed two men. Indeed, he stated then that *he* "always had a distaste" for degenerates, and had killed Rescigno partly "for the satisfaction of" killing a degenerate, and partly to steal money. It may also be noted that the "God's emissary" delusion and degeneracy had nothing to do with his previous three murders.

Moreover, he did not just kill Rescigno when he ascertained the latter was a degenerate, but first had to "figure out the angles", made sure his intended victim was drunk, and then distracted him by offering a cigarette. After the killings, defendant did not tarry long, being apprehensive that Sess' dying noises and the barking of a dog would alert neighbors to the fact "that something was *wrong*" (emphasis supplied). The People's psychiatrist, Dr. D'Angelo, supported Dr. Winkler in his view that defendant knew the nature and quality of his acts and that they were wrong.

In People v. Schmidt, . . . Judge Cardozo, discussing the meaning of the word "wrong" as used in section 1120, Consol.Laws, c. 40 of the Penal Law, held that there are certain circumstances in which the word "ought not to be limited to legal wrong." Continuing: "Knowledge that an act is forbidden by law will in most cases permit the inference of knowledge that, according to the accepted standards of mankind, it is also condemned as an offense against good morals. Obedience to the law is itself a moral duty. If, however, there is an insane delusion that

God has appeared to the defendant and ordained the commission of a crime, we think it cannot be said of the offender that he knows the act to be wrong. It is not enough, to relieve from criminal liability, that the prisoner is morally depraved [citation]. It is not enough that he has views of right and wrong at variance with those that find expression in the law. The variance must have its origin in some disease of the mind. . . . * * * Cases will doubtless arise where criminals will take shelter behind a professed belief that their crime was ordained by God * * *. We can safely leave such fabrications to the common sense of juries." . . .

As defendant concedes in his brief, the Trial Judge correctly charged the jury on the meaning of the word "wrong" when he stated: "When it speaks of the defendant's ignorance of his act as wrong, the law does not mean to permit the individual to be his own judge of what is right or wrong. It says that the individual has sufficient knowledge that an act was wrong if its perpetrator knows that his act is against the law and against the commonly accepted standards of morality and conduct which prevail in the community of mankind. He must know that his act was contrary to the laws of God and man." The Trial Judge then stated an example which is so strikingly parallel to defendant's claim that the jury could not have failed to see the point.

Of course the question as to whether Wood knew it was wrong to kill when he killed Sess and Rescigno was a question of fact for the jury, and, as we stated in People v. Horton, . . . "if the record in its entirety presents a fair conflict in the evidence, or if conflicting inferences can properly be drawn from it, ' * * * the determination of the jury will not be interfered with, unless it is clearly against the weight of evidence, or appears to have been influenced by passion, prejudice, mistake or corruption.' . . . We see nothing in the record to take the instant case out of this general rule. Of course the fact that a defendant was suffering from some type of mental disorder . . ., or that he had a psychopathic personality . . ., or that his "moral perceptions were of low order" . . ., or that he had an irresistible impulse to commit the crime . . ., does not immunize him from criminal responsibility. . . .

There was abundant evidence here upon which the jury reasonably could have rejected entirely the defense that Wood considered himself to be "God's emissary". Moreover, the jury, having been properly instructed, could reasonably have found that defendant was operating under a standard of morality he had set up for himself and which applied only to him. The law does not excuse for such moral depravity or "views of right and wrong at variance with those that find expression in the law" . . . While the very nature and circumstances of the present homicides, as well as the expert testimony on both sides, make clear that Wood was not well balanced mentally, the weight of evidence clearly supports the determination, implicit in the verdict, that he knew not only the nature and quality of his acts, but also that they were wrong, as that term was correctly defined and exemplified by the trial court. Under these circumstances we have no right to interfere with the verdict. . . .

Defendant also contends that he was denied a fair trial on the issue of insanity by reason of various rulings of the court and certain conduct and comment of the prosecutor. One of these contentions relates to the remarks of the prosecutor in his summation concerning two of the defense psychiatrists. Specifically he referred to them as "the two happiness boys", as "those two idiots—I am sorry, those two psychiatrists"; he "charged" them with being "ignorant, stupid, incompetent", and scoffed at their titles of "Diplomate". These remarks were clearly improper, and cannot be justified or excused by anything that transpired earlier in the trial. Although we have been disturbed by this aspect of the case, we have concluded that these remarks, now complained of, did not deprive defendant of a fair trial. Only the first of these comments was objected to at the trial, and it was stricken. Counsel did not object to the summation upon the ground that it or any part thereof was inflammatory, nor make a motion for a mistrial. While objection need not be voiced in a capital case to preserve a question for our review, we are of the opinion, on the present record, that the prosecutor's remarks had no influence upon the jury.

We have examined the other contentions of the defendant and find no merit to them.

The judgment appealed from should be affirmed.

FULD, JUDGE (dissenting). I agree with the court that, upon the record before us, the People have established that the defendant was legally sane under the law of this State as it now stands . . ., but I cannot refrain from observing that the result demonstrates the unreality, if not the invalidity, of our present standards for determining criminal responsibility. This case serves to confirm the view, frequently expressed over the years, that section 1120 of the Penal Law should be amended and the "right-wrong" test which now controls our decisions changed.

However, since the issue of the defendant's insanity under section 1120 seems to me so extremely close, I do not believe that we may disregard the prosecutor's concededly inexcusable and improper remarks, relating to the defense psychiatrists, as technical error under section 542 of the Code of Criminal Procedure.

DESMOND, C. J., and VAN VOORHIS, J., dissent and vote to reverse and to dismiss the indictment upon the ground that by the clear weight of evidence this defendant is insane under the rule of section 1120 of the Penal Law in which connection we express our strong disapproval of the prosecutor's inexcusable ridicule of the court-appointed psychiatrists.

NOTES

1. Subsequently, the New York legislature changed the test of insanity. See New York Penal Law § 40.15.

2. Consider the following statement of the Supreme Court of North Carolina in State v. Cooper, 286 N.C. 549, 213 S.E.2d 305, 321 (1975):

"We may take judicial notice of the well known fact that a dog, a wild animal or a completely savage, uncivilized man may have the mental capacity to intend to kill and patiently to stalk his prey for that purpose. The law, however, does not impose criminal responsibility upon one who has this level of mental capacity only. For criminal responsibility it requires that the accused have, at the time of the act, the higher mental ability to distinguish between right and wrong with reference to that act. It requires less mental ability to form a purpose to do an act than to determine its moral quality. The jury, by its verdict, has conclusively established that this defendant, at the time he killed his wife and the four little children, had this higher level of mental capacity. It necessarily follows that he had the lesser, included capacity. The jury also determined that he did, in fact, premeditate and deliberate upon the intended killings. It made these determinations in the light of proper instructions as to what constitutes premeditation and deliberation. Premeditation and deliberation do not require a long, sustained period of brooding."

B. THE IRRESISTIBLE IMPULSE TEST

As a supplement to the M'Naghten test, a number of jurisdictions have adopted the so-called "irresistible impulse" test. Under that test, the jury is instructed that it must acquit the defendant if it finds that the diseased mind of the accused rendered him incapable of exercising the normal governing power of the will so as to control his actions under the compulsion of an insane impulse to act. The rule is not a recent one, since an instruction based on the same concept was given as early as 1844 in a Massachusetts case. Chief Justice Shaw's jury instruction in Commonwealth v. Rogers [1] read, in part:

> If then it is proved, to the satisfaction of the jury, that the mind of the accused was in a diseased and unsound state, the question will be, whether the disease existed to so high a degree, that for the time being it overwhelmed the reason, conscience, and judgment, and whether the prisoner, in committing the homicide acted from an irresistible and uncontrollable impulse, if so, then the act was not the act of a voluntary agent, but the involuntary act of the body, without the concurrence of a mind directing it.

Consider the following paragraph from Moenssens & Inbau, Scientific Evidence in Criminal Cases (2d ed. 1978), Chapter 3 on "Forensic Psychiatry", § 3.03(2):

> The motivation for formulating the irresistible impulse rule arose from the psychiatrist's difficulty in perceiving the

1. 48 Mass. (7 Metc.) 500, 502 (1844).

various forms of compulsive behavior within the M'Naghten definition of legal insanity. Compulsive behavior such as kleptomania, pyromania, and dipsomania occurs when the actor does know right from wrong and does contemplate the consequences of his normative violation, knowing it is wrong, but nevertheless persists in the act because of an inner force which he is powerless to resist. Psychiatrists might not categorize this individual as insane in the right-wrong sense; consequently, if such behavior is to be exempted from responsibility, the irresistible impulse is a necessary adjunct to *M'Naghten.* It should also be observed that if the named dysfunctions do not qualify as an irresistible impulse, they would under the next test. [The Durham Test, infra]

NOTES

1. Can a person have a true "irresistible impulse" without his being, at the same time, deficient or defective with respect to the nature and quality of his act or his ability to distinguish between right and wrong? Consider the following viewpoints:

(a) ". . . there are no clinical data which support, the hypothesis that a person's intelligence may be quite normal but that he may nonetheless be unable to keep from killing or robbing or committing some other serious harm . . . The assumption that kleptomania and pyromania are psychoses expressing irresistible impulses is also untenable. Recent studies have shown that they are usually neuroses, and also that the claim of concomitant unimpaired intelligence is fallacious. Thus, a psychiatrist reporting on his study of kleptomaniacs states, 'One thing is certain. Every patient who has ever been investigated extensively showed some faults in the critical appreciation of the factors of reality'." Hall, General Principles of Criminal Law (2d ed. 1960), 488.

(b) ". . . while it is true that the effective, cognitive and co-native processes of the mind are interrelated, certain forms of mental disorder may affect one more than the others. A disorder manifesting itself in impulsions which can be said to have been 'irresistible', may affect intelligence *somewhat,* but not necessarily to such extent as to obliterate knowledge of right and wrong." Weihofen, Mental Disorder as a Criminal Defense 96 (1954).

2. As to whether kleptomania is a legal defense in those jurisdictions which recognize the "irresistible impulse" doctrine, see Weihofen, supra, p. 124, n. 15.

3. Irresistible impulse is not the same as "temporary insanity." In State v. Kolisnitschenko, 84 Wis.2d 492, 267 N.W.2d 321 (1978), the Court said, "[W]e are not willing to hold . . . that a temporary psychotic state which lasts only for the period of intoxication and which is brought into existence by the interaction of a stormy personality and voluntary intoxication constitutes a mental disease which is a defense to the crime charged [murder]."

C. THE PRODUCT TEST

In Durham v. United States, 94 U.S.App.D.C. 228, 214 F.2d 862 (1954) defendant Durham, an individual with a long history of mental illness, appealed from his conviction for housebreaking on the grounds that the existing tests in the District of Columbia for determining criminal responsibility (the right-wrong test supplemented by the irresistible impulse test) were not satisfactory criteria for determining criminal responsibility.

The Court of Appeals for the District of Columbia accepted the argument of a large number of medico-legal writers that the right-wrong test is based upon an entirely obsolete and misleading conception of the nature of insanity. It accepted the view of psychiatry that man is an integrated personality of which reason is only one element, not the sole determinant of his conduct. Therefore the right-wrong test, because it considers knowledge or reason alone, is an inadequate guide to mental responsibility for criminal behavior. The fundamental objection to the right-wrong test is that it is made to rest upon any particular symptom. In attempting to define insanity in terms of a symptom, courts have assumed an impossible role.

Turning to the "irresistible impulse test", the court found that test inadequate because based upon the misleading implication that "diseased mental condition(s)" produce only sudden, momentary or spontaneous inclinations to commit unlawful acts. Such a test gives no recognition to mental illness characterized by brooding and reflection.

Finally, the court concluded that a broader test should be adopted and formulated the rule that an accused is not criminally responsible if his unlawful act was the "product of mental disease or mental defect". It went on to say, "We use 'disease' in the sense of a condition which is considered capable of either improving or deteriorating. We use 'defect' in the sense of a condition which is not considered capable of either improving or deteriorating and which may be either congenital or the result of injury or the residual effect of a physical or mental disease." [1]

In essence this test permits a jury to find a defendant not guilty by reason of insanity if it believes beyond a reasonable doubt that the accused suffered from a mental disease or defect and that there was sufficient causal connection between the mental abnormality and the accused's unlawful act to excuse the defendant from criminal responsibility for it. [2]

An excellent analysis of the various arguments for and against adoption of the *Durham* test is found in Sauer v. United States, 241

---

1. A similar "product" test had previously been formulated by New Hampshire in State v. Pike, 49 N.H. 399 (1870) and State v. Jones, 50 N.H. 369 (1871).

2. It should be noted here that the District of Columbia has abandoned the Durham-Product test in United States v. Brawner, 471 F.2d 969 (D.C.Cir. 1972), discussed infra.

F.2d 640 (9th Cir. 1957), where the court was called upon to decide whether the traditional right-wrong test, supplemented by the irresistible impulse test, would continue to be used, or whether the *Durham* test should be adopted. The court expressed doubt that the question was an open one for it to decide; it was of the opinion that the United States' Supreme Court had tacitly endorsed the "right-wrong" and irresistible impulse tests in the two cases of Davis v. United States, 160 U.S. 469, 16 S.Ct. 353 (1895), and 165 U.S. 373, 17 S.Ct. 360 (1897). Nevertheless it stated the following:

"At the beginning it is appropriate to state that even if we were free to decide this question anew—the same result would be reached. The rule of the Durham case would be rejected. . . .

"A.   Advantages Seen in the Durham Rule

"The chief advantage of the Durham test, according to its proponents, is that under it the jury is no longer required to rely on specific and particular mental symptoms in determining criminal responsibility, but that all relevant evidence as to mental condition goes to the jury on the ultimate question of fact. The court pointed out that psychiatry now recognizes that man is an integrated personality; that the forces that drive him cannot be compartmentalized. Hence, it is urged that the M'Naghten test, which emphasized the intellect or cognitive element and consequently de-emphasizes the volitional and emotional facets of personality, is not only misleading and inadequate, but an impossible guide. The Durham decision is said to have the further effect of permitting the expert witness to carry out his proper role of informing the jury of the nature of the mental disorder suffered by the accused, without limiting him to the 'moral' question of right and wrong.

"One evident consequence of the Durham decision is to shift the entire question of criminal responsibility to the jury. Some say this is as it should be, viewing the question of responsibility as solely one of fact. Under the M'Naghten rules, a division of authority exists. It is the function of the court to develop a standard of criminal responsibility, based on the moral and ethical standards of the community, and it is for the jury to ascertain, first, whether the accused is in fact a victim of mental disorder, and secondly, whether his affliction meets the criteria established by the courts.

"The Durham opinion has generally been regarded as a response by the law to progress achieved in the field of psychiatry. It has been the recipient of much favorable comment. But it is far from having obtained universal acceptance.

"B.   Disadvantages Seen in the Durham Rule

"The Durham rule has been subjected to articulate and persuasive criticism by distinguished commentators. Though the psychiatrists view the Durham opinion as their Magna Carta, it appears that it may raise almost as many questions as it resolves. . . .

". . . [T]he release of psychiatrists from the 'strait jacket' of M'Naghten's Rules can hardly be regarded as a panacea for the problem of communication from medical expert to layman. This communication is a semantic problem that faces judges and attorneys daily. It is difficult to solve, but the solution may better lie, not in the layman accommodating the specialist, but rather in the adjustment by the specialist of his technical vocabulary to the language of the layman. It should be added that some of the 'strait jacket' argument is based on a lack of a real understanding of the operation of trial courts. There appear to be some who believe that the expert witness is asked but one question: 'Did the accused know right from wrong?' Nothing could be further from the truth. The inquiry quoted is but the ultimate question. For example, in the instant matter, Dr. Vernon Miller, the court appointed psychiatrist, testified at length regarding the appellant's disorders before he was asked the critical question. The appellant's entire mental condition was brought to the attention of the jury. Dr. Miller cogently and concisely described appellant's abnormality in language that could be clearly understood by the jury. If he was verbally confined in a 'strait jacket,' it is apparent that he did not know it and that no one took the effort to inform him of it.

"The abdication of responsibility for determining the standard of criminal responsibility by the court in the Durham case exposes the court to the same criticism levied against the New Hampshire decisions. . . . The resulting uncertainty would breed disrepute of the law. Moreover, the plea of insanity, presently under heavy criticism as a frequently used ruse in homicide cases, would thus be made even more attractive to an accused.

"Most importantly, however, the Durham case must be examined in the light of the purposes of the criminal law. It is here that the new rule must face its final test. . . .

"Whatever we may conclude to be the objectives of the criminal law, one traditional result has been punishment. Functioning under such a system, our society does not assess punishment where it cannot ascribe blame. It is inimical to the morals and ideals of an organized social order to impose punishment where blame cannot be affixed. Man is regarded as a moral being. Modern psychiatry to the contrary, the criminal law is grounded upon the theory that, in the absence of special conditions, individuals are free to exercise a choice between possible courses of conduct and hence are morally responsible. Thus, it is moral guilt that the law stresses.

"At least one purpose of the penal law is to express a formal social condemnation for forbidden conduct, and buttress that condemnation by sanctions calculated to prevent that which is forbidden. The ultimate goal is deterrence. In attempting to achieve this end we employ means which secondarily satisfy the retributive feelings of society.

Any theory of criminal responsibility must be evolved in light of these purposes, else it will be unacceptable to some considerable segment of society.

"Much of the conflict over the rules of criminal responsibility is attributable to a basic misconception as to the nature of the problem. Criminal responsibility is a legal not a medical question. Involved is legal consequence, not medical diagnosis, Indeed, we are told by recognized authorities that the word 'insanity' has no medical significance; that no such condition has been found; and that there are serious doubts that such condition exists. This information is transmitted by voices tinged with alarm. The fears are misplaced. The law is not endeavoring to pioneer in medical science. When the word 'insanity' is used, it can be no more and no less than a shorthand legal expression to describe the consequences which certain symptoms of various mental diseases or defects produce in the law. Its meaning may vary with the purpose at hand. It may mean one thing in respect to capacity to make a valid contract and a far different thing as it pertains to criminal responsibility. Perhaps the confusion would be alleviated if the term 'insanity' could be relegated to the wastebasket. . . .

"Perhaps a revision of the rules of criminal responsibility would be forthcoming if the law felt it could place greater trust and confidence in psychiatry. The spectacle not only of individual psychiatrists in disagreement, but also entire divergent schools of thought is not an inspiring one. As one authority stated, '[P]sychiatry is still more of an art than a science.'

"But there is another, and possibly the most significant reason, why this court must refuse to modify existing law. Many observers implicitly assume in their criticism of present law that if the accused is set free on the criminal side that he will be confined on the civil. Unfortunately, that is not the case. If it were, this court might be much more disposed to alter its current views. The choice today in this jurisdiction is not between confinement and commitment, but rather between confinement and freedom.

"This, however, is not the situation in the District of Columbia, nor was it at the time Durham was decided. In fact, Judge Bazelon carefully noted that the decision would not set Durham free. Under the then existing D.C. Code provision, Sec. 24–301, if the jury found the accused not guilty solely by reason of insanity, it was required to so state. The statute further provided that the court 'may' then have him committed. Congress, however, was obviously concerned that commitment was discretionary, and so by an amendment passed on August 9, 1955, commitment was made mandatory.

"Unlike the District of Columbia, and the procedure in some State courts, there is no similar provision governing the conduct of trials in other Federal courts. The defense of insanity comes under the 'not guilty' plea, and the jury is not required to state specifically its grounds

for acquittal. Thus there is no way for the Government to determine
the basis of the jury verdict. It therefore sets the accused free. As a
case in point, consider the instant matter. One could hardly find a
factual situation in which there is less dispute as to what transpired.
Yet if the jury found the appellant not guilty, how could the court, the
Government or anyone ever know that it was because of insanity, or
because the jury believed he lacked the necessary specific intent at the
time he entered the bank?

"Dr. Miller testified in this case that appellant suffers from an
epileptic condition characterized by grand mal seizures, petit mal
episodes, and psychomotor episodes. However, he stated that appellant
did not suffer an attack from this condition while committing the
offense charged. Dr. Miller also stated that appellant has a mental
disorder which he termed a schizophrenic reaction of the hebephrenic
type. In essence, this means that the individual is silly, has poor
control of his emotional responses, and poor reasoning power. He was
of the opinion that appellant is a passive dependent personality, and
that such a person 'finds it rather difficult to make decisions regarding
their adult responsibilities. They don't handle adult problems very
well.' He testified that appellant has a 'dependent' and 'inadequate'
personality, and he recommended that appellant be institutionalized.
Yet, if the jury acquitted appellant on the ground of insanity, there is
no provision in the United States Code which would authorize the
Government to have appellant committed. That a regrettable void
exists in the law today in this respect is readily apparent. . . .

". . . [I]t is not for this court to undertake a drastic revision in
the concept of criminal responsibility, a task which would necessitate a
searching analysis of philosophies, purposes, and policies of the criminal law, and which might substitute freedom of insane persons for
either confinement or commitment. If change there is to be, it must
come from a higher judicial authority, or from the Congress.

"The judgment of the District Court is affirmed."

D. THE AMERICAN LAW INSTITUTE (A.L.I.) TEST, AND ITS RECENT MODIFICATIONS

The response of other jurisdictions to *Durham* was less than
enthusiastic. Perhaps this was due in part to the increasing popularity
of the A.L.I. test. The American Law Institute, in Tentative Draft No.
4 of its Model Penal Code, proposed the following insanity test:

(1) A person is not responsible for criminal conduct if at
the time of such conduct as a result of mental disease or defect
he lacks substantial capacity either to appreciate the criminality of his conduct or to conform his conduct to the requirements
of law.

(2) The terms "mental disease or defect" do not include an abnormality manifested only by repeated criminal or otherwise anti-social conduct.

As the A.L.I. test became adopted in more jurisdictions, the *Durham* rule lost what little stature it had achieved. Then on June 23, 1972, the Court of Appeals for the District of Columbia, in United States v. Brawner, 471 F.2d 969 (D.C.Cir. 1972), abandoned *Durham* and accepted the A.L.I. test. The court continued to adhere, however, to the definition of "mental disease or defect" it had earlier articulated in McDonald v. United States, 114 U.S.App.D.C. 120, 312 F.2d 847 (1962): "mental disease or defect includes any abnormal condition of the mind which substantially affects mental or emotional processes and substantially impairs behavior controls." The principal reason for the *Brawner* departure from *Durham* was the undue dominance gained by experts giving testimony on insanity. This dominance occurred because of the broad area of relevance encompassed by the *Durham's* "product" concept which "did not signify a reasonably identifiable common ground that was also shared by the nonlegal experts, and the laymen serving on the jury as the representatives of the community. Accordingly, the court decided:

> The experts have meaningful information to impart, not only to the existence of mental illness or not, but also on its relationship to the incident charged as an offense. In the interest of justice this valued information should be available, and should not be lost or blocked by requirements that unnaturally restrict communication between the experts and the jury. The more we have pondered the problem the more convinced we have become that the sound solution lies not in further shaping of the *Durham* "product" approach in more refined molds, but in adopting the ALI's formulation as the linchpin of our jurisprudence.

> The ALI's formulation retains the core requirement of a meaningful relationship between the mental illness and the incident charged. The language in the ALI rule is sufficiently in the common ken that its use in the courtroom, or in preparation for trial, permits a reasonable three-way communication—between (a) the law-trained, judges and lawyers; (b) the experts and (c) the jurymen—without insisting on a vocabulary that is either stilted or stultified, or conducive to a testimonial mystique permitting expert dominance and encroachment on the jury's function. There is no indication in the available literature that any such untoward development has attended the reasonably widespread adoption of the ALI rule in the Federal courts and a substantial number of state courts.

With respect to the caveat paragraph in subsection (2) of the Model Penal Code test, which excludes from the concept of mental disease or defect abnormalities that are manifested only by repeated criminal or otherwise anti-social conduct, the *Brawner* court took notice of the fact that there was a split among the jurisdiction which had adopted the ALI test concerning this provision. Some courts had concluded to adopt the caveat, which excluded the defense of insanity for the so-called psychopathic personalities or sociopaths, while other jurisdictions had specifically decided to omit it from the test. *Brawner* pragmatically adopted the caveat paragraph as a rule for application by the judge, to avoid miscarriage of justice, but not for inclusion in instructions to the jury. The court stated in this regard:

> . . . The introduction or proffer of past criminal and anti-social actions is not admissible as evidence of mental disease unless accompanied by expert testimony, supported by a showing of the concordance of a responsible segment of professional opinion, that the particular characteristics of these actions constitute convincing evidence of an underlying mental disease that substantially impairs behavioral controls.

In an appendix to its opinion the Court of Appeals for the District of Columbia in *Brawner* suggested the following instruction on insanity to be given at trial:

"The defendant in this case asserts the defense of insanity.

"You are not to consider this defense unless you have first found that the Government has proved beyond a reasonable doubt each essential element of the offense. One of these elements is the requirement [of premeditation and deliberation for first degree murder] [or of specific intent for _____], on which you have already been instructed. In determining whether that requirement has been proved beyond a reasonable doubt you may consider the testimony as to the defendant's abnormal mental condition.

"If you find that the Government has failed to prove beyond a reasonable doubt any one or more of the essential elements of the offense, you must find the defendant not guilty, and you should not consider any possible verdict relating to insanity.

"If you find that the Government has proved each essential element of the offense beyond a reasonable doubt, then you must consider whether to bring in a verdict of not guilty by reason of insanity.

"The law provides that a jury shall bring in a verdict of not guilty by reason of insanity if, at the time of the criminal conduct, the defendant, as a result of mental disease or defect, either lacked substantial capacity to conform his conduct to the requirements of the law, or lacked substantial capacity to appreciate the wrongfulness of his conduct.

"Every man is presumed to be sane, that is, to be without mental disease or defect, and to be responsible for his acts. But that presumption no longer controls when evidence is introduced that he may have a mental disease or defect.

"The term insanity does not require a showing that the defendant was disoriented as to time or place.

"Mental disease [or defect includes any abnormal condition of the mind, regardless of its medical label, which substantially affects mental or emotional processes and substantially impairs behavior controls. The term 'behavior controls' refers to the processes and capacity of a person to regulate and control his conduct and his actions.

"In considering whether the defendant had a mental disease [or defect] at the time of the unlawful act with which he is charged, you may consider testimony in this case concerning the development, adaptation and functioning of these mental and emotional processes and behavior controls.

"[The term 'mental disease' differs from 'mental defect' in that the former is a condition which is either capable of improving or deteriorating and the latter is a condition not capable of improving or deteriorating.]

"[Burden of proof—alternate versions:

"(b) The burden of proof is on the defendant to establish by a preponderance of the evidence that, as a result of mental disease or defect, he either lacked substantial capacity to conform his conduct to the requirements of the law or lacked substantial capacity to appreciate the wrongfulness of his conduct. If defendant has met that burden you shall bring in a verdict of not guilty by reason of insanity. If he has not met that burden you shall bring in a verdict of guilty of the offenses you found proved beyond a reasonable doubt.

"(b) The burden is on the Government to prove beyond a reasonable doubt either that the defendant was not suffering from a mental disease or defect, or else that he nevertheless had substantial capacity both to conform his conduct to the requirements of the law and to appreciate the wrongfulness of his conduct. If the Government has not established this beyond a reasonable doubt, you shall bring in a verdict of not guilty by reason of insanity.]

"Evaluation of Testimony

"In considering the issue of insanity, you may consider the evidence that has been admitted as to the defendant's mental condition before and after the offense charged, as well as the evidence as to defendant's mental condition on that date. The evidence as to the defendant's mental condition before and after that date was admitted solely for the purpose of assisting you to determine the defendant's condition on the date of the alleged offense.

"You have heard the evidence of psychiatrists [and psychologists] who testified as expert witnesses. An expert in a particular field is permitted to give his opinion in evidence. In this connection, you are instructed that you are not bound by medical labels, definitions, or conclusions as to what is or is not a mental disease [or defect]. What psychiatrists [and psychologists] may or may not consider a mental disease [or defect] for clinical purposes, where their concern is treatment, may or may not be the same as mental disease [or defect] for the purpose of determining criminal responsibility. Whether the defendant had a mental disease [or defect] must be determined by you under the explanation of those terms as it has been given to you by the Court.

"There was also testimony of lay witnesses, with respect to their observations of defendant's appearance, behavior, speech, and actions. Such persons are permitted to testify as to their own observations and other facts known to them and may express an opinion based upon those observations and facts known to them. In weighing the testimony of such lay witnesses, you may consider the circumstances of each witness, his opportunity to observe the defendant and to know the facts to which he has testified, his willingness and capacity to expound freely as to his observations and knowledge, the basis for his opinion and conclusions, and the nearness or remoteness of his observations of the defendant in point of time to the commission of the offense charged.

"You may also consider whether the witness observed extraordinary or bizarre acts performed by the defendant, or whether the witness observed the defendant's conduct to be free of such extraordinary or bizarre acts. In evaluating such testimony, you should take into account the extent of the witness's observation of the defendant and the nature and length of time of the witness's contact with the defendant. You should bear in mind that an untrained person may not be readily able to detect mental disease [or defect] and that the failure of a lay witness to observe abnormal acts by the defendant may be significant only if the witness had prolonged and intimate contact with the defendant.

"You are not bound by the opinions of either expert or lay witnesses. You should not arbitrarily or capriciously reject the testimony of any witness, but you should consider the testimony of each witness in connection with the other evidence in the case and give it such weight as you believe it is fairly entitled to receive.

"You may also consider that every man is presumed to be sane, that is, to be without mental disease [or defect], and to be responsible for his acts. You should consider this principle in the light of all the evidence in the case and give it such weight as you believe it is fairly entitled to receive.

"Effect of Verdict of Not Guilty by Reason of Insanity

"If the defendant is found not guilty by reason of insanity, it becomes the duty of the court to commit him to St. Elizabeths Hospital. There will be a hearing within 50 days to determine whether defendant is entitled to release. In that hearing the defendant has the burden of proof. The defendant will remain in custody, and will be entitled to release from custody only if the court finds by preponderance of the evidence that he is not likely to injure himself or other persons due to mental illness.

"Note: If the defendant so requests this instruction need not be given."

NOTES

1. The A.L.I. test, sometimes with omissions or slight revisions, was adopted in the following federal cases: United States v. Freeman, 357 F.2d 606 (2d Cir. 1966); Government of Virgin Islands v. Fredericks, 578 F.2d 927 (3d Cir. 1978); United States v. Chandler, 393 F.2d 920 (4th Cir. 1968); Blake v. United States, 407 F.2d 908 (5th Cir. 1969); United States v. Smith, 404 F.2d 720 (6th Cir. 1968); United States v. Shapiro, 383 F.2d 680 (7th Cir. 1967); Pope v. United States, 372 F.2d 710 (8th Cir. 1967); Wade v. United States, 426 F.2d 64 (9th Cir. 1970); Wion v. United States, 325 F.2d 420 (10th Cir. 1963); United States v. Brawner, supra, (D.C.Cir. 1972); United States v. Frederick, 3 M.J. 230 (1977). The First Circuit, in Amador Beltran v. United States, 302 F.2d 48 (1st Cir. 1962), suggested, in reversing a conviction of perjury where the judge had applied the M'Naghten rule, that on re-trial the court be guided by the ALI test as used in United States v. Currens, 290 F.2d 751 (3d Cir. 1961).

2. Many states, too, have patterned their insanity test upon the A.L.I. formulation, whether by statute (e.g., Illinois, Maryland, Vermont), or by judicial decision. A 1981 annotation, "Modern Status of Test of Criminal Responsibility—State Cases," listed 29 states as having adopted the A.L.I. test, in its original or modified form, as against 15 states still adhering to M'Naghten, and another 5 states as adopting M'Naghten + irresistible impulse. See 9 A.L.R.4th 526.

3. In People v. Wolff, 61 Cal.2d 795, 40 Cal.Rptr. 271, 394 P.2d 959 (1964), the defendant unsuccessfully attempted to have the M'Naghten test declared unconstitutional. In September, 1978, however, the Supreme Court of California in its 4/3 decision in People v. Drew, 22 Cal.3d 333, 149 Cal.Rptr. 275, 583 P.2d 1318 (1978), discarded the M'Naghten rule it had followed for over a century and, instead, adopted the American Law Institute test, in a lengthy opinion by Justice Tobriner. The dissenting opinion of Justice Richardson felt that "a major change of the type contemplated by the majority should be made by the Legislature." How valid is that argument?

The ALI test embraced in People v. Drew was effectively nullified when California voters, in 1982, passed Proposition 8. Subsequently there was enacted California Penal Code §§ 25(b) which provides:

> In any criminal proceeding, including any juvenile court proceeding, in which a plea of not guilty by reason of insanity is entered, this defense shall be found by the trier of fact only when the accused person proved by a preponderance of the evidence that he or she was incapable of knowing or understanding the nature and quality of his or her act *and* of distinguishing right from wrong at the time of the commission of the offense.

Since the statutory language used the conjunctive "and" rather than the disjunctive "or" between the two prongs of the test, does this mean that California's earlier M'Naghten test was reinstated? In People v. Horn, 158 Cal. App.3d 1014, 205 Cal.Rptr. 119 (1984), defendant would have been insane under both the A.L.I. and the Durham tests; nevertheless, the trial court found him legally sane on the ground that the new statute was stricter than M'Naghten, in that it required both prongs to be met. The appeals court reversed, holding that Proposition 8 reinstated the M'Naghten rule and did not intend to employ a more difficult test for insanity than existed prior to its enactment. Accord: People v. Weber, 170 Cal.App.3d 139, 215 Cal.Rptr. 827 (1985). When a different appeals court came to a contrary result, the California Supreme Court resolved the issue in People v. Skinner, 39 Cal.3d 765, 217 Cal.Rptr. 685, 704 P.2d 752 (1985), holding, as a matter of judicial construction, that § 25(b) was intended to restore the law to "the pre-Drew California version of the M'Naghten test." The court concluded that the conjunctive "and" in the Proposition and in the statute was a "drafting error," and that to literally apply the conjunctive "and" would pose a serious problem. In dissent, Chief Justice Bird, despite her opposition to capital punishment commented that "there is nothing in the statute, in Proposition 8 as a whole, or in the ballot arguments that implies that the electorate intended 'and' to be 'or.' However unwise that choice, it is not within the court's power to ignore the expression of popular will and rewrite the statute."

4. For tactical measures available to the prosecution in instances involving suspected spurious assertion of the insanity defense consult Flannery, Meeting the Insanity Defense, 51 J.Crim.L., C. & P.S. 309 (1960), and Goulett, The Insanity Defense in Criminal Trials (1965).

5. Consider the following recommendation that the word "wrongfulness" should be used instead of "criminality" urged by Professor Henry Weihofen, 58 J.C.L., C. & P.S. 27 (1967):

"If we are to hold a person mentally responsible for his criminal act unless he is so disordered as to be unable to appreciate its criminality, we shall have to condemn as responsible and fit for punishment some of the most wildly disordered persons ever seen—for example, persons with elaborately developed delusions who hear 'voices' and who kill while believing that the deed was commanded by God. Such a person may know full well that the act was a violation of the temporal law. He may even commit it precisely because he knows it is criminal: believing that he is the reincarnation of Jesus Christ, ordained again to suffer execution, he commits an act that will bring about that result. As long ago as 1800, just such a case was tried in England. That was the famous case of Hadfield, a war veteran who had been discharged from the British army on the ground of insanity. He was suffering from systematized delusions that, like Christ, he was called upon to sacrifice himself for the world's salvation. He therefore shot at King George III, so that by the appearance of crime he might be condemned, and thereby lay down his life as he felt divinely called upon to do. Hadfield was acquitted on the ground of insanity, largely because of the brilliant handling of the case by his counsel, Lord Erskine. Under the 'criminality' wording of the Model Code formula, it would seem that latter-day Hadfields would have to be condemned."

6. The court's opinion in United States v. Brawner, 471 F.2d 969 (D.C.Cir. 1972), was written by Circuit Judge Leventhal. Chief Judge Bazelon, who had written the Durham v. United States opinion in 1954 (94 U.S.App.D.C. 228, 214 F.2d 862), wrote a separate opinion in *Brawner,* concurring in part and dissenting in part. He stated, in part: "We are unanimous in our decision today to abandon the formulation of criminal responsibility adopted eighteen years ago in Durham. . . . But the adoption of this new test [ALI] is largely an anticlimax, for even though *Durham's* language survived until today's decision, the significant differences between our approach and the approach of

the ALI test vanished many years ago". Chief Judge Bazelon then proceeds to dispel the notion that the court's action achieved "uniformity" in the federal courts and also expresses the pessimistic view that the ALI test will not produce significantly better results than those obtained under *Durham*. The two opinions, read together (and some 70 pages long) provide an excellent analysis of the insanity defense problem. For law review discussion of *Brawner* see 47 N.Y.U.L.Rev. 962 (1972).

E. THE FEDERAL TEST

In the aftermath of the acquittal, in 1982, on grounds of insanity, of John W. Hinckley, Jr., for the attempted assassination of President Reagan, Congress, for the first time, passed a statute to formulate a uniform test for insanity for use in federal criminal trials. The Insanity Defense Reform Act of 1984 (18 U.S.C.A. § 20) provides:

§ 20. Insanity Defense

(a) Affirmative Defense. It is an affirmative defense to a prosecution under any Federal statute that, at the time of the commission of the acts constituting the offense, the defendant, as a result of severe mental disease or defect, was unable to appreciate the nature and quality of the wrongfulness of his acts. Mental disease or defect does not otherwise constitute a defense.

(b) Burden of Proof. The defendant has the burden of proving the defense of insanity by clear and convincing evidence.

Under previous federal practice, once the presumption of sanity had been overcome by evidence of insanity produced by the defendant, the burden of proving sanity beyond a reasonable doubt then shifted to the government. The Insanity Defense Reform Act shifts the burden of proving insanity to the defendant by clear and convincing evidence, and further requires that proof of the underlying disabling illness show "severe" mental disease or defect. Does such a shifting of the burden of proof run afoul of the cases discussed in Chapter 2–D on constitutional requirements related to the presumption of innocence?

F. THE WEIGHT OF PSYCHIATRIC TESTIMONY

PEOPLE v. WOLFF
Supreme Court of California, 1964.
61 Cal.2d 795, 40 Cal.Rptr. 271, 394 P.2d 959.

SCHAUER, JUSTICE. * * *

Defendant, a fifteen year old boy at the time of the crime, was charged with the murder of his mother. The juvenile court found him to be "not a fit subject for consideration" under the Juvenile Court Law, and remanded him to the superior court for further proceedings in the criminal action. To the information accusing him of murder defendant entered the single plea of "not guilty by reason of insanity," thereby admitting commission of the basic act which, if not qualified under the special plea, constitutes the offense charged. . . After considering reports of three alienists appointed to examine defendant . . . the court declared a doubt as to his mental capacity to stand trial . . . At a hearing on that issue, however, the court found defendant to be "mentally ill but not to the degree that would preclude him from cooperating with his counsel in the preparation and presentation of his defense." The plea of not guilty by reason of insanity was then tried to a jury and resulted in a verdict that defendant was legally sane at the time of the commission of the jurisdictional act of killing. . . . The court determined the crime to be murder in the first degree; . . .

         *   *   *

The Sufficiency of the Evidence of Sanity

Turning now to defendant's more specific contentions, it is first urged that "As a matter of law, [defendant] was legally insane at the time of the commission of the offense." In support of this proposition defendant stresses the fact that each of the four psychiatrists who testified at the trial stated (1) that in his *medical* opinion defendant suffers from a permanent form of one of the group of mental disorders generically known as "schizophrenia" and (2) that defendant was also *legally* insane at the time he murdered his mother. Much confusion has been engendered in this and similar cases by failure to distinguish between these two branches of the testimony and by uncritical acceptance of both as equally "expert." The bases of the psychiatrists' "legal" opinion will be explored hereinafter; on the purely medical question these witnesses agreed (and in this litigation no one disputes their findings) that defendant's illness is characterized by a "disintegration of the personality" and a "complete disassociation between intellect and emotion," that defendant "is not capable of conceptual thinking" but only of "concrete" thinking, and that although his memory is not impaired his judgment is affected "to a considerable degree."

However impressive this seeming unanimity of expert opinion may at first appear (and we give it due consideration not only on the issue of sanity, but also in a subsequent portion of this opinion wherein we discuss the degree of the crime), our inquiry on this just as on other factual issues is necessarily limited at the appellate level to a determination whether there is substantial evidence in the record to support the jury's verdict of sanity (and the trial court's finding as to the degree of the murder) under the law of this state. . . . It is only in the rare case when "the evidence is uncontradicted and entirely to the effect that the accused is insane" . . . that a unanimity of expert testimony could authorize upsetting a jury finding to the contrary. While the jury may not draw inferences inconsistent with incontestably established facts . . . nevertheless if there is substantial evidence from which the jury could infer that the defendant was legally sane at the time of the offense such a finding must be sustained in the face of any conflicting evidence, expert or otherwise, for the question of weighing that evidence and resolving that conflict "is a question of fact for the jury's determination" . . . Indeed, *the code specifically requires that the jury be instructed* (and they were so instructed in the case at bench) that "The jury is not bound to accept the opinion of any expert as conclusive, but should give to it the weight to which they shall find it to be entitled. The jury, may, however, disregard any such opinion if it shall be found by them to be unreasonable." (Pen.Code, § 1127b.)

The question of what may constitute substantial evidence of legal sanity cannot be answered by a simple formula applicable to all situations. . . .

[I]t is settled that "the conduct and declarations of the defendant occurring within a reasonable time before or after the commission of the alleged act are admissible in proof of his mental condition at the time of the offense." . . . In the present case such evidence was introduced, both of defendant's conduct and of his declarations.

Conduct of Defendant as Evidence of Legal Sanity. Among the kinds of conduct of a defendant which our courts have held to constitute evidence of legal sanity are the following: "an ability on the part of the accused to devise and execute a deliberate plan" . . .; "the manner in which the crime was conceived, planned and executed" . . .; the fact that witnesses "observed no change in his manner and that he appeared to be normal" . . .; the fact that "the defendant walked steadily and calmly, spoke clearly and coherently and appeared to be fully conscious of what he was doing" . . .; and the fact that shortly after committing the crime the defendant "was cooperative and not abusive or combative" . . ., that "questions put to him * * * were answered by him quickly and promptly" . . ., and that "he appeared rational, spoke coherently, was oriented as to time, place and those persons who were present" . . ..

In the case at bench there was evidence that in the year preceding the commission of the crime defendant "spent a lot of time thinking about sex." He made a list of the names and addresses of seven girls in his community whom he did not know personally but whom he planned to anesthetize by ether and then either rape or photograph nude. One night about three weeks before the murder he took a container of ether and attempted to enter the home of one of these girls through the chimney, but he became wedged in and had to be rescued. In the ensuing weeks defendant apparently deliberated on ways and means of accomplishing his objective and decided that he would have to bring the girls to his house to achieve his sexual purposes, and that it would therefore be necessary to get his mother (and possibly his brother) out of the way first.

The attack on defendant's mother took place on Monday, May 15, 1961. On the preceding Friday or Saturday defendant obtained an axe handle from the family garage and hid it under the mattress of his bed. At about 10 p.m. on Sunday he took the axe handle from its hiding place and approached his mother from behind, raising the weapon to strike her. She sensed his presence and asked him what he was doing; he answered that it was "nothing," and returned to his room and hid the handle under his mattress again. The following morning . . . He returned to the kitchen, approached his mother from behind and struck her on the back of the head. She turned around screaming and he struck her several more blows. They fell to the floor, fighting. She called out her neighbor's name and defendant began choking her. She bit him on the hand and crawled away. He got up to turn off the water running in the sink, and she fled through the dining room. He gave chase, caught her in the front room, and choked her to death with his hands. Defendant then took off his shirt and hung it by the fire, washed the blood off his face and hands, read a few lines from a Bible or prayer book lying upon the dining room table, and walked down to the police station to turn himself in. Defendant told the desk officer, "I have something I wish to report. * * * I just killed my mother with an axe handle." The officer testified that defendant spoke in a quiet voice and that "His conversation was quite coherent in what he was saying and he answered everything I asked him right to a T."

Defendant's counsel repeatedly characterizes as "bizarre" defendant's plan to rape or photograph nude the seven girls on his list. Certainly in common parlance it may be termed "bizarre;" likewise to a mature person of good morals, it would appear highly unreasonable. But many a youth has committed—or planned—acts which were bizarre and unreasonable. This defendant was immature and lacked experience and judgment in sexual matters. But it does not follow therefrom that the jury were precluded as a matter of law from finding defendant *legally* sane at the time of the murder. From the evidence set forth hereinabove the jury could infer that defendant had a motive for his actions (gratification of his sexual desires), that he planned the attack on his mother for some time (obtaining of the axe handle from the garage several days in advance; abortive attempt to strike his mother with it on the evening before the crime), that he knew that what he was doing was wrong (initial concealment of the handle underneath his mattress; excuse offered when his mother saw him with the weapon on the evening before the crime; renewed concealment of the handle under the mattress), that he persisted in the fatal attack (pursuit of his fleeing mother into the front room; actual infliction of death by strangling rather than bludgeoning), that he was conscious of having committed a crime (prompt surrender to the police), and that he was calm and coherent (testimony of desk officer and others). We need not determine whether such conduct would alone constitute substantial evidence from which the jury could find defendant legally sane at the time of the murder, for as will next be shown the record contains further evidence on this issue.

Declarations of Defendant as Evidence of Legal Sanity. Oral declarations made by a defendant during the period of time material to his offense may constitute evidence of legal sanity. . . . In People v.

Darling (1962) . . . we referred *inter alia* to statements made by a defendant relating to his "reason for first committing the homicide and later surrendering himself," and held that "such evidence firmly establishes that defendant was aware at all times that his actions were wrong and improper." . . .

In the case at bench defendant was questioned by Officers Stenberg and Hamilton shortly after he came to the police station and voluntarily announced that he had just killed his mother. The interrogation was transcribed and shown to defendant; he changed the wording of a few of his answers, then affixed his signature and the date on each page. When asked by Officer Hamilton why he had turned himself in, defendant replied, "Well, for the act I had just committed." Defendant then related the events leading up to and culminating in the murder, describing his conduct in the detail set forth hereinabove. With respect to the issue of his state of mind at the time of the crime, the following language is both relevant and material: When asked how long he had thought of killing his mother, defendant replied, "I can't be clear on that. About a week ago, I would suppose, the very beginning of the thoughts. First I thought of giving her the ether. * * * Then Thursday and Friday I thought of it again. Q. Of killing your mother? A. Not of killing. Well, yes I think so. Then Saturday and Sunday the same." After stating that he struck her the first blow on the back of the head, defendant was asked: "Q. Did you consider at the time that this one blow would render her unconscious, or kill her? A. I wasn't sure. I was hoping it would render her unconscious. Q. Was it your thought at this time to kill her? A. I am not sure of that. Probably kill her, I think." Defendant described the struggle in which he and his mother fell to the floor, and was asked: "Q. Then what happened. * * * A. She moved over by the stove, and she just laid still. She was breathing, breathing heavily. I said 'I shouldn't be doing this'— not those exact words, but something to that effect, and laid down beside her, because we were on the floor. Q. Were you tired? A. Yes." After defendant had choked her to death he said, "God loves you, He loves me, He loves my dad, and I love you and my dad. It is a circle, sort of, and it is horrible you have done all that good and then I come along and destroy it."

Detective Stenberg thereafter interrupted Officer Hamilton's interrogation, and asked the following questions: "Q. (Det. W.R. Stenberg) You knew the wrongfulness of killing your mother? A. I did. I was thinking of it. I was aware of it. Q. You were aware of the wrongfulness. Also had you thought what might happen to you? A. That is a question. No. Q. Your thought has been in your mind for three weeks of killing her? A. Yes, or of just knocking her out. Q. Well, didn't you feel you would be prosecuted for the wrongfulness of this act? A. I was aware of it, but not thinking of it." . . . Officer Hamilton asked: "Q. Can you give a reason or purpose for this act of killing your mother? Have you thought out why you wanted to hurt her? A. There is a reason why we didn't get along. There is also the reason of sexual intercourse with one of these other girls, and I had to get her out of the way. Q. Did you think you had to get her out of the way permanently? A. I sort of figured it would have to be that way, but I am not quite sure."

Thus, contrary to the misunderstanding of counsel and amicus curiae, Officer Stenberg's question ("You knew the wrongfulness of killing your mother?") related unequivocally to defendant's knowledge *at the time of the commission of the murder;* and defendant's equally unequivocal answer ("I did. I was thinking of it. I was aware of it.") related to the same period of time. This admission, coupled with defendant's uncontradicted course of conduct and other statements set forth hereinabove, constitutes substantial evidence from which the jury could find defendant legally sane at the time of the matricide.

It is contended that the foregoing evidence of defendant's conduct and declarations is equally consistent with the type of mental illness (i.e., a form of "schizophrenia") from which according to the psychiatric witnesses, defendant is said to be suffering. But this consistency establishes only that defendant is suffering from the diagnosed mental illness—a point that the prosecution readily concedes; it does not compel the conclusion that on the very different issue of legal sanity the evidence is insufficient as a matter of law to support the verdict. To hold otherwise would be in effect to substitute a trial by "experts" for a trial by jury, for it would require that the jurors accept the psychiatric testimony as conclusive on an issue—the legal sanity of the defendant—which under our present law is exclusively within the province of the trier of fact to determine.

To guard against misunderstanding of our rules it is pertinent to observe that we do not reject expert testimony simply or solely because it may *also* answer the ultimate question the jury is called upon to decide . . .; but strictly speaking, a psychiatrist is not an "expert" at all when it comes to determining whether the defendant is *legally* responsible under the terms of the California rule. Thus Dr. Alfred K. Baur, psychiatrist and Chief of Staff of the Veteran's Administration Hospital at Salem, Virginia, has recently warned that the question of a defendant's "insanity" (which he defines as *legal* irresponsibility) should not even be asked of members of his profession: "As psychiatrists, we can testify as to our findings regarding the 'mental condition' of the person in question * * *; but, to ask the psychiatric witness, 'Doctor, in your opinion is this person insane (or sane)?' is the same as asking an expert witness in a criminal trial, 'In your opinion, is the accused guilty or not guilty?' Yet, many lawyers ask psychiatrists to state opinions on the sanity of the accused and, unfortunately, many psychiatrists perpetuate the problem by accepting the role of oracle and answering the question, even thinking it properly within their functions." (Baur, Legal Responsibility and Mental Illness (1962) 57 Nw. U.L.Rev. 12, 13; for similar views, see Address of Dr. Karl Menninger to the Judicial Conference of the 10th Circuit (1962) 32 F.R.D. 566, 571;

Glueck, Law and Psychiatry (1962) pp. 65–67; cf. People v. O'Brien (1932) 122 Cal.App. 147, 150–154 [2], 9 P.2d 902.)

In the light of the authorities which have been brought to our attention it thus appears that a psychiatrist's conclusion as to the *legal* insanity of a schizophrenic is inherently no more than tentative. As Dr. Manfred S. Guttmacher observes, "in the most malignant type of psychosis schizophrenia, the decision is often extremely difficult and the psychiatrist, conscientiously attempting to assay the individual's capacity to distinguish right and wrong will be able to do little more than conjecture. Much, indeed is known about the schizophrenic disorders at a descriptive level and valid generalizations about the symptomatology can be made. But our methods of examination do not permit us to particularize convincingly in regard to the individual patient." (Guttmacher, Principal Difficulties with the Present Criteria of Responsibility and Possible Alternatives, in Model Pen.Code, Tent. Draft No. 4 (1955), p. 171.) In this uncertain state of knowledge, the fact that the four psychiatrists in the case at bench happened each to diagnose defendant's *medical* condition as "schizophrenia" did not preclude the jury from weighing, as they were required to do, these witnesses' further opinions that defendant was *legally* insane at the time of the murder. Nor is this case unusual in this respect: in accordance with the just mentioned principle, jury verdicts of legal sanity have been upheld in a long line of cases in which the expert medical testimony was unanimous that the defendant was suffering from schizophrenia [Citations omitted] . . ..

To the extent, moreover, that the psychiatric witnesses in the case at bench were asked their opinion as to defendant's legal sanity, a close examination of their responses discloses still further grounds in support of the verdict. . . . Dr. Nielsen testified on direct examination that at the time of the murder defendant "knew right from wrong" but was "acting impulsively" and "didn't think it through"; that during the period of the final outburst "He knew what he was doing after all. He studied his mother to see whether she was dead and when she wasn't, he went ahead and finished it." On cross-examination Dr. Nielsen was asked whether defendant's compulsion to kill his mother resembled an "irresistible impulse"; he replied, "It was not resisted and it was an impulse." The doctor further agreed that defendant "was capable at the time of knowing the difference between right and wrong, but that he didn't bother to think about it"; . . .

The next psychiatric witness, Dr. Smith, testified that when defendant killed his mother "He was acting on an impulse"; that "his expressions of intention to go out and have intercourse and his intention to knock out his mother and the aunt, if she came, are evidence of his ability to think because of his ability to plan. Now beyond that point of having struck his mother, this is an impulsive schizophrenic piece of behavior which is entirely separated in my opinion from some planned piece of activity."

The final psychiatric witness, Dr. Skrdla, testified on direct examination that at the time of the killing defendant "knew that he had committed a wrong act, at least morally wrong, and possibly legally wrong, because, according to the story he gave me, he washed the blood from himself and changed his clothes, and, a few minutes after the murder, went to the police station to report it. This would indicate that he recognized that his act was wrong." On cross-examination Dr. Skrdla testified that when defendant killed his mother "he probably did know the difference between right and wrong" but that he was one of this schizophrenics who "because of their emotional problems, their own conflicts, * * * are not able to prevent themselves from going ahead and acting on whatever ideas or compulsions they may have."

. . .

The doctrine of "irresistible impulse" as a defense to crime is, of course not the law of California; to the contrary, the basic behavioral concept of our social order is free will. . . .

It is true that certain other psychiatric testimony was to the effect that at the time of the murder defendant did not know the nature and quality of his acts and that what he was doing was wrong. But this created only a conflict in the evidence, which was for the jury to resolve. From the testimony quoted above the jury could infer that even though some or all of the psychiatric witnesses concluded that defendant was "legally insane," there was no basis for that conclusion under the California M'Naghten rule.

Finally, to accept defendant's thesis would be tantamount to creating by judicial fiat a new defense plea of "not guilty by reason of schizophrenia." To do so (assuming *arguendo* that it were within our power) would be bad law and apparently still worse medicine. It would require the jurors to accept as beyond dispute or question the opinions of the psychiatric witnesses as to the defendant's *legal* sanity. But it is doubtful that any reputable psychiatrist today would claim such infallibility; clearly the four who testified in the case at bench did not do so. Thus, Dr. Daryl D. Smith agreed with counsel's assertion with respect to schizophrenia that "there is quite a bit of divergence of [psychiatric] opinion relative to this disease." Indeed, it is often acknowledged that the causes and cure of schizophrenia are unknown (e.g., Diamond, From M'Naghten to Currens, and Beyond (1962) 50 Cal.L.Rev. 189, 195; Weihofen, Mental Disorder as a Criminal Defense (1954) p. 16), and that "schizophrenia" is not even a single disease as such but merely a label or term of convenience encompassing a variety of more or less related symptoms or conditions of mental disorder; thus in the case at bench Dr. J.M. Nielsen agreed that "schizophrenia" is "just a psychiatric classification, * * * simply an abstract definition as applied to the behavior pattern."

Such a classification covers a broad spectrum of mental conditions. As Dr. Alfred K. Baur emphasizes, "Some people are sophisticated enough to know that schizophrenia is one of the 'major psychoses' and contributes to many in the 'insane' category. But it is very difficult to get across to lay people the idea that a person diagnosed schizophrenic may be quite competent, responsible, and not dangerous, and, in fact, a valuable member of society, albeit at times a personally unhappy one. The same can be said of every psychiatric diagnosis or so-called mental illness." (Baur, Legal Responsibility and Mental Illness (1962) 57 Nw. U.L.Rev. 12, 16–17.) The argument for defendant, in short, ignores our often-repeated admonition that " 'sound mind' and 'legal sanity' are not synonymous."   . . .

[The court's further discussion on the contention that the evidence was insufficient to support the trial court's finding that the murder was of the first, rather than the second degree follows in Section F on Diminished Responsibility.]

HOLLOWAY v. UNITED STATES

United States Court of Appeals, District of Columbia Circuit, 1945.
80 U.S.App.D.C. 3, 148 F.2d 665.

[Defendant was convicted of rape. He appealed on the sole ground that the record disclosed such substantial doubt of his sanity that the verdict should be set aside. The record disclosed that in 1940 the defendant was held in Gallinger Hospital for mental observation. Later he was confined in a federal hospital as a mental patient. And, in 1943, he was again committed to Gallinger Hospital as a mental patient. He was later released, not as recovered, in the custody of his mother, with further directions for the treatment of his mental disorders. Some months after this release he raped two women on the same day. Following is the Court of Appeals' opinion affirming the defendant's conviction.]

ARNOLD, J. The application of [the tests for insanity], however they are phrased, to a borderline case can be nothing more than a moral judgment that it is just or unjust to blame the defendant for what he did. Legal tests of criminal insanity are not and cannot be the result of scientific analysis or objective judgment. There is no objective standard by which such a judgment of an admittedly abnormal offender can be measured. They must be based on the instinctive sense of justice of ordinary men. . . .

[W]hen psychiatrists attempt on the witness stand to reconcile the therapeutic standards of their own art with the moral judgment of the criminal law they become confused. Thus it is common to find groups of distinguished scientists of the mind testifying on both sides and in all directions with positiveness and conviction. This is not because they are unreliable or because those who testify on one side are more skillful or learned than those who testify on the other. It is rather because to the psychiatrist mental cases are a series of imperceptible gradations from the mild psychopath to the extreme psychotic, whereas criminal law allows for no gradations. It requires a final decisive moral judgment of the culpability of the accused. For purposes of conviction there is no twilight zone between abnormality and insanity. An offender is wholly sane or wholly insane.

A complete reconciliation between the medical tests of insanity and the moral tests of criminal responsibility is impossible. The purposes are different; the assumptions behind the two standards are different. For that reason the principal function of a psychiatrist who testifies on the mental state of an abnormal offender is to inform the jury of the character of his mental disease. The psychiatrist's moral judgment reached on the basis of his observations is relevant. But it cannot bind the jury except within broad limits. To command respect criminal law must not offend against the common belief that men who talk rationally are in most cases morally responsible for what they do.

The institution which applies our inherited ideas of moral responsibility to individuals prosecuted for crime is a jury of ordinary men. These men must be told that in order to convict they should have no reasonable doubt of the defendant's sanity. After they have declared by their verdict that they have no such doubt their judgment should not be disturbed on the ground it is contrary to expert psychiatric opinion. Psychiatry offers us no standard for measuring the validity of the jury's moral judgment as to culpability. To justify a reversal circumstances must be such that the verdict shocks the conscience of the court.

G. COMPETENCY TO STAND TRIAL

Competency to stand trial presents a different issue than insanity at the time of the criminal act. The test of competency is succinctly stated in one state statute in the following terms: ". . . a defendant is unfit to stand trial or be sentenced if, because of a mental or physical condition, he is unable: (1) to understand the nature and purpose of the proceedings against him; or (2) to assist in his defense.

The issues which may arise with respect to competency are many and, on occasions, very difficult to resolve. Since they entail procedural rather than substantive criminal law, a treatment of the subject is reserved for the casebooks on criminal procedure.

H. MODERN CHANGES IN THE INSANITY DEFENSE

For a long time neither the Supreme Court nor Congress played a major role with respect to the insanity defense. However, in the wake of the successful insanity defense on behalf of John W. Hinckley, Jr. at his 1982 federal trial for the attempted assassination of President Ronald Reagan in 1981, Congress and a number of state legislatures have focused attention on the perceived need for a change in the law regarding that defense. Over thirty separate bills were introduced in Congress. The proposals ranged from total abolishment of the defense to such modifications as the one earlier discussed in the first set of Notes in this chapter, whereby the burden of proving insanity, and beyond a reasonable doubt, rests upon the defense. Ironically, in the

Hinckley case, had he been prosecuted for violation of a law of the District of Columbia (attempted murder, for example) the burden would have been upon him to prove insanity by a preponderance of the evidence; however, because he was tried for violating the Presidential Assassination Statute, a Congressional nationwide offense, the general federal law imposed upon the prosecution the burden of proving sanity beyond a reasonable doubt.

At the mid-year meeting of the American Bar Association House of Delegates in February, 1983, that policy making body adopted a resolution that the insanity defense henceforth be used only where the defendant "as a result of mental disease or defect, was unable to appreciate the wrongfulness of his or her conduct at the time of the offense charged." This is a repudiation of the American Law Institute (A.L.I.) test which the ABA had publicly supported since 1975, and a turn to the "cognitive" approach, which is itself an outgrowth of the M'Naghten test. The ABA recommendation, which was opposed by that body's Criminal Justice Section, would leave the burden of disproving sanity on the prosecution, but suggests that if the A.L.I. formulation is retained, then the burden ought to be on the defendant to prove his insanity by a preponderance of the evidence. In the wake of the ABA action, the Reagan Administration abandoned its abolitionist stance and supported the ABA recommendation on the test for insanity, but remained determined in wanting the burden of proof on the defendant in all cases.

A movement in the states toward abolition of the defense of insanity, while not entirely new,[1] took on new momentum in recent years.[2] Three states abolished the defense of insanity altogether. Montana passed a statute abolishing the defense,[3] and providing that evidence of "insanity" would be excluded unless relevant to the mental

---

1. See, e.g., Rood, Abolition of the Defense of Insanity in Criminal Cases, 9 *Mich.L.Rev.* 126 (1910); Keedy, Insanity and Criminal Responsibility, 30 *Harv.L. Rev.* 535 (1917); Wilbur, Should the Insanity Defense to a Criminal Charge be Abolished?, 8 *A.B.A.J.* 631 (1922).

2. E.g., Goldstein & Katz, Abolish the "Insanity Defense"—Why Not?, 72 *Yale L.J.* 853 (1963); Morris, Madness and the Criminal Law, 1982; Dershowitz, Abolishing the Insanity Defense; The Most Significant Feature of the Administration's Criminal Code—An Essay, 9 *Crim.L.Bull.* 434 (1973); Morris, Psychiatry and the Dangerous Criminal, 41 *So.Cal.L.Rev.* 514 (1968); Thomas, Breaking of the Stone Tablet: Criminal Law Without the Insanity Defense, 19 *Idaho L.Rev.* 239 (1983); Morris, The Criminal Responsibility of the Mentally Ill, 33 *Syrac.L.Rev.* 477 (1982). Taking a different position, see e.g., Wexler, An Offense-Victim Approach to Insanity Defense Reform, 26 *Ariz.L.Rev.* 17 (1984); Arenella,

Reflections on Current Proposals to Abolish or Reform the Insanity Defense, 8 *Am. J.L. & Med.* 271 (1982); Morse, Excusing the Crazy: The Insanity Defense Reconsidered, 58 *So.Cal.L.Rev.* 777 (1985).

3. Mont.Rev.Codes Ann. § 40–14–201 provide, in part:

"(1) Evidence of mental disease or defect is not admissible in a trial on the merits unless the defendant . . . files a written notice of his purpose to rely on a mental disease or defect to prove that he did not have a particular state of mind which is an essential element of the offense charged. . . .

"(2) When the defendant is found not guilty of the charged offense or offenses or any lesser included offense for the reason that due to a mental disease or defect, he could not have a particular state of mind that is an essential element of the offense charged, the verdict and judgment shall so state."

state requirement for the offense charged. Idaho [4] and Utah followed this example. Other states have an insanity defense but combine with it a sentencing scheme that permits a finding of not guilty by reason of insanity, which leads to civil commitment, or a finding of guilty but mentally ill (GBMI), which leads to a sentencing procedure that is not that different from the one adopted in Montana, where the defense was abolished.[5]

STATE v. KORELL

Supreme Court of Montana, 1984.
213 Mont. 316, 690 P.2d 992.

HASWELL, CHIEF JUSTICE.

Jerry Korell appeals the judgment of the Ravalli County District Court finding him guilty of attempted deliberate homicide and aggravated assault. Korell was sentenced to concurrent sentences of thirty-five and fifteen years at the Montana State Prison. Korell's defense at trial was that he lacked the requisite criminal mental state by reason of his insanity. On appeal his primary contention is that the Montana statutory scheme deprived him of a constitutional right to raise insanity as an independent defense.

Jerry Korell is a Viet Nam veteran who had several disturbing experiences during his tour of duty. The exact nature of the trauma was never fully documented. Friends and family agree that he was a different person when he returned from the service. Between Korell's honorable discharge in 1970 and the present events, he was twice admitted to VA hospitals for psychological problems and treated with anti-psychotic drugs. In 1976 he was jailed briefly in Boise, Idaho, for harassing and threatening the late Senator Frank Church.

The basic nature of Korell's problems was that he would periodically slip into paranoid phases during which he had trouble relating to male authority figures. His mental health varied dramatically. In the poorer times his family entertained thoughts about having him civilly committed. His VA hospitalizations were voluntary and neither of the stays were of such length that he was fully evaluated or treated.

---

4. 4 Idaho Code § 18–207 provides as follows:

(a) Mental condition shall not be a defense to any charge of criminal conduct.

(b) If . . . the court finds that one convicted of crime suffers from any mental condition requiring treatment, such person shall be committed . . . in an appropriate facility for treatment, having regard for such conditions of security as the case may require. . . .

(c) Nothing herein is intended to prevent the admission of expert evidence on the issues of mens rea or any state of mind which is an element of the offense, subject to the rules of evidence.

5. E.g., Mich.Comp.Laws Ann. § 768.36. See also, Smith & Hall, Evaluating Michigan's Guilty But Mentally Ill Verdict: An Empirical Study, 16 U.Mich.J.L.Ref. 77 (1982).

Attacks on constitutional grounds on statutes that create special verdicts in insanity cases have been warded off. Thus, in Taylor v. State, 440 N.E.2d 1109 (Ind. 1982), the Indiana Supreme Court upheld a state statute that established alternative verdicts of "Not Responsible by Reason of Insanity" and "Guilty But Mentally Ill."

In 1980 Korell entered a community college program for echocardiology in Spokane, Washington. Echocardiology is the skill associated with recording and interpreting sonograms of the heart for diagnostic purposes. In March 1982 he was sent to Missoula to serve a clinical externship at St. Patrick's Hospital. Korell's supervisor at the hospital was Greg Lockwood, the eventual victim of this crime.

Korell's relationship with Lockwood deteriorated for a variety of work-related reasons. Foremost was Korell's belief that he was worked excessively by Lockwood. At this time Korell was subjected to what expert testimony labeled psychological stressors: a divorce by his wife, financial problems and the pressures of graduation requirements.

In April 1982 Korell wrote a letter to the hospital administrator complaining about his supervisor, Lockwood. Korell was transferred to an externship in Spokane, and Lockwood was placed on probation. Both men retained very bitter feelings about the incident. Lockwood stated to friends he would see to it that Korell was never hired anywhere in echocardiology. Korell may have learned of Lockwood's statements.

Korell's actions in the next two months indicate a great deal of confusion. He set fire to a laundromat because he lost nine quarters in a machine and was tired of being ripped off. He set fire to a former home of his wife because she had bad feelings about it.

Released on bail from these incidents, he returned to Missoula in June 1982. Psychiatric testimony introduced at trial indicates that Korell felt he had to kill Lockwood before Lockwood killed him. He removed a handgun from a friend's home, had another acquaintance purchase ammunition, and on the evening of June 25, 1982, drove to the Lockwood home in the Eagle Watch area of the Bitterroot Valley. Shirley Lockwood, Greg's wife, saw the unfamiliar vehicle approach the house. Greg Lockwood was lying on the living room floor at the time watching television. Korell entered the house through a side door and began firing. Although wounded, Greg Lockwood managed to engage the defendant in a struggle. A shot was fired in the direction of Lockwood's wife. Korell grabbed a kitchen knife and both men were further injured before Lockwood was able to subdue Korell.

Korell was charged with attempted deliberate homicide and aggravated assault. The defendant gave notice of his intent to rely on a mental disease or defect to prove that he did not have the particular state of mind which is an essential element of the offense charged. Prior to trial he sought a writ of supervisory control declaring that he had a right to rely on the defense that he was suffering from a mental disease or defect at the time he committed the acts charged. The writ was denied by this Court on December 20, 1982, and the case proceeded to trial.

Several psychologists and psychiatrists testified on Korell's mental condition. The defense sought to establish by its expert witnesses and numerous character witnesses that Korell was a disturbed man who was psychotic at the time the crimes were committed. It was argued that his actions when he entered the Lockwood home were not voluntary acts. The State produced its own expert witnesses who testified on Korell's mental condition. Four doctors testified in all, two for the prosecution and two for the defense. Three of the four stated Korell had the capacity to act knowingly or purposely, the requisite mental state for the offenses, when he entered the Lockwood home.

Without giving prior notice, the State produced Cedric Hames as a rebuttal witness who testified that he purchased ammunition for the defendant several days before the shooting. A motion for mistrial was made by the defense. The court denied the motion but offered the defense a continuance. The offer was refused by defendant's counsel.

In keeping with Montana's current law on mental disease or defect, the jury was instructed that they could consider mental disease or defect only insofar as it negated the defendant's requisite state of mind. The jury returned guilty verdicts for the attempted deliberate homicide and aggravated assault.

On appeal the defendant presents the following issues:

1. Is there a constitutional right to raise insanity as an independent defense to criminal charges?

2. Was the State's rebuttal testimony of Cedric Hames properly admitted?

3. Was the jury properly instructed on the issue of voluntariness?

4. Did the District Court fail to consider defendant's mental condition at sentencing?

5. Did the District Court act within its discretion in awarding fees to defendant's court-appointed attorney?

I. CONSTITUTIONAL CHALLENGE

A. *Background*

In 1979 the Forty–Sixth Session of the Montana Legislature enacted House Bill 877. This Bill abolished use of the traditional insanity defense in Montana and substituted alternative procedures for considering a criminal defendant's mental condition. Evidence of mental disease or defect is now considered at three phases of a criminal proceeding.

Before trial, evidence may be presented to show that the defendant is not fit to proceed to trial. Anyone who is unable to understand the proceedings against him or assist in his defense may not be prosecuted.

During trial, evidence of mental disease or defect is admissible when relevant to prove that, at the time of the offense charged, the defendant did not have the state of mind that is an element of the crime charged, e.g., that the defendant did not act purposely or knowingly. The State retains the burden of proving each element of the offense beyond a reasonable doubt. Defendant may, of course, present evidence to contradict the State's proof that he committed the offense and that he had the requisite state of mind at that time.

Whenever the jury finds that the State has failed to prove beyond a reasonable doubt that the defendant had the requisite state of mind at the time he committed the offense, it is instructed to return a special verdict of not guilty "for the reason that due to a mental disease or defect he could not have a particular state of mind that is an essential element of the offense charged. . . ."

Finally at the dispositional stage following the trial and conviction, the sentencing judge must consider any relevant evidence presented at the trial, plus any additional evidence presented at the sentencing hearing, to determine whether the defendant was able to appreciate the criminality of his acts or to conform his conduct to the law at the time he committed the offense for which he was convicted.

The sentencing judge's consideration of the evidence is not the same as that of the jury. The jury determines whether the defendant committed the offense with the requisite state of mind, e.g., whether he acted purposely or knowingly. The sentencing judge determines whether, at the time the defendant committed the offense, he was able to appreciate its criminality or conform his conduct to the law.

If the court concludes the defendant was not suffering from a mental disease or defect that rendered him unable to appreciate the criminality of his conduct or to conform his conduct to the requirements of law, normal criminal sentencing procedures are invoked.

Whenever the sentencing court finds the defendant was suffering from mental disease or defect which rendered him unable to appreciate the criminality of his conduct or to conform his conduct to the requirements of law, mandatory minimum sentences are waived. The defendant is committed to the custody of the director of institutions and placed in an appropriate institution for custody, care and treatment not to exceed the maximum possible sentence. As a practical matter, this means the defendant may be placed in the Warm Springs State Hospital under the alternative sentencing procedures. The institutionalized defendant may later petition the District Court for release from the hospital upon a showing that the individual has been cured of the mental disease or defect. If the petition is granted, the court must transfer the defendant to the state prison or place the defendant under alternative confinement or supervision. The length of this confinement or supervision must equal the original sentence.

In summary, while Montana has abolished the traditional use of insanity as a defense, alternative procedures have been enacted to deal with insane individuals who commit criminal acts.

Much has been written concerning criminal responsibility and insanity. Professor Norval Morris commented that "[r]ivers of ink, mountains of printer's lead, forests of paper have been expended on this issue. . . ." Morris, Psychiatry and the Dangerous Criminal, 41 S.Cal.L.R. 514, 516 (1968). Yet there is a paucity of judicial opinions construing the constitutional parameters of the traditional insanity defense or the various reform proposals. This case is the first direct constitutional challenge to Montana's abolition of the affirmative insanity defense and adoption of alternative procedures in its place.

* * *

While some jurisdictions, most notably the federal courts, have given the prosecution the burden of proving the defendant's sanity beyond a reasonable doubt, such practice is not the rule in Montana. Prior to 1979, insanity was treated as an affirmative defense that had to be established by the accused by a preponderance of the evidence. As the above discussion and our [previous] holding . . . states, it is sufficient that the State prove beyond a reasonable doubt the requisite mental state, e.g., purposely or knowingly, that is an element of the offense charged.

* * *

Review of our case law reveals that the constitutionality of the legislature's abolition of the affirmative defense of insanity has not previously been decided. Korell's present challenge is based on the Fourteenth Amendment guarantee of due process of law and the Eighth Amendment prohibition against cruel and unusual punishment.

B. *Due Process Considerations*

1. Fundamental Rights

The due process clause of the Fourteenth Amendment was intended in part to protect certain fundamental rights long recognized under the common law. Appellant contends that the insanity defense is so embedded in our legal history that it should be afforded status as a fundamental right. He argues that the defense was firmly established as a part of the common law long before our federal constitution was adopted and is essential to our present system of ordered liberty.

The United States Supreme Court has never held that there is a constitutional right to plead an insanity defense. Moreover, the Court has noted that the significance of the defense is properly left to the states:

> "We cannot cast aside the centuries-long evolution of the collection of interlocking and overlapping concepts which the common law has utilized to assess the moral accountability of an individual for his antisocial deeds. The doctrines of *actus reus, mens rea,* insanity, mistake, justification, and duress have historically provided the tools for a constantly shifting adjustment of the tension between the evolving aims of the criminal law and changing religious, moral, philosophical, and medical views of the nature of man. This process of adjustment has always been thought to be the province of the States." Powell v. Texas (1968), 392 U.S. 514, 535–536, 88 S.Ct. 2145, 2156, 20 L.Ed.2d 1254, 1269.

An examination of the common law in a search for fundamental rights can be misleading. When looking at concepts of insanity and criminal responsibility, one discovers a continuum of changing societal values and views. Commentators and courts have reached differing conclusions on the role of the insanity defense in the history of jurisprudence.

The English jurist Stephen observed:

". . . in very ancient times proof of madness appears not to have entitled a man to be acquitted, at least in case of murder, but to a special verdict that he committed the offense when made. This gave him a right to a pardon. The same course was taken when the defence was killing by misadventure or in self-defence." 2 Stephen, A History of the Criminal Law of England 151 (1883).

This early thirteenth century practice of pardoning the insane was acknowledged in our *Watson* decision and the historical discussion therein. Pardons were liberally granted and the practice represented a humane departure from earlier times of absolute liability for criminal acts.

Development of the *mens rea* concept preceded recognition of the insanity defense. The Latin phrase *mens rea* literally translates as "evil mind." It has also been interpreted as guilty mind, evil intent or criminal intent. Enlightened medieval jurists developed the *mens rea* doctrine: without criminal intent, there can be no moral blameworthiness, crime or punishment. In the words of Henrici Bracton (d. 1268): "For a crime is not committed unless the will to harm be present." This principle has played a central role in all subsequent considerations of capacity, insanity, and moral and legal culpability.

For centuries evidence of mental illness was admitted to show the accused was incapable of forming criminal intent. Insanity did not come to be generally recognized as an affirmative defense and an independent ground for acquittal until the nineteenth century. Morris, The Criminal Responsibility of the Mentally Ill, 33 Syracuse L.R. 477, 500 (1982); American Medical Association, The Insanity Defense in Criminal Trials and Limitations of Psychiatric Testimony, Report of the Board of Trustees, at 27 (1983). The defense grew out of the earlier notions of *mens rea*.

We reject appellant's contention that from the earliest period of the common law, insanity has been recognized as a defense. What we recognize is that one who lacks the requisite criminal state of mind may not be convicted or punished.

Three older state court decisions have found state statutes abolishing the insanity defense to be unconstitutional. State v. Lange (1929), 168 La. 958, 123 So. 639; Sinclair v. State (1931), 161 Miss. 142, 132 So. 581; State v. Strasburg (1910), 60 Wash. 106, 110 P. 1020. These decisions are distinguishable in that they interpret statutes that precluded *any* trial testimony of mental condition, including that which would cast doubt on the defendant's state of mind at the time he committed the charged offense. The Montana statutes in question expressly allow evidence of mental disease or defect to be introduced to rebut proof of defendant's state of mind.

The United States Supreme Court refused in 1952 to accept the argument that the Due Process Clause required the use of a particular insanity test or allocation of burden of proof. Leland v. Oregon (1952). The Oregon statute upheld in *Leland* required the defendant to prove insanity beyond a reasonable doubt. This allocation of proof was found constitutionally sound because the State retained the burden to prove the requisite state of mind and other essential criminal elements. The State's due process burden of proof was further emphasized in In Re Winship (1970). *Winship* established that the prosecution must prove beyond a reasonable doubt every element constituting the crime charged.

The Montana statutory scheme is consistent with the dictates of *Leland* and *Winship*. The 1979 amendments to the criminal code do not unconstitutionally shift the State's burden of proof of the necessary elements of the offense. The State retains its traditional burden of proving all elements beyond a reasonable doubt.

2. The Delusional Defendant

In addition to asserting that the insanity defense is a fundamental constitutional right, the appellant contends that insanity is a broader concept than *mens rea*. Korell argues that individuals may be clearly insane yet also be capable of forming the requisite intent to commit a crime. For example, an accused may form intent to harm under a completely delusional perception of reality or act without volitional control. It is defendant's position that the due process of these defendants is compromised by state law which permits conviction of delusional defendants and those who act without volitional control.

Addressing the delusional defendant first, we note that planning, deliberation and a studied intent are often found in cases where the defendant lacks the capacity to understand the wrongfulness of his acts. Fink & Larene, In Defense of the Insanity Defense, 62 Mich.B.J. 199 (1983). Illustrations include the assassin acting under instructions of God, the mother drowning her demonically-possessed child, and the man charging up Montana Avenue on a shooting spree believing he is Teddy Roosevelt on San Juan Hill. Defendant contends that these people could properly be found guilty by a jury under current Montana law.

As some commentators have noted, the 1979 amendments to the law on mental disease or defect may actually have lowered the hurdle mentally disturbed defendants must clear to be exculpated. In order to be acquitted, the defendant need only cast a reasonable doubt in the minds of the jurors that he had the requisite mental state. See, Bender, After Abolition: The Present State of the Insanity Defense in

Montana, 45 Mont.L.R. 133, 141 (1984). As a practical matter, the prosecutor who seeks a conviction of a delusional and psychotic defendant will be faced with a heavy burden of proof.

Assuming the delusional defendant is found guilty by a jury, factors of mitigation must be considered by the sentencing judge in accordance with section 46–14–311, MCA. The fact that the proven criminal state of mind was formed by a deranged mind would certainly be considered. In addition, a defendant can be sentenced to imprisonment only after the sentencing judge specifically finds that the defendant was *not* suffering, at the time he committed the offense, from a mental disease that rendered him unable to appreciate the criminality of his conduct or to conform his conduct to the requirements of law.

3. The Volitionally–Impaired Defendant

The test of mental disease or defect that was afforded defendants prior to 1979 read as follows:

> "A person is not responsible for criminal conduct if at the time of such conduct as a result of mental disease or defect he is unable either to appreciate the criminality of his conduct or to conform his conduct to the requirements of the law." Section 46–14–101, MCA (1978).

It is the second prong of this standard, the volitional aspect of mental disease or defect, that appellant claims has been eliminated. He argues that there are those who lack the ability to conform their conduct to the law and that elimination of the involuntariness defense is unconstitutional.

The volitional aspect of mental disease or defect has not been eliminated from our criminal law. Consideration of a defendant's ability to conform his conduct to the law has been moved from the jury to the sentencing judge. The United States Supreme Court found in *Leland,* that the "irresistible impulse" test of insanity was not implicit in the concept of ordered liberty. Additionally, the minimum requirements of any criminal offense are still a voluntary act and companion mental state. Section 45–2–202, MCA, provides that "[a] material element of every offense is a voluntary act. . . ."

This Court has not judicially recognized the automatism defense. Applications of the defense may exist where a defendant acts during convulsions, sleep, unconsciousness, hypnosis or seizures. See, *People v. Grant* (1978). Our criminal code's provisions requiring a voluntary act and defining involuntary conduct adequately provide for such defenses. See sections 45–2–202 and 45–2–101(31), MCA.

To the extent that the 1979 criminal code revisions allegedly eliminated the defense of insanity-induced volitional impairment, we find no abrogation of a constitutional right.

C. *Eighth Amendment Considerations*

Appellant next contends that abolition of the affirmative defense of insanity violates the Eighth Amendment's prohibition of cruel and unusual punishment. In *Robinson v. California* (1962), the Supreme Court held that punishment for the status crime of drug addiction violated the Eighth Amendment prohibition. The Court declared that any law which created a criminal offense of being mentally ill would also constitute cruel and unusual punishment. The Court noted that had the California statute under which Robinson was convicted required proof of the actual use of narcotics, it would have been valid. In *Powell v. Texas,* a statute imposing a fine for public intoxication was found to not violate the Eighth Amendment. There the Court reasoned that although alcoholism might be a disease, the statute was valid because it punished an act, not the status of being an alcoholic.

The Montana Criminal Code does not permit punishment of a mentally ill person who has not committed a criminal act. As such, the statutes avoid the constitutional infirmities discussed in *Robinson v. California,* supra, and *Powell v. Texas,* supra.

Prior to sentencing, the court is required to consider the convicted defendant's mental condition at the time the offense was committed. This review is mandatory whenever a claim of mental disease or defect is raised. The plain language of the statute reads: ". . . the sentencing court *shall* consider any relevant evidence. . . ." Section 46–14–311, MCA (emphasis added). Whenever the sentencing court finds the defendant suffered from a mental disease or defect, as described in section 46–14–311, MCA, the defendant must be placed in an ". . . appropriate institution for custody, care and treatment. . . ." Section 46–14–312(2), MCA.

These requirements place a heavy burden on the courts and the department of institutions. They serve to prevent imposition of cruel and unusual punishment upon the insane. Since the jury is properly preoccupied with proof of state of mind, it is imperative that the sentencing court discharge its responsibility to independently review the defendant's mental condition.

It is further argued that subjecting the insane to the stigma of a criminal conviction violates fundamental principles of justice. We cannot agree. The legislature has made a conscious decision to hold individuals who act with a proven criminal state of mind accountable for their acts, regardless of motivation or mental condition. Arguably, this policy does not further criminal justice goals of deterrence and prevention in cases where an accused suffers from a mental disease that renders him incapable of appreciating the criminality of his conduct. However, the policy does further goals of protection of society and education. One State Supreme Court Justice who wrestled with this dilemma observed: "In a very real sense, the confinement of the insane is the punishment of the innocent; the release of the insane is the punishment of society." State v. Stacy (Tenn.1980), 601 S.W.2d 696, 704 (Henry, J., dissenting).

Our legislature has acted to assure that the attendant stigma of a criminal conviction is mitigated by the sentencing judge's personal consideration of the defendant's mental condition and provision for commitment to an appropriate institution for treatment, as an alternative to a sentence of imprisonment.

For the foregoing reasons we hold that Montana's abolition of the insanity defense neither deprives a defendant of his Fourteenth Amendment right to due process nor violates the Eighth Amendment proscription against cruel and unusual punishment. There is no independent constitutional right to plead insanity.

* * *

[The opinion of JUSTICE MORRISON, concurring in part and dissenting in part, is omitted.]

SHEEHY, JUSTICE, dissenting:

It is a matter of coincidence that I dictate this dissent on Sunday, November 11, 1984. This used to be called Armistice Day, and the television news is full of reports of a reunion of Viet Nam war veterans in Washington, D.C. Coincident with their reunion is the dedication of a memorial statuary to Viet Nam war veterans, the seven-foot tall representation of three Viet Nam war servicemen who seem to be peering intently at an earlier Viet Nam war memorial on which is inscribed the names of more than 58,000 servicemen who lost their lives in that war.

It was a war in which nothing was won and much was lost. A part of that loss, not recognized or admitted by the authorities at first, was the damaging effect to the cognitive abilities of some that served in the war. Only recently has there been positive acceptance that there does exist in some ex-servicemen a post-Viet Nam war traumatic syndrome.

Jerry Korell, the evidence is clear, is a victim of that syndrome. Before his term of service, he was a mentally functional citizen. After his return from service, he is mentally dysfunctional. We can measure our maturity about how we meet such problems by the fact that Jerry Korell now will inevitably spend a great part of his life in jail for his actions arising out of that dysfunction.

Jerry Korell's dysfunction can be traced almost directly to the Viet Nam war. There are thousands of others whose mental aberrations have no such distinct origins. From genes, from force of environment, from physical trauma, or from countless other causes, their actions do not meet the norm. You know them well—the strange, the different, the weird ones.

Sometimes (not really often it should be said) these mentally aberrant persons commit a criminal act. If the criminal act is the product of mental aberration, and not of a straight-thinking cognitive direction, it would seem plausible that society should offer treatment, but if not treatment, at least not punishment. The State of Montana is not such a society.

I would hold that Montana's treatment of the insanity defense is unconstitutional for at least two reasons: One, it deprives the insane defendant of due process by depriving him of a trial by jury for each element of the crime for which he is charged; and two, it invades the insane defendant's right against self-incrimination.

In this dissent I use the terms "insanity" and "insane" in their universal sense. They include the broad spectrum of mental aberration from the maniacal to those deprived of their reasoning processes by such vague forces as prolonged melancholia, depression, paranoia and the like. I use the terms in the sense of those persons who meet the American Law Institute formulation of insanity for criminal purposes:

> "A person is not responsible for criminal conduct if at the time of such conduct as a result of mental disease or defect he lacks substantial capacity to appreciate the criminality of his conduct or to conform his conduct to the requirements of the law."
> Model Penal Code, section 4.01(1), proposed official draft (1962).

Before 1979, it was clear in Montana that persons suffering from a mental disease or defect were not responsible for their criminal conduct. Former section 95–501, R.C.M. 1947, provided:

> "(1) A person is not responsible for criminal conduct if at the time of such conduct as a result of mental disease or defect he is unable either to appreciate the criminality of his conduct or to conform his conduct with the requirements of law."

> "(2) As used in this chapter, the term 'mental disease or defect' does not include an abnormality manifested only by repeated criminal or other antisocial conduct."

The provisions of former section 95–501, R.C.M. 1947, reflected the American Law Institute position with respect to the insanity defense. The language found in subsection (2) of section 95–501, R.C.M. 1947, was a caveat formed by the ALI to restrict the definition of mental disease or defect.

In 1979, the legislature acted to repeal and eliminate what was subdivision (1) of section 95–501, R.C.M. 1947. What remains are only the provisions of present section 46–14–101, MCA, which defines mental disease or defect in the same manner as subdivision (2) of former section 95–501, supra.

Thus, the 1979 legislature removed any statutory direction that a person is not responsible for criminal conduct if at the time of the conduct, as a result of mental disease or defect, he was unable to appreciate the criminality of his conduct or to conform his conduct to the requirements of law.

The 1979 legislature went further. While one may not use the defense of mental disease or defect unless within ten days of entering plea one files a written notice of a purpose to rely on such mental disease or defect to prove that one did not have a particular state of mind which is the essential element of the offense charged (section 46–14–201, MCA), once one has filed such a notice, the court thereupon appoints a psychiatrist or requests the superintendent of the Montana State Hospital to designate a qualified psychiatrist to examine and report upon the mental condition of the defendant.   Section 46–14–202, MCA.

Under section 46–14–202(3), in the examination of the defendant any method may be employed which is accepted by the medical profession for the examination of those alleged to be suffering from mental disease or defect.   Under section 46–14–212, the psychiatrist is to be permitted to have reasonable access to the defendant for the purpose of the examination.   Chemical injection, if accepted by the medical profession, is one of the methods that may be used in such an examination. There can be no question that, regardless of the method of the examination, the insane defendant's right against self-incrimination is at once imperiled.

I would not, however, on the grounds of self-incrimination alone, hold the process unconstitutional.   I recognize the necessity, in cases where insanity is pleaded as a defense, that the State have equal right to psychiatric testimony to the same extent that is enjoyed by the defendant.   What is more serious constitutionally, however, is what our statutes provide with respect to the testimony at trial from the examining psychiatrist.

Section 46–14–213, MCA, provides that when the psychiatrist who has examined the defendant testifies, his testimony may include his *opinion* "as to the ability of the defendant *to have a particular state of mind* which is an element of the offense charged."   The statute takes away from the psychiatrist, and from the jury, the previous test of whether the defendant lacked the capacity to appreciate the criminality of his conduct or his ability to conform his conduct to the requirements of the law.   The statute instead places in the power of the psychiatrist, and takes from the jury, the determination of *whether the defendant had the particular state of mind* which is an element of the offense charged.   Thus is the defendant deprived of his right of trial by jury as to every element of the crime charged against him.   See, *In Re Winship* (1970), 397 U.S. 358, 90 S.Ct. 1068, 25 L.Ed.2d 368.

The elements of the crime of deliberate homicide in Montana are a voluntary act (section 45–2–202, MCA), coupled with either purpose or knowledge (section 45–5–102, MCA).   Thus the jury must be instructed, even where the insanity is an issue, that if the defendant acted purposely, or with knowledge, he is guilty of the offense.   The jury is then instructed that a person acts knowingly if, with respect to the conduct, he is aware of his conduct.   Section 45–2–101(33), MCA.

The jury is also instructed that the defendant acted purposely if it is his conscious object to engage in that conduct or to cause that result. Section 45–2–101(58), MCA.   No consideration is given by the jury as to whether the defendant lacks substantial capacity to appreciate the criminality of his conduct, or whether he is unable to conform his conduct to the requirements of the law. If the psychiatrist has testified that the defendant had the state of mind required as an element of the crime, that is, in the case of deliberate homicide, purpose or knowledge, the defendant is criminally guilty. The jury never gets to determine if the defendant acted by force of mental aberration.

In a case under present Montana law, therefore, when the defendant relies on insanity to explain the crime of deliberate homicide, the jury is led to the inevitable conclusion by *managed testimony* that he is indeed guilty of the crime.

Montana's statutory scheme seeks to ameliorate the managed conviction of the insane defendant by providing that at his *sentencing,* he having been convicted of a criminal act, the sentencing judge may take into consideration his insanity! At the sentencing, the judge, and not the jury, shall for the first time consider whether the defendant was suffering from a mental disease or defect which rendered him unable to appreciate the criminality of his conduct or to conform his conduct to the requirements of law. Section 46–14–311, –312, MCA.

For the reasons foregoing, I would hold the statutory scheme pertaining to insane defendants in Montana unconstitutional. I do not hold with the majority that there is no independent constitutional right to plead insanity. I consider that position the ultimate insanity. I would hold that he has an independent constitutional right to trial by jury of the fact of his ability to commit a crime by mental aberration.

* * *

Unfortunately, our criminal code does not define a "voluntary act." It does define an "involuntary act" to include reflexes or convulsions, unconscious sleep movements, hypnosis and such. Section 45–2–101(31), MCA. The majority has changed the definition of an involuntary act to limit the scope of a voluntary act which, to me, is not the intent of the criminal code and is improperly restrictive.

I would reverse and remand for a new trial, and direct the District Court to instruct the jury on the ALI formulations respecting insanity as applied to criminal acts.

I suggest a retrial on the basis of the ALI formulations not because I consider those formulations the last word on the subject, but because we do have remaining in our statutes some recognition of the ALI formulations with respect to the insanity defense. Under present law the District Court must look to the ALI formulations to determine the extent of the sentence to be imposed, section 46–14–311, MCA. The real problem facing this Court is that the abolition by the legislature in 1979 of mental disease or defect as an exculpatory defense leaves a cavity in our criminal law that is the obligation of the legislature to fill. Unless we now recognize the ALI formulations on the basis that there is legislative recognition of their validity in the sentencing process, we have no legislative direction in the statutes for the insanity defense.

It is curious that Montana abolished the insanity defense in 1979, before the onset of the Hinckley trial. Hinckley's attack on President Reagan, and the subsequent acquittal of Hinckley in June 1982, prompted a rash of enactments and proposals for enactments with respect to the insanity defense. The Standing Committee on Association Standards for Criminal Justice of the American Bar Association at the time of the Hinckley verdict had been considering mental health law and criminal justice issues for close to a year and a half. The Hinckley verdict triggered the Committee's consideration of key issues in order to advise Congress, state legislatures and the public in the aftermath of the concern arising from the Hinckley verdict. At least part of the credit must be given to that Standing Committee for the fact that Congress has refused so far to abolish the insanity defense.

The Standing Committee on Association Standards has since promulgated its proposed criminal justice mental health standards for consideration by the Bar and by legislatures. It proposes that the insanity defense be considered as "the defense of mental nonresponsibility," and further proposes that such a condition be exculpatory to a criminal charge. The Committee examined enactments such as Montana's and in comment had this to say:

> "This approach, which would permit evidence of mental condition on the requisite mental element of the crime but eliminate mental nonresponsibility as an independent, exculpatory doctrine, has been proposed in several bills in Congress, and adopted in Montana, Idaho and Utah. The ABA has rejected it out of hand. Such a jarring reversal of hundreds of years of moral and legal history would constitute an unfortunate and unwarranted overreaction to the Hinckley verdict.
>
> ". . .
>
> "Yet the issue of criminal blameworthiness should require a deeper inquiry. Implicit in this concept is a certain *quality* of knowledge and intent, going beyond a minimal awareness and purposefulness. Otherwise, for example, a defendant who knowingly and intentionally kills his son under the psychotic delusion that he is the biblical Abraham and his son, the biblical Isaac, could be held criminally responsible. The Montana, Idaho and Utah enactments, on their face, would deny a defense to such a defendant." American Bar Association, Standing Committee on Association Standards for Criminal Justice, Report to the House of Delegates, August, 1984, Standard 7–6.1, Commentary P. 327.

Thus has Montana's abolition of the insanity defense in 1979 been held up for criticism and disrespect by national authorities and scholars. It behooves our legislature, which will be meeting in a few months, to reexamine its mental health laws as they pertain to criminal justice and to revamp the same. It could do nothing finer than to adopt the standard of exculpatory definition proposed by the Standing

Committee on Association Standards of the American Bar Association which follows:

> "Standard 7–6.1. The defense of mental nonresponsibility [insanity].
>
> "(a) A person is not responsible for criminal conduct if, at the time of such conduct, and as a result of mental disease or defect, that person was unable to appreciate the wrongfulness of such conduct.
>
> "(b) When used as a legal term in this standard 'mental disease or defect' refers to:
>
> "(i) impairments of mind, whether enduring or transitory; or, (ii) mental retardation either of which substantially affected the mental or emotional processes of the defendant at the time of the alleged offense."

There are accompanying standards proposed by the Standing Committee which the legislature should also adopt, which would soften the aspects of self-incrimination which I have described above, and especially a proposed standard which would prevent the experts from invading the province of the jury. Particularly applicable, in my opinion, would be Standard 7–6.–6:

> "Standard 7–6.6. Limitation on opinion testimony concerning mental condition.
>
> "Expert opinion testimony as to how the development, adaptation and functioning of the defendant's mental processes may have influenced defendant's conduct at the time of the offense charged should be admissible. Opinion testimony, whether expert or lay, as to whether or not the defendant was criminally responsible at the time of the offense charged should not be admissible."

It is clear that the Standing Committee, by proposing Standard 7–6.6, recognized the impropriety of handing to medical or other persons the ultimate question to be determined by the jury, whether the defendant is entitled to be exculpated because of his mental processes at the time of the crime charged. The Report of the Standing Committee points out that the issue is jurisprudential, and not medical, and for that reason we should provide an exception to section 704 of the Montana Rules of Evidence, which allows opinion testimony on the ultimate question in the ordinary case.

In the meantime, I would reverse the conviction of Jerry Korell, and return this cause for a trial on his insanity defense.

SHEA, JUSTICE, dissenting:

I join in the dissent of Justice Sheehy and I also will be filing my own dissent setting forth in more detail my own reasons.

NOTES

1. According to Kermani, Handbook of Psychiatry and the Law, 1989, retention of the insanity defense is essential to the moral integrity of the law. He states, at p. 174:

> The insanity defense, according to the American Psychiatric Association (APA), helps maintain one of the fundamental premises of the criminal law, namely that punishment for wrongful deeds should be predicated upon moral culpability. This renders retention of the insanity defense essential to the moral integrity of criminal law and the criminal justice system. Therefore, the APA officially stands behind the belief that the insanity defense should be retained in some form.
>
> The APA is extremely skeptical regarding the concept of the guilty but mentally ill verdict, or any similar indeterminate verdicts. Presented by judges as an alternative to the traditional insanity verdict, GBMI usually ends up being a compromise verdict instead which the jury can grasp when the going gets tough. Not to doubt the intentions of juries who choose this middle-ground verdict, still, GBMI lessens the pressure on the jurors, offering them an 'easy out,' and makes it unnecessary for them to undergo the emotional and intellectual strain of choosing among the definitive verdicts of not guilty, not guilty by reason of insanity, or guilty.

2. Contrast the view of the APA, above, with that of the American Medical Association (AMA), which House of Delegates voted, on December 6, 1983, to support the abolition of the special defense of insanity. Staunchly opposed by the APA, the continuing debate in the medical groups eventually led to a joint statement approved by both groups in 1985. Dr. Kermani, op. cit. supra, at p. 177, said that "In the joint statement, the organizations politely criticize each other, while exchanging compliments, and resolving that they share a concern over the role of medical testimony in the legal system." He stated further that the joint statement "failed to reach a definite formulation or guidelines for the legislatures and courts," largely because the positions of both organizations, in favor of retaining the defense of insanity (APA position) and in favor of abolishing it (AMA) remained essentially unchanged.

3. In creating, in 1981, the guilty but mentally ill disposition and placing the burden of proving sanity on the state, and in 1984 shifting the burden of proving insanity, in an ordinary insanity defense case, on the defendant, the Illinois legislature had made it next to impossible to properly instruct the juries on burdens of proof. As a result, a GBMI verdict was struck down by the Illinois Supreme Court in People v. Fierer, 124 Ill.2d 176, 124 Ill.Dec. 855, 529 N.E.2d 972 (1988). Believing that the existing jury instructions for GBMI and insanity cannot be reconciled, a bill was introduced in the legislature in 1989 to abolish GBMI. See, Loeb, Let's Abolish the Guilty But Mentally Ill Verdict, Illinois Bar J., Nov. 1989, p. 802.

4. Consider Weintraub, Criminal Responsibility: Psychiatry Alone Cannot Determine It, 49 A.B.A.J. 1075 (1963), in which the Chief Justice of the New Jersey Supreme Court expresses the following viewpoint:

> My thesis is that insanity should have nothing to do with the adjudication of guilt, but rather should bear only upon the disposition

of the offender after conviction, and that the contest among M'Naghten and its competitors is a struggle over irrelevancy. * * *

M'Naghten is denounced as unjust to the defendant. It is called arbitrary in the light of modern psychiatric knowledge, and I agree that it is. But the proposal to replace it with another definition of legal insanity contains two flaws. One is the naked assumption that insanity should bear on the determination of guilt as distinguished from the postconviction disposition of the offender. The other is that the very thesis of the attack upon M'Naghten demonstrates that the proposed substitutes are equally arbitrary and incompatible with the psychiatric view of man. * * *

For all practical purposes the furor over M'Naghten is confined to the disposition of offenders convicted of murder. It is the death penalty which sparks the quarrel.

For views similar to those of Chief Justic Weintraub, see the following articles by two psychiatrists: Scher, Expertise and the Post Hoc Judgment of Insanity or the Antegnostician and the Law, 57 Nw.U.L.Rev. 4 (1962), and Baur, Legal Responsibility and Mental Illness, ibid. 12. In the same publication consider also Schmideberg, The Promise of Psychiatry: Hopes and Disillusionment, at p. 19. See also, Wilbur, Should the Insanity Defense to a Criminal Charge be Abolished?, 8 A.B.A.J. 631 (1922); Hart, Punishment and Responsibility, 1968; Goldstein & Katz, "Abolish the Insanity Defense"—Why Not?, 72 Yale L.J. 853 (1963); Morris, Psychiatry and the Dangerous Criminal, 41 So. Cal.L.Rev. 514 (1968).

APPENDIX—RELEVANT PROVISIONS OF THE UNITED STATES CONSTITUTION AND ITS AMENDMENTS

Provisions of the Constitution of the United States, and certain Amendments thereto, of particular significance in the administration of criminal justice:

Preamble

We the People of the United States, in Order to form a more perfect Union, establish Justice, insure domestic Tranquility, provide for the common defense, promote the general Welfare, and secure the Blessings of Liberty to ourselves and our Posterity, do ordain and establish this Constitution for the United States of America.

Article I.

. . .

Section 8. The Congress shall have Power To lay and collect Taxes, Duties, Imposts and Excises, to pay the Debts and provide for the common Defence and general Welfare of the United States; but all Duties, Imposts and Excises shall be uniform throughout the United States; . . .

To regulate Commerce with foreign Nations, and among the several States and with the Indian Tribes; . . .

To provide for the Punishment of counterfeiting the Securities and current Coin of the United States; . . .

To constitute Tribunals inferior to the supreme Court;

To define and punish Piracies and Felonies committed on the high Seas, and Offences against the Law of Nations;

To declare War, grant Letters of Marque and Reprisal, and make Rules concerning Captures on Land and Water; . . .

To make Rules for the Government and Regulation of the land and naval Forces;

To provide for calling forth the Militia to execute the Laws of the Union, suppress Insurrections and repel Invasions;

To provide for organizing, arming, and disciplining, the Militia, and for governing such Part of them as may be employed in the Service of the United States, reserving to the States respectively, the Appointment of the Officers, and the Authority of training the Militia according to the discipline prescribed by Congress;

To exercise exclusive Legislation in all Cases whatsoever, over such District (not exceeding ten Miles square) as may, by Cession of particular States, and the Acceptance of Congress, become the Seat of the Government of the United States, and to exercise like Authority over all Places purchased by the Consent of the Legislature of the State in which the Same shall be, for the Erection of Forts, Magazines, Arsenals, dock-Yards, and other needful Buildings;—And

To make all Laws which shall be necessary and proper for carrying into Execution the foregoing Powers, and all other Powers vested by this Constitution in the Government of the United States, or in any Department or Officer thereof.

Section 9.

. . .

No Bill of Attainder or ex post facto Law shall be passed.

Article III.

Section 1.   The judicial Power of the United States, shall be vested in one supreme Court, and in such inferior Courts as the Congress may from time to time ordain and establish.   The Judges, both of the supreme and inferior Courts, shall hold their Offices during good Behaviour, and shall, at stated Times, receive for their Services, a Compensation, which shall not be diminished during their Continuance in Office.

Section 2.

. . . the supreme Court shall have appellate Jurisdiction, both as to Law and Fact, with such Exceptions, and under such Regulations as the Congress shall make.

The Trial of all Crimes, except in Cases of Impeachment, shall be by Jury; and such Trial shall be held in the State where the said Crimes shall have been committed; but when not committed within any State, the Trial shall be at such Place or Places as the Congress may by Law have directed.

Section 3.   Treason against the United States, shall consist only in levying War against them, or in adhering to their Enemies, giving them Aid and Comfort.   No Person shall be convicted of Treason unless on the Testimony of two Witnesses to the same overt Act, or on Confession in open Court.

The Congress shall have Power to declare the Punishment of Treason, but no Attainder of Treason shall work Corruption of Blood, or Forfeiture except during the Life of the Person attainted.

Article VI.

. . .

This Constitution, and the Laws of the United States which shall be made in Pursuance thereof; and all Treaties made, or which shall be made, under the Authority of the United States, shall be the supreme Law of the Land; and the Judges in every State shall be bound thereby, any Thing in the Constitution or Laws of any State to the Contrary notwithstanding.

AMENDMENTS

Amendment I.

Congress shall make no law respecting an establishment of religion, or prohibiting the free exercise thereof; or abridging the freedom of speech, or of the press; or the right of the people peaceably to assemble, and to petition the Government for a redress of grievances.

Amendment II.

A well regulated militia, being necessary to the security of a free State, the right of the people to keep and bear arms, shall not be infringed.

Amendment III.

No Soldier shall, in time of peace be quartered in any house, without the consent of the owner, nor in time of war, but in a manner to be prescribed by law.

Amendment IV.

The right of the people to be secure in their persons, houses, papers, and effects, against unreasonable searches and seizures, shall not be violated, and no warrants shall issue, but upon probable cause, supported by oath or affirmation, and particularly describing the place to be searched, and the persons or things to be seized.

Amendment V.

No person shall be held to answer for a capital, or otherwise infamous crime, unless on a presentment or indictment of a Grand Jury, except in cases arising in the land or naval forces, or in the militia, when in actual service in time of war or public danger; nor shall any person be subject for the same offence to be twice put in jeopardy of life or limb; nor shall be compelled in any criminal case to be a witness against himself, nor be deprived of life, liberty, or property, without due process of law; nor shall private property be taken for public use, without just compensation.

Amendment VI.

In all criminal prosecutions, the accused shall enjoy the right to a speedy and public trial, by an impartial jury of the State and district wherein the crime shall have been committed, which district shall have been previously ascertained by law, and to be informed of the nature and cause of the accusation; to be confronted with the witnesses against him; to have compulsory process for obtaining witnesses in his favor, and to have the assistance of Counsel for his defence.

Amendment VII.

In Suits at common law, where the value in controvery shall exceed twenty dollars, the right of trial by jury shall be preserved, and no fact tried by a jury, shall be otherwise re-examined in any Court of the United States, than according to the rules of the common law.

Amendment VIII.

Excessive bail shall not be required, nor excessive fines imposed, nor cruel and unusual punishments inflicted.

Amendment IX.

The enumeration in the Constitution, of certain rights, shall not be construed to deny or disparage others retained by the people.

Amendment X.

The powers not delegated to the United States by the Constitution, nor prohibited by it to the States, are reserved to the States respectively, or to the people. . . .

Amendment XIII.

SECTION 1. Neither slavery nor involuntary servitude, except as a punishment for crime whereof the party shall have been duly convicted, shall exist within the United States, or any place subject to their jurisdiction.

SECTION 2. Congress shall have power to enforce this article by appropriate legislation.

Amendment XIV.

SECTION 1. All persons born or naturalized in the United States, and subject to the jurisdiction thereof, are citizens of the United States and of the State wherein they reside. No State shall make or enforce any law which shall abridge the privileges or immunities of citizens of the United States; nor shall any State deprive any person of life, liberty, or property, without due process of law; nor deny to any person within its jurisdiction the equal protection of laws. . . .

SECTION 5. The Congress shall have power to enforce, by appropriate legislation, the provisions of this article.

Amendment XV.

SECTION 1. The right of citizens of the United States to vote shall not be denied or abridged by the United States or by any State on account of race, color, or previous condition of servitude.

SECTION 2. The Congress shall have power to enforce this article by appropriate legislation.

Amendment XVI.

The Congress shall have power to lay and collect taxes on incomes, from whatever source derived, without apportionment among the several States, and without regard to any census or enumeration. . . .

INDEX

References are to Pages

†

0-88277-937-0

90000

9 780882 779379